UNITED STATES Coast Pilot®

7

Pacific Coast: California, Oregon, Washington, Hawaii and Pacific Coast

2013 (45th) Edition

This edition cancels the 44th Edition, 2012, and has been corrected through 11th Coast Guard District Local Notice to Mariners No. 44/12, the 13th Coast Guard District Local Notice to Mariners No. 44/12, the 14th Coast Guard District Local Notice to Mariners No. 44/12, and includes all previously published corrections.

Weekly updates to this edition are available at:
http://nauticalcharts.noaa.gov/nsd/cpdownload.htm
They are also published in the National Geospatial-Intelligence Agency (NGA) Notice to Mariners.

U.S. Department of Commerce
Dr. Rebecca M. Blank, Acting Secretary

National Oceanic and Atmospheric Administration (NOAA)
Jane Lubchenco, Ph.D., Under Secretary of Commerce for Oceans and Atmosphere, and Administrator, NOAA

National Ocean Service
David M. Kennedy, Assistant Administrator, National Ocean Service

www.TheBoatBookShop.com

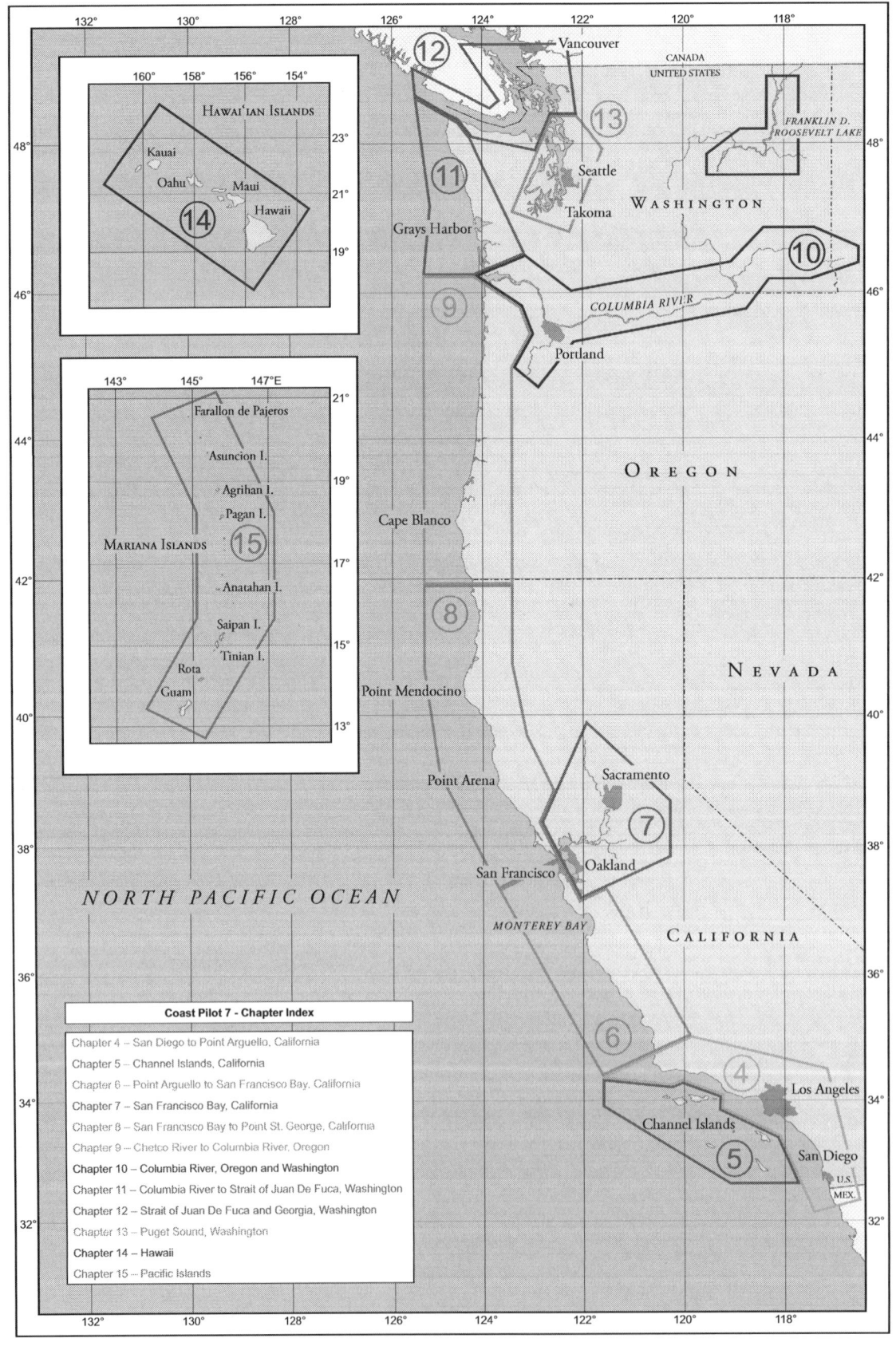

Preface

The United States Coast Pilot is published by the National Ocean Service (NOS), National Oceanic and Atmospheric Administration (NOAA), pursuant to the Act of 6 August 1947 (33 U.S.C. 883a and b), and the Act of 22 October 1968 (44 U.S.C. 1310).

The Coast Pilot supplements the navigational information shown on NOAA nautical charts. The Coast Pilot is continually updated and maintained from inspections conducted by NOAA survey vessels and field parties, corrections published in Notices to Mariners, information from other Federal agencies, State and local governments, maritime and pilots' associations, port authorities, and concerned mariners.

NOAA's Office of Coast Survey encourages public feedback regarding its suite of nautical charting products and services through the Nautical Inquiry/Discrepancy Reporting System. This system allows comments, inquiries and chart discrepancies to be submitted directly to NOAA's nautical charting program. Inquiries are typically acknowledged by email within one day, and ninety percent are answered or resolved within five days.

General comments or inquiries can be made at http://nauticalcharts.noaa.gov/inquiry. Detailed nautical chart or Coast Pilot discrepancies can be reported at http://nauticalcharts.noaa.gov/discrepancy.

Coast Survey also maintains a toll free phone line for public comments or inquiries. Customers may contact the charting program by telephone on weekdays from 8:00 a.m. to 4:00 p.m. (Eastern Time) at 888-990-6622.

Keep your Coast Pilot up-to-date

Check for weekly critical updates for this edition at
http://nauticalcharts.noaa.gov/nsd/cpdownload.htm
(See **33 CFR 164.33 Charts and Publications**, chapter 2, for regulations.)

You may print the specifically affected paragraphs to revise this book, or download an updated .pdf of the entire volume.

A *Weekly Record of Updates* is provided for your convenience directly preceding the index.

---

www.TheBoatBookShop.com

Contents

California, Oregon, and Washington •5

San Diego to Point Arguello, Cal •18

Channel Islands, California •55

Point Arguello to San Francisco Bay, California •67

San Francisco Bay, California •83

San Francisco Bay to Point St. George, California •131

Chetco River to Columbia River, •158

Oregon •153

Columbia River, Oregon and Washington •177

Columbia River to Strait of Juan De Fuca, Washington •209

Strait of Juan De Fuca and Georgia, Washington •227

Puget Sound, Washington •261

Hawaii •301

Pacific Islands •369

California, Oregon, and Washington

(1) The California-Oregon-Washington coast of the United States, between Mexico on the S and Canada's British Columbia on the N, is mostly rugged and mountainous, with high land rising abruptly from the sea in many places. S of San Francisco Bay the mountains are usually bare or covered with chaparral and underbrush. N of the bay the mountains are generally well timbered, and in some places, especially N of the Columbia River, the timber is particularly dense and heavy.

Disposal Sites and Dumping Grounds

(2) These areas are rarely mentioned in the Coast Pilot, but are shown on the nautical charts. (See Disposal Sites and Dumping Grounds, chapter 1, and charts for limits.)

Aids to navigation

(3) Lights are numerous along the coast; there are only a few places where a vessel is not in sight of one or more lights. Sound signals are at most of the principal light stations. Many coastal and harbor buoys are equipped with radar reflectors, which greatly increase the range at which the buoys may be detected. The critical dangers are buoyed and are generally marked by kelp.

(4) There are many aerolights along the coast that are useful for navigation purposes, but they should not be confused with the marine lights. (See the Light List for a complete description of navigational aids.)

(5) The frequent occurrence of fog along this coast makes radar an invaluable aid in detecting other traffic and obtaining a line of position and/or fix. Bridge-to-bridge radio communication (VHF-FM) is another useful aid, regardless of weather, in waters where maneuvering room is limited or restricted. The primary advantages of this radio system are its line-of-sight characteristic and relative freedom from static interference.

COLREGS Demarcation Lines

(6) Lines have been established to delineate those waters upon which mariners must comply with the International Regulations for Preventing Collisions at Sea, 1972 (72 COLREGS) and those waters upon which mariners must comply with the Inland Navigational Rules Act of 1980 (Inland Rules). The waters inside of the lines are **Inland Rules Waters**, and the waters outside of the lines are **COLREGS Waters**. (See **Part 80,** chapter 2, for specific lines of demarcation.)

Ports and Waterways Safety

(7) (See **Part 160,** chapter 2, for regulations governing vessel operations and requirements for notification of arrivals, departures, hazardous conditions, and certain dangerous cargoes to the Captain of the Port.)

Channels

(8) **Federal project depth** is the dredging depth of a channel as authorized by an Act of Congress upon recommendation of the Chief of Engineers, U.S. Army. **Controlling depth** in a channel is its least depth; it restricts use of the channel to drafts less than that depth.

(9) Where deepwater channels are maintained by the Corps of Engineers and the controlling depths are printed on the charts, the Coast Pilot usually gives only the project depth. Because of constant shoaling in places, depths may vary considerably between maintenance dredgings. (See Notice to Mariners and latest editions of charts for controlling depths.)

(10) Where secondary channels are maintained regularly by the Corps of Engineers, the Coast Pilot gives the controlling depths together with the dates of the latest surveys.

(11) In the case of other channels, the controlling depths printed in the Coast Pilot are from the latest available reports, which may, however, be several years old.

Depths alongside wharves

(12) In general, depths given alongside wharves are those reported by owners and/or operators of the waterfront facilities, and have not been verified by government surveys. Since these depths may be subject to change, local authorities should be consulted for current controlling depths.

(13) Depths are in feet below the low-water tidal datum of the charts; deck heights where given are in feet above the chart datum for water depths.

(14) **Traffic Separation Schemes (Traffic Lanes)** have been established from the Gulf of Santa Catalina to the vicinity of Point Conception, off the entrance to San Francisco Bay, and in the Straits of Juan de Fuca and Georgia and Haro Straits. (See chapters 4, 7, and 12, respectively, for details.)

(15) **Vessel Traffic Services (VTS)**, have been established in the San Francisco Bay area and in the Strait of Juan de Fuca, E of Port Angeles and in the waters of Rosario Strait, Admiralty Inlet, Puget Sound and the

Low Sulfur Distillate Fuel Oil Regulations

GENERAL INFORMATION

The California Air Resources Board (ARB) created regulations for vessel emissions reductions for California's ports as part of its continued mission to improve air quality around the state. The requirements came into effect in July 2009, under California Code of Regulations(CCR), Section 2299.2, *Fuel Sulfur and Other Operational Requirements for Ocean Going Vessels within California Waters and 24 Nautical Miles of the California Baseline.*

Since 01 August 2012, the regulations require that vessels burn either marine gas oil with maximum 1.0% sulfur, or marine diesel oil with maximum 0.5% sulfur, in their main and auxiliary engines.

Following the implementation of the regulations, California continues to experience loss of propulsion (LOP) incidents within state waters at a much higher rate than was seen prior to July 2009.

This advisory focuses upon reducing the probability of an LOP incident occurring on vessels due to the use of Low Sulfur Distillate Fuel Oil (LSDFO).

OPERATIONS
Initial Entry

For vessels intending to enter the California ARB Emissions Control area for the first time, California advises the crew should conduct a "TRIAL" (actual) fuel switching within 45 days prior to entering California waters. Run main and auxiliary engines no less than four (4) hours on LSDFO. This will help identify any specific change over or operational issues or problems.

Repeat and Initial Entry
  Part One-TRAINING:
- Within 45 days prior to entering the Ports of California it is strongly advised ship engineers should exercise:
    A. Operating main engine from the engine control room.
    B. Operating main engine from engine side (local).
- Crew should become familiar with "Failure to Start" procedures while maneuvering and establish corrective protocols for "Failure to Start" incidents.

Part Two-While Underway after Fuel Switching Completed (HFO to Low Sulfur Distillate):
- Ships should ensure one of the senior* engineering officers is in the engine control room while the vessel is in pilotage waters and be:
    A. able to operate the ship main engine from the engine control room.
    B. able to operate the ship main engine from engine side (local).
    *Special Attention to International Standards of Training, Certification and Watchkeeping (STCW) Rest Requirements

Part Three-Engine Guidelines:
- Consult engine and boiler manufacturers for fuel switching guidance.
- Consult fuel suppliers for proper fuel selection.
- Exercise strict control when possible over the quality of the fuel oils received.
- Consult manufacturers to determine if system modifications or additional safeguards are necessary for intended fuels.
- Develop detailed fuel switching procedures.
- Establish a fuel system inspection and maintenance schedule.
- Ensure system pressure and temperature alarms, flow indicators, filter differential pressure transmitters, etc., are all operational.
- Ensure system purifiers, filters and strainers are maintained.
- Ensure system seals, gaskets, flanges, fittings, brackets and supports are maintained.
- Ensure that the steam isolation valves on fuel lines, filters, heaters etc. are fully tight in closed position while running on Low Sulfur Distillate Fuel Oil.
- Ensure that the fuel oil viscosity and temperature control equipment is accurate and operational.
- Ensure detailed system diagrams are available and engineers are familiar with systems and troubleshooting techniques. Senior engineering officers should know the location and function of all automation components associated with starting the main engine.

navigable waters adjacent to these areas. The services have been established to prevent collisions and groundings and to protect the navigable waters from environmental harm.

(16) The Vessel Traffic Services provide for a **Vessel Traffic Center (VTC)** that may regulate the routing and movement of vessels by radar surveillance, movement reports of vessels, VHF-FM radio communications, and specific reporting points. The systems consists of traffic lanes, separation zones, precautionary areas and reporting points.

(17) Participation in the **Vessel Traffic Service San Francisco** is mandatory for certain vessels within navigable waters of the United States and within the 12-mile boundary of the U.S. territorial sea. (See chapter 7, for details.) The Vessel Traffic Service in the Strait of Juan de Fuca, E of Port Angeles, and in the waters of Rosario Strait, Admiralty Inlet, and Puget Sound is mandatory. (See **161.1 through 161.60**, chapter 2, for rules governing vessel operations in the Vessel Traffic Service, and, chapter 12, for details.)

(18) **Offshore Vessel Movement Reporting System San Francisco** has been established in the ocean approaches to San Francisco; the system is mandatory. (See chapter 7 for details.)

(19) **Vessel Traffic Information Service Los Angeles/Long Beach** has been established for the approaches to Los Angeles and Long Beach. The Service is **voluntary.** (See chapter 4 for details.)

Drawbridges

(20) The general regulations that apply to all drawbridges are given in **117.1 through 117.49**, chapter 2, and the specific regulations that apply only to certain drawbridges are given in **Part 117, Subpart B,** chapter 2. Where these regulations apply, references to them are made in the Coast Pilot under the name of the bridge or the waterway over which the bridge crosses.

(21) The drawbridge opening signals (see **117.15**, chapter 2) have been standardized for most drawbridges within the United States. The opening signals for those few bridges that are nonstandard are given in the specific drawbridge regulations. The specific regulations also address matters such as restricted operating hours and required advance notice for openings.

(22) The mariner should be acquainted with the general and specific regulations for drawbridges over waterways to be transited.

(23) **Depths**, along most of the Pacific coast decrease much too rapidly from seaward to be of any practical use as an aid to navigation. The 100-fathom curve lies at an average distance of less than 10 miles from shore, but this distance is exceeded in the approaches to San Francisco Bay, Heceta Bank, Columbia River, and the Strait of Juan de Fuca.

Anchorages

(24) Anchorages, affording shelter for large vessels from the severe NW winds of summer, may be had in a number of places along the coast. In SE and SW weather there are few places where shelter is available; San Diego Bay, Los Angeles Harbor, the lee side of the Channel Islands, and Monterey Bay are the only places S of San Francisco Bay. N of San Francisco, good shelter is found in Humboldt Bay, Coos Bay, Columbia River, Willapa Bay, and Grays Harbor; but most of these places must be made before the sea rises, as afterward the bars become impassable. Neah Bay, just inside the entrance to the Strait of Juan de Fuca, is used considerably by small vessels in W or S weather. Many anchorages have been established in the area covered by this Coast Pilot. (See **Part 110**, chapter 2, for limits and regulations.)

Dangers

(25) There are few outlying dangers, the principal ones being Bishop Rock, W of San Diego; Noonday Rock and the Farallon Islands, off San Francisco Bay; and Blunts, St. George, Rogue River, Orford, and Umatilla Reefs, N of San Francisco. The Channel Islands, off southern California, are the largest, most prominent, and the farthest offshore of any islands along the coast.

Oil well structures

(26) Offshore drilling and exploration operations are increasing in the waters off California, especially in Santa Barbara Channel.

(27) Obstructions in these waters consist of submerged wells and oil well structures (platforms), including appurtenances thereto, such as mooring piles, anchor and mooring buoys, pipes, and stakes.

(28) Pacific offshore platforms are regulated by **safety zones** administered and enforced by the United States Coast Guard. (See **33 CFR 147**, chapter 2, for limits and regulations.) If, for safety reasons, a vessel must approach an offshore platform, it is essential to notify the operator of the platform and/or the Captain of the Port on VHF-FM channel 16 for permission to enter the safety zone. Boarding or mooring to a platform is strongly discouraged and may be considered trespass unless permission is given in advance from the platform operator or Captain of the Port, or access to the platform is required as a result of emergency circumstances.

(29) In general, the oil well structures (platforms), depending on their size, depth of water in which located, proximity of vessel routes, nature and amount of vessel traffic, and the effect of background lighting, may be marked in one of the following ways:

(30) Quick flashing white light(s) visible at least 5 miles: sound signal sounded when visibility is less than 5 miles.

(31) Quick flashing white light(s) visible at least 3 miles: sound signal sounded when visibility is less than 3 miles.

(32) Quick flashing white or red lights visible at least 1 mile: may or may not be equipped with sound signal.

(33) Structures on or adjacent to the edges of navigable channels and fairways, regardless of location, may be required to display lights and sound signals for the safety of navigation.

(34) Associated structures within 100 yards of the main structure, regardless of location, are not normally lighted but are marked with red or white retro-reflective material. Mariners are cautioned that uncharted submerged pipelines and cables may exist in the vicinity of these structures, or between such structures and the shore.

(35) During construction of a well or during drilling operations, and until such time as the platform is capable of supporting the required aids, fixed white lights on the attending vessel or drilling rig may be shown in lieu of the required quick flashing lights on the structure. The attending vessel's foghorn may also be used as a substitute.

(36) Submerged wells may or may not be marked depending on their location and depth of water over them.

(37) All obstruction lights and sound signals, used to mark the various structures, are operated as privately maintained aids to navigation. (See **33 CFR 67**, for detailed regulations for the marking of offshore structures.)

(38) Information concerning the establishment, change, or discontinuance of offshore oil-well structures and their appurtenances is published in the Local Notice to Mariners or by Broadcast Notice. Additional information may also be obtained from the Coast Guard Commander. Mariners are advised to navigate with caution in the vicinity of these structures and in those waters where oil exploration is in progress, and to use the latest and largest scale chart of the area.

(39) During the continuing program of establishing, changing, and discontinuing oil-well structures, special caution should be exercised when navigating the inshore and offshore waters of the affected areas in order to avoid collision with any of the structures.

(40) Information concerning seismographic operations is not published in Notice to Mariners unless such operations create a menace to navigation in waters used by general navigation. Where seismographic operations are being conducted, casings (pipes), buoys, stakes, and detectors are installed. Casings are marked with flags by day and fixed red lights by night; buoys are colored international orange and white horizontal bands; and stakes are marked with flags.

Pipelaying barges

(41) With the increased number of pipeline laying operations, operators of all types of vessels should be aware of the dangers of passing close aboard, close ahead, or close astern of a jetbarge or pipelaying barge. Pipelaying barges and jetbarges usually move at 0.5 knot or less and have anchors which extend out about 3,500 to 5,000 feet in all directions and which may be marked by lighted anchor buoys. The exposed pipeline behind the pipelaying barge and the area in the vicinity of anchors are hazardous to navigation and should be avoided. The pipeline and anchor cables also represent a submerged hazard to navigation. It is suggested, if safe navigation permits, for all types of vessels to pass well ahead of the pipelaying barge or well astern of the jetbarge. The pipelaying barge, jetbarge, and attending vessels may be contacted on VHF-FM channel 16 for passage instructions.

Fish havens

(42) Fish havens, some marked by private buoys, are numerous along the Pacific coast. Navigators should be cautious about passing over fish havens or anchoring in their vicinity.

Kelp

(43) Kelp grows on nearly every danger with a rocky bottom and is particularly heavy at various points in Santa Barbara Channel and in the vicinity of San Diego Bay. It will be seen on the surface of the water during the summer and autumn; during the winter and spring it is not always to be seen, especially where it is exposed to a heavy sea. Many rocks are not marked by kelp, because a heavy sea will occasionally tear it away and a moderate current will draw it under water so that it will not be seen. When passing on the side of a kelp patch from which the stems stream away with the current, care should be taken to give it a good berth. Dead, detached kelp floats on the water curled in masses, while live kelp, attached to rocks, streams away level with the surface. Live kelp is usually an indication of depths less than 10 fathoms.

Logs and deadheads

(44) Mariners are cautioned that a large number of logs and deadheads are adrift in the navigable water of Washington and Oregon at all times, particularly after storms, spring freshets, and unusually high tide. Mariners are urged to be alert for the presence of such logs and deadheads, as they constitute a serious menace to craft of small and moderate size.

River entrances

(45) Along the Oregon and Washington coast, bars build up at the mouths of the many rivers and streams that empty into the Pacific Ocean. The tidal currents at these entrances can obtain considerable velocity, especially when the ebb tide is reinforced by the river runoff. The most dangerous condition prevails when a swift ebb current meets the heavy seas rolling in from the Pacific at the shallow river entrances. The water piles up and breaks and creates a bar condition too rough for small craft. In a bar area, sea conditions can change rapidly and without warning. Always cross it with caution.

Regulated Boating Areas

(46) The U.S. Coast Guard has provided for the termination of the use of boats during especially hazardous conditions on certain river bars and coastal inlets along the Pacific coastline of Oregon and Washington. The hazardous bar areas are depicted in the Coast Guard "Bar Guides" or in a pamphlet entitled "Boating in Coastal Waters," published by the Oregon Marine Board. It is important for the small-craft operator to know when he is operating in the general vicinity of a regulated boating area, and be prepared for any changing tidal or sea conditions which may be hazardous to his vessel.

Danger zones

(47) **Danger zones** and **Restricted areas** are along the Pacific coast, around the Channel Islands, in the Straits of Juan de Fuca and Georgia, and in Puget Sound. (See **334**, chapter 2, for limits and regulations.)

Caution

(48) Heavy concentrations of fishing gear may be expected off Drakes Bay, Grays Harbor, Columbia River, Coos Bay, Humboldt Bay and Destruction Island between December 1 and August 15, from shore to about 30 fathoms.

(49) To reduce the destruction of fishing gear by vessels and to reduce the fouling of propellers and shafts by fishing gear, Washington Sea Grant, Washington State University Extension has coordinated an agreement between towboaters and crab fishermen for the establishment of towboat lanes along the Pacific coast between San Francisco, California and Cape Flattery, Washington. Copies of the agreement showing fishing areas and towboat lanes may be obtained from Washington Sea Grant, Washington State University Extension, Box 88, South Bend, WA 98586; telephone 360–875–9331. The tow lanes can be viewed online at http://graysharbor.wsu.edu/marine/lane.html.

Tides

(50) A very important characteristic of the tides along the W coast of the United States is the large inequality in the heights of the two high waters and of the two low waters of each day. On the outer coast the average difference between the heights of the two high waters of the day is from 1 to 2 feet, and the average difference in the heights of the two low waters from 2 to 3 feet. It was because of this large difference in the low-water heights that the mean of the lower low waters, rather than the mean of all low waters, was adopted as the plane of reference for the charts of this region.

(51) This inequality changes with the declination of the Moon. When the Moon is near the Equator the inequality is relatively small; but when the Moon is near its greatest N or S declination, the difference in the heights of the two high waters or of the two low waters of each day reaches a maximum. The tides at this time are called **Tropic tides**.

(52) Off the outer coast, the mean rise of the tide varies from 5 feet off southern California to about 7.5 feet off the coast of Washington. Extreme variations from 3 feet below to 10 feet above the datum may reasonably be expected.

(53) At the entrance to San Francisco Bay the mean rise of the tide is about 5 feet. At the S end of the bay the tide occurs about 1½ hours later, and the mean rise is about 2.5 feet greater than at the entrance of the bay. Passing N into San Pablo Bay, the tide occurs from 1 to 2 hours later than at the Golden Gate, with a mean rise of about 0.5 foot greater than at the latter place. In Suisun Bay the time of tide is about 3 hours later than at the Golden Gate, with a mean rise about the same. It requires about 4 hours for high water to pass from Suisun Bay to Stockton, on the San Joaquin River, and about 5 hours from Suisun Bay to Sacramento, on the Sacramento River. The mean rise of the tide at Stockton is 3.6 feet, and at Sacramento is 2.6 feet.

(54) In Humboldt Bay the tide is from ½ to 1 hour later than on the outer coast. The mean rise is about 6 feet.

(55) In Coos Bay the tide is from ½ to 1½ hours later, and the rise of high water about same as in Humboldt Bay.

(56) In Yaquina Bay the mean rise is about 7 feet.

(57) At the entrance to Columbia River the mean rise is about 7 feet. It requires about 6 hours for high water to pass from the entrance to the Columbia River to the mouth of the Willamette River. In passing up the Columbia River the range of tide decreases until it is only 1.4 feet at the mouth of the Willamette. Above this point the tidal range becomes too small to be of practical importance. There are, however, large fluctuations in the level due to meteorological conditions. An extreme variation of 24.5 feet has been noted at St. Johns on the Willamette River. Columbia River is usually highest during May, June, and July, and lowest during September, October, and November.

(58) In Willapa Bay and in Grays Harbor the mean rise is about 9 feet.

(59) Passing through the Strait of Juan de Fuca, the tide occurs about 3 hours and 40 minutes later at Port Townsend than at Cape Flattery. The mean rise increases from 7.2 feet above the datum at Cape Flattery to 7.9 feet at Port Townsend. There is an increase in the average inequality between the two low waters of each day from 3 feet at Cape Flattery to 5 feet at Port Townsend. The average inequality between the two high waters of each day at both places is about 1.5 feet.

(60) In Puget Sound the tide is about ½ to 1 hour later than at Port Townsend. The mean rise increases from 7.5 feet at Port Townsend to 13.5 feet at Olympia. In Puget Sound the average difference between the two low waters of each day is 6 feet. At Seattle an extreme range from 4.5 feet below the datum of mean lower low water to 15 feet above the same datum has been observed. At

Olympia, in the S part of the sound, an extreme high water 18 feet above the datum has been noted.

(61) In the San Juan Islands, the mean rise of the tide varies from 6.5 to 8 feet. An extreme range from 4.5 feet below to 12 feet above the same datum may reasonably be expected.

Caution

(62) In using the Tide Tables, high or low water should not be confused with slack water. For ocean stations there is usually little difference between the time of high or low water and the beginning of ebb or flood currents; but for places in narrow channels, landlocked harbors, or on tidal rivers the time of slack water may differ by several hours from the time of high or low water stand. The relation of the times of high and low water to the turning of the current depends upon a number of factors, hence no simple rule can be given. (See the Tidal Current Tables for predicted times of slack water or strength of current.)

Currents

(63) A current, the outer limit of which extends offshore more than 300 miles, flows approximately parallel to the U.S. Pacific coast from latitude 50° to 30°N. The direction of the current is generally S throughout the year except as noted below. Its velocity, which averages about 0.2 knot, is greatly influenced by prevailing winds; N winds increase it, and S winds diminish it. North of latitude 45°N. the set is usually N from November through February.

(64) Along the coast during certain periods there is a weak N flow known as the **Davidson Inshore Current**, which is evident between San Diego and Point Conception from July through February and between Point Conception and Cape Flattery from November through February.

(65) Along the coast of Vancouver Island there is usually a NW flow, which as measured at Swiftsure Bank (48°32.0'N., 124°59.7'W.) has a velocity of nearly 0.5 knot at all seasons.

(66) The above statements apply to general or average conditions. The currents, particularly offshore, at a specific time depend largely upon prevailing winds, whereas alongshore and off the entrances to inland waterways they depend also upon tidal and drainage effects. (See the Tidal Current Tables for detailed information.)

Tsunamis (seismic sea waves)

(67) Although the coasts of California, Oregon, and Washington are not generally subject to waves of the magnitude which strike the Hawai'ian Islands and other Pacific areas, widespread damage to shipping and to waterfront areas occasionally occurs. The tsunami of March 28, 1964, originating in the Gulf of Alaska, caused 16 deaths and several million dollars damage to ships and property in California, Oregon, and Washington. The loss of life and property can be lessened if shipmasters and others acquaint themselves with the behavior of these waves so that intelligent action can be taken when they become imminent. (See chapter 1 for details about these waves.)

(68) The Warning System operated by the National Oceanic and Atmospheric Administration and described in chapter 14 supplies warnings to the Civil Defense authorities in California, Oregon, and Washington who are responsible for disseminating this information to the affected areas. The warnings are also broadcast by the National Weather Service on NOAA Weather Radio.

(69) When a warning is received, persons should vacate waterfront areas and seek high ground. The safest procedure for ships will depend on the amount of time available, and this may not always be known. A ship well out at sea would ride such waves safely, and hence if time is available to put to sea, that would be the safest action. On the other hand, the crew of a ship in harbor may have a difficult time averting serious damage. The ship may be washed ashore by incoming waves or grounded because of excessive withdrawal of water between crests. Much of the damage in the Los Angeles area during the 1960 Chilean tsunami was caused by rapid currents and the swift rise and fall of the water level that parted mooring lines and set floating docks and ships adrift.

Blue, fin and humpback whales

(70) All whales are protected under the Marine Mammal Protection Act (MMPA) and, when in Sanctuary waters, under the National Marine Sanctuaries Act (NMSA). Certain large whales, including blue, fin and humpback whales, are also listed as endangered under the Endangered Species Act (ESA). Blue, fin and humpback whales migrate through, or may be found in large aggregations, feeding in the nutrient-rich and highly productive waters along the continental shelf of California, Oregon and Washington. Whales may not react to approaching vessels, increasing the risk of collision. A collision could result in significant damage to the vessel and death or serious injury to the whale. Collisions with vessels in these waters may be affecting the recovery of blue, fin and humpback whales. NOAA is responsible for providing protection to whales under the MMPA, ESA and NMSA and provides the following species information and precautionary measures for mariners to reduce risk of vessel collisions.

(71) **Descriptions of blue, fin and humpback whales:**

(72) **Blue whales**: body is mottled bluish-gray; up to 85 feet in length; blow is tall and columnar; relatively small dorsal fin is usually not seen during surfacing (but can be seen prior to a dive); tail flukes are often raised before a dive. The most recent population estimate for blue whales off the U.S. west coast is approximately 2,500.

(73) **Fin whales**: body is solid gray to black above and white below, with a chevron pattern behind head often visible from above; up to 79 feet in length; blow is tall and shaped like an inverted cone; the dorsal fin is usually sickle shaped and visible during surfacing; tail

flukes are rarely raised before a dive. The most recent population estimate for fin whales off the U.S. west coast is approximately 3,000.

(74) **Humpback whales**: body is dark gray with black and white patches on underside; up to 52 feet in length; blow is round and bushy; long white and black flippers; head covered with knobs or nodules; relatively prominent dorsal fin relative to body size; flukes are often raised before deep dives. The most recent population estimate for humpback whales off the U.S. west coast is approximately 2,000.

(75) **Occurrence of blue, fin and humpback whales:** Though these large whales are found along the western coast of the United States year-round, overall abundance is highest from May to November, when whales are feeding on dense aggregations of krill and other forage fish. Blue whales are most commonly seen in California from May through September. Fin whales are most common in summer and winter, and humpback whales are most common in summer and fall. These whales regularly occur in large feeding groups around the Channel Islands and off of Long Beach and Orange County in southern California and in the waters off of San Francisco and Monterey Bay in central California.

(76) **Precautions when transiting whale habitat:**

(77) Vessel operators and observers are advised to keep a sharp lookout for whales when transiting near the coast, especially near the 100-fathom curve and offshore islands. NOAA has established two whale advisory zones to alert mariners of the seasonal presence (May through November) of blue, fin and humpback whales and to encourage vessel operators to keep a sharp lookout for whales and proceed with caution within these areas. One whale advisory zone, in southern California, includes the waters from Point Arguello to Dana Point; a second, in Central California, extends from Point Piedras Blancas to Bodega Bay. NOAA works with the U.S. Coast Guard and the National Weather Service to broadcast and publish this information annually.

(78) NOAA may make recommendations to large vessels to reduce speed in specific areas to reduce the risk of lethal ship strikes. NOAA's recommendations are broadcast via the Coast Guard Notice to Mariners (and appear in the published Local Notice to Mariners) and NOAA Weather Radio. To receive current advisories and other whale-related information, mariners can sign up for e-mail announcements here: http://www.rain.org/mailman/listinfo/noaa-whale-advisory-l.

(79) Please report any collisions with whales or any observed injured, entangled or dead whales to NOAA at 877–SOS–WHALe (877–767–9425) or to the U.S. Coast Guard on VHF Channel 16. For more information, visit: http://sanctuaries.noaa.gov/protect/shipstrike/welcome.html.

(80) **Precautions when in the presence of whales:**

(81) NOAA has established additional guidelines to help keep both mariners and whales safe. In the presence of whales, mariners should:

(82) Maintain a distance of at least 100 yards from any marine mammal

(83) Never pass in front of a whale's path

(84) Avoid sudden speed or directional changes around whales

(85) Never get between two whales, especially a cow and her calf

(86) Always travel parallel to whales and at or below their speed

(87) Never chase whales

(88) Civil and criminal penalties could apply if these guidelines are not observed. NOAA's National Marine Fisheries Service (NMFS) has regulatory responsibility for implementing the MMPA and ESA. Whales in a national marine sanctuary are also protected under the National Marine Sanctuaries Act (NMSA), which prohibits unauthorized take or possession of any marine mammal in sanctuary waters, including harassment and disturbance.

Weather, West Coast and Hawaii

(89) This section presents an overall, seasonal picture of the weather that can be expected in the offshore waters along the entire west coast of the United States as well as coastal and near-coastal sites and the Hawai'ian and Pacific Islands. Detailed information, particularly concerning navigational weather hazards, can be found in the weather articles in the following chapters.

(90) All weather articles in this volume are the product of the **National Oceanographic Data Center (NODC)** and the **National Climatic Data Center (NCDC).** The meteorological and climatological tables are the product of the NCDC. Both centers are entities of the **National Environmental Satellite, Data, and Information Service (NESDIS)** of the **National Oceanic and Atmospheric Administration (NOAA).** If further information is needed in relation to the content of the weather articles, meteorological tables or climatological tables, contact the National Climatic Data Center, Attn: Customer Service Division, Federal Building, 151 Patton Avenue, Room 120, Asheville, NC 28801-5001. You may also contact the CSD at 704–271–4994, or fax your request to 704–271–4876.

(91) Climatological tables for coastal locations, meteorological tables for the coastal ocean areas, and a table of mean surface water temperatures and densities relevant to locations discussed within this volume, Appendix B. The climatological tables are a special extraction from the International Station Meteorological Climate Summary. The ISMCS is a CD-ROM jointly produced by the National Climatic Data Center, Fleet Numerical Meteorology and Oceanography Detachment-Asheville, and the U.S. Air Force Environmental Technical Applications Center, Operating Location–A. The meteorological tables for the ocean areas are compiled from observations made by ships in passage and extracted from the National Climatic Data Center's Tape Deck-1129, Surface Marine Observations. Listed in Appendix

A are National Weather Service offices and radio stations which transmit weather information.

(92) **Marine Weather Services Charts** published by the National Weather Service show radio stations that transmit marine weather broadcasts and additional information of interest to mariners. These charts are for sale by the National Ocean Service Distribution Division (N/ACC3). (See Appendix A for address.)

(93) The Pacific coastal region of the United States and the adjacent ocean areas are located along the east portion of the Pacific high-pressure system. This high, when well developed, forms the principal circulation control forcing most of the low-pressure systems to follow a course to the north of the contiguous United States. This is reflected in the presence of the Aleutian low in the Gulf of Alaska. This action damps out weather changes that might otherwise occur and brings a stability factor that would not otherwise exist. Air which reaches the coast as a result of the prevailing westerly winds has acquired much moisture during its ocean passage, resulting in high humidities along the coast. The marine influence is also evidenced in a cooling effect in summer and a warming influence in winter.

(94) Two features of the climate in these waters, while not commonplace, warrant the mariner's attention because of their severity. One is the tropical cyclones and the other a local wind known as the Santa Ana.

(95) **Tropical cyclones** originate south of the area, off the west Mexican coast, in summer and autumn. About 15 form each season, of which eight reach hurricane intensity. Few come far enough north to affect U.S. coastal waters. The ones that do have usually lost their hurricane intensity and are short-lived. However, these storms can be dangerous and have generated winds of more than 120 knots. Further reference is made to tropical cyclones in the seasonal description.

(96) The **Santa Ana** is an offshore desert wind that occurs in or near San Pedro Bay. While infrequent, it may be violent; speeds have been measured at more than 50 knots. These winds diminish little, if any, immediately after passing over water, and can extend up to 50 miles (93 km) out to sea. They are most likely in late autumn or winter. (See Weather articles, chapter 4, for more details.)

(97) A third feature, the **El Nino/Southern Oscillation (ENSO)**, sporadically influences these waters. **ENSO** is a two-phased weather phenomenon with roots in the equatorial Pacific and coastal South America; El Nino is the warm water phase and **La Nina**, the cool water phase.

(98) El Nino is an abnormally warm, eastward-moving, Equatorial Pacific current which is thought to have a pronounced influence on the global atmospheric circulations. It is known that during an El Nino event, the normal southeast trade winds of the near Equatorial Pacific region break down allowing for near-global-wide altered weather patterns. During a strong El Nino, this typically means an unusually strong subtropical jet stream that brings storms from central and southern California eastward through the gulf coast and southeast states. If the El Nino is weaker, drought to California and rains to the gulf coast and southeast states may be expected.

(99) Following an El Nino event, the near-equatorial trade winds return to normal. On occasion, the southeast trade winds become stronger than normal. If this occurs, a La Nina is present, the opposite of El Nino. It is believed that a strong La Nina leads to drought across much of North America.

(100) Winter, like an incoming tide, creeps over the northeastern North Pacific. Subtle changes begin in September. Seas off central and southern California come under the protection of a weak, good-weather subtropical high centered near 35°N and 145°W. Only enough storms penetrate this protective barrier to make winter a distinguishable season off southern California. This same high pressure system in conjunction with a strengthening Aleutian Low, bodes differently for points further north. Summer breezes become gales. Rain is commonplace. Winds and cool temperatures make the air feel damp and chilly. Storms become routine and onshore flow is near-persistent. Choppy seas turn rough.

(101) Winter storms usually work their way from the central Pacific northward into the Gulf of Alaska or to the coast of British Columbia, trailing their frontal systems across the area. Two or three times a month, on an average, a storm will move directly through the seas off the Washington-Oregon coast. The more seaward storms generate the moderate to strong southeast through west winds that prevail over northern waters and influence the weather as far south as central California. The stronger winds that blow over a long fetch of water whip up rough seas. Seas of 12 feet (3.7 m) or more are generated 15 to 20 percent of the time. In addition, the warm south flow brings cloudiness, drizzle, and sometimes fog. Drizzle occurs about 5 to 8 percent of the time, and there are about 2 to 4 days a month when dense fog reduces visibilities to 0.5 mile (0.9 km) or less at sea. These conditions can persist for a week or more if one of these big storms stalls in the Gulf of Alaska. The south flow is also responsible for air temperatures in the upper forties and fifties (8.9° to 15°C). Cold temperatures are unusual and are most likely when cold Arctic air is fed into a low in the Gulf by a large high in the Bering Sea or when a rare outbreak of Arctic air occurs over the area from the north or northeast. Temperatures at these times may drop below freezing (<0°C) off the Washington coast and into the upper thirties (3.3° to 3.9°C) farther south. The infrequency of cold temperatures lessens the chances for snow, which is observed less than 2 percent of the time off Washington and less than 1 percent of the time off Oregon.

(102) When a storm moves close or through these northern waters, weather changes rapidly. The center is preceded by a strong southeast to southwest flow that may reach gale force (gales occur on about 3 to 5 days per winter month) and may whip seas up to 20 feet (6.1 m)

or more; seas of these heights occur up to 4 percent of the time. These conditions are often accompanied by clouds and rain, with temperatures in the fifties (10° to 15°C). After the center passes, winds will veer to the west through north and remain strong for a while. Brief showers soon end, the clouds break, and temperatures drop into the low forties (5° to 6.7°C). A high-pressure system from the central Pacific may follow and bring a brief period of clear conditions. If a storm stalls or it is followed by a series of storms, bad weather can be prolonged for a week or more. Rain falls on 18 to 28 days per winter month in these north waters, and skies are overcast or obscured 40 to 50 percent of the time.

(103) About once or twice a month, a storm moves into northern California offshore waters. While these lows are often weaker than those farther north, some cause gales and rough seas. Gales blow on 4 to 5 days per month, and seas reach 12 feet (3.7 m) or more about 8 to 16 percent of the time. These conditions can also be generated by the interaction of a low to the north and a high to the south. The south winds can raise temperatures into the sixties (16.1° to 20.6°C) off northern and central California. Clouds and rain accompany these systems. Rain falls on about 10 to 15 days per month.

(104) Off northern and central California, storms bring a preponderance of southeast through southwest winds, but this is matched by northwest and north winds that blow around the subtropical highs. These highs either form in the Pacific or migrate from Asia. They dominate the weather off the southern California coast, where west through north winds blow more than 60 percent of the time. However, these highs are weakest during winter, and occasionally storms move close enough to bring some clouds, rain, and wind. Rain occurs on about 5 to 10 days per month off central and southern California. Gales and rough seas are rare south of Los Angeles. Between Los Angeles and San Francisco, gales blow on about 1 to 4 days per month, while seas of 12 feet (3.7 m) or more occur about 4 to 8 percent of the time.

(105) Fog is a problem in the offshore waters between Los Angeles and San Francisco. Visibilities less than 2 miles (4 km) occur 5 to 7 percent of the time, while dense fog reduces visibilities to less than 0.5 mile (0.9 km) on 2 to 5 days per month.

(106) Spring brings change. March is an epilogue to winter, while May provides a prologue to summer. Cold rainy days alternate with mild sunny ones. The gradual changeover takes place under the forceful prodding of the expanding good-weather Pacific high. In March the center approximates 30°N and 140°W. As the high expands, it forces the increasingly weak and infrequent storms north into the western Gulf of Alaska and Bering Sea. Since the high is not yet a permanent feature, storms will occasionally penetrate the area, particularly in early spring, when they sometimes move into the Pacific northwest or even across the northern California coast. Southern California waters remain protected by the high. This expanding high-pressure system, which brings good weather, creates a problem in the offshore waters of central and northern California. It causes a tightening of the pressure gradient, which increases wind strength. In other areas, winds and waves are becoming less of a problem. A change is taking place in the direction of prevailing winds. Off southern California, prevailing northwest and north winds are becoming increasingly persistent. With the expansion of the high, north and northwest winds are becoming the prevailing directions throughout the area. This is a slow change. In March, south and north winds share equal billing.

(107) Storms to the W and NW of the Washington-Oregon offshore waters, while not as frequent as in winter, still generate SE to W winds as they work their way N. The prevailing storm track is shifting northward so not as many lows move directly through the area, and they are often less intense. Gales from these near and distant storms blow on about 2 days in March, and they are rare by May. Seas also calm down. In March, waves of 12 feet (3.7 m) or more occur 15 to 20 percent of the time; this drops to 10 percent by April and to around 5 percent by May. The general south flow from these storms still bring rain, drizzle, and fog. Rain or drizzle can be expected on about 15 to 18 days in March and 9 to 15 days in May. Dense fog (visibilities less than 0.5 mile (0.9 km)) forms on less than 2 days per month, while visibilities drop below 2 miles (4 km), 2 to 4 percent of the time. Because of the clouds and rain associated with this S flow, it is not always responsible for the warmest spring temperatures. Usually, it is accompanied by temperatures in the forties and low fifties (5° to 11.1°C) in March and 50°F (10°C) readings during May. An occasional cold N outbreak, usually following a storm, can drop March temperatures into the mid- to upper thirties (0.6° to 3.9°C).

(108) Occasionally a low will move close enough to bring some clouds, rain, and drizzle; distant lows often account for some of the cloudy days. This is more likely in early spring, when rain falls on about 4 to 5 days in the S, and 5 to 15 days in central and Northern waters. By May, storms are less frequent, and rain occurs on just 1 or 2 days S of Los Angeles and 3 to 10 days to the N.

(109) Fog is a problem in the offshore waters between Los Angeles and San Francisco. In April and May, visibilities drop below 2 miles (4 km) 8 percent of the time, and fog reduces visibilities to less than 0.5 mile (0.9 km) on about 2 to 3 days per month. It occurs mostly with winds from the SW through NW, when they bring warm air over the cooler waters.

(110) Two important features are responsible for the summer weather in these offshore waters, the subtropical Pacific high and the cold California Current.

(111) The influence of high-pressure systems becomes increasingly frequent in these northern waters during spring. In fact, a principal path of highs from the central and western Pacific runs through this area and onto the Washington-Oregon coast. These systems bring clearing conditions, W through N winds, and sometime mild

temperatures. Temperatures can, on occasion, get up into the upper fifties and low sixties (14.4° to 16.7°C) in March and into the upper sixties (19.4° to 20.0°C) in May. Clear to partly cloudy skies occur most often with W to N winds. Wind speeds are less than 10 knots most often with W to N winds.

(112) High-pressure systems dominate the weather in California offshore waters, although an occasional storm disrupts the good weather, particularly in early spring. Wind and sea conditions are not so good, however, in waters from off San Francisco northward. In this region, the pressure gradient between highs and lows is often very tight, creating strong N winds which blow at speeds that average near 20 knots and whip up seas of 12 feet (3.7 m) or more from 8 to 20 percent of the time. This situation continues throughout spring.

(113) Conditions improve rapidly toward the S, where winds are lighter and seas calmer. The high-pressure systems are responsible for W through N winds, clear skies, and cool temperatures. Winds become increasingly persistent during spring, as the highs become more frequent. By May, NW through N winds are blowing close to 70 percent of the time N of San Francisco, and W through NW, about the same to the S. These winds blow over cold water and help keep temperatures in the fifties (10.6° to 15.0°C) throughout the spring, N of San Francisco. Even to the S, temperatures in the fifties (10.6° to 15°C) in March only climb into the mid-fifties to mid-sixties (11.7° to 19.4°C) by May. This compares with temperatures in the 70° to 80° (21.1° to 26.7°C) range at the same latitudes in North Atlantic offshore waters, where the Gulf Stream helps warm the air. The high-pressure systems are also responsible for the clear skies (about one-quarter cloud cover) that occur 25 to 50 percent of the time in these offshore California waters.

(114) The high is made up of high-pressure systems, which either form in the Eastern Pacific or move into the area from Western Pacific waters, the Bering Sea, or the Gulf of Alaska. By July the mean center of the Pacific High is located around 40°N and 150°W. The S flowing California Current is partially driven by the clockwise circulation of these high-pressure systems. Upwelling also contributes to cool water temperatures. Sea-surface temperatures run 10° to 15°F (-12.2° to -9.4°C) cooler than they do off the Atlantic coast. Its influence is so great that average air temperatures off Eureka never get out of the fifties (10.6° to 15.0°C), and extremes have only reached 87°F (30.6°C), just 9°F (-12.8°C) warmer than the January extreme. The California Current and coastal upwelling are responsible for the poor visibilities of summer and fall. The most dense and frequent fog occurs over the narrow stream of coldest water, just off the coast, and is often limited to a band of 50 miles (81 km) or less. At other times, fog covers large areas, both in latitude and longitude, and may extend for hundreds of miles (>161 km). Its effect is even more pronounced onshore, as you can read in the Weather articles in the chapters following. The effect of the California Current in summer extends along the entire coast.

(115) When a high sits to the W, which is most of the time in summer, W through N winds blow over the offshore waters. Between Point Arguello and Portland, this warm moist air is being chilled by the California Current. This results in not only cool temperatures but low clouds and fog. W through N winds blow 70 to 80 percent of the time. In the offshore waters, where merchant ships are trying to avoid poor visibilities, fog and haze are still encountered 30 to 40 percent of the time between Point Arguello and San Francisco. The fog reduces visibilities to below 0.5 mile (0.9 km) up to 5 days per month. Skies are obscured by fog, or are overcast, up to 50 percent of the time in these offshore waters. Temperatures are often in the midfifties to midsixties (11.7° to 19.4°C) at these times.

(116) Between San Francisco and Portland, fog and haze occur 15 to 25 percent of the time. Fog reduces visibilities to below 0.5 mile (0.9 km) on about 3 to 8 days per month. Skies are obscured or overcast about 30 to 40 percent of the time. In addition to fog, this offshore area is often plagued by gales and rough seas created by a tight pressure gradient between a high off the coast and a heat low over the southwestern United States and Mexico. Gales blow on about 4 to 6 days per month. Strong winds whip up seas of 12 to 20 feet (3.7 to 6.1 m) about 3 to 10 percent of the time.

(117) As storms become less frequent during summer, so does rain. By August, rain falls 3 to 7 percent of the time in the offshore waters from Point Arguello to Vancouver Island.

(118) In the offshore waters between Portland and Vancouver Island, W and NW winds blow more than one-half of the time, skies are clear 20 to 30 percent of the time, and temperatures are frequently in the sixties (16.1° to 20.6°C). Gales are rare; and, while it rains 5 to 10 percent of the time, this a lot less frequent than during any other season. W through N winds often bring poor visibilities to this area. Fog and haze are encountered 8 to 15 percent of the time. Fog drops visibilities below 0.5 mile (0.9 km) on about 2 to 5 days per month and is most frequent from midsummer on.

(119) South of Point Arguello, weather is fair. Visibilities are usually better than 5 miles, winds and seas are calmer, but temperatures are cool. These offshore waters are almost always under the influence of a high. W through NW winds, which blow 70 to 75 percent of the time, keep temperatures mostly in the sixties (16.1° to 20.6°C) and bring haze and fog about 15 percent of the time. These warm, moist winds blowing over the California Current also help keep the sky overcast or obscured almost one-half of the time. Skies are clear about one-quarter of the time. Gales are rare, as are rough seas. Winds blow at about 10 knots.

(120) The subtropical high-pressure system forces most tropical storms S of southern California. There is a threat of tropical cyclones from June through November. An

average tropical cyclone season sees about 15 tropical cyclones (winds of about 34 knots), of which an average of 8 reach hurricane strength. These storms seldom move N of 30°N. They are most likely to reach the latitudes of 30° to 35°N in August or September. However, by this time, they are usually weak and either well out to sea or well inland over Arizona. The eastern North Pacific season peaks in July, August, and September. About three to five tropical cyclones can be expected each month, with an average of one to two reaching hurricane strength. The last damaging tropical cyclone to affect southern California was the September 1939 storm which moved inland near Los Angeles. In September 1972, the remains of a hurricane moved inland between San Diego and Los Angeles; it carried only 20-knot winds at the time of landfall. Several other tropical storms have completed the decaying process in the California coastal waters near the Channel Islands.

(121) Fall arrives subtly in September N of Point Arguello. It is delayed a month or so to the S by the subtropical high. High-pressure systems still bring some sunny, mild days with light west through N winds off Oregon and Washington, but even on these days, swells from distant storms often cast an ominous mood over these waters. Some storms move close enough to generate a SE through SW flow off Oregon and Washington. They also bring rain to offshore Washington waters about 8 to 13 percent of the time. A tightening of pressure gradients, off northern California and Oregon in September, is responsible for gales on 2 to 5 days, and for seas of 12 feet (3.7 m) or more, 2 to 4 percent of the time. Meanwhile, off central California, gales blow less often and seas are calmer than they were last month. September is usually the driest month in offshore waters from Oregon southward. Precipitation frequencies range from 6 percent off Oregon to less than 1 percent off southern California. Poor visibilities continue to plague the offshore waters N of Point Arguello. Fog reduces visibilities to less than 0.5 mile (0.9 km) on about 4 to 6 days in September. September temperatures usually range from the upper fifties and low sixties (14.4° to 16.7°C) in the N, to the mid- and upper sixties (18.3° to 20.6°C) off southern California.

(122) During October and particularly November, storms become more frequent, more intense, and move closer to the area than those of summer and early autumn. As the subtropical high weakens and retreats southward and the Aleutian Low is at its deepest, these storms move to the NW and N, most affecting the vulnerable waters off Washington and Oregon. They frequently sweep these seas with strong SE through SW winds, which carry rain and sometimes fog. These winds average 15 to 20 knots. Gales occur on about 2 to 4 days in October and 3 to 6 days in November, off Washington and Oregon. Strong winds whip up seas of 12 feet (3.7 m) or more about 10 to 16 percent of the time. Rain falls more often as autumn progresses. It occurs about 8 to 20 percent of the time in October, increasing to 16 to 30 percent by November in these N seas. This is about as much as it rains in any month. Fog continues to plague this area, and often rides in on a strong, warm S flow that accompanies a low-pressure system. It reduces visibilities to below 0.5 mile (0.9 km) on about 2 to 5 days per month. Temperatures of Washington and Oregon are often in the fifties (10.6° to 15°C) in October and mid-forties to mid-fifties (8.9° to 13.9°C) the following month.

(123) The winter transition comes later to California offshore waters. High-pressure systems remain influential, so winds often blow out of the N and NW through late autumn, particularly in the S. Even off northern California, winds out of the N are only slightly less frequent than southerlies as late as November. Storms move closer and occasionally break through the protective barrier in November. In offshore northern California waters, they are responsible for about 3 to 5 gale days per month, and for seas of 12 feet (3.7 m) or more, 6 to 10 percent of the time. They also dump rain up to 10 percent of the time. Weather generally improves to the S, where rain falls as little as 3 percent of the time. Gales occur on about 2 days or less. Seas of 12 feet (3.7 m) or more occur about 8 percent of the time in central waters, and about 1 percent in the S. Temperatures change slowly over offshore waters. In October, they frequently run in the fifties (10.6° to 15.0°C) in the N, and in the sixties (16.1° to 20.6°C) to the S. Temperatures drop just a few degrees in November.

(124) Fog continues to be the most frequent navigational weather hazards in the waters of offshore northern and central California. Fog reduces visibilities to below 0.5 mile (0.9 km) on about 5 to 7 days during October, the worst month. Fog and haze are reported about 15 to 20 percent of the time, except off Los Angeles, where they occur about 40 percent of the time.

Routes

(125) The route along the California-Oregon-Washington coast frequently must be navigated in thick weather. Most of the courses are long, and the effect of currents is uncertain.

San Diego to Strait of Juan de Fuca

(126) Vessels can proceed on rhumb lines through the following positions:
(127) 32°37'N., 117°16'W.; off San Diego.
(128) Thence to the Traffic Separation Scheme off San Pedro Bay, then follow the Traffic Separation Scheme between Point Fermin and Point Conception.
(129) 34°33'N., 120°42'W.; off Point Arguello.
(130) 37°38'N., 123°12'W.; off Farallon Islands (San Francisco).
(131) 38°55'N., 123°50'W.; off Point Arena.
(132) 40°26'N., 124°32'W.; off Blunts Reef.
(133) 42°50'N., 124°44'W.; off Cape Blanco.
(134) 46°11'N., 124°12'W.; off Columbia River.
(135) 48°10'N., 124°52'W.; off Umatilla Reef.

(136) 48°26'N., 124°47'W.; off Cape Flattery.
(137) **Caution:** Route W of Farallon Islands crosses San Francisco-Honolulu and other Pacific courses of vessels using the San Francisco Traffic Separation Scheme.

San Diego to San Francisco

(138) Vessels can follow San Diego-Strait of Juan de Fuca route to position off Point Arguello, thence rhumb lines through the following positions:
(139) 36°17'N., 121°57'W.; off Point Sur.
(140) 37°10'N., 122°26'W.; off Pigeon Point.
(141) Thence by prescribed San Francisco Traffic Separation Scheme route to vicinity of San Francisco Approach Lighted Whistle Buoy SF.

San Francisco to Strait of Juan de Fuca

(142) Follow prescribed San Francisco Traffic Separation Scheme route to a position off Point Reyes, thence to Point Arena and other positions on the San Diego-Strait of Juan de Fuca route.

Caution

(143) Strict adherence to tracks through positions listed above could result in collision of meeting vessels. It is suggested that southbound vessels shape courses through positions 1 mile farther off the mainland.

San Diego to Panama

(144) Proceed on rhumb lines through the following positions:
(145) 32°38'N., 117°13'W.
(146) 28°00'N., 116°00'W.
(147) 24°40'N., 112°30'W.
(148) 20°00'N., 107°30'W.
(149) 07°05'N., 81°45'W.

San Diego to Honolulu

(150) Rhumb line from 32°37'N., 117°16'W., to 21°14'N., 157°39'W.

Los Angeles to Honolulu

(151) Follow the Traffic Separation Scheme route through the Gulf of Santa Catalina, thence proceed on rhumb lines through the following positions:
(152) 32°48'N., 118°16'W.
(153) 21°14'N., 157°39'W.

San Francisco to Honolulu

(154) Follow prescribed San Francisco Traffic Separation Scheme route to a position S of Farallon Islands, thence rhumb line to
(155) 21°14'N., 157°39'W.

Strait of Juan de Fuca to Honolulu

(156) Great circle from
(157) 48°26'N., 124°47'W., to
(158) 21°14'N., 157°39'W.

Strait of Juan de Fuca to Unimak Pass

(159) Great circle from
(160) 48°31'N., 125°00'W., to
(161) 54°00'N., 163°00'W.; thence on rhumb line to
(162) 54°20'N., 164°45'W.

Offshore Vessel Traffic Management Recommendations

(163) Based on the **West Coast Offshore Vessel Traffic Risk Management Project**, which was co-sponsored by the **Pacific States/British Columbia Oil Spill Task Force** and **U.S. Coast Guard Pacific Area**, it is recommended that, where no other traffic management areas exist such as Traffic Separation Schemes, Vessel Traffic Services, or recommended routes, vessels 300 gross tons or larger transiting along the coast anywhere between Cook Inlet and San Diego should voluntarily stay a minimum distance of 25 nautical miles offshore. It is also recommended that tank ships laden with persistent petroleum products and transiting along the coast between Cook Inlet and San Diego should voluntarily stay a minimum distance of 50 nautical miles offshore. Vessels transiting short distances between adjacent ports should seek routing guidance as needed from the local Captain of the Port or VTS authority for that area. This recommendation is intended to reduce the potential for vessel groundings and resulting oil spills in the event of a vessel casualty.

Principal ports

(164) The principal deep-draft commercial ports within the area of this Coast Pilot are: San Diego, Long Beach, Los Angeles, San Francisco, Oakland, Richmond, Stockton, Humboldt Bay, Coos Bay, Portland, Vancouver, Grays Harbor, Seattle, Tacoma, and Honolulu.
(165) Other ports are Port Hueneme, Port San Luis, Redwood City, Sacramento, Astoria, Longview, Port Angeles, Anacortes, Bellingham, Olympia, and Hilo.

Pilotage, general

(166) In the area covered by this Coast Pilot, pilotage, with a few exceptions, is compulsory for all foreign vessels and for U.S. vessels under register in the foreign trade. It is optional for U.S. vessels in the coastwise trade, provided they are under the control and direction of a pilot duly licensed by Federal law for the waters which that vessel travels.
(167) Only at San Francisco do pilot boats cruise on station continuously. At the other ports the pilots must be notified in advance in order for the pilot boat to meet the vessel at the proper time. Most of the pilot boats and stations may be contacted by radio; though ships' agents normally arrange for pilots, a vessel may notify the pilot station of its estimated time of arrival by radio. Specific information is given in the description of the various ports.

Towage

(168) Tugs of various sizes are available at all the deep-draft ports. Arrangements for their use are usually made by the ship's agent, but in some cases may be made from the vessel by radio. For further information, refer to the description of the port.

Vessel Arrival Inspections

(169) Quarantine, customs, immigration, and agricultural quarantine officials are stationed in most major U.S. ports. (See Appendix A for addresses.) Vessels subject to such inspections generally make arrangements in advance through ships' agents. Unless otherwise directed, officials usually board vessels at their berths.

Harbormasters and wharfingers

(170) Harbormasters and wharfingers are mentioned in the text when applicable. They generally have charge of the anchorage and berthing of vessels.

Supplies

(171) Supplies of all kinds are available at San Diego, Los Angeles, Long Beach, San Francisco Bay, Portland, Seattle, and Tacoma. Limited quantities can be obtained at many other ports.

Repairs

(172) Large ocean-going vessels may be drydocked for complete repairs at Los Angeles, Long Beach, San Francisco Bay, Portland, and Seattle. Smaller ships of up to about 7,000 tons may also be drydocked at San Diego. Fishing boats and yachts can be hauled out and can have hulls and engines repaired at numerous other places. The Coast Pilot gives information on many of these facilities; usually the largest repair facility in each area is mentioned. Additional information may be obtained from the series of small-craft charts published for many places.

(173) **Salvage** equipment is available at Los Angeles, San Francisco Bay, Portland, and Seattle.

Small-craft facilities

(174) There are numerous places where fuel, supplies, protected berths, repairs, and shore facilities are available for small craft. For isolated places and small cities, the Coast Pilot describes the more important of these facilities; for large port areas, where individual facilities are too numerous to mention, the information given is more general. Additional information may be obtained from the series of small-craft charts published for the many places, and from various local small-craft guides.

(175) **A vessel of less than 65.6 feet (20 meters) in length or a sailing vessel shall not impede the passage of a vessel that can safely navigate only within a narrow channel or fairway. (Navigation Rules, International-Inland Rule 9(b).)**

(176) Southern California has many small-craft harbors with excellent facilities, but N of San Francisco the distances between protected harbors having facilities increases considerably until in the Puget Sound area. Temporary moorage is usually available for transients at most of the harbors. The intense yachting activity of California as far N as San Francisco, however, makes transient moorage more difficult along this section of the coast, even with its numerous harbors built especially for such craft.

Standard time

(177) California, Oregon, and Washington use Pacific standard time, which is 8 hours slow of Greenwich mean time. Example: When it is 1000 at Greenwich, it is 0200 in the three coastal States. Hawaii uses Hawaii-Aleutian standard time (H.A.s.t.), which is 10 hours slow of Greenwich mean time. Example: When it is 1000 at Greenwich, it is 0000 in Hawaii.

Daylight saving time

(178) In California, Oregon, and Washington, clocks are advanced 1 hour on the second Sunday of March and are set back to standard time on the first Sunday of November. Daylight saving time is not observed in the State of Hawaii, American Samoa, or the U.S. territory of Guam.

Legal public holidays

(179) The following are legal holidays in the area covered by this Coast Pilot: New Year's Day, January 1; Martin Luther King, Jr.'s Birthday, third Monday in January; Washington's Birthday, third Monday in February; Memorial Day, last Monday in May; Independence Day, July 4; Labor Day, first Monday in September; Columbus Day, second Monday in October; Veterans Day, November 11; Thanksgiving Day, fourth Thursday in November; and Christmas Day, December 25. The national holidays are observed by employees of the Federal Government and the District of Columbia, and may not be observed by all the States in every case.

(180) In addition, the following holidays are also observed in the area covered by this Coast Pilot: Lincoln's Birthday, February 12, in California and Washington, first Monday in February, in Oregon; Presidents Day, first Monday in February, in Hawaii; Kuhio Day, March 26, in Hawaii; Good Friday, in Hawaii, in California from 1200 to 1500; Kamehameha Day, June 11, in Hawaii; Admission Day, third Friday in August, in Hawaii; Admission Day, September 9, in California; General Election Day, first Tuesday after first Monday in November, in California and Washington.

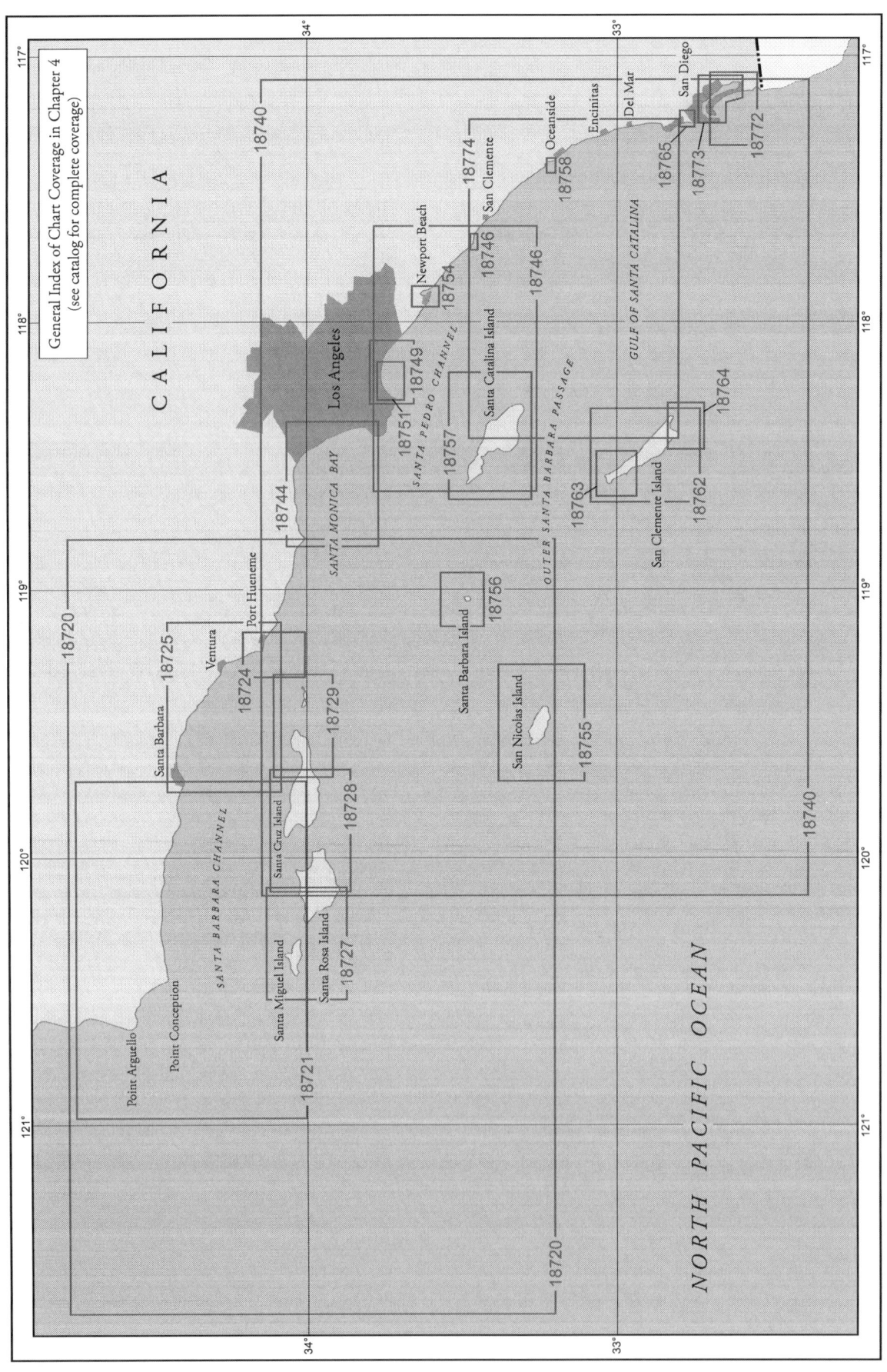

San Diego to Point Arguello, California

(1) This chapter describes the 240-mile irregular coast of southern California from the Mexican border to Point Arguello. The coast extends in a general NW direction and includes the major ports of San Diego, Long Beach, Los Angeles, and Port Hueneme. This chapter also describes the recreational and fishing ports of Oceanside, Newport Beach, Ventura, Santa Barbara, and the many other ports on San Pedro and Santa Monica Bays and along the Santa Barbara Channel.

COLREGS Demarcation Lines

(2) The lines established for this part of the coast are described in **80.1104 through 80.1126**, chapter 2.

Chart 18022

(3) There are several islands and dangers from 7 to 100 miles off the southern California coast; they are described in chapter 5.

(4) Many restricted and danger areas are in these waters. (See **334.860, 334.870, 334.880, and 334.890**, chapter 2 for limits and regulations.) In addition, missile firing, gunnery, and bombing operations are conducted on and over offshore waters not included in the areas defined in chapter 2, and at times endanger surface vessels. Information about these areas is published in Local Notice to Mariners issued by Commander, Eleventh Coast Guard District, Alameda, CA, and Notices to Mariners issued by National Geospatial-Intelligence Agency, Washington, D.C.

(5) Submerged submarine operations are conducted at various times in the waters off the coast of southern California; proceed with caution. (For information on submarine emergency identification signals, see chapter 1.)

Weather, San Diego to Point Arguello

(6) The mild climate from San Diego to Point Arguello is controlled by the Pacific high-pressure system. Aided by the sea breeze, it brings winds from off the water, mainly S through N, which help keep coastal temperatures up in winter and down in summer. Coldest average temperatures range from the middle to upper fifties (12° to 16°C), while summertime readings are most often in the seventies (22° to 27°C). Occasionally a hot dry flow off the land in autumn will cause temperatures to soar into the nineties (33° to 38°C), and a rare winter outbreak from the E can drop temperatures to below freezing (<0°C). Winter is the rainy season, although not much rain falls along these coasts.

(7) Strong winds and rough seas, while less frequent than farther N, can be a problem from the middle of fall through late spring. Strong pressure gradients, distant storms, and infrequent close storms account for most of the gales and seas of 12 feet (3.7 m) or more, particularly off Point Arguello and in the Santa Barbara Channel. Strong local winds (Santa Ana) also generate gales along sections of this coast.

(8) Advection or sea fog, formed by warm moist air flowing over cool water, frequently confronts mariners in these waters. It is a persistent and widespread problem, particularly in the summer and fall N of Santa Monica, and in fall and winter S of Santa Monica.

Blue, fin and humpback whales

(9) All whales are protected under the Marine Mammal Protection Act (MMPA) and, when in Sanctuary waters, under the National Marine Sanctuaries Act (NMSA). Certain large whales, including blue, fin and humpback whales, are also listed as endangered under the Endangered Species Act (ESA). See chapter 3 for more information.

Charts 18740, 18765

(10) In clear weather, vessels coming from S will sight Table Mountain, and its surrounding high land, and Los Coronados before picking up the San Diego landmarks.

(11) **Table Mountain** (chart 18022), conspicuous and flat-topped, is in Mexico, 25 miles SE of Point Loma and 6 miles inland.

(12) **Los Coronados (Coronado Islands)** are four bare, rocky islands, extending 4.5 miles in a NW direction, 7 miles offshore in Mexican waters, and 15 miles S of Point Loma. These islands are prominent in clear weather, and the passage E of them is commonly used by vessels. Depths in the vicinity of the islands are irregular, and in thick weather or at night caution must be observed when near them.

(13) A light is shown from a white cylindrical masonry tower on the S end of the S island; it is obscured from certain directions by the N islands. Another light is shown from a white square masonry tower near the N end of the S island; local fog sometimes obscures it.

(14) The boundary between the United States and Mexico is marked by a 14-foot white marble obelisk on a pedestal 41 feet above the water near the edge of a low table

bluff. The visible marker is 200 yards from the beach and 10 miles 142° from Point Loma Light. A large circular concrete arena is conspicuous just S of the marker. A stone mound, 365 feet above the water and 1 mile E of the obelisk, marks another point on the boundary line. Directly N of the obelisk the mesa falls to the low marshy land S of San Diego Bay.

(15)   About 1.5 miles N of the border at Imperial Beach is a fishing pier extending 400 yards to seaward.

(16)   In the approach from seaward in clear weather, San Clemente Island, the southernmost of the off-lying islands, will be sighted before the distinguishing features of the coast are seen. This will check the vessel's position and indicate subsequent shaping of the course for Point Loma. Upon a nearer approach, Cuyamaca Peak and the high land of the interior, Los Coronados, and Point Loma will be distinguished. Several aerolights in the vicinity of San Diego are visible at night from seaward.

(17)   When making the approach to San Diego, useful radar targets are San Clemente Island, Los Coronados, the pleasure piers at Imperial Beach and Ocean Beach, the jetties of Mission Bay, Point Loma, and Ballast Point.

(18)   When entering the harbor, the buoys marking the channel and Ballast Point are easily identified targets, thence Shelter Island, the radar reflector on North Island, and the various piers on either side of the channel; thence Harbor Island, the Coast Guard station pier, B Street Pier, and the Tenth Avenue Marine Terminal.

Charts 18773, 18772

(19)   **San Diego Bay**, where California's maritime history began in 1542, is 10 miles NW of the Mexican boundary. In September of that year, Juan Rodriquez Cabrillo, the Spanish explorer, sailed his frail bark into the bay. The bay is considered one of the finest natural harbors in the world, and affords excellent protection in any weather; it is free of excessive tidal current movements. A low, narrow sandspit, which expands to a width of 1.6 miles at North Island on its NW end, separates the bay from the ocean.

(20)   The city of **San Diego** is on the NE shore of the bay. **Coronado** is on the sandspit opposite San Diego. **National City** and **Chula Vista** are S of San Diego on the SE shore of the bay. The principal wharves are at San Diego and National City. Coronado, connected to San Diego by a highway bridge, is a residential and resort area of little commercial importance.

Prominent features

(21)   **Point Loma**, on the W side of the entrance to San Diego Bay, is a ridged peninsula with heights of about 400 feet. The ridge is bare of trees except in the gullies and where planted around the houses near the summit, and is sparsely covered with grass, sagebrush, and cactus. The tanks and buildings of a sewage treatment plant are conspicuous about 0.9 mile N of the point. At a distance the point usually has the appearance of an island. **Point Loma Light** (32°39'54"N., 117°14'33"W.), 88 feet above the water, is shown from a black house on a 70-foot white square pyramidal skeleton tower at the S end of the point. The light has a sound signal. Thick kelp beds extend more than 1.5 miles S of the point, and a sunken wreck is about 0.5 mile S of the light.

(22)   On the nearer approach, an abandoned lighthouse will be seen on the highest part of the hill immediately back of Point Loma Light. The old lighthouse and grounds form the **Cabrillo National Monument**, honoring the discoverer of San Diego Bay. The statue of Cabrillo, about 300 yards NE of the abandoned lighthouse, is reported to be an excellent mark when fog obscures the old lighthouse. From inside the bay, prominent objects along the crest of the ridge are a large red and white checkered elevated tank, a green standpipe, and a tall lookout tower all about 2.5 miles N from the light.

(23)   **Ballast Point**, low and sandy, projects 0.4 mile NE from the E side of Point Loma, 1.3 miles N from Point Loma Light. **Ballast Point Light B** (32°41'11"N., 117°13'58"W.), 16 feet above the water, is shown from a dolphin with a green and white diamond-shaped daymark off the end of the point; the light has a sound signal. Three piers of the Naval Submarine Base are just N of Ballast Point.

(24)   **North Island**, the filled NW end of the sandspit on the E side of the bay entrance, is Naval Base Coronado. On its SE side is the City of Coronado. Prominent features that show up well from the entrance are the tall condominiums at Coronado Shores 2.7 miles E of the entrance, the cupola of Hotel del Coronado 3 miles E of the entrance, and the tower of the Naval Air Station Administration Building, which is marked by an aerolight and is operated intermittently with varying characteristics. In clear weather the skyline of the city of San Diego is very prominent on the S approach.

COLREGS Demarcation Lines

(25)   The lines established for San Diego Harbor are described in **80.1104**, chapter 2.

Channels

(26)   A **Federal project** provides for a dredged channel with depths of 47 feet in the entrance and through North San Diego Bay to the turning basin on the NE side of North Island (near Pier K), thence 42 feet to just NW of the San Diego-Coronado Bay bridge, thence 37 feet to a basin SW of the National City Marine Terminal. (See Notice to Mariners and the latest editions of charts for controlling depths.)

Anchorages

(27)   General anchorages, special anchorages, and anchorages for Government vessels have been established in San Diego Bay. (See **110.1, 110.90, and 110.210**, chapter 2, for limits and regulations.) The Port of San

Diego has temporarily prohibited anchoring or mooring in **Special Anchorage A-8** (Sweetwater Anchorage), in South San Diego Bay, through the end of 2011. The anchorage is currently undergoing environmental restoration and clean-up.

(28) Permission to use anchorage berths 212 through 216 and Mooring Buoy 19, S of Harbor Island, must be obtained from Navy Afloat Training Group Pacific at 619–556–0900.

(29) Vessels waiting outside the entrance for a pilot will find good anchorage in 36 feet or more SE of the entrance to the channel, although permission to anchor in the restricted area must be obtained from the local naval authorities. For permission to use anchorage berths 125, 126, 147, 158, and 171, contact Navy Afloat Training Group Pacific at 619–556–0900. For permission to use anchorage berths 124, 135, 146, and 170, contact Navy Region Southwest Port Operations at 619–556–1433. For permission to use all other anchorage berths off Silver Strand, contact COMNVBEACHGRU at 619–437–2476. The area in the lee of Point Loma, S of Ballast Point and W of the E line of the project channel, is reserved for pilot boats and harbor patrol or U.S. Government craft. (See **334.880**, chapter 2, for limits and regulations.)

Dangers

(30) A submerged jetty, marked by lights and a sound signal at the seaward end, extends 1 mile S along **Zuñiga Shoal** from **Zuñiga Point**, the SW extremity of North Island. The outer two-thirds of the jetty has only small sections visible at high water. The lights marking the jetty have a white daymark with orange border and the words "DANGER SUBMERGED JETTY."

(31) A submerged jetty, marked by lights with daymarks that read "DANGER SUBMERGED JETTY," extends about 220 yards W from Zuñiga Point.

(32) There are numerous wrecks and obstructions in the shallow area of SE San Diego Bay. Caution should be exercised when navigating outside the marked channels.

Regulated Navigation Areas

(33) **Restricted areas** are: in the waters off the entrance to San Diego Bay; in the lee of Point Loma and S of Ballast Point; between Ballast Point and Zuñiga Point (degaussing station); adjacent to the W side of North Island; 0.4 mile N of Ballast Point, W of the dredged channel; off the NE side of North Island surrounding the Navy Pier; adjacent to and extending SE from the entrance channel to Glorietta Bay. (See **33 CFR 334.860, 334.865, 334.870, 334.880 and 334.890**, chapter 2, for limits and regulations.)

(34) **Security zones** are: on the W side of the entrance to San Diego Bay surrounding the Naval Base, extending from Ballast Point to just S of the entrance to Shelter Island Yacht Basin (**165.1102**, chapter 2); adjacent to the W and NE sides of North Island (**165.1105 and 165.1104**, chapter 2); around the Navy Pier adjacent to Broadway Pier (**165.1121**, chapter 2); surrounding the Naval Amphibious Base just S of the entrance channel to Glorietta Bay (**165.1120**, chapter 2); surrounding the Naval Station along the waterfront of National City from Chollas Creek to Pier 14 (**165.1101**, chapter 2); within 25 yards of all piers, abutments, fenders, and pilings of the Coronado Bay Bridge (**165.1110**, chapter 2). (See **33 CFR 165.1101, 165.1102, 165.1104, 165.1105, 165.1110, 165.1120, and 165.1121**, chapter 2, for limits and regulations.)

(35) A series of floating protection barriers, anchored by lighted buoys, surrounds the Naval facilities within the security zones: on the W side of the entrance to San Diego Bay; just N of Ballast Point, on the NE side of North Island; and of the Naval Station along the waterfront of National City.

(36) **Security zones** are in effect around all cruise ships entering, leaving, or anchored in the Port of San Diego Bay. (See **33 CFR 165.1108**, chapter 2, for limits and regulations.)

(37) **Regulated navigation areas** have been established in all waters of San Diego Bay, Mission Bay, and their approaches, and adjacent to the Naval Submarine Base just N of Ballast Point, extending E across the channel to the W shore of North Island. (See 33 **CFR 165.1122** and **165.1107**, chapter 2, for limits and regulations.)

(38) A **safety zone** is E of Harbor Island on the N side of the bay. (See **33 CFR 165.1106**, chapter 2, for limits and regulations.)

Bridges

(39) A fixed highway bridge linking San Diego and Coronado crosses San Diego Bay 0.3 mile SE of the Tenth Avenue Marine Terminal.

San Diego-Coronado Bay Bridge Clearances (feet)		
Span	Horizontal	Vertical
Piers 14 and 15	194	156
Piers 18 and 19	660	195
Piers 19 and 20	660	214
Piers 21 and 20	500	175
RACONS mark the center of the spans between piers 18-19 and 19-20 and a sound signal is on pier 19.		

Currents

(40) The currents set generally in the direction of the channels. In the vicinity of the entrance the usual velocity varies from 0.5 to 5 knots depending upon the stage of the tide. S of the end of the jetty there is a slight set toward Zuñiga Shoal on the ebb. Great care should be taken while passing Ballast Point as a vessel may take a sudden sheer because of a crosscurrent deflected from Ballast Point.

(41) The eddy usually encountered along the ends of the municipal piers makes docking difficult. The velocity and direction of the eddy are irregular, and the greatest care must be exercised by even the most experienced.

Strangers should not attempt to dock large vessels without a pilot. (See the Tidal Current Tables for daily predictions.)

Weather, San Diego

(42) In the San Diego Bay area, visibilities are reduced to less than 0.5 mile (0.9 km), mostly by radiation fog, on about 3 to 7 days per month from September through April. December is the foggiest month. This fog is worst during the late night and early morning hours. Dense soundis as frequent at North Island as it is at Imperial Beach. However, sound signals indicate that in general it is foggier around the entrance to the bay than it is in the N sections. For example, in December, the sound signal at Point Loma is operating about 20 percent of the time, compared to 10 percent at Ballast Point.

(43) Temperatures are moderate. The average high is 71°F (21.7°C) and the average low, 57°F (14°C). August is the warmest month with an average temperature of 72.2°F (22.3°C). Absolute extremes range 82°F (27.8°C) from an all-time high of 111°F (43.8°C) recorded in September 1963 to an absolute minimum of 29°F (1.7°C) in January 1949. Every month has seen temperatures of 90°F (32°C) or greater except January and December. Only January has recorded below freezing (0°C) temperatures.

(44) Precipitation is light and falls, on average, only 71 days each year. January is the wettest month when an average of just over two inches (51 mm) can be expected. January through March is the rainiest period where an average of eight days each month records precipitation. July is the driest month and June through October comprise the dry season. On average, only two one-hundredths (0.5 mm) of an inch falls in July while August is the most rain-free month when an average of only two days during the month records measurable rainfall. Annual precipitation measures less than ten inches (<254 mm) each year. The wettest year on record, 1978, documented 19.48 inches (495 mm) of precipitation and the driest year, 1953, saw only 3.41 inches (87 mm) of rainfall. Only trace amounts of snowfall have occurred on several occasions during the months of December and January.

(45) Winds in the area are strongest from March through September, when they blow 17 knots or more about 2 percent of the time. Gales are unheard of. Wind gusts have reached 50 knots or more during January. Strong winds often have a southerly component, but they also blow from the W and E. Winds along the coast are often affected by local topography, particularly when the flow is off the land. For example, at Imperial Beach, E winds blow 15 to 20 percent of the time from November through March. At Lindbergh Field Municipal Airport, prevailing winds are out of the N through NE during this period. W through NW winds are also common at both places. They become increasingly more frequent by March. During the late spring and summer, SW through NW winds prevail at both locations. However, at the more exposed Imperial Beach, W winds occur up to 25 percent of the time, whereas the flow is more variable at San Diego. By October, the winter wind regime begins to reestablish itself.

(46) No vessel over 1,600 designed displacement tons should transit the Coronado Bay Bridge in low visibility conditions if the bridge is not held visually within stopping distance. Tank ships or barges carrying petroleum products, explosive or other hazardous materials should not commence a movement in the approaches to or within the outer or inner harbor of San Diego when visibility of less than 0.5 mile or 1,000 yards is prevalent.

(47) The National Weather Service maintains an office at Lindbergh Field Municipal Airport; barometers may be compared there or by telephone.

(48) (See Appendix B for **San Diego climatological table**.)

Pilotage, San Diego

(49) All foreign vessels and vessels from a foreign port or bound thereto, and all vessels over 300 gross tons sailing under register between the port of San Diego and any other U.S. port, are subject to pilotage. Further information regarding pilotage requirements are detailed in the Pilotage section of the **Port of San Diego Tariff**, available through the ship's agent or directly from the Port District at (619) 686–6343.

(50) Vessels sailing under enrollment and licensed, and engaged in the coasting trade, between the port of San Diego and other U.S. ports, are exempt from all pilotage, unless a pilot is actually employed.

(51) Pilotage and berthing requirements for naval vessels are coordinated by Navy Region Southwest Port Operations, 619–556–1433.

(52) San Diego Bay is served by the San Diego Bay Pilots Association, Inc., which maintains an office at the Tenth Avenue Marine Terminal. 626 Switzer Street, San Diego, CA 92101. The pilot boat monitors VHF-FM channels 16 and 12, 1 hour prior to scheduled vessel arrivals; VHF-FM channel 12 is used as a working frequency. If contact with the pilot is needed prior to 1 hour in advance of arrival, information should be relayed via the ship's agent.

(53) The San Diego Bay Pilots have two pilot boats; a 65-foot white vessel with the word PILOT on the front of the fly bridge and a 38-foot white monohull with the word PILOT on the front of the wheelhouse. Both boats display the International Code flag 'H' while engaged in pilotage duties during daylight hours and white over red lights at night.

(54) Arrangements for pilots are made via ship's agent and boarding information via radio by calling "San Diego Pilots" on VHF-FM channel 12. Pilots request incoming vessels contact them at least 1 hour prior to arrival and provide estimated time of arrival and draft.

(55) Pilots board vessels in the vicinity of San Diego Bay Approach Lighted Whistle Buoy SD (32°37'20"N., 117°14'45"W.) When approaching San Diego, vessels should pass to the S and E of the buoy leaving it on the

	Name	Location	Berthing Space (feet)	Depths* (feet)	Deck Height (feet)	Mechanical Handling Facilities and Storage	Purpose	Owned/ Operated by:
1	B Street Pier Cruise Ship Terminal	32°43'03"N., 117°10'36"W.	2,400	35-37	13	Passenger terminal	• Mooring cruise ships • Boarding passengers	San Diego Unified Port District
2	Broadway Pier	32°42'57"N., 117°10'36"W.	2,030	35	13	n/a	• Mooring cruise ships • Mooring miscellaneous excursion vessels and craft for US Customs	San Diego Unified Port District
3	Tenth Avenue Marine Terminal (Berths 1 and 2)	32°42'05"N., 117°09'32"W.	1,120	30-32	13	• Tank storage (167,850 barrels) • Pipelines extend from storage tanks to berths	• Receipt and shipment of conventional and containerized general cargo and perishable food • Bunkering vessels	San Diego Unified Port District/Jankovich & Son
4	Tenth Avenue Marine Terminal (Berths 3, 4, 5 and 6)	32°41'55"N., 117°09'28"W.	2,580	35-36	13	• Covered storage (40,000 tons) • Open storage (3.5 acres) • Tank storage (3 million gallons) • One traveling gantry cement unloader served by a conveyer	• Receipt and shipment of conventional and containerized general cargo and perishable food • Receipt of bulk fertilizer and cement • Bunkering vessels	San Diego Unified Port District/Jankovich & Son/Pacific Coast Cement Corp.
5	Tenth Avenue Marine Terminal (Berths 7 and 8)	32°41'48"N., 117°09'12"W.	920	20-42	13	• Tank/Silo storage (33,000 metric tons) • One traveling bulk shiploader served by a belt conveyer	• Receipt and shipment of miscellaneous dry bulk commodities and conventional/containerized general cargo • Bunkering vessels	San Diego Unified Port District/Jankovich & Son/North American Terminals, Inc.
6	National City Marine Terminal (Berths 24-1 and 24-2)	32°39'25"N., 117°07'18"W.	1,400	20-35	13	• Open storage (107 acres) • Covered storage (40,320 square feet) • Tank storage (348,000 barrels)	• Receipt and shipment of general cargo and automobiles • Occasional reciept of fuel oil	San Diego Unified Port District
7	National City Marine Terminal (Berths 24-3 and 24-4)	32°39'14"N., 117°07'18"W.	1,000	35-37	13	• One traveling container crane (40 long tons) • One mobile straddle carrier (40 tons)	• Receipt and shipment of conventional and containerized general cargo and automobiles • Occasional reciept of fuel oil	San Diego Unified Port District
8	National City Marine Terminal (Berths 24-10 and 24-11)	32°38'56"N., 117°06'54"W.	1,500	35	13	Open storage (76 acres)	• Receipt and shipment of conventional general cargo and automobiles • Receipt of lumber • Shipment of cattle	San Diego Unified Port District

*The depths given above are reported. For information on the latest depths contact the port authorities or the private operators.

port side when making the approach, unless otherwise directed by the pilot. When boarding, pilots request vessels maintain a speed of 7 knots and rig the pilot ladder 6 feet above the water on the lee side.

The San Diego Unified Port District operates a VHF-FM radio station from Harbor Control Headquarters at Shelter Island for contacting merchant ships, port pilots, and other nearby stations. Channel 16 is for calling; channels 12 and 17 are for port operations. The station call sign is KJC-824.

Towage

Tugs to 3,500 hp are available from commercial operators in the San Diego area. Naval tugs handle navy vessels, but will assist commercial vessels in emergencies.

Quarantine, customs, immigration, and agriculture quarantine

(See chapter 3, Vessel Arrival Inspections, and Appendix A for addresses.) U.S. Customs requires that all non-commercial vessels, including corporate yachts, less than 130 feet in length returning from a foreign port or place, report directly to the Harbor Police Dock (32°42'30"N., 117°14'05"W.) on Shelter Island. When space is unavailable at the dock, vessels should utilize one of the three quarantine buoys located across from the dock until space is available. Commercial and non-commercial vessels greater than 130 feet in length returning from a foreign port or place, must contact the Harbor Police Communications Center at 619–686–6272, eight hours prior to arrival and request dock space. Only the master may leave the vessel to contact the U.S. Customs Service in order to request an inspector respond to Shelter Island. All persons aboard the clearing vessel are quarantined to the vessel until cleared by Customs. Additionally, no visitors are allowed aboard the vessel. Persons of foreign nationality should identify themselves to make arrangements to declare entry into the county with the Immigration and Naturalization Service. Officials usually board documented vessels at their berths. United States Customs can be reached at 619–685–4300, 24-hours a day.

(59) **Quarantine** is enforced in accordance with regulations of the U.S. Public Health Service. (See Public Health Service, chapter 1.)

(60) San Diego is a **customs port of entry**.

Coast Guard

(61) Coast Guard Sector San Diego is on the mainland just NE of the E end of Harbor Island. Coast Guard Sector San Diego is a consolidated unit that includes an air station, a small boat station, cutters, an aids-to-navigation team, a command center and other personnel. The Prevention Department handles the business of the former Marine Safety Office (see Appendix A for address); telephone, 619–278–7000. On San Diego Bay adjacent to the base is a **safety zone** for Coast Guard search and rescue and law enforcement missions.

Harbor regulations

(62) The Port of San Diego is under control of the San Diego Unified Port District. Rules and regulations are enforced by a Port Director, who is appointed by the Board of Port Commissioners. The general offices of the port district are at 3165 Pacific Highway, San Diego. The manager of marine operations and the chief wharfinger have offices at the Tenth Avenue Marine Terminal, 687 Switzer Street, San Diego. The office of wharfinger can be reached by telephone at 619–686–6346 or fax 619–686–6354.

(63) The Coast Guard Captain of the Port, San Diego, has designated the ship channels in San Diego Harbor as "narrow channels" for the purposes of enforcing Rule 9 of the Navigation Rules. Vessels of less than 20 meters (65.6 feet), sailing vessels, vessels engaged in fishing, and crossing vessels shall not impede the passage of a vessel that can safely navigate only within a narrow channel.

(64) The State of California, with the approval of the Environmental Protection Agency, has established a No-Discharge Zone (NDZ) in San Diego Bay. The NDZ is comprised of the portion of San Diego Bay that is less than 30 feet deep at mean lower low water (MLLW), as determined from the most recent NOAA nautical chart.

(65) Within the NDZ, discharge of sewage, whether treated or untreated, from all vessels is prohibited. Outside the NDZ, discharge of sewage is regulated by **40 CFR 140** (see Chapter 2).

(66) In addition to the **No-Discharge Zone** and concurrent with the federal regulations above, the **San Diego Unified Port District Code** (section 8.50) prohibits the discharge of any material, including sewage, into San Diego Bay without written permission by the Port Director.

Wharves

(67) The **San Diego Unified Port District** owns the deepwater commercial facilities in the bay and operates them either independently or in conjunction with private firms. The port piers and wharves have water, rail, and highway connections. There are a number of smaller privately operated wharves and piers used for receiving oil, repairing vessels, and for mooring and fueling small craft. Only the deep-draft commercial facilities are listed in the table. The alongside depths given for each facility listed are reported depths. (For information on latest depths, contact the Port of San Diego.) For a complete description of the port facilities, refer to Port Series No. 27, published and sold by the U.S. Army Corps of Engineers. (See Appendix A for address.)

(68) General cargo at the port is usually handled by ship's tackle; special handling equipment, if available, is listed in the table for the particular facility.

(69) In the port area, the San Diego Unified Port District and private companies operate warehouses having a total of 764,500 square feet of dry storage space and 1,997,400 cubic feet of cold storage space. A large amount of transit shed space and open storage is available.

Supplies

(70) Marine supplies of all kinds are available in San Diego. Bunker fuel, diesel oil, and lubricants are available. Large vessels can be bunkered via pipeline at the Tenth Avenue Marine Terminal, or arrangements can be made to fuel at all commercial berths from barges. Water is available at most of the berths.

Repairs

(71) There are shipbuilding and repair yards in San Diego with floating drydocks, the largest of which has a lifting capacity of 25,000 tons. The largest marine railway can handle craft up to 1,000 tons. Complete shipyard facilities are available for all types of repair work.

(72) A U.S. Navy graving dock, located at the naval station near the foot of 32nd Street, may be used by local repair firms by prior arrangements with the San Diego Unified Port District and local naval authorities. The dock has a clear inside length of 693 feet and an entrance width of 90 feet. The dock is served by a 27½-ton full portal traveling crane. The graving dock at National Steel and Shipbuilding Co., about 0.9 mile NW of the Navy graving dock, has a clear length of 998 feet and an entrance width of 176 feet.

Communications

(73) San Diego has transcontinental railroad connections to the N and E. Major airline service is available at San Diego International Airport, Lindbergh Field. San Diego is the port of call for many steamship and cruise lines. Major bus, railroad, and motor freight lines serve the city.

Small-craft facilities

(74) **Shelter Island**, across the channel from North Island and 1.5 miles above Ballast Point, includes the **Shelter Island Yacht Basin** on the S and the **Americas**

Cup Harbor on the N. Shelter Island is the most important small-boat area in San Diego Bay. The yacht basin has several large marinas and yacht clubs. It can accommodate more than 2,000 boats at its piers, floats, and moorings. The entrance channel has depths of 20 feet to inside the entrance, thence 15 feet to most of the facilities; the least depth is 9 feet. The entrance is marked by lights. The **354°** lighted range marking the entrance to San Diego Bay also marks the approach to the entrance to Shelter Island Yacht Basin. The **harbor police** are at the Harbor Control Headquarters just inside the entrance to the yacht basin. The police dock is also the boarding station for the inspection of small craft by Customs, Public Health, Immigration and Agricultural quarantine personnel when such inspections are necessary. Harbor police boats, providing fire protection, law enforcement, and assistance to small boats in distress, operate from this facility on a 24-hour basis. Overnight berths for transient vessels are usually available at one of the marinas; if no such berth is available, temporary mooring or berthing may be made available through the harbor police. The Americas Cup Harbor has accommodations for over 600 vessels and is the home port for many commercial fishing vessels. Repair yards in the basin have marine railways that can handle craft up to 800 tons. All kinds of repairs to small vessels may be obtained here. Both the yacht basin and the Americas Cup Harbor have fueling docks, a launching ramp, and marine supplies.

(75) **Harbor Island**, about 0.5 mile NE of Shelter Island, is in the northernmost part of the bay. **Harbor Island West Basin** has berthing and mooring accommodations for nearly 1,600 craft. A number of marinas, hotels, restaurants, and shops are along the shore of the basin. A light shows from atop a building near the W end of the island.

(76) A **090°–270° measured nautical mile** is off the S side of Harbor Island. Each range is marked by two diamond-shaped markers.

(77) **Glorietta Bay**, on the S side of Coronado and 6 miles from Ballast Point, is a small-craft harbor occupied by a yacht club and a small marina. The facilities include berths for over 215 yachts and small craft. A channel marked by lighted and unlighted buoys and a **232°** lighted range leads from the main channel in San Diego Bay to the basin in Glorietta Bay. In 2004, the controlling depth in the channel was 15 feet; thence in 1993, depths of 15 to 17 feet were reported in the basin with lesser depths along the edges. A 5 mph **speed limit** is enforced in Glorietta Bay. Water, ice, and a launching ramp are available.

(78) A **restricted area**, marked by buoys, is outside the SE limit of the channel into Glorietta Bay. (See **334.860**, chapter 2, for limits and regulations.)

(79) A **security zone** is also outside the SE limit of the channel into Glorietta Bay, within the restricted area off the Naval Amphibious Base. (See **165.1 through 165.8, 165.30, 165.33, and 165.1120**, chapter 2, for limits and regulations.)

(80) **Speed Control Lights** cross South San Diego Bay, near the head, N of Chula Vista.

(81) **Chula Vista Harbor** is on the E side near the head of South San Diego Bay at Chula Vista. The entrance is protected by breakwaters marked at the outer ends by private lights. The entrance channel and basin channel are marked by private buoys, lights, and daybeacons. In 2002, the approach to the basin had a reported depth of 18 feet with 16 feet reported alongside the piers. Berthing, electricity, water, ice, sewage pump-out, nautical supplies, and a launching ramp are available.

Chart 18740

(82) The 80-mile coast between San Diego Bay and San Pedro Bay is thickly settled, and the buildings of numerous towns and resorts are prominent from offshore. Several small-boat harbors and the port of Newport Bay are along the coast.

(83) The first 11 miles of the coast, between Point Loma and Point La Jolla, is extremely rocky, and the kelp beds extend up to 2 miles from shore; vessels should stay well offshore.

(84) About 1 mile N of Point Loma Light is a submerged sewer outfall line extending about 1 mile to the W.

(85) **Ocean Beach**, 5 miles N of Point Loma, has a large Y-shaped fishing pier with a private sound signal on the end.

Weather, Gulf of Santa Catalina

(86) Over the Gulf of Santa Catalina and along its shores, fog is a problem during fall and winter. This is most often a land (radiation) fog that drifts out over the gulf at night. By late morning, conditions begin to clear, particularly along the coast. Offshore, fog reduces visibilities to less than 0.5 mile (0.9 km) on about 4 to 9 days per month, from September through February and in May. September and October are the worst months. Along the coast, visibilities drop below 0.5 mile (0.9 km) on about 2 to 8 days per month from August through April. November, December, and February are the worst months.

(87) Gale force winds never occur as much as 1 percent of the time in the Gulf of Santa Catalina. They are infrequently encountered from November through April. Wind speeds of 17 knots or more occur about 1 to 3 percent of the time from December through May. Winds on the coast are often light. At Camp Pendleton, winds less than 3 knots occur 40 to 50 percent of the time from September through March. Seas are most likely to get choppy from November through April, when distant storms S of 40°N. generate W swells. These swells are 6 feet (1.8 m) or more, about 2 to 5 percent of the time. In winter, they occasionally exceed 9 feet (2.7 m) and some 12-foot (3.7 m) swells have been reported.

Chart 18765

(88) **Mission Bay**, entered between two jetties 5.5 miles N of Point Loma, is a recreational small-craft harbor administered by the city of San Diego. Lights mark the entrance to the bay as well as a sound signal on the outer end of the N jetty. The mariner radio activated sound signal is initiated by keying the microphone five times on VHF-FM channel 79A. A prominent feature when approaching the harbor is the municipal fishing pier at Ocean Beach, 0.3 mile S of the entrance. The lighted 338-foot tower at Sea World is prominent 1.8 miles E of the entrance. Sound signals are sounded from the fishing pier. A dredged channel leads from deep water in the Pacific Ocean to the highway bridge about 1.3 miles above the entrance. **Quivira Basin** and **Mariners Basin**, on the E and W sides of the channel, respectively, are entered about 1 mile above the entrance.

(89) In 2010, the controlling depth was 10 feet (20 feet at midchannel) in the dredged channel to the highway bridge; general depths of 15 to 18 feet were available in Mariners Basin with lesser depths along the edges and a depth of 20 feet was available in Quivira Basin. A jetty marked on its outer end by a light, extends about 125 yards NW from the S side of the entrance to Quivira Basin. The inner bay has depths of about 6 feet.

(90) The entrance to Mission Bay can be difficult to navigate under certain conditions. Large swells in any season and from virtually any direction can break completely across the entrance channel. With a rough sea outside, a heavy surge exists inside the bay, especially in Quivira Basin. Boats must be securely moored to prevent damage from this surge condition. Mission Bay contains an enormous amount of water which is funneled in and out of the narrow entrance channel with tidal changes. During periods of unusually large tidal flow, an extremely strong current may be present in the channel; mariners are urged to use caution when transiting the entrance.

No-Discharge Zone

(91) The State of California, with the approval of the Environmental Protection Agency, has established a No-Discharge Zone (NDZ) in Mission Bay. It encompasses the entire by (see NOAA chart 18765 for the zone limits).

(92) Within the NDZ, discharge of sewage, whether treated or untreated, from all vessels is prohibited. Outside the NDZ, discharge of sewage is regulated by **40 CFR 140** (see Chapter 2).

COLREGS Demarcation Lines

(93) The lines established for Mission Bay are described in **80.1106**, chapter 2.

(94) Two fixed highway bridges cross Mission Bay. The first, crossing above the entrance between Ventura Point and Sunset Point, has a clearance of 38 feet. The second, connecting Vacation Isle with Crown Point to the N and Dana Landing to the S, has a clearance of 31 feet under the N span and 38 feet under the S span.

(95) An aerial tramway cable, with a clearance of 42 feet, crosses the entrance to **Perez Cove**, immediately SE of Dana Landing.

(96) The San Diego City Lifeguard Headquarters and the San Diego Police Department, Mission Bay Harbor Unit, are on the S side of the entrance to Quivira Basin. Harbor regulations are enforced and emergency assistance is provided by the two units. The Lifeguard Service maintains a 24-hour watch on VHF-FM Channel 16 and handles all dispatches. Police matters are dispatched to the Police Harbor Patrol. Calls for assistance in Mission Bay and within 3 miles of the coastline, from Point Loma to the S, to Blacks Beach, about 3 miles N of Point La Jolla to the N, are the responsibility of the Lifeguard Service. Both units have patrol boats and make safety inspections. Water skiing, swimming, sailing, fishing and speed regulations are enforced in Mission Bay. Most regulations are posted; complete regulations are available from the City Lifeguard Headquarters Office. A full service repair facility is available in Quivira Basin. A 100-ton hoist for hull and engine repairs, gasoline, diesel fuel, water, ice, and marine supplies are available. There are numerous launching ramps and parking areas around the bay. The inner bay has several marinas and many private moorings.

Anchorages

(97) **Special anchorages** are along the W side of Mission Bay in **San Juan Cove**, **Santa Barbara Cove**, **Bonita Cove**, Mariners Basin, and Quivira Basin. (See **110.1 and 110.91**, chapter 2, for limits and regulations.)

(98) **Mission Beach**, 6.5 miles N of Point Loma, is an amusement place with prominent buildings. From seaward the highest part of the roller coaster looks like a dome.

(99) **Pacific Beach**, 8 miles N of Point Loma, has a pleasure pier extending about 260 yards from the beach. The pier was partially destroyed in the winter of 1984, and submerged piles are reported within 90 yards of the seaward end; caution is advised.

(100) A 2-mile rounding rocky point, 9 miles N of Point Loma, is the first high land N of San Diego Bay. The point is a spur from 822-foot **Soledad Mountain**. The S end of this headland is called **False Point**, and the N end is **Point La Jolla**. In the vicinity of Point La Jolla, rock cliffs with caves rise abruptly from the water to heights of 80 feet. The buildings at **La Jolla** and Pacific Beach, and the television towers on Soledad Mountain are prominent.

(101) **Scripps Institution of Oceanography**, one of the leading institutions in research in oceanography and marine biology, has extensive facilities 12 miles N of Point Loma. The institution maintains a long pier for observation purposes.

(102) Just N of Scripps Institution the bluffs rise to a height of 300 feet, then decrease gradually for the next 5 miles to heights of 20 to 80 feet.

(103) A **000°–180° measured nautical mile** has been established 13.5 miles N of Point Loma; each range is marked by two steel towers.

(104) **Del Mar**, 18 miles N of Point Loma, is a resort city.

(105) The coast from Del Mar N for 31 miles to San Mateo Point is a low, flat tableland with abrupt cliffs 60 to 130 feet high and with broad beaches. The tableland is intersected by numerous deep valleys with streams that usually dry in the summer. In the N part, the high ridges of the interior are much nearer the coast. Paralleling this coast are U.S. Highway 101 and a Class I railroad.

Charts 18740, 18774, 18758

(106) **Carlsbad**, 30 miles N of Point Loma, is a resort area with a number of hotels and motels. The stack of the San Diego Gas and Electric Co. near the S end of town is very prominent. The stack is marked by flashing white lights during the day and by fixed and flashing red lights at night. The company maintains a lighted bell buoy about 0.9 mile offshore. Mariners are cautioned to pass W of the lighted bell buoy because it marks the seaward end of a submerged pipeline. Near the N edge of town the low white square tower on the W end of the San Diego Army and Navy Academy is distinctive.

(107) The pleasure pier at **Oceanside**, 32.5 miles N of Point Loma, has a fish haven covered 10 feet around its seaward end. The pier is marked by lights.

(108) **Oceanside Harbor**, at the N end of the city, 1.2 miles NW of the pleasure pier, is a small-craft harbor administered by the City of Oceanside, Department of Harbor and Beaches. The harbor, which can accommodate about 950 small craft, shares a common entrance with Del Mar Boat Basin (**Camp Pendleton Marine Corps Base**) to the N.

(109) Prominent features when approaching the harbor include a large lighted sign reading "OCEANSIDE" in white letters on a blue background located on a grassy bluff overlooking the middle of the harbor, a tall condominium on the E side of the harbor, a lighted tower on the SE side of the harbor resembling a lighthouse, and a hotel in the vicinity of the harbor entrance.

(110) The common entrance to Oceanside Harbor and Del Mar Boat Basin is between two jetties. The long W jetty is marked by a single light at the seaward end, and the short E jetty has a N and S extension. The S extension has a light and sound signal at the seaward end; a light is at the outer end of the N extension. Inside the common entrance is a lighted junction buoy separating the entrance channels to Oceanside Harbor and Del Mar Boat Basin. The entrance channel for Oceanside Harbor is marked by lighted buoys, lights and a daybeacon. A submerged jetty, just N of the entrance channel to Oceanside Harbor, is marked by a danger buoy at its outer end.

No-Discharge Zone

(111) The State of California, with the approval of the Environmental Protection Agency, has established a No-Discharge Zone (NDZ) in Oceanside Harbor. It encompasses the entire harbor including Del Mar Boat Basin.

(112) Within the NDZ, discharge of sewage, whether treated or untreated, from all vessels is prohibited. Outside the NDZ, discharge of sewage is regulated by **40 CFR 140** (see Chapter 2).

COLREGS Demarcation Lines

(113) The lines established for Oceanside Harbor are described in **80.1108**, chapter 2.

Channels

(114) A dredged channel leads from deep water through the entrance jetties, thence branches E to Oceanside Harbor and N to Del Mar Boat Basin. Strangers should not attempt the entrance at night in rough seas without assistance. The entrance channel is subject to severe wave action and shoaling, and buoys are frequently shifted with changing conditions. Mariners are requested to contact the harbor patrol on VHF-FM channel 16 before entering.

Harbor regulations

(115) The harbor is under the control of the City of Oceanside, Department of Harbor and Beaches. The harbor headquarters building is on the E side of the harbor opposite the entrance. About 50 berths for transient craft are available at the harbor headquarters. All moorage must be arranged with the harbor office in the headquarters building. Prepaid reservations are accepted for 24 guest slips, with the remainder available on a first come, first served basis. The **Oceanside Harbor Police** operates from the headquarters building. The police boats are equipped with rescue and fire fighting equipment. The police boats monitor VHF-FM channel 16, 24 hours a day, and work on channel 12.

Weather, Oceanside

(116) Wind speeds at Oceanside rarely get above 28 knots; they are most likely to occur from December through April. Fog is sometimes a late night and early morning navigational hazard from August through March. During this period, visibilities drop below 0.5 mile (0.9 km) on 2 to 8 days per month; November is usually the foggiest month. The worst time of day is between midnight and 0500.

(117) Swells are most frequent from January through April.

Supplies

(118) Gasoline and diesel fuel are pumped at the fuel dock. Marine supplies, ice, and pumpout facilities are available.

Repairs

(119) A repair yard just N of the harbor district headquarters has a mobile lift that can handle craft to 42 feet and 14 tons. Hull, engine, and electronic repairs are available.

(120) **Del Mar Boat Basin (Camp Pendleton)**, just N of Oceanside Harbor, is part of the U.S. Marine Corps reservation. (See **334.910**, chapter 2, for limits and regulations of the **restricted area**.) The boat basin shares a common entrance with Oceanside Harbor. The channel is marked by buoys and daybeacons. A **restricted area** is off the outer breakwater. (See **334.900**, chapter 2, for limits and regulations.)

(121) A **military exercise area** extends about 3 miles seaward from about 2 miles NW of the boat basin northwestward to San Clemente. Mariners are advised to consult Eleventh Coast Guard District Local Notice to Mariners for scheduled exercise dates and times.

(122) A **restricted area** is within the military exercise area and centered about 4.5 miles NW of Del Mar Boat Basin entrance. (See **334.905**, chapter 2, for limits and regulations.)

(123) A red and white checkered elevated tank, 1.7 miles NE of the boat basin, is prominent from well offshore. The highway bridge and the trestlework of the railroad crossing of the **Santa Margarita River**, 1.7 miles W of the tank, also are prominent. A large white building nearly 7 miles NW of the boat basin is conspicuous from seaward.

(124) **San Onofre Mountain**, 44 miles N of Point Loma and 1.5 miles inland, is the highest of the coastal range in the area.

(125) **San Mateo Point**, locally known as **Cottons Point** and 47 miles NW of Point Loma, ends in cliffs 60 feet high and is the N head at the mouth of **San Mateo Creek**. Both San Mateo Creek and **Arroyo San Onofre**, a mile SE, are crossed by a trestle. Two large domes of a nuclear powerplant are 2.3 miles SE of San Mateo Point. A smaller dome-shaped building is on top of the bluff a few hundred yards SE.

(126) **San Mateo Point Light** (33°23'18"N., 117°35'45"W.), 63 feet above the water, is shown from a pole with a red and white diamond-shaped daymark on San Mateo Point.

Charts 18740, 18774, 18746

(127) From San Mateo Point to Dana Point, 7.5 miles NW, the land is higher and more rugged, and is broken by **San Juan Creek** about 1.5 miles E of Dana Point. The railroad and the highway run close together along the beach under the bluffs in this stretch of the coast to San Juan Creek, where the railroad turns inland.

(128) **San Clemente**, 2 miles N of San Mateo Point, has many white houses with red-tiled roofs, making the place conspicuous from the sea. There is a small pleasure pier at the town; a fish haven covered 10 feet is off its seaward side. A reef that uncovers 3 feet is about 700 yards NW of the pier.

(129) **Dana Point**, 8 miles NW of San Mateo Point, is the seaward end of a high ridge. The spur forming the point ends in a moderately bold sandstone cliff 220 feet high with a precipitous broken face. Outlying rocks and ledges marked by a lighted whistle buoy extend offshore for 350 yards. **San Juan Rock**, 10 feet high and about 50 feet in extent, is 340 yards S of the highest point on the cliff, and a rock covered 2 fathoms is 2.4 miles SE of the point.

Charts 18740, 18746

(130) **Dana Point Harbor** is a small-craft harbor in the lee of Dana Point. The harbor, administered by the Orange County Harbor, Beaches, and Parks District, is entered from the E between two breakwaters each marked by a light on the seaward end. A sound signal is at the S light. The sound signal can be activated upon request to the Coast Guard by radiotelephone VHF-FM channel 16. A church with a giant cross is very visible on the hill above the harbor. A submerged sewer outfall line extends about 0.6 mile from shore, passing about 300 yards E of the S breakwater light. A rock, covered 7½ feet and marked by a lighted buoy, is about 300 yards NE of the S breakwater light. When entering the harbor care should be taken to remain clear of these dangers, especially during low stages of the tide and/or periods of heavy SE swell.

(131) Numerous uncharted private racing buoys are off the entrance to the harbor.

(132) The harbor's E and W basins are separated by a fixed highway bridge with a 45-foot channel span and a clearance of 20 feet. Berths in the E basin can accommodate over 1,400 vessels, and berths in the W basin can accommodate over 1,000 vessels. A **harbormaster** assigns berths in the harbor.

(133) The Dana Point Harbor Patrol has an office in the most southeasterly building observed after passing through the breakwater. Patrol craft equipped with rescue and fire fighting equipment are stationed here. The patrol maintains a 24-hour radio watch on 2182 kHz and VHF-FM channel 16. Berthing assignments for about 42 transient craft are available at the harbor patrol office.

(134) A **speed limit** of 5 mph is enforced in Dana Point Harbor. A swimming area, marked by private buoys, is in the NW corner of the harbor.

Anchorage

(135) A **special anchorage** is in the W part of the harbor. (See **110.1 and 110.93**, chapter 2, for limits and regulations.)

No-Discharge Zone

(136) The State of California, with the approval of the Environmental Protection Agency, has established a No-Discharge Zone (NDZ) in Dana Point Harbor. It encompasses the entire harbor (see NOAA chart 18746 or 18774 for the zone limits).

(137) Within the NDZ, discharge of sewage, whether treated or untreated, from all vessels is prohibited. Outside the NDZ, discharge of sewage is regulated by **40 CFR 140** (see Chapter 2).

COLREGS Demarcation Lines

(138) The lines established for Dana Point Harbor are described in **80.1110**, chapter 2.

Supplies and repairs

(139) Most supplies and repairs are available at the marinas and service facilities at the harbor. Lifts to 25 tons are available.

(140) **San Juan Capistrano**, a small town about 4 miles inland from Dana Point, is the site of the old mission founded in 1776. The grounds and the buildings have undergone extensive preservation, and services are held regularly in the chapel used by founding Father Junipero Serra. This mission is famous for the return of the swallows each March 19.

(141) The 11.5-mile coast from Dana Point to Newport Bay is bold with rocky cliffs 40 to 100 feet high; these are the seaward ends of ridges separated by narrow, deep valleys. The community of **Laguna Beach** is midway along this stretch. A fishing and pleasure pier is near the mouth of **Aliso Creek** about 3.5 miles NW of Dana Point.

(142) **Santiago Peak**, 17.5 miles NE of Dana Point and visible 80 miles, is the dominant feature of this part of the coast; the peak is double-headed and dark in contrast with the immediate coastal range.

Chart 18754

(143) **Newport Bay**, 64 miles NW of Point Loma, is an extensive lagoon bordered on the seaward side by a 3-mile sandspit. The bay is an important yachting and sport fishing center, and offers excellent anchorage for large yachts and small craft under all weather conditions. The city of **Newport Beach** embraces the districts of **Newport** and **Balboa**, on the sandspit, and **Corona del Mar**, E of the entrance.

Prominent features

(144) The numerous houses and buildings along the beach and on the hills back of the bay are prominent from seaward. The tall office buildings at the Newport Center, 1.4 miles N of the harbor entrance, are the most conspicuous. The memorial hospital building, 0.3 mile N of the turning basin, and the light-colored concrete school buildings on the high ground 1 mile back from the beach are also conspicuous.

(145) The entrance to Newport Bay is between jetties 275 yards apart with lights at their outer ends. A sound signal is at the W jetty light. The sound signal can be activated upon request to the Coast Guard by radiotelephone VHF-FM channel 16. A lighted bell buoy is off the entrance.

(146) A **111°37'–291°37' measured nautical mile** is in San Pedro Channel, about 1.3 miles W of the entrance to Newport Bay. The E range is marked in front by a daymark on an 800-foot pleasure pier and in the rear by a daymark on shore at Balboa Beach. The W range is marked by daymarks on shore at Newport Beach. Another 950-foot pleasure pier is 2.8 miles NW of the W jetty.

COLREGS Demarcation Lines

(147) The lines established for Newport Bay are described in **80.1112**, chapter 2.

Channels

(148) A **Federal project** provides for a 20-foot main channel from the entrance to a turning basin of the same depth NW of Lido Isle and a 10-foot Balboa Island North Channel extending N from the entrance along the E and N sides of Balboa Island. (See Notice to Mariners and latest editions of charts for controlling depths.)

Anchorages

(149) Special anchorages are in Newport Bay. (See **110.1 and 110.95**, chapter 2, for limits and regulations.) Assignments are made by the harbormaster.

Dangers

(150) A **speed limit** of 5 m.p.h. in Newport Bay has been established by the Orange County Harbors, Beaches, and Park District. The upper reaches of the bay are extremely shoal.

Bridges

(151) There are no bridges over the main channel. None of the bridges to the islands in the bay restrict passage to the anchorage areas.

Weather, Newport Bay

(152) Severe storms are rare. The Santa Ana is an exceptional wind that blows from the NE or E with great violence, although of short duration. (See Weather, Los Angeles, indexed as such, this chapter for discussion of Santa Ana winds.)

Harbor regulations

(153) The Orange County Harbors, Beaches, and Parks District controls the movement and berthing of vessels under the direction of a harbormaster, who has an office on the E side of the bay about 0.8 miles from the entrance. Patrol and assistance craft operate from the harbor office on a 24-hour basis. The harbor office may be contacted by telephone 949–723–1002 or VHF-FM channels 12 and 16. The patrol boats monitor VHF-FM channel 16.

Coast Guard

(154) A search and rescue craft of the U.S. Coast Guard is stationed at the pier adjacent to the Harbor District Headquarters.

Wharves

(155) The numerous small wharves and landings in the bay are mostly for the use of local yachts and fishing craft. Five berths and several offshore moorings are available for transient craft at the Harbor District Headquarters pier. The harbormaster must be consulted before mooring. Five other transient berths are usually available at a marina at the NW end of the turning basin.

Supplies

(156) Fuel, water, and marine supplies are available at most of the facilities in the bay.

Repairs

(157) The largest marine railway in Newport Bay has a capacity of 325 tons and can handle craft up to 150 feet. Machine shops are available. Several shipyards can haul out small boats for general repairs.

Chart 18746

(158) The 20-mile coast from Newport Bay to Point Fermin is low, and there are several lagoons near the beach. There are no trees near the shore; towns and resorts are almost continuous along the beach.

(159) **Huntington Beach State Park** is a recreational area that extends 2 miles NW along the coast from the mouth of **Santa Ana River**, which is 4.5 miles NW of Newport Bay entrance. The trestle crossing the mouth of this river is conspicuous. A buoy marks the seaward end of a terminal structure of a water conduit extending from shore 1.4 miles NW of Santa Ana River. The twin stacks of the Southern California Edison Co. plant on shore and a spire about 1 mile back from the beach are conspicuous from any direction.

(160) A submerged oil pipeline extends nearly 1.2 miles seaward, 2 miles NW of Santa Ana River; mooring buoys are off the end of the pipeline. **Huntington Beach**, a resort 5 miles NW of Newport Beach, is identified by its many oil derricks. The city has a fishing and pleasure pier which has a fish haven covered 10 feet around its seaward end. **Sunset Beach** is a small town 5 miles NW of Huntington Beach. An elevated tank is near the W extremity of the town.

Charts 18746, 18749

(161) **Anaheim Bay**, 14 miles NW of Newport Bay, is the site of the U.S. Naval Weapons Station. Jetties protect the entrance to the bay. Waters inside the jetties are within a **restricted area**, and **explosive anchorages** have been established on the E and W sides of the channel. (See **334.930 and 110.215**, chapter 2, for limits and regulations.) The Navy has implemented a protection barrier at the Naval Weapons Station in the bay. This barrier consists of alternating orange and white spherical buoys connected by wire rope. All boating traffic is required to stay within the small craft channel at all times.

(162) An entrance channel leads NE between converging jetties to a turning basin inside Anaheim Bay. (See Notice to Mariners and the latest editions of the chart for depths.) The channel is marked by lighted and unlighted buoys, lights, and a **036°48'** lighted range. The outer ends of the jetties are marked by lights; a sound signal is at the W jetty light. The sound signal can be activated upon request to the Coast Guard by radiotelephone VHF-FM channel 16.

(163) In Anaheim Bay, during a flooding tide, the current 50 to 75 yards from the Naval Weapons Station's pier flows E to W as opposed to the normal flow of W to E. This causes a ship approaching the berth for a portside mooring to experience difficulty in twisting to starboard. An ebbing tide has an opposite effect. After a heavy rain, runoff water from the area N of Anaheim Bay during an ebbing tide increases the rate of ebb up to 5 knots with resultant swirls and countercurrents.

COLREGS Demarcation Lines

(164) The lines established for Anaheim Bay are described in **80.1114**, chapter 2.

(165) **Huntington Harbour**, a small-boat basin, is just S of Anaheim Bay. The harbor is a private development, and, with the exception of two small marinas, consists of private docks adjacent to waterfront homes.

(166) The harbor is entered through the restricted waters of Anaheim Bay, and permission to pass must be obtained from the Commanding Officer, U.S. Naval Weapons Station, Seal Beach, CA. (See **334.930**, chapter 2, for regulations governing passage.)

(167) The **Harbor Patrol** office is adjacent to the boat launch ramp in the NW corner of the harbor. A repair yard can handle craft to 50 feet and 25 tons for engine and hull repairs. Gasoline, diesel fuel, and marine supplies are available in the harbor. Launching ramps are in the NW and SE corners of the harbor.

(168) **Seal Beach**, just NW of Anaheim Bay, has several resort structures and a 1,650-foot pleasure pier, which has a fish haven covered 9 feet at its seaward end.

(169) **Alamitos Bay**, 15 miles NW of Newport Bay, is the site of the **Long Beach Marina**, a small-craft harbor administered by the city of Long Beach Marine Department. The harbor is entered from the S between two jetties each marked by a light on the seaward end; a sound signal is at the W jetty light. The sound signal can be activated upon request to the Coast Guard by radiotelephone VHF-FM channel 16. In 2010, depths of 13 to 17 feet were available in the entrance channel.

(170) A dangerous wreck (33°43'45"N., 118°07'26"W.) is in the approach to the entrance of Alamitos Bay and a dangerous wreck (33°44'10"N., 118°07'35"W.), covered 19 feet, is just W of the entrance.

(171) A **general anchorage** has been designated around the entrance channel to Alamitos Bay. (See **33 CFR 110.214**, chapter 2, for limits and regulations.)

(172) The fixed bridge across Marine Stadium, which forms the inner part of the bay, has a fixed span with a clearance of 32 feet. A fixed bridge with a clearance of 13 feet crosses the junction of the W waterway and Marine Stadium. A fixed bridge, with a clearance of 11 feet, crosses the E waterway off Marine Stadium that leads to a NE basin. A fixed bridge, with a clearance of 4 feet, crosses the W waterway between Naples and Belmont Shore. The five fixed bridges crossing the Rivo Alto Canal on Naples Island have a least clearance of 7 feet, and the power cable has a reported clearance of 55 feet.

(173) Berths in Long Beach marina are limited to about 1,800 boats, but extensive parking and ramp-launching areas are provided for trailer-drawn craft. Visiting yachts may obtain temporary berthing on a first-come first-served basis. All mooring is controlled by a **harbormaster**, who has an office on the E side of the entrance channel near the end of the point about 500 yards above the bend in the channel.

Supplies and repairs

(174) All types of supplies and services are available at the marinas and service facilities in the bay. The largest repair yard can handle craft up to 40 tons and 60 feet.

(175) A pleasure pier on the W side of Belmont Shore, 1.7 miles NW of Alamitos Bay entrance, extends about 340 yards from the beach; a fish haven is 100 feet off the seaward end. A reported wreck covered 16 feet is about 940 yards S of the end of Belmont Pier.

Charts 18751, 18749

(176) **San Pedro Bay**, between Seal Beach on the E and Point Fermin on the W, is 82 miles NW of San Diego. On the shores of the bay are the cities and port areas of **Long Beach** and **Los Angeles. Terminal Island**, in the NW part of San Pedro Bay, separates the outer bay from Los Angeles and Long Beach inner harbors. The bay is protected by breakwaters and is a safe harbor in any weather.

(177) **Long Beach Harbor**, in the E part of San Pedro Bay, includes the City of Long Beach and part of Terminal Island.

(178) **Los Angeles Harbor**, at the W end of San Pedro Bay, includes the districts of **San Pedro, Wilmington**, and a major part of Terminal Island.

(179) Long Beach and Los Angeles Harbors are connected by Cerritos Channel. The distance between the seaward entrance to the two harbors is about 4 miles.

(180) Four oil production islands, marked by lights, are to the N and E of Long Beach Pier J. A sound signal is sounded from the S end of each island.

(181) The **Port of Long Beach**, one of the largest ports on the Pacific coast, has the reputation of being America's most modern port. It has extensive foreign and domestic traffic with modern facilities for the largest vessels. It is a major container cargo port with several of the largest and most efficient container terminals on the Pacific coast. Some of the principal exports are bulk petroleum, bulk coke, steel and steel products, bulk potash, grains, fresh fruits, scrap steel, animal feed, and copper concentrate. Some of the principal imports are crude petroleum, steel and steel products, motor vehicles and parts, machinery, bulk gypsum, newsprint, lumber, bulk salt, bananas, plywood, and bulk molasses.

(182) The **Port of Los Angeles**, also one of the largest ports on the Pacific coast, has a history of leading the Pacific coast ports in terms of tonnage handled. It has extensive facilities to accommodate all types of traffic. Some of the principal exports are crude minerals, iron and steel scrap, inorganic chemicals, animal feed, cotton, manufactured fertilizers, and fresh fruits and nuts. Some of the principal imports are iron and steel products, motor vehicles and parts, organic chemicals, fresh fruits/nuts, paper/paperboard, sugar, molasses and syrups, glass, and fresh/frozen fish.

Prominent features

(183) **San Pedro Hill** (chart 18746), 3.3 miles NW of Point Fermin, is the distinguishing feature for making San Pedro Bay from SE or W. The hill terminates seaward in steep, rocky cliffs about 60 feet high, with several horizontal terraces between them and the summit. On top of the summit are two large white radar domes.

(184) Because it is high above the usual low-lying fog area, the lighted tower atop Santa Catalina Island is reported a useful guide for vessels approaching the Los Angeles-Long Beach area; the light can be seen for about 16 miles.

(185) **Point Fermin**, the SE extremity of San Pedro Hill, is a bold cliff about 100 feet high. **Point Fermin Light** (33°42'17"N., 118°17'38"W.), 120 feet above the water, is shown from a pole on the southern extremity of the point. A prominent pavilion (The Bell of Friendship) is on the high ground about 0.3 mile N of the light.

Vessel Operating Procedures for Los Angeles/Long Beach
(Best Maritime Practices)

Anchoring Procedures

In addition to observing all port tariffs and U.S. Coast Guard regulations, the Master of any commercial vessel at anchor shall implement the following Standards of Care:
1. Maintain a 24-hour bridge watch by an English speaking licensed deck officer monitoring VHF-FM Channel 16.
2. Make frequent checks to assure vessel is not dragging anchor.
3. When winds exceed 40 knots, have the propulsion plant ready to bring on line on short notice and make another anchor ready to let go.
4. Provide 15-minute advance notice to the respective pilot station (inside anchorages) or to VTS (outside anchorages) before heaving anchor to get underway.

General Anchoring Guidelines

Outside the Federal breakwaters:
1. All anchorages outside the Federal breakwater will be managed and monitored by the Vessel Traffic Service (VTS).
2. Any vessel desiring to use one of these anchorages must advise their intentions to VTS on VHF-FM Channel 14 and receive clearance to do so from VTS.

Inside the Federal breakwaters:
1. All anchorages inside the Federal breakwater will be managed and monitored by the Long Beach and/or Los Angeles Pilot Station.

Under-Keel Clearance

Minimum clearances (between the deepest point on the vessel and the bottom in still water conditions) are established for these ports and depend upon transit/anchor location.
1. Between **Los Angeles Lighted Whistle Buoy 3** and **Los Angeles Main Channel Lighted Buoy 11**, and between **Long Beach Channel Approach Lighted Whistle Buoy** and **Long Beach Channel Lighted Buoy 3**, minimum under-keel clearance before correction for roll and pitch is 10 percent of vessel's draft.
2. In the channel between **Los Angeles Main Channel Lighted Buoy 11** and position off of designated berth, and in the channel between **Long Beach Channel Lighted Buoy 3** and position off of designated berth, minimum under-keel clearance is 1.5 feet (.46 meter).
3. Shifts via outer harbor between Los Angeles and Long Beach, minimum under-keel clearance is 3 feet (.91 meter).
4. Larger vessels require more under-keel clearance.
5. In the final approach to the berth, and while at berth, the vessel must always remain afloat.
6. Terminal or vessel operators may require minimum under-keel clearances that are more restrictive than the above guidelines.

Reduced Visibility

In Los Angeles/Long Beach harbors Standards of Care exist for movements in reduced visibility. The definition of reduced visibility is dependent upon vessel type and size, but generally ranges from 0.5 nautical mile to 1.0 nautical mile. Special provisions providing equivalent safety levels may permit some operation in reduced visibility. Whenever visibility inside the Federal breakwater is less than 0.5 mile, the respective Vessel Traffic Center (VTC) will impose one-way traffic where appropriate.

General guidelines for movements in reduced visibility without a pilot are:
1. Masters must make a positive evaluation of factors including, but not limited to, traffic in the harbors, planned transit speeds, vessel maneuverability, quality of the vessel's navigation systems, availability of assist tugs, and other special circumstances.
2. Vessels 1600 GT or greater shall make the following broadcast to the VTS on VHF-FM channel 14 at least 15 minutes prior to getting underway: *"Vessel name/call sign, making our inclement weather COTP notification, as per guidance within the Harbor Safety Plan, that we intend to transit from vessel location to intended destination."*
3. A safety broadcast shall also be made on VHF-FM Channel 13, and the vessel shall coordinate its movement with the appropriate Vessel Traffic Center (VTC).

(186) **Signal Hill**, Long Beach, rises to a height of 355 feet about 2 miles from the beach, and is readily recognized because of several radio towers around it.

(187) In Long Beach Harbor, prominent charted objects are a green hotel tower (marked by a large blue letter "b") located just N of the Municipal Auditorium, and the white stone tower of another hotel 0.4 mile E, and the lighted large white dome on the S side of the entrance to Queensway Bay. The derricks on the artificial oil islands E of Long Beach Pier J are constructed to appear as high-rise apartment buildings.

(188) Prominent charted objects in Los Angeles Harbor which are of use to the navigator are the green and white tank near the S end of Pier 1, the lighted radio tower atop San Pedro City Hall, and the stack on Terminal Island.

(189) **Long Beach Light** (33°43'23"N., 118°11'13"W.), 50 feet above the water, is shown from a 42-foot white rectangular tower on a white building on the E end of Middle Breakwater; a sound signal is at the light.

(190) **Note:** The Long Beach Pilots have established a current meter in about 57 feet of water 0.41 mile and bearing 198.5° from Long Beach Light. A cable runs from the meter to the Long Beach Light. Mariners are requested to avoid anchoring or bottom fishing in this area.

(191) **Los Angeles Light**, (33°42'31"N., 118°15'06"W.), 73 feet above the water, is shown from a white

cylindrical tower with black stripes on a concrete block on the outer end of the San Pedro breakwater; a sound signal is at the light.

COLREGS Demarcation Lines

(192) The lines established for San Pedro Bay are described in **80.1114**, chapter 2.

Traffic Separation Scheme

(193) **Traffic Separation Scheme, Los Angeles/Long Beach**, also known as **Traffic Separation Scheme, Gulf of Santa Catalina**, is in the approaches to Los Angeles/Long Beach. The Scheme leads from the Gulf of Santa Catalina through San Pedro Channel and Santa Barbara Channel to Point Arguello. (See charts 18022, 18740, 18720, 18725, 18746, 18721.) This Traffic Separation Scheme is recommended for use by all vessels traveling between the points involved, and is composed basically of four elements; **(1) Northbound Lanes, (2) Separation Zone, (3) Southbound Lanes, and (4) a Precautionary Area**. Traffic Lanes have been designed to aid in the prevention of collisions at the approaches to major harbors and along heavily traveled waters, but are not intended in any way to supersede or to alter the applicable Navigation Rules. Separation zones are intended to separate N and S traffic lanes, to be free of ship traffic, and should not be used except for crossing purposes. Mariners should use extreme caution when crossing traffic lanes and separation zones. Rule 10 of the collision regulations apply to this Traffic Separation Scheme.

(194) Extreme caution must be exercised in the Precautionary Area off the entrances to Los Angeles and Long Beach Harbors as both incoming and outgoing vessels use this area. (See also Traffic Separation Schemes, chapter 1, for additional information.)

(195) **Ferry Routes** in the Gulf of Santa Catalina and San Pedro Channel differ from the Traffic Separation Scheme in that area. Mariners using the area's Traffic Separation Scheme are advised to **use caution and beware of crossing ferries** enroute between local coastal ports and ports at Santa Catalina Island.

Vessel Traffic Service

(196) The **Vessel Traffic Service (VTS) Los Angeles/Long Beach**, operated by the Marine Exchange in cooperation with the U.S. Coast Guard, has been established within the approaches to the ports of Los Angeles and Long Beach.

(197) The Vessel Traffic Service is a California State mandatory service and a federally mandated Vessel Movement Reporting System (VMRS), and is designed to enhance navigational safety in the main approaches to the ports of Los Angeles and Long Beach. Mandatory participation and monitoring of VHF-FM channel 14 is required by state and federal law for participating vessels.

(198) **VTS Area:** The VTS Area consists of Los Angeles and Long Beach Harbors (inside the breakwater), and the waters of San Pedro Bay and San Pedro channel, including Santa Monica Bay, within a 25 nautical mile radius of Point Fermin Light. This includes all of the Precautionary Area and portions of the Traffic Separation Scheme Lanes.

(199) **VTS Communications:** The responsibility of information exchange in the VTS Area outside the breakwater will be handled by the Marine Exchange Vessel Traffic Center (VTC), and inside the breakwater by the appropriate Pilot Station.

(200) All reports and communications made to the VTC (voice call "**San Pedro Traffic**") shall be on VHF-FM channel 14, to Los Angeles Pilots on VHF-FM channel 73, and to Long Beach Pilots on VHF-FM channel 12 or 74. All stations monitor VHF-FM channels 16 and 13.

(201) If arrival/departure information has been given and new data is received by the VTS, the VTS will attempt to contact vessels to pass the updated information. In addition, a traffic advisory broadcast is given on VHF-FM channel 14 every hour on the quarter hour. Other navigational information may be given on a case by case basis.

(202) The **Marine Exchange** of Southern California records, classifies, and disseminates information on ship arrivals to, departure from, and movement within the Los Angeles/Long Beach harbors. The Exchange, about 0.4 mile N of Point Fermin, is manned 24-hours a day. It has a visual lookout, VHF-FM radiotelephone, visual communication capability, and a battery of landline telephones. The station, call sign KGW-299, monitors VHF-FM channel 16 and 13, and uses channel 14 for working.

Active User (VMRS)

(203) The following vessels are required to comply with Vessel Movement and Reporting Procedures:

(204) (a) Every power driven vessel 40 meters (approximately 131 feet) or more in length while navigating;

(205) (b) Commercial towing vessels 8 meters (approximately 26 feet) or more in length that are towing alongside, astern, or by pushing ahead;

(206) (c) Every vessel certified to carry 50 or more passengers for hire while engaged in trade, under sail or power.

Passive User (VTS)

(207) These vessels are required to monitor VHF-FM channel 14 and must respond when hailed by the VTS and must comply with operating rules;

(208) (a) Power driven vessels of 20 meters (approximately 65 feet) or more in length;

(209) (b) Vessels of 100 gross tons or more carrying one or more passengers for hire, while engaged in trade, regardless of length, whether under sail or power;

(210) (c) Every dredge or floating plant.

Non Participant

(211) Vessels that do not fall into the active or passive user categories such as fishing boats, yachts, and recreational boats can greatly enhance the safety of navigation in the VTS area by listening on VHF-FM channel 14 and by maintaining a sharp lookout. It is not necessary to participate actively.

Vessel Movement and Reporting Procedures:

(212) All participating vessels when underway and entering the VTS Area from sea shall contact the VTC on VHF-FM channel 14 and report the following information:
(213) (a) Vessel name/call sign.
(214) (b) Course and speed.
(215) (c) Vessel destination.
(216) (d) State whether taking on a pilot or being piloted by master/commanding officer.
(217) (e) ETA breakwater sea buoy/pilot station.

Entering the Precautionary Area:

(218) Prior to entering the Precautionary Area, all participating vessels shall:
(219) (a) Contact the VTC and report that the master/commanding officer is on the bridge and the vessel is being steered by hand.
(220) (b) Vessels under 40 meters subject to USCG/IMO standards shall have the senior licensed or certified person on board to be in charge of the navigation of the vessel when underway within the Precautionary Area.
(221) (c) Vessels of 40 meters or greater, when in the Precautionary Area, shall not exceed 12 knots.
(222) (d) Vessels when underway within the Precautionary Area should maintain a minimum vessel separation of .25 nautical mile (460 meters).
(223) (e) Vessels crossing the Precautionary Area, maneuvering in an unusual manner (i.e. compass/RDF calibration or drills/exercises), and arriving/departing anchorages outside the breakwater shall notify the VTC and advise of their intentions.

Entering the Pilot Areas:

(224) (a) All vessels shall contact the appropriate pilot stations prior to entering the pilot areas to receive vessel traffic information inside the breakwater. Vessels shall provide the following information to pilot stations:
(225) (1) Vessel name/call sign.
(226) (2) ETA breakwater or sea buoy/pilot station.
(227) (3) Vessel destination.

Departing Berth or Anchorage:

(228) (a) All vessels shall contact the appropriate pilot station prior to departing a berth or anchorage to receive vessel traffic information inside the breakwater. Provide the following information to the pilot station:
(229) (1) Vessel name/call sign.
(230) (2) Advise who is piloting vessel.
(231) (3) Vessel destination, whether to sea or destination within harbor.

(232) (b) All outbound vessels shall notify VTC on VHF-FM channel 14 at least 15 minutes prior to passing breakwater entrance, including Anaheim Bay, and provide the following information:
(233) (1) Vessel name/call sign.
(234) (2) Vessel destination port or direction of departure, and advise if the vessel will be using or crossing the Traffic Separation Scheme.
(235) (3) Advise VTC when leaving the Precautionary Area and when leaving the VTS Area.
(236) All vessels shall comply with Navigation Rules (having particular regard for rules for vessels operating in and near Traffic Separation Schemes) and with the rules of the Regulated Navigation Area in San Pedro Bay (See **165.1 through 165.13 and 165.1152**, chapter 2, for limits and regulations.)
(237) Participating vessels are to ensure that a copy of the **VTS Users Manual** is available on board the vessel when operating within the VTS area. The manual is available at no charge from Executive Director, Marine Exchange of Southern California, P.O. Box 1949, San Pedro, CA 90733, phone 310–832–6411 or can be viewed and downloaded at http://www.mxsocal.org.
(238) The State of California has established Tank Vessel Escort Regulations for tank vessels underway in the Los Angeles/Long Beach Harbor and their approaches. The full text of the regulations can be found at http://www.dfg.ca.gov/ospr or can be obtained from the California Office of Spill Prevention and Response 24-hour Communications Center at 916–445–0045. .
(239) Tug Escort Applicability: All laden tank vessels (tankers or barges carrying as cargo a total volume of oil greater than or equal to 5,000 metric tons of oil) entering the port should ensure proper implementation of either the Tanker Force Selection Matrix or the Tank Barge and Tug Matching Criteria listed below. In addition, except for tank barge/primary towing units that have total displacements of 20,000 metric tons or less, escort tugs must be tethered.
(240) Three Tank Vessel Escort Zones are established as follows:
(241) Zone 1: Upon all waters within 2.0 nautical miles to seaward of the Federal Breakwater, escort tugs required for all laden tank vessels.
(242) Zone 2: Upon all waters in the approaches to the Port of Long Beach within 3.5 nautical miles to seaward of the Federal Breakwater, escort tugs required for all laden tank vessels with static deep draft greater than 16.5 meters.
(243) Zone 3: Upon all waters in the approaches to the Port of Los Angeles within 4.0 nautical miles to seaward of the Federal Breakwater, escort tugs required for all laden tank vessels with static deep draft greater than 14.0 meters.
(244) Inbound, laden Oil and Chemical Tank Vessels shall not proceed closer than the seaward limit of the applicable Tank Vessel Escort Zone, unless the prescribed escort tug(s) are in position at the seaward limit of the

applicable Tank Vessel Escort Zone. Masters shall also ensure the anchors are ready for letting go prior to entering the applicable Tank Vessel Escort Zone. The tank vessel master/pilot shall hold a "pre-escort conference" that should at a minimum include:

(245) 1. Contacting the escort tug operator to confirm the number and position of the escort tug(s); and

(246) 2. Establishing the radio frequency to be used; and

(247) 3. Establishing the destination of the tank vessel; and

(248) 4. Discussing any other pertinent information that the master/pilot and escort tug operator deem necessary.

(249) An "Escort Tug," as defined by California regulations, is a tug that is designed primarily for pushing or pulling ahead or astern, or towing alongside another vessel. A tug is considered to be designed for escort work whether or not it is involved in such activity. In the harbors of Los Angeles/Long Beach, an "Assist/Escort Tug" means any tug that is accepted by the tank vessel master and/or pilot to escort a tank vessel that is transiting waters where an assist/escort is required. Arrangements should be made via the vessel agent, tug company and appropriate pilot service. Outbound laden tank vessels are not required to use tugs once they have safely cleared the breakwater. All tank vessels shifting within the harbor(s) (including dock to anchor, anchor to anchor, and dock to dock) shall comply with the escort requirements. Arrangements should be made via the vessel agent, tug company or appropriate pilot service to ensure compliance.

TANKER FORCE SELECTION MATRIX

Tanker Displacement	Forces For Tug(s) Tethered at the Stern (see notes below)
Metric Tons	**Short Tons**
0 to < 60,000	10
60,000 to < 100,000	20
100,000 to < 140,000	30
140,000 to < 180,000	40
180,000 to < 220,000	50
220,000 to < 260,000	62
260,000 to < 300,000	75
300,000 to < 340,000	87
340,000 to < 380,000	105
380,000 to < 420,000	128

Note 1: Ahead forces for tugs using stern lines (e.g., Voith-Schneider propeller – VSP tugs). Astern forces for tugs using headlines (e.g., azimuth stern drive – ASD tugs)

Note 2: The *Forces For Tugs* described in the Tanker Force Selection Matrix were evaluated in a water depth equal to 1.2 times the tanker's deep draft for tankers with a displacement of less than 260,000 metric tons, and in a water depth equal to 1.1 times the tanker's deep draft for tankers with a displacement equal to or greater than 260,000 metric tons.

Small Tank Barge Matrix

Total Displacement Tonnage of the Tank Barge and the Primary Towing Tug	Minimum Required Escort Tug(s) Static Bollard Pull tethered escort tug(s)/ un-tethered escort tug(s)
0 to 20,000 displacement tons	10 short tons/15 short tons
> 20,000 displacement tons	A total astern static bollard pull (in pounds) equal to or greater than the sum of both the primary towing tug(s) and barge(s) total displacement tonnage. (e.g., where the total towing tug and tank barge displacement is 25,000 displacement tons, the escort tug(s) astern static bollard pull shall be at least 25,000 pounds or 12.5 short tons.)

(250) All the escort tugs required to satisfy the Tanker Force Selection Matrix shall be tethered on the tanker's stern.

(251) These force requirements reflect favorable circumstances and conditions. The tanker master/pilot shall arrange for additional escort tug(s) should adverse weather conditions, unusual port congestion, the contemplated movement of the vessel or other conditions or circumstances so require.

(252) (See **33 CFR 157**, chapter 2, for regulations for Tank Vessels Carrying Oil in Bulk and Maneuvering Performance Capability.)

(253) **Vessel Speed Reductions**, in addition to the mandatory 12 knot speed limit in the Los Angeles/Long Beach Vessel Traffic Service (VTS) Precautionary Area, the following excerpt is from Rule 402 from the South Coast Air Quality Management District (SCAQMD):

(254) The Port of Long Beach asks every vessel entering or leaving the port to observe the **voluntary 12-knot speed limit** that extends seaward 20 nautical miles from Point Fermin. Reducing ship speed will reduce exhaust emissions into Southern California's air, which will result in better air quality. The speed of every vessel in the speed reduction zone is measured and recorded by the Marine Exchange of Southern California; please contact the Marine Exchange for more information. Your cooperation with this important air quality improvement program is greatly appreciated.

(255) Vessels making the breakwater entrances should proceed at speeds no greater than is necessary for steerage. Vessels that approach the entrance close in and attempt to turn at or near the entrance are in danger of collision with outbound vessels, especially with smaller craft at night when their lights are not easily distinguishable at low tide or against the background of lights in the harbor.

(256) Vessels awaiting a pilot should stay well to seaward and E of the outer fairway buoys.

(257) **San Pedro Breakwater** extends about 0.9 mile in a SE direction from the E side of Point Fermin, then turns ENE for another 0.9 mile to Los Angeles Light. **Middle Breakwater** extends ENE for 2.1 miles from the Los Angeles entrance, thence E for 1 mile to the Long Beach entrance, and is marked at both ends by lights. **Long Beach Breakwater** extends E 2.2 miles from Long Beach entrance and is marked by lights on both ends. Ranges for a 090°–270° measured nautical mile are on

the Long Beach Breakwater. They are yellow diamond-shaped daymarks on iron pipes.

(258) Kelp beds are along the inside edge of the W end of Middle Breakwater and a shallow water habitat is on the inside edge of San Pedro Breakwater; the shallow water habitat is surrounded by a submerged dike and is marked by lights.

(259) **Fish Harbor**, on the S side of Terminal Island near its W end, is protected by two sets of breakwaters and the mole of Pier 300, the outer ends of which are marked by lights. A dredged channel with a controlling depth of about 14 feet leads between the outer and inner breakwaters to Fish Harbor, which has depths of about 16 to 18 feet. The seawall is lined with canneries and other fish works. The outer breakwaters enclose the Yacht Club Anchorage, sometimes called the Fish Harbor Extension. This anchorage has depths of 17 to 20 feet E and depths of 11 to 14 feet W of the dredged channel.

Channels

(260) **Long Beach Channel** leads NW from W of Long Beach Breakwater for 2.2 miles to **Middle Harbor**, thence N to **Back Channel** and the **Inner Harbor**. A **restricted harbor** entrance area has been designated in the channel and side areas which extends from about 1 mile N of the breakwater to inside Middle Harbor; regulations of the Board of Harbor Commissioners, Port of Long Beach, grant priority to outbound vessels and stipulate a **6-knot speed limit** in this restricted area.

(261) Most of the channels in Long Beach Harbor are maintained at more than the project depth of 35 feet. (See Notice to Mariners and latest editions of charts for depths.)

(262) **Los Angeles Main Channel** leads NW from E of the San Pedro Breakwater for about 1 mile, thence N to the Inner Harbor turning basin, thence NE through **East Basin Channel** and **Cerritos Channel**. About 0.6 mile NW of the breakwater, **Super Tanker Channel** leads W from the Main Channel to the deep-draft facilities at Berths 45–50. Los Angeles Main Channel from the breakwater to the Super Tanker Channel and the Super Tanker Channel are maintained at more than the project depth of 45 feet and 40 feet, respectively. (See Notice to Mariners and latest editions of charts for depths.)

(263) Los Angeles Main Channel is marked by a **296°** lighted range.

(264) The Los Angeles and Long Beach main channels are considered narrow channels. Vessels less than 20 meters in length, sailing vessels, vessels engaged in fishing, or any vessel attempting to cross these channels shall not impede a vessel that can only safely navigate within a narrow channel per Inland Navigation Rules, Rule 9. To obtain information on the movement of deep draft vessels inside the Federal Breakwater, contact the Los Angeles Pilot Station on VHF-FM channel 73 or Long Beach Pilot Station of VHF-FM channel 74.

Anchorages

(265) Limits and regulations of general, naval, explosives, and special anchorage areas in San Pedro Bay are given in **110.1, 110.100, and 110.214**, chapter 2. When inside the breakwaters, vessels are required to anchor in the anchorage area prescribed in the regulations except in cases of great emergency. The Santa Ana is the only wind dangerous to vessels anchored inside the breakwaters.

(266) The shallow water habitat along the E side of Pier 400 and about 0.4 mile S of the Naval Base Mole extends into Special Anchorage B-1 (**33 CFR 110.100**), however, there are no boating or anchorage restrictions associated with the shallow water habitat.

(267) Vessels are cautioned against anchoring in the vicinity of pipeline and cable areas shown on the charts.

Dangers

(268) A shoal area, with a rock covered 3 feet and a rock awash near the outer end, extends about 0.3 mile S of the shore just E of Point Fermin Light. A lighted whistle buoy is about 300 yards SW from the S end of the shoal area.

Regulated navigation areas

(269) A **regulated navigation area** has been established in the waters S of the Los Angeles-Long Beach breakwater encompassing the approaches to both Los Angeles and Long Beach harbors, the pilot areas, and Commercial Anchorage G. (See **165.1 through 165.13 and 165.1152**, chapter 2, for limits and regulations.)

(270) **Safety zones** have been established in San Pedro Bay, including around the oil drilling platforms, in

(271) 33°35'45"N., 118°08'27"W (**Platform Edith**);

(272) 33°35'00"N., 118°07'40"W (**Platform Elly**);

(273) 33°34'57"N., 118°07'42"W (**Platform Ellen**); and

(274) 33°33'50"N., 118°07'00"W (**Platform Eureka**). (See **147.1 through 147.20, 147.1104, 147.1108, and 147.1111**, chapter 2 for limits and regulations and chapter 3 under 'Oil well structures' for additional information.)

(275) A **naval restricted area** is in the West Basin off the S shore of Terminal Island inside the jetty of the Naval Base Mole (See **334.990**, chapter 2, for limits and regulations.)

(276) A **restricted area** is off the E side of Reservation Point. (See **334.938**, chapter 2, for limits and regulations.)

Bridges

(277) The Vincent Thomas Bridge, a highway suspension span with a clearance of 185 feet over the center 500-foot width, crosses Los Angeles Main Channel just below the turning basin, 3.2 miles above the entrance breakwater.

(278) Two bridges cross Cerritos Channel on the N side of Terminal Island: Schuyler F. Heim Highway Bridge, under construction (2012), consult Local Notice to

Mariners, or contact Caltrans at 213-444-1171 for latest conditions; and Henry Ford (Badger) Avenue railroad bridge 25 yards W with authorized span clearances of 6 feet down and 165 feet up. The Henry Ford (Badger) Avenue railroad bridge is maintained in the down position. The bridgetender of the Schuyler F. Heim bridge monitors VHF-FM channel 13; call sign WHX-947. (See **117.1 through 117.59 and 117.147**, chapter 2, for drawbridge regulations.)

(279) It is reported that clearance gages have been established on a pier flanking the navigable span of the Schuyler F. Heim Bridge and on the dolphins flanking the Henry Ford Avenue railroad bridge. The gages indicate the vertical navigational clearance beneath each of the bridges at any height of tide.

(280) Near the E end of Cerritos Channel are several power cables that have a clearance of 155 feet. Vessels are required to have a clearance of at least 6 feet under the cables to avoid the danger of arcing.

(281) The Gerald Desmond Bridge, across Back Channel between Long Beach Inner Harbor and Middle Harbor, has a fixed span with a clearance of 155 feet.

(282) The Queen's Way (Magnolia Avenue) Bridge, crossing **Queensway Bay** 0.8 mile W of oil **Island Grissom**, is a fixed span connecting downtown Long Beach with the terminal facilities of Piers F, G, H, and J; clearances are 36 feet for the 500-foot main channel span or 45 feet at the center, and 31 feet elsewhere.

Currents

(283) The tidal currents follow the axis of the channels and rarely exceed 1 knot.

Surge

(284) Both Los Angeles and Long Beach Harbors are subject to seiche and surge. The most persistent and conspicuous oscillation has a period of approximately 1 hour. In the vicinity of Reservation Point and near the E end of Terminal Island, the hourly surge is very prominent, causing velocity variations which at times may be as great as 1 knot, and which often overcome the lesser tidal current so that the current floods and ebbs at half-hour intervals. Because of the more restricted channel, the surge through Back Channel at the E end of Terminal Island usually reaches a greater velocity than through the channel W of Reservation Point. In Back Channel, the hourly variation may sometimes be 1.5 knots or more. The hourly surge, together with other oscillations of shorter period and of more irregular occurrence, at times causes a very rapid change both in height of the water and the velocity and direction of the current and may endanger vessels tied up at the piers. A 3-minute surge is reported to be responsible for major ship movements and damage. Pilots advise taut lines to reduce the effect of the surge.

Weather, Los Angeles

(285) Fog is most likely from October through February. Out over the bay, it drops visibilities below 0.5 mile (0.9 km) on about 11 days per month during this period. It is mostly a land (radiation) fog that drifts out and is worst in the late night and early morning. Smoke from nearby industrial areas often adds to the thickness and persistence of the fog. There are times when it will hang over the inner channels for several days and along the coast can be very local in occurrence. For example, at Long Beach, which is particularly susceptible to cold air drainage, fog reduces visibilities to less than 0.5 mile (0.9 km) on an average of 18 more days annually than at nearby Los Angeles International Airport. Along the shores, visibilities drop to less than 0.5 mile (0.9 km) on about 3 to 8 days per month from August through April; December is usually the worst month.

(286) Winds are variable particularly in fall and winter. They are also strongest during this period when the **Santa Ana wind** can blow. This is an offshore desert wind which, though infrequent, may be violent. It occurs when a strong high-pressure system sits over the plateau region and generates a NE to E flow over southern California. The air streams through Cajon Pass into the Great Valley, swings toward the SW, and follows either the Santa Ana River Canyon through the Santa Ana Mountains or moves directly over the low mountains S of the canyon and then follows a well-defined path over the plains of Orange County to reach the ocean near Newport. It diminishes little in intensity immediately after passing over the bay, and some reports credit it with blowing far out to sea. However, beyond 50 miles (93 km) from shore, Santa Anas are of little concern. These winds have reached speeds of 50 knots or more along the coast.

(287) Aside from weather forecasts, there is little warning of the onset of a Santa Ana. For some hours preceding its arrival, good visibility and unusually low humidity often prevail. Shortly before its arrival on the coast, the Santa Ana may be observed as an approaching dark-brown dust cloud. This will often give from 10 to 30 minutes warning, and is a positive indication. The Santa Ana may come at any time of the day. It can be reinforced by a land breeze in the early morning or weakened by a sea breeze during the afternoon.

(288) Winter storms are also responsible for strong winds over San Pedro Bay, particularly from the SW through NW. Winds of 17 knots or greater occur about 1 to 2 percent of the time from November through May. Winter winds often have an E component, although WNW winds are most frequent at Long Beach. At Los Angeles International Airport, W and NE winds are the most common, while at Los Alamitos, NE, E, and SW winds are frequent. However, at both locations, calm conditions are as common or more so from fall through spring. SW through W winds begin to prevail in spring, and this lasts through the summer and into early fall. Gales are rare and have occurred occasionally during

Facilities in the Port of Los Angeles

Name	Location	Berthing Space (feet)	Depths* (feet)	Deck Height (feet)	Mechanical Handling Facilities and Storage	Purpose	Operated by:
POLA Liquid Bulk Terminal (Berths 45-47)	33°42'53"N., 118°16'31"W.	1063	47	16	Two hydraulic unloading arms	Crude oil	Port of Los Angeles
POLA Breakbulk Terminal (Berths 49-53)	33°43'08"N., 118°16'26"W.	2100	35-51	14.6	Open storage (24 acres)	Breakbulk steel	Port of Los Angeles
SSA (Berths 54-55)	33°43'29"N., 118°16'34"W.	1340	35	14	Transit shed (211,000 sq feet)	Imported meats, Imported fruits	Stevedoring Services of America
Westway (Berths 70-71)	33°43'29"N., 118°16'29"W.	800	35	14.8	Tank storage (593,000 barrels)	Liquid bulk	Westway Terminal Company
World Cruise Center (Berths 91-93)	33°44'51"N., 118°16'34"W.	2850	37	15	Terminal buildings and warehouses	Handling passenger vessels	Pacific Cruise Ship Terminals
West Basin Container Terminal (Berth 100)	33°45'09"N., 118°16'30"W.	1200	45-53	15	• Four Panamax cranes • Open storage (75 acres)	General cargo in containers	West Basin Container Terminal LLC
Kinder Morgan Liquid Terminal	33°45'22"N., 118°16'51"W.	825	35	13	Tank storage (498,000 barrels)	Petroleum products	Kinder Morgan, Inc.
West Basin Container Terminal (Berths 121-131)	33°45'39"N., 118°16'33"W.	3500	35-45	15	• Eight Panamax cranes • Open storage (186 acres)	General cargo in containers	West Basin Container Terminal LLC
TraPac Terminal (Berths 135-139)	33°46'00"N., 118°16'25"W.	4050	35-53	15.7	• Eleven Panamax cranes • Open storage (173 acres)	General cargo in containers	Trans Pacific Container Service Corp.
ConocoPhillips Terminal (Berths 148-151)	33°45'18"N., 118°16'22"W.	1328	37	15.2	Tank storage (825,000 barrels)	Petroleum products	ConocoPhillips
Warehouse Terminal (Berths 153-155)	33°45'23"N., 118°16'12"W.	1781	34	12.8	Covered storage (26,880 sq ft)	General cargo	Port of Los Angeles
Valero (Berths 163-164)	33°45'36"N., 118°16'03"W.	888	40	13.7	Tank storage (1.5 million barrels)	Petroleum products	Valero
Ultramar (Berth 164)	33°45'35"N., 118°16'03"W.	888	40	13.7	Tank storage (947,000 barrels)	Petroleum products	Ultramar
Borax (Berths 165-166)	33°45'30"N., 118°16'05"W.	679	37	14.2	Storage for (350 tons)	Industrial borates	U.S. Borax Inc.
Shell Oil (Berths 167-169)	33°45'18"N., 118°16'04"W.	1238	40	13	Tank storage (580,000 barrels)	Petroleum products	Shell Oil
Pasha (Berths 174-181)	33°45'43"N., 118°15'40"W.	3300	35-45	15	• Three cranes (40 tons) • Transit shed (235,000 sq feet)	Steel	Pasha Properties Inc.
Vopak (Berths 187-191)	33°45'50"N., 118°15'35"W.	2336	38	15	• Tank storage (700,000 barrels) • Covered storage (86,000 sq feet)	Liquid bulk chemical products	Vopak
WWL Vehicle Services (Berths 195-199)	33°46'07"N., 118°15'09"W.	2250	32-34	16-18	Storage for up to 8000 vehicles	Automobiles	WWL Vehicle Services Americas, Inc.
POLA Container Terminal (Berths 206-209)	33°45'46"N., 118°14'55"W.	2180	40-45	15.5	• Four gantry cranes • Open storage (86 acres)	General cargo in containers	Port of Los Angeles
Hugo Neu-Proler (Berths 210-211)	33°45'40"N., 118°15'12"W.	1500	35	13.7	Open storage (26.7 acres)	Scrap metal (ferrous/non-ferrous)	Hugo Neu-Proler Co.
Yusen Terminal (Berths 212-225)	33°45'16"N., 118°15'46"W.	5800	35-45	15	• 10 Panamax cranes • Open storage (185 acres)	General cargo in containers	Yusen Terminals Inc.
Seaside Terminal (Berths 226-236)	33°44'32"N., 118°16'26"W.	4700	38-45	13-15	• Eight Panamax cranes • Open storage (205 acres)	General cargo in containers	Seaside Transportation Services, LLC
ExxonMobil (Berths 238-240C)	33°44'01"N., 118°16'21"W.	903	37	14	Tank storage (2.3 million barrels)	Petroleum products	ExxonMobil
LAXT (Berth 301)	33°43'51"N., 118°15'46"W.	1000	72	16	•Open and domed storage •Enclosed conveyor sysytem	Petroleum coke	Los Angeles Export Terminal, Inc.
APL Terminal/Global Gateway South (Berths 302-305)	33°44'00"N., 118°15'14"W.	4000	50	15	• 12 Panamax cranes • Open storage (292 acres)	General cargo in containers	Eagle Marine
APM Terminals/Pier 400 (Berths 401-406)	33°43'44"N., 118°15'30"W.	7190	55	15.2	• 14 Panamax cranes • Open storage (484 acres)	General cargo in containers	APM Terminals

* The depths given above are reported. For information on the latest depths contact the port authorities or the private operators.

March and November. March, April, and May are the windiest months and December the most calm. An all-time peak gust of 54 knots was recorded in March 1952.

(289) The average temperature for Los Angeles is 63°F (17.2°C). The average high is 70°F (21.1°C) and the average low is 55°F (12.8°C). Every month has recorded temperatures in excess of 90°F (32.2°C) except January. The all-time maximum is 110°F (43.3°C) recorded in September of 1963. The all-time minimum is 27°F (-2.8°C) recorded in January of 1949. April, June, September, October, and November have each had temperatures in excess of 100 F (37.8°C). August is the warmest month and January the coolest.

(290) The average annual precipitation at Los Angeles is just under twelve inches (305 mm). The average number of days with precipitation is 60 each year. The driest month is July when only 0.02 inches (0.51 mm) can be expected and the wettest month is January with an average monthly rainfall of 2.88 inches (71.1 mm). July and August each average only two days per month with measurable precipitation while January and March average eight days each with measurable rainfall. The driest year on record is 1947 when only 3.11 inches (79 mm) of rain fell and the wettest year on record is 1983 when 29.46 inches (748 mm) of precipitation was recorded. Only trace amounts of snowfall have been recorded in Los Angeles and January is the only month of this occurrence.

(291) The National Weather Service maintains an office at Long Beach Airport, Los Angeles International Airport, and downtown Los Angeles (see Appendix A for address). Barometers may be compared at these locations or by telephone.

(292) (See Appendix B for **Los Angeles climatological table**.)

Pilotage, Port of Los Angeles

(293) All vessels 300 gross registered tons and over and all foreign vessels leaving, entering, or shifting within the Port of Los Angeles are subject to pilotage. Vessels licensed and engaged in the fishing trade and enrolled vessels of the United States under the direction of an officer federally licensed for the port are exempt from pilotage.

(294) The Port of Los Angeles Pilot Service boards vessels in the vicinity of Los Angeles Approach Channel Lighted Whistle Buoy 3. Tank vessels will be boarded at least two miles from the Los Angeles entrance. Deep-draft vessels (draft more than 55 feet) will be boarded in the vicinity of Los Angeles Approach Channel Lighted Buoy 1. The pilot boats, STEPHEN M. WHITE and PHINEAS BANNING, have black hulls and white cabins with L.A. PILOTS displayed on each side. The pilot station is at the SE end of Pier 1. Pilotage can be arranged through the pilot station, telephone 310–732–3805, or VHF-FM channels 73 and 16; call sign KEB-260. The pilot station and boats monitor and use as working frequencies VHF-FM channels 73, 14, and 16. The pilot boats display the standard day and night signals. The pilot station requests 2 hours advance notice of estimated time of arrival on VHF-FM channel 73. The pilots normally board the vessels on the starboard side with the ladder about 1 meter above the water. Vessels may not be boarded during periods of poor visibility or severe weather.

Pilotage, Port of Long Beach

(295) All foreign vessels and U.S. vessels of 300 gross registered tons and over sailing under register are subject to a pilotage fee whether or not a municipal pilot is actually employed. Vessels sailing under U.S. enrollment and licensed and engaged in coastwise, intercoastal, or fishing trades under the direction of an officer federally licensed for the port are exempt from pilotage unless a municipal pilot is employed.

(296) The Jacobsen Pilot Service, Inc., handles pilotage for San Pedro Bay, Los Angeles Harbor, Anaheim Bay, and primarily Long Beach Harbor. The pilots board vessels 1 mile S of Long Beach Approach Lighted Whistle Buoy LB. Large deep-draft vessels are boarded 2 miles or more S of the approach buoy. The pilot boats, POLARIS and VEGA, have yellow hulls and white cabins with LONG BEACH PILOTS displayed on each side. The pilot station is at the NW end of Pier F. Pilotage can be arranged by telephone (562–432–0664), fax (562–432–3597) and VHF-FM channels 12 and 74. The pilot station monitors VHF-FM channels 12 and 16; the pilot boats monitor VHF-FM channels 12, 13, 14, and 16. The pilot boats display the standard day and night signals. The pilot station requests 2 hours advance notice of estimated time of arrival (ETA) by radiotelephone; call sign, KMA-372. Vessels should state name, call sign, ETA at the pickup station, and draft, and for vessels equipped with bow or stern thrusters, the operational status of the thrusters. Vessels will be given information regarding the desired lee for boarding. In normal weather, pilots board on the starboard side, with the ladder about 2 meters above the water, and a moderate speed. Accommodation ladders must not be used outside the breakwater. In very thick fog vessels may be requested to anchor outside the breakwater in Anchorage F.

Towage

(297) Several tugboat companies operate in the Los Angeles-Long Beach area with tugs up to 5,000 hp available. Large vessels usually have one or more tugs in attendance while berthing at or departing from the wharves along the inner channels.

Quarantine, customs, immigration, and agricultural quarantine

(298) (See chapter 3, Vessel Arrival Inspections, and Appendix A for addresses.)

(299) **Quarantine** is enforced in accordance with regulations of the U.S. Public Health Service. (See Public Health Service, chapter 1.)

Facilities in the Port of Long Beach

Name	Location	Berthing Space (feet)	Depths* (feet)	Deck Height (feet)	Mechanical Handling Facilities and Storage	Purpose	Operated by:
Pier J (Berths 266-270)	33°44'11"N., 118°11'24"W.	2711	47-56	15	• 16 gantry cranes • Open storage (64 acres)	General cargo in containers	SSA Marine
Pier J (Berths 243-247)	33°44'36"N., 118°11'44"W.	3300	36-40	16	• Open storage (57 acres) • Covered storage (100,000 sq feet)	General cargo in containers	SSA Marine
Pier G (Berths 226-236)	33°44'39"N., 118°11'56"W.	6379	36-42	15	• 16 gantry cranes • Open storage (160 acres) • Container freight station (70,000 sq feet)	General cargo in containers	International Transportation Service
Pier G (Berths 212-215)	33°44'52"N., 118°12'23"W.	1900	50	18-19	• Two traveling shiploaders • Covered storage (540 tons)	Petroleum Coke, Coal, Potash, Borax, Soda ash, Concentrates, Prilled sulfer	Metropolitan Stevedore Company
Pier F (Berths 211A and 209)	33°45'02"N., 118°12'24"W.	800	43	19	• Pipeline system • Tank storage (425,000 barrels)	Petroleum products	Chemoil Marine Terminal
Pier F (Berth 211)	33°45'02"N., 118°12'28"W.	1100	40	19	• Terminal services for bulk materials	Petroleum coke	Koch Carbon, Inc.
Pier F (Berth 210)	33°44'59"N., 118°12'34"W.	700	40	19	Belt conveyor system	Bulk salt	Morton Salt Company
Pier F (Berth 208)	33°44'54"N., 118°12'44"W.	420	29-33	19	• Storage space (50,000 sq feet) • Belt conveyor system	Bulk cement	MCC-Lucky Cement Company
Pier F (Berths 206-207)	33°44'46"N., 118°12'43"W.	1200	32	18.5	• Open storage (12.2 acres) • Covered storage (190,000 sq feet)	Steel products, Plywood, Lumber, Large machinery	Crecent Terminal (SSA)
Pier F (Berths 204-205)	33°44'38"N., 118°12'32"W.	1265	36	18.5	• Open storage (5.5 acres) • Covered storage (180,000 sq feet)	Steel products, Plywood, Lumber	Cooper/T. Smith Stevedoring
Pier F (Berths 6-10)	33°45'15"N., 118°12'40"W.	2750	50	14.4	• Seven gantry cranes • 240 reefer outlets	General cargo in containers	Long Beach Container Terminal, Inc.
Pier E (Berths 24-26)	33°45'35"N., 118°12'50"W.	2100	48	17.7	• Five gantry cranes • Open storage (58 acres) • 400 reefer outlets	General cargo in containers	California United Terminals
Pier D (Berths 30-31)	33°45'31"N., 118°12'55"W.	700	43	19.5	• Tank storage (6.7 million gallons)	Tallow, Vegetable oils	Baker Commodities, Inc.
Pier D (Berths 32-33)	33°45'31"N., 118°13'00"W.	680	36	13.8	• Silo storage (50k tons) • Open storage (87k sq. feet)	Bulk cement	Pacific Coast Cement Corp.
Pier T (Berths 132-140)	33°45'13"N., 118°14'08"W.	5000	55	14.7	• 14 gantry cranes • Open storage (237 acres) • 1088 reefer outlets	General cargo in containers	TTI-Hanjin Shipping Co.
Pier T (Berth 122)	33°45'17"N., 118°13'08"W.	600	40	23	• Open storage (7.7 acres) • Covered storage (15,000 sq feet)	Lumber and Lumber products	Fremont Forest Group Corp.
Pier T (Berth 121)	33°45'24"N., 118°13'11"W.	1140	76	20	• Tank storage available in Carson	Crude oil and Petroleum products	BP
Pier T (Berth 118)	33°45'39"N., 118°13'14"W.	900	36	22	• Vessel loading crane • Open storage (13.5 acres)	Recyclable metal & steel products	Pacific Coast Recycling Co.
Pier T (Berths 116-117)	33°45'47"N., 118°13'17"W.	600	32-35	23	• Open storage (9.9 acres)	Lumber and Lumber products	Weyerhaeuser Company
Pier D (Berth 46)	33°46'10"N., 118°12'44"W.	640	40	17.2	• Belt-conveyor system • Storage shed (40,000 tons)	Gypsum	G-P Gypsum Corp.
Pier D (Berths 50-54)	33°46'16"N., 118°12'36"W.	2370	36	10-17	• Open storage (6.9 acres) • Transit shed (495,000 sq feet)	Newsprint and Lumber	Forest Terminals
Pier C (Berths 60-62)	33°46'13"N., 118°13'00"W.	1800	42	14.5	• Three gantry cranes • Open storage (57 acres)	General cargo in containers & Automobiles	SSA Marine-Matson Terminal
Pier B (Berths 76-78)	33°46'33"N., 118°12'47"W.	2200	46	14.4	Tank storage (1.8 million barrels)	Petroleum products	BP
Pier B (Berths 82-83)	33°46'28"N., 118°13'05"W.	1060	38	14.4	• Tank storage (410k barrels) • Open storage (110 acres) • Transit shed (150k sq. feet)	Petroleum products and Automobiles	Petro-Diamond and Toyota
Pier B (Berths 84-87)	33°46'20"N., 118°13'21"W.	1980	52	16.8	Tank storage (254k barrels)	Crude oil, Petroleum products, Bunker fuel	Tesoro Refining and Marketing Company

		Facilities in the Port of Long Beach					
Name	Location	Berthing Space (feet)	Depths* (feet)	Deck Height (feet)	Mechanical Handling Facilities and Storage	Purpose	Operated by:
Pier A (Berths 88-96)	33°46'09"N., 118°13'54"W.	3600	50	14.2	• Ten gantry cranes • Open storage (90 acres) • 652 reefer outlets	General cargo in containers	SSAT Long Beach Terminal

* The depths given above are reported. For information on the latest depths contact the port authorities or the private operators.

(300) Los Angeles and Long Beach are both **customs ports of entry**

Coast Guard

(301) A **sector office** is located in the Los Angeles/Long Beach Harbor complex. (See Appendix A for addresses.)
(302) **Los Angeles/Long Beach Coast Guard Station** is on the E side of Main Channel at **Reservation Point**.

Harbor regulations

(303) Local rules and regulations for the Port of Los Angeles are enforced by the Port Warden of the Harbor Department. The Los Angeles Harbor Department Headquarters are at 425 South Palos Verdes Street, San Pedro.
(304) Similar regulations for the Port of Long Beach are enforced by the Executive Director of the Harbor Department assigned by a Board of Harbor Commissioners. The Long Beach Harbor Department Administration Building is on Pier "G" at 925 Harbor Plaza, Long Beach. The **speed limit** for Middle Harbor and Inner Harbor is 6 knots.
(305) Permits are required from the Port Warden for any method of underwater diving within Los Angeles Harbor. Similarly, a permit from the Port Manager is required in Long Beach Harbor.
(306) Copies of the regulations may be obtained from the local office concerned.

Wharves

(307) All land of the Port of Los Angeles is owned by the City of Los Angeles. This land is leased to various facilities listed in the table; only the major deep-draft facilities are listed. For a complete description of the port facilities refer to Port Series No. 28, published and sold by the U.S. Army Corps of Engineers. (See Appendix A for address.) The alongside depths given in the table are reported. (For information on the latest depths contact the port authorities or the private operators.) Most of the piers and wharves have shore connections (electrical/water), highway and railroad connections.
(308) General cargo at the port is usually handled by ship's tackle. Special handling equipment, if available, is noted in the table. Floating cranes to 350 tons are available.
(309) The office of the chief wharfinger is at 425 South Palos Verdes Street, San Pedro

Wharves

(310) All land of the Port of Long Beach is owned by the City of Long Beach. This land is leased to various facilities listed in the table; only the major deep-draft facilities are listed. For a complete description of the port facilities refer to Port Series No. 28, published and sold by the U.S. Army Corps of Engineers. (See Appendix A for address.) The alongside depths given in the table are reported. (For information on the latest depths contact the port authorities or the private operators.) Most of the piers and wharves have shore connections (electrical/water), highway and railroad connections.
(311) The famous passenger liner QUEEN MARY, retired in 1967 and purchased by the Port of Long Beach, is moored on the NE side of Pier H, parallel to the skyline of the city of Long Beach. The ship is used as a floating museum, hotel, and convention center.
(312) The large lighted white dome S of the QUEEN MARY was once the exhibit center for Howard Hughes' famous flying boat SPRUCE GOOSE. The dome is now used by Carnival Cruise Lines to support the Long Beach Cruise Terminal.

Supplies

(313) Fuel oil, water, and marine supplies can be had in any quantity at both Los Angeles and Long Beach. Fuel oil can be supplied at the oil docks or by barge.

Repairs

(314) Los Angeles Harbor is well equipped with marine repair plants. The largest marine railway, at Berth 264 in the NE end of Fish Harbor in East San Pedro, has a hauling power of 1,000 tons. There are a number of smaller facilities. There are no graving docks. The port is well equipped with salvage facilities. A trained salvage crew and a corps of expert divers are ready at all times to render aid in any disaster to shipping along the coast and at distant localities.
(315) Long Beach Harbor is also well equipped for marine repairs. A variety of barge cranes are available in the 40- to 275-ton capacity range. There are several marine railways for small craft at Long Beach Harbor.

Communications

(316) Los Angeles and Long Beach Harbors have connections to the extensive freeway system which connects the cities of Los Angeles and Long Beach and their

suburbs; four U.S. or Interstate highways extend from the area freeway system to the N, S, and E. The harbors are served by three major railroads and many airlines. The harbors are ports of call for many foreign and domestic steamship lines and by coastal barge lines.

(317) While the Ports of Los Angeles and Long Beach are separate entities, their harbor facilities are closely interrelated.

Small-craft facilities

(318) The major small-craft facilities in Long Beach are Long Beach Marina in Alamitos Bay and the Downtown Marina on Queensway Bay, W of oil Island Grissom. Other facilities in Long Beach Harbor are just inside the entrances to both Channel Two and Channel Three. All repair facilities, supplies, fuel, moorage, and related yacht requirements may be had at individual private marinas or from other establishments in the Middle Harbor. Several boatyards are in Channel Two and Channel Three.

(319) Los Angeles Harbor has small-craft facilities on both sides of Cerritos Channel from the Heim lift bridge to East Basin, on the E side of East Basin, in Watchhorn Basin, and along the W side of West Channel. All the berths, fuel, supplies, and services required for small boats are available at the individual private marinas or may be obtained nearby.

Chart 18746

(320) From Point Fermin the coast trends in a general W direction 6.5 miles to Point Vicente, and forms the N shore of San Pedro Channel, which is discussed in chapter 5. From Point Vicente the shoreline curves N. The coast is free of off-lying dangers and is well marked by kelp.

(321) The Traffic Separation Scheme between Point Fermin and Point Conception is discussed earlier in this chapter.

(322) Several submarine sewers extend 1.3 miles offshore near **White (Whites) Point**, 1.3 miles NW from Point Fermin.

(323) **Point Vicente**, 6.3 miles NW of Point Fermin, is a steep rocky cliff, 120 feet high, white and red in color, with red predominating. A rock awash is 250 yards SW from the point with kelp extending 100 yards farther to seaward. A small black 25-foot high pyramidal rock is close inshore 0.3 mile E of the point.

(324) **Point Vicente Light** (33°44'31"N., 118°24'38"W.), 185 feet above the water, is shown from a cylindrical tower on the SW end of the point.

Danger zone

(325) A **danger zone** for practice firing extends off Point Vicente. (See **334.940**, chapter 2, for limits and regulations.)

Charts 18740, 18744

(326) **Palos Verdes Point**, 2 miles NNW of Point Vicente, is a bold, bluff point, 120 feet high, rising abruptly to the W extremity of Palos Verdes Hills. There are no dangers off the point, but heavy kelp extends 0.6 mile offshore and is marked by a lighted bell buoy 0.7 mile W of the point.

(327) **Lunada Bay** is a small bight on the S side of Palos Verdes Point. **Resort Point** forms the S side of this bay.

(328) **Flat Rock Point**, 1.7 miles NE of Palos Verdes Point, is on the S side of Santa Monica Bay. A narrow spur protrudes from the otherwise rounded point. **Flat Rock**, 6 feet high, and **Bit Rock**, 5 feet high, are 175 yards and 250 yards, respectively, off the end of the spur. **Bluff Cove** is a shallow bight on the S side of Flat Rock Point. The beach is covered with boulders.

(329) **Santa Monica Bay** is formed by the curving coast between Point Vicente and Point Dume. From Flat Rock Point to Santa Monica the shore is comparatively low with a sand beach backed by a continuous city area to the inland mountains. The depths of Santa Monica Bay are comparatively shoal, the 10-fathom curve in general lying about 1 mile from shore, except at Redondo Beach where a deep submarine valley, **Redondo Canyon**, heads close to the shore.

(330) **Malaga Cove**, just N of Flat Rock Point, is used occasionally by fishing boats with local knowledge, but it is open to the prevailing W winds. Boats enter through a break in the kelp and anchor inside in 6 to 7 fathoms, with the S point of the cove bearing 207°.

(331) **King Harbor**, 4.5 miles NNE of Palos Verdes Point, is a large small-craft harbor at **Redondo Beach**. The harbor is used mostly by pleasure craft and accommodates upwards of 1,400 boats.

Prominent features

(332) At the N end of King Harbor and about 200 yards inshore is a large power plant with five large smokestacks approximately in-line and parallel with the beach. A private light is shown from atop the power plant.

COLREGS Demarcation Lines

(333) The lines established for Redondo Harbor are described in **80.1116**, chapter 2.

(334) The entrance is between two lights at the ends of the breakwaters at the S end of the harbor. A sound signal is at the light on the E side of the entrance. The sound signal can be activated upon request to the Coast Guard by radiotelephone VHF-FM Channel 16. A lighted bell buoy is 230 yards SSW of the S end of the W breakwater. The channel is marked by private buoys, with lights at the entrances to Basins 1 and 2. Natural depths through the entrance are 27 to 30 feet with a depth of 8 feet in the three basins, except for an isolated depth of 6 feet in the northeasternmost channel of Basin 1. In 1977, shoaling was reported on the S side of the entrance to

Basin 3, and in 1989, rocks awash were reported near the N side of the entrance to the basin.

(335) In 1988, numerous uncharted sunken wrecks were reported in the harbor.

Harbor regulations

(336) The harbor is administered by the city of Redondo Beach and is under the control of a harbormaster, who has an office near the entrance to Basin 2. Transients should contact the **harbormaster** for berth assignments. The harbor patrol operates from Basin 2. Both the harbor office and the patrol monitor radiotelephone VHF-FM channel 16 and can be reached be telephone at 310–318–0632.

Supplies

(337) There is a fuel dock that has gasoline and diesel fuel; most other small-craft supplies are available.

(338) A yacht club is in Basin 3.

Repairs

(339) A boatyard here can handle craft up to 50 feet and 60 tons for all general repairs.

Caution

(340) The city of Los Angeles advises that under certain tidal conditions, underwater installations between King Harbor and Marina del Rey, seaward to 9 fathom depths, present possible hazards to surface navigation.

(341) Sport fishing barges usually anchor 1 or 2 miles offshore during the summer; caution is advised to avoid them.

Submarine oil seepage

(342) About 1.5 miles off Redondo Beach, in the deep water of Redondo Canyon, there is a submarine oil seepage and the water surface is often covered with a film of petroleum. Gas bubbles have been reported in several locations in this vicinity. A second seepage 3.5 to 4 miles to the NW is more noticeable and more continuously in action. On calm days, globules and large blobs of oil have been seen projected clear of the water surface. Gas also escapes continuously in large bubbles often 3 to 6 inches in diameter.

Charts 18740, 18744, 18748

(343) **Hermosa Beach** and **Manhattan Beach** are between Redondo Beach and El Segundo; both have public fishing piers with fish havens covered 9 feet around their seaward ends. The pier at Hermosa Beach is about 1.3 miles N of Redondo Beach and extends about 275 yards from shore; a private sound signal is at the outer end. The Manhattan Beach pier, 2.5 miles N of Redondo Beach, extends almost 175 yards from shore.

(344) **El Segundo**, about 2 miles N of Manhattan Beach, has extensive oil refineries with several large oil tanks on high ground being prominent. Other prominent features are: an aero light N of El Segundo at Los Angeles International Airport, two 334-foot striped stacks in about 33°55'06"N., 118°25'39"W., and a power plant with four stacks about 0.6 mile SSE of the striped stacks. A rock groin, marked at its outer end by a private light, extends seaward from the N end of the power plant.

(345) An offshore oil terminal with two multi-buoy sea berths is about 1.3 miles W of El Segundo. The terminal, operated by Chevron USA, loads and discharges tankers through several submerged hoses and pipelines. A private lighted bell buoy is W of the offshore terminal and a safety zone surrounds the terminal. (See **33 CFR 165.1156**, chapter 2, for limits and regulations.) Two anchorages are WSW of the offshore terminal for vessels awaiting berthing assignments at the terminal. Vessels intending to use these anchorages must first contact the Vessel Traffic Information Service on VHF-FM channel 14 for assignment and further instruction.

Caution

(346) Mariners should exercise caution when navigating over the sewer outfalls and submerged pipelines that extend seaward from El Segundo. Numerous uncharted buoys and other potential hazards to navigation exist within this area.

(347) A **restricted area** extends about 7 miles offshore at El Segundo. (See **162.195**, chapter 2, for limits and regulations.)

(348) **Marina del Rey**, 7.6 miles NNW of Redondo Beach and King Harbor, is a large manmade small-craft harbor. It has a capacity for over 6,000 pleasure craft.

COLREGS Demarcation Lines

(349) The lines established for Marina del Rey are described in **80.1118**, chapter 2.

(350) A detached breakwater parallel to the shore is just to seaward of the jetties protecting the entrance channel.

Channels

(351) A dredged entrance channel leads NE from the detached breakwater for about 0.7 mile, then the harbor channel continues N for about 0.6 mile to the N end of the harbor. There are two openings between the jetties and the detached breakwater; the chart is the best guide for navigating the openings. In 2011, the controlling depths were 13 feet in the entrance channel to just past Basins B and H; thence in 2006-2009, 10 feet to Basin E at the head of the harbor. The N and S ends of the detached breakwater and the outer ends of the jetties are marked by lights. A sound signal is at the light on the outer end of the N jetty. The sound signal can be activated upon request to the Coast Guard by radiotelephone VHF-FM channel 16.

(352) A **restricted area** governing navigation inside the detached breakwater has been established. (See **162.200**, chapter 2, for limits and regulations.)

(353) **Traffic separation lanes** have been established in the entrance channel to Marina del Rey. These lanes are marked by State Waterway Regulatory Buoys with the words "No Sail." All vessels under power, or power and sail, shall keep these buoys to their port when entering or departing the harbor. The center lane between the buoys is used by vessels solely under sail, both entering or departing the harbor.

Anchorage

(354) A **special anchorage** is in the upper reach of the harbor channel. Anchoring is permitted only during storm, stress, or other emergency. (See **110.1 and 110.111**, chapter 2, for limits and regulations.)

Coast Guard

(355) A search and rescue craft is stationed at the pier just S of the harbor office, on the E side of the bend in the entrance channel.

Harbor regulations

(356) The harbor is administered by the Los Angeles County Department of Beaches and Harbors. The Harbormaster, under the Los Angeles County Sheriffs Department, has an office on the E side of the bend in the entrance channel. Guest berths are available further down the channel at Burton Chace Park.

(357) The Sheriff's Harbor Patrol operates the office on the E side of the entrance channel, providing 24-hour service. Radiotelephone VHF-FM channel 16 is monitored on a 24-hour basis, and the Sheriff's Department can be reached by telephone at 310–823–7762.

Supplies

(358) Marine supplies of all kinds can be obtain at most of the marinas and repair yards. Gasoline and diesel fuel are available at the fuel docks. Several yacht clubs are on the shores of the various basins. Medical facilities are available at the harbor, and a hospital is nearby.

Repairs

(359) There are two boatyards in the harbor that have hull and engine repair facilities. The largest lift can handle vessels to 100 tons.

(360) Fish havens, marked by private buoys, are about 1.1 miles W of the light at the N end of the detached breakwater.

Charts 18740, 18744

(361) About 1 mile N of the entrance to Marina del Rey is the 1,100-foot-long Los Angeles city public fishing pier at Venice; a fish haven covered 10 feet surrounds its seaward end.

(362) A **144°40'-324°40' measured nautical mile** is off Marina del Rey. The S range is two triangular white and orange markers located at the midpoint of Marina del Rey detached breakwater. The N range is an orange and white triangle located on the centerline of Los Angeles city public fishing pier.

(363) **Santa Monica**, 3.5 miles NW of Marina del Rey, has a large pleasure pier, but there is no water commerce. A private sound signal is on the outer end of the pier. A 0.3-mile-long breakwater, submerged at high tide, is off the outer end of the pier and parallel to the beach. A lighted bell buoy is about 550 yards S of the breakwater.

(364) The city of Santa Monica Harbor Patrol maintains a temporary office on the large pleasure pier. VHF-FM channels 12 and 16 are monitored on a 24-hour basis. A rescue boat is on call for emergencies.

(365) The buildings and structures along the beach are prominent. Most conspicuous from offshore are the tall General Telephone Building with a red and white antenna on top, and the clock tower atop a bank building.

(366) The 16-mile coast between Santa Monica and Point Dume is bold, rocky, and rugged. Steep cliffs rise abruptly from the water's edge, ascending gradually within 3 or 4 miles to the summits of the Santa Monica Mountain Range, about 3,000 feet high. The seaward termination of this range is at Point Mugu, 14 miles W of Point Dume.

(367) **Kellers Shelter**, 9 miles W of Santa Monica at **Malibu Beach**, is an open bight offering protection from N and W winds in 2 to 7 fathoms, sandy bottom. A reef marked by kelp extends a short distance offshore about 0.5 mile W of the anchorage.

(368) A fishing and pleasure pier, 700 feet long with 15 feet of water at its outer end, is on the W side of Kellers Shelter. Twin white buildings are prominent marks at the outer end of the pier. Private mooring buoys are maintained E of the pier for the use of sport fishing boats which leave for the nearby fishing grounds. Frequently the headlights of automobiles on the highway along the beach are directed toward the sea.

(369) **Paradise Cove**, 2 miles NE of Point Dume, affords protection similar to Kellers Shelter. The anchorage is abreast the fourth break or arroyo in the cliffs from Point Dume, and is immediately outside the kelp line, in 6 to 7 fathoms, sand bottom, with Point Dume bearing 240°. Kelp should be avoided because of possible dangers. A 300-foot sport fishing pier is on the NW side of Paradise Cove. A rescue vessel is moored in Paradise Cove.

(370) In 1985, hazardous submerged pilings were reported about 300 yards SSW of the fishing pier in about 34°01.1'N., 118°47.1'W.

(371) **Point Dume** is the seaward end of a rather low plateau that terminates in a dome-shaped head, about 200 feet high, rising from a bold rocky bluff. The bluff is reddish, with white cliffs E and W. A small bare rock is 150 yards S of the point, and a reef that uncovers is 150 yards farther out. Foul ground extends about 500 yards E of the reef. A lighted bell buoy is 0.5 mile off the point.

(372) A rescue boat is moored at **Zuma Beach**, about 1 mile NW of Point Dume. The rescue boat can be

(373) **Dume Canyon** (see also chart 18740) is a submarine valley with extremely steep slopes running about 0.3 mile offshore from Point Dume, and extending NW roughly parallel to the beach. Moderately strong currents of a confused directional nature have been observed in the vicinity of this submarine valley.

Chart 18720

(374) The 14-mile coast between Point Dume and Point Mugu is very rugged, and there are no known outlying dangers. About 2 miles E of Point Mugu, on the beach at the foot of a very high bluff, is a 140-foot sand dune. This is quite prominent and can be made out on clear moonlit nights. The dune is charted as a "prominent slide."

(375) **Point Mugu**, the seaward termination of the Santa Monica Mountains, is prominent because of the lowland of the Santa Clara Valley to the W. The cuts and fills of the highway which skirt the shore from Point Mugu E are prominent. Aluminum-colored twin tanks, 1.5 miles NW of the point and on the W slopes of Laguna Peak, show well from SE through W. A pipeline runs from the tanks to a prominent white radar structure atop Laguna Peak. The tanks and the pipeline are marked by flashing red lights.

Weather, Point Mugu

(376) Fog hampers visibilities most often from July through December, when the visibility drops below 0.5 mile on about 5 to 8 days per month; September is usually the worst month. N through NE winds are common from October through March, while W winds prevail from April through September. While gales are infrequent, wind gusts have reached 50 to 60 knots from fall through spring. These strong winds often blow out of the ENE. Calm conditions are frequent all year round, but particularly from May through October.

Caution

(377) The U.S. Navy advises navigation interests and others that continuous hazardous operations may take place on the Pacific Missile Test Range, Point Mugu, CA, Monday through Sunday. The test range extends for 180 miles in a SW direction from Point Mugu and is up to 210 miles wide. The specific danger portions of the firing area are broadcast daily Monday through Friday at 0900 and 1200 on 2638 kHz and 2738 kHz (See Eleventh Coast Guard District Local Notice to Mariners for additional information). The U.S. Navy will make broadcast every 30 minutes on VHF-FM Marine bridge-to-bridge radio channels 11 and 16 during hazardous operations. For information regarding the current hazardous operations status contact "PLEAD CONTROL" on VHF-FM channels 11 or 16, or at 805–989–8841/8843 from 0600-1800, or 805–816–0792 RODO (Range Operation Duty Officer) after 1800. A recorded message is available at 805–989–1470. If PLEAD CONTROL cannot be reached, contact "San Pedro Traffic" on VHF-FM channel 14 or 310–832–6411.

(378) The U.S. Navy requests all vessels transiting through the Pacific Missile Test Range submit a notification to PLEAD CONTROL indicating the vessel name, destination and estimated time of entry into and departure from the test range. Notifications can be faxed to 805–989–0102. This is for information only and does not constitute approval to enter the range. When inbound, contact PLEAD CONTROL or "San Pedro Traffic" to determine when and where an exercise is scheduled. Communicate in sufficient time to divert or adjust vessel speed to avoid naval operations. When outbound, advise "San Pedro Traffic" intention to transit "Northbound" (through the Santa Barbara Channel) or "Westbound" (south of the Channel Islands) when reporting fifteen minutes prior to departing the federal breakwater. San Pedro Traffic will provide the most recent information regarding hazardous naval operations.

Danger zone

(379) **Danger zones** for Navy small-arms firing ranges extend about 2 miles offshore at Point Mugu and about 3 miles offshore at Laguna Point. (See **334.1120** and **334.1125**, chapter 2, for limits and regulations.)

(380) **Mugu Canyon** is a submarine valley with its head near Mugu Lagoon. The 50-fathom curve is about 0.5 mile offshore.

(381) **Santa Barbara Channel** is discussed in chapter 5.

Chart 18724

(382) **Point Hueneme** (pronounced: y-nee-me), 22 miles WNW of Point Dume is low, rounding, and sandy. It is the outermost point of the low land of the Santa Clara Valley.

(383) **Point Hueneme Light** (34°08'43"N., 119°12'36"W.), 52 feet above the water, is shown from a 48-foot white square tower on the point. A sound signal is on the point about 70 yards SW of the light and can be activated upon request to the Coast Guard by radiotelephone VHF-FM channel 16. A sewer outfall line, about 1.4 miles SSE of Point Hueneme Light, extends about 1 mile from shore.

Weather, Point Hueneme

(384) In the coastal waters from Point Hueneme to Santa Barbara, sea fog hampers navigation most often from July through October. It is generally more widespread and often more persistent than land (radiation) fog. Visibilities fall below 0.5 mile (0.9 km) on about 5 to 10 days per month during these months; August and September are usually the worst.

(385) **Port Hueneme** is an inland basin, about 1,400 feet long by 1,200 feet wide, located at the head of a

submarine canyon, **Hueneme Canyon**. It is under the control of the U.S. Navy, Naval Base Ventura County. The SE part of the basin is owned by the Oxnard Harbor District and is operated as a deep-draft commercial terminal. The commercial terminal is used by cargo vessels, commercial and sport fishing craft, and offshore supply vessels operating from here to offshore drilling rigs.

Prominent features

(386) The most prominent objects around the shores of the harbor are two red and white striped stacks at a powerplant, 2.4 miles SE of the harbor, are prominent, and the aerobeacon at Oxnard, 3 miles N of the harbor, is a good night mark.

COLREGS Demarcation Lines

(387) The lines established for Port Hueneme are described in **80.1120**, chapter 2.

(388) A **Safety Fairway** leading to the channel has been established. (See **166**, chapter 2, for limits and regulations.)

Channel

(389) The dredged channel leads between two jetties and through a land cut into the basin. The outer ends of the jetties are marked by lights. A lighted whistle buoy is about 800 yards SW of the outer end of the E jetty. Lighted buoys and a **037°** lighted range mark the channel.

(390) A **Federal project** provides for a depth of 36 feet in the entrance channel and 35 feet in the basin. Mariners are advised that between periodic dredging, depths in the channel and basin are subject to change due to minor silting. Vessels with deep drafts are advised to consult with the Port Hueneme Pilots Association (805–986–3213) concerning the available depths prior to vessel arrival. General guidelines call for under-keel clearances of 3 feet for inbound vessels and 2 feet for outbound vessels, taking tidal height into consideration. The narrowest width of the entrance channel is 330 feet. However, because of prevailing fresh winds only one-way traffic is permitted for large ships. The pilots control the traffic direction.

Anchorage

(391) There is no anchorage area in the harbor basin because of space limitations. The recommended anchorage for deep-draft vessels is about 1.7 miles S of Port Hueneme Light. This location offers no protection in heavy weather.

Dangers

(392) A **naval restricted area** is in Port Hueneme. (See **334.1 through 334.6 and 334.1127**, chapter 2, for limits and regulations.)

Currents

(393) The harbor is not affected by tidal streams or currents, however, cross currents do occur near the entrance to the harbor, and are not predictable.

Pilotage, Port Hueneme

(394) All commercial vessels 300 gross registered tons and over, entering, leaving, or shifting within the Port of Hueneme, including the area of the Oxnard Harbor District, must be piloted by a port pilot duly licensed to perform the services of piloting vessels within the Port. The Oxnard Harbor district does not maintain pilots. Requests for pilots may be made by calling the Port Hueneme Pilots Association, telephone 805–986–3213. Pilots are available on a 24-hour basis and board vessels from a tug at a point 1.5 to 2.0 miles from the sea buoy. When pilots are boarding, vessels should stay on the range line and reduce speed to 5 knots or less.

(395) Pilot ladder should be rigged on the lee side (normally starboard while inbound, port side outbound) amidship, about 5 feet (1.5 m) above the water. Pilot ladder should be rigged well away from any overboard discharge. At night, the ladder must be properly lighted.

(396) Access to and from the ladder to the deck of the ship should be through a break in the rail, or if the ladder tends over the rail, then steps should be provided on the inboard side to permit access back to the deck level. Manropes should NOT be rigged, when boarding a Pilot, coming from sea.

(397) A proper ring-buoy (with light and line attached) should be provided at the boarding area. The harbor pilots guard VHF-FM channel 16. Vessels are cautioned to remain a safe distance off-shore when calling pilots because dock space must often be cleared.

Towage

(398) Tug service for the port is furnished by a private tug company. Requests for service may be made by telephone, 805–986–1600. Tugs up to 4,000 hp are available on a 24-hour basis.

Quarantine, customs, immigration, and agricultural quarantine

(399) (See chapter 3, Vessel Arrival Inspections, and Appendix A for addresses.)

(400) **Quarantine** is enforced in accordance with regulations of the U.S. Public Health Service. (See Public Health Service, chapter.)

(401) Port Hueneme is a **U.S. Customs port of entry**, telephone 805–488–8574.

Agricultural quarantine

(402) All vessels from outside of California that dock at Port Hueneme, except those specifically exempt, must be inspected by U.S. Department of Agriculture and/or the Ventura County Department of Agriculture. There are local representatives in the Oxnard area.

Harbor regulations

(403) The U.S. Navy exercises overall Port Control Authority. Port Hueneme, Control One, is on duty at all times, and monitors VHF-FM channel 6; the Oxnard Harbor District is responsible for its commercial operations. The Wharfinger is on duty at all times and guards VHF-FM channel 14; the Wharfinger office is at the E end of Slip A, along with the pilot and tugboat offices. Entrance to Naval Base Ventura County is restricted, and no photography is permitted without clearance.

(404) No garbage, waste, or refuse shall be discharged in any manner from any vessel in accordance with the California Administrative Code, a copy of which is available at the port's main administrative building. A 5-knot **speed limit** is enforced in the harbor.

Wharves

(405) Oxnard Harbor District has three 600-foot long deep-draft berths (Wharf No. 1) and two 700 foot -long deep- draft berths (Wharf No. 2). There is also a shallow depth wharf at the W end of the port property adjacent to the entrance channel. It is 379 feet long with 15 to 18 feet alongside.

(406) Wharf No. 1: 1,800 feet long; 35 feet alongside; deck height, 14 feet; three refrigerated warehouses providing 210,000 square feet of covered storage; 20 acres of open storage; three 60-ton vehicular weight scales; and Central Gate; operated by Oxnard Harbor District.

(407) Wharf No. 2: 1,450 feet long; 35 feet alongside; deck height, 14 feet; 96,000 square feet of warehouse; 23 acres of open storage; operated by Oxnard Harbor District.

Supplies

(408) Water and most marine supplies are available. Bunker fuel from dockside pipeline at commercial berths and diesel oil are obtainable.

Repairs

(409) Minor repairs may be made in the port. Machine shops in Ventura and Oxnard are qualified for normal voyage repair work.

Communications

(410) Oxnard has good rail, air, and highway connections with Los Angeles and points N.

Chart 18725

(411) **Channel Islands Harbor**, 1 mile NW of Port Hueneme and 5.8 miles SE of Ventura Marina, is a small-craft harbor. It is used by pleasure and sport fishing vessels and has existing berthing facilities for over 2,400 boats.

No-Discharge Zone

(412) The State of California, with the approval of the Environmental Protection Agency, has established a No-Discharge Zone (NDZ) in Channel Islands Harbor. It encompasses the entire harbor (see NOAA chart 18725 for the zone limits).

(413) Within the NDZ, discharge of sewage, whether treated or untreated, from all vessels is prohibited. Outside the NDZ, discharge of sewage is regulated by **40 CFR 140** (see Chapter 2).

COLREGS Demarcation Lines

(414) The lines established for Channel Islands Harbor are described in **80.1122**, chapter 2.

Channels

(415) The entrance to Channel Islands Harbor is between two jetties protected by an offshore breakwater. Each end of the breakwater and both the seaward and inshore ends of both jetties are marked by lights. A sound signal is at the seaward end of the S jetty. The sound signal can be activated upon request to the Coast Guard by radiotelephone VHF-FM channel 16.

(416) The areas SE of the entrance channel and NW of the N jetty are subject to rapid and uncertain shoaling. Mariners are advised to approach the entrance channel from the S and to exercise caution when approaching the harbor at night.

(417) A Federal project provides for a 20-foot entrance channel that leads NE from the breakwater and between the jetties, then turns N into an entrance basin of the same depth, thence to a 10-foot inner basin just N of the entrance basin. (See Notice to Mariners and latest editions of charts for depths.)

Coast Guard

(418) The Channel Islands Harbor Coast Guard Station is just S of the harbormaster's office. Search and rescue vessels are stationed here.

Harbor regulations

(419) The harbor is administered by the Harbor County Department, Ventura County, and is under control of a **harbormaster**, who has an office on the E side of the harbor about 400 yards N of the first bend in the channel. The harbor office maintains guest berths for 70 craft. Transients should report to the harbormaster for berth assignments. The harbormaster guards VHF-FM channel 16, 24 hours a day. Harbor patrol boats operate from the office.

Supplies

(420) Gasoline and diesel fuel are pumped at a fueling dock on the E side of the harbor just N of the harbor office. Water, ice, and most marine supplies are available.

Repairs

(421) Two full-service marine repair yards are on the E side of the channel, about 0.5 mile N of the harbormaster's

(422) A **147°51'–327°51' measured nautical mile** is off the breakwater and beach just N of the harbor entrance. The S range is marked by the breakwater S light and the S jetty light. The N range is marked by less visible poles on the beach.

(423) A row of cottages extends NW along the beach for 2 miles from Point Hueneme. From the point, low sand beaches and dunes trend NW for 9 miles to the mouth of **Ventura River**.

(424) A striped 209-foot stack having a bright flashing red light on top is 0.6 mile N of **Mandalay Beach** and is conspicuous throughout the area.

(425) **Ventura** is 8.5 miles N of Point Hueneme on **Pierpont Bay**. It has a 1,960-foot fishing pier with about 19 feet of water at the outer end, and about 18 feet at the inner end of a 250-foot loading face.

(426) Freshwater is piped to the pier, and gasoline is available in the town.

(427) Two fish havens are about 2.3 miles SW and 1.7 miles S, respectively, from Ventura Pier.

(428) Small craft may anchor anywhere in Pierpont Bay, but the anchorage is unprotected and is not recommended except for short day use. Boats may obtain moorage at Ventura Harbor.

(429) The most prominent features around Ventura are the lighted microwave tower, atop a hill 1.8 miles NE of the seaward end of Ventura Pier, and the tall motel, about 300 yards W of the pier. Also prominent are the railroad trestle crossing Ventura River, just W of town, and **Padre Junipero Serra Cross**, on a 350-foot hill immediately NW of the center of town. There are several aluminum-colored tanks and many oil derricks high up the slopes of the hills NW of town.

(430) **Ventura Harbor**, 6.7 miles N of Point Hueneme and just N of Santa Clara River, is a small-craft harbor used by pleasure craft and commercial fishing vessels. It has existing berthing facilities for about 1,500 boats. Commercial fish handling facilities are available in the harbor. In 2001, a submerged rock was reported in about 34°15.3'N., 119°16.4'W. Caution is advised.

COLREGS Demarcation Lines

(431) The lines established for Ventura Harbor are described in **80.1124**, chapter 2.

(432) The entrance to Ventura Harbor is between two jetties protected by a 1,800-foot detached breakwater. The S end of the breakwater and the seaward ends of both jetties are marked by lights. A sound signal is at the S jetty light. The sound signal can be activated upon request to the Coast Guard by radiotelephone VHF-FM channel 16.

(433) Dangerous breakers can develop in the approach area to the entrance channel in winter when the prevailing winds are from the W. Inbound and outbound vessels are advised by local interests to run a direct course between Ventura Marina Entrance Lighted Whistle Buoy 2V and the breakwater entrance.

Channels

(434) The dredged entrance channel leads NE between the jetties, then turns E into the harbor. The private buoys in the entrance channel and harbor are not charted because the positions are changed frequently due to the shifting shoals. Mariners are advised to exercise extreme caution and to contact the harbormaster for the latest channel and harbor conditions prior to entering.

(435) A channel leads NE from the N part of the harbor to a private waterfront home development called **Ventura Keys**. In 2000, depths of 14 feet were reported in the development.

Harbor regulations

(436) Ventura Harbor is administered by the Ventura Port District and is under the control of a **harbormaster**, who has an office on the point N of the entrance basin. Transients should report to the harbormaster for guest slip assignments. The harbormaster monitors VHF-FM channels 16 and 12, from 0600 to 0200 daily.

Supplies

(437) Gasoline and diesel fuel are available just E of the harbormaster's office and at the S end of the harbor. Water, ice, and marine supplies are available. Two yacht clubs are on the shores of the harbor.

Repairs

(438) Boatyards in the harbor have mobile lifts that can haul out vessels to 150 tons for hull and engine repairs. Electronic service is also available.

(439) From Ventura River, the **Santa Ynez Mountains** extend to Point Conception and Point Arguello. For 11 miles W from the river to Rincon Point the coast is very rugged; elevations of over 2,000 feet being found within 1 mile of the beach. The dangers do not extend over 0.5 mile from the beach which is well fringed with kelp. Between Ventura and Santa Barbara are several small towns, and the highway and railroad skirt the shore; retaining walls are a common feature.

(440) **Pitas Point**, 5.5 miles NW of Ventura, is the first bold point W of Ventura River. A very steep gulch is on the W side. E of the point is 1 mile of beach cottages. High on the steep slopes above the cottages are the derricks and tanks of an oil field. Aluminum-colored tanks and oil-processing plants are prominent 1 mile E of the point.

(441) A fish haven, marked by a buoy, is about 1.4 miles SE of Pitas Point.

(442) **Punta Gorda**, 9 miles NW of Ventura, is low at its outer extremity, but rises rapidly to prominent **Rincon Mountain**. E of the point is a long pier supporting several oil pumps. Oil tanks are conspicuous on the outer end of the pier. Tanks and numerous derricks are along the highway just E of the pier. W of this pier a causeway

office. Mobile lifts can handle craft to 25 tons, and a fixed lift can handle vessels to 60 tons.

extends S from Punta Gorda for 0.5 mile to an artificial island used for oil operations. A private light and sound signal are on the island.

(443) **Rincon Point,** 11 miles NW of Ventura, is low and sandy. **Sand Point,** 3.5 miles W of Rincon Point, is low and rounding, with the narrow opening to **El Estero,** a lagoon of no importance lying close under and E of it. A rock that uncovers is 550 yards offshore from Sand Point. Oil-drilling platforms are off Sand Point.

(444) A Standard Oil installation is prominent on the E side of **Carpinteria,** 8 miles E of Santa Barbara. A submerged pipeline leads to offshore oil drilling platforms and to mooring buoys about 0.6 mile offshore where tankers are loaded. A pier is used to load support boats operating to and from the oil platforms. Many storage tanks are back of and on each side of the pier. One tank with an aluminum-colored dome may be seen from seaward.

(445) **Ortega Hill,** just W of **Summerland** and 18 miles NW of Ventura, is 250 feet high and conspicuous because of the extensive cuts for the highway; from offshore it has the appearance of a large slide.

(446) **Santa Barbara,** 29 miles NW of Point Hueneme, is a resort city and popular yachting harbor. The harbor is used mostly by pleasure craft and fishing vessels. There are about 1,200 slips in the harbor.

(447) **Santa Barbara Light** (34°23'47"N., 119°43'21"W.), 142 feet above the water, is shown from a 24-foot white tower about 2 miles W of the harbor entrance. **Lavigia Hill,** 0.6 mile NE of the light is 459 feet high and the distinguishing feature in approaching Santa Barbara from the E or W.

(448) Submerged shellfish structures are about 0.7 mile SE of Santa Barbara Light in about 34°23'15"N., 119°42'45"W.

(449) **Santa Barbara Point,** 1 mile E of the light, is a high cliff at the SE limit of the narrow tableland extending from Lavigia Hill. The point is the beginning of a sand beach extending 0.6 mile E to **Point Castillo,** the W point of the breakwater forming Santa Barbara Harbor.

(450) Conspicuous landmarks are the neon-lighted hotel tower on the beach 1 mile E of the town, the several radio towers, and the many residences on the hillsides back of the town. At night the lights of Santa Barbara are prominent from the channel, but they are obscured from the W by Lavigia Hill.

COLREGS Demarcation Lines

(451) The lines established for Santa Barbara Harbor are described in **80.1126,** chapter 2.

(452) The harbor has a 500-yard breakwater extending NE from **Point Castillo** to an extensive sandbar which forms the S side of the harbor. A jetty extends across the sandbar about 400 yards N from the NE end of the breakwater. A light is at the end of the jetty and a light and sound signal mark the connection between the breakwater and jetty. The sound signal is activated by the Santa Barbara Harbor Patrol. The NE side of the harbor is formed by Stearns Wharf; the wharf is marked by a light at the S end. A groin, about 125 yards long, extends S from shore about 0.3 mile W of Stearns Wharf. At night, sometimes the lights are difficult to see against the background of city lights.

Channels

(453) A dredged entrance channel leads NW between the breakwater and Stearns Wharf then turns SW into the harbor. The channel is marked by buoys. The harbor buoys are not charted because their positions are frequently changed. The entrance and harbor are subject to rapid shoaling. The harbormaster advises that the entrance channel has a tendency to shoal after SE storms. Mariners should contact the harbormaster on 2182 kHz or on VHF-FM channel 16 for channel conditions and assistance in entering.

Anchorage

(454) A special anchorage area is in the basin behind the breakwater. (See **110.1 and 110.115,** chapter 2, for limits and regulations.) Anchoring inside the harbor is usually prohibited by the harbormaster. A seasonal anchorage area (April-October) and a permitted mooring area are E of Stearns Wharf; the mooring area contains several mooring buoys. Anchorage is prohibited within 300 feet E of Stearns Wharf. Large vessels should anchor outside the anchorage and mooring areas in better holding ground. The harbormaster desires advanced requests for permission to anchor (805–564–5530).

Regulated Navigation Area

(455) A security zone exists within a 100-yard radius of any cruise ship located within 3 nautical miles of the Santa Barbara Harbor Breakwater Light. (See **33 CFR 165.1157,** chapter 2, for limits and regulations.)

Caution

(456) The long sandbar N of the breakwater light is inconspicuous on a high-tide night, but the masts of boats moored in the harbor are quite visible over the breakwater. The **harbormaster** reports that these circumstances have caused several groundings on the sandbar when strangers making for the harbor at night failed to identify the breakwater light, failed to see the sandbar, but sighted the masts in the harbor and steered toward them, consequently going hard aground on the sandbar. The shoreline of the sandbar is subject to continual change.Caution should be exercised when entering at night; the buoyed channel should be carefully followed.

Weather, Santa Barbara

(457) Fog plagues the harbor most often from August through November, when it reduces visibilities to less than 0.5 mile (0.9 km) on 4 to 7 days per month. Morning

is usually the worst time. Winds are often calm at Santa Barbara. Winds of 3 knots or less occur 18 percent of the time or more year round, and 25 to 40 percent of the time from September through March. The sea breeze helps reduce this percentage. These spring and summer winds are mainly out of the E through WSW. NE winds, common throughout the year, are the most frequent winds from November through February, though a distant second to calm conditions.

Coast Guard

(458) A Coast Guard rescue vessel is stationed at the city pier in the SW part of the harbor; Marine Safety Detachment is nearby.

Harbor regulations

(459) Santa Barbara Harbor is administered by the City of Santa Barbara Water Front Department and is under the control of a **harbormaster**, who has an office at the SW corner of the harbor. Transients should report to the harbormaster for guest slip assignments. The office monitors VHF-FM channel 16, and can be reached by telephone 805–564–5530.

(460) The harbor patrol is on 24-hour duty and monitors VHF-FM channel 16. Strangers desiring assistance entering the harbor will be assisted by a patrol boat as needed when requested.

Supplies

(461) The City Pier, inside the harbor, has diesel fuel, gasoline, commercial ice, water, and other marine supplies.

Repairs

(462) The City Pier has a hoist with a maximum lift of 2 tons. There is a boatyard on the SW side of the basin that can handle craft up to 25 tons and 50 feet for hull and engine repairs. A small floating drydock in the harbor can lift craft up to 20 tons for hull maintenance and repair. There are several other boat builders and repair yards in the city of Santa Barbara.

Communication

(463) Communication is by rail, motor vehicle, and by airplane. The Santa Barbara Municipal Airport is at **Goleta**, 7 miles W of the harbor.

Chart 18721

(464) The 8-mile coast from Santa Barbara W to Goleta Point consists of bluffs 30 to 100 feet high with short stretches of sand beach and is fringed with kelp 0.2 mile offshore.

(465) **Goleta Point**, 6.2 miles W of Santa Barbara Light, is low and terminates in a cliff about 30 feet high. The buildings of the University of California at Santa Barbara are conspicuous just N of the point and are dominated by a lone tower. The aerolight 1.5 miles N and the two lighted radio towers 1.5 miles NE of the point are good marks at night. A 1,475-foot pleasure pier is in the bight E of the point. A 4-ton hoist is available.

(466) The 32-mile coast from Goleta Point to Point Conception is more rugged than that Eastward. **Cañada de la Gaviota**, 12 miles E of Point Conception, is a conspicuous break in the mountains back of this coast. A railroad skirts the shore over trestles and embankments which cross the mouths of numerous gulches and arroyos. The kelp grows quite heavily, and in some places extends over a mile offshore. The Pacific Coast Highway parallels the coast from Santa Barbara to Gaviota, where it turns inland.

(467) Oil well production heads covered 6 fathoms or more and submerged pipelines to shore extend as much as 3 miles offshore between Goleta Point and Point Conception. Several oil-well structures in the area are lighted and equipped with racons and fog signals.

Safety zones

(468) Safety zones have been established around oil drilling platforms and an offshore storage and treatment vessel mooring area, about 13 miles W of Goleta Point, in

(469) 34°23'27"N., 120°07'14"W. (**Platform Hondo**);

(470) 34°22'36"N., 120°10'03"W. (**Platform Harmony**);

(471) 34°21'01"N., 120°16'45"W. (**Platform Heritage**); and

(472) 34°24'19"N., 120°06'00"W. (**vessel mooring area**). (See **147.1 through 147.20, 147.1105, 147.1106, 147.1114 and 147.1115**, chapter 2 for limits and regulations and chapter 3 under **'Oil well structures'** for additional information.)

(473) Temporary drilling platforms can be found along this coastline and may be moved periodically. Mooring buoys for tankers are SW of Coal Oil Point and S of Gaviota.

(474) **Coal Oil Point**, 1.8 miles W of Goleta Point, is low and may be distinguished by the strong odor of petroleum discharged by a spring. This odor is noticeable over 2 miles offshore.

(475) Pilings of former piers and ruins of a drilling rig may exist from Coal Oil Point for about 2.5 miles NW to the pier at **Ellwood**. The private 2,300-foot pier is owned by Arco Oil. Passage without local knowledge is not advisable.

(476) A rock covered 14 feet is at 34°25'18"N., 119°57'06"W., about 4.3 miles W of Coal Oil Point and 0.9 mile offshore; it is surrounded by kelp.

(477) **Capitan**, 7.5 miles W of Coal Oil Point, is in a small bight which offers little protection to small craft. A lone tank stands on a bare hill 500 feet high and 0.3 mile inland.

(478) **Refugio Beach** at **Orella**, 2.5 miles W of Capitan, is a state park for camping at the mouth of the canyon. A

(478) small bight here offers some protection for small boats in northwesterly winds in about 15 feet.

(479) Oil is loaded from a submerged pipeline at **Gaviota**, 13.5 miles E of Point Conception. A number of large green storage tanks mark the inshore end of the pipeline. About 1 mile W of Gaviota is a State beach park with a 545-foot pleasure-fishing pier. An electric hoist for launching skiffs is available. The railway trestle along the beach is quite prominent.

(480) **Cojo Anchorage**, 1.5 miles E of Point Conception, affords protection off the mouth of the Cojo Valley from moderate W and NW winds. The suggested anchorage is opposite a culvert under the railroad tracks in 5 to 10 fathoms, hard sandy bottom. The cove 1.7 miles E of this anchorage known as Little (Old) Cojo, is foul and affords little protection.

(481) **Point Conception**, 118 miles NW of Point Fermin and at the W end of Santa Barbara Channel, is a bold headland 220 feet high that marks an abrupt change in the trend of the coast. There is comparatively low land immediately behind it. At a distance from N or E, it usually looks like an island.

(482) Point Conception has been called the **Cape Horn of the Pacific** because of the heavy NW gales encountered off it during the passage through Santa Barbara Channel. A marked change of climatic and meteorological conditions is experienced off the point, the transition often being remarkably sudden and well defined. When the northwesterly winds are strong they blow down the canyons between Point Conception and Capitan and cause heavy offshore gusts.

(483) **Point Conception Light** (34°26'55"N., 120°28'15"W.), 133 feet above the water, is shown from a 52-foot white tower behind a building near the W part of the point. A low black rock, nearly awash at high tide, is 220 yards offshore, SW of the light.

Danger and Safety zones

(484) **Danger zones** extend offshore from Point Conception to Point Sal. (See **334.1130**, chapter 2, for limits and regulations.) For additional information on Vandenberg Danger Zones, contact 800–648–3019 or 805–606–8825.

(485) **Safety zones** have been established around oil drilling platforms in

(486) 34°27'19.0"N., 120°38'47.0"W. **(Platform Hermosa)**;

(487) 34°28'09.5"N., 120°40'46.1"W. **(Platform Harvest)**; and

(488) 34°29'42.0"N., 120°42'08.0"W. **(Platform Hidalgo)**. (See **147.1 through 147.20, 147.1109, 147.1110, and 147.1112**, chapter 2 for limits and regulations and chapter 3 under **'Oil well structures'** for additional information.)

(489) From Point Conception, the coast trends in a gentle curve NW for 12 miles to Point Arguello and consists of bold rocky cliffs, 100 to 400 feet high. The coast railroad runs along these cliffs and through several tunnels.

(490) The 100-fathom depth curve off Point Arguello, and to a lesser extent off Point Conception, is characterized by a succession of indenting deeps or gorges. In following the curve during thick weather with an echo sounder, these submarine features should be found extremely useful.

(491) **Espada Bluff** is a prominent cliff 378 feet high, 5.5 miles NNW of Point Conception. The cliffs on each side drop sharply to less than 100 feet in height.

(492) **Tranquillon Mountain**, near the seaward end of the Santa Ynez Mountains, is prominent in clear weather. It terminates in Rocky Point, Point Arguello, and Point Pedernales.

(493) **Rocky Point**, 1.2 miles S of Point Arguello, has numerous detached rocks extending in some cases 300 yards offshore.

(494) **Point Arguello** is a narrow, jagged, rocky projection, extending about 800 yards W of the general trend of the coast. An outlying rock is about 200 yards seaward. The extremity of the point overhangs the water's edge, and about 200 yards inshore the point is nearly divided by gullies on the N and S sides. These form a saddle which, from N and S, looks like two heads. **Point Arguello Light** (34°34'37"N., 120°38'50"W.), 100 feet above the water, is shown from a 20-foot high post on the W end of the point.

Weather, Point Arguello

(495) Off Point Arguello, sea fog becomes a persistent and frequent navigational hazard. The cool California Current is responsible for a sudden increase in fog frequencies. These fogs are often thick, and Point Arguello is considered by mariners to be one of the most dangerous areas along the coast. The observing station at Point Arguello, 371 feet (113 m) above mean sea level, records an annual average of twice as many days with visibilities less than 0.5 mile (0.9 km) as at any location farther S. From June through October, visibilities drop below 0.5 mile (0.9 km) on about 12 to 20 days per month; July and August are the worst months.

Chart 18687

(496) **Lake Mead**, Arizona-Nevada, is a National Recreation Area on the **Colorado River** impounded by **Hoover Dam** (36°01.0'N., 114°44.2'W.).

Anchorage areas

(497) Restricted and anchorage areas established by Federal regulations are in Lake Mead. (See **110.1**, 110.127, and 162.220, chapter 2, for limits and regulations.) Additional information may be obtained from the local office of the National Park Service, U.S. Department of the Interior, 601 Nevada Highway, Boulder City, NV 89005.

(498) Eleventh Coast Guard District Local Notice to Mariners contains information concerning boating

events, boating safety, bridge construction and lighting, aids to navigation, and anchorages on the Colorado River, Lake Mead National Recreation Area, and Glen Canyon National Recreation Area. These notices may be obtained, free of charge, by making application to Commander, Eleventh Coast Guard District. (See Appendix A for address.)

| TIDAL INFORMATION ||||||
Chart	Station	LAT/LONG	Mean Higher High Water*	Mean High Water*	Mean Low Water*
18721	Point Arguello	34°35'N/120°39'W	5.2	4.5	1.0
18721	Bechers Bay, Santa Rosa Island	34°01'N/120°03'W	5.1	4.4	1.0
18724	Port Hueneme, Santa Barbara Channel	34°09'N/119°12'W	5.4	4.7	1.0
18725	Ventura, Santa Barbara Channel	34°16'N/119°17'W	5.4	4.7	1.0
18725	Santa Barbara	34°25'N/119°41'W	5.4	4.6	1.0
18744	Santa Monica (Municipal Pier)	34°01'N/118°30'W	5.4	4.7	0.9
18746	Catalina Harbor, Santa Catalina Island	33°26'N/118°30'W	5.2	4.5	0.9
18748	El Segundo, Santa Monica Bay	33°55'N/118°26'W	5.3	4.6	0.9
18748	King Harbor, Santa Monica Bay	33°51'N/118°24'W	5.3	4.6	0.9
18751	Los Angeles, Outer Harbor	33°43'N/118°16'W	5.5	4.8	0.9
18751	Los Angeles Harbor, Mormon Island	33°45'N/118°16'W	5.4	4.7	1.0
18754	Newport Bay Entrance (Corona del Mar)	33°36'N/117°53'W	5.4	4.7	0.9
18754	Balboa Pier, Newport Beach	33°36'N/117°54'W	5.3	4.6	0.9
18758	Oceanside Harbor	33°13'N/117°24'W	5.4	4.6	--.--
18765	Crown Point, Mission Bay	32°47'N/117°14'W	5.5	4.8	0.9
18765	La Jolla, Scripps Institution Wharf	32°52'N/117°15'W	5.3	4.6	0.9
18772	Point Loma	32°40'N/117°14'W	5.3	4.6	0.9
18773	San Diego, Quaratine Station	32°42'N/117°14'W	5.6	4.8	0.9
18773	National City, San Diego Bay	32°40'N/117°07'W	5.9	5.2	0.9
18773	San Diego (Broadway), San Diego Bay	32°43'N/117°10'W	5.7	5.0	0.9
18774	San Clemente	33°25'N/117°37'W	5.3	4.6	0.9
18774	Avalon, Santa Catalina Island	33°21'N/118°19'W	5.3	4.6	0.9

* Heights in feet referred to datum of sounding MLLW.
Real-time water levels, tide predictions, and tidal current predictions are available at:
http://tidesandcurrents.noaa.gov
To determine mean tide range subtract Mean Low Water from Mean High Water.
Data as of September 2012

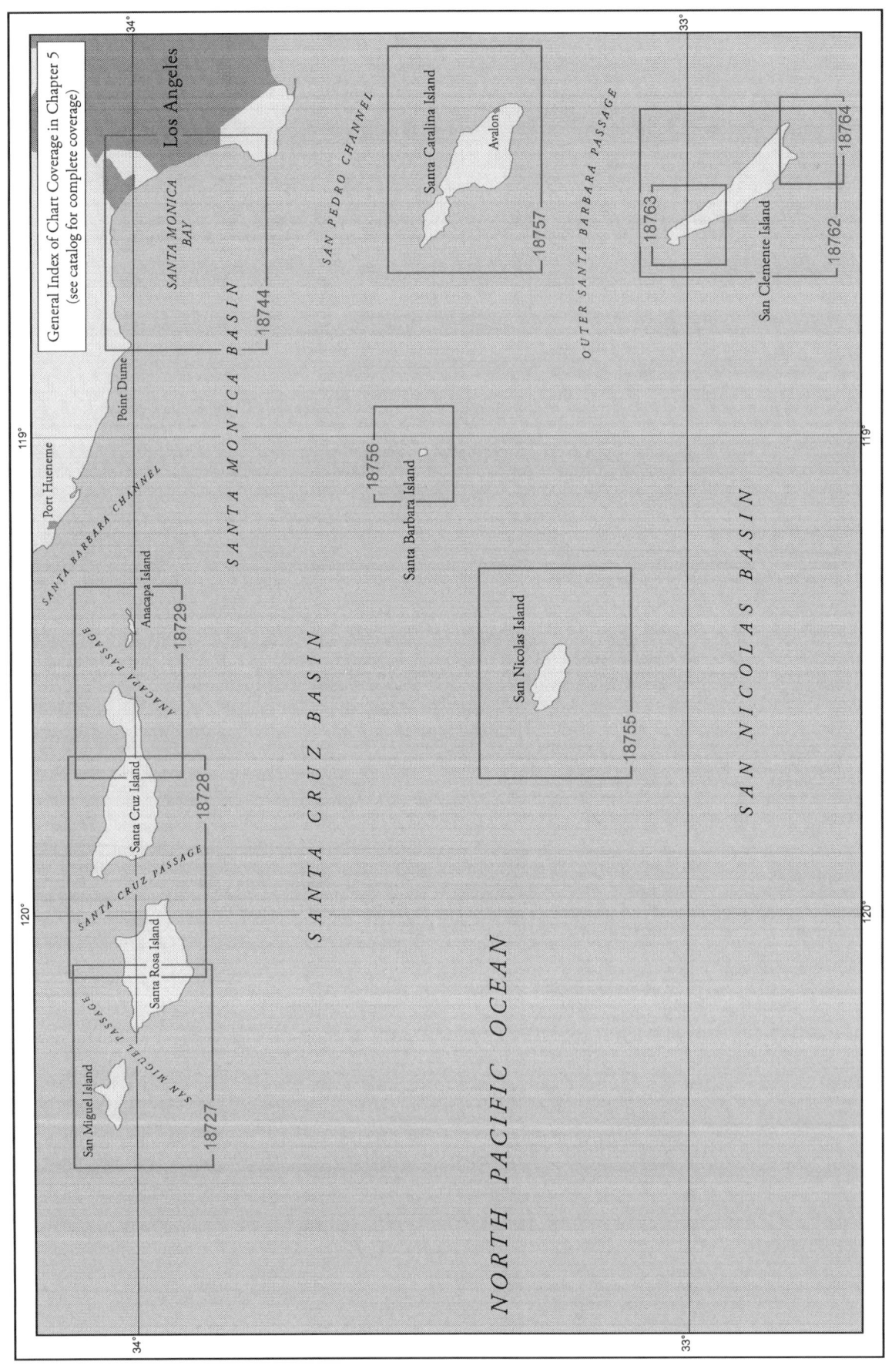

Channel Islands, California

(1) This chapter describes the eight **Channel Islands** that extend for 130 miles in a NW direction off the coast of southern California from San Diego to Point Conception. They include the four islands of the southern group–San Clemente, Santa Catalina, San Nicolas, and Santa Barbara; and the four islands of the northern group also referred to as the **Santa Barbara Islands**–Anacapa, Santa Cruz, Santa Rosa, and San Miguel. Also described are the passages and channels between these islands including Outer Santa Barbara Passage, San Pedro Channel, Anacapa Passage, Santa Cruz Channel, San Miguel Passage, and Santa Barbara Passage, and Avalon Bay, the most active harbor in the area, as well as many smaller harbors and landings.

COLREGS Demarcation Lines

(2) The lines established for this part of the coast are described in **80.1102**, chapter 2.

Chart 18022

(3) San Clemente, San Nicholas, and San Miguel Islands are military reservations and, except for San Miguel Island, off limits to the public.

(4) Santa Barbara, Anacapa, Santa Cruz, Santa Rosa, and San Miguel Islands form **Channel Islands National Park.** The park was created in 1980 to protect the extensive flora and fauna of the islands. The park is under the supervision of the National Park Service, Department of the Interior.

(5) In the approach from the S, several banks are encountered before reaching the Channel Islands. **Sixtymile Bank**, 62 miles SSW of Point Loma (32°39.9'N., 117°14.5'W.), has a least depth of 53 fathoms over it.

(6) **Channel Islands National Marine Sanctuary** has been established to protect and preserve the natural, cultural and historical resources in the waters surrounding the northern Channel Islands and Santa Barbara Island. The sanctuary encompasses the waters within six nautical miles of Santa Barbara Island and the northern Channel Islands (Anacapa, Santa Cruz, Santa Rosa and San Miguel Islands), including Castle and Richardson Rocks. Visitor use is encouraged for boating, diving, snorkeling, fishing, swimming, kayaking, and wildlife viewing. (See **15 CFR 922.70** through **922.74**, chapter 2, for limits and regulations.)

Area to be Avoided–Channel Islands

(7) The International Maritime Organization (IMO) has adopted the waters surrounding the Channel Islands as areas to be avoided. In order to avoid risk of pollution in the area designated as the Channel Islands National Marine Sanctuary, all ships, except those bound to and from ports on one of the islands within the area, engaged in the trade of carrying hazardous cargo, including but not limited to tankers and other bulk carriers and barges, should avoid the areas in the region of San Miguel, Santa Rosa, Santa Cruz, and Anacapa Islands bounded by a line connecting the following points:

(8) 33°58.7'N., 119°12.8'W.
(9) 33°54.0'N., 119°17.0'W.
(10) 33°46.3'N., 120°07.8'W.
(11) 33°59.0'N., 120°39.5'W.
(12) 34°10.4'N., 120°39.5'W.
(13) 34°14.0'N., 120°31.3'W.
(14) 34°10.0'N., 119°56.4'W.
(15) 34°01.4'N., 119°18.6'W., and the area surrounding Santa Barbara Island contained within a circle of radius 7.5 nautical miles, centered on the following point:
(16) 33°28.6'N., 119°02.2'W.

Blue, fin and humpback whales

(17) All whales are protected under the Marine Mammal Protection Act (MMPA) and, when in Sanctuary waters, under the National Marine Sanctuaries Act (NMSA). Certain large whales, including blue, fin and humpback whales, are also listed as endangered under the Endangered Species Act (ESA). See chapter 3 for more information.

Local Magnetic Disturbance

(18) Differences of 4° or more from the normal magnetic variation have been observed within a radius of 8 miles of Sixtymile Bank.

Chart 18740

(19) **Bishop Rock**, in about 32°27'N., 119°08'W. and which the clipper ship BISHOP struck in 1855, is awash and marked by a lighted bell buoy. The rock, about 40 miles SW of San Clemente Island, is the farthest outlying danger along the coast. A wreck, covered ½ fathom and about 0.1 mile SE of the rock, is the shallowest point on **Cortes** Bank. The currents are largely nontidal in character; velocities between 1 and 2 knots have been measured. These currents cause considerable swell, and

(20) even in moderate weather the sea usually breaks at this rock.

The area for about 2.5 miles ESE of Bishop Rock should be avoided because of the broken bottom. Deep-draft vessels should also avoid a 9-fathom spot 5 miles WNW of the rock where the bottom is extremely broken, although no breakers have been reported.

(21) **Tanner Bank** covers an area about 12 miles long in a WNW direction and about 5 miles wide. The least survey depth over it is 9 fathoms. The NW end of the bank is about 28 miles SE of San Nicolas Island.

(22) A bank covered 45 to 70 fathoms is 18 miles NW of Tanner Bank. The bank extends 9 miles in a NW-SE direction and has an average width of 2 miles. The bottom is hard with fine gray sand and shells. The bank is fished extensively during the winter.

Chart 18762

(23) **San Clemente Island**, 43 miles SSW of Point Fermin and 57 miles WNW of Point Loma, is 18 miles long in a NW direction and 4 miles wide at its widest part, and reaches an elevation of 1,965 feet. The island is a U.S. Naval Reservation and is closed to the public. Vessels including yachts and fishing craft are warned that the vicinity of the island may be dangerous at any time because of naval activities, including gunfire, bombing, and rocket fire. (See **165.1131, 165.1141, 334.920, 334.921, 334.950, 334.960, and 334.961**, chapter 2, for limits and regulations.)

Local magnetic disturbance

(24) Differences of as much as 5° from normal variation have been observed up to 3 miles offshore along the N, E, and S coasts of the island.

(25) The top of the island appears as a tableland from a distance. A prominent white radar dome (32°53.1'N., 118°27.0'W.), on the highest part of the island, is visible from both the E and W sides of the island.

(26) The NE side of the island is bold, with rocky cliffs. The water is generally deep close inshore, and kelp grows close to the beach. On this side of the island a prominent white rock is close inshore, 6 miles NW of Pyramid Head. On the beach behind this rock is a freshwater spring, the only one available during the dry season.

(27) The SW side of the island is more irregular, but it is lower and has more gentle slopes. Here the kelp extends several hundred yards offshore, and generally to or beyond the 10-fathom curve. Rocks are numerous close inshore and inside the kelp, but outside the kelp line, the bottom slope is more gradual than on the other side of the island, and there are many places where vessels might anchor safely in the lee of the island during the NE storms, known as the Santa Anas.

(28) **Seal Cove**, on the SW side of the island midway between the two ends, affords a boat landing and indifferent anchorage for small craft in NW weather.

(29) **Outer Santa Barbara Passage** lies between San Clemente and Santa Catalina Islands.

Chart 18764

(30) **China Point** is the SW extremity of San Clemente Island and on the W side of Pyramid Cove. A light is shown from a white pyramidal structure on the point.

(31) **Pyramid Cove**, the deep bight in the S end of San Clemente Island, is used as a naval shore bombardment area and included in a **danger zone**. (See **334.950**, chapter 2, for limits and regulations.) The cove, closed to the public, offers protected anchorage in 10 fathoms or more in NW weather to authorized vessels and vessels in distress. Vessels should not enter the kelp as there are indications of other dangers in addition to those already charted. Some swell makes into the cove most of the time. Authorized landing on the beach is usually not difficult, but can be extremely hazardous because of unexploded ordnance.

(32) **Pyramid Head**, the SE point of San Clemente Island and the E side of Pyramid Cove, is about 900 feet high, sharp, jagged, and prominent. **Pyramid Head Light** (32°49'13"N., 118°21'12"W.), 226 feet above the water, is shown from a post with red and white diamond-shaped daymark.

Chart 18763

(33) **Wilson Cove**, on the NE shore of San Clemente Island, 15.5 miles NW of Pyramid Head, is a fair anchorage in the prevailing W weather, but is uncomfortable at times as the swells make around the point from the NW. A strong wind usually blows down off the hills in the afternoon. A **restricted anchorage area** and a **naval restricted area** and **security zone** are in the vicinity of the cove. (See **110.218, 165.1131, and 334.920**, chapter 2, for limits and regulations.)

(34) **Wilson Cove Light** (33°00'14"N., 118°33'10"W.), 125 feet above the water, is shown from a post with a red and white diamond-shaped daymark; a sound signal is at the light.

(35) Wilson Cove should be approached from the NE to avoid the numerous buoys N and S of the cove.

(36) The buildings on the hill overlooking Wilson Cove are prominent from the SE. The best anchorage for small craft is in the lee of the kelp making off from a point nearly a mile NW of the pier.

(37) The Navy pier in the middle of Wilson Cove is of steel construction and extends 550 feet from shore. A landing section at the outboard end of the pier is 38 feet wide and 210 feet long, and has a deck height of 18 feet. Depths alongside the landing section range from 14 feet inboard to 24 feet outboard. The two breasting mooring

(38) buoys on each side opposite the landing should be used to avoid danger of damage from surge. Time of the tide is about the same as that for Los Angeles.

(38) **Northwest Harbor**, on the NW end of the island, affords shelter in S weather and is a comfortable anchorage in the prevailing W weather, as the large beds of kelp and the low islet to the N of the anchorage afford protection. It is open N and is unsafe in heavy NW weather.

(39) **San Clemente Island Light** (33°01'50"N., 118°35'47"W.), 202 feet above the water, is shown from a post with red and white diamond-shaped daymark on the headland at the N end of the island.

(40) A line of rocks extends W from the NW extremity of San Clemente Island, terminating about 0.4 mile off the point in bold and rocky **Castle Rock**. A **danger area** for aerial bombing, rocket firing, and strafing extends 300 yards around this prominent islet.

(41) **West Cove**, on the NW side of San Clemente Island, 1.5 miles SE of Castle Rock, offers some shelter from Santa Ana winds; holding ground is good. A **safety zone, naval restricted area, and a danger zone** extend off the W coast of San Clemente Island from West Cove. (See **334.921, 334.960, and 334.961**, chapter 2, for limits and regulations.)

(42) A **150°-330°** measured nautical mile is 1.3 miles S from West Cove. The 70-foot towers of the front and rear markers on San Clemente Island are more than 500 feet high.

Chart 18757

(43) **Santa Catalina Island**, 18 miles S of Point Fermin, is 18.5 miles long in a SE direction and has a greatest width of 7 miles. The island is privately owned. Arrangements for overnight permits and the leasing of the many mooring buoys found throughout the area may be made through Two Harbors Enterprises at Two Harbors. Except at Avalon, permits are required for activities other than day use on the other islands.

(44) The island is almost divided by a deep N cut about 6 miles from the W end. The cut forms coves less than 0.5 mile apart at their heads, and because the isthmus separating these coves is low, the island appears as two from a few miles off. Rugged and mountainous, the island has steep, precipitous shores intersected occasionally by deep gulches and valleys, and is covered with a thick growth and some scrub oak. The highest peak, 2,125 feet, is near the middle of the E part of the island.

(45) Much of the N shore is free from kelp, but the S side in general has a narrow fringe of kelp close to the beach. The island rises abruptly from deepwater, the 30-fathom curve being close inshore. Most of the dangers in the approaches to the island are inside the kelp.

(46) Lights are shown from a pole with a red and white diamond-shaped daymark on the S end, **Long Point** (E side), and **West End** (NW point) of the island.

(47) **Ribbon Rock**, on the W side of Santa Catalina Island, 2.9 miles SE of West End, shows as a dark vertical rock wall with a gigantic ribbon of quartz veining that is visible for many miles.

(48) **Farnsworth Bank**, 9.2 miles SSE of West End and 1.6 miles offshore, has a least known depth of 9 fathoms over it.

(49) Shelter from Santa Ana winds can be had by anchoring in the bight near the **Palisades** on the S side of the island, 2 to 3 miles NW of the S extremity.

(50) Two prominent rock quarries are on the island; one is on the E end of the island, about 1.5 miles SE of Avalon Bay, and the other is about 1.5 miles SE of Isthmus Cove. Private lighted mooring buoys are off the quarry at the E end of the island.

(51) **White Cove**, 3.5 miles NW of Avalon, affords anchorage in 8 fathoms and provides almost the same protection as that found at Avalon. The beach in White Cove is known as **Whites Landing**.

COLREGS Demarcation Lines

(52) The lines established for Santa Catalina Island are described in **80.1102**, chapter 2.

(53) **Avalon Bay**, on the N shore of Santa Catalina Island, 2.5 miles from its SE extremity is entered between **Casino Point**, breakwater on the N and the breakwater extending from **Cabrillo Peninsula**, on the S. The breakwaters are marked by lights on their seaward ends.

(54) The small bay has depths of 2 to 13 fathoms; a depth of 20 fathoms is immediately outside the points of the bay. The **harbormaster** reports that shelter is good during SW, NW, and SE weather if the wind does not exceed 20 knots. The breakwater provides limited protection in the NW and SE ends of the harbor during NE Santa Ana winds that occasionally blow during the fall and winter.

(55) A large white circular building, brilliantly illuminated for about half the night during summer, is on Casino Point.

(56) **Avalon**, an incorporated city and part of Los Angeles County, is an extensive resort and the principal settlement of the island. Daily ferry and helicopter service is maintained year round to San Pedro, Long Beach, Newport Beach, Marine del Rey, and Dana Point. A road along the beach extends some distance on each side of the cove, and at night the lights along this road are conspicuous from San Pedro Channel.

(57) The bay is extremely popular as a yacht haven and vacation resort during the summer. Yachting and fishboat supplies, limited engine and underwater repair facilities, and towing service are available at Avalon.

(58) A pleasure pier with various loading floats, concessions, equipment rental firms and a 2-ton hoist are in the S part of Avalon Bay. There are three, 100-foot floating docks, with reported depths of 30 feet alongside, on the E side of the **Cabrillo Mole** (Cabrillo Peninsula.) The Cabrillo Mole floats are used by passenger vessels that

(59) operate to the mainland, and are available to any vessel through prior arrangement with the harbormaster.

Yachts and other small craft moor to buoys in the bay; there are no alongside berths. The mooring buoys in the bay are privately owned. The harbormaster will rent mooring buoys that are not reserved by the owner to vessels on a daily basis. The **harbormaster**, located on the pleasure pier, offers 24 hour service year round and can be reached on VHF-FM channel 12 and 16 or call 310–510–0535. A harbor patrol boat will meet visiting yachts at the harbor entrance upon arrival and will assign them to a mooring if desired; a fee is collected for the daily use of moorings. Shoreboats can be reached on VHF-FM channel 9.

(60) Emergency rescue services are available at Avalon. The fire and rescue boat can be contacted through the Coast Guard or the harbormaster at Avalon on VHF-FM channel 16, 24 hours a day; the call sign is "Baywatch Avalon."

(61) Weather information for Avalon is broadcast by NOAA weather radio channel 1.

Anchorage

(62) A **small-craft anchorage** is in Descanso Bay, just N of Casino Point. Three **anchorage areas**, used for large passenger vessels and assigned by VTS Los Angeles/Long Beach, are just outside Avalon Bay. (See **33 CFR 110.1 and 110.216**, chapter 2, for limits and regulations.) In 1978, it was reported that the holding ground was poor, and that heavy concentrations of kelp made anchoring difficult in the Descano Bay anchorage.

(63) **Isthmus Cove**, on the N shore 6 miles from the W end of the island, affords shelter for small vessels in S and W weather, but is dangerous in N and NE weather. Several prominent buildings are on shore. Isthmus Cove and Avalon are connected by a road, and during the tourist season launch service is maintained between the two points. Two Harbors Enterprises manages and leases all coves and moorings outside the City of Avalon. Isthmus Harbor Base can be reached on VHF-FM channel 9 or call 310–510–4254.

(64) A pier at the head of the cove extends out to a depth of about 12 feet; a fuel dock is on the E side of the pier. Water, ice, marine supplies, and limited repairs are available; a general store and restaurant are ashore.

(65) Emergency rescue service is available at Two Harbors. The fire and rescue boat can be contacted through the Coast Guard or on VHF-FM channel 16 from 0900 to 1700 daily; the call sign is "Baywatch Isthmus."

(66) **Fourth of July Cove** and **Cherry Cove**, just NW of Isthmus Cove, are popular overnight mooring destinations for yachts using the facilities at Two Harbors. There are a number of leased moorings in both coves. The shore areas are leased by camps or yacht clubs with restricted shore access.

Anchorage

(67) A **restricted** and **nonrestricted anchorage** area is in Isthmus Cove. (See **110.1 and 110.216**, chapter 2, for limits and regulations.)

(68) The approach to Isthmus Cove alongshore from the E is clear, but W of the entrance is **Eagle Reef**, covered 3 feet. The reef is marked by growing kelp and by a buoy about 100 yards to the E. In the approach from the N, **Ship Rock**, about 1 mile N of the cove, is the guide. A light is shown from a pole on the rock. From the channel the rock resembles a black haystack; the top is mostly white because of bird droppings. A reef extends about 120 yards S of Ship Rock, ending in a rock that uncovers 3 feet.

(69) **Bird Rock**, 37 feet high and about 150 yards long, is about 500 yards off the beach N from the E part of the cove entrance. The rock is covered with sand and grass. In places, reefs extend off the rock more than 100 yards, but it may be approached close-to on the E side.

(70) **Harbor Reefs**, about 400 yards SW of Bird Rock, are about 450 yards long, orientated in a NW direction, and about 250 yards wide. They are usually well marked by kelp. A rock near the SE end uncovers about 2 feet. The reef is marked by a light on the E side and a lighted buoy on the W side.

(71) **Fisherman Cove**, in the E part of Isthmus Cove, is small, but is said to be the only shelter against Santa Ana winds on the N shore of Santa Catalina Island. The cove is privately operated by the USC Marine Science Center with restricted access for visiting boaters.

(72) **Catalina Harbor**, on the S side of the isthmus separating it from Isthmus Cove, affords excellent shelter for small vessels in all but S weather. **Catalina Harbor Light** (33°25'24"N., 118°30'50"W.), 400 feet above the water, is shown from a pole on **Catalina Head**, on the W side of the harbor entrance. The harbor, a popular yacht anchorage, is funnel-shaped, open to the S, and easy of access. Small and bare **Pin Rock**, close inside the E head of the harbor, is 150 yards offshore and has deep water around it. The anchorage is in 4 to 5 fathoms, soft bottom, abreast **Ballast Point**, the long low point on the E shore. The head of the harbor is shoal. The 3-fathom curve is marked by kelp, and vessels entering should give the shores a berth of 150 yards. The facilities on Ballast Point are leased by a yacht club. From the head of the harbor it is only about 0.3 mile overland to Two Harbors.

Chart 18740

(73) **San Pedro Channel** is about 17 miles wide between the mainland, Point Fermin to Point Vicente, and Santa Catalina Island. Current observations have been made 7 miles S of San Pedro Breakwater. Two periodic currents occur at this location: a tidal current, and a daily current apparently due to a land and sea breeze. Both are rotary,

turning clockwise, and each is weak, having a velocity of 0.2 knot. The tidal current is very complicated, but the daily current is simple, maintaining on the average an approximately constant velocity and shifting direction to the right about 15° each hour. It sets N about 0900, E at 1500, S at 2100, and W at 0300.

Currents

(74) Currents due to winds and oceanic drifts vary in velocity and direction. The average current for the period of observations sets 112° with a velocity of 0.1 knot. Currents greater than 1 knot occur infrequently. The greatest velocity during 5 months of observations was 1.5 knots.

Chart 18755

(75) **San Nicolas Island**, the outermost of the group off southern California, is 53 miles off the nearest point of the mainland, 43 miles WNW of San Clemente Island, and 24 miles SW of Santa Barbara Island. The island is a military reservation and off limits to the public.

(76) A **naval restricted area** extends 3 miles from the shoreline around the island. (See **334.980**, chapter 2, for limits and regulations.)

(77) The island is 8 miles long in an E direction, 3 miles wide, and 907 feet high at its highest point; it is visible about 38 miles. The island has a gently rounding profile from a distance. The W part is covered with sand, some of which has drifted to the middle N shore. The rest of the island is cut by deep arroyos, and the top of the mesa is spotted with patches of burr clover and bunch grass. With the exception of the rocky points, the beaches are all sand. The island is practically surrounded by kelp. At the W end the kelp extends W about 3 miles over very irregular bottom. Two reefs in the kelp extend 1.6 miles W from the W extremity of the island. In thick weather great caution must be exercised in approaching from W and vessels should in no case pass inside the kelp. No dangers are known to exist outside the kelp.

(78) An aerolight, 981 feet above the water, is near the center of San Nicholas Island. A light is on the E side of the island and a lighted bell buoy is about 1.3 miles SE of the E sandspit.

(79) **Begg Rock**, 15 feet high, is 8 miles NW of the W point of San Nicolas Island. A reef extends N and S of the rock over 100 yards in each direction. The rock rises abruptly from depths of 50 fathoms. A lighted whistle buoy is 500 yards N of the rock.

(80) A bank covered 30 to 50 fathoms extends 7.8 miles E from the E point of San Nicolas. From the 50-fathom curve the depths increase rapidly to the E and S.

(81) **Restricted anchorage areas** are off the NW, SW, and SE ends of San Nicolas Island. (See **110.1 and 110.220**, chapter 2, for limits and regulations.) Upon approval by naval authorities, indifferent anchorage may be had on the S side of the 0.6-mile-long sandspit on the E end of the island. Small craft anchor in 8 fathoms, hard sand bottom, near the inshore edge of the kelp. Larger vessels anchor farther offshore in 10 to 17 fathoms, hard sand bottom. The anchorage is often uncomfortable because the island tends to split the W seas and they break with equal force on both sides and meet off the end of the spit in a maelstrom of breakers. This condition tends to move the sand from the W end of the island and builds up the sandspit. After sunset a strong wind frequently blows off the mesa, making holding difficult. In a blow, local fishermen usually leave this anchorage, preferring the one at Santa Barbara Island. A landing can usually be made at the E end on the S side of the island during the summer without difficulty.

Chart 18740

(82) **Osborn Bank**, about 22 miles ENE of San Nicolas Island and 6.5 miles S of Santa Barbara Island, is 5 miles long in a WNW-ESE direction and has an average width of 1 mile. The least depth found over it is 19 fathoms.

(83) A submerged pinnacle rock of very small area covered by at least 17 fathoms is 16 miles NNW of Santa Barbara Island.

Channel Islands National Park

(84) Santa Barbara Island, Anacapa Island, Santa Cruz Island, Santa Rosa Island, San Miguel Island and areas within 1 mile of the shoreline of these islands, except for certain described parcels of land, have been reserved as Channel Islands National Park, and are subject to rules and regulations prescribed by the Secretary of the Interior and administered by the National Park Service. Landing on rocks and islets is prohibited. Additional information may be obtained from Channel Islands National Park, 1901 Spinnaker Drive, Ventura, CA 93001.

Chart 18756

(85) **Santa Barbara Island**, 33 miles SSW of Point Dume and 21 miles W from the W end of Santa Catalina Island, is 1.5 miles long in a N direction and has a greatest width of 1 mile. The profile of the island is saddle-shaped, and at a considerable distance it appears to be two islands. The greatest elevation is 635 feet on the S side of the saddle, and the island is visible for over 25 miles in clear weather. The shores are bold and precipitous and well marked by kelp extending to about 10 fathoms at irregular distances from the shore. W of the island the kelp makes out more than a mile over very irregular bottom; a rock that breaks in moderate swells is 0.7 mile W of the point. This rock may not break in a calm sea and is dangerous, even for small craft. The water around the island is deep except where the kelp indicates foul or rocky bottom.

(86) **Santa Barbara Island Light** (33°29'15"N., 119°01'49"W.), 195 feet above the water, is shown from a post located on the NE point of the island.

(87) **Sutil Island**, a rocky islet 300 feet high and surrounded by kelp, is 0.4 mile W from the S point of Santa Barbara Island; its N face is steep. A smaller 145-foot-high rock islet is 200 yards offshore about 0.2 mile W from the N point of Santa Barbara Island.

Anchorage

(88) A **general anchorage area** extends 2 miles off the E coast of Santa Barbara Island. (See **110.1 and 110.222**, chapter 2, for limits and regulations.) For yachtsmen desiring to go ashore, an anchorage reported to give fair protection for small craft in the prevailing W weather is in the small cove about 700 yards W of Santa Barbara Island Light. (If the water is too deep or too rough to anchor off the cove, anchor inside, but maintain an anchor watch.) Swinging room on a single anchor is restricted in the cove. The cove affords no landing beach; yachtsmen can debark from a dinghy onto rock steps in the side of the cliff. Large vessels can anchor within the 30-fathom curve with hard gray sand bottom.

Chart 18729

(89) **Anacapa Island**, 11 miles SW of Point Hueneme, is the easternmost of the northern group of Channel Islands and consists of three islands separated by two very narrow openings that cannot be used as passages. The E opening is filled with rocks and is bare. The W opening is only 50 feet wide and is blocked by sand. **Anacapa Island Light** (34°00'57"N., 119°21'34"W.), 277 feet above the water, is shown from a 55-foot white cylindrical tower on the E end of the island. A sound signal is at the light.

(90) From its E point the island extends 4.5 miles in a general W direction. The E and lowest island of the Anacapa group is 1 mile long, 0.2 mile wide, 250 feet high, and rather level on top. The middle one is 1.5 miles long, 0.2 mile wide, and 325 feet high. The W and largest island is 2 miles long and 0.6 mile wide, and rises to a 930-foot peak. The westernmost island is visible at a distance of 35 miles in clear weather; the other two at 15 to 20 miles. The shores of Anacapa Island are perpendicular and filled with numerous caves. The E extremity terminates in 80-foot **Arch Rock**, with a 49-foot arch and a pyramidal rock just S of its E end. The island is surrounded by kelp except in a few small places.

(91) The National Park Service rangers are on Anacapa Island. Seals and pelicans are present in large numbers. The cream-colored houses with tile roofs of the park service rangers are 300 to 400 yards W of the light. A single large white building is 100 yards farther to the W.

Anchorages

(92) The best anchorage in SE storms is on the N side about 0.2 mile N of the center of the middle island in depths of 9 to 12 fathoms. In NW weather the best anchorage is 0.3 mile S of the E opening in depths of 8 to 12 fathoms. However, it is best for larger vessels to lie at Smugglers Cove, on the E side of Santa Cruz Island, where the bottom is not so steep-to. Small boats anchor in 5 to 7 fathoms in **East Fish Camp**, a bight about 0.4 mile SW of the E opening. About the only protection from northeasters is to anchor as close as possible in the bight immediately W of **Cat Rock**, on the S side of the W island. The National Park Service maintains a boat landing and kayak hoist on the N side near the E extremity. Landings can also be made on either side of the island near the W opening and at East Fish Camp. In thick weather, vessels in the area should stay in 50 fathoms or more, because the island rises abruptly from deep water.

(93) **Anacapa Passage**, between Anacapa and Santa Cruz Islands, is 4 miles wide and free of dangers. It is steep-to on the Anacapa Island side and has a gradual slope to the shore of Santa Cruz Island. The passage is seldom used, and should not be attempted in thick weather as soundings give no warning of a close approach to the islands. Tide rips are strong under certain conditions of wind and current, especially during SE storms and northeasters.

Charts 18729, 18728

(94) **Santa Cruz Island**, 17 miles WSW of Point Hueneme, is the largest of the Channel Islands. The Nature Conservancy, a private, non-profit organization dedicated to preserving unique islands, owns most of Santa Cruz Island. It is considered an inholding within the National Park. Landing permits may be obtained from Santa Cruz Island Preserve, 213 Sterns Wharf, Santa Barbara, CA 93101, (Telephone 805–964–7839). The eastern quarter of the island is public land administered by the National Park Service.

(95) The island is about 21 miles long in a W direction and has an average width of 5 miles. The highest peak, in the W part of the island, rises to 2,434 feet; in the E part the land attains an elevation of about 1,800 feet. The E part is very irregular and barren; the W part has a few trees, is well covered with grass, and has several springs. The shores are high, steep, and rugged, with deep water close inshore, and there is considerably less kelp than around the other islands. The reefs, extending a mile offshore on the S coast at Gull Island, are the only outlying dangers.

(96) **San Pedro Point** is the E extremity of the island. There is a small-boat landing in **Scorpion Anchorage**, a shallow bight 1.8 miles NW of San Pedro Point; it consists of a cribbed area with a float and gangway at the end of the roadway. Several large buildings are along the roadway. Large clumps of trees are near the houses.

(97) **Chinese Harbor**, in the E part of the broad bight on the N shore, 4.5 miles W of San Pedro Point, affords anchorage in the kelp in 5 to 6 fathoms. The NE part of the harbor is an excellent anchorage in SE to SW weather in 9 to 10 fathoms. This harbor affords the best shelter on the island from NE winds.

(98) **Prisoners Harbor**, in the W part of the bight on the N shore 8 miles W of San Pedro Point, affords shelter from all winds except from NE to W. Some protection from NW weather is afforded by the kelp, but a heavy swell rolls in. In NE weather the anchorage is unprotected and dangerous. A wharf with 16 feet at its face is in the harbor. There are buildings back of the wharf. The best anchorage is in 12 to 15 fathoms, sandy bottom, abreast a white rock on the W shore of the bight, and the outer end of the wharf in range with the buildings at the inner end.

(99) **Pelican Bay**, a small indentation in the N shore of Santa Cruz Island, 1 mile WNW of Prisoners Harbor, is used as a yacht anchorage during the summer. In NW weather small boats anchor close to the cliff that forms the W shore of the bay.

(100) **Painted Cave**, 3 miles E of **West Point**, the NW extremity of the island, is a large cave into which dinghies may be rowed for a considerable distance. The entrance is over 150 feet high. The inner end of the first chamber, 600 feet from the entrance, has depths of more than 2 fathoms.

(101) **Forney Cove**, 1 mile E of **Fraser Point** at the W end of the island, affords shelter in N weather in 7 to 8 fathoms. The surf is heavy on the beach, but the rocky islet W and the reef connecting it with the shore lessen the swell at the anchorage.

(102) **Gull Island**, 65 feet high and about 0.2 mile in extent, is the largest and outermost of a group of small rocky islets, 0.7 mile S of **Punta Arena**, on the S side of Santa Cruz Island. Kelp surrounds Gull Island, and the bottom in the vicinity of the group is foul.

(103) **Willows Anchorage**, on the S shore 3.6 miles E of Gull Island, can be used by small craft in NW weather and affords a good boat landing.

(104) **Smugglers Cove**, 1.2 miles SW of San Pedro Point, affords shelter in NW weather in 5 fathoms, sandy bottom.

Charts 18728, 18727

(105) **Santa Rosa Island**, 24.5 miles SW of Goleta Point on the mainland, is 15 miles long in a W direction and has a greatest width of nearly 10 miles. No landing fee or permit is required.

(106) The highest point, near the middle of the island, is 1,589 feet high and visible over 40 miles. The island has some water and is partially covered with vegetation. The shores are bold, high, and rocky; kelp surrounds most of the island. Depths in the approaches to the island shoal more abruptly from S than from N, where the 100-fathom curve is over 5 miles and the 20-fathom curve about 2 miles from the beach.

(107) There are no harbors, but anchorage may be made in Bechers Bay and Johnsons Lee. There are several good boat landings and a pier near Northwest Anchorage.

(108) **East Point**, the E extremity of Santa Rosa Island, is moderately high, sharp, and bold. A rock covered 2¾ fathoms is in the kelp 0.7 mile N from the point, and a shoal covered 3½ fathoms is 2 miles N of the point.

(109) Numerous rocks and pinnacles covered 5¾ fathoms are in an area centered 1.5 miles S of the point and extend 0.8 mile NW and SE.

(110) **Skunk Point**, 2.5 miles N of East Point, is formed of drifts of sand; it is difficult to see on dark nights. There are sand beaches W and S, and the sand dunes behind the point are as much as 300 feet high. Care should be taken to avoid the sandspit off the point where the sea breaks heavily in bad weather. The current is sometimes strong in the vicinity of the point.

(111) **Bechers Bay**, a broad semicircular bight on the NE side of Santa Rosa Island, is 4.5 miles wide between Skunk and Carrington Points and 1.5 miles in depth. **Southeast Anchorage**, 1.3 miles W of Skunk Point, affords protection in SE weather in about 6 fathoms, sandy bottom. **Northwest Anchorage**, in the W part of the bight and 1.5 miles S from Carrington Point, affords fair shelter in NW weather.

(112) A **naval operating area** is in Bechers Bay bounded by the following:
(113) 34°02'12"N., 120°01'34"W.,
(114) 34°00'58"N., 120°02'17"W.,
(115) 34°00'04"N., 120°02'02"W.,
(116) 33°59'18"N., 120°00'32"W.,
(117) 33°59'33"N., 119°59'02"W.,
(118) 34°00'32"N., 119°59'05"W.,
(119) 34°01'40"N., 120°00'25"W.

(120) Anti-ship mining operations take place at frequent and irregular intervals, including weekends, throughout the year. They are conducted as air drops from low-flying aircraft or released from submarines. Submerged metallic remains from these operations may pose a hazard to fishing operations conducted along the seabed. Particular operations are published in Eleventh Coast Guard District Local Notices to Mariners. Announcements are also made locally on VHF-FM channel 16, at 0800 local time, 1200 local time, and/or 1 hour prior to mining operations. Status of the zone and/or permission to enter, may be requested by calling PLEAD CONTROL on VHF-FM channel 16, or by telephone to the Pacific Marine Test Center at 805–989–8280/8841, or 805–816–0792 RODO (Range Operation Duty Officer) after 1800; fax 805-989–0102.

(121) **Carrington Point**, the N point of the island, has a seaward face 0.8 mile in length. It is bold and rocky, and rises rapidly to an elevation of 452 feet.

(122) Foul ground extends about 0.3 mile N from Carrington Point and terminates in **Beacon Reef**, which

(123) covers 2¼ fathoms. The reef rarely breaks, and there is no safe passage behind it.

Brockway Point, high, bold, and rounding, is about midway along the N shore of Santa Rosa Island. **Rodes Reef**, marked by kelp, is a patch of three submerged rocks 1.6 miles ENE from Brockway Point and 0.8 mile offshore. It breaks in nearly all weather.

(124) **Sandy Point**, the W extremity of the island, is moderately bold and rocky, with a detached rock lying close inshore and sand dunes more than 400 feet high extending inland. These white dunes are prominent when approaching from S or W. Shallow water extends off the point. During the general NW weather, swells form at a considerable distance from the shore. The swell also reaches the point from the SW direction.

(125) **Talcott Shoal**, covered 1¾ fathoms, is on the edge of the kelp 1.5 miles NNE from Sandy Point. Depths surrounding the shoal range from 4 to 12 fathoms. The shoal breaks only in heavy weather. In calm weather there is little indication of the shoal as the kelp is light and there is very little lumping of the water. A detached kelp patch is 1 mile N of the shoal.

(126) **Bee Rock**. 0.8 mile offshore 3.6 miles SSE of Sandy Point, is 5 feet high, but is not easily seen. It is surrounded by kelp that stretches from South Point to Sandy Point. A smaller rock, 10 feet high, is about 100 yards SE of the rock. In ordinary weather there is a lumping of the water with an occasional break on the rock, covered 2 fathoms, 0.3 mile NW of Bee Rock. Another rock, covered 1¼ fathoms, is close S of Bee Rock. Several other rocks and shoals exist inside the kelp. Vessels should not go inside the kelp in this area.

(127) **South Point**. the S point of Santa Rosa Island, terminates in a rocky bluff 100 feet high, and rises rapidly to a height of 460 feet, then to 603 feet. Cliffs, several hundred feet high and about 0.5 mile in extent, form the SW face of the point. A light is shown from a small white house on the point.

(128) **Johnsons Lee**, an open roadstead immediately E of South Point, affords fair shelter from W and NW winds, but is dangerous in S weather. The Coast Guard makes landings on the W shore of Johnsons Lee with supplies for South Point Light.

(129) **San Miguel Passage**, between Santa Rosa and San Miguel Islands, is 2.5 miles wide between the ledges which project from Sandy Point and Cardwell Point, the closest points between the two islands. There is much broken water with many current rips near these ledges. To avoid Talcott Shoal, vessels making the passage from the SW should not allow the outer rock off the W point of Santa Rosa Island to bear W of S until clear of the shoal. Sailing vessels should avoid this passage as the light airs and calms under the lee of San Miguel Island and the currents frequently combine to set a vessel toward Talcott Shoal.

Danger zone

(130) A **naval danger zone** is around San Miguel Island and extends into San Miguel Passage. (See **334.1140**, chapter 2, for limits and regulations.)

Chart 18727

(131) **San Miguel Island**, 23 miles SSE of Point Conception, is the westernmost of the Channel Islands and the most dangerous to approach. The island is irregular in shape and 7.6 miles long in a E-W direction, with an average width of 2 miles; the highest points, 831 and 817 feet, are near the middle of the island and are visible about 35 miles. The island is covered with grass, but there are no trees. The W part has more sand dunes on it than any of the other islands in the group. The shores are bold, broken, and rocky, with a few short stretches of beach; the S shore is more precipitous than the N.

(132) San Miguel Island, although a military reservation, is administered on a day to day basis by the National Park Service. Cuyler Harbor is the only place landing is allowed. A permit is required for other than beach use.

Danger zone

(133) A **naval danger zone** has been established around San Miguel Island. (See **334.1140**, chapter 2, for limits and regulations.)

(134) **Cardwell Point** is the E extremity of the island. A low sandy area which uncovers extends 0.5 mile E of the point and a dangerous reef extends an additional 0.4 mile from the tip of the area. In 1994, a shoal with breakers was reported near the reef in about 34°01'06"N., 120°17'24"W. A submerged rock and rock awash are about 400 yards S of the middle of the sandy point. During prevailing weather, breakers off this point are caused by the meeting of the seas.

(135) **Prince Island**, 296 feet high, is 2.6 miles NW of Cardwell Point and 0.4 mile off the E head of Cuyler Harbor. The island is dark in color and rocky, with a precipitous seaward face.

(136) **Cuyler Harbor** is a bight 1.2 miles long and 0.6 mile wide on the N shore SW of Prince Island. The anchorage is in the W part of the harbor; the E part is foul. Good shelter may be had in S weather, but the holding ground is poor. In strong NW weather the heavy swells that sweep around the N shore and into the harbor make the anchorage dangerous. The harbor is not safe in rare N or E winds. Water may be obtained at a small spring abreast the anchorage. Prince Island and Harris Point are prominent in the approaches.

(137) **Middle Rock**, 0.5 mile WSW of Prince Island, uncovers about 4 feet; foul ground surrounds the rock for a distance of 100 yards. **Can Rock**, 4 feet high, is 0.3 mile SW of Prince Island; there is foul ground between the rock and the S shore of the harbor. Kelp grows all over the bight.

(138) To enter Cuyler Harbor, bring Harris Point to bear **261°**, distant 1.7 miles, and the W point of Prince Island to bear **186°**, distant 1.3 miles; thence steer **209°**, heading midway between Middle Rock and the W point at the entrance, and when the S point of Prince Island bears **084°**, anchor in 5 to 7 fathoms. The course heads for **Judge Rock**, small and black, near the W end of the sand beach. The W point at the entrance off **Bat Rock** should be given a berth of about 0.3 mile to avoid the shoal extending E for over 300 yards. Anchorage may be made about 0.2 mile S of Bat Rock where better protection is afforded in NW weather. The passage between Prince Island and the E head should be attempted only by small craft.

(139) **Harris Point**, the N extremity of the island, is bold and precipitous, rising to a hill, 485 feet high, 1 mile S of the point.

(140) **Wilson Rock**, 2.2 miles NW of Harris Point, is 19 feet high and black. A reef, extending about 1 mile WNW from the rock, uncovers in two places; foul ground is a short distance N of the reef. It breaks in any light swell from the NW. There is foul ground S and SW of the rock. The covered rock 0.3 mile S of Wilson Rock breaks. This locality should not be approached in thick weather, as the dangers rise abruptly from deep water and are not marked by kelp; soundings give no positive warning of their proximity.

(141) **Simonton Cove**, on the NW side of San Miguel Island, is a very shallow bight 2.4 miles long and 0.6 mile wide. This cove has considerable kelp and a few covered rocks. From the SW head of Simonton Cove, foul ground extends NW for nearly 1 mile.

(142) **Castle Rock**, 180 feet high, is a three-headed islet 1.6 miles NNE from Point Bennett, in the middle of the kelp field, and 0.5 mile offshore. A shoal spot 0.5 mile W of the rock is near the edge of the kelp. Submerged rocks have been reported to extend about 100 to 200 yards SW of Castle Rock.

(143) **Westcott Shoal**, covered 4¾ fathoms, is 0.8 mile N from Castle Rock. A 2¾ fathom spot near an oil spring is about 0.6 mile N from the shoal.

(144) **Point Bennett**, the W point of the island, is a long, narrow, jagged bluff, 74 feet high, rising rapidly to 337 feet. High sand dunes extend from the point for 2 miles. There are two rocky islets S of and close under the point, and foul ground extends about 0.5 mile W and 1 mile N of the point but inside the limit of the kelp.

Caution

(145) Navigation in this area should not be attempted without local information.

(146) **Richardson Rock**, 5.5 miles NW from Point Bennett, is 53 feet high, white-topped, and small in area. Two smaller and lower rocks are close-to on the E side. Richardson Rock rises abruptly from deep water, 30 to 40 fathoms being found within 0.3 mile. The rock is prominent in clear weather, but in thick weather the locality should be avoided, as soundings give no warning of a near approach.

(147) **Tyler Bight** is on the S shore 1.8 miles E of Point Bennet and has a sand bottom. In moderate NW weather, the winds may attain velocities up to 45 knots 0.5 mile offshore; the sea in the bight, however, is quite smooth.

(148) **Wyckoff Ledge**, 1.4 miles W from Crook Point and 0.5 mile offshore, is covered 1½ fathoms.

(149) **Crook Point**, the S point of the island, is low and irregular. A boat landing may be made on the S shore of the island in a small cove immediately W of the point, but there is no anchorage.

Chart 18720

(150) **Santa Barbara Channel** is 63 miles long and increases gradually in width from 11 miles at the E end to 23 miles at the W end. The channel is free of dangers and has depths of 40 to more than 300 fathoms along the recommended track from San Diego and Los Angeles to northern ports.

(151) Offshore oil wells and oil drilling platforms, some privately marked by lights, buoys, and sound signals, extend as much as 10 miles offshore between Point Hueneme and Point Conception.

Safety zones

(152) **Safety zones** have been established around the oil drilling platforms and an offshore storage and treatment vessel mooring area in:

(153) 34°07'02"N., 119°16'35"W. (**Platform Gina**);
(154) 34°07'30"N., 119°24'01"W. (**Platform Gail**);
(155) 34°10'56"N., 119°25'07"W. (**Platform Gilda**);
(156) 34°10'47"N., 119°28'05"W. (**Platform Grace**);
(157) 34°23'27"N., 120°07'14"W. (**Platform Hondo**);
(158) 34°24'19"N., 120°06'00"W. (**an offshore storage and treatment vessel mooring area**);
(159) 34°22'36"N., 120°10'03"W. (**Platform Harmony**);
(160) 34°21'01"N., 120°16'45"W. (**Platform Heritage**);
(161) 34°27'19"N., 120°38'47"W. (**Platform Hermosa**);
(162) 34°28'09.5"N., 120°40'46.1"W. (**Platform Harvest**);
(163) 34°29'42"N., 120°42'08"W. (**Platform Hidalgo**); and
(164) 34°36'37.5"N., 120°43'46.0"W. (**Platform Irene**).

(165) (See **147.1** through **147.20**, **147.1102**, **147.1103**, **147.1105** through **147.1107**, **147.1109**, **147.1110**, and **147.1112** through **147.1116**, chapter 2, for limits and regulations and chapter 3 under **Oil well structures** for additional information.

(166) On the N side of Santa Barbara Channel is the mainland between Point Hueneme and Point Conception. On the S side is the northern group of the Channel Islands–Anacapa, Santa Cruz, Santa Rosa, and San Miguel–which break the force of the heavy westerly

Pacific swell and afford a lee in winter from the full force of the SE gales.

(167) The E entrance to Santa Barbara Channel has a clear width of 2 miles between the 100-fathom curves, and lies between Anacapa Island and Point Hueneme. On the N side of this entrance is deep **Hueneme Canyon**, which extends from Point Hueneme in a SSW direction across the channel. The W entrance to the channel has a clear width of 10 miles between the 100-fathom curves, and lies between Richardson Rock and Point Conception. (See chapter 4 for details about the **Traffic Separation Scheme** between Point Fermin and Point Conception.)

Weather, Channel Islands

(168) The prevailing winds are W and NW and blow nearly every day, especially in the afternoon. Strong SE winds occur in the winter, and at times the sea is too rough for several days to permit the passage of small vessels.

(169) In the summer the winds in the channel are wholly different from those outside the islands and off the coast to the NW. Under the N shore, which is protected by the bold range of the Santa Ynez Mountains, the W winds do not reach far E of Point Conception with much strength but are felt towards the islands, a strong NW wind and heavy swell coming in from the open ocean. The climate in the Santa Barbara Channel, because of this blocking of the winds, is much milder than to the N along the coast. However, during NW weather boats crossing the channel from the mainland usually encounter heavier seas as the islands are approached. The belt of rough seas, locally known as **Windy Lane**, lies along the N shores of the islands and is about 6 miles (11 km) wide. This sea condition is the opposite to that experienced in the crossing from Los Angeles-Long Beach to Santa Catalina Island. Strangers are cautioned that good seamanship sometimes calls for returning to the mainland rather than attempting Windy Lane when rough seas are encountered. These W winds usually begin about 1000 and grow progressively stronger until sundown.

(170) During heavy NW weather strong squally winds draw down the canyons between Point Conception and Capitan and pass directly offshore, causing a severe choppy sea. Heavy NW gales are often encountered off Point Conception on coming through Santa Barbara Channel, and great changes of climatic and meteorological conditions are experienced; the transition is often remarkably sudden and well defined.

(171) In the fall and winter, stiff northeasters are occasionally experienced at and near the E end of the channel. They come up without warning, usually at night in clear dry weather, and when the barometer is either high or rising rapidly. At such times small boats should be prepared to seek shelter at a moment's notice.

(172) During the summer heavy fogs are a common occurrence in the Santa Barbara Channel and envelop the main shore, channel, and islands. Sometimes the mainland and channel are clear while the islands alone are hidden. At other times all are clear during the day, but wrapped in dense wet fog nights and mornings. This condition, the fog lying offshore during the day and enveloping the land at night, is characteristic of the whole southern California coast. The fogs occur mostly during calm weather and light winds, and are generally dissipated by the strong NW winds.

(173) Winds at **San Nicolas Island**, located about 75 miles (140 km) southwest of Los Angeles, average 12 knots from the northwest on an annual basis. A peak wind of 57 knots was recorded in both July and August 1979. The average annual temperature for San Nicolas is 61°F (16.1°C). The average maximum is 66°F (18.9°C) and the average minimum is 55°F (12.8°C). An extreme maximum temperature of 103°F (39.4°C) was recorded in August 1976 and an extreme minimum of 30°F (-1.1°C) was recorded in January 1978. San Nicolas Island averages only 34 days each year with measurable precipitation. Snowfall has never been reported on the island.

(174) At **San Clemente Island**, about 60 miles (111 km) northwest of San Diego, west winds dominate at a lower average speed of only seven knots. The average annual temperature for San Clemente is 61°F (16.1°C). The average maximum temperature is 66°F (18.9°C) and the average minimum is 56°F (13.3°C). An extreme maximum temperature of 97°F (36.1°C) was recorded in April 1989 and extreme minimum of 33°F (0.6°C) was recorded in January 1976. San Clemente averages only 49 days each year with measurable precipitation. Snowfall has never been reported on the island.

Currents

(175) Currents in Santa Barbara Channel are variable, depending to a great extent upon the wind. It appears that a weak nontidal flow sets E in the spring and summer, and W in autumn and winter.

(176) It has been observed that a strong inshore set prevails on a rising tide in the deep waters of Hueneme Canyon. In general, there are conflicting currents, at times quite strong, around the slopes of the submarine valleys both here and off Point Mugu.

(177) The tidal current sets along the N shore of Santa Barbara Channel with velocities of 0.5 to 1 knot. In heavy NW weather, the current and heavy swells make into the S side of the W entrance to the channel and along the N shore of San Miguel Island.

(178) The currents in the vicinity of the Channel Islands frequently follow the direction of the wind, with eddies under the lee of the islands and projecting points. Tidal currents of about 1 knot set through the passages between the islands.

TIDAL INFORMATION					
Chart	Station	LAT/LONG	Mean Higher High Water*	Mean High Water*	Mean Low Water*
18727	Cuyler Harbor, San Miguel Island	34°03'N/120°21'W	5.2	4.5	1.0
18728	Prisoners Harbor, Santa Cruz Island	34°01'N/119°41'W	5.0	4.3	0.9
18728	Bechers Bay, Santa Rosa Island	34°01'N/120°03'W	5.1	4.4	1.0
18740	Point Loma, California	32°40'N/117°14'W	5.3	4.6	0.9
18740	Newport Bay Entrance (Corona del Mar)	33°36'N/117°53'W	5.4	4.7	0.9
18740	Port Hueneme, Santa Barbara Channel	34°09'N/119°12'W	5.4	4.7	1.0
18740	La Jolla, Scripps Institution Wharf	32°52'N/117°15'W	5.3	4.6	0.0
18740	Los Angeles, Outer Harbor	33°43'N/118°16'W	5.5	4.8	0.9
18755	San Nicolas Island	33°16'N/119°30'W	4.9	4.2	0.9
18756	Santa Barbara Island	33°29'N/119°02'W	5.1	4.4	0.9
18757	Avalon, Santa Catalina Island	33°21'N/118°19'W	5.3	4.6	0.9
18757	Catalina Harbor, Santa Catalina Island	33°26'N/118°30'W	5.2	4.5	0.9
18763	Wilson Cove, San Clemente Island	33°00'N/118°33'W	5.2	4.5	0.9

* Heights in feet referred to datum of sounding MLLW.
Real-time water levels, tide predictions, and tidal current predictions are available at:
http://tidesandcurrents.noaa.gov
To determine mean tide range subtract Mean Low Water from Mean High Water.
Data as of September 2012

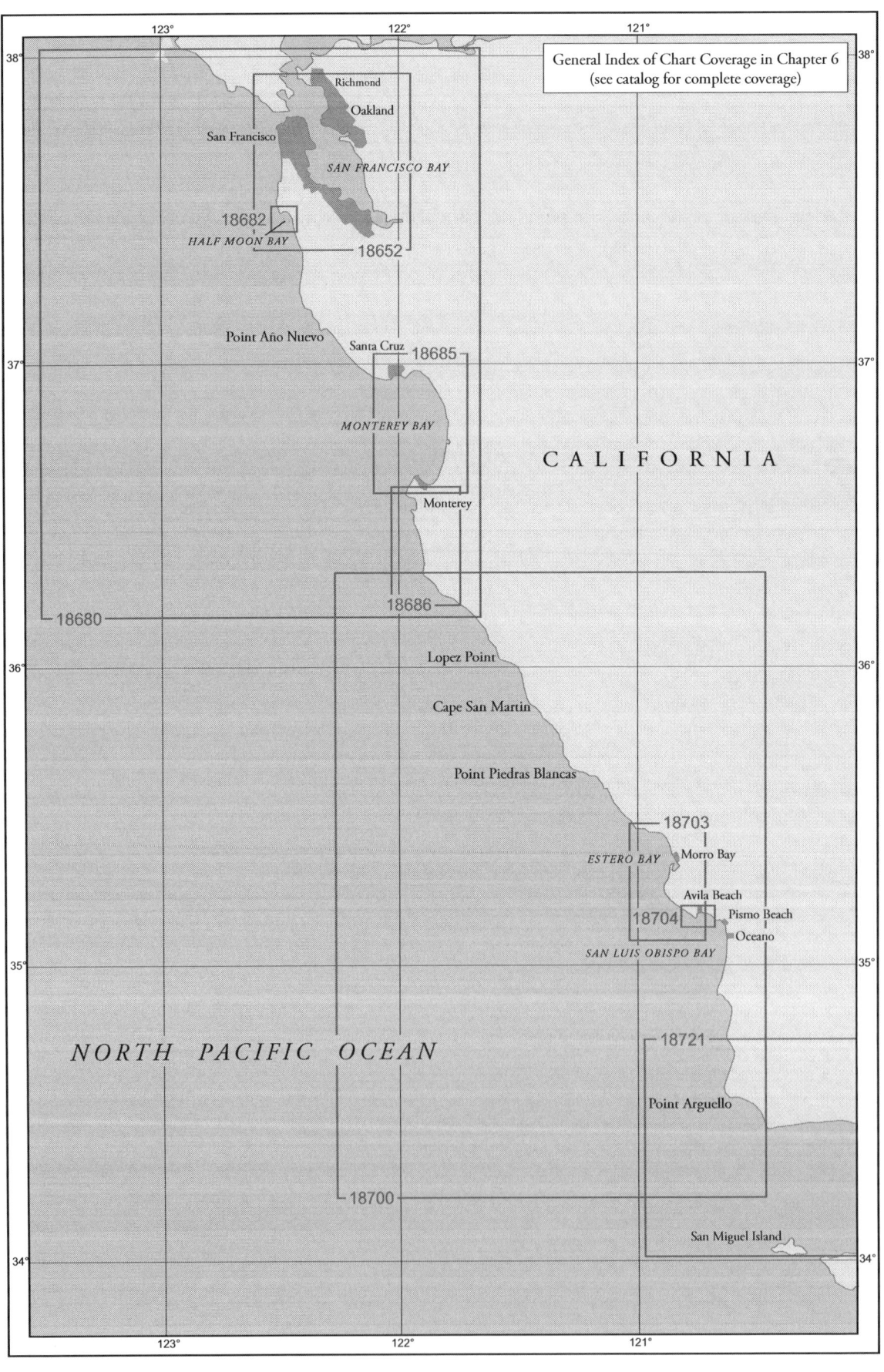

Point Arguello to San Francisco Bay, California

(1) This chapter describes the waters of San Luis Obispo, Estero, Morro, Monterey, and Half Moon Bays; also, the port of Port San Luis, and the small-craft and commercial fishing harbors of Morro Bay, Monterey, Moss Landing, Santa Cruz, and Pillar Point. The coast, except for the bays, is rugged with many detached rocks close inshore and other dangers extending no more than 2 miles offshore. However, in 1975, shoaling to 10 fathoms was reported in 37°00.0'N., 122°30.1'W., about 12 miles SW of Pigeon Point. The area is well marked with navigational aids.

COLREGS Demarcation Lines

(2) The lines established for this part of the coast are described in **80.1130 through 80.1140,** chapter 2.

Sea Otter Refuge

(3) The State of California Fish and Game Code prohibits the discharge of firearms or bows and the trapping of birds or mammals in the California Sea Otter Game Refuge. The refuge extends as a continuous band between the coastline and the three nautical mile limit for the state of California extending offshore from the mouth of the Santa Rosa Creek (35°34'N.) in the N. (See charts 18700 and 18680.) Additional information may be obtained by writing the Department of Fish and Game, Marine Region, 20 Lower Ragsdale Drive, Suite 100, Monterey, CA 93940, telephone 831 649 2870.

Weather, Point Arguello to San Francisco Bay

(4) The weather along this coast is mostly cool, damp, and foggy in the summer, becoming mild and wet in winter. Summer afternoons on the coast are often clear and pleasant. The dominant weather feature is the semipermanent Pacific high. In summer, it is big and strong and covers the entire region. Storms and fronts are forced to move along the N side, so few affect this coast. In winter, the high weakens and retreats SE. This allows storms or frontal systems to pass through the area about every 7 to 10 days, on the average. Sometimes a series of these systems may result in a prolonged period of strong winds and heavy rains along the central and southern California coast. This situation is rare and occurs about every 2 to 3 years.

(5) The clockwise flow around the highs results in a NW flow along the coast in summer. These winds are enhanced by the formation of a thermal low over land, to the SE. The combination of these two features results in a sea breeze that can reach 20 knots during the afternoon and persist, at lower speeds, until midnight. Daytime temperatures often climb to near 70°F (21.1°C); nighttime lows drop to the low fifties (10.6° to 11.7°C) in summer. Occasionally a hot flow from the land will push temperatures into the nineties (32.8° to 37.2°C). This is as likely in early fall as it is in summer. The winds blowing across the cool **California Current** produce low clouds and sea fog. These conditions are prevalent close to the coast in the early morning hours. They improve during the day, particularly close to and on the shore. August and September are the worst months; fog reduces visibilities to below 0.5 mile (0.9 km) on more than 15 days per month at some locations.

(6) Winds are more variable, but often NW, in winter, becoming WNW in midwinter. Weak E winds often occur when a warm-type high centers itself over the **Great Basin** to the NE. (The Great Basin is the desert plateau comprising most of Nevada, western Utah and portions of northern Arizona.) This warm high pressure system produces clear skies and ideal conditions for land fog, which may drift out over coastal waters. This fog, while often dense, is shallow and usually burns off during the morning hours. Occasionally following a passage of a cold front, a cold-type high will move into the Great Basin. This can result in a foehn wind, over central and southern California, known as a **Santa Ana**. This NE wind flows down the canyons and into certain coastal basins. Its effect varies from place to place, but speeds may reach 50 knots. In some areas, an intensified sea breeze counterflow is observed. The most severe conditions are normally observed in late fall, but may occur from fall through spring, which is also considered the rainy season. From about November through April, precipitation occurs on about 6 to 12 days per month. Average maximum temperatures in winter range from the middle fifties (11.7° to 13.9°C) around San Francisco, to the low sixties (16.1° to 17.2°C) at Point Arguello, while nighttime lows drop to the low to middle forties (5.0° to 8.3°C). Occasionally a cold outbreak will send temperatures below freezing (<0°C).

Charts 18700, 18721

(7) From Point Arguello to Point Sal, the coast trends N for 19.5 miles in two shallow bights separated by Purisima Point. From Point Sal the coast continues N for 14 miles, then bends sharply W for 6 miles to Point San Luis, forming San Luis Obispo Bay. Soundings are useful along this stretch of the coast, and between Point

Arguello and Point San Luis the 20-fathom curve can be followed with safety in thick weather. In clear weather, the headlands and other natural features can be easily recognized.

(8) **Danger and restricted areas** extend 3.5 miles offshore from S of Point Arguello to Point Sal. (See **334.1130**, chapter 2, for limits and regulations.)

(9) **Point Pedernales**, 1.5 miles N of Point Arguello, and the largest of the numerous rocks as far as 300 yards offshore, are very dark and conspicuous alongside the sand dunes immediately N of the point.

(10) **La Honda Canyon**, 2 miles N of Point Arguello, is a deep gulch crossed by a railroad trestle easily distinguished when abreast the mouth. From here the coast to Purisima Point consists of a low tableland and sand dunes that contrast strongly with the dark cliffs S.

(11) **Surf**, 7 miles N of Point Arguello, is a station along the railroad. The yellow station house and a black tank are conspicuous. A white elevated water tank, 1.3 miles NE of the station house, and several launching gantries at the Vandenberg Air Force Base are conspicuous along this section of the coast.

Chart 18700

(12) **Purisima Point**, 10.6 miles N of Point Arguello, is low and rocky, with reefs extending SE for 0.3 mile. The N side of the point is bare sand. It has been reported that an inshore set is experienced off the coast in the vicinity of the point. From Purisima Point to Point Sal, the coast is sandy and lower than that S.

(13) **Point Sal**, 19.5 miles N of Point Arguello, is a bold dark headland marked by stretches of yellow sandstone. From the NW the headland looks like a low conical hill with two higher conical hills immediately behind it. It rises gradually to a ridge, 1,640 feet high, 3 miles to the E. From the S the hills are not so well defined. **Lion Rock**, 54 feet high, is a rocky islet 200 yards off the S face of Point Sal. A small rock is close to the point. Breakers and reefs extend nearly 600 yards S and W from Point Sal and 200 yards SW of Lion Rock.

Anchorage

(14) Anchorage under Point Sal affords some protection from NW winds in 7 to 9 fathoms, sandy bottom, but is subject to swells. Shoal water extends nearly 0.5 mile W from the SE point of the anchorage. The best anchorage is in 7 fathoms 500 yards 123° from Lion Rock and with the northern end of the rock just open of the extremity of Point Sal.

(15) From Point Sal north the coast is a sand beach backed by low dunes for 14 miles and then changes to bold rocky cliffs that curve sharply W to Point San Luis and form the N shore of San Luis Obispo Bay.

(16) **Oceano** is a small resort 12 miles N of Point Sal. The county airport is here.

(17) **Pismo Beach** is a resort 14 miles N of Point Sal. The pleasure pier is 1,200 feet long and has 12 feet at the outer end. In 1983, the pier was partially destroyed by storms, and submerged pilings are reported to exist at the outer end. Caution is advised in the area near the pier. **Shell Beach** is a small residential settlement, 1.5 miles NW of Pismo Beach. An aerolight, 6 miles N of Pismo Beach, is visible from seaward.

Charts 18703, 18704

(18) **San Luis Obispo Bay**, 35 miles N of Point Arguello, is a broad bight that affords good shelter in N or W weather. S gales occur several times during the winter. The E shore is a narrow tableland that ends in cliffs 40 to 100 feet high to within 0.5 mile of **San Luis Obispo Creek** where a sand beach fronts **Avila Beach**. W of the creek the shore is high with rocky bluffs extending to **Point San Luis**.

(19) **Port San Luis**, on the W shore of the bay, is the seaport for San Luis Obispo which is 10 miles inland. The port is primarily a base for commercial fishing boats, sport-fishing boats, and recreational craft.

Prominent features

(20) Point San Luis, a bold prominent headland, and the pier in about 35°10'13"N., 120°44'27"W. are reported to be useful radar targets.

(21) **San Luis Obispo Light** (35°09'37"N., 120°45'38"W.), 116 feet above the water, is shown from a cylindrical structure on Point San Luis; a sound signal is at the light. **San Luis Hill**, 0.5 mile NW of the light, is prominent from the S.

COLREGS Demarcation Lines

(22) The lines established for San Luis Obispo Bay are described in **80.1130**, chapter 2.

Anchorage

(23) The general anchorage is inside a line extending SW from Fossil Point to the outer end of a breakwater which extends SE from Whaler Island. Mariners should contact the harbormaster's office for anchorage information.

(24) **Special anchorages** are E of Avila Pier 1 (County Wharf) and in the W end of the harbor. (See **110.1 and 110.120**, chapter 2, for limits and regulations.) All anchorages are exposed to weather from the S and SE which cause heavy swells.

(25) The dangers off the entrance to San Luis Obispo Bay are buoyed; the E part of the bay has many rocks and heavy growths of kelp. **Souza Rock**, 2.1 miles SE of San Luis Obispo Light, is covered 16 feet and rises abruptly from 19 fathoms. **Westdahl Rock**, 1.3 miles SW of the light, is covered 18 feet and rises abruptly from 10 fathoms. **Howell Rock**, 1.6 miles E of the light, is

(26) covered 13 feet. **Lansing Rock** covered 18 feet and **Atlas Rock** covered 13 feet are 0.7 and 0.5 mile E of the light, respectively.

(26) A 2,400-foot breakwater, extending SE from Point San Luis through **Whalers Island** to a ledge partly bare at low water, provides some protection to vessels at anchor or at the wharves. **Smith Island**, 44 feet high and about 90 yards wide, is 0.2 mile N of Whalers Island.

Routes

(27) San Luis Obispo Bay may be entered from S by passing 100 yards W of the lighted gong buoy marking Souza Rock, thence a **000°** course for about 2 miles until past Lansing Rock, and thence to anchorage or to the wharves. From N stay outside the lighted bell buoy marking Westdahl Rock and the lighted whistle buoy off Point San Luis breakwater, then head into the bay as previously mentioned.

Quarantine, customs, immigration, and agricultural quarantine

(28) (See chapter 3, Vessel Arrival Inspections, and Appendix A for addresses.) Vessels subject to inspection are requested to contact the harbormaster's office.

(29) **Quarantine** is enforced in accordance with the regulations of the U.S. Public Health Service. (See Public Health Service, chapter 1.)

(30) Port San Luis is a **customs port of entry**.

Harbor regulations

(31) The port of Port San Luis is administered by the Port San Luis Harbor District and under the control of a harbormaster. The office is at the foot of Harford Pier 3. The harbormaster monitors VHF-FM channel 16 and can be contacted by phone at 805–595–5435. Transients should report to the harbormaster for guest mooring assignments.

Wharves

(32) Harford Pier 3, 0.5 mile N of Point San Luis, is used by commercial and sport fisherman. The berthing space at the end has 17 to 20 feet alongside. In 1990, shoaling to an unknown extent was reported along the pier. The pier is lighted at night. A fuel dock is at the bulkhead just N of the pier. The pier is operated by the Port San Luis Harbor District.

(33) The California Polytechnic State University Pier, 1 mile NE of Point San Luis, has 31 feet along both sides. The entire length of the pier is lighted at night. It is not safe to moor alongside in strong S to SE weather; vessels usually leave the pier on the approach of a storm and anchor until it moderates.

(34) Avila Pier 1 (County Wharf), 1.4 miles NE of Point San Luis, was damaged by a winter storm in 1983. Submerged obstructions are reported to be in the area near the pier. A submarine sewer line is about 40 feet E and parallel to the pier.

Supplies and repairs

(35) Gasoline, diesel fuel, water, marine supplies, a launching ramp, and a 50-ton mobile hoist are available. Some repairs can be made.

Communications

(36) Transportation is by automobile to San Luis Obispo where rail, bus, and air connections can be made.

Charts 18703, 18700

(37) From Point San Luis to Point Buchon, the coast trends NW for 9 miles and consists of cliffs 40 to 60 feet high. The land rises rapidly from the cliffs to Mount Buchon. There are numerous outlying rocks and submerged ledges that extend more than a mile from the shore in some places.

(38) Point San Luis and Point Buchon, both bold prominent headlands, are reported to be useful radar targets when navigating this section of the coast.

(39) **Mount Buchon**, a rugged mountain mass between San Luis Obispo Bay, Estero Bay, and the valley of San Luis Obispo, is prominent from either N or S. **Saddle Peak**, 4.1 miles NNW of San Luis Obispo Light, is visible for over 40 miles.

(40) **Santa Rosa Reef**, 1.4 miles WSW from San Luis Obispo Light, is covered 2¾ fathoms and rises abruptly from 13 fathoms. **Lone Black Rock**, 2 feet high and of small extent, is 0.5 mile W from the light and 0.2 mile offshore.

(41) **Pecho Rock**, 40 feet high, is 3 miles WNW from the light and 0.5 mile offshore. Two smaller rocks, 0.3 mile E (2 feet high) and 0.4 mile SE, are in the vicinity of Pecho Rock. Foul ground, marked by kelp, is between the rocks and shore.

(42) A fish haven with a least depth of 9 fathoms is about 0.7 mile NW of Pecho Rock.

(43) **Diablo Canyon**, 5.8 miles NW of San Luis Obispo Light, is the site of a large nuclear powerplant. The two concrete dome-shaped structures and other large buildings are conspicuous from well offshore. A **security zone** has been established in the waters of the Pacific Ocean off Diablo Canyon. (See **165.1155**, chapter 2, for limits and regulations.)

(44) A sharp prominent dark gray rock, 111 feet high, is 0.1 mile offshore from the powerplant.

(45) **Lion Rock**, 0.9 mile NW from the powerplant and 0.2 mile offshore, is 240 yards long in a NW direction and 136 feet high. A high rock lies between it and the shore, and a small low rock is 200 yards W.

(46) **Point Buchon** ends in an overhanging cliff 40 feet high, with a low tableland behind that rises rapidly to a bare hill a mile to the E. There are a few detached rocks close under the cliffs. A lighted whistle buoy is 1 mile SW of the point and about 400 yards WSW of a rock covered 3¾ fathoms.

(47) **Estero Bay** is formed by a curve in the coast between Point Buchon and **Point Estero**, 13.5 miles NNW. The shore of the bay follows a general N direction from Point Buchon for 11 miles, then turns sharply W for 5 miles to Point Estero. The N part of Estero Bay is fringed with covered rocks and scattered kelp. The seaward faces of Cayucos Point and Point Estero are cliffs 50 to 90 feet high.

(48) The coast drops abruptly from bold Mount Buchon to a sandy spit bordering Morro Bay and then rises to a bluff-bordered treeless country of rolling hills.

(49) Point Estero, Morro Rock, and Cayucos Point are reported to be useful radar targets in the vicinity of Estero and Morro Bays.

(50) **Morro Bay**, 6 miles N of Point Buchon, is a shallow lagoon separated from Estero Bay by a narrow strip of sand beach. The port facilities at the city of Morro Bay, a mile inside the entrance, are used by commercial fishing, sport-fishing, and recreational craft.

(51) **Morro Rock**, the tall cone-shaped mound on the N side of the entrance to Morro Bay, is the dominant landmark in this area. A breakwater, extending 600 yards S from the rock, is marked at its outer end by **Morro Bay West Breakwater Light** (35°21'46"N., 120°52'11"W.), 36 feet above the water and shown from a white column. A sound signal is at the light. Sections of the S end of the breakwater are reported to be frequently awash under heavy seas and high tides, but have never been observed completely submerged.

(52) The three 450-foot powerplant stacks 0.5 mile E of Morro Rock are visible from far offshore. The standpipe about 500 yards E of the stacks is prominent from close in. **Hollister Peak**, 4.2 miles ESE of Morro Rock, is the most prominent of a row of peaks behind Morro Bay because of its jagged outline.

COLREGS Demarcation Lines

(53) The lines established for Estero-Morro Bay are described in **80.1132**, chapter 2.

Channels

(54) The entrance to Morro Bay is through a buoyed channel between the protective breakwaters. Due to continual shifting of the channel, buoy positions are frequently shifted to mark the best water.

(55) Mariners are advised to use extreme caution when entering the bay and to contact the harbormaster or Coast Guard Sector Los Angeles/Long Beach on VHF-FM channel 16 for current entrance and channel conditions.

(56) From Fairbank Point, on the E side of the bay, a privately maintained channel leads S to the Morro Bay State Park Basin at **White Point**. Vessels heading for the basin should approach White Point close inshore as the channel narrows at this point. In 1993, shoaling to 1 foot was at the entrance to the basin. Swells from North Pacific winter storms sometimes break across the entire entrance.

Anchorages

(57) **Special anchorages** are in Morro Bay, 1 and 2 miles above the entrance. (See **110.1 and 110.125**, chapter 2, for limits and regulations.)

(58) Extremely high waves created by the sandbars in the entrance to Morro Bay make dangerous navigation conditions.

Currents

(59) Currents in the entrance channel and around the breakwaters are strong at times. It is advisable to approach the entrance from the SW because of the currents and sea conditions. Sharp turns should be avoided in the vicinity of the breakwaters, especially in heavy weather. It is reported that currents in the N part of the bay, especially flood currents, have a tendency to set vessels toward the city north T-pier.

Weather, Estero Bay

(60) Estero Bay is one of the foggiest areas along the Pacific Coast. The fog is most common in the mornings and evenings. (See Weather, West Coast and Hawaii, indexed as such, chapter 3, for further information.)

Coast Guard

(61) A Coast Guard station is at the foot of the city north T-pier. The station maintains motor lifeboats and monitors VHF-FM channel 16.

Harbor regulations

(62) Morro Bay Harbor is owned by the city of Morro Bay and is under the control of a **harbormaster**, who maintains an office at the foot of the city north T-pier. The harbormaster monitors VHF-FM channels 16 and 12 and can be reached by telephone at 805–772–6254. Harbor patrol boats operate from the city north T-pier and monitor VHF-FM channel 16. The boats are manned during daylight, and a patrolman is on call at all other times.

(63) Yachts and small craft may tie up to the yacht club dock; otherwise they must either anchor in the bay or check with the harbormaster for other accommodations

Wharves

(64) The city north T-pier, at the city of Morro Bay, is on the N side of the harbor about 0.8 mile above the entrance; depths alongside are about 22 feet. The pier is owned and operated by the city of Morro Bay.

(65) The city south T-pier, SE of the city north T-pier, is owned and operated by the city. It has about 20 feet alongside.

Supplies and repairs

(66) Gasoline, diesel fuel, water, ice, a launching ramp, and marine supplies are available in the port.

(67) A boat works has a crane that can handle craft up to 20 tons and 50 feet long; hull, engine, and rigging repairs can be made.

(68) For 3 miles N of Morro Rock, submerged pipelines extend up to 0.6 mile offshore in Estero Bay. A rock covered 5¼ fathoms, 1.3 miles NW of Morro Rock, is marked by a gong buoy. An unmarked fish haven, covered 6¾ fathoms, is about 1.4 miles NNW of Morro Rock in about 35°23'36"N., 120°52'32"W.

(69) **Cayucos**, 4.5 miles N of Morro Rock and in the NE part of Estero Bay, has a fishing and pleasure pier; a depth of 12 feet is at the outer end.

(70) Anchorage with fair shelter from the N and NW may be had in 11 fathoms, sandy bottom, with the prominent white concrete tank on a hill W of Cayucos bearing 017°.

(71) **Mouse Rock**, 0.7 mile W of Cayucos, is covered ½ fathom and breaks heavily in all but smooth weather; it is marked by a bell buoy.

(72) **Cayucos Point**, 2 miles W of Cayucos, is a low rocky promontory. **Constantine Rock**, 0.5 mile S of the point, is covered 1 fathom and breaks heavily in a moderate swell; it is marked on the S side by a buoy.

Chart 18700

(73) From Point Estero N for 8 miles to the village of Cambria, the bluffs increase in height and the range of grassy hills is close to shore. The shore is well fringed with kelp; several rocks are close inshore. **White Rock**, 6 miles NW of Point Estero, is the most prominent. A pinnacle rock, 0.7 mile SW of White Rock, is covered 5½ fathoms.

(74) **Von Helm Rock**, 7.2 miles NW of Point Estero and nearly a mile offshore, is covered 2½ fathoms. The rock is very sharp and breaks only in the roughest weather.

(75) **Cambria** is about 1 mile inland in a grove of pine trees. Some of the streets and buildings are visible from seaward. No landing or anchorage is recommended.

(76) From Cambria for 6.5 miles to San Simeon, rocks continue close inshore, but the bluffs decrease in height and the hills recede from the shoreline. Thick groves of pine trees scatter the hillsides. Of the several rocks offshore, **Cambria Rock**, 10 feet high, and **Pico Rock**, 12 feet high, are the largest, but they are not prominent from seaward. Shoal patches up to 360 yards surround Cambria Rock, and there is foul ground NW and S of Pico Rock. A shoal, 580 yards SW of Pico Rock, is covered 3¾ fathoms.

(77) **San Simeon Bay**, 14 miles NW of Point Estero, is formed by the shoreline curving sharply to the W, and on the W side by **San Simeon Point**, a low wooded projection extending SE. The trees show well from W, but from S the warehouses and buildings in San Simeon are more prominent. From W the point itself is not easily recognized by those not familiar with it.

(78) A lighted bell buoy, 0.4 mile SE of the point, marks the entrance to San Simeon Bay. The bay offers good shelter in N weather, but is exposed to S gales in winter. The best anchorage is in the middle of the bight in 5 to 8 fathoms, hard sand bottom. A small ravine due W of the anchorage can be used to go ashore.

(79) **San Simeon**, 1.7 miles ESE of San Simeon Point, is a small town with a 995-foot sport fishing pier. A number of motels are in the town to handle the many tourists that visit Hearst Castle.

(80) Prominent **Hearst Castle**, 2.7 miles NE of San Simeon, is the former palace of the late William Randolph Hearst; it is now a State Historical Monument. The structure is lighted at night.

(81) The coast from San Simeon Point for 5 miles NW to Point Piedras Blancas, is low, with numerous detached rocks lying in some cases over 0.5 mile offshore and usually well marked by kelp.

(82) **Point Piedras Blancas** is a low rocky point projecting about 0.5 mile from the general trend of the coast. **Piedras Blancas Light** (35°39'56"N., 121°17'04"W.), 142 feet above the water, is shown from a white conical tower with a flat top at the point.

(83) **Piedras Blancas** are two large white rocks, 74 and 31 feet high, 500 yards offshore and about 0.8 mile E of the point. From the S they look like one rock.

(84) **Outer Islet**, a large and prominent white rock 110 feet high, is 0.25 mile W of the point. In hazy weather this rock is sometimes visible from the NW and W when the light cannot be seen.

(85) Anchorage for a small vessel, with protection from NW winds, may be had under Point Piedras Blancas in 4 to 5 fathoms, sandy bottom, with the light about 0.2 mile bearing 280°.

(86) A bank covered 11 fathoms, 3 miles WNW from Piedras Blancas Light, has been reported breaking in a heavy W swell.

(87) From Point Piedras Blancas for 6 miles NNW to the mouth of the San Carpoforo Valley, the coast is low, with small bluffs and rolling treeless hills. Numerous rocks, fringed with kelp, extend well offshore. **Harlech Castle Rock**, 0.7 mile offshore and 1.5 miles NW of Piedras Blancas Light, is the outermost rock and uncovers 1 foot; it is not usually marked by kelp. A shoal covered 2¾ fathoms, 0.5 mile NW of this rock, is surrounded by 10 to 12 fathoms.

(88) **La Cruz Rock**, 48 feet high and fairly prominent, is 3 miles NNW of Piedras Blancas Light and just S of Point Sierra Nevada. A sandy beach inshore from the rock is a fair landing place in heavy NW weather. This stretch of beach is relatively free from breakers in NW weather. There is a suitable anchorage for small boats E of the N limits of the rock in heavy NW or light S weather.

(89) **Point Sierra Nevada**, a low inconspicuous bluff, is named for the steamship SIERRA NEVADA, which stranded on the rock 400 yards NW of the point.

(90) About 1.8 miles N of Point Sierra Nevada is a group of isolated buildings inland from **Breaker Point**; the point is not prominent nor easily identified.

(91) **Ragged Point**, 6 miles N of Point Piedras Blancas, is a low projection readily identified, being the first point S of prominent San Carpoforo Valley; visible rocks and ledges extend about 0.3 mile W of the point.

(92) From Ragged Point NW for 41 miles to the Big Sur River, the coast is very bold and rugged. The cliffs are 200 to 500 feet high, and the land rises rapidly to elevations of 2,500 to 5,000 feet within 2 to 3 miles from the coast. There are few beaches and few outlying rocks. The highway along the coast is plainly visible from seaward.

(93) Two conspicuous landmarks lie between Ragged Point and Cape San Martin. **White Rock No. 1**, 39 feet high and rather sharp, is 0.5 mile offshore and 3.8 miles NW of Ragged Point, about 200 yards W of White Rock No. 1 is a rock awash. **White Rock No. 2**, 64 feet high and with a rounded top, is 0.2 mile offshore and 5.8 miles NW of Ragged Point.

(94) **Salmon Cone**, 500 feet high, is a rocky butte close to the shore and 0.5 mile NE of White Rock No. 1. The cone is not conspicuous as it blends into the background.

(95) Several deep narrow gulches indent the coast between Salmon Cone and Cape San Martin. Two of the most prominent are **Villa Creek** and **Alder Creek**. Villa Creek is crossed by a conspicuous white bridge.

(96) A pinnacle rock, covered 1¾ fathoms, is 1.7 miles SE of Cape San Martin and 0.5 mile offshore.

(97) **Whaleboat Rock**, which uncovers 5 feet, and **Bird Rock**, 5 feet high, are about a mile SE of Cape San Martin; they are conspicuous only when close inshore. A group of buildings is on the bluff just N of these rocks.

(98) **Cape San Martin**, 16 miles NW of Point Piedras Blancas, has a ragged precipitous seaward face and is readily identified by the **San Martin Rocks**. From S, the inner rock, which is 100 yards offshore, is the most prominent, being 144 feet high and white in appearance. The middle rock is 34 feet high and triangular. The outer and northernmost rock is cone-shaped, 44 feet high, and 0.5 mile offshore.

(99) **Willow Creek** bridge, about 0.3 mile N of Cape San Martin, is prominent from W.

(100) From Cape San Martin for 9.5 miles to Lopez Point, the coast forms an open bight with rugged shores intersected occasionally by deep narrow valleys. There are a few detached rocks, but only two extend far from the shoreline.

(101) **Plaskett Rock** is a large prominent white rock, 110 feet high, 2 miles N of Cape San Martin and 0.3 mile offshore.

(102) **Tide Rock**, 4 miles N of Cape San Martin and 0.7 mile offshore, is awash and quite sharp; it is a menace in smooth weather as there is no breaker to indicate its position.

(103) **Lopez Point**, 9.5 miles NW of Cape San Martin, is a narrow tableland, 100 feet high, projecting a short distance from the highland. **Lopez Rock**, 51 feet high with a prominent cleft in the middle, is 0.3 mile offshore and 0.8 mile NW of Lopez Point. A shoal covered 6 fathoms is 0.3 mile SW of Lopez Rock.

(104) An open anchorage affording some protection from NW weather may be had about 1 mile SE of Lopez Point in 10 fathoms, sandy bottom. Smaller vessels may obtain better shelter by anchoring inside the kelp bed in about 5 fathoms, sandy bottom, with Lopez Point bearing about 287°. A rock covered 1¾ fathoms is in the kelp beds 0.5 mile SE of Lopez Point.

(105) **Harlan Rock**, 10 feet high, is 0.3 mile offshore and 1.7 miles ESE of Lopez Point. The rock is conspicuous only when approaching the anchorage. A shoal covered ¾ fathom is 680 yards SE of Harlan Rock.

(106) Several peaks are prominent behind Lopez Point. **Junipero Serra Peak**, 10 miles NE of Lopez Point, has pines on and near the summit. **Twin Peak** and **Cone Peak**, 4 miles NE of Lopez Point, are known as the twin peaks; they have scattered trees on their summits and are good landmarks even at night. An observation tower on the summit of Cone Peak is lighted when occupied.

(107) From Lopez Point for 17.5 miles to Pfeiffer Point, the coast is rugged, and high mountains rise precipitously from the shore. The coastline makes in slightly, forming a shallow bight. Several hundred feet above the beach, the slopes are marked by numerous highway cuts, and the highway bridges over these are conspicuous from offshore.

(108) **Square Black Rock**, 4 miles NNW of Lopez Point, is 62 feet high.

(109) **Dolan Cone**, 4.5 miles NNW of Lopez Point, is white in appearance and 77 feet above the water.

(110) **Little Slate Rock**, 7.5 miles NNW of Lopez Point, is 4 feet high; **Slate Rock** is 18 feet high. Both rocks are discernible only when close inshore.

(111) Two major landslides are prominent in the vicinity of **Partington Point**, about 6.5 miles ESE of Pfeiffer Point.

(112) A prominent dwelling, visible from the W and N, is on a bluff 5.5 miles ESE of Pfeiffer Point. Several conspicuous highway bridges cross the canyons. The highway leaves the coast about 3.5 miles ESE of Pfeiffer Point and does not appear again until N of Point Sur.

(113) A deep submarine valley makes in from the S in the bight 13.5 miles NW of Lopez Point and 4.5 miles SE of Pfeiffer Point. The head of the canyon parallels the shore for about a mile and the 100-fathom curve lies only 500 yards from the shore.

Chart 18686

(114) **Pfeiffer Point**, 17.5 miles NW of Lopez Point and 6 miles SE of Point Sur, is 400 to 500 feet high; it is the seaward end of a long ridge 2,000 feet high, 1.5 miles NE of the point. The point presents a bold, precipitous, light-colored face to seaward. It is distinguished from

the S by its color, and from N the pointed summit stands out. The point is more prominent from N than from S. **Sycamore Canyon** is immediately NW of the point.

Anchorage

(115) Anchorage, affording fair protection in N and NW weather, may be had for small vessels about 0.9 mile ESE of Pfeiffer Point and 500 yards offshore in 8 fathoms, sandy bottom, with chain sufficient to clear the kelp line. This anchorage is used extensively by local fishermen. Access by land is difficult as the road is poor.

(116) **Cooper Point**, 1.5 miles NW of Pfeiffer Point, is marked by a prominent pinnacle 172 feet high and an off-lying rock 18 feet high.

(117) From the mouth of **Big Sur River**, 3.5 miles NW of Pfeiffer Point, to Point Sur, the shore is low, with sand beaches and dunes extending E. Submerged rocks and ledges extend 1 mile or more offshore in some places between Cooper Point and Point Sur.

(118) **False Sur**, 1.2 miles SE of Point Sur Light, is a 209-foot rounded hillock of somewhat similar appearance to Point Sur, and during fog and low visibility may be mistaken for it.

(119) **Point Sur**, 121 miles NW of Point Arguello and 96 miles SSE of San Francisco Bay entrance, is a black rocky butte 361 feet high with low sand dunes extending E from it for over 0.5 mile. From N or S, it looks like an island and in clear weather is visible about 25 miles. The buildings on the summit of Point Sur may confuse the stranger. **Point Sur Light** (36°18'23"N., 121°54'06"W.), 250 feet above the water, is shown from a white tower on a gray stone building on the seaward face of the point. The buildings of a U.S. Naval Facility for oceanographic research are about 0.5 mile E from the light.

(120) **Pico Blanco**, 4.5 miles E of Point Sur, rises from the long ridge bordering the S side of Little Sur River. The pointed and white-topped peak is prominent in clear weather.

(121) **Sur Rock**, 1.8 miles SSE from Point Sur Light and nearly 0.8 mile offshore, is awash. A shoal covered 2 fathoms, 0.3 mile W of Point Sur, breaks heavily in all but very smooth weather. About 0.5 mile SW from Sur Rock is a shoal covered 4½ fathoms that breaks in heavy weather. Extending 0.9 mile from Sur Rock toward Point Sur are many covered rocks that show breakers in moderately smooth weather. Foul ground lies between the rocks and the beach. These dangers are usually well marked by kelp, but it is a dangerous locality in thick or foggy weather, and vessels should stay in depths greater than 30 fathoms.

Chart 18680

(122) The coast trends NNW from Point Sur for 17 miles to Cypress Point, then NE for 4 miles to Point Pinos.

(123) Monterey Bay is a broad open bight 20 miles wide between Point Pinos and Point Santa Cruz. The shores decrease in height and boldness as Point Pinos is approached, while those of Monterey Bay are, as a rule, low and sandy. The valleys of Salinas and Pajaro Rivers, which empty into the E part of Monterey Bay, are marked depressions in the coastal mountain range and are prominent as such from a considerable distance seaward. From Point Santa Cruz the coast curves W and N for 23 miles to Pigeon Point, and then extends for 25 miles in a general NNW direction to Point San Pedro, the S headland of the Gulf of the Farallones.

(124) Between Cypress Point and Point Pinos the coast is bold and the 30-fathom curve is less than 1 mile from shore in many places; deep submarine valleys extend into Carmel Bay and Monterey Bay. N of Monterey Bay, depths are more regular and the few dangers extend less than 1 mile from shore.

(125) **Monterey Bay National Marine Sanctuary** was established to protect and manage the conservation, ecological, recreational, research, educational, historical and esthetic resources and qualities of the coastal and ocean waters and submerged lands in and surrounding Monterey Bay. (See **15 CFR 922,** chapter 2, for limits and regulations.)

Routes

(126) **Routes** or **recommended tracks** for vessels **300 gross tons and higher** transiting the vicinity of Monterey Bay National Marine Sanctuary are from a position (36°18.31'N., 122°12.79'W.) 15 miles off Point Sur, to a position (37°10.86'N., 122°39.74'W.) 12.7 miles off Pigeon Point, for N bound vessels; and from a position (37°10.85'N., 122°43.87'W.) 16 miles off Pigeon Point, to a position (36°18.29'N., 122°18.98'W.) 20 miles off Point Sur, for **S bound vessels.**

(127) Vessels carrying **hazardous bulk cargo** recommended tracks are further offshore, beginning at a position (36°18.27'N., 122°25.16'W.) 25 miles off Point Sur, to a position (37°10.81'N., 122°55.14'W.) 25 miles off Pigeon Point, for N bound vessels; and from a position (37°10.78'N., 123°01.39'W.) 30 miles off Pigeon Point, to a position (36°18.24'N., 122°31.35'W.) 30 miles off Point Sur, for S bound vessels.

(128) **Tank vessels** are recommended to transit the Monterey Bay National Marine Sanctuary area well offshore (at least 50 miles). Tank vessels and vessels **carrying hazardous cargo** transiting San Francisco Golden Gate are recommended to use the Main (W) Traffic Lanes when proceeding to and from S of San Francisco Traffic Separation Scheme.

Chart 18686

(129) Just N of Point Sur (36°18.4'N., 121°54.0'W.), a sandy beach and bluff continue for 1.8 miles to **Little Sur River**, where the coast becomes bold, the 30-fathom

curve lying in many cases less than 1 mile from shore. The highway returns to the coast just N of Point Sur and is visible from seaward until it reaches Pinnacle Point. It is marked by several bridges.

(130) **Ventura Rocks**, 2.2 miles N of Point Sur, are two rocks close together about 0.6 mile offshore. The N rock is conical-shaped and 12 feet high. It is fairly conspicuous when seen from the N with the sand bluff N of Point Sur as a background, but when seen from the S it is confused with the rocks near the beach and to the N. The S rock uncovers.

(131) From the conspicuous valley of the Little Sur River for more than 7 miles to Soberanes Point, the coast, although moderately straight, is bold, rugged, and broken, with numerous detached rocks and covered ledges close inshore.

(132) **Bixby Landing**, 4 miles N of Point Sur, is identified by a prominent concrete arch bridge across Bixby Creek; the bridge shows well to the W, but is obscured to the N. Less prominent is another concrete arch bridge across Rocky Creek, which is just N of Bixby Creek.

(133) **Soberanes Point** projects slightly from the general trend of the coast. An isolated 200-foot grassy hillock lies immediately back of the point, and a grassy ridge extends inland to heights of 1,600 feet.

(134) The 4.6-mile coastline from Soberanes Point to Pinnacle Point is rugged and broken, but becomes less precipitous and the mountain ridges lessen in height as Pinnacle Point is approached. Innumerable rocks and ledges extend in some cases over 0.3 mile offshore.

(135) **Lobos Rocks**, a group of small rocky islets, are nearly 0.5 mile W of Soberanes Point. The two larger islets are white-topped, and each is about 40 feet high. From seaward they rise abruptly from 20 fathoms, but there is foul ground between them.

(136) **Mount Carmel** (chart 18680), 7.3 miles NE of Point Sur, is round and bare on the summit. This peak and **Pico Blanco**, 4.5 miles E of Point Sur, sometimes can be seen when the lower land is covered by fog or haze.

(137) **Yankee Point**, 2.5 miles N of Soberanes Point, projects 0.3 mile from the general trend of the coast. The seaward face is irregular and broken, with numerous detached rocks. **Yankee Point Rock**, 6 feet high, is 125 yards W of the point. A covered rock that generally breaks is 0.4 mile S of the point and the same distance offshore.

(138) **Pinnacle (Carmel) Point**, the outer tip of **Point Lobos** and the S point at the entrance to Carmel Bay, is an irregular, jagged, rocky point 100 feet high. **Whalers Knoll**, the 200-foot-high hill 0.5 mile ESE of Pinnacle Point, is one of the prominent knobs on Point Lobos. **Sea Lion Rocks** are a group of rocks off the point. A rock, formerly known as Whalers Rock, is the farthest offshore of the group and is 0.5 mile SW of the point. It is 12 feet high, the most conspicuous of the group, and more prominent from the N than from the S.

(139) The entire Point Lobos area is included in a state ecological reserve. Regulations prohibit landing anywhere within its boundaries. **Whalers Cove**, the bight on the N shore 0.8 mile ESE of Pinnacle Point, may be used as a harbor of refuge only. Kelp growth is quite heavy in the cove.

(140) **Carmel Bay** is a 2.8-mile-wide open bight between Pinnacle Point and Cypress Point. The beach in front of the city of Carmel is low, but the land on the S side of the bay is bare and mountainous, and the N side is hilly and heavily wooded.

(141) Carmel Bay affords shelter in N and S weather to small craft having local knowledge. In N weather anchorage may be had in two coves on the N shore, **Pebble Beach** on the W and **Stillwater Cove** on the E. These are shallow kelp-filled bights, with rock and gravel bottom. Anchorage is in 1 to 3 fathoms, but local knowledge is necessary to avoid the dangers. In S weather, anchorage may be had in Whalers Cove in 3 to 4 fathoms, rock or gravel bottom, but there is a rock covered 1¾ fathoms near the middle of the cove.

(142) **Carmel Canyon**, a deep submarine valley, heads in the SE part of Carmel Bay and has depths of 50 fathoms less than 0.2 mile from the beach. The bay is not recommended for strangers.

(143) On the NE shore of Carmel Bay, and N of **Carmel River**, is the city of **Carmel**. The lights of Carmel are prominent on a clear night. The tower of Carmelite Monastery, 1.5 mile E of Pinnacle Point, is a conspicuous structure.

(144) **Cypress Point**, on the N side of the entrance to Carmel Bay, is comparatively low and extends about 2 miles beyond the general trend of the coast. The cliffs are steep, and numerous detached rocks are close under them. The point is heavily wooded to within 400 yards of its tip. **Cypress Point Rock**, 12 feet high, is 450 yards NW of Cypress Point and is prominent from either N or S. A lighted gong buoy is NW of the point.

Chart 18685

(145) From Cypress Point to Point Pinos, the coast trends NE for 4 miles. Numerous small rocks and ledges closely border the shoreline. The land is low, with the height of the cliff decreasing toward **Point Joe**, a rocky extension of the shoreline where the surf breaks heavily. From this point to Point Pinos, white sand dunes are conspicuous against the dark trees behind them, even in moonlight.

(146) **Point Pinos**, on the S side of Monterey Bay, is low, rocky, and rounding with visible rocks extending offshore for less than 0.3 mile. The point is bare for about 0.2 mile back from the beach, and beyond that is covered with pines. **Point Pinos Light** (36°38'00"N., 121°56'01"W.), 89 feet above the water, is shown from a 43-foot white tower on a dwelling near the N end of the point. A lighted bell buoy is about 0.7 mile off the point.

(147) **Monterey Bay**, between Point Pinos and Point Santa Cruz, is a broad 20-mile-wide open roadstead. The shores are low with sand beaches backed by dunes or

low sandy bluffs. **Salinas Valley**, the lowland extending E from about the middle of the bay, is prominent from seaward as it forms the break between the Santa Lucia Range S and the high land of the Santa Cruz Mountains N. The bay is free of dangers, the 10-fathom curve lying at an average distance of 0.7 mile offshore. The submarine **Monterey Canyon** heads near the middle of the bay with a depth of over 50 fathoms about 0.5 mile from the beach near Moss Landing. Shelter from NW winds is afforded at Santa Cruz Anchorage and Soquel Cove, off the N shore of the bay, and from SW winds at Monterey Harbor, off the S shore. The tidal currents are reported to be generally weak except at the Deep-draft Mooring Facility about 0.8 mile NW from Moss Landing harbor entrance.

Weather, Monterey Bay

(148) Sea fog is a problem on the bay from about July through September. It is worse over open waters and along the exposed E shore. Around Monterey Harbor in the S and Santa Cruz Anchorage in the N, fog reduces visibility to less than 0.5 mile (0.9 km) on 4 to 8 days per month during the worst period. Close to shore, cloudiness begins to increase and descend in the evening by 2100 or 2200. Low clouds or fog cast a pall over the E shore. Around sunrise, conditions begin to improve, and, by 0900, visibilities are usually better than 0.5 mile (0.9 km). The best conditions occur in the early afternoon, when visibilities are less than 3 miles (6 km) and cloud ceiling are less than 1,500 feet (458 m) only 10 to 20 percent of the time. Clear skies and excellent visibility occur 15 to 20 percent of the time. Poor conditions can be expected over the bay and along exposed coasts on 10 to 15 days per month during July, August, and September. Moss Landing is an exposed location, and sound signals operate about 25 percent of the time in August. Radiation fog occurs infrequently from the fall through spring.

(149) Gales are rare over Monterey Bay; extreme gusts have been reported at 40 to 50 knots from October through May. The maximum gust for Monterey Peninsula was a gust of 60 knots from the NE in January 1989. Winds of 17 knots or more occur 1 to 4 percent of the time from November through March; they are rare during July, August, and September. Prevailing winds are W averaging seven knots, except in late fall and early winter, when E winds are as frequent. W through NW winds remain the predominant directions into October, when winds become more variable again.

(150) Winter winds over the bay are variable. Winds from the ESE are as common as winds from the WNW, and, along the shore, calms occur more than 20 percent of the time. In late winter, WNW winds prevail. Strongest winter winds are often out of the S. During spring and summer, they are most likely from the NW.

(151) The average annual temperature at Monterey is 57°F (13.9°C). The average maximum is 65°F (18.3°C) and the average minimum is 48°F (8.9°C). The all-time warmest temperature is 104°F (40°C) recorded in October of 1987. The coolest thermometer reading is 20°F (-6.7°C), recorded in December 1990. The average annual precipitation for Monterey is 18.6 inches (472 mm). Trace amounts of snow have fallen during February in Monterey.

Pilotage, Monterey Bay

(152) Pilotage in and out of Monterey Bay is compulsory for all vessels of foreign registry and U.S. vessels under enrollment not having a federal licensed pilot on board. The San Francisco Bar Pilots provide pilotage to harbors in Monterey Bay (see Pilotage, San Francisco, chapter 7 for contact information.) The pilot boarding area is within a 1-mile radius centered around a point located at 36°40'00"N., 121°58'00"W., about 2.5 miles NW of Point Pinos Light.

(153) A **restricted and a prohibited area** for an army firing range is in the SE part of the bay, and a naval operating area is in the NE part of the bay. (See **334.1150**, chapter 2, for limits and regulations.)

(154) **Pacific Grove**, a summer resort just SE of Point Pinos, has no commercial wharves, but a small solid-concrete jetty with low-level landing usable only on a seasonal basis, is just S of **Lovers Point**.

(155) **Monterey Harbor**, 3 miles SE of Point Pinos, is a compact resort harbor with some commercial activity and fishing. The harbor can accommodate over 800 vessels.

(156) Depths of more than 20 feet are available in the outer harbor and entrance, and 10 to 6 feet in the small-boat basin. There are many sport-fishing landings, and the small-craft basin provides good shelter for over 500 boats. There are four public launch ramps available in the harbor. The municipal marina has transient berths available and can provide electricity, pump-out, ice, and marine supplies; a 3-ton and 70-ton lift is available for hull, engine, and electrical repairs. The marina monitors VHF-FM channels 16 and 5. The boat yard, located just inside the breakwater has a 70-ton travel lift.

(157) **Monterey**, a colorful and picturesque city on the W side of the harbor, was the capital of California under Mexican rule and for sometime after it became a State. The old adobe custom house is still standing near the waterfront and is now used as a historical museum.

Prominent features

(158) Prominent features include the granite **Presidio Monument** on the brow of a hill on the W side of the harbor and a radio tower 0.6 mile N of the monument.

(159) Two radio towers just inshore from the sand dunes at **Marina**, 6.5 miles NE from the breakwater, are conspicuous in the S part of Monterey Bay. An aerolight at Monterey Peninsula Airport is 1.9 miles ESE of Monterey Harbor Light 6. Another aerolight is 7.3 miles NE of Light 6.

Moss Landing Harbor, California
Image courtesy of U.S. Army Corps of Engineers

COLREGS Demarcation Lines

(160)   The lines established for Monterey Harbor are described in **80.1134**, chapter 2.

(161)   Monterey Harbor breakwater is on the N side of the entrance to Monterey Harbor. The breakwater extends seaward from the Coast Guard pier for a combined length of about 1,700 feet. This affords excellent protection in NW weather. However, in heavy weather there may be a strong surge in the harbor. The outer end of the breakwater is marked by a light. A sound signal is at the light. The outer harbor is marked by a private lighted junction buoy. The N channel at the junction buoy leads to a private marina and fuel dock. Loud-barking sea lions occupy the breakwater during the day and should not unnecessarily be disturbed.

Anchorages

(162)   A **special anchorage** is just S of the breakwater. (See **110.1** and **110.126**, chapter 2, for limits and regulations.) A **seasonal special anchorage and mooring area** is just E of Municipal Wharf No. 2. Mariners operating in the vicinity of Monterey Harbor are requested to avoid transiting through this area. Mooring or anchoring is restricted based on current weather conditions. Permission to moor or anchor may be obtained through the Office of the Harbormaster.

Currents

(163)   A very strong current is reported to exist at the small-boat basin entrance when swells run following winter storms. The current runs mainly from the breakwater towards Municipal Wharf No. 1; caution is advised.

Quarantine, customs, immigration, and agricultural quarantine

(164)   (See chapter 3, Vessel Arrival Inspections, and Appendix A for addresses.)

(165)   **Quarantine** is enforced in accordance with regulations of the U.S. Public Health Service. (See Public Health Service, chapter 1.)

(166)   Monterey is a **customs station**.

Coast Guard

(167)   Monterey Coast Guard Station is at the foot of the Coast Guard pier.

Harbor regulations

(168)   The harbor is owned by the city of Monterey and under the control of a harbormaster. His office is in a building on shore about midway between the two municipal wharves. Transients requesting berth assignments should contact either the harbormaster's office or the privately-owned Monterey Bay Boatworks Company on VHF-FM channel 16. The harbormaster can be

contacted by phone at 831–646–3950 or at http://www.monterey.org.

(169) The **speed limit** in the harbor is 3 knots.

Wharves

(170) Municipal Wharf No. 2, the most easterly pier, is 1,600 feet long and 86 feet wide at the outer end; depths alongside the outer E and W sides are 24 feet. Freight and supplies are handled by trucks directly to the pier; a 3-ton hoist is at the pier on the marina side.

(171) Municipal Wharf No. 1, frequently called Fishermans Wharf, is 300 yards W of Wharf 2. It is lined with restaurants and shops.

(172) A marina is just S of the foot of the Coast Guard dock. A 60-ton boat lift is available; complete hull, electrical, and electronic repairs are available.

Supplies

(173) Gasoline and diesel fuel are available at Municipal Wharf No. 2. Water, ice, and marine supplies, are available at the marina S of the Coast Guard dock and Municipal Wharf No. 2.

Communications

(174) Monterey has good air and highway connections with San Francisco and points S.

(175) **Moss Landing Harbor**, on the E shore of Monterey Bay 12.5 miles NE of Point Pinos and just N of the small town of **Moss Landing**, is a good harbor of refuge. The harbor is used by pleasure craft and a fishing fleet of about 300 boats. The harbor has 500 berths.

Prominent features

(176) The two huge stacks at a large powerplant near the harbor are the dominating landmarks on Monterey Bay. The stacks are 528 feet high and are marked by flashing red lights. Other stacks at the powerplant and at the nearby mineral processing plant are less conspicuous.

(177) An area of turbulent water, caused by water discharge from the power plant, is about 250 yards SW of the S jetty light; the turbulence may be dangerous to small craft.

COLREGS Demarcation Lines

(178) The lines established for Moss Landing Harbor are described in **80.1136**, chapter 2.

Channels

(179) A **Federal project** for Moss Landing Harbor provides for a 15-foot jettied entrance channel leading NE to an outer turning basin, and thence an inner channel of the same depth leading S to an inner turning basin about 0.8 mile above the entrance. (See Notice to Mariners and latest editions of charts for controlling depths.) The approach to the harbor is marked by a lighted bell buoy. The entrance channel is marked by a buoy, lights and a **052°** lighted range. The jetties are marked by lights on their outer ends, and the inner channel is marked by lights, buoys, and a daybeacon. A sound signal is at the S jetty light. Shoaling usually occurs on the S side of the entrance between the jetties; vessels should favor the N side of the channel when entering.

(180) A channel, marked by private buoys, leads N from the outer turning basin to Moss Landing Harbor's North Harbor basin; a private yacht club is adjacent to the basin. In 2004, the reported controlling depth was 10 feet, thence the North Harbor basin had depths of 10 to 16 feet. Because of frequent shoaling, local knowledge is advised prior to entering the channel. A surfaced launching ramp is on the E side of the channel, S of the North Harbor basin.

Anchorage

(181) The anchorage off Moss Landing Harbor is unprotected, but the holding ground is good for larger vessels in fair weather.

Weather, Moss Landing

(182) The prevailing winds are NW, but there are a few SE winds and N gales during the winter. Mariners in the area should be aware of reported unique environmental conditions. Vessels have experienced sudden wind shifts during the late morning to early afternoon hours. At this time the new wind begins to generate its own waves from the W and NW, dissipating existing swells, and creating a cross pattern of waves giving the sea a "choppy" or confused appearance. During the first few hours following the wind shift, the appearance of the sea surface may not provide a reliable indication of the wind speed. This condition has effected ship handling by setting deep-draft vessels. Occasionally, when there is a southwesterly wind during an ebb tide, slight breaking seas cross the harbor entrance. (See Weather, West Coast and Hawaii, indexed as such, chapter 3, for further information.)

Harbor regulations

(183) The harbor is administered by the Moss Landing Harbor District and is under the control of a harbormaster. The office is near the inner turning basin. Transients should report to the harbormaster for mooring assignments. Contact the harbormaster on VHF-FM channel 9, 16 or telephone 831–633–2461 for local weather conditions.

Supplies and Repairs

(184) Gasoline, diesel fuel, water, ice, and some marine supplies can be obtained; bilge and sewage pumpout is available; a 70-ton mobile hoist is available for repair work.

Monterey Wind Gap

(185)　The great mountain barriers N and S of Monterey Bay and the receding shoreline to the E offer a broad entrance to the cold foggy NW winds of the summer, and they drive over the bay and well into Salinas Valley to the S.

(186)　**Soquel Cove** is in the NE part of Monterey Bay, E of Santa Cruz Anchorage. Fair shelter is afforded in NW weather, but the cove is open to S weather. The best anchorage is SE of the mouth of **Soquel Creek** in 5 to 6 fathoms, sandy bottom.

(187)　At **Seacliff Beach**, 0.5 mile W of **Aptos Creek**, a concrete ship has been beached and filled with sand. The pleasure pier for sport fishing extends from ship to the shore.

(188)　A small fishing and pleasure wharf at **Capitola**, on the NW side of Soquel Cove, has 11 feet alongside the landing at the outer end. There are facilities to hoist out small boats. Houses on the bluffs about 1.5 miles E of Capitola are prominent. Three radio towers 0.6 mile NW of **Soquel Point** are conspicuous from the E and S.

(189)　**Point Santa Cruz**, 20 miles N of Point Pinos and 2.5 miles W of Soquel Point, consists of cliff heads about 40 feet above the water. The area back of the point is flat, but rises in terraces to higher land. There are two flat rocks close under the point; the outer one is the higher.

(190)　**Santa Cruz Light** (36°57'05"N., 122°01'36"W.), 60 feet above the water, is shown from a 39-foot white lantern house on a square brick tower attached to a brick building near the S extremity of the point. A lighted whistle buoy is 1.1 miles SE of the light.

(191)　The city of **Santa Cruz** is on the NW shore of the bay. **Seabright, Twin Lakes**, and **Soquel**, suburbs of Santa Cruz, are along the beach to the E.

(192)　**Santa Cruz Anchorage**, on the NW shore of Monterey Bay between Point Santa Cruz and Soquel Point, has a municipal pier and small-craft harbor.

(193)　The Santa Cruz small-craft harbor is just E of Seabright and has slips and end-ties for about 1,200 small craft.

Prominent features

(194)　The Casino building and the roller coaster immediately E of the town are prominent.

COLREGS Demarcation Lines

(195)　The lines established for Santa Cruz Anchorage (Santa Cruz Harbor) are described in **80.1138**, chapter 2.

Channels

(196)　The entrance to the small-craft harbor is protected by jetties; a light, and sound signal are at the end of the W jetty. The least clearance for the bridges between the north and south basins is 18 feet.

(197)　The Santa Cruz harbormaster advises that extensive shoaling occurs at the harbor entrance from November through May. Persons unfamiliar with the area should contact the harbormaster's office prior to entering the harbor; a radio guard on VHF-FM channel 16 is maintained 24 hours a day or telephone 831–475–6161 between 0830 and 1700 daily. The Santa Cruz harbormaster further recommends that mariners without local knowledge should not attempt to enter the harbor during periods of high ground swells.

Anchorage

(198)　Good anchorage can be had anywhere off the pier in 5 fathoms, sand bottom. Santa Cruz Anchorage provides good shelter in N weather, but in NW weather a heavy swell is likely to sweep into the anchorage. In S weather there is no protection in the harbor; vessels must run for Monterey or Moss Landing Harbor or take refuge in Santa Cruz Municipal small-craft harbor.

Harbor regulations

(199)　The harbor is administered by the Santa Cruz Port District Commission. Transient vessels should report to the harbor office at the SE corner of the small-craft harbor, for berth assignments.

(200)　A patrol boat operates in the harbor and monitors VHF-FM channel 16. The patrol boat will guide vessels into the harbor on request.

Wharves

(201)　The municipal pier, 0.8 mile W of the entrance to the small-craft harbor, is over 0.4 mile long with 26 feet alongside at its outer end; a private seasonal sound signal in on the outer end of the pier. Landings can be made in all but heavy S weather, but few vessels land except fishing boats. Due to the ocean swell sweeping around the point, there is usually considerable surge. The pier is lined with restaurants and stores. A small-boat hoist is on the pier.

Supplies

(202)　Gasoline, diesel fuel, and marine supplies are available. A launching ramp and a yacht club are in the harbor.

Repairs

(203)　A repair yard at the harbor has a 40-ton mobile lift that can handle vessels for hull and engine repairs. Electronic repairs are also available.

Communications

(204)　Santa Cruz has highway and rail connections with San Francisco and the interior.

Chart 18680

(205) From Point Santa Cruz the coast trends W about 4 miles to Needle Rock Point and thence NW to Point Ano Nuevo. The shoreline rises from high bluffs, with a few intervening beaches, to a low flat tree-covered mountain range.

(206) **Needle Rock Point** is 4 miles W of Santa Cruz Light; a slender pillar of rock stands a short distance seaward from the face of the cliffs; another lower pinnacle is about 200 yards E. Neither is distinguishable when abreast it.

(207) **Sand Hill Bluff**, 6.5 miles W of Santa Cruz Light, is composed of sandstone cliffs about 50 feet high with a rounding irregular hillock of white sand near the edge of the cliffs; this hillock is white on the NW side, and is covered with brush and grass on the SE side. Neither this bluff nor Needle Rock Point is a good landmark.

(208) The buildings of a large cement works at **Davenport**, 9 miles NW of Point Santa Cruz, are conspicuous. A steel tower is prominent by day, and many lights are visible at night. The ruins of an old cement loading wharf are at the plant.

(209) In 1975, shoaling to 10 fathoms was reported in 37°00.0'N., 122°30.1'W., about 14.5 miles W of Davenport.

(210) **Loma Prieta**, a prominent flat-topped peak surmounting the high mountainous ridge 13 miles NE of Santa Cruz Light, is the predominating mountain feature of this section. A fire observation tower is on the top of the peak.

(211) **Waddell Creek**, 14.5 miles NW of Point Santa Cruz, is in a narrow steep-sided valley. The high whitish bluffs, immediately N, are quite prominent.

(212) **Point Ano Nuevo**, 18 miles NW of Point Santa Cruz, is formed by sand dunes 20 to 100 feet high. A low black rocky islet is 0.3 mile off the point. Foul ground extends NW and SE from the islet. A group of white houses on the islet is conspicuous. A lighted whistle buoy is about 0.8 mile S of the tower.

(213) Anchorage with protection from N and NW winds can be had in the bight S of the point. The kelp bed and reef, extending a little over 0.5 mile SE from the islet, break the force of the swell.

(214) The 5-mile coast between Point Ano Nuevo and Pigeon Point is low and rocky. **Pigeon Point**, 22.5 miles NW of Point Santa Cruz, is 50 feet high and rises in a gentle slope to the coastal hills. Several moderately large detached rocks extend 350 yards SW. Pigeon Point was named from the wreck at this place of the clipper ship CARRIER PIGEON.

(215) **Pigeon Point Light** (37°10'54"N., 122°23'38"W.), 148 feet above the water, is shown from a 110-foot white conical tower on the end of the point. The light cannot be seen in the bight E of a line joining Pigeon Point and Pillar Point, 20 miles to the N. The light station buildings on Pigeon Point are white with red roofs. A group of farm buildings is about 0.5 mile E. A row of trees, conspicuous against a background of barren hills is about 500 yards NE of the light.

(216) From Pigeon Point for 4 miles to **Pescadero Point**, the coast is nearly straight and is composed of reddish cliffs with numerous outlying submerged and visible rocks. A rocky patch covered 3 feet is about 0.8 mile S of Pescadero Point; a 6¼-fathom rocky patch is about 0.7 mile WSW of the point.

(217) From **Pescadero Creek**, 1.5 miles N of Pescadero Point, the coast for 8 miles N becomes more broken and rugged, with yellow or white vertical cliffs. A prominent whitish cliff over 100 feet high is 7.5 miles N of Pescadero Point. About 9 miles N of the point is a pale yellow building surrounded by numerous antenna poles.

(218) The coast is broken by several small streams in deep steep-sided valleys. N of the high cliff, a low flat tableland extends N for 9 miles and then bends sharply W to Pillar Point, forming Half Moon Bay. The land consists generally of grass-covered rolling hills with ranch houses and cultivated ground in the foreground.

Chart 18682

(219) **Pillar Point**, 18 miles S of San Francisco entrance, is the S extremity of a 2.5-mile low ridge. Several black rocks extend over 300-yards S of the point; from N these appear as three or four, but from S as only one. **Half Moon Bay** comprises the bight from **Miramontes Point** on the S to Pillar Point on the N.

(220) **Pillar Point Harbor**, in the N part of Half Moon Bay E of Pillar Point, is used by fishing vessels and pleasure craft. The harbor is well protected by breakwaters. The entrance, 200-yards wide, is between the E and W breakwaters. A light marks the end of the E breakwater, and a light and sound signal are on the end of the W breakwater. The entrance has a depth of about 20 feet with depths of 2 to 17 feet inside the harbor. Shoaling has been reported along N side of the breakwaters inside the harbor. The harbor provides good holding ground for anchored and moored vessels. Two breakwaters and a detached breakwater, protect a marina on the N side of the harbor. The detached breakwater is marked by lights on the E and W ends.

Prominent features

(221) Several buildings and a white radar antenna at the U.S. Air Force radar site about 0.2 mile N of Pillar Point are conspicuous when approaching the harbor. The lights of the radar site are conspicuous at night. A rotating aero beacon located 1 mile NW of the marina is visible from the south.

(222) **Caution** is necessary in approaching Pillar Point Harbor because of the foul ground off the entrance. Rocks and reefs, marked by kelp and a lighted bell buoy, extend SE for over 1 mile from Pillar Point. **Southeast**

Reef, extending from 1.5 to over 2 miles SE of Pillar Point, is covered 4 to 20 feet and has a pinnacle rock awash at extreme low water at the SE end. Mariners are advised to exercise caution in the vicinity of Pillar Point in dense fog.

COLREGS Demarcation Lines

(223) The lines established for Pillar Point Harbor are described in **80.1140,** chapter 2.

Routes

(224) Vessels from the S approach the harbor E of the lighted gong buoy marking Southeast Reef; vessels from the N use the buoyed opening between the Pillar Point foul ground and Southeast Reef.

Harbor regulations

(225) Pillar Point Harbor is administered by the San Mateo County Harbor District and under the control of a harbormaster. The harbormaster's office is at the head of the L-shaped pier in the marina. The harbormaster can be contacted on VHF-FM channel 16 or telephone 650–726–4382.

(226) There are only private mooring floats in the harbor so transients must anchor. The harbormaster should be consulted before tying alongside piers.

Wharves

(227) An L-shaped pier, 590 feet long with 13 feet alongside the 275-foot outer face, is on the N side of Pillar Point Harbor. Water, ice, and electricity are at the pier, and gasoline and diesel fuel are pumped at the landing. A skiff hoist is on the end of the pier. Marine railways are in the harbor W of the marina and are capable of hauling vessels up to 50 tons.

(228) The 660-foot pier W of the L-shaped pier has about 5 feet at the outer end. A surfaced launching ramp and parking area are near the inshore end of the E breakwater.

Chart 18680

(229) **Montara Mountain**, 4 miles N of Pillar Point and 2.5 miles inland, is covered with grass and bare trees. From S it shows as a long ridge with several small elevations upon it, but from NW it appears as a flat-topped mountain with four knobs on the summit. It is a prominent feature in approaching the entrance to San Francisco Bay.

(230) **Point Montara**, 2.8 miles N of Pillar Point, is the seaward end of a spur from Montara Mountain and the NW extremity of the ridge forming Pillar Point. It terminates in cliffs about 60 feet high with numerous outlying rocks. Covered rocks and ledges lie 0.8 mile W of the point and extend in a NW direction for about 1.5 miles. This is a dangerous locality in thick weather, and extreme caution should be used when inside the 30-fathom curve.

(231) **Point Montara Light** (37°32'11"N., 122°31'09"W.), 70 feet above the water, is shown from a 30-foot white conical tower on the point. A group of white buildings with red roofs is prominent on the point.

(232) From Point Montara for 2.5 miles to Point San Pedro the coast is bold and rugged, rising sharply from the sea to the spurs extending from Montara Mountain. **Devils Slide** is light-colored and is the highest bluff in this locality. The highway cuts are distinctive features in the bluffs. There are no outlying rocks or dangers other than those off Point Montara.

(233) **Point San Pedro** is a dark, bold, rocky promontory, 640 feet high. It is the seaward termination of Montara Mountain and is an excellent mark in clear weather from either N or S. A large triple-headed rock, about 100 feet high and white on its S face, projects 0.3 mile W from the point. A rocky area, which breaks in a heavy swell, is reported to exist about 1 mile N of the point.

(234) A 200-yard-long Municipal fishing pier is about 2.5 miles NE of Point San Pedro.

TIDAL INFORMATION					
Chart	Station	LAT/LONG	Mean Higher High Water*	Mean High Water*	Mean Low Water*
18682	Princeton, Half Moon Bay	37°30'N/122°29'W	5.5	4.9	1.1
18685	Moss Landing, Ocean Pier	36°48'N/121°47'W	5.2	4.5	1.0
18685	Santa Cruz, Monterey Bay	36°58'N/122°01'W	5.3	4.6	1.1
18685	Monterey, Monterey Bay	36°36'N/121°53'W	5.3	4.6	1.1
18686	Carmel Cove, Carmel Bay	36°31'N/121°56'W	5.2	4.6	1.1
18704	Port San Luis Wharf	35°10'N/120°45'W	5.3	4.6	1.0
18721	Point Arguello	34°35'N/120°39'W	5.2	4.5	1.0
18721	Bechers Bay, Santa Rosa Island	34°01'N/120°03'W	5.1	4.4	1.0

* Heights in feet referred to datum of sounding MLLW.
Real-time water levels, tide predictions, and tidal current predictions are available at:
http://tidesandcurrents.noaa.gov
To determine mean tide range subtract Mean Low Water from Mean High Water.
Data as of September 2012

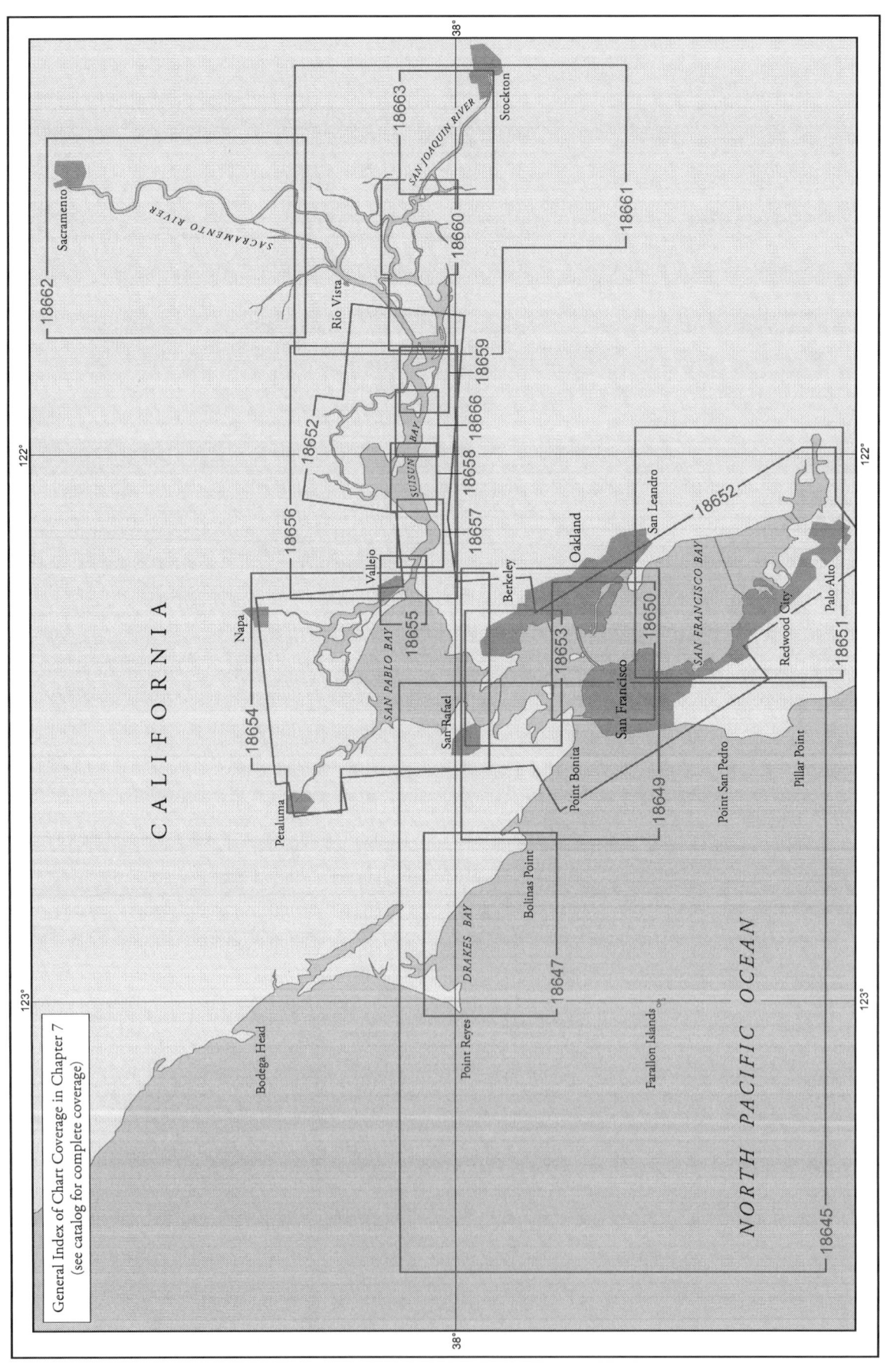

San Francisco Bay, California

Chart 18640

(1) **San Francisco Bay**, the largest harbor on the Pacific coast of the United States, is more properly described as a series of connecting bays and harbors of which San Francisco Bay proper, San Pablo Bay, and Suisun Bay are the largest. Depths of 29 to 40 feet are available for deep-draft vessels to San Francisco, Oakland, Alameda, Richmond, and Redwood City in San Francisco Bay proper; to Stockton on the San Joaquin River; and to Sacramento through the lower Sacramento River and a deepwater channel. Much of the local navigation is by light-draft vessels and barges.

(2) The extensive foreign and domestic commerce of San Francisco Bay is handled through the several large ports which are the terminals for many transpacific steamship lines, airlines, and transcontinental railroads.

(3) The E shore of San Francisco Bay proper is low except for rolling grassy hills in the N part and extensive marshes intersected by numerous winding sloughs in the S part. The W shore N of the entrance is much bolder than the E shore where there are only a few stretches of low marsh. Below San Francisco, marshes and flats intersected by numerous sloughs extend to the S end of the bay.

(4) The Coast Guard Captain of the Port, San Francisco, has ordered that all ships greater than 300 gross tons, anchored in San Francisco Bay maintain a radio listening watch on VHF-FM channels 13 and 14 when the wind is 25 knots or greater. Any ship not equipped with channel 13 shall maintain a listening watch on VHF-FM channel 16. This radio watch must be maintained by a person who can speak the English language.

(5) The Coast Guard considers the following areas to be narrow channels or fairways for the purpose of enforcing the International and Inland Rules of the Road:

(6) a. All traffic lanes and precautionary areas in the San Francisco Bay eastward of the San Francisco Approach Lighted Whistle Buoy SF to the San Francisco-Oakland Bay Bridge and the Richmond-San Rafael Bridge.

(7) b. Oakland Harbor Bar Channel including the Outer Harbor Entrance Channel and the Inner Harbor Entrance Channel.

(8) c. Oakland Outer Harbor.

(9) d. Oakland Inner Harbor from Inner Harbor Channel Light 7 to, and including, the Brooklyn Basin South Channel.

(10) e. Alameda Naval Air Station Channel in its entirety.

(11) f. South San Francisco Bay Channels between the central Bay Precautionary Area and Redwood Creek Entrance Light 2.

(12) g. Redwood Creek between Redwood Creek Entrance Light 2 and Redwood Creek Light 21.

(13) h. San Pablo Straight Channel from the Richmond-San Rafael Bridge to San Pablo Bay Channel Buoy 7.

(14) i. Pinole Shoal Channel in San Pablo Bay between San Pablo Bay Channel Buoy 7 and San Pablo Bay Channel Light 14.

(15) j. Carquinez Strait between San Pablo Bay Channel Light 14 and the Benicia-Martinez Highway Bridge.

(16) k. Mare Island Strait between Mare Island Strait Light 2 and Mare Island Causeway Bridge.

(17) l. Suisun Bay Channels between the Benicia-Martinez Highway Bridge and Suisun Bay Light 34.

(18) m. New York Slough between Suisun Bay Buoy 30 and San Joaquin River Light 2.

(19) n. Sacramento River Deep Water Ship Channel from Suisun Bay Light 34 to the Port of Sacramento.

(20) o. San Joaquin River from San Joaquin River Light 2 to the Port of Stockton.

(21) The above listing of narrow channel or fairway areas is not intended to be exhaustive. Rather it identifies deep-draft navigation areas where commercial and public vessels routinely operate and where small craft can impede the safe transit of larger vessels if extreme care is not exercised. Narrow Channels, Inland-Navigation Rule 9, applies.

COLREGS Demarcation Lines

(22) The lines established for San Francisco Bay are described in **80.1142**, chapter 2.

Chart 18645

(23) The entrance to San Francisco Bay is through **Gulf of the Farallones** and the narrow Golden Gate. The gulf extends from Point San Pedro on the S for 34 miles to Point Reyes on the N, and has a greatest width of 23 miles from Farallon Islands on the W to the mainland.

(24) In clear weather many prominent features are available for use in making San Francisco Bay, but in thick weather the heavy traffic and the currents, variable in direction and velocity, render the approaches difficult and dangerous. Point San Pedro, Montara Mountain, Farallon Islands, Mount Tamalpais, and Point Reyes

(25) are prominent in clear weather and frequently can be seen when the land near the beach is shut in by low fog or haze. Radar navigation on the approach to San Francisco Bay is not difficult because of the numerous distinctive and high relief of targets available. Southeast Farallon Island, Point Reyes, Double Point, Bolinas Point, Duxbury Point, Rocky Point, Point Bonita, San Pedro Rock and Point, and Pillar Point are good radar targets.

(25) The first 8 miles of coast from Point San Pedro to San Francisco Bay entrance consists of whitish bluffs that reach a height of 600 feet, then a 3-mile sand beach extends to the entrance. **Shelter Cove**, on the N side of Point San Pedro, provides shelter from the E storms with good holding ground in gray sand bottom. **San Pedro Rock**, close to the point and 100 feet high, also gives some protection in S weather.

(26) The **Gulf of the Farallones National Marine Sanctuary** has been established to protect and preserve the natural, cultural and historical resources in the waters surrounding the Farallon Islands, including offshore of the Marin and Sonoma county coasts to Bodega Head. The sanctuary boundary includes the estuarine waters of Bolinas Lagoon, Tomales Bay, Estero Americano, Estero de San Antonio and Bodega Bay but not Bodega Harbor. Visitor use is encouraged for boating, diving, snorkeling, fishing, swimming, kayaking and wildlife viewing. (See **15 CFR 922.80** through **922.84**, chapter 2, for limits and regulations.)

(27) **Farallon Islands**, 23 miles W of San Francisco Bay entrance, are rocky islets extending NW for 7 miles. **Southeast Farallon**, the largest of the group, actually consists of two islands separated by a narrow impassable gorge. The larger E island is pyramidal in shape and 350 feet high; a small-boat landing is on the S side. **Farallon Light** (37°41'57"N., 123°00'07"W.), 358 feet above the water, is shown from a white conical tower on the highest peak of the island. Dwellings are on the lowland on the S side of the island. **Fisherman Bay**, just N of Farallon Light, is somewhat protected by several rocky islets on the W side and affords anchorage in 8 fathoms in the outer part. Boats can be landed on a small sand beach on the largest islet.

(28) **Hurst Shoal**, 0.6 mile SE of Farallon Light, is covered 22 feet and breaks only in heavy weather.

(29) **Middle Farallon**, 2.3 miles NW of the light, is a 20-foot single black rock 50 yards in diameter; several rocks covered 5 to 7 fathoms are within 0.7 mile S and SW of it.

(30) **North Farallon**, 6.5 miles NW of Farallon Light, consists of two clusters of bare precipitous islets and rocks from 91 to 155 feet high, 0.9 mile in extent, and 0.3 mile wide; submerged rocks surround them.

(31) **Fanny Shoal**, 9.8 miles NW of Farallon Light and 14 miles SW of Point Reyes, is 2 miles in extent and covered 2 to 30 fathoms. **Noonday Rock**, covered 3 1/4 fathom, rises abruptly from 20 fathoms and is the shallowest point of the shoal; it is the principal danger in the N approach to San Francisco Bay. A lighted bell buoy is about 0.7 mile W of the rock. Noonday Rock derives its name from the clipper ship that struck it in 1862 and sank within an hour, in 40 fathoms.

(32) **Cordell Bank**, 27 miles NW of Farallon Light and 20 miles W of Point Reyes, is about 6 miles long and 3 miles wide; the bank is covered 20 to 40 fathoms, but depths increase rapidly outside it.

(33) The **Cordell Bank National Marine Sanctuary** has been established to protect and conserve the special, discrete, highly productive marine area of Cordell Bank and its surrounding waters and to ensure the continued availability of the areas ecological, research, educational, aesthetic, historical, and recreational resources. (See **15 CFR 922,** chapter 2, for limits and regulations.)

Blue, fin and humpback whales

(34) All whales are protected under the Marine Mammal Protection Act (MMPA) and, when in Sanctuary waters, under the National Marine Sanctuaries Act (NMSA). Certain large whales, including blue, fin and humpback whales, are also listed as endangered under the Endangered Species Act (ESA). See chapter 3 for more information.

Chart 18647

(35) **Point Reyes**, 18 miles N of Farallon Light, is a bold, dark, rocky headland 612 feet high at the W and higher extremity of a ridge running in an E direction for 3 miles. It is an excellent radar target in thick weather. There is lowland N of the point, so that from N and S, and from seaward in hazy weather, it usually appears as an island. The point is visible for over 25 miles.

(36) **Point Reyes Light** (37°59'44"N., 123°01'23"W.), 265 feet above the water, is shown from a platform on top of a square building on the W extremity of the point. A sound signal is at the light. Two rocks, 275 yards W of the light, are covered about 3 feet and break in a moderate swell.

(37) **Drakes Bay**, named after English explorer Sir Francis Drake, who anchored here in 1579, is NE of the 1-mile-long 200-foot-high, narrow peninsula that forms the easternmost part of Point Reyes. White cliffs commence at the SW angle of the bay and curve round to the NE for about 6 miles, ending at high white sand dunes. This curving shoreline forms Drakes Bay, which affords good anchorage in depths of 4 to 6 fathoms, sandy bottom, in heavy NW weather. Several lagoons back of the N shore empty into the bay through a common channel which is navigable by shallow-draft vessels with local knowledge.

(38) **Chimney Rock** lies close under the outer end of the Drakes Bay peninsula. The area between Chimney Rock and the 5-fathom curve, 0.4 mile E and SE, breaks in moderate weather. A lighted whistle buoy is moored 0.6 mile SE of the rock.

(39) Drakes Bay is used extensively in heavy NW weather and many fishing vessels operate from here during the season. A fish wharf is about midway along the inner side of the peninsula. A visible wreck is about 100 feet E of the fish wharf in about 37°59'41"N., 122°58'19"W. Visible and submerged piles W of the fish wharf are a hazard.

(40) From the sand dunes near the E part of Drakes Bay, cliffs 100 to 200 feet high extend 5 miles SE to **Double Point**, which has two high spurs, 0.4 mile apart, projecting 200 to 300 yards from the general coastline. A small 47-foot-high island is 300 yards off the NW spur, and a 54-foot-high rock is close under the longer and lower SE spur. From Double Point to Bolinas Point, about 3.5 miles SE, the coast is bold with high cliffs behind narrow sand beaches.

(41) **Bolinas Point**, 15.3 miles SE of Point Reyes Light, is 160 feet high and the W extremity of the comparatively level tableland extending E to Bolinas Lagoon. An aerolight and numerous radio towers are 0.6 mile N of the point.

(42) **Duxbury Point**, 16.5 miles SE of Point Reyes Light, is 160 feet high and yellow in color. The point is the S edge of the tableland W of Bolinas Lagoon.

(43) **Duxbury Reef**, extending 1.2 miles SE of Duxbury Point, is long, narrow, and partly bare at low water. A ledge covered 9 to 36 feet extends from the reef to about 1.4 miles S of the point; a lighted whistle buoy is about 2 miles S of the point. Great care must be exercised in passing this area.

Warning

(44) It was reported that in heavy weather strong N currents resulting from prolonged S winds may exist in the area from Duxbury Reef to Golden Gate.

Charts 18645, 18649

(45) **Bolinas Bay**, E of Duxbury Point, is an open bight 3.5 miles wide between Duxbury Point and Rocky Point. The bay affords shelter in NW weather in 24 to 36 feet, sandy bottom. Care must be taken to avoid Duxbury Reef and the dangers extending up to 0.7 mile E of it. **Bolinas Lagoon** is separated from the bay by a narrow strip of sandy beach that is cut by a narrow shifting channel. The lagoon is shoal and entered only by small boats with local knowledge. The entrance has a depth of less than 3 feet.

(46) **Rocky Point** is 100 feet high and shelving. Numerous detached rocks are within 200 yards of the high and precipitous cliffs on the S side of the point.

(47) The 6-mile coast between Rocky Point and Point Bonita is very rugged and broken. The cliffs, which are seaward ends of spurs from Mount Tamalpais, rise to heights of over 500 feet and are cut by deep narrow valleys stretching inland.

(48) **Point Bonita**, on the N side of the entrance to Golden Gate, is a sharp black cliff 100 feet high, increasing to 300 feet on its seaward face, 0.3 mile N. From NW it shows as three heads. **Point Bonita Light** (37°48'56"N., 122°31'46"W.), 124 feet above the water, is shown from a 33-foot white tower on the S head. A sound signal is at the light. A tower and radar antenna operated by the San Francisco Vessel Traffic Service is prominent on the N head about 0.3 mile from the light. In summer the cliffs are white with bird droppings, but the first heavy rain restores them to their natural black color. There are a few detached rocks surrounding the point, but these do not extend over 200 yards offshore.

(49) **Bonita Cove**, E of Point Bonita, is occasionally used as an anchorage by small vessels. The anchorage is close under Point Bonita in about 36 feet.

(50) **Mount Tamalpais**, 7 miles N of Point Bonita, is visible for over 60 miles in clear weather. From S and W it shows three summits, the westernmost with two radar domes is the highest and the easternmost with a lookout tower is the sharpest. The mountain is covered with bushes and scrub trees, giving it a dark appearance which contrasts strongly with the surrounding hills, especially in summer when the hills assume a light reddish color.

(51) **San Francisco Approach Lighted Whistle Buoy SF** (37°45'00"N., 122°41'34"W.) is 9 miles WSW of San Francisco Bay entrance. The buoy is red and white and is equipped with a racon.

(52) **San Francisco Bar**, a semicircular shoal with depths less than 36 feet, is formed by silt deposits carried to the ocean by the Sacramento and San Joaquin River systems. The bar extends from 3 miles S of Point Lobos to within 0.5 mile of Point Bonita off the southern coast of Marin Peninsula; the extreme outer part is about 5 miles WSW of San Francisco Bay entrance. **Potatopatch Shoal**, the N part of the bar on **Fourfathom Bank**, has depths from 24 to 28 feet.

Warning

(53) Very dangerous conditions develop over the bar whenever large swells, generated by storms far out at sea, reach the coast. A natural condition called shoaling causes the large swells to be amplified and increase in height when they move over the shallow water shoals. This piling up of the water over the shoals is worsened during times when the tidal current is flowing out (ebbing) through the Golden Gate. Outbound tidal current is strongest about 4 hours after high water at the Golden Gate Bridge and attains a velocity in excess of 6 knots at times. The incoming large swells are met by outbound tidal current causing very rough and dangerous conditions over the bar. Steep waves to 20 or 25 feet have been reported in the area. Mariners should exercise extreme caution as the bar conditions may change considerably in a relatively short period of time.

(54) **The most dangerous part of the San Francisco Bar is considered to be Fourfathom Bank. Bonita Channel,**

Golden Gate and San Francisco Bay, California
Image courtesy of U.S. Army Corps of Engineers

between the shoal and the Marin coast, can also become very dangerous during large swell conditions. The safest part of the bar is the Main Ship Channel through the center of the bar. But even that area can be extremely dangerous when the tidal current is ebbing.

(55) **Golden Gate**, the passage between the ocean and San Francisco Bay, is 2 miles wide at the W end between Point Bonita and Point Lobos, but the channel is reduced in width to 1.5 miles by Mile Rocks and to less than 0.7 mile by the Golden Gate Bridge pier. Depths in the passage vary from 108 feet to over 300 feet.

(56) **Point Lobos**, the S entrance point to the Golden Gate, is high, rocky, and rounding with black rugged cliffs at its base. A large water tank is on the summit. The **Cliff House** is near the S part of the W face of the point; high and rocky **Seal Rocks** are just offshore.

(57) **Mile Rocks**, 700 yards NW of the sharp projecting point off **Lands End** on the N face of Point Lobos, are two small 20-foot-high black rocks about 100 feet apart. **Mile Rocks Light** (37°47'34"N., 122°30'37"W.), 49 feet above the water, is shown from an orange and white horizontally banded tower on the outer and larger rock; a sound signal is at the light.

(58) Passage between Mile Rocks and Point Lobos should not be attempted because of the covered and visible rocks extending over 300 yards from shore and the rocks covered 6 and 14 feet S of Mile Rocks Light.

(59) The S shore of the Golden Gate extends in a gentle curve NE for 2 miles to Fort Point, forming a shallow bight called **South Bay**. The cliffs rise abruptly from narrow beaches, except near the middle of the bight where a valley terminates in a sand beach 0.3 mile long. Sailing craft are sometimes obliged to anchor here when becalmed, or when meeting an ebb current, to avoid drifting onto Mile Rocks, but the anchorage is uncomfortable and it is difficult to get underway from it.

(60) **Fort Point** projects slightly from the high cliffs and is marked by a square red brick fort with a stone seawall in front. The fort, which is obscured by the S end of the Golden Gate Bridge, and 29 acres of land adjacent to the fort are part of the Fort Point National Historic Site. The fishing wharf at Fort Point is unsafe for mooring because of surge conditions.

(61) The N shore of the Golden Gate is bold and rugged, with reddish cliffs rising abruptly from the water's edge to over 600 feet.

(62) **Point Diablo**, 1.4 miles E of Point Bonita, rises abruptly from a 0.1-mile sharp projection to a height of over 200 feet with deep water on all sides. A light is shown from a white house on the end of the point; a sound signal is at the light.

(63) The mile-long shore between Point Diablo and Lime Point forms a shallow bight with steep cliffs. Near the middle of the bight the cliffs are cut by a narrow valley which ends in a low beach at the shore.

(64) **Lime Point**, 2.5 miles E of Point Bonita, is high and precipitous, and rises abruptly to a height of nearly 500 feet in less than 0.3 mile. A light is shown from a pole at the end of the point.

(65) **Golden Gate Bridge**, crossing the Golden Gate from Fort Point to Lime Point, has a clearance of 225 feet at the center of the 4,028-foot-wide channel span between the 740-foot-high supporting towers; the least clearance of 211 feet at the S pier. Two scaffolds located in the main navigation channel span and one scaffold in the southern span reduce vertical clearance by approx 12 feet and are lighted at night with red lights. The Golden Gate Bridge District will move the scaffolding upon 48 hours advance notice for the passage of vessels. Scaffolding is moved to the piers when not in use. Mariners should contact the Golden Gate Bridge at 415–923–2230. The center of the span is marked by a fixed green light with three fixed white lights in a vertical line above it and by a private sound signal and racon; a private light and sound signals are on the S pier. When approaching Golden Gate Bridge in the eastbound traffic lane in fog, channel Buoy 2 sometimes provides a radar image that indicates the location of the S pier of the bridge. Aero obstruction lights mark the tops of the bridge towers.

Traffic Separation Scheme

(66) **Traffic Separation Scheme San Francisco** has been established off the entrance to San Francisco Bay. (See chart 18645.) The scheme is composed of **directed traffic areas** each with one-way inbound and outbound **traffic lanes** separated by defined **separation zones; a precautionary area;** and a **pilot boat cruising area.** The Scheme is recommended for use by vessels approaching or departing San Francisco Bay, but is not necessarily intended for tugs, tows, or other small vessels which traditionally operate outside of the usual steamer lanes or close inshore.

(67) **The Traffic Separation Scheme has been designed to aid in the prevention of collisions at the approaches to major harbors, but is not intended in any way to supersede or alter the applicable Navigation Rules. Separation zones are intended to separate inbound and outbound traffic lanes and to be free of ship traffic, and should not be used except for crossing purposes. Mariners should use extreme caution when crossing traffic lanes and separation zones.** (See **167.1 through 167.15** and **167.400 through 167.451**, chapter 2, for limits and regulations and Traffic Separation Schemes, chapter 1, for additional information.)

(68) When not calling at San Francisco mariners are urged to sail direct between Point Arguello and Point Arena so as to pass the San Francisco Bay area to the W of the Farallon Islands and clear of the San Francisco Traffic Separation Scheme. In this manner through coastwise traffic will avoid crossing the directed traffic areas and/or precautionary area.

(69) The **precautionary area** off the entrance to San Francisco Bay is inscribed by a circle with a radius of 6 miles centered on San Francisco Approach Lighted Whistle Buoy SF (37°45'00"N., 122°41'34"W.) with the traffic lanes fanning out from its periphery. The W half of the circle has depths of 15 to 30 fathoms, the E half has lesser depths of 4 to 21 fathoms. Extreme caution must be exercised in navigating within the precautionary area inasmuch as both incoming and outgoing vessels use the area in making the transition between San Francisco Main Ship Channel and one of the established directed traffic areas as well as maneuvering to embark and disembark pilots. It is recommended that all vessels in the precautionary area guard VHF-FM channels 13 and 14.

(70) A circular area to be avoided, with a 0.5 mile radius centered on the San Francisco Approach Lighted Whistle Buoy SF, has been established in the precautionary area of the San Francisco Traffic Separation Scheme. This zone has been established for the protection of the lighted whistle buoy.

(71) Mariners are cautioned that San Francisco Approach Lighted Whistle Buoy SF cannot be safely used as a leading mark to be passed close aboard, and are requested to stay outside that area.

(72) The **pilot boat cruising area** is about 1 mile NE of the San Francisco Approach Lighted Whistle Buoy SF. (See pilotage for San Francisco Bay, this chapter.)

Northern Traffic Lanes:

Traffic Lane, Inbound

(73) The N approach to San Francisco is between Point Reyes and the Farallon Islands through the N inbound traffic lane that tapers from 1.7 miles to 1 mile wide in its length of about 15.4 miles. Entering the traffic lane at a point in about 37°55.0'N., 123°05.2'W., a course of **120°** follows the centerline of the traffic lane to the junction with the precautionary area; thence an ESE course for about 7 miles leads to the pilot boat cruising area. The least known depth in the traffic lane is 29 fathoms.

Traffic Lane, Outbound

(74) The N exit from San Francisco Bay by outbound vessels is 6 miles, 312° from the San Francisco Approach Lighted Whistle Buoy SF through the N outbound traffic lane that expands from 1 mile to 1.7 miles wide in its length of about 15.4 miles. A course of **305°** follows the centerline of the traffic lane to its end; thence steer usual courses to destination. Least known depth in the traffic lane is 25 fathoms.

Separation Zone

(75) The N separation zone between the inbound and outbound traffic lanes tapers from 1.7 miles wide at its outer end to 1 mile wide at its junction with the

precautionary area and is centered on a line bearing **302½°** and passing through San Francisco Approach Lighted Whistle Buoy SF and San Francisco Northern Traffic Lane Lighted Bell Buoy N (37°48'00"N., 122°47'55"W.).

Western Traffic Lanes:

Traffic Lane, Inbound

(76) The SW approach to San Francisco Bay is SE of the Southeast Farallon Island through the main inbound traffic lane which tapers from 1.7 miles to 1 mile wide in its length of about 9.4 miles. Entering at a point in about 37°35.8'N., 122°56.9'W., a course of **058½°** follows the centerline of the traffic lane to the junction with the precautionary area; thence a NE course for about 6.7 miles leads to the pilot boat cruising area. The least known depth in the traffic lane is 28 fathoms, except for the charted wreck 6.7 miles **226°** from San Francisco Approach Lighted Whistle Buoy SF which has a minimum depth of at least 9½ fathoms.

Traffic Lane, Outbound

(77) The SW exit from San Francisco Bay by outbound vessels is 6 miles, 244° from the San Francisco Approach Lighted Whistle Buoy SF through the main outbound traffic lane that expands from 1 mile to 1.7 miles wide in its length of about 8.8 miles. A course of **247°** follows the centerline of the traffic lane to its end; thence steer usual courses to destination. The least known depth in the traffic lane is 27 fathoms.

Separation Zone

(78) The main separation zone between the inbound and outbound traffic lanes tapers from 1.7 miles wide at its outer end to 1 mile wide at its junction with the precautionary area and is centered on a line bearing 242½° from San Francisco Main Traffic Lane Lighted Gong Buoy W (37°41'28"N., 122°47'40"W.).

Southern Traffic Lanes:

Traffic Lane, Inbound

(79) The S approach to San Francisco Bay is through the 1-mile wide Southern Traffic Lane (Inbound) that has a length of about 12 miles. Entering at a point in about 37°27.0'N., 122°39.5'W., a **000°** course follows the centerline of the traffic lane to the junction with the precautionary area; thence a NNW course for about 6 miles leads to the pilot boat cruising area. Least known depth in the traffic lane is about 21 fathoms.

Traffic Lane, Outbound

(80) The S exit from San Francisco Bay for outbound vessels is about 6 miles **195°** from the San Francisco Approach Lighted Whistle Buoy SF through the 1-mile wide Southern Traffic Lane (Outbound) that has a length of about 12 miles. A course of **180°** follows the centerline of the traffic lane to its end. Least known depth in the traffic lane is about 25 fathoms.

Separation Zone

(81) The S separation zone between the inbound and outbound traffic lanes is about 2 miles wide and 12 miles long, centered on a line bearing **000°** from San Francisco South Traffic Lane Lighted Bell Buoy S (37°39'00"N., 122°41'42"W.).

(82) An additional **Traffic Separation Scheme** has been established through the Main Ship Channel and Golden Gate into San Francisco Bay. The scheme consists of one-way **traffic lanes** separated by a **separation line** and, after entry into San Francisco Bay, includes a **precautionary area**, a **regulated navigation area**, and **recreation areas**. For purposes of INTERNATIONAL NAVIGATION Rule 10, this scheme has been adopted by IMO seaward of the demarcation line. (See Traffic Separation Schemes, chapter 1, for additional information).

Vessel Traffic Service

(83) **Vessel Traffic Service San Francisco** serves San Francisco Bay, its seaward approaches and its tributaries as far inland as Stockton and Sacramento. Participation is mandatory for certain vessels within navigable waters of the United States. (See **161.1 through 161.23 and 161.50**, chapter 2, for limits and regulations.)

(84) The purpose of the San Francisco Vessel Traffic Service (VTS) is to coordinate the safe, secure, and efficient transit of vessels in San Francisco Bay including its approaches and tributaries in an effort to prevent accidents with the possible associated loss of life, damage to property and the environment. VTS also fully supports Coast Guard and other public service missions through its unique communications and surveillance capabilities. The Vessel Traffic Center (VTC), located on Yerba Buena Island in San Francisco, is staffed 24 hours a day, seven days a week by Coast Guard personnel.

(85) The VTS uses radar, closed-circuit television and VHF-FM radiotelephone to gather information, and uses VHF-FM radiotelephone to disseminate information. Information provided by the VTS is mostly generated from vessel reports; this information can therefore be no more accurate than the reports received from mariners coupled with the ability of VTS equipment to verify those reports. The VTS may not have first hand knowledge of hazardous circumstances existing in the VTS area. Unreported hazards may still confront mariners at any time. This service does not in any way supersede or alter applicable Navigation Rules. The owner, operator, charterer, master, or person directing the movement of the vessel remains at all times responsible for the manner in which the vessel is operated and maneuvered, and is responsible for the safe navigation of the vessel under all circumstances.

(86) The VTS maintains a continuous radiotelephone watch on VHF-FM channels 12, 13, 14, and 16. The

VTS is also equipped to communicate on all VHF-FM radiotelephone channels. The radio call sign is "San Francisco Traffic Service." After communications have been established, the abbreviated call sign "Traffic" may be used. Mariners may also contact VTS by cellular or land-line telephone at 415–556–2760.

(87) The VTS area is divided into two sectors: offshore and inshore. The **Offshore Sector** consists of the ocean waters within a 38 nautical mile radius of Mount Tamalpais (37°55.8'N., 122°34.6'W.) excluding the San Francisco Offshore Precautionary Area. (The San Francisco Offshore Precautionary Area is the area within a six-mile radius of the San Francisco Approach Lighted Whistle Buoy SF.) Channel 12 VHF-FM is the designated working frequency for the Offshore Sector. At minute 15 and minute 45 of each hour, VTS makes broadcasts giving the positions, courses, and speeds of participating vessels in the sector.

(88) The **Inshore Sector** consists of the waters of the San Francisco Offshore Precautionary Area eastward to San Francisco Bay and its tributaries extending inland to the ports of Stockton, Sacramento, and Redwood City. VHF-FM Channel 14 is the designated working frequency for the Inshore Sector.

Reporting points for the San Francisco VTS area are as follows:

Offshore Sector Procedures

Initial Check-in and Sailing Plan Report

(89) The Offshore Sector area is formally defined as the ocean waters within a 38 nautical mile radius of Mount Tamalpais (37°55.8'N., 122°34.6'W.) excluding the San Francisco Offshore Precautionary Area (the area within a six mile radius of the San Francisco Sea Buoy).

(90) This translates roughly to an arc starting at the shoreline near Bodega Head, crossing Cordell Bank, then circling southward to pass about 30 nautical miles W of the San Francisco Sea Buoy, and curving eastward to the shoreline near Pescadero Point (see charts 18640 and 18680).

(91) The eastern boundary of the Offshore Sector is a line from Duxbury Point due S to the boundary of San Francisco Offshore Precautionary Area, then following the boundary of the Precautionary Area past the "N" "W" and "S" buoys, and then due E to Mussel Rock.

(92) When approaching from sea, check in with VTS 15 minutes from the outer boundary on VHF-FM channel 12 and report your Sailing Plan.

Sailing Plan

(93) Give the following information in your Sailing Plan:
(94) Vessel name
(95) Vessel type
(96) Position; latitude and longitude (if unable to provide coordinates then provide your bearing and range from the San Francisco Sea Buoy)
(97) ETA at next reporting point
(98) ETA at the San Francisco Sea Buoy (if inbound) or the outermost reporting point on your route (if outbound or transiting across the Offshore Sector)

Sailing Plan Amplification Reports

(99) When your vessel is at the next reporting point, call VTS. Give the following information:
(100) Vessel name and position of the Offshore reporting point you are passing
(101) Vessel's course and speed
(102) ETA at the San Francisco Sea Buoy if you are inbound
(103) ETA to the outermost reporting point if you are outbound

Other reports

(104) When conducting research, engaged in naval exercises, or conducting other special operations in the Offshore Sector, report your Sailing Plan to VTS and include the nature of your operation. Report any emergency on board your vessel or other vessels to VTS immediately.

(105) When you are engaged in fishing you may report this fact to VTS. However, you are not required to do so unless your vessel fits into one of the categories as described in **161.2**, chapter 2 of this Coast Pilot.

Transiting across the offshore sector

(106) When you are transiting across the Offshore Sector and will not enter the San Francisco Offshore Precautionary Area, call VTS on VHF-FM channel 12 and report your Sailing Plan when you reach the first Offshore Sector reporting point on your route. (See below list of reporting points in the Offshore Sector).

Offshore vessel traffic advisories

(107) VTS broadcasts the positions, courses, speeds, and estimated times of arrivals at reporting points of all VTS users who have reported to VTS in the Offshore Sector. VTS makes these advisories at minute 15 and minute 45 each hour. VTS strongly recommends that vessels in the area of the Offshore Sector listen to these broadcasts.

Offshore Reporting Point Inbound

North

(108) Bodega Head or Cordell Bank;
(109) Point Reyes (or entering the Traffic Separation Scheme);
(110) "N" Buoy or Duxbury Reef Buoy.

West

(111) Approximately 30 nautical miles from the San Francisco Sea Buoy or at longitude 123°20'W.;

(112) Southeast Farallon Island (entering the Traffic Separation Scheme);

(113) "W" Buoy.

South

(114) Pescadero Point or approximately 30 nautical miles from the San Francisco Sea Buoy or at latitude 37°15'N.;

(115) Pillar Point (entering the Traffic Separation Scheme);

(116) "S" Buoy or Mussel Rocks.

Inshore Sector:

(117) • Pilot Area/Point of Entry into VTS area
(118) • San Mateo Bridge
(119) • Redwood Creek Entrance Light 2
(120) • Dumbarton Bridge
(121) • Richmond-San Rafael Bridge
(122) • "E" buoy in San Pablo Bay
(123) • Petaluma Channel Daybeacon 19
(124) • Mare Island Strait Lighted Buoy 1
(125) • Mare Island Causeway Bridge (when inbound/outbound Mare Island Strait)
(126) • Carquinez Bridge
(127) • Military Ocean Terminal Concord (MOTCO)
(128) • New York Point
(129) • Antioch Bridge
(130) • Prisoners Point
(131) • Rio Vista Bridge
(132) • Sacramento Deep Water Channel Lights 51 and 65
(133) • when secured at the destination or when departing the VTS area

(134) For detailed information about the VTS, go to http://www.uscg.mil/d11/vtssf. The site contains links to the Users Manual, Communications Guide, Regulated Navigation Areas, and other information particularly useful to commercial and recreational mariners. Vessels operating within the VTS Area defined as VTS Users are reminded of the requirement to carry a copy of the National VTS Regulations aboard their vessel and are recommended to carry a copy of the San Francisco VTS User's Manual.

Routes

(135) The routes for approaching San Francisco Bay are described in chapter 3 and at the beginning of this chapter under San Francisco Traffic Separation Scheme.

(136) Taking care to avoid the circular 0.5-mile-radius area centered on San Francisco Approach Lighted Whistle Buoy SF, steer a course to enter the charted eastbound San Francisco Bay traffic lane. The recommended route for outbound vessels is via the charted westbound San Francisco Bay traffic lane to the precautionary area of the San Francisco Traffic Separation Scheme.

(137) Vessels with a draft of 45 feet or greater bound for the deepwater anchorages S of the San Francisco-Oakland Bay Bridge or N to San Pablo Bay and Carquinez Strait should use the charted **Deep Water Route** E of the Golden Gate Bridge. Vessels intending to use the Deep Water Route should notify San Francisco Traffic before passing Mile Rocks. Deep draft vessels will neither meet nor overtake in the Deep Water Route. Deep draft vessels bound for Anchorage 9, S of San Francisco-Oakland Bay Bridge, should pass E of Blossom Rock then through the C-D or D-E spans of the bridge.

(138) From the Golden Gate Bridge, vessels with drafts less than 45 feet bound for San Pablo Bay and Carquinez Strait set a course to follow the charted Traffic Separation Scheme to the precautionary area E of Alcatraz Island, thence N through the charted Traffic Separation Scheme to San Pablo Bay and Carquinez Strait.

(139) Mariners are cautioned that the traffic lanes between Angel Island and North Point are frequently crossed by tugs with barges, and self-propelled dredges. These vessels normally transit to and from the dumping ground S of Alcatraz Island.

Channels

(140) The principal approach to San Francisco Bay is through the buoyed **Main Ship Channel** over the bar on bearing **070°** toward Alcatraz Light. The project depth is 55 feet in the 2,000-foot wide channel. (See Notice to Mariners and latest edition of chart for controlling depths.) A wreck covered 62 feet lies near the middle of the channel at 37°47'23"N., 122°33'16"W.

(141) From N, coasters and other vessels use buoyed **Bonita Channel**, between the E end of Potatopatch Shoal and the shore N of Point Bonita. The channel is narrowed to 0.2 mile by several rocky patches including **Sears Rock**, covered 22 feet, 1.2 miles NW of Point Bonita.

Regulated navigation areas

(142) **Security zones** have been established in the entrance to San Francisco Bay (Main Ship Channel) and Golden Gate. (See **165.1183 and 165.1187**, chapter 2, for limits and regulations.)

(143) A **Regulated Navigation Area** has been established in Golden Gate and San Francisco Bay. (See **165.1181**, chapter 2, for limits and regulations.)

Caution

(144) Vessels departing San Francisco Bay through Bonita Channel on the ebb current must use extreme caution when crossing the tide rip off Point Bonita. When the bow passes the rip the stern is thrown to port and, unless promptly met, the vessel will head straight for the rocks off the point. Vessels favoring Potatopatch Shoal too closely have reported a set toward it.

(145) Bonita Channel should not be used by large vessels. Strangers wishing to cross the bar in thick weather

should either wait for clearing or take a pilot. Fog is prevalent in the Golden Gate; radar is a great aid here.

(146) It has been reported, however, that radar targets at the entrance to San Francisco Bay may be difficult to identify at times because of ghost echoes.

Currents

(147) The currents at the entrance to San Francisco Bay are variable, uncertain, and at times attain considerable velocity. Immediately outside the bar there is a slight current to the N and W, known as the **Coast Eddy Current**. The currents at San Francisco Approach Lighted Whistle Buoy SF are described in some detail in the Tidal Current Tables. The currents most affecting navigation in this vicinity are the tidal currents. Across the bar the flood current converges toward the entrance and is felt sooner around Point Lobos and Point Bonita than across the Main Ship Channel. The ebb current spreads from the entrance over the bar, but the main strength is WSW, parallel with the S edge of the Potatopatch Shoal, and through the Main Ship Channel. In the Bonita Channel the ebb current is weak and of short duration; the flood current begins so early that during the last half of the ebb in the Golden Gate the current in Bonita Channel forms an eddy flowing SE around Point Bonita into Bonita Cove.

(148) In the vicinity of Mile Rocks the currents attain considerable velocity within a few minutes after slack on both flood and ebb.

(149) In the Golden Gate the flood current sets straight in, with a slight tendency toward the N shore, with heavy overfalls both at Lime Point and Fort Point when strong. It causes an eddy in the bight between Point Lobos and Fort Point. The ebb current has been observed to have a velocity of more than 6.5 knots between Lime Point and Fort Point, and it sets from inside the bay on the N side toward the latter point. Like the flood current, it causes an eddy in the bight between Fort Point and Point Lobos, and a heavy rip and overfall reaching about 0.25 mile S from Point Bonita. At the Golden Gate Bridge, large current eddies near the foundation piers cause ships to sheer off course. Daily current predictions are given in the Tidal Current Tables.

Weather, San Francisco Bay

(150) The climate of the San Francisco Bay Area is classified as a Mediterranean Climate, which generally means that summers are dry, sunny, and warm and winters are wet and occasionally stormy. However, the Mediterranean Climate classification is somewhat of a simplification and in reality the Bay Area has several climate regimes, sometimes referred to as microclimates. Significant differences in temperature, winds, and fog patterns over relatively short distances are due to variations in air mass between land and sea and to the complex terrain of the coastal mountain ranges. Gaps in the coastal mountain ranges further modify weather conditions on a local scale.

Spring

(151) Storms that periodically affect the region during the winter months often continue with regularity into March, but by April the storm track begins to shift N and storms rolling inland off the pacific become less frequent. The rainy season is typically over by mid-April and the variation in wind direction that occurs with passing storms mostly ends by May. During spring, an area of high pressure over the Pacific gradually strengthens and moves N. Meanwhile, longer days and a more direct sun angle result in increased warming over land, particularly in the interior valleys. Warming near the surface causes air to rise and air pressures near the surface to fall. The resulting difference between high pressure over the ocean and low pressure over land bring about increased W to NW onshore winds during the spring months. In fact, spring is generally the windiest time of the year. However, springtime weather can be highly variable and onshore breezes do not blow as consistently as they do in the summer months. The region can experience several days of generally light winds before the next round of brisk W to NW winds kick up. Wind speeds with the stronger springtime wind events sometimes reach gale force over the coastal waters outside the Golden Gate, and approach Gale Force locally in northern San Francisco Bay. W to NW winds during the spring months decrease farther inland and are generally lighter in the delta and into the Central Valley.

(152) Strong springtime winds over the coastal waters kick up rough and choppy seas with short period swells. The large, long-period swells that are common during the winter months still roll through the coastal waters quite often during the early spring, but taper off significantly by late spring as the storm track across the pacific becomes less active.

(153) Persistent NW winds along the California coast during the spring months enhance the river of surface water flowing S and parallel to the coast known as the California current. In the northern hemisphere, oceanic currents are deflected to the right by the Coriolis force. The deflection caries surface water offshore and causes cold nutrient-rich water from the bottom of the ocean to surge up along the coast. As moist air blowing across the Pacific comes into contact with the cold waters near the coast, condensation occurs and a layer of low clouds and/or fog develops. The low clouds that form in this situation are called stratus clouds. Stratus clouds are gray with generally uniform bases. They usually do not produce precipitation, although drizzle can sometimes occur if the stratus layer is sufficiently thick. When stratus and fog are present along the coast, meteorologists often use the term "marine layer." The marine layer is a moist and cool layer near the surface that is capped by an inversion (a very stable atmospheric condition where warm air lies above cold air). The marine layer ranges in depth from just a few hundred feet to as much as 4000 feet. The depth of the marine layer depends on the height of the inversion above the surface, and the

inversion height is regulated by various atmospheric conditions as well as land-sea interaction. The marine layer can exists without low clouds and fog, but typically clouds and/or fog are present when there is a marine layer. In the spring and summer months, fog and low clouds typically form first over the coastal waters and are then swept inland with onshore breezes through the Golden Gate or other low spots in the coastal ranges. This type of fog is referred to as "advection fog." People often mistakenly refer to stratus clouds as fog or "high fog." By definition, fog is composed of tiny water droplets that are in contact with the surface, essentially a cloud in contact with the ground. The distinction between stratus clouds and fog is important because fog reduces visibility and makes marine navigation more difficult or even dangerous. Stratus clouds, on the other hand, do not by themselves reduce the visibility at the water's surface.

(154) Dense fog is defined as a fog that reduces visibility to one-half mile or less on San Francisco Bay or to one mile or less over the coastal waters. Advection fog is not usually dense over the bays and into the Delta and Central Valley. However, this type of fog can often be dense over the coastal waters when the marine layer is shallow. Under those circumstances the fog is usually confined to the coastal waters and moves only locally into San Francisco Bay, usually around the Golden Gate. Because the marine layer typically is not as shallow in the spring months as in summer, episodes of coastal dense fog are not as common in spring as in summer. Also, the low levels of the atmosphere are more stable in summer than in spring which is another factor contributing to a greater incidence of dense coastal fog in summer compared to the spring months.

(155) Dense fog is more common in San Francisco Bay, and especially in the delta and central valley, during the winter months. That type of fog is called "radiation fog." Radiation fog is covered in more detail in the winter section.

Summer

(156) During the months of June, July and August the Eastern Pacific high is well established offshore while a trough of low pressure is a nearly a constant feature over California's interior. The inland low pressure is often referred to as a "thermal trough" because its formation and strength is primarily driven by strong surface heating that persists throughout the great Central Valley during the dry and sunny summer months. The pressure difference between the eastern pacific high and thermal trough over the interior maintain both northwesterly winds over the coastal waters and onshore winds through the coastal gaps and across the bays. Persistent NW winds over the coastal waters in turn maintain cold upwelling near the coast. Meanwhile subsidence under the strengthening eastern Pacific high produces additional warming aloft and strengthens the low level inversion, effectively placing a "cap" on the marine layer. Because these meteorological conditions are in place nearly every day in the summer, the marine layer is a semi-permanent fixture along the California coast from June through August. Fog and low clouds can remain entrenched along the coast for days, sometimes weeks, at a time.

(157) Marine layer fog and low clouds generally begin to roll in off the ocean and spread into San Francisco Bay through the Golden Gate and gaps in the coastal mountains during the late afternoon or early evening hours, when surface heating by the sun diminishes. The fog and low clouds then typically travel E toward the Berkeley hills where they spread both N and S, eventually covering the bay and adjoining land areas. Fog and stratus are most widespread around the bay from late night until a few hours after sunrise. By mid morning the strong summer sun provides enough heating to begin dissipating the fog and stratus. Clearing typically occurs in the bay by midday, but often remains over the coastal waters through the day.

(158) How far inland the stratus and fog develop overnight depends primarily on the depth of the marine layer, but also on the strength of the onshore flow. If the marine layer is shallow (i.e., less than 1000 feet) low clouds will spread only locally inland around San Francisco Bay, but seldom reach farther inland into the Delta and never into the Central Valley. A shallow marine layer typically results in more fog and reduced visibilities, especially over the coastal waters and locally into San Francisco Bay from the Golden Gate E to Alcatraz or Angel Island.

(159) A deeper marine layer and stronger onshore flow will allow stratus to surge well inland through the delta overnight and sometimes as far inland as Sacramento and Stockton by sunrise. Inland marine surges such as these typically are characterized by low overcast conditions and lack of fog. Daytime clearing is gradual, and low clouds often persist near the Golden Gate and locally around the Bay well into the afternoon.

(160) During the summer months winds throughout the area follow a daily cycle that is most heavily influenced by inland heating during the day and cooling at night. The general tendency during the summer is for winds to blow from high pressure offshore to low pressure over land. This sea to land wind flow is referred to as "onshore flow." The magnitude of the onshore flow is regulated by the daily cycle of differential heating between land and sea. Because ocean temperatures remain nearly constant from day to night, the most important factor in driving the daily wind cycle is inland heating. Daytime heating over land causes surface air pressure to drop during the afternoon hours, and the difference between high pressure over the ocean and low pressure over land increases. Onshore winds begin to increase by early afternoon and reach a peak by late afternoon into the early evening hours. Winds then gradually subside during the evening as surface heating over land decreases. Wind speeds reach their lowest point late at night and remain

relatively light through mid morning before the cycle starts over again. Wind direction is generally W to E (from sea to land), but wind direction exhibits a great deal of variation on a local scale; that variation is due primarily to mountain/valley location and orientation and gaps in the coastal mountain ranges. Of course the most prominent gap in the coastal ranges is the Golden Gate and it is here the onshore winds funnel inland with the least amount of resistance. Once the airflow moves through the Golden Gate, it fans out across the northern San Francisco Bay, deflected to the SE toward the southern part of the bay and the warm Santa Clara Valley, to the NE toward Carquinez Strait and delta and the heat of the Central Valley beyond, and toward the N into the Petaluma and Napa Valleys of the North Bay. The strongest afternoon and evening summer sea breezes occur along the route from the Golden Gate to the Central Valley, specifically past Alcatraz and the southern end of Angel Island, Point Blunt, E to Berkeley and then N past Pinole Point, NE to the Carquinez Strait and finally E into the Delta and Central Valley where the airflow spreads out and diminishes. Afternoon and evening wind speeds frequently reach 20 to 25 knots (meeting small craft advisory criteria) in northern San Francisco Bay from mid afternoon through mid evening during the summer months. In fact, small craft advisory conditions occur nearly every day in summer through this area and wind speeds sometimes reach 30 knots locally. Gales are rare in summer, but can occur during an unusually intense onshore push. Marine air spills inland through other gaps in the coastal ranges including the San Bruno gap just to the WNW of San Francisco Airport (SFO). Some of the strongest sea breezes occur on the W side of the Bay from Hunters Point S through the area around SFO, and small craft conditions are common here as well. Elsewhere in the Bay, summer sea breezes generally do not exceed 20 knots. Wind speeds gradually taper off throughout the Bay after sunset and reach a low point from the late night hours through late morning. On many days winds can be variable at less than 10 knots during this time. But once surface heating increases in the interior around midday, the daily cycle begins again and onshore winds began to increase.

(161) Over the coastal waters outside of the Golden Gate, in the Gulf of the Farallones, summer winds are predominantly from the NW, parallel to the coast and the coastal mountain ranges. Maximum wind speeds here occur from mid afternoon to mid evening, similar to the time of maximum sea breeze winds in San Francisco Bay. Wind speeds generally range from 5 to 15 knots during the night and morning hours, and increases to 10 to 20 knots in the afternoon and early evening hours, but can often reach 25 knots. Strongest NW winds over the coastal waters in summer typically occur to the S of points and capes.

(162) During the summer months seas in the coastal waters are mostly generated from local winds and therefore have a short period and tend to be choppy. Large long period swell from the open ocean contribute much less to the overall wave spectrum than in the late autumn to early spring time frame. Swell direction is predominantly from the NW, but during the late summer swell with an S to SW direction become more frequent. The southerly swells are generated from tropical storms over the pacific. Because these swells originate a long distance from our coast, they typically have long periods, generally 15 seconds or more.

(163) Although summer time wind patterns over the coastal waters and through the Bays and into the Central Valley are consistent in their direction and diurnal patterns, occasionally the typically wind patterns are disrupted. This disruption occurs when high pressure builds inland over the Pacific Northwest and over the Great Basin. At the same time, the trough of low pressure that usually resides over the interior of California drifts to the W and sets up over the coastal waters. Under this scenario, the usual pattern of high pressure over the ocean and low pressure over land is reversed and winds then blow from land to see. This is called offshore flow. Because these winds originate over land, they are typically hot and dry. Also, the air mass undergoes further warming as it descends mountain ranges on its journey from inland areas to the sea. Strongest winds during offshore wind events typically occur in the hills of the northern and eastern San Francisco Bay Area during the late night and morning hours, but offshore winds can sometimes reach 20 knots or more through Carquinez Strait to the Golden Gate. Even during offshore wind events, a weak late afternoon and early evening sea breeze often develops. Often too, the start of an offshore wind event is characterized by strong and gusty northerly winds down the Sacramento Valley and across the Delta. Winds over the coastal waters during offshore wind events are usually light, except locally moderate just outside the Golden Gate.

(164) Offshore flow events usually last no more than two or three days before the inland high pressure breaks down and onshore flow returns. Often, offshore events are followed by a phenomenon known as a "southerly surge." A southerly surge occurs when surface air pressure over the coastal waters on the lee side of the coastal ranges drop. When the pressure along the northern California coast drops lower than along the southern California coast, a southerly wind develops. Usually, the onset of southerly winds is also accompanied by a fog bank that surges up along the coast in a very shallow marine layer. During southerly surge events, weather conditions over the coastal waters can change rapidly from light winds with clear skies, to 15 to 20 knots of southerly winds accompanied by thick fog reducing visibilities to less than a half mile. Once the leading edge of the southerly surge reaches the Golden Gate, the colder fog-ladden airmass surges inland across northern San Francisco Bay towards Carquinez Strait. Here too, weather conditions can change rapidly from light winds to SW winds reaching 25 knots or greater. After

several hours, the shallow marine layer deepens and onshore breezes spread out across a more widespread area, and locally strong winds gradually subside.

Autumn

(165) Weather in and around San Francisco Bay is most tranquil during the months of September, October and November. The Pacific high gradually weakens while heating over the interior subsides and weakens the inland thermal trough. Pressure gradients relax and wind speeds ease over the ocean and bays. The trend toward lighter winds starts in late summer (August) and continues through autumn. Gales are almost nonexistent from August through October. Offshore wind events are most common during the autumn months. Because of the weakened sea breezes, and more frequent offshore wind events, the marine layer becomes less prominent during the autumn and low clouds and fog are less prevalent than in summer. Wave heights are also at a minimum during the autumn months. Storms over the northern Pacific become stronger and more common by late October and early November. This is when long period swells from the W and NW begin to increase along the northern and central California coast.

Winter

(166) The storm track across the Pacific becomes increasingly active in November and also migrates to the S. By the second half of the month weather systems begin to roll through the San Francisco Bay Area. Most rainfall in the Bay Area falls between mid-November and lasts until early April, with the stormiest months being December, January, and February. Late November and much of March can also have active stormy times. Some storms during the winter months can produce powerful winds and seas, conditions that can be very hazardous to the mariner.

(167) As frontal systems approach the coast, winds from the S and SE increase in magnitude. Typically, strongest winds in the winter occur in the hours prior to a cold frontal passage. Depending on the strength of the storm, southerly winds ahead of the cold front can easily reach 20 knots across the region, often 25 knots and sometimes gale force. Although rare, storm force winds of 48 knots or greater can occur with the strongest of these winter storms. A few notable cases of storm force winds over San Francisco Bay are December 12, 1995 and January 4, 2008. Strong south winds occur on a large scale and are not as dependent on topography and microclimates as the summer sea breeze is. Gale force winds can occur anywhere from the coastal waters E through the delta and into the Central Valley.

(168) After frontal passage winds veer to the SW and eventually W and NW. Generally wind speeds decrease significantly after frontal passage, but can remain quite strong and gusty for several hours after frontal passage. On occasion, winds will veer from SE to SW after frontal passage, only to swing back to the S or SE a few hours later before gradually veering back to the W and NW.

(169) Winter is the season with the most significant seas, both in terms of locally driven wind waves and open ocean swells that are built by long fetches of strong winds over the eastern Pacific. Seas can be confused ahead of a front with wind waves moving from S to N on top of long period swells coming in from the W or NW. Seas can often build enough to produce breakers across the San Francisco bar, several miles offshore of the Golden Gate. These breaking waves in the open ocean present a significant danger to mariners, especially those unfamiliar with the area. Breakers across the bar are most common with a W long period swell, during maximum ebb current through the Golden Gate.

(170) Although the strongest winds occur during the winter months, there are often long periods of tranquil weather in the winter when the storm track can shift to the N for weeks at a time. During this time, high pressure dominates the area and sets up conditions where the low levels are very stable and an inversion develops over the inland valleys. Widespread fog will develop if the surface is sufficiently moist during these times (after soaking rains), particularly in the Central Valley. This type of radiation fog can be particularly dense and persistent and is often referred to as "tule fog." Visibilities often fall to near zero in the southern Sacramento Valley, northern San Joaquin Valley, and through the Delta, making marine navigation in these areas dangerous. Lowest visibilities occur late at night through the mid morning hours. Visibilities improve by late morning and often the fog layer lifts into a low overcast during the afternoon. Sometimes if there is a light offshore flow during a tule fog event, dense fog can develop W into northern San Francisco Bay and even spread S into the S part of the bay. It is during these times that San Francisco Bay realizes its worst visibility problems.

(171) Offshore winds during the winter months are generally light. However, locally strong and gusty easterly winds can occur through Carquinez Strait and also over the coastal waters below coastal canyons. On some clear winter mornings when winds are light from the E across most of the region, locally strong winds have been reported along the San Mateo and Marin county coasts.

(172) Winter can be highly variable in terms of weather. Long periods of dry weather with light winds can be followed by weeks of stormy weather with only short breaks in between individual storms. Years of studies have concluded that sea surface temperature anomalies in the equatorial Pacific can have an impact on the overall amount of precipitation and storminess across California during the winter months. When El Nino conditions exist, sea surface temperatures in the eastern tropical Pacific are above normal. Strong or moderately strong El Nino winters are characterized by higher than normal precipitation across central and southern California. However, this does not mean that individual

storms with the heaviest rain and strongest winds occur during El Nino winters. In fact, two of the most powerful winter storms to pummel the region in the past 20 years occurred during non El Nino winters. The upshot is that mariners need to be prepared for the possibility of dangerous storms in any winter, and not assume that navigating the open ocean and bays will be easier during non El Nino winters.

Pilotage, San Francisco

(173) Pilotage in and out of San Francisco is compulsory for all vessels of foreign registry and U.S. vessels under enrollment not having a federal licensed pilot on board. The San Francisco Bar Pilots provide pilotage to ports in San Francisco Bay and to ports on all tributaries to the bay, including Stockton and Sacramento.

(174) The San Francisco Bar Pilots keep one of two vessels on station at all times, the SAN FRANCISCO or the CALIFORNIA. The pilot boats are 85 feet long with a blue waterline band, international orange hull, and white superstructure. The top of the cabin houses, the mast, and after deck covers are orange. The word "PILOT" is shown on the fore part as well as the port and starboard sides of the midship house. The boat displays the standard day and night signals. The pilot vessel cruises on station 24 hours a day near the San Francisco Approach Lighted Whistle Buoy SF, or, in foul weather, seaward of it. Prior arrangements with the bar pilots' office can be made by telephone 415–393–0457, telex (SF Pilot 415–371–5595), fax messages 415–982–4721, or cable (BARPILOTS, San Francisco). If prior arrangements have not been made with the pilots' office on Pier 9, masters may give these signals upon approaching the San Francisco Approach Whistle Buoy SF:

(175) **Clear visibility:** by day, hoist code flag "G"; by night, four long flashes on the signal lamp. **Limited visibility:** four long blasts and lay to. The pilot boat monitors VHF-FM channels 10, 13, and 16. The pilot boats' radio calls are SAN FRANCISCO WYZ-8288 and CALIFORNIA WYK-4689; the pilot office call is KMG-389; cable address: BARPILOTS, San Francisco. The office monitors VHF-FM channel 10. Masters or agents are requested to advise the pilots whenever there is a change in the draft, arrival or sailing time, or maneuvering or equipment limitations.

(176) The pilots board directly from the pilot boat. Pilot ladders should be rigged clear of all discharges and spouts about 10 feet from the waterline and amidship of the vessel at all times. The ladder must comply with International Maritime Organization (IMO) and IMPA recommendations and be made in one length and not consist of two lengths shackled or lashed together, and should be equipped with spreaders about ten feet apart to comply with SOLAS Regulation 17, Chapter 5, (not in this text). A light must be ready to illuminate the ladder if necessary. Contact pilot boat about 30 minutes prior to arrival to determine on what side the ladder should be rigged. No lines should be attached to the lower end of the ladder. A manrope, heaving line, and a ring buoy with a self-igniting light must be provided; vessel speed, 6 to 8 knots.

(177) Pilot boarding is usually conducted in all but the most severe conditions. Extensive fog conditions are often experienced. Strong currents, accelerated by river freshets in the winter and spring months, often exist and greatly alter the predicted current calculations.

(178) The preferred anchorage for deep-draft vessels in the vicinity of the bar pilots pickup station (San Francisco Approach Lighted Whistle Buoy SF) is an area with a 1 mile radius centered in 37°49'N., 122°42'W. Anchoring offshore is strictly forbidden. Exceptions may be made for vessel engine casualties or severe weather preventing transit into port. Any vessel anchoring outside of established anchorages is required to notify the VTS immediately.

(179) **Inbound tank vessels under escort embark pilots about 1 mile W of San Francisco Approach Lighted Whistle Buoy SF.**

Coast Guard

(180) Golden Gate Coast Guard Station is about 0.4 mile NNE of the bridge at the entrance to Horseshoe Bay. Station Golden Gate is participating in the Coastal Weather Display Program. A 35-foot flag pole is located near the S end of the Coast Guard Station, visible to mariners exiting San Francisco Bay. Coastal warning flags will be flown from one hour before sunrise to one hour after sunset. (See illustration; Chapter 1.)

(181) Weather flags are flown only at select Coast Guard stations to supplement other weather notification sources. Light signals corresponding to these flags are not displayed at night. In all cases mariners should rely upon National Weather Service broadcasts as their primary source of government provided weather information.

State regulations

(182) **Tank Vessel Escort Regulations** have been established by the State of California for San Francisco, San Pablo, and Suisun Bays. Tank vessel masters, owners, and operators are expected to be familiar and in compliance with the regulations. Failure to be in compliance may result in unsafe transit delays, and fines. The regulations can be found at http://www.dfg.ca.gov, or may be obtained by calling the California Office of Spill Prevention and Response 24-hour Communications Center at 916–445–0045. Tank vessel masters should contact their agent or vessel manager/owner for additional information. The San Francisco Marine Exchange may also be able to provide mariners with additional information and can be contacted at 915–441–6600.

Chart 18650

(183) **San Francisco**, one of America's great cities, occupies the N portion of the peninsula forming the S entrance to the bay. The 3-mile N shore of San Francisco from the Golden Gate Bridge to the main waterfront includes the **Presidio of San Francisco**; several yacht harbors; Government buildings and piers on Black Point; Aquatic Park; and Fisherman's Wharf. Shoals with depths less than 10 feet extend up to 0.2 mile from the shore.

(184) The charted **recreation area** extending along this shore is intended primarily for use by recreation vessels. It should not be utilized by vessels 300 tons or more for through passage or for any other purpose, except in case of emergency or special circumstances.

(185) **Alcatraz Island**, 2.5 miles E of the Golden Gate Bridge, is one of the leading marks in entering San Francisco Bay. The small island is 148 feet high and has many buildings on it. Near the NW end of the island is a water tower, which is reported to be usually the only landmark visible when that area is in fog. **Alcatraz Light** (37°49'34"N., 122°25'20"W.), 214 feet above the water, is shown from a gray, octagonal pyramidal tower on the SE part of the island. A sound signal is on the extreme NW end of the island.

(186) A rock awash, marked on its W side by a bell buoy, is 125 yards W of the NW end of Alcatraz Island. The rocks and tide pools, which extend about 100 feet from the S tip of the island, are reported to cover at high water.

(187) Mariners are advised that surveys indicate shoaling tends to build to the NW of the disposal area S of Alcatraz Island and caution should be used in the area. A shoal oriented SW to NE with a least depth of 34 feet extends off the E shore of the island.

(188) Alcatraz Island, a part of the Golden Gate National Recreation Area, is administered by the Department of Interior's National Park Service.

(189) Federal regulations require that prior permission to land at Alcatraz, or to berth vessels at Fort Mason, Black Point, and Aquatic Park must be obtained from the General Superintendent, Golden Gate National Recreation Area, Fort Mason, San Francisco, CA 94123.

(190) A passenger ferry, which operates frequently, uses a dock on the SE side of the island. In 1979, 28 feet was reported off the dock.

(191) **Yerba Buena Island**, 345 feet high and 2.5 miles SE of Alcatraz Island, is of small extent, irregular in shape, and covered with a scrubby growth of trees. On its summit is a former lookout tower and the Coast Guard operated San Francisco Vessel Traffic Service Operation Center and radar antenna site. **San Francisco Coast Guard Station** is on the E side of the island.

(192) **Treasure Island** is a low filled area N of and connected by a causeway to Yerba Buena Island. Built originally for the San Francisco International Exposition of 1939-40, Treasure Island now belongs to the city of San Francisco. A light is on the N end of the island and a shoal, covered 15 feet, is off the N end of the island.

(193) When the prevailing W winds are blowing, deep-draft vessels proceeding to the berthing area on the E side of the island may have extreme difficulty making the 90° turn from the narrow channel between the 30-foot curves SE of Yerba Buena Island.

(194) **Naval restricted areas**, are off the N end of Treasure Island and between this island and Yerba Buena Island. (See **334.1070 and 334.1080**, chapter 2, for limits and regulations.) A **restricted area** surrounds the Coast Guard Station off the E side of Yerba Buena Island. (See **334.1065**, chapter 2, for limits and regulations.)

(195) The **San Francisco-Oakland Bay Bridge**, one of the longest bridges in the world, crosses the bay from **Rincon Point** in San Francisco to Yerba Buena Island, thence to Oakland. Racons mark the main bridge spans. The recommended passage for southbound traffic is under the NE half of span A-B (midspan clearance 204 feet). Northbound traffic should use the SW half of span D-E (midspan clearance 204 feet). The midspan clearance of spans B-C and C-D are each 220 feet. In 2010, a fixed highway bridge between Yerba Buena Island and Oakland was under construction just N of the existing span, with a design clearance of 112 feet. The Coast Guard requests that mariners use the temporary main channel designated between piers I and J on the existing bridge, and piers E-3 and E-4 on the bridge under construction. These clearances are approximate; they may be reduced by several feet due to heavy traffic on the bridge and prolonged periods of extremely high temperature, and as much as 10 feet under extreme conditions. Maintenance scaffolding located in each span reduces vertical clearance by approximately 5 feet and is lighted at night with red lights. Caltrans will move the scaffolding if requested for the passage of vessels. Mariners should contact Caltrans Toll Sergeant at 510–286–1148.

(196) The **Port of San Francisco** is the oldest on the Pacific coast. Though primarily a general cargo port, grain, bulk liquids, containers, newsprint, automobiles, bananas, copra, cotton, and other commodities are handled here. San Francisco is a popular port of call for passenger vessels on regular scheduled and special cruises.

Prominent features

(197) The skyline of the city of San Francisco is unmistakable, with several dominant landmarks: the 980-foot television tower supporting three antennas, the pyramid-shaped Transamerica Building, the Coit Tower on Telegraph Hill 3.4 miles E of the bay entrance, and the Bay Bridges with their freeway elevated approaches. Inside the bay, the Bank of America Building, the Bank of America Clock Tower, the clock tower at the S end of the San Francisco-Oakland Bay Bridge, the old Ferry Building with its 240-foot clock tower on the waterfront S of

Pier 1, and the U.S. Coast Guard radar tower on Yerba Buena Island are prominent.

(198) The **Ferry Building**, terminal of many ferry boats, also houses the **San Francisco Port Authority** offices, the offices of the Marine Exchange, Inc., and the many offices and exhibits of the World Trade Center.

Channels

(199) Depths of 45 feet or more are available from the Golden Gate Bridge to most of the anchorages; depths ranging from 29 to 40 feet can be taken to most of the San Francisco piers.

Anchorages

(200) General, naval, and explosives anchorages are in San Francisco Bay. (See **110.1 and 110.224**, chapter 2, for limits and regulations.)

Warning

(201) Two submarine pipeline areas cross San Francisco Bay within General Anchorage 9; one crosses between Metropolitan Oakland International Airport and **Brisbane**, and the other about 1.5 miles to the S. Mariners are cautioned not to anchor in these areas. (See chart 18651.)

Dangers

(202) **Anita Rock**, 1.1 miles E of Fort Point and 300 yards from shore, is covered 3 feet and marked by a light.

(203) There are several rocky patches with depths of 33 to 35 feet W and NW of Alcatraz Island that must be avoided by deep-draft vessels. The northwesternmost of these shoals is **Harding Rock**, marked by a lighted buoy equipped with a racon.

(204) **Blossom Rock**, covered 40 feet and marked on the W side by a lighted bell buoy, is about 1 mile SE of Alcatraz Island. Another rock, covered 43 feet, is 0.3 mile S of Blossom Rock.

(205) The Trans-Bay Tube of the Bay Area Rapid Transit District crosses San Francisco Bay from the vicinity of the Ferry Tower to Oakland. Mariners are **prohibited** from dropping or dragging anchors when in the vicinity of the tunnel crossing.

(206) Heavy tide rips occur in the vicinity of Alcatraz Island.

Regulated navigation areas

(207) **Regulated navigation areas** have been established in the waters of San Francisco Bay. (See **165.1181** and **165.1185**, chapter 2, for limits and regulations.)

Currents

(208) Inside the Golden Gate the flood current sets into all parts of the bay and causes swirls from the Golden Gate as far E as Alcatraz and Angel Islands and through Raccoon Strait, N of Angel Island. The ebb current, inside the Golden Gate, is felt first along the S shore. In the Golden Gate, the average duration of the ebb stream is somewhat greater than that of the flood. The Sacramento and San Joaquin Rivers have weak flood currents during periods of freshets.

(209) The San Francisco-Oakland Bridge has large current eddies near the foundation piers that cause ships to sheer off course.

(210) Strong currents due to heavy spring runoffs have been reported along the San Francisco waterfront between pier 39 (37°48'36"N., 122°24'38"W.) and pier 94 (37°44'34"N., 122°22'13"W.)

Caution

(211) Oakland's Seventh Street Marine Terminal, about 1 mile E of Yerba Buena Island, forms a current lee on both the flood and the ebb current. Vessels making for Middle Harbor and Oakland Inner Harbor on a flood current will encounter a lee on the S side of the terminal; when the bow enters the slack water, the vessel will tend to sheer to the left. Similarly, vessels bound for the Outer Harbor on an ebb current will encounter slack water on the N side of the terminal, with a tendency to sheer to the right. This condition may be dangerous to deep-draft, loaded vessels, and should be anticipated.

(212) See the Tidal Current Tables for daily predictions for San Francisco Bay area.

Weather, San Francisco

(213) San Francisco enjoys a marine-type climate characterized by mild and moderately wet winters and by dry, cool summers. Winter rains (December through March) account for about three-fourths of the average annual rainfall of just over 19 inches (483 mm), and measurable precipitation occurs on an average of 13 days per month during this period. Snowfall occurs, but is infrequent. The greatest amount is 1.5 inches (38 mm) recorded in January 1962. Flurries have occurred in each month, December through March. There are frequent dry periods lasting well over a week. Severe winter storms with gale winds and heavy rains occur only occasionally. December is the month most likely to experience gales followed by January. Thunderstorms average five a year and may occur in any month, but are usually very mild.

(214) The daily and annual range in temperature is small ranging from an average annual maximum of 65.2°F (18.4°C) and an average annual minimum of 48.7°F (9.3°C). A few frosty mornings occur during the winter, but the temperature seldom drops below freezing. The coldest temperature on record at the International Airport is 24°F recorded in December 1972. Each month, November through March, has recorded temperatures below freezing (0°C). Winter temperatures generally rise to the high fifties (13.9° to 15°C) in the early afternoon.

(215) The summer weather is dominated by a cool sea breeze resulting in an average summer wind speed of nearly 13 knots. Winds are light in the early morning,

					Facilities in the Port of San Francisco		
Name	Location	Berthing Space (feet)	Depths* (feet)	Deck Height (feet)	Mechanical Handling Facilities and Storage	Purpose	Owned/ Operated by:
Pier No. 45 (Sheds B and D)	37°48'36"N., 122°25'06"W.	1,200	14-25	12	• Covered storage (88,150 square feet) • Six mast-and-boom derricks	• Receipt of seafood • Mooring fishing vessels	Port of San Francisco
Pier No. 35	37°48'35"N., 122°24'23"W.	2,055	35	12	Passenger terminal (32,000 square feet)	• Mooring cruise ships • Boarding passengers	Port of San Francisco/ Metropolitan Stevedore Company
Pier No. 33	37°48'32"N., 122°24'15"W.	1,624	15	12	Covered storage (66,900 square feet)	• Receipt of seafood • Mooring fishing vessels and excursion boats	Port of San Francisco
Pier Nos. 17 and 15	37°48'09"N., 122°23'48"W.	2,085	17-35	12	• Covered storage (173,700 square feet) • Open storage (33,000 square feet)	Mooring floating equipment	Port of San Francisco/ Baydelta Maritime
Pier No. 9	37°48'05"N., 122°23'44"W.	1,754	15	12	Covered storage (61,200 square feet)	Mooring floating equipment and pilot boats	Port of San Francisco/ Blue and Gold Fleet and San Francisco Bar Pilots
Pier No. 50 Mission Rock Terminal	37°46'25"N., 122°22'54"W.	4,155	35-45	12	Covered storage (231,700 square feet)	Mooring vessels and equipment	Port of San Francisco/ Westar Marine Services and Clean Bay Cooperative
Pier No. 54	37°46'11"N., 122°23'01"W.	1550	18-20	12	Covered storage (15,000 square feet)	• Mooring vessels • Receipt of seafood	Port of San Francisco/ Crowley Maritime Corperation
Pier No. 70	37°45'43"N., 122°22'47"W.	2,480	35	12	Tank storage (404,000 barrels)	Mooring vessels	Port of San Francisco
North Container Terminal (Pier No. 80)	37°45'02"N., 122°22'33"W.	5,091	38	13	• Covered storage (393,000 square feet) • Four traveling container cranes (up to 40 long tons)	• Receipt and shipment of conventional, containerized, and roll-on/roll-off general cargo	Port of San Francisco/ Marine Terminals Corp.
Pier No. 92	37°44'50"N., 122°22'48"W.	868	35	12	• Tank storage (2.9 million gallons) • Open storage (20,000 tons of sand) • Belt conveyor	• Shipment of tallow • Receipt of sand	Port of San Francisco/ Darling International, Inc. and Mission Valley Rock
Pier Nos. 94 and 96	37°44'34"N., 122°22'13"W.	2,456	40	14	• Open storage (76 acres) • Four traveling container cranes (up to 40 long tons)	Mooring vessels	Port of San Francisco

* The depths given above are reported. For information on the latest depths contact the port authorities or the private operators.

but normally reach 17 to 22 knots in the afternoon, depending on location. Where topography and man-made structures funnel the winds, higher gusts may occur in those areas.

(216) A sea fog, arriving over the station during the late evening or night as a low stratified cloud, is another persistent feature of the summer weather. This "high" fog, occasionally producing drizzle or mist, usually disappears during the late forenoon. Despite the morning overcast, summer days are remarkably sunny. On the average a total of only 15 days during the 4 months from June through September are classified as cloudy.

(217) Daytime temperatures are held down both by the morning low overcast and the afternoon strengthening sea breeze, resulting in daily maximum readings averaging in the lower- to middle seventies (21.7° to 23.9°C) from May through August. However, during these months occasional "hot" spells lasting a few days are experienced without the usual "high" fog and sea breeze. September, when the sea breeze becomes less pronounced, is the warmest month with an average maximum of 73°F (22.8°C). Minimum temperatures during the summer are in the lower- to middle fifties (10.6° to 12.8°C). The all-time high temperature recorded at the International Airport is 106°F (41.1°C) recorded in June 1961.

(218) A strong temperature inversion with its base usually at a height of 1,500 feet (458 m) persists throughout the summer. Inversions close to the ground are infrequent in summer, but rather common in fall and winter. As a consequence of these factors and the continued population and economic growth of the area, atmospheric pollution has become a problem of increasing importance.

(219) The National Weather Service maintains offices in Oakland, Redwood City, and at San Francisco International Airport; barometers may be compared there or by telephone. (See Appendix A for addresses.)

(220) (See Appendix B for **San Francisco climatological table**.)

Towage

(221) Tugboats are available in sufficient quantity for the traffic in the greater harbor.

Quarantine, customs, immigration, and agricultural quarantine

(222) (See chapter 3, Vessel Arrival Inspections, and Appendix A for addresses.)

(223) San Francisco–Oakland is a **customs port of entry**.

(224) **Quarantine** is enforced in accordance with regulations of the U.S. Public Health Service. (See Public Health Service, chapter 1.)

Coast Guard

(225) **Sector Office San Francisco** is located on Yerba Buena Island. (See Appendix A for addresses.) **San Francisco Coast Guard Air Station** is at San Francisco International Airport. A Coast Guard base and station are on the E side of Yerba Buena Island.

(226) The **Marine Exchange** of the San Francisco Bay region reports and records all Golden Gate ship arrivals and departures and conducts communications to serve the bay area commercial traffic. The station can be called 24 hours a day for relay of messages and other marine related services on VHF-FM channels 10 and 18. The station also monitors channels 13 and 16. The ship spotting station is located in Building B, Fort Mason, about 2.5 miles E of the Golden Gate Bridge.

Harbor regulations

(227) The Port of San Francisco is under control of the city of San Francisco, and its management is vested in the San Francisco Port Commission, in direct charge of the port director of that body. The office of the **Chief Wharfinger** is in the Ferry Building.

(228) The harbor regulations are prescribed by the San Francisco Port Authority and enforced by the Chief Wharfinger.

(229) In addition to the San Francisco Port Authority regulations, the Coast Guard Captain of the Port has issued the following supplemental regulations for vessels carrying explosives and certain hazardous bulk cargoes. Vessels entering or leaving San Francisco Bay laden with explosives (Class A or Military) having a net explosive weight in excess of 100 short tons for ships and in excess of 5 short tons for barges, or carrying certain dangerous cargo as listed in **33 CFR 160.204**, may be escorted by a Coast Guard patrol craft while underway within the bay. These escorts are at the discretion of the Captain of the Port (COTP). Each vessel shall coordinate all movements with the Captain of the Port and ensure:

(230) (a) Speed of transit shall not exceed 12 knots.

(231) (b) No Vessel movement will occur unless visibility is a minimum of 1,000 yards, in/out or within the San Francisco Bay area.

(232) (c) A 96 hour advance notice of arrival is required.

(233) (d) Vessels shall participate in the Vessel Traffic Service (VTS) and adhere to the traffic separation scheme, except as permitted by VTS or COTP.

Wharves

(234) The general cargo and specialized terminals of the Port of San Francisco are on the bay and on Islais Creek. All of the piers listed are owned by the San Francisco Port Authority and leased to private concerns. Only the major piers are listed in the table. The alongside depths given for each facility are reported depths. (For information on the latest depths, contact the Port of San Francisco.) Cargo at the port is handled mostly by ship's tackle, but hoisting and heavy lift equipment is available in the port. Most piers have electrical shore power and water connections.

(235) The Port of San Francisco is served by a Class I railroad. The port offers wharf side intermodal transfer of containers between ship and rail at both the San Francisco Container Terminals North (Pier 50) and South (Piers 94 and 96), and has a dedicated Intermodal Container Transfer Facility located adjacent to Container Terminal South with direct access to both terminals. Most of the port's inbound and outbound cargo moves to and from the piers by truck. The Embarcadero, a four-lane thoroughfare, provides access to most of the piers. For a complete description of the port facilities refer to Port Series No. 30, published and sold by the U.S. Army Corps of Engineers. (See Appendix A for address.)

(236) **China Basin**, 1.1 miles S of the Ferry Building, is a canal extending about 0.6 mile SW from San Francisco Bay. The 3rd and 4th Street bascule bridges across the canal have a least clearance of 1 foot. (See **117.1 through 117.59 and 117.149**, chapter 2, for drawbridge regulations.) The bridgetender monitors VHF-FM channel 9 and works on channels 13, 17, and 65A; call sign WXY–959, San Francisco Drawbridges. China Basin is a no anchorage zone.

(237) **Islais Creek Channel** is entered 2.9 miles S of the Ferry Building. A dredged approach area with a project depth of 35 feet is off the entrance. Two bascule bridges, the Illinois Street Bridge and the 3rd Street Bridge, cross the creek about 0.6 mile above the mouth; both have clearances of 4 feet. (See **117.59** and **117.163**, chapter 2, for drawbridge regulations.) The bridgetender at the 3rd Street Bridge monitors VHF-FM channel 16 and uses channel 9 for working; call sign WXY-977, San Francisco Drawbridges.

Supplies

(238) Fuel oils, gasoline, and all other marine supplies and services may be had in any desired quantity. Fuel oil is usually delivered by barge. Water can be obtained on the piers or by barge.

Repairs

(239) San Francisco, Oakland, Richmond, and Alameda have facilities for making repairs to vessels and machinery of all kinds and sizes. The largest commercial floating drydock in San Francisco has a length of 900 feet, width of 148 feet, and a lifting capacity of 65,000 tons. There are several small drydocks on the San Francisco

side, and several marine railways and floating docks on the Oakland side.

Ferries

(240) High-speed commuter ferries frequently operate in central/south San Francisco Bay and San Pablo Bay. Concentrations of these ferries are highest around the San Francisco Ferry Building (37°47'45"N., 122°23'35"W.) where most central bay routes terminate. Mariners are cautioned when transiting these waters that ferries may maneuver quickly when approaching and departing the dock. Departing ferries from the Ferry Building often back away from the dock. Charted ferry routes can be seen on applicable charts of the area; however, mariners are cautioned that these ferries may deviate from their routes due to inclement weather, traffic conditions, navigational hazards, or other emergency conditions.

(241) In San Francisco Bay charted ferry routes run N and S in North Channel (E of Angel Island) and in the Precautionary Area just E of Alcatraz Island. They generally run E and W in the waters between Alcatraz Island and Angel Island. The routes cross each other in the Precautionary Area (37°49'30"N., 122°24'10"W.) and about 1.2 miles S of the Richmond-San Rafael Bridge. In these areas all vessels should maintain a close watch for ferries. In San Pablo Bay, ferry routes run in both directions just S of Pinole Shoal Channel between the Richmond-San Rafael Bridge and Mare Island; one route runs E of East Brothers Island. Many ferries also operate between San Francisco's north shore, Alcatraz and Sausalito/Tiburon. These ferries do not run along charted ferry routes. They too may back away when departing San Francisco docks and may maneuver rapidly when approaching San Francisco.

(242) The **San Francisco Harbor Safety Committee**, in conjunction with the Coast Guard, has established a **Ferry Traffic Routing Protocol** for: the area surrounding the Ferry Building terminal along the waterfront of San Francisco, the waters of central San Francisco Bay, and the waters of San Pablo Bay. The protocol is intended to increase safety in the area by reducing traffic conflicts and, while not compulsory, the guidelines set forth in the protocol are strongly recommended. The Harbor Safety Committee also recommends that recreational and fishing vessels keep a close lookout when near ferry routes, and avoid ferry routes whenever possible. For additional information, see the San Francisco Vessel Traffic Service website http://www.uscg.mil/d11/vtssf and San Francisco Marine Exchange website http://www.sfmx.org.

Communications

(243) San Francisco is the terminus of several transpacific steamship lines and the port of call for numerous lines of foreign, coastal, and intercoastal vessels. It is served directly by a major highway and is connected by the Bay Bridge to several others. The city is served by three transcontinental railroads; connections to two of the railroads are by barge, while one has tracks extending S and E around the S bay. San Francisco International Airport is on the W shore of the bay about 5 miles S of the city; it is served by many airlines.

Small-craft facilities

(244) San Francisco Municipal Yacht Harbor, 1.8 miles E of the Golden Gate Bridge with a W and E basin about 0.3 mile apart, has depths of 8 to 12 feet to the berths. A light near the end of a point marks the N side of the entrance to W basin; a prominent stone tower is 0.2 mile W of the light. The E basin is protected on the N by a breakwater extending E from the W shore, and on the E by a pier of **Fort Mason**. The seaward end of the breakwater is marked by a light. E basin is entered between the breakwater light and the pier. The harbor accommodates about 700 boats in the W and E basins. Guest berths are available; transients should report to the harbormaster's office on the S side of the W basin for berth assignment.

(245) **Aquatic Park**, 2.6 miles E of the Golden Gate Bridge, is a recreation area protected on the W by a curved pier extending out from Black Point and on the E by a pier that berths historic ships of the National Maritime Museum. The basin is closed to power vessels, and other vessels must stay offshore away from buoys marking a swimming area. The **speed limit** is 3 knots. Depths of 9 to 16 feet are inside the basin. Small craft can find anchorage in about 13 feet. Permission to anchor for more than 24 hours must be obtained from the Aquatic Park Ranger Station.

Charts 18651, 18652

(246) S of San Francisco, **Point Avisadero**, which is the E extremity of Hunters Point, **Sierra Point**, Oyster Point, **Point San Bruno**, and Coyote Point, all on the W shore of the bay, are prominent natural features. The Bayshore Freeway extends S on a filled area from the vicinity of **Candlestick Point**, and cuts back inland at Sierra Point. Sierra Point is the site of a small-boat harbor which can accommodate about 500 boats. **Oyster Point Channel**, marked by private lights, has depths of about 5 feet, except for a 2-foot shoal in about 37°40'09.5"N., 122°22'47.5"W., and leads to a small basin. A spur channel, marked by private lights, branches off the N side of Oyster Point Channel and leads to the entrance to the small-boat harbor at Sierra Point. The basin at the end of Oyster Point Channel has two private wharves in ruins and sheds on the W side; a marina that can accommodate about 200 boats is on the S side.

(247) **Oyster Point**, a low filled area, is the site of a small-boat harbor accommodating about 570 boats. Depths of about 8 feet are in the harbor. An entrance channel E of the harbor is marked by private lights. In 2006, the channel had a reported depth of 10 feet. Transients

should report to the harbormaster's office for berth assignment. A prominent sculptured tower is on the hill 0.7 mile S of Oyster Point; the tower is floodlighted.

(248) The area between Point San Bruno and Coyote Point is occupied by **San Francisco International Airport.** A **security zone** has been established in the waters surrounding the airport. (See **165.1192**, chapter 2, for limits and regulations.)

(249) **Coyote Point** is covered by a heavy growth of trees and is raised as an island. It is the most prominent point on the S bay. A small-craft harbor accommodating about 580 boats is on the E side of the point. The approach channel, marked by two private lights, had a depth of 8 feet in 2010. The harbor, operated by San Mateo County, is composed of two basins with depths of 6 to 8 feet. Transients should report to the harbormaster's office on the NW side of the harbor for berth assignment; guest berths are usually available. A harbor patrol boat is maintained.

(250) (See the small-craft facilities tabulation on chart 18652 for services and supplies available at the small-craft facilities at Oyster Point and Coyote Point.)

(251) The **San Mateo-Hayward Bridge** crossing the lower part of San Francisco Bay near **San Mateo** has a fixed span with a clearance of 135 feet over the main channel. The bridge is marked at mid span by a racon. An overhead power cable with a clearance of 160 feet over the main channel crosses the bay just S of the bridge.

(252) A section of the old San Mateo lift bridge, now used as a fishing pier, extends 4,135 feet from the San Mateo shore just S of the new bridge. A part of the fishing pier extends into the W part of the main channel.

(253) In 1983, a 34-foot shoal was reported to extend from under to just SE of the bridge in about 37°35'N., 122°15'W.

(254) **Redwood Creek**, 4 miles SE of San Mateo Bridge, is entered through a marked channel that leads to the municipal wharves at the **Port of Redwood City**, 2.5 miles above the mouth. Turning basins are to the N and S of the wharves. Federal project depths are 30 feet in the channel and basins. (See Notice to Mariners and latest editions of charts for controlling depths.)

(255) Traffic in the waterway is in bulk cement, gypsum, rock salt, sand, and scrap metal. Overhead power cables across the waterway have a clearance of 155 feet. Prominent silos of a cement plant are at the junction with **Westpoint Slough**, just N of the port.

Wharves

(256) The Port of Redwood City operates five deepwater municipal wharves. Only the wharves with shiphandling facilities are described. For a complete description of the port facilities refer to Port Series No. 30, published and sold by the U.S. Army Corps of Engineers. (See Appendix A for address).

(257) Wharves 1 and 2 (37°30'47"N., 122°12'35"W.): 1,651 feet of berthing space with dolphins; 32 to 35 feet alongside; deck height, 15 feet; storage silos with a total capacity of 58,000 tons; open storage for 85,000 tons of sand; receipt of sand and bulk cement; various operators.

(258) Wharf 3 (37°30'42"N., 122°12'40"W.): just S of Wharves 1 and 2; 750 feet of berthing space with dolphins; 34 feet alongside; deck height, 15 feet; conveyor systems with up to 500-ton-per-hour capacity; two 40-ton, diesel crawler cranes; open storage for 50,000 tons of scrap metal and 60,000 tons of gypsum; receipt of bauxite, mill scale, gypsum, and sand; shipment of scrap metal; various operators.

(259) Wharf 4 (37°30'34"N., 122°12'43"W.), just S of Wharf 3, is operated by the U.S. Geological Survey, Department of the Interior, and is used for mooring research vessels. Wharf 5 (37°30'25"N., 122°12'44"W.), just S of Wharf 4, is operated by the Port of Redwood City and is used for mooring cruise vessels.

(260) Cargill Salt, Redwood City Wharf (37°30'16"N., 122°12'55"W.): 620 feet of berthing space; 30 feet alongside; deck height, 16 feet; occasional shipment of liquid magnesium chloride; owned and operated by Cargill Salt Inc.

(261) **Redwood City** is 2 miles S of the port facilities. Redwood City Municipal Marina, just S of the port in about 37°30'08"N., 122°12'45"W., can accommodate about 225 small craft. Other small-craft facilities are further upstream in Redwood Creek. A full service marina on the S side of Westpoint Slough can accommodate vessels up to 120 feet.

(262) **Ravenswood Point** and **Dumbarton Point** are at the head of the bay and the mouth of Coyote Creek. Two bridges and an aqueduct cross the bay at this point. The **Dumbarton Highway Bridge**, the NW bridge, has a fixed span with a clearance of 85 feet. About 1,100 yards SE of the Dumbarton bridge, an aqueduct, used to supply the city of San Francisco with water, crosses the bay. On the W shore, the aqueduct is carried on a trestle to a concrete building (charted) where it tunnels the channel to the E shore. The **Dumbarton Railroad Bridge**, just S, has a swing span with a clearance of 13 feet. The bridge is maintained in the open position. (See **117.1 through 117.49**, chapter 2, for drawbridge regulations.)

(263) **Coyote Creek** has many tributary sloughs. The main channel is marked as far as **Calaveras Point**, about 4 miles above the railroad bridge at Dumbarton Point. The power cables, 1.3 miles above Calaveras Point, have a clearance of 65 feet.

(264) A channel, marked by a daybeacon at the entrance, leads for about 3 miles through **Guadalupe Slough.** In 1985, a submerged obstruction with 3 feet over it was about 150 yards NNW of Daybeacon 20; caution is advised when transiting the area. An overhead power cable with a clearance of 65 feet crosses the slough about 1 mile above the entrance.

Oakland, California
Image courtesy of U.S. Army Corps of Engineers

(265) Just S of the Metropolitan Oakland International Airport, a dredged channel leads to a small-craft harbor operated by the city of San Leandro. The channel is marked by lights and daybeacons; a seasonal sound signal is at the entrance. In 2011-2012, the controlling depth was 4 feet in the entrance channel to the basin, thence 2 feet in the access channel through the basin. The access channel branching E from the entrance to the basin had a depth of 5 feet.

(266) The harbor accommodates about 500 small craft; 15 guest slips are maintained. The harbormaster's office is on the SW side of the basin. A high-speed patrol boat is maintained. (See the small-craft facilities tabulation on chart 18652 for services and supplies available.)

Charts 18650, 18652

(267) **Alameda** is on an island separated from the mainland by **San Leandro Bay** on the E, and Oakland Inner Harbor and Tidal Canal on the N. A ferry terminal owned by the City of Alameda and operated by the Blue and Gold Fleet LP, is at Alameda (37°47'28"N., 122°17'38"W.) The ferry service operates daily to Oakland and San Francisco.

Coast Guard

(268) The Coast Guard Shore Infrastructure Logistics Center is on **Coast Guard Island** (Government Island). A **security zone** has been established along the SW side of the island surrounding the Coast Guard pier. The security zone extends into the navigation channel about 10 to 20 yards at each end and is outlined by a floating security barrier. (See **33 CFR 165.1190**, chapter 2, for limits and regulations.)

(269) **Ballena Bay Yacht Harbor**, a large small-craft harbor, is on the E side of an island along the S shore of Alameda. This harbor offers safe refuge in storms. A private light marks the entrance to the harbor. (See the small-craft facilities tabulation on chart 18652 for services and supplies available.) A depth of 9 to 10 feet is available in the channel between the island and Alameda. A fixed bridge, with a clearance of 5 feet, crosses the channel about midway along the N shore of the island.

(270) **Oakland**, on the E or mainland shore opposite San Francisco, is the second largest city on San Francisco Bay. It is the main-line terminus of the transcontinental railroads entering the San Francisco Bay area.

(271) The **Port of Oakland** is entirely distinct from the Port of San Francisco; it is a separate customs **port of entry**. The Port of Oakland is the largest general cargo port on the bay, and a leading container-ship terminal on the Pacific coast.

(272) The Port of Oakland encompasses two areas: Outer and Inner Harbors. **Oakland Outer Harbor** is between

Facilities in the Port of Oakland							
Name	Location	Berthing Space (feet)	Depths* (feet)	Deck Height (feet)	Mechanical Handling Facilities and Storage	Purpose	Owned/ Operated by:
Burma Road Terminal (Berth 7)	37°49'12"N., 122°19'03"W.	1,459	35	14	• Covered storage (80,000 square feet) • One 100-ton gantry crane	Receipt and shipment of break bulk general cargo	Port of Oakland/ Marine Terminals Corp.
Outer Harbor Container Terminal (Berths 20, 21 and 22)	37°49'09"N., 122°18'39"W.	2,241	42	14	• Open storage (59 acres) • Three container cranes (30 long tons)	Receipt and shipment of containerized cargo	Port of Oakland/ Maersk Pacific, Ltd.
Outer Harbor Container Terminal (Berth 23)	37°49'02"N., 122°18'56"W.	900	42	14	• Open storage (46 acres) • Two container cranes (50 long tons)	Receipt and shipment of containerized cargo	Port of Oakland/ Yusen Terminals, Inc.
Outer Harbor Container Terminal (Berth 24)	37°48'53"N., 122°19'04"W.	1,138	42	14	• Open storage (57 acres) • Three container cranes (50 long tons)	Receipt and shipment of containerized cargo	Port of Oakland/ Maersk Pacific, Ltd.
Outer Harbor Container Terminal (Berths 25 and 26)	37°48'43"N., 122°19'15"W.	1,138	42	14	• Open storage (40 acres) • Two container cranes (40 long tons)	Receipt and shipment of containerized cargo	Port of Oakland/ TransBay Container Terminal Company
Outer Harbor Container Terminal (Berth 30)	37°48'37"N., 122°19'31"W.	1,075	42	14	• Open storage (33 acres) • Three container cranes (40 long tons)	Receipt and shipment of containerized cargo	Port of Oakland/ TransBay Container Terminal Company
Outer Harbor Container Terminal (Berths 32, 33 and 34)	37°48'39"N., 122°19'53"W.	2,481	38	14	• Open storage (65 acres) • Three container cranes (40 long tons)	• Receipt and shipment of containerized cargo • Receipt and shipment of roll-on/roll-off cargo	Port of Oakland/ Stevedoring Services of America Terminals
Ben E. Nutter Container Terminal (Berths 35, 37 and 38)	37°48'26"N., 122°20'23"W.	2,480	35	12	• Open storage (58 acres) • Five container cranes (50 long tons)	Receipt and shipment of containerized cargo	Port of Oakland/ Marine Terminals Corp.
Middle Harbor Container Terminal (Berths 55 and 56)	37°47'52"N., 122°19'15"W.	2,400	42	14	• Open storage (120 acres) • Four container cranes (60 long tons)	Receipt and shipment of containerized cargo	Port of Oakland/ Hanjin Shipping Co.
Middle Harbor Container Terminal (Berths 60, 61, 62 and 63)	37°47'37"N., 122°18'01"W.	2,743	42	14	• Open storage (81 acres) • Five container cranes (45 long tons)	Receipt and shipment of containerized cargo	Port of Oakland/ American President Lines
Schnitzer Steel Products 7th Street Pier	37°47'38"N., 122°17'33"W.	875	36	12	• Open storage (33 acres) • One traveling container crane (30 long tons)	Shipment of ferrous scrap metal	Schnitzer Steel Products Co.
Schnitzer Steel Products 6th Street Pier	37°47'39"N., 122°17'30"W.	700	36	11	Belt-conveyor and vessel loading spout (500 tons per hour)	Shipment of shredded scrap metal	Schnitzer Steel Products Co.
Schnitzer Steel Products Bulkhead Wharf	37°47'43"N., 122°17'22"W.	500	31	10	Barge mounted cranes and crawler cranes	Receipt of scrap metal	Schnitzer Steel Products Co.
Charles P. Howard Container Terminal (Berths 67 and 68)	37°47'41"N., 122°17'03"W.	2,016	42	14	• Open storage (50 acres) • Four traveling container crane (50 long tons)	Receipt and shipment of conventional, containerized, and roll-on/roll-off general cargo and heavy lift items	Port of Oakland/ Stevedoring Services of America Terminals

* The depths given above are reported. For information on the latest depths contact the port authorities or the private operators.

the Ben E. Nutter Container Terminal (Seventh Street Marine Terminal) on the S and the San Francisco-Oakland Bay Bridge approach on the N. A **restricted area** is in the N end of Oakland Outer Harbor adjacent to the Oakland Army Base. (See **334.1050 and 334.1060**, chapter 2, for limits and regulations.)

(273) **Oakland Inner Harbor** is that part of Inner Harbor Channel extending E from San Francisco Bay to **Tidal Canal**. It is adjacent to the most highly developed section of the city, bordering Oakland to the N and Alameda to the S. At the E end of the harbor, the artificial Tidal Canal leads to San Leandro Bay where a channel continues to the Metropolitan Oakland International Airport. Mariners should exercise caution when transiting Oakland Inner Harbor to prevent wake damage to boats moored at marinas along the waterway.

(274) A **restricted area** is in Oakland Inner Harbor from the entrance to the E boundary of the Naval Air Station. (See **334.1020 and 334.1030** chapter 2, for limits and regulations.)

Channels

(275) A **Federal project** provides for a depth of 50 feet from the Bar Channel to and including the Oakland Outer Harbor, 50 feet in the Inner Harbor Reach, thence 35 feet from the Grove Street Pier to the Park Street Bridge Reach, thence 18 feet to Tidal Canal. (See Notice to Mariners and latest editions of charts for controlling depths.)

Bridges

(276) The fixed highway bridge across Brooklyn Basin at the E end of Coast Guard Island has a clearance of 11

feet. The three highway drawbridges across Tidal Canal have a least clearance of 15 feet. The vertical lift railroad bridge across Tidal Canal has a clearance of 13 feet down and 135 feet up. The bridgetenders monitor VHF-FM channel 16 and work channel 9. (See **117.1 through 117.59 and 117.181**, chapter 2, for drawbridge regulations.)

Quarantine, customs, immigration, and agricultural quarantine

(277) (See chapter 3, Vessel Arrival Inspections, and Appendix A for addresses.)

(278) **Quarantine** is enforced in accordance with regulations of the U.S. Public Health Service. (See Public Health Service, chapter 1.)

Harbor regulations

(279) The Port of Oakland is under the jurisdiction of the Board of Port Commissioners of the City of Oakland, and is managed by an executive director. The port's general offices are at 530 Water Street, Oakland, CA 94607.

Wharves

(280) The Port of Oakland owns the facilities engaged in handling general cargo in the port, and their operation is carried out through private companies. The port also has a number of smaller piers and wharves that are used for mooring small vessels, repair work, and for other purposes. Most major deep-draft facilities are listed in the table. The alongside depths given for each facility are reported depths. (For information on the latest depths contact the Port of Oakland or the facility operator.) General cargo at the port is usually handled by ship's tackle; special handling equipment, if available, is mentioned in the description of the particular facility. Floating cranes with lifting capacities to 350 tons are available.

(281) The port is served by two transcontinental Class I railroads. Truck connections are also available to the city's freeway system. For a complete description of the port facilities, refer to Port Series No. 31, published and sold by the U.S. Army Corps of Engineers. (See Appendix A for address.)

Supplies

(282) Bunker fuel, diesel oil, gasoline, water, and most other marine supplies and services are available in Oakland. Bunker fuel is usually delivered by barge.

Repairs

(283) A drydock and repair firm in Oakland has a maximum drydock capacity of 2,800 tons; marine railways here are capable of hauling out to 500 tons. All kinds of repairs are made to both hulls and engines.

Small-craft facilities

(284) There are many small-craft facilities on both sides of the channel from Oakland Inner Harbor entrance to the airport at the S end of San Leandro Bay. Mariners should exercise caution when transiting Oakland Inner Harbor to prevent wake damage to boats moored at marinas along the waterway.

Communications

(285) Oakland is served directly by three major highways, with connections to several others. The city is the main-line terminus of three transcontinental railroads. Metropolitan Oakland International Airport, on the bay about 5 miles SE of the city, is served by many airlines.

Chart 18650

(286) **San Leandro Channel** connects San Leandro Bay with San Francisco Bay. The channel is very narrow with shallow uneven depths at the E end. Mariners should seek local knowledge before transiting the channel. Three bascule bridges, operating simultaneously, with a minimum clearance of 20 feet at the S side of the draw, cross the channel at its E end. The bridgetender for the San Leandro Bay bridges at Alameda monitors VHF-FM channel 16, and works on channel 9; call sign: WHX 870, Bay Farm Island Bridge. (See **117.1 through 117.59 and 117.193**, chapter 2, for drawbridge regulations.)

Charts 18649, 18653, 18652

(287) **Berkeley**, the site of the University of California, adjoins Oakland and **Emeryville** to the N. The long pier extending into the bay is marked by a light; the 1.7-mile offshore section of the pier is in ruins, and the inshore 3,000-foot section is used for fishing. In clear weather the Campanile (bell tower) at the university shows prominently from the bay.

(288) **Berkeley Yacht Harbor**, on the N side of the long pier, is protected at the entrance by two detached breakwaters. The S breakwater is marked by lights on the ends and at the center. The N breakwater is marked by a light on the NE and SW ends. The N side of the entrance into the harbor is marked by a private light, and the S side by a private light and sound signal. **Berkeley Reef**, awash, is 0.9 mile NW from the inner harbor entrance; it is marked by a light. About 925 boats can be accommodated in the harbor, including 20 guest berths. Transients should report to the harbormaster's office on the S side of the harbor.

(289) Two marinas are at Emeryville, about 1.5 miles S of Berkeley Yacht Harbor. The enclosed basin can accommodate about 730 small craft.

(290) (See the small-craft facilities tabulation on chart 18652 for services and supplies available at Berkeley Yacht Harbor and at Emeryville.)

Richmond Harbor, California
Image courtesy of U.S. Army Corps of Engineers

(291) **Southampton Shoal Light** (37°52'55"N., 122°24'01"W.), 32 feet above the water, is shown from a white cylindrical tower near the S end of the 1.6-mile-long shoal. A sound signal (bell) is at the light. A wreck covered 4 feet lies 0.6 mile to the NE at 37°53'16"N., 122°23'18"W.

(292) Vessels going from San Francisco Bay proper bound for Richmond usually use the 45-foot project channel through the shoal area NW of Southampton Shoal Light.

(293) **Red Rock**, 3.2 miles NNW of Southampton Shoal Light, is 169 feet high and prominent in the S approach. Buoyed **Castro Rocks**, 0.6 mile ENE of Red Rock, are small and low.

(294) **Richmond Harbor**, on the E shore of San Francisco Bay 1.5 miles N of Southampton Shoal Light, includes the port facilities to Point San Pablo. The harbor is served by two Class I railroads, and is an important oil refining center and oil shipping port.

Channels

(295) A **Federal project** provides for a depth of 45 feet in Southampton Shoal Channel and in the maneuvering area off Richmond Long Wharf, thence 38 feet in the channels leading to the port facilities at the Port of Richmond, to a point about 2,000 feet in Sante Fe Channel, thence 30 feet in the remainder of Sante Fe Channel and the turning basin. The channel is well marked by navigational aids. (See Notice to Mariners and latest editions of charts for controlling depths.) A 10,000-foot training wall is S of the dredged channel and extends W from Brooks Island.

(296) A **Federal project** further provides for an approach area 32 feet deep to the wharves at Point Orient and Point San Pablo. (See latest editions of charts for controlling depths.)

Regulated Navigation Areas

(297) A **security zone** has been established around the Chevron Long Wharf. (See **165.1197**, chapter 2, for limits and regulations.) A **restricted area** extends 0.3 mile offshore at Molate Point, site of a Navy fuel depot 0.8 mile N of Richmond-San Rafael Bridge. (See **334.1090**, chapter 2, for limits and regulations.) In 2000, shoaling to 16 feet was off the end of the Navy depot in about 37°56'47"N., 122°25'40"W. **Regulated navigation areas** are in the entrance channel and between Point Richmond and Point Potrero. (See **165.1181**, chapter 2, for limits and regulations.)

Quarantine, customs, immigration, and agricultural quarantine

(298) (See chapter 3, Vessel Arrival Inspections, and Appendix A for addresses.)

Name	Location	Berthing Space (feet)	Depths* (feet)	Deck Height (feet)	Mechanical Handling Facilities and Storage	Purpose	Owned/ Operated by:
Facilities in the Port of Richmond							
Port of Richmond Terminal No. 4 Wharf	37°57'47"N., 122°25'46"W.	1,047	32-35	14	• Tank storage (504,500 barrels) • One 5-ton mobile crane	Receipt and shipment of liquid bulk products (petroleum products, petrochemicals, chemicals, vegetable oils)	City of Richmond/ Paktank Corp.
Cheveron Products Richmond Long Wharf	37°55'19"N., 122°24'39"W.	3,065	40-50	15	• Tank storage (20.2 million barrels) • Pipelines extend from wharf to refinery	• Receipt of crude oil • Receipt and shipment of petroleum products	Cheveron Products Co.
Port of Richmond Point Potrero Marine Terminal No. 7 Wharf	37°54'27"N., 122°21'50"W.	1,615	38	12	• Open storage (40 acres with an additional 50 acres available if needed)	Occasional receipt and shipment of general cargo	City of Richmond/ Pasha Group
ARCO Products Richmond Tanker Wharf	37°54'43"N., 122°21'53"W.	710	38	12	• Tank storage (737,000 barrels) • Pipelines extend from wharf to tanks	Receipt and occasional shipment of petroleum products	ARCO Products Co.
Tosco Refining Richmond Tanker Wharf	37°54'54"N., 122°21'55"W.	836	37	12	• Tank storage (857,300 barrels) • Pipelines extend from wharf to tanks	Receipt and shipment of petroleum products and liquid bulk products (solvents, vegtable oils, coconut oil, caustic soda)	Tosco Refining Co./ Tosco Refining Co. and GATX Terminals Corp.
Tosco Refining Richmond Barge Wharf	37°54'58"N., 122°21'56"W.	836	37	12	• Tank storage (5,000 barrels) • Pipelines extend from wharf to tanks in Ref. No 5	Shipment and occasional receipt of petroleum products	Tosco Refining Co.
National Gypsum Richmond Dock	37°55'10"N., 122°22'06"W.	600	38	9-11	• Covered storage (40,000 tons of gypsum) • Belt conveyor (1,400 tons per hour)	Receipt of gypsum rock	National Gypsum Co., Gold Bond Building Products
Castrol North America Richmond Wharf	37°55'21"N., 122°22'26"W.	700	32	7	• Tank storage (85,000 barrels) • Pipelines extend from wharf to tanks	Receipt and shipment of petroleum products	Castrol North America, Incorporated
IMTT-Richmond Richmond Wharf	37°55'16"N., 122°22'09"W.	650	38	8	Tank storage: (441,200 barrels petroleum products) (4.2 million gal. caustic soda) (2.5 million gal. paraffin wax)	• Receipt and shipment of petroleum products • Receipt of caustic soda and paraffin wax	IMTT-Richmond-CA
Levin-Richmond Terminal Richmond Wharf (Berths A, B and C)	37°55'16"N., 122°22'01"W.	1,450	34-37	13	• Open storage (15 acres) • Five gantry cranes (25-50 tons) • Belt-conveyors (600 tons per hour)	• Shipment of scrap metal and petroleum coke • Receipt of miscellaneous dry bulk commodities	Levin-Richmond Terminal Corporation
Shore Terminals Richmond Wharf	37°55'05"N., 122°21'51"W.	700	33	12	• Tank storage (618,000 barrels) • Pipelines extend from wharf to tanks	Receipt and shipment of petroleum products	Shore Terminals LLC
Port of Richmond Terminal No. 2 Upper Wharf	37°54'59"N., 122°21'44"W.	300	38	13	• Tank storage (2 million gallons) • Pipelines extend from wharf to tanks	Receipt and shipment of edible oils	City of Richmond/ California Oils Corp.
Port of Richmond Terminal No. 3 Wharf	37°54'47"N., 122°21'42"W.	1,109	38	13	• Open storage (18 acres) • Two traveling container cranes (37 ton)	Receipt and shipment of conventional general cargo (steel, wood products and heavy lift items)	City of Richmond/ Stevedoring Services of America

* The depths given above are reported. For information on the latest depths contact the port authorities or the private operators.

(299) **Quarantine** is enforced in accordance with regulations of the U.S. Public Health Service. (See Public Health Service, chapter 1.)

Wharves

(300) Commodities handled at the Port of Richmond consist primarily of crude oil, petroleum products and miscellaneous dry and liquid bulk cargoes. All major deep-draft facilities are listed in the table. The alongside depths given for each facility are reported; the operators of the wharves should be contacted for information on the latest depths. Most of the large oil wharves have hose-handling cranes. Of the facilities listed, all have truck access and most have railconnections to Class I railroads. Water and electrical shore power are available at most piers.

(301) General cargo at the port is usually handled by ship's tackle; special handling equipment, if available, is mentioned in the table under 'Mechanical Handling Facilities'. For a complete description of the port facilities refer to Port Series No. 31, published and sold by

the U.S. Army Corps of Engineers. (See Appendix A for address.)

Repairs

(302) Repairs to fishing boats, recreational craft and other types of small vessels can be made at three marine repair yards on the Santa Fe Channel. A marine railway at one of the yards has a 20-ton hauling capacity and boat lifts to 88 tons are also available. There are no floating drydocks for public use at the port; the nearest such facilities are located at Oakland.

Small-craft facilities

(303) A marina and yacht club are in **Richmond Marina Bay** and a private yacht harbor is on the E side of Point Richmond. Available services include: transient berths, gasoline, diesel fuel, electricity, water, ice, pump-out and a launching ramp.

Bridge

(304) The 21,343-foot **Richmond-San Rafael Highway Bridge**, 8.8 miles above the Golden Gate Bridge, is one of the longest fixed high level double deck bridges. The E 970–foot fixed channel span clearance is 135 feet; the W fixed span has a 1,000–foot opening with a clearance of 185 feet. The centerline of both channels through the bridge spans is marked by a racon. The bridge is well lit, and the channels leading to it are marked with navigational aids.

(305) **Invincible Rock**, 1.3 miles N of Richmond-San Rafael Bridge, is covered 7 feet. **Whiting Rock**, covered 13 feet, is 0.2 mile NNE of Invincible Rock. Both rocks are buoyed. The buoy marking Whiting Rock is reported to submerge during strong ebb currents caused by the heavy spring runoffs in the area. Large vessels changing course and other craft in this area are advised to use caution.

(306) **The Brothers**, 1.7 miles N of Richmond-San Rafael Bridge, are two small low flat-topped islands. **East Brother Island Light** (37°57'48"N., 122°26'01"W.), 61 feet above the water, is shown from a buff square tower on the E island; a seasonal sound signal is at the station.

(307) **Point San Pablo**, 0.3 mile NE of East Brother Island Light, is the NW extremity of a low ridge of hills on the E shore of San Francisco Bay at its junction with San Pablo Bay. The point rises abruptly to a height of 140 feet. A dredged channel off the NE shore of the point is used by commercial and sport fishermen. Depths of 8 feet were reported in the channel to the fishery and the former whaling station docks.

(308) A small-boat basin used by commercial and sport fishermen is 0.5 mile SE from Point San Pablo.

(309) A private yacht basin is 1 mile SE from Point San Pablo. A channel leading to the basin has reported depths of about 2 feet.

(310) **Point Cavallo**, on the W side of San Francisco Bay 0.5 mile NE of the Golden Gate Bridge, is sharp and rocky with some visible and covered rocks under its face. **Horseshoe Bay** is a shallow bight W of the point.

Coast Guard

(311) From Point Cavallo the steep rocky shore tends N for 0.3 mile to **Yellow Bluff**, thence NW for 1 mile to Sausalito. A rock, covered 5 feet, is about 100 yards ESE of Yellow Bluff in about 37°50.2'N., 122°28.2'W.

(312) **Richardson Bay**, 2 miles N of the Golden Gate Bridge, is shoal except for the S part fronting Sausalito. In the N part of Richardson Bay, a wildlife sanctuary, established by the National Audubon Society, provides safe refuge for migratory fowl that arrives each fall. The sanctuary is closed to marine traffic from October to March. Seasonal buoys N of a line approximately **097°** True from Strawberry Point to Belvedere, mark the perimeter of the sanctuary. Three concrete piles topped by white cones, also mark the southern edge of the sanctuary. A special anchorage is in Richardson Bay. Local authorities control the anchoring of vessels and placement of moorings in Richardson Bay. Mariners should contact the Richardson Bay Regional Agency at (415) 289-4143 for specific information. Richardson Bay is a no-discharge zone; it is illegal for vessels to discharge any form of waste into the bay. (See **110.1 and 110.126a**, chapter 2, for limits and regulations.) A channel leading NW through Richardson Bay to facilities at Sausalito is marked by lights, daybeacons, and buoys.

(313) A **no-wake speed limit** is in all channels in Richardson Bay.

(314) **Sausalito** harbors some commercial fishing boats and many pleasure craft. Several boatbuilding and repair yards have marine ways, the largest of which can handle craft up to 350 tons. (See the small-craft facilities tabulation on chart 18652 for services and supplies available.)

(315) The Corps of Engineers has an operations base and model current-flow basin at Sausalito.

(316) **Belvedere Cove,** 3 miles NNE of the Golden Gate Bridge, is entered between **Peninsula Point** on the S and **Point Tiburon** on the N. Two private yacht clubs are in the cove. There are several small piers used by ferry boats about 0.2 mile W of Point Tiburon. Passenger ferry service is available between Tiburon and San Francisco and between Tiburon and Angel Island. The ruins of an abandoned railroad ferry slip is just W of Point Tiburon.

(317) **Angel Island**, 3 miles NE of the Golden Gate Bridge, is partially wooded and level on top. The irregular-shaped island is separated from the mainland by Raccoon Strait. The island, formerly an immigration detention station, is now a State park. A ferry operates from the island to Tiburon and just S of Pier 1 in San Francisco.

(318) **Point Blunt**, the SE extremity of Angel Island, terminates in a 60–foot-high knob, and is connected with the island by a low neck of land. **Point Blunt Light** (37°51'12"N., 122°25'09"W.), 60 feet above the water, is shown from a white house on the point; a sound signal is at the station. A shoal with visible and covered rocks extends SSE for 0.1 mile. Tide rips and swirls are heavy around the point, especially with a large falling tide.

(319) **Quarry Point**, the E end of Angel Island, is a bold bluff with deepwater close-to. The wharf 0.6 mile N of the point is in ruins. The point is marked by a light.

(320) A lighted buoy is off **Point Stuart**, the W extremity of Angel Island. A shoal area covered 14 to 30 feet, extending SW from **Point Knox**, is marked by a lighted buoy.

(321) **Ayala Cove**, indenting the N side of Angel Island, about 0.6 mile NE of Point Stuart, is reported to afford good anchorage in depths of 10 to 12 feet, mud bottom, and protection from S and W winds. Slips are available for day use only; mooring buoys are available for overnight stays. A pier at the State park facility in the cove is used by ferries and State park personnel.

(322) **Raccoon Strait**, nearly 0.5 mile wide between Angel Island and the mainland, is used by ferry boats and pleasure craft. The tidal currents in the strait have considerable velocity, and rips and swirls are heavy at times. A midchannel course can be followed. **Raccoon Shoal**, covered 29 feet, is 500 yards N of Raccoon Strait Lighted Buoy 4. A strong ebb current sets directly across the channel at the E entrance.

(323) The charted **recreation area** extending SW of Angel Island and including all of Raccoon Strait and Richardson Bay is intended primarily for use by recreation vessels. It should not be utilized by vessels 300 tons or more for through passage or for any other purpose, except in case of emergency or special circumstances.

(324) **Bluff Point**, on the mainland and marked by a light, is the E extremity of Tiburon Peninsula 1.2 miles N of Point Stuart. Point Chauncey, 0.8 miles NW of Bluff Point, is the site of the University of San Francisco Romberg Fisheries Laboratory as well as NOAA's Tiburon Fisheries Laboratory. Pier ruins at the site are marked by lights.

(325) **Paradise Cay**, a filled real estate project 2.6 miles NW of Bluff Point, has a small-boat harbor that accommodates about 200 boats. The harbor is on the N side of the project.

(326) **Corte Madera Creek**, at the head of a marshy bight about 2 miles NW of Paradise Cay, is the site of a ferry terminal with frequent service to and from San Francisco.

(327) **Corte Madera Channel** leads NW from deep water in the bay over the flats to a turning basin at the mouth of the creek. In 2011, the controlling depth in the entrance channel was 11 feet, thence 13 to 14 feet in the turning basin. The channel and turning basin are marked by lights.

(328) A railroad bridge, 0.4 mile above the turning basin, has a 38-foot bascule span with a clearance of 10 feet. (See **117.1 through 117.59 and 117.153**, chapter 2, for drawbridge regulations.) The bridge remains in the open position except when trains or rail maintenance equipment are crossing the creek. The fixed highway bridges, 0.1 mile above the railroad bridge, have 35-foot channel spans with a clearance of 21 feet. Submerged obstructions that protrude 3 to 4 feet from the bottom are under the fixed bridges. The obstructions are marked by signs on either side of the bridges. In 1984, a submerged obstruction was reported on the N edge of the channel about 400 yards W of the fixed bridges. The power cables over the turning basin and creek have a least clearance of 120 feet.

(329) **Point San Quentin**, at the W end of the Richmond-San Rafael Bridge, has low land on either side. The buildings of the State Prison S of the bridge and the long wharf N of it are prominent. A State **security zone** extends off the SE side of Point San Quentin. The buoys are orange and white and display the words "San Quentin Prison."

(330) **San Rafael Creek**, 1.8 miles NW of Point San Quentin, is used by many small craft basing at the city of **San Rafael**. A dredged channel leads across the flats of **San Rafael Bay** into San Rafael Creek to the Grand Avenue bridge, about 1.2 miles above the mouth; a turning basin is on the S side of the channel just below the bridge. In 2011-2012, the controlling depth was 4 feet at midchannel from the channel entrance to mouth of the creek, thence 2 feet at midchannel to the turning basin, with 2 feet in the basin. The channel entrance is marked by lights and a **293°** lighted range. The overhead power cables near the entrance to the creek have a clearance of 125 feet. The Grand Avenue Bridge has a 30–foot fixed span with a clearance of 4 feet.

(331) The municipal yacht harbor is on the S side of San Rafael Creek, about 400 yards E of the turning basin, and there are numerous small-craft facilities elsewhere along the creek. (See the small-craft facilities tabulation on chart 18652 for services and supplies available.)

(332) **Point San Pedro**, 3 miles N of Point San Quentin at the W entrance to San Pablo Bay, extends 100 yards E of 356-foot-high **San Pedro Hill**. Three charted brick stacks are just S from the point. There is a large quarry just N from the point.

Charts 18654, 18652, 18658

(333) **San Pablo Bay**, is nearly circular, 10 miles long in a NE direction, with a greatest width of 8 miles. The N part consists of low marshes intersected by numerous sloughs and a large area of shoal water and mudflats that bare at extreme low water. The S shore is bolder, except between Point San Pablo and Pinole Point, where it is low and marshy for about 3 miles. Carquinez Strait joins San Pablo Bay with Mare Island Strait and Suisun Bay

at its E extremity. There is considerable traffic through the bay. Deep-draft oil tankers and sugar-laden vessels pass through the bay bound for Crockett and Martinez. Lighter draft vessels pass through bound for points on Suisun Bay, and the Sacramento River to Sacramento, and on the San Joaquin River to Stockton.

(334) Mariners are advised that winds and currents in San Pablo Bay may be particularly strong and must be taken into consideration by tankers bound for the oil terminals. Vessels transiting the Pinole Shoal Regulated Navigation Area westbound on an ebb current should use extra caution to avoid being set down on the aids to navigation following the turn at San Pablo Bay Channel Light 11.

(335) The marked channel through San Pablo Bay extends in a gentle curve N and E from the entrance to the E end. The Federal project depth is 35 feet across Pinole Shoal. (See Notice to Mariners and latest editions of charts for controlling depths.) A **regulated navigation area** has been established in Pinole Shoal Channel. (See **33 CFR 165.1181(e)(2)**, chapter 2, for limits and regulations.) Vessels that do not meet the tonnage requirements to transit the Pinole Shoal Regulated Navigation Area (**165.1181**) follow an informal transit pattern along the 25-foot curve just to the south of Pinole Shoal between San Pablo Bay Channel Lighted Buoy E and the entrance to Carquinez Strait.

(336) A **regulated navigation area** has been established in San Pablo Bay N of the Pinole Shoal Channel. (See **33 CFR 165.1184**, chapter 2, for limits and regulations.)

(337) **General and naval anchorages** are in San Pablo Bay. (See **110.1 and 110.224**, chapter 2, for limits and regulations.)

(338) Shoals and flats, which uncover, extend from Point San Pablo to Pinole Point, thence NE to Lone Tree Point.

(339) **Pinole Point** is a moderately high, rocky bluff, projecting about 1 mile from the SE shore of San Pablo Bay. A T-head fishing pier extends NW from the E side of the point. Piles and a light are off the face of the pier. The ruins of a former wharf extend from the E side of the point, and numerous oil tanks are on the hills about 2 miles in back of it. About 3.5 miles E of Pinole Point, the black and white tank at a chemical fertilizer plant is prominent. A pleasure fishing pier and a small-craft harbor are at **Lone Tree Point,** 4.6 miles E from Pinole Point. (See the small-craft facilities tabulation on chart 18652 for services and supplies available.) A steel skeleton tower is 0.6 mile S of Lone Tree Point. **Oleum,** on **Davis Point,** is an oil town. There are many prominent oil tanks, painted in pastel colors, on the hills back of the town. Six stacks in a line SE of Davis Point are also prominent.

(340) The Conoco-Phillips Wharf, a T-shaped wharf, extends out from the Oleum refinery on Davis Point. In 2005, a least depth of 40 feet was alongside the 1,250-foot wharf; 1,375 feet of berthing space is available with dolphins. All four corners of the wharf are marked by private lights, and a private sound signal is at the E end; the trestle leading to the wharf is lighted at night. The deck height is 17 feet. Pipelines extend from the wharf to nearby storage tanks. The wharf is used for receipt and shipment of petroleum products and for bunkering vessels. A **security zone** has been established surrounding the wharf. (See **165.1197**, chapter 2, for limits and regulations.)

(341) Shore Oil Terminal Wharf, about 1 mile E of the Conoco-Phillips wharf, has a 72-foot face with 980 feet of berthing space with dolphins and 40 to 45 feet alongside; deck height, 20 feet. The wharf is used for receipt of petroleum products

(342) **Gallinas Creek** enters San Pablo Bay about 1.5 miles NW of Point San Pedro. The entrance channel, marked by private markers on the N side, leads across flats to the mouth of the creek. In 1983, the channel had a controlling depth of 2 feet. Local knowledge is advised. Overhead cables crossing the creek have a minimum clearance of 65 feet.

(343) A dredge offloading facility and booster pump facility are about 1.43 miles NE of Point San Pedro in about 38°00'22"N., 122°25'53"W. and 38°01'15"N., 122°27'04"W., respectively. The two facilities consist of several pilings with permanently moored barges. A marked, submerged pipeline and power cables connect the two facilities, thence runs NW to the shoreline in about 38°02'47"N., 122°29'36"W. Mariners are advised to use caution when transiting the area.

(344) **Petaluma River** enters San Pablo Bay on the NW side. The city of **Petaluma**, 12 miles above the mouth, is the center of an extensive dairy and egg industry. The river is used by pleasure craft and by barges handling gravel, oyster shell, heavy construction equipment, and prestressed concrete products.

(345) A dredged channel leads from deep water in San Pablo Bay to the mouth of the Petaluma River and continues upstream to the city of Petaluma. A Federal project provides for depths of 8 feet in the entrance and through the river to a turning basin at Petaluma, thence 4 feet to the upstream limit of the project. (See Notice to Mariners and latest edition of the chart for controlling depths.)

(346) Least clearances over Petaluma River are: drawbridges, 4 feet; fixed bridges, 8 feet; and power cables, 70 feet. The bridgetender for the D Street highway bridge at Petaluma monitors VHF-FM channel 16, and works channel 9; call sign: WQX 644, D Street Bridge. When not in use, the drawspans of the railroad bridges at Black Point and Haystack Landing are maintained in the open to navigation position. (See **117.1 through 117.59 and 117.187**, chapter 2, for drawbridge regulations.)

(347) A privately dredged channel with private markers leads SSW from the dredged entrance channel to Petaluma River just below the entrance to the river and

thence to **Novato Creek**. In 1985, the reported controlling depth was 2 feet.

Danger zones

(348) Danger zones are in the E part of San Pablo Bay adjacent to the W shore of Mare Island and in the N central part of the bay. (See **334.1160 and 334.1170**, chapter 2, for limits and regulations.)

Charts 18655, 18652

(349) **Mare Island Strait**, at the mouth of the Napa River, is between the mainland and **Mare Island**. The project depth for the Mare Island Strait Channel, from the entrance to just S of the Vallejo-Mare Island Causeway Bridge, about 2.9 miles above the entrance, is 30 feet. (See Notice to Mariners and latest editions of charts for controlling depths.)

(350) The waters around Mare Island are included in a **restricted area.** (See **334.1100**, chapter 2, for limits and regulations.)

(351) In 2010, shoaling to 14 feet was in the NW corner of Naval Anchorage 21, with shoaling to 5 feet in the adjacent Disposal Area.

(352) A power cable crossing lower Mare Island Strait between Vallejo and Mare Island has a clearance of 206 feet. If the clearance between the masthead and the cable is less than 10 feet or if the clearance is not known, vessels shall not move under the cable without authority.

(353) The entrance to Mare Island Strait is between two dikes. On the E side of the entrance, Dike No. 9 extends about 700 yards SW from the mainland and on the W side, Dike No. 14 extends about 500 yards SE from Mare Island; both dikes have submerged outer sections. Dike No. 9 is marked at the outer end by a light and Dike No. 14 is marked at the outer end by a lighted buoy.

Coast Guard

(354) **Coast Guard Station Vallejo**, about 2.5 miles above the entrance to Mare Island Strait just below the Vallejo-Mare Island causeway lift bridge, is on the E side of the strait.

(355) **Vallejo**, on the E shore of Mare Island Strait, is the terminal of a railroad connecting interior N points. A large flour mill is prominent S of the railroad yard. A passenger ferry operates between Vallejo and San Francisco.

(356) Two small-craft facilities are also on the E side of the Mare Island strait. (See the small-craft facilities tabulation on chart 18652 for services and supplies available.)

(357) The Vallejo-Mare Island causeway and lift bridge connects Mare Island with the city of Vallejo. It has a lift span with a clearance of 100 feet up and 12 feet down. (See **117.1 through 117.59 and 117.169**, chapter 2, for drawbridge regulations.) The bridge is equipped with radiotelephone. The bridgetender monitors VHF-FM channel 16 and works on channel 13; voice call, Mare Island Causeway Bridge. Just above **Sears Point**, 1 mile above Vallejo, a fixed highway bridge with a clearance of 100 feet crosses the strait. A public fishing pier is close S of this bridge and extends about 350 yards from the E side of the strait. A Navy reserve fleet pier is on the W side of the strait between Vallejo-Mare Island causeway lift bridge and the fixed bridge just above Sears Point. If practical, approach the bridges only when running against the current. No passage should be attempted during the periods of peak flood or ebb current.

Charts 18654, 18652

(358) **Napa River**, the continuation of Mare Island Strait above the Vallejo-Mare Island Causeway Bridge, is used by barges and pleasure boats. Barge traffic on the river is in crushed rock, salt, and steel. A dredged channel leads from the causeway bridge to a turning basin at **Jacks Bend**, thence to the head of navigation at the 3rd Street Bridge in **Napa,** 13 miles above the causeway bridge. A **Federal project** provides a depth of 10 feet from **Horseshoe Bend** to the upstream limit of the channel. (See Notice to Mariners and latest editions of charts for controlling depths.) Napa River is marked to Horeshoe Bend by lights and a daybeacon; above Horseshoe Bend, the river is marked by lights and daybeacons to the 3rd Street Bridge in Napa. A visible wreck, marked by a buoy, is on the E side of the channel just N of Slaughterhouse Point. In 2004, a submerged obstruction was reported in the channel E of Knight Island in about 38°08'16.5"N., 122°16'57.2"W.

(359) The railroad bridge across Napa River at **Brazos**, about 6.8 miles above the Vallejo-Mare Island Causeway, has a vertical lift span with a clearance of 2 feet down and 97 feet up. When not in use, the drawspan is maintained in the open to navigation position. (See **117.1 through 117.59 and 117.169**, chapter 2, for drawbridge regulations.) The channel through the bridge crosses from one bank to the other causing a hazardous condition, particularly for downbound loaded barges, because the direction of the ebb current is as much as 50° from the axis of the channel.

(360) A fixed highway bridge with a clearance of 107 feet crosses the Napa River at Suscol, about 9.7 miles above the Vallejo-Mare Island Causeway.

(361) Near **Imola**, 12 miles above Vallejo-Mare Island Causeway bridge, a fixed highway bridge crosses the river with a clearance of 60 feet. The three fixed bridges in Napa have a minimum width of 47 feet and a clearance of 3.7 feet. The minimum clearance of the power cables crossing the river below Napa is 125 feet, and in Napa, 40 feet.

(362) A small-craft basin is on the W side of Napa River opposite **Bull Island**, 8 miles above the Vallejo-Mare

Carquinez Strait, California
Image courtesy of U.S. Army Corps of Engineers

Island Causeway, and several other small-craft facilities are elsewhere on the river. (See the small-craft facilities tabulation on chart 18652 for services and supplies available.)

Charts 18656, 18652

(363) Six-mile-long **Carquinez Strait** connects San Pablo and Suisun Bays. For the first 3.5 miles it is a little less than 0.5 mile wide, and then widens to about 1 mile. It is deep throughout with the exception of a small stretch of flats on the N shore, and a small shoal area in the bight on the S shore near the E end.

Anchorages

(364) **General anchorages** are in Carquinez Strait. (See **110.1 and 110.224**, chapter 2, for limits and regulations.)

Charts 18655, 18652

(365) The **California State Maritime Academy** and pier are in **Morrow Cove**, on the N shore of the W entrance to Carquinez Strait.

(366) Interstate Route 80 fixed highway bridges cross Carquinez Strait near its W entrance at **Semple Point**. The channel on each side of the center pier is 998 feet wide; the least clearance is 146 feet through the N span and 132 feet through the S span. Private sound signals are sounded at the bridge piers and racons are at the center of each span of the E bridge.

(367) Power cables cross the strait 0.3 mile W of the highway bridges and 1.2 miles E of it; the minimum clearance is 179 feet.

(368) **Crockett**, on the S shore just E of the highway bridges, is built around The California and Hawai'ian Sugar Co. Refinery. The refinery's wharf has a 2,715-foot face with 2,815 feet of berthing space with dolphins, and a deck height of 12 feet. A depth of 30 feet is alongside. Four cranes and a conveyor system serve the wharf, maximum unloading rate is 250 tons per hour each; water is available. The wharf is used for receipt and shipment of sugar products and the transfer of bulk liquid molasses; it is owned and operated by California and Hawai'ian Sugar Co.

(369) A marina is on the S shore just W of the highway bridges, and a small-boat basin is in **Elliot Cove** on the N side of the strait opposite Crockett. (See the small-craft facilities tabulation on chart 18652 for services and supplies available.)

Charts 18657, 18652

(370) A light is 130 yards off the S side of Carquinez Strait, 1.5 miles E of Interstate Route 80 fixed highway bridges; a light is off **Port Costa**, 0.6 mile to the E. On

the N side of the strait, a light is on **Dillon Point** and another is off **Benicia Point**.

(371) The Defense Fuel Supply Center Support Point, Ozol Oil Wharf, at **Ozol**, is about 1.6 miles SE of Port Costa. The 270-foot offshore wharf, marked by lights on the E and W ends, has 880 feet of berthing space with dolphins; 37 feet alongside; deck height is 8 feet; water and electrical shore power connections are available; it is owned by the U.S. Government and operated by Blaiz Co., Inc.

(372) There are three wharves extending out to deep water at **Martinez**, 2 miles SE of Point Carquinez.

(373) The westernmost of these facilities is the municipal fishing pier with a tugboat slip on its W side. A small-boat harbor, protected by breakwaters, is on the E side of the pier. A private light is on the channel end of both breakwaters. In 1994, shoaling to a depth of about 4 feet was reported at the entrance to the marina.

(374) The Shell Oil Co., Martinez Refinery Wharf, E of the municipal fishing pier, is a 900-foot offshore wharf, 1,850 feet usable with dolphins; depth of 42 feet alongside decreasing to 39 feet at the W end; deck height is 15 feet; water and electrical shore power connections are available; owned and operated by Shell Oil Co. The wharf is marked by private lights and a sound signal. A **security zone** has been established around the wharf. (See **165.1197**, chapter 2, for limits and regulations.)

(375) The Tesoro Amorco Pier, Upper and Lower Wharves, 400 yards E of the Shell Oil Co. Wharf, have depths of 35 feet alongside and both are used for bunkering vessels as well as the receipt and shipment of petroleum products. The W wharf is a 76-foot offshore wharf with 281 feet usable with dolphins; depth of 35 feet alongside; deck height is 15 feet. The E wharf is a 76-foot offshore wharf with 512 feet usable with dolphins; deck height is 17 feet. The wharves provide 978 feet of continuous berthing space; owned and operated by Tesoro Corporation. Both wharves are marked by private lights. A **security zone** has been established around the wharves. (See **165.1197**, chapter 2, for limits and regulations.)

(376) **Benicia** is on the N shore at the E end of Carquinez Strait. Most of the smaller piers around the town are in ruins.

(377) A marina, protected by breakwaters, is at Benicia. Private lights on the breakwater mark the entrance. (See the small-craft facilities tabulation on Chart 18652 for services and supplies available.)

(378) In 1988, a sunken wreck with a least depth of 21 feet was reported about 600 yards WSW of the Port of Benicia in about 38°02'17.5"N., 122°08'39.6"W.

(379) The **Port of Benicia** is at Army Point at the E end of the town. Highway and railroad connections, and water and electrical shore power connections are available at all of the facilities.

(380) Valero-Benicia Refinery (38°02'41"N., 122°07'45"W.): 1,100 feet of berthing space; 40.4 feet alongside; deck height, 15 feet; receipt and shipment of petroleum products; receipt of crude oil; owned and operated by Valero Energy Corporation. A **security zone** has been established around the wharf. (See **165.1197**, chapter 2, for limits and regulations.)

(381) Benicia Industries, Wharf No. 95 (38°02'28"N., 122°08'05"W.): 2,404 feet of berthing space; 38 feet alongside; deck height, 11 to 15 feet; receipt of automobiles and crude oil; receipt and shipment of general cargo; shipment of bagged rice, petroleum coke, and petroleum products; owned by Benicia Industries, Inc., and operated by various companies.

(382) Three bridges cross Carquinez Strait at the E end from **Army Point** to **Suisun Point**. The Benicia-Martinez Highway Bridge has a fixed span with a clearance of 135 feet over Suisun Point Reach. A sound signal and RACON are over the main channel span between piers 10 and 11 and a sound signal is between piers 6 and 7. The Union Pacific Railroad Bridge, just E of the fixed bridge, has a lift span with clearances of 70 feet down and 135 feet up over the main channel. The I-680 Highway Bridge, 0.1 mile E of the railroad bridge, has a fixed span with a clearance of 153 feet over Bulls Head Channel. (See **117.1** through **117.49**, chapter 2 for drawbridge regulations.) The bridgetender monitors VHF-FM channel 13 and works on channel 14; call sign KQ-7193, Union Pacific Railroad Bridge. All mariners intending to transit underneath the Union Pacific Railroad Bridge should be familiar with the communications protocol established specifically for vessel-to-bridge radiotelephone communications at the bridge. The protocol addresses procedures for requesting an opening of the bridge as well as special emergency communication procedures for all vessels transiting underneath the bridge. For a complete explanation of the San Francisco communications protocol, or to contact the Training Director, go to http://www.uscg.mil/d11/vtssf/.

(383) **Bulls Head Point**, just E of the S end of the bridge, shows as a 100-foot rounding hill with a prominent high white stack.

(384) The Tesoro Corporation, Avon Refinery Wharf extends across the flats at **Avon**, 1.5 miles E of the Suisun Point bridges. Total berthing space is 1,320 feet; depths alongside the channel face are 32 feet; deck height is 19 feet, with 14 feet at the center section. Tankers berth along the channel side of the face, and barges along the inshore side of the face; receipt and shipment of petroleum products; owned and operated by Tesoro Corporation. Private lights and sound signals are on the outer ends of the pier. A **security zone** has been established around the wharf. (See **165.1197**, chapter 2, for limits and regulations.)

(385) The Shore Oil Terminal Wharf, 970 feet of berthing space with dolphins, is 0.5 mile W of the Tesoro Wharf; depth alongside, 34 feet; receipt and shipment of petroleum products. The wharf is owned and operated by Shore Terminals Oil Corp.

Charts 18656, 18652

(386) **Suisun Bay** is a broad shallow body of water with marshy shores and filled with numerous marshy islands, many of which have been reclaimed and are now under cultivation. It is practically the delta of the Sacramento and San Joaquin Rivers which empty into the E part of the bay. Two narrow winding channels lead to the mouths of the rivers. They are marked by lights. The rivers and the channels near the mouths have been improved by the Government to increase the depth, remove obstructions, and provide relief during freshet seasons. A **Federal project** provides for a main channel 35 feet deep through the bay to the San Joaquin River. (See Notice to Mariners and latest editions of charts for controlling depths.)

(387) The bay is used by many light-draft vessels having local knowledge. It is recommended that large vessels take a pilot if bound above Crockett. For information on obtaining an inland pilot contact the San Francisco Marine Exchange or San Francisco Bar Pilots.

Anchorages

(388) **General anchorages** are in Suisun Bay. (See **110.1 and 110.224,** chapter 2, for limits and regulations.) Mariners are advised that a cable area runs through Anchorage No.23.

(389) **Suisun Slough** empties into the NW side of Suisun Bay 5.5 miles N of Benicia. A dredged channel leads from Suisun Bay into the entrance to the slough. In 1990, the controlling depth was 6½ feet. The entrance channel is marked by lights. Above the dredged channel, river channel had a reported depth of 6.3 feet in 2001, from the mouth to **Suisun City**, 12 miles above the entrance. Traffic on the slough includes gasoline, jet fuel, and residual fuel oil. Petroleum products are barged to an oil distributor at Suisun City. A power cable with a clearance of 110 feet crosses the slough just S of the city.

(390) A **restricted berthing area** for Maritime Administration Reserve Fleet vessels is along the W side of Suisun Bay. (See **162.270,** chapter 2, for limits and regulations.)

(391) (See **117.1 through 117.59, 117.151, and 117.185,** chapter 2, for drawbridge regulations for the bridges over the minor tributaries of Suisun Bay.)

Charts 18658, 18652

(392) The site of the **Concord U.S. Naval Weapons Station** is on the S side of the bay. A **restricted area** has been established along the waterfront of the Naval Station (See **33 CFR 334.1110,** chapter 2, for limits and regulations.) A **security zone** has also been established around the piers of the Naval Station. (See **33 CFR 165.1199,** chapter 2, for limits and regulations.)

Charts 18656, 18652

(393) Two adjacent small-craft basins are on the S side of the flats about 1.6 miles E of **Middle Point**, the E boundary of the Navy weapons station. The basins are connected to the bay by twin canals cut through the flats.

Charts 18659, 18661, 18652

(394) **Pittsburg**, on the S side of New York Slough 12 miles E of Suisun Point bridges, is a manufacturing city with several deepwater berths.

(395) The PGE-Pittsburg Fuel Pier, about 0.3 mile W of **New York Point**, is an offshore wharf with 1,070 feet of berthing space, 35 feet alongside, and a deck height of 14 feet. It is used for receiving and transshipping petroleum products.

(396) The Diablo Service Corp. Wharf, about 0.6 mile E of New York Point is an offshore wharf with 1,154 feet of berthing space with dolphins, 35 feet alongside, and deck height of 12 feet. There is a conveyer system and crawler tractors. Rail and highway connections, and water and electrical shore-power connections are available. It is owned by Tosco Corp. and is used for the receipt of petroleum coke.

(397) USS-Posco Industries, Pittsburg Wharf, about 1.3 mile E of New York Point, is a 891-foot marginal wharf with depths of 33 feet alongside and a deck height of 11 feet. Three 37½-ton cranes are available, and there are rail and highway connections, and water and electrical shore power connections. It is used for receipt of semi-finished steel.

(398) The Dow Chemical Co., Pittsburg Plant Wharf, about 2 miles E of New York Point, is an offshore wharf with 672 feet of berthing space with dolphins, 40 feet alongside and a deck height of 20 feet. It is used for shipment and receipt of caustic soda.

(399) **Antioch** on the S side of San Joaquin River 16 miles E of Suisun Point bridges, is a manufacturing city with waterborne commerce.

(400) Georgia-Pacific Corp., Antioch Plant Wharf, about 38°00'56"N., 121°47'08"W., is a 197-foot offshore wharf, 780 feet usable with dolphins, with 31 feet alongside and a deck height of 11 feet. A conveyor system is available for the receipt of gypsum rock. Highway connections, and water and electrical shore power connections are available.

(401) Gaylord Container Corp., California Mill Wharf, about 0.5 mile E of Kaiser Gypsum Co. Pier, is a 291-foot offshore wharf, 766 total berthing space, with depths of 35 feet alongside. Receipt of miscellaneous dry bulk commodities.

(402) There are also barge facilities at Antioch.

(403) The Fulton Shipyard, on the E edge of the city, has a marine railway that can haul out vessels up to 350 tons

for general repairs. The yard repairs auxiliary vessels such as towboats and barges.

(404) Several small-craft facilities are at Pittsburg and Antioch. (See the small-craft facilities tabulation on chart 18652 for services and supplies available.)

Charts 18661, 18662

(405) The **Delta Region**, the combined deltas of the San Joaquin and Sacramento Rivers, comprises the feeder rivers, sloughs, and canals that directly or indirectly connect with one or both of the rivers. Hundreds of miles of navigable waterways for small boats are available in the Delta; both local and visiting small craft use these waterways extensively. Common types of pleasure craft peculiar to the Delta include pontoon boats and houseboats, but many conventional powerboats and sailboats use these waters also, especially in summer when San Francisco Bay is foggy and choppy. Some of the more important sloughs are used by tugs and barges.

(406) Bordering the various waterways are levees which are 12 feet or more higher than the land behind them. The levees are built up from dredged material taken from the adjacent waterway, and because of the settlement of the levees, dredging has been done periodically to keep the tops at height and grade. As material is needed for levee work, the dredge pays more attention to the requirements of the levee than to the depth of the channel for navigation purposes. This leaves an uneven bottom. The tops of the levees generally have dirt roads. **Tule** is often found on the channel side of the levees. Tule is the name given to a tall aquatic plant growth similar to bulrush.

(407) Many public and private small-boat harbors, marinas, and boating resorts are spread over the Delta region. All types of facilities and services for small craft are available, though some areas in the Delta are much more developed than others. Groceries are one of the most difficult items to obtain in this region; groceries in any quantity must be obtained from the larger towns on the Sacramento River, at Antioch or Stockton on the San Joaquin River, or at one of the larger resorts. Diesel oil is similarly rather scarce, since most craft on these waters use gasoline. Diesel oil may be obtained at the junction of the Mokelumne and San Joaquin Rivers, on the W side of King Island, at or near the cities of Antioch and Stockton, and at Bethel Island.

(408) Some areas in the Delta in which small-craft facilities are especially concentrated are: most of the perimeter of **Bethel Island (Bethel Tract)**, 3.4 miles E from Antioch Bridge; the S side of San Joaquin River on both sides of Antioch Bridge; the W side of the Mokelumne River from its junction with the San Joaquin River to Georgiana Slough; and the San Joaquin River from Fourteenmile Slough through Stockton. (See the small-craft facilities tabulation on charts 18661 and 18662 for services and supplies available at the small-craft facilities in the Delta Region.)

Cable ferries

(409) The Sacramento and San Joaquin Rivers, including some of the feeder rivers, sloughs, and canals that directly or indirectly connect with one or both of the rivers, are crossed by cable ferries (see charts 18661 and 18662). These ferries in the delta region are guided by cables and sometimes propelled by a cable rig attached to the shore. Cables to the ferries, which extend from both banks of the waterway, may be at, near, or above the water surface. Operating procedures vary and mariners are advised to use extreme caution and seek local knowledge. In 1978, the U.S. Coast Guard advised that cable ferries were not operating in many charted locations in the delta region. These ferries may operate intermittently, so caution is advised while operating in their vicinity. **DO NOT ATTEMPT TO PASS A MOVING CABLE FERRY.**

(410) **Clearances for structures** (bridges, cables, pipelines, etc.) across all navigable waterways throughout the **Delta Region** (except the San Joaquin River) are listed on structure-crossing tables. These tables are located near the waterways being discussed in the text. Mariners are advised that **low water datum** listed on the tables is **mean lower low water** at **low-river stage**; overhead cable clearances reference **high water datum**. During **flood stage levels**, bridge and overhead cable clearances may be **reduced** as much as 29 feet or more. See chapter 1 for more information about bridges and overhead cables.

Charts 18661, 18660, 18663

(411) **San Joaquin River** rises in the Sierra Nevada, flows 275 miles in a W direction, and enters Suisun Bay through **New York Slough**. The winding river is navigable for deep-draft vessels to Stockton. The water is generally fresh at Antioch. Major floods in the river valley may occur from November to April, caused by intense general storms of several days' duration. At the mouth of the river an ordinary flood will cause a rise of 8 feet and an extreme flood a rise of 10 feet in the river level. At Stockton, ordinary flood will cause a rise of 8.5 feet, and extreme flood a rise of 13.5 feet in the river level. The delta of the river is formed of many marshy islands intersected by sloughs and channels. The islands are reclaimed tule and cattail marshes which have been converted to agriculture. Bordering the river are levees that are 12 feet or more higher than the land behind them.

(412) Reports of gage heights of the San Joaquin River delta can be obtained from the Sacramento National Weather Service Office at any time. The information is published in the Sacramento Bee and, in addition, is

Structures Across the Principal Tributaries of the San Joaquin River

Name·Description·Type	Location	Clear Width of Draw or Span Opening (feet)	Clear Height above Water Datum (feet) Low	Clear Height above Water Datum (feet) High	Information
Mokelumne River					
Mokelumne River highway swing bridge	38°07'34"N., 121°34'47"W.	100	11	8	Bridgetender monitors VHF-FM channel 16 and works channel 9; call sign KMJ-382 Mokelumne River Bridge. **(Note 1)**
South Fork Mokelumne River					
Overhead power cable	38°07'04"N., 121°29'44"W.			110	
Overhead power cable	38°13'32"N., 121°29'30"W.			110	
San Joaquin County highway bridge (removable span)	38°13'32"N., 121°29'30"W.	58	16	13	**(Note 1)**
North Fork Mokelumne River					
Millers Ferry highway swing bridge	38°13'25"N., 121°30'25"W.	85	15	12	Bridgetender monitors VHF-FM channel 16 and works channel 9; call sign WBE-8326 Millers Ferry Bridge. **(Note 1)**
Wilson Bridge/Deadhorse Island Bridge (removable span)	38°13'28"N., 121°30'17"W.	56	14	11	
Mokelumne River					
Interstate 5 fixed highway bridges	38°15'18"N., 121°26'52"W.	65	24	21	
Franklin Road swing bridge	38°15'20"N., 121°26'23"W.	80	21	18	Clearances are for the south draw only. **(Note 1)**
Union Pacific Railroad swing bridge	38°15'17"N., 121°25'54"W.	61	19	16	Clearances are for the south draw only. **(Note 1)**
Galt-New Hope Road fixed bridge	38°14'12"N., 121°25'07"W.	62	18	2	
Little Potato Slough					
Potato Slough Bridge (swing, highway)	38°06'56"N., 121°29'52"W.	100	37	35	Bridgetender monitors VHF-FM channel 16 and works channel 9; call sign KSK-278 Potato Slough Bridge. **(Note 2)**
Georgiana Slough					
Overhead power cable	38°08'47"N., 121°36'03"W.			85	
Tyler Island Bridge Road (swing)	38°09'43"N., 121°35'05"W.	80	13	10	Bridgetender monitors VHF-FM channel 16 and works channel 9; call sign WHU-246 Tyler Island Bridge. **(Note 3)**
Old River					
Overhead power cable	38°04'16"N., 121°34'32"W.			110	
Overhead power cable	37°58'57"N., 121°34'53"W.			110	
BNSF Railroad Bascule Bridge	37°56'24"N., 121°33'38"W.	95 (75 feet open)	14	11	Bridgetender monitors VHF-FM channel 16 and works channel 9; call sign WHU-322 Santa Fe Railroad Bridge.
Overhead power cable	37°55'44"N., 121°33'32"W.			125	
State Route 4 highway swing bridge	37°53'28"N., 121°34'13"W.	98	16	12	**(Note 4)**
Overhead power cable	37°53'13"N., 121°34'32"W.			50	Cable is temporary with estimated duration through April 2011; vertical clearance is approximate.
Old River Fixed Bridge	37°50'36"N., 121°32'16"W.	24	18	14	
Overhead power cable	37°50'36"N., 121°32'16"W.			110	
Overhead power cable	37°50'21"N., 121°32'20"W.			115	
Overhead power cable	37°49'44"N., 121°33'09"W.			110	
Overhead power cable	37°49'08"N., 121°33'15"W.			data unavailable	
Overhead power cable	37°48'54"N., 121°33'11"W.			26	
Overhead power cable	37°47'26"N., 121°30'51"W.			data unavailable	
Tracy Boulevard Fixed Bridge	37°48'16"N., 121°26'59"W.	46	18	15	
Overhead power cable	37°48'28"N., 121°24'36"W.			110	
Junction with San Joaquin River	37°48'30"N., 121°19'39"W.				
Middle River					
Bacon Island Swing Bridge	37°57'23"N., 121°31'41"W.	37[1] 90[2]	18[1] 11[2]	15[1] 8[2]	[1]Clearances for west span [2]Clearances for east span Bridgetender monitors VHF-FM channel 16 and works channel 9; call sign WHU-8326 Bacon Island Bridge. **(Note 5)**

Structures Across the Principal Tributaries of the San Joaquin River					
Name·Description·Type	Location	Clear Width of Draw or Span Opening (feet)	Clear Height above Water Datum (feet) Low	High	Information
Overhead power cable	37°56'33"N., 121°31'57"W.			110	
BNSF Railroad Bascule Bridge	37°56'23"N., 121°32'00"W.	85 (79 feet open)	14	11	(Note 5)
Overhead power cable	37°56'09"N., 121°31'52"W.			125	
Overhead power cable	37°54'24"N., 121°30'26"W.			114	
State Route 4 Highway Fixed Bridge	37°53'28"N., 121°29'21"W.	105	14	11	(Note 5)
Overhead power cable	37°53'04"N., 121°28'15"W.			110	
Tracy Boulevard Fixed Bridge	37°52'56"N., 121°27'23"W.	68	15	12	
Overhead power cable	37°53'28"N., 121°26'25"W.			110	
Overhead power cable	37°53'35"N., 121°25'51"W.			70	
Howard Road Fixed Bridge	37°52'39"N., 121°23'00"W.	24	18	15	
Undine Road Fixed Bridge	37°50'05"N., 121°23'02"W.	45	18	15	
Overhead power cable	37°49'57"N., 121°23'07"W.				data unavailable
Overhead power cable	37°49'45"N., 121°23'11"W.			110	
Junction with Old River	37°49'20"N., 121°22'30"W.				
Turner Cut					
Zuckerman Bridge (retractable span)	37°58'35"N., 121°28'30"W.	30	19	16	Bridgetender monitors VHF-FM channel 16 and works channel 9; call sign WHV-959 Zuckerman Brothers Bridge (202-464-1253). (Note 6)

Note 1 – See **117.1 through 117.59 and 117.175**, chapter 2 for limits and regulations
Note 2 – See **117.1 through 117.59 and 117.167**, chapter 2 for limits and regulations
Note 3 – See **117.1 through 117.59 and 117.157**, chapter 2 for limits and regulations
Note 4 – See **117.1 through 117.59 and 117.183**, chapter 2 for limits and regulations
Note 5 – See **117.1 through 117.59 and 117.171**, chapter 2 for limits and regulations
Note 6 – bridge maintained in the open position except when being crossed by a vehicle. If it is necessary for the bridge to be in the closed position for an extended period, the bridgetender may be contacted.

reported on radio broadcasts from station KFBK (1530 kHz) whenever the gage heights are sufficient to be of general interest.

(413) Information on gage heights can also be obtained from the State Department of Water Resources, 1416 9th Street, Sacramento, CA 95814 or by recorded message at (916) 653-6416.

(414) A **Federal project** provides for a 35-foot channel from the mouth of the San Joaquin River to a turning basin at Stockton, and for suitable passing and turning basins. (See Notice to Mariners and latest editions of charts for controlling depths.)

Anchorages

(415) **General and explosives anchorages** are in the San Joaquin River on the W side of Sherman Island near the mouth, and just N of Venice Cut between Mandeville Island and Venice Island. (See **110.1 and 110.224**, chapter 2, for limits and regulations.)

(416) (See **162.205**, chapter 2, for rules and regulations governing maximum speed, passing, right-of-way, collision, and wrecks in the San Joaquin River.)

(417) **Antioch Bridge**, (State Route 160), a fixed highway bridge with a clearance of 142 feet, crosses San Joaquin River about 3 miles E of Antioch. There are no other bridges over the main channel below the turning basin at Stockton. Power cables over the main channel of San Joaquin River from the mouth to the turning basin at Stockton have a minimum clearance of 140 feet.

(418) There are small-craft facilities on the S side of San Joaquin River on both sides of Antioch Bridge. (See the small-craft facilities tabulation on chart 18661 for services and supplies available.)

(419) The main channel in San Joaquin River to Stockton is marked by a daybeacon, buoys, lights, and lighted ranges. At **Mandeville Cut** and **Venice Cut**, 15 miles above Antioch Bridge, the river still follows its old channel and violent sheers are experienced if the navigator is not prepared to meet the river current when passing from the cuts into the river and from the river into the relatively quiet waters of the dredged channel. Under freshet conditions, vessels tend to sheer off course at the junction of the San Joaquin River and the main ship channel at Channel Point near Stockton.

(420) **Stockton**, 28 miles above Antioch Bridge, is in the center of the fertile San Joaquin Valley. The deep-draft harbor is near the W city limits.

Bridges

(421) A fixed highway bridge with a clearance of 45 feet at high water (50 feet at low water) crosses the upper Stockton channel 0.2 mile E of the turning basin.

Weather, Stockton

(422) Stockton, the county seat of San Joaquin County, is near the center of the great **Central Valley** of California, on the SE corner of the broad delta formed by the confluence of the San Joaquin and Sacramento Rivers. The surrounding terrain is flat, irrigated farm- and orchard-land, near sea level, with the rivers and canals of the delta controlled by a system of levees.

(423) About 25 miles (46 km) E and NE of Stockton lie the foothills of the Sierra Nevada, rising gradually to an elevation of about 1,000 feet (305 m). Beyond the foothills, the mountains rise abruptly to the crest of the Sierra, at a distance of about 75 miles (139 km), with some peaks here exceeding 9,000 feet (2745 m) in elevation. On a few days during the year, when atmospheric conditions are favorable, the "downslope" effect of a N or NE wind can bring unseasonably dry weather to the delta area; but on the whole the Sierra Nevada has little or no effect on the weather of San Joaquin County. The Sierra Nevada does affect the area, however, to the extent that the entire economy of the Central Valley depends upon the underground water supplies and rivers which are fed in summer by the melting snows which have piled up during the winter on the windward (W) slopes of the mountains.

(424) To the W and SW, the Coast Range, with peaks above 2,000 feet (610 m), form a barrier separating the Central Valley from the marine air, which dominates the climate of the coastal communities. Several gaps in the Coast Range in the San Francisco Bay Area, however, permit the passage inland of a sea breeze which fans out into the delta and has a moderating effect on summer heat, with the result that Stockton enjoys slightly cooler summer days than communities in the upper San Joaquin and Sacramento Valleys.

(425) Stockton's climate is characterized in summer by warm, dry days and relatively cool nights, with clear skies and no rainfall; and in winter by mild temperatures and relatively light rains, with frequent heavy fogs. The annual average temperature is 62°F (16.7°C) with an average daily maximum of 74°F (23.3°C) and an average daily minimum of 49°F (9.4°C).

(426) The annual rainfall averages between 13 and 14 inches (330 to 356 mm), with 90 percent of this precipitation falling in the winter-half year, i.e., November through April. Thunderstorms are infrequent, occurring on 3 or 4 days a year, generally in the spring, and occasionally in summer, although rainfall with summer thunderstorms is negligible. Measurable rain can be expected on about 52 days a year, and rain exceeding 0.5 inch (13 mm) on about 7 days a year. Since the Pacific storms that bring rainfall to this area are associated with above-freezing temperatures (>0°C) at sea-level elevations, snowfall is practically unknown in the Stockton area with trace amounts happening a few times and measurable snowfall happening only one time; February 1976.

(427) In summer, temperatures exceeding 100°F (37.8°C) can be expected on 6 days in July and about 14 days during the entire summer. During these hot afternoons the air is extremely dry, with relative humidities running generally less than 20 percent. Even on these hot days, however, temperatures will fall into the low sixties (16.1° to 17.2°C) at night. In winter the nighttime temperature on clear nights will fall to, or slightly below, freezing (0°C), and will rise in the afternoon into the low fifties (10.6° to 11.7°C). The all-time recorded maximum for Stockton is 114°F (45.5°C) recorded in July 1972 while the all-time minimum is 16°F (-8.9°C) recorded in January 1949. Each month, April through October, has recorded temperatures in excess of 100°F (37.8°C) while each month, November through April, has recorded temperatures of freezing (0°C) or lower.

(428) In late autumn and early winter, clear still nights give rise to the formation of dense fogs, which normally settle in during the night and burn off sometime during the day. In December and January, the so-called fog season, under stagnant atmospheric conditions the fog may last for as long a 4 or 5 weeks, with only brief and temporary periods of clearing.

Pilotage, San Joaquin River

(429) River pilots, commissioned by the Port of Stockton, are obtained by ship's agents, through the office of the Port of Stockton, or the San Francisco Bar Pilots.

Towage

(430) It has not been necessary for towage companies to operate at this port because all vessels operate under their own power; however, tugs up to 1,200 hp are available.

Quarantine, customs, immigration, and agricultural quarantine

(431) (See chapter 3, Vessel Arrival Inspections, and Appendix A for addresses.)

(432) **Quarantine** is enforced in accordance with regulations of the U.S. Public Health Service. (See Public Health Service, chapter 1.)

Wharves

(433) Deep-draft facilities at the Port of Stockton are on the S side of Stockton Deep Water Channel from the junction with the San Joaquin River E to the turning basin (East Complex). All facilities have highway connections and the facilities operated by the Port of Stockton are served by the port's beltline railroad, which connects with two major railroads. All facilities have water connections and most have electrical. Warehouse storage is available in the port for general merchandise and dry bulk materials. General cargo is usually handled by ship's tackle or by shore side traveling cranes; special handling equipment, if available, is listed under 'Mechanical Handling Facilities' in the table. Shore-based hoisting facilities with lifting capacities to 150 tons are

		Facilities in the Port of Stockton					
Name	Location	Berthing Space (feet)	Depths* (feet)	Deck Height (feet)	Mechanical Handling Facilities and Storage	Purpose	Owned/ Operated by:
Port of Stockton Wharves 12 and 13	37°57'02"N., 121°20'05"W.	843	40	13.4	• 130,000-ton Open storage area • Tank storage (19.2 million gallons) • Loading tower and belt conveyor system	• Shipment of miscellaneous dry bulk commodities (clay, sulphur, and petroleum coke) • Receipt and shipment of liquid fertilizer	Port of Stockton/ Metropolitan Stevedoring Co., Hydro Agri North America, Inc., Rice Terminals, Bay Sulfur Co.
Port of Stockton Wharves 10 and 11	37°57'05"N., 121°19'55"W.	1,011	35	15.5	• Open storage (18.5 acres) • Two 30-ton container cranes • Three 30-ton bridge cranes • One 150-ton crawler crane	• Receipt and shipment of conventional and containerized general cargo • Receipt and shipment of steel products and liquid fertilizer	Port of Stockton/ The Learner Co., Hydro Agri North America, Inc., Rice Terminals
Port of Stockton Wharf 9	37°57'06"N., 122°19'46"W.	645	35	15.5	• Covered storage (56,800 square feet) • Open storage (175 acres)	Receipt and shipment of conventional general cargo and miscellaneous dry bulk commodities	Port of Stockton
Port of Stockton Wharf 8	37°57'00"N., 121°19'30"W.	484	35	15.5	• Tank storage: (8 million gal. molasses) (14 million gal. ammonia) • Open storage (30,000 square feet) • Covered storage (36,150 square feet)	• Receipt and shipment of conventional general cargo • Reciept of molasses and anhydrous ammonia	Port of Stockton/ Brusco Tug & Barge, Inc., California Ammonia Co., Cargill Inc., PM Ag Products Inc.
Port of Stockton Wharf 7	37°57'07"N., 121°19'35"W.	516	35	15.5	Covered storage (25,100 square feet)	Receipt and shipment of conventional general cargo	Port of Stockton
Port of Stockton Wharf 6	37°57'06"N., 121°19'34"W.	418	35	15.5	Covered storage (17,650 square feet)	Receipt and shipment of conventional general cargo	Port of Stockton
Port of Stockton Wharf 5	37°57'06"N., 121°19'30"W.	429	35	15.5	Covered storage (41,000 square feet)	Receipt and shipment of conventional general cargo	Port of Stockton
Port of Stockton Wharf 4	37°57'07"N., 121°19'22"W.	461	35	15.5	• Covered storage (41,300 square feet) • Open storage (62,800 square feet)	• Receipt and shipment of conventional general cargo • Receipt of dry bulk fertilizer	Port of Stockton
Port of Stockton Wharf 3	37°57'07"N., 121°19'16"W.	461	35	15.5	• Covered storage (30,000 square feet) • One 30-ton container crane • Belt-conveyor system	• Receipt and shipment of miscellaneous dry bulk material • Receipt of dry bulk fertilizer and cement	Port of Stockton/ Viridian Fertilizer Inc., Calaveras Cement Co.
Port of Stockton Wharf 2	37°57'05"N., 121°19'12"W.	585	35	15.5	• Covered storage (75,000 tons) • Open storage (175 acres) • Two 30-ton gantry cranes	• Receipt and shipment of miscellaneous dry bulk material • Receipt of dry bulk fertilizer and cement	Port of Stockton/ Viridian Fertilizer Inc., Calaveras Cement Co.
Continental Grain Corp. Stockton Elevator Wharf	37°57'04"N., 121°18'59"W.	564	37	15.5	• Covered storage (6.8 million bushels) • Two grain towers with loading spouts (1,000 tons per hour)	Shipment and occasional receipt of grain	Continental Grain Corperation

* The depths given above are reported. For information on the latest depths contact the port authorities or the private operators.

available. Additional rental cranes are available locally. Floating cranes for heavy lifts are available at Alameda. Depths alongside are reported; for information on the latest depths contact the Stockton Port District. Only the deep-draft facilities are listed in the table. For a complete description of the port facilities refer to Port Series No. 32, published and sold by the U.S. Army Corps of Engineers. (See Appendix A for address.)

Supplies

(434) Supplies may be had in any quantity, and water is piped to the wharves. Ships may fuel from barges; alongside bunkering of large vessels may be done at the oil terminals in San Pablo Bay and Carquinez Strait.

Repairs

(435) Some dockside facilities are available here, but major repairs to oceangoing vessels must be done at the drydocks in San Francisco, Oakland, Alameda, and Richmond. Several facilities make repairs to small craft; marine railways up to 200–ton capacity are available.

Small-craft facilities

(436) Several small-craft facilities are at Stockton or nearby.

San Joaquin River above Stockton

(437) From its junction with Stockton Channel, the river has a controlling depth of about 3 feet for 70 miles to

Hills Ferry, and is used only by small pleasure craft, fishermen, and an occasional small barge. The only facilities available are those dispensing gasoline, lubricants, and water at a few points.

Bridges

(438) More than 15 bridges cross San Joaquin River between Stockton and Hills Ferry. The minimum clearance for bridges crossing the river between Stockton and Mossdale, about 13 miles above Stockton, is 17 feet. (See **117.1 through 117.59 and 117.191**, chapter 2, for drawbridge regulations.)

Charts 18661, 18662

(439) The principal tributaries of the San Joaquin River are described as the river is ascended. Bridge clearances are at low water. (See **117.1 through 117.59, 117.143, 117.150, 117.157, 117.159, 117.161, 117.167, 117.171, 117.175, and 117.183**, chapter 2, for drawbridge regulations.)

(440) **Threemile Slough**, meets the San Joaquin River 5.8 miles above Antioch Bridge and joins the Sacramento River at the N end of Decker Island. The slough is a route frequently used by tugs and barges making passage between Sacramento and Stockton. Near the junction with the Sacramento River is a highway lift bridge with clearances of 16 feet down and 110 feet up at low water. The bridgetender monitors VHF-FM channel 16 and works on channel 9; call sign KMJ–385, Threemile Slough Bridge. (See **117.1 through 117.49**, chapter 2, for drawbridge regulations.) The power cable E of the bridge has a clearance of 108 feet.

Anchorage

(441) A **restricted anchorage area** is along the E side of **Decker Island**. (See **162.205**, chapter 2, for limits and regulations.)

(442) **Mokelumne River**, one of the principal tributaries of the San Joaquin River, rises in the Sierra Nevada and empties into it 11.8 miles above Antioch Bridge. The river separates, 3.5 miles above its mouth, into two branches, the **North Mokelumne River (North Fork)** and the **South Mokelumne River (South Fork)** The branches continue in a N direction and rejoin 9 miles NNE from the mouth. The river then describes a semicircular route for 7 miles to the N and E to the head of navigation at the Galt-New Hope Bridge.

(443) Corps of Engineers project maps for 1978 show the following controlling depths for Mokelumne River: 12 feet from the mouth to the lower junction of the North and South Mokelumne Rivers, thence 7 feet by North Mokelumne River to Snodgrass Slough; thence 2 feet to upper junction of the North and South Mokelumne Rivers; 7 feet from the lower junction by South Mokelumne River to the upper junction; and thence 2 feet to the Galt–New Hope bridge. Mokelumne River is subject to shoaling; local knowledge is advised.

(444) **Little Potato Slough** (38°06'00"N., 121°29'30"W.) enters the South Fork of the Mokelumne River about 6 miles E of the confluence of the north and south forks and connects the river with other tributaries of the San Joaquin River.

(445) **Georgiana Slough** enters Mokelumne River about 3 miles above the mouth, and connects that river with the Sacramento River at Walnut Grove. The controlling depth through the slough is about 13 feet. Tugs and barges formerly used the slough in making the run from Sacramento to Stockton, but to avoid the snags and sharp turns they now favor the route through Threemile Slough.

(446) **Old River** flows into the San Joaquin River about 13 miles above the Antioch Bridge after diverging from the latter river about 38 miles above the bridge. It is the most W branch of the interconnecting tidal channels into which San Joaquin River divides in crossing its delta. Old River has many sloughs and canals that connect with Middle River to the E.

(447) In 1978, the controlling depths in Old River were: 10 feet for 10 miles from the mouth to Orwood; thence 10 feet for 9 miles to the lower end of Grant Line Canal; thence 7 feet for 9 miles to the Holly Sugar Factory near Tracy; and from the other end of Grant Line Canal to the head of Old River in San Joaquin River, 5 feet.

(448) The Holly Sugar Co. refinery and terminal near Tracy has a large wharf and an unloading basin; a passing basin is about 0.5 mile downstream from the terminal.

(449) **Middle River** enters the San Joaquin River 15.3 miles above Antioch Bridge. The river and connecting channels are a part of a complicated network of tidal canals, some natural and some artificial, in the delta of the San Joaquin River. One of the principal channels, Middle River leaves Old River at the SW corner of Roberts Island about 7 miles SSW of Stockton and roughly parallels Old River to the San Joaquin River.

(450) The controlling depth in Middle River is about 6 feet to the Bacon Island swing bridge, about 15.5 miles below the junction with Old River. The channel is not maintained above the bridge, and navigation is obstructed by many snags and shoals.

Cable ferry

(451) Woodward Island Ferry crosses Middle River about 12.5 miles below the junction with Old River. The ferry carries passengers and vehicles, and operates from 0800 to 1700 daily. White warning signs, with black letters and orange borders, are posted about 500 feet on either side of the ferry crossing. Flashing red beacons are shown by the ferry when underway. When the ferry is underway, the cables are 6 to 7 feet above the water surface; when docked, the cables are on or within 1 or 2 feet of the bottom. **DO NOT ATTEMPT TO PASS A MOVING CABLE FERRY.**

Structures Across the Sacramento Deep Water Ship Channel, Sacramento River and its Principal Tributaries

Name·Description·Type	Location	Clear Width of Draw or Span Opening (feet)	Clear Height above Water Datum (feet) Low	Clear Height above Water Datum (feet) High	Information
Sacramento River					
Overhead power cable	38°03'55"N., 121°47'09"W.			125	
Overhead power cable	38°04'56"N., 121°45'10"W.			140	
Overhead power cable	38°05'07"N., 121°44'45"W.			130	Clearance of 160 feet over ship channel
Rio Vista/State Highway 12 Vertical Lift Bridge (highway)	38°09'31"N., 121°40'57"W.	270	22 (down) 149 (up)	18 (down) 144 (up)	Bridgetender monitors VHF-FM channel 16 and works on channels 9 and 13; call sign KMJ-384, Rio Vista Bridge. **(Note 1)**
Overhead power cable	38°10'04"N., 121°37'43"W.			125	
Overhead power cable	38°09'52"N., 121°37'16"W.			125	
Isleton Bascule Bridge (highway)	38°10'19"N., 121°35'38"W.	200 (166 open)	18	15	Bridgetender monitors VHF-FM channel 16 and works on channel 9; call sign KMJ-383, Isleton Bridge. **(Note 2)**
Walnut Grove Bascule Bridge (highway)	38°14'33"N., 121°30'53"W.	199 (187 open)	24	21	Bridgetender monitors VHF-FM channel 16 and works on channel 9; call sign KMJ-491, Walnut Grove Bridge. **(Note 2)**
Overhead power cable	38°17'34"N., 121°33'45"W.			110	
Paintersville Bascule Bridge (highway)	38°19'07"N., 121°34'40"W.	198	27	24	Bridgetender monitors VHF-FM channel 16 and works on channel 9; call sign KMJ-381, Paintersville Bridge. **(Note 2)**
Overhead power cable	38°20'45"N., 121°32'56"W.			125	
Freeport Bascule Bridge (highway)	38°27'21"N., 121°30'07"W.	199 (190 open)	32	29	Bridgetender monitors VHF-FM channel 16 and works on channel 9; call sign KMJ-490, Freeport Bridge. **(Note 2)**
Overhead power cable	38°28'02"N., 121°30'17"W.			125	
Interstate 80 Fixed Bridges	38°34'18"N., 121°30'57"W.	214	84	81	
Tower Vertical Lift Bridge (highway)	38°34'50"N., 121°30'30"W.	170	32 (down) 98 (up)	30 (down) 96 (up)	Bridgetender monitors VHF-FM channel 16 and works on channel 9; call sign KDO-739, Tower Bridge. **(Notes 2 and 7)**
I Street Swing Bridge (highway & railway)	38°35'11"N., 121°30'23"W.	148	32	30	**(Note 2)**
Overhead power cable	38°35'11"N., 121°30'23"W.			80 (east draw) 74 (west draw)	Clearances reference the draws of the I Street Swing Bridge
Junction with American River	38°35'50"N., 121°30'32"W.				
Overhead power cable	38°35'33"N., 121°30'28"W.			125	
Interstate 80 Fixed Bridges	38°35'54"N., 121°32'53"W.	250	85	82	
Overhead power cable	38°35'58"N., 121°33'00"W.			80	
Interstate 5 Fixed Bridges	38°40'24"N., 121°37'35"W.	175	84	55	
Overhead power cable	38°47'00"N., 121°37'06"W.			125	
Junction with Feather River	38°47'06"N., 121°37'16"W.				
Overhead power cables	38°45'49"N., 121°41'00"W.			80	
Overhead power cables	38°45'49"N., 121°41'15"W.			125	
State Highway 113/Knights Landing Bascule Bridge	38°48'08"N., 121°43'12"W.	199 (160 open)	23		**(Note 2)**
Overhead power cables	38°48'13"N., 121°43'23"W.			125	
Overhead power cable	38°49'09"N., 121°43'27"W.			124	
Overhead power cable	38°51'34"N., 121°43'52"W.			125	
Overhead power cable	38°51'35"N., 121°43'52"W.			125	
Overhead power cable	38°53'58"N., 121°48'12"W.			80	
Overhead power cable	39°00'51"N., 121°49'32"W.			125	
Overhead power cable	39°02'27"N., 121°50'02"W.			80	
Overhead power cable	39°04'00"N., 121°52'13"W.			125	
Overhead power cable	39°04'25"N., 121°53'26"W.			60	
Meridian/State Highway 20 Swing Bridge	39°08'44"N., 121°55'04"W.	143	39	10	**(Note 2)**
Overhead power cable	39°08'45"N., 121°55'04"W.			120	
Overhead power cable	39°10'12"N., 121°56'15"W.			106	

Structures Across the Sacramento Deep Water Ship Channel, Sacramento River and its Principal Tributaries					
Name·Description·Type	Location	Clear Width of Draw or Span Opening (feet)	Clear Height above Water Datum (feet)		Information
			Low	High	
River Road Bridge (removable span)	39°12'51"N., 122°00'02"W.	100	32		Vertical clearance is 6 feet (25 feet when raised) above flood level. **(Note 2)**
Overhead telephone cable	39°12'52"N., 121°00'04"W.			75	
Overhead power cable	39°12'53"N., 121°00'07"W.			75	
Sacramento Deep Water Ship Channel at Cache Slough					
Overhead power cable	38°11'16"N., 121°39'36"W.			137	
Overhead power cable	38°15'58"N., 121°39'52"W.			140	
Overhead power cable	38°19'17"N., 121°39'02"W.			140	
Overhead power cable	38°28'26"N., 121°35'01"W.			140	
Overhead power cable	38°33'08"N., 121°34'43"W.			140	
Overhead power cable	38°33'40"N., 121°33'33"W.			140	
Industrial Boulevard Fixed Bridge	38°33'41"N., 121°32'20"W.	130	32	29	
Jefferson Boulevard Bascule Bridge (highway/railway)	38°33'41"N., 121°31'43"W.	86 (73 open)	20	17	
Steamboat Slough					
Overhead power cable	38°13'49"N., 121°36'09"W.			125	
Steamboat Slough Bascule Bridge	38°18'17"N., 121°34'28"W.	200 (184 open)	24	21	Bridgetender monitors VHF-FM channel 16 and works on channel 9; call sign WHX-295, Steamboat Slough Bridge. **(Note 3)**
Lindsey Slough					
Hastings Farm Highway Bridge (removable span)	38°14'49"N., 121°52'09"W.	53	22	19	**(Note 4)**
Overhead power cable	38°14'51"N., 121°42'24"W.			110	
Overhead power cable	38°15'30"N., 121°43'37"W.			85	
Miner Slough					
Overhead power cable	38°15'56"N., 121°38'37"W.			114	
State Route 84 Swing Bridge	38°17'32"N., 121°37'51"W.	72	21	17	**(Note 5)**
Overhead power cable	38°17'12"N., 121°36'27"W.			110	
Sutter Slough					
Overhead power cable	38°16'00"N., 121°36'08"W.			93	
Overhead power cable	38°19'44"N., 121°34'42"W.			93	
State Route 160 Swing Bridge	38°19'40"N., 121°34'35"W.	75	22	19	**(Note 6)**

Note 1 – See **117.1 through 117.59**, chapter 2 for limits and regulations
Note 2 – See **117.1 through 117.59 and 117.189**, chapter 2 for limits and regulations
Note 3 – See **117.1 through 117.59 and 117.199**, chapter 2 for limits and regulations
Note 4 – See **117.1 through 117.59 and 117.165**, chapter 2 for limits and regulations
Note 5 – See **117.1 through 117.59 and 117.173**, chapter 2 for limits and regulations
Note 6 – See **117.1 through 117.59 and 117.201**, chapter 2 for limits and regulations
Note 7 – The decorative lighting on the bridge will be extinguished upon request of the mariner.

(452) **Empire Cut** enters Middle River about 16.5 miles below the latter's junction with Old River.

Cable ferries

(453) Mildred Island Ferry crosses Empire Cut about 0.6 mile E of the junction with Middle River. This private cable ferry carries passengers, vehicles and farm equipment, and operates during daylight hours. When the ferry is underway, the cables are suspended at an unknown depth below the water surface; when docked, the cables are dropped to the bottom. A sign on each side of the ferry warns of the cables; a flashing red signal is shown when underway. **DO NOT ATTEMPT TO PASS A MOVING CABLE FERRY.**

(454) Gasoline and fishing supplies may be obtained at the town of **Middle River**, about 8.5 miles above the mouth.

(455) **Little Connection Slough** enters the San Joaquin River about 1 mile above the mouth of Middle River.

Cable ferry

(456) Venice Island Ferry crosses Little Connection Slough about 1 mile above the entrance. The ferry carries passengers and vehicles and operates from 0800 to 1700 daily. White warning signs, with black letters and orange borders, are posted about 500 feet on either side

of the ferry crossing. Flashing red beacons are shown by the ferry when underway. When the ferry is underway, the cables are 6 to 7 feet above the water surface; when docked, the cables are dropped to the bottom. **DO NOT ATTEMPT TO PASS A MOVING CABLE FERRY.**

(457) **Turner Cut** enters the San Joaquin River about 7.5 miles below Stockton and is crossed about 2 miles above the entrance by a highway bridge with a 30-foot retractable span. The bridge is normally maintained in the open position except when it is being crossed by a vehicle.

(458) **Sacramento River** rises in the Trinity Mountains in N central California, flows S for 325 miles, and enters Suisun Bay on the N side of **Sherman Island**. Deep-draft vessels follow the lower Sacramento River to **Cache Slough**, 1.5 miles above Rio Vista Bridge, thence through a deepwater ship channel to Sacramento, a distance of 37 miles above the mouth of the river. Barges and other small craft also use Sacramento River all the way to Sacramento, a distance of 50 miles. Above Sacramento, small craft go to Colusa, 125 miles above the mouth, but there is no regular navigation above this point.

Cable ferry

(459) **Steamboat Slough** enters Cache Slough about 1.8 miles above Rio Vista bridge. A cable ferry crosses the Steamboat Slough about 5 miles above the junction with Cache Slough. The ferry carries passengers and vehicles, and operates 24 hours daily. When the ferry is underway, the cable is suspended below the water surface at varying depths. When the ferry is docked, the cable is about 5 feet below the surface of the water. Warning signs are posted at the crossing. When underway, the ferry shows flashing red lights. **DO NOT ATTEMPT TO PASS A MOVING CABLE FERRY.**

Channels

(460) **Sacramento River Deep Water Ship Channel** extends from Suisun Bay through lower Sacramento River, Cache Slough, and a 22-mile land cut to a triangular harbor and turning basin at the Port of Sacramento. The **William G. Stone Lock** is on the barge canal that once connected the Deep Water Ship Channel with the Sacramento River; the lock is closed to all navigation.

(461) The project depth in the ship channel is generally maintained. (See Notice to Mariners and latest editions of charts for controlling depths.) The controlling depth in the river route is about 10 feet. Above Sacramento, the controlling depth is about 6 feet to Colusa. The sounding datum is **mean lower low water at low-river stage.**

(462) Numerous uncharted piles, snags, pumps, and pipes, some submerged, may exist along the edges of the river. Mariners are advised to exercise extreme caution while navigating close to the banks of the river.

Currents

(463) Currents in Sacramento River depend on the river stage. During high-river stages, there is little or no flood current and the ebb current is strong to Sacramento. During the dry season a flood current can be carried to Paintersville and from there slack water to Freeport, 30 and 41 miles above the mouth, respectively. At times of extreme low-river stages, flood current may be evident as far as Sacramento. Local knowledge is required to estimate current conditions for a particular time.

(464) Major floods in the Sacramento River valley usually occur from November to April and are generally caused by intense general storms of several days' duration, the runoff from which may be augmented by the melting of snow in the mountains. At the mouth of the river an ordinary flood will cause a rise of 8 feet and an extreme flood a rise of 10 feet in the river level. At Sacramento, ordinary flood will cause a rise in the river level of 20 feet and extreme flood, a rise of 30 feet.

(465) Reports of gage heights of the Sacramento River can be obtained from the Sacramento National Weather Service Office at any time of the year. The information is published in the **Sacramento Bee** and, in addition, is reported on the radio broadcast from station KFBK (1530 kHz) whenever the gage heights are of sufficient magnitude to be of general interest. Information on gage heights can also be obtained from the State Department of Water Resources, 901 "P" Street, Sacramento, CA 95814 or by recorded message at 916–651–0725.

(466) The upper 20 miles of Sacramento River Deep Water Ship Channel are free of river current and flood waters. However, the area is still affected by tidal currents.

Weather, Sacramento Valley

(467) The climate of the lower Sacramento Valley is mild, with plenty of sunshine year round. Cloudless skies prevail during the spring, summer, and fall. Winter is the rainy season, with measurable amounts falling on about 10 days per month. Snow is rare, since freezing temperatures are rare. The valley is protected from most severe winter storms by the mountains to the W, N, and E. Sometimes, torrential rains on the slopes can cause flooding along the Sacramento River. The average annual precipitation for the Sacramento Airport is about 17.5 inches (445 mm) with about 90% of this amount falling from November through April.

(468) The mountains are responsible for the predominantly S winds throughout the valley. These are oceanic winds that have moved through the Carquinez Strait and been turned N by the Sierra ranges. At the port of Sacramento, SE through SW winds prevail, particularly during spring and summer. NW through N winds are also frequent, and bring warm, dry air down the mountains. These winds cause brief heat waves, with temperatures rising to over 100°F (37.8°C) in summer, and they modify cool weather in winter. Strongest winds occur in winter although gales occur less than 1 percent of the time, even in midwinter. Winds of 17 to 28 knots occur

6 to 10 percent of the time from December through March, and less than 5 percent of the time during July, August, and September. Extreme winds have reached 60 knots, with gusts of more than 70 knots; these are most likely during fall or winter.

(469) Dense fog is common in winter, infrequent during spring and fall, and rare in summer. It is a radiation type fog that occurs during the late night and early morning hours. It usually clears by noon. Occasionally stagnant weather conditions will cause the fog to hang on for a few days. Visibilities at Sacramento drop below 0.5 mile (0.9 km) on about 5 to 10 nights per month, from November through February. During this same period, they fall below 7 miles (13 km) on about 10 to 20 occasions per month. During the summer, visibilities are almost always better than 7 miles (13 km). Twenty-two out of 31 days during each month, December and January, can expect fog. This number drops to less than one day for both June and July.

Routes

(470) The deep-draft channel to the Port of Sacramento through Sacramento River Deep Water Ship Channel is marked with navigational aids.

(471) The shallow-draft route continues in Sacramento River from 1.5 miles above the Rio Vista Lift Bridge to Sacramento, and for the most part is marked by leading lights.

(472) From Ida Island for a distance of 3.5 miles upstream there are shifting shoals. After passing Ida Island work gradually over to the W half of the channel and favor that side around the next bend. From this point to Clarksburg the channel is clear, and midchannel courses may be followed favoring the falling tide bends. At Clarksburg favor the E shore a little until just past the town, then swing into midchannel again. From just below Freeport the channel is rather shoal and wing dams have been built at several places to scour out the channel. These are covered at high-water stages and may be struck if the shore is approached too closely. By favoring the ebbtide bends no trouble should be encountered from here to Sacramento.

(473) **NOTE:** Care should be exercised at all times to keep clear of the levees, as most of them are faced with rock which may damage vessels that drag along them.

Pilotage, Sacramento River

(474) River pilots, commissioned by the Port of Sacramento, are arranged for by the ship's agents, but may be obtained through the office of the port of Sacramento or the San Francisco Bar Pilots

Towage

(475) Tugs up to 1,500 hp are available.

Chart 18661

(476) **Rio Vista**, on the NW bank, 10.5 miles above the mouth of the Sacramento River, is commercially the most important town below Sacramento. The **Rio Vista Coast Guard Station** is just S of the town. A small-craft harbor on the S side of the town has gasoline, diesel fuel, water, and berths available. A 20 ton lift here can handle craft up to 40 feet for hull and engine repairs. A large dredging facility is on the NW side of the river just N of the Rio Vista Bridge.

(477) **Ida Island**, on the S bank 13.5 miles above the mouth of the river, is the site of a resort and small-boat basin. Gasoline, water, and moorage are available. A full marine service with marine railway can handle vessels up to 40 feet.

(478) **Isleton**, on the S bank 15 miles above the mouth of the river, has a 140-foot public landing. Gasoline, diesel fuel, and some supplies are available in town. A large grain elevator is on the SE side of the river, 0.75 mile above Isleton.

Chart 18662

(479) **Walnut Grove**, 24 miles above the mouth of Sacramento River, is at the junction with Georgiana Slough. Gasoline, and marine supplies may be obtained in moderate quantities. A wharf and a large wooden shed are on the E side of the river 1.2 miles above Walnut Grove; gasoline and some repair work is available. A **measured nautical mile** along the NE side of the river begins 1.2 miles above Walnut Grove. A resort is at the junction of Steamboat Slough with the river. Gasoline and water are available. Five miles above Walnut Grove at the small village of **Paintersville**, a highway bridge with a double-bascule span across the river has a clearance of 24 feet. (See **117.1 through 117.59 and 117.189**, chapter 2, for drawbridge regulations.) The bridgetender monitors VHF-FM channel 16 and works on channel 9; call sign: KMJ–381, Paintersville Bridge.

(480) **Courtland**, 31 miles above the mouth of the river, has supplies in moderate quantities; gasoline, oil, water, and ice are available.

(481) At **Clarksburg**, 37.5 miles above the mouth of the river, there are two abandoned oil company landings.

(482) **Freeport**, 41.5 miles above the mouth of the river, has gasoline. A water intake facility at 38°28'21"N., 121°30'24"W. is marked by four private white lights.

(483) A paved highway between Antioch and Sacramento runs along the levee of the river for nearly its entire distance.

(484) **Sacramento** the State capital, is the head of navigation for most of the shipping on the river, and is a distribution and transportation center for N California and parts of Nevada and Oregon. The **Port of Sacramento**, 79 miles above the Golden Gate Bridge and at the head of the deepwater channel, is an important point for

interchange of cargo between rail, highway, and water transportation. The port has a 124 metric ton capacity mobile harbor crane that will handle container cargo.

Weather, Sacramento

(485) The lower Sacramento Valley, where Sacramento is located, enjoys a mild climate and abundance of sunshine throughout the year. Cloudless skies prevail during the summer and largely in the spring and autumn. The summers are remarkably dry, with warm days and pleasant nights. In the winter "rainy season" (December, January, and February) over one-half of the total annual precipitation falls, yet rain in measurable amounts occurs only on about 10 days monthly during winter. Snow is rare since freezing temperatures are rare, with trace amounts falling several times and measurable snowfall having fallen on only one occasion, two inches (51 mm) in February 1976. Mountains surround the valley to the W, N, and E. The Sierra Nevada snow fields are only 70 miles E of Sacramento and usually provide a plentiful supply of water in the valley streams during the dry season. Because of the shielding influence of the high mountains around the valley, winter storms reach valley districts in modified form. However, torrential rain and heavy snow frequently fall on the western Sierra slopes, the southern Cascades, and to a lesser extent the Coastal Range. As a result, flood conditions occasionally occur along the Sacramento River and its tributaries. Excessive rainfall and damaging windstorms are rare in the valley. The average annual precipitation for the Sacramento Airport is about 17.5 inches (445 mm) with about 90% of this amount falling from November through April.

(486) Prevailing winds at Sacramento are S all year, due to the N-S direction of the valley and the deflecting effect of the towering Sierra Ranges on the prevailing oceanic winds that move through the Carquinez Strait at the junction of the Sacramento and San Joaquin Rivers. No other tidewater gap exists in the coastal mountains to admit marine air into the Sacramento or the San Joaquin Valley. Occasionally a steep northerly barometric pressure gradient develops and air is forced over the Siskiyou Mountains to the N, warmed dynamically with descent, and reaches the valley floor as a warm, dry, N wind. These occasionally disagreeable winds, known as "northers" in the valley, are the counterpart of the well-known "chinook" winds of the Rocky Mountains, and they, or modifications of them, produce the pronounced heat waves in summer. Fortunately, they are of infrequent occurrence and produce an unstable atmospheric condition that is usually followed within 2 or 3 days by the normally cool S breezes, especially at night. Summer nights in the lower Sacramento Valley are, with few exceptions, cool and invigorating, the result of a prevailing oceanic influence. While it is true that "northers" cause dry, hot weather for brief periods during the summer, it is equally true they are the modifications of cold waves in the winter. Winter northers, with only a few exceptions, are comparatively warm, drying winds. The average annual temperature for Sacramento is 61°F (16.1°C) with an average maximum of 74°F (23.3°C) and an average minimum of 48°F (8.9°C). The all-time maximum occurred in June 1961 when the mercury climbed to 115°F (46.1°C). The all-time minimum of 18°F (-7.8°C) was recorded in December 1990. Each month, May through October, has seen temperatures in excess of 100°F (37.8°C) while every month, November through April, has recorded temperatures at or below freezing (0°C).

(487) The average annual thunderstorm occurrence is three. They are usually mild and are most likely in February and March. However, they have been documented in each of the twelve months. Snow falls so rarely, and in such small amounts, that its occurrence may be disregarded as a climatic feature. Heavy fog occurs mostly in midwinter, rarely in summer, and seldom in spring or autumn. Light and moderate fog are more frequent and may come anytime during the wet, cold season. The fog is usually the radiational cooling type, and confined to the early morning hours. An occasional winter fog, under stagnant atmospheric conditions, may continue for several days.

(488) (See Appendix B for **Sacramento climatological table**.)

Pilotage, Sacramento

(489) See Pilotage, Sacramento River, indexed as such, earlier in this chapter.

Towage

(490) Tugs up to 1,500 hp are available.

Quarantine, customs, immigration, and agricultural quarantine

(491) (See chapter 3, Vessel Arrival Inspections, and Appendix A for addresses.)

(492) **Quarantine** is enforced in accordance with regulations of the U.S. Public Health Service. (See Public Health Service, chapter 1.)

Coast Guard

(493) **Sacramento Coast Guard Air Station** is NE of Sacramento at McClellan Air Force Base.

Harbor regulations

(494) Copies of the harbor regulations are available from the Port of Sacramento located at 1110 West Capital Avenue, West Sacramento, CA 95691.

(495) The port radio station KPB–386 VHF-FM channel 18A is monitored 24 hours a day.

Wharves

(496) The deepwater facilities of the Port of Sacramento consist of six berths, each of which has a berthing length of at least 600 feet with a deck height of 19 feet and

		Facilities in the Port of Sacramento					
Name	Location	Berthing Space (feet)	Depths* (feet)	Deck Height (feet)	Mechanical Handling Facilities and Storage	Purpose	Owned/ Operated by:
Port of Sacramento Berth 8	38°33'56"N., 121°33'04"W.	840	35	19	• Covered storage (308,000 square feet) • Open storage (27.3 acres)	Shipment of miscellaneous dry bulk commodities	Port of Sacramento
Port of Sacramento Berth 7	38°33'53"N., 121°32'58"W.	840	35	19	Covered storage (86,400 square feet)	Receipt and shipment of general cargo	Port of Sacramento
Port of Sacramento Berth 6	38°33'50"N., 121°32'54"W.	600	35	19	Open storage (6 acres)	Receipt and shipment of general cargo and miscellaneous dry bulk	Port of Sacramento
Port of Sacramento Berth 5	38°33'46"N., 121°32'48"W.	600	35	19	• Silo storage (1.2 million bushels) • Vessel loading spouts	Shipment of grain, feed pellets, miscellaneous dry and liquid bulk	Port of Sacramento/ Cargill, Inc.
Port of Sacramento Berth 2	38°33'42"N., 121°32'38"W.	600	35	19	Covered storage (86,400 square feet)	Receipt and shipment of general cargo	Port of Sacramento
Port of Sacramento Berth 1	38°33'42"N., 121°32'31"W.	613	35	19	• Silo storage (21,500 tons) • Vessel loading spouts	Receipt and shipment of bulk rice	Port of Sacramento

* The depths given above are reported. For information on the latest depths contact the port authorities or the private operators.

reported depths alongside of 35 feet. All berths are served by railroad and highway connections, and all berths have water and electrical shore power connections. General cargo at the port is usually handled by ship's tackle; mechanical handling equipment, if available, is mentioned in the facilities table. All of these facilities are owned and most are operated by the Sacramento-Yolo Port District. For a complete description of the port facilities refer to Port Series No. 32 published and sold by the U.S. Army Corps of Engineers. (See Appendix A for address.) or visit the website http://www.portofsacramento.com for additional information.

Supplies

(497) Provisions are available in any quantity. Some marine supplies may be obtained. Fuel oil may be obtained by tank truck or barge. Ships do not normally take on fuel or provisions in Sacramento.

Repairs

(498) There are no repair facilities for large oceangoing vessels in Sacramento; the nearest shipyards with large drydocks are at Richmond, Oakland, Alameda, and San Francisco.

Small-craft facilities

(499) There are several small-craft facilities along the Sacramento River at Sacramento. (See the small-craft facilities tabulation on chart 18662 for services and supplies available.) Mariners are advised that there are no facilities serving small craft along the Sacramento Deep Water Ship Channel and at the Port of Sacramento. Once at the head of navigation on the channel, there is no way to pass through the locks to the Sacramento River.

Communications

(500) Sacramento is served by four railroads, several highways, and two airports.

Chart 18664, 18667

(501) Above Sacramento the prevailing flood conditions are as follows: At Verona at the junction of Feather River, 70 miles above the mouth, 20 feet at ordinary floods and 24 feet at extreme floods; at Colusa, 125 miles above the mouth, 25 feet at ordinary floods and 32 feet at extreme floods.

(502) Between Sacramento and Colusa are numerous warehouses and small landings.

(503) **Feather River** rises in the Sierra Nevada and empties into Sacramento River at **Verona**, 18 miles above Sacramento. The river has been improved by snagging and the construction of wing dams at **Marysville**, 26 miles above the mouth. The controlling depth is usually 3 feet from about February 15 to June 15. Ordinary flood fluctuation is 20 feet, and extreme flood fluctuation is about 25 feet. With the exception of several small privately owned landings, all loading is handled on the banks. There has been no commercial navigation on the Feather River in recent years.

Chart 18665

(504) **Lake Tahoe** (39°06'N., 120°00'W.), California-Nevada, is a recreation area almost surrounded by Tahoe, Toiyabe, and Eldorado National Forests. **Restricted areas** established by Federal regulations are given in **162.210 and 162.215**, chapter 2. Lake Tahoe is to be navigated by leaving all red buoys to starboard when transiting in a counterclockwise direction. Safe water will always be found toward the center of the lake from red federal buoys. Information about facilities may be

obtained from one of the local offices of the Forest Service, U.S. Department of Agriculture.

Coast Guard

(505) **Lake Tahoe Coast Guard Station** is on the W shore of the lake about 1.2 miles NE of Tahoe City.

TIDAL INFORMATION					
Chart	Station	LAT/LONG	Mean Higher High Water*	Mean High Water*	Mean Low Water*
18645	Princeton, Half Moon Bay	37°30'N/122°29'W	5.5	4.9	1.1
18645	Southeast Farallon Island	37°42'N/123°00'W	5.6	4.9	1.1
18647	Point Reyes, Drakes Bay	38°00'N/122°59'W	5.8	5.1	1.2
18649	Oakland Inner Harbor, San Francisco Bay	37°48'N/122°17'W	6.5	5.8	1.1
18649	Point Orient, San Francisco Bay	37°58'N/122°26'W	6.0	5.4	1.1
18649	Hunters Point, San Francisco Bay	37°44'N/122°21'W	6.8	6.2	1.1
18649	Yerba Buena Island, San Francisco Bay	37°49'N/122°22'W	6.2	5.5	1.1
18650	San Leandro Channel, San Francisco Bay	37°42'N/122°12'W	7.2	6.6	1.1
18650	San Francisco (Golden Gate)	37°48'N/122°28'W	5.8	5.2	1.1
18650	Rincon Point, Pier 22 1/2, San Francisco Bay	37°47'N/122°23'W	6.3	5.7	1.1
18650	Alameda (Naval Air Station), San Francisco Bay	37°46'N/122°18'W	6.6	5.8	1.1
18650	Alcatraz Island, San Francisco Bay	37°50'N/122°25'W	5.8	5.2	1.1
18650	Oakland Middle Harbor, Pier 40	37°48'N/122°20'W	6.2	5.6	1.1
18651	San Mateo Bridge (east end)	37°37'N/122°11'W	7.7	7.1	1.2
18651	San Mateo Bridge (west end)	37°35'N/122°15'W	7.7	7.1	1.2
18651	Dumbarton Highway Bridge, San Francisco Bay	37°30'N/122°07'W	8.5	7.9	1.2
18651	Mud Slough Railroad Bridge, San Francisco Bay	37°28'N/121°59'W	7.5	6.9	0.5
18651	Redwood City, Wharf 5, San Francisco Bay	37°30'N/122°13'W	8.2	7.6	1.2
18652	Oyster Point Marina, San Francisco Bay	37°40'N/122°23'W	7.1	6.4	1.1
18652	Petaluma River entrance, San Pablo Bay	38°07'N/122°30'W	6.1	5.6	1.0
18653	Sausalito, San Francisco Bay	37°51'N/122°29'W	5.7	5.1	1.1
18653	Berkeley, San Francisco Bay	37°52'N/122°18'W	5.9	5.3	1.1
18653	Angel Island (west side), San Francisco Bay	37°52'N/122°27'W	5.6	5.0	1.1
18653	Angel Island, East Garrison, San Francisco Bay	37°52'N/122°25'W	5.9	5.3	1.2
18653	Point Chauncey, San Francisco Bay	37°54'N/122°27'W	5.7	5.1	1.1
18653	Richmond Inner Harbor, San Francisco Bay	37°55'N/122°21'W	6.0	5.4	1.1
18653	Point San Quentin, San Francisco Bay	37°57'N/122°29'W	5.8	5.2	1.1
18654	Hercules, Refugio Landing, San Pablo Bay	38°01'N/122°18'W	6.1	5.5	1.0
18654	Mare Island, Carquinez Strait	38°04'N/122°15'W	5.8	5.2	0.9
18654	Sonoma Creek, San Pablo Bay	38°09'N/122°24'W	5.6	5.0	0.8
18655	Selby, Carquinez Strait	38°03'N/122°15'W	6.3	5.8	1.1
18655	Crockett, Carquinez Strait	38°04'N/122°13'W	5.9	5.4	1.0
18655	Mare Island Strait, San Francisco Bay	38°07'N/122°16'W	5.9	5.4	0.9
18656	Suisun City (Suisun Slough)	38°14'N/122°02'W	5.4	4.9	0.7
18656	Suisun Slough entrance	38°07'N/122°04'W	4.7	4.2	0.7
18656	Montezuma Slough Bridge	38°11'N/121°59'W	4.9	4.4	0.7
18657	Benicia, Carquinez Strait	38°03'N/122°08'W	5.3	4.8	0.9
18658	Port Chicago, Suisun Bay	38°03'N/122°02'W	4.9	4.4	0.7
18659	Pittsburg	38°02'N/121°53'W	4.1	3.6	0.6
18659	Antioch, San Joaquin River	38°01'N/121°49'W	3.9	3.4	0.6
18659	Mallard Island Ferry Wharf, Suisun Bay	38°03'N/121°55'W	4.1	3.6	0.6
18659	Collinsville, Sacramento River	38°04'N/121°51'W	4.0	3.5	0.6
18660	Threemile Slough entrance, San Joaquin River	38°05'N/121°41'W	3.6	3.1	0.5
18660	Prisoners Point, San Joaquin River	38°04'N/121°33'W	3.7	3.2	0.5
18660	Wards Island, Little Connection Slough	38°03'N/121°30'W	3.5	3.0	0.5
18660	Irish Landing, San Joaquin River	38°02'N/121°35'W	3.6	3.2	0.5
18660	False River	38°03'N/121°39'W	3.3	2.9	0.5

* Heights in feet referred to datum of sounding MLLW.
Real-time water levels, tide predictions, and tidal current predictions are available at:
http://tidesandcurrents.noaa.gov
To determine mean tide range subtract Mean Low Water from Mean High Water.
Data as of September 2012

| TIDAL INFORMATION ||||||
Chart	Station	LAT/LONG	Mean Higher High Water*	Mean High Water*	Mean Low Water*
18661	Stockton, San Joaquin River	37°58'N/121°17'W	4.0	3.5	0.5
18661	Georgiana Slough entrance, Mokelumne River	38°07'N/121°35'W	3.3	2.9	0.4
18661	Rio Vista, Saeramento River	38°08'N/121°41'W	4.3	3.8	0.6
18662	Snodgrass Slough, Sacramento River	38°17'N/121°29'W	2.5	2.1	0.3
18662	Clarksburg, Sacramento River	38°25'N/121°31'W	2.9	2.6	0.3
18663	Bishop Cut, Disappointment Slough	38°03'N/121°25'W	3.9	3.4	0.5
18664	Sacramento, Sacramento River	38°35'N/121°30'W	2.9	2.6	0.3
18667	Montezuma Slough, Suisun Bay	38°05'N/121°53'W	4.2	3.7	0.6

* Heights in feet referred to datum of sounding MLLW.
Real-time water levels, tide predictions, and tidal current predictions are available at:
http://tidesandcurrents.noaa.gov
To determine mean tide range subtract Mean Low Water from Mean High Water.
Data as of September 2012

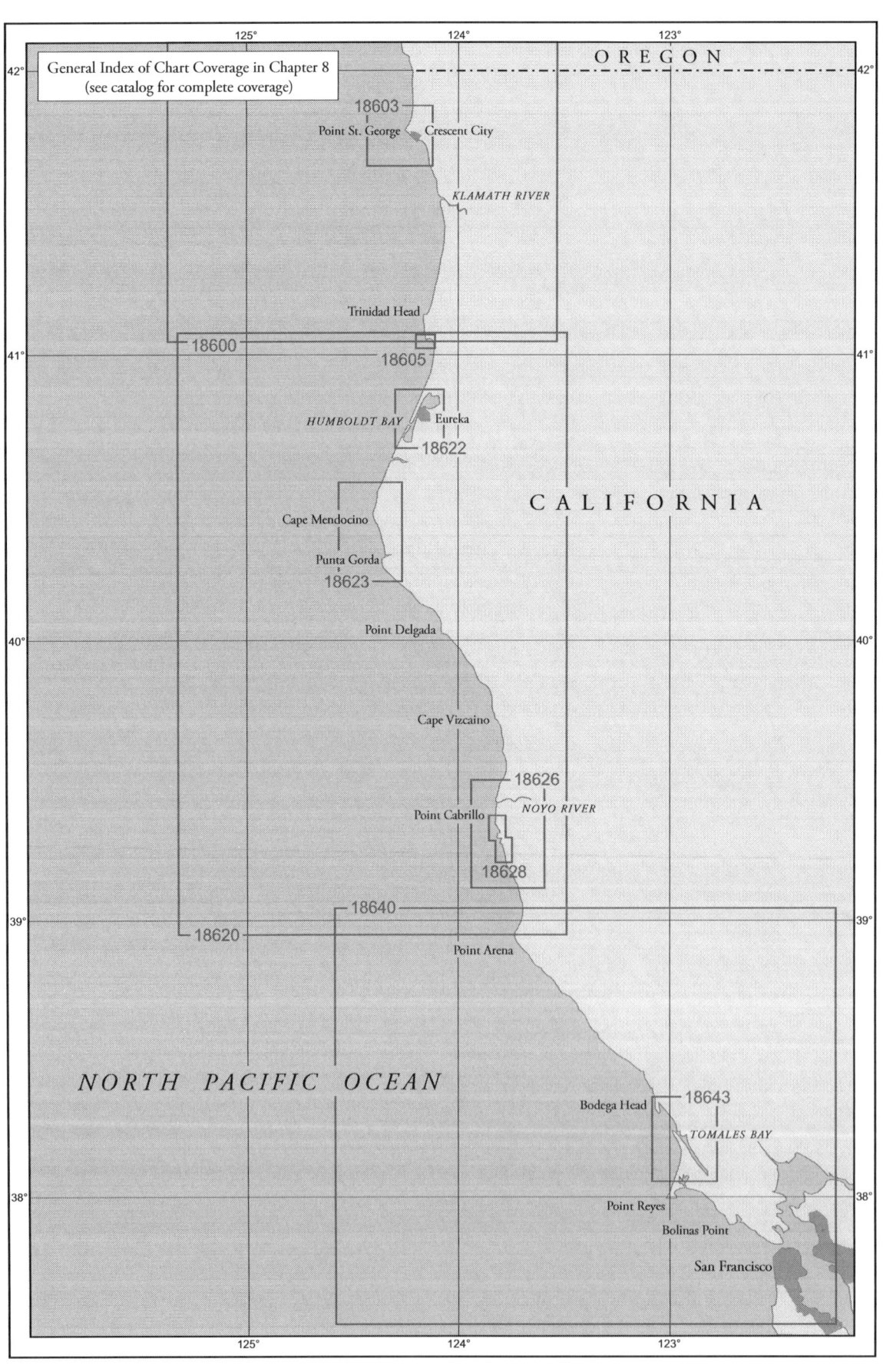

San Francisco Bay to Point St. George, California

Chart 18010

(1) This chapter describes Bodega Bay, Tomales Bay, Noyo River and Anchorage, Shelter Cove, Humboldt Bay, and numerous other small coves and bays. The only deep-draft harbor is Humboldt Bay, which has the largest city along this section of the coast, Eureka. The other important places, all for small craft, are Bodega Harbor, Noyo River, Shelter Cove, and Crescent City Harbor. The coast is rugged and often mountainous, with many detached rocks. The principal dangers, all marked, are Blunts Reef, Redding Rock, and St. George Reef.

COLREGS Demarcation Lines

(2) The lines established for this part of the coast are described in **80.1144 through 80.1152, chapter 2**.

Weather, San Francisco Bay to Point St. George

(3) Winter storms and a strong spring pressure gradient between the subtropical high and the Aleutian Low make these two seasons very windy. Speeds of 20 to 30 knots occur 15 to 20 percent of the time. Gales occur about 5 percent of the time off Point Arena and N of Cape Mendocino. Fronts and storms cause varying wind directions, but since many lows pass well offshore and to the N, winds are often out of a Southerly direction. Strong winds inhibit radiation or winter fog formation. It is most likely S of Eureka in the early morning after a night of clear skies and light winds. At times, this type of fog can plague Humboldt Bay. S winds help keep winter temperatures mild for these latitudes. Daytime highs in the mid-fifties (11.7° to 13.9°C) and nighttime lows around 40°F (4.4°C) are common; this compares with highs in the upper thirties (3° to 4°C) and lows in the mid-twenties (-5° to -2.8°C) along the East Coast. The storms that pass near or through the area make winter the rainy season. December through January is the height of the season, and precipitation of 0.1 inch (2.54 mm) or more can be expected on about 10 to 11 days per month S of Cape Mendocino and on up to 20 days to the N. Snow falls occasionally along this N coast.

(4) Winds in spring are more variable than in winter, as the subtropical high builds and the Aleutian Low shrinks. The change takes place gradually from N to S. NW through N winds become more common while S winds are not quite so prevalent. With the decrease in storm activity, rain falls on only about 6 or 7 days per month. Temperatures rise by about 4° or 5°F (-15.6° or -15.0°C) over winter averages by April. Visibilities are at their best during March and April. The pressure gradient keeps strong winds frequent.

(5) By summer, the high has taken control along this coast. However, S winds continue to occur frequently in the N. NW through N winds are most common and are reinforced by the sea breeze. Wind speeds of 20 to 30 knots occur 10 to 20 percent of the time, attesting to this reinforcement. They are most likely N of Cape Mendocino, where gales occur 5 to 10 percent of the time. These speeds do not inhibit the formation of advection fog, which plagues the area from July through September. Visibilities drop below 1 mile (2 km) on about 10 to 15 days per month S of Point Delgada and 5 to 10 days per month to the N. Sound signals fill the air 30 to 50 percent of the time during August, which is the worst month. At coastal stations, visibilities drop below 0.5 mile (0.9 km) on 10 to 20 days per month. Fog is particularly dangerous in shoal-ridden Humboldt Bay. Point Reyes and Point Arena are the foggiest spots, while Point St. George appears to be the least foggy. Fog and low stratus often blanket the waters around Point Reyes for weeks at a time, permitting little sunshine. As a result, Point Reyes has close to the lowest average midsummer temperature of any observing site in the United States. In general along the coast, daytime temperatures average in the low to midsixties (16.7° to 19.4°C), while nighttime lows drop into the low fifties (11° to 12° C). This compares with an average July high of 85°F (29°C) and a low of 67° F (19°C) in New York. Rain is of little concern.

(6) Autumn brings a gradual return to winter conditions. Fog becomes less frequent. This is a gradual change in sheltered regions like Humboldt Bay, where radiation fog is likely. Temperatures fall off by 2° or 3°F (-17.2° or -16.7°C) on the average by October. Winds become a mix of S and N, with N gaining the edge, as fall turns toward winter. Gales are infrequent, and winds blow 20 to 30 knots 10 to 15 percent of the time.

Charts 18640, 18643

(7) From Point Reyes, the coast trends in a general N direction for 10 miles as a broad white sand beach backed by high grassy sand dunes, and then curves NW for 6 miles in high yellow cliffs, terminating in **Tomales Point**. The large white building at the radio station, 7 miles NE of Point Reyes, is prominent.

(8) The **Gulf of the Farallones National Marine Sanctuary** has been established to protect and preserve the marine birds and mammals, their habitats, and other natural resources in the waters surrounding the Farallon Islands and Point Reyes, and to ensure the continued availability of the area as a research and recreational resource. The sanctuary encompasses the waters off Bodega Head and Point Reyes, and the waters surrounding Farallon Islands. The sanctuary includes Bodega Bay but not Bodega Harbor. Recreational use of the area is encouraged. (See **15 CFR 922**, chapter 2, for limits and regulations.)

(9) The Gulf of the Farallones National Marine Sanctuary regulations prohibit operation of any vessel engaged in carrying cargo – including but not limited to tankers and other bulk carriers and barges – or engaged in the trade of servicing offshore installations within 2 miles from the Farallon Islands, Bolinas Lagoon, or any Area of Special Biological Significance (ASBS). Exception: vessels transporting persons or supplies to or from islands or mainland areas adjacent to Sanctuary waters, or fishing, recreational or research vessels.

(10) Areas within the sanctuary include:

(11) – **Farallon Island** ASBS, San Francisco County; waters within 1 mile of Southeast Farallon (including Maintop Island), Middle Farallon, North Farallon, and Noonday Rock.

(12) – **Duxbury Reef Reserve and Extension ASBS**, Marin County; waters 2,000 feet beyond the mean high tide line.

(13) – **Point Reyes Headland Reserve and Extension ASBS**, Marin County (including areas off the Point Reyes lighthouse and Chimney Rock); waters 2,000 feet beyond the mean high tide line.

(14) – **Double Point ASBS**, Marin County; the area enclosed by the 5-fathom contour and the mean high tide line, N and S along the shore about 1,900 feet from the point where Pelican Lake Creek enters the Pacific.

(15) – **Bird Rock ASBS**, Marin County; waters 1,000 feet in all directions from Bird Rock, W of Tomales Point.

(16) **Bodega Bay,** a broad opening between Tomales Point and Bodega Head, affords shelter from NW weather at its N end, but is dangerous in S or W weather. The summit of **Bodega Head** is rounding and grassy, with steep rocky cliffs on the S and W ends. Low **Bodega Rock** and foul ground extend from 0.2 to 0.7 mile SE of the S face of Bodega Head.

(17) **Bodega Marine Life Refuge** is just north of Bodega Head. Its sea perimeter begins at 38°18'40"N., 123°04'04"W. and extends offshore around **Mussel Point** to 38°19'23"N., 123°04'22"W. The refuge extends from the shoreline, at the line of mean high water (tide), a distance of 1,000 feet offshore. Within these perimeters all marine plants and invertebrates are protected. Established by an act of the California legislature in 1965, the refuge is managed by the University of California at Davis.

(18) **University of California Bodega Marine Laboratory is on Horseshoe Cove** about 1.3 miles NW of Bodega Head Light. Two large white buildings at the site are reported to be prominent and lighted at night.

(19) **Bodega Head Light** (38°18'01"N., 123°03'14"W.), 110 feet above the water, is shown from a post with a red and white diamond-shaped daymark on the SE end of Bodega Head.

(20) Lighted buoys mark the entrance to Bodega Bay.

Danger

(21) In good weather small boats having local knowledge sometimes use the passage between Bodega Head and Bodega Rock. The passage is unsafe whenever breakers from heavy ground swells reduce the width of the passage. Large breaking waves can occur inside the 30-foot depth contour line NW and SW of Bodega Rock. The safest part of the passage between Bodega Head and Bodega Rock is along the deeper part of the passage. When the width of the passage is reduced by breakers, mariners entering Bodega Bay should pass S of Bodega Harbor Approach Lighted Gong Buoy BA.

COLREGS Demarcation Lines

(22) The lines established for Bodega and Tomales Bays are described in **80.1144**, chapter 2.

(23) **Tomales Bay** enters the S part of Bodega Bay E of Tomales Point, and extends SE for 12 miles with an average width of 0.5 mile. The channel with depths of 3 to over 10 feet is marked by buoys and daybeacons for about 4 miles to deeper water inside the bay. The shoals and channels within the bay are subject to continual change, local knowledge is advised. An unmarked rock covered 10 feet is near the center of the bay, 0.8 mile SE of Pelican Point in about 38°10'47"N., 122°55'08"W. In 2006, a partially submerged metal pipe was reported near the entrance to Tomales Bay in about 38°14'21"N., 122°59'09"W. Mariners are advised to transit the area with caution.

(24) **The entrance bar is dangerous and should not be attempted by strangers**. A 6-knot current may be encountered on a spring tide at the entrance to the bay. The shallow area on the entrance bar frequently becomes rough, and it is reported that the sudden appearance of breakers in a calm sea is common. Because such waves appear with little warning, they are called "sneaker waves." These waves occur primarily during the ebb tide, but the entire bar area can become rough owing to strong afternoon winds. Boatmen should plan to leave the area before the tide turns or be prepared to remain outside until the rough water subsides, or to go to another harbor such as Bodega.

(25) Fish, clams, mussels, and oysters are taken from Tomales Bay by commercial and sport fishermen. Oyster farms occupy large sections of tide flats south of Toms Point. A small-craft facility on the bay can make hull and

(26) Tomales Bay is part of the Point Reyes/Farallon Islands National Marine Sanctuary.

(27) **Bodega Harbor**, in the N part of Bodega Bay, is an important commercial fishing base and, in season, an active sports fishing and recreation harbor. During salmon season more than 500 fishing craft either anchor just outside in the shelter of the N part of the bay or dock at the numerous marinas inside the harbor.

(28) A **Federal project** provides for a 12-foot channel, protected by entrance jetties, which leads from Bodega Bay to facilities along the N and NE sides of the harbor at the town of Bodega Bay. The channel has a turning basin just inside the entrance, at the N end of the harbor and along the NE side of the harbor. (See Notice to Mariners and latest editions of charts for controlling depths.) The channel is marked by buoys, daybeacons, and lights; lighted ranges also mark the channel from the entrance to the turning basin at the N end of the harbor.

(29) Transient berths with electricity, gasoline, diesel fuel, ice, water, and some marine supplies and provisions can be obtained in the harbor. The marina at Spud Point on the W side of the harbor has the largest lift in the area, which can handle boats up to 20 tons. Hull, engine, and electronic repairs, launching ramps, and winter dry and wet storage are available in the harbor. A channel marked by private buoys and a light, leads from the main channel just SW of the outer turning basin to a marina at the NW side of the harbor.

Coast Guard

(30) **Bodega Bay Coast Guard Station** is on the E side of the channel, 0.8 mile above the entrance.

Chart 18640

(31) The coast from Bodega Head for 52 miles to Point Arena trends in a general NW direction. There are some dangers, but they do not extend over a mile offshore, and in thick weather the 30-fathom curve may be followed with safety. In the summer the rocks are generally marked by kelp, which extends in some cases to the 10-fathom curve, but during the winter gales much of the kelp is torn away.

(32) In clear weather the mountains may be readily seen, and at times are visible when the lower land is shut in by haze or fog. In thick weather soundings should be taken frequently, as the currents are extremely irregular both in direction and velocity.

(33) Protection from the prevailing NW winds of summer may be had at several places, but there is no shelter from the winter winds, which are usually accompanied by a heavy W swell.

(34) N of Bodega Head, the cliffs are about 200 feet high for 2 miles, and then are succeeded by a broad sand beach 2 miles long backed by sand dunes 120 feet high. From this point the coast N consists of abrupt rocky cliffs, broken by gulches, to the mouth of the Russian River, 10 miles N of Bodega Head.

(35) Numerous rocks, 20 to 130 feet high, are within 0.3 miles of the shore, but some extend as much as a mile offshore. **Gull Rock**, 100 feet high, is 1.7 miles SE of the mouth of Russian River and 0.3 mile offshore. About 0.5 mile NW of Gull Rock and 400 yards offshore is a large arched rock, 85 feet high, with a flat top. This is the largest arched rock on this part of the coast.

(36) **Duncans Landing**, 6 miles N of Bodega Head, is a fair small-boat landing in NW weather.

(37) The spit making out from the S point of **Russian River** has been partially reinforced by a short rock jetty, but the mouth of the river is closed by a shallow bar. The bold sharp point immediately to the S of the river appears as an island from the S; it is connected to the mainland by a roadway. Many summer resorts are on the shores of Russian River; at the settlement of **Jenner** there is a landing. Gasoline and water can be obtained nearby.

(38) **Ross Mountain**, 3 miles inland and N of Russian River, is the highest knob on the ridge. A few clusters of trees are near its summit; the slopes are bare of trees and the gulches are wooded.

(39) From Russian River for 6.5 miles to Fort Ross Cove, the coast is high, consisting of bare steep spurs from Ross Mountain. **Sunken Reef** extends 0.8 mile from shore 4.5 miles NW of Russian River; it is marked by a bell buoy.

(40) **Fort Ross Reef**, 5.7 miles NW of Russian River and nearly 1 mile SE of Fort Ross Cove, consists of pinnacle rocks 35 feet high, 600 yards offshore, and connected with the beach by a reef which is partially marked by kelp.

(41) **Fort Ross Cove**, 15.5 miles N of Bodega Head and 33 miles N of Point Reyes, affords good shelter in NW weather. The holding ground is poor, and the anchorage is constricted by a rock that uncovers in the middle of the cove and a rock about 50 yards N of it that is covered 14 feet. The cove is divided into two bights, the W one being slightly the larger. The anchorage is suitable for small vessels only, and if used by strangers should be entered with caution.

(42) **Fort Ross** was first settled by the Russians in 1812, and the old Russian church is still standing. The buildings have been restored, and the area is now a State Historical Monument. There are no landing facilities.

(43) From Fort Ross Cove the coast extends NW and is nearly straight. It is bold and wooded to the crests of the hills which closely approach the coast, and is cut by numerous gulches and bordered by many inshore rocks. The 30-fathom curve is at an average distance of

(44) **Salt Point**, 5 miles N of Fort Ross Cove, is 35 feet high, very rocky, and bare of trees; it is bordered by outlying rocks for 200 yards. The 30-fathom curve is less than 0.5 mile off this point. 0.7 mile offshore from Fort Ross Cove for 20 miles to near Gualala River.

(45) **Fisk Mill Cove**, 2.5 miles N of Salt Point, affords fair shelter for small vessels in NW weather. The bottom is rocky, but there are no hidden dangers.

(46) **Horseshoe Point**, 3 miles N of Salt Point, is a cliff 180 feet high, with a depression of 60 feet immediately behind it. It is bare of trees and the summit is marked by several projecting rocks.

(47) From Horseshoe Point the coast trends NW for 12.5 miles to Gualala River and consists of cliffs, about 60 feet high, bordered by numerous outlying rocks. The tree line is from 0.1 to 0.5 mile back from the edge of the cliffs.

(48) **Fisherman Bay**, 26.5 miles NW of Bodega Head, is a fair shelter for small craft in NW weather. There are two covered rocks marked by kelp 350 yards off the S point of the bay. There is a general store at the village of **Stewarts Point** on the N side of the bay.

(49) **Gualala Point**, 16 miles SE of Point Arena and 1 mile S of Gualala River, is 42 feet high, about 300 yards offshore, and connected with the bluff by a rocky reef covered with sand. Sand dunes extend behind the bluff for 600 yards.

Local magnetic disturbance

(50) Differences of as much as 8° from normal variation have been reported near Gualala Point, and a difference of as much as 4° near Saunders Reef.

(51) **Gualala River** intersects the coast 15 miles SE of Point Arena. A long sand beach extends a mile S from the mouth. The white hotel building at **Gualala** can be seen from the W and SW.

(52) **Robinson Reef** lies N of the mouth of Gualala River and 1.1 miles N of Gualala Point. It consists of a cluster of 25 or more visible rocks about 600 yards offshore, with a covered rock 70 yards WNW of the outer rock.

(53) **Bourns Landing** is 1.5 miles NW of Gualala River. The anchorage here is exposed and can be used only in the summer. Local knowledge is necessary because the approaches have several covered rocks. Lumber from the Gualala mills was formerly shipped from here.

(54) **Havens Anchorage**, 12 miles SE of Point Arena and 4 miles NW of Gualala Point, offers shelter for small vessels from the prevailing NW winds S of Fish Rocks. The cove is constricted by rocks and ledges extending 250 yards SE from the W head. Strangers should approach the anchorage with caution. During the summer the anchorage is used extensively by fishing boats in NW weather.

(55) **Fish Rocks**, two rocky islets 4.2 miles NW of Gualala Point, are connected at low water with the shore and surrounded by numerous smaller rocks. The outer rock is 150 feet high and the inner 100 feet high and 100 yards offshore. A rock 40 feet high lies 175 yards SE of the outer rock.

(56) **Havens Neck**, 145 feet high and prominent, is 0.6 mile NW of Fish Rocks. It is bare of trees and connected with the bluffs by a narrow neck.

(57) **Gualala Mountain**, 5 miles inland NE of Havens Neck, is heavily wooded and prominent in clear weather. **Sail Rock**, 44 feet high, is a sharp, pyramidal rock 800 yards offshore, 2.8 miles NW of Fish Rocks. From off Point Arena it resembles a small vessel under sail. **Saunders Reef**, 4.5 miles NW of Fish Rocks, is 0.5 mile offshore. It shows several rocks that uncover and is well marked by kelp. Foul ground extends between it and the shore. A lighted gong buoy is 0.4 mile SW of the outer rock and 7.5 miles SE of Point Arena.

(58) **Arena Cove**, 2.5 miles SE of Point Arena, is a slight indentation affording shelter to small vessels in NW weather. The S head is a high yellow cliff that under favorable circumstances is visible for a considerable distance. A wharf is at the head of the cove. A 3-ton hoist is on the wharf; gasoline, diesel fuel, and water are available. Some groceries may be had. A white lookout tower with a red roof on a steel structure is prominent. A lighted bell buoy is 0.6 mile SW from the end of the wharf. To enter, make the lighted bell buoy, then bring the end of the wharf to bear **074°** and stand in on this course. This leads about 150 feet S of a rock covered 16 feet that lies 300 yards 264° from the end of the wharf. In thick weather during the summer in approaching the cove from N or S, the edge of the kelp may be followed which will lead to within 300 yards of the lighted bell buoy. The town of **Point Arena** is on the highway 1 mile E of the landing.

(59) A breaker is reported in a heavy SW swell 0.8 mile WSW of the N point of Arena Cove, and scattered kelp extends almost out to that position.

(60) **Point Arena**, 68 miles NW of Point Reyes, consists of a long level plateau, diminishing in height to the end of the 60-foot-high point. It is the first prominent point N of Point Reyes. The point is bare of trees for about a mile from the shore.

(61) **Point Arena Light** (38°57'17"N., 123°44'26"W.), 155 feet above the water, is shown from a 115-foot white cylindrical tower with black gallery at the extremity of the point. A reef that usually shows breakers extends about 0.6 mile NW from the extremity of the point.

(62) **Arena Rock**, 1.4 miles N of Point Arena Light, is covered 13 feet and shows a breaker except in very smooth weather. A covered rock which rises abruptly from deep water and breaks only in heavy weather is 200 yards N of Arena Rock.

Caution

(63) Vessels approaching Point Arena from N in thick weather are advised to keep outside the 40-fathom curve

because Arena Rock is only 0.8 mile inside the 30-fathom curve and shoaling near it is abrupt.

Chart 18620

(64) From Point Arena the coast extends in a general NNW direction for 50 miles and then trends NW for nearly 35 miles to Punta Gorda, thence NNW for 10 miles to Cape Mendocino. The S portion is less bold and rugged than the N portion, and the mountains are neither as high nor as close to the coast. The dangers are all included within the 30-fathom curve, and except for Blunts Reef and the other reefs in the vicinity of Cape Mendocino, do not extend more than a mile offshore. Several submarine valleys with depths greater than 50 fathoms come within 0.5 to 2 miles of the shore between Point Delgada and Cape Mendocino; the currents are irregular in this area.

(65) From Cape Mendocino to Trinidad Head, the coast trends in a NNE direction for 40 miles and, with the exception of the rocks off False Cape, the dangers are within 0.5 mile of the shore. The land is generally low with sandy beaches, broken by the mouths of the Eel and Mad Rivers and the entrance to Humboldt Bay. The only marked elevations N of False Cape are Table Bluff and Buhne Point.

(66) In clear weather the mountains are good landmarks and can frequently be seen when the lower land is obscured by fog or haze.

(67) Between Point Arena and Cuffeys Cove, protection from the prevailing NW winds of summer may be had in a few places, but there is none from S or W.

(68) From Point Arena the cliffs of the point extend 0.5 mile NE to the mouth of **Garcia River,** from which sand dunes and beaches extend N for 4 miles. Beyond this point for 40 miles to **Ten Mile River Beach** the coast is rugged, with high, bold cliffs bordered by numerous outlying rocks.

(69) **Mal Pass** is a steep gulch 5.2 miles N of Point Arena; the bluffs on each side are nearly 280 feet high. **Red Bluff**, 8 miles N of Point Arena, is a prominent reddish 200-foot-high cliff. **Elk Rock**, 8.5 miles N of Point Arena, is 95 feet high and 0.5 mile offshore.

Chart 18626

(70) **Nose Rock**, 10.3 miles N of Point Arena and 0.7 mile offshore from Elk, is 24 feet high. **Casket Rock**, 700 yards NE of Nose Rock, is the outermost of three large rocks W of a 150-foot cliff fronting the village of **Elk**.

(71) **Cuffeys Cove**, 11 miles N of Point Arena, is a small anchorage affording fair shelter in NW winds. **Cuffeys Inlet**, just W of the cove, is an excellent anchorage for small boats in N and W weather. Caution is necessary to avoid the many covered and visible rocks in the approaches to the cove and inlet. A small kelp-covered rock that uncovers lies near the center of the entrance to the inlet. The cove is covered with patches of kelp during most of the year.

(72) From Cuffeys Cove for 3 miles to **Navarro River,** the coast consists of cliffs 200 feet high, bordered by outlying rocks. Although the mouth of the river is nearly always closed by a bar with only 1 or 2 feet of water over it, the entrance has fair shelter from NW winds. **Navarro Head**, 405 feet high, is on the N bank of the river.

Chart 18628

(73) **Salmon Point**, the S entrance point to **Whitesboro Cove**, 1.2 miles N of Navarro River, is a treeless cliff 109 feet high. Detached rocks extend W of the point for 0.2 mile, with **Bull Rock**, a covered ledge, usually showing a breaker 0.5 mile NW of the extremity of the point. In a heavy swell, breakers show between it and the visible rocks off the point. Whitesboro Cove is rocky, exposed to NW and W winds, and seldom used as an anchorage.

(74) **Albion Cove**, 16.5 miles N of Point Arena, affords good shelter in N weather. The S point at the entrance rises to a knoll 179 feet high; low rocks extend nearly 500 yards W of the point. The N point is a rocky islet 80 feet high lying close to the point which has the same elevation; both are bare. Small visible rocks lie 200 yards W of the islet, and covered rocks, showing breakers in a moderate swell, extend out more than 500 yards WSW from it. **Mooring Rock**, in about the middle of the cove, is 30 feet high, pyramidal in shape, and marked by a light and a mariner radio activated sound signal, initiated by keying the microphone five times on VHF-FM channel 81A. Small rocks extend from Mooring Rock to the N shore. A lighted whistle buoy marks the entrance to the cove.

(75) The village of **Albion** is on both high banks of **Albion River.** Several small piers on the river serve the commercial and sport fishermen. Gasoline, diesel oil, water, ice, fishing supplies, and a launching ramp are available. The river is crossed by a fixed highway bridge that has a clearance of 118 feet, 0.1 mile above the mouth.

COLREGS Demarcation Lines

(76) The lines established for the Albion River are described in **80.1146**, chapter 2.

(77) Between Albion Cove and Colby Reef, breakers are seen in a heavy swell nearly 0.5 mile from shore; vessels should not approach closer than 1 mile.

(78) **Stillwell Point**, 1.6 miles N of Albion Cove, is a bold, sharp 190-foot cliff. A 141-foot-high rocky islet lies close inshore on its NW side. A yellow slide is on the S face of Stillwell Point. **Colby Reef**, 0.5 mile offshore W of Stillwell Point, is a shoal rocky patch. Numerous other dangers are just inside the 20-fathom curve along this stretch of coast.

(79) **Little River**, 19 miles N of Point Arena, offers shelter in the entrance cove. The reefs and rocks surrounding

the cove are well marked by kelp, and a heavy undertow is felt when in the vicinity of the rocks. The NW shore of the cove is bluff, rocky, and bare of trees for over 0.5 mile. The entrance is marked by a bell buoy, but the channel narrows to 60 yards by covered rocks N of the inner visible rock. The beach area at Little River is a State Park.

(80) The 2-mile coast between Little River and Mendocino Bay is a broad tableland with a seaward face of cliffs, 40 to 60 feet high, bordered by numerous low rocks. The tree line is over 0.5 mile from the cliffs.

(81) **Mendocino Bay**, 21 miles N of Point Arena, affords fair shelter in NW weather, but vessels are obliged to leave in S or W weather. In heavy SW gales the sea breaks clear across the entrance. The S point at the entrance is a rocky, irregular cliff 100 feet high, bordered by numerous rocks extending 150 yards offshore. A knoll 156 feet high is 300 yards inshore from the point. A reef covered 3 fathoms extends 500 yards NW of the outermost visible rock. This area should be avoided when there is any swell running. The N point is a broken cliff 60 feet high, bordered by numerous rocks close inshore. A whistle buoy marks the entrance to the bay.

(82) **Big River** enters in the NE part of Mendocino Bay. The town of **Mendocino** is on the N shore of the bay. Water is available.

(83) **Russian Gulch**, 2 miles N of Mendocino, is a small cove occasionally used as an anchorage by small craft with local knowledge as it affords excellent protection. A State Park is at the head of the cove. The concrete arch highway bridge across Russian Gulch should show well from S to W. An important danger is a submerged rock 400 yards NW of the S entrance point, surrounded by a reef covered 1¼ fathoms.

(84) **Point Cabrillo**, 3 miles N of the town of Mendocino and 24 miles N of Point Arena, is a flat-topped point 50 to 60 feet high terminating seaward in nearly vertical cliffs; numerous low rocks extend offshore over 200 yards, and the 30-fathom curve is barely 0.2 mile outside of them. The point is bare except for a few trees at the houses near the light.

(85) **Point Cabrillo Light** (39°20'55"N., 123°49'34"W.), 81 feet above the water, is shown from a 47-foot white octagonal frame tower on a dwelling on the point.

(86) From Point Cabrillo the coast trends N for 9 miles to Laguna Point as a nearly straight line of bluffs, with numerous rocks close under the cliffs. It is moderately high, partly wooded to the face of the cliffs, and is broken by several indentations and small streams. The 30-fathom curve is an average distance of 1 mile from shore.

(87) **Caspar Anchorage**, a mile N of Point Cabrillo, is a small cove at the mouth of **Caspar Creek**. Fair shelter, except from W, is afforded, but the anchorage is constricted and seldom used. The village of **Caspar** is on the N bank of the creek near its mouth.

Chart 18626

(88) From Caspar Creek for 4 miles to Noyo Anchorage the coast consists of broken irregular cliffs, 40 to 60 feet high, with numerous rocks extending 400 yards offshore. These are fairly well fringed by kelp, especially in summer.

(89) **Noyo Anchorage**, 5 miles N of Point Cabrillo, affords fair shelter from N or S. The anchorage is limited to an area about 400 yards long and less than 200 yards wide, with depths of 3½ to 6½ fathoms. Buoys mark the entrance to the anchorage.

(90) **Noyo River** enters at the head of Noyo Anchorage. A jetty with a light and sound signal is on the N side of the entrance, and a small jetty, with a light off the seaward end, is on the S side of the entrance. A fixed highway bridge with a clearance of 97 feet crosses the river about 300 yards E of the mouth. The river above the first sharp bend affords excellent protection for small boats.

(91) A dredged channel leads between the jetties to **Noyo Basin**, about 0.6 mile above the entrance. In 2007, the controlling depth was 6.7 feet with lesser depths to 3.4 feet along the edges of the channel. Noyo Basin had reported depths of 10 feet. The basin is protected by a breakwater which is marked on its outer end by a light. The river channel is marked by lights, a buoy, and a directional light. **Dolphin Cove** is about 0.5 mile above Noyo Basin just past the federally maked channel; local knowledge is advised. Overhead power cables crossing the river have a least clearance of 80 feet.

(92) **Hazardous bar conditions** are common at the entrance to Noyo River. Mariners should monitor VHF-FM channel 16 for safety broadcast/advisories concerning the Noyo River and are encouraged to contact the Coast Guard prior to transiting the entrance.

(93) The Coast Guard has established Noyo River Entrance Small Boat Warning Light on the N side of the river in about 39°25'40"N., 123°48'20"W. The light is equipped with two quick flashing yellow lights that will be activated when seas exceed 4 feet in height and are considered hazardous for small boats. Mariners are cautioned that if the lights are not flashing, there is no guarantee that sea conditions are favorable.

(94) Caution is necessary in entering to avoid the reefs and a rock on the S side of the entrance. Heavy W or SW swells form breakers at the entrance to the river; once inside there is good shelter. With W winds and seas, heavy surge is felt in the river as far as Noyo Basin.

COLREGS Demarcation Lines

(95) The lines established for the Noyo River are described in **80.1148**, chapter 2.

Coast Guard

(96) The Noyo River Coast Guard Station is located on the S bank of the river, just below Noyo Basin. The

(97) station monitors VHF-FM channel 16 or can be reached at 707–964–6612.

A **Storm Warning Flag System** consisting of a series of square flags and triangular pennants, will be displayed on a pole that is located on the SW end of the Noyo River Coast Guard Station dock and will be visible to mariners from both directions. The flags will indicate that winds and/or sea conditions forecast for the area may pose a hazard to boaters. (See illustration; Chapter 1.) Flags are flown at select Coast Guard stations to supplement other weather notification sources. Light signals corresponding to these flags are not displayed at night. In all cases, mariners should rely upon National Weather Service Broadcasts as their primary source of government provided weather information.

(98) The lower section of Noyo River is the principal commercial and sport fishing center of this section of the coast. Many fishing boats are based here. Most of the facilities extend along both banks of the river to about 0.5 mile above the entrance. Water and ice can be obtained at several fishhouses with wharves having depths from 4 to 8 feet alongside. Berths, gasoline, diesel fuel, water, ice, marine supplies, and launching ramps are available at the facilities along the river and at Fort Bragg. Machine shops and marine railways can handle vessels up to 45 feet for hull and engine repairs. The phone number for the Noyo Basin Harbormaster is 707–964–4719.

(99) From Noyo River, for 0.7 mile to Fort Bragg, the coast consists of rocky cliffs, 40 to 60 feet high, bordered by rocks and sunken ledges extending 100 to 400 yards offshore.

(100) **Fort Bragg**, 30 miles N of Point Arena, is the largest coast town between San Francisco and Eureka. It is near the head of a cove formerly known as **Soldiers Harbor**. The former loading wharf has been removed; lumber is now shipped out by rail and truck. Groceries can be obtained, and minor repairs made.

(101) The cove is constricted by the rocks and ledges extending from both the N and S, leaving only a limited area for small boats to anchor. A rocky reef, partly bare at high water, extends SW from the N head and breaks the force of the swell from NW. In W weather the cove is wide open. Since Noyo River gives better protection, the cove is seldom used.

(102) For 3 miles from Fort Bragg to Laguna Point, the coast is moderately low and rocky and cut by two small streams; the tree line is within 0.2 mile of the beach.

(103) **Laguna Point**, 8.5 miles N of Point Cabrillo, is near the S end of Ten Mile River Beach. It is a small, projecting cliff, 30 feet high, flat-topped, and bare of trees for 600 yards. It is noticeable only when close inshore. A bare reef extends 300 yards NW from the point. The cove immediately N of Laguna Point is exposed and only available for small boats. It affords fair protection in S weather and is occasionally used in winter.

(104) **Bald Hill** (chart 18620), 2.5 miles SE of Laguna Point, is a prominent landmark; its summit and SW slope are bare of timber.

Chart 18620

(105) For 0.5 mile N of Laguna Point the bluffs are low, thence a straight sand beach extends for 3 miles to the mouth of **Ten Mile River**. The beach is backed by sand dunes for 0.5 mile inland; the tree line is about 1.5 miles from the beach. The concrete highway bridge over Ten Mile River is conspicuous from the W.

(106) From Ten Mile River the coast extends in a general NW direction for 52 miles to Punta Gorda. This stretch of the coast is particularly bold and rugged, bordered by numerous rocks, and is heavily timbered as far as Point Delgada. N of Point Delgada the tops of the ridges are generally bare or only partly covered with trees and brush. The cliffs along the shore range from 40 to 100 feet in height. The high, rugged mountains in the vicinity of the coast, which reach elevations of 3,000 to 4,000 feet, are prominent.

(107) **Kibesillah Rock**, 1.2 miles N of Ten Mile River and 0.4 mile off the line of the cliffs, is the outermost danger for many miles N and S. It is small and washed over almost continuously even in ordinary weather. Other rocks and rocky islets up to 80 feet high are inside of Kibesillah Rock.

(108) **Bells Mountain**, 4.5 miles N of Ten Mile River and 0.5 mile inland, is bare on top with a few trees on the oceanside.

(109) **Switzer Rock**, 5.5 miles N of Ten Mile River and 0.3 mile offshore, is small with deep water close around it; every large swell washes over the rock. A covered rock marked by a breaker is 170 yards SE of Switzer Rock.

(110) **Gordon Hill**, 6.5 miles N of Ten Mile River, is bare to the summit and terminates seaward in 60-foot-high **Abalone Point**, which is bordered by low outlying rocks.

(111) **Hardy Rock**, 9.5 miles N of Ten Mile River and 0.4 mile offshore, is a small 47-foot-high islet.

(112) From Abalone Point the coast trends NW for 4 miles to **Cape Vizcaino**, which is a broad, irregular line of precipitous cliffs, 100 feet high, very broken, and bordered by low rocks, 200 to 300 yards offshore.

(113) **Island Knob**, a rocky lime-covered islet, lies close-to and almost connected with Cape Vizcaino. A covered rock marked by a breaker is 275 yards W of the islet. **Cottaneva Rock**, 20 feet high, is 500 yards SE of Island Knob and 275 yards offshore. Several smaller rocks lie inside of it and two others about 160 yards NW.

(114) **Cahto Peak**, 11.5 miles E of Cape Vizcaino, is prominent in clear weather.

(115) Between Cape Vizcaino and Point Delgada are several small exposed landings available for use only in the summer and in smooth weather.

(116) **Sea Lion Rock**, a mile N of Cape Vizcaino and 500 yards offshore, is 5 feet high and inhabited by sea lions.

(116) **Cottaneva Needle**, 0.5 mile N of Sea Lion Rock, is a prominent black pinnacle rock 55 feet high.

(117) **Double Cone Rock** is 3.5 miles N of Cape Vizcaino and 300 yards offshore.

(118) **Usal Rock**, 5 miles N of Cape Vizcaino, is 45 feet high and black in color. It lies 200 yards off a small point of rocks.

(119) The mouth of **Usal Valley** is about a mile N of Usal Rock, and is a narrow, steep gulch, in front of which is a small area of flat land with a low beach. A small grassy hillock is just inside the gulch. The view up the valley is open for a very short time while passing.

(120) **Big White Rock**, 95 feet high, lies 7.7 miles N of Cape Vizcaino, and 125 yards offshore from the steep cliffs, which are bordered by numerous rocks. The rock is a prominent feature when the higher points of the land are in fog.

(121) **Anderson Cliff**, 10 miles N of Cape Vizcaino, is a projecting rocky spur 715 feet high, with one large rock and numerous smaller ones close inshore. **Jackson Pinnacle**, 1.1 miles N of Anderson Cliff, is a black rock 45 feet high, so close to the rocky beach that from seaward it is hard to distinguish from the bluff behind it. When seen from along shore, it is prominent.

(122) **Cluster Cone Rock**, a prominent 68-foot pinnacle, is the largest and whitest of a small cluster of 6 rocks, 200 yards offshore, lying 12.5 miles N of Cape Vizcaino.

(123) **Morgan Rock**, a large white-topped, block-shaped rock 57 feet high and 0.5 mile NW of Cluster Cone Rock, shows prominently. It is the largest of a group of rocks extending some 200 yards from a high rocky cliff and is particularly valuable as a landmark when higher land is covered by fog.

(124) **Bear Harbor Ridge**, a detached coastal ridge about a mile NW of Cluster Cone Rock, has two peaks; the S one, 375 feet high, is the higher. It is the most prominent feature in this vicinity when viewed from the NW. The seaward face of the ridge is marked by steep, loose slides.

(125) **Needle Rock**, 46 feet high, is 14.5 miles N of Cape Vizcaino; the rock blends into the bluff from offshore. A group of old mill buildings, a few houses, and an old landing platform about midway up the flat mark the abandoned landing.

(126) **Small White Rock**, 37 feet high, lies 5 miles N of Cluster Cone Rock and 4 miles S of Point Delgada. It is close inshore and just outside the low-water beach; once identified, this rock makes a valuable landmark.

(127) From just below Small White Rock to Point Delgada, the country is not timbered, but is covered with dense, low brush, which presents a uniform dark green appearance.

(128) A submarine ridge known as **Tolo Bank** extends S from Point Delgada for about 7 miles. The depths are quite irregular; the least depth found is 9 fathoms.

Caution

(129) The area just S of Shelter Cove is subject to slides which might deposit rocks along the shore.

(130) **Point Delgada**, 66 miles N of Point Arena, and nearly 20 miles S of Punta Gorda, is a cliff-faced plateau making out about a mile from the general trend of the coast. The seaward face of the plateau is a mile long and bordered by numerous rocks. A lighted horn buoy is 1.1 miles SW from the point, and a bell buoy is 0.8 miles SE from the point. A paved airplane landing strip, approximately 3,500 feet and a 43-foot high lighthouse (unlit) which can be observed offshore during the day are on the point.

(131) **Shelter Cove** lies under the S face of Point Delgada and affords fair shelter in NW weather, but is exposed and dangerous with S or SE winds. Occasionally a swell runs in the cove. There are no wharves in the cove. Water may be obtained ashore, but must be carried down from the plateau. A marine supply store is on the bluff on the W side of the cove. Gasoline, diesel fuel, lubricants, ice, marine supplies, and provisions are available. A launching ramp is at the head of the cove. Shelter cove is used extensively as an offshore moorage for fishing boats. A pump-out station and dry winter storage are at Shelter Cove. Local boat launch service monitors VHF-FM channel 68. A paved road is maintained to the cove. Telephone service is available.

(132) The rocks covered 1 to 5 fathoms S of Point Delgada can be avoided in approaching Shelter Cove by staying over 200 yards S of the lighted whistle buoy and E of the bell buoy.

(133) From Point Delgada the coast extends NW for 19 miles to Punta Gorda, and is backed by steep mountains covered with chaparral and trees. A black-sand beach, 0.8 miles N of Point Delgada, extends N for 4 miles. **Kaluna Cliff** overlooks the S end of the sand beach, and its steep face, scarred by frequent slides, is a noticeable landmark.

(134) **King Peak**, 4,090 feet high, the highest of three, is the well-known landfall generally called **Three Peaks**. It lies 8.5 miles N of Point Delgada, 2.5 miles from the coast, and in clear weather is visible seaward for about 75 miles.

(135) About 6 miles N from Point Delgada is the head of **Delgada Canyon**, a submarine valley; the 100-fathom curve lies within 0.5 mile of the beach. This valley extends in a N direction with an average width of 1 mile between the 100-fathom curves for 3.5 miles, and then expands, funnel-shaped, for 3 miles more. Over 400 fathoms are found at its mouth and 300 fathoms within 4 miles of the beach. The side slopes are steep.

(136) **Big Flat** is a narrow strip of low, flat land 7 miles NW of Point Delgada. It is 2 miles long and is bordered by sand beaches. A few abandoned ranch houses and barns are at the S end of the flat. **Shubrick Rock**, low and small, lies 300 yards off the S end.

(137)   About 11.5 miles NW of Point Delgada is the head of **Spanish Canyon**, a submarine valley. The 100-fathom curve lies within 2 miles of the shore.

(138)   **Reynolds Rock**, 10 feet high, is 14.5 miles NW of Point Delgada. It is 550 yards offshore and, when seen from close inshore, appears as a double-headed rock over which the swell breaks in nearly all weather.

(139)   **Rodgers Break**, 0.5 mile W of Reynolds Rock, is covered 1¾ fathoms. This pinnacle rock lies 4 miles SE of Gorda Rock and 6.8 miles WNW of Big Flat; it seldom breaks and the top is occasionally seen in a heavy swell. A pinnacle rock covered 2½ fathoms lies about 0.5 mile NW about the same distance offshore. It probably breaks in very heavy weather. This pinnacle and Rodgers Break are the outermost known dangers in this stretch of the coast.

(140)   From Reynolds Rock NW to Punta Gorda the shore is bordered by numerous rocks extending about 0.3 mile offshore. The sharp depression in the hills near the coast, caused by the gulch of **Cooskie Creek**, 3.5 miles S of Punta Gorda, is sometimes useful on dark nights to vessels close inshore in making the point from S.

Chart 18623

(141)   **Punta Gorda** is a high, bold, rounding cape, 83 miles NW of Point Arena and 11 miles S of Cape Mendocino. The seaward face rises to about 900 feet, 400 yards back from the beach, and terminates in a spur, 140 feet high, almost overhanging the sea. It is bare of trees except in the gulches. The gray rectangular structure of an abandoned lighthouse, 25 feet high, is S of the point. For over 1.5 miles N and about 2 miles S of the point, the beach is bordered by numerous rocks and shoals extending in some cases 0.6 mile offshore.

(142)   The wind, sea, and currents off Punta Gorda are probably as strong as off any point on the coast; frequent and strong tide rips have been noted. Many times when the weather at Shelter Cove and even at Big Flat is clear and calm and the sea smooth, both the wind and the sea will pick up as Punta Gorda is approached, until just N of this point where strong breezes to moderate gales will be experienced. At other times clear weather S of this point will lead to fog N, or vice versa.

(143)   **Gorda Rock**, 10 feet high and conical in shape, is 0.7 mile S of Punta Gorda and 0.6 mile offshore. A lighted whistle buoy is 300 yards SW from the rock.

(144)   **Conical Rock**, 20 feet high, is 100 yards off the point, and another 20-foot rock is 350 yards N from it; these rocks have foul ground between them.

(145)   From Punta Gorda to Cape Mendocino the hills back of the coast are lower than those S; they are bare of trees and bordered by stretches of low, narrow, sandy flats with a narrow, low-water beach. The outlying rocks are not more than 0.7 mile offshore until about 2.5 miles S of Cape Mendocino, where they extend offshore to Blunts Reef, 2.5 miles W of the cape. **Mattole Canyon**, a narrow submarine valley, is 3 miles N of Punta Gorda where the 100-fathom curve is about 1 mile from the beach. **Mendocino Canyon** is 4.5 miles S of Cape Mendocino where the 100-fathom curve is about 2 miles from the beach.

(146)   **Christmas Rock**, covered 1½ fathoms, is 0.9 mile NW of Punta Gorda.

(147)   **Mattole River**, 2 miles N of Punta Gorda, is not navigable. The N 360-foot-high head is bare and the S head, about the same height, is partly covered with oak trees. A prominent sand dune is on the S side at the entrance to the valley. Another large sand dune, 3.5 miles to the N, marks the N side of **McNutt Gulch** and should not be confused with the one at Mattole River.

(148)   **Mattole Point** is 0.3 mile N of the river at the base of **Moore Hill**. **Sea Lion Rock**, 8 feet high, is 0.3 mile N of Mattole Point and 250 yards off the beach at the head of Mattole Canyon. A rock covered ½ fathom lies 0.4 mile NW of Mattole Point.

(149)   A rock, 16 feet high, is the largest of a cluster of small rocks 0.5 mile offshore and nearly 4 miles N of Punta Gorda. **The Brothers**, 8 feet high, consist of two small rocks, close together, 800 yards offshore and 1.5 mile NNW of Sea Lion Rock. **Mussel Rocks**, 0.9 mile N of The Brothers, form a ledge that projects 400 yards from the shore.

(150)   **Devils Gate Rock**, 20 feet high, lies nearly 2.8 miles S of Cape Mendocino and 0.5 mile offshore. It is low and pyramidal, with a smaller rock close under the NW face. A reef extends 200 yards W from the rock; numerous rocks lie inshore. A rocky shoal covered 3½ fathoms lies 1.4 miles W of Devils Gate Rock.

(151)   A rock which bares 1 foot is about 1.1 miles NNW of Devils Gate Rock and 0.8 mile offshore.

(152)   **Steamboat Rock**, 30 feet high, lies 1.5 miles S of Cape Mendocino and 600 yards offshore. The upper part of the rock is white and the lower black, somewhat resembling a steamer with a low black hull and white upper works.

(153)   **Cape Mendocino**, 185 miles N of San Francisco Bay entrance and 367 miles S of Columbia River entrance, is a mountainous headland, the famous landmark of the old Spanish navigators and the galleons from the West Indies. The cape is the turning point for nearly all vessels bound N or S. In view of the dangers in the vicinity, it should be approached with considerable caution in thick weather; the bottom and the currents are very irregular. It is in the latitude of great climatic change; the winds do not blow home so violently in the bight S of it, and the amount of rainfall increases rapidly to the N. Fog is more prevalent S. The strong NW winds of summer are less violent S of the cape, which forms a parallel lee for vessels working their way N.

(154)   The seaward face of Cape Mendocino is steep, rocky, and water worn toward the shoreline. NE of the light the general appearance is rolling and grass-covered, except in the deep ravines and upon some of the steep hillsides where the N exposure is covered with forest or brush.

(155) **Cape Mendocino Light** (40°26'23"N., 124°24'22"W.), 515 feet above the water, is shown from a post on the W slope of the cape. For about 3 miles S of the cape, the beach is bordered by numerous rocks and sunken ledges extending in some cases to over 0.5 mile offshore.

(156) **Sugar Loaf**, 326 feet high, is 250 yards W of Cape Mendocino and is connected with it at low water by a narrow neck of rocks and shingle beach. This rock is a prominent feature in making the cape from either N or S, but in thick or hazy weather care should be taken to avoid mistaking it for False Cape Rock, which it somewhat resembles, that is in a similar position off False Cape, 4.5 miles N of Cape Mendocino. False Cape Rock is about 216 feet high and is not so regular in outline as the Sugar Loaf, and, from the W or NW, shows two large rocks, 95 and 54 feet high, immediately inside it, whereas the Sugar Loaf stands solitary and compact. As seen from the SW, Sugar Loaf shows a cave on its SW face, extending about one-third the height of the rock.

(157) **Blunts Reef**, 2.9 miles W of Cape Mendocino Light, is one of the outermost visible dangers off Cape Mendocino. The reef consists of two small black rocks awash about 230 yards apart. **Blunts Reef Lighted Bell Buoy 40** (40°26'24"N., 124°30'19"W.), is 2 miles WSW of the outer rock. The currents at the buoy are described in the Tidal Current Tables.

(158) The area as far W as Blunts Reef Lighted Buoy 40 and for about 4 miles N and S of Cape Mendocino includes dangerous rocks and covered ledges. Vessels should not attempt the passage between Blunts Reef Lighted Bell Buoy 40 and the cape under any circumstances. A heavy W swell breaks even in 9 to 10 fathoms in this locality.

(159) From Cape Mendocino for 4.5 miles to False Cape, the coast is straight, bold, and bordered by a broad low-water beach.

(160) **False Cape** is a steep, bold headland, rising to a height of over 600 feet in less than 0.2 mile from the beach; it projects slightly from the general trend of the coast. It is covered with grass, but the gulches on its sides are wooded. The base of the cape is bordered by a narrow, low-water beach of shingle and sand. For about a mile on each side of the cape are numerous rocks and ledges, the outermost of which are about a mile from the beach.

(161) **False Cape Rock**, 216 feet high, lies 0.4 mile W of the cape; other rocky islets are between it and the shore. It is not as regularly shaped nor as high as the Sugar Loaf off Cape Mendocino, and the top is much flatter. **Mussel Rock**, 7 feet high, is 0.8 mile N of False Cape Rock.

Chart 18620

(162) N of False Cape the hills decrease in height; 4 miles beyond the cape is the beginning of a stretch of sand beach and dunes, broken only by Table Bluff and Buhne Point, that extend to Trinidad Head.

(163) **Centerville Beach**, 4 miles N of False Cape, is not prominent from seaward. A white cross is on the 120-foot bluff just S of Centerville Beach. A number of buildings from a former U.S. Naval facility are on the bluffs 0.8 mile S of the village.

(164) **Eel River** empties 8 miles N of False Cape. This is a stream of considerable size and is occasionally entered by light-draft vessels, but the channel over the bar is continually shifting. The depth on the bar varies largely with the amount of water in the river, depending upon the character of the winter, and has been at times as much as 14 feet, but generally the depth is about 8 or 9 feet. The river is seldom entered except by fishing boats and other very small craft, and then only by those with local knowledge of the bar.

(165) **Eel Canyon** is a submarine valley extending in a NW direction. It comes to a head 10 miles NW of Cape Mendocino. Vessels are cautioned against mistaking this valley for one of those S of the cape.

Chart 18622

(166) **Table Bluff**, 12 miles N of False Cape and 4.5 miles S of Humboldt Bay entrance, is a prominent feature from seaward. The W face is 0.5 mile long, 165 feet high, and very steep, and has a narrow sand beach under it.

(167) From Table Bluff for 4 miles to Humboldt Bay entrance the coast consists of a narrow sand spit.

(168) **Humboldt Bay**, 21 miles N of Cape Mendocino Light, is the first important harbor N of San Francisco and is used by vessels drawing up to 38 feet. Humboldt Bay is the second largest natural bay on the coast of California and as such contains many environmentally and economically important wetland habitats. In addition to being a nursery area for many species of commercially and recreationally important fish and invertebrates, Humboldt Bay also produces more than 50 percent of the oysters harvested in California. Due to Humboldt Bay's location on the Pacific Flyway, it is also an important feeding, resting and nesting area for thousands of migratory shorebirds and waterfowl. Along Humboldt Bay's shoreline, thousands of acres have been set aside by State, Federal and local agencies as wildlife habitat for a variety of threatened and endangered species. Humboldt Bay can be used as a harbor of refuge in impending bad weather, providing a vessel can get inside before the bar becomes impassable. The bay consists of two shallow basins, South Bay in the S and Arcata Bay in the N part, connected by a narrow channel about 5 miles long. Due to the sensitive nature of Humboldt Bay's environment, extreme care should be taken to utilize all best management practices when transiting Humboldt Bay, fueling or transferring fuels or lubricants and transferring cargo.

Humboldt Bay, California
Image courtesy of U.S. Army Corps of Engineers

(169) The redwood timber industry dominates Humboldt Bay. Large quantities of lumber and wood products are shipped to both foreign and domestic ports. General merchandise, gasoline, and fuel oil are received.

(170) Coast Guard Captain of the Port considers the following channels to be narrow channels or fairways for the purpose of enforcing the International and Inland Rules of the Road, Rule 9.

(171) a. Humboldt Bay Bar Channel.
(172) b. Humboldt Bay Entrance Channel.
(173) c. Fields Landing Channel.
(174) d. North Bay Channel.
(175) e. Eureka Channel; Outer and Inner Reaches.
(176) f. Samoa Channel.
(177) g. All other government maintained channels and turning basins.

Routes

(178) A pilot should be engaged by deep-draft vessels and by strangers if there is any sea on the bar. Because the bar is subject to change, the entrance ranges may not always mark the deepest channel.

From South

(179) From a position 1.5 miles 260° from Blunts Reef Lighted Bell Buoy 40, steer **356½°** for 5 miles, when Cape Mendocino Light bears 126°; thence a **038½°** course made good for 20 miles leads to Humboldt Bay Entrance Lighted Whistle Buoy HB. In thick weather, after passing False Cape Rock, all dangers will be cleared by keeping in a depth of over 15 fathoms until up with the lighted whistle buoy, where anchorage should be made until a pilot is obtained.

From North

(180) From a position 3 miles W of Trinidad Head Light, a **187°** course, made good for 17 miles, leads to Humboldt Bay Entrance Lighted Whistle Buoy HB. In thick weather the depths should not be shoaled to less than 20 fathoms between Turtle Rocks and Trinidad Head and, when S of the head, the depths should not be shoaled to less than 15 fathoms until up with the lighted whistle buoy, where a vessel should anchor until a pilot is obtained.

From seaward

(181) In clear weather the high land of Cape Mendocino and Punta Gorda S, and Trinidad Head N of the entrance, are good landmarks. At night, the lights are a good guide. In thick weather soundings should be taken frequently, and upon getting depths of 30 fathoms or less great caution must be exercised until sure of the vessel's position, when the course should be shaped for the lighted whistle buoy.

(182) Sailing craft during the prevailing NW winds of summer should try to make the land in the vicinity of

(183) Trinidad Head; this gives a fair slant for the entrance and is an additional precaution against the irregular S set of the current. In thick weather soundings should be taken constantly when inside of 50 fathoms. Making the land N of the entrance avoids the irregular bottom and dangerous currents in the vicinity of Cape Mendocino.

(183) From the Humboldt Bay Entrance Lighted Whistle Buoy HB, make good a course of **105°** following the Humboldt Bay Approach Range to the intersection with Humboldt Bay Entrance Range, thence a course of **141.5°** on the entrance range into the bay. The entrance range parallels the S jetty and is only about 150 yards from it. The turn from the approach to the entrance range, 200 yards off the outer end of the S jetty, is rather abrupt and is difficult under certain conditions of wind, sea, and current. Inside the bay the channels are well marked by navigational aids.

(184) The approach to the bay is marked by a lighted whistle buoy and a bell buoy off the entrance, and approach range lights and a sound signal on the outer end of the North Spit. A light is shown near the seaward ends of the N and S jetties. The S jetty light has a sound signal. Range lights and lighted buoys mark the entrance channel inside the bar.

(185) **NOTE:** The approach range should not normally be used beyond its intersection with the entrance range. The entrance range should not normally be used seaward of the outer ends of the jetties. Both ranges are lighted 24 hours a day.

(186) Two jetties are at the entrance to the bay, 700 yards apart. The bar NW of the S jetty is subject to considerable shifting and shoaling at times, especially during the winter.

(187) In the past **Humboldt Bar** was considered treacherous and dangerous, and many disasters have occurred there. Even with present improvements, mariners are still advised to use extreme caution on the bar and, because strong currents may be encountered, when approaching the abrupt turn at the outer end of the S jetty. The bar is smoothest during the last of the flood current, and it is often passable at this time and impassable 2 hours later, when the ebb current has set in. Mariners are advised to contact Coast Guard Station Humboldt Bay on VHF-FM channel 16 or 22A prior to transitting the bar. Caution should also be exercised inside the jetties due to the rapid change in the channel conditions. Deep-draft vessels are usually taken in and out of the bay at high tide if there is any swell on the bar because of the shoaling in the entrance channel.

(188) The Coast Guard has established Humboldt Bay Entrance Small Boat Warning Sign at **Coast Guard Station Humboldt Bay** (40°45'59"N., 124°13'02"W.). The north-facing sign is equipped with two flashing yellow lights that will be activated when seas exceed 4 feet in height and are considered hazardous for small boats. Boaters are cautioned, however, that if the lights are not flashing, it is no guarantee that sea conditions are favorable.

COLREGS Demarcation Lines

(189) The lines established for Arcata–Humboldt Bay are described in **80.1150**, chapter 2.

Channels

(190) **Federal project** depths for Humboldt Bay are 48 feet over the bar and in the entrance channel, thence 38 feet in North Bay Channel to Eureka, thence 38 feet in the Eureka Channel outer reach and 26 feet in the inner reach. Project depth in Samoa Channel, including the turning basin, is 38 feet, and in Fields Landing Channel leading to South Bay, including the turning basin, is 26 feet. Maintenance dredging is performed regularly. (See Notice to Mariners and latest chart edition for controlling depths.)

Prominent features

(191) **Humboldt Bay Light** (40°45'51"N., 124°13'48"W.), 100 feet above the water and shown from a white column on North Spit, is the best landmark by night; the approach range rear light also is shown from the Humboldt Bay Light structure. By day the tall stacks and the smoke from the pulp mill in the bay can usually be seen. North Spit has clumps of trees along the bay shore near the channel while South Spit is barren. The red bluff at **Buhne Point** on the east shore of the bay and a lighted radio tower about 1.0 mile E are conspicuous in entering the bay.

(192) **South Bay**, in the S part of Humboldt Bay, is about 3 miles long and 2 miles wide. A marked channel on the E side of the bay leads to a lumber wharf on the E side of the channel at **Fields Landing**.

(193) **Bucksport** is on the E shore about 3 miles above the entrance. The two oil piers at Bucksport are used mainly by barges.

(194) **Fairhaven** is a small town on the W shore, about 3.5 miles above the entrance. The pier of a pulp company is here.

(195) **Eureka**, the principal town on the bay, is on the E shore, 4 miles N of the entrance. It handles much of the waterborne commerce on the bay. Eureka is the terminus of the North Coast Railroad Co.; a branch of the railroad continues to Arcata and Samoa.

(196) **Samoa** is a small settlement on the W shore opposite Eureka, about 5.5 miles above the entrance. A large pulp mill here ships a considerable amount of pulp.

(197) **Arcata Bay**, the N part of Humboldt Bay, is about 3 miles in diameter with low, marshy shore cut by sloughs. **Arcata** is on the N shore of the bay. The town has no serviceable wharves. The ruins of several old wharves are near the head of abandoned Arcata Channel.

Anchorages

(198) There are no authorized anchorages in Humboldt Bay.

Regulated navigation areas

(199)　The Bar Channel and Entrance Channel of Humboldt Bay are included in a **regulated navigation area.** (See **33 CFR 165.1195**, chapter 2, for limits and regulations.)

Bridges

(200)　A fixed highway bridge crosses Humboldt Bay from Eureka to a point just above Samoa on the Samoa Peninsula. Clearances of the fixed spans are 40 feet from Eureka to Woodley Island; 30 feet from Woodley Island to Indian Island; and 45 feet from Indian Island to the Samoa Peninsula.

Currents

(201)　The tidal currents follow the general direction of the channels. In the main channel, the average velocity is less than 2 knots and the maximum does not exceed 3 knots. Between the jetties, the average velocity is about 2 knots, with a maximum of about 4 knots; during storm conditions, velocities can reach up to 5.5 knots. Current predictions are given in the Tidal Current Tables.

Weather, Eureka

(202)　The climate of Eureka is completely maritime, and high humidity prevails the entire year, which is divided into the "rainy" season and the "dry" season. The rainy season begins in October and continues through April. About 90 percent of the year's precipitation falls during this period. The dry season extends from May through September and is marked by considerable fog or low cloudiness. On average, 23 of the 31 days in August will record fog where only 10 of the 31 days in March will note fog. Usually, however, the fog clears in the late forenoon and the early afternoons are generally sunny. On average, better than 38 inches (965 mm) of precipitation falls on an annual basis in Eureka and 152 of the 365 days of the year record some sort of precipitation. January is the wettest month and July, the driest. Snowfall is light and averages less than one-half inch annually (13 mm) however, snowfall has been recorded in each of the months November through April. The greatest daily snowfall was two inches (51 mm) in February 1989.

(203)　Temperatures are moderate the entire year. Although the highest ever recorded was 87°F (30.6°C) in October 1993, and the lowest 21°F (-6.1°C) in December 1972, the usual range is from a low of about 47°F (8.3°C) to a high of about 58°F (14.4°C). The daily range of temperature averages from about 10°F (-12.2°C) in the summer to 13°F (7°C) in the winter, and is occasionally not over 2° to 3°F (1° to 2°C).

(204)　The principal industries are lumbering, fishing, and dairy farming. Owing to the low temperatures and lack of sunshine, there is very little truck farming, but the climate is nearly ideal for berries and flowers.

(205)　The National Weather Service is on **Woodley Island. Barometers** may be compared there or by telephone. (See Appendix A for address.)

(206)　See Appendix B for **Eureka climatological table**.

Pilotage, Humboldt Bay

(207)　Pilotage is compulsory for foreign vessels under registry and U.S. vessels under registry and enrollment. Pilotage is voluntary for all other vessels.

(208)　Pilotage for ports in Humboldt Bay is available from **Humboldt Bar Pilots Association**, P.O. Box 3555, Eureka, CA 95502-3555.

(209)　The pilots monitor VHF-FM channel 16. The pilot boat monitors VHF-FM channels 13 and 16, and the pilot office and tug boat use 13, 18, and 77 as working frequencies. The pilot boat, TUG KOOS KING, is 65 feet long and has a black hull, buff and white house, and red stack with a white K.

(210)　Arrangements for pilots are made by ships' agents or by telephone through Westfall Stevedore Co., PHONE (707) 443-5688, FAX (707) 443-4672, cable WESTFALLEUREKA, VHF-FM channel 10. The operational status of the engines, draft, and estimated time of arrival are required within 24 hours and 4 hours of arrival. E-mail: westfall@northcoast.com.

(211)　Pilots board vessels within 0.5 mile radius of Humboldt Bay Entrance Lighted Whistle Buoy HB (40°46.4'N., 124°16.2'W.) or 1.5 miles W of Humboldt Bay Entrance Jetties. When boarding, pilots request vessels maintain a speed not to exceed 5 knots and rig the pilot ladder on the leeward side about 3 meters above the water; no man ropes.

(212)　In the summer, vessels are entered on flood and ebb tidal currents; in the winter, vessels usually are entered on the first or last of the flood or first of the ebb. Vessels depart on flood tidal currents only, regardless of the time of year. Vessels with drafts over 30 feet, enter or depart on the last of the flood from November through March 30; night sailing depends on the bar condition before dark.

(213)　Pilots report that strong currents create a N set in the Bar Channel from October to April. When vessels enter the jetties, this current has a tendency to twist vessels by setting the stern N and turning the bow S toward the S jetty. During or shortly after SE, S, and SW storms, currents in the Bar Channel and Entrance Channel are reported to attain a velocity of about 4 to 5.5 knots. Heavy swells about 8 to 10 feet high occur well inside the jetties when seas from the SW are deflected, about midway along the N jetty.

Towage

(214)　Tugs up to 2,000 hp are available.

Quarantine, customs, immigration, and agricultural quarantine

(215)　(See chapter 3, Vessel Arrival Inspections, and Appendix A for addresses.)

(216)　**Quarantine** is enforced in accordance with regulations of the U.S. Public Health Service. (See Public Health Service, chapter 1.) The city has several hospitals.

Name	Location	Berthing Space (feet)	Depths* (feet)	Deck Height (feet)	Mechanical Handling Facilities and Storage	Purpose	Owned/ Operated by:
Chevron Products Co. Eureka Terminal Wharf	40°46'41"N., 124°11'42"W.	400	24-30	10.5	• Tank storage (105,000 barrels) • Pipelines extend from wharf to storage tanks	Receipt of petroleum products by barge	Chevron Products Co.
Sierra Pacific Industries Eureka Wharf	40°47'42"N., 124°11'15"W.	470	32-35	10	• Open storage (15 acres) • Wood chip loader and belt conveyor	Shipment of logs, lumber and wood chips	Eureka Forest Products, Inc/Sierra Industries, Inc.
Pacific Affiliates Eureka Wharf	40°47'51"N., 124°11'12"W.	1,000	35	11	Open storage (17 acres)	Receipt and shipment of conventional general cargo	David L Schneider/ Pacific Affiliates, Inc.
City of Eureka Humboldt Dock B	40°48'05"N., 124°10'58"W.	200	23	11	Three mast-and-boom derricks with 15-foot booms	Receipt of seafood	City of Eureka
Louisiana-Pacific Corp. Samoa Chemical Wharf	40°48'13"N., 124°11'18"W.	1,147	35	20	Tank storage (645,000 barrels)	Receipt of caustic soda	Louisiana-Pacific Corp.
Louisiana-Pacific Corp. Samoa Chip Export Wharf	40°47'55"N., 124°11'26"W.	1,260	38	20	• Open storage • Pneumatic chip loader (1,200 tons per hour)	Shipment of wood chips	Louisiana-Pacific Corp.
Fairhaven Terminal Co./ Westfall Stevedore Co. Simpson Mill Wharf	40°47'18"N., 124°11'41"W.	700	38	15	• Open storage (10 acres) • Covered storage (5 acres)	• Receipt and shipment of conventional general cargo and wood pulp • Receipt of lumber	Simpson Investment Co./Fairhaven Terminal Co. and Westfall Stevedore Co.
Humbolt Bay Forest Products Fields Landing Wharf	40°43'57"N., 124°13'09"W.	600	36	12	• Open storage (50 acres) • Three 12-ton crawler cranes	Receipt and shipment of logs, lumber and wood chips	Humboldt Bay Forest Products, Inc.

* The depths given above are reported. For information on the latest depths contact the port authorities or the private operators.

(217) Eureka is a **customs port of entry.**

Coast Guard

(218) Humboldt Bay Coast Guard Station is on North Spit.

Harbor regulations

(219) These regulations are prescribed by the Humboldt Bay Harbor Recreation and Conservation District. The District operates a large marina on the S side of Woodley Island, just N of Eureka on the N side of Eureka Channel Inner Reach. A wharfinger, located at the Eureka Public Marina, has jurisdiction over fishing and pleasure craft using the facilities at the city-owned boat basin.

Wharves

(220) The deep-draft facilities at Humboldt Bay are alongside the channels leading to Arcata Bay and at Fields Landing in South Bay. Only the deep-draft facilities are listed in the table. The alongside depths for the facilities are reported; for the latest depths, contact the private operators. All facilities have direct highway connections. One facility (Pacific Affiliates, Eureka Wharf - reference #3) has a railway connection. All facilities have water connections and some have electrical connections. For a complete description of the port facilities refer to Port Series No. 30 published and sold by the U.S. Army Corps of Engineers. (See Appendix A for address.)

Supplies

(221) Deep-draft vessels are usually bunkered at the berths by tank truck. Marine supplies and provisions, including water, are available at the port.

Repairs

(222) There are no facilities for making major repairs to deep-draft vessels; the nearest such facilities are at the Port of San Francisco. Complete hull and engine repairs are available for small craft. The Humboldt Bay Harbor, Recreation and Conservation District has a lift to 150 tons. The largest marine railway, located on the W side of the channel opposite Eureka, can handle craft up to 300 tons, 100 feet long, 30 feet wide, and with a 10-foot draft.

Small-craft facilities

(223) Transient berths with electricity are available at the marina on the S side of Woodley Island and at Eureka Public Marina (40°48'14"N., 124°10'36"W.). Additional berthing space is available at marinas on Fields Landing and behind Buhne Point. Water, gasoline, diesel fuel, marine supplies, and launching ramps are available at most marinas in Humboldt Bay.

(224) Wet winter storage is at the marina at the S side of Woodley Island.

Chart 18620

(225) N of the entrance to Humboldt Bay, the coast consists of sand dunes partly covered with timber for 11

(226) miles to the mouth of **Mad River**. The first 7 miles forms the W shore of Humboldt Bay, and then the land behind the dunes is low and marshy as far as the river.

(226) From the mouth of Mad River, the sand dunes are 20 to 60 feet high and continue for 5.5 miles to **Little River**, a small shallow stream. The N point at the mouth of the stream is rocky, and from this point the coast consists of rocky cliffs extending beyond Trinidad Head.

Coast Guard

(227) **Humboldt Bay Coast Guard Air Station** is at McKinleyville about 2.5 miles N of the mouth of Mad River.

Chart 18605

(228) **Little River Rock**, 126 feet high, is 0.8 mile NW of the mouth of Little River, and 0.3 mile offshore. Several rocks and foul ground are between it and the beach, and a rock 4 feet high is about 100 yards NW.

(229) From Little River Rock to Trinidad Head, the shore is bordered by numerous rocks and ledges extending 0.3 mile offshore.

(230) **Pilot Rock,** 93 feet high, is 0.5 mile S of Trinidad Head. It is of small extent, conical, and whitish in color, rising abruptly from depths of 48 to 50 feet on all sides. Pilot Rock is marked on its W side by a gong buoy.

(231) **Trinidad Head** is nearly 39 miles NNE of Cape Mendocino and 17.5 miles N of the entrance to Humboldt Bay. It rises to a height of 380 feet. The sides are steep and covered with chaparral. From N or S the head is generally raised as a dark, round-topped island. Near the N end it is joined to the mainland by a narrow neck, from the S side of which **Little Head**, a rocky knoll 125 feet high, projects into Trinidad Harbor. The white cross 200 yards N of the S point of Trinidad Head is fairly prominent.

(232) **Trinidad Head Light** (41°03'07"N., 124°09'05"W.), 196 feet above the water, is shown from a lighthouse near the SW side of the head; a sound signal is at the light. A lighted whistle buoy is 1 mile W of the head.

(233) **Trinidad Harbor**, a small cove E of Trinidad Head, affords shelter in NW weather, but is dangerous in W or S weather. The cove is small and is further constricted by several rocks, and, as a rule, there is always a swell even in N weather. It is used by fishing boats to a considerable extent during the summer, even though the holding ground is only fair. A white lighthouse structure, a memorial containing the original oil-burning light used at Trinidad Head until 1948, is at the center of the bluff on the N side of the harbor. A pier with a bait and tackle shop, and restaurant is located in the bight W of Little Head. A small marine railway near the foot of the pier is used for launching and retrieving small craft up to 25 feet long and 8½ feet wide. A beach boat launch is located on the E side of the marine railway. A water taxi is available during the summer months and a floating pier is provided to access the main pier during the months of May through September. Gasoline, marine supplies, and ice are available in **Trinidad**, a town on the N shore of the cove. The harbor monitors VHF-FM channel 78.

(234) **Prisoner Rock**, 220 yards E of Trinidad Head, is 42 feet high and the most prominent of the rocks in the cove. It consists of two rocks so close together that they are usually taken for one. From S they resemble an animal lying down with its head toward the W. A rock covered 7 feet is 150 yards NNW from them.

(235) **Flat Rock**, low and small, lies 350 yards ENE from Prisoner Rock; a rock covered 5 feet lies 150 yards SSE from it. A bell buoy is 175 yards W of a rock covered 9 feet, which lies 400 yards SSE of Prisoner Rock.

Anchorage

(236) The best anchorage is in 42 feet, muddy bottom, about halfway between Prisoner Rock and Trinidad Head, with Flat Rock, bearing 073°, just open S of Prisoner Rock. A **special anchorage** is on the E side of Trinidad Head. (See **110.1 and 110.127c**, chapter 2, for limits and regulations.)

(237) **Blank Rock**, 111 feet high, lies 0.3 mile W of Trinidad Head. Foul ground is between it and the head. A smaller rock is 150 yards N of Blank Rock. A rock awash and a ledge covered 15 feet are 275 yards SSE of Blank Rock.

(238) **Flatiron Rock**, 72 feet high, lies 0.3 mile NW of Blank Rock. It is considerably larger than Blank Rock, with two rocky heads of about the same height. A covered rock lies 300 yards off its SW face, and numerous ledges extend SE toward the head.

Chart 18600

(239) From Trinidad Head for 5.5 miles to Rocky Point, the coast is rocky, with numerous outlying islets and ledges extending as much as 1.2 miles offshore and cliffs reaching elevations of over 100 feet. The mountains back of Trinidad Head are good landmarks for vessels approaching from seaward. N of Rocky Point, the beach is low and sandy, with several lagoons behind it, for nearly 11 miles to the S end of the Gold Bluffs. From this point to Point St. George, the coast is rocky, the cliffs being from 100 to 500 feet high and bordered by numerous rocks. The Klamath River breaks through the cliffs 16 miles S of Point St. George. From Point St. George for 65 miles to Cape Blanco, the coast trends in a general NW direction with a shallow bight known as Pelican Bay immediately N of Point St. George. The beach is fringed by numerous rocks and ledges, but, with the exception of St. George, Rogue River, and Orford Reefs, these in general do not extend over a mile from shore. The 30-fathom curve follows the general trend of the coast, and in thick weather may be considered as the

(240) **Green Rock**, 108 feet high and of small extent, lies 1.5 miles N of Trinidad Head and nearly 600 yards offshore. The top is covered with grass. Numerous rocks lie inshore, and a rock awash lies 700 yards W of it. A rock covered 2¾ fathoms lies 0.5 mile W of Green Rock. It seldom breaks and rises abruptly from 15 fathoms. Two covered rocks lie 0.5 and 0.8 mile NNE of Green Rock.

(241) **White Rock**, 118 feet high, lies 1.9 miles N of Trinidad Head. It is of small extent and is 250 yards off a wooded projecting head about the same height. Another rocky islet 129 feet high is 1 mile N of White Rock.

(242) **Cone Rock**, 17 feet high, is 3.8 miles N of Trinidad Head and over 1 mile offshore. It is conical in shape and of small extent. A smaller rock, 15 feet high, lies 0.5 mile E.

(243) **Turtle Rocks**, two rocks of small extent 20 and 29 feet high, are 1.5 miles N of Cone Rock and abreast of Rocky Point. E of Turtle Rocks the ground is foul, with two breakers 600 and 800 yards from the outer rock and numerous visible rocks extending to the beach. A bell buoy is 0.5 mile W of Turtle Rocks.

(244) **Rocky Point**, 5.5 miles N of Trinidad Head, is a bold feature with cliffs about 200 feet high, bordered by numerous rocks and ledges extending 200 to 300 yards offshore. The point is covered with oak and scrub pine for 0.5 mile back to the redwood forest; through this oak growth two rocky pinnacles about 250 feet high are visible.

(245) **Rodgers Peak**, 2,800 feet high and 6.3 miles E of Rocky Point, is heavily wooded and easily identified.

(246) N of Rocky Point the cliffs are succeeded by a low sandy beach for 4.5 miles to the N end of **Big Lagoon**, which is immediately behind the sand beach. Above Big Lagoon the cliff formation is resumed and extends 2 miles to **Stone Lagoon**.

(247) **Sharp Point**, 6.2 miles N of Rocky Point, is a sharp-pointed conical rock cliff about 400 feet high. Its light-gray color makes it readily distinguishable for a distance of 15 miles in clear weather from any direction. The beach in this area is bordered by numerous rocks extending about 0.8 mile offshore.

(248) **Gold Bluffs**, a 9-mile stretch of gravel and sand 100 to 500 feet high, begin about 9 miles N of Rocky Point. The S part is comparatively low and bordered by several outlying rocks; in about the middle the buffs are broken by two valleys.

(249) **Mussel Point**, 11.2 miles N of Rocky Point, is a light gray cliff about 300 feet high, with a small, flat top distinguishable at 10 to 12 miles in clear weather.

(250) **Reading Rock**, 94 feet high and of small extent, is 4.5 miles offshore W of Mussel Point. It is dark for about one-third the height and white above with a cleft on the S face. It is marked by a light, 98 feet above the water, shown from a house with a red and white diamond-shaped daymark.

(251) N of Gold Bluffs the coast becomes rocky, irregular, and broken, the bold cliffs being bordered by many rocks.

(252) A yellow clay slide extending from the top of a 900-foot slope to the beach is 9 miles N of Mussel Point. It is sharp at the top, broad at the base, and the highest and most prominent of the bluffs in that vicinity. It may be seen in clear weather for a distance of 15 to 18 miles.

(253) **Split Rock** is a slightly projecting head 3.5 miles N of the N end of Gold Bluffs; it is so named because of the cut on the N face.

(254) **High Bluff** is a slightly projecting head 0.8 mile N of Split Rock. It is prominent because of an enormous split or chasm on its N face; at the S edge of the cut the bluff is 340 feet high.

(255) **White Rock**, 107 feet high, lies 600 yards N of High Bluff and 300 yards offshore. Numerous rocks, covered and visible, lie between it and the beach. Its S face is very precipitous, and its W face is steep, sloping N. It can be distinguished by its color for several miles.

(256) **Flint Rock Head**, 177 feet high, is a detached rocky head connected with the cliffs by a low sandspit. It is at the S end of the Klamath River sand beach, 1.8 miles N of Split Rock. Its SW face is precipitous. A rock awash lies 0.6 mile NW from Flint Rock Head and 0.5 mile offshore.

(257) **Klamath River** mouth is 16 miles S of Point St. George and 30 miles N of Trinidad Head. It is a large river draining an extensive mountainous area. The entrance is no longer navigable, but there is small-craft traffic on the river. There are several float landings where sport fishing craft berth. Gasoline, water, ice, launching ramps, and marine supplies are available.

(258) The coast highway crosses the river at **Klamath**, a small town 2 miles inland. A fixed highway bridge, 3 miles above the mouth, has a clearance of 13 feet.

(259) **Requa** is a small village on the N shore of the river just inside the mouth with a hotel and private landings.

(260) **Red Mountain**, 8 miles E of the mouth of Klamath River, is visible for about 60 miles in clear weather.

(261) From the mouth of the Klamath River the coast curves NW for 3 miles to the mouth of **Wilson Creek**. The cliffs are high, irregular, and jagged, and the hills above are covered with grass and chaparral. Numerous rocks extend about 300 yards offshore.

(262) A covered rock 0.6 mile offshore is 1.4 miles NW of the mouth of Klamath River. A rock, 37 feet high, is 1 mile offshore, 2.6 miles NW of the mouth of Klamath River, and about 1.5 miles S of Wilson Creek.

(263) **False Klamath Rock**, 203 feet high, reddish, and round-topped, is the most prominent rock on this part of the coast. It lies 650 yards W of the S point of the small cove into which Wilson Creek empties. **Wilson Rock**, awash, is 0.5 mile W of False Klamath Rock. A rock awash is 0.9 mile NW of False Klamath Rock. Numerous covered rocks lie E and NE of the line from this rock to another rock, 37 feet high, SW of False Klamath Rock.

Crescent City Harbor, California
Image courtesy of Rick Hiser/Crescent City Harbor District (2008)

(264) From False Klamath Rock for 7 miles N the coast consists of bold rocky cliffs, much broken and bordered by numerous covered and exposed rocks. Beyond these, extending 3 miles to Crescent City, is a broad sand beach backed by flat cultivated land.

(265) **Midway Point**, 4 miles N of False Klamath Rock, is bold, rising to a height of 820 feet, 800 yards from the beach.

(266) **Sister Rocks**, a cluster of prominent rocks, 0.5 mile W of Midway Point, consist of three large and several smaller rocks covering a limited area; the outer one is 69 feet and the inner one 72 feet high.

Chart 18603

(267) **Crescent City Harbor**, protected by breakwaters, is midway between San Francisco Bay and the entrance to Columbia River. Commercial and sport fishing boats operate out of the harbor. Waterborne traffic in the harbor is in the receipt of gasoline and fuel oils. **Crescent City** is on the N side of the harbor.

(268) **Crescent City Entrance Light** (41°44'11"N., 124°11'28"W.), 55 feet above the water, is shown from a pile at the seaward end of the W breakwater. A sound signal is at the light. A historic private light is on the islet S of **Battery Point**. The entrance to the harbor is marked by lighted buoys, lights, and a lighted range.

(269) The entrance range should not be followed past a point approximately abeam of Whaler Island, as it leads close to the end of the breakwater extending N from this island.

COLREGS Demarcation Lines

(270) The lines established for Crescent City Harbor are described in **80.1152**, chapter 2.

(271) A dredged entrance channel leads N into the harbor to an inner harbor basin which extends around the outer end of the inner breakwater. In 2008, the controlling depth was 14 feet in the entrance channel; thence in 2008-2011, 12 feet in the basin.

(272) The W breakwater gives good protection from NW winds for vessels anchored in the outer harbor, but the harbor is open to the S. The basin N of **Whaler Island** provides excellent anchorage for small craft.

(273) Vessels anchored in the harbor should take precaution against a local SE wind known as the **kick back** or **back draft**, which frequently blows with considerable violence. This wind follows only periods of strong NW winds outside. It usually starts in the early afternoon and ends about midnight.

Caution

(274) Care should be exercised in approaching Crescent City Harbor because of the many rocks and shoals.

(274) **Chase Ledge,** covered 21 feet, lies 0.9 mile S of **Round Rock**. **Mussel Rock,** only a few feet high, is 0.6 mile SE of Round Rock; a rock covered 8 feet, 700 yards to the S, breaks only in a heavy swell. Other covered rocks extend N to Whaler Island. Foul ground with many bare and covered rocks extends nearly a mile offshore along the low but rocky coast NW of Crescent City Harbor for 3.5 miles to Point St. George. This area should be avoided.

(275) The long wharf in the W part of the harbor is used by fishing vessels to offload fish. The remains of two other wharves, just E, were almost completely wiped out by the seismic sea wave which struck the harbor following the March 27, 1964, Alaska earthquake. The seismic wave caused considerable damage and changes to the harbor shoreline.

(276) The basin just N of Whaler Island is formed by the inner breakwater extending NW from the island and the sand barrier from the island to the E shore. Citizens Dock, the Y-shaped pier at the N side of the harbor, extends out to a depth of about 9 feet. Several fishhouses are on the pier. Fishing boats unload their catch along both of the outer spurs of the pier. Water and ice are available on the pier. Gasoline and diesel fuel are available. Many mooring floats for commercial fishing boats are in the inner basin N of Citizens Dock. Berths with electricity, gasoline, diesel fuel, water, ice, wet and dry winter storage, a pump-out station, a launching ramp, and marine supplies are available.

(277) The **harbormaster** has an office at the basin N of Whaler Island. The harbormaster assigns berths and monitors VHF-FM channels 9 and 16, Monday through Friday from 0700 to 1700.

(278) A boatyard in the basin has lifts that can handle boats up to 110 feet, 270 tons. Engine repairs are available from several local firms.

(279) A Coast Guard vessel is stationed in the basin N of Whaler Island.

(280) The inner small-craft basin just N of Citizens Dock can accommodate about 250 boats with an additonal 100 boats at the small sport dock. In 2002, the controlling depths were 8.7 feet (12.3 feet at midchannel) in the entrance channel to the basin.

(281) **Castle Rock**, 2.3 miles NW of Battery Point and 0.5 mile S of the S point of Point St. George, has a rather flat top, with a small knob near the E edge.

(282) **Point St. George**, 3 miles NW of Battery Point, is low with several irregular and rocky hillocks near the beach. The seaward face is about a mile long in a NW direction, with sand dunes and low land immediately behind it. The tree line is about 0.6 mile inland, with a few trees near the S end of the point. Numerous conspicuous rocks fringe the point up to 0.5 mile offshore. **Brown Rock**, 28 feet high, is near the outer end of the exposed rocks extending NW from the point.

(283) **St. George Channel**, over a mile wide, is clear between the visible rocks fringing Point St. George and the E rocks of St. George Reef. It is frequently used in clear weather by coastwise vessels.

(284) **St. George Reef** is composed of rocks and covered ledges extending 6.5 miles NW and W from Point St. George. Nine visible rocks are in the group.

(285) **St. George Reef Lighted Whistle Buoy 46** (41°50'13.8"N., 124°23'11.3"W.), is about ½ mile W of **Northwest Seal Rock** and Little Black Rock, the outermost rocks of St. George Reef.

(286) **Star Rock,** the SE rock of the group, is 64 feet high. It is 1.7 miles W of the S tip of Point St. George. Between Star and Northwest Seal Rocks are three rocks, **Hump Rock, Whale Rock**, and **Southwest Seal Rock**, almost in line, varying in height from 18 to 45 feet. S of these visible rocks are two covered ledges, **Mansfield Break**, and **Jonathan Rock**. The latter is 2.5 miles NW of Star Rock and 3.2 miles SE of Northwest Seal Rock. It breaks only in a heavy swell, and not continuously then; deep water surrounds it. Mansfield Break lies 2.3 miles S of Northwest Seal Rock and nearly 3.5 miles NW of Star Rock. It is about 100 yards in extent, with 20 fathoms close-to and around it.

(287) **Great Break**, 0.5 mile SE of Southwest Seal Rock, is about 150 yards in extent. A covered ledge that breaks at low water is 125 yards SW of Southwest Seal Rock.

(288) **Dragon Channel**, which leads N of Jonathan Rock and between Mansfield Break and Great Break, is not recommended.

(289) **East Rock** and **Long Rock** are 2.1 and 1.6 miles, respectively, N of Star Rock.

(290) **Flat Rock** lies nearly midway between Long and Whale Rocks, and about 0.6 mile from the former. **Mussel Rock** is nearly 0.5 mile W of Long Rock; a covered ledge showing a breaker is 200 yards N of the rock. A covered rock that breaks in moderate swells is 330 yards NE of Hump Rock.

(291) All the rocks of St. George Reef rise abruptly; soundings made in the vicinity give no warning of their presence. In thick weather, the greatest caution should be observed and the reef given a wide berth.

Chart 18600

(292) For about 10 miles N of Point St. George, the shores of **Pelican Bay** are composed of sand dunes, with a broad beach extending to the mouth of **Smith River. Lake Talawa** and **Lake Earl** are surrounded by low marshy land behind this stretch of dunes.

(293) A small rock about 10 feet high is 1.8 miles S of the mouth of Smith River, and nearly 0.5 mile offshore. A cluster of three low rocks is nearly a mile offshore and 0.9 mile NNE of the 10-foot rock.

Chart 18602

(294) From Smith River for 3.2 miles to the California-Oregon boundary, the coast is composed of low rocky

cliffs, bordered by numerous rocks and ledges, covered and awash, and backed by a low narrow tableland. Several prominent rocky knolls rise from 100 to 200 feet above this tableland.

(295) **Pyramid Point**, a rocky knoll 222 feet high, marks the N point of Smith River.

(296) **Prince Island**, of small extent and 171 feet high, lies 0.1 mile offshore abreast Pyramid Point. **Hunter Rock**, 177 feet high, double-headed and somewhat smaller, is 0.3 mile N of Prince Island. Several other smaller rocks are in the vicinity.

(297) **Cone Rock**, 1.3 miles N of Prince Island and 0.6 mile offshore, is the most prominent of the visible dangers in this vicinity. It is 68 feet high and of small extent.

TIDAL INFORMATION					
Chart	Station	LAT/LONG	Mean Higher High Water*	Mean High Water*	Mean Low Water*
18602	Brookings, Chetco Cove, Oregon	42°03'N/124°17'W	6.9	6.3	1.2
18603	Crescent City	41°44'N/124°11'W	6.9	6.2	1.2
18605	Trinidad Harbor	41°03'N/124°09'W	6.7	6.0	1.2
18620	Shelter Cove	40°02'N/124°04'W	6.0	5.4	1.2
18622	Samoa, Humboldt Bay	40°49'N/124°11'W	7.3	6.6	1.3
18622	Fields Landing, Humboldt Bay	40°43'N/124°13'W	6.8	6.2	1.2
18622	Humboldt Bay, North Spit	40°46'N/124°13'W	6.9	6.2	1.3
18622	Bucksport, Humboldt Bay	40°47'N/124°12'W	7.0	6.2	1.3
18622	Eureka, Humboldt Bay	40°48'N/124°10'W	7.3	6.6	1.3
18622	Arcata Wharf, Humboldt Bay	40°51'N/124°07'W	7.0	6.3	1.3
18628	Mendocino, Mendocino Bay	39°18'N/123°48'W	5.8	5.1	1.1
18643	Tomales Bay entrance	38°14'N/122°59'W	5.2	4.5	1.0
18643	Inverness, Tomales Bay	38°06'N/122°51'W	5.3	4.6	0.9
18643	Bodega Harbor entrance	38°18'N/123°03'W	5.7	5.0	1.2

* Heights in feet referred to datum of sounding MLLW.
Real-time water levels, tide predictions, and tidal current predictions are available at:
http://tidesandcurrents.noaa.gov
To determine mean tide range subtract Mean Low Water from Mean High Water.
Data as of September 2012

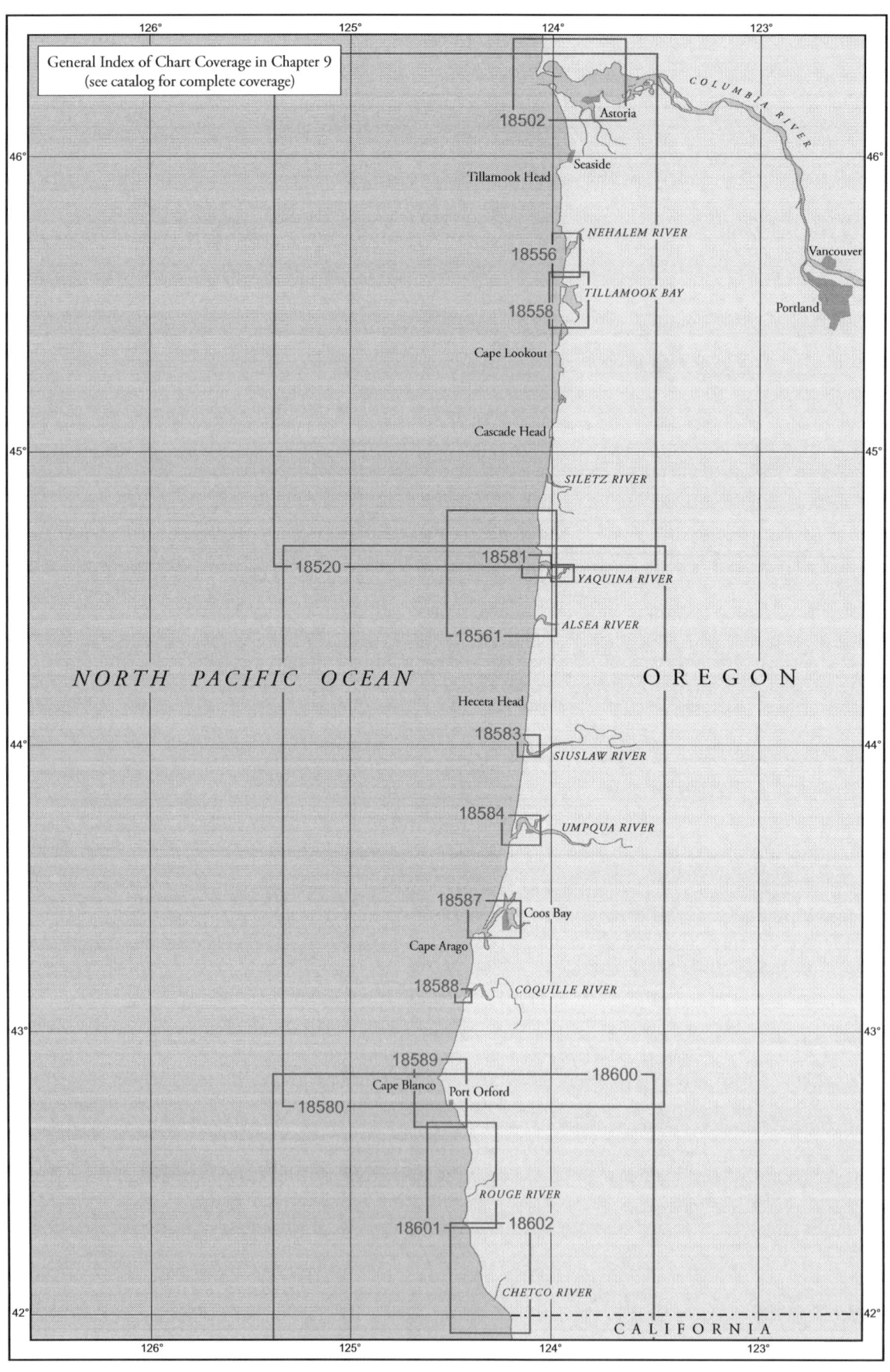

Chetco River to Columbia River, Oregon

(1) This chapter describes 200 miles of the Oregon coast from the mouth of the Chetco River to the mouth of the Columbia River. Also described are the Chetco and Rogue Rivers, Port Orford, Coquille River, Coos Bay, Umpqua and Siuslaw Rivers, Yaquina Bay and River, Nehalem River, and Tillamook Bay. The cities of Coos Bay and North Bend on Coos Bay and Newport on Yaquina Bay are the only deep-draft ports on the Oregon coast. The principal dangers are unmarked Rogue River Reef, and Orford Reef, which is marked by a light.

COLREGS Demarcation Lines

(2) The lines established for this part of the coast are described in **80.1305 through 80.1360**, chapter 2.

Weather, Chetco River to Columbia River

(3) Fog and rain are the major weather headaches to the mariner along the Oregon coast. Summer and early fall bring light winds, mild temperatures, clear or partly cloudy skies, and frequent fog. While fog is a problem all along the coast, its frequency increases as you head S. Around Astoria, visibilities drop below 0.5 mile (0.9 km) on 4 to 6 days per month from August through October. At North Bend, this happens on 6 to 13 days per month from July through December. August is usually the worst month. Fog is thickest at night and in the morning. Conditions often improve by midafternoon, when skies clear or become partly cloudy. Temperatures climb into the mid-sixties (16.7° to 19.4°C) in summer and low sixties (16.1° to 17.2°C) in fall. At night, they drop into the low fifties (10.6° to 11.7°C) in summer and mid-forties (6.1° to 8.3°C) in autumn. Winds are generally light in summer and early fall. Northwesterlies and southwesterlies through southerlies are frequent, the latter becoming increasingly so in fall. Winds at North Bend on Coos Bay are an exception, and strongest in June, July, and August. They blow at 17 knots or more 15 to 20 percent of the time and at 28 knots or more 1 to 2 percent of the time.

(4) Rain (0.1 inch or more) falls on less than 10 days per month from May through September. It becomes more frequent in October and reaches a peak in January, when 15 to 20 rainy days occur on the average. Snow is uncommon, since temperatures are usually mild. Winter temperatures reach the low fifties (10.6° to 11.7°C) during the day and fall into the upper thirties (3° to 4°C) at night; extremes have dipped into the low teens (-11.7° to -10.6°C). Fog can occur in winter with fronts or under rare clear skies; it is more likely in early winter. Winter and spring winds are moderately strong, particularly S of Newport. From North Bend southward, winds reach 17 knots or more about 5 to 15 percent of the time and 28 knots or more about 1 to 3 percent of the time. Extreme wind speeds usually occur in either winter or early spring, and have climbed to around 50 knots. They are most common from a S direction. Winter winds along the entire coast are generally out of the SE through S. Northwesterlies are also common. It is not until May that these directions switch roles and northwesterlies become more or as frequent. Spring warming is also a slow process. By April, temperatures are about 4° to 7° above January levels.

Charts 18602, 18600

(5) From the California-Oregon boundary for 3.8 miles to Chetco River, the coast is composed of low rocky cliffs, bordered by numerous rocks and ledges, covered and awash, and backed by a low narrow tableland. Several prominent rocky knolls rise from 100 to 200 feet above this tableland. Due to the numerous dangers, the coast should not be approached closer than 1.5 miles. The sea boundary between the Eleventh and Thirteenth Coast Guard Districts is at the state boundary between California and Oregon.

(6) **Chetco Cove**, 15.5 miles N of Point St. George, affords some protection from NW winds, but is exposed in S weather. **Chetco Point** marks the NW side of the cove. There are numerous visible and covered rocks fringing the shore of the cove and its approaches. **Chetco River** empties into the N side of the cove. The river is entered through a dredged channel which leads between two stone jetties to the **Port of Brookings** turning basin, about 0.3 mile above the jetties. The turning basin and a small-craft basin just N of it are protected to the W by a 1,800-foot-long dike. Another small-craft basin is about 250 yards SE of the turning basin. A barge slip, just E of the turning basin, is at the N side of the mouth of the entrance channel to the lower small-craft basin. The river entrance channel is marked by a **030°** lighted range. A light is on the outer end of the W jetty and a mariner radio activated sound signal is on the inner end of the E jetty, initiated by keying the microphone five times on VHF-FM channel 83A.

(7) A **Federal project** provides for a 14-foot entrance channel and turning basin from deep water in Chetco Cove to the turning basin just inside the breakwater protecting the Port of Brookings; access channels with

project depths of 12 feet, lead N and S from the turning basin. (See Notice to Mariners and latest editions of charts for controlling depths.) An overhead power cable crossing the river about 0.6 mile above the jetties has a clearance of about 46 feet. The highway bridge has a clearance of 59 feet.

COLREGS Demarcation Lines

(8) The lines established for the Chetco River are described in **80.1305**, chapter 2.

Coast Guard

(9) **Chetco River Coast Guard Station** is on the E side of the river 450 yards inside the entrance. A lookout tower atop a building at the station is used to observe the bar during heavy weather. The Coast Guard has established Chetco River Regulated Navigation Area Warning Sign, a **rough bar advisory sign** 13 feet above the water, visible from the channel looking seaward, on the N end of the Coast Guard moorings, to promote safety for small-boat operators. The sign is diamond-shaped, painted white with an international orange border, and with the words "Rough Bar" in black letters. The sign is equipped with two quick flashing amber lights that will be activated when hazardous conditions exist and the bar is restricted to recreational and uninspected passenger vessels. Boaters are cautioned, however, that if the lights are not flashing, it is no guarantee that sea conditions are favorable.

(10) A **heavy weather flag**, a square RED flag with a square BLACK center, will be displayed on a pole that is located near the N end of the Coast Guard station and is visible to mariners from both directions to indicate that winds 48 knots and above are forecast for the area. Display of flags are required from one hour before sunrise to one hour after sunset. Weather flags are flown at select Coast Guard stations to supplement other weather notification sources. Light signals corresponding to these flags are not displayed at night. In all cases mariners should rely upon National Weather Service broadcasts as their primary source of government provided weather information.

(11) The upper and lower small-craft basins are used primarily by commercial fishing boats and pleasure craft. The upper basin has over 500 berths, most with electricity; gasoline, diesel fuel, water, ice, marine supplies, and a launching ramp are available. Berths with electricity and water are reported to be available in the lower basin. A 60-ton lift and wet and dry winter storage are available.

(12) From Chetco Cove for 4.5 miles to Cape Ferrelo, the coast is composed of high broken cliffs, bordered by numerous rocky islets and ledges extending, in some cases, over 0.5 mile offshore.

(13) **Goat Island**, locally known as Bird Island, is 1.9 miles NW of Chetco Point and 500 yards offshore. It has deep water off its W and SW faces, but rocks and foul ground extend 350 yards S from the SE point. The island is readily identified; its profile closely resembles that of Prince Island off Pyramid Point.

(14) **Cape Ferrelo**, 4.4 miles NW of Chetco Point, is the prominent headland N of St. George Reef and, though not projecting seaward to any extent, is conspicuous because of its bold, rugged face. Several rocks and islets lie up to 0.5 mile directly off the cape.

(15) From Cape Ferrelo for 9.5 miles to Crook Point, the coast is very rugged and rocky, with several large and prominent islets and reefs extending well offshore. In some cases, these form anchorages for small vessels in N weather.

(16) **Whalehead Island**, the outer of two rocky islets 2.3 miles N of Cape Ferrelo, is 107 feet high. The inner of the two islets is 128 feet high. A rock awash lies 800 yards S of the highest point of the island.

(17) A rugged cliff from 200 to 300 feet high is 3.3 miles N of Cape Ferrelo. The face is about 1 mile long, and behind it rises a treeless triple-headed hill to heights of 700 to 800 feet.

(18) **Thomas Creek**, 3.7 miles N of Cape Ferrelo, is crossed by the highest bridge in Oregon; the bridge stands 345 feet above the creek.

(19) **Leaning Rock**, 49 feet high, is 0.5 mile offshore and 3.5 miles N of Whalehead Island. It has a perpendicular face on its NW side and slopes gradually SE. Several other rocks are near it.

(20) Between Whalehead Island and Crook Point are two prominent grassy areas in the forest near the crest of the hills about 2 miles apart and situated at an elevation of nearly 2,000 feet; the S one is known as **Rocky Prairie**.

(21) **Yellow Rock**, 84 feet high, is 4.5 miles N of Whalehead Island and 0.5 mile offshore. The rock is yellowish in color and can be recognized from 4 miles offshore.

(22) **Bosley Butte**, 8.5 miles NE of Cape Ferrelo, shows above the coast ridges from the W and NW as flat-topped with two summits separated by a slight depression. The NE summit is rounded and somewhat larger, but is slightly lower than the E summit.

(23) **Mack Arch** is a double-headed rocky islet 0.8 mile offshore, 1.5 miles S of Crook Point and 8 miles NNE of Cape Ferrelo. The W head is 231 feet high and the E a little lower; both are black to near the summits, which are generally white from bird droppings. The arch, about 100 feet high, is under the E summit and shows prominently from S. A rock awash lies 125 yards S of the E point.

(24) The bight to the ESE of Mack Arch has been used as a temporary anchorage during moderate NW weather. The rocks and reefs break the swell. In approaching the bight, pass to the S of Mack Arch about midway between it and Yellow Rock. Anchor in 11 fathoms, sand bottom, with Mack Arch bearing 296° and Yellow Rock bearing 155°. No breakers have been observed, but caution

(25) **Mack Reef** extends from Mack Arch to Crook Point and comprises many rocks, visible or sunken, varying in height from awash to 133 feet. From S these rocks stand out conspicuously when seen against the white sand dunes N of Crook Point. Mack Arch, because of its size and height, is the most prominent.

(26) **Mack Arch Cove** lies immediately E of Mack Reef and affords fair shelter in NW weather in 6 to 7 fathoms, sandy bottom. In entering from S, pass E of Mack Arch, giving it a berth of about 150 yards, but taking care to avoid the rock 125 yards S of its E point. Then bring the 125-foot rock, in the N part of the reef, to bear 352° and steer for it on that bearing until up to the area abreast the group of rocks 0.5 mile N of Mack Arch.

(27) **Crook Point** is moderately low, but terminates seaward in a rocky knoll 175 feet high, with a slight depression immediately behind it. The rocks close to the point often show up during moderately thick weather; several have a very noticeable pinnacle formation.

(28) From the vicinity of Crook Point to the mouth of the **Pistol River** are sand dunes which show up prominently in clear weather and distinctly mark this section. In thick weather these dunes are not readily distinguished. From the mouth of the river to Cape Sebastian are numerous rocks and rocky islets extending 0.3 mile offshore, reaching in some cases a height of 150 feet. The Pistol River bar opens in the rainy season; its location varies from year to year.

(29) **Hunters Cove**, a small constricted cove under the SE face of Cape Sebastian, is formed partly by the cape and partly by **Hunters Island** in the entrance. The island is 0.2 mile in extent, rocky, flat-topped, and 113 feet high. Shoal water extends from it E to the beach. The cove is used occasionally by launches and small craft. During strong NW weather the sea at the entrance is rather lumpy for small boats. With moderate SW weather a heavy sea piles up across the entrance between the cape and Hunters Island.

Charts 18601, 18589

(30) **Cape Sebastian**, 33.5 miles N of Point St. George, is conspicuous from either N or S. It is the seaward termination of a ridge transverse to the coast, and rises abruptly from seaward to a height of 694 feet, with a depression behind it, and then more gradually to a height of about 2,000 feet. The seaward face is precipitous and broken, and has a few trees; southward the lower part is grass covered. A rock covered 1¾ fathoms that seldom breaks is 0.5 mile offshore, 0.9 mile NW of the W extremity of the cape.

(31) From Cape Sebastian for 6 miles to the mouth of Rogue River, the coast is considerably broken, quite rugged, and low near the beach, and has a few outlying rocks.

(32) The outer of three exposed rocks off the entrance to **Hunter Creek**, 3.7 miles N of Cape Sebastian, lies nearly 0.5 miles offshore.

(33) **Rogue River**, 6 miles N of Cape Sebastian, is an important sport fishing stream. Several float landings and a hoist for trailer-drawn craft are just above the old lumber dock on the N side of the river near the mouth. **Gold Beach**, on the opposite side of the river from **Wedderburn**, is the larger town. The entrance to Rogue River is protected by stone jetties; buoys mark the approach. A seasonal light and sound signal are on the seaward end of the NW jetty. A **Federal project** provides for a 13-foot entrance channel from the ocean along the N jetty to a point about 0.4 mile above the NW jetty light. At this point, a dredged access channel continues ENE from the entrance channel then turns sharply SSE and leads between two jetties to a boat basin at Gold Beach. (See Notice to Mariners and latest editions of charts for controlling depths.)

Coast Guard

(34) The Coast Guard has a seasonal lifeboat station in the boat basin that operates from June to mid-September and can be reached on VHF-FM channel 12.

(35) The Coast Guard has established Rogue River Regulated Navigation Area Warning Sign, a seasonal **rough bar advisory sign**, on the N side of the river, 0.6 mile upstream of the entrance, to promote safety for small-boat operators. The sign is diamond-shaped, painted with an international orange border, and with the words **"Rough Bar"** in black letters. The sign is equipped with two quick flashing amber lights that will be activated when hazardous conditions exist and the bar is restricted to recreational and uninspected passenger vessels. Boaters are cautioned, however, that if the lights are not flashing, it is no guarantee that sea conditions are favorable.

(36) A **heavy weather flag**, a square RED flag with a square BLACK center, will be displayed on a pole that is located near the S side of the Coast Guard lifeboat station and is visible to mariners from both directions to indicate that winds 48 knots and above are forecast for the area. Display of flags are required from one hour before sunrise to one hour after sunset. Weather flags are flown at select Coast Guard stations to supplement other weather notification sources. Light signals corresponding to these flags are not displayed at night. In all cases mariners should rely upon National Weather Service broadcasts as their primary source of government provided weather information.

Caution

(37) The controlling depths in Rogue River channel and basin are usually considerably less than project depth and are subject to continual and pronounced change; vessels are advised not to enter the river without local knowledge.

Port Orford, Oregon
Image courtesy U.S. Army Corps of Engineers (1990)

COLREGS Demarcation Lines

(38) The lines established for the Rogue River are described in **80.1310**, chapter 2.

(39) About 200 berths, some with electricity, gasoline, diesel fuel, water, ice, launching ramps, wet and dry winter storage, and marine supplies, are available in Gold Beach.

(40) A concrete arch highway bridge across Rogue River, 0.8 mile above the mouth, has a fixed span with a clearance of 30 feet. An overhead power cable with a clearance of 77 feet crosses the river about 0.2 mile E of the highway bridge. The bridge is prominent when off the mouth of the river.

(41) The N head at Rogue River entrance that reaches a height of 700 feet a mile N of the river, the marked depression in the coast range made by the river valley, and the rocks of Rogue River Reef are prominent from seaward.

(42) **Rogue River Reef**, extending over 4 miles NW from Rogue River entrance, includes many visible and covered rocks; because of the broken bottom, vessels should stay over 5 miles offshore when passing this area. A 0.5-mile-wide channel separates the reef from the beach, but it is not safe to use without local knowledge. **Northwest Rock**, 4 miles NW of Rogue River entrance, is the outermost visible rock of the reef. A rock, covered 2½ fathoms, is 0.3 mile W of Northwest Rock. **Needle Rock**, 1.1 miles SE of Northwest Rock, is the most prominent of the rocks in the reef; the needle is on the S side.

(43) N of Rogue River the coast trends N for 10 miles and then NW to Cape Blanco. The mountains are high, irregular, dark, and covered with chaparral. The beach is bordered by numerous rocks for 5 miles, then is comparatively clear with the exception of Orford and Blanco Reefs.

(44) A group of covered and visible rocks, 1 mile long and 0.5 mile wide, lies 5 miles N of Rogue River and nearly 2 miles offshore; these rise abruptly from 12 fathoms. **North Rock**, 7 feet high, is the largest and nearest to the beach. A rock, covered 1¼ fathoms, lies about 0.6 mile NW of North Rock.

(45) The channel between Rogue River Reef and the mainland, and North Rock and the mainland, is sometimes used by coastwise freighters in clear weather. This channel should not be attempted by strangers.

(46) **Brushy Bald Mountain**, nearly 9 miles NE of Rogue River entrance and 3 miles inland, shows up in hazy weather as a flat rounded peak, with a gentle slope from a W and S direction.

(47) **Sisters Rocks** are a group of three rocky islets 10.5 miles N of Rogue River entrance. The smallest, 0.8 mile offshore, is the outermost. There is fairly smooth water in NW weather under the lee of the largest islet.

(48) **Colebrooke Butte**, 2 miles E of Sisters Rocks, appears from the W as a cone with gentle sloping sides.

(49) **Lookout Rock**, 2.3 miles N of Sisters Rocks, is a prominent projecting cliff, with a marked depression behind it. The seaward face is precipitous.

(50) **Bald Mountain**, 3.2 miles NE of Lookout Rock, appears from offshore as an irregular knob at the NW end of a long ridge. **Rocky Peak**, on the SE end of the ridge, is a sharp conical peak. From a SW direction, three peaks or knobs show; from a NNW direction, two peaks show almost in range. These peaks were used by the early navigators as a landfall for Port Orford in coming from the N.

(51) Prominent **Humbug Mountain**, 3.3 miles N of Lookout Rock and 4 miles S of Port Orford, is conical in shape, and its seaward face is steep and rugged.

Chart 18589

(52) **Island Rock**, 1.3 miles off the seaward face of Humbug Mountain, is flat on top. A needle rock is 200 yards off its NW end. These rocks are prominent when approaching Port Orford from S. Except for two small rocky patches, covered 6¾ and 10 fathoms, within 0.5 mile of the N end of Island Rock, there is deep water around these islands and between them and the beach.

(53) **Redfish Rocks** are a group of islets covering an area 0.5 mile square, lying 2 miles N of Island Rock and nearly 1 mile offshore. They are six in number and range from 10 to 140 feet in height. Many covered rocks lie within this area.

(54) **Port Orford**, 6.5 miles S of Cape Blanco and 19 miles N of Rogue River, is a cove that affords good shelter in NW weather, but is exposed and dangerous in S weather. It is easy of access and is probably the best natural NW lee N of Point Reyes.

(55) The town of **Port Orford**, on the N side of the cove, is the home of the famous yellow cedar; lumber is trucked from the town.

(56) **The Heads**, forming the W point of the cove, appear from S as a long ridge with three knobs. The inner two are slightly higher and covered with trees. **Tichenor Rock** lies 175 yards S of The Heads.

(57) **Klooqueh Rock**, 0.3 mile off the NW face of The Heads, is black and conical in shape. It is prominent, especially when coming from the NW inside Orford Reef. Rocky ledges are between this rock and shore.

(58) Anchorage may be had in about the center of Port Orford in 5 to 10 fathoms, sand bottom, however, it is reported that many anchors have been lost near the rocky 1¾-fathom shoal 0.2 mile E of the S end of the breakwater. The cove is marked by a lighted bell buoy and a light, 0.5 mile S and 0.8 mile ENE of Tichenor Rock, respectively. Small craft may anchor closer to The Heads where better protection is afforded against the NW winds, which sweep with considerable force through the depression at the head of the cove.

(59) **Battle Rock**, in the N part of the cove close to shore, is high, narrow, and black; it is detached only at extreme high tides. Visible and covered rocks extend up to 0.5 mile from shore around the cove.

(60) A wharf E of **Graveyard Point** is used mostly for commercial fishing. Fishing boats are lifted to cradles on the wharf with two large hoists. The wharf can accommodate vessels that are a maximum of: 44 feet in length, 15 feet in width, and no more than 19 tons. Gasoline, diesel fuel, water, marine supplies, ice, and dry boat storage is available on the wharf; minor repairs can be made. A **Federal project** provides for a depth of 16 feet in the channel leading to the wharf. (See Notice to Mariners and latest editions of charts for controlling depths.) At times, shoaling causes the water depth alongside the wharf to be less than adequate for docking. Mariners are urged to contact the wharf office at 541–332–1306 for the latest conditions. A 550-foot breakwater, with a light on the outer end, extends SE from Graveyard Point and provides some protection for the wharf.

(61) From The Heads for 6.5 miles to Cape Blanco, the coast extends in a general NNW direction. N of The Heads the shore is a narrow sand ridge, rising at one point to 160 feet, covered with grass, fern, and brush, and ending abruptly nearly 3 miles from The Heads at the edge of the Elk River Valley. N of this point are sand dunes extending to the mouth of **Elk River**, a small unimportant stream. Beyond the mouth of Elk River to Cape Blanco, the coast consists of vertical cliffs, wooded to the edge, and in some places over 150 feet high.

(62) **Orford Reef**, from 2 to 5 miles offshore between The Heads and Cape Blanco, is composed of a group of irregular rocks up to 149 feet high and ledges, many of which are awash or show a break. Kelp extends from Orford Reef to within 1.3 miles of the shore.

(63) **Fox Rock** and **Southeast Black Rock**, 1.3 miles apart, about 5 miles SW of Cape Blanco, are the southernmost rocks of Orford Reef; they usually show a heavy break. **Northwest Rock**, 3 miles SW of Cape Blanco, is the northernmost visible rock of Orford Reef, although several rocks, covered 5 fathoms, are 1.2 miles NE of Northwest Rock.

(64) **Blanco Reef**, extending 1.5 miles SW from Cape Blanco, consists of numerous rocks and ledges, some of which are marked by kelp. **Black Rock**, 1.2 miles SW of Cape Blanco Light, is the southernmost visible rock of Blanco Reef. **Pyramid Rock**, 1 mile W of the light, is the northernmost visible rock of the reef, although a rocky patch uncovers about 3 feet 0.4 mile to the N. Rocky patches, covered ½ to 6 fathoms, extend from 0.5 mile SW of Black Rock to 0.4 mile W of Pyramid Rock.

(65) In clear weather small vessels with local knowledge sometimes use the passage inside Orford Reef and between Orford Reef and Blanco Reef.

(66) **Cape Blanco** projects about 1.5 miles from the general trend of the coast. It is a small bare tableland, terminating seaward in a cliff 203 feet high, with low land behind it. A large high rock lies close under the S side of the cape. From seaward the cape is not prominent, but, from N or S, it appears like a moderately low bluff islet. The group of buildings at Cape Blanco is very prominent.

(67) **Cape Blanco Light** (42°50'13"N., 124°33'49"W.), 245 feet above the water, is shown from a 59-foot white conical tower near the center of the flat part of the cape.

(68) Numerous covered and visible rocks extend 0.5 mile or more NW from the cape.

(69) **Gull Rock**, 1 mile N of Cape Blanco Light, is surrounded by covered rocks. Its seaward face is black and rugged, and the summit has two knobs, the higher being to the S. A rocky patch, covered 3 fathoms, lies 0.5 mile W of Gull Rock.

(70) **Castle Rock**, 1.5 miles NE of Cape Blanco Light and 300 yards off the mouth of **Sixes River**, rises abruptly from the sea and is readily made out 10 miles to seaward. Many low rocks and ledges are within 400 yards, and several rocky islets are to the W and NW.

(71) **Blacklock Point** is a precipitous rocky point 2.5 miles NNE of Cape Blanco. The cliff is 157 feet high. A sharp high point, bordered by rocks, stretches out nearly 300 yards. A narrow curved line of rocks extends 0.8 mile WSW from the point. A rock that breaks in heavy weather is 1 mile NW of the point. Rocky patches, covered 4 fathoms, are within 1.3 miles of the point in a W and NW direction.

Chart 18580

(72) From Cape Blanco for 112 miles to Yaquina Head, the coast is remarkably straight and trends in a NNE direction. It differs considerably from the coast to the S. The coastal mountains are much lower, the difference being more marked because of the high mountains inland. The shore consists of high yellow sand dunes and cliffs broken by bold rocky headlands of moderate height and backed by low pine-covered hills. There are few outlying dangers, the outermost being Blacklock Point, Coquille Rock, and Cape Arago.

(73) From Blacklock Point the shore continues rocky with cliffs gradually decreasing in height for 1.5 miles N, thence for about 11 miles the shore is a broad sandy beach backed by dunes and long narrow lakes. The tree line is at an average distance of 0.2 mile from the sea. From the end of the sand beach for 2 miles to the mouth of Coquille River, the shore again consists of rocky cliffs, 40 to 80 feet high, with several outlying rocks as much as 0.5 mile from shore. Covered dangers extend 1.6 miles W from Coquille Point. The land directly behind this stretch of coast is comparatively flat and wooded, rising to heights of 1,000 feet in 2.5 to 3 miles.

Charts 18588, 18580

(74) **Coquille River** is 18 miles N of Cape Blanco. Some fishing boats operate from **Bandon**, about 0.8 mile above the mouth.

(75) **Coquille Point** is 0.6 mile S of Coquille River entrance. Several rocky islets extend 0.5 mile off the point and rocks showing breakers in any swell extend 1.2 miles W and a mile NW of the point.

(76) **Coquille Rock**, 1.6 miles NW of the point, is covered 28 feet and breaks in heavy weather.

(77) A long, low area of shifting dunes is N of the Coquille River entrance. The conical tower and dwelling of an abandoned lighthouse is near the inner end of the N jetty.

COLREGS Demarcation Lines

(78) The lines established for the Coquille River are described in **80.1315**, chapter 2.

(79) The entrance to Coquille River is protected by jetties; a light and sound signal are on the S jetty. A **Federal project** provides for a depth of 13 feet from the entrance to Bandon. (See Notice to Mariners and latest editions of charts for controlling depths.) The channel is subject to frequent change, and the deepest water is not always on the entrance range. Local knowledge is essential when the bar is rough. It is reported that the bar breaks even in calm seas and mariners should favor the N in approaching the entrance range. The reported depth above Bandon is about 6 feet to Coquille, 21 miles above the entrance.

Coast Guard

(80) A Coast Guard motor lifeboat is stationed at the mooring basin at Bandon on the S side of the river about 0.8 mile above the entrance.

(81) The Coast Guard has established Coquille River Regulated Navigation Area Warning Sign, a seasonal **rough bar advisory sign**, 29 feet above the water, visible from the channel looking seaward on the S shore just N of the Coast Guard station, to promote safety for small-boat operators. The sign is diamond-shaped, painted with an international orange border, and with the words **"Rough Bar"** in black letters. The sign is equipped with two quick flashing amber lights that will be activated when hazardous conditions exist and the bar is restricted to recreational and uninspected passenger vessels. Boaters are cautioned, however, that if the lights are not flashing, it is no guarantee that sea conditions are favorable.

(82) A small-craft basin, on the S side of the river about 0.9 mile above the entrance, has about 180 berths and

a launching ramp; marine supplies are available. Fuel is available by truck. In 1999, the controlling depth was 12 feet from the main channel to the basin, with depths of 5 to 8 feet in the basin. The 310-foot wharf of a former lumbermill, NE of the small-craft basin, has reported depths of 12 feet alongside. A machine shop is at Bandon.

(83) A highway bridge, 3 miles above the entrance, has a lift span with clearances of 28 feet down and 74 feet up. (See **117.1 through 117.59 and 117.875**, chapter 2, for drawbridge regulations.) In 2003, the lift span was inoperable and in the closed position. An overhead cable E of the bridge has a clearance of 72 feet.

(84) The village of **Prosper** is 4 miles above Coquille River entrance.

(85) Several power cables cross the river between Prosper and Coquille; the least clearance is 68 feet.

(86) **Coquille**, 21 miles above the entrance, is the distributing center for several agricultural communities of the river valley and has railway connections with the interior.

Chart 18580

(87) N of the entrance to the Coquille River the sand dunes extend for about 4 miles and are then succeeded by cliffs. **Fivemile Point**, 6 miles N of the river entrance, is a rocky cliff 60 feet high with a cluster of rocks, 10 to 40 feet high, extending more than 0.3 mile offshore.

(88) N of Fivemile Point the coast consists of cliffs, 40 to 80 feet high, which rise to heights of 100 to 250 feet 2 miles S of Cape Arago and are cut by deep gulches, named the **Seven Devils**. Numerous rocks of varying shapes and sizes border the beach.

(89) **South Cove**, immediately under the S point of Cape Arago, is used extensively as a summer anchorage by small craft and fishing boats with local knowledge.

(90) **Cape Arago**, 29 miles NNE of Cape Blanco, is an irregular jagged point projecting about a mile from the general trend of the coast. There are no high mountains immediately behind the cape, and it is conspicuous only when the mountains in the interior are obscured. The seaward face of the cape, 2.5 miles long in a N direction, is a narrow wooded tableland 50 feet high, with rugged and broken cliffs and outlying rocks of the same height as the cliff. Immediately off the cape are reefs extending NW for about a mile. A small cove near the N end, inside the reefs, is sometimes used by small boats with local knowledge.

Charts 18587, 18580

(91) **Baltimore Rock**, 3.2 miles NNE of Cape Arago, is covered 9 feet and usually breaks. It is the outermost rock of a covered ledge extending NW from the shore. A lighted buoy is 0.2 mile N of the rock. E of Baltimore Rock, **Mussel Reef** extends about 0.8 mile NW from **Yoakam Point** and has a least depth of 18 feet; mariners should exercise caution in this area.

(92) **Coos Head**, 229 feet high, is on the S side of the entrance to Coos Bay. The cliffs of Coos Head are about 100 feet high and terminate in several small rocky points with sand beaches between them. The buildings of a former government facility are conspicuous on the bluffs just SW of Coos Head.

(93) **Coos Bay**, 33 miles N of Cape Blanco, is used as a harbor of refuge and can be entered at any time except in extreme weather. Coos Bay is one of the most important harbors between San Francisco and the Columbia River, and one of the largest forest products ports in the world. Principal foreign exports are logs, woodchips, lumber, and plywood. The coastwise trade consists mainly of logs.

(94) From the entrance the bay extends NE for 8 miles with widths of 0.3 to 1 mile, then bends SE for about 4 miles to the mouth of Isthmus Slough. The dredged channel through the bay is bordered by marshland and intersected by several sloughs.

Prominent features

(95) Coos Head and Umpqua River Light are good guides to the entrance. The sand dunes N toward Umpqua River are prominent. The entrance to the bay is protected by jetties. A light with a seasonal sound signal marks the N jetty. A lighted whistle buoy is 1.8 miles WNW of the entrance. The channels are marked with lighted ranges, lights, buoys, and daybeacons.

Routes

(96) Vessels should make sure of the entrance range before standing close in. There is usually a current sweeping either N or S just off the jetties, and this current should be guarded against. The entrance ranges should be watched carefully until clear of all dangers. The S current is often encountered during the summer. With strong S winds during the winter, the current sometimes sets to the N.

(97) Approaching from any direction in thick weather, great caution is essential. The currents are variable and uncertain. Velocities of 3 to 3.5 knots have been observed offshore between Blunts Reef and Swiftsure Bank, and greater velocities have been reported. The most favorable time for crossing the bar is on the last of the flood current, and occasionally it is passable only at this time.

COLREGS Demarcation Lines

(98) The lines established for Coos Bay are described in **80.1320**, chapter 2.

Channels

(99) A **Federal Project** provides for a 37-foot channel across the bar to a point 1.1 miles above the mouth of Isthmus Slough, and thence, 22 feet to Millington, 14.7

miles above the entrance to the bay. Turning basins at North Bend and Coos Bay have project depths of 37 feet. (See Notice to Mariners and latest editions of charts for controlling depths.)

Coast Guard

(100) The Coast Guard has established Coos Bay South Slough Regulated Navigation Warning Sign, a **rough bar advisory sign**, on the E end of the breakwater at Charleston Boat Basin in about 43°20'48"N., 124°19'18"W., to promote safety for small-boat operators. The sign is diamond-shaped, painted white with an international orange border, and with the words **"Rough Bar"** in black letters. The sign is equipped with two quick flashing amber lights that will be activated when hazardous conditions exist and the bar is restricted to recreational and uninspected passenger vessels. Boaters are cautioned, however, that if the lights are not flashing, it is no guarantee that the sea conditions are favorable.

Anchorage

(101) Anchorage for small craft can be had almost anywhere in the bay outside the dredged channels and below the railroad bridge.

Caution

(102) Due to the rapid and severe onset of weather from the North Pacific Ocean, anchorage in the ocean outside of Coos Bay is reported not safe and is dangerous during the winter months. Like all unprotected areas along the Oregon coast, large swells and heavy winds characterize the area during the winter. These conditions can suddenly and unexpectedly besiege the unwary with catastrophic results. The prevailing direction of both swell and wind will drive disabled or improperly handled vessels onto the shore.

Dangers

(103) **Guano Rock**, on the S side of the entrance channel and 280 yards NW of Coos Head, uncovers only at extreme low water.

(104) A submerged section of the N entrance jetty extends about 300 yards W of the visible jetty; and a submerged section of the S entrance jetty extends about 100 yards W of the visible jetty. Because of the submerged jetties, it is reported that there are breakers in these areas most of the time. Extreme care must be exercised at all times.

(105) A submerged jetty extends 500 yards off the E shore of Coos Bay just inside the entrance, 0.8 mile NE of Coos Head. In entering with a strong NW wind, large vessels have difficulty in making the turn and may find themselves being set toward the submerged jetty.

Bridges

(106) The Coos Bay Railroad bridge across Coos Bay, 7.5 miles above the entrance, has a swing span with a vertical clearance of 12 feet. Mariners should use extreme caution when passing through the bridge because of unpredictable changing winds, currents, and sea conditions reported in this area. The bridgetender monitors VHF-FM channel 18A and works on channel 13; call sign KT-2006. A fixed highway bridge, 8.1 miles above the entrance, has a clearance of 123 feet across the main channel. A power cable, 100 yards W of the fixed bridge, has a clearance of 167 feet. (See **117.1 through 117.59 and 117.871**, chapter 2, for drawbridge regulations.)

Currents

(107) Current observations in the entrance to Coos Bay indicated a velocity of about 2 knots. The greatest observed ebb velocity was a little over 3 knots. Predictions for the entrance may be obtained from the Tidal Current Tables. During long runouts an ebb current of 5 knots has been reported at Guano Rock.

Pilotage, Coos Bay

(108) Pilotage is compulsory for all foreign vessels and all U.S. vessels under registry. Pilotage is optional for U.S. vessels in the coastwise trade that have onboard a pilot licensed by the Federal Government for these waters.

(109) Pilotage for Coos Bay, its tributaries and Yaquina Bay is available from **Coos Bay Pilots Association**, 686 N Front Street, Coos Bay, OR 97420; telephone 541–267–6555; Fax 541–267–5256.

(110) The pilot boats monitor VHF-FM channels 13 and 16 and use channels 12 and 18A as working frequency.

(111) The pilot boats, COOS BAY and NORTH BEND, are 75-foot-long tugs with black hulls, orange pilothouses, and white stacks. The pilot boats used the standard pilot lights at night. Vessels are handled 24 hours a day, weather permitting.

(112) Arrangements for pilots are usually made by ships' agents or by telephone. A 24-hour notice of time of arrival is requested. The pilots usually board vessels about 1 mile NW of Coos Bay Approach Lighted Whistle Buoy K. Vessels are requested to maintain a speed of about 4 to 5 knots and rig the ladder, without manropes, about 3 meters above the water.

Towage

(113) Tugs to 2,000 hp are available and are used for docking and mooring. The two pilot boats, the largest tugs available, do most of the dock assist work in the port.

Quarantine, customs, immigration, and agricultural quarantine

(114) (See chapter 3, Vessel Arrival Inspections, and Appendix A for addresses.)

(115) **Quarantine** is enforced in accordance with regulations of the U.S. Public Health Service. (See Public Health Service, chapter 1, for details.)

(116) Coos Bay is a **customs port of entry.**

Facilities at Coos Bay

Name	Location	Berthing Space (feet)	Depths* (feet)	Deck Height (feet)	Mechanical Handling Facilities and Storage	Purpose	Owned/ Operated by:
Roseburg Forest Products Wood Chip Dock	43°25'32"N., 124°15'28"W.	1,430	40	17	• Open storage (40 acres) • Steel loading tower and belt-conveyor system	Shipment of wood chips	Roseburg Forest Products Co.
Ocean Terminals North Bend Wharf	43°24'37"N., 124°13'12"W.	750	38	10	• Open storage (32 acres) • Four 30-ton log loaders	Receipt and shipment of logs and lumber	Ocean Terminals Co.
Oregon Chip Terminal Wharf	43°23'20"N., 124°13'10"W.	1,086	36	12	• Open storage • Steel loading tower and belt-conveyor system	Shipment of wood chips	Pacific Chip Terminal Inc./Oregon Chip Terminal Inc.
Dolphin Terminals Wharf	43°22'49"N., 124°13'02"W.	825	36	10	N/A	Occasional shipment of logs	Oregon International Port of Coos Bay/ Dolphin Terminals
Georgia Pacific Coos Bay Wood Chip Wharf	43°21'42"N., 124°12'09"W.	500	35	12	• Open storage • Steel loading tower and chain-conveyor system	Shipment of wood chips	Georgia Pacific Corp.
Coos Bay Dock Wharf	43°21'43"N., 124°12'02"W.	726	36	12	• Open storage (20 acres) • Covered storage (115,000 square feet)	• Shipment of logs, finished lumber, plywood and paper products • Receipt of conventional and containerized general cargoq	Georgia Pacific Corp./ Knutson Towboat Co.
Knutson Log Yard Dock	43°19'55"N., 124°11'37"W.	500	17	-	Open storage (45 acres)	Receipt of logs	Knutson Transportation Co.

* The depths given above are reported. For information on the latest depths contact the port authorities or the private operators.

Coast Guard

(117) **Coos Bay Coast Guard Station** is on the S side of Charleston Boat Basin, 0.7 mile SE of Coos Head. **North Bend Coast Guard Air Station** is at the North Bend Municipal Airport.

Harbor regulations

(118) The port authority, Oregon International Port of Coos Bay, is controlled by a Board of Port Commissioners and a port manager. Harbor regulations are prescribed by the Port Commissioners and enforced by the port manager. The port manager's office is at 125 Central Avenue, Suite 300, Coos Bay.

Wharves

(119) Most of the deep-draft facilities in the Port of Coos Bay are at the cities of Coos Bay and North Bend; only these facilities are listed in the table. For a complete description of the port facilities refer to Port Series No. 33, published and sold by the U.S. Army Corps of Engineers. (See Appendix A for address.) The alongside depths are reported depths; for information on the latest depths contact the port manager or the private operators. All the facilities described have direct highway connections and most have connections to a Class I railroad. Water is available at most of the wharves, but electrical shore power connections are only available at reference numbers 1 and 6 in the table. Special handling equipment, if available, is mentioned under 'mechanical handling facilities' in the table.

Supplies

(120) Most marine supplies and services are available at Coos Bay. Fuel oil is available at one fuel pier. Diesel oil and water are available.

Repairs

(121) There are no facilities for major repairs to large oceangoing vessels in Coos Bay; the nearest such facilities are in Portland, OR. Above-the-waterline repairs can be made at several machine shops on the waterfront. There are two 1,000-ton drydocks at Coos Bay which can handle vessels up to 180 feet in length and 45 feet in width. The largest marine railway can handle vessels to 1,200 tons, 137 feet long, 45 feet wide, and 12 feet in draft. Hull and engine repairs can be made here. Electronic repairs can be arranged for. (See Charleston Boat Basin, this chapter, for small-craft facilities and repairs.)

Communications

(122) The cities of Coos Bay and North Bend are served by U.S. Highway 101 and a Class I railroad. Two state highways connect to Interstate Highway 5 inland. North Bend Municipal Airport, served by a major airline, is just NW of North Bend.

(123) **South Slough**, shoal and navigable only for small boats, extends 4 miles S from its junction with Coos Bay near the entrance. A **Federal project** provides for a 17-foot entrance channel extending S from the junction for about 0.6 mile to the Charleston Boat Basin, thence a 16-foot channel continues to a highway bascule bridge. (See Notice to Mariners and latest editions of chart for controlling depth information.) The channel

Umpqua River, Oregon
Image courtesy U.S. Army Corps of Engineers (1990)

from junction with Coos Bay to Charleston Boat Basin is subject to shoaling. Mariners are advised to seek local knowledge when transiting this area.

(124) **Charleston Boat Basin**, operated and maintained by the Port of Coos Bay, is 0.3 mile N of Charleston, across the slough from **Barview**. The basin is used by commercial and sport fishermen. About 500 berths with electricity, gasoline, diesel fuel, water, ice, a launching ramp, and marine supplies are available. A pumpout station and wet and dry winter boat storage are available in the basin. A repair facility at the basin has a drydock that can handle vessels to 300 tons, 90 feet long, and 30 feet wide, and a marine railway that can handle craft 70 feet long, 22 feet wide, and 6 feet draft for hull and engine repairs. Electronic repairs can also be made at the basin. Four fish piers are in the basin, and three fish packing facilities are just S of the basin on South Slough. **Coos Bay Coast Guard Station** is on the S side of the basin.

(125) A Coast Guard buoy storage area is in Coos Bay about 150 yards E of the channel and about 2.5 miles above the entrance jetties.

(126) The highway bridge over South Slough, 1 mile S of the entrance, has a bascule span with a clearance of 22 feet. (See **117.1 through 117.59 and 117.892**, chapter 2, for drawbridge regulations.) Power and television cables S of the bridge have a least clearance of 71 feet.

(127) The W shore of Coos Bay as far as the bend is formed by a sandspit covered with dunes, partly wooded, and in some places as much as 90 feet high. On the E shore and above the bend are low rolling hills with houses and several prominent buildings.

(128) **Haynes Inlet** and **North Slough**, which join the bay through a common entrance on the N side, are navigated by small boats. Haynes Inlet and North Slough channels are marked by private daybeacons. A causeway with a fixed bridge over North Slough has a clearance of 15 feet. The causeway extends E and joins the State highway fixed bridge over Haynes Inlet, which has a clearance of 20 feet (27 feet at center).

(129) **North Bend**, 9.5 miles above the entrance, is a city with many sawmills and factories; considerable lumber is shipped from here. North Bend Fire Department has a fire boat and launches dock along the city. **Coos Bay**, 12 miles above the entrance, is the principal city on the bay and is the distributing center for the area, which is primarily devoted to lumbering, fishing, and agriculture. Coos Bay also includes the **Empire** district, which is 4 miles above the entrance. North Bend and Coos Bay form practically one continuous city extending along the shore from North Point to the mouth of Coalbank Slough.

(130) Three sloughs empty into Coos Bay between the city of Coos Bay and Coos River. **Coalbank Slough** is unused. **Isthmus Slough** is used for logging operations to **Millington**. The highway bridge across the slough has a bascule span with a clearance of 18 feet. (See **117.1 through 117.59 and 117.879**, chapter 2, for drawbridge regulations.) The overhead power and television cables

(130) just N of the bridge, and the overhead power cable 0.9 mile S of the bridge, have clearances of 100 and 150 feet, respectively. **Catching Slough** is navigable for several miles by light-draft vessels. The fixed highway bridge across the mouth has a clearance of 40 feet. The power cable for about 1.7 miles above the bridge have a least clearance of 57 feet; other overhead cables upstream have a least known clearance of 13 feet.

(131) **Coos River** empties through two channels into the bay at its head. The N unmarked channel follows the E side of the bay and empties abreast of North Bend. **Marshfield Channel**, marked by a lighted range, lights, and buoy, crosses the flats and empties abreast the city of Coos Bay.

(132) Coos River divides at a point 3.2 miles above **Graveyard Point** into **South Fork** and **Millicoma River**. A highway bridge across the river, 0.9 mile above Graveyard Point, has a lift span with clearances of 28 feet down and 54 feet up. (See **117.1 through 117.59 and 117.873**, chapter 2, for drawbridge regulations.) The least clearance of the overhead power cables crossing Millicoma River is 40 feet. **Allegany**, 7.5 miles above the confluence, is the head of navigation on Millicoma River. **Dellwood**, 8.2 miles above the confluence, is the head of navigation on South Fork.

(133) In 2002, depths of 4 to 5 feet were available in Coos River through Marshfield Channel to Graveyard Point; thence in 1990, the controlling depth was 2 feet to the lift bridge about 0.9 mile above Graveyard Point, thence 5 feet to the confluence of the Millicoma River and South Fork. In 1990, the controlling depth in South Fork was 3 feet to Dellwood. In 1990, the controlling depth in the Millicoma was 4 feet to Allegany. Numerous snags and deadheads exist in the South Fork and the Millicoma River.

(134) A fixed highway bridge crossing South Fork 0.5 mile above the confluence has been removed; two concrete piers remain. A fixed highway bridge crossing South Fork 1.9 miles above the confluence has a clearance of 38 feet. Several overhead power and telegraph cables cross South Fork; least clearance is 42 feet.

Chart 18580

(135) From Coos Bay for 19.5 miles to Umpqua River, the coast consists of sand beaches and dunes backed by moderately low hills. The mouth of **Tenmile Creek** is 13.7 miles N of Coos Head.

Charts 18584, 18580

(136) **Umpqua River** is entered 22.7 miles N of Coos Bay. Some lumber, sand, crushed rock, and oil are barged on the river, but commercial traffic is very light. The **customs port of entry** is at Coos Bay.

(137) The S point at the entrance to the river is marked by sand dunes, partly covered with trees, that reach elevations of 300 feet. About a mile below the entrance is a bright bare spot in the dunes that shows prominently among the trees. Shifting sand dunes about 100 feet high are on the spit on the N side of the entrance.

(138) **Umpqua River Light** (43°39'44"N., 124°11'55"W.), is shown from a white conical tower just S of the mouth of the river. Trees surround the light, but the lantern shows over the tops.

(139) The entrance to the river is protected by jetties. The S jetty extends 1,200 yards seaward from the shoreline and is marked by a light with a seasonal sound signal and radar reflector. About 160 yards of the outer end of the jetty is submerged. A lighted whistle buoy, about 0.9 mile W of the S jetty light, marks the approach. A 086° lighted range and a buoy mark the entrance channel which is subject to frequent changes. The middle jetty extends from the shoreline and connects with the outer section of the S jetty. The N jetty extends 1,100 yards seaward from the shoreline. The river channels are marked by lighted ranges, lights, buoys, and daybeacons. A Coast Guard lookout tower is about midway out on the middle jetty.

COLREGS Demarcation Lines

(140) The lines established for the Umpqua River are described in **80.1325**, chapter 2.

Channels

(141) A **Federal project** provides for depths of 26 feet in the entrance channel, thence 22 feet to Gardiner and Reedsport, and 22 feet in the turning basin at Reedsport. (See Notice to Mariners and latest edition of chart for controlling depths.)

(142) The channel over the bar is reported shoalest usually during September. Later in the season the river cuts a deeper channel through the bar. Depths in the channels and basins may vary considerably between dredging operations.

Coast Guard

(143) The Coast Guard has established Umpqua River Regulated Navigation Area Warning Sign, a **rough bar advisory sign**, visible from the channel looking seaward, on Winchester Point about 1.5 miles inside the river entrance, to promote safety for small-boat operators. The sign is diamond-shaped, painted white with an international orange border, and with the words **"Rough Bar"** in black letters. The sign is equipped with two quick flashing yellow lights that will be activated when hazardous conditions exist and the bar is restricted to recreational and uninspected passenger vessels. Boaters are cautioned, however, that if the lights are not flashing, it is no guarantee that conditions are favorable.

(144) A **heavy weather flag**, a square RED flag with a square BLACK center, will be displayed on a pole that is located on the N side of the Coast Guard lookout

tower at the Umpqua River entrance and is visible to mariners from both directions to indicate that winds 48 knots and above are forecast for the area. Display of flags are required from one hour before sunrise to one hour after sunset. Weather flags are flown at select Coast Guard stations to supplement other weather notification sources. Light signals corresponding to these flags are not displayed at night. In all cases mariners should rely upon National Weather Service broadcasts as their primary source of government provided weather information.

(145) **Umpqua River Coast Guard Station** is in East Basin about 2.3 miles from the entrance.

Supplies

(146) Gasoline, diesel fuel, water, and fuel oil for launches may be obtained at Reedsport.

Repairs

(147) A machine shop is at Reedsport; a marine railway here can handle craft to 150 feet. A tidal graving dock for barges, 260 feet long and 60 feet wide, is operated by this firm across the river. Hull and engine repairs for small craft can be made at East Basin.

(148) **West Basin** and **East Basin**, 1.8 and 2.3 miles above the entrance respectively, are small-craft basins entered through dredged channels that lead from the main river channel. The entrance channel to West Basin is marked by a light and daybeacon and the entrance to East Basin is marked by two lights. (See Notice to Mariners and the latest edition of chart for controlling depths.)

(149) The village of **Winchester Bay** is a fishing resort on the E side of East Basin. A fish wharf with cold storage and ice plant on its outer end is on the W side of the basin. Berths with electricity, gasoline, diesel fuel, water, ice, launching ramps, marine supplies, and an 8-ton crane are available in East Basin.

(150) **Gardiner**, on the NE bank of the river 8.5 miles inside the entrance, is the site of a large papermill and a lumbermill. A dredged channel serves these mills. Barges unload fuel oil at the papermill wharf, 0.8 mile N of the town. Depths of 18 feet are reported alongside. The wharf is marked by a private light. There is a public small-craft launching ramp in Gardiner.

(151) **Reedsport**, on the SW bank of the river, 10 miles inside the entrance, is a station on the railroad and the principal town on the river. A plywood plant and a sawmill are in the town. The plywood plant wharf, at the entrance to Scholfield Creek, is in ruins and not used. The sawmill barges lumber intermittently from the port wharf, which is between the swing bridges; the wharf has about 18 feet along the loading face. A lumber wharf, used occasionally, is on the NW end of Bolon Island.

(152) The U.S. Route 101 highway bridge crossing the river at the upper end of the turning basin at Reedsport has a swing span with a clearance of 36 feet. Just W of the bridge is a power cable with a clearance of 152 feet; the least clearance of cables above the highway bridge is 95 feet. The railroad bridge, 500 yards above the highway bridge, has a swing span with a clearance of 16 feet. (See **117.1 through 117.59 and 117.893**, chapter 2, for drawbridge regulations.)

(153) At high tide Umpqua River is navigable by vessels of 6-foot draft to **Scottsburg**, 14.8 miles above Reedsport.

(154) **Scholfield Creek** enters Umpqua River N of Reedsport. The entrance to the creek is marked by daybeacons. A fixed highway bridge with a clearance of 20 feet crosses the creek 0.9 mile above the mouth and a railroad bridge with a 30-foot fixed span and clearance of 16 feet crosses the creek 2 miles above the mouth. Overhead power cables with a least clearance of 41 feet cross the creek between the two bridges.

(155) **Smith River** enters Umpqua River from the NE at Reedsport. The controlling depth is about 5 feet for 5 miles above the mouth, thence 2 feet to **Sulphur Springs Landing**, 18 miles above the mouth. The highway bridge, 2.7 miles above the mouth, has a retractable span with a clearance of 22 feet. (See **117.1 through 117.49**, chapter 2, for drawbridge regulations.) An overhead telephone cable with a clearance of 67 feet crosses the river just below the bridge.

Chart 18580

(156) From Umpqua River for 21 miles to Siuslaw River, the coast is straight and consists of sand dunes broken only by the mouths of **Threemile Creek**, **Tahkenitch Creek**, **Siltcoos River** and the stream from **Cleawox Lake**.

Charts 18583, 18580

(157) **Siuslaw River**, 8.3 miles S of Heceta Head Light, has some logging operations, and finished lumber is barged to Pacific ports. Prominent from offshore is wooded **Cannery Hill**, on the E side of the river 1.4 miles above the entrance. The **customs port of entry** is at Coos Bay.

COLREGS Demarcation Lines

(158) The lines established for the Siuslaw River are described in **80.1330**, chapter 2.

(159) The river is entered through a dredged channel between two partially submerged jetties; caution is advised. The river then leads S to a turning basin off the town of Florence, 4.4 miles above the entrance, thence E for about 2 miles to Cushman. A light, seasonal sound signal, and a Coast Guard tower are on the N jetty. The channel is marked by a **096°** lighted entrance range that favors the N side of the channel, and by other ranges and navigational aids to 1 mile above Florence. The uncharted buoys at the mouth of the river are frequently

shifted to mark the best water. The bar at the entrance is narrow, and the depths vary greatly because of storms and freshets. The entrance and south jetty shoals tend to build during late winter and spring. Mariners are advised to contact **Siuslaw River Coast Guard Station** on VHF-FM channel 16 before attempting to cross the bar. A **Federal project** provides for an 18- to 16-foot depth in the entrance channel to the highway bridge at Florence; thence 16 feet in the turning basin; thence 12 feet to Cushman. (See Notice to Mariners and latest editions of the chart for controlling depths.)

(160) The Coast Guard has established Siuslaw River Regulated Navigation Warning Sign, a **rough bar advisory sign**, 37 feet above the water, visible from the channel looking seaward, on the Coast Guard lookout tower on the N jetty, to promote safety for small-boat operators. The sign is diamond-shaped, painted white with an international orange border, and with the words **"Rough Bar"** in black letters. The sign is equipped with two quick flashing amber lights that will be activated when hazardous conditions exist and the bar is restricted to recreational and uninspected passenger vessels. Boaters are cautioned, however, that if the lights are not flashing, it is no guarantee that sea conditions are favorable.

(161) A **heavy weather flag**, a square RED flag with a square BLACK center, will be displayed on a pole that is located on the SW corner of the Coast Guard station and is visible to mariners from both directions to indicate that winds 48 knots and above are forecast for the area. Display of flags are required from one hour before sunrise to one hour after sunset. Weather flags are flown at select Coast Guard stations to supplement other weather notification sources. Light signals corresponding to these flags are not displayed at night. (See illustration, Chapter 1.) In all cases mariners should rely upon National Weather Service broadcasts as their primary source of government provided weather information.

(162) **Siuslaw Coast Guard Station** is on the E side of the river, 1.3 miles above the entrance.

(163) **Florence** is a small town on the N bank of Siuslaw River 4.4 miles above the entrance. A bascule highway bridge with a clearance of 17 feet crosses the river from Florence to **Glenada**, a small settlement on the S bank of the river opposite Florence. (See **117.1 through 117.59 and 117.889,** chapter 2, for drawbridge regulations.) An overhead power cable with a clearance of 23 feet crosses the river about 150 yards E of the bridge; the cable is submerged at the main channel. Another overhead power cable with a clearance of 88 feet crosses the river about 1 mile above the bridge.

(164) A cannery wharf, and a small port-operated boat basin, and marina are at Florence; fish are shipped by truck. Another marina, about 0.15 mile W of the bridge, has about 80 berths, dockside electricity, gasoline, water, ice, launching ramp, and marine supplies; minor engine repairs can be made. The Port of Siuslaw Marina, about 0.3 mile E of the bridge, has over 250 berths, gasoline, diesel fuel, water, ice, some marine supplies, and launching ramps. Wet and dry winter storage is also available.

(165) **Cushman**, on the N bank of the river 2 miles above Florence, has lumber and shingle mills. The products from these mills are shipped by rail and barge. A small-craft repair facility here has a marine railway that can handle craft to 60 feet long, for engine and hull repairs. A 50-ton hoist is also available for handling small craft. About 50 berths with electricity, water, and a launching ramp are available. Wet and dry winter storage is also available at this facility. A large marine supply firm is at Cushman. An overhead power cable with a clearance of 75 feet crosses the river at Cushman. The railroad bridge across the river, 1 mile above Cushman, has a swing span with a clearance of 15 feet. (See **117.1 through 117.59 and 117.889**, chapter 2, for drawbridge regulations.) An overhead power cable with a clearance of 80 feet crosses the river at Mapleton.

(166) Light-draft vessels can go to **Mapleton**, 17 miles above the mouth, but the channel is narrow and crooked. A barge facility, about 14 miles above the mouth of the river, ships wood products and some perishable goods downriver.

Chart 18580

(167) From Siuslaw River for 7.5 miles to Heceta Head, the coast is composed of sand dunes that are quite conspicuous in contrast with the dark trees partly covering them.

(168) **Heceta Head**, 28.5 miles N of Umpqua River Light, has a seaward face 2.5 miles long with nearly vertical cliffs 100 to 200 feet high. The summit of the head reaches an elevation of 1,000 feet 0.5 mile from the cliffs and is covered with grass and a few pines. A sharp black conical rock, 180 feet high, marks the extreme W and N part of the head, and is easily made out from either N or S. **Cox Rock**, 1.5 miles S of the S part of the head, is conical and usually white on top with bird droppings.

(169) **Heceta Head Light** (44°08'15"N., 124°07'42"W.), 205 feet above the water, is a private light (currently extinguished for repairs; 2012) shown from a 56-foot white conical tower on a bench cut in the high bluff near the W extremity. Because of the high bluff N of the light, vessels from N will not make out the tower or buildings until abreast of the station.

(170) **Heceta Bank**, 70 miles NNW of Cape Blanco and 30 miles offshore W of Heceta Head, covers an irregular area about 30 miles long and 10 miles wide. The least depth on the bank is 25 fathoms, but the depths are irregular. The depths N and S of the bank are considerably greater.

(171) From Heceta Head to Cape Perpetua, a distance of 9 miles, the coast consists of high broken rocky cliffs, except for the first 2 miles which are composed of much

lower sloping sandy cliffs, backed by a strip of clear land. The hills behind reach an elevation of over 800 feet in less than 0.5 mile from the beach, and are heavily wooded.

(172) **Tenmile Creek**, 5 miles N of Heceta Head, is marked by a sand beach about 0.3 mile long at its mouth.

(173) **Cape Perpetua**, 9 miles N of Heceta Head, consists of two projecting points, the N of which is the bolder and marked by **Cleft of the Rock Light** (44°17'30"N., 124°06'30"W.), a private light 110 feet above the water and shown from a gray square tower attached to a dwelling. The cape reaches a height of 800 feet a short distance from the beach and 1,000 feet at a distance of 0.8 mile. The rocky cliff forming the face of the N point is reddish. A few rocks that uncover are close to its face.

(174) **Yachats River**, navigable only for canoes, breaks through the coast hills immediately N from Cape Perpetua.

(175) The coast for 2.5 miles N of Cape Perpetua consists of cliffs, 15 to 30 feet high, with a narrow strip of grassy land 0.2 to 1 mile wide behind them. Thence for 5.5 miles to Alsea Bay there are low bluffs, with a broad sand beach in front and comparatively low wooded country behind them.

(176) **Table Mountain**, 11 miles NE of the mouth of Alsea Bay, is flat-topped, covered with dead trees, and looks whitish. Another summit is 0.6 mile SW of Table Mountain.

(177) **Mary Peak**, a prominent mountain 24 miles E of the entrance to Yaquina Bay, is wooded on its sides, but its summit is covered with grass.

Chart 18561

(178) **Alsea Bay** is 68 miles N of Cape Arago. The N point is low, broad, and sandy, but the S point is an abrupt sandstone cliff about 100 feet high, covered with trees. The entrance has a shifting bar with a depth of about 6 feet. With a rising tide, the bar fills in with sand and the full effect of the tide cannot be counted on. There are considerable fishing and crabbing in the bay and river, but boats rarely cross the bar. **Waldport**, a mile inside the entrance, is the principal settlement. A marina with about 100 berths, gasoline, and a launching ramp is on the NE side of the town. The river, marked by seasonal private buoys, is navigable by small craft to about 10 miles above the mouth. There are several marinas along the river above Waldport; most have berths and gasoline. Outboard engine repairs can be made at a marina about 3 miles above the mouth.

(179) The fixed bridge of the Oregon Coast Highway crossing Alsea Bay, a mile inside the entrance, has a clearance of 66 feet.

COLREGS Demarcation Lines

(180) The lines established for Alsea Bay are described in **80.1335**, chapter 2.

(181) The 11.5-mile coast between Alsea Bay and Yaquina Bay is nearly straight, and consists of a low sand beach backed by dunes at each end with bluffs up to 100 feet high between; the land behind is low and wooded with areas of second-growth timber. Rocks covered 2 to 4 fathoms extend almost 2 miles offshore. **Seal Rocks**, abreast the highest part of the bluffs about 5 miles N of Alsea Bay entrance, extend up to 0.5 mile offshore for 2 miles; the tallest is 20 feet high.

(182) **Stonewall Bank**, 17 miles SW of Yaquina Head Light and 14 miles offshore, is 9 miles long in a N direction and 2.5 miles wide. There is a least depth of 13 fathoms on the bank. An unmarked submerged obstruction is close SW of Stonewall Bank in about 44°29.8'N., 124°24.9'W.

(183) **Yaquina Head**, 32.5 miles N of Heceta Head, is distinguished by two conical hills covered with grass. The outer one is 356 feet high and the inner 390 feet high, with a low saddle between them. The extremity of the point, which projects about a mile from the general trend of the coast, is broken and rocky, but comparatively low. One mile inland from the point, the grass-covered land changes to a dense forest and the hills rise rapidly. Two covered ledges lie N of the point 0.6 mile from the beach. There is a covered rock and considerable kelp about a mile S of the point. A patch of rocks that uncovers 8 feet is about a mile N of Yaquina Head Light. S to Yaquina Bay, the coast consists of broken yellow cliffs, bordered on the S part by broad sand beaches.

(184) **Yaquina Head Light** (44°40'36.3"N., 124°04'46.0"W.), 162 feet above the water, is shown from a 93-foot white conical tower on the flat bench projecting at the W extremity of the head.

(185) **Yaquina Reef** and its continuation N is a ridge of hard sand and rock covered 4 to 25 feet and marked by breakers. The reef extends from the submerged outer end of the N jetty and parallel to the shore to Yaquina Head. The submerged wreck of the ship JOHN ASPIN is about 0.65 mile N from the outer end of the N jetty.

(186) **South Reef**, with a least depth of 8 feet, is a continuation of Yaquina Reef, the two being separated by the entrance channel.

Chart 18581

(187) **Yaquina Bay** entrance is 4 miles S of Yaquina Head Light. The bay is a tidal estuary, the harbor itself being merely the widening of **Yaquina River** just inside the entrance.

(188) The N point of Yaquina Bay entrance is a sandy bluff, 120 feet high. A lighthouse and a Coast Guard lookout tower are on the high part of the point. When viewed from the NW, the circular lighthouse tower on the roof of a two-story frame dwelling obscures the lower portion of the lookout tower. The S entrance point is a low sand beach backed by dunes rising to 150 feet.

(189) The entrance to Yaquina Bay is protected by jetties 330 yards apart. The long N jetty, with the outer 100 yards submerged, extends out to Yaquina Reef. A seasonal sound signal is near the seaward end of the S jetty and a light is about 200 yards inside the seaward end. A lighted whistle buoy is 1.5 miles SW of the entrance. The channels are marked by lighted ranges, lights, and buoys. Between the jetties, numerous submerged rocks lie along the outside of the charted entrance channel limits.

(190) During the summer, when the swell is approximately parallel with the coast, the bar is comparatively smooth, being partially sheltered by Yaquina Head. In winter, however, the heavy W swell makes the bar very rough. A smooth bar and a favorable tide are necessary for large vessels leaving Yaquina Bay.

Coast Guard

(191) The Coast Guard has established Yaquina Bay Regulated Navigation Warning Sign, a **rough bar advisory sign**, 25 feet above the water, on the Coast Guard station, to promote safety for small-boat operators. The sign is diamond-shaped, painted white with an international orange border, and with the words "**Rough Bar**" in black letters. The sign is equipped with two quick flashing amber lights that will be activated when hazardous conditions exist and the bar is restricted to recreational and uninspected passenger vessels. Boaters are cautioned, however that if the lights are not flashing, it is no guarantee that sea conditions are favorable.

(192) A **heavy weather flag**, a square RED flag with a square BLACK center, will be displayed on a pole that is located on the western corner of the Coast Guard station and is visible to mariners from both directions to indicate that winds 48 knots and above are forecast for the area. Display of flags is required from one hour before sunrise to one hour after sunset. Weather flags are flown at select Coast Guard stations to supplement other weather notification sources. Light signals corresponding to these flags are not displayed at night. (See illustration, Chapter 1.) In all cases mariners should rely upon National Weather Service broadcasts as their primary source of government provided weather information.

COLREGS Demarcation Lines

(193) The lines established for Yaquina Bay are described in **80.1340**, chapter 2.

Channels

(194) A **Federal project** provides for a 40-foot entrance channel, thence 30 feet from the first turn in the channel to and in the turning basin at McLean Point, thence 18 feet to Yaquina, thence 10 feet to Toledo at the head of the project. Controlling depths may be considerably less than these project depths. (See Notice to Mariners and latest editions of the charts for controlling depths.)

(195) At the entrance to Yaquina Bay and River, the buoys cannot be relied upon to indicate the best water, and in the river, depths are subject to frequent change. Recreational boaters unfamiliar with the area are advised to contact the Coast Guard on VHF-FM channel 16 or telephone 541–265–5381 for the latest bar conditions, advisory, or to arrange an escort when unfamiliar with bar conditions. Professional mariners desiring to enter Yaquina Bay and River should employ a pilot or someone with local knowledge.

(196) A fixed highway bridge across the channel, about 1.3 miles above the entrance, has a clearance of 129 feet. **Yaquina Bay Coast Guard Station** is on the N side of the bay, 400 yards NE of the bridge.

(197) NOAA's **Marine Operations Center-Pacific** operates a pier on the S side of Yaquina Bay, one-quarter mile E of the highway bridge, which serves as the shipbase for the Administration's Pacific Fleet. The N face of the pier has a 520-foot berth, 260-foot berth and another 520-foot berth, from W to E, with 24 to 27 feet alongside. The E end of the S face of the pier has a 230-foot berth with 22 to 26 feet alongside. The berths are marked by four private lights. There is a 215-foot floating dock inshore at the E end of the pier. The waters inside the pier are restricted to authorized traffic only. To report emergencies or suspicious activity at this pier contact the Facilities Manager at (541) 867-8735.

(198) **Newport**, just inside the N entrance point, is the principal town on the bay and river. The town has a considerable fishing industry with several small fish-processing plants. Lumber, logs, paper and plywood, either barged from upper river mills or delivered by truck, are shipped from the wharves at **McLean Point**, just E of Newport.

Currents

(199) The current velocity is about 2.4 knots on the flood, and 2.3 knots on the ebb, in Yaquina Bay entrance. Near Newport docks the velocity is about 0.5 knot. Off Yaquina, and 1 mile S of Toledo, the velocity is about 1.4 knots. (See the Tidal Current Tables for predictions.)

Pilotage, Yaquina Bay

(200) Pilotage is compulsory for all foreign vessels and U.S. vessels under register. Pilotage is optional for U.S. vessels in the coastwise trade that have onboard a pilot licensed by the Federal Government for these waters. Pilotage for Yaquina Bay is available from Coos Bay Pilots Association. See Pilotage, Coos Bay, indexed as such, earlier this chapter for details.

(201) Pilots usually board vessels about 0.5 mile W of Yaquina Bay Approach Lighted Whistle Buoy Y (44°35'52"N., 124°06'47"W.).

Towage

(202) Tugs are available from Toledo and Coos Bay.

Quarantine, customs, immigration, and agricultural quarantine

(203)   (See chapter 3, Vessel Arrival Inspections, and Appendix A for addresses.)

(204)   **Quarantine** is enforced in accordance with regulations of the U.S. Public Health Service. (See Public Health Service, chapter 1.)

(205)   Newport is a **customs port of entry**.

Wharves

(206)   There are two deep-draft wharves in Yaquina Bay. The wharf at McLean Point, about 1 mile E of the highway bridge has two berths. Berth 1, just N of the turning basin, has 465 feet of berthing space, 30 to 32 feet reported alongside, and a deck height of 21 feet. Berth 1 was reported under construction until June 2011. Berth 2 (barge dock), just NE of the turning basin, has 250 feet of berthing space, 25 feet reported alongside, and a deck height of 15 feet. A concrete Ro/Ro extension connected to Berth 2 has 140 feet of berthing space in line with Berth 1, 30 feet reported alongside, and a deck height of 14 feet. Logs, lumber, plywood, and paper are shipped from both berths. The wharf is owned and operated by the Port of Newport.

Small-craft facilities

(207)   The Port of Newport operates a boat basin on the S side of the bay about 350 yards E of the bridge. The basin is protected to the N and W by jetties marked on the outer ends by a daybeacon and a light, respectively. A dredged entrance channel leads through the jetties, thence S along the W jetty turning E at the foot and terminating at a boat ramp at the head of the boat basin. In 2008, the controlling depth was 6 feet. Gasoline berths, diesel fuel, electricity, water, ice, and a pumpout facility are available. Hull, engine, and shaft repairs can be made. Facilities can be contacted on VHF-FM channel 12 by hailing the Port of Newport South. The Port of Newport Internet address is http://www.portofnewport.com.

(208)   The Port of Newport operates a commercial moorage on the N shore about 0.7 mile above the highway bridge; a marina is also in this area. The moorage area is protected from the main channel by a detached breakwater marked by a light at each end. Berths for about 206 vessels, gasoline, diesel fuel, electricity and water are available; marine supplies can be obtained in Newport. The marina can be contacted on VHF-FM channel 12 by hailing "Port of Newport North". A marine repair facility is just N of **Oneatta Point**, 3.8 miles above the highway bridge at the entrance to the bay. The facility has two travel lifts, one 15-ton and one 70-ton, and two 60-ton cranes.

Communication

(209)   Communication is by highway and air. The municipal airport is about 4 miles S of Newport. A U.S. highway extends N and S along the coast, and a State highway leads to the interior.

(210)   **Yaquina** is a small settlement 4.2 miles above the entrance. A power cable across Yaquina River, 0.5 mile above Yaquina, has a clearance of 77 feet. At Yaquina, there is moorage and a 6,000 pound hoist. Fuel and supplies can be purchased. Several small marinas are along the river between Newport and Toledo. (See Newport small-craft facilities description.)

(211)   **Toledo**, about 11.5 miles above the entrance has large lumbermills and a papermill. The least depths alongside the wharves are 10 feet. Toledo also has a moorage capability for about 20 boats 65 feet or less. There is access to a 40-ton travel lift and a 300-ton marine dry dock. The fixed highway bridge, 0.5 mile above Toledo, has a clearance of 34 feet. An overhead pipeline with a clearance of 54 feet crosses **Depot Slough** just above the mouth. Overhead pipelines 0.3 mile above the mouth of the slough have a clearance of 18 feet.

Chart 18520

(212)   From Yaquina Head to the mouth of Columbia River, the coast is fairly straight. The headlands are Cape Foulweather, Cascade Head, Cape Lookout, Cape Meares, Cape Falcon, and Tillamook Head. The 30-fathom curve follows the general trend of the coast about 3.5 miles offshore, without indicating the several headlands. When about opposite Tillamook Head, the curve swings W and is about 7.5 miles off the end of Clatsop Spit.

Chart 18561

(213)   From Yaquina Head for 5.5 miles to Cape Foulweather, the coast consists of yellow and white sandstone cliffs, low and broken. **Iron Mountain**, 1.5 miles NE of Yaquina Head Light, is a 654-foot-high hill. When viewed from the S, the highest third of the hill is bare and composed of a red rock formation, the N side and lower part of the hill are covered with thick brush.

(214)   A low flat rock, 8 feet high, is 0.4 mile offshore 2.8 miles N of Yaquina Head.

(215)   **Otter Rock**, 11 feet high, is 3.2 miles N of Yaquina Head and 0.6 mile offshore. **Gull Rock**, 56 feet high, is 1.2 miles N of Otter Rock and 0.4 mile offshore. In line between the two rocks is a kelp field with several rocks, covered and awash. Covered rocks that break are 0.5 to 1 mile N of Gull Rock.

(216)   **Cape Foulweather** is a prominent headland with about 6 miles of seaward face consisting of rocky cliffs over 60 feet high. The cape is formed by several grass-covered headlands, separated by densely wooded gulches. Near the middle of the cape is a strip of flat land, 0.5 mile long and 0.2 mile wide, bare of trees. The highest point of the cape is near the S part. A grassy patch is

conspicuous on the SW slope. A white building with a red roof, 0.7 mile NNE of Gull Rock, is prominent on the high bluff just S of Cape Foulweather. About 0.9 mile SE of the extreme W point of the cape is a rocky point 445 feet high, and E of the point the hills rise to 1,100 feet in 0.6 mile. Dangers extend for nearly 2 miles N of the N point of Cape Foulweather and about 600 yards offshore.

(217) The coast highway follows the shoreline closely at Cape Foulweather.

(218) **Depoe Bay**, 8 miles N of Yaquina Head, has one of the best small-boat shelters along this part of the coast. The bay proper has foul ground on both the N and S sides, but the channel leading to the narrow dredged channel to the inner basin is deep and well marked. The foul areas break in moderate seas and are marked by kelp. Prominent from seaward is the concrete arch bridge over the entrance to the basin. A lighted whistle buoy is 1.1 miles W of the entrance to the bay. A lighted bell buoy and **085.5°** lighted range mark the entrance to the bay and the approach to the dredged channel to the basin, respectively. A mariner radio activated sound signal, located on the S side of the entrance is about 50 yards SW of the bridge, and is initiated by keying the microphone five times on VHF-FM channel 83A.

COLREGS Demarcation Lines

(219) The lines established for Depoe Bay are described in **80.1345**, chapter 2.

(220) In 1986, the reported controlling depth in the dredged channel to the fixed arched bridge was 8 feet; thence in 2009, depths of 6 to 8 feet were available in the basin with lesser depths to 3 feet in the SE corner. In 1994, shoaling to 4 feet was reported near the W edge of the channel under the bridge.

(221) The fixed concrete arched bridge over the entrance is unusual in that its width of 30 feet is less than the clearance of 42 feet. The navigator is cautioned against the dangerous surge in the narrow entrance to the basin. Boats over 50 feet long cannot enter the basin without a special waiver from the harbormaster, and then only at highwater. The entrance should not be attempted at night or in rough weather without local knowledge. **Depoe Bay Coast Guard Station**, at the inner basin, monitors VHF-FM channel 16 or may be contacted at 541–765–2123.

Coast Guard

(222) The Coast Guard has established Depoe Bay Regulated Navigation Area Warning Sign, a **rough bar advisory sign**, 25 feet above the water, visible from the channel looking seaward, on a building on the N side of the basin entrance channel, to promote safety for small-boat operators. The sign is diamond-shaped, painted white with an international orange border, and with the words "**Rough Bar**" in black letters. The sign is equipped with two quick flashing amber lights that will be activated when hazardous conditions exist and the bar is restricted to recreational and uninspected passenger vessels. Boaters are cautioned, however, that if the lights are not flashing, it is no guarantee that sea conditions are favorable.

(223) A **heavy weather flag**, a square RED flag with a square BLACK center, will be displayed on a pole that is located approximately 50 yards north of the bridge across the entrance to Depoe Bay, on the west side of highway 101 to indicate that winds 48 knots and above are forecast for the area. Display of flags are required from one hour before sunrise to one hour after sunset. Weather flags are flown at select Coast Guard stations to supplement other weather notification sources. Light signals corresponding to these flags are not displayed at night. (See illustration, Chapter 1.) In all cases mariners should rely upon National Weather Service broadcasts as their primary source of government provided weather information.

(224) The town of **Depoe Bay** is on the N side of the basin. The basin has a concrete bulkhead, mooring floats, and a tidal grid for minor hull repair work. Also available are berths with electricity, gasoline, diesel fuel, water, ice, launching ramp, and marine supplies. Hull and engine repairs can be made.

Chart 18520

(225) From Cape Foulweather for 9.5 miles to the entrance of Siletz Bay, the coast continues as yellow broken bluffs, 40 to 100 feet high, bordered by about 3 miles of sandy beaches. From the N point of the bluffs to the bay entrance are sand dunes covered with low brush.

(226) The entrance to **Siletz Bay** is 15 miles N of Yaquina Head. The entrance channel is subject to frequent change, and drafts of 4 or 5 feet are considered the deepest that can be safely taken in at high water.

(227) The N point at the entrance is a low bluff with a narrow sand beach. The S point is a low sandspit about 250 yards wide. The dunes on the spit are thinly wooded near the shore, but become thickly wooded inland. Several houses are on the spit. The bay inside the entrance is shoal. **Siletz River** enters the bay at the SE end.

(228) **Taft** and **Cutler City** are communities on the bay; both are parts of **Lincoln City**, which is 1.8 miles N. There are several marinas on the bay; a facility just above the highway bridge at the mouth of Siletz River has gasoline, water, ice, a launching ramp, and some marine supplies. Outboard engine repairs can be made here. The highway bridge just below the marina has a clearance of 31 feet.

(229) From Siletz Bay the coast extends 7 miles N to the Salmon River. For 2.5 miles of this stretch to the outlet of **Devils Lake**, the yellow standstone cliffs are 80 to 100 feet high. The lake is a large body of freshwater, 10 feet

(230) above sea level, that empties through a narrow stream. At 0.5 mile WSW of the mouth of the stream is a covered rock that generally breaks. For 3 miles N from the outlet of the lake, the bluffs are 20 to 60 feet high, rising to grassy hills. A broad beach and ledges of rocks are along the shore.

(230) **Salmon River** empties at the S extremity of Cascade Head; the entrance is nearly closed by sandbars.

(231) Immediately S of Salmon River is a rocky cliff whose seaward face is 0.6 mile long. The summit is a dome-shaped butte 510 feet high. From here a rolling grassy plateau with a few trees extends S and E to the river. A rock, 46 feet high, is 700 yards W of this cliff, and about a mile S is a covered rock 630 yards off the beach. Immediately S of and in line with Cascade Head, opposite the mouth of the river, are three grayish rocks about 765 yards offshore. These have heights of 56 feet on the N, 25 feet in the center, and 47 feet on the S.

(232) **Cascade Head**, 23 miles N of Yaquina Head, is very jagged and heavily wooded. The face of the cliff is 3 miles long, is over 700 feet high in places, and is cut by several deep gorges through which the waters of three creeks are discharged in cascades 60 to 80 feet high. Several rocks are about 0.1 mile offshore.

(233) **Two Arches**, 30 feet high, is a rock 0.9 mile N of the S point of Cascade Head. The arches are visible from N; the inner is the larger.

(234) From Cascade Head for 9.5 miles to Cape Kiwanda, the coast is a low sand beach with a narrow marsh behind the S part. Rolling hilltops, occasionally wooded, rise to an elevation of 500 feet behind the beach.

(235) **Neskowin Rock**, at the high-water line about 0.3 mile N of the N extremity of the cliffs marking Cascade Head, rises abruptly from the sand beach to 113 feet in height. The rock is dark brown and wooded on top.

(236) N of Neskowin Rock the Oregon Coast Highway is about 0.5 mile inland. At night the headlights of automobiles traveling this road cause intermittent flashes as they make the turns and might be mistaken for lights of vessels.

(237) **Nestucca River** empties into **Nestucca Bay** 5.5 miles N of Cascade Head. The channel over the bar changes frequently in position and depth, and only light-draft vessels having local knowledge are able to cross. A fixed highway bridge at Pacific City has a clearance of 10 feet. The river has many snags that change the depths and shift the channel. Even in a moderate sea, the bar is extremely dangerous. The point on the S side of the entrance consists of several low-rolling, grassy hillocks, about 400 to 500 feet high, which approach very close to the beach. The N point is the S extremity of the sandspit and dunes that extend to Cape Kiwanda.

(238) **Pacific City** is a summer resort about 3 miles above the entrance to Nestucca Bay. Gasoline and supplies are available in the community.

(239) **Haystack Rock**, 327 feet high, 0.5 mile SW of Cape Kiwanda and 0.5 mile offshore, is a prominent landmark. The rock is conical and dark for about half its height, and in summer the top is whitened by bird droppings.

(240) **Cape Kiwanda**, 33 miles N of Yaquina Head, is a low yellow rocky point, much broken and eroded, that projects about 0.5 mile from the general trend of the coast. Behind the cape are bright sand dunes, 500 feet high, which are prominent from seaward. Just S of Cape Kiwanda is a beach resort area; a public launching ramp is here. A bell buoy is about 0.5 mile W of the cape.

(241) From Cape Kiwanda the coast extends 7.5 miles in a general N direction to Cape Lookout. It is broken about halfway by the entrance to **Sand Lake**, which is shallow and not navigable. The coast consists of sand beaches and dunes until about a mile N of Sand Lake where it changes to vertical sandstone cliffs, 50 to 100 feet high. These continue to Cape Lookout.

(242) **Cape Lookout**, 40 miles N of Yaquina Head, projects W for 1.5 miles, forming a narrow rocky promontory 432 feet in height at its seaward extremity. The S face is nearly straight, and its precipitous cliffs have numerous caves. The N face is sloping and covered with a thick growth of timber. The ridge that forms the cape runs at about right angles to the coast, reaching an elevation of some 2,000 feet, 3.8 miles inland. The N face of the cape is smooth and bold for the first mile, and then is much broken and marked by caves and several cascades. Fair shelter in NW winds may be had under the S side of the cape in 6 to 8 fathoms, sandy bottom.

(243) N of Cape Lookout for 4.5 miles, the land falls to a low narrow sandy peninsula, separating Netarts Bay from the ocean. The sand dunes on the peninsula are visible for 10 or 12 miles.

(244) **Netarts Bay** is a shallow lagoon most of which is bare at low water. The village of **Netarts** is on the N shore a mile inside the entrance. Only light-draft boats with local knowledge can enter. A small-boat basin with two floating piers and a launching ramp are at Netarts. N of the entrance to Netarts Bay, for 1.5 miles to the rocks forming the S part of Cape Meares, the coast is a sandy beach, backed by cliffs 50 to 120 feet high. These cliffs, topped by sand dunes varying in height from 150 to 200 feet, are good landmarks.

COLREGS Demarcation Lines

(245) The lines established for Netarts Bay are described in **80.1350**, chapter 2.

Chart 18558

(246) **Cape Meares**, 48 miles N of Yaquina Head, is high and rocky, with a 2-mile-long seaward face. The N part is the higher, with nearly vertical cliffs 640 feet high. The W point is narrow, covered with fern and brush, and terminates seaward in a cliff 200 feet high.

(247) **Three Arch Rocks** are the largest of a cluster extending 350 yards off the S point of the cape. They range in height from 204 to 275 feet. The largest arch is in the

Tillamook Bay, Oregon
Image courtesy U.S. Army Corps of Engineers (1993)

middle of the lowest rock, and is about half the height of the rock above water. These rocks are the favorite resort of sea lions, whose barking can be heard a considerable distance with a favorable wind.

(248) **Cape Meares Light** (45°29'11"N., 123°58'42"W.), 232 feet above the water, is shown from a 17-foot white masonry building on the summit of the cliff.

(249) **Pillar Rock**, 75 feet high, is 0.2 mile NW of Cape Meares Light, and 0.4 mile farther NW is **Pyramid Rock**, 110 feet high, which leans seaward. A submerged rock covered 34 feet, lies 0.4 mile NW of Pyramid Rock.

(250) From Cape Meares to Kincheloe Point, the coast is a low partly wooded sandspit, with dunes 40 to 50 feet high. It forms the W shore of Tillamook Bay. A sand dike prevents a breakthrough N of Cape Meares, at **Pitcher Point**.

(251) **Tillamook Bay** entrance is 42 miles S of the Columbia River, 25.5 miles S of Tillamook Rock, and 5.7 miles N of Cape Meares Light. The bay has a tidal area of about 13 square miles, most of which, at low tide, presents a succession of sand and mud flats. There is no commercial traffic in the bay except for fishing boats and pleasure craft.

(252) **Kincheloe Point** is low and sandy and appears to be an island from a distance to the N. The N side of the entrance is the termination of a high wooded ridge extending between the bay and Nehalem River. **Green Hill**, opposite Kincheloe Point, is a 400-foot spur that terminates in a bluff rounded point. The prominent hill is covered by ferns, grass, and dense brush with trees on top.

(253) **Tillamook Bay Coast Guard Station** is on the N shore W of Garibaldi. A lookout tower is near the intersection of the N entrance jetty and the shore.

COLREGS Demarcation Lines

(254) The lines established for Tillamook Bay are described in **80.1355**, chapter 2.

(255) The entrance to Tillamook Bay is protected by jetties. The N jetty extends about 600 yards offshore; the westernmost 150 yards of the jetty is submerged. The S jetty extends 1000 yards offshore with the westernmost 100 yards submerged. Extreme caution should be taken in the vicinity of the jetties. A **Federal project** provides for an 18-foot entrance channel that crosses the bar and leads eastward between the jetties through the N part of Tillamook Bay to an inactive turning basin just W of Miami Cove. An access channel leads to a 12-foot small boat basin at the town of Garibaldi. (See Notice to Mariners and latest editions of charts for controlling depths.)

(256) A lighted whistle buoy is 1.35 miles about SSW of the seaward end of the N jetty. The N jetty is marked by a light and seasonal sound signal. The main approach to Tillamook Bay is from the S. There is a leading light marking the center of the jetties which signals when

the mariner is clear of the S jetty and safe to make the approach into the bay. Mariners should use caution while making the approach to the jetties due to frequent shoaling and heavy breakers in the vicinity of the approach channel. The entrance and channel to Garibaldi is marked by buoys and lights. Caution is advised during periods of heavy seas.

(257) Several visible and covered rocks are on the N side of the dredged channel. **Sow and Pigs**, across the channel from Kincheloe Point and nearly 500 yards off the N shore, is a rocky ledge that uncovers 1 to 6 feet. The ledge is dangerous when entering with a flood current, as the current sets toward it.

Currents

(258) The current velocity is 3 knots in the entrance to Tillamook Bay.

Coast Guard

(259) The Coast Guard has established Tillamook Bay Regulated Navigation Area Warning Sign, a **rough bar advisory sign**, on the N side of the channel near the beginning of Garibaldi Channel, visible from the channel, to promote safety for small-boat operators. The sign is diamond-shaped, painted white with an international orange border and with the words **"Rough Bar"** in black letters. The sign is equipped with two quick flashing amber lights that will be activated when hazardous conditions exist and the bar is restricted to recreational and uninspected passenger vessels. Boaters are cautioned, however, that if the lights are not flashing, it is no guarantee that sea conditions are favorable.

(260) **Garibaldi**, a lumber and fishing town, is on the N shore 2 miles inside the entrance. A grey concrete stack and a silver elevated tank are conspicuous. There are several small fish companies at Garibaldi.

(261) The town has a boat basin for commercial and sport fishing vessels. Berths for about 250 craft, electricity, gasoline, diesel fuel, water, ice, a launching ramp, and marine supplies are available at the basin. A drydock in the basin can handle craft to 100 tons, 68 feet long, or up to 9 feet in. draft. Repair work must be arranged for independently of the drydock operator; complete marine repairs can be made.

(262) S of Garibaldi, unmarked **Bay City Channel** follows the E side of Tillamook Bay to the S end where it continues through narrow and crooked **Hoquarten Slough** to Tillamook, 11 miles above Tillamook Bay entrance. The channel has a depth of about 6 feet to Bay City, 4.4 miles above Tillamook Bay entrance, but S of this point depths are less than 3 feet to Tillamook. During freshets, snags are carried into the upper part of the bay where they form a menace to navigation.

(263) **Bay City** has a small oyster cannery on an earth-fill pier. Fishing and crabbing are carried on in the vicinity, but all shipments are made by truck or rail.

(264) **Tillamook** is noted for the production of cheese. It is the distributing center for a rich farming and dairying section.

(265) **Tillamook River** empties into the S part of Tillamook Bay just W of the entrance to Hoquarten Slough. A fixed highway bridge with a clearance of 15 feet crosses the river about 0.7 mile above the mouth. A small marina is just S of the bridge on the W bank of **Trask River**, just inside the mouth; berths with electricity, water, ice, gasoline, a launching ramp, and marine supplies are available. Outboard engine repairs can be made. This marina is open only during the summer. Depths of about 2 feet can be carried in Tillamook River to the highway bridge. Wet and dry winter boat storage is available at the marina.

Chart 18520

(266) From Tillamook Bay to Nehalem River, the coast is nearly straight for about 5 miles. Several lakes in this stretch are separated from the beach by wooded sand dunes. The heavily wooded hills begin to rise 0.5 mile to 0.8 mile from the beach and in 1 mile reach elevations of 1,000 to 1,600 feet.

(267) **Twin Rocks** are 700 yards offshore and 2 miles N of the entrance to Tillamook Bay. Their bases are so close together that they usually look like one rock. The S and larger has an arch in it.

Chart 18556

(268) **Nehalem River**, 5 miles N of Tillamook Bay entrance, is tidal for about 10 miles from the entrance. Above this point the river is a mountain stream full of riffles and obstructed by boulders. The river constitutes a natural outlet for an extensive area of heavily timbered country. Lumbering and fishing are the principal industries. Sawmills are along the lower river.

COLREGS Demarcation Lines

(269) The lines established for the Nehalem River are described in **80.1360**, chapter 2.

(270) **Nehalem Beach**, the N point at the entrance, is a narrow sandspit, bare of trees, and with dunes of moderate elevation over the N part. The S side of the entrance is a low broad sand beach, backed by wooded country rising to elevations of 400 feet.

(271) The entrance is protected by jetties extending 600 yards from the shoreline, though there are a number of breaks in the jetties. A whistle buoy is nearly 1 mile W of the entrance and a private range marks the entrance channel. Mariners are advised to seek local knowledge before using the entrance channel because of seasonal changes.

(272) The depths on the bar and within the bay are not sufficient for coastwise shipping. The controlling depth

(273) is about 4 feet on the bar, and 3 to 8 feet to Wheeler. The channel is changeable.

(273) A marina is on the E side of the river just inside the entrance. Berths with electricity, gasoline, water, ice, launching ramp, and marine supplies are available. Engine repairs can be made; wet winter boat storage is also available.

(274) **Brighton** is a small settlement on the E shore, 1 mile inside the entrance to the river. A marina is at Brighton. Berths with electricity, gasoline, water, ice, and a launching ramp is at the marina. Dry winter storage and engine repairs are available. **Wheeler**, 4.7 miles above the entrance, has an abandoned sawmill, a launching ramp, and wharf in ruins. All traffic is by truck.

(275) **Nehalem** is a small settlement on the W shore of the river, 6.3 miles above the entrance. A fixed highway bridge over the river just below Nehalem has a clearance of 30 feet. Close N of this bridge is an overhead power cable with a clearance of 52 feet. A surfaced launching ramp is on the E side of the river about 0.1 mile below the highway bridge.

Charts 18520, 18003

(276) The coast is low and sandy for about 3 miles N of Nehalem River entrance, then a dense forest begins which rises gradually to the S slope of Neahkahnie Mountain. There are grassy hillocks, 40 to 100 feet high, in the vicinity of the beach.

(277) **Cape Falcon**, 17 miles N of Cape Meares and 10 miles S of Tillamook Rock, projects about 2 miles from the general trend of the coast. The seaward face, less than 0.5 mile in extent, is very jagged with numerous rocks under the cliffs. The SW point of the cape is composed of nearly vertical cliffs, 200 feet high, and is partially timbered. **Falcon Rock**, 0.7 mile W of the cape, is small and not very conspicuous.

(278) **Smuggler Cove**, a small bight just S of Cape Falcon, is an excellent anchorage for small boats. The best anchorage is close to the N shore in 4 to 5 fathoms, protected from all except SW winds. Care should be taken to avoid two rocks, bare at extreme low water, that are about 150 yards from the N shore of the cove and rise abruptly from deep water.

(279) **Neahkahnie Mountain**, 2.8 miles inland of Cape Falcon, is a prominent landmark, and the most important feature for locating Nehalem River. The W summit of the double-headed mountain is rounded and 1,900 feet high, but the E summit is serrated and divided into three peaks of nearly equal height. The entire SE slope is bare of timber, but is covered with grass and fern. The seaward face terminates in rocky broken cliffs over 500 feet high, and there are a few rocks about 100 feet from the beach. The two summits are visible from S; from N, the W summit hides the E and is very conspicuous.

(280) NE of Cape Falcon, and 2 to 3 miles back from the shoreline, is a group of peaks; the highest and most prominent has a rounded summit, with a very gentle slope to the S and a more marked and abrupt drop to the N. It is very conspicuous from W in clear weather.

(281) **Arch Cape**, rocky and precipitous, projects slightly from the general trend of the coast. It is the termination of a mountain ridge rising to 2,775 feet about 3 miles E. The cape is bare of timber. A high rock is close to the cape and connected with it at low water. A smaller rock is about 100 yards seaward of the larger. There are several other high rocks in the vicinity of the cape.

(282) **Castle Rock** derives its name from its remarkable resemblance to a medieval castle with two towers, the taller of which is on the seaward end. It is about 0.8 mile W of the highest part of Arch Cape, and is the outermost bare rock. The upper part of the rock is covered with bird droppings and shows up very distinctly in sunlight. A rock awash is about 0.9 mile off the cape and 0.4 mile SW of Castle Rock; another rock, bare at lowest tides, is 0.5 mile offshore and 1 mile S of Castle Rock.

(283) **Hug Point** is a small cliff close to the beach, 1.8 miles N of Arch Cape; the cliffs in its vicinity are above 180 feet high.

(284) **Double Peak**, halfway between Cape Falcon and Tillamook Head, is the seaward end of a ridge extending E that reaches a height of 1,050 feet in less than 0.7 mile from the shore. It is heavily wooded and pitches abruptly to the sea, ending in a rocky broken cliff 100 feet high and 0.2 mile long. A rock is close to and abreast of the S end of the cliff; another rock is close to and abreast the N end. A ledge, with two rocks that uncover about 4 feet, is about a mile WSW of the highest part of the cliff.

(285) From Double Peak, the coast extends N for 2.7 miles to the mouth of **Ecola Creek**, and then turns sharply NW for the same distance to the W point of Tillamook Head. The coast is high and wooded with broken cliffs bordered by numerous rocks, except at Cannon Beach at the mouth of Ecola Creek.

(286) **Haystack Rock**, 1.5 miles N of Double Peak, is the largest of a cluster of rocks stretching out from the low-water line to 10 fathoms. A rock awash at low water and surrounded by about 9 fathoms is 0.8 mile SW of Haystack Rock.

(287) **Tillamook Head**, 76 miles N of Yaquina Head, ends in two points which are 0.5 mile apart. The cliffs are 560 feet high at the S point and 1,000 feet high at the N point. A pinnacle rock is at the foot of the N cliffs, and extending offshore from it for 300 yards is a cluster of rocks, 45 to 150 feet high, the outer one being the lowest. The summit of the head is flat and densely wooded, with slightly lower land behind it.

(288) **Tillamook Rock**, nearly 1.2 miles W of the S point of Tillamook Head, has an abandoned lighthouse and buildings on it. The W face leans a little seaward. A rock awash is between Tillamook Rock and the nearest part of Tillamook Head.

(289) N of Tillamook Head the coast is a broad sand beach extending for 17 miles to Clatsop Spit, on the S side of the entrance to Columbia River. Low sandy ridges, covered with grass, fern, and brush, extend parallel with and back of the beach. **Necanicum River**, a small stream, empties at the summer resort of **Seaside**, 2.5 miles from the N side of Tillamook Head.

(290) **Saddle Mountain**, double-headed and 3,283 feet high, is the landfall for the approach to the Columbia River. The mountain is 14 miles E of Tillamook Rock and is visible 50 miles offshore. From NW, the mountain appears to be triple-headed; the NE peak appears cone shaped, sharp, and lowest; the middle peak is irregularly cone shaped; and the S and highest peak is a flat-topped cone.

TIDAL INFORMATION					
Chart	Station	LAT/LONG	Mean Higher High Water*	Mean High Water*	Mean Low Water*
18520	Nestucca Bay entrance	45°10'N/123°58'W	7.6	6.9	1.1
18520	Garibaldi, Tillamook	45°34'N/123°55'W	7.8	7.1	1.2
18520	Columbia River entrance (North Jetty)	46°16'N/124°04'W	7.5	6.8	1.2
18520	Bar at entrance, Yaquina Bay	44°37'N/124°05'W	7.9	7.2	1.3
18556	Brighton, Nehalem River	45°40'N/123°56'W	7.8	7.1	1.2
18556	Nehalem, Nehalem River	45°43'N/123°53'W	7.2	6.5	0.9
18558	Miami Cove, Tillamook Bay	45°33'N/123°54'W	7.4	6.7	1.1
18558	Tillamook, Hoquarten Slough, Tillamook Bay	45°28'N/123°51'W	6.6	5.9	0.7
18558	Bay City, Tillamook Bay	45°31'N/123°54'W	7.1	6.4	1.0
18558	Barview, Tillamook Bay	45°34'N/123°57'W	7.5	6.8	1.1
18561	Waldport, Alsea Bay	44°26'N/124°04'W	7.7	7.0	1.2
18580	Umpqua River entrance	43°41'N/124°12'W	6.9	6.3	1.2
18581	Yaquina, Yaquina River	44°36'N/124°01'W	8.2	7.5	1.3
18581	Toledo, Yaquina River	44°37'N/123°56'W	8.1	7.4	1.1
18581	Newport, Yaquina Bay	44°38'N/124°03'W	8.0	7.3	1.3
18583	Suislaw River entrance	44°01'N/124°08'W	7.3	6.7	1.2
18587	Coos Bay, Coos Bay	43°23'N/124°13'W	7.3	6.7	1.1
18587	Empire, Coos Bay	43°24'N/124°17'W	6.7	6.0	1.1
18588	Bandon, Coquille River	43°07'N/124°25'W	7.1	6.4	1.2
18601	Wedderburn, Rogue River	42°26'N/124°25'W	6.7	6.0	1.1
18602	Brookings, Chetco Cove	42°03'N/124°17'W	6.9	6.3	1.2

* Heights in feet referred to datum of sounding MLLW.
Real-time water levels, tide predictions, and tidal current predictions are available at:
http://tidesandcurrents.noaa.gov
To determine mean tide range subtract Mean Low Water from Mean High Water.
Data as of September 2012

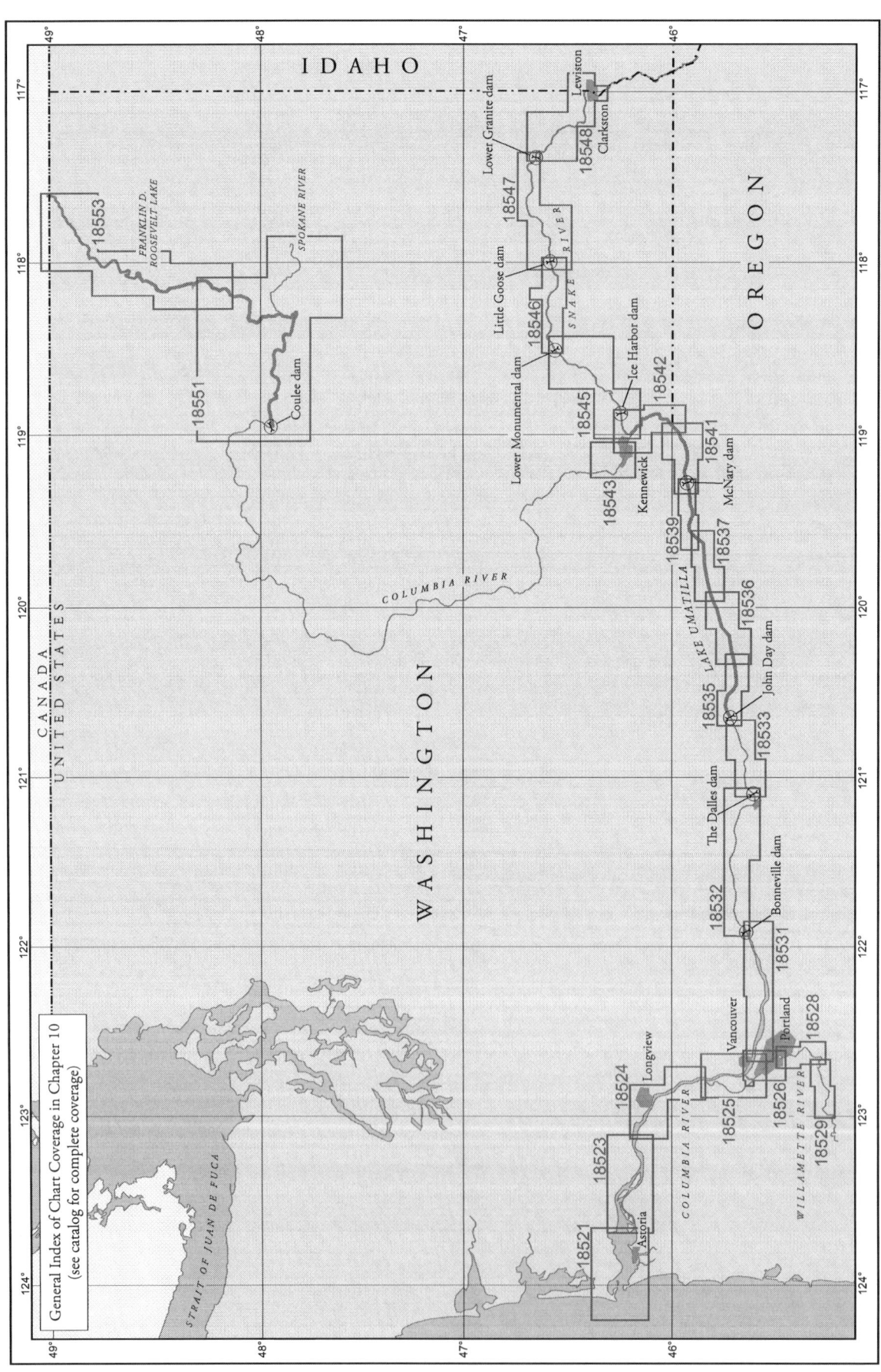

Columbia River, Oregon and Washington

(1) This chapter describes the Columbia River from its mouth at the Pacific Ocean to the head of navigation above Richland, WA. Also described are its two major tributaries, the Willamette River in Oregon and the Snake River in Washington and Idaho. The deep-draft ports of Astoria, Longview, Portland, and Vancouver are described as well as many smaller ports.

(2) **Note:** The nautical charts covering the Columbia, Willamette, and Snake Rivers show statute mile designations. However, the **distances** given in the text for these waterways are the **nautical miles** above their respective mouths with the statute mile equivalents shown in parentheses. Unless otherwise indicated, all other distances are given in nautical miles.

(3) **Mile 0.0**, on the Columbia River, is at the junction of the Main Channel Range and a line joining the outer ends of the jetties. The distance to the mouth of the Columbia River from a position 0.5 mile W of the Columbia River Approach Lighted Whistle Buoy CR is 5.8 (6.6) miles.

(4) Conversion tables, nautical miles to statute miles, and statute miles to nautical miles are in Appendix B. Mileage conversion scales are also shown on the nautical charts.

COLREGS Demarcation Lines

(5) The lines established for the Columbia River are described in **80.1365**, chapter 2.

Caution

(6) The volcanic eruptions of Mount Saint Helens in mid-1980 caused extensive flooding with resulting heavy siltation in the lower Columbia River. Large amounts of mud, logs, and other debris entered Columbia River from Cowlitz River, just E of Longview at Mile 59 (68). In late 1980, dredging was done in the aforementioned area, however, mariners are advised to use caution in the Columbia River and its tributaries. Self-propelled hopper dredges, dredge barges and pipeline dredges may be encountered throughout the transit from sea to Bonneville Dam. Mariners should contact these vessels on VHF-FM channel 13 to make passing arrangements, and navigate with due caution through these areas.

(7) Rice Island, Miller Sands, Jim Crow Sands and Cottonwood Islands are used for dredging disposal sites. Elevations of these islands constantly change, as well as the overall shape and dimensions.

Charts 18003, 18007

(8) **Columbia River** rises in British Columbia, Canada, through which it flows for some 370 (425) miles before entering the continental United States in NE Washington. Thence it flows S to its junction with Snake River, from which it curves W and forms the boundary between the States of Washington and Oregon for the remainder of its course to the Pacific Ocean. Its entrance is 548 miles N of San Francisco and 145 miles S of the Strait of Juan de Fuca. The length of the river is 647 (745) miles in the United States. Between the Cascade Mountains, the river flows through a canyon averaging about 5 miles wide between high cliffs on each side; of this width, the river occupies about 1 mile, the rest being marsh, low islands, and lowlands. Near the mouth, the river becomes wider, and in some places is 5 miles across.

(9) Columbia and Willamette Rivers are navigable by deep-draft vessels to Vancouver, WA, and Portland, OR. Barges navigate the Columbia River to Pasco and Kennewick, WA, 286 (329) miles above the mouth.

(10) Navigation on the tributary Snake River, which joins the Columbia at Pasco, is possible to Lewiston, Idaho. The hydro-electric powerplants at the dams on the Columbia provide the major supply of electricity for the entire Northwest.

(11) The commerce, both foreign and domestic, is extensive. The exports are principally logs, lumber, and forest products, grain, flour, chemicals, fruit, fish, general and containerized cargo, and general merchandise; the imports are coal, petroleum products, bulk salt, bulk cement, alumina, manufactured, and general and containerized cargo.

(12) There are numerous settlements and landings, but Astoria, OR; Longview, WA; Vancouver, WA; and Portland, OR are the principal shipping points. The distances above the mouth of the Columbia River to these ports are, respectively, 12 (14) miles, 58 (66) miles, 92 (106) miles, and 97 (112) miles; Portland is on the Willamette River 9 (10.5) miles above its junction with the Columbia. The Columbia River has major highways (State, U.S., and Interstate) on the S and N sides connecting principal cities and the towns in between.

Prominent features

(13) **Columbia River Approach Lighted Whistle Buoy CR** (46°11'05"N., 124°11'03"W.), about 5.3 miles SW of

Washington State Requirements

Reports of Oil Spills and Vessel Emergencies
All vessels must report oil spills or potential oil spills to both:
1. Washington State   800–258–5990
2. National Response Center 800–424–8802

Tank vessels and cargo and passenger ships 300 gross tons or larger must make notifications to Washington State for vessel emergencies, including a loss or serious degradation of propulsion, steering, means of navigation, electrical generating capability and seakeeping capability constituting a substantial threat of pollution affecting Washington state natural resources. In addition to any notifications to the USCG, the owner or operator must notify the state of any vessel emergency that results in the discharge or substantial threat of a discharge of oil to state waters or that may affect the natural resources of the state within one hour of the onset of the emergency.

Washington State Vessel Inspections
The Washington State Department of Ecology regulates cargo and passenger vessels and tank vessels operating in Washington waters.
• A cargo vessel is any self-propelled vessel in commerce that is 300 gross tons or more.
• A passenger vessel is any vessel 300 gross tons or more with a fuel capacity of at least 6,000 gallons that carries passengers for compensation.
• A tank vessel is a ship that is constructed or adapted to carry, or that carries, oil in bulk as cargo or cargo residue.

Washington State Ecology inspectors may conduct vessel inspections on regulated cargo, passenger, and fishing vessels when in Washington waters. Additional information is available at:
http://www.ecy.wa.gov/programs/spills/prevention/VesselTechAssist/AISsubstantialrisk.html/

Oil Transfer Requirements
Safe bunkering procedures must be followed during fueling operations. For vessels 300 gross tons or greater, Washington State Ecology inspectors may conduct inspections of these regulated oil transfers on vessels receiving fuel for propulsion within Washington waters. Details can be found in state regulations at Washington Administrative Code (WAC) 317-40. Additional information is also available at:
http://www.ecy.wa.gov/programs/spills/prevention/VesselTechAssist/Bunkering.html/

Tank vessels delivering oil in bulk to a non-recreational vessel or facility within Washington waters must meet state oil transfer requirements. They may also be subject to Washington State oil transfer inspections for these regulated oil transfers. Details can be found in WAC 173-184. Additional information is available at:
http://www.ecy.wa.gov/programs/spills/prevention/VesselTechAssist/vessel_otr.html/

• For a transfer of more than 100 gallons of bulk oil to a facility or non-recreational vessel, the delivering vessel must submit an Advance Notice of Transfer (ANT) report to Ecology. This ANT must be submitted 24 hours prior to the transfer for facilities or within the timeframe required by local USCG Captain of the Port.
• For convenience, the ANT report can be made either: online using the Ecology website at
https://secureaccess.wa.gov/ecy/ants, by
e-mail: OilTransferNotifications@ecy.wa.gov, or by
fax: 360–407–7288 or 800–664–9184.

Contingency Plan Requirements
Tank vessels and cargo and passenger ships 300 gross tons or larger transiting Washington waters must either have a Washington State Department of Ecology approved oil spill contingency plan or be a member of a non-profit corporation that provides oil spill response capabilities consistent with their Washington State approved contingency plan. The non-profit corporation for the Columbia River is the Maritime Fire & Safety Association (MFSA). Additional information is available at:
http://www.ecy.wa.gov/programs/spills/preparedness/cplan/cplans.html/

---

(14) the entrance to Columbia River, has red and white vertical stripes and is equipped with a racon.

Mount Saint Helens, nearly 8,500 feet high with a truncated-cone shape, is about 75 miles E of the entrance to the river. On a clear day it is visible when looking up the valley from seaward. **Mount Hood** and **Mount Adams** are lofty snow-covered peaks, which are also visible from parts of Columbia River on a clear day.

(15) In 1980, several volcanic eruptions occurred from Mount Saint Helens. Mount Saint Helens' eruptions were the first in the continental United States since the volcanic eruption of Mount Lassen in northern California in 1915; both volcanoes are part of the Cascade Range.

Chart 18521

(16) **Clatsop Spit**, on the S side of the entrance, is a low sand beach, extending about 2.5 miles NW from Point Adams. There is a tendency for the shoal N of the spit to build up to the NW because of spring freshets and NW storms; vessels are cautioned to keep informed about conditions at the spit.

(17) **Point Adams**, just inside Clatsop Spit, is a low sandy point covered with spruce and undergrowth to the edge of the sand beach and low dunes. The point usually shows well from seaward, particularly if it is hazy inside.

(18) **Cape Disappointment**, the rugged N point at the Columbia River entrance, is the first major headland along the 20 miles of sand beach N from Tillamook

Head. It comprises a group of rounding hills covering an area 2.5 miles long and 1 mile wide, divided by a narrow valley extending NNW. The seaward faces of these hills are precipitous cliffs with jagged, rocky points and small strips of sand beach. **Cape Disappointment Light** (46°16'33"N., 124°03'08"W.), 220 feet above the water, is shown from a 53-foot white conical tower with white horizontal band at top and bottom, and black horizontal band in the middle, on the S point of the cape. **Cape Disappointment Coast Guard Station** is at Fort Canby on the E side of the cape.

(19) From the S, Cape Disappointment shows as three low knobs, separated by low flat ridges. North Head Light shows on the W slope of the W knob. From the W, the cape is not prominent, but it stands out clearly when there is fog, haze, or smoke inside the cape. From NW, the cape appears as a flat island with a slight depression in the center and a timbered knob at each end. From this direction, a low, flat hill with gently sloping sides between the cape and high ridges E appears as an island from a distance.

(20) **McKenzie Head**, 0.8 mile NW of Cape Disappointment Light, is 190 feet high and nearly round. On its seaward face it is covered with grass and fern; bare of trees. On its E face it is heavily wooded with spruce.

(21) **North Head**, the extreme W point of the cape, is 270 feet high, with a very jagged, precipitous cliff, backed by a narrow grassy strip; the higher ground behind it is covered with trees. **North Head Light** (46°17'56"N., 124°04'41"W.), 194 feet above the water, is shown from a 65-foot white conical tower on the W point.

(22) The entrance to Columbia River is marked by two jetties. The S jetty extends 2.7 miles seaward from the NW end of Clatsop Spit; the westernmost mile of the jetty is submerged. The N jetty extends 800 yards seaward from the shoreline on the N side of the entrance. Lighted ranges, lights, buoys, and daybeacons mark the channels.

Channels

(23) Federal project depths in the Columbia River are 55 feet (48 feet in southern quarter) over the bar, thence 43 feet past the confluence of the Willamette and Columbia Rivers to the lower turning basin at Vancouver; and thence 35 feet through the upper turning basin at Vancouver. (See Notice to Mariners for controlling depths.) Additional information can be obtained from the Corps of Engineers, Portland, OR. (See Appendix A for address.)

(24) Above Vancouver the Federal project depth is 27 feet for about 75 (86) miles to The Dalles, thence 14 feet for about 87 (100) miles to McNary Dam. The **Federal project** also provides for a 15-foot barge channel which extends SE from the S side of the upper turning basin at Vancouver and connects with the 27-foot channel about 1 mile upriver. An alternate barge channel, just S of and running parallel to the barge channel, extends SE to the 27-foot channel. Controlling depths throughout the river channels and basins may be considerably less than project depths. The depths over the lower sills of the locks at The Dalles, John Day, and McNary Dams may be the controlling depth for this stretch of the river; the least sill depth (at McNary Dam) will usually exceed 12 feet at normal pool level. In the pool above McNary Dam to Pasco and Kennewick, depths range from 14 to 115 feet. Navigation on the Snake River is possible to Lewiston, ID. (See Notice to Mariners for controlling depths.) Additional information can be obtained from the U.S. Army Corps of Engineers, Portland, OR and Walla Walla, WA. (See Appendix A for addresses.)

Depths

(25) Minimum depths are given at mean lower low water from the entrance of the Columbia River to Harrington Point, thence at Columbia River Datum to Bonneville Dam on the Columbia River, and Willamette Falls Locks at Oregon City on the Willamette River. **Columbia River Datum** is the mean lower low water during lowest river stages. The staff gage at the Columbia River Pilots' Office, at the foot of 14th Street at Astoria, OR, is set with zero at mean lower low water. The staff gages on the bars from Harrington Point to Portland, OR, are set with zero at Columbia River Datum. Above the Willamette Falls Locks, at Oregon City, depths of the Willamette River are at **Willamette River Datum**. Above Bonneville Dam depths of the Columbia River are referred to the normal pool level of the various dams on the Columbia River.

Anchorages

(26) **General anchorages** are in the Columbia River. (See **110.1 and 110.228**, chapter 2, for limits and regulations.)

Bridges and cables

(27) Clearances of bridges and cables over Columbia River and its tributaries are at **mean lower low water** below Harrington Point and at **Columbia River Datum** between Harrington Point and Bonneville Dam. Above Bonneville Dam the clearances are referred to the normal pool level of the various dams on the Columbia River. On the Willamette River above the Willamette Falls Locks, at Oregon City, clearances are referred to the datum of **Newburg Pool**. Minimum clearance of cable crossing the main channel of the Columbia and Willamette Rivers to Portland and Vancouver is 216 feet.

Caution regarding aids to navigation

(28) During the seasonal high-water conditions, aids to navigation may be destroyed or rendered unreliable. Mariners are warned to exercise caution in navigating the river and to obtain the latest information regarding aids to navigation by local inquiry and through local Notice to Mariners, available upon request to the Commander, 13th Coast Guard District, Seattle, (see

Appendix A for address). Every effort is made to restore the aids to operating condition as soon as possible.

Weather, Columbia River, Oregon and Washington

(29) The maritime climate near the Columbia River's mouth slowly turns continental as you head upstream. Temperatures become warmer in summer and colder in winter. Daily temperatures vary more. Rain and fog are less frequent, but the chance of snow is greater. In the Columbia River Gorge, winds are deflected and channeled by topography.

(30) Average winter daytime temperatures vary from the upper forties (8.9° to 9.4°C) near the mouth to the upper thirties (3.3° to 3.9°C) near the Snake River junction. At night, this range is from the mid-thirties (0.6° to 2.8°C) to the mid-twenties (-5.0° to -2.8°C). Cold spells occur with an outbreak of frigid Canadian air. Extreme temperatures range from the low teens (-11.7° to -11.1°C) near the coast to below zero upriver (-18.3°C). Snow, of a significant amount, falls on 2 to 5 days each year, and is most likely upriver. Occasionally, an ice storm or "silver thaw" will occur; this happens most often between the Gorge and Vancouver. While winds are strongest in late fall and winter, they seldom reach gale force along the Columbia. Extremes of 75 knots have occurred; strongest winds are usually out of the south or southwest. Wind flow is generally from the east through southeast in winter, and wind speeds reach 17 knots or more about 5 to 10 percent of the time. However, locally at Troutdale, winds blow at 17 knots or more up to 30 percent of the time. Fog drops winter visibilities below 0.5 mile (0.9 km) on about 3 to 6 days per month.

(31) Spring temperatures rise slowly near the mouth of the Columbia, compared to the rise upriver. By April, daytime temperatures upriver average in the midsixties (17.2° to 19.4°C), while those near the mouth are in the midfifties (11.7° to 13.9°C). Average low temperatures are near 40°F (4.4°C) everywhere. Rain and fog become less frequent than they were in winter. Gales are rare and winds of 17 knots or more blow less than 5 percent of the time except locally around The Dalles, where winds of 17 knots or more occur 18 to 25 percent of the time from April through August. By April, winds are generally out of the W through NW. Flooding on the Columbia is most likely to occur from April through June, when snow melt at its headwater is most rapid. While flooding is kept under control, to a great extent, by multi-purpose dams, heavy rains during the melting season can trigger floods.

(32) Summer winds remain W through NW and generally light. Near the mouth of the river, these maritime winds have a cooling effect. They keep average daytime temperatures below 70°F (21.1°C) at Astoria and below 80°F (26.7°C) at Portland. This effect diminishes upstream, and E of the Cascades daytime temperatures average close to 90°F (32.2°C). Lows at night fall into the low fifties near the coast and upper fifties (14.4° to 15.0°C) inland. Rain falls on only a few days per month, usually in the form of showers or thunderstorms. Toward late summer, fog becomes a hazard near the mouth. At Astoria, visibilities fall below 0.5 mile (0.9 km) on about 4 days in August.

(33) Fog spreads upstream to Portland and Troutdale by September. During the fall, fog reduces visibilities to less than 0.5 mile (0.9 km) on 4 to 8 days per month, W of the Columbia River Gorge. The difference in fog E and W of the Gorge does not extend to temperatures. The temperature range is smallest in fall. In October, daytime high temperatures range from the low sixties (16.1° to 16.7°C) near the mouth to the midsixties (17.2° to 19.4°C) upriver, while average low temperatures vary from the mid-forties (6.1° to 8.3°C) near the coast to the low forties inland (5.0° to 5.6°C. By October, winds begin to blow more out of the E through SE and become stronger. While gales are infrequent, winds of 17 knots or more occur 4 to 10 percent of the time. Rain falls on about 5 to 15 days per month W of the Cascades and 2 to 6 days per month to the E.

Lower Columbia Region Harbor Safety Plan

(34) The Lower Columbia Region Harbor Safety Committee has developed a **Lower Columbia Region Harbor Safety Plan** that formally establishes Standards of Care for the Columbia River and its navigable tributaries from the seaward approaches to the Columbia River Entrance to Bonneville Dam. The standards contained in the Lower Columbia Region Harbor Safety Plan complement and supplement existing federal, state, and local laws. These standards were developed and adopted by local experts to improve maritime safety but do not replace the good judgment of a ship's master in the safe operation of a vessel. The Harbor Safety Plan provides important safety information and good marine practices for professional and recreational mariners transiting the Lower Columbia Region. The Harbor Safety Plan is available at http://www.lcrhsc.org.

Routes, Columbia River approach

(35) The lights at the entrance and at Willapa Bay 28 miles N, are distinguishing marks for determining a vessel's position and subsequent shaping of her course.

(36) In thick weather, great caution is essential on the approach from any direction. The currents are variable and uncertain. Velocities of 3 to 3.5 knots have been observed between Blunts Reef and Swiftsure Bank, and velocities considerably in excess of those amounts have been reported. Under such conditions, vessels should keep outside the 30-fathom curve until Columbia River Approach Lighted Whistle Buoy CR has been made.

(37) In clear weather, vessels should have no difficulty in entering the river as the aids to navigation are numerous. In thick weather, however, when aids cannot be seen, strangers should not attempt to enter without a pilot.

(38)   Dredges will usually be found at work in the channels; these dredges should be passed with caution and reduced speed. (See **162.225**, chapter 2, for navigation regulations.)

Weather, Cape Disappointment

(39)   An estimate of bar conditions, visibility, and weather may be obtained by radio from the Coast Guard station at Cape Disappointment.

Currents

(40)   The currents in the Columbia River and approaches are described in the Tidal Current Tables.

Caution

(41)   The Columbia River bar is reported to be very dangerous because of sudden and unpredictable changes in the currents often accompanied by breakers. It is reported that ebb currents on the N side of the bar attain velocities of 6 to 8 knots, and that strong NW winds sometimes cause currents that set N or against the wind in the area outside the jetties.

(42)   In the entrance the currents are variable, and at times reach a velocity of over 5 knots on the ebb; on the flood they seldom exceed a velocity of 4 knots. The current velocity is 3.5 knots, but this tidal current is always modified both as to velocity and time of slack water by the river discharge. On the flood there is a dangerous set toward Clatsop Spit, its direction being approximately ESE; on the ebb the current sets along the line of buoys. Heavy breakers have been reported as far inside the entrance as Buoy 20, N of Clatsop Spit.

(43)   (See the Tidal Current Tables for daily predictions.)

Freshets

(44)   The annual high water freshet stage on the Columbia occurs in the latter part of May, but on Willamette River the peak-flow period usually begins mid-December and continues through February, according to measurements taken by the U.S. Geological Survey over the past 70 years. Thus, the Willamette is low or nearly so at the time of the peak flow on the Columbia in late May. This causes the Willamette to apparently change direction under the influence of the stronger flow or "backup" from the Columbia, which change is apparent at least as far up the Willamette as the city of Portland.

(45)   On Columbia River, the freshet flow causes some shoaling in the dredged cuts, but redredging is done to maintain project depths.

(46)   Since logging is one of the main industries of the region, free floating logs and submerged deadheads or sinkers are a constant source of danger in the Columbia and Willamette Rivers. The danger is increased during spring freshets. **Deadheads** or **sinkers** are logs which have become adrift from rafts or booms. One end of the sinker settles to the bottom while the other end floats just awash, rising and falling with the tide.

Ice

(47)   Ice forms occasionally in both the Willamette and Columbia Rivers, but it is seldom heavy enough to affect navigation seriously.

Pilotage, Columbia River and Bar

(48)   Pilotage across the Columbia River bar and up or down the river is compulsory for U.S. vessels enrolled or sailing under Registry and all foreign vessels, except foreign recreational or fishing vessels not more than 100 feet in length or 250 gross tons international.

(49)   Columbia River Pilots and Columbia River Bar Pilots serve Columbia River and its tributaries, from the entrance over the bar to the head of navigation. Larger ports served are Astoria and Portland, OR; Vancouver, Kalama, and Longview, WA.

(50)   Pilotage is provided by the Columbia River Bar Pilots for the river entrance, from the open sea 5 miles from shore by a line described in ORS 776.025 to a line across the Columbia River along longitude 123°44'00" W., and by the Columbia River Pilots from the line across the Columbia River along longitude 123°55'00" W., to the head of navigation on the Columbia or Willamette Rivers and their tributaries. The State of Oregon has also established a Columbia River bar precautionary zone, 7 miles seaward of the Columbia River bar pilotage ground out to 12 miles from shore described in ORS 776.030 of which no person shall pilot any vessel intending to enter or depart the Columbia River bar pilotage ground, except pursuant to instructions from the Columbia River bar pilots. The Columbia River Pilots office address is: 13225 N. Lombard, Portland, OR 97203; telephone 503–289–9922; Fax 503–289–9955. The Columbia River Bar Pilots office address is: 100 16th Street, Astoria, OR 97103; telephone 503–325–2641; Fax 503–325–5630; email pilotast@pacifier.com.

(51)   All vessels requesting the service of the Columbia River Bar Pilots are requested to give notification of their time of arrival directly to the Columbia River Bar Pilots, Astoria (not through agent) at least 12 hours in advance by telephone or fax, or email to the pilot office in Astoria. The Columbia River Bar Pilots office is capable of communicating by VHF radio with vessels offshore at distances greater than 60 miles. If the arrival time changes due to weather or other causes, the Columbia River Bar Pilots are to be notified no later than 4 hours before the original ETA expires. Failure to communicate in a timely manner directly to the Columbia River Bar Pilots may result in delay. Marine exchange, vessel agents and Columbia River Pilots are advised of information received by the Columbia River Bar Pilots. When incoming from sea without the service of a Columbia River Bar Pilot, vessels or agents must give notice to the Columbia River Pilots between the hours of 0800 and 1600, and at least 12 hours prior to estimated time of arrival at Astoria. The call may be placed to the Columbia River Bar Pilots office in Astoria, OR.

(52) When ordering a Columbia River Bar Pilot, the following information is required:
(53) 1. Complete name and type of vessel.
(54) 2. The date and time of vessel ETA at the Pilot Station.
(55) 3. Maximum fresh water draft. If vessel is not even keel, provide fore and aft fresh water drafts.
(56) 4. Any pertinent special information or instructions about the vessels and its arrival.
(57) Embarking and disembarking Columbia River Bar Pilots is accomplished by helicopter or boat. All vessels are required to contact Columbia River Bar Pilots via VHF channel 9, 13, or 16 at least two hours before their ETA. The call sign for the Bar Pilot office is KOK-360. Vessels will be asked to confirm arrival time and are advised to call in again when 15 miles from the CR buoy via VHF channels 9 or 13. At that time vessels will be advised of pilot boarding instructions. The primary method of pilot boarding is by helicopter. The Bar Pilots also keep one of 2 pilot boats on standby at all times. Vessels should not approach the CR buoy until advised by a pilot. While awaiting a pilot boarding by helicopter or pilot boat, vessels should stay within a marshaling area approximately 5 miles west of the CR buoy. Pilots boarding by helicopter will generally board within 4 to 10 miles northwest to southwest of the CR buoy. Boarding by pilot boat generally takes place in the vicinity of the CR buoy.

Helicopter Transfer Procedures

General:
(58) Operations will be in accordance with ICAO regulations and with the International Chamber of Shipping's Guide to Helicopter/Ship Operations rules. The pilot helicopter SEAHAWK is 43 feet long with a rotor span of 36 feet and has a yellow body with the word PILOT prominently displayed on the side. Vessel configuration, sea state and wind force will determine if a hoist or landing will be conducted. To provide the highest degree of safety for boarding, the Master may be requested to alter course or speed of the vessel, if safe to do so. The objective is to provide **minimum roll of the vessel** at the time of transfer.

Communication:
(59) 1. After initial contact, the arriving vessel shall call in to Columbia River Bar Pilots on VHF channel 9 when 15 miles from the CR buoy.
(60) 2. Pilot helicopter "SEAHAWK" will then be dispatched to the vessel with the Marine Pilot.
(61) 3. The arriving vessel must remain on VHF channel 9 for helicopter operations until the marine pilot is safely transferred and the helicopter has departed the area.

Masters, prior to helicopter arrival must confirm the following:
(62) 1. Check that no wires or aerials are above the helicopter maneuvering zone.
(63) 2. Check that no loose objects are in or near the helicopter maneuvering zone.
(64) 3. **At night**, the vessel should be illuminated with all available deck lighting, but not in such a way as to blind the helicopter crew. Deck lights must remain ON until the helicopter has departed the area.
(65) 4. Assisting crewman should wear eye protective goggles.
(66) 5. Camera flashlight equipment must not be used as it will interfere with the helicopter crew's night vision.
(67) 6. If requested by helicopter-pilot, switch ship's radar to "stand-by".
(68) 7. DO NOT CHANGE COURSE OR SPEED unless instructed by helicopter.
(69) 8. If conditions are rough, a trail/tag line may be used:
(70) a. The vessel crew tending the trail line must ensure that the line is not tied to the vessel and does not become fouled with the vessel.
(71) b. The vessel crew tending the trail line shall use it to guide the Marine Pilot to the intended hoist area using only enough force to stabilize and keep the Pilot from swinging into hazards.
(72) c. The trail line, when used, must **NOT** be fastened to the vessel.

Land on Deck operations:
(73) 1. All vessel crew assisting with the transfer must remain clear of designated helicopter maneuvering zone.
(74) 2. No vessel crew should ever approach the helicopter unless directed.
(75) 3. Never pass in back or in front of the helicopter while it approaches or is on deck.

Pilot Boat Transfer Procedures
(76) If the arriving vessel is advised that the pilot boat be utilized for pilot transfer, one of two boats will be used, as follows:
(77) The pilot boat CHINOOK is 72 feet long and has a yellow hull and yellow super structure with the word PILOT prominently displayed on the side of the house. The pilot boat COLUMBIA is also 72 feet long and has an orange hull and orange superstructure with the word PILOT prominently displayed on the side of the house. When either the CHINOOK or COLUMBIA are used, speed of the vessel should be approximately 10 to 12 knots and the pilot ladder should be rigged 2 meters above the waterline. With either boat, the ladder should be rigged on the side indicated by the pilot boat, as close to midship as possible, with no manropes, and clear of all discharges and obstructions. The ladder must be rigged in accordance with SOLAS requirements, and

(78) must be well lighted at night. When regulations require a combination ladder, it must be rigged as close to 7 meters above the water as possible. Manropes are required on outbound vessels.

(78) When transferring pilots off Astoria, pilot boat CONNOR FOSS is used. It is 63 feet in length with a dark green hull and white superstructure. The word PILOT is prominently displayed on the superstructure. When using the CONNOR FOSS, the pilot ladder should be rigged midship, 2 meters above the waterline, in accordance with SOLAS requirements. Maximum speed of the vessel should be 9 knots.

(79) Inbound vessels with drafts of 36 feet or greater are requested to arrive at Astoria 2 hours prior to Astoria high tide in order to take advantage of tidal conditions. Outbound vessels with drafts of up to 36 feet but less than 38 feet can generally sail at any time, but occasionally sailing times must be delayed to avoid transiting the river during extremely low tides. Outbound vessels with drafts of 38 feet or greater must have sailing times set to take advantage of optimum tidal conditions.

(80) Masters of vessels arriving at the Columbia River when the bar is not passable are advised to stand offshore at least 10 miles west of the Columbia River Approach Buoy "CR" and await instructions from the Columbia River Bar Pilots. Using the open roadstead in the vicinity of the Columbia River entrance as an anchorage is dangerous in any weather, and IS NOT recommended by the Columbia River Bar Pilots.

(81) A fixed amber light is maintained by the Columbia River Bar Pilots atop the pilot office at Astoria. When this light is exhibited it will inform outward bound vessels that desire a Bar Pilot that the bar is not passable and that the vessel should remain in port.

(82) **Baker Bay** is a shoal open bight, E of Cape Disappointment, formed by the cape and the recession of the land N. **Sand Island**, low and flat, fronts the bay on the SW side.

(83) A dredged channel leads N from the Columbia River along the W side of Sand Island thence to the Port of Ilwaco mooring basin about 3 miles above the entrance. The entrance is between two detached jetties marked at the channel ends by lights. The channel is marked by lights and daybeacons. The entrance usually has swells and is subject to continual change; the channel should be navigated only at high water with local knowledge. (See Notice to Mariners and the latest edition of the chart for controlling depths.) The rest of Baker Bay is covered with shoals and abandoned fish traps.

(84) **Ilwaco** is the base for a large commercial and sport fishing fleet. Berths with electricity, gasoline, diesel fuel, ice, water, and other supplies are available. The largest marine railway can handle vessels up to 75 feet long for all types of repairs. Lifts up to 50 tons are also available. Wet winter boat storage is available at this port. Machine and carpentry shops are at this boatyard.

The **Port of Ilwaco** administers the docks and facilities of the port. For information about the channel or facilities, contact the port manager or harbormaster at 360–642–3143 or on VHF-FM channel 16.

(85) **Desdemona Sands**, marked by a light near the W end, is a shoal area extending SE for about 8 (9.2) miles from just inside the entrance to Columbia River. Desdemona Sands has the main river channel to the S and a secondary channel to the N. The southern section of Desdemona Sands is composed of shifting sand shoals that dry at low water. Only shallow draft vessels should attempt to navigate Desdemona Shoals; mariners are urged to use caution in the area.

(86) A boat basin is at **Hammond**; the entrance is marked by a light and a daybeacon on the E and W jetties, respectively. In 2008, a reported depth of 5 feet was available in the basin channel with shoaling to lesser depths at the S end. Berths with electricity, for about 140 craft, gasoline, diesel fuel, water, ice, marine supplies, and a launching ramp are available at the basin. Wet winter storage and minor repairs are available in the basin.

(87) A packing plant wharf is about 0.5 mile SE of the boat basin at Hammond.

(88) **Warrenton**, on the **Skipanon Waterway** at Mile 9.5 (11), is the base of a large sport fishing fleet. About 1 mile above the entrance to the waterway is a basin with a marina on the S side. Berths with electricity, gasoline, diesel fuel, water, ice, marine supplies, and a launching ramp are available. A marine railway that can handle boats up to 80 feet long is at the marina for hull repairs.

(89) In 2011, the midchannel controlling depth was 10 feet to the turning basin, thence 5 in the turning basin, thence 6 feet to the end of the project. There are general depths of about 5 feet above the railroad bridge; this part of the **Skipanon River** is used for logging operations. The channel to the turning basin is marked by a **198°30'** lighted range; lights mark the channel entrance.

(90) Above the waterfront area, the river is crossed by a fixed highway bridge with a clearance of 17 feet. A power cable upstream from the bridge has a clearance of 21 feet.

(91) **Scarboro Hill**, 820 feet high, is on the Washington side about 7 (8) miles E of Cape Disappointment. It is a long, gradually rising ridge, covered with grass, fern, and some trees. A number of conspicuous light-colored buildings of the historical Fort Columbia State Park may be seen near the base of the hill.

(92) A dredged marked channel leads from Columbia River near the E end of Baker Bay to a basin at **Chinook**, on the Washington side. In 2011, the midchannel controlling depth was 8 feet. Berths with electricity, gasoline, diesel fuel, water, ice, a launching ramp, and some marine supplies are available at the basin. A packing company wharf is at the basin. A 6-ton hoist is available for engine repair work. Wet winter storage is available in the basin.

(93) **Smith Point**, at Mile 11.3 (13.0) on the Oregon side, is the W termination of a high, wooded ridge; it

is the first prominent point on the S bank SE of Point Adams. The ridge culminates in **Coxcomb Hill**, 595 feet high, behind Astoria. The Astoria Column on the top of the hill is prominent.

(94) **Youngs Bay** is a shoal body of water just W of Smith Point. It receives the waters of **Youngs River** and **Lewis and Clark River**. The docks of a marine repair yard are 0.5 mile above the Old Route 101 highway bridge crossing the Lewis and Clark River. The yard can handle vessels up to 350 tons for hull and engine repairs. Traffic on the two rivers is confined chiefly to tugs handling log rafts just above the highway bridges. Small tugs operate to the town of **Olney** on Youngs River at high tide.

(95) A dredged channel leads from Columbia River through Youngs Bay to naturally deep water at the mouth of Youngs River. In 2007, the controlling depth in the dredged channel was 4 feet. A channel, marked by buoys and daybeacons, leads S from the dredged channel in Youngs Bay to the mouth of the Lewis and Clark River. In 1992, the mouth of the river had shoaled to bare.

(96) Youngs Bay is crossed by U.S. Route 26/101 vertical-lift highway bridge with clearances of 39 feet down and 74 feet up, about 0.3 mile above the mouth. The bridgetender monitors VHF-FM channel 16 and works on channel 13, call sign WHG-914. The highway bascule bridge, 2.1 miles above the bay entrance at the entrance to Youngs River, has a clearance of 24 feet. (See **117.1 through 117.59 and 117.899**, chapter 2, for drawbridge regulations.) In 2003, the N draw leaf of the bascule span was disabled. The least clearance of overhead cables across Youngs River to about 4 miles above the mouth is 103 feet.

(97) Over Lewis and Clark River, 0.8 miles above the mouth, is a highway bascule bridge with a clearance of 25 feet. The power cable at the bridge and the two about 1.8 miles above the mouth have a least clearance of 64 feet. The highway bridge, 4.8 miles above the mouth, has a fixed span 18 feet wide with clearance of 10 feet. (See **117.1 through 117.59 and 117.899**, chapter 2, for drawbridge regulations.) Clearances and depths on Youngs River and Lewis and Clark River are at **mean lower low water.**

(98) **Point Ellice**, on the Washington side 11 (12.7) miles inside the entrance, is the termination of a spur from the mountain ridge back of Scarboro Hill. The point is rounding and rocky, but not high. Two high hillocks lie behind the point. In this area there are many abandoned fish traps and pile structures that extend into the river.

(99) **Astoria**, at Mile 12 (14) on the Oregon side, extends from Youngs Bay to Tongue Point. It is the principal city on the Columbia River below Longview, WA. It has connections with the interior by both rail and highway.

Anchorages
(100) **General anchorages** are N and W of Tongue Point. (See **110.1 and 110.228**, chapter 2, for limits and regulations.)

(101) The fixed highway bridge between Astoria and Point Ellice has a clearance of 205 feet at the center over the main channel and 48 feet over the N channel. A racon is on the bridge support pier just N of the main ship channel.

Currents
(102) Above Astoria the current velocity is 1 to 3 knots except during the freshet period when the ebb is considerably increased although not enough to affect navigation seriously.

Weather, Astoria and vicinity
(103) Astoria's perennially verdant landscape is hemmed by rather low mountains on the N, E, and S. On the W it is open to the Pacific Ocean over 4 miles (7 km) or more of low green dunelands and the last 10 miles (19 km) of the Columbia River.

(104) The average temperature in Astoria is 51°F (10.6°C). The average maximum is 58°F (14.4°C) while the average minimum is 44°F (6.7°C). Ninety degree-plus readings have been recorded only during the June through September period and the all-time high is 100°F (37.8°C) recorded in July 1961. Temperatures less than 40°F (4.4°C) have been recorded in every month and only June through September have escaped below-freezing temperatures. The extreme minimum is 6°F (-14.4°C) recorded in December of 1972 and 1990.

(105) The average precipitation for Astoria is just over 67 inches (1702 mm). December is the wettest month averaging 10.50 inches (267 mm) while July is the driest month averaging only 1.10 inches (27.94 mm). An average of 240 days each year record precipitation. Snowfall is unusual. The average annual snowfall total is only 4.3 inches (109.2 mm) but every month except June through September has recorded at least a trace. An average of 191 days each year has fog and it is somewhat evenly distributed throughout the year. May is the most fog-free month while October records the most foggy days.

(106) Weather hazards occasionally occur. Storms may sink or wreck ships. Even in fair weather, wind and wave may combine to produce a type of breaker known as the "widow-maker" and swamp a boat. Heavy rains inundate lowlands, and high tides aggravated by gales may push seawater across highways and up beaches. Rains may cause earthslides, mostly in highway cuts. Storms may fell trees or break power and phone lines. Lightning strikes are rare. Showers of small hail may briefly whiten the ground during many of the months. Occasionally in winter there may be rather brief periods of freezing temperatures, with snow or ice.

(107) The climate of Astoria is generally characterized by summers with cool breezes and waters, moderate temperatures and periods of fog. Heat waves are uncommon and usually brief. Winters often bring dampness,

Facilities at Hammond, Warrenton and Astoria

Name	Location	Berthing Space (feet)	Depths* (feet)	Deck Height (feet)	Mechanical Handling Facilities and Storage	Purpose	Owned/ Operated by:
Point Adams Packing Co. Hammond Wharf	46°12'01"N., 123°56'26"W.	180	41	20	Two ¾-ton mast-and-boom derricks	Receipt of seafood	California Shellfish, Inc.
Nygaard Brothers Logging Company Warrenton Wharf	46°11'29"N., 123°55'24"W.	460	40	15	• Open storage (80 acres) • One 200-ton crawler crane • Log stackers/loaders	Receipt of logs	City of Warrenton/ Nygaard Brothers Logging Co. and Warrenton Fiber Co.
Warrenton Fiber Company Wharf	46°11'25"N., 123°55'25"W.	470	12	20	• Open storage area • One loading tower and spout • Electric belt-conveyor	Shipment of wood chips	City of Warrenton/ Warrenton Fiber Co.
Pacific Coast Seafoods Warrenton Wharf	46°10'10"N., 123°54'52"W.	390	16	15	• Two ½-ton mast-and-boom derricks • Tank storage (475 barrels)	Receipt of seafood	Pacific Coast Seafood, Inc.
Port of Astoria Pier No. 2	46°11'21"N., 123°51'44"W.	425 (face) 1,307 (lower) 1,250 (upper)	35-40 35 22	16	• Tank storage (101,500 barrels) • Open storage (10.8 acres) • Covered storage (46,000 square feet) • One 250-ton mobile crane • One 50-ton crawler crane	• Receipt and shipment of conventional general cargo • Shipment of logs and lumber • Receipt of petroleum products	Port of Astoria/ Cavenham Forest Industries; McCall Oil and Chemical Co.; Marine Spill Response Corp.
Port of Astoria Pier No. 1 (West Side)	46°11'23"N., 123°51'34"W.	1,100	40	16	• Open storage (5 acres) • Cranes are available from reference No. 1	• Receipt and shipment of conventional general cargo and logs • Shipment of wood chips	Port of Astoria/ Cavenham Forest Industries
Port of Astoria Pier No. 1 (Face)	46°11'26"N., 123°51'31"W.	875	40	16	• Open storage (5 acres) • Cranes are available from reference No. 1	• Receipt and shipment of conventional general cargo and wood chips • Shipment of logs	Port of Astoria
Astoria Warehousing Wharf	46°11'35"N., 123°50'40"W.	320	40	16	• Covered storage (121,000 square feet) • Eleven 2½-ton forklifts	Receipt of canned salmon	Astoria Warehousing, Inc.
Fishhawk Fisheries Astoria Wharf	46°11'33"N., 123°50'18"W.	45	40	16	Two ¼-ton electric hoists	Receipt of seafood	Fishhawk Fisheries, Inc.
Ocean Foods of Astoria Wharf	46°11'30"N., 123°49'58"W.	260	30	15	One 2-ton derrick and two 1-ton derricks	Receipt of seafood	Ocean Foods of Astoria, Inc.
Tongue Point Piers 3, 4, and 5	46°12'00"N., 123°45'28"W.	2,300 (Pier 3) 2,300 (Pier 4) 2,300 (Pier 5)	12-24	15	Open storage (4.5 acres)	• Shipment of steel products • Mooring vessels for construction and shipbreaking	State of Oregon/ Cresmont Inc., Pacific Marine and Steel Inc., The Ogilvie Co.
James River Corp. Wauna Mill Transit Shed Dock	46°09'38"N., 123°24'20"W.	1,090	30	11	• Open storage (25,000) • Covered storage (120,000 square feet)	Shipment of paper products and wood pulp	James River Corp.
James River Corp. Wauna Mill Peco Wharf	46°09'25"N., 123°24'01"W.	762	20-40	15	• Open storage area • One electric crane • Belt-conveyor system	Receipt of wood chips and sawdust	James River Corp.

* The depths given above are reported. For information on the latest depths contact the port authorities or the private operators.

increased precipitation, storms, winds and cloudiness with brief periods of freezing temperatures, snow and ice. (See Appendix B for Astoria **climatological table**.)

Pilotage, Astoria

(108) See Pilotage, Columbia River and Bar, indexed as such, earlier this chapter.

Towage

(109) Tugs to 3,600 hp are available at Astoria with 12 hours notice. Arrangements for tugs are usually made in advance by ships' agents. Barges of various size and application are available with prior arrangement.

Quarantine, customs, immigration, and agricultural quarantine

(110) (See chapter 3, Vessel Arrival Inspections, and Appendix A for addresses.)

(111) **Quarantine** is enforced in accordance with regulations of the U.S. Public Health Service. (See Public Health Service, chapter 1.)

(112) Astoria is a **customs port of entry**.

Coast Guard

(113) Two Coast Guard cutters are stationed at Astoria. A Coast Guard Air Station is at Warrenton-Astoria Regional Clatsop County Airport.

Harbor regulations

(114) Harbor regulations are prescribed by the Port of Astoria Board of Commissioners. The direct operation of the port is controlled by a port manager who is appointed by the Board.

Wharves

(115) The Port of Astoria is a municipal corporation embracing all of Clatsop County as a port district. The district extends from the mouth of the Columbia River to Westport (46°07'55"N., 123°22'07"W.), and includes the towns of Hammond, Warrenton and Astoria. The port owns a substantial part of the waterfront at Smith Point, and operates a well-equipped modern terminal with three piers. The port offices are at the head of Pier 2. For the latest information about depths alongside the piers, contact port authorities at 503–325–4521. Water and electrical shore power connections are available at most of the berths. General cargo at the port is usually handled to and from vessels by ships' tackle. Additional equipment, if available, is listed under 'mechanical handling facilities' in the table. For a complete description of the port facilities refer to Port Series No. 34, published and sold by the U.S. Army Corps of Engineers. (See Appendix A for address.)

Supplies

(116) Most marine supplies and services are available at Astoria. Facilities for bunkering ocean-going vessels are maintained at Pier 2, about 0.3 mile E of the bridge. Bunkering is available at anchorage, arrangements can be made at least 12 hours in advance through the ships agent or Brix Maritime on VHF-FM Channel 10. Fishing vessels are fueled at Carmichael-Columbia Oil Inc. wharf, about 0.5 mile E of the bridge.

Repairs

(117) The largest marine railway in the Astoria area can handle vessels to 400 tons. Complete hull, engine, and electronic repairs can be made. Complete salvage equipment is available in Astoria.

Small-craft facilities

(118) Two mooring basins for small craft and fishing vessels are maintained by the Port of Astoria. The West Basin, 0.3 (0.3) mile W of the S end of the Astoria Bridge, has 15 feet reported through the entrance and depths of about 5 feet at the floats. The entrance to the basin is marked by private lights. Berths with electricity, gasoline, diesel fuel, water, ice, and some marine supplies are available. All types of repairs can be made at several private firms on the basin. A 10–ton hoist at a packing company just W of the basin can handle small craft in emergencies. The East Basin, 2 (2.3) miles E of the Astoria Bridge, has berths and a launching ramp; however, no services are available. Reported depths of 15 feet through the entrance and 10 feet at the floats are available. West Basin has wet winter storage, and East Basin has wet and dry winter storage.

Communications

(119) U.S. Highway 101 extends N and S from Astoria, and U.S. Highway 30 extends inland to Portland, OR. Astoria is served by a Class I railroad. The Clatsop County Airport, S of Youngs Bay, is served by a charter airline that handles passengers and freight.

(120) **Tongue Point**, at Mile 16 (18) on the Oregon side, is a bold, rocky peninsula, 308 feet high, covered with trees and connected with the S bank by a low, narrow neck; it projects into the river for 0.8 mile. A buoy depot of the Coast Guard is on the W side of the peninsula near its inner end. On the E side are the concrete piers of the former naval base.

(121) **Cathlamet Bay** is E of Tongue Point and S of the main ship channel. The bay is subject to frequent change with shifting shoals and channels. There are many islands which are covered with tule in the summer, but in the winter they are almost indiscernible. Protected anchorage for small craft can be found in the area between Mott Island and Lois Island in 12 to 17 feet. A submerged obstruction with a least depth of 5 feet is close to the middle of this area in about 46°11'24"N., 123°44'18"W. The **John Day Channel** extends between Tongue Point and **John Day Point**. At the junction with the **John Day River**, just N of the point, the name changes to **South Channel**, which follows the shore closely to and around **Settler Point** to **Svensen**; these channels are marked by lights and daybeacons. A railroad swing bridge crosses John Day River near the mouth and has a reported clearance of 8 feet. (See **117.1 through 117.59 and 117.881**, chapter 2, for drawbridge regulations.) Several power cables cross the river and have a least clearance of 30 feet at mean lower low water. Many houseboats are moored along John Day River. The E part of Cathlamet Bay (chart 18523) is used mostly for logging operations and log storage.

(122) **Grays Bay** on the Washington side extends from **Grays Point** to **Harrington Point** N of the Main Ship Channel. Extensive mud flats are in the NE section of the bay and are subject to frequent change. Privately maintained buoys mark the preferred channel from Harrington Point to Rocky Point. A dangerous submerged rock is off Rocky Point in 46°17'15"N., 123°43'40"W. **Deep River** flows into the N part of the bay. The channel is marked and follows the shore from Grays Point around **Portuguese Point** and **Rocky Point**. This river is used only by small pleasure craft and sport fishermen and for logging operations. Depths of about 6 feet are available for about 2 miles above the mouth, above which it is shoal and probably good for no more than 2 feet.

(123) **Grays River**, entered just E of Deep River, is another small stream used only by pleasure craft. Depths

are not more than 2 feet, and much of the stream is blocked by snags and sunken logs.

Chart 18523

(124) Between **Harrington Point**, Mile 20.5 (23.6), and **Crims Island**, Mile 47.5 (54.6), Columbia River main channel follows the N bank to **Three Tree Point**, thence swings around the bend, holding to the NE shore as far as **Hunting Islands**, where it swings along the S shore until off the SE end of **Puget Island;** thence it follows the N bank from **Cape Horn** past **Abernathy Point** and N of Crims Island and **Gull Island**.

Currents

(125) In this section the current velocity is about 1 knot. Because of the river flow, which combines with the current, the upstream flow is weak or nonexistent and the downstream flow attains velocities of 2 to 3 knots.

Local magnetic disturbance

(126) Differences of as much as 3° from the normal variation have been observed along this section of the river.

(127) **Steamboat Slough**, NE of **Price Island** at Mile 29.3 (33.7) on the Washington side, and **Elochoman Slough**, on the E side of Hunting Islands at Mile 31.3 (36), are used by fishing boats, tugs, and for log storage. Gasoline and diesel fuel are available at **Skamokawa** just above the NW end of Steamboat Slough. A small marine railway, owned by a private packing firm, can be used if prior arrangements are made. In 2000, the controlling depth was 1 foot along the SE edge of the entrance channel (shoaling to bare across the remainder of the entrance) and in the channel bend off Skamokawa.

(128) At Mile 35 (39.9), a power cable with a least clearance of 230 feet crosses the main channel to Puget Island. The tower on the E side of the channel on Puget Island is prominent.

(129) **Cathlamet Channel** joins the main channel at Mile 32.3 (37.2) on the Washington side. It is used by fishing boats, tugs, log rafts, and barges, and for some log storage above the city of **Cathlamet**. A mooring basin is at Cathlamet with its entrance on Elochoman Slough; 190 berths (some with electricity), gasoline, diesel fuel, water, ice, wet and dry winter boat storage, a pumpout station, a launching ramp, and marine supplies are available. A fixed highway bridge crosses the channel from Cathlamet to Puget Island; the clearance is 75 feet for the N span. A power cable, 0.5 mile above the bridge, has a clearance of 310 feet.

(130) Three wharves, owned and operated by Fort James, are at **Wauna**, on the Oregon side at Mile 36.2 (41.7). The wharves are in line and together provide a total of 3,000 feet of continuous berthing space. Depths alongside are 20 to 50 feet and deck heights are 11 to 15 feet. A clamshell bucket unloads wood chips into a receiving hopper served by a conveyor system. Wood chips, sawdust, and fuel oil are received, and paper products are shipped.

(131) **Westport Slough**, at Mile 37.4 (43) on the Oregon side, leads to a ferry dock at the village of **Westport**. A lumbermill wharf, in ruins, is just E of the ferry slip. In 1989-2009, the midchannel depth was 4 feet to the ferry dock. The ferry operates between Westport and the ferry landing 0.5 mile N of **Pancake Point** on Puget Island, and carries passengers and automobiles. Above Westport the slough was used for log storage; decaying and submerged piling may present hazards to vessels operating close to shore. About 7 feet can be carried to **Kerry**, 2.4 miles above the mouth. Overhead power cables 0.8 and 1 mile above the mouth of the slough have clearances of 74 and 76 feet, respectively.

(132) **Wallace Slough**, at Mile 41 (47) S of Wallace Island, is used by fishing boats and house floats. A depth of 4 to 5 feet can be carried through the slough.

(133) **Beaver Slough** enters Wallace Slough near the SE end of Wallace Island. The slough is used by fishing boats and house floats. A fixed bridge with a 30–foot span and clearance of 8 feet crosses the W arm of the slough near its mouth. An overhead power cable with a clearance of 68 feet crosses the slough about 2 miles above the mouth.

(134) **Clatskanie River** is a tributary of Beaver Slough. A railroad swing bridge, about 0.6 mile above the mouth, has a clearance of 16 feet through the E draw. (See **117.1 through 117.59 and 117.865**, chapter 2, for drawbridge regulations.) There is a wharf at Clatskanie. Gasoline, diesel fuel, and water are available in cans from the town; mariners supplies, ice, and a launching ramp are also available. Several sawmills once operated along the river. Logs were stored throughout the area, and remnants of piling and related structures may present hazards close to shore. In 1998, depths of about 2 feet could be carried through Beaver Slough to the mouth of Clatskanie River; thence 2 feet could be carried in the river to the town of Clatskanie; local knowledge is advised. Numerous shoals and snags have been reported in Beaver Slough and Clatskanie River.

(135) **Port Westward**, a former Army ammunition terminal, is the site of a general cargo terminal. The main wharf, just W of the entrance to Bradbury Slough, is 1,200 feet long, has 40 feet reported alongside and a deck height of 20 feet, and can be used for shipment and receipt of general cargo.

(136) **Bradbury Slough**, at Mile 46.6 (53.6) SW of Crims Island, has depths of 9 feet as far as the upper end where it shoals to 3 feet. There once was extensive log storage along the Crims Island shore. Remnants of pilings and log storage related structures may present hazards close to shore.

| Facilities at Longview ||||||||
Name	Location	Berthing Space (feet)	Depths* (feet)	Deck Height (feet)	Mechanical Handling Facilities and Storage	Purpose	Owned/ Operated by:
Reynolds Metals Company Longview Reduction Plant Alumina Dock	46°08'08"N., 123°00'03"W.	700	38	15	• Tank storage (64,000 tons) • One traveling electric unloading tower and belt-conveyor	Receipt of alumina	Reynolds Metals Co.
Weyerhaeuser Company Longview Plant Salt Dock	46°07'44"N., 122°59'20"W.	1,160	32	26	• Tank storage (100,000 barrels) • Open storage (23,000 tons of salt)	Receipt of salt	Weyerhaeuser Co.
Weyerhaeuser Company Longview Plant Lumber Barge Dock	46°07'40"N., 122°59'10"W.	200	35	20	Open storage (2½ acres)	Shipment of lumber and newsprint	Weyerhaeuser Co.
Weyerhaeuser Company Longview Plant Wood Pulp Export Dock	46°07'32"N., 122°58'57"W.	1,185	35	26	• Covered storage (93,000 square feet) • Open storage (250,000 square feet)	Shipment of lumber, paper products, and wood pulp	Weyerhaeuser Co.
Weyerhaeuser Company Longview Plant Barge Slip	46°06'49"N., 122°57'48"W.	320	13	20	Open storage (12 acres)	Receipt of wood chops by barge	Weyerhaeuser Co.
Weyerhaeuser Company Longview Plant Log Export Dock	46°06'33"N., 122°57'40"W.	1,320	35	21	Open storage (20 acres)	Shipment of logs	Weyerhaeuser Co.
Port of Longview Berth No. 1	46°06'23"N., 122°57'23"W.	792	40	30	• Open storage (28 acres) • Covered storage (637,000 square feet) • One 50-ton gantry crane • One bulk loading spout and belt-conveyor	Receipt and shipment of conventional general cargo and dry bulk materials	Port of Longview
Port of Longview Berths Nos. 2 and 3	46°06'21"N., 122°57'17"W.	845	40	30	• Open storage (2.8 acres) • Covered storage (11,000 tons of dry bulk) • One 600-ton shear-leg derrick • One loading spout and belt-conveyor	• Receipt and shipment of conventional general cargo and heavy lift items • Shipment of dry bulk materials	Port of Longview
Port of Longview Petroleum Coke Wharf Berth No. 5	46°06'12"N., 122°56'52"W.	722	40	20	• Tank storage (44,000 tons) • One electric-hydraulic shiploader	Shipment of petroleum coke and logs	Port of Longview
Port of Longview Berth Nos. 6 and 7	46°06'08"N., 122°56'41"W.	1,500	40	29	• Open storage (38 acres) • One 33-ton electric traveling crane	• Receipt and shipment of general cargo and logs • Receipt of miscellaneous bulk materials	Port of Longview
International Paper Co. Longview Wood Chip Export Dock	46°06'01"N., 122°56'20"W.	1,440	35	29	• Open storage (144,000 tons of wood chips) • One 15-ton derrick • Telescopic pipeline and loading spout	Shipment of wood chips	International Paper Co.
Longview Fibre Co. Wood Chip Dock	46°05'58"N., 122°55'16"W.	2,360	12	20	• Open storage area • Two fixed unloaders with belt-conveyors	Receipt of wood chips and hogged fuel	Longview Fibre Co.

* The depths given above are reported. For information on the latest depths contact the port authorities or the private operators.

Chart 18524

(137)　Between Crims Island and Saint Helens, Mile 75 (86), the main channel starts its SE swing, passing S of **Fisher Island** and **Hump Island**, and N of **Walker Island** and **Lord Island**; thence, under the Longview fixed bridge, thence W of **Cottonwood Island**, E of **Sandy Island**, and W of **Martin Island** and **Burke Island**. Numerous jetties along this stretch are usually marked by lights or daybeacons.

Currents

(138)　In this section, the average velocity on the ebb is 2.0 knots. Flood currents can be experienced at low river levels after spring freshet and until the fall rainy season.

Local magnetic disturbance

(139)　Differences of as much as 8° from the normal variation have been observed along this section of the Columbia River.

(140)　**Coal Creek Slough**, at Mile 48.9 (56.3) on the Washington side, empties into the river at **Stella**. The slough is used for moorage of small craft. It was also used for log storage, and piling and related structures present hazards close to shore. Power cables over the deeper part of the slough have a least clearance of 65 feet.

(141)　**Fisher Island Slough**, N of Fisher Island, is used as the Longview Yacht Basin, by small fishing vessels, and as log-storage grounds. A depth of 7 feet may be carried

(142) Power cables over the main channel at Mile 54.2 (62.4), at Lord Island, have a least clearance of 216 feet.

(143) The channel between Walker Island and the Oregon shore is used for log-raft storage. The power cables S of Lord Island have a least clearance of 115 feet.

(144) The **Lewis and Clark Bridge**, at Mile 57.3 (66.0) between Longview and Rainier, has a fixed span with a clearance of 187 feet. The bridge piers are marked by buoys.

(145) **Longview**, at Mile 57.3 (66) on the Washington side is a major river port. Papermills, lumbermills, and an aluminum plant are in the city. Waterborne commerce includes lumber and wood products, flour, alumina and aluminum ingots, and general cargo.

Prominent features

(146) The Lewis and Clark Bridge with its high towers is easily the most prominent feature in approaching Longview from either up or down the river. Upon closer approach, the many stacks and tanks of the mills can be identified; most are charted.

Anchorages

(147) Deep-draft vessels may anchor NW of Lewis and Clark Bridge between the main ship channel and the smaller channel N of the main ship channel. (See **110.1** and **110.228**, chapter 2, for limits and regulations.) A secondary anchorage, SE of the bridge and just S of the main ship channel, may also be used. Depths in these anchorages range from 30 to 38 feet. Care should be exercised not to obstruct the dredged channels.

Currents

(148) Average current velocity, on the ebb, at Longview is 2.0 knots.

Pilotage, Longview

(149) See Pilotage, Columbia River and Bar, indexed as such, early this chapter.

Towage

(150) Tugs to 3,600 hp are available at Longview.

Quarantine, customs, immigration, and agricultural quarantine

(151) (See chapter 3, Vessel Arrival Inspections, and Appendix A for addresses.)

(152) **Quarantine** is enforced in accordance with regulations of the U.S. Public Health Service. (See Public Health Service, chapter 1.)

(153) Longview is a **customs port of entry**.

Harbor regulations

(154) The Port of Longview is a municipal corporation governed by a board of commissioners and administered by a port manager.

Wharves

(155) The deep-draft facilities at Longview include six berths owned and operated by the Port of Longview, and the privately owned and operated facilities of two large paper companies and an aluminum plant. Only the deep-draft facilities are listed in the table. For a complete description of the port facilities refer to Port Series No. 34, published and sold by the U.S. Army Corps of Engineers. (See Appendix A for address.) Depths alongside the port-owned wharves are reported to be maintained at 40 feet; for information on the latest depths contact the port authorities or private operators. All the facilities described have direct highway connections and plant trackage with direct railroad connections. The port-owned properties have a total covered storage area of 1 million square feet and open storage area of 75 acres. Water and electrical shore power connections are available at the port wharves and some of the private facilities. Special handling equipment, if available, is mentioned under 'mechanical handling facilities' in the table.

(156) The Weyerhaeuser facilities (Table Ref. Nos. 2-4) NW of the Lewis and Clark Bridge are reached by a side channel. The channel is marked by a 115° private lighted range.

Supplies

(157) Provisions and some marine supplies and services are available. Fuel oil and water are available at the wharves.

Repairs

(158) There are no facilities for major repairs to large oceangoing vessels in Longview; the nearest such facilities are in Portland. Some above-the-waterline repairs can be made, and there are several machine shops in the city. The Port of Longview has cranes to 65-ton capacity which can be used to lift private craft if prior arrangements are made.

Communications

(159) Longview is served by Interstate Highway 5 and U.S. Highway 30, and by three transcontinental railroads.

(160) **Cowlitz River** flows into Columbia River at Mile 59 (68), just E of Longview. The mouth of the river is heavily silted as a result of the volcanic eruptions of Mount Saint Helens in 1980. Large amounts of mud, logs, and other debris entered Columbia River from Cowlitz River. In 1980, dredging was done in the area but the **Federal project** is no longer maintained by the

Facilities at Kalama							
Name	Location	Berthing Space (feet)	Depths* (feet)	Deck Height (feet)	Mechanical Handling Facilities and Storage	Purpose	Owned/ Operated by:
Port of Kalama Bulk Materials Dock	46°02'36"N., 122°52'36"W.	800	40	-	Open storage (100 acres)	Receipt and shipment of bulk materials and steel products	Port of Kalama/ BHP Steel
Peavy Company Kalama Grain Elevator Wharves	46°01'36"N., 122°52'05"W.	800	40	25	• Silo storage (2 million bushels) • Electric belt-conveyors • One electric bucket-type marine leg	Receipt and shipment of grain	Peavy Co.
Kalama Chemical Kalama Wharf	46°01'17"N., 122°51'38"W.	680	40	23	Tank storage (5 million gallons)	Receipt of toluene	Kalama Chemical, Inc.
RSG/Forest Products Kalama Wharf	46°00'55"N., 122°51'13"W.	300	25	16	Open storage (40 acres)	Shipment of lumber	Port of Kalama/ RSG/Forest Products, Inc.
Harvest States Cooperatives, Kalama Grain Elevator Wharf	45°59'03"N., 122°50'05"W.	840	40	25	• Silo/Tank storage (6.4 million bushels) • Seven vessel loading spouts • Electric belt-conveyors • One electric bucket-type marine leg	Receipt and shipment of grain	Port of Kalama/ Harvest States Cooperative

* The depths given above are reported. For information on the latest depths contact the port authorities or the private operators.

U.S. Army Corps of Engineers. Mariners are advised to use extreme caution and seek local knowledge prior to entering Cowlitz River. The tide varies from 4 feet at the mouth to zero at **Ostrander**, 7.8 miles above the mouth. At Kelso a stage of 20 feet is reached during ordinary freshets and a stage of 25 feet at extreme floods.

(161) Five fixed bridges and several overhead power/television cables cross the river between the mouth and Ostrander; least clearances for the bridges are 10 feet and for the cables are 67 feet. A bascule bridge, 1.4 miles above the mouth of the river, has a clearance of 25 feet. (See **117.1 through 117.59 and 117.1037**, chapter 2, for drawbridge regulations.)

(162) At **Kelso** there are several private wharves including a sand and gravel wharf, a public landing, and several small craft floats, at one of which gasoline is available.

(163) **Rainier** is on the Oregon side opposite Longview. The town of Rainier operates a small-craft basin; berths, gasoline, water, ice, a launching ramp, a pumpout station, wet winter boat storage, and marine supplies are available. Diesel fuel may be obtained at the tugboat moorage just E of the city basin.

(164) **Carrolls Channel**, between Cottonwood Island and the Washington shore of Columbia River, is used for log storage and fishing boats.

(165) Two State fish hatcheries are on **Kalama River** at Mile 63.5 (73.1). **Kalama**, on the E bank about 3 (3.5) miles above Cottonwood Island, is the site of two lumber mills.

(166) A marina and mooring basin are at Kalama. Berths with electricity, gasoline, diesel fuel, water, a launching ramp, a pumpout station, and wet and dry winter boat storage are available at the marina.

(167) The channel circling the W side of **Sandy Island** is used by tugs hauling log rafts and barges.

(168) **Martin Slough**, between Martin Island and Burke Island and the Washington shore, formerly a booming and log storage area, as was **Burke Slough** between Burke Island and the Washington shore. Mariners are cautioned that submerged piling and hazardous structures may exist throughout the area close to shore.

(169) **Columbia City** is a municipality at Mile 73 (84) on the Oregon side. The main channel follows along the waterfront.

(170) At the S end of **Deer Island Slough**, about 1.5 miles N of Columbia City, is the pier of a chemical plant.

(171) **Saint Helens**, at Mile 75 (86) opposite the mouth of Lewis River, is the site of a pulp and paper mill.

(172) Berths with electricity, gasoline, water, ice, and some marine supplies are available at the marina at Saint Helens. Engine repairs can be made. There are a large number of houseboats and boathouses in the vicinity of the marina. A launching ramp and wet winter boat storage are available at the marina.

(173) A dredged channel with a reported controlling depth of 6 feet in 1986 leads to a marina in **Scappoose Bay**, SW of Saint Helens. This marina, owned by the Port of Saint Helens, has berths with electricity, gasoline, water, and ice available. Some supplies, a launching ramp, and wet winter storage are at the marina.

(174) **Lewis River** enters Columbia River at **Austin Point**, Mile 75.7 (87.0), on the Washington side. Depths are about 3 feet over the mouth, but just below the first bridge a bar reduces the depth to less than 1 foot. Some recreational traffic moves up to **Woodland**, 5.7 miles above the mouth, at high water. The railroad swing bridge 1.8 miles above the mouth remains in the closed position and has a clearance of 28 feet. (See **117.1053**, chapter 2, for drawbridge regulations.) The other bridges, all fixed, have clearances of 34 feet or more.

Willamette River and Portland, Oregon
Image courtesy U.S. Army Corps of Engineers (1988)

(175) From Saint Helens, Columbia River follows a S course to the mouth of the Willamette River, Mile 88 (101.2), and then turns SE to Vancouver, Mile 92 (106).

Chart 18525

(176) **Multnomah Channel** is a 19-mile waterway separated from the Columbia River near Saint Helens and from the Willamette River near Portland by **Sauvie Island**. A power cable about midway through the channel has a clearance of 100 feet. A fixed highway bridge, near the S end, has a clearance of 77 feet. There are several full service marinas and yacht clubs along the channel. Covered berths, electricity, gasoline, diesel fuel, water, ice, marine supplies, launching ramps, and pump-out stations are available. Hull, engine, and electronic repairs can be made and an 80-ton marine lift and 60-ton marine railway are available. There are several houseboats along the channel, and most of the channel S of **Coon Island**, is designated a **no wake zone**.

(177) **Warrior Rock**, the point on the E side of **Warrior Point** at the N end of Sauvie Island, is marked by a light. In thick fog vessels seldom attempt to pass the light; they anchor either above or below the point until the weather clears.

Local magnetic disturbance

(178) Differences of as much as 6° from the normal variation have been reported between Warrior Rock and Duck Club Light 6 off **Duck Club**, 1.5 miles S.

(179) **Lake River**, the outlet for **Vancouver Lake**, flows N for 9.5 miles to its junction with Columbia River at the N end of **Bachelor Island**, Mile 76 (88). The reported controlling depth was 6 feet in 1973 to the small-craft harbor at **Ridgefield**, 2.5 miles above the mouth. A marina is at Ridgefield; berths, water, ice, a launching ramp, and some marine supplies are available. The town of Ridgefield operates a public small-craft dock and launching ramp just S of the marina. Wet winter boat storage is at the marina.

(180) A marina, in the channel behind the elongated island W of Shillapoo Lake, has berths, with electricity, gasoline, water, ice, a launching ramp, and marine supplies. A 2½-ton hoist is available for launching small craft. Reported depths of 5 feet can be carried through the channel and to the river N of the marina, however, the channel S of the marina is closed by shoals.

Charts 18526, 18527

(181) At Mile 88 (101.2), Columbia River is joined by **Willamette River**, its largest tributary below the Cascade

Structures Across the Willamette River *(statute miles 0 through 15)*				
Name·Description·Type	Location	Clear Width of Draw or Span Opening (feet)	Clear Height above Low Water Datum (feet)	Information
Overhead power cables (three)	45°36'54"N., 122°47'20"W.		230	
St. Johns Bridge (highway, fixed)	45°35'07"N., 122°45'51"W.	1068	205	
Burlington Northern Railroad Lift Bridge	45°34'37"N., 122°44'50"W.	499	54 (down), 200 (up)	Bridgetender monitors VHF-FM channel 16 and works on channel 13; call sign KQ-9050.
Fremont Bridge (highway, fixed)	45°32'17"N., 122°41'00"W.	928	163	
Broadway Bridge (highway, bascule)	45°31'55"N., 122°40'27"W.	251	90	Bridgetender monitors VHF-FM channels 16 and 13 and answers on channel 13; call sign KLU-724. **(Note 1)**
Steel Bridge (highway/railroad, vertical lift)	45°31'39"N., 122°40'09"W.	205	26 (down), 161 (up) 71 (up, lower deck only)	Bridgetender monitors VHF-FM channel 16 and works on channel 13; call sign KQU-534. **(Note 1)**
Burnside Bridge (bascule)	45°31'23"N., 122°40'03"W.	205	64	Bridgetender monitors VHF-FM channels 16 and 13 and works on channel 13; call sign KTD-520. **(Note 1)**
Morrison Bridge (bascule)	45°31'05"N., 122°40'12"W.	209 (185 open)	69	**(Note 1)**
Hawthorne Bridge (vertical lift)	45°30'47"N., 122°40'15"W.	200	49 (down), 159 (up)	Bridgetender monitors VHF-FM channels 16 and 13 and works on channel 13; call sign KTD-521. **(Note 1)**
Marquam Bridge (fixed)	45°30'29"N., 122°40'08"W.	350	(see information)	Clearances: 120 feet for central 220 feet 102 feet for central 350 feet
Ross Island Bridge (fixed)	45°30'04"N., 122°39'51"W.	490	(see information)	Clearances: 120 feet for central 100 feet 90 feet for central 330 feet
Overhead power cables	45°29'50"N., 122°39'50"W.		(see information)	Clearances: 123 feet (main channel) 83 feet (east channel)
Overhead power cables	45°29'25"N., 122°39'27"W.		75	Cable crosses east channel

Note 1 – See **33 CFR 117.1 through 117.59 and 117.897**, chapter 2, for drawbridge regulations.

Mountains. The Willamette drains a large territory and is important as the site of the city of Portland, 9 (10.4) miles above its mouth.

(182) The Federal project depth in Willamette River is 40 feet to the Broadway Bridge in Portland, thence, maintained by the Port of Portland, 30 feet between Broadway Bridge and Ross Island. (See Notice to Mariners and latest editions of charts for controlling depths on the Willamette River to the Broadway Bridge.) Additional information can be obtained from the Corps of Engineers, Portland, OR. (See Appendix A for address.) Contact the Port of Portland for the controlling depths of the section of the channel maintained by the port.

(183) (See **162.225**, chapter 2, for navigation regulations on Willamette River.)

(184) From the entrance of the Willamette River to the Willamette Falls Locks at Oregon City, overhead clearances and depths are at Columbia River Datum. Above the Willamette Falls Locks depths of the Willamette River are at **Willamette River Datum** and clearances are at the datum of **Newburg Pool**.

(185) **Kelley Point Junction Light** (45°39'11"N., 122°45'46"W.), 39 feet above the water, is shown from a pile structure with a red and green triangular daymark on the end of the dike extending from **Kelley Point** on the E side of the entrance to the river.

(186) **Columbia Slough**, a narrow back channel roughly parallel to Columbia River, empties into the Willamette about 0.4 (0.5) mile above its mouth. Least depth in the slough is usually less than 2 feet. A dam has been constructed across the slough about 7.3 miles above the mouth.

(187) The fixed bridges over the slough have a least clearance of 15 feet. The least clearance of the overhead power and telephone cables is 42 feet.

(188) In the vicinity of **Post Office Bar Range**, 2 (2.4) miles above the mouth of Willamette River, deep-draft vessels favor the W side of the river, while smaller vessels and tows usually hug the E side because of lesser current. Overhead power cables with a least clearance of 230 feet cross the river 0.3 mile above the junction with Multnomah Channel. The twin towers supporting the cables are the most conspicuous features in this area.

(189) **Portland**, on Willamette River about 9 (10.4) miles from its mouth, is the principal city of the Columbia River system and one of the major ports on the Pacific coast. The port has several deep-draft piers and wharves on both sides of the Willamette River between its junction with the Columbia and Ross Island. In addition there are extensive facilities for small vessels and barges S of Hawthorne Bridge and at North Portland Harbor, S of Hayden Island. It has extensive commerce, both

foreign and domestic, and is the port of call for many lines of coastwise, intercoastal, and transpacific vessels.

(190) The **Port of Portland** created by the State in 1891, is controlled by a Port Commission and administered by an executive director. The port owns several marine terminals, Port of Portland Ship Repair Yard, and dredges the channel between Broadway and Ross Island Bridges; it also assists the Corps of Engineers with other dredging in the Willamette and Columbia Rivers. The port also operates an international airport and three general aviation airports. A 30-inch hydraulic pipeline dredge is owned by the port. In addition to dredging the port waterfront and river channel, the port conducts hydrographic surveys periodically along all port-owned piers and wharves.

Anchorages

(191) The anchorage areas that are generally used in the Columbia River are Kelley Point Anchorage, E of Kelley Point and on the SW side of Vancouver Lower Channel and Hayden Island Anchorage, between the N end of Hayden Island and Vancouver Range (See **110.1** and **110.228**, chapter 2, for limits and regulations.) Hayden Island anchorage has two anchor buoys for use by bulk carriers/large vessels. In 2004, an anchor was reported to have been lost in Hayden Island Anchorage in about 45°38'32"N., 122°44'01"W.

(192) A **special anchorage** in the Columbia River is between Tri-Club Island (Sand Island) and Lemon Island about 6.5 miles above the railroad bridge. (See **110.1** and **110.128**, chapter 2, for limits and regulations.)

Regulated navigation areas

(193) Regulated navigation areas have been established in the waters of the Willamette River in the Port of Portland's Terminal 4 and above Marquam Bridge, extending above Ross Island Bridge. (See **165.1 through 165.3, 165.1326 and 165.1337**, chapter 2, for limits and regulations.)

Weather, Portland and vicinity

(194) The coast range provides limited shielding from the maritime influence of the Pacific Ocean. The Cascade Range provides a steep high slope for the lifting moisture-laden westerly winds which produces heavy rainfall in the western Cascade piedmont region. They also form the barrier for the Columbia River basin region and dry continental air masses. Airflow is usually NW in Portland in spring and summer and SE in fall and winter, interrupted occasionally by outbreaks of dry continental air E through Cascade passes and across ridge tops. When such an outbreak occurs, extreme high or low temperatures are usually experienced in the Portland area.

(195) Portland has a very definite winter rainfall climate. About 88 percent of the annual total occurs in October through May, nine percent in June and September, while only 3 percent comes in July and August. The average annual precipitation is 37.33 inches (948.2 mm). December is the wettest month and July, the driest. Precipitation is mostly rain; on the average only 17 days each year have snow. Snowfall is seldom more than a couple of inches, and it generally lasts only a few days. The annual average is only seven inches (178 mm) with January having the most. Snowfall has fallen in every month from November through May. The greatest measured snowfall in 24-hours was just under 11 inches (279 mm) recorded in January 1971.

(196) Each season is clearly marked. Winter is mild, cloudy, and wet with southeast surface winds predominating. Summer is marked by mild temperature, with prevailing northwest winds and very little precipitation. Fall and spring are transitional in nature, with frequent periods of ground fog. An average of 18 days during October record foggy conditions while only three days during July can expect fog. At all times, incursions of marine-tempered air are a frequent moderating influence. Outbreaks of continental air from east of the Cascade Mountains flow through the Columbia Gorge at near sea level and spread into the Portland area associated with the movement of Pacific storms offshore on a northeast storm track. In winter this brings the coldest weather and the extremes of low temperature are registered in the cold airmass. Freezing rain and ice glaze often are transitional effects. In summer the hot, dry, continental air brings the highest temperatures. Extreme temperatures below zero are very infrequent. The absolute lowest ever reached is 3°F below zero (-19.4°C) recorded in February 1950. Extreme temperatures above 100°F (37.8°C) have occurred during each month from May through September; the absolute highest temperature is 107°F (41.6°C) recorded in July 1942, July 1965 and August 1981. Temperatures 90°F (32.2°C) or higher are reached every year, but seldom persist for more than 2 or 3 days before the warm spell is broken by a flow of cool, moist air from the ocean. The average annual temperature for Portland is 53.9°F (12.1°C). The average maximum is 63°F (17.2°C) while the average minimum is 45°F (7.2°C).

(197) Destructive storms are infrequent in the Portland area. Surface winds seldom exceed gale force. Thunderstorms are infrequent occurring, on average, only seven days each year. Tornadoes with the funnel cloud reaching the ground are rare and there are rare occurrences of heavy rain even though winter rains may persist for days at a time.

(198) Ice forms occasionally, but it is seldom heavy enough to affect navigation seriously, although navigation by small craft may be difficult.

(199) (See Appendix B for **Portland climatological table**.)

Pilotage, Portland

(200) See Pilotage, Columbia River and Bar, indexed as such, earlier this chapter.

Facilities at Portland

Name	Location	Berthing Space (feet)	Depths* (feet)	Deck Height (feet)	Mechanical Handling Facilities and Storage	Purpose	Owned/ Operated by:
Facilities on the Willamette River							
Port of Portland Terminal 5 (Berth 501) Grain Terminal Dock	45°38'33"N., 122°46'20"W.	900	40	25	• Three loading towers • One marine leg • Electric belt-conveyors • Silo/Tank storage (4.1 million bushels)	Receipt and shipment of grain	Port of Portland/ Columbia Grain, Inc.
STC Submarine Systems Dock	45°38'25"N., 122°46'31"W.	680	35-40	32	• Steel roller conveyors	Shipment of fiber optic cable	Port of Portland/ STC Submarine Systems, Inc.
Unocal Rivergate/Portland Agricultural Terminal Dock	45°37'33"N., 122°47'18"W.	1,164	35	35	• Covered storage • Tank storage: (7.8 million gal./ammonia) (19,200 gal./caustic soda) (15,600 gal./sulfuric acid)	• Receipt of granulated bulk urea • Receipt and shipment of anhydrous ammonia • Shipment of caustic soda and sulfuric acid	Unocal Petroleum Products & Chemicals Division, Unocal Corp.
Ash Grove Cement Co. Rivergate Plant Dock	45°37'22"N., 122°47'18"W.	230	25	30	• One 90-ton pedestal crane • Electric belt-conveyor • Open storage (80,000 tons of limestone)	Receipt of limestone	Ash Grove Cement Co.
James River Corporation Western Transportation Rivergate Barge Wharf	45°37'14"N., 122°47'18"W.	1,587	20-30	33	• Three 7-ton elevators and electric transfer system • Open storage (1.1 acres) • Covered storage (600,000 square feet)	• Receipt and shipment of general cargo • Receipt of starch and woodpulp • Shipment of paper products	James River Corp., Western Transportation
Time Oil Company Rivergate Terminal Wharf	45°36'54"N., 122°47'10"W.	750	40	26	• One 10-ton pedestal crane • Tank storage (750,000 barrels)	Receipt and shipment of petroleum products	Time Oil Co.
Premier Edible Oils Corporation Dock	45°36'47"N., 122°47'08"W.	670	42	32	• One ½-ton hose-handling derrick • Tank storage (7 million gallons)	• Receipt of crude palm, coconut and palm kernal oil • Occasional shipment of coconut oil	Schnitzer Steel Products Co./Premier Edible Oils Corp.
Georgia-Pacific Corp. Linnton Wood Chip Dock	45°36'45"N., 122°47'27"W.	1,200	36	28.5	• Tower on platform with shiploading chute • Electric belt-conveyor system • Open storage	Shipment of wood chips	Georgia-Pacific Corp.
International Terminals Berths 1, 2 and 3	45°36'39"N., 122°46'46"W.	1,900	35-40	25	• Three 60-ton gantry cranes • Two crawler cranes • Six 40-ton locomotive cranes • One 25-ton mobile crane • Open storage (20 acres) • Covered storage (65,000 square feet)	• Shipment of scrap metal • Receipt and shipment of steel products and miscellaneous dry bulk materials (pig iron, magnesite)	Schnitzer Steel Products Co./International Terminals
International Terminals Berth 4 Bulk Loader Dock	45°36'26"N., 122°46'50"W.	700	35	25	• Electric belt-conveyor system with loading spout • Open storage area	Shipment of miscellaneous bulk commodities (scrap metal, ore, sand, petroleum coke)	Schnitzer Steel Products Co./International Terminals
Port of Portland Terminal 4 (Berth 401) Grain Elevator	45°36'19"N., 122°46'47"W.	950	40	35	• Two traveling gantry towers with loading spouts • Electric belt-conveyor system • Covered storage (44,886 square feet)	Shipment of grain	Port of Portland/ Cargill, Inc.
GATX Tank Storage Terminals Corporation Portland Dock	45°36'15"N., 122°47'09"W.	740	32	28	• Four electric hose-handling derricks • Tank storage (484,000 barrels)	Receipt and shipment of liquid bulk commodities and petroleum products	GATX Tank Storage Terminals Corp.
Port of Portland Terminal 4, Pier 1 (Berths 403, 404 and 405)	45°36'16"N., 122°46'36"W.	1,500	35	35	• Steel tower with marine leg • Electric belt-conveyor system • Silo/Tank storage (7.6 million bushels) • Tank storage (5 million gal.) • Covered storage	• Receipt and shipment of molasses and liquid fertilizer • Receipt of grain	Port of Portland/ PM Ag Products, Inc. and Cargill, Inc.
Port of Portland Terminal 4 (Berths 406, 407 and 408)	45°36'16"N., 122°46'36"W.	1,500	35	30	• One 35½-ton container crane • Open storage (13 acres)	Receipt and shipment of conventional and containerized general cargo	Port of Portland/ Oregon Terminal Co.
Port of Portland Terminal 4 (Berths 411 and 410)	45°36'04"N., 122°46'31"W.	1,140	40	33	• One traveling tower crane • One fixed loading tower • Covered storage (33,600 tons of soda ash)	• Receipt and shipment of miscellaneous bulk commodities (coal tar pitch and alumina) • Shipment of soda ash, bentonite clay, talc, sodium sulphite and soybean meal	Port of Portland/ Hall-Buck Marine, Inc.

Facilities at Portland

Name	Location	Berthing Space (feet)	Depths* (feet)	Deck Height (feet)	Mechanical Handling Facilities and Storage	Purpose	Owned/ Operated by:
Port of Portland Terminal 4 (Berths 414 and 415)	45°35'50"N., 122°46'27"W.	1,344	40	25	• One 36-ton gantry crane • Open storage (38 acres) • Covered storage (205,000 square feet)	Receipt and shipment of conventional general cargo, steel and lumber	Port of Portland/ Oregon Terminal Co.
ARCO Products Co. Linnton Terminal Wharf	45°35'40"N., 122°46'41"W.	830	35	32	• One hose-handling derrick • Tank storage (497,000 barrels)	Receipt and shipment of petroleum products	ARCO Products Co.
Mobil Oil Corporation Linnton Terminal Wharf	45°35'34"N., 122°46'37"W.	672	36	32	Tank storage (675,000 barrels)	• Receipt and shipment of petroleum products • Loading barges for bunkering vessels at berth	Mobil Oil Corp.
Time Oil Company Linnton Terminal Wharf	45°35'22"N., 122°46'21"W.	450	35	30	• One pedestal crane • Tank storage (350,000 barrels)	Receipt and shipment of petroleum products	Time Oil Co.
Port of Portland Terminal 4 (Berth 416) Automobile Unloading Dock	45°35'38"N., 122°46'18"W.	1,014	40	14	Open storage (73 acres)	Receipt of automobiles	Port of Portland/ Toyota Vehicle Processors, Inc.
Pacific Northern Oil Corp. Portland Terminal Wharf	45°34'50"N., 122°45'33"W.	750	40	30	• One 9-ton pedestal crane • Tank storage (270,000 barrels)	Receipt and shipment of petroleum products	Northwest Natural Gas Co./Pacific Northern Oil Corp.
Elf Atochem North America Portland Plant Dock 2	45°34'20"N., 122°44'36"W.	410	30	30	• One hose-handling derrick • Tank storage: (8 million gal./caustic soda) (300,000 gal./sodium chlorate) (124,800 gal./chlorine)	Shipment and occasional receipt of liquid caustic soda, chlorine and sodium chlorate solutions	Elf Atochem North America, Inc.
Elf Atochem North America Portland Plant Dock 3	45°34'12"N., 122°44'24"W.	900	30	30	• Hopper and belt-conveyor • Open storage (90,000 tons of salt)	Receipt of salt	Elf Atochem North America, Inc.
GATX Terminals Corp. Willbridge Plant Pier	45°34'03"N., 122°44'19"W.	1,008	33	32	• Four hose-handling derricks • Tank storage (834,000 barrels)	Receipt and shipment of petroleum products	GATX Terminals Corp.
Chevron U.S.A. Willbridge Terminal Pier	45°34'01"N., 122°44'17"W.	1,312	40	32	• Two hose-handling derricks • Two hose-handling cranes • Tank storage: (1.6 million barrels) (1.3 million barrels/crude oil)	• Receipt and shipment of petroleum products • Receipt of crude oil	Cheveron U.S.A., Inc.
Unocal Petroleum Products and Chemicals Division Portland Terminal Pier	45°33'58"N., 122°44'14"W.	1,152	34-37	32	• Four hose-handling derricks • Tank storage (760,000 barrels)	Receipt and shipment of petroleum products	Unocal Petroleum Products and Chemicals Division, Unocal Corp.
McCall Oil and Chemical Company Portland Terminal Wharf	45°33'54"N., 122°44'02"W.	922	37	30	• Two pedestal cranes • Tank storage (930,000 barrels)	• Receipt and shipment of petroleum products • Loading barges for bunkering vessels at berth	McCall Oil and Chemical Co.
Lone Star Northwest Front Avenue Plant Pier	45°33'48"N., 122°43'56"W.	225	20	28	• Hopper and belt-conveyor • Open storage (60,000 tons of aggregate)	Receipt of sand and gravel	Lone Star Northwest, Inc.
Texaco Refining and Marketing Portland Terminal Wharf	45°33'25"N., 122°43'16"W.	670	31	29	• Two ½-ton hose-handling derricks • Tank storage (580,000 barrels)	Receipt and shipment of petroleum products	Texaco Refining and Marketing, Inc.
Waterway Terminals Co. Portland Front Avenue Wharf	45°33'01"N., 122°42'13"W.	1,540	35	33	• Seven freight elevators • Covered storage (1 million square feet)	Receipt and shipment of conventional general cargo	Waterway Terminals Co.
Port of Portland Terminal 2 (Berth 203)	45°32'43"N., 122°42'02"W.	400	25	20	• One 36-ton gantry crane • Covered storage (39,000 square feet)	Receipt and shipment of wood pulp and paper products	Port of Portland/James River Corp., Western Transportation Division
Port of Portland Terminal 2 (Berths 204, 205 and 206)	45°32'56"N., 122°42'01"W.	2,295	40	26	• Two 50-ton container cranes • Open storage (27½ acres) • Covered storage (261,000 square feet)	• Receipt and shipment of conventional, containerized, roll-on/roll-off general and refrigerated cargo • Shipment of lumber and wood pulp	Port of Portland/ Stevedoring Services of America, Inc.
Columbia Aluminum Portland Wharf	45°32'59"N., 122°41'38"W.	1,350	40	27	• Traveling ship unloader • Hopper and belt-conveyor • Silo storage (46,000 tons)	Receipt of alumina	Columbia Aluminum Corp.
Ash Grove Cement Co. Portland Plant Wharf	45°32'42"N., 122°41'17"W.	250	20	31	• Two pneumatic pipelines • Silo storage (19,500 tons of cement)	Receipt of bulk cement	Ash Grove Cement Co.
Port of Portland Terminal 1 (Berths 101, 102 and 103)	45°32'29"N., 122°41'27"W.	1,650	22-35	29	• Open storage (5.3 acres) • Covered storage (125,900 square feet)	Receipt and shipment of wood pulp and paper products	Port of Portland/James River Corp., Western Transportation Division

Towage

(201) Dock assist tugs to 3,600 hp are available in Portland. No lighterage is necessary, but occasionally lumber is transferred by barge from lumbermills to vessels.

Quarantine, customs, immigration, and agricultural quarantine

(202) (See chapter 3, Vessel Arrival Inspections, and Appendix A for addresses.)

(203) **Quarantine** is enforced in accordance with regulations of the U.S. Public Health Service. (See Public Health Service, chapter 1.)

(204) Portland is a **customs port of entry**.

Coast Guard

(205) A marine safety unit and station are located in the Swan Island Industrial Park at Portland. (See Appendix A for address.)

Harbor regulations

(206) The regulations are enforced by the City of Portland **harbormaster** and Multnomah County Sheriff River Patrol; copies of the regulations (Title 19) may be obtained on the Internet at http://www.portlandonline.com or, for a nominal fee, by contacting the City Auditors Office at 1221 SW 4th Avenue, Room 140, Portland, OR 97204. The harbormaster may be contacted by phone 503–823–3767 or by writing Portland Fire Bureau, Attn: Harbormaster, 55 SW Ash Street, Portland, OR 97204.

Wharves

(207) The Port of Portland operates several modern marine terminals. In addition to the port-owned piers and wharves there are many privately owned deepwater facilities and many barge wharves in the harbor. Only the deep-draft facilities are listed in the facilities table. For a complete description of the port facilities refer to Port Series No. 34, published and sold by the U.S. Army Corps of Engineers. (See Appendix A for address.) The alongside depths are reported depths. (For information on the latest depths contact the port authorities or the private operators.) All the Port of Portland operated facilities have rail trackage, water, and electrical shore power connections, as well as many of the privately operated facilities. All wharves have highway connections. Floating and shore-based mobile cranes of up to 65-ton capacity are available, but most general cargo is handled by ship's tackle. Special handling equipment, if available, is mentioned under 'Mechanical Handling Facilities' in the table.

Supplies

(208) Marine supplies of all kinds are available in Portland. Bunker fuel, diesel oil, and lubricants are available. Most large vessels are bunkered at their berths by barge. Water is available at most of the berths.

Repairs

(209) Portland is a major ship repair center on the Pacific coast. The Port of Portland, Swan Island Ship Repair Yard, on **Swan Island** on the E side of Willamette River, is the major repair facility at the Port of Portland. There are three floating drydocks here with a maximum lift capacity of 87,000 tons. Complete repair facilities and services are available at the yard, including construction, conversion and above and below waterline repairs. The yard has over 9,500 feet of ship repair berths to a maximum alongside draft of 40 feet (depending on river stage). There is a 157,050-barrel ballast treatment plant for the offloading of oily slops.

(210) Several firms are available for undertaking outfitting and repair work. Marine railways with hauling capacities to 1,000 tons and cranes to 70 tons are available for full repairs and to any type of vessel.

Communications

(211) Portland is served by several major railroads and airlines. Portland International Airport is about 2 miles N of the city. Many barge lines provide service up the Columbia River to Richland, WA., 214 (246) miles from Portland; barge service is also available on the Willamette River to Salem, OR, 73.6 (84.7) miles above the mouth, and on the Snake River to Lewiston, ID, 324 (373) miles from Portland.

Small-craft facilities

(212) Most of the small-craft facilities, including practically all of the moorage, is in North Portland Harbor and along the S bank of the Columbia River between Interstate 5 highway bridge and the W end of Government Island. Complete facilities are available. Berths with electricity, gasoline, diesel fuel, water, ice, marine supplies, launching ramps, pumpout stations, and wet and dry winter boat storage can be obtained at many marinas. Hull, engine, and electronic repairs can be made. Drydocks to 70 tons, 55 feet long, and 16 feet wide are available in North Portland Harbor.

Chart 18528

(213) Navigation of Willamette River above Portland is hazardous due to the rocks, shoaling bars, and strong currents. Local knowledge and midchannel courses are recommended. Present chart coverage extends only to Newberg, 43.4 (50) miles above the mouth. Many of the daybeacons in the Willamette River are seasonal. The navigational aids above Newberg are not maintained. Navigation should be with local knowledge only. The Portland Coast Guard should be contacted for the latest information concerning navigation of Willamette River above Salem.

(214) Below the falls at Oregon City, ordinary fluctuation of stage of water is 15 feet and extreme fluctuation due to flood conditions is 30 to 50 feet. Above Oregon City,

					Facilities at Portland		
Name	Location	Berthing Space (feet)	Depths* (feet)	Deck Height (feet)	Mechanical Handling Facilities and Storage	Purpose	Owned/ Operated by:
Lone Star Northwest River Street Terminal Dock	45°32'12"N., 122°40'39"W.	600	34	30	• Two pneumatic pipelines • One 10-ton mobile crane • Silo storage (58,000 tons of bulk cement)	Receipt of bulk cement	Lone Star Northwest, Inc.
Cargill Portland Wharf	45°32'07"N., 122°40'32"W.	950	40	30	• Grain gallery with five loading spouts served by belt-conveyor • Silo storage (1.5 million bushels)	Shipment of grain	Cargill, Inc.
Cargill Portland Barge Dock	45°32'03"N., 122°40'27"W.	240	17	30	• One marine leg served by a belt-conveyor • Silo storage (See Ref. No. 36)	Receipt of grain	Cargill, Inc.
Louis Dreyfus Corporation Portland Barge Dock	45°31'46"N., 122°40'12"W.	200	40	20	• One marine leg served by a belt-conveyor • Silo storage (See Ref. No. 39)	Receipt of grain	Louis Dreyfus Corp.
Louis Dreyfus Corporation Portland Wharf	45°31'43"N., 122°40'09"W.	750	40	31	• Grain gallery with six loading spouts served by two belt-conveyors • Silo storage (1.8 million bushels)	Shipment of grain	Louis Dreyfus Corp.
James River Corporation Lake Oswego Wood Chip Transfer Dock	45°25'11"N., 122°39'22"W.	840	16	30	• One barge loading spout and electric belt-conveyor • Open storage (15 acres)	Shipment of wood chips	Port of Portland/ James River Corp.
Facilities at North Portland							
Port of Portland Terminal 6 (Berth 601) Automobile Unloading Dock	45°38'51"N., 122°45'29"W.	1,000	12	12	Open storage (75 acres)	Receipt of motor vehicles	Port of Portland/ Hyundai Motor America
Port of Portland Terminal 6 (Berths 603, 604 and 605)	45°38'26"N., 122°44'54"W.	2,850	40	26	• Seven traveling container cranes to 85 tons • Open storage (68.2 acres)	Receipt and shipment of containerized general cargo and heavy-lift items	Port of Portland
Port of Portland Terminal 6 (Berth 607) Automobile Unloading Dock	45°38'02"N., 122°44'22"W.	1,014	35	12	Open storage (50 acres)	Receipt and shipment of automobiles	Port of Portland/ American Honda Motor Co.

* The depths given above are reported. For information on the latest depths contact the port authorities or the private operators.

ordinary fluctuation is 12 to 20 feet and extreme is 20 to 27 feet.

(215) Depths and clearances of bridges and cables are at **Columbia River Datum** below the Willamette Falls Locks. Above the Willamette Falls Locks depths of the Willamette River are at **Willamette River Datum** and clearances are at the datum of **Newberg Pool**.

(216) The minimum clearances of the overhead power cables crossing the river from Portland to Newberg are: 77 feet to Willamette Falls Canal; 72 feet over Willamette Falls Canal; and 75 feet to Newberg.

(217) Between Portland and Willamette Falls most of the terminals are privately owned mill wharves and oil-receiving facilities. Above the falls are small privately owned wharves or natural landings.

(218) A public launching ramp is on the W side of the river at a park about 13.5 (15.7) miles above the entrance.

(219) Sellwood fixed highway bridge, 14.5 (16.7) miles above the mouth, is under construction (2011). Consult Local Notice to Mariners or USCG for latest conditions. A public mooring is on the E side of the river at a park just N of the bridge. A repair facility is directly across the river from the park; gasoline, water, and a launching ramp are available. A lift to 7 tons are available for all types of repairs to light- draft boats.

(220) A launching ramp is at **Milwaukie**, 16.2 (18.6) miles above the mouth. Minor engine and hull repairs can be made on light-draft boats. Dry winter boat storage is available.

(221) A fixed railroad bridge, 17.4 (20) miles above the mouth, has a clearance of 74 feet.

(222) A wharf on the W bank of the river, 0.3 (0.3) mile above the railroad bridge, has 840 feet of berthing space with a depth of 16 feet alongside; the deck is 30 feet high and marked by private lights. Electric belt conveyors serve barge-loading spouts and a 15-acre open storage area in the rear. The wharf ships wood chips by barge and is owned by the Port of Portland and operated by James River Corporation.

(223) The channel passes E of **Hog (Rocky) Island**, 1.6 (1.8) miles above the railroad bridge. **Copeleys Rock**, 150 yards E of the S end of the island, is covered 10 feet and should be avoided.

(224) **Oregon City**, on the E bank 22.6 (26) miles above the mouth, is connected with **West Linn** by two fixed highway bridges; one, about 0.2 (0.2) mile below the Willamette Falls canal locks, has a vertical clearance of 74 feet. The second, 0.6 (0.7) miles below the N end of the locks, has a clearance of 76 feet.

(225) A marina, on the E bank just above the lower highway bridge, has about 350 berths, electricity, gasoline,

(226) A large papermill is on each bank of the river at Willamette Falls Canal.

(227) **Willamette Falls Canal,** on the W bank 22.8 (26.2) miles above the mouth, has four locks with a total lift of 50 feet; usable lock dimensions are 175 feet long, 37 feet wide, and 5 feet deep over the miter sills at low water. A bascule highway bridge across the canal has a vertical clearance of 27 feet closed. The least clearance of the power cables and pipeline that cross the canal is 67 feet. (See **207.680**, chapter 2, for regulations concerning administration and navigation of the canal and locks.) Upbound vessels may expect a delay at the approach to the locks and through the locks during weekdays because of the downbound traffic from the papermills. The lock is equipped with a radiotelephone. The lockmaster can be contacted on VHF-FM channel 14; call sign WUJ–363.

(228) A warehouse and other buildings of a papermill are on the W bank alongside the canal locks. An 850-foot timber wharf is on the E side of the canal.

(229) A marina, on the E bank opposite **Willamette** and 24.3 (27.9) miles above the mouth, has about 50 berths, with electricity, gasoline, diesel fuel, and water available. This marina has an elevator lift that can handle craft to 5 tons or 30 feet for hull and engine repairs.

(230) From the entrance to **Tualatin River**, 24.8 (28.5) miles above the mouth, for over 4 miles, Willamette River is shallow and winding; buoys and unlighted ranges mark the channel.

(231) **Walnut Eddy** is on the E bank 29.4 (33.8) miles above the mouth.

Cable ferry

(232) The Canby ferry crosses the river about 1.1 (1.3) miles above Walnut Eddy. The ferry carries passengers and vehicles, and operates from 0645 to 2115 daily except during periods of high water. When the ferry is underway, the cable is suspended below the water surface at varying depths. When the ferry is docked, the cable is dropped to the bottom. **DO NOT ATTEMPT TO PASS A MOVING CABLE FERRY.**

(233) Near **Wilsonville**, 33.7 (38.8) miles above the mouth, there are twin fixed highway bridges and a fixed railroad bridge, with clearances of 74 feet and 76 feet, respectively. A marina, on the S bank under the railroad bridge, has about 115 berths, with electricity, gasoline, water, ice, and marine supplies. The marina has a launching ramp and can make hull and engine repairs. Marine towing service for small craft is also available at this marina.

(234) A quarry is on the N side of the river about 300 yards W of the railroad bridge. Mariners are advised to exercise caution because barges and tugs may be operating in the area.

(235) Near **Butteville**, 37.3 (43.0) miles above the mouth, there is a small-craft marina with about 35 berths, electricity, gasoline, water, ice, a launching ramp, and some marine supplies available. Minor engine repairs can be made. The fixed highway bridge, 42.1 (48.4) miles above the mouth, has a clearance of 68 feet at the main span. At **Newberg**, 43.4 (50.0) miles above the mouth, there is a fixed highway bridge with a clearance of 88 feet. An overhead power cable with a clearance of 55 feet, crosses the river 44.9 (51.7) miles above the mouth.

(236) From Newberg to Corvallis, Willamette River is more tortuous and turning, and can be difficult for the small craft; the stretch contains numerous gravel bars, pools and snags. Mariners should exercise due caution for shallow water transits. The tributary **Yamhill River** empties into Willamette River about 3 miles above Newberg. Depths in Yamhill River of about 3 feet are reported to Dayton, 4 miles above its mouth.

Cable ferry

(237) The Wheatland ferry crosses Willamette River about 63 (72.5) miles above the mouth. The ferry carries passengers and vehicles, and operates between 0530 and 2145 daily except when the river level exceeds 16 feet. Warning signs and warning lights mark the crossing. The ferry is guided by two cables. The upper cable, 80 feet above the river level, controls the ferry during normal conditions. The low water cable, near the bottom at all times, controls the ferry when the river level drops below 12 feet. The low water cable is dropped to the bottom when the ferry is not operating. **DO NOT ATTEMPT TO PASS A MOVING CABLE FERRY.**

(238) **Salem**, capital of the State of Oregon, is 74.4 (85.6) miles above the mouth. Several moorings and floats for log-rafts and small craft are here; berths, gasoline, diesel fuel, water, ice, launching ramps, and marine supplies are available at several small marinas. Hull engine, and electronic repairs can be made in Salem.

(239) A power cable at the N city limits of Salem has a clearance of 86 feet. Minimum clearance of the bridges is 64 feet at the fixed highway bridges, and 42 feet down and 87 feet up at the railroad lift bridge. The railroad lift bridge is maintained in the closed position. (See **117.897**, chapter 2, for bridge regulations.)

(240) At **Independence**, 83 (95.5) miles above the mouth, there is a small-craft launching ramp, but no facilities.

(241) The town of **Buena Vista** is 92 (106) miles above the mouth of the river.

Cable ferry

(242) A cable ferry crosses the river near Buena Vista. The self-propelled ferry carries passengers and vehicles, and operates from 0700 to 1700 (Wednesday-Friday), 0900 to 1900 (Saturday and Sunday), and is closed Monday and Tuesday. The ferry is seasonal and operates between April and October. Both when the ferry is underway and

Facilities in the Port of Vancouver						
Name	Location	Berthing Space (feet)	Depths* (feet)	Deck Height (feet)	Mechanical Handling Facilities and Storage	Purpose	Owned/ Operated by:
Vanalco, Vancouver Alumina Dock	45°38'44"N., 122°43'57"W.	840	40	30	Tank storage (70,000 tons)	Receipt of alumina	Alumina Co. of America/Vanalco, Inc.
Terminal 4 (Berth 10)	45°38'26"N., 122°42'56"W.	1145	40	-	Open storage (45 acres)	Receipt of automobiles	Port of Vancouver
Terminal 3 (Berths 8 and 9)	45°38'18"N., 122°42'30"W.	1350	40	28-30	• Open storage (34 acres) • Covered storage (289,900 sq ft)	Receipt and shipment of conventional and containerized general cargo	Port of Vancouver
Dry Bulk Materials Wharf (Berth 7)	45°38'14"N., 122°42'21"W.	960	40	34	• Covered storage (55,000 tons) • Electric belt conveyor	Shipment of dry bulk materials	Port of Vancouver
Oil Terminal Dock (Berth 5)	45°38'05"N., 122°42'06"W.	450	40	30	Tank storage: (gallons) • Chemical (3.3 million) • Petroleum (560,000) • Ethanol (336,000) • Fertilizer (2.3 million)	• Receipt and shipment of petroleum products • Receipt of liquid fertilizer	Port of Vancouver/ GATX Terminals, Tesoro Refining, and CENEX
Terminal 2 (Berths 1-4)	45°37'58"N., 122°41'52"W.	2035	40	30	• Open storage (35 acres) • Gantry cranes (two)	Receipt and shipment of conventional and containerized general cargo, dry bulk commodities and automobiles	Port of Vancouver
Vancouver Grain Elevator Wharf	45°37'49"N., 122°41'34"W.	1678	40	34.5	• Silo storage (5 million bushels) • Gantry spout • Belt conveyors	Receipt and shipment of grain	Port of Vancouver/ United Grain Corporation
Boise Cascade Vancouver Dock	45°37'25"N., 122°40'49"W.	275	25	-	Tank storage (480 tons)	Receipt of wood pulp	Boise Cascade Corperation

* The depths given above are reported. For information on the latest depths contact the port authorities or the private operators.

when docked the guide cables are suspended approximately 80 feet above the water. When underway, the ferry shows the required navigation lights. **DO NOT ATTEMPT TO PASS A MOVING CABLE FERRY.**

(243)　　The river is crossed at **Albany**, 104 (119.8) miles above the mouth, by three bridges: a railroad swing bridge with a clearance of 40 feet, a fixed highway bridge with a clearance of 55 feet, and a fixed highway bridge with a clearance of 60 feet in the center of the N span and 58 feet in the center of the S span. The railroad swing bridge is maintained in the closed position. (See **117.1 through 117.59 and 117.897**, chapter 2, for drawbridge regulations.)

(244)　　**Corvallis**, 114.6 (131.9) miles above the mouth, is the limit of the **Federal project** of the river. Navigation above Corvallis is dangerous and should not be attempted.

(245)　　There are small-craft finger piers, ramps, and marginal facilities at Corvallis; gasoline and water are available. A highway bridge has a swing span with a clearance of 35 feet. (See **117.1 through 117.59 and 117.897**, chapter 2, for drawbridge regulations.)

Chart 18526

(246)　　The main channel of the Columbia River favors the Washington shore, N of **Hayden Island** and **Tomahawk Island**, from **Mathews Point** to Ryan Point. Overhead clearances are at **Columbia River Datum**. Overhead power cables with a least clearance of 220 feet cross at Mile 90.6 (104.2). The Burlington Northern Railroad swing bridge at Mile 91.8 (105.7) has a clearance of 39 feet. The bridgetender monitors VHF-FM channels 13 and 16 and works on channel 13 (call sign KQ-9049.) The interstate 5 highway bridge at Mile 92.5 (106.5) has twin spans that cross three separate channels. The clearances are: lift spans across the Tomahawk Bar Channel, 39 feet down and 178 feet up; fixed spans across the barge channel, 46 feet (58 feet at the center); fixed spans across the alternate barge channel, 72 feet. The bridgetender monitors VHF-FM channels 13 and 16 and works on channel 13; call sign, KBM Interstate. (See **117.1 through 117.59 and 117.869**, chapter 2, for drawbridge regulations.)

(247)　　**North Portland Harbor** is that portion of the river channel between the Oregon shore and Hayden Island. The lower or W entrance is at Mile 89.0 (102.5); the upper or E entrance is at Mile 94.5 (108.8).

(248)　　A **Federal project** provides for a 40-foot turning basin at the W entrance to North Portland Harbor, a 40-foot channel for about 1.3 miles above the W entrance, and thence a 20-foot channel to the project limit about 2 miles farther upstream. The **Federal project** for the E entrance to North Portland Harbor provides for a channel 10 feet deep from the main channel in Columbia River SW to just S of the E end of Tomahawk Island. (See Notice to Mariners and latest edition of chart for depths.) A **241°** lighted range marks the E entrance channel for about 0.6 mile from the junction with Columbia River. Two bridges cross North Portland Harbor. The railroad bridge, 2.6 miles E of the W entrance, has a swing span with a clearance of 39 feet. (See **117.1 through 117.59 and 117.887**, chapter 2, for drawbridge regulations.) A fixed highway bridge (Interstate 5) about 0.8 mile E has a clearance of 35 feet.

(249) **Vancouver** is on the Washington side of the Columbia River at Mile 92 (106). The port is a water outlet for a large lumber-producing section in SW Washington, as well as a distributing point for a fair share of the grain produced in the interior of Washington and Oregon. Bulk bentonite clay, paper, petroleum products, fertilizer, and general merchandise are also shipped. Steel, wood products, chemicals, and automobiles are the major imported items at Vancouver.

(250) The Port of Vancouver is controlled by a board of three commissioners and a general manager.

Anchorages

(251) Anchorages for Vancouver are the same as those used for Portland. (Refer to that section under the discussion of the Port of Portland.)

Pilotage, Vancouver

(252) See Pilotage, Columbia River and Bar, indexed as such, earlier this chapter.

Towage

(253) Tugs to 3,600 hp are available at Vancouver.

Quarantine, customs, immigration, and agricultural quarantine

(254) (See chapter 3, Vessel Arrival Inspections, and Appendix A for addresses.)

(255) **Quarantine** is enforced in accordance with regulations of the U.S. Public Health Service. (See Public Health Service, chapter 1.)

Wharves

(256) The Port of Vancouver owns and operates three deep-draft terminals; a grain wharf and oil dock, owned by the port, are managed by private companies. There are several private facilities which, with two exceptions, handle barge traffic only. Only the deep-draft facilities are listed. For a complete description of the port facilities refer to Port Series No. 34, published and sold by the U.S. Army Corps of Engineers. (See Appendix A for address.) The alongside depths given in the table are reported. (For information on the latest depths contact the port authorities or the private operators.) Most of the piers and wharves have shore connections (electrical/water). All the facilities described have direct highway connections and plant trackage with direct railroad connections.

Supplies

(257) Complete marine supplies and services are available from Portland. Fuel oil must be delivered by barge. Small-craft supplies are available in North Portland Harbor and at other places on the Columbia River E of Vancouver.

Repairs

(258) Complete repairs for large and small vessels are available at Portland. Vancouver has no facilities for repair work on large oceangoing vessels. Small-craft repairs on craft up to 70 tons or 55 feet can be made in North Portland Harbor; there are no repair facilities on the N side of the river at Vancouver.

Communications

(259) Vancouver is served by Interstate Highway 5 and by several State routes. Three major railroads have connections to the city. Portland International Airport is on the S side of the river about 3.5 miles ESE of Vancouver.

Chart 18531

(260) From Vancouver to Bonneville, Mile 126 (145), Columbia River passes through the impressive **Columbia River Gorge**, flanked on each side by railroads and highways. Commerce on the river in this section consists mostly of pleasure craft and barges.

(261) There are more than 35 dike dolphins along this portion, some are marked with lights at their ends. All the dikes are completely covered at higher stages, but bare about 6 feet at datum level.

(262) **Ryan Point**, 1.4 miles ESE of the Interstate 5 highway bridge, is the site of a former shipyard and is now an industrial park. A public launching ramp is at the park.

(263) There are many full service marinas, yacht clubs, and moored houseboats along the Oregon shore from Interstate 5 highway bridge to the W end of Government Island.

(264) At Mile 97.9 (112.7), the river is crossed by a fixed highway bridge with a clearance of 136 feet (144 feet for the center 300 feet) over the channel.

Anchorage

(265) A special anchorage is between **Tri-Club Island (Sand Island)** and **Lemon Island,** the W end of **Government Island**. (See **110.1 and 110.128**, chapter 2, for limits and regulations.)

(266) **Camas**, at Mile 104.3 (120.0) on the Washington side, has a large papermill which maintains its own wharf on **Camas Slough**, N of **Lady Island**. About 8 feet can be taken from the Columbia River through the W entrance to the papermill wharf near the E end of the slough; the channel is marked by a light, a daybeacon, and a lighted range. The E entrance to the slough is foul and bares at low water. Most of the traffic in the slough is for the papermill, which barges its products to Portland for reshipment. At high flood stages a current of as much as 5 knots prevails in the slough.

(267)	Two fixed highway bridges cross Camas Slough from the mainland to Lady Island; the W one has a clearance of 69 feet, and the E one has a clearance of 37 feet.

(268)	A marina at mile 105.7 (121.6) just E of Camas, has about 250 berths, open and covered and with electricity, gasoline, water, a launching ramp, and complete marine supplies. A marine sales and repair facility adjacent to the marina has a 12-ton hoist that can handle craft to 42 feet for hull and engine repairs. A sawmill is just E of the marina.

(269)	There are five power cables crossing at **Ione Reef**, S of Lady Island. The least clearance is 133 feet.

(270)	The entrance to **Sandy River**. on the Oregon side opposite Camas, bares at low water. At higher flood stages, passage up Sandy River as far as **Troutdale** is possible.

Local magnetic disturbance

(271)	Differences of as much as 8° from the normal variation have been observed between **Tunnel Point** and **Point Vancouver**, E of **Reed Island.**

Dangers

(272)	In this section of the river, the principal hazards to navigation are the strong currents, rocks and rocky banks, winds, and an accumulation of ice.

Currents

(273)	In general, currents run fair with the main channels with considerable intensity, increasing in regions upstream toward Bonneville. Exceptions are the turn in the channel at Washougal Light 50, where a NW set prevails; SW of **Cape Horn**, where a W set is experienced; and the region between Fashion Reef and Multnomah Falls, where a S set is experienced.

Weather, Corbett

(274)	Between **Corbett**, Mile 110.3 (127), and The Dalles, Mile 165 (189.8), the river flows between the bold mountains of the **Cascade Range**. In this stretch, winds of considerable force prevail during much of the time; generally they blow upstream in summer and downstream in winter. Daily peak velocities vary from 6 to 42 knots, but Corps of Engineers officials at Bonneville Dam measured gusts as high as 76 knots during 1960-62.

(275)	Near **Warrendale**, Mile 123 (141.5), the river becomes very constricted within less than a mile and continues so almost to the approach to the locks of Bonneville Dam, at the lower end of **Bradford Island**.

(276)	**Beacon Rock**, 840 feet high and 300 yards inshore, is on the Washington side opposite Warrendale. It is a prominent dark gray rock outcropping of volcanic origin. A State park of the same name surrounds the rock. The park maintains a mooring float just inside the entrance to the channel W of **Pierce Island**; moorage is restricted to pleasure boats and to periods not to exceed 5 nights. Water, electricity, and pump-out facility are available at the park.

(277)	**Bonneville**, on the Oregon side at Mile 126 (145), is the headquarters of the U.S. Army Corps of Engineers in charge of the Bonneville Lock and Dam.

(278)	**Bonneville Lock** and **Dam**, 126.3 (145.3) miles above the mouth of the Columbia River, is in four parts. Powerhouse No. 2 is between the Washington shore and Cascade Island; the spillway is between Cascade Island and Bradford Island; Powerhouse No. 1 and the old lock are between Bradford Island and Robins Island; and the new lock is between Robins Island and the Oregon shore. The new navigation lock has a vertical lift of about 59 feet, a width of 86 feet and a length of 675 feet. Overhead power cables over the lock have a clearance of 210 feet. The old lock has been placed in mothball status. Restricted areas are above and below the spillway and powerhouse. (See **207.718**, chapter 2, for information concerning use, administration, and navigation of Bonneville Lock and Dam.)

(279)	The strong current toward the powerhouse makes it difficult to approach Bonneville Lock from upstream, particularly if the lock is approached at an angle and if a turn is to be executed in time to avoid an accident. Therefore, all craft approaching the lock from the E and pushing one or more barges should steer as close to the Oregon mainland shore as safety will permit, should be in line with the lock upon reaching the E end of the guide wall, and should continue at a steady but reduced speed if the lock is prepared for entrance and the signal for entrance has been given.

(280)	From Bonneville to The Dalles, the channel is through the pool created by Bonneville Dam, which extends 40 (46) miles to The Dalles Dam. Depths and overhead clearances are at **normal pool level**.

(281)	Although there is deep water in much of the pool, the controlling depth to The Dalles Dam navigation lock is about 20 feet. The channels are marked by aids to navigation.

(282)	An overhead power cable with a clearance of 190 feet crosses the river 1 (1.1) mile above the dam.

(283)	Tugs use the dolphins on the S side of the river 1.2 (1.5) miles above the lock for mooring and shifting barges and log rafts. Small craft can find refuge in the mouth of **Eagle Creek,** 0.6 (0.7) miles above the lock, if the creek is not in flood.

Currents

(284)	From the lock at Bonneville through Cascade Rapids, constant piloting is necessary because of the strong currents. From Cascade Rapids E, a set of 1° to 3° may be experienced depending on the angle that the course makes with the general direction of the river, the strength of the current, and the direction and strength of the wind.

Local magnetic disturbance

(285) Differences of as much as 6° from normal variation have been observed along this section of Columbia River.

Chart 18532

(286) **Bridge of the Gods**, 2.6 (2.8) miles above the Bonneville Dam, has a fixed span with a clearance of 135 feet over a middle width of 284 feet.

(287) **Cascade Locks** 3 (3.3) miles above the Bonneville Dam, have been drowned out. At normal stages of pool level the sides of the old chamber of the lock bare about 3 feet. A strong current flows through the lock. A marina, just E of the lock, has berths, gasoline, and a launching ramp.

(288) Along this section are several inlets or rivers, generally used for log storage, where small craft may find refuge. Most are behind fixed bridges. These places, and their distances above the Bonneville Dam are:

(289) **Rock Creek** at **Stevenson**, WA, 4.2 (4.8) miles; the bridge clearance is 19 feet. **Government Cove,** on the Oregon side, 5.6 (6.4) miles. **Wind River** at **Home Valley**, WA, 8.1 (9.3) miles; the minimum bridge clearance is 26 feet. **Drano Lake**, near **Cook**, WA, 14.5 (16.7) miles; the bridge clearance is 15 feet. **Ruthton**, OR, 17.8 (20.4) miles. **White Salmon River** at **Underwood**, WA, 20.9 (24) miles; the bridge clearance is 26 feet.

(290) Rock Creek, Wind River, and Drano Lake have log rafts and booms used by nearby sawmills.

(291) **Hood River**, OR, 21.7 (25) miles above the Bonneville Dam, is a town at the junction of Columbia and Hood Rivers. There are two boat basins at Hood River; the W basin is privately owned and is used by a repair yard for building and repairing steel barges and tugs. The E basin, operated by the Port of Hood River Commission, has about 55 berths; gasoline and water are available. A daybeacon is at the outer E end of the W basin and private lights mark the entrance to the E basin. In 1976, depths of 7 to 12 feet were reported to be available in the E basin. A large shoal area extends NW from the E basin around the mouth of the Hood River to about 0.2 mile N of the W basin.

(292) The highway bridge over Columbia River just above the small-craft basin has a lift span with a clearance of 67 feet down and 148 feet up. The bridgetender monitors VHF-FM channel 16 and works on channel 13; call sign KTD-562. (See **117.1 through 117.59 and 117.869**, chapter 2, for drawbridge regulations.)

(293) There are power cables with clearance of 155 feet over the river at **Stanley Rock**, 22.9 (26.4) miles above Bonneville Dam, and at **Crates Point,** 13 (15) miles above Stanley Rock.

(294) At **Bingen**, on the Washington side 23 (26.4) miles above the Bonneville Dam, there are two barge basins with adjacent sawmills. A light and a daybeacon mark the entrance to the E basin, which has a launching ramp and about 20 berths for small craft. In 1976, the controlling depth was 7 feet at midchannel in the entrance to the E basin with 5 to 10 feet in the basin, except for shoaling along the edges. The entrance to the W basin is unmarked; reported depths of 10 feet are in this basin.

(295) **The Dalles** on the Oregon side of Columbia River, 39 (44.8) miles above the Bonneville Dam. River traffic, between the town and Vancouver, consists mainly of petroleum products and general freight bound upstream, and wheat, wool, and rafted logs bound downstream.

(296) A small-boat mooring basin with a breakwater and sheer boom protection is just E of the city wharf. Depths inside are 4 to 8 feet. The basin has a small-craft launching ramp. Gasoline, ice, and marine supplies are available. Engine repairs can be made.

(297) The city wharf is over 1,000 feet long and has two warehouses; depths alongside are about 20 feet. There are also private facilities for handling petroleum products, bulk grain, and fresh fruit. An aluminum mill is at West The Dalles.

Charts 18533, 18535

(298) **The Dalles Lock and Dam**, 40 (46) miles above Bonneville Dam, has a single lift lock with a vertical lift of about 87.5 feet. **Restricted areas** are above and below the dam. (See **207.718**, chapter 2, for information concerning use, administration, and navigation of The Dalles Lock and Dam.) **Lake Celilo**, the pool created by The Dalles Dam, provides slack water navigation with a controlling depth of about 14 feet for 22 (25.3) miles upstream to the John Day Dam. Depths and overhead clearances are at **normal pool level.**

(299) Traffic above The Dalles Dam consists mostly of grain and petroleum products.

Ice

(300) Ice occasionally interferes with navigation for 2 weeks or more, usually in January or February.

(301) A fixed highway bridge across the downstream approach to the lock at The Dalles Dam has a clearance of 100 feet.

(302) A railroad bridge, 7 (8.1) miles above The Dalles Dam, has a lift span with clearance of 20 feet down and 79 feet up. The bridgetender monitors VHF-FM channel 16 and works on channel 13; call sign KQ-9048. (See **117.1 through 117.59 and 117.869**, chapter 2, for drawbridge regulations.)

(303) The Celilo Park basin 7.7 (8.9) miles above The Dalles Dam, offers shelter to small boats, but there are no facilities except a launching ramp. The entrance to the basin is marked by a light.

(304) At **Miller Island**, 10.5 (12) miles above The Dalles Dam, the N and S channels are marked by ranges. The main channel is along the N side of the island; however it is reported that the S channel is more frequently used.

In 1994, submerged obstructions with depths of 1 to 3 feet were reported in the S channel in about 45°38'17"N., 120°54'56"W. and 45°38'14"N., 120°54'54.5"W.

(305) On the Oregon side just S of Miller Island is **Deschutes River**, crossed by a fixed bridge with clearance of 20 feet. Small craft occasionally seek shelter here during unfavorable weather.

(306) A grain elevator with a barge loading chute extending to the river is at **Biggs**, OR.

(307) The **Biggs Bridge**, 13.6 (17) miles above The Dalles Dam, has a clearance of 88 feet at the center of the fixed highway span. The bridge joins **Maryhill**, WA, and **Biggs Junction**, OR.

Charts 18535, 18536, 18537, 18539

(308) **John Day Dam**, 188 (216.3) miles above the mouth of the Columbia and 21 miles above The Dalles Dam, has a single lift lock with a vertical lift of about 105 feet. **Restricted areas** are above and below the dam. (See **207.718**, chapter 2, for information concerning use, administration, and navigation of John Day Dam.) Depths and overhead clearances are at **normal pool level**.

(309) The rock awash near the E approach to John Day Locks in 45°43'25"N., 120°41'20"W. is marked by a light and sign; mariners are urged to exercise caution when passing N of Lake Umatilla Lighted Buoy 2, so as to avoid being carried to the NW and striking the rock awash.

(310) **Lake Umatilla**, the pool created by John Day Dam, extends 65 (75) miles to McNary Dam. Depths are generally great, but there are many shoals. The winding channel through the lake has a controlling depth of about 19 feet and is marked by aids to navigation. The chart is the best guide. An overhead power cable with a clearance of 95 feet is about 41 (47.2) miles above John Day Dam.

(311) **John Day River** is 2.3 miles above John Day Dam on the S side of the Columbia. Just S of the highway bridges over the entrance to the river is the **John Day River Recreation Area**. There are floats here for about 40 craft and a launching ramp. The fixed highway bridges have a clearance of 19 feet.

(312) A grain elevator with barge-loading facilities is at **Arlington**, OR, 21.5 (24.7) miles above John Day Dam. A loading tower for the elevator is marked by a light. Small-craft moorage and a launching ramp are available at Arlington.

(313) At **Boardman**, 45.6 (52.5) miles above the John Day Dam, there is a small-craft basin protected by a stone breakwater and a jetty. Berths and a launching ramp are available here.

(314) There are two woodchip docks, a general cargo dock, and a grain elevator dock at a port about 1.2 miles NE of the small-craft basin at Boardman.

(315) A grain elevator dock and barge loading pier is on the Oregon side of the river, about 3 miles NW of Irrigon, OR.

(316) **Umatilla** is on the Oregon side 62 (71.3) miles above the John Day Dam.

(317) There is a small-craft basin about 500 yards W of the highway bridge. The E side of the entrance is marked by a light. About 125 covered and uncovered berths, electricity, gasoline, diesel fuel, water, and ice are available. A concrete launching ramp is at the basin.

(318) The fixed parallel highway bridges across the river, 63 (72.5) miles above the John Day Dam near Umatilla, each has two navigational spans with a least clearance of 71 feet. The N openings are generally used during high water because there is less current, but during low water it is unsafe. The power cables E of the fixed parallel highway bridges have a least clearance of 82 feet.

Charts 18541, 18542, 18543

(319) **McNary Lock and Dam**, 254.5 (292.9) miles above the mouth of the Columbia River and just above Umatilla, has a single lift lock with a vertical lift of about 75 feet. A **restricted area** is above the dam. (See **207.718**, chapter 2, for information concerning use, administration, and navigation of McNary Lock and Dam.) Depths and overhead clearances are at **normal pool level.**

(320) **Lake Wallula**, the pool created by McNary Dam, provides slack-water navigation from McNary Dam to the junction with the **Yakima River**, a distance of about 37(43) miles. Depths in the lake are generally deep, however, there are several isolated shallow spots and rocky areas along the length of the lake. The channel through the lake is marked by aids to navigation from the Walla Walla River to Richland, 40 (46) miles above McNary Dam.

(321) The **Port of Umatilla**, on the Oregon side, about 0.4 mile above the McNary Lock and Dam, owns a 230-foot port wharf with 800 feet of berthing space; reported depths of 20 feet are available alongside; a private company operates the wharf. A grain elevator, owned and operated by Pendleton Grain growers, Inc., has a loading rate of 20,000 bushels per hour; the grain elevator is just E of the port wharf. A barge wharf, used for receipt and shipment of petroleum products and liquid fertilizer, is just E of the grain elevator; the oil wharf is owned and operated by the Tidewater Barge Lines.

(322) **Hat Rock State Park,** on the S side about 5.5 (6.3) miles above McNary Dam, has a public launching ramp and offers excellent protection for small craft. Gasoline is available here.

(323) **Port Kelley**, on the E side of Columbia River, 16 (19.5) miles above McNary Dam, has a large grain elevator and facilities for handling bulk grain by rail, truck, or water. The elevator loading rate is 30,000 bushels per hour. Unlighted ranges lead clear of the rock and shoal area in the middle ground 0.4 mile W of the facility.

(324) A small boat moorage is in the bight just NE of Port Kelley. Berths, electricity, gasoline, and water are available.

(325) **Walla Walla River** enters Columbia River on the E side 18.4 (21.2) miles above McNary Dam. There is a public launching ramp on the S side of the river just E of the highway bridges at the entrance.

(326) A grain wharf, at **Wallula Junction** just S of the Walla Walla River, has a grain elevator and barge loading spout with a loading rate of 20,000 bushels per hour; a reported depth of 20 feet is alongside the wharf. The wharf is owned and operated by Walla Walla Grain Growers, Incorporated. A barge wharf, at the **Port of Walla Walla** just S of **Attalia**, is owned and operated by Boise Cascade Corporation. The wharf ships wood pulp and receives caustic soda. A reported depth of 12 feet is alongside.

(327) About 1.9 miles S of the Snake River mouth, on the W side of Lake Wallula, is the Unocal Corporation chemical plant; anhydrous ammonia and urea are received here by barge. The dock has 480 feet of berthing space and has a reported depth of 30 feet alongside. Two white ammonia storage tanks at this plant are prominent.

(328) The Union Pacific Railroad bridge crossing Columbia River, 27 (31) miles above McNary Dam, has a vertical lift span with a clearance of 11 feet down and 72 feet up. The bridgetender monitors VHF-FM channel 16 and works on channel 13; call sign KTD-561. (See **117.1 through 117.59 and 117.1035**, chapter 2, for drawbridge regulations.)

Charts 18545, 18546, 18547, 18548

(329) **Snake River**, 283 (325.2) miles above the mouth of Columbia River, rises in Yellowstone National Park, from which it winds S past the Grand Tetons, and thence for some 868 miles to its junction with the Columbia at Pasco, WA.

(330) From that junction for 119 (137) miles to Lewiston, ID there are few small-craft facilities. (See small-craft facilities tabulation on charts 18545, 18546, 18547, and 18548 for supplies and services available.) There are several marinas along the river at **Clarkston**, WA and **Lewiston**, ID where berths, gasoline, diesel fuel, water, ice, and marine supplies may be obtained. The Ports of Clarkston and Lewiston at the confluence of the Snake and Clarkford Rivers are the primary ports along the Snake River and serve the inland agricultural and logging communities of Washington, Idaho, and Oregon. Barge loading facilities and grain terminals are available at both ports.

(331) Near its mouth, at the village of **Burbank**, Snake River is crossed by the Burlington Northern Railroad lift bridge with a clearance of 14 feet down and 60 feet up. The bridgetender monitors VHF-FM channel 16 and works on channel 13; call sign KQ-9047. About 0.6 (0.7) mile above the railroad bridge, there are dual spans of a fixed highway bridge with a least clearance of 61 feet. Numerous overhead cables with a reported minimum clearance of 43 feet cross Snake River between the fixed highway bridge and Ice Harbor Lock and Dam.

(332) **East Pasco**, on the N side of Snake River 1 mile above the mouth, has privately owned facilities for receipt and shipment of petroleum products and liquid fertilizer. Burbank, on the S side of the river has two grain facilities owned by the Port of Walla Walla and operated by private companies. From East Pasco to Lewiston there are several facilities used for shipment of grain and wood chips. Other facilities along the river specialize in the receipt and shipment of logs, general cargo, petroleum products, anhydrous ammonia, and liquid fertilizer.

(333) **Ice Harbor Lock and Dam**, 8.4 (9.7) miles above the mouth of the Snake River, has a single lift lock with a vertical lift of about 100 feet. A **restricted area** is above and below the dam; the area is marked by buoys above the dam. (See **207.718**, chapter 2, for information concerning use, administration, and navigation of Ice Harbor Lock and Dam.) **Lake Sacajawea**, the lake formed by the waters behind Ice Harbor Dam, provides depths at slack water of 10 feet or more for a distance of 27.8 (32) miles to Lower Monumental Dam.

(334) **Lower Monumental Lock and Dam**, 27.6 (31.8) miles above Ice Harbor Dam and about 36 (41.5) miles above the mouth of the Snake River, has a single lift lock with a vertical lift of about 100 feet. A **restricted area** is above and below the dam; the area is marked by buoys above the dam. (See **207.718**, chapter 2, for information concerning use, administration, and navigation of Lower Monumental Lock and Dam.)

(335) The Snake River between Lower Monumental Dam and Little Goose Dam, 25 (28.8) miles above Lower Monumental Dam, is crossed by three fixed bridges with a least clearance of 52 feet; overhead power cables crossing the river between the two dams have a least clearance of 90 feet.

(336) **Little Goose Lock and Dam**, about 25 (28.8) miles above Lower Monumental Dam and about 61.1 (70.3) miles above the mouth of the Snake River, has a single lift lock with a vertical lift of about 98 feet. A **restricted area** is above and below the dam; the area is marked by buoys above the dam. (See **207.718**, chapter 2, for information concerning use, administration, and navigation of Little Goose Lock and Dam.)

(337) **Lake Bryan**, the pool formed by Little Goose Dam is crossed by a fixed highway bridge with a clearance of 60 feet about 10.7 (12.3) miles above the dam; overhead power cables with a least clearance of 75 feet cross the lake between Little Goose Dam and Lower Granite Dam.

(338) **Lower Granite Lock and Dam**, about 31.5 (36.8) miles above Little Goose Dam and about 93.4 (107.5) miles above the mouth of the Snake River, has a single lift navigation lock 675 feet long and 86 feet wide. The dam, completed in 1975, permits navigation to **Lewiston**, ID, 120 (138) miles above the mouth of the Snake River. A **restricted area** is above and below the dam; the area is marked by buoys above the dam. (See **207.718**,

(339) A fixed highway bridge with a clearance of 60 feet crosses Snake River about 1.5 miles below its junction with Clearwater River. A highway lift bridge with clearances of 7 feet down and 60 feet up crosses **Clearwater River** about 0.35 mile above the junction with Snake River (See **117.1 through 117.59 and 117.381**, chapter 2, for lift bridge regulations.) A fixed highway bridge, about 1.15 miles above the lift bridge, has a clearance of 21 feet. A vertical lift highway bridge with a clearance of 10 feet down and 42 feet up crosses the Snake River between Lewiston, ID and **Clarkston**, WA. (See **117.1 through 117.59 and 117.385**, chapter 2, for drawbridge regulations.) A fixed highway bridge with a clearance of 60 feet is about 1.5 miles above the lift bridge. Overhead power cables with a minimum clearance of 80 feet cross the river between the dam and Lewiston.

Charts 18542, 18543

(340) **Pasco**, on the N side of the Columbia River 286 (329) miles above its mouth, is 32 (36.8) miles above McNary Dam. The Port of Pasco Marine Terminal Wharf (46°13'10"N., 119°05'52"W.), operated by Continental Grain Company, has reported depths of 16 to 20 feet alongside with a total berthing space of 970 feet. A grain elevator, with a capacity for 450,000 bushels, serves the wharf and can load barges at a rate of 15,000 bushels per hour. The port also owns a Container Terminal Wharf at the barge slip in about 46°12'50"N., 119°04'14"W. The wharf is used for receipt and shipment of containerized general cargo and has a total berthing space of 840 feet; depths alongside the wharf are reported to be 20 feet. The Port of Pasco is a municipal corporation consisting of a Board of Commissioners and a General Manager. In addition to the marine terminals, the port operates an airport. The Pasco-Kennewick-Richland area is the most important commercial barging center above Portland.

(341) The Pasco Yacht Basin, on the E side just below the railroad lift bridge, has berths, gasoline, diesel fuel, and marine supplies. Engine and electronic repairs can be made. An 8-ton hoist and a launching ramp are available at the basin.

(342) **Kennewick**, on the S side of Columbia River opposite Pasco, has a grain elevator dock with 500 feet of berthing space and a reported depth of 14 feet alongside. At **Clover Island**, there is a large small-craft harbor. About 80 berths with electricity, gasoline, diesel fuel, water, and marine supplies are available. Hull, engine, and electronic repairs can be made. A 12-ton crane is at a marina occupying the center section of the island. A private yacht club is on the S side of the island.

(343) A railroad lift bridge crosses the Columbia River between Pasco and Kennewick, about 0.4 mile below Clover Island, and has a clearance of 18 feet down and 70 feet up. (See **117.1 through 117.59 and 117.1035**, chapter 2, for drawbridge regulations.) The fixed highway bridge just SE of Clover Island has a clearance of 56 feet and another fixed bridge, 0.9 mile above Clover Island, has a clearance of 61 feet. Interstate Route 182 fixed bridge crosses the Columbia River at Richland and has a clearance of 73 feet. Overhead cables cross the Columbia River just above the junction with Snake River and at the E end of Clover Island; clearances are 85 and 54 feet, respectively.

(344) **Columbia Park Recreation Area**, just above the upper fixed highway bridge at Pasco, has a small-craft marina at which berths, electricity, gasoline, water, a launching ramp, and marine supplies are available. Engine repairs can be made. Diesel fuel is available in the town of **Richland**, just above the recreation area.

(345) The **Hanford Works**, a huge U.S. Department of Energy reservation, is on the S and W sides of the Columbia River about 13 (15) miles above Richland. The facility is devoted to energy research, development, and demonstration; production of nuclear materials; management of defense nuclear waste; and commercial nuclear fuel cycle research. The original site was created in 1943 under the direction of the Manhattan District of the U.S. Army Corps of Engineers for the production of materials for nuclear weapons such as those which helped to end World War II.

(346) **Priest Rapids Dam**, 68 (78.3) miles above McNary Dam and 353 (407) miles above the mouth of Columbia River, completed and dedicated in 1962, is the head of navigation, although in its construction provision was made for later building of a navigational lock if needed. However, Richland is the present practical head of navigation.

Charts 18551, 18553

(347) **Franklin D. Roosevelt Lake**, WA, is a National Recreation Area on the upper Columbia River impounded by the **Grand Coulee Dam** (47°57.5'N., 118°59.0'W.). Information about facilities and services is available at the recreation area headquarters in the town of Coulee Dam, the visitors' center at Fort Spokane, and the ranger station at Kettle Falls.

(348) A **restricted area** has been established in the discharge channel of the Grand Coulee Dam, and extending about 2.5 miles downstream from the dam. (See **162.230**, chapter 2, for limits and regulations.)

Chart 18554

(349) **Lake Pend Oreille** (48°10'N., 116°25'W.), Idaho, is a recreation area nearly surrounded by the Kaniksu National Forest. The charted depths are based on a lake level of 2048.15 feet above mean sea level. Normal winter and summer lake levels are about 3 feet and 14

(350) Marina services at **Sandpoint**, on the N side of the **Pend Oreille River** at its junction with Lake Pend Oreille, include berthing, gasoline, a launching ramp, winter storage, and hull and engine repairs. The drawspan of the railroad bridge across the Pend Oreille River, at the river and lake junction, is in the permanently closed position. (See **117.1 through 117.59 and 117.383**, chapter 2, for drawbridge regulations.) U.S. Route 95 fixed highway bridge crosses the river just above the railroad bridge; the least clearance for both bridges is 14 feet. At **Bayview** (47°59'N., 116°34'W.), at the SW end of the lake just W of Scenic Bay, has several marinas that can provide transient berthing, gasoline, diesel fuel, launching ramps, winter storage, marine supplies, water, and pump-out stations; complete marine services are available. Additional information about facilities and services may be obtained from the Sandpoint Chamber of Commerce, Sandpoint, ID 83864.

TIDAL INFORMATION						
Chart	Station	LAT/LONG	Mean Higher High Water*	Mean High Water*	Mean Low Water*
18521	Columbia River entrance (North Jetty)	46°16'N/124°04'W	7.5	6.8	1.2
18521	Ilwaco, Baker Bay, Columbia River	46°18'N/124°02'W	7.6	7.0	1.0
18521	Harrington Point, Columbia River	46°16'N/123°39'W	7.7	7.0	0.9
18521	Point Adams, Columbia River	46°12'N/123°57'W	8.3	7.6	1.2
18521	Astoria (Tongue Point), Colombia River	46°13'N/123°46'W	8.6	7.9	1.2
18521	Chinook, Baker Bay	46°16'N/123°58'W	8.1	7.4	1.3
18523	Cathlamet, Columbia River	46°12'N/123°23'W	6.7	6.1	0.6
18523	Settlers Point, Columbia River	46°10'N/123°41'W	8.0	7.3	1.0
18523	Wauna, Columbia River	46°10'N/123°24'W	6.3	5.9	0.6
18523	Skamokawa, Steamboat Slough, Columbia River	46°16'N/123°27'W	6.9	6.5	0.8

* Heights in feet referred to datum of sounding MLLW.
Real-time water levels, tide predictions, and tidal current predictions are available at:
http://tidesandcurrents.noaa.gov
To determine mean tide range subtract Mean Low Water from Mean High Water.
Data as of September 2012

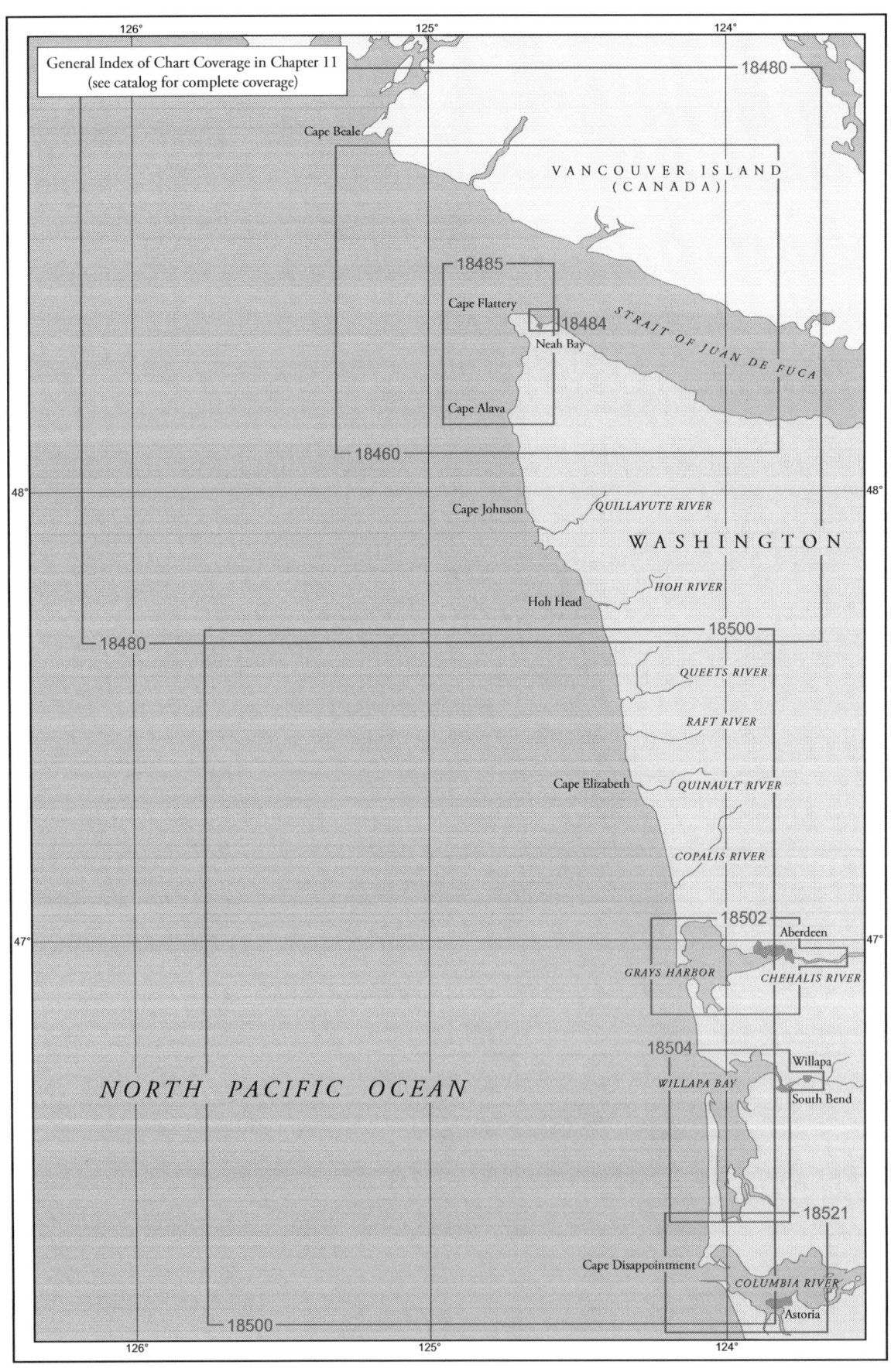

Columbia River to Strait of Juan De Fuca, Washington

(1) This chapter describes the Pacific coast of the State of Washington from the Washington-Oregon border at the mouth of the Columbia River to the northwestern-most point at Cape Flattery. The deep-draft ports of South Bend and Raymond, in Willapa Bay, and the deep-draft ports of Hoquiam and Aberdeen, in Grays Harbor, are described. In addition, the fishing port of La Push is described. The most outlying dangers are Destruction Island and Umatilla Reef. A U.S. Navy operating/exercise area parallels the coastline from about 10 miles N of Point Brown to Cape Alava, extending from 3 miles offshore to about 50 miles offshore.

(2) The **Olympic Coast National Marine Sanctuary,** off the Olympic Peninsula of Washington State, including the waters of the Strait of Juan de Fuca, extends from Koitlah Point due north to the international boundary seaward to the 100 fathom isobath, thence southward to a point due west of the mouth of the Copalis River cutting across the heads of Nitnat, Juan de Fuca, and Quinault Canyons. (See **15 CFR 922**, chapter 2, for limits and regulations.)

Area to be Avoided-Washington Coast

(3) The International Maritime Organization (IMO) has adopted the waters off the Washington Coast as an area to be avoided. (See IMO SN circular 309.) In order to reduce the risk of a marine casualty and resulting pollution and damage to the environment of the Olympic Coast National Marine Sanctuary, all ships and barges that carry oil or hazardous materials in bulk as cargo or cargo residue and all ships 400 gross tonnage and above solely in transit should avoid the area bounded by a line connecting the following points:

(4) 48°23.30'N., 124°38.20'W.
(5) 48°24.17'N., 124°38.20'W.
(6) 48°26.15'N., 124°44.65'W.
(7) 48°26.15'N., 124°52.80'W.
(8) 48°24.67'N., 124°55.71'W.
(9) 47°51.70'N., 125°15.50'W.
(10) 47°07.70'N., 124°47.50'W.
(11) 47°07.70'N., 124°11.00'W.

COLREGS Demarcation Lines

(12) The lines established for this part of the coast are described in **80.1370 through 80.1380**, chapter 2.

Chart 18500

(13) From Cape Disappointment, the coast extends N for 22 miles to Willapa Bay as a low sandy beach, with sandy ridges about 20 feet high parallel with the shore. Back of the beach, the country is heavily wooded. Numerous summer resorts and cottages are along the beach. Landmarks along this section of the coast are few. The 10-fathom curve averages a distance of about 2.5 miles from the shore. There are no known offlying dangers S of the Willapa Bay entrance bar.

Weather, Columbia River to Strait of Juan De Fuca

(14) The weather along this coast is usually mild, windy, and rainy in winter, cool and pleasant in summer, with some periods of fog. Close to shore, and particularly in Willapa Bay and Grays Harbor, wind and fog conditions are often local and different from conditions offshore. Radiation fog often blankets these bodies of water, as well as rivers and shore points, in fall and winter. It can form any time when nights are clear and calm.

(15) Storms that move along this coast or a distance out to sea bring cloudy days with highs in the mid-forties (6.1° to 8.3°C) and lows in the middle to upper thirties (3.3° to 3.9°C). In winter, they cause rain on about 15 to 25 days per month and significant snow on 2 or 3 days. They are responsible for predominantly E to SE winds from October through March; these winds reach gale force 3 to 6 percent of the time. In the intermittent periods of settled weather, sound becomes an early morning hazard over rivers and protected bays. Visibilities drop below 0.5 mile (0.9 km) on 3 to 4 days per month, from October to February. sound signals in waters like Grays Harbor operate up to 35 percent of the time.

(16) With the coming of spring, conditions improve. Storms become less frequent. Winds diminish and blow more from a W direction. Temperatures often rise into the low to middle fifties (11° to 13°C) during the day and fall to the low forties (5.0° to 5.6°C) at night. Visibilities are usually good, and rain falls on just 8 to 15 days per month.

(17) Summer is the true fog season along these shores. In general, advection fog reduces visibilities to below 0.5 mile (0.9 km) on 3 to 10 days per month; up to 16 days per month at Tatoosh Island. Sound signals blow 15 to 30 percent of the time. Conditions are worst in Grays Harbor and near the entrance to the Strait of Juan de Fuca. Temperatures are often in the sixties (16.1° to 20.6°C) during the day and around 50°F (10°C) at

Washington State Requirements

Reports of Oil Spills and Vessel Emergencies

All vessels must report oil spills or potential oil spills to both:
1. Washington State   800–258–5990
2. National Response Center   800–424–8802

Tank vessels and cargo and passenger ships 300 gross tons or larger must make notifications to Washington State for vessel emergencies, including a loss or serious degradation of propulsion, steering, means of navigation, electrical generating capability and seakeeping capability constituting a substantial threat of pollution affecting Washington state natural resources. In addition to any notifications to the USCG, the owner or operator must notify the state of any vessel emergency that results in the discharge or substantial threat of a discharge of oil to state waters or that may affect the natural resources of the state within one hour of the onset of the emergency.

Emergency Response Tug at Neah Bay

An industry-funded emergency response tug is located at Neah Bay at the entrance to the Strait of Juan de Fuca. The tug is available 24 hours a day and can be underway within twenty minutes of a decision to deploy. The purpose of the tug is to assist vessels having propulsion and steering failures or that are directed by either the US or Canadian Coast Guards to obtain towing assistance. Among other capabilities, the tug is intended to be able to make up to, stop, hold, and tow a drifting or disabled vessel of 180,000 metric dead weight tons in severe weather conditions. The tug can be contacted through the USCG VTS or the Puget Sound Marine Exchange.

Washington State Vessel Inspections

The Washington State Department of Ecology regulates cargo and passenger vessels and tank vessels operating in Washington waters.
- A cargo vessel is any self-propelled vessel in commerce that is 300 gross tons or more.
- A passenger vessel is any vessel 300 gross tons or more with a fuel capacity of at least 6,000 gallons that carries passengers for compensation.
- A tank vessel is a ship that is constructed or adapted to carry, or that carries, oil in bulk as cargo or cargo residue.

Washington State Ecology inspectors may conduct vessel inspections on regulated cargo, passenger, and fishing vessels when in Washington waters. Additional information is available at:

http://www.ecy.wa.gov/programs/spills/prevention/VesselTechAssist/AISsubstantialrisk.html/

Oil Transfer Requirements

Safe bunkering procedures must be followed during fueling operations. For vessels 300 gross tons or greater, Washington State Ecology inspectors may conduct inspections of these regulated oil transfers on vessels receiving fuel for propulsion within Washington waters. Details can be found in state regulations at Washington Administrative Code (WAC) 317-40. Information is also available at:

http://www.ecy.wa.gov/programs/spills/prevention/VesselTechAssist/Bunkering.html/

Tank vessels delivering oil in bulk to a non-recreational vessel or facility within Washington waters must meet state oil transfer requirements. They may also be subject to Washington State oil transfer inspections for these regulated oil transfers. Details can be found in WAC 173-184. Additional information is available at:

http://www.ecy.wa.gov/programs/spills/prevention/VesselTechAssist/vessel_otr.html/

- For a transfer of more than 100 gallons of bulk oil to a facility or non-recreational vessel, the delivering vessel must submit an Advance Notice of Transfer (ANT) report to Ecology. This ANT must be submitted 24 hours prior to the transfer for facilities or within the timeframe required by local USCG Captain of the Port.
- For convenience, the ANT report can be made either: online using the Ecology website at
https://secureaccess.wa.gov/ecy/ants, by
e-mail:OilTransferNotifications@ecy.wa.gov, or by
fax: 360–407–7288 or 800–664–9184.

Contingency Plan Requirements

Tank vessels and cargo and passenger ships 300 gross tons or larger transiting Washington waters must either have a Washington State Department of Ecology approved oil spill contingency plan or be a member of a non-profit corporation that provides oil spill response capabilities consistent with their Washington State approved contingency plan. In Washington State, the non-profit corporation for Puget Sound and Grays Harbor is the Washington State Maritime Cooperative (WSMC). The non-profit corporation for the Columbia River is the Maritime Fire & Safety Association (MFSA). Additional information is available at:

http://www.ecy.wa.gov/programs/spills/preparedness/cplan/cplans.html/

(17) night. Winds are from a W to NW direction and usually less than 17 knots; calms occur up to 12 percent of the time. It rains on about 5 to 10 days per month.

(18) Fog remains a problem in autumn, although it is less frequent. Temperatures drop slowly with daytime readings often in the low to midsixties (16.1° to 19.4°C), dropping to the upper forties (8.9° to 9.4°C) at night. Rain falls more often. Winds become stronger and return to an E direction.

Chart 18504

(19) **Willapa Bay** entrance is 24 miles N of the Columbia River entrance. The bay is used primarily by fishing and oyster boats. No deep-draft vessels have entered Willapa Bay since 1976. Oyster beds cover much of the shoaler areas of the bay. Lumber, fish, and other sea foods are shipped by rail and truck from South Bend and Raymond.

Prominent features

(20) **Leadbetter Point**, the N extremity of **North Beach Peninsula**, is the S point of the entrance to Willapa Bay. It is low and sandy, and has no distinctive feature to mark its extremity; the chart limit of the trees is 2.2 miles S.

(21) **Cape Shoalwater**, the N point at the entrance, terminates in a low bluff about 50 feet high. The cape is sandy, and N portion is covered with trees to within 300 yards of the point.

(22) The N shore of the entrance to the bay is marked by timbered bluffs and ridges, several hundred feet high. In the daytime, scars on the cliffs often are visible before the light can be seen. The termination of the tree line on Leadbetter Point is sharply defined.

(23) The entrance is in the N part of the bay, which consists of two arms; the S, 18 miles long, and the E, 10 miles long. Both arms are filled with extensive shoals, large areas of which bare at low water. The S arm is separated from the ocean by a strip of low sand and sand dunes, averaging 1.5 miles in width and covered with trees until within 2.2 miles of Leadbetter Point. Numerous cottages and summer resorts are along the seaward face of the narrow peninsula. The shore of the bay elsewhere is composed of low, rolling hills, 100 to 200 feet high, covered with dense growths of timber.

(24) **Willapa Bar** extends about 3 miles outside of a line joining Cape Shoalwater and Leadbetter Point. The bar channel is continually shifting, and depths over it vary from season to season. Because of the frequent changes in the position of the bar and difficulty in dredging the bar to project depth, depths have consistently been less than the 26-foot project depth. The buoys marking the channel over the bar are non lateral and moved from time to time because of the shifting sands and changing channel. Dredging range lights are temporarily established at the entrance at times during dredging operations. The entrance buoys and the dredging range lights do not necessarily mark the best water. The major channels in the bay are marked by aids to navigation.

(25) **Willapa River** flows into the E arm of the bay. Lights, buoys, daybeacons, and lighted and unlighted ranges mark the channel through the E arm and Willapa River to South Bend and Raymond.

COLREGS Demarcation Lines

(26) The lines established for Willapa Bay are described in **80.1370**, chapter 2.

Channels

(27) A **Federal project** provides for a 26-foot channel over the bar at the mouth of Willapa Bay, and a 24-foot channel from deep water in Willapa Bay to just above both forks of Willapa River at Raymond. The channel over the bar into Willapa Bay is subject to frequent change. (See Notice to Mariners and latest editions of charts for controlling depths.)

Anchorage

(28) Anchorage with good holding ground may be had at almost any point inside the bay. The anchorage generally used is off Toke Point in 30 to 40 feet.

Dangers

(29) An underwater dike, 18 feet below the surface, extends about 800 yards into the North Channel from a rock groin along the shore between Cape Shoalwater and North Cove in about 46°43'35"N., 124°03'30"W.

Currents

(30) In the entrance the current velocity is about 2.5 knots. Currents of 4 to 6 knots occur at times; the velocity is greatest on the ebb, particularly with S wind.

(31) In the channel at South Bend, the velocity is about 1.2 knots on the flood and 1.4 knots on the ebb. (See Tidal Current Tables for predictions for South Bend.)

Routes

(32) From N or S, the course to Willapa Bay should be shaped to make the outermost lighted whistle buoy. From seaward in clear weather, the lights at the entrance of Grays Harbor, 14 miles N, and at North Head, 22 miles S, are distinguishing marks for fixing a vessel's position and the subsequent shaping of the course.

(33) Approaching from any direction in any weather, great caution is essential. The currents are variable and uncertain. Velocities of 3 to 3.5 knots have been observed between Blunts Reef and the Swiftsure Bank, and velocities considerably in excess of these amounts have been reported. Under such conditions, vessels should not shoal the water to less than 20 fathoms until the lighted whistle buoy off the entrance has been made.

(34) Navigators of deep-draft vessels should bear in mind the changeable nature of the bar. Strangers should not navigate the bay in thick weather.

(35) **South Bend** is on the S bank of Willapa River, 8 miles above Toke Point. The principal industries are lumbering, oystering, and fishing; two canneries are operating here. Willapa Harbor Airport is on the N bank of the river about 2.5 miles NW of South Bend. **Raymond**, the principal town, is on the S bank of Willapa River at the junction of the South Fork, 3 miles above South Bend. There are sawmills here, and large quantities of lumber are shipped out.

Bridges

(36) There are no bridges over the main channel. The Burlington Northern railroad swing bridge across South Fork, 0.3 mile above its mouth, has a clearance of 8 feet. (See **117.1 through 117.59 and 117.1063(b)**, chapter 2, for drawbridge regulations.) Two fixed highway bridges over South Fork about 0.5 mile above the railroad swing bridge have a least clearance of 15 feet. The fixed highway bridge over North Fork at Raymond has a clearance of 20 feet. A railroad fixed bridge over **Ellis Slough** has a clearance of 24 feet.

(37) At The Narrows, 1 mile below the Port of Willapa Harbor wharf, the river is crossed by power cables with a minimum clearance of 165 feet.

(38) **Pilotage** for Grays Harbor, discussed later in this chapter, also pertains to Willapa Bay.

Towage

(39) Tugs to 2,200 hp are available at Hoquiam in Grays Harbor. Arrangements should be made in advance through ships' agents or through the pilots.

Quarantine, customs, immigration, and agricultural quarantine

(40) (See chapter 3, Vessel Arrival Inspections, and Appendix A for addresses.)

(41) **Quarantine** is enforced in accordance with regulations of the U.S. Public Health Service. (See Public Health Service, chapter 1, for details.)

(42) South Bend and Raymond are **customs ports of entry**.

Supplies

(43) Diesel oil, gasoline, water, ice, and some marine supplies are available in South Bend and Raymond. Both South Bend and Raymond have small-craft moorages operated by the respective towns.

Repairs

(44) The largest of two marine railways at South Bend can handle vessels 60 feet long and 19½ feet wide for hull repairs. A nearby machine shop and foundry does some engine repair work.

(45) **Tokeland** on **Toke Point**, is a summer resort. There is a dredged entrance channel and small-craft basin on the N side of the point. A light is on the outer end of a jetty on the S side and a daybeacon is on the N side of the entrance. In 2002, the controlling depth was 13.1 feet in the entrance channel to the basin; thence in 2000, the basin had depths of 9 to 13 feet, except for lesser depths along the SW edge. Berths, gasoline, diesel fuel, water, and ice are available either at the basin or nearby. A launching ramp is at the basin.

(46) **North River**, which enters the E arm 2 miles E of Toke Point, is navigated by small logging launches. The channel is marked by private daybeacons, and is navigable at high water to **Eatons Ranch**, 3 miles above the last daybeacon.

(47) The S part of Willapa Bay is used by light-draft vessels. **Bay Center** is a village just S of **Goose Point** (46°38.2'N., 123°57.5'W.). It is one of the many oyster places in this bay; there is also some fishing and crabbing. There are floats here for mooring fishing vessels; gasoline is available.

(48) The channel to Bay Center leads from deep water in Willapa Bay about 1.4 miles WNW of Goose Point, thence N of Goose Point, and thence S into Palix River to the basin at Bay Center. The channel is marked by lights and buoys. The channel is subject to continual change and buoys are frequently shifted to mark the best water. (See the Notice to Mariners and the latest edition of the chart for controlling depths.)

(49) **Palix River**, on the E side of the bay, is navigable for small logging tugboats and fishermen for about 1 mile up each of the three forks above their junction. The fixed highway bridge, about 1 mile below the forks, has a clearance of 25 feet.

(50) **Nemah River Channel**, 5 miles S of Goose Point, is marked by private aids. Controlling depths are about 4 feet to Daybeacon 20, thence 2 feet to Lynn Point, thence 1 foot to the junction of South and Middle Nemah Rivers.

(51) **Nahcotta Channel**, about 4.5 miles S of Goose Point, leads S between North Beach Peninsula on the W and Long Island Shoal and Long Island on the E to Shoalwater Bay. The channel is well marked and has depths greater than 20 feet.

(52) **Stanley Channel** leads from Nahcotta Channel at Long Island Junction Light, thence E of Long Island and **Stanley Peninsula** to the mouth of Naselle River. Shallow-draft boats with local knowledge can cross **Long Island Shoal**.

(53) **Long Island**, 5.5 miles long in a NW direction and of irregular width, wooded, and rising to over 100 feet in elevation, lies in the S arm of the bay near the head and nearly fills it. The waters surrounding Long Island encompass the Willapa National Wildlife Refuge, and its boundary is marked by numerous piles.

(54) **Nahcotta**, on the E side of North Beach Peninsula, is a small village 9 miles S of Leadbetter Point. There

(55) are several large oyster plants here. The boat basin at Nahcotta has floats for small craft; diesel fuel and dry winter boat storage are available. In 2004, the channel leading from deep water in Nahcotta Channel to the basin had a controlling depth of 5 feet, thence depths of 4 to 6 feet were available in the basin except for lesser depths along the N edge and shoaling to bare in the NW corner. The entrance to the basin is marked by lights.

(55) **Naselle River**, on the E side of the bay, is navigable by boats of 5 feet or less draft, at half tide or higher water, as far as the bridge at the village of **Naselle**, 10 miles above the mouth. This bridge marks the head of tide water at ordinary high tides. The river has numerous snags and submerged logs, and is crossed by power cables with least clearance of 60 feet; passage should not be attempted without local knowledge. Small logging and fishing boats operate on the river.

(56) **Bear River** enters at the SE corner at the head of **Shoalwater Bay**. A long, tortuous, unmarked channel across the flats makes entrance to the river difficult. Vessels of 5-foot draft or less can make the fixed bridge about 1.5 miles above the mouth at half tide.

Chart 18500

(57) From Cape Shoalwater to Point Chehalis, the S point at the entrance to Grays Harbor, the coast extends for 11 miles as a low sand beach, backed by a heavy growth of timber.

Chart 18502

(58) **Grays Harbor** entrance is about 40 miles N of Cape Disappointment and 93 miles S of Cape Flattery. The bay and its tributaries furnish an outlet to an extensive timber area. Grays Harbor is an important lumber port in the foreign and domestic trade. Oil is delivered by tanker; logs, lumber, pulpwood, woodchips, and biodiesel are shipped out.

(59) The bay at the entrance is about 1 mile wide, but shoals extending S from Damon Point and N from Westport reduce the navigable channel to a width of 0.6 mile. From its entrance the bay extends E for 15 miles to the mouth of Chehalis River. The bay is filled by shoals and flats; thence bare at low water and are cut by numerous channels with a marked maintained channel.

(60) **Point Chehalis** is low and sandy and is bare of trees for 1.5 miles S of its extremity. A jetty extends seaward from the end of the point. A Coast Guard lookout tower is prominent on the point.

(61) **Grays Harbor Light** (46°53'18"N., 124°07'01"W.), 123 feet above the water, is shown from a 107-foot white truncated octagonal pyramidal tower on the seaward side of Point Chehalis.

(62) **Point Brown**, the N entrance point is 1.8 miles NW of Point Chehalis; it is low, rounding, and sandy, with shoals extending S and W which, together with those extending W from Point Chehalis, form the bar at the entrance. The point is wooded to within 0.5 miles of the extremity. A jetty extends W from the point. A wreck covered 24 feet is about 1.1 miles W of the jetty at 46°55'38"N., 124°12'30"W.

(63) A small-craft basin is NE of the point. The entrance to the basin is marked by lights; the approach channel is marked by a line of lighted and unlighted dolphins. A submerged jetty extends about 0.6 mile NE from the N side of the basin entrance. Reported depths of 5 feet are available through the natural channel leading to the basin with depths of 3 feet or less inside the basin due to silting.

Prominent features

(64) The country about Grays Harbor is flat and featureless, with few conspicuous objects. **Saddle Hill** (chart 18500), about 310 feet high, 8 miles N of the entrance and 2 miles inshore, is the most conspicuous feature.

(65) Grays Harbor Light shows prominently on a closer approach to the entrance. A micro tower, painted a red and white checkerboard pattern, is 3.6 miles NNE of the N jetty and a large rust-colored standpipe, lighted at night by floodlights, is 2.5 miles SSE of Point Chehalis. Both these objects are prominent on a closer approach, and the standpipe is reported to be visible for a considerable distance at night. In clear weather, **Brackenridge Bluff**, on the N shore 6 miles inside the entrance, is quite prominent. It is a reddish cliff about a mile long, rising in two places to a height of 80 feet; from seaward it is visible only through the entrance.

(66) In clear weather **Neds Rock**, off Brackenridge Bluff, shows prominently from inside the entrance; it is reddish.

COLREGS Demarcation Lines

(67) The lines established for Grays Harbor are described in **80.1375**, chapter 2.

(68) Grays Harbor is served by the Marine Exchange of Puget Sound. (See Marine Exchange of Puget Sound, chapter 13, for details).

Channels

(69) The entrance to Grays Harbor, between two jetties, is marked by two lighted ranges and buoys. Inside the bay, a **Federal project** channel provides depths of 46 feet across the bar, thence 42 to 40 feet in the entrance, thence 36 feet inside the bay to Cow Point, thence 32 feet to Cosmopolis, about 9 miles above the bay entrance. The channel inside the bay to Cosmopolis is well marked. There is no deep-draft navigation above Cosmopolis. (See Notices to Mariners and latest editions of the charts for controlling depths for the dredged channel.)

(70) The jettied entrance has a tendency to shoal at the curve on the Point Chehalis side. Submerged sections of the N and S jetties extend seaward about 0.2 and 0.9 mile, respectively, from the visible sections. Both N and

S jetties should be given a wide berth during periods of heavy weather due to hazardous breakers. Lighted whistle, bell, and gong buoys mark the approach and entrance to the bay. A seasonal sound signal is about mid-length of the visible section of the S jetty.

Anchorage

(71) The best anchorage is N of Westport and SE of **Damon Point** in 30 to 60 feet. The holding ground is good, and there is more swinging room here than elsewhere in the harbor.

Currents

(72) In the entrance, the average current velocity is about 1.9 knots on the flood and 2.8 knots on the ebb, but velocities may reach 5 knots. In the channels through the bay, the velocities seldom exceed 3 knots. It was reported that currents in the vicinity of the bar are very erratic, setting N close inshore and S offshore. (See Tidal Current Tables for daily predictions at the entrance to Grays Harbor.)

Routes

(73) From N or S, the course should be shaped to make the entrance buoy. From seaward in clear weather, Saddle Hill, 8 miles N of the entrance, and Grays Harbor Light on Point Chehalis will be seen.

(74) Approaching from any direction in thick weather, great caution is essential. The currents are variable and uncertain. Velocities of 3 to 3½ knots have been observed between Blunts Reef and Swiftsure Bank, and velocities in excess of these amounts have been reported. Because of the possibility of a strong onshore set, especially in SW weather, vessels should not shoal the depths to less than 20 fathoms unless sure of the position.

(75) The bar channel is subject to change. Deep-draft vessels should not enter without knowledge of conditions at the time of entering. The deepest water is not always on the range. Information concerning conditions on the bar can be obtained from the Grays Harbor Pilots Association or from the Coast Guard on VHF-FM channel 16. The bar channel and harbor should not be attempted in thick weather.

Pilotage, Grays Harbor

(76) Pilotage is compulsory for all foreign vessels, and U.S. vessels under enrollment and registered in foreign trade.

(77) Grays Harbor Bar Pilots serve Grays Harbor, Chehalis River, and Willapa Bay, and maintains an office at Aberdeen, WA, and a station at Westhaven Cove, Westport, WA.

(78) The office address is: Port of Grays Harbor, P.O. Box 660, 111 S. Wooding Street, Aberdeen, WA 98520; telephone 360–533–9564.

(79) The station and pilot boat monitor VHF-FM channels 12 and 16, and use 12 as working channel. The pilot boat, CHEHALIS, is 65 feet long and has an orange and green hull. The word 'PILOT' is displayed on both sides of the boat, and the standard day and night signals are used when vessels are approaching from seaward.

(80) Arrangements for pilots can be made by ships' agents by telephone or radiotelephone. A 24-hour advance notice of arrival is requested; any change in the estimated time of arrival requires a 4-hour advance notice to the pilots via the Marine Exchange, Seattle, WA or radiotelephone.

(81) Pilots board vessels near Grays Harbor Approach Lighted Whistle Buoy GH (46°51'55"N., 124°14'26"W.). To assist pilots in boarding from the bow of the pilot boat, the ship is requested to maintain a speed of 6 knots. A pilot ladder should be rigged amidships on the leeward side clear of the gangway or other obstructions, and about 3 meters above the water with no manropes. In rough weather, pilots may board during daylight.

(82) **Westhaven Cove**, on the inner side of the N tip of Point Chehalis, is protected by breakwaters marked by lights. The harbor is a large sport and commercial fishing center operated by the Port of Grays Harbor.

(83) In 2003, a depth of 19.6 feet was available in the N entrance and a depth of 14.1 feet was available in the S entrance, thence depths of 9 to 16 feet were available in the cove (except for shoaling along the SW edge of the breakwater.) Lesser depths are near both entrance channel edges and breakwaters.

(84) **Grays Harbor Coast Guard Station** is on the S side of Westhaven Cove. The town of **Westport**, a summer resort and fishing town, is about a mile S of Westhaven Cove.

(85) Westhaven Cove has about 1,000 berths, with electricity, about 20 transient berths, gasoline, diesel fuel, water, ice, a launching ramp, pump-out facilities, and marine supplies. Dry winter boat storage is available in the cove. A boatyard at the S end of the harbor has a mobile lift that can handle craft to 60 tons for hull or engine repairs; the yard includes a ship chandlery. Electronic repair service is available at the harbor. The Grays Harbor pilot boat is berthed at Westhaven Cove.

(86) The Coast Guard has established Grays Harbor Regulated Navigation Area Warning Sign, a **rough bar advisory sign**, 20 feet above the water, visible from the channel looking seaward, on the N side of Westhaven Cove, to promote safety for small-boat operators. The sign is diamond shaped, painted white with an international orange border, and with the words "Rough Bar" in black letters. The sign is equipped with two quick flashing amber lights that will be activated when hazardous conditions exist and the bar is restricted to recreational and uninspected passenger vessels. Boaters are cautioned, however, that if the light is not flashing, it is no guarantee that sea conditions are favorable.

(87) The Coast Guard displays **heavy weather warning flags**, square RED flags with square BLACK centers, at two locations in Grays Harbor; one flag is on the

Facilities in Grays Harbor (Hoquiam, Aberdeen, Cosmopolis)							
Name	Location	Berthing Space (feet)	Depths* (feet)	Deck Height (feet)	Mechanical Handling Facilities and Storage	Purpose	Owned/ Operated by:
Port of Grays Harbor Terminal 1	46°57'59"N., 123°51'19"W.	450	30	18	• Open storage (5 acres) • Electric belt conveyor (500 tons/hour)	Shipment of wood chips by barge	Port of Grays Harbor/ Olympic Fibre, Inc. (360-533-6588)
Port of Grays Harbor Terminal 2	46°57'53"N., 123°51'08"W.	900	41	18	• Open storage (51 acres) • 50,000 square foot storage building	Receipt and shipment of bulk agricultural commodities	Port of Grays Harbor/ AGP Inc. (360-533-9513)
Port of Grays Harbor Terminal 4	46°57'39"N., 123°50'19"W.	1400	41	18	• Open storage (100 acres) • Two 50-ton gantry cranes	Receipt and shipment of logs, lumber, and conventional general cargo	Port of Grays Harbor (360-533-9513)
Willis Enterprises, Aberdeen Wharf	46°57'57"N., 123°49'19"W.	650	20	16	• Open storage (17 acres) • Electric belt conveyor (510 tons/hour)	Shipment of wood chips	Quigg Bros., Inc./Willis Enterprises (360-249-5244)
Sierra Pacific Industries, Junction City Wharf	46°58'20"N., 123°46'39"W.	825	27-28	19.5	• Open storage (45 acres)	Shipment of wood chips; receipt and shipment of logs	Sierra Pacific Industries (360-532-2323)
Weyerhaeuser Co., Bay City Log Export, Berths 1 and 2	46°58'01"N., 123°46'43"W.	725	35	16	• Open storage (27 acres)	Shipment of logs and occasional shipment of lumber	Weyerhaeuser Co. (360-537-8216)
Weyerhaeuser Co., Aberdeen Saw Mill, Wood Chip Wharf	46°58'30"N., 123°47'38"W.	480	21-24	-	• Open storage (20,000 tons of wood chips) • Electric conveyor (400 tons/hour)	Shipment of wood chips	Weyerhaeuser Co. (360-537-8216)
Weyerhaeuser Co., Aberdeen Saw Mill, Lumber Wharf	46°58'26"N., 123°47'57"W.	900	24-33	16	• Open storage (16 acres)	Shipment of lumber	Weyerhaeuser Co. (360-537-8216)

* The depths given above are reported. For information on the latest depths contact the port authorities or the private operators.

Coast Guard lookout tower 70 feet above the water on the S side of Point Chehalis and the other is on the NW side of the Coast Guard station boat house 50 feet above the water. These displays will be based on current weather warnings issued in the following National Weather Service forecast areas; Cape Flattery to Cape Shoalwater. Display of flags are required from one hour before sunrise to one hour after sunset. Weather flags are flown at select Coast Guard stations to supplement other weather notification sources. Light signals corresponding to these flags are not displayed at night. (See illustration Chapter 1.) In all cases mariners should rely upon National Weather Service broadcasts as their primary source of government provided weather information.

(88) **Bay City**, 3.7 miles SE from Westhaven Cove, on the E shore of **South Bay** formerly was a whaling station. The wharf, built originally for the old fertilizer factory, is now in ruins, and there are no marine facilities now at Bay City. The fixed highway bridge at Bay City has a clearance of 39 feet.

(89) For the rest of the 2.6-mile distance, South Bay is crooked and full of shoals to the mouth of **Elk River**, which is used some for logging.

(90) **Markham**, site of a large cranberry plant and a small seafood company, is on the S side of the bay at the mouth of **Johns River**, a shallow stream crossed by a fixed highway bridge with clearance of 33 feet, near the entrance. Above the bridge, the stream is navigable only for rowboats.

(91) **Hoquiam** and **Aberdeen** are twin cities about 14 miles above the harbor entrance. Hoquiam is on the river of that name, and Aberdeen is on Chehalis River. South Aberdeen is across the river, but is part of the city of Aberdeen.

(92) **Cosmopolis** is a small town on the S side of Chehalis River just above South Aberdeen. There is a large pulpmill here.

(93) **Chehalis River** enters at the E end of Grays Harbor and is marked by lights to Cosmopolis. It is navigable by small boats to **Elma**, 24 miles above the mouth. The upper portion of the river, for a distance of about 45 miles above Elma, is used for floating logs.

(94) **Montesano**, about 14 miles above Aberdeen, has several mills. This stretch of the river is used only by log tows and outboard motorboats. A small-boat moorage is on the N bank of the river just W of the highway bridge at South Montesano; a launching ramp is near the moorage.

Towage

(95) Tugs up to 2,200 hp are available at Hoquiam. Arrangements for a tug should be made in advance either through the Grays Harbor Pilots Association or ships' agents. Tugs monitor and use as working frequency VHF-FM channel 9.

Bridges

(96) The main channel of Chehalis River is crossed by U.S. Route 101 highway drawbridge at Aberdeen, about 1.4 miles above Cow Point. The bridge has a clearance

of 35 feet. The bridgetender of the highway bridge monitors VHF-FM channel 16 and works on channel 13; call sign KJA-289. (See **117.1 through 117.59 and 117.1031**, chapter 2, for drawbridge regulations.) A fixed bridge with a clearance of 29 feet is at South Montesano.

(97) In the 6-mile stretch between Montesano and Elma there are three fixed bridges having least clearance of 8 feet. At Cosmopolis, 5.5 miles above the mouth, is a power cable with a clearance of 125 feet. Between this point and Montesano the least clearance of power cables is 54 feet.

Quarantine, customs, immigration, and agricultural quarantine

(98) See chapter 3, Vessel Arrival Inspections, and Appendix A for addresses.)

(99) **Quarantine** is enforced in accordance with regulations of the U.S. Public Health Service. (See Public Health Service, chapter 1, for details.)

(100) Aberdeen is a **customs port of entry**.

Harbor regulations

(101) The Port of Grays Harbor Commission appoints a port manager who directs the facilities and port affairs of the harbor district, which is coextensive with Grays Harbor County. The Port of Grays Harbor general offices are at 111 South Wooding Street, about 500 yards from the inshore end of Terminal Pier 1.

Wharves

(102) The Port of Grays Harbor operates three marine terminals. In addition to the port-operated facilities listed in the table, there are several private deep-draft piers and wharves in the Hoquiam, Aberdeen, and Cosmopolis area. Only the major deep-draft facilities are listed. For a complete description of the port facilities refer to Port Series No. 35, published and sold by the U.S. Army Corps of Engineers. (See Appendix A for address.) The alongside depths given in the table are reported. (For information on the latest depths contact the port authorities or the private operators.)

Supplies

(103) Bunker fuel, diesel oil, lubricants, water, and some marine supplies are available for large vessels at Grays Harbor. Complete service and repair facilities for small craft are available at Westhaven Cove, Aberdeen, and Hoquiam.

Repairs

(104) There are no facilities for major repairs to large oceangoing vessels in Grays Harbor; the nearest such facilities are in Portland, OR. There are several marine railways in Grays Harbor, the largest of which is at a shipyard on the W bank of the Hoquiam River 1 mile above its mouth. This railway can handle vessels to 400 tons, 80 feet long or 34 feet wide for hull repairs. Machine shops and foundries are nearby and can make some engine repairs. Electronic repair service is available.

Communications

(105) Grays Harbor is served by two Class I railroads. Two U.S. highways serve Aberdeen and Hoquiam. Bowerman Airport, owned and operated by the Port of Grays Harbor, is on an extensive filled area just W of Hoquiam; there are flights to Seattle, Portland, Astoria, and points beyond.

(106) **North Bay**, immediately E of Point Brown, is a shallow bight about 6 miles long. It is filled with shoals and flats that bare at low water. There is some oyster culture in the bay, which is used considerably by small oyster boats. The entrance to the bay is marked by buoys.

(107) **Hoquiam River** empties into Grays Harbor about 2 miles W of the mouth of Chehalis River. It is practically a tidal slough 11 miles long. In 1980, the midchannel controlling depth was 6 feet from the mouth of Hoquiam River to the junction of the Hoquiam River and the East Fork of the Hoquiam River, a distance of about 2.5 miles. Traffic on the river consists of log tows, tugs, and other small craft.

(108) The Hoquiam River is crossed by a railroad swing bridge, the Simpson Avenue/U.S. Route 101 bascule bridge, and the 6th Avenue lift bridge within 0.7 mile of the mouth. Clearances are: 11 feet for the swing bridge; 25 feet for the bascule bridge; and 4 feet down and 65 feet up for the lift bridge. The railroad swing bridge about 2 miles above the mouth has a clearance of 5 feet. In 2004, the lift bridge was stuck in the down position. (See **117.1 through 117.59 and 117.1047**, chapter 2, for drawbridge regulations.) Overhead power and television cables along the river have a least clearance of 43 feet.

(109) The **Wishkah River** empties into the N side of Chehalis River in the E part of Aberdeen; it is little used. The river is crossed by two swing bridges and one bascule bridge within 0.4 mile of the mouth; least clearance is 8 feet. A fixed bridge about 1 mile above the mouth has a clearance of 15 feet. (See **117.1 through 117.59 and 117.1065**, chapter 2, for drawbridge regulations.) Overhead power cables crossing the river have a least clearance of 30 feet.

Chart 18500

(110) From Point Brown the coast extends N for 23 miles to Point Grenville as a low, sandy beach, broken occasionally by small streams and in some places by bluffs. A few small towns and settlements, connected by roads or trails, are scattered along this stretch.

(111) **Copalis Head**, 13 miles N of Point Brown, is a bright yellow bluff 2 miles long and 200 feet high. It is 1.5 miles

N of **Copalis River**. **Copalis Rocks**, two small rocks the larger 34 feet high, lie 500 yards off the head, and a rock awash is about 0.5 mile WSW of the head.

(112) Two small bluffs mark the mouth of **Joe Creek**, 3.5 miles N of Copalis Head.

(113) **Moclips River** entrance is 6 miles N of Copalis Head. The S point at the mouth is bare and sandy; on the N bank is a bright yellowish bluff 50 feet high. **Moclips**, near the mouth of this river, is connected by a branch of the Burlington Northern Railroad with Hoquiam on the N shore of Grays Harbor. A triangular-shaped yellowish bluff about 110 feet high on the S bank of **Wreck Creek**, which empties about 2.5 miles N of Moclips, is prominent from offshore.

(114) **Point Grenville**, 10 miles N of Copalis Head, is a broken rocky promontory with nearly vertical whitish cliffs over 100 feet high. Numerous rocks extend for some distance off the point. **Grenville Arch**, dark in color, 83 feet high, is the outer and more prominent of two rocks lying W of the point; it is over 0.5 mile SW of the inner extremity of the point. The arch lies E and W. A rock that uncovers is 400 yards NW of Grenville Arch. The W rock, off the W end of the point, is 200 yards off the cliff and 92 feet high. There are several rocks inside of it, but none outside. Two rocks, over 90 feet high, are 400 yards S of the S extremity of the point.

(115) An indifferent anchorage in NW weather may be had under Point Grenville by vessels of moderate draft, but the depths compel anchoring at such a distance from the beach that little shelter is afforded. The anchorage is in 4 fathoms, sandy bottom, with the inner extremity of the point bearing **338°**, and Grenville Arch bearing **239°**. This anchorage is not recommended for ordinary use.

(116) N of Point Grenville is a series of cliffs; the upper part appears light gray, the lower part dark, separated by a well-defined line of demarcation. This formation disappears near the S end of the cliffs where they are broken up and present a stratified appearance. The strata slope downward to the N of the cliffs is a shingle beach followed by irregular bluffs and cliffs terminating near Taholah in white cliffs of uniform height, which from offshore do not present the stratified appearance noticeable to the S.

(117) **Quinault River** breaks through the cliffs about a mile SE of Cape Elizabeth. **Taholah** is an Indian village on the banks of the river. The shoreline in this section is low. The river is navigable only by skiffs and outboard motorboats. Some gasoline and supplies are available. A piling dike has been built along the spit in front of the village. In the background is a ridge with three long, flat summits. The road serving the beach settlements, and connecting them with Hoquiam, terminates at Taholah.

(118) From Taholah to Cape Elizabeth the cliffs present an almost unbroken face seaward and in places are about 200 feet high. They appear either white or bright yellow, and from offshore present a very noticeable stratification, sloping downward to the S; an important difference from the direction of slope around Point Grenville.

(119) **Sonora Reef** extends SSE from Cape Elizabeth for over 2 miles, its S end lying 1.1 miles offshore.

(120) **Cape Elizabeth** projects about a mile from the general trend of the coast, and when seen from seaward appears as a bright yellow, rocky cliff reaching in places a height of 200 feet. There are no high or large rocks off the cape; numerous rocks awash extend to the S. The houses of the Quinault Indian Reservation are at the E end of the cliffs.

(121) From Cape Elizabeth for 20 miles to Destruction Island, the coast is nearly straight, with low shores and rocky cliffs heavily wooded to the edges. Numerous rocks lie offshore, but these are inshore of the usual track of vessels.

(122) **Flat Rock**, low and black, is 1.6 miles NW from Cape Elizabeth and 0.9 mile offshore. A covered rock which breaks in ordinary weather is 400 yards S of it. A small rock is halfway between Flat Rock and Cape Elizabeth, with a smaller one inside halfway to the beach.

(123) **Pratt Cliff**, 3 miles N of Cape Elizabeth, is a sharp point backed by cliffs, 139 feet high. **Split Rock**, 70 feet high, is 1 mile offshore, abreast of the N end of Pratt Cliff. It is split in two, and the division shows when seen from W to NW. A small, low, black rock is 0.5 mile S of it, and a larger one is 0.4 mile S of Split Rock.

(124) **Willoughby Rock**, 120 feet high, 0.4 mile NE of Split Rock, is nearly round with an abrupt seaward face. A cluster of rocks is between Willoughby and Split Rock and a little S of them; one is black and conical, with a rock awash 200 yards SW from it.

(125) **Sealion Rock**, 8 feet high, small and black, is 3 miles NW of Split Rock and 2.6 miles offshore.

(126) From Pratt Cliff to **Raft River**, 3.5 miles, the coast consists of broken cliffs over 100 feet high bordered by rocks extending over 0.5 mile offshore. Midway between these points are three rocky heads covered with trees to the edges projecting beyond the cliffs and almost detached from them.

(127) **Tunnel Island**, 157 feet high, is in the entrance to Raft River, and at low water is connected with the S point of the river. A vertical pillar, 108 feet high, stands 150 yards NNW of the rock, and a cluster of rocks is close-to under its SE point.

(128) From Raft River to Queets River, 4.5 miles, the coast consists of cliffs about 80 feet high, broken occasionally by small streams.

(129) **Queets River** is the largest stream between Grays Harbor and Cape Flattery. The S point is a low, sandy spit about 0.1 mile long, projecting from an abrupt cliff, 80 feet high, and densely wooded. The N point is 1.3 miles long, low, and sandy, with some trees at the mouth of the river, and a narrow lagoon between it and the bluff.

(130) From Queets River for 10 miles to abreast Destruction Island, the coast is rather low and is broken by cliffs about 50 feet high with broad low-water beaches.

Kalaloch Rocks are about 4.5 miles N of the river, close inshore.

(131) A **U.S. Navy Underwater Tracking Range** is W of the mouth of Queets River, about 6 to 10 miles offshore. Underwater cables, several feet above the ocean bottom and over an area about 1 mile wide, extend NE from the upper E side of the tracking range, at about 47°32.5'N., 124°30'W., to the shore at about 47°36.3'N., 124°22.5'W. Mariners are cautioned against anchoring or dragging in these areas.

(132) **Destruction Island**, 90 feet high, is 20 miles NNW of Cape Elizabeth and 3 miles offshore. It is flat-topped and covered with brush, with a few clumps of trees. The island is 0.5 mile long and 300 yards wide at its S part. From the N end rocks and ledges extend about a mile from the cliffs; these are bordered by a line of kelp on the inshore side.

(133) An indifferent anchorage, affording shelter from NW winds, may be had off the SE face of the island in 10 fathoms, sandy bottom, with the light bearing between **293°** and **315°**. Vessels must leave if the wind hauls W or S. During the fishing season many small fishing boats anchor for the night under Destruction Island; it is the only shelter from offshore winds between Grays Harbor and Cape Flattery.

Chart 18480

(134) For 5.5 miles from Destruction Island to Hoh Head, the coast trends in a general NW direction. The cliffs are 50 to 100 feet high, and many rocks and ledges extend 1.2 miles offshore in some places.

(135) **Abbey Islet**, 3.5 miles NE of Destruction Island, is over 100 feet high and covered with trees. It is 200 yards off the cliffs. Many rocks are close S of it, the most distant of which is **South Rock**, 46 feet high, 1 mile S, and 0.5 mile offshore.

(136) At the mouth of **Hoh River**, 2 miles SE of Hoh Head, is a broad sand beach; the absence of cliffs for 0.5 mile is noticeable for a considerable distance offshore. In smooth weather the river can be entered by canoes, but the channel shifts. An Indian village is on the S bank at its mouth.

(137) **Hoh Head**, 200 feet high, is a bright yellow cliff covered with a dense forest. It projects a little over 0.5 mile from the general trend of the coast. A large cluster of rocks is off the S cliff of the head and covered rocks extend to about 1.6 miles offshore between the head and North Rock. A rock covered 2¼ fathoms lies 1.8 miles WNW of Hoh Head.

(138) **Middle Rock, North Rock,** and **Perkins Reef** are other dangers within 1.5 miles off Hoh Head. Middle Rock, 65 feet high and black with vertical sides, is 0.8 mile off the mouth of Hoh River. North Rock, a mile S of Hoh Head, is 107 feet high and grayish in color, with steep sides; in the afternoon sun this rock shows white, which makes it a very distinct landmark. Perkins Reef is a long, bold, and jagged islet, 1.1 miles W of Hoh Head. This area has numerous other rocks, covered and bare.

(139) The coast continues rugged and rocky from Hoh Head to La Push, 11 miles to the NW. The cliffs are 100 to 120 feet high, broken here and there by small streams. Several rocky islets 25 to 120 feet high and covered ledges extend in some places as much as 2 miles offshore.

(140) **Alexander Island**, 121 feet high, is 2 miles NNW of Hoh Head and 1 mile offshore. It is covered with low vegetation, and is flat-topped with steep sides. The island is prominent in hazy or smoky weather. A small clump of trees in its center makes it easily distinguishable from the other rocks and islands in the area. A covered rock, 1.8 miles WNW of Alexander Island, is the outermost known danger in this vicinity.

(141) **Toleak Point**, 4.7 miles NW of Hoh Head, is a narrow point terminating in a small knob with an abrupt seaward face. A high wooded islet lies 400 yards W of the point, to which it is connected by an extensive bare reef. **Rounded Islet**, a grassy rock 130 feet high with rounded top and steep sides, is 0.3 mile seaward of Toleak Point. A low black rock is 0.7 mile S of the islet.

(142) **Giants Graveyard**, 1.5 miles N of Toleak Point, consists of very irregular rocks; the largest are up to 210 feet high. The farthest offlying rock is about 0.8 mile from shore.

(143) **Teahwhit Head**, 8 miles NW of Hoh Head and 2.4 miles SSE of La Push, is a jagged double point 100 feet high and heavily wooded. **Strawberry Bay**, on the SE side of the head, is a small bight in which fishing boats find shelter from NW winds. There are numerous rocks in and around the bight.

(144) **Quillayute Needle**, 103-foot high pinnacle, 1.3 miles WNW of Teahwhit Head, is the outermost of many rocks, visible or covered, that are within a mile of the shore. Some are as high as 100 to 195 feet, and many are awash or covered by a fathom or less. The foul area continues to within 1 mile S of James Island, at the entrance to La Push.

(145) **James Island**, 15 miles NNW of Destruction Island on the N side of Quillayute River mouth, is 183 feet high, bold and wooded, and joined to the beach at low water. Numerous smaller wooded islands, immediately N, are prominent. An indifferent anchorage affording some shelter from NW winds may be had close SE of James Island, in 5 to 6 fathoms, sandy bottom, about 600 yards from the beach. Sea swell makes this anchorage unsafe.

(146) **James Island Light** (47°54'17"N., 124°38'51"W.), 150 feet above the water, is shown from a white house on the S part of the Island.

(147) **La Push**, an Indian village on the E bank and about 0.4 mile above the entrance of **Quillayute River**, is an important sport fishing center.

(148) The river channel is protected by a jetty on the SE side and a dike on the NW side; a lighted whistle buoy is about 1.8 miles SW from the outer end of the jetty.

About 250 feet of the outer end of the jetty is awash at high water.

COLREGS Demarcation Lines

(149) The lines established for the Quillayute River are described in **80.1380**, chapter 2.

(150) The river channel leads from the sea to a small-craft basin at La Push. The entrance channel is marked by a directional light. The channel to the basin is marked by a light and seasonal buoys. Buoys are not charted because they are frequently shifted in position; local knowledge is advised. In 2011, depths of 4 to 10 feet were available in the basin. The N and S sides of the entrance to the basin are marked by lights.

(151) The channel, which passes close to the SE shore of James Island, is sometimes dangerous, especially in heavy S weather. Weather conditions which make the entrance hazardous normally occur only in the winters, usually in December and January. When there are breakers of any size making across the entrance, it should not be attempted except at better than half tide and with a well-powered boat. Mariners unfamiliar with the area may contact **Quillayute River Coast Guard Station** on Channel 16 VHF-FM or via telephone at 360–374–6469 for assistance. A tank, E of the entrance, is prominent.

(152) In late summer and fall mariners are advised to use caution when transiting the channel because fish nets may be present.

Weather, Quillayute, Tatoosh Island, and vicinity

(153) Maritime air from over the Pacific has an influence on the climate throughout the year. In the late fall and winter, the low-pressure center in the Gulf of Alaska intensifies and is of major importance in controlling weather systems entering the Pacific Northwest. At this season of the year, storm systems crossing the Pacific follow a more S path striking the coast at frequent intervals. The prevailing flow of air is from the SW and W. Air reaching this area is moist and near the temperature of the ocean water along the coast which ranges from 45°F (7.5°C) in February to 57°F (13.9°C) in August. The wet season begins in late September to October. From October through January, rain may be expected on about 22 days per month; from February through March, on 21 days; from April to June, on 20 days; and from July to September, on 15 days. Precipitation falls an average of 239 days each year.

(154) As the weather systems move inland, rainfall is usually of moderate intensity and continuous, rather than heavy downpours for brief periods. Gale force winds are not unusual. Most of the winter precipitation over the coastal plains falls as rain; however, snow can be expected each year. Snow is seldom deeper than 10 inches (254 mm) or remains on the ground longer than 2 weeks. The average annual snowfall is only 13 inches (330 mm) but snow has fallen during every month except June, July, and August. Annual precipitation increases from about 90 inches (2286 mm) near the coast, to more than 120 inches (3048 mm) over the coastal plains, to 200 inches or more (>5080 mm) on the wettest slopes of the Olympic Mountains. The average annual precipitation at Quillayute airport is nearly 102 inches (2591 mm). December is the wettest month averaging nearly 15 inches (381 mm) and July is the driest with an average of only 2.37 inches (61 mm).

(155) During the rainy season, temperatures show little diurnal or day to day change. Maximums are in the forties (5.0° to 9.4°C) or minimums in the mid-thirties (0.6° to 2.8°C). A few brief outbreaks of cold air from the interior of Canada can be expected each winter. Clear, dry, cold weather generally prevails during periods of east winds. Maximum temperatures range from 25°F (-3.9°C) to 35°F (1.7°C) and minimums from 10° to 25°F (-12.2° to -3.9°C). The coolest temperature on record is 5°F (-15°C) recorded November 1985. Every month except June, July, and August has seen below freezing (<0°C) temperatures.

(156) In the late spring and summer, a clockwise circulation of air around the large high-pressure center over the North Pacific brings a prevailing northwest and west flow of cool, comparatively dry, stable air into the northwest Olympic Peninsula. The dry season begins in May with the driest period between mid-July and mid-August. The total rainfall for July is less than 0.5 of an inch (13 mm) in 1 summer out of 10; also, it exceeds 5.0 inches (127 mm) in 1 summer out of 10. During the warmest months, afternoon temperatures are in the upper sixties and lower seventies (20.0° to 22.2°C), reaching the upper seventies and the lower eighties (25.6° to 27.8°C) on a few days. Occasionally, hot, dry air from the east of the Cascade Mountains reaches this area and maximum temperatures are in the mid- or upper-nineties (34° to 38°C) for 1 to 3 days. Minimum temperatures are in the upper forties and the lower fifties (8.9° to 11.1°C). The lowest relative humidity and greatest danger of forest fires occur with east winds. The warmest temperature on record is 99°F (37°C) recorded in August 1981. Each month, May through September, has recorded temperatures in excess of 90°F (32.2°C).

(157) In summer and early fall, fog or low clouds form over the ocean and frequently move inland at night, but generally disappear by midday. In winter, under the influence of a surface high-pressure system, centered off the coast, fog, low clouds, and drizzle occur daily as long as this type of pressure pattern continues. An average of 236 days each year has fog. It is fairly evenly distributed throughout the year but the months of October through January have a slightly greater occurrence. The average frost-free season is from the last of April until mid-October.

(158) See Appendix B for **Quillayute climatological table**.

(159) In the vicinity of **Tatoosh Island** (see Tatoosh Island further on, this chapter), gales occur frequently with December and January being the favored months. Rainfall

is moderate averaging nearly 80 inches (2032 mm) each year. December is the rainiest month followed closely by January and February. July is the driest. An average of 251 days each year record measurable precipitation. Snowfall is light due to the extreme maritime influence and averages only 13.5 inches (343 mm) each year. It is most likely in January. The daily range in temperature is narrow, seldom exceeding ten degrees (-12.2°C). The average temperature on Tatoosh Island is 49°F (9°C). The average maximum is 53°F (11.7°) while the average minimum is 45°F (7.2°C). January is the coolest month and August the warmest. Extremes on Tatoosh Island include an extreme maximum temperature of 82°F (27.8°C) recorded in June 1955 and an extreme minimum of 14°F (-10°C) recorded in January 1950 and December 1964.

(160) The Coast Guard has established Quillayute River Regulated Navigation Area Warning Sign, a **rough bar advisory sign**, 34 feet above the water, visible from the channel looking seaward, on the NW corner of the old Coast Guard boathouse, to promote safety for small-boat operators. The sign is diamond shaped, painted white with an international orange border, and with the words "**Rough Bar**" in black letters. The sign is equipped with two quick flashing amber lights that will be activated when hazardous conditions exist and the bar is restricted to recreational and uninspected passenger vessels. Boaters are cautioned, however, that if the lights are not flashing, it is no guarantee that sea conditions are favorable.

(161) About 96 berths, electricity, gasoline, diesel fuel, water, ice, a launching ramp, and some marine supplies are available at the basin at La Push. A good highway connects La Push with U. S. Highway 101 N of Forks.

(162) From James Island NNW for 16.4 miles to Cape Alava, the rugged coast continues, with rocks and foul ground extending as much as 2 miles offshore; the land side consists of steep wooded bluffs and narrow beaches. The cliffs, however, are not continuous. The once densely timbered country ascends gradually E to the snow-capped mountains of the Olympic Range, which can be seen for many miles in clear weather. In 1974, areas of heavy logging activity were in evidence inland for many miles from this coastal area.

(163) **Cake Rock**, 116 feet high, is 2 miles NW of James Island and 1.5 miles offshore. This rock, about 200 yards long, has steep sides and its flat top is surmounted by a 20-foot mound. There are several other visible rocks between Cake Rock and the shore.

(164) **Cape Johnson**, small and not particularly prominent, projects less than 0.5 mile from the coastline, terminating in a vertical cliff 100 feet high.

(165) **Sea Lion Rock**, 78 feet high, 2.6 miles NW of Cape Johnson, is large, brown, covered with guano, and irregular in outline. A low black rock is 200 yards E of Sea Lion Rock. **Carroll Island**, 225 feet high, is 0.8 mile N of Sea Lion Rock. It has vertical whitish sides and a grassy top. A pillar rock, 134 feet high, lies 200 yards W, and a low black rock is 200 yards off the SE side. Carroll Island and the pillar rock are quite prominent, especially in the sunlight.

(166) **Jagged Island** is the larger of two high bare rocks, inside of Sea Lion Rock and Carroll Island, about 0.8 mile offshore. It is 320 feet high with steep sides. The smaller rock is 183 feet high. They are 200 yards apart, and between them are two pinnacle rocks close together. Many other rocks are shoreward of the island.

(167) **Hand Rock**, 33 feet high, is 1.5 miles N of Carroll Island and 1.5 miles offshore. So named from its shape, the rock is black with a white cap of guano on top. A larger rock lies 0.5 mile toward shore and is sometimes mistaken for Hand Rock.

(168) **White Rock**, 161 feet high, 1.7 miles S of Cape Alava and about 0.8 mile offshore, has nearly vertical sides and a rounded top; it is whitish, and in the sunlight is visible for a long distance. A group of large, low, black rocks lie 0.8 mile SSE of White Rock and 0.8 mile offshore.

Charts 18485, 18460

(169) **Cape Alava**, the westernmost point of the State of Washington, is 13 miles S of Cape Flattery. The seaward face is about 0.6 mile in extent. **Tskawahyah Island**, a steep rocky island, 142 feet high and with trees on top, is off its NW extremity. The shore is bordered by numerous rocks and covered ledges.

(170) **Flattery Rocks** and Umatilla Reef are rocks and islets extending W from Cape Alava for 2.3 miles. **Ozette Island**, 236 feet high, is 0.8 mile SW of the cape. The island, 0.5 mile long, is flat-topped with steep sides. About 0.3 mile off the S and SE sides are low, black rocks. **Bodelteh Islands**, 1.2 miles WNW of the N end of Cape Alava, have high bold seaward faces. The outer one is 198 feet high.

(171) In season, a few fishermen find shelter in an anchorage off the SE end of Ozette Island. The area is small and requires local knowledge to enter. It affords fair protection from the prevailing NW wind.

(172) **Umatilla Reef**, 2.3 miles NW of Cape Alava, the greatest danger to navigation off this section of the coast, is 0.7 mile W of the outer Bodelteh Island. It extends for 200 yards in a W direction and is about 75 yards wide. The reef consists of small, low, black rocks and some breakers. A rock covered 4½ fathoms is N of the reef at 48°11'44"N., 124°46'57"W., and a rock covered 2½ fathoms is S of the reef at 48°10'18"N., 124°47'02"W. There is a rock covered ½ fathom, 0.3 mile E of Umatilla Reef, which endangers passage inside, sometimes used by small boats. Umatilla Reef is difficult to make out, especially in thick weather.

(173) Between Cape Alava and Cape Flattery, the coast curves slightly in a series of bights, but continues as rugged as before. There are alternate stretches of wooded

(173) bluffs and high rocky cliffs. The country immediately back of the beach is not high, but it is densely wooded.

(174) **Point of Arches**, 5 miles NNE of Cape Alava, is the N point of the cliffs that extend some 1.5 miles S. Numerous rocks and ledges are offshore as far as about a mile.

(175) **Father and Son**, two rocks connected by a low reef, lie 0.6 mile offshore abreast the S end of the cliffs. The outer rock is 167 feet high, and the inner one 65 feet high. From the outer rock to Spike Rock there are several exposed rocks.

(176) **Spike Rock**, 35 feet high, sharp and bare, is 0.8 mile NW of the Point of Arches. It is the outermost of a chain of rocks, the largest of which is 185 feet high; there are three arches in these rocks. A rock that uncovers 5 feet is 0.3 mile WSW of Spike Rock.

(177) **Portage Head**, 2.5 miles N of Point of Arches, has a mile-long seaward face of bold irregular cliffs over 410 feet high. **Anderson Point**, at the N end of the cliffs, has a height of about 270 feet. A reef extends from the point toward Cape Flattery for 1.5 miles showing several low, black rocks awash, and one small rock 45 feet high. A rock covered 5 feet, is 1.3 miles NW of Portage Head.

(178) **Makah Bay** is a shallow bight included between Portage Head and Waatch Point. It affords indifferent shelter in N and E weather and a smooth sea, but is little used. The shores are low and sandy. **Waatch River** enters in the N part of the bight immediately E of Waatch Point. It is a tidal slough, and the valley through which it runs extends about 2 miles to Neah Bay on the Strait of Juan de Fuca. This low depression is one of the features for recognizing Cape Flattery.

(179) **Waatch Point**, 3 miles SE of Cape Flattery, is the SE extremity of the cliffs extending to the cape. This stretch is bordered by numerous rocks and ledges.

(180) **Fuca Pillar**, 0.2 mile S of the W point of Cape Flattery, is a rocky column 157 feet high and 60 feet in diameter, leaning slightly NW. It is 150 yards off the face of the cliff, and is more prominent from N than from S.

(181) **Cape Flattery**, a bold, rocky head with cliffs 120 feet high, rises to nearly 1,500 feet about 2 miles back from the beach. From S it looks like an island because of the low land in the valley of Waatch River. Numerous rocks and reefs border the cliffs E and S of the cape. Tide rips are particularly heavy off Cape Flattery.

(182) A large radar dome, highest and most prominent structure in the area, is on **Bahokus Peak**, the part of Cape Flattery about 2 miles back from the beach that rises to nearly 1,500 feet. This inflated plastic dome, about 50 feet in diameter, is on top of a tower, and was reported to be a very good landmark over low dense fog for vessels coming from the S.

(183) **Tatoosh Island**, 0.4 mile NW of Cape Flattery, is about 0.2 mile in diameter, 108 feet high, flat-topped, and bare. It is the largest of the group of rocks and reefs making out about 0.9 mile NW from the cape. The passage between Tatoosh Island and the cape is dangerous and constricted by two rocks awash near its center. Although sometimes used by local small craft, it cannot be recommended. The currents are strong and treacherous. Breakers may be in the area, especially during maximum currents.

(184) (See Appendix B for **Tatoosh Island climatological table**.)

(185) **Cape Flattery Light** (48°23'31"N., 124°44'13"W.), 165 feet above the water, is shown from a 35-foot skeleton tower, adjacent to the old white conical tower lighthouse on the W end of Tatoosh Island.

(186) A rocky patch, covered 7½ fathoms, on which the sea breaks occasionally in a W swell, is 1.4 miles SW of the light.

(187) **Duncan Rock** and **Duntze Rock**, the two principal dangers NNW of Tatoosh Island, are respectively, 1 mile and 1.3 miles from the light. Duncan Rock is small, low, and black; Duntze Rock is covered 2¾ fathoms. A lighted whistle buoy is 500 yards NW of Duntze Rock. Ledges and rocks constrict the passage between Duncan Rock and Tatoosh Island to less than 0.5 mile, and strong currents and tide rips make it hazardous.

Charts 18460, 18480

(188) **Swiftsure Bank**, about 3.5 miles in extent, is off the mouth of the Strait of Juan de Fuca, NW of the submarine valley making into the strait. The bank has a least depth of 18 fathoms.

(189) During the summer, large numbers of fishing vessels may be trolling or at anchor on Swiftsure Bank. During periods of low visibility, which are not uncommon in this vicinity, extreme caution must be exercised to avoid collision with fishing boats; most of these craft tend to defy radar detection.

(190) U.S. Navy operating areas are SW of the entrance to the Strait of Juan de Fuca. Mariners should exercise caution when navigating in this vicinity while exercises are in progress.

Carmanah Point to Amphitrite Point, Canada

(191) The coast from Carmanah Point to Cape Beale is very dangerous and, except during fine weather and offshore winds, should be given a wide berth.

(192) **Carmanah Point** is on the Vancouver Island shore, 13 miles N of Tatoosh Island. A light, 175 feet above the water, is shown from a white octagonal concrete tower on the point.

(193) **Clo-oose**, an abandoned village, is 4 miles NW of Carmanah Point in the small cove at the mouth of the Cheewhat River, E of the entrance to Nitinat Lake.

(194) A reef 0.8 mile long in a NW direction, with a rock awash in its center, is off this cove. It is marked by a lighted whistle buoy 0.8 mile SW of the rock.

(195) **Tsusiat Lake** is 8.5 miles NW of Carmanah Light. At the seaward end of the lake is a conspicuous waterfall which is visible far off even in hazy weather, and may help fix a vessel's position as it is the only waterfall on

(196) **Pachena Point**, 25 miles NW of Cape Flattery, is marked by a light.

(197) **Seabird Rocks** are off the entrance to Pachena Bay, 3 miles NW of Pachena Point. The largest is about 48 feet high, bare, and of small extent; it is marked by a light. There is no safe passage between Seabird Rocks and the shores NE, and the rocks should not be approached closer than 1.5 miles.

(198) **Cape Beale** is a bold rocky point, 120 feet high. A reef with rocks above and below water extends about 0.8 mile SW from it. **Cape Beale Light** (48°47'11"N., 125°12'56"W.), 167 feet above the water, is shown from a red trapezoidal skeleton tower with a white rectangular daymark near the W extremity of the cape.

(199) **Barkley Sound**, an extensive arm of the sea 35 miles NW of Cape Flattery, lies between Cape Beale and Amphitrite Point. It is 15 miles wide at its entrance, and though encumbered by numerous islands and rocks, it maintains a breadth of 13 miles for 8 miles inland, above which it separates into several narrow inlets. The shores are low, except in the N part and among the inlets, where they become high, rugged, and mountainous.

(200) In the W part of the sound are innumerable rocks and islands with navigable channels between them. Entrance should not be attempted without local knowledge or a pilot. **Imperial Eagle Channel** is the easiest of access.

(201) **Amphitrite Point** is the W entrance point of Barkley Sound. A light, 49 feet above the water, is shown from a white rectangular tower on the end of the point; a sound signal is at the light. A lighted Whistle buoy is 0.6 mile S of the point.

(202) A more detailed description of Canadian waters is given in Pub. No. 154, Sailing Directions (Enroute) for British Columbia, published by the National Geospatial-Intelligence Agency, and the Sailing Directions, British Columbia Coast, (South Portion) Vol. I, published by the Canadian Hydrographic Service.

Routes

(203) In clear weather no difficulty will be experienced in approaching the entrance to the Strait of Juan de Fuca from any direction, as the land on both sides is high and Cape Flattery is readily distinguished, particularly from S, owing to the low land between Makah and Neah Bays. Lights are available on both sides of the strait to assist in obtaining a fix.

(204) In thick weather soundings will assist in estimating the distance from shore. Vessels should pick up the 100-fathom curve and be guided by the soundings. The relationship between the 100- and 50-fathom curve is a good indication for fixing the position; vessels should not proceed inside the 50-fathom curve until a fix has been obtained. The mountain peaks in the interior sometimes can be seen when the coast is obscured by fog.

Depths

(205) The depths in the approaches to the Strait of Juan de Fuca are very irregular, especially outside the 50-fathom curve. There is a deep submarine valley with depths of over 100 fathoms and a width of 2 to 4 miles, between the 100-fathom curves, which leads from about 37 miles SSW of Cape Flattery, rounds this cape at a distance of 2 miles, and extends about 32 miles into the strait. The 100-fathom curve on the W side of this submarine valley is very irregular, but on the E side it is more regular. Within the strait the curve is regular on both sides of the valley.

Currents

(206) The current on Swiftsure Bank is described in the Tidal Current Tables. Off the entrance of the Strait of Juan de Fuca the coastal current is influenced by the flow into and out of the strait. On the flood there is a set into all the sounds on the Vancouver Island shore, and this, combined with the prevailing NW current and light S winds, with possibly some swell from the same direction, makes the coast in the vicinity and W of Carmanah Light dangerous, especially for small vessels. Many strandings have occurred on the Vancouver Island shore.

(207) The flood current entering the Strait of Juan de Fuca sets with considerable velocity over Duncan and Duntze Rocks, but instead of running in the direction of the channel there is a continued set toward the Vancouver Island shore, which is experienced as far as Race Rocks. The flood current also has more velocity on the N shore of the strait than on the S.

(208) The ebb current is felt most along the S shore of the strait, and between New Dungeness Light and Crescent Bay there is a decided set S and W, especially during large tides. With wind and swell against the current, a short choppy sea is raised near the entrance to the strait. (For additional information on currents in the Strait of Juan de Fuca, see chapter 12.)

(209) Sailing craft approaching the strait should keep well off the mainland coast S of Cape Flattery, unless working to windward against a fine N wind, which is frequently found during the summer. In this case the coast may be approached to within 3 miles. At other times there is no inducement to hug the coast, on which a long rolling swell frequently sets, and this swell, meeting the SE gales of winter, causes a confused sea. The cape and its offlying dangers should be given a berth of at least 3 miles, as the tidal current sometimes sets with great velocity toward Duncan and Duntze Rocks. It is equally necessary when entering or leaving the strait to avoid the coast of Vancouver Island between Port San Juan and Bonilla Point, when there is any appearance of bad weather.

(210) Sailing vessels making the strait during the winter, especially during November and December, and

(211) experiencing the E and SE winds prevalent at that season, should endeavor to hold a position S or SW of Cape Flattery, and should on no account open the entrance of the strait until an opportunity offers of getting well inside. It is also important to remember that, though it may be blowing strongly from the S or SSW outside, on rounding Cape Flattery, an E wind may be found blowing out of the strait, and a vessel would then find the Vancouver Island coast a dangerous lee shore.

(211) Coming from the W with a heavy W or NW gale and thick weather, vessels uncertain of their positions should lie-to on soundings at not less than 30 miles from the entrance or on the edge of the bank. These gales seldom last more than 12 hours, and if they veer toward the SW the weather will clear and vessels may bear up for the strait.

Fog

(212) The fog is generally heavier near the entrance, decreasing in density and frequency up the strait. Near the entrance the fog sometimes stands like a wall, and vessels entering the strait run out of it into clear bright weather, even before passing Tatoosh Island. The fog frequently extends a long distance seaward. The wind gradually works the fog into the strait, and it will follow the N shore past Port San Juan to the Sombrio River; occasionally it will reach as far as Sooke Inlet and at times to Race Rocks. As a rule, however, the fog moves farther into the strait along the S shore, at times reaching Port Townsend; frequently the N shore is clear when the S shore is enveloped in fog.

(213) During the spring, fog is frequent in the strait. With the W wind it often stops at the headland between Crescent and Freshwater Bays, the fog then extending W while it is clear to E. When fog extends past Freshwater Bay the small area about the W bight will often be clear.

Weather, Strait of Juan de Fuca and vicinity

(214) In summer, the prevailing NW winds draw into the strait, increasing toward evening and at times blowing 25 knots before midnight. This occurs, however, only when the winds are strong outside. In light winds, sailing vessels may be a week from Cape Flattery to Admiralty Inlet, and vice versa.

(215) In winter, SE winds draw out of the strait, causing a confused cross-sea off the entrance, the heavy SW swell meeting that coming out. Under these conditions small outboard vessels, especially sail, often make Neah or Clallam Bays and await more favorable weather. The weather off the entrance as a rule is exceptionally severe, and wrecks are of frequent occurrence. The heavy broken seas are probably due to the shoaling off the entrance, the irregularity and velocity of the currents, and the conflict between the wind drawing out of the strait and that along the outer coast.

(216) The rainfall in the vicinity of the entrance is considerable, even during the summer, although the heaviest rains occur between December and March.

TIDAL INFORMATION					
Chart	Station	LAT/LONG	Mean Higher High Water*	Mean High Water*	Mean Low Water*
18460	Sekiu, Clallam Bay, Strait of Juan de Fuca	48°16'N/124°18'W	7.5	6.7	1.8
18480	La Push, Quillayute River	47°55'N/124°38'W	8.4	7.7	1.4
18485	Tatoosh Island, Cape Flattery	48°24'N/124°44'W	8.0	7.2	1.5
18485	Neah Bay, Strait of Juan de Fuca	48°22'N/124°37'W	8.0	7.1	1.6
18502	Montesano, Chehalis River, Grays Harbor	46°58'N/123°36'W	8.2	7.7	0.9
18502	Aberdeen, Grays Harbor	46°58'N/123°51'W	10.1	9.4	1.5
18504	Naselle River, Willapa Bay	46°23'N/123°50'W	10.8	10.0	1.3
18504	Long Island, Paradise Point, Willapa Bay	46°28'N/123°57'W	10.2	9.4	1.4
18504	Nahcotta, Willapa Bay	46°30'N/124°02'W	10.0	9.3	1.4
18504	Bay Center, Palix River, Willapa Bay	46°37'N/123°57'W	9.2	8.5	1.4
18504	South Bend, Willapa River, Willapa Bay	46°40'N/123°48'W	9.8	9.1	1.4
18504	Raymond, Willapa River	46°41'N/123°45'W	10.0	9.3	1.4
18504	Toke Point, Willapa Bay	46°43'N/123°58'W	8.9	8.2	1.4

* Heights in feet referred to datum of sounding MLLW.
Real-time water levels, tide predictions, and tidal current predictions are available at:
http://tidesandcurrents.noaa.gov
To determine mean tide range subtract Mean Low Water from Mean High Water.
Data as of September 2012

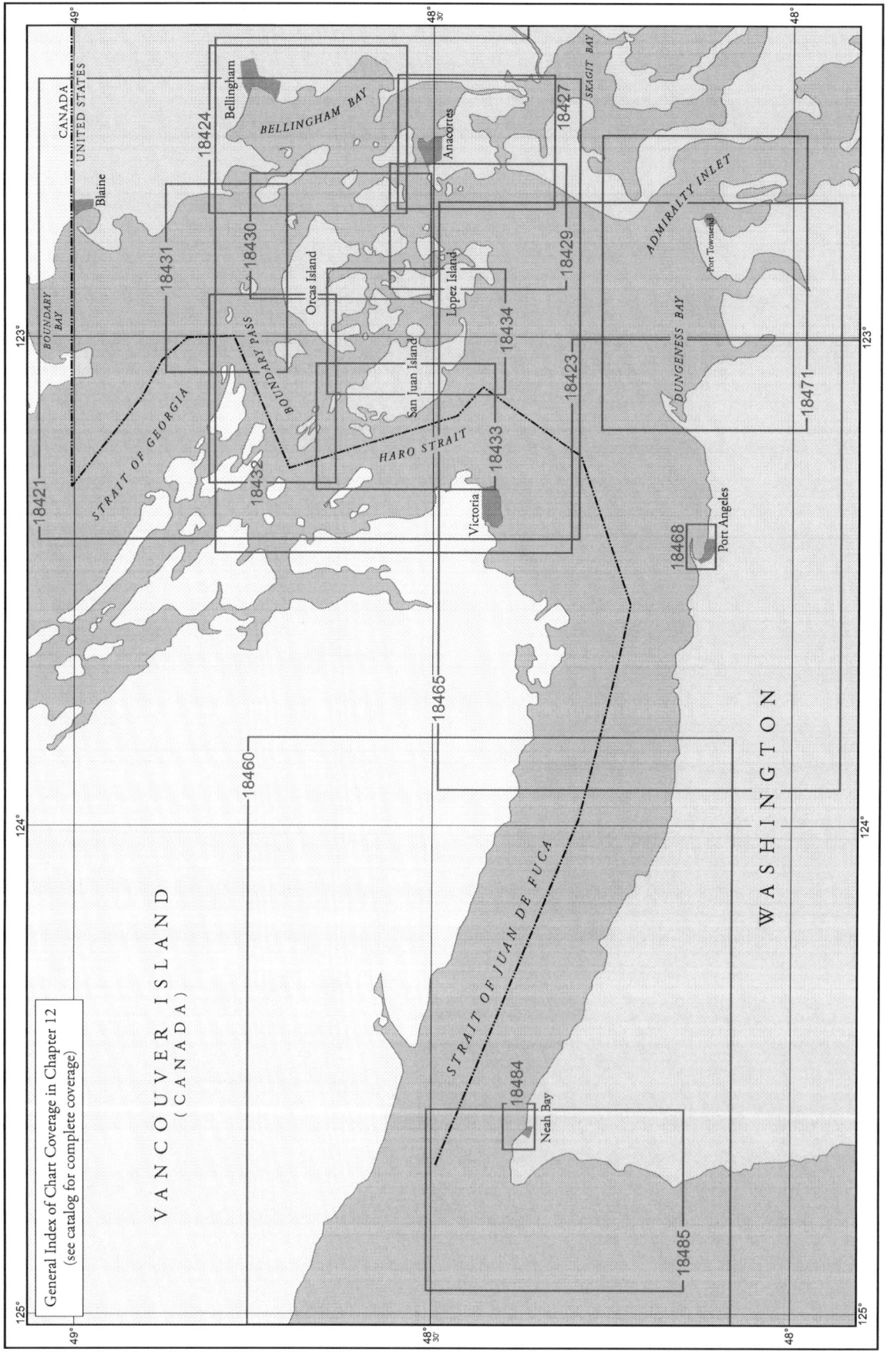

Strait of Juan De Fuca and Georgia, Washington

Chart 18400

(1) This chapter includes the Strait of Juan de Fuca, Sequim Bay, Port Discovery, the San Juan Islands and its various passages and straits, Deception Pass, Fidalgo Island, Skagit and Similk Bays, Swinomish Channel, Fidalgo, Padilla, and Bellingham Bays, Lummi Bay, Semiahmoo Bay and Drayton Harbor, and the Strait of Georgia as far N as Burrard Inlet. The more important U.S. harbors described are Neah Bay, Port Angeles, Friday Harbor, La Connor, Anacortes, Bellingham, and Blaine Harbor. Deep-draft vessels use the harbors at Port Angeles, Anacortes, and Bellingham, the principal cities in the area. The Canadian coasts are only briefly described. (See Pub. 154, Sailing Directions (Enroute) for British Columbia, published by the National Geospatial-Intelligence Agency, and the Sailing Directions, British Columbia Coast, (South Portion) Vol. 1, published by the Canadian Hydrographic Service, for detailed information on Canadian waters.)

(2) **Strait of Juan de Fuca** separates the S shore of Vancouver Island, Canada, from the N coast of the State of Washington. The entrance to the strait lies between parallels 48°23'N., and 48°36'N., on the meridian of 124°45'W. This important body of water is the connecting channel between the ocean and the interisland passages extending S to Puget Sound and N to the inland waters of British Columbia and southeastern Alaska.

(3) The commerce of this region is extensive, both foreign and domestic. Vast quantities of lumber, fish, grain, and general merchandise are exported, while the manufacturing and shipbuilding industries are important. Several transcontinental railroads have their terminals on Puget Sound. There are many steamer lines, foreign and domestic, operating from this area to places across the Pacific or through the Panama Canal, in addition to the coastal vessels.

(4) At its entrance and for 50 miles E to Race Rocks, the strait is about 11 miles wide and then widens to about 16 miles for 30 miles E to Whidbey Island, its E boundary. The waters as a rule are deep until near the shore with few outlying dangers, most of which are in the E part. The shores on both sides are heavily wooded, rising rapidly to elevations of considerable height, and, except in a few places, are bold and rugged.

(5) The navigation of these waters is relatively simple in clear weather. The aids to navigation are numerous. In thick weather, because of strong and irregular currents, extreme caution and vigilance must be exercised. Strangers should take a pilot.

COLREGS Demarcation Lines

(6) The International Regulations for Preventing Collisions at Sea, 1972 (72 COLREGS) apply on all the waters of the Strait of Juan de Fuca, Haro Strait, and Strait of Georgia. (See **80.1385** and **80.1390**, chapter 2.)

Traffic Separation Scheme

(7) The **Strait of Juan de Fuca Traffic Separation Scheme** has been established in the Strait of Juan de Fuca. The separation scheme consists of five sets of traffic lanes: the **Western Approach** and the **Southwestern Approach** from the ocean; the **Western Lanes** in the Strait; the **Southern Lanes** to Port Angeles; the **Northern Lanes** to Victoria; and two precautionary areas, one WNW of Cape Flattery and the other N of Port Angeles. Each set of lanes consists of **inbound** and **outbound traffic lanes** with **separation zones**. Each precautionary area is marked by lighted yellow buoys. The lighted buoy marking the precautionary area WNW of Cape Flattery is equipped with a racon. The purpose of these buoys is to assist in the separation of inbound and outbound vessels transiting the Strait of Juan de Fuca to eliminate as much as possible the cross vessel traffic that now occurs between the entrance to the Strait of Juan de Fuca at Cape Flattery and the pilot stations at Port Angeles and Victoria, BC. It is recommended that all vessels navigate so as to leave these buoys to port.

(8) The **Haro Strait and Strait of Georgia Traffic Separation Scheme**, consisting of **inbound** and **outbound traffic lanes** with **separation zones**, continues E from the Victoria Approach segment of **Strait of Juan de Fuca Traffic Separation Scheme** to Victoria, BC, thence through Haro Strait, Boundary Pass, and the Strait of Georgia, to Vancouver, BC.

(9) Two abbreviated traffic separation schemes, also consisting of inbound and outbound traffic separation lanes, with separation zones, connect the Haro Strait and Strait of Georgia Scheme with the **Puget Sound Traffic Service** (described later in this chapter.) One leads NW from the precautionary area E of Hein Bank into Haro Strait, and the other leads NW from the precautionary area S of Alden Bank into the Strait of Georgia. All Traffic Separation Schemes within the Strait of Juan de Fuca and Strait of Georgia have been adopted by the IMO. (See **167.1 through 167.15**, chapter 2, for additional information.)

Washington State Requirements

Reports of Oil Spills and Vessel Emergencies
All vessels must report oil spills or potential oil spills to both:
1. Washington State   800–258–5990
2. National Response Center 800–424–8802

Tank vessels and cargo and passenger ships 300 gross tons or larger must make notifications to Washington State for vessel emergencies, including a loss or serious degradation of propulsion, steering, means of navigation, electrical generating capability and seakeeping capability constituting a substantial threat of pollution affecting Washington state natural resources. In addition to any notifications to the USCG, the owner or operator must notify the state of any vessel emergency that results in the discharge or substantial threat of a discharge of oil to state waters or that may affect the natural resources of the state within one hour of the onset of the emergency.

Tug Escorts for Laden Tankers
Any laden oil tanker, whether enrolled or registered, proceeding east of a line extending from Discovery Island Light (British Columbia, CN) south to New Dungeness Light (Washington State, US) must be escorted by a tug or tugs with an aggregate shaft horsepower equivalent to five percent of the deadweight tons of that tanker. For additional details see Washington state law at 88.16 Revised Code of Washington (RCW).

Emergency Response Tug at Neah Bay
An industry-funded emergency response tug is located at Neah Bay at the entrance to the Strait of Juan de Fuca. The tug is available 24 hours a day and can be underway within twenty minutes of a decision to deploy. The purpose of the tug is to assist vessels having propulsion and steering failures or that are directed by either the US or Canadian Coast Guard to obtain towing assistance. Among other capabilities, the tug is intended to be able to make up to, stop, hold, and tow a drifting or disabled vessel of 180,000 metric dead weight tons in severe weather conditions. The tug can be contacted through the USCG VTS or the Puget Sound Marine Exchange.

Washington State Vessel Inspections
The Washington State Department of Ecology regulates cargo and passenger vessels and tank vessels operating in Washington waters.
- A cargo vessel is any self-propelled vessel in commerce that is 300 gross tons or more.
- A passenger vessel is any vessel 300 gross tons or more with a fuel capacity of at least 6,000 gallons that carries passengers for compensation.
- A tank vessel is a ship that is constructed or adapted to carry, or that carries, oil in bulk as cargo or cargo residue.

Washington State Ecology inspectors may conduct vessel inspections on regulated cargo, passenger, and fishing vessels when in Washington waters. Additional information is available at:
http://www.ecy.wa.gov/programs/spills/prevention/VesselTechAssist/AISsubstantialrisk.html/

Oil Transfer Requirements
Safe bunkering procedures must be followed during fueling operations. For vessels 300 gross tons or greater, Washington State Ecology inspectors may conduct inspections of these regulated oil transfers on vessels receiving fuel for propulsion within Washington waters. Details can be found in Washington Administrative Code (WAC) 317-40. Information is also available at:
http://www.ecy.wa.gov/programs/spills/prevention/VesselTechAssist/Bunkering.html/

Tank vessels delivering oil in bulk to a non-recreational vessel or facility within Washington waters must meet state oil transfer requirements. They may also be subject to Washington State oil transfer inspections for these regulated oil transfers. Details can be found in WAC 173-184. Additional information is available at:
http://www.ecy.wa.gov/programs/spills/prevention/VesselTechAssist/vessel_otr.html/

- For a transfer of more than 100 gallons of bulk oil to a facility or non-recreational vessel, the delivering vessel must submit an Advance Notice of Transfer (ANT) report to Ecology. This ANT must be submitted 24 hours prior to the transfer for facilities or within the timeframe required by local USCG Captain of the Port.
- For convenience, the ANT report can be made either:
online using the Ecology website at:
https://secureaccess.wa.gov/ecy/ants, by
e-mail: OilTransferNotifications@ecy.wa.gov, or by
fax: 360–407–7288 or 800–664–9184.

Contingency Plan Requirements
Tank vessels and cargo and passenger ships 300 gross tons or larger transiting Washington waters must either have a Washington State Department of Ecology approved oil spill contingency plan or be a member of a non-profit corporation that provides oil spill response capabilities consistent with their Washington State approved contingency plan. The non-profit corporation for Puget Sound and Grays Harbor is the Washington State Maritime Cooperative (WSMC). Additional information is available at:
http://www.ecy.wa.gov/programs/spills/preparedness/cplan/cplans.html/

(10) Vessels so desiring, may while transiting the Strait of Juan de Fuca, contact the Puget Sound Vessel Traffic Service by calling SEATTLE TRAFFIC on VHF-FM channel 5A to receive desired information on known traffic, aids to navigation discrepancies, and locally hazardous weather conditions. In Admiralty Inlet, S of a line between Nodule Point on Marrowstone Island and Bush Point on Whidbey Island, vessels should use VHF-FM channel 14 to contact SEATTLE TRAFFIC. VHF-FM channel 13 should be used to make passing arrangements in U.S. waters and is Seattle Traffic's secondary frequency, however because channel 13 is not used in Canadian waters as the primary bridge-to-bridge radiotelephone channel, vessels are encouraged to use channel 5A to make passing arrangements in the Strait of Juan de Fuca. Preliminary calls to SEATTLE TRAFFIC on VHF-FM channel 16 are not required or desired. (See Traffic Separation Schemes, chapter 1, for additional information.)

(11) The Canadian Government recommends that ships conduct themselves in accordance with the navigational procedures set forth in the Ship Routing Regulations when navigating in or near the traffic separation scheme in Canadian waters. Mariners are advised that the Canadian Ship Routing Regulations are based upon the International Maritime Organization's "General Principles of Ships' Routing", except for a relaxation that permits vessels engaged in fishing to proceed in any direction in or near traffic lanes and on the high seas. (Canadian Ship Routing Regulations are published in the Annual Edition of Canadian Notices to Mariners.)

(12) The Canadian waters SE and E of Vancouver Island are a **Vessel Traffic Management Zone**.

(13) Complete details of the traffic separation schemes and the vessel traffic management and information system for the coastal waters of southern British Columbia are given in Pub. No. 154, Sailing Directions Enroute, British Columbia, published by the National Geospatial-Intelligence Agency, Sailing Directions, British Columbia Coast (South Portion), Volume 1, published by the Canadian Hydrographic Service, and the Annual Edition of Canadian Notices to Mariners, published by the Canadian Coast Guard.

Vessel Traffic Service

(14) The U.S. Coast Guard operates a mandatory Vessel Traffic Service (VTS) in the Strait of Juan de Fuca, Rosario Strait, Admiralty Inlet, Puget Sound and navigable waters adjacent to these areas. Vessel operating procedures and designated radiotelephone frequencies are published in **33 CFR 161**, chapter 2, and/or the VTS User's Manual. Mariners should consult these sources for applicable rules and reporting requirements. 'Seattle Traffic' is a full service VTS providing Information Service, Traffic Organization Service and Navigation Assistance Services to vessels operating in the VTS area. The System is designed to prevent collisions and groundings and to protect the navigable waters concerned from environmental harm resulting from such collisions and groundings.

(15) The **Puget Sound Vessel Traffic Service** comprises three major components: a Traffic Separation Scheme, a Vessel Movement Reporting System, and radar surveillance. The Traffic Separation Scheme comprises a network of one-way traffic lanes, separation zones in between, and precautionary areas. Most traffic lanes are 1,000 yards wide and are separated by 500-yard-wide separation zones.

(16) The Vessel Movement Reporting System is based upon a VHF-FM communications network maintained continuously by the Coast Guard Vessel Traffic Center in Seattle. This center will process information received from vessels in required and voluntary reports, and will, in turn, disseminate navigational safety information to vessels participating in the service. The mariner is cautioned that information provided by the vessel traffic center is, with the exception of AIS, radar, or closed circuit television camera information, largely generated from these reports by vessels and can be no more accurate than that received. Additionally, the Coast Guard may not have first-hand knowledge of hazardous circumstances existing in the Vessel Traffic Service Area, and unreported hazards may confront the mariner at any time. The Vessel Traffic Service is shown on the appropriate nautical charts of the area.

(17) The rules governing vessels operating in the Vessel Traffic Service are given in **161.1 through 161.23 and 161.55**, chapter 2. In addition, the proper operating procedures are contained in the Puget Sound Vessel Traffic Service User Manual, available at no charge from Commander, U.S. Coast Guard Sector Puget Sound, 1519 Alaskan Way South, Seattle, WA 98134-1192.

(18) A **Cooperative Vessel Traffic Service (CVTS)** has been established in the Strait of Juan de Fuca region, based on an agreement between the United States and Canada. Operated by the U.S. Coast Guard and the Canadian Coast Guard, the system is intended to enhance safe and expeditious vessel movement, and to minimize risk of pollution to the marine environment; the system is **mandatory**. The appropriate Vessel Traffic Center (VTC) (Tofino Traffic, Seattle Traffic, Victoria Traffic) administers the rules issued by both nations, however, it will enforce only its own set of rules within its jurisdiction. The CVTS Exchange lines delineating the sector boundaries and frequency change lines between Vessel Traffic Center management authorities are published below and in the VTS User's Manual. Useful information for operating in the CVTS area is available via http://www.uscg.mil/d13/cvts.

CVTS Sector Boundary and Exchange Lines

(19) **Part 1** – The 124°40' west meridian of Longitude in Juan de Fuca Strait from the Canadian low-water line to the U.S. low-water line as depicted on official charts. **Part 2** – Church Point on Vancouver Island, to Race Rocks Light, due easterly to the intersection of the

U.S./Canadian border at 48°17'53.0"N., 123°14'06.0"W, north-easterly to Hein Bank in position 48°21'05.62"N., 123°02'45.72"W, northerly to Cattle Point Light on San Juan Island, along the shoreline to Lime Kiln Light, to Kellet Bluff Light on Henry Island, along the shoreline to the tip of McCracken Point at the northernmost point of Henry Island, to the southernmost point on Stuart Island in position 48°39'28"N., 123°11'05"W, along the shoreline to Turn Point Light, to Sandy Point on Waldron Island, along the shoreline to Point Hammond, to Patos Island Light, to Alden Bank in position 48°50'23.39"N., 122°52'13.67"W, then due north to Boundary Bay in position 49°00'07.5"N., 122°52'13.67"W, then due east along the international boundary to the shoreline in Semiahmoo Bay.

(20) Mariners are advised that **Ferry Routes** may differ from the established Vessel Traffic Services, Traffic Separation Schemes, and Cooperative Vessel Traffic Management Systems for the entire Strait of Juan de Fuca and Puget Sound area.

(21) All vessels 30 meters or greater, including tug and tows, when inbound and crossing longitude 127°W, latitude 48°N, or within 50 nautical miles of Vancouver Island, whichever occurs first, are requested to contact **Tofino Traffic** on VHF-FM Channel 74.

(22) In accordance with the Cooperative Vessel Traffic Service, the United States and Canada, in cooperation with industry and the British Columbia Coast Pilots have established a **Special Operating Area (SOA)** at the intersection of Haro Strait and Boundary Pass in the vicinity of Turn Point Light (48°41'20"N., 123°14'15"W.). This special area will help reduce the risk of incidents between both commercial and recreational vessels transiting the boundary waters of Haro Strait and Boundary Pass. The **Turn Point Special Operating Area** consists of those Canadian and United States waters contained within a four sided area connected by the following co-ordinates:

(23) (1) 48°41'20"N., 123°14'15"W. (Turn Point Light);
(24) (2) 48°42'24"N., 123°13'54"W.;
(25) (3) 48°41'05"N., 123°17'37"W. (Arachne Reef Light);
(26) (4) 48°39'44"N., 123°16'26"W. (Tom Point Light).

(27) The **Turn Point SOA** applies to participating vessels of **100 meters/328 feet or longer** operating within or approaching the **Turn Point SOA** from Boundary Pass, southbound for Haro Strait, northbound for Boundary Pass or Swanson Channel. These vessels are requested not to enter the **Turn Point SOA** when another VTS participant of 100 meters or more in length is already located in the area, unless:

(28) (a) When following astern, maintain a minimum of 0.5 mile separation with the vessel ahead.

(29) (b) When overtaking in the **SOA**, with the concurrence of Victoria Traffic that there is no opposing traffic and a Closest Point of Approach (CPA) of at least 0.5 mile is maintained.

(30) (c) If outbound from Boundary Pass and meeting an inbound vessel from Haro Strait already in the **SOA**, enter only after the outbound vessel is past the heading of the inbound vessel engaged in the turn and maintain at least a 0.5 mile CPA.

(31) (d) If inbound from Haro Strait and meeting an outbound vessel from Boundary Pass already in the **SOA**, enter only after the outbound vessel has crossed a bearing line between Turn Point and Arachne Reef and maintain at least a 0.5 mile CPA.

(32) All vessels should maintain a distance of at least 0.3 mile off Turn Point. Special circumstances are considered to exist when more than two vessels, greater than 100 meters or more, are interacting around the **SOA** at the same time. All 100 meter vessels in a special circumstance should maintain a CPA of at least 0.5 mile, continuing to maintain a distance of 0.3 mile off Turn Point.

(33) All VTS participants will verbally communicate with Victoria Traffic on VHF-FM channel 11 when 3 miles from Turn Point. VTS participants are expected to make safe arrangements with other VTS participants within or near the SOA.

Regulated navigation area

(34) Due to heavy vessel concentrations, the waters of the Strait of Juan de Fuca, the San Juan Islands, the Strait of Georgia, and Puget Sound, and all adjacent waters, are a regulated navigation area. (See **165.1 through 165.13 and 165.1301**, chapter 2, for regulations.)

Caution

(35) Since logging is one of the main industries of the region, free-floating logs and submerged deadheads or sinkers are a constant source of danger in the Strait of Juan de Fuca and Puget Sound. The danger is increased during freshets, after storms, and unusually high tides. **Deadheads** or **sinkers** are logs which have become adrift from rafts or booms, have become waterlogged, and float in a vertical position with one end just awash, rising and falling with the tide.

Currents, Cape Flattery to Race Rocks

(36) The currents may attain velocities of 2 to 4 knots, varying with the range of tide, and are influenced by strong winds. E of Race Rocks, in the wider portion of the strait, the velocity is considerably less. At Race Rocks and Discovery Island the velocity may be 6 knots or more.

(37) The **flood current** entering the Strait of Juan de Fuca sets with considerable velocity over Duncan and Duntze Rocks, but, instead of running in the direction of the channel, it has a continued set toward the Vancouver Island shore which is experienced as far as Race

Rocks. The flood current velocity is greater on the N shore of the strait than on the S.

(38) The **ebb current** is felt most along the S shore of the strait, and between New Dungeness Light and Crescent Bay there is a decided set S and W, especially during large tides. With the wind and swell against the current, a short choppy sea is raised near the entrance to the strait.

(39) The current movement is complicated by a large daily inequality. The Tidal Current Tables should be consulted for times and velocities.

(40) **Tide rips** occur off the prominent points and in the vicinity of the banks. These are particularly heavy off Cape Flattery, Race Rocks, Dungeness Spit, and Point Wilson, at times becoming dangerous to small vessels.

Weather (Winds and visibility), Straits of Juan De Fuca and Georgia

(41) Winds are strongest from October through March. This results from the numerous winter storms that move through these waters; this is also an area where storms tend to intensify. As low-pressure systems approach the coast, winds strengthen and back to the SE quadrant, sometimes reaching gale force. After the storm passes, winds veer to the SW or NW. Gales usually last less than 1 day whereas the interval between storms normally varies from 1 to 5 days or up to 2 weeks when a strong high-pressure system settles in. These systems can also present local wind problems in the Georgia Strait. The mountainous terrain of this region plays an important part in determining the direction and speed of the wind. There are normally two wind seasons; winter lasts from October through March, while a summer regime covers the other 6 months.

(42) From October through March, winds at the Pacific entrance to the Strait of Juan de Fuca blow mostly out of the SE through SW. Gales blow on 4 to 6 days per month. They can come from any direction, however, SE winds are consistently the strongest, averaging about 18 knots. Strong SE winds raise dangerous confused seas off Cape Flattery, when they meet the long, rolling SW swells that frequent these waters. The frequent strong winds from a S quarter make the Vancouver coast between Cape Cook and Port San Juan a dangerous lee shore. When gales blow from the SW through W, it is usually safer inside the Strait than out. In general, winds are strongest and gales more frequent in the W end of the Strait. In the open water of the middle of the Strait, winter winds blow mostly out of the E through SE. Gales occur on about 2 to 4 days per month in the E half. The S shore is protected from the SE gales; Port Angeles provides good shelter. An approaching storm often sets up strong E winds in the central part of the Strait. This, in turn, sets up a drainage of air from the Georgia Strait, so that winds near the E entrance are frequently from the N through NE. As the storm moves inland, it produces a reversal of this flow. Winds blow from the W through most of the strait, backing to the SW in the E. Winds near the W entrance have reached 65 knots with gusts to 90 knots. In the strait, 50-knot winds and 80-knot gusts have been reported.

(43) Summer winds at sea blow mainly from the SW through NW around the subtropical Pacific high. Heating of the North American continent helps draw air into the Strait of Juan de Fuca. This sea breeze reinforces the prevailing flow and results in winds up to 30 knots in the late afternoon. The land breeze opposes the normal flow, and calms are often the rule in early morning. SW through W winds are most frequent in the Strait of Juan de Fuca.

(44) In few parts of the world is the vigilance of the mariner more called upon than when entering the Strait of Juan de Fuca from the Pacific in fog. Sea fog is the most common type, and it is at its worst from about July through October. Local land fog extends the visibility hazard into the winter. Fog is most frequent at the W end of the Strait. Here, visibilities drop to less than 0.75 mile (1.4km) on about 55 days annually, compared to about 35 days in the E end. Dense fog sometimes hangs over the ocean entrance to the Strait for days at a time; this is most likely during calms or light breezes. It gives the appearance of a wall, and ships entering often run into clear, bright weather before they pass Tatoosh Island. Often the fog is carried E on the W sea breeze. When this happens, the fog usually penetrates farther E along the S shore. It is much more likely to reach Port Angeles or Port Townsend than Victoria. In spring, the E penetration of an infrequent fog is usually limited to Crescent or Freshwater Bays. Often when thick weather prevails in the Strait of Juan de Fuca, skies are clear N of Race Rocks.

Pilotage, Strait of Juan de Fuca and Puget Sound

(45) Pilotage is compulsory for all foreign vessels and U.S. vessels engaged in foreign trade. Pilotage is optional for U.S. vessels engaged in the coastwise trade with a federally licensed pilot on board.

(46) Puget Sound Pilots serve all U.S. ports and places E of 123°24'W., including Port Angeles, Puget Sound, and adjacent inland waters. The office address is: Puget Sound Pilots, 101 Stewart Street, Suite 900, Seattle, WA 98101; telephone, 206–448–4455 (24 hours), 206–728–6400; Fax 206–448–3405. Pilot station address is: 305 Ediz Hook Road, P.O. Box 788, Port Angeles, WA 98362; telephone, 800–221–0234, 360–457–7944; fax 360–452–8566.

(47) Port Angeles has been designated as the pilotage station for all vessels enroute to or from the sea. The pilot station is located on Ediz Hook about 0.7 mile W of Ediz Hook Light (see chart 18468). There are two pilot boats, both are 22 meters in length with white hulls and orange houses. The standard day and night signals are displayed. The pilot station and pilot boats are equipped with radar to locate and track vessels, radio communication can be made by calling "Puget Sound Pilots" on VHF-FM channel 13.

(48) Pilotage should be arranged between 0800 and 1700 at least 24 hours in advance of inbound ETA through the vessel's agent, by direct telephone communication with Puget Sound Pilots at the previously mentioned telephone numbers, or the Marine Exchange of Puget Sound (telephone: 206–443–3830 or Telex 6734358 "Matex"). If subsequent conditions make it necessary, an amended estimated time of arrival should be made. Inbound vessels are requested to reaffirm their estimated time of arrival to the pilot boarding station when they are passing Cape Flattery, and again when they are one hour away.

(49) Loaded petroleum tankers requiring a pilot should proceed to position 48°09'54"N.,123°24'19"W., (1.5 miles N of the E end of Ediz Hook); all other vessels to position 48°09'24"N.,123°24'00"W., (1.0 mile N of the E end of Ediz Hook). A pilot ladder should be rigged in compliance with SOLAS regulations on the leeward side about 1 meter above the water. When approaching the boarding area, vessels are requested to monitor VHF-FM channel 13, and maintain a steady course and speed of about 6 knots when the pilot boat comes alongside.

Towage

(50) Tugs are stationed at Port Angeles. Arrangements are usually made in advance through ships' agents.

Quarantine, customs, immigration, and agricultural quarantine.

(51) (See chapter 3, Vessel Arrival Inspections, and Appendix A for addresses.)

(52) Quarantine is enforced in accordance with regulations of the U.S. Public Health Service. (See Public Health Service, chapter 1.)

Charts 18480, 18460

Strait of Juan de Fuca, N shore (Canada)

(53) Carmanah Point is described in the previous chapter. **Bonilla Point**, the N entrance point at the W end of the strait, is about 1.8 miles ESE from Carmanah Light. Inland of Bonilla Point, which slopes gradually to the sea, the mountains attain heights of over 3,500 feet and are heavily wooded. A reef extends 0.5 mile off the point, and the shores should be given a berth of at least 1.5 miles.

(54) From Bonilla Point the coast trends in a SE direction for 9.5 miles to Owen Point. It is nearly straight, rocky, and bluff, with high mountains rising immediately behind it; all are heavily wooded.

(55) **Port San Juan** offers the first anchorage on the N shore within the entrance to the Strait of Juan de Fuca. The port is conspicuous from seaward, appearing as a deep gap between two mountain ranges.

(56) The entrance between **Owen Point** and **San Juan Point**, 1.7 miles wide and 3.5 miles long, is 13 miles NE of Cape Flattery Light. It is marked by a lighted whistle buoy.

(57) The port is open to SW winds, and a heavy sea rolls in when a moderate gale is blowing from that direction. Though it is possible that a vessel with good ground tackle could ride out a gale if anchored in the most sheltered part, it is recommended that with any indication of SW gales a vessel should weigh anchor immediately and, if the vessel's draft is 16 feet or less, seek shelter in Neah Bay; vessels of deeper draft should proceed to Port Angeles.

(58) Anchorage may be had in 6 to 9 fathoms anywhere in Port San Juan; a good position is in 5½ fathoms about 1 mile from the beach at the head of the port.

(59) **Cerastes Rocks**, about 300 yards SW from San Juan Point, include several high pinnacle rocks with a few trees growing on them. About 800 yards N of these rocks and 300 yards from shore is another reef partly uncovered.

(60) **Port Renfrew** is a settlement on the SE side of Port San Juan, about 2 miles NE of San Juan Point. A T-head pier has depths of 15 feet alongside.

(61) From Port San Juan the coast trends SE for 23.5 miles to Sheringham Point. This stretch of coast presents no prominent features. The country is thickly wooded, and the land rises to a considerable elevation. The points, some of which are bare on their extremities, are not prominent nor are they easily identified, except from close inshore.

(62) A Canadian Armed Forces **firing** and **practice exercise area** is established in the vicinity of Sheringham Point and San Simon Point about 8 miles to the W. (See Annual Edition of Canadian Notices to Mariners for area limits, types of practices, warning signals, etc.)

(63) Between Port San Juan and Race Rocks, fish traps and broken piles are reported to extend 0.5 mile offshore in places.

Chart 18465

(64) **Sheringham Point** is marked by a light. Victoria marine radio station VAK is at Sheringham Point.

(65) From Sheringham Point the coast continues in a series of bays and inlets for 16.5 miles to Race Rocks.

(66) **Beechey Head**, 11.5 miles ESE of Sheringham Point, is bold, wooded, and steep-to. Vessels bound up the strait and passing outside Race Rocks should give Beechey Head a berth of 2 miles.

(67) **Race Rocks**, 5 miles E of Beechey Head, are a cluster of bare low rocks from 0.5 mile to almost 1.5 miles from shore. Foul ground extends for 0.5 mile in all directions from the light; dangerous overfalls and races occur during bad weather. A light and sound signal are on the largest rock of the group, and a lighted buoy marks the SE rock of the group. The tidal currents in Race Passage and in the vicinity of Race Rocks attain a

(67) velocity of 4 to 6 knots at times, and dangerous tide rips are formed.

(68) **Firing practice** and **exercise areas** of the Canadian Armed Forces are E of Race Rocks in the approaches to Esquimalt and Victoria Harbors. (See the Annual Edition of Canadian Notices to Mariners.)

(69) Foul ground, due to dumping of heavy steel wire mesh material, is 3.2 miles W from Race Rocks Light.

(70) E of Race Rocks the Strait of Juan de Fuca expands to a width of about 16 miles, and extends for 30 miles ENE to the entrance to Admiralty Inlet on the S and Rosario Strait on the N.

(71) A 25-fathom bank lies 8.5 miles SE of Race Rocks along the steamer track from Race Rocks Light to Point Wilson Light. The W edge of this bank is sometimes sharply defined by a line of ripples with glassy calm water to the E.

(72) **Bentinck Island**, 1 mile NW of Race Rocks Light, is fringed with kelp on its S and E sides. **Pedder Bay, Parry Bay**, and **Royal Roads**, separated by William Head and **Albert Head**, form the coast between Bentinck Island and the W entrance to Esquimalt Harbor.

(73) A **027°43'–207°43' measured nautical mile** has been established on the NW shore of Parry Bay. Range beacons, consisting of fluorescent orange diamond-shaped daymarks, mark the NE and SW ends of the measured course.

(74) A **prohibited area** has been established in Parry Bay by the Canadian Government. No vessel may anchor in the area without permission.

(75) **William Head** is a comparatively low promontory extending about 0.5 mile NE of **Ned Point**. Close W of William Head is **Quarantine Cove**, on the E shore of which are the conspicuous red brick buildings of the former quarantine station, now used as a penitentiary. Unauthorized vessels should not approach William Head within 200 yards.

(76) Anchorage affording protection from W weather may be had in 7 fathoms about 0.5 mile N of William Head and about 1,200 yards from the mainland.

(77) **Constance Bank**, 6.8 miles E of William Head Light, has general depths of 8 to 13 fathoms. It is about 2 miles long and 1 mile wide, within the 20-fathom curve. The bottom is rocky, and tide rips form in this vicinity. Vessels should not attempt to anchor on the bank.

(78) **Albert Head**, 3.3 miles NE of William Head. **Fisgard Island**, on the W side of the entrance to Esquimalt Harbor, is marked by a light. Its red sector covers **Scroggs Rocks** off the E entrance point. Scroggs Rocks are marked by a light.

(79) **Esquimalt Harbor**, about 3 miles NNE of Albert Head, affords safe and ample anchorage and can be entered at any time. The entrance channel has general depths of 8 fathoms. Depths within the entrance gradually decrease for 1.5 miles N to **Cole Island**, above which the head of the harbor dries.

(80) **Victoria Harbor**, landlocked and well protected, is about 2 miles ESE of Esquimalt Harbor, and can accommodate large vessels. A U.S. Immigration station is in Victoria.

(81) Victoria Harbor is entered between **Macaulay Point** on the W and the breakwater extending from **Ogden Point** on the E; the breakwater is marked by a light. Vessels requiring a pilot are requested to notify **"Pilots Victoria"** by radio station **VAK** at least 6 hours in advance of their estimated time of arrival. The harbor extends for more than 0.5 mile N to **Shoal Point** on the E side, and thence trends E to **James Bay**. From the N part of James Bay, the upper harbor, which is crossed by three bridges, extends about 0.8 mile NNW to **Selkirk Water**, the W extremity of which is connected to **Portage Inlet**.

(82) **Brotchie Ledge**, the only outlying danger, about 200 yards long within the 5-fathom curve, lies 0.6 mile S of Ogden Point. The ledge has a least depth of 12 feet, and is marked by a light.

(83) **Clover Point**, 2 miles ESE of the entrance to Victoria Harbor, is low, bare of trees, and steep-to. Strong tide rips form off the point.

(84) **Trial Islands**, 4 miles E of Victoria Harbor, are bare and rocky; from most directions the two islands appear as one. The islands are marked by a light. The S and larger island is 80 feet high, and from **Staines Point**, its S extremity, a rocky ledge that uncovers 2 feet extends about 100 yards. Severe tide rips form off Staines Point, especially on the flood tidal current, which attains a velocity of 3 to 6 knots during large tides. The point should be given a wide berth.

(85) **Discovery Island**, 2 miles ENE of **Gonzales Point**, lies off the junction of Haro Strait and the Strait of Juan de Fuca. The island is wooded, and near its SE tip, **Pandora Hill** attains a height of about 125 feet. The island is marked by a light on the E side. The shores on all sides of the island are fringed with rocks in some places extending as far as 600 yards offshore.

Charts 18465, 18421, 18429

Strait of Juan de Fuca, E end

(86) **Hein Bank**, with a least depth of 2½ fathoms, lies 8.5 miles SE of Discovery Island; it is about 2 miles long in a N direction, within the 10-fathom curve, and 0.8 mile wide. The shoalest part of the bank is covered with thick kelp in the summer. It is marked by two lighted buoys, the northernmost is equipped with a racon.

(87) **Smith Island**, 5 miles W of Whidbey Island and 8 miles ESE of Hein Bank, is irregular in shape and about 0.5 mile long. The E end is low, but rises abruptly to an elevation of 55 feet at its W end, terminating in a white perpendicular cliff composed of sand and gravel. A rocky bank, covered with kelp, extends about 2 miles W of the island over depths of 3 to 6 fathoms. A rock that bares at lowest tides is about 0.3 mile W of Smith Island. Strong currents set in and around the shoal area, especially on the flood, and deep-draft vessels should keep well

(87) outside the 10-fathom curve to avoid being set into danger. **Smith Island Light** (48°19'06"N., 122°50'38"W.), 97 feet above the water is shown from a 50-foot skeleton tower near the W extremity of the island.

(88) A **restricted area** of an air-to-surface weapon range is W of Smith Island. (See **334.1180**, chapter 2, for limits and regulations.)

(89) **Minor Island**, small, low, and rocky, lies 1 mile NE of Smith Island, and at lowest tide is connected with it by a gravel and boulder spit. A light is on the island.

(90) The northernmost part of the western shore of **Whidbey Island** forms the E end of the Strait of Juan de Fuca. This part of the island has a uniform sandy shore backed by low and rolling upland of farm and wooded areas. A marina at Oak Harbor, on the E side of the island, has electricity, gasoline, diesel fuel, and pumpout facility.

(91) **Naval restricted areas** are adjacent to the northernmost part of the W shore of Whidby Island. (See **334.1200**, chapter 2, for limits and regulations.)

(92) The aerolight (48°20.9'N., 122°40.2'W.) at Ault Field is conspicuous.

Charts 18485, 18484

(93) On the S side of the Strait of Juan de Fuca the coast trends E for 4 miles from Cape Flattery to **Koitlah Point**, the W point of Neah Bay. The shores are rugged, and the country is heavily timbered.

(94) **Neah Bay**, about 5 miles E of Cape Flattery, is used extensively by small vessels as a harbor of refuge in foul weather. Its proximity to Cape Flattery and ease of access at any time make the anchorage very useful. It is protected from all but E weather.

(95) **Baada (Baadah) Point**, the E entrance point to Neah Bay, is rocky and grass-covered for some distance back from the shore. **Waadah Island**, 0.3 mile N of Baada Point, is 0.5 mile long, high, and wooded. A light marks the N and S end of the island. A stone breakwater extends from the W side of the bay to about the middle of Waadah Island. A reef and foul ground extend 0.2 mile from the SW side of the island. A reef that bares, marked by a lighted bell buoy, extends 500 yards NW from **Dtokoah Point**, SE of the entrance.

(96) The buildings of **Neah Bay Coast Guard Station**, 0.4 mile SW of Baada Point, are prominent from the entrance.

(97) The entrance to the bay is between Waadah Island and Baada Point. A depth of 17 feet can be carried into the bay. Anchorage is in 20 to 35 feet, mud bottom.

(98) The W shore of Neah Bay is high and precipitous, and bordered by craggy rock outcroppings. The shore E of the village of Neah Bay is a low sand beach to Baada Point. Unmarked sunken wrecks are in the W part of the bay in about 48°22'22"N., 124°37'15"W., and in the NE corner of the bay in about 48°22'39"N., 124°36'20"W. Caution is advised when anchoring in the vicinity of the wrecks.

(99) The Indian village of **Neah Bay**, on the SW shore of the bay, is the site of considerable sport fishing.

(100) Neah Bay is a **customs port of entry**. The customs officer also performs **immigration** duties.

(101) The Makah Indian T-head pier with a 300-foot face, and the ruins of a T-head pier no longer visible, are about 375 and 500 yards SW of Baada Point. Caution is advised in the vicinity of the pier in ruins, as submerged piles may exist. The Coast Guard pier is 0.5 mile SW of Baada Point.

(102) Two cooperative fish piers, 1 mile and 1.2 miles SW of Baada Point, have facilities for icing and supplying fishing boats. Limited berthage, electricity, gasoline, diesel fuel, water, and ice are available. Both piers have reported depths of 12 feet off the ends. There are many small-craft floats extending along the S shore of the bay. A marina is about 1 mile SW of Baada Point on the S shore and has 200 slips; gasoline, diesel fuel, water, electricity, pump-out, and a launching ramp are available.

(103) A paved highway extends along the Strait of Juan de Fuca to Port Angeles; telephone service is available.

Chart 18460

(104) From Neah Bay to Clallam Bay, the coast for more than 14 miles is rugged and the back country high and heavily wooded.

(105) **Seal Rock** and **Sail Rock**, about 2 miles E of Neah Bay and about 600 yards offshore, are very prominent. Seal Rock, the W one, is 100 feet high with a flat top showing E, and light in color. Sail Rock, 0.2 mile E of Seal Rock, is lower and more pointed. Covered rocks extend from Seal Rock to shore, and there are patches of kelp in this area.

(106) The wreck of the steamer ANDALUCIA, once partially visible but now completely covered, is just off Seal and Sail Rocks.

(107) A marina is along the shore near Sail Rock. Berths, gasoline, water, ice provisions, and a 3-ton lift are available. Mariners are advised to exercise caution in approaching the marinas because of the numerous rocks and ledges. The floats at the marina bare at low water. **Sail River** empties near Seal and Sail Rocks. **Sekiu River**, about 6.5 miles SE of Sail River, has some logging operations. The bridge over the river shows prominently through the trees.

(108) **Clallam Bay**, about 15 miles SE of Neah Bay, is a broad open bight about 2 miles long and 1 mile wide. It affords anchorage in 6 to 10 fathoms, sandy bottom, and is used to some extent in S or thick weather.

(109) **Slip Point**, the E point of the bight, is high and wooded; there is a light-colored streak like a landslip down its face, which is visible for a long distance. A reef,

extending 0.2 mile W of the point, is marked by a bell buoy.

(110) **Sekiu** is a resort and sport fishing town on the W end of Clallam Bay and S of Sekiu Point. The town has berths, gasoline, water, ice, launching ramps and limited marine supplies. A marine railway that can handle craft to 24 feet long is at the town. **Clallam Bay**, a small town on the E side of Clallam Bay, has no waterfront facilities.

(111) In entering Clallam Bay, give Slip Point a berth of more than 0.2 mile to avoid the reef projecting W of it. Storm-bound vessels generally anchor abreast the rocky point near the middle of the long semicircular beach on the S shore of the bay.

(112) **Pillar Point**, 6.7 miles ESE of Slip Point, is bold, 700 feet high, wooded up to its summit, with a dark pillar-shaped rock more than 100 feet high lying close under its E face. The rock shows prominently from W. Good anchorage may be had in 9 to 12 fathoms, sticky bottom, about 0.8 mile SE of Pillar Point. This anchorage offers good shelter from the heavy W swell, but gives no protection from the brisk E and NE winds that prevail in winter.

(113) **Twin Rivers** are two small streams that flow into the strait about 7 miles E of Pillar Point. An earthfilled barge-loading facility, 0.3 mile W of West Twin River, has a reported depth of 15 feet alongside. The facility is owned by a cement company and used for barging clay to Seattle.

Chart 18465

(114) Shoal water makes out a considerable distance from **Low Point** (48°09.6'N., 123°49.5'W.), 5 miles E of Twin Rivers, and vessels should not approach this point closer than 0.8 mile. Many boulders that uncover are W of the point. A salmon pen, about 2.4 miles W of the point and 0.6 mile from the nearest shore, is marked by two private lighted buoys.

(115) **Agate Bay**, 3.5 miles E of Low Point, is clear and deep; 10 fathoms can be carried to within 0.2 mile of the shore.

(116) **Crescent Bay**, 4.2 miles E of Low Point, is a small semicircular bight 1 mile in diameter. The E part is shoal and near the W shore the remains of a wharf should be avoided. This is not a good landing place in N weather. The anchorage is of limited extent and suitable only for small vessels. **Crescent Rock**, covered ¼ fathom and marked by a buoy, is 0.4 mile N of the W entrance point of Crescent Bay. The rock extends 0.4 mile in E direction, with a narrow channel between it and the point. The channel has a reported depth of 10 fathoms and is not recommended without local knowledge. A reef extends about 400 yards NW from **Tongue Point**, the E entrance point of Crescent Bay. A shoal, covered 1¼ fathoms, is about 0.3 mile W of Tongue Point. Except for crabs and fish, the 1¼-fathom shoal is a marine sanctuary for other shellfish and sealife. A wreck is off the entrance about 0.3 miles N of Tongue Point.

(117) **Observatory Point** is 3 miles E of Tongue Point. Between these points is a wooded ridge which, because of the lower land behind it, makes this area appear as an island when raised from E or W. The ridge attains an elevation of 1,135 feet, and is known as **Striped Peak**. A rock, 20 feet high, is close off Observatory Point; the rock and the point are almost joined at low water.

(118) **Freshwater Bay**, about 4 miles E of Crescent Bay, is a broad open bight, affording anchorage in 6 to 10 fathoms. The bay and adjacent waters are designated as an **emergency explosives anchorage**. (See **110.1 and 110.230 (a)(1) and (b)**, chapter 2, for limits and regulations.) A park with a launching ramp is along the SW shore of Freshwater Bay.

(119) **Angeles Point**, on the E side of Freshwater Bay, is low, sandy, and covered with alders. The **Elwha River** empties into the strait at this point.

(120) A microwave tower, marked by aircraft warning lights and a good landmark by day and night, is on Angeles Point.

Caution

(121) The U.S. Navy advises that the precautionary area, located within a 1 mile radius centered around a point in about 48°15'36"N., 123°15'48"W., approximately 9 miles NNE of Ediz Hook, is used by naval vessels to conduct equipment calibration tests. Surface vessels or submerged submarines will occasionally be maneuvering in circles in this area for several hours or days. When these operations are in progress, the test facility located on the east end of Ediz Hook will be manned and reference lights consisting of a lazy "T" bar, 1 sec flashing yellow, 2/sec flashing red, and a high intensity spot will be lit. The group of lights is visible from the N side of Ediz Hook with the "T" bar to the W and spot light to the E. The naval vessels will be participating in the Seattle Vessel Traffic System on VHF-FM channel 5A. The Navy Test Facility Port Angeles will monitor VHF-FM channels 16 and 69. Mariners transiting this area are requested to proceed with caution.

(122) A **Vessel Traffic Service** has been established in the Strait of Juan de Fuca, E of Port Angeles, and in the adjacent waters. (See **161.1 through 161.55**, chapter 2, for regulations, and the beginning of this chapter for additional information.)

Chart 18468

(123) **Port Angeles**, 6.5 miles E of Freshwater Bay and 56 miles from Cape Flattery, is entered between **Ediz Hook**, a low and narrow sandspit 3 miles long, and the main shore to the S. The harbor, about 2.5 miles long, is easy of access by the largest vessels, which frequently use it when refueling, making topside repairs, waiting for orders or a tug, and when weather-bound.

(124) The harbor is protected from all except E winds, which occasionally blow during the winter. During SE winter gales, the wind is not usually felt but some swells roll in. The depths are greatest on the N shore and decrease from 30 to 15 fathoms in the middle of the harbor; from the middle, the depths decrease regularly to the S shore, where the 3-fathom curve in some places in the E part is nearly 0.2 mile from the beach. A rock covered 5 fathoms is at 48°07'22"N., 123°13'18"W. A shoal with a least depth of 2¼ fathoms is 330 yards NW of the NW corner of the easternmost pier on the waterfront; a buoy is 200 yards E of the shoal.

(125) Extra caution in navigating the waters inside Ediz Hook should be exercised because of the large number of submerged deadheads or sinkers in the area. Deadheads or sinkers are logs that have become adrift from rafts or booms, have become waterlogged, and float in a vertical position with one end just awash, rising and falling with the tide.

Anchorage

(126) Puget Sound Vessel Traffic Service requires advance notification of watch supervisor for all vessels using Port Angeles anchorage; telephone 206-217-6050. The best anchorage is off the wharves, in 7 to 12 fathoms, sticky bottom.

(127) A **nonanchorage area** has been established in the E part of Port Angeles Harbor. (See **110.1 and 110.229**, chapter 2, for limits and regulations.)

(128) Extensive log booming grounds in the N part of the harbor extend more than 1 mile from the W shore. Care must be taken when anchoring at night to avoid the rafted logs; the booming grounds are charted.

(129) **Ediz Hook Light** (48°08'25"N., 123°24'08"W.), 50 feet above the water, is shown from a skeleton tower, 0.3 mile W of the E extremity of Ediz Hook; a mariner radio activated sound signal is at the light, initiated by keying the microphone five times on VHF-FM channel 83A. A 170-foot Coast Guard VTS radar tower is about 0.1 mile WSW of the light. Shoals extend to about 75 yards E of the E extremity of Ediz Hook. A lighted buoy is about 150 yards E of the outer limits of the shoals. Coast Guard radio station **NOW** is at the air station. A shoal, with a least depth of 7 fathoms and marked by a lighted buoy, is about 3.4 miles WNW of Ediz Hook Light. An aquaculture site, marked by private lights, is off the S side of Ediz Hook about 800 yards WSW of the light.

(130) **Port Angeles** is on the S shore of the harbor. Logs, lumber, plywood, newsprint, pulp, shakes and shingles, and petroleum products are the principal commodities handled.

Pilotage, Port Angeles

(131) Pilotage is compulsory for all vessels except those under enrollment or engaged exclusively in the coasting trade on the W coast of the continental United States (including Alaska) and/or British Columbia. Pilotage for Port Angeles is provided by the Puget Sound Pilots. They monitor VHF-FM channel 13. (See Pilotage, Strait of Juan de Fuca and Puget Sound, indexed as such, early this chapter.) The pilot station is about 0.7 mile W from Ediz Hook Light. A pier for berthage of the pilot boats is on the S side of Ediz Hook, adjacent to the pilot station.

Towage

(132) Tugs to 1,200 hp are stationed at Port Angeles, and tugs to 5,000 hp are available from Seattle with advance notice.

Quarantine, customs, immigration, and agricultural quarantine

(133) (See chapter 3, Vessel Arrival Inspections, and Appendix A for addresses.)

(134) **Quarantine** is enforced in accordance with regulations of the U.S. Public Health Service. (See Public Health Service, chapter 1.)

(135) Port Angeles is a **customs port of entry**.

Coast Guard

(136) Port Angeles Coast Guard Air Station/Sector Field is on Ediz Hook, about 0.3 mile W of the E extremity.

Harbor regulations

(137) The Port of Port Angeles Terminal Manager's office is in Port Angeles at the foot of Cedar Street.

Wharves

(138) The major piers described, both private and port operated, extend along the S and W sides of the harbor. For a complete description of the port facilities refer to Port Series No. 37, published and sold by the U.S. Army Corps of Engineers. (See Appendix A for address.) The alongside depths of the facilities described are reported depths. (For information on the latest depths contact the port authorities or the private operators.)

Port-operated facilities:

(139) Port Terminal No. 1 (48°07'30"N., 123°26'24"W.): 956-foot berthing space on N side with an additional 425 feet to dolphins; 610 foot berthing space on S side, 42 feet at the end; deck height, 17 feet; 17,000 square feet covered storage; 96,000 square feet open storage; shipment of general cargo, lumber, logs, pulp, and other forest products; berthing space for top side repair of large ocean going vessels.

(140) Port of Port Angeles, Terminal No. 3 (W of Port Terminal 1): 480-foot berthing space; 41 to 45 feet alongside; deck height, 17 feet; receipt and shipment of general cargo, shipment of logs and lumber.

Privately operated facilities:

(141) Black Ball Ferry Transport (48°07'21"N., 123°25'45"W.): Terminus of passenger and automobile ferry connecting Port Angeles and Victoria, BC; ferry makes two trips daily from March to May and October to January. From May to October it makes 4 trips daily. Visit "http://www.northolympic.com/coho" for the current schedule. Operated by Black Ball Transport, Inc.

(142) Diashowa America, Port Angeles Mill Dock (48°07'57"N., 123°27'33"W.): 640-foot total berthing space with dolphins; 28 feet alongside; deck height, 10 feet; shipment of lumber; owned and operated by Merrill and Ring, Inc. **Note:** Vessels moor portside-to at this wharf; a tug is recommended for both docking and undocking.

(143) Diashowa America, Port Angeles Barge Dock (48°08'08"N., 123°27'37"W.): 570-foot berthing space with dolphins; 36 to 40 feet alongside; deck height, 17½ feet; approximately 28,000 square feet covered storage; receipt of fuel oil for plant consumption; shipment of paper products; owned by Diashowa; operated by Diashowa America and BP Marine Americas. A 25-foot shoal is charted about 100 feet E of the face of the Wharf; a tug is recommended when undocking.

(144) In addition to the facilities mentioned, there are several small piers and wharves at which tugs and other floating equipment moor. Many log dumps are in the harbor.

Supplies

(145) Water, ice, and marine supplies are available. Groceries are nearby. Diesel oil and gasoline are available at the port boat haven. Bunkering is available by barge.

Repairs

(146) Port Angeles has several companies and facilities to perform major topside repairs to large oceangoing vessels; the nearest drydocking facilities are in Seattle/Tacoma or Bellingham.

Small-craft facilities

(147) **Port Angeles Boat Haven**, operated by the port, is a large, well-equipped small-craft basin in the SW part of the harbor that can accommodate a large fleet of fishing boats and pleasure craft. The basin is marked by lights. In 2007, the controlling depth in the entrance and basin was 16 feet with 12 feet alongside the berths. About 660 berths, electricity, gasoline, diesel fuel, water, ice, a pump-out station, launching ramps, marine supplies, and winter wet storage are available. A boatyard at the E end of the basin has a marine railway that can handle craft to 100 tons; a 225-ton lift is also available. Hull and engine repairs can be made at the yard, and electronic repair work can be arranged. The **harbormaster** controls the moorings in the basin (360–457–4505).

(148) A **121°16'-301°16' 200-yard measured course** is in the SW part of the harbor close N of Port Angeles Boat Haven.

Communications

(149) Port Angeles is served by U.S. Highway 101. It is connected by ferry to Victoria, BC. The airport is 2.5 miles W of the city.

Charts 18465, 18471

(150) From Port Angeles the coast trends E for 13 miles to the end of **Dungeness Spit**, which borders the W side of **Dungeness Bay**. This bay affords shelter in W winds, but is open E; in N weather, the protection afforded is only fair. It is a dangerous place in winter gales, especially from the SE. The bay is formed by a sandspit extending NE 4 miles and forming, in addition to Dungeness Bay, a small lagoon at the head of the harbor that can be entered by light-draft vessels with local knowledge.

(151) A **075°–255° measured nautical mile** has been established on the strait side of Dungeness Spit; the range markers are in the small lagoon at the head of the harbor.

(152) **New Dungeness Light** (48°10'54"N., 123°06'37"W.), 67 feet above the water, is shown from a 63-foot white conical tower on a dwelling on the outer end of the spit.

(153) From the end of the spit a shoal extends NE for 0.8 mile from the light. This has been reported as extending farther N, and it should be passed with caution. A lighted buoy marks the shoal but it may be submerged during periods of strong current; vessels should not pass between the buoy and the light. A shoal makes out about 1 mile from the S side of the bay.

(154) The best anchorage is in 5 to 9 fathoms, sticky bottom, about 1 mile SE of the light, clear of the cable area.

(155) **Dungeness** is a small town on the S shore of the bay. The ruins of a former wharf extend about 1,000 yards out across the flats.

(156) **Sequim Bay**, 6 miles SE of Dungeness Bay, is a landlocked bay 3.8 mile long. The bay is separated from the Straits by **Travis Spit**, a sandspit that extends W from the NE corner of the bay almost to the W shore. A long, narrow channel marked by lighted and unlighted buoys leads around Travis Spit and W of a shoal area called The Middle Ground into the bay. Depths of about 9 feet are available with local knowledge in the marked channel. The area between the lighted buoy at the entrance and Gibson Spit on the W shore reportedly bares at minus tide and several groundings are known to occur; caution is advised. Strong currents that tend to follow the channel have also been reported. Anchorage inside Sequim Bay can be had anywhere in 6 to 21 fathoms, muddy bottom. A marina is located on the W side of the bay just N of **Pitship Point**. Lights mark the breakwater entrance. In 2011, the reported alongside depth was 8 feet. Services include transient berths, electricity,

(156) gasoline, diesel fuel, water, ice, marine supplies, launching ramp and a pump-out station. The harbormaster controls moorage in the basin and can be contacted at 360–417–3440; VHF-FM is not monitored. A marine research center of the Battelle Memorial Institute, is on the W side of the entrance to the harbor abreast the sandspit. Some log rafts are made up in the bay. **Sequim Bay State Park** is at the SW end of the bay. A seasonal mooring float is at the park.

(157) **Protection Island**, a prominent feature in approaching Discovery Bay, is 200 feet high near its W extremity, 1.5 miles long and sparsely wooded; its N shore consists of bare, light bluffs. The E end and S shore are clear of dangers, but off **Kanem Point**, its SW end, a shoal extends SW for over 0.2 mile, and depths of 5 fathoms and less are found 0.5 mile W of the point. **Dallas Bank** extends N from Protection Island; the 10-fathom curve lies about 2.5 miles from the N point. N of the 10-fathom curve the bank drops off abruptly to depths of over 20 fathoms. **Miller Peninsula**, about 6 miles long and 3 to 5 miles wide, separates Sequim Bay and Discovery Bay.

(158) **Discovery Bay** is 2 miles SSE of Protection Island. George Vancouver, the English explorer, anchored and refitted his ships here for his exploration of these regions in 1792. The bay trends in a SE direction for about 8 miles. The entrance is masked from seaward by Protection Island, which protects it from NW winds. There are no outlying dangers, and the depths are great. **Cape George** is at the E entrance point of Discovery Bay. A marina here can provide water, electricity, a launching ramp, and has about 80 slips that can accommodate vessels up to 40 feet in length with a maximum beam of 12 feet. The entrance has a reported depth of 3½ feet. The entrance jetty is marked by a light.

(159) A dangerous sunken wreck is on the W side of the bay about 300 yards S of Mill Point in 48°00'53"N., 122°51'27"W.

(160) In 1980, a sunken wreck was reported on the E side of the bay in about 48°03'17"N., 122°51'12"W.

(161) **Diamond Point** is the W point at the entrance to Discovery Bay. A wharf in ruins is just inside the point.

(162) The shore from Cape George for 3 miles to **McCurdy Point**, consists of high, bare, clay bluffs, sparsely wooded on top, attaining a height of 400 feet near the NE end. A shoal covered 11 feet extends 0.6 mile NW of McCurdy Point; it is marked by a buoy. Vessels are cautioned not to pass between the buoy and the point.

(163) From McCurdy Point, the shore trends E for 3.5 miles to **Point Wilson**, the W point at the entrance to Admiralty Inlet, and consists of high, bare, clay bluffs, sparsely wooded on top, decreasing in height near McCurdy Point, and ending abruptly close W to Point Wilson.

(164) **Point Wilson Light** (48°08'39"N., 122°45'17"W.), 51 feet above the water, is shown from a white octagonal tower on a building on the E extremity of the low point.

(165) Shoals extend 0.5 mile NW of Point Wilson to the 5-fathom curve over irregular bottom; these are generally indicated by kelp. The E edge of the shoals rises rather abruptly from deep water. Heavy tide rips extend N of these shoals, being especially heavy with a W wind and ebb current. A lighted buoy marking the shoals is about 0.7 mile NW of Point Wilson Light.

(166) In approaching Point Wilson in thick or foggy weather, soundings should be taken continuously.

(167) **Point Partridge**, the Westernmost point of Whidbey Island, has a yellow face and is prominent from the N or S; it is rounding and not easily identified from the W. **Point Partridge Light** (48°13'29"N., 122°46'10"W.), 105 feet above the water, is shown from a skeleton tower on the W extremity of the point. A rocky ledge, marked by a lighted bell buoy, extends 0.5 mile W from the point. In the summer, the ledge is usually marked by kelp.

(168) The W shore of Whidbey Island, between Admiralty Head and Point Partridge, is mostly a sandy beach rising sharply to bluffs 100 to 250 feet high, backed by pine trees. The shoreline is generally strewn by logs.

(169) **Admiralty Head**, 80 feet high, on Whidbey Island, is the E entrance point of Admiralty Inlet and the SE extremity of a succession of light bare bluffs which extend N of Point Partridge, where they attain their highest elevation. About 0.5 mile N of Admiralty Head an abandoned lighthouse tower 39 feet high stands on top of a bluff.

(170) From Point Partridge the NW coast of Whidbey Island extends NNE for 11.5 miles to Deception Pass. It is free of offlying dangers, but should not be approached closer than 1 mile.

(171) A **Small Arms Safety Zone** operated by Naval Air Station Whidbey Island, is located about 5 miles NNE of Point Partridge. The zone is in operation 7 days a week; red flashing lights and flags are displayed during live exercises. Mariners should exercise extreme caution when transiting the area.

(172) **Partridge Bank**, within the 10-fathom curve, is about 3 miles long and 1.5 miles wide; the SE end reaches within 2 miles of Point Partridge. The N and E sides fall off abruptly to 20 and 30 fathoms. The shallowest part, 2½ fathoms, is near the N side about midway between the ends; it is marked by a buoy. A lighted bell buoy is about 0.6 mile SSE of the 2½ fathom spot. A considerable part of the bank is covered with kelp, which is usually drawn under by currents. The kelp generally extends to the 7-fathom curve, except toward the E end where the shoal narrows, and no kelp exists beyond a depth of 4 fathoms; kelp density varies by season.

Charts 18421, 18432, 18433, 18434

(173) The waters of the **San Juan Islands** embrace the passages and bays N of the E end of the Strait of Juan de Fuca. These passages are used extensively by pleasure craft, especially in July, August, and September. Some

tugs and barges use the larger passes. Automobile ferries, operated by the State of Washington, are on regular round-trip runs from Anacortes through Thatcher Pass, Harney Channel, Wasp Passage, San Juan Channel, Spieden Channel, and across Haro Strait to Sidney, B.C. The island ferry landings are at Upright Head, Lopez Island; on the E side of the entrance to Blind Bay, Shaw Island; Orcas, Orcas Island; and Friday Harbor, San Juan Island. Oceangoing vessels normally use Haro and Rosario Straits and do not run the channels and passes in the San Juan Islands. Many resorts and communities have supplies and moorage available for the numerous pleasure craft cruising in these waters. Well-sheltered anchorages are numerous.

(174) The directions which follow are intended for use only in clear weather; in thick weather or at night strangers should take a pilot for large vessels. Small craft should not attempt navigation under these conditions without local knowledge. Sailing craft should not attempt the passages against the current unless the wind is fair and fresh. A reliable auxiliary engine for sailboats is an absolute necessity. The tidal currents have great velocity in places, causing heavy tide rips that are dangerous. Because of the variable direction and velocity of the currents, compass courses are of little value, and, where followed, allowance must be made for the set of the current.

(175) **Haro Strait** and **Boundary Pass** form the westernmost of the three main channels leading from the Strait of Juan de Fuca to the SE end of the Strait of Georgia; it is the one most generally used. Vessels bound from the W to ports in Alaska or British Columbia should use the Haro Strait/Boundary Pass channel, as it is the widest channel and is well marked. Vessels bound N from Puget Sound may use Rosario Strait or Haro Strait; the use of San Juan Channel by deep-draft vessels is not recommended.

(176) A **Vessel Traffic Service** has been established in the Strait of Juan de Fuca, E of Port Angeles, and in the adjacent waters. (See **161.1 through 161.55**, chapter 2, for regulations, and the beginning of this chapter for additional information.)

(177) Haro Strait extends N from the S end of San Juan Island for about 18 miles to Turn Point Light on Stuart Island, thence Boundary Pass leads NE for 13 miles to its junction with the Strait of Georgia between East Point, the E end of Saturna Island, BC, and the W end of Patos Island, the small United States island; both of which are marked by lights. These waterways have widths from 1.5 to 5 miles, and the depths are generally great.

(178) No difficulty will be experienced in navigating Haro Strait and Boundary Pass in clear weather; strangers should take a pilot in thick weather.

(179) The E shore of the passage will be described in detail, with only a brief general description of the W shore. More complete detail of the W shore is contained in Pub. 154, Sailing Directions (Enroute) for British Columbia, published by the National Geospatial-Intelligence Agency Hydrographic/Topographic Center, and the Sailing Directions, British Columbia Coast (South Portion) Vol. 1, published by the Canadian Hydrographic Service.

(180) The International Boundary between the United States and Canada passes through Haro Strait and Boundary Pass.

(181) In accordance with the Cooperative Vessel Traffic Service, the United States and Canada, in cooperation with industry and the British Columbia Coast Pilots have established a **Special Operating Area** at the intersection of Haro Strait and Boundary Pass in the vicinity of Turn Point Light (48°41'18"N., 123°14'12"W.). This special area will help reduce the risk of incidents between both commercial and recreational vessels transiting the boundary waters of Haro Strait and Boundary Pass. For the boundaries and rules regarding the **Special Operating Area**, see **Cooperative Vessel Traffic Service (CVTS)** at the beginning of this chapter.

Tidal currents

(182) In Haro Strait and Boundary Pass, the flood current sets N; the ebb current sets in the opposite direction. The ebb usually runs longer and has a greater velocity. At the N entrance to Boundary Pass, the flood sets E along the N and S sides of Sucia Islands and across Alden Bank; the velocity is about 1 to 2 knots. The current has moderate velocity between Sucia and Orcas Islands. There is a large, daily inequality in the current (see Tidal current Tables for predicted times and velocities). Heavy, dangerous tide rips occur between East Point on Saturna Island and Patos Island, and for two miles N in the Strait of Georgia. Tide rips also occur on the ebb between Henry Island and Turn Point, as well as around Turn Point where the ebb may attain a velocity of 6 knots during large tides. The flood current sets E from Discovery Island across the S end of Haro Strait until close to San Juan Island. This E set especially noticeable during the first half of the flood. Heavy tide rips occur N of Middle Bank as well as on the Bank and around Discovery Island.

(183) Rocky **Middle Bank**, with a least depth of 10 fathoms, is in the S approach to Haro Strait. The bank is about 3.5 miles long, and the least depth is in its NE part and 5.7 miles SW of Cattle Point Light on the southernmost tip of San Juan Island. Heavy tide rips, dangerous to small craft, form in the vicinity of this bank in bad weather.

(184) **Beaumont shoal**, covered 9 fathoms, lies 3 miles NW of the NW corner of Middle Bank and is marked by a lighted buoy. A second small bank with a least depth of 7 fathoms lies 1 mile to the north. In bad weather, heavy tide rips form over these banks.

(185) **San Juan Island**, the largest of the group, is about 13 miles long, rugged, and partly wooded. **Mount Dallas**, the highest of several hills on the island, rises abruptly from the middle of the W side to a height of 1,080 feet.

In most places the shores are free of outlying dangers. The N end of the island is indented by several small bays that, with the exception of Roche Harbor, are shoal and of no commercial importance.

(186) From **Eagle Point**, the W shore of San Juan Island trends NW and forms the E side of Haro Strait. This shore is steep-to and rocky, and beyond 400 yards offshore it is free of danger; however, the depths off this shore are too great for anchoring.

(187) **Kanaka Bay**, a small cove used by fishing boats, is 2.5 miles NW of Eagle Point.

(188) **Lime Kiln Light** (48°30'57"N., 123°09'08"W.), 55 feet above the water, is shown from a 25 foot white octagonal tower attached to a building on the W side of San Juan Island. Two dwellings are about 150 yards SE of the light. Rocks awash lie close inshore about 1 mile SE of the light.

(189) **Smallpox Bay** and **Andrews Bay**, 1.5 miles NW of Lime Kiln Light, offer protection for small craft from N and E weather.

Local magnetic disturbance

(190) Differences from the normal variation of as much as 4° have been observed in the vicinity of **Bellevue Point**, 1 mile N of Lime Kiln Light.

(191) During the June-October fishing season, many purse seiners operate in this area. At night these vessels anchor close inshore, generally between Cattle Point and Pile Point.

(192) **Hanbury Point** (48°34.7'N., 123°10.3'W.), 3.8 miles N of Lime Kiln Light, is the N entrance point to **Mitchell Bay**, one of a series of well-sheltered bays on the NW coast of the island. A small islet 3 feet high is in the center of the bay about 350 yards SE of the entrance. A rock about 100 yards W of the islet uncovers 6 feet. The only safe passage into the bay is N of the islet. **Snug Harbor**, a resort and yacht haven on the S side of Mitchell Bay, has about 70 berths with electricity, gasoline, water, ice, and limited marine supplies. A launching ramp is available; engine repairs can be made to small craft. **Mosquito Pass**, available only to small craft with local knowledge, leads N from Hanbury Point to **Garrison Bay, Westcott Bay**, and Roche Harbor.

(193) A large aquaculture facility, covered 3 feet and consisting of clam beds and suspended oyster racks, is in the middle of Westcott Bay about 1 mile above the entrance. Mariners should use caution in the area.

(194) **Henry Island** is close W of the N point of San Juan Island, from which it is separated by Mosquito Pass and Roche Harbor.

(195) **Kellett Bluff**, at the S end of Henry Island, is steep and rocky and prominent from either S or N. It is marked by a light. **Open Bay**, E of Kellett Bluff, offers good holding ground and protection for small boats from W, N, and E weather.

(196) **Roche Harbor** has its main entrance between the N end of Henry Island and the W end of **Pearl Island**, which is marked by a light. Sandspits covered 17 and 18 feet extend into the channel from the islands on each side of the entrance. Entrance to the harbor can also be made from the S through Mosquito Pass between Henry Island and Bazalgette Point. The harbor has depths of 4 to 9 fathoms. It affords good anchorage and in the summer is used extensively by yachts. The harbormaster can be contacted on VHF-FM channel 78A.

(197) A large resort is on the E side of Roche Harbor. The resort operates a wharf with shed, floats with berths for over 450 craft, including over 150 transient berths, a hotel, cabins, a general store, and restaurant. Electricity, gasoline, diesel fuel, water, ice, a launching ramp, pump-out station, and marine supplies are available. The site was once the largest lime works W of the Mississippi, and quarry tunnels and the ruins of the old mill are still prominent.

(198) A **customs office** is on the N side of the main dock. Two to three customs officers are here full time in the summer and on call from Friday Harbor in the winter to inspect visiting Canadian yachts. The customs officer also performs **immigration** and **agricultural quarantine** inspections. Weekend and after-hours custom service can be obtained from Blaine; a toll-free phone number is posted. Roche Harbor has a paved and lighted airstrip; daily air service is available year-round to Seattle. A paved road leads to Friday Harbor.

(199) **Battleship Island**, small and 30 feet high, is about 0.2 mile WNW of McCracken Point, the N extremity of Henry Island, and is the W point in the approaches to Roche Harbor.

(200) **Danger Shoal**, with a least depth of 1 fathom, is in the fairway to Spieden Channel about midway between Battleship Island and Spieden Bluff. A lighted buoy is close SW of the shoal, which is marked by kelp.

(201) A rock, marked by kelp and covered 11 feet, is about 200 yards NW of **Barren Island**, 0.7 mile E of McCracken Point; it is marked by a buoy. Another rock (48°37'27"N., 123°09'31"W.), marked by kelp and covered 9 feet, is about 350 yards E.

(202) **Spieden Channel** leads E between Spieden Island on the N and Battleship, Henry, and San Juan Islands on the S; the channel leads from Haro Strait to President Channel and San Juan Channel. The E entrance, the narrowest part, is 0.6 mile wide, and for 2 miles W of it the channel is free of danger. However, in the W entrance, which has an irregular bottom, are several dangers, but the fairway is deep throughout. The meeting of the flood currents, which flow E from Haro Strait and W from San Juan Channel, cause heavy tide rips and eddies. This channel is not recommended for sailing craft.

(203) **Spieden Island** lies with **Spieden Bluff**, its NW end, 1.6 miles NNE of Battleship Island. The island is 2.5 miles long in an E direction with an extreme width of 0.5 mile. **Green Point**, the E end of which is marked by

(204) a light, is low and grassy. The S side of the island has few trees, but the N face is well wooded.

There are several dangers SE of Spieden Bluff. **Center Reef**, which bares, is 0.7 mile S of the bluff; it is marked off its S side by a buoy. **Sentinel Rock** and **Sentinel Island** are closer inshore; a rock midway between them is covered 5 feet.

Charts 18421, 18431, 18432, 18433, 18434

(205) **Stuart Island** is NW of Spieden Island and has two prominent hills near the middle, 640 feet high. **Turn Point** is the W extremity of Stuart Island. It is bold, steep-to, and marked by **Turn Point Light** (48°41'20"N., 123°14'15"W.), 44 feet high on a 16-foot white concrete tower.

(206) **Reid Harbor** indents the SE shore of Stuart Island and trends NW about 1.5 miles. The harbor, which is landlocked and 400 yards wide, affords good anchorage in 4 to 5 fathoms, soft bottom. The State Parks and Recreation Commission maintains a small-craft pier and floats here. The harbor is free of danger, but from the E entrance point foul ground extends about halfway across the entrance. Enter in midchannel and anchor anywhere in the middle of the wider portion of the harbor. In 1996, a visible wreck was reported in the harbor entrance in about 48°40'12"N., 123°11'19"W.

(207) **Prevost Harbor**, on the N shore of Stuart Island about 1.5 miles E of Turn Point, affords good shelter and anchorage. A pier used by the Coast Guard and the county is on the W shore of the harbor. Mail is delivered to the island by air. The State Parks and Recreation Commission maintains a float landing for small boats.

(208) **Satellite Island** lies within Prevost Harbor, with reefs and shoals extending off its SE extremity. Vessels should not pass E of the island. Enter in midchannel W of Satellite Island and anchor in 6 to 7 fathoms, muddy bottom, in the middle of the wider portion just within the entrance, keeping clear of a rock that uncovers 6 feet, 200 yards off the S shore.

(209) **Johns Pass**, between Stuart Island and **Johns Island** close E, is much used by fishing vessels and small boats. At the S end of the pass foul ground extends about 0.6 mile SE from Stuart Island.

(210) **Waldron Island**, 6.5 miles E of Turn Point, is steep and rocky on the E side, but flat with sandy beaches on the N and W sides. It is irregular in shape and 3 miles long. The highest point, 612 feet, is near **Point Disney**, its S end. On the N and E sides of the island is a high yellow sand bluff, terminating abruptly in **Point Hammond**.

(211) **Cowlitz Bay**, which indents the SW shore of Waldron Island, is a broad, open bight affording anchorage in fair weather. Shoal water extends 0.5 mile S of **Sandy Point**, the W end of the island. **Mouatt Reef**, with a least depth of 3 feet and marked by kelp, is 0.4 mile offshore and 0.5 mile N of Point Disney. A wharf built out to a depth of 7 feet, is on the shore NE of Mouatt Reef.

(212) **Bare Island**, small, grassy, and bare of trees, is 0.5 mile NNW of Point Hammond, and **Skipjack Island**, 120 feet high and wooded, is about 1.2 miles NW of Point Hammond. The passage between them should be avoided because of its high current velocity. A small, bare rock is off the E end of Skipjack Island, and a group of rocks awash, are about midway between it and Bare Island. **Skipjack Island Light** (48°43'58"N., 123°02'21"W.), 18 feet above the water, is shown from a steel tower on the W side of the island.

(213) A rocky shoal with a least depth of 6 fathoms is about 2 miles NNE of Skipjack Island and is marked by an isolated danger lighted bell buoy.

(214) **Patos Island**, 4.3 miles NNE of Point Hammond, is 60 feet high and wooded except at its W end toward which it gradually decreases in height; the island is a state park. **Active Cove**, between Patos Island and Little Patos Island, is reported to be a good anchorage for small vessels. There are several public mooring buoys available in the cove. Vessels without local knowledge should enter Active Cove from the W, as the southern-facing entrance experiences strong, swirling currents at almost all stages of tide. **Patos Island Light** (48°47'20"N., 122°58'17"W.), 52 feet above the water, is shown from a 38-foot white square frame tower on **Alden Point**, the W point of the island.

(215) **Sucia Islands**, consisting of one large and several smaller islands, are SE of Patos Island and 2.5 miles N of Orcas Island. The large island, 200 feet high and heavily wooded, is horseshoe-shaped; its W side is a series of steep, wooded cliffs. It is a state park. **Echo Bay** indents the E side of the island. In W weather small vessels with local knowledge can find good anchorage in 4 to 5 fathoms near the head of the bay. At the head of **Fossil Bay**, on the S side of **Sucia Island**, there is a State Parks and Recreation Commission small-craft anchorage and float pier; water is available. The bays and coves around Sucia Island have been designated as Sensitive Eelgrass Areas. Vessels are encouraged to avoid anchoring in less than 30 feet of water. Numerous mooring buoys are available for recreational vessels.

(216) Reefs extend about 1.5 miles W of Sucia Islands to **West Bank**, which has a minimum depth of 8 feet. Strong tidal currents exist between West Bank and the Sucia Islands; only vessels with local knowledge should transit the area.

(217) **Clements Reef**, 0.5 mile N of Sucia Islands, is about 1.2 miles long and 0.3 mile wide. The NW end and the SE end of the reef are marked by buoys.

(218) The tidal currents are particularly strong and dangerous between Patos Island and East Point on Saturna Island, BC, and for 2 miles N in the Strait of Georgia. Tidal currents between Patos Island and Sucia Islands are less extreme and more regular than Boundary Pass.

Haro Strait, SW approach (Canada)

(219) The several channels and passages leading between the islands and dangers off the coast of British Columbia from Gonzales Point to **Cadboro Point**, 2.8 miles NNE, constitute the SW approach to Haro Strait. These passages and channels should be used only by vessels with local knowledge.

(220) The side of Haro Strait W of the international line is bordered by several islands and reefs, the most important of which are, from S to N: **Kelp Reefs**, marked by a light, about 7 miles N of Discovery Island; **Sidney Island**, about 3 miles NW of the light on Kelp Reefs; **Moresby Island**, marked by a light, about 16 miles N of Baynes Channel and Discovery Island, and the smaller islands and reefs in between.

(221) **Swanson Channel,** used sometimes as an alternate route by vessels bound for Alaska points, extends NW between Moresby Island and the **Pender Islands**, and connects ultimately with Active Pass to reach the Strait of Georgia in 48°53'N.

(222) **Active Pass** is deep but tortuous and in its narrowest part is about 600 yards wide. The dangers do not extend over 200 yards from shore. Vessels should enter the pass at slack water, if possible, but a vessel with a speed of 10 knots can always get through. A vessel with local knowledge can take advantage of the eddies and variations of the tidal currents, but others should keep in midchannel. Great care should be taken to avoid the shoals on either side of the N entrance to the pass.

(223) **Enterprise Reef**, in the S approach to Active Pass, consists of two rocky heads about 400 yards apart. The W head uncovers 3 feet, and the E head is awash. Foul ground extends between the heads and 200 yards W of the W head. A light is on the W head, and a buoy marks the E head.

(224) **South Pender Island**, 3 miles N of Stuart Island, is marked by a light on **Gowlland Point**, its SE extremity. The last of the Canadian lights in this stretch is on **East Point**, the E point of **Saturna Island**, 6.2 miles ENE of Gowlland Point.

(225) **Rosenfeld Rock**, 1.2 miles NNE of East Point, is marked by a lighted buoy. The rock is covered by 1¼ fathoms, and rocks that bare are within 900 yards of it. Close E of the rock, overfalls and dangerous tide rips are formed.

(226) (See Pub. 154, Sailing Directions (Enroute) for British Columbia, published by the National Geospatial-Intelligence Agency, and Sailing Directions, British Columbia Coast, (South Portion) Vol. 1, published by the Canadian Hydrographic Service for more details of the islands and features on the Canadian side.)

(227) **San Juan Channel**, the middle one of three principal channels leading from the Strait of Juan de Fuca to the Strait of Georgia, separates San Juan Island from the islands E. It is 13 miles long from its S end to its junction with President Channel at the N end. San Juan Channel is deep throughout and, except near its S entrance, has few off-lying dangers.

Currents

(228) In the S end of San Juan Channel, between Goose Island and Deadman Island, the average current velocity is 2.6 knots on the flood and ebb, however, maximum flood currents of 5 knots or more cause severe rips and eddies. Daily current predictions for this location may be obtained from the Tidal Current Tables.

(229) **Cattle Point** is the SE extremity of San Juan Island and forms the W point at the S entrance to San Juan Channel. **Cattle Point Light** (48°27'02"N., 122°57'48"W.), 94 feet above the water, is shown from a white octagonal tower on the point. Cattle were once loaded here for shipment to and from Victoria.

(230) **Salmon Bank**, S of Cattle Point and on the W side of **Middle Channel**, is an extensive shoal covered 1½ to 3 fathoms; it is marked by a lighted gong buoy. Kelp grows on the rocks. **Whale Rocks**, two dark rocks about 5 feet high, are on the E side of Middle Channel 0.6 mile NW of Long Island. A reef, with a least depth of 8 feet, extends 0.4 mile S of Whale Rocks.

(231) **Long Island**, 1.5 miles NW of Iceberg Point, is the largest of a group of islands on the E side of the entrance to San Juan Channel.

(232) **Lopez Island** is the southeasternmost one of the San Juan Islands; **Lopez Hill**, 488 feet high, is near the S midsection of the island. **Iceberg Point**, 3.3 miles SE of Cattle Point, is at the W extremity of the S part of Lopez Island and is marked by **Iceberg Point Light 2** (48°25'19"N., 122°53'39"W.), shown from a white square concrete house with red daybeacon, 35 feet above the water.

(233) **Richardson** is a small settlement on the N shore of the cove N of Iceberg Point, and close N of **Charles Island**. Five fuel tanks are prominent from seaward. A wharf directly below the fuel tanks has a face 120 feet long and extends over rocks to a depth of 17 feet. Gasoline and diesel fuel may be obtained; moor alongside a high pier when fueling.

(234) **Mackaye Harbor**, N of Iceberg Point, has several private piers used by seafood company vessels. The harbor affords good shelter in 5 to 6 fathoms, soft mud; small craft with local knowledge can obtain excellent shelter in **Barlow Bay**, on the S side of the harbor. Vessels approaching Mackaye Harbor or Richardson should pass at least 0.3 mile S and E of the off-lying islands and islets. Local vessels, by keeping close to the N shore to avoid rocks near midchannel, use a small passage between Lopez and Charles Islands, but this should not be attempted without local knowledge. **Twin Rocks**, in midchannel of this small passage, are marked by a daybeacon.

(235) **Davis Point**, the SW end of Lopez Island, is on the E side of the S entrance to San Juan Channel. **Deadman**

Island is close off the E side of the entrance, and several rocks are within 600 yards N of the island. **Goose Island**, small and low, is about 0.5 mile N of Cattle Point and close off the W side of the entrance to San Juan Channel.

(236) **Shark Reef**, awash, is over a mile N of Deadman Island and close off some white cliffs on the E side of San Juan Channel.

(237) From Goose Island N to **Pear Point**, the W side of San Juan Channel is foul with many rocks covered and awash within 0.7 mile of the shore. However, good anchorage for small vessels can be had W of **Harbor Rock**, at the S end, between the 10 and 20-fathom curves.

(238) **North Bay** is entered between Pear Point and **Dinner Island**. Gravel is barged from pits on the NW shore of the bay to Vancouver Island. **Little Island**, at the head of North Bay, is connected to the mainland by a narrow spit. Just N of Little Island, on the W side of the spit, is a park with a launching ramp. The bay affords fair anchorage in 7 to 10 fathoms, about 800 yards N of Dinner Island. Two dangers are in the approaches to the bay; a rocky shoal covered ¾ fathom 0.7 mile E of Dinner Island, and another rock shoal covered ¾ fathom 0.4 mile SE of Dinner Island. In 2005, a shoal with a depth of 7 feet was reported inside the bay in about 48°31'01"N., 123°00'08"W. The passage W of Dinner Island should not be attempted.

(239) **Fisherman Bay**, on the E side of San Juan Channel abreast North Bay, is a shallow lagoon entered by a marked, narrow, and tortuous channel. A rock awash is on the E side of the channel at the mouth of the bay. Good anchorage with shelter from all winds may be had in 10 to 12 feet, soft bottom, for small craft with local knowledge. The tidal currents have considerable velocity. The village of **Lopez**, located near the entrance, is the largest community on Lopez Island. A resort in the bay has a pier and floats with berths for about 66 craft; electricity, gasoline, diesel fuel, water, ice and overnight facilities are available. A marina adjacent to the resort has 100 berths, water, electricity, marine supplies, and a 15-ton lift is available.

Charts 18433, 18434

(240) At **Turn Island**, off the E side of San Juan Island, San Juan Channel turns NW for about 7.5 miles and connects at its N end with Spieden Channel and President Channel.

(241) **Turn Rock**, about 0.2 mile E of Turn Island, is a ledge bare at half tide; it should be given a berth of at least 100 yards. A light is on the rock. **Reid Rock**, 1.4 miles NW of Turn Rock, is in midchannel off the entrance to Friday Harbor. The rock, covered 2¼ fathoms, rises abruptly from deep water and is marked by a lighted buoy.

(242) **Friday Harbor**, 1.4 miles W of Turn Island, is a small cove about 1 mile long and nearly as wide. **Brown Island**, locally known as Friday Island because of the housing development here, occupies the middle of the harbor, with shoals nearly 200 yards wide off both its E and S shores. A shoal, covered 3¼ fathoms and marked by a buoy, extends nearly into midchannel from the W shore of the island. Shoals off the SE end of the island are marked by a daybeacon. The harbor may be entered either E or W of Brown Island. Anchorage may be had off the wharves in 6 to 7 fathoms, and city floats provide berthing space for pleasure craft.

(243) **Friday Harbor**, the town on the W shore of the cove, is the county seat and the population center of San Juan Island, which has some farming in the interior of the island. Commercial fishermen and recreational boaters frequent Friday Harbor, especially in the summer months.

(244) The University of Washington maintains a marine biological laboratory 0.4 mile NNW of the N end of Brown Island. The E pier, a high structure cantilevered about 35 feet out from shore, makes a prominent landmark in entering Friday Harbor. Near the main building is the landing wharf with a 32-foot face and depths of 11 to 13 feet alongside. The wharf is exposed to winds from the NE, but is easily approached. It is marked by private lights.

(245) Friday Harbor is a **customs port of entry**. The customs office is about 75 yards W of the port's office, at the yacht club building. The customs officer also performs **immigration** and **agricultural quarantine** inspections.

(246) The Interisland Medical Center at Friday Harbor is the only complete medical facility in the San Juan Islands. In addition, Orcas and Lopez Islands have small clinics with resident physicians and paramedics. Air ambulance service to Seattle, Anacortes, or Bellingham is available on all the larger islands.

(247) The Port of Friday Harbor small-craft harbor, protected on the S and E sides by a long floating breakwater is marked at the N end by a light. Berths with electricity for over 500 craft are available. At least 150 of this total capacity is used for transient berthing. Water and pump-out station are available. **Note:** Vessels should not anchor within 100 yards of the floating breakwater because of the danger of fouling with the breakwater's anchor cables. A seaplane float is near the customs float at the port's small-craft harbor. There are three amber strobe signal lights in the harbor. They are located at the NE end of the Port of Friday Harbor Docks, on the University of Washington Laboratory shore, and at the NW end of Brown Island, respectively. It is reported that when activated, these strobe lights signal the takeoff or landing of seaplanes in the harbor. Gasoline, diesel fuel, water, ice, and marine supplies are available at Friday Harbor. SE of the Port of Friday Harbor are a charter dock and ferry slip. SE of the ferry slip are condominiums with private docks.

(248) A shipyard is at the S end of Friday Harbor. A 35-ton lift is available; complete hull and engine repairs can be made.

(249) Freight and passengers reach Friday Harbor by airplane or by State ferry. The town has an airport with surfaced and lighted runways; twin-engine aircraft can be accommodated. Mail is transported by air.

(250) **Point George**, the W point at the entrance to **Parks Bay**, is across the channel from Friday Harbor. Good anchorage for small craft in 6 to 8 fathoms, soft bottom, can be had in the bay. The head of the bay, however, is foul with submerged piles.

(251) **Wasp Islands** are in the W approach to West Sound between **Neck Point**, the NW tip of Shaw Island, and **Steep Point**, the SW extremity of Orcas Island. Several narrow channels lead between the islands; the channels in general use are the North and Pole Passes, close under the Orcas Island shore. The tidal currents have considerable velocity in the channels, which should be attempted only by vessels with local knowledge.

(252) **North Pass**, between Steep Point on Orcas Island and the Wasp Islands, leads E from San Juan Channel to Deer Harbor and into Pole Pass. The pass is about 0.2 mile wide between Steep Point and **Reef Island**, and is free of outlying dangers, except for a rock covered 10 feet, 0.3 mile E of the N end of Reef Island.

(253) **Deer Harbor**, E of Steep Point, has good anchorage in 6 to 7 fathoms about 0.2 mile from the head. **Fawn Island** is near the entrance of the harbor and about 200 yards from the W shore; vessels may pass on either side. The E shore of Deer Harbor should be given a berth of at least 300 yards because of a shoal which in some places extends more than 200 yards off.

(254) **Deer Harbor**, on the E side of the harbor, is a village with stores, a marina, and an inn. Pleasure boats call here frequently in the summer. The marina has about 100 berths, including 65 transient berths that can accommodate craft up to 100 feet. Services available include: electricity, gasoline, diesel fuel, water, ice, pump-out facility, launching ramp, marine supplies, a 40-ton marine railway and full repairs can be made.

(255) A private light is on the end of a pier about 0.8 mile SSE of the town of Deer Harbor.

(256) **Crane Island** is off the entrance to Deer Harbor and about 1 mile SE of Steep Point. The N shore of the island is foul with bare and covered rocks within 250 yards of it. A shoal covered ½ fathom is 350 yards N of the center of the N side of the island, and a rock that uncovers 5 feet is 200 yards off the E point, with foul ground between it and the shore.

(257) **Pole Pass** leads from North Pass to West Sound and separates Crane Island from Orcas Island; the fairway is 75 yards wide in its narrowest part. A 7-knot speed limit is enforced through Pole Pass and should not be attempted without local knowledge. A light is on the NE side of the pass at its narrowest part.

(258) **Wasp Passage** leads from San Juan Channel to West Sound and separates Crane Island from the N shore of Shaw Island. A light is on the rock 300 yards E of Bell Island at the E end of the pass, and on Cliff Island and **Shirt Tail Reef**, at the W end of the pass.

(259) **Bell Island**, small and wooded, is about 0.3 mile E of Crane Island. When transiting Pole Pass, vessels should pass Bell Island close-to in order to avoid the reef and shoals extending S from **Caldwell Point** on Orcas Island.

(260) **Cliff Island**, the southernmost of the Wasp Islands, is 0.4 mile SW of Crane Island, and is marked by a light on its S side. **Low Island**, small and 10 feet high, is about 700 yards W of Cliff Island, and **Nob Island**, 40 feet high, is close-to and NW of Cliff Island. Local vessels bound from Friday Harbor to Deer Harbor use a clear deep channel about 70 yards wide through the rocks and shoals lying between Cliff Island and Low Island.

(261) **Yellow Island**, the westernmost of the Wasp Islands, is about 0.8 mile WNW of Neck Point and about 3.5 miles NNW of Friday Harbor. The island is small, grassy, and nearly bare of trees. A shoal extends 300 yards W of the island and terminates in a rock that uncovers 3 feet and is marked by kelp. This island should be given a berth of not less than 0.5 mile. **McConnell Island**, NE of Yellow Island, is the largest of the group. **Coon Island**, is close to and SE of McConnell Island. **Bird Rock**, which uncovers, is between McConnell and Crane Islands, and is marked by a light.

(262) **Jones Island**, 2 miles N of Wasp Passage, is on the E side of the N entrance to San Juan Channel; the island is wooded. Small pleasure craft anchor in the bights of the N and S shores. A State marine park in the bight of the N shore has a small seasonal pier, campground, and mooring facilities; limited water is available. A buoy marks the N side of a rocky area on the N side of Jones Island near the entrance of the N bight. **Spring Passage** separates Jones Island from the SW part of Orcas Island; in general, the passage is free of danger.

(263) **Rocky Bay** is an open bight in the E side of San Juan Island. **O'Neal Island**, surrounded by a shoal, is almost in the middle of the bay.

(264) **Limestone Point**, about 1.2 miles NNW of O'Neal Island forms the W point of the N entrance to San Juan Channel, and is the NE portion of San Juan Island. Heavy tide rips and eddies form off Limestone Point and Green Point on Spieden Island, 0.7 mile N.

(265) **Lonesome Cove**, 0.2 mile W of Limestone Point, has a resort with cabins. Limited berthage and gasoline are available.

(266) **Flattop Island**, prominent in the N approaches to San Juan Channel, is 1 mile NE of the E end of Spieden Island. It is about 174 feet high, flat on top, and sparsely covered with underbrush and trees. **Gull Rock**, 33 feet high and bare, is about 0.3 mile NW of the NW shore of the island.

Charts 18421, 18431, 18432

(267) **White Rock**, 35 feet high, is about 2.7 miles N of the junction of Spieden and San Juan Channels and about midway between Flattop and Waldron Islands. Rocks,

bare and covered, marked by kelp, extend nearly 0.3 miles NW from White Rock. **Danger Rock**, covered 3 feet and marked by kelp, is 0.3 mile SE of White Rock.

(268) The NW approach to San Juan Channel from Boundary Pass extends between Waldron Island on the E and Stuart Island, Johns Island, and Spieden Island to the W and S.

(269) **President Channel**, between Waldron and Orcas Islands, is about 5 miles long. Depths are generally great, and the passage is free of dangers. The tidal currents have a velocity of 2 to 5 knots, and heavy swirls and tide rips, especially with an adverse wind, are off the N point of Waldron Island and between Waldron and Patos Islands. The rips are generally heaviest with the ebb current. Rips and swirls are also heavy off Limestone Point and the E end of Spieden Island.

(270) **Orcas Island** is wooded and mountainous. **Mount Constitution**, a 2,402-foot peak on the island's E side, is marked by a stone lookout tower and a lighted radio tower. **Turtleback Mountain (Turtle Back Range)** and **Orcas Knob**, conical, and bare on the summit, in the W part of the island, are prominent and easily recognized.

(271) **Point Doughty**, the NW tip of Orcas Island, is bare and terminates in a small knob on its outer end. A resort in the bight, 1.5 miles SSW of Point Doughty, has seasonal floats with about 40 berths, gasoline, water, ice, a concrete launching ramp, and some marine supplies. In 2006, a reported depth of 3 feet at mean lower low water was at the gas dock floats.

Local magnetic disturbances

(272) Differences from the normal variation of 2° or more have been observed in the vicinity of Point Doughty.

(273) **Parker Reef,** marked by a light, is about 0.7 mile off the N shore of Orcas Island and uncovers. The rocky reef extends about 110 yards in all directions from the light, except on the E side, where it extends about 160 yards from the light. Kelp covers the reef and the area between it and the shore. There are several shoal spots of 1¾ to 2¾ fathoms in the area within the 10-fathom curve SSW and W of Parker Reef.

(274) A passage between Sucia Islands on the N and Orcas Island on the S connects the N end of President Channel with the junction of the Strait of Georgia and Rosario Strait.

Chart 18434

Minor passages, San Juan Islands

(275) **Upright Channel**, between Lopez Island and Shaw Island, is about 3 miles long. **Canoe Island**, off **Flat Point**, constricts the passage to a width of less than 400 yards. Flat Point is marked by a light. General depths in the channel range from 20 to 25 fathoms. A shoal, covered 7½ fathoms, is 700 yards SSW, and a rock awash is 250 yards SW of the SW end of Canoe Island. Anchorages for small craft may be had in **Indian Cove**, W of Canoe Island, in 4 to 7 fathoms, soft bottom.

(276) **Harney Channel**, between Shaw and Orcas Islands, is the approach to West Sound from the E. General depths in the channel range from 11 to 30 fathoms with a 9-fathom shoal 700 yards E of Broken Point, the northernmost extremity of Shaw Island.

(277) **Orcas**, a village located on the N shore in a cove at the W end of Harney Channel, has a public wharf with about 9 feet alongside. Several year-round stores are located at Orcas. Water, ice, and some marine supplies are available. The ferry slip just E of the wharf serves the interisland ferry that operates from Anacortes. A rock, covered 2½ fathoms, is about 125 yards S of the wharf; deep water is between the rock and the shore.

(278) **Blind Bay**, a small cove indenting Shaw Island just opposite Orcas, has depths of 2 to 6 fathoms. There are several reefs at its NW entrance and along the SW side of the bay. **Blind Island** is in the entrance. A private daybeacon marks a rock that uncovers 3 feet on the E side of the entrance. **Shaw Island**, a village at the E entrance, is served by the ferry. **Broken Point**, 1.6 miles W of the Shaw Island landing, projects some 0.3 mile N from the N side of the island. It is quite prominent.

(279) **West Sound** indents the W part of the S shore of Orcas Island for about 2.8 miles. **Massacre Bay** is in the N part. The depths range from 7 to 20 fathoms. Anchorage in 7 to 12 fathoms may be had anywhere N of **Double Island**, which consists of two small islands connected at low water; it is close to the W shore near the entrance.

(280) **West Sound**, a village on the E shore, is about 2 miles N of the entrance. A few pilings remain of an old sawmill wharf; care should be taken to avoid submerged pilings about 100 feet SW of the wharf. A marina with the largest moorage facility on Orcas Island and largest repair facility in the San Juan Islands, is at West Sound. The marina has 180 berths and guest moorage is available on a 250-foot float on the S side of the marina. Gasoline, diesel fuel, water, pump-out station, a 30-ton travel lift, hull and engine repairs, and marine supplies are available.

(281) **Picnic Island**, is a low islet in the S part of the cove, close S from West Sound settlement. A shoal extends about 150 yards W from the island. In the bight E of the island is a marina with berths for about 80 small craft. An 11-ton hoist here can handle craft to 36 feet for hull and engine repairs. Marine supplies and a salvage and retrieval tug are available. In 1969, a channel with a depth of 1½ feet was reported to exist between Picnic Island and Orcas Island; local knowledge is advised.

(282) **Harbor Rock**, 4 feet high, lies in midchannel about 1.9 miles above the entrance to the sound; it is just inside Massacre Bay. The rocky patch marked by a daybeacon, is of small extent and is surrounded by depths of 1¾ to 10 fathoms.

Charts 18421, 18429, 18430

(283) **East Sound** indents Orcas Island NNW for about 6 miles. Depths vary from 15 fathoms at the entrance to 9 fathoms less than 0.2 mile from the head. There are no outlying dangers, and the shores may be approached to within 0.2 mile; however, a shoal covered less than 5 fathoms extends some 700 yards off the W shore, 0.8 mile inside the entrance. Anchorage may be had anywhere in the sound.

Local magnetic disturbance

(284) Differences from the normal variation of about 2° have been reported in the upper end of East Sound.

(285) **Olga** is a village on the W shore of **Buck Bay**, a small cove on the E shore of the sound just inside the entrance.

(286) **Cascade Bay**, a small cove on the E side of the sound, about 3 miles N of the entrance, is the site of a large resort with floats having berths with electricity for about 60 craft. Gasoline, diesel fuel, water, ice, and a restaurant are available. Depths of 15 feet are reported alongside the floats. The large white resort hotel on **Rosario Point,** the W point of the bay, is conspicuous.

(287) **Eastsound**, the largest village on Orcas Island, lies in the W of two small adjacent coves at the head of the sound. The wharf is built out to a depth of 7½ feet; gasoline and water are available. A medical clinic is at Eastsound; air ambulance service to Anacortes, Bellingham, or Seattle is available.

(288) **Obstruction Pass**, with a least width of 350 yards, separates **Obstruction Island** from Orcas Island, and leads W from Rosario Strait to the inner passages and sounds of the San Juan Islands. A launching ramp and float are on the N side of the pass about 0.6 mile NW of Deer Point; depths alongside the float are about 4 feet. Caution is advised because of the numerous private pilings and moorings in the area. Obstruction Pass is marked by a light on the NE side of Obstruction Island.

(289) **Peavine Pass**, safer and straighter than Obstruction Pass, separates Blakely Island from Obstruction Island. The pass is a little over 200 yards wide at its narrowest part, and in midchannel the least depth is 6 fathoms. Peavine Pass Light 1, on the SW point of Obstruction Island, marks the W entrance to the pass. **Spindle Rock**, marked by a daybeacon, lies about 0.2 mile offshore from Blakely Island at the E entrance to Peavine Pass.

Currents

(290) The currents through Obstruction and Peavine Passes have estimated velocities of 5.5 to 6.5 knots at times. Heavy tide rips occur E of Obstruction Island.

(291) **Blakely Island Shoal**, rocky and covered 11 feet, is 0.5 mile off the W side of Blakely Island and is marked on its S side by a lighted buoy. The passage between the shoal and Blakely Island is deep and clear.

(292) **Blakely Island**, E of Lopez and Shaw Islands, is privately owned and maintained but open to the public. At its N end, bordering on Peavine Pass, is a small-craft basin and channel. About 65 berths are at the cove dock and inside the basin. An airplane landing strip and lodging are nearby. Gasoline, diesel fuel, water, ice, and some marine supplies are available.

(293) **Thatcher Pass**, between Blakely Island and **Decatur Island**, is about 0.5 mile wide in its narrowest part. The pass is deep and free of danger with the exception of **Lawson Rock**, in midchannel, 0.4 mile N of Fauntleroy Point. The S point of Blakely Island and Lawson Rock are marked by lights. Thatcher Pass serves as the primary route for ferries transiting from Anacortes to the San Juan Island terminals.

(294) **Fauntleroy Point**, the NE end of Decatur Island, is marked by a light. With a S wind and ebb current, heavy rips will be encountered off the E entrance to Thatcher Pass.

(295) **Leo Reef**, in the entrance to **Swifts Bay** on the NE end of Lopez Island, uncovers and is marked by a light.

(296) In 1981, a rock covered 3 feet was reported about 350 yards WNW of Leo Reef Light. **Port Stanley** is a small village on the shores of Swifts Bay.

(297) **Upright Head**, the northernmost point of Lopez Island, is a narrow peninsula that attains an elevation of 260 feet. A ferry slip is in the small cove at the tip of this peninsula. A private light is 50 yards out from the slip. There is daily ferry service with the other islands and the mainland.

(298) **Lopez Sound**, on the E side of Lopez Island, may be entered from Rosario Strait by Thatcher Pass. The depths in the greater part of the sound are 3 to 5 fathoms, muddy bottom, but a narrow and deeper channel is along the E shore.

(299) Fair protection in SE weather can be had in the area W of Decatur Island and N of **Center Island** in 3 to 5 fathoms, mud bottom. Strong winds blow across the low neck at the S end of Decatur Island and may make the area W uncomfortable for small craft. Good anchorage in W weather can be had in the large bight on the W side of the sound.

(300) **Decatur** is a small village on the W side of Decatur Island. A wharf with depths of 8 feet at its end is here.

(301) **Lopez Pass**, S of Decatur Island, leads from Rosario Strait into Lopez Sound. The pass has depths of 9 to 12 fathoms, but is very narrow and little used. A light is at the S end of Decatur Island.

(302) **Rosario Strait**, the easternmost of the three main channels leading from the Strait of Juan de Fuca to the Strait of Georgia, is 20 miles long and from 1.5 to 5 miles wide. The water is deep, and the most important dangers are marked. A bank with a least depth of 7 fathoms is located 0.3 mile E of Orcas Island and one mile WSW of Strawberry Island at about 48°33'19.4"N., 122°45'39.6"W.

(303) The strait is in constant use by vessels bound for Cherry Point, Bellingham, Anacortes, and the San Juan Islands. Vessels bound for British Columbia or Alaska also frequently use it in preference to the passages farther W, when greater advantage can be taken of the tidal currents.

(304) A **Vessel Traffic Service** has been established in the Strait of Juan de Fuca, E of Port Angeles, and in the adjacent waters. (See **161.101 through 161.187**, chapter 2, for regulations, and the beginning of this chapter for additional information.)

Tides and Currents

(305) For times and velocities of current in Rosario Strait and vicinity, the Tidal Current Tables should be consulted. The currents in Lopez, Thatcher, and Obstruction Passes are reported to attain velocities of 3 to 7 knots. This should be kept in mind when proceeding through Rosario Strait, particularly at night or in thick weather. On the ebb of a large tide off the entrance to the passes, a S wind causes tide rips that are dangerous to small craft.

(306) Small craft can get good protection from W and S weather by anchoring near the head of **Watmough Bay**, at the extreme SE end of Lopez Island.

(307) **Colville Island**, 64 feet high, small and bare of trees, is off the SE end of Lopez Island. Heavy kelp extends W of Colville Island. **Davidson Rock**, 0.3 mile E of Colville Island, bares and is marked by a light. Mariners should give Colville Island and Davidson Rock a good berth. The southbound lane of the Traffic Separation Scheme is close S and E of Davidson Rock.

(308) **Aleck Bay**, the W and largest of three small bays on the S shore of Lopez Island, affords good anchorage except in heavy SE winds for small vessels in 4 to 7 fathoms, mud bottom. Rocks, awash and covered, and reefs abound in these waters; caution is advised.

(309) A bank covered 10 to 20 fathoms extends across the S entrance to Rosario Strait. A shoal in the W part of the bank, 1.6 miles E of Davidson Rock, is covered 4 fathoms and marked by a lighted bell buoy on the W edge. **Lawson Reef**, 0.6 by 0.3 mile in extent, in the E part of the bank, is 1.7 miles W of Deception Island. The reef has a least depth of 2.2 fathoms and is marked by a lighted bell buoy.

Charts 18427, 18429, 18421

(310) **Deception Pass**, the impressive 2-mile passage between Whidbey Island and **Fidalgo Island**, provides a challenging route that connects the N end of Skagit Bay with the S end of Rosario Strait. Near its middle the width is reduced to 150 yards by **Pass Island**. A fixed highway bridge over the pass between Pass Island and Whidbey Island has a clearance of 144 feet at the center and 104 feet elsewhere. Overhead telephone and power cables 50 yards and 0.2 mile E of the bridge have a minimum clearance of 220 feet.

(311) Deception Pass is used frequently by local boats bound from Seattle to Anacortes, Bellingham, and the San Juan Islands. The pass should be negotiated at the time of slack, since the velocity of the stream at other times makes it prohibitive to some craft. However, many fast boats run it at all stages of the tide. The pass is also used by log tows from the N bound to Everett or Seattle, which prefer this route to avoid the rough weather W of Whidbey Island.

(312) Currents in the narrows of Deception Pass attain velocities in excess of 8 knots at times and cause strong eddies along the shores. With W weather, heavy swells and tide rips form and make passage dangerous to all small craft. (See the Tidal Current Tables for daily predictions.)

(313) **Canoe Pass**, N of Pass Island, is not recommended except for small craft with local knowledge.

(314) **Deception Island**, 1 mile W of Pass Island, is 0.4 mile NW of **West Point**, the NW end of Whidbey Island. A shoal which bares at low water extends 175 yards (160 meters) S of Deception Island. Foul ground extends 262 yards (240 meters) NW of West Point. The passage between these two hazards is 200 yards (183 meters) wide with a least depth of 2.5 fathoms and great care should be taken when navigating in this area. **Northwest Pass**, N of Deception Island, is the preferred route. The Northwest Pass channel is deeper, but narrows and follows close to Lighthouse Point; a light is on the point.

(315) **Strawberry Island** lies almost in the middle of Deception Pass, 0.4 mile E of Pass Island. **Ben Ure Island** is 0.2 mile S of Strawberry Island at the entrance to Cornet Bay; a light is at the NE end of the island.

(316) **Cornet Bay**, shallow and suitable for small craft only, indents the N end of Whidbey Island, in Deception Pass. A marina with a privately dredged entrance channel and mooring basin is in the bay; the channel is marked by private daybeacons. The marina has about 85 open and covered berths at the floats; gasoline, diesel fuel, electricity, water, ice, and marine supplies are available. Two marine service and repair facilities are W of the marina. A public small-craft facility with berthing, pump-out station, and a launching ramp is E of the marina.

Routes

(317) From W the best water through Deception Pass will be found 0.3 mile W of **Rosario Head**, a point 0.5 mile N of Deception Island. Steer a SE course to pass about 100 yards SW of the light on Lighthouse Point; then follow an E course through the middle of the pass, being careful to guard against sets from the current when running partly across it. After passing under the bridge, favor slightly the N shore so as to avoid the pinnacle rocks and ledges making out from the S shore. After leaving Pass Island, steer to pass about midway between Ben Ure and Strawberry Islands. Strawberry Island should not

be approached within 125 yards because a reef, marked by kelp, extends S of the island. From a position off Ben Ure Island Light 2, steer a NE course to pass about midway between **Hoypus Point** and **Yokeko Point**. The flood current N and W of Strawberry Island sets NE and should be guarded against.

(318)　**Bowman (Reservation) Bay**, a small bight between **Reservation Head** and Rosario Head, offers anchorage for small craft in 2¼ fathoms, mud bottom. **Northwest Island** between Rosario Head and Sares Head, is 28 feet high and grass-covered. **Sares Head**, 1 mile N of Deception Island, is steep-to and 480 feet high.

(319)　**Burrows Bay** indents the W shore of Fidalgo Island between **Biz Point** and **Fidalgo Head**. Burrows Bay is a broad open bight affording anchorage in the N part, in 15 to 16 fathoms, soft bottom. Protection from W and N is afforded by **Burrows Island** and **Allan Island**, but the bay is exposed to S weather. In the SE part, the depths are less than 6 fathoms, and in places shoals extend almost 0.4 mile off the E and S shores of the bay. E of the passage between Allan and Burrows Islands is a middle ground with a least depth of 5 fathoms. Small craft using Deception Pass, bound to or from points in the islands or from Bellingham Bay, pass through Burrows Bay and the passage N of Burrows Island.

(320)　**Burrows Island Light** (48°28'41"N., 122°42'49"W.), 57 feet above the water, is shown from a 34-foot white square tower on a building at the W end of the island; a mariner radio activated sound signal is at the station; initiated by keying the microphone five times on VHF-FM channel 83A.

Local magnetic disturbance

(321)　Differences from normal variation of 4° have been observed on the E shore of Burrows Bay.

(322)　**Williamson Rocks**, a group of small, grass-covered islets and rocks, are 0.5 mile S of Allan Island and are marked on the S side by a lighted gong buoy. **Dennis Shoal**, 500 yards off the S shore of Allan Island and 0.6 mile NW of Williamson Rocks, bares and is marked on its W side by a buoy.

(323)　**Flounder Bay**, a well-sheltered basin and popular yachting harbor at the N end of Burrows Bay, is the site of a large marina. The entrance channel is protected by jetties and marked by private lights. In 2007, a depth of 3 feet was reported in the entrance channel. The E side of the entrance is subject to shoaling. Gasoline, diesel fuel, water, ice, about 250 berths with electricity, transient berths, dry storage facilities, two 1½-ton hoists, a 24-ton lift, and marine supplies are available at the marina. Hull, engine, and electronic repairs can be made. A private company located at the W end of the marina provides heavy transport service to the islands. A road connects the bay with a highway, providing access to the State ferry terminal in Ship Harbor, the Anacortes airport, and the city of Anacortes.

Charts 18421, 18424, 18429, 18430, 18431

(324)　**Bird Rocks**, consisting of three rocks close together, are near the middle of Rosario Strait, about 2 miles WNW of Burrows Island Light. The southernmost and largest is 37 feet high. There is deep water close-to, and passage may be made on either side of the rocks.

(325)　**Belle Rock**, bare at extreme low water and marked by a light, is about 0.5 mile NE of Bird Rocks. Belle Rock can be passed about 0.6 mile to the E by keeping **Tide Point**, the W extremity of Cypress Island, and **Lawrence Point**, the E end of Orcas Island, in range on a bearing of about 359°.

(326)　Rosario Strait is generally clear, with great depths, except for the following principal offshore dangers:

(327)　**Kellett Ledge**, 2 miles N of Point Colville, extends 700 yards off **Cape St. Mary**, on the SE part of Lopez Island. The ledge is marked by kelp and a buoy, and uncovers at the lowest tides. In 2000, two shoal spots were reported E of the ledge. The first shoal was about 550 yards E in about 48°26'58"N., 122°47'13"W. with a depth of about 7 fathoms. The second shoal about 700 yards E in about 48°26'57"N., 122°47'05"W. with a depth of about 8 fathoms.

(328)　**James Island** is close off **Decatur Head**, the E end of Decatur Island, and between the two is a deep but narrow passage; on the island are two hills with heights of 260 and 219 feet.

(329)　**Pointer Island**, 16 feet high, is 0.3 mile off the SE shore of Blakely Island, and **Black Rock**, 4 feet high and marked by a light, is 0.5 mile off the E shore of the island.

(330)　**Cypress Island**, 1,530 feet high, steep on the lower slopes and gently rounding at the top, is on the E side of Rosario Strait and opposite Blakely Island. From S the island appears to lie in the middle of Rosario Strait.

(331)　A shoal extends about 0.4 mile S from **Reef Point**, the SW tip of Cypress Island. A lighted buoy is about 0.7 mile S of Reef Point. Vessels rounding the point should not attempt to pass between the buoy and the point as submerged piles and heavy kelp may exist in that area.

(332)　**Strawberry Island**, small, low, and wooded, is about 400 yards off the W shore of Cypress Island. Passage E of it is not recommended. An indifferent anchorage may be had in **Strawberry Bay** in 7 fathoms; it is seldom used.

(333)　**Lydia Shoal**, covered 4 fathoms and marked on its S side by a lighted gong buoy, is 1 mile E of Obstruction Pass Light. **Peapod Rocks**, marked by a light on the largest rock of the group at the N end, are 1 mile S of Lawrence Point on Orcas Island. This group of islands extends about 1 mile in a NE direction, some 0.5 mile from the Orcas Island shore, which is fringed with rocks and reefs.

(334) **Buckeye Shoal**, with a least depth of 3½ fathoms, is 1.2 miles SSE from **North Peapod**, and is marked by a lighted bell buoy. Between this and the N end of Cypress Island are **Cypress Reef**, a dangerous rocky patch marked by a daybeacon at the S end, and **Towhead Island**, 0.3 mile to the SE and about 400 yards N of the N end of Cypress Island. The passage between the two is used by local vessels, especially those plying between Obstruction Pass and Bellingham Bay.

(335) **Doe Bay** indents the SE shore of Orcas Island abreast Peapod Rocks. **Doe Bay (Doebay)**, a village on the bay, has a wharf with 12 feet at its end; during strong S winds the wharf should not be approached. Doe Island, 0.6 mile SSW of Doe Bay, is a State park.

(336) **Sinclair Island**, N of Cypress Island, is wooded and comparatively low in places; dangerous reefs extend 0.8 mile off the N shore. Portions of **Boulder Reef**, the outermost danger, uncover at half tide; kelp marking the reef is frequently drawn under by the current. The outer end of the reef is marked by a lighted bell buoy. **Urban**, a village at the SW end of the island, has a pier with depths of 12 feet at the end.

(337) **Lummi Island**, wooded and about 8 miles long, forms the E side of the N end of Rosario Strait, opposite Orcas Island. The N part is low, but in the S part **Lummi Peak** attains an elevation of over 1,600 feet.

(338) **Lummi Rocks** are off the SW shore of Lummi Island about 3 miles NW of **Carter Point**, the S tip. They are marked by a light.

(339) Shoals extend over 0.5 mile from **Point Migley**, the NW extremity of Lummi Island; the NW edge of the shoals is marked by a lighted buoy. **Village Point** on the NW side of Lummi Island is marked by a light. **Legoe Bay** is an open bight SE of Village Point. A small seasonal marina and boat launch is located in Legoe Bay.

(340) **Clark Island** and **Barnes Island**, and the several adjacent rocks and islets, lie almost in the middle of Rosario Strait, about 2.5 miles NNW of Lawrence Point on Orcas Island. These islands may be passed on either side, giving them a berth of 0.5 mile. A light, 40 feet above water, is on the easternmost island.

(341) **Matia Island**, a wildlife refuge about 4 miles W of Point Migley, is 120 feet high and wooded. The mooring float of a State marine park is **Rolfe Cove** on the NW side of the island; water is available. **Puffin Island**, 40 feet high, is about 0.2 mile E of Matia Island. A reef, marked at its SE extremity by a light, extends E from the SE end of Matia Island to a point about 0.2 E of Puffin Island. Mariners should not attempt to pass between the islands.

(342) **Alden Bank**, 3 miles N of Matia Island, within the 10-fathom curve is about 3 miles long in a SE direction. The shallowest part is near the SE end of the bank with depths of 2¾ to 4 fathoms covering a considerable area and marked by kelp. The bank is marked by a lighted gong buoy off its NW end, a lighted bell buoy off its SE end, and by a buoy on its E edge. Caution is advised due to the heavy concentrations of crab pots and marker buoys, especially in the southern part of the bank.

Chart 18427

(343) **Skagit Bay**, N part, between the N part of Whidbey Island and the mainland, is entered from the N through Deception Pass and from the S through Saratoga Passage. Skagit River, described in chapter 13, empties into the SE part of the bay.

(344) The greater portion of Skagit Bay is filled with flats, bare at low water. Shoals extend 100 to 300 yards off the Whidbey Island shore.

(345) Along the shore of Whidbey Island, between it and the edge of the flats, is a natural channel varying in width from 0.2 to 0.5 mile, except at Hope Island, where it narrows to 150 yards. The channel is marked with lights and buoys from Deception Pass to the N entrance of Saratoga Passage. The main channel from Deception Pass S through Skagit Bay has depths of 6 fathoms or more.

(346) Velocity and direction of the current vary throughout this channel. The flood current enters through Deception Pass and sets in a generally S direction. The ebb flows in a general N direction. SW of Hope Island, the velocity is 2.3 knots on the flood and 2.0 knots on the ebb. S of Goat Island the velocity is 1.8 knots on the flood and 1.4 knots on the ebb. N of Rocky Point the velocity is 0.6 knot on the flood and 1.0 knot on the ebb. (See the Tidal Current Tables for predictions.)

(347) **Similk Bay**, at the N end of Skagit Bay, is used for log-rafting operations and is unsafe for navigation due to numerous submerged piles. **Skagit Island** and **Kiket Island**, 111 feet and 194 feet high, respectively, are just S of Similk Bay opposite the E entrance to Deception Pass. **Hope Island**, 1 mile S of Skagit Island, is fringed with rocks off its E side, and marked by a light on its W point. An aquiculture site, marked by private lights, is 0.4 mile NNE of Hope Island in about 48°24'28"N., 122°33'33"W. **Ben Ure Spit**, across the channel from Hope Island, is a low projecting point within a shoal extending about 350 yards E.

(348) Good anchorage may be had in **Kiket Bay**, N of Hope Island, and vessels at times make use of this anchorage area while waiting for slack water in Deception Pass.

(349) The narrow channel E of Hope Island is used by small craft with local knowledge. This channel, with a controlling depth of 5 fathoms, passes 130 yards off the Hope Island shore. The bottom is rocky and very irregular, and numerous dangers marked by heavy kelp are between the channel and the Fidalgo Island shore. A summer anchorage for pleasure craft is S of **Snee-oosh (Hunot) Point**.

(350) **Seal Rocks**, 1.4 miles S of Hope Island, are on the E side of the main channel. They are marked by a light.

(351) **Swinomish Channel** is a dredged channel that connects the waters of Skagit Bay with those of Padilla Bay, about 10 miles to the N. The entrance channel from Skagit Bay leads ENE between two jetties, thence N of **Goat Island**, which is rocky, steep, and timber covered, thence through **Hole in the Wall**, in the S part of Fidalgo Island, and thence N to Padilla Bay. The S jetty, submerged except for a small section near Goat Island, extends about 0.6 mile W of Goat Island and is marked by buoys; the N jetty, submerged and marked by a light off its W end, extends W about 1.1 miles from the S end of Fidalgo Island. A **072°–252° lighted range** marks the entrance channel from Skagit Bay, and other navigational aids mark the channel to Padilla Bay. In 2004-2010, the midchannel controlling depth was 6.4 feet in the channel from Skagit Bay to Padilla Bay.

(352) Several bridges and overhead power and telephone cables cross Swinomish Channel; minimum clearance of the power cables is 72 feet. Just S of La Conner, the highway fixed bridge has a clearance of 75 feet for a center width of 275 feet. At the Padilla Bay entrance, the railroad swing bridge has a clearance of 5 feet; the span is left in the open position until a train approaches. Twin fixed highway bridges 0.2 mile S of the swing bridge have a clearance of 75 feet.

(353) Most of the yachts going between Bellingham and Seattle prefer Swinomish Channel to Deception Pass because of the calmer water and shorter run. The channel is used extensively for towing logs. Two floats and a launching ramp are under the E end of the highway bridge at the N end of Swinomish Channel.

(354) **La Conner**, near the S end of Swinomish Channel, is the center of a rich agricultural district, and has several fish canneries. Many commercial fishing boats operate from here. Piers, wharves, and mooring floats are along the entire waterfront, much of which is bulkheaded. A marina at La Conner operates a S and N basin along the E side of the channel about 0.6 and 0.8 mile N of the highway fixed bridge, respectively. The marina has 500 covered and uncovered berths, including about 60 transient berths, and can also provide dry storage. Services available include: electricity, gasoline, diesel fuel, water, ice, pump-out facility, launching ramp, marine supplies, an 82-ton marine lift and complete repairs (hull, engine, electrical) can be made. An extensive log storage and sorting yard is on the W side of the channel opposite the marina basins.

(355) **Guemes Channel**, between Guemes Island on the N and Fidalgo Island on the S, leads E from Rosario Strait to Padilla Bay. The channel, which is about 3 miles long and 0.5 mile wide at its narrowest point, has depths of 8 to 18 fathoms. Lighted buoys mark the channel at the W end.

Local magnetic disturbance

(356) Differences from normal variation of as much as 14° have been observed off the SE point of Guemes Island.

(357) **Shannon Point**, the S point at the W entrance of Guemes Channel, is low and rounding, and marked by a light and a mariner radio activated sound signal, initiated by keying the microphone five times on VHF-FM channel 81A. A shoal extends to the NW from the point.

(358) The current velocity in Guemes Channel exceeds 5 knots at times. It is reported that the flood (E current) is accompanied by an eddy between the E end of Guemes Island and Cap Sante with the W countercurrent extending about 200 yards from the shore along the N side of Fidalgo Island. (See the Tidal Current Tables for predictions.)

(359) **Ship Harbor** is a bight close E of Shannon Point, at the W entrance to Guemes Channel. Washington State ferries to the San Juan Islands and Sydney, BC depart frequently from facilities on the W side of the bight. Vessels anchoring here in heavy weather should be cautious of dragging anchor because the bottom is not good holding ground.

(360) **City of Seattle Rock**, covered 1½ fathoms, is 200 yards offshore on the S side of the channel, 2 miles E of Shannon Point.

(361) **Anacortes**, is on the S shore of Guemes Channel. The port is incorporated as the **Port of Anacortes**. Commerce includes logs and petroleum products.

(362) **Cap Sante Waterway**, a dredged channel leading to the E waterfront of Anacortes, is marked by daybeacons and lights. The ends of the breakwaters forming the boat haven are marked by lights. In 2010, the controlling depth was 11 feet in the entrance channel to the basin, thence depths of 11 to 12 feet in the basin. Vessels should give the S breakwater a berth of at least 40 feet to stay in good water.

(363) A dredged channel, marked by lights and buoys, extends about 0.7 mile SW from the entrance of Cape Sante Waterway to the waterfront area of Anacortes Industrial Park. In 2010, the controlling depth was 13 feet in the channel. A marina is at the N end of the industrial waterfront area. Private berthing with water, electricity, storage boxes, and telephone connections are available. A haul out and repair yard with a 35-ton lift is at the S end of the marina.

Anchorage

(364) General Anchorages have been established off Anacortes. (See **33 CFR §110.1** and **§110.230**, chapter 2, for limits and regulations.)

Pilotage, Anacortes

(365) Pilotage is compulsory for all vessels except those under enrollment or engaged exclusively in the coasting trade on the W coast of the continental United States (including Alaska) and/or British Columbia. Pilotage is available from the Puget Sound Pilots. See Pilotage, Strait of Juan de Fuca and Puget Sound, indexed as such, early this chapter.

Towage

(366) Tugs may be arranged through the Marine Exchange of Puget Sound, which monitors radiotelephone VHF-FM channels 9 and 20.

Quarantine, customs, immigration, and agricultural quarantine

(367) (See chapter 3, Vessel Arrival Inspections, and Appendix A for addresses.)

(368) **Quarantine** is enforced in accordance with regulations of the U.S. Public Health Service. (See Public Health Service, chapter 1.)

(369) Anacortes is a **customs port of entry**,

Harbor regulations

(370) The port is controlled by a port commission and a manager, whose office is on the port wharf at the foot of Commercial Avenue.

Wharves

(371) The Port of Anacortes operates three deep-draft wharves. For a complete description of the port facilities refer to Port Series No. 37, published and sold by the U.S. Army Corps of Engineers. (See Appendix A for address.) The alongside depths are reported depths. (For information on the latest depths contact the port authorities.) Water is available at the three port wharves.

(372) **Port of Anacortes, Pier No. 1** (48°31'20"N., 122°36'40"W.): wooden pilings, 540-foot berthing space; 33 feet alongside; deck height, 16 feet; forklifts; receipt and shipment of general cargo.

(373) **Port of Anacortes, Pier No. 2** (48°31'20"N., 122°36'24"W.): concrete piling with concrete surface, 1,113-foot berthing space with dolphins; 44 feet reported alongside; deck height, 16 feet; 13½ acres open storage; shipment of petroleum coke and logs; mooring vessels. The wharf is marked on each end by a private light.

(374) **Port of Anacortes, Curtis Wharf** (48°31'20"N., 122°37'00"W): steel piling with concrete surface, 313-foot berthing with dolphins; 28 feet reported alongside; deck height, 16 feet; one acre of unpaved open storage.

(375) **Note:** Considerable current sets along the faces of these wharves (E flood, W ebb); it is advisable to dock at slack water or against the current.

Supplies

(376) Gasoline, diesel fuel, and other small-craft supplies may be obtained at the port boat haven. Ice and marine supplies are available in the city.

Repairs

(377) The largest repair facility in the area is on the S side of Guemes Channel (48°31'18"N., 122°36'35"W.) The yard has a 5,000-ton capacity lift; a 314-foot dry dock with a 9,000-ton capacity, and a 600-ton marine railway. Machine and carpentry shops are also available and complete hull and engine repairs can be made. A marina on the E waterfront of Anacortes, S of Cap Sante Boat Haven can provide complete repairs (hull, engine, electrical) and has a 55-ton marine lift. A large boatyard about 1.5 miles E of Shannon Point (48°30'43"N., 122°38'44"W.) is also equipped for complete repairs with two marine railways having a maximum capacity of 2,000 tons. Complete repairs can also be found at a repair shop in the Cap Sante Boat Haven.

Small-craft facilities

(378) Cap Sante Boat Haven (Port of Anacortes) has up to 200 permanent and transient berths. Services available include electricity, gasoline, diesel fuel, water, ice, pump-out facility, marine supplies and a 50-ton marine lift. A harbormaster assigns berths, and can be contacted on VHF-FM channel 66A.

Communications

(379) The port has an airport about five miles W of the city center. A private automobile ferry provides regular service to Guemes Island. Washington State Ferries provide service to the San Juan Islands and Sydney, BC. from facilities at Ship Harbor Bight.

(380) **Fidalgo Bay**, a shallow arm of Padilla Bay, extends S from the E end of Guemes Channel.

(381) **Padilla Bay**, between the mainland and the N part of Fidalgo Island, is largely occupied by drying flats, but deep water is E of Anacortes and Guemes Island. Entrance to the bay from Rosario Strait is through Guemes Channel; a passage E of Guemes Island leads into Padilla Bay from the N.

(382) **March Point** is a low peninsula between Fidalgo and Padilla Bays. The two long Tesoro and Shell Refinery piers extend N to deep water from the N end of the point. The W pier, owned by Shell Oil, has a 7,150-foot approach trestle, deck height of 22 feet, and is marked at the E and W ends by private lights. The N side of the pier has 1,130 feet of berthing space with dolphins and depths of 45 feet alongside; the S side of the pier has 735 feet of berthing space with dolphins and depths of 45 feet reported alongside.

(383) The Tesoro Pier, 0.5 mile E of the Shell Pier, has a 3,466-foot approach trestle, deck height of 22 feet, and is marked at the E end by a private light and at the W end by a private light and sound signal. The N side of the pier has 974 feet of berthing space with dolphins and a depth of 45 feet reported alongside; the S side of the pier has 820 feet of berthing space with dolphins and a depth of 38 feet reported alongside.

(384) About 200 yards from the Tesoro Pier, when making a starboard landing, a vessel is set by the current onto the pier and great care must be taken to avoid being set hard onto the pier. The use of an anchor in docking is advisable. The current is at times pronounced when docking at the inside berth, and care must be taken to

avoid being set onto the shoal to the S. Range markers facilitate docking. Less current is generally experienced at the Tesoro Pier; however, the use of an anchor is recommended when making a starboard landing.

Local magnetic disturbance

(385) Differences from normal variation of 2° have been observed in the vicinity of March Point.

(386) **Bay View**, a village across the flats of Padilla Bay ESE from March Point, has no facilities except for a small boat repair shop.

Chart 18424

(387) **William Point**, 100 feet high and marked by a light, is the W point of **Samish Island**, which forms the N side of Padilla Bay. The point is wooded and, because of the low land E of it, appears as an island although it is connected with the mainland. It is marked by a light.

(388) **Bellingham Channel**, deep between Cypress and Guemes Island, is the most direct route to Bellingham Bay from Anacortes. Between Cypress, Guemes, and Sinclair Islands the tidal currents have considerable velocity, however, between Sinclair and Vendovi Islands the velocities are considerably less. In 1983, Bellingham Channel Lighted Buoy 6, about 300 yards NW of Clark Point, was reported to submerge during periods of strong currents. Lighted buoys mark the E side of Bellingham Channel and a light is on the W side of the channel off the E side of Cypress Island. A submerged wreck, covered 4¼ fathoms, is 1 mile W of **Kellys Point**, the SW tip of Guemes Island, in about 48°31'48"N., 122°40'12"W.

(389) **Deepwater Bay**, on the W side of Bellingham Channel S of **Cypress Head**, has several aquiculture pens marked by private lights. **Cone Islands**, a group of five islets on the W side of Bellingham Channel are 0.4 mile E of the NE side of Cypress Island.

(390) **Clark Point**, at the northern end of Bellingham Channel, is a steep bluff forming the N point of Guemes Island. A reef extends 300 yards N from the point. A marina, about 1.6 miles SE of Clark Point, has gasoline. A launching ramp and a hoist that can handle small craft to 18 feet is available. **Vendovi Island** is 1.8 miles NE of Clark Point. Shoaling to 4 fathoms, 0.4 mile SW of Vendovi Island, is marked by a buoy. A light marks the E side of the island. A private light is in a small cove on the NW side of Vendovi Island.

(391) Deep-draft vessels approaching Bellingham Bay from N use the channel between Lummi and Sinclair Islands. With the exception of Viti Rocks and the dangers N of Sinclair Islands, this channel is free of danger. The fairway is deep and has a width of 0.6 mile at its narrowest part, between **Viti Rocks** and **Carter Point**, the S tip of Lummi Island. The northwesternmost Viti Rock is 35 feet high, 200 yards long, and marked by a light. A lighted bell buoy marks the shoal extending SSE from the southernmost rock.

(392) **Smugglers Cove**, on the E side of Lummi Island, is 2.5 miles N of Carter Point. A large stone quarry with mooring facilities for rock barges is prominent.

(393) **Hale Passage**, 6 miles long, separates Lummi Island from the mainland to the NE. Depths in the passage vary from 2 fathoms on the bar near the NW end to 20 fathoms in the SE end of the channel.

(394) **Lane Spit**, on the W side of Hale Passage 1.5 miles SE of Point Migley, is marked by a lighted buoy. A light is on the E side of Lummi Island 3 miles SE of Lane Spit.

(395) **Lummi Island**, a village on the W side of Hale Passage, is 1 mile S of Lane Spit. The village and island are linked to the mainland at **Gooseberry Point** by an automobile ferry. The ferry dock at Lummi Island is marked by a private light. A pier, adjacent to the ferry slip at Gooseberry Point, has a 6-ton hoist that can handle craft 28 feet long; gasoline, water, ice, marine supplies, and hull and engine repairs are available. Depths of 4 feet are reported off the end of the pier at the hoist.

(396) From **Point Francis**, the rounded high bluff on the SE side of **Portage Island**, a shoal and broken ground extend SSE to Eliza Island. The depths range from 5 to less than 1½ fathoms about midway between the point and the island. A lighted buoy is about 300 yards S of the 1½ fathom spot.

(397) **Bellingham Bay**, from William Point to the head, is about 12 miles long and 4 miles wide. Anchorage may be obtained almost anywhere in the bay S of the flats; the depths, over the greater portion, range from 6 to 15 fathoms. Because of the mud bottom, vessels are apt to drag anchor in heavy weather. Recreational and commercial fishing is popular in this area. Numerous crab pots fill the bay during crabbing season.

(398) **Samish Bay**, separated from Padilla Bay by Samish Island, with flats bare for a considerable distance at low water, forms the SE part of Bellingham Bay. Extensive oyster culture is carried on in the E portion of the bay.

(399) **Eliza Island**, low and partly wooded, is 1 mile NE of Carter Point. The island is well populated with numerous private boat facilities along its shores. Shoals fringe most of the island, which should not be approached closer than about 400 yards. A rock covered 1 fathom is some 500 yards N of the W tip of the island.

(400) Vessels anchoring between Lummi Island and Eliza Island during heavy weather should be cautious of dragging anchor because of the poor holding ground.

(401) **Eliza Rock**, marked by a light, is off the S end of Eliza Island.

(402) **Chuckanut Bay** which indents the E shore of Bellingham Bay, is a cove affording shelter to small craft. Relatively free of obstructions, the bay does include an island and a dangerous chain of rocks near the entrance. **Chuckanut Rock** is located in the N part of the bay and has rocks awash to the N and S. Shoal areas surround **Chuckanut Island** to the W and S; the island should not be approached closer than 200 yards. The

small-craft launching ramp of **Larabee State Parkis** at **Wildcat Cove**, 0.6 mile SE of **Governors Point** at the SW entrance to Chuckanut Bay.

(403) **Post Point**, on the NE side of Bellingham Bay, is 1.5 miles NNW of the N entrance point of Chuckanut Bay. A shoal, marked by a lighted buoy, extends about 450 yards W from the point. Starr Rock, covered 1 fathom, is about 200 yards offshore and is marked by a buoy. Vessels should not pass inside the buoy.

(404) **Bellingham** is at the head of Bellingham Bay on the E shore. As of 2006, the Port of Bellingham's waterfront was in the transition stages from import/export of industrial products to mixed use commercial. Wharves and port facilities are still present, but will be undergoing changes within the next five years. Debris and several submerged pilings and dolphins exist along the formerly industrialized areas of the Bellingham waterfront between Squalicum Creek Waterway and the piers of South Bellingham; mariners are urged to use caution when navigating in or around this area.

(405) The S terminal of the Port of Bellingham, on the N side of Post Point at South Bellingham, includes the Alaska State Ferry Terminal Dock, a boatbuilding plant, and a boat ramp. Bornstein Seafoods is on the I and J Street Waterway; fishing boats unload at this wharf. There are several other light industry and commercial facilities around the harbor.

(406) **Whatcom Creek Waterway** at the SE end of Bellingham Harbor, **Squalicum Creek Waterway** at the NW end of the harbor, and **I and J Street Waterway** in between, provide dredged channel access to the port facilities at Bellingham. Bellingham Yacht Harbor is adjacent to and SE of Squalicum Creek Waterway; the yacht harbor is described later in this chapter.

Prominent features

(407) Particularly prominent at night is the lighted sign HERALD on the newspaper building (48°44'51"N., 122°28'44"W.) and the lighted sign ICE on the Bellingham Cold Storage building (48°45'28"N., 122°30'37"W.) Also prominent are the stack at the cement plant 1.5 miles NW of I & J Street Waterway Light 1 and the stack 0.3 mile to the E, and the church spire near the Bellingham waterfront.

Channels

(408) A **Federal project** provides for a depth of 30 feet in Whatcom Creek Waterway Outer and Middle Reaches; thence 18 feet through the Inner Reach, 26 feet in Squalicum Creek Waterway, and 18 feet in I and J Street Waterway. Depths in Whatcom Creek Waterway are usually near project depth to the port wharf; the controlling depth for Middle and Inner Reach of this waterway may be considerably less than project depth. The controlling depth for Squalicum Creek Waterway and I and J Street Waterway may also be considerably less than project depth. (See Notice to Mariners and latest editions of the chart for controlling depths.)

(409) Squalicum Creek Waterway is marked by lighted buoys and a lighted range. I and J Street Waterway is marked by lights and buoys. Whatcom Creek Waterway is marked by a lighted range. The port authority maintains depths of more than 30 feet alongside the Whatcom Creek Waterway port wharf, and also dredges the small-craft basin.

Anchorages

(410) The bottom mud is a thin accumulation over hardpan, and is not good holding ground in heavy weather. A **general anchorage** and an **explosives anchorage** are in the bay. (See **110.1 and 110.230**, chapter 2, for limits and regulations.) Good holding ground may be found just N of **Governors Point**, near the S end of Chuckanut Bay.

Pilotage, Bellingham

(411) Pilotage is compulsory for all vessels except those under enrollment or engaged exclusively in the coasting trade on the W coast of the continental United States (including Alaska) and/or British Columbia. Pilotage for Bellingham is provided by the Puget Sound Pilots. (See Pilotage, Strait of Juan de Fuca and Puget Sound, indexed as such, early this chapter.)

Towage

(412) Tugs to 4,000 hp are available at Bellingham, and larger tugs at Seattle. Arrangements for tugs should be made in advance through ships' agents or through the Marine Exchange of Puget Sound. Tugs monitor and use as a working frequency VHF-FM channel 7.

Quarantine, customs, immigration, and agricultural quarantine

(413) (See chapter 3, Vessel Arrival Inspections, and Appendix A for addresses.)

(414) **Quarantine** is enforced in accordance with regulations of the U.S. Public Health Service. (See Public Health Service, chapter 1.)

(415) Bellingham is a **customs port of entry**.

Coast Guard

(416) Bellingham Coast Guard Station is on the I and J Street Waterway.

Harbor regulations

(417) The city fire chief is responsible for the prevention of hazardous fire conditions in the harbor. The Port of Bellingham directs the operation of the North Terminal on Whatcom Creek Waterway, the South Terminal at Post Point, and the yacht harbor E of Squalicum Creek Waterway. The port's general offices are located N of the I and J Street Waterway near the boat ramp (360–676–2500).

Wharves

(418) The Port of Bellingham operates two deep-draft terminals, one at South Bellingham (Fairview) and one on Whatcom Creek Waterway. For a complete description of the port facilities refer to Port Series No. 37, published and sold by the U.S. Army Corps of Engineers. (See Appendix A for address.) The alongside depths of the facilities described are reported depths. (Contact the Port of Bellingham or the private operator for the latest depths.)

(419) **Port of Bellingham, Whatcom International Shipping Terminal, Main Wharf** (48°44'43"N., 122°29'39"W.): berthing space, 1,370 feet; depth alongside, 31 feet; deck height, 15½ feet; owned by Port of Bellingham and operated by Port of Bellingham and Bellingham Stevedoring Co.

(420) **Note:** If a tug is not furnished, the use of anchor in docking is recommended when winds prevail. Vessels backing out of the Whatcom Creek Waterway channel must stay in the axis of the channel until abeam of Starr Rock Buoy to avoid shoal water on either side.

(421) **Georgia-Pacific West, Bellingham Operations Wharf** (48°44'56"N., 122°29'19"W.): berthing space, 1,400 feet; depth alongside, 36 feet (outer side), 18 feet (inner side); deck height, 16 feet; owned and operated by the Port of Bellingham.

(422) **Note:** vessels docking with the assistance of a tug should use an anchor. Shoal water is at the NE end of the wharf.

(423) Bellingham Cold Storage and several seafood facilities are on the E side of Squalicum Creek Waterway. Fishing boats and an occasional ship unload fish in the area. A plywood mill is on the W side of the waterway.

Supplies

(424) Complete marine supplies are available for small craft, and some for large vessels. Fuel oil is available by truck from Seattle.

Repairs

(425) Two floating drydocks, 1,600-ton and 3,000-ton capacities, and a 700-ton marine railway are available for ship repairs at Fairhaven Shipyard and Drydock in South Bellingham. Other facilities for oceangoing vessel repair are located in Seattle, WA and Vancouver, BC. Complete repair facilities are available for small craft. A propeller works, several machine shops, engine and deck-gear suppliers, and an electronic repair company are along the Bellingham waterfront. The larger of two repair yards is just W of the Port of Bellingham South Terminal. This yard has a machine shop and a marine railway that can handle vessels up to 700 tons, 120 feet long or 34 feet wide for hull repairs. Another repair yard, at Squalicum Boat Harbor has a marine railway that can handle vessels up to 290 tons, 125 feet long or 24 feet wide for hull repairs. Several local machine shops in the area do engine repair work for the two repair yards.

(426) **Squalicum Boat Harbor**, adjacent to and SE of the Squalicum Creek Waterway, is protected by breakwaters on its SE and SW sides. The harbor can be entered from the SE between the two breakwaters, or from the NW from the Squalicum Creek Waterway. The ends of the breakwaters at the SE entrance are marked by lights. The entrance from Squalicum Creek Waterway is marked by a light. Depths inside the harbor are 10 to 15 feet.

(427) Berths for about 1800 pleasure craft and fishing boats are in the harbor. A guest float is maintained near the **harbormaster's** office on the NE side of the harbor (360–676–2542). Gasoline, diesel fuel, electricity, water, ice, and marine supplies are available. Several marine equipment repair and fishing supply firms are in the area N of the SE entrance to the harbor.

(428) A small-craft basin, protected by a breakwater on its S side, is N of I & J Street Waterway. The basin can be entered from I & J Street Waterway. Depths of 9 to 12 feet are in the basin. A boat ramp is on the E side of the basin.

Communications

(429) Bellingham is served directly by one major railway and has connections to another. It is on U.S. Interstate Highway 5 and is a hub for three State highways. The airport is about 2.5 miles NW of the city.

Chart 18400

(430) The **Strait of Georgia** extends some 115 miles NW from its S end, in the vicinity of Alden Bank, and is bordered on the W by Vancouver Island, BC, and on the E by the mainland of Canada. General depths are great and in many places exceed 200 fathoms.

(431) Vessels bound to the Strait of Georgia from Puget Sound should give the SW shore, between Boundary and Active Passes, a berth of at least 2 miles because it is fringed with dangers. Point Roberts, on the N shore, affords an excellent landmark.

(432) A **Vessel Traffic Service** has been established in the Strait of Juan de Fuca, E of Port Angeles, and in the adjacent waters. (See **161.1 through 161.55**, chapter 2, for regulations, and the beginning of this chapter for additional information.)

Currents

(433) The tidal currents in the Strait of Georgia are not nearly as strong as those in the channels leading to it from the Strait of Juan de Fuca. The currents in the Strait of Georgia attain a velocity of 3 knots at times, particularly during the freshets of the summer, when the Fraser River discharges a large volume of freshwater. This freshwater, which has a peculiar milky color, flows across the banks at the mouth of the river and almost directly toward Active Pass. Frequently this water

extends entirely across the strait and at times reaches into the inner channels along the shore of Vancouver Island; at other times, it reaches only to the middle of the strait and forms a striking contrast with the deep blue water of the Strait of Georgia.

(434) In the middle of the strait N of Patos and **Saturna Islands**, the velocity of the current varies from 1 to 3 knots, seldom exceeding the latter. The velocity is still less NW of the mouth of the Fraser River, where the strait is about 15 miles wide. The tidal currents SE of the mouth of Fraser River are slightly stronger off the S shore than off the N shore. The currents within a line joining Point Roberts and Sandy Point are scarcely felt, and vessels can take advantage of this, especially since good anchorage can be obtained in this vicinity.

(435) The tidal currents are stronger close to the S shore which is swept by the rapid currents out of Active, Porlier, and Gabriola Passes. The south-going tidal current in the Strait of Georgia sets strongly SW into Active Pass.

Weather, Georgia Strait and vicinity

(436) In the open waters of the Georgia Strait, winds are usually either northwesterlies or southeasterlies. Southeasterlies are more frequent from October through March. Close to the British Columbia coast, they are often deflected and become easterlies. While the Georgia Strait is somewhat sheltered from the sea by the mountains of Vancouver Island, gales still occur three or four times per month. While some are associated with the intense storms of winter, particularly dangerous gales occur in clear weather. These are locally known as **Squamish winds**. They occur periodically in most of the main inlets in winter. They come up suddenly and may exceed 50 knots. Squamishes occur when a vast pool of very cold air accumulates on the interior plateau of British Columbia. A pressure fall at sea will trigger a movement of this air toward the coast. This flow is intensified by the direction and narrowness of the inlets. As the air reaches the mouths of these inlets, it spreads out over the strait and the wind speeds diminish. Winds rarely remain strong 15 to 20 miles away. Howe Sound, Jervis, Toba, and Bute Inlets all experience squamishes each winter.

(437) In summer, winds in the Rosario and Haro Straits are usually southwesterlies. Summer breezes are variable and baffling in the San Juan Islands. N of Point Roberts, in the middle of the Georgia Strait, the prevailing winds are northwesterlies. Gales are uncommon, particularly in mid-summer, when storm activity reaches a lull.

(438) Georgia Strait is more affected by land fogs than sea fogs. These fogs form on cool nights under clear skies and light winds, and usually dissipate by early afternoon. These conditions are most prevalent from September through February. During prolonged periods of cold, clear, calm weather, these fogs may persist for several days at a time. Land fog is more local than sea fog. Visibilities fall below 0.75 mile (1.4 km) on about 20 days annually, but this can increase to 60 days in preferred locations like the flat land in the delta of the Fraser River where the low water temperatures of the river help produce the fog.

Charts 18421, 18424, 18431

(439) **Sandy Point**, about 2.5 miles N of Lummi Island and at the NW side of **Lummi Bay**, is the site of an extensive housing development fronting a privately dredged basin. The entrance to the basin is marked by two lights.

(440) Between Sandy Point and **Cherry Point**, about 4.5 miles NW, the shore of the mainland forms a bight in which there are no off-lying dangers. The piers of two large oil refineries and an aluminum smelter are in the bight. A **general anchorage** is off Cherry Point. (See **110.1 and 110.230**, chapter 2, for limits and regulations.)

(441) The 1,800-foot pier of the Tosco Refining Co. (formerly British Petroleum Co.) is at **Ferndale**, 2.4 miles N of Sandy Point. The L-shaped pier has 883 feet of berthing space and reported depths of 42 to 53 feet at the outer face, and 722 feet of berthing space and depths of 35 feet at the inner face. Deck height is 18 feet. The pier is used for the receipt of crude oil and shipment of petroleum products, and for bunkering vessels. The pier is marked by private lights and a sound signal. An oil refinery tower 0.8 mile inshore is prominent. **Note:** A portside-to landing is preferred when docking at the outer berth during S winds and a flood tide; the use of an anchor is advisable.

(442) The long loading wharf and pier of the Intalco Aluminum Corp. is 0.8 mile N of the Tosco Refining Co. pier and 3.2 miles N of Sandy Point. The wharf has 950 feet of berthing space with dolphins and depths of 36 feet alongside. Deck height is 22 feet. The wharf is used for the receipt of alumina and liquified petroleum gas. Private lights and a sound signal are on the wharf, and two private lighted mooring buoys are just off the wharf. **Note:** Vessels normally dock starboardside-to; however, a portside-to landing is required for vessels having their bridge forward of a cargo hold and with less than 30 feet between the hold and the rear of the pilothouse.

(443) The BP/Amoco pier (formerly Atlantic Richfield Co.) with a 2,400-foot angular approach trestle is at Cherry Point, about 4.5 miles NNW of Sandy Point. The pier has 1,000 feet of berthing space at the face with dolphins, and reported depths of 65 feet alongside. Deck height is 22 feet. The dolphins are marked by private lights. The facility is used for receipt of crude oil, shipment of petroleum products, and bunkering vessels. **Note:** The pier has rigid loading arms for the transfer of liquid cargo; chicksan rigs are not required on vessels. Some vessels prefer to drag an anchor in approaching the pier; however, tugs are available on advance notice from Bellingham. Three oil boom deployment buoys are

off the face of the pier, one on either end and one 600 feet off the center of the face of the pier. Water and electrical shore power connections are available. A special gangway is provided in lieu of the ship's gangway.

(444) **Point Whitehorn**, about 2.8 miles NW of Cherry Point, is a conspicuous, bold bluff about 150 feet high; its seaward face is a steep cliff of white clay.

(445) **Birch Bay**, on the E side of the Strait of Georgia between Point Whitehorn and **Birch Point**, is an open bight. It affords some protection, in 4 to 5 fathoms, from N, but is open to the SW. Flats that bare occupy a considerable area at the head of the bay. A number of resorts are along the shore. A mooring basin and private marina are on the N side of the bay; the basin entrance is marked by lights and daybeacons.

(446) The **International Boundary** between the United States and Canada is marked by a series of lights where it crosses Semiahmoo Bay and Boundary Bays.

(447) The **Peace Monument** on the boundary is a white masonry arch, facing N and S, about 28 feet above the ground. It is a distinctive landmark as it stands alone and shows offshore against a background of dark trees.

Caution

(448) The International Navigation Rules govern in all Canadian waters.

(449) **Point Roberts** is the prominent feature in approaching from either N or S. The E face is about 180 feet high and is composed of white, vertical bluffs. The point is well wooded, and because of the low land behind it, is usually made as an island, especially from S. The SW extremity of the point is marked by a light. Extensive night drift-fishing in the area from Point Roberts to Blaine makes night navigation difficult. A marina at Point Roberts provides transient berths, gasoline, diesel fuel, ice, and pump-out. An alongside depth of 6 feet was reported in 2010. Complete repair services with a 35-ton marine lift are available.

(450) Point Roberts is a **customs port of entry**.

(451) Temporary anchorage may be obtained W of Point Roberts in 8 fathoms, good holding ground, about 1 mile 321° from Point Roberts Light. The position is about 0.3 mile from the edge of Roberts Bank; vessels should not anchor any farther N.

(452) **Semiahmoo Bay** has its entrance between Birch Point and Kwomais Point, about 5 miles NNW. It is connected with Drayton Harbor by a narrow channel. The E part of the bay is shoal with extensive sand flats in the SE part. Anchorage may be had in the bay in 3½ to 9 fathoms on the NW side of Semiahmoo Spit, affording protection from S and SE storms.

(453) **Drayton Harbor** is a small cove formed by **Semiahmoo Spit**, the extension of a sandspit N of Birch Point. It is about 2 miles long, but flats that bare at low water occupy a large area in the E and S parts of the harbor. A light and a buoy about 700 yards to the WSW are near the N end of the extensive sand flats off the NW side of Semiahmoo Spit.

(454) The channel from Semiahmoo Bay to the cannery wharf on Semiahmoo Spit and to Blaine Harbor, E of the cannery wharf, has a controlling depth of about 21 feet; greater depths are possible with local knowledge. The 15-foot spot about 130 yards N of the cannery wharf, and the 9-foot spot about 300 yards E of the E end of the wharf should be avoided.

(455) **Blaine Harbor**, at Blaine, is a large and well-equipped small-boat basin near the entrance on the N shore of Drayton Harbor. The harbor is an active fishing center operated by the Port of Bellingham. A light marks the outer end of the breakwater that protects the basin on the S side. In 1981, depths through the entrance and in the basin were 11 feet except for shoaling along the edges. In 1999, the channel was reported as not being maintained. The harbor has berths for about 400 boats; 200 additional berths are being planned by the Port of Bellingham. A **harbormaster** is on duty in the harbor. Fish-processing plants and a fish reduction plant are in operation. Gasoline, diesel fuel, electricity, water, ice, launching ramp, dry storage facilities, marine supplies, and pump-out facility are available in the harbor. A repair yard with a marine railway that can handle vessels to 300 tons, 80 feet long, or 21 feet wide is also available; hull repairs can be made. A depth of 2 feet has been reported at the entrance to the marine railway.

(456) **Blaine,** a small town on the NE shore of Drayton Harbor, is a **customs port of entry.**

Quarantine, customs, immigration, and agricultural quarantine

(457) (See chapter 3, Vessel Arrival Inspections, and Appendix A for addresses.)

(458) **Quarantine** is enforced in accordance with regulations of the U.S. Public Health Service. (See Public Health Service, chapter 1.)

(459) The United States-Canadian boundary line passes through the N edge of town. The Burlington Northern Railroad serves the town.

Tides and currents

(460) The mean range of **tide** at Blaine is 5.9 feet, and the diurnal range of tide is 9.5 feet.

(461) The average velocity of the **current** in Drayton Harbor entrance is 1.0 knot. The flood sets SE and the ebb NW.

(462) Several buildings, an elevated tank, and a small-boat basin, constituting the town of **Semiahmoo**, are at the N end of the sandspit.

(463) To enter Drayton Harbor and Blaine Harbor from Semiahmoo Bay, pass about 300 yards N of Semiahmoo Bay Light 4, and steer a course about midway between the cannery wharf and the Blaine Harbor boat basin taking care to avoid the 15-foot spot about 130 yards N

of the cannery wharf. After passing the cannery wharf, favor the N side of the channel to avoid the 9-foot spot E of the E end of the cannery wharf, and the spit ESE of the cannery, and make Blaine Harbor or anchor as convenient in Drayton Harbor. Anchoring in the shoal water of Drayton Harbor is not recommended because the floating debris and vegetation may clog a vessel's underwater intakes.

(464) The depths in Drayton Harbor and its entrance are subject to change.

Chart 18400

Strait of Georgia, E shore (Canada)

(465) **Boundary Bay** indents the mainland between **Kwomais Point**, the N entrance point of Semiahmoo Bay, and Point Roberts. The greater portion of the bay is filled with flats, bare at low water.

(466) Anchorage in 5 fathoms with good holding bottom is available about 1 mile ENE of the SE point of Point Roberts, affording protection from W and NW storms.

(467) Except for **English Bluff** about 1.5 miles N of **Boundary Bluff**, the coast N to Point Grey is low, featureless, and barely discernible from the Strait of Georgia.

(468) A causeway extends about 1.8 miles SW from English Bluff and terminates in a ferry landing; a light and sound signal are at the landing. A breakwater, about 0.2 mile long and marked by a light at its W end, is just S of the ferry landing. Just NW of the ferry landing are the long pier and facilities used for bulk loading and export of coal by bulk carriers. These facilities, although operated by private interests, are owned by the Port of Vancouver.

(469) **Roberts Bank** and **Sturgeon Bank** are formed by the alluvial deposits of the Fraser River. These banks dry in patches, and in places extend 4.5 miles offshore. They are steep-to: soundings of 50 fathoms will be found very close to the edge of the bank. Vessels proceeding along the edge of Roberts Bank should not bring the S extremity of Point Roberts to bear more than 114°.

(470) The cooperation of ships' masters is requested to avoid navigating their vessels between the charted traffic separation scheme and Sturgeon Bank. This is in the interest of the fishing industry and the reduction of damage to nets and fishing vessels by ships passing close to the fishing ground.

(471) **Fraser River** enters the Strait of Georgia about 10 miles NW of Point Roberts.

Caution

(472) The channels in Fraser River are constantly changing, and the aids to navigation that mark them are moved accordingly.

(473) **Pilotage** for the Fraser River is discussed at the beginning of this chapter.

(474) The main entrance to Fraser River is between the two lighted buoys W of Sand Heads Light, which is near the outer end of Steveston Jetty; a shorter jetty is on the S side of the main entrance. (See the Sailing Directions, British Columbia Coast (South Portion), Vol. 1, and British Columbia Small Craft Guide, Vol. 2, for detailed information on Fraser River and other local Canadian waters.)

(475) **Steveston** on **Lulu Island**, about 1.0 mile N of **Pelly Point**, the S entrance point to Fraser River, extends along the bank of the river for about 1 mile. Several canneries and wharves are here.

(476) The tidal **currents** in Fraser River are affected by the weather in the Strait of Georgia, the rains, and the amount of water in the river. In the channel above Pelly Point during freshets, the flow, which may be checked by the rise of the tide, is almost continuously toward the mouth of the river. During the freshets the greatest velocity occurs 2 to 3 hours before low water and may amount to 5.5 knots. After the freshets are over, the greater velocity occurs on the average about 1½ hours before low water and is reduced to 3 or 4 knots. During the low stage of the river there is a flood and ebb on all the larger tides; the flood begins soon after high water and commences first along the bottom.

(477) At New Westminster the flood current is unable to reverse the river current except in the autumn. The river is seldom frozen over here; loose pieces of ice, which do no damage to shipping, occasionally come down the river.

(478) **New Westminster** is on the N bank about 20 miles above the entrance. Several canneries and sawmills are here, and a conspicuous grain elevator stands about 1 mile below the city, which now has grown into the expanded Vancouver suburbs. New Westminster Harbor is a major Canadian port. The port is mainly used by bulkcarriers and cargo vessels. The principal exports are lumber, plywood, general cargo, concentrates, wheat, zinc, lead, fertilizer, paper products, and salmon. There are many wharves; most of them have warehouses and rail connections. Depths alongside range from 25 to 35 feet.

(479) New Westminster is a **Canadian customs port of entry**.

(480) **North Arm** of Fraser River is entered 0.5 mile SW of Point Grey. Depths of 15 feet are maintained from the mouth to the NE extremity of Sea Island, and 10 feet from this point to Poplar Island. From Poplar Island (49°12'N., 122°56'W.), to the main river channel the depth is again 15 feet.

(481) **Point Grey**, the S entrance point of **Burrard Inlet**, is a rounded bluff forming the W termination of a wooded promontory. The point is very conspicuous from S. The buildings of the University of British Columbia are conspicuous on the high land above the point. **Point**

Atkinson, the N entrance point of Burrard Inlet, is comparatively steep-to. It is marked by a light.

(482) Tide rips occur frequently off Point Atkinson, caused by the meeting of the tidal currents from Burrard Inlet and Howe Sound.

(483) **Spanish Bank** extends 0.6 mile N from the W half of the promontory terminating in Point Grey. The bank, which dries, is composed of hard sand and is steep-to. It is marked by lights. W winds when it is marked by a line of small breakers.

(484) **Vancouver Harbor** includes all the tidal waters in Burrard Inlet E of a line drawn from Point Grey to Point Atkinson. A secure, deep harbor, easily entered by the largest vessel, is formed between First and Second Narrows, and on its shores is the city of Vancouver, the third largest city of Canada and the commercial metropolis of British Columbia. A U.S. Immigration station is in the city. Vancouver is a **Canadian customs port of entry**. Complete marine supplies, repair facilities, and services for small craft and the largest ships are available.

(485) The three principal anchorages in Vancouver Harbor are English Bay, the outer anchorage; Vancouver, above the first narrows; and in Indian Arm.

Chart 18421

(486) **Strait of Georgia**, W shore (Canada). The coast between East Point and Active Pass should be given a berth of at least 2 miles because it is fringed with dangers.

(487) **Belle Chain Islets** is a narrow rocky ridge 2 miles long lying parallel with several islets and drying rocks along the NE shore of **Samuel Island**. Foul ground extends about 0.3 mile SE from **Edith Point,** the NE extremity of **Mayne Island**. A rocky patch with two heads, each of which covers 4 feet, is about midway between Edith Point and the NW end of Belle Chain Islets.

Chart 18400

(488) **Salamanca Point**, on the SE side of **Galiano Island**, is conspicuous from both SE and NW. The point is rocky, and the trees on it grow down nearly to the highwater mark.

(489) **Porlier Pass**, 12 miles NW of Salamanca Point, separates Galiano Island and **Valdes Island** and connects **Trincomali Channel** with the Strait of Georgia. The pass has a minimum width of about 800 yards, but the navigable channel is narrow and the tidal currents attain velocities up to 9 knots. Current predictions may be obtained from the Tidal Current Tables. It is advisable to employ a pilot on the first visit to this pass.

(490) **Gabriola Pass** is between the NW end of Valdes Island and Gabriola Island, connecting the NW end of **Pylades Channel** to the Strait of Georgia. This pass is not recommended for general navigation, but only for those with local knowledge. The velocity of the current in the pass is 4.0 knots, setting E on the flood and W on the ebb. The current may attain a velocity of 8 knots. (See the Tidal Current Tables for predictions.)

(491) The outermost danger off Gabriola Pass, **Thrasher Rock**, a detached steep-to rock that dries, is 2.3 miles NE of the pass entrance. A light is on the rock. Shoreward of it are many rocks and reefs, including **Gabriola Reefs**; caution is essential.

(492) **Entrance Island**, 0.4 mile N of Orlebar Point, the NE point of Gabriola Island, is marked by a light. It is the guide to the entrance to **Nanaimo**, a Canadian port of entry. **Fairway Channel**, the easternmost of the channels in the N approach to Nanaimo, is deep and has a navigable width of 0.8 mile.

(493) Off the entrance to **Nanoose Harbor**, 13 miles WNW of Entrance Island, there are many islets and reefs and, unless making for Nanoose, the navigator should keep 3 miles offshore until he raises the **Ballenas Islands** 5.5 miles NW of the Nanoose Harbor entrance.

(494) Details of local Canadian ports and features are given in Pub. No. 154, Sailing Directions (Enroute) for British Columbia, published by the National Geospatial-Intelligence Agency, and the Sailing Directions, British Columbia Coast, (South Portion) Vol. 1, and British Columbia Small Craft Guides, Vol. 1 and 2, published by the Canadian Hydrographic Service.

| TIDAL INFORMATION ||||||
Chart	Station	LAT/LONG	Mean Higher High Water*	Mean High Water*	Mean Low Water*
18421	Bellingham, Bellingham Bay	48°45'N/122°30'W	8.5	7.8	2.4
18421	Blaine, Semiahmoo Bay, Strait of Georgia	49°00'N/122°46'W	9.5	8.7	2.7
18424	Eagle Harbor, Cypress Island, Rosario Strait	48°35'N/122°42'W	8.2	7.4	2.4
18424	Point Migley, Hale Passage, Rosario Strait	48°45'N/122°43'W	8.6	7.8	2.6
18427	Yokeko Point, Deception Pass	48°25'N/122°37'W	10.5	9.5	2.6
18427	Deception Pass State Park, Fidalgo Island	48°25'N/122°39'W	7.7	7.1	2.5
18429	Armitage Island, Thatcher Pass, Rosario Strait	48°32'N/122°48'W	7.8	7.2	2.3
18430	Eagle Harbor, Cypress Island, Rosario Strait	48°35'N/122°42'W	8.2	7.4	2.4
18430	Upright Head, Lopez Island	48°34'N/122°53'W	7.8	7.1	2.5
18430	Tide Point, Cypress Island, Rosario Strait	48°35'N/122°44'W	8.1	7.3	2.4
18430	Village Point, Lummi Island	48°43'N/122°42'W	8.6	7.8	2.6
18431	Echo Bay, Sucia Islands	48°45'N/122°54'W	8.6	7.8	2.6
18431	Patos Island Wharf, Haro Strait	48°47'N/122°58'W	8.6	7.9	2.6
18431	Cherry Point, Strait of Georgia	48°52'N/122°45'W	9.2	8.3	2.6
18432	Turn Point, Stuart Island, Haro Strait	48°41'N/123°14'W	7.5	6.9	2.5
18433	Roche Harbor, San Juan Island	48°37'N/123°09'W	7.6	7.0	2.5
18433	Kanaka Bay, San Juan Island	48°29'N/123°05'W	7.3	6.7	2.4
18434	Rosario, East Sound, Orcas Island	48°39'N/122°52'W	8.1	7.4	2.5
18434	Friday Harbor, San Juan Island	48°32'N/123°01'W	7.8	7.1	2.3
18460	Sekiu, Clallam Bay, Strait of Juan de Fuca	48°16'N/124°18'W	7.5	6.7	1.8
18465	Sooke, Vancouver Island, B.C.	48°22'N/123°44'W	9.4	8.4	4.8
18465	Victoria, Vancouver Island, B.C.	48°26'N/123°23'W	8.6	8.0	4.6
18465	Crescent Bay, Strait of Juan de Fuca	48°10'N/123°44'W	6.7	6.1	2.0
18468	Port Angeles, Strait of Juan de Fuca	48°08'N/123°26'W	7.1	6.5	1.9
18471	Oak Bay, Admiralty Inlet	48°01'N/122°43'W	9.4	8.6	2.6
18471	Port Townsend, Admiralty Inlet	48°07'N/122°45'W	8.5	7.8	2.5
18480	La Push, Quillayute River	47°55'N/124°38'W	8.4	7.7	1.4
18484	Neah Bay, Strait of Juan de Fuca	48°22'N/124°37'W	8.0	7.1	1.6
18485	Tatoosh Island, Cape Flattery	48°24'N/124°44'W	8.0	7.2	1.5

* Heights in feet referred to datum of sounding MLLW.
Real-time water levels, tide predictions, and tidal current predictions are available at:
http://tidesandcurrents.noaa.gov
To determine mean tide range subtract Mean Low Water from Mean High Water.
Data as of September 2012

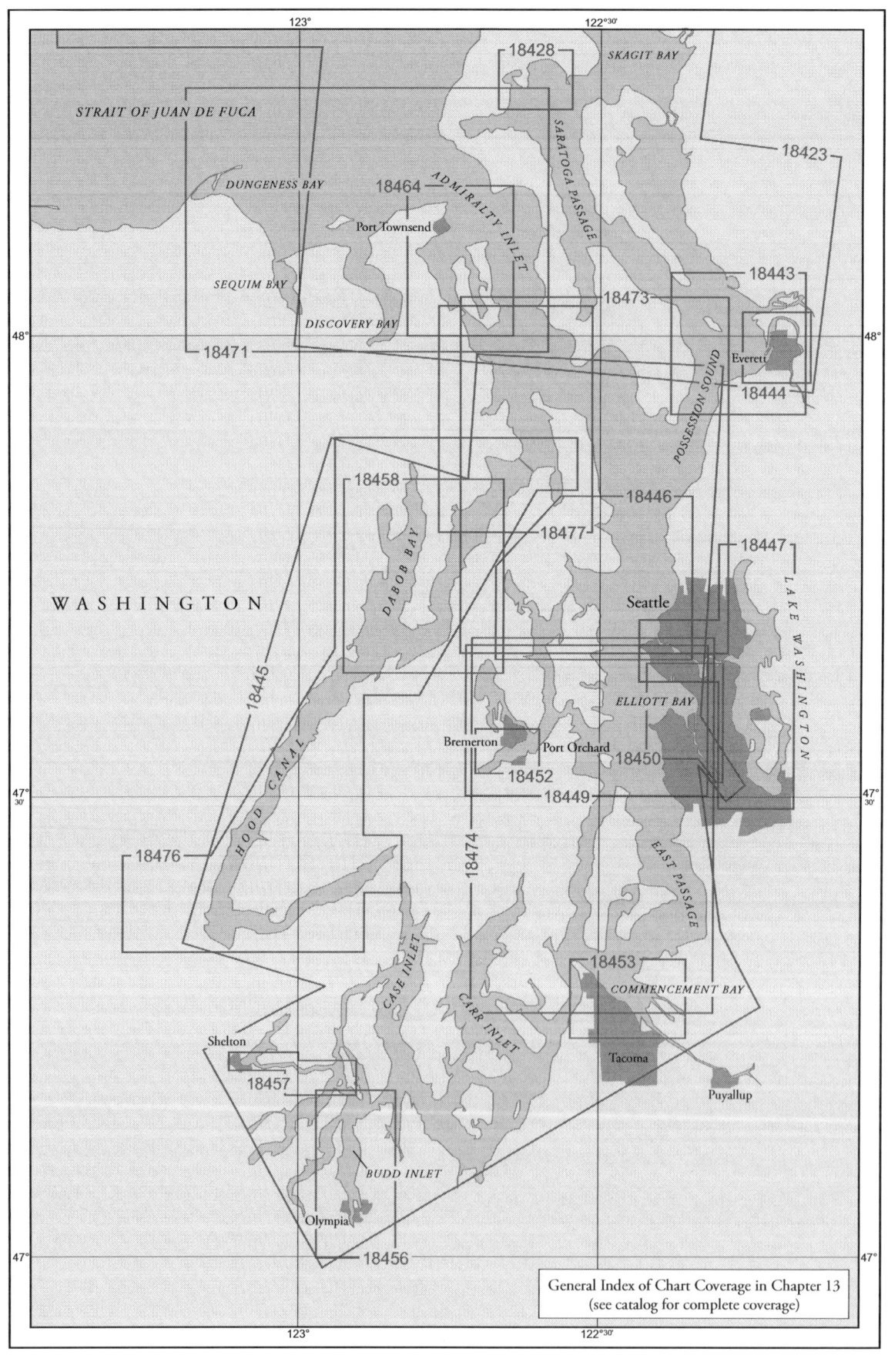

Puget Sound, Washington

(1) This chapter describes Puget Sound and its numerous inlets, bays, and passages, and the waters of Hood Canal, Lake Union, and Lake Washington. Also discussed are the ports of Seattle, Tacoma, Everett, and Olympia, as well as other smaller ports and landings.

COLREGS Demarcation Lines

(2) The International Regulations for Preventing Collisions at Sea, 1972 (72 COLREGS) apply on all the waters of Puget Sound and adjacent waters, including Lake Union, Lake Washington, Hood Canal, and all tributaries. (See **80.1395**, chapter 2.)

Chart 18440

(3) **Puget Sound**, a bay with numerous channels and branches, extends about 90 miles S from the Strait of Juan de Fuca to Olympia. The N boundary of the sound is formed, at its main entrance, by a line between Point Wilson on the Quimper Peninsula and Point Partridge on Whidbey Island; at a second entrance between West Point on Whidbey Island, Deception Island, and Sares Head on Fidalgo Island; at a third entrance, at the S end of Swinomish Channel between Fidalgo Island and McGlinn Island. Puget Sound was named by George Vancouver for Lieutenant Peter Puget, who explored the S end in May 1792. Deep-draft traffic is considerable in the larger passages, and small craft operate throughout the area. Unusually deep water and strong currents characterize these waters.

(4) Navigation of the area is comparatively easy in clear weather; the outlying dangers are few and marked by aids. The currents follow the general direction of the channels and have considerable velocity. In thick weather, because of the uncertainty of the currents and the great depths which render soundings useless in many places, strangers are advised to take a pilot.

(5) The **Marine Exchange of Puget Sound**, located in Seattle, has a Vessel Monitoring/Vessel Reporting service which tracks the arrival of a vessel from a time prior to arrival at the pilot station to a berth at one of the Puget Sound ports. Constant updates of the ship's position and estimated time of arrival are maintained through a variety of sources. This information is available to and is passed to the vessel's agents and to other interested activities. These services continue until the vessel passes the pilot station on her outbound voyage.

(6) Other services offered by the Marine Exchange include a daily newsletter about future marine traffic in the Puget Sound area, communication services, and a variety of coordinative and statistical information. The office monitors VHF-FM channels 20 for Grays Harbor traffic, 9 for Strait of Juan de Fuca traffic to Protection Island, and 20 for Puget Sound traffic from Protection Island, 24 hours a day. The Marine Exchange may also be contacted by phone, 206–443–3830 or toll free 800–562–2856.

(7) **Vessel Traffic Service Puget Sound**, operated by the U.S. Coast Guard, has been established in the waters of the Strait of Juan de Fuca, Rosario Strait, Admiralty Inlet, Puget Sound, and the navigable waters adjacent to these areas. (See **161.1 through 161.23** and **161.55**, chapter 2, for regulations, and the beginning of chapter 12 for additional information.)

(8) The **U.S. Coast Guard** and the **Puget Sound Harbor Safety Committee** have developed and adopted a Harbor Safety Plan that formally establishes a set of Standards of Care for Puget Sound and surrounding waters. The standards and protocols contained in the **Puget Sound Harbor Safety Plan** complement and supplement existing federal, state, and local laws. The Harbor Safety Plan is not intended to take the place of or otherwise intended to replace the good judgement of a ship's master in the safe operation of his/her vessel. These standards and protocols were developed and adopted by local experts for insuring greater safety. Some sections of the plan provide important safety info for professional mariners transiting Puget Sound, while the Standards of Care formalize and document good marine practice. The Harbor Safety Plan can be obtained from the Marine Exchange of Puget Sound website at http://www.marexps.com or contact 206–443–3830.

Regulated navigation area

(9) Due to heavy vessel concentrations, the waters of the Strait of Juan de Fuca, the San Juan Islands, the Strait of Georgia, and Puget Sound, and all adjacent waters, are a regulated navigation area. (See **165.1 through 165.13 and 165.1301**, chapter 2, for regulations.)

(10) Floating logs and **deadheads** or **sinkers** may be encountered anywhere in Puget Sound; caution should be exercised.

Washington State Requirements

Reports of Oil Spills and Vessel Emergencies
All vessels must report oil spills or potential oil spills to both:
1. Washington State   800–258–5990
2. National Response Center 800–424–8802

Tank vessels and cargo and passenger ships 300 gross tons or larger must make notifications to Washington State for vessel emergencies, including a loss or serious degradation of propulsion, steering, means of navigation, electrical generating capability and seakeeping capability constituting a substantial threat of pollution affecting Washington state natural resources. In addition to any notifications to the USCG, the owner or operator must notify the state of any vessel emergency that results in the discharge or substantial threat of a discharge of oil to state waters or that may affect the natural resources of the state within one hour of the onset of the emergency.

Tug Escorts for Laden Tankers
Any laden oil tanker, whether enrolled or registered, proceeding east of a line extending from Discovery Island Light (British Columbia, CN) south to New Dungeness Light (Washington State, US) must be escorted by a tug or tugs with an aggregate shaft horsepower equivalent to five percent of the deadweight tons of that tanker. For additional details see Washington state law at 88.16 Revised Code of Washington (RCW).

Emergency Response Tug at Neah Bay
An industry-funded emergency response tug is located at Neah Bay at the entrance to the Strait of Juan de Fuca. The tug is available 24 hours a day and can be underway within twenty minutes of a decision to deploy. The purpose of the tug is to assist vessels having propulsion and steering failures or that are directed by either the US or Canadian Coast Guard to obtain towing assistance. Among other capabilities, the tug is intended to be able to make up to, stop, hold, and tow a drifting or disabled vessel of 180,000 metric dead weight tons in severe weather conditions. The tug can be contacted through the USCG VTS or the Puget Sound Marine Exchange.

Washington State Vessel Inspections
The Washington State Department of Ecology regulates cargo and passenger vessels and tank vessels operating in Washington waters.
- A cargo vessel is any self-propelled vessel in commerce that is 300 gross tons or more.
- A passenger vessel is any vessel 300 gross tons or more with a fuel capacity of at least 6,000 gallons that carries passengers for compensation.
- A tank vessel is a ship that is constructed or adapted to carry, or that carries, oil in bulk as cargo or cargo residue.

Washington State Ecology inspectors may conduct vessel inspections on regulated cargo, passenger, and fishing vessels when in Washington waters. Additional information is available at:
   http://www.ecy.wa.gov/programs/spills/prevention/VesselTechAssist/AISsubstantialrisk.html/

Oil Transfer Requirements
Safe bunkering procedures must be followed during fueling operations. For vessels 300 gross tons or greater, Washington State Ecology inspectors may conduct inspections of these regulated oil transfers on vessels receiving fuel for propulsion within Washington waters. Details can be found in state regulations at Washington Administrative Code (WAC) 317-40. Additional information is also available at:
   http://www.ecy.wa.gov/programs/spills/prevention/VesselTechAssist/Bunkering.html/

Tank vessels delivering oil in bulk to a non-recreational vessel or facility within Washington waters must meet state oil transfer requirements. They may also be subject to Washington State oil transfer inspections for these regulated oil transfers. Details can be found in WAC 173-184. Additional information is available at:
   http://www.ecy.wa.gov/programs/spills/prevention/VesselTechAssist/vessel_otr.html/

- For a transfer of more than 100 gallons of bulk oil to a facility or non-recreational vessel, the delivering vessel must submit an Advance Notice of Transfer (ANT) report to Ecology. This ANT must be submitted 24 hours prior to the transfer for facilities or within the timeframe required by local USCG Captain of the Port.
- For convenience, the ANT report can be made either: online using the Ecology website at:
   https://secureaccess.wa.gov/ecy/ants, by e-mail: OilTransferNotifications@ecy.wa.gov, or by fax: 360–407–7288 or 800–664–9184.

Contingency Plan Requirements
Tank vessels and cargo and passenger ships 300 gross tons or larger transiting Washington waters must either have a Washington State Department of Ecology approved oil spill contingency plan or be a member of a non-profit corporation that provides oil spill response capabilities consistent with their Washington State approved contingency plan. The non-profit corporation for Puget Sound is the Washington State Maritime Cooperative (WSMC). Additional information is available at:
   http://www.ecy.wa.gov/programs/spills/preparedness/cplan/cplans.html/

Anchorages

(11) General, explosives, and foul weather anchorages have been established. (See **110.1 and 110.230**, chapter 2, for limits and regulations.)

Dangers

(12) Restricted areas have been established. (See **334.1200**, chapter 2, for limits and regulations.)

(13) The large tides of Puget Sound are very complex and variable; use of the Tide Tables is advised.

Currents

(14) In Admiralty Inlet and Puget Sound, the tidal currents are subjected to daily inequalities similar to those of the tides. Velocities of 2 to 7 knots occur from Point Wilson to Point No Point. In the more open waters of the sound S of Point No Point the velocities are much less.

(15) At Point Wilson and at Marrowstone Point, slack water occurs from one-half to 1 hour earlier near shore than in midchannel.

(16) In the winter, when S winds prevail, there is generally a N surface drift which increases the ebb current and decreases the flood current. This effect is about 0.5 knot between Nodule and Bush Points.

(17) The tidal currents in the S entrance of Possession Sound are weak and variable.

(18) Between Foulweather Bluff and Misery Point, the tidal currents have a velocity of about 0.8 knot, while in the S part of Hood Canal, the velocity is only about 0.5 knot; at times of tropic tides, however, the greater ebbs may attain velocities more than double these values.

(19) The tidal currents have velocities up to about 6 knots or more in Agate Passage and in The Narrows.

Weather (Winds and Visibility), Puget Sound

(20) Puget Sound is open to the N and S and protected to the W and E by mountains. Winds are mainly SE through SW from September through April and NW through N in late spring and summer. However, winter directions are still common in summer, as are summer directions in winter. From fall through spring, lows moving through or near the Puget Sound are responsible for the mainly S flow. Intense storms can generate sustained winds of 40 knots with 50-knot gusts over the area. These strong winds are almost always from a S direction. In the Seattle area, sustained winds of 56 knots and gusts of 60 knots have been recorded. Winds are strongest in winter and early spring, on the average. Also, calm conditions are frequent in fall and winter, reflecting the lull between storm passages. In late spring and summer, winds flow into Puget Sound from the Pacific High. Often, winds are light and variable at night, then pick up to 8 to 15 knots during the afternoon, reflecting a sea breeze effect over the sound. Occasionally, a low or front will bring a return to a Southerly flow during the summer, and these winds remain the strongest, on the average.

(21) Fog in the Puget Sound area causes visibility problems on about 25 to 40 days each year. It most likely hinders navigation in autumn and again during January and February. This fog is mainly a land type that forms on cool, clear, calm nights, drifts out over the water, then dissipates during the day. It can hang on for several days if a stagnant condition develops. Fog can form in any month, but is least likely during May, June, and July.

(22) Poor visibilities are encountered more often N and S of Puget Sound than in the sound itself. In Admiralty Inlet, fog lowers visibilities on this part of the coast to less than 0.5 mile (0.9 km) on about 4 to 8 days per month. South of Point Robinson, in the East Passage, the sound signals operate about 8 to 15 percent of the time in fall and mid-winter. In Puget Sound, sound signals, even during the heart of the season, blow less than 8 percent of the time; less than 5 percent in Elliot Bay. Waters of Point Wells and Three Tree Point are among the most fog free in the area; sound signals there operate just a few hours a month for most of the year. In the Seattle area, visibility falls below 0.5 mile (0.9 km) on about 3 to 6 days per month during the foggy season. Detailed information on heavy weather to Puget Sound ports may be found in the **Puget Sound Area Heavy Weather Port Guide** published by the Marine Meteorology Division, Naval Research Laboratory, Monterey, CA 93943 and available on the internet at https://www.npmod.navy.mil/PSAPG/PSAPG.htm.

Charts 18471, 18464

(23) **Point Wilson** is the W point to Admiralty Inlet and Puget Sound.

(24) **Point Wilson Light** (48°08'39"N., 122°45'17"W.), 51 feet above the water, is shown from a white octagonal tower on a building on the E extremity of the low point.

(25) Shoals extend 0.5 mile NW of Point Wilson to the 5-fathom curve over irregular bottom; these are generally indicated by kelp. The E edge of the shoals rises rather abruptly from deep water. Heavy tide rips extend N of these shoals, being especially heavy with a W wind and ebb current. A buoy marking the shoals is about 0.7 mile NW of Point Wilson Light.

(26) In approaching Point Wilson in thick or foggy weather, vessels should obtain soundings constantly.

(27) **Fort Worden State Park**, formerly an Army base, is about 0.8 mile SSW of Point Wilson. An unused 438-foot pier, with reported depths of 14 feet and shoaling along the face, is in good condition. A launching ramp is just N of the pier.

(28) **Port Townsend**, immediately S of Point Wilson, is entered between Point Hudson and Marrowstone Point. It extends in a general SSW direction for 2.5 miles, and then turns SSE for 3 miles, with a reduced width to its head. Inside Point Hudson, depths generally range from

5 to 20 fathoms. It is an excellent harbor and is easily entered, however, mariners are warned to be aware of strong side currents that exist in Admiralty Inlet. The prevailing winds in summer are from W to SW, and in winter are generally in the SE quadrant.

(29) **Point Hudson**, on the W shore 1.7 miles SSE of Point Wilson, is low, sandy, and marked by a light. The outer limits of the shoal making out from the point are marked by a lighted bell buoy NE of the light.

(30) **Marrowstone Point,** the E point at the entrance to Port Townsend, is low at its extremity, but rises abruptly to a bluff about 120 feet high. The buildings of the former Fort Flagler, now a recreation area of the Washington Parks system, are about 0.5 mile to the S. The fort pier, with depths of about 20 feet at its face, is in poor condition. A fish haven is near the pier in about 48°05'28"N. 122°41'23"W. **Marrowstone Point Light** (48°06'06"N., 122°41'16"W.), 28 feet above the water, is shown from a 20-foot white square structure on the E edge of the point. Pilings from former piers and anchor pilings for wartime submarine nets extend up to 500 yards offshore 0.6 and 1.6 miles W of the light.

(31) **Midchannel Bank**, covered 4¾ to 10 fathoms, extends NW from Marrowstone Point about 2 miles toward Point Wilson. The bank has several submerged obstructions and large boulders on the bottom. Due to the nature of the bottom and the existence of cross currents from Admiralty Inlet, the bank is unsuitable for safe anchorage.

(32) **Port Townsend**, the principal town, is on the W shore immediately W of Point Hudson. The depths at the wharves range from 8 to 30 feet along the faces. The only commercial traffic, other than fishing boats and ferries, is at Port Townsend Paper Corporation papermill SW of the town at Glen Cove.

Anchorage

(33) The usual anchorage is about 0.5 to 0.7 mile S of the railroad ferry landing in 8 to 10 fathoms, muddy bottom. In S gales better anchorage is afforded closer inshore off the N end of Marrowstone Island or near the head of the bay in moderate depths, muddy bottom. Two **explosives anchorages** are in the bay. (See **110.1 and 110.230**, chapter 2, for limits and regulations.)

Pilotage, Puget Sound

(34) Pilotage is compulsory for all vessels except those under enrollment or engaged exclusively in the coasting trade on the W coast of the continental United States (including Alaska) and/or British Columbia. Pilotage for Puget Sound is provided by the **Puget Sound Pilots** (See Pilotage, Strait of Juan de Fuca and Puget Sound, indexed as such, chapter 12, for detail.)

Towage

(35) Tugs are not available at Port Townsend, but may be obtained on advance notice from Port Angeles or Seattle through ships' agents.

Quarantine, customs, immigration, and agricultural quarantine

(36) (See chapter 3, Vessel Arrival Inspections, and Appendix A for addresses.)

(37) **Quarantine** is enforced in accordance with regulations of the U.S. Public Health Service. (See Public Health Service, chapter 1.)

(38) Port Townsend is a **customs port of entry**.

(39) The graystone Custom House-Post Office Building, built in 1893, is conspicuous on the bluff overlooking the waterfront. This building was the customs headquarters for Puget Sound until 1913, when headquarters was moved to Seattle. Deep-draft vessels and tugs are inspected alongside the pulpmill wharf. Small craft report their arrival by telephone (800–562–5943).

(40) **Point Hudson Harbor**, just W of Point Hudson, is leased by the Port of Port Townsend to a private company. The entrance, protected by jetties, is marked by a private light on the end of the S jetty. About 100 small-craft berths, electricity, water, pump-out station, launching ramp, and a 25-ton lift are available. Hull and engine repairs for small craft can be made. Reported depths of 9 feet were available in the approach to the harbor, with 12 feet alongside the berths. The town business district is adjacent to the harbor.

(41) The terminus of the Port Townsend-Keystone ferry is 0.4 mile WSW of Point Hudson Harbor.

(42) **Port Townsend Boat Haven**, 1.1 miles SW from Point Hudson, is operated by the Port of Port Townsend. The entrance is marked by lights; in 2000, the controlling depths were 11.3 feet in the entrance channel and 10 to 12 feet in the basins. There are floats for about 600 small craft. A seafood packing company and several boat building and boat repair firms are at the basin. Electricity, gasoline, diesel fuel, water, ice, marine supplies, winter dry boat storage, and a pumpout station are available. Travel lifts up to 300-ton capacity are at the basin for launching and hauling out vessels. A launching ramp is at the NW end of the basin.

Supplies

(43) Gasoline and diesel are available at Port Townsend Boat Haven. Water, ice, groceries, marine supplies are available at these facilities and in the town.

Repairs

(44) Only minor above-the-waterline repairs can be made to large vessels. Travel lifts to 300 tons are available at Port Townsend Boat Haven; a 20-ton travel lift is at Point Hudson Harbor. Hull, engine, and electronic repairs can be made.

Communications

(45) A passenger and automobile ferry operates between Port Townsend and Keystone Harbor, just E of Admiralty Head, Whidbey Island. Another ferryboat operates

between Port Townsend, Victoria, BC, Friday Harbor, and Seattle from late April through mid-October.

(46) **Glen Cove**, about 2.2 miles SW of Point Hudson, is the site of the Port Townsend papermill, at the N end of the cove. The 480-foot-long pier has reported depths of 30 feet alongside and a deck height of 18 feet. A private light and sound signal, on the seaward end of the pier, are maintained by the mill. A slight current may be encountered, and the use of an anchor is recommended in docking. Fuel oil tankers use the N side of the wharf; paper products are shipped from the S side. The large white building and tall stacks of the mill are prominent, as is the smoke.

(47) A floating security barrier, marked by private lights, surrounds a naval restricted area in the E part of the harbor off **Walan Point** on **Indian Island** (48°04'18"N., 122°44'47"W.). (See **334.1270**, chapter 2, for limits and regulations.)

(48) **Irondale**, on the W shore about 1.5 miles from the head of the bay, is the site of a former iron foundry. Shoal water extends up to 0.3 mile from the shoreline near the town.

(49) **Port Hadlock**, a village at the head of the harbor, has landings with depths of 10 and 12 feet. The Port of Port Townsend maintains a mooring float during the summer. Gasoline is available in the town. Submerged pilings are in the vicinity of the mooring float, and local knowledge is necessary to avoid them.

(50) A marina, 0.4 mile SW of the N entrance to Port Townsend Canal, has 5 to 10 transient berths; water, and electricity are available.

(51) **Port Townsend Canal**, a dredged passage giving access to Oak Bay to the SE, is subject to considerable shoaling. In 1995, the controlling depth was 13 feet. There are jetties on both sides of the S entrance. Lights and daybecons mark the N and S entrances.

(52) Currents through the canal are strong at times, although there is no particular danger from them as the channel is wide and straight; there are, however, strong eddies at the S end on the ebb current.

(53) The canal is crossed by a fixed highway bridge with a clearance of 58 feet. Power cables nearby have clearances of 90 feet. (See **162.235**, chapter 2, for rules, regulations, and use of the canal.)

(54) **Kilisut Harbor**, between Indian Island on the W and **Marrowstone Island** on the E, is a narrow inlet extending about 4 miles in a SSE direction. The entrance to Kilisut Harbor is 2.5 miles WSW of Marrowstone Point. The entrance channel is winding. In 1981, a reported depth of 5 feet was in the entrance channel. A submerged pile is N of the entrance in about 48°05'13"N., 122°44'24"W.; caution is advised when approaching Kilisut Harbor from N. **Fort Flagler State Park** is on the NE side of the entrance channel. Two boat ramps and a small-craft float are at the park. Water is available. Inside the harbor is good anchorage in 4 to 5 fathoms.

At the S end of the harbor the two islands are connected by an earth-filled causeway and narrow strip of beach. The village of **Nordland** is on the E side of **Mystery Bay**, a small shallow cove midway on the E side of Kilisut Harbor. A small-craft float is maintained in the cove by the Washington State Park System. Water and pump-out station are available. The short pier of an oyster company is just SE of the State Park float. The head of the cove is used as a log dump. Caution should be exercised to avoid two concrete blocks located 20 to 30 feet off the E end of the State Park pier.

Charts 18441, 18471, 18477

(55) **Admiralty Inlet** extends from the Strait of Juan de Fuca to Foulweather Bluff. A **naval restricted area** is at the N entrance of Admiralty Inlet, extending W and NW from Admiralty Head. (See **334.1210**, chapter 2, for limits and regulations.)

(56) **Admiralty Head**, 80 feet high, on Whidbey Island, is the E entrance point of Admiralty Inlet and the SE extremity of a succession of light bare bluffs which extend N of Point Partridge, where they attain their highest elevation. About 0.5 mile N of Admiralty Head an abandoned lighthouse tower 39 feet high stands on top of a bluff.

(57) **Admiralty Bay**, E of Admiralty Head, is used only occasionally as an anchorage as it is exposed to SW winds and has a hard bottom and strong currents.

(58) **Keystone Harbor** (see also chart 18464) is entered through a dredged channel just NE of Admiralty Head. A state ferry landing is at the head of the harbor. This landing is the Whidbey Island terminus of the passenger and automobile ferry that operates to Port Townsend. In 2001, the controlling depth in the dredged entrance channel was 23 feet, thence 15 feet in the harbor basin with lesser depths along the sides. A breakwater, marked by a light, protects the E side of the entrance. A private light on a concrete pile marks the W side of the entrance. A launching ramp is on the E side of the harbor.

(59) A tall, narrow, grayish green tank is prominent on **Lagoon Point**, 5.5 miles SSE of Admiralty Head. Dredged canals give access to private moorings.

(60) **Bush Point**, 8 miles SSE of Admiralty Head, is marked by a light at the end of a low sandspit. Back of the spit the land shows as a low timbered point from N or S. The flood current is reported to set strongly toward Bush Point. In 1983, Puget Sound Traffic Lane Separation Lighted Buoy SC, about 1.1 miles W of Bush Point, was reported to submerge during periods of strong currents. Tidal Current Charts for this area should be consulted. Several rocks lie nearly 0.2 mile offshore 1.1 miles SE of Bush Point.

(61) **Oak Bay** is a cove on the W side of Admiralty Inlet, W of the S ends of Marrowstone and Indian Islands. A 1½-fathom shoal, marked by a light, extends S from Kinney Point.

(62) **Mutiny Bay**, between Bush Point and Double Bluff, affords temporary anchorage near the center in 10 to 20 fathoms. This anchorage is useful if overtaken by fog. The extremities are clay bluffs, and the center is low with extensive flats. Several sport fishing resorts are in the bay. Some have marine railways and can make minor repairs to outboard engines, and most have gasoline, water, and ice. Strong tide rips, at times dangerous for small craft, occur off Double Bluff, particularly on the ebb with strong NW winds. There is frequently an eddy in Mutiny Bay; tidal current charts should be consulted.

(63) **Double Bluff**, marked by a light, consists of bare, white cliffs, 300 to 400 feet high on its SE face, but much lower on its NW face. A lighted buoy marks the extremity of the shoals 600 yards W of the bluff. The shoals are usually marked by kelp.

Chart 18477

(64) **Foulweather Bluff**, on the E side of the entrance to Hood Canal, is one of the most prominent cliffs in Puget Sound. The N face, which is bare, is 0.5 mile broad and consists of vertical, grayish sand and clay bluffs, 225 feet high, sloping off on the E side to a bluff 40 feet high, but on the Hood Canal side the point is steep and high. A marsh, enclosed by a sandspit and marked by a light, extends about 500 yards from the base of the bluff on the Hood Canal side. The top of the bluff is fir and underbrush. There are several boulders which bare within 100 yards N of the highest part of the bluff, and a shoal covered 2 to 18 feet extends 200 yards E from the extremity and in line with the face of the bluff. If overtaken by fog, a vessel can find temporary anchorage 0.5 mile N of Foulweather Bluff, in not less than 60 feet. A lighted bell buoy marks the shoal 0.4 mile N of the bluff.

(65) At times the tide rips N of and around Foulweather Bluff are sufficiently heavy to be dangerous to small craft and to break up log rafts. This is most dangerous when the ebb current from the main body of Puget Sound meets that of Hood Canal off the point, and particularly so with the ebb against a strong N or NW wind.

(66) **Klas Rock**, 0.2 mile from the W shore and 0.7 mile SSE of **Olele Point**, marks the entrance to Mats Mats Bay to the W and to **Port Ludlow** to the S. It is of small extent and awash at high water. The rock, marked by kelp, is surrounded by deep water with depths up to 100 feet between it and the shore. Klas Rock is marked on the E side by a lighted bell buoy.

(67) **Mats Mats Bay**, SW of Klas Rock, is a small, nearly landlocked lagoon offering excellent protection from the wind to small craft. The entrance to the bay is about 100 yards wide at high water. A dredged channel, marked by a **261.3°** lighted range, buoys, and lights, leads from the entrance to the NE corner of the bay. In 1977, the controlling depth in the entrance channel was 5 feet for a midwidth of 100 feet. Good anchorage may be had in the bay with general depths of 4 to 12 feet.

(68) A boat ramp and 200 feet of transient moorage, maintained by the Port of Port Townsend, are on the SE side of the bay.

(69) The three **Colvos Rocks**, 0.7 mile S of Klas Rock and about 0.3 mile off the W shore, mark the N extremity of the bank covered by 7 to 28 feet which extends in an arc S to **Tala Point**. The NW rock, 28 feet high and of small extent with deep water around it, is marked by a light. The SE point of the shoal extending SE from the rocks is also marked by a light. Tala Point is a bluff, wooded, and about 310 feet high. A light is about 200 yards NE of the point.

(70) **Snake Rock** is 0.4 mile SW of the W Colvos Rock and 300 yards offshore.

(71) The entrance to **Port Ludlow**, in the W part of Admiralty Inlet, is just W of Colvos Rocks on the W side at the entrance to Hood Canal. From the broad entrance the bay extends in a general S direction 2.5 miles, terminating in a basin 0.5 mile in diameter. The basin affords good anchorage in 40 to 50 feet, soft bottom; the shores are fairly steep.

(72) **Burner Point**, marked by a light, is on the N side of the entrance to the inner portion of the bay. A **speed limit** of 5 knots is enforced southerly of a line extending due east from Burner Point to the east shore.

(73) The town of **Port Ludlow**, once a major Puget Sound lumber port, is on the N shore of the inner portion of the bay. The former Port Ludlow townsite is now occupied by a housing development and resort of the same name. A series of exposed piles are on the NW side of the inner bay. Several private small-craft floats are in the bay.

(74) A marina, on the N side of the bay and just W of Burner Point, has berths for nearly 300 craft; electricity, gasoline, diesel fuel, water, ice, pumpout facilities and some marine supplies are available. Reported depths of 15 feet can be taken to the floats. The entrance to the fuel dock is reported to shoal on the right side at low tide.

(75) **The Twins** are two islands at the extreme SW end of Port Ludlow. The small bay S of The Twins is sometimes used as an anchorage for small craft in rough weather. A reported depth of 10 feet is in the entrance to the bay between the islands.

(76) **Hansville**, about 2.5 miles ESE of Foulweather Bluff, is a small village with a general store. Berthage and dock facilities are not available.

(77) **Norwegian Point**, low and rounding, is about 0.2 mile NW of Hansville. A conspicuous privately owned lighthouse, 210 feet above the water and built from plans of the original lighthouse at Mukilteo, is about 1 mile W of Hansville.

(78) **Point No Point**, on the W shore of the sound about 3.5 miles SE of Foulweather Bluff, is a low sandspit. **Point No Point Light** (47°54'44"N., 122°31'37"W.), 27

feet above the water, is shown from a 20-foot white octagonal tower on the end of the point.

Chart 18441

(79) **Useless Bay**, indenting Whidbey Island E of Double Bluff, is open to the SW. The shores are bluff, brush covered, and low with a marshy area surrounding the bay. The N and SE sides of the bay are spotted with homes. At night, the lighted antenna about 2 miles NE of the head of Useless Bay is prominent.

(80) **Scatchet Head** and **Possession Point**, at the S end of Whidbey Island, are both prominent, especially from S; the white bluffs are visible for a considerable distance. A lighted bell buoy is 0.5 mile S of Possession Point. A fish haven is close W of the lighted bell buoy. Shoals extend 0.5 mile offshore immediately W of Scatchet Head and over 0.2 mile offshore from the head to Possession Point. A lighted gong buoy is about 0.5 mile off Scatchet Head. **Cultus Bay**, just W of Possession Point, is shoal; much of the bay bares at low water. A channel, marked by lights at the entrance, leads to a private mooring basin on the E side of the bay. The channel has a reported depth of 3 feet. A mooring float and launching ramp are just N of the mooring basin on the E side of the bay.

(81) Possession Sound and its tributaries are described later in this chapter.

Charts 18446, 18473

(82) **Apple Cove Point** is a low sandspit projecting 220 yards from the high, wooded land of the peninsula. The point is steep-to, but a shoal makes out nearly 0.5 mile SE from it. Just off the point is a light. Heavy tide rips caused by strong NW winds and a strong ebb current are encountered in the vicinity of the light.

(83) A microwave tower on the high ground about 0.6 mile SW from Apple Cove Point Light, is prominent from offshore.

(84) **Appletree Cove** is the open bight on the W side of the sound about 1.5 miles S of Apple Cove Point. It affords anchorage in 30 to 60 feet inside the line of the entrance points, with some shelter from winds drawing in or out of the sound, but not from N and SE.

(85) **Kingston**, a town on the N side of the cove, has a large, well-equipped small-craft basin, a 420-foot long fishing pier, and a pier with a ferry slip at its end. The ferry runs between Kingston and Edmonds. The basin is used by tugs, fishing boats, and pleasure craft. The harbor is protected by a stone breakwater that extends about 340 yards SW from the ferry pier; the end of the breakwater is marked by a light. In 2009, the marina had a reported depth of 12 feet in the entrance and 6 feet alongside the berths. Services available include: electricity, gasoline, diesel fuel, water, ice, pump-out facility, surfaced launch ramp and marine supplies. The marina has space for 275 small-craft including about 49 transient berths.

(86) **Edwards Point** is a high, wooded point on the E side of Puget Sound 3.6 miles ESE of Apple Cove Point. It is a turning point for vessels running from Seattle N into Possession Sound and adjoining waters.

(87) **Edmonds** is an incorporated city 1 mile NE of Edwards Point with a small boat basin and marina under the administration of the **Port of Edmonds**. The protected basin is entered from the NW at about the midpoint of the marina; the entrance is marked by lights and a light is on the SW corner. The reported depth is 9 feet alongside the piers. There are open and covered berths for about 600 craft up to 50 feet, including 20 transient moorings; berth assignments are made by the harbormaster. Services available include: electricity, gasoline, diesel fuel, water, ice, marine supplies, pump-out station and full repairs can be made. A 50-ton marine travel lift and 10-ton fork lift are also available at the marina. The marina monitors VHF-FM channels 16 and 69.

(88) Just N of the boat basin are a fish haven and fishing pier, the Edmonds and Kingston ferry landing, and a scuba diving area N of the landing. The fish haven is marked by private buoys near the boat basin breakwater N section; private buoys also mark the W side of the scuba diving area.

(89) A **037°01'-217°01' measured nautical mile** is on the shoreline 1 mile NE of Edmonds. The front markers are on short metal poles atop the seawall which protects the railroad tracks; the rear markers are about 20 yards SE of the front markers. The bluff is 60 feet high behind the NE pair of markers and 12 feet high behind the SE pair of markers. All four markers are white wooden triangular daymarks.

(90) **Point Wells** is a low, sandy point projecting 450 yards from the high land 1.5 miles S of Edwards Point on the E side of the sound. It is distinguished by prominent oil tanks. It is a water terminal and storage plant of Chevron USA, Inc. There are two wharves here, however, only the S wharf is in use. The wharf is 1,054 feet long and has a deck height of 21 feet. In 1983, reported depths of 40 to 70 feet were alongside. A conveyor serving this wharf is used for outloading drummed petroleum products. Barges are loaded on the inside of both the N and S extensions of the wharf.

(91) The current at Point Wells is unpredictable being inconsistent for similar tidal conditions; however, a vessel making a port landing on a flood tide may expect to be set off the pier. The use of an anchor is recommended when docking in high wind. The Manager of the Marine Department of Chevron USA, Inc. prefers that vessels not be docked without the use of tugs when conditions are such that damage might be done to the wharf. Deep-draft vessels approaching the wharf for a starboard landing during a flood tide must guard against being set on to the shoal S of the wharf. A company-maintained sound signal is on the S wharf.

(92) **Richmond Beach** is a community on the E shore just S of Point Wells. A tall, charted radio tower (KCIS), marked by aircraft warning lights, is about 1.5 miles inshore from Richmond Beach; it is an excellent landmark, especially at night. A fish haven is off the mouth of **Boeing Creek**, about 1.9 miles S of Point Wells.

Charts 18446, 18449

(93) **Bainbridge Island**, 9 miles long and heavily wooded, forms part of the W shore of Puget Sound. There are several towns on the island.

(94) **Port Madison** indents the W shore between the N end of Bainbridge Island and **Point Jefferson**. It is about 2.5 miles long and very deep; not until within 0.5 mile of the beach can anchorage be found in 90 to 100 feet, sticky bottom. Its SW part connects with Port Orchard through Agate Passage.

(95) The N shore is formed by broken white bluffs, with low beaches between, and bordered by sand and shingle beaches that bare in some cases as much a 0.2 mile offshore. **Indianola**, a village on the N shore, has a long pier. The water E of the end of the pier is shoal. The bluffs on the W shore are moderately low; the buildings of the small town of **Suquamish** near the entrance to Agate Pass are prominent.

(96) **Miller Bay**, in the NW part of Port Madison, is used by shallow-draft pleasure craft. The channel should not be used at low tide because of the very irregular bottom. In 2002, the reported depth in the channel along the docks at the S end of the bay was 5 feet.

(97) **Point Monroe**, the S point at the entrance of Port Madison, is a low, narrow sandspit, curving W and S. A small cove is between the sandspit and the shore to the S. The entrance dries at low water.

(98) The S shore of Port Madison is composed of broken bluffs, except where it is indented by the narrow arm extending 1 mile S. The entrance to this narrow arm is 0.7 mile W of Point Monroe. The town of **Port Madison**, has many private piers but no fueling facilities. The narrow channel through the arm has a least depth of 16 feet, and local knowledge is necessary to keep in the best water. Two submerged rocks, covered 7 feet and marked by a daybeacon (47°41'51"N., 122°32'08"W.), about 220 yards SSW of **Treasure Island**; caution should be exercised. An old ballast dump, nearly bare at low water, is 75 yards offshore 400 yards in from the E entrance point. Care should be taken to avoid the cluster of covered rocks 100 yards off the E entrance point. Sheltered anchorage for small craft may be had in up to 21 feet, mud bottom.

(99) **Meadow Point**, on the E side of Puget Sound nearly opposite Point Monroe, is a low, grassy point, with a high tree and brush-covered bluff behind it. A lighted buoy is about 0.2 mile NW of the point.

(100) **Murden Cove** is an open bight on the W side of the sound about 3.5 miles S of Point Monroe. An extensive flat which bares extends almost 0.5 mile from the head of the cove, and outside of it the depth increases rapidly. **Skiff Point**, the N entrance point, has low yellow bluffs to the S. A shoal, covered by kelp, extends about 250 yards from the point; this shoal is reported to be building out and should be given a wide berth. **Yeomalt Point**, the S entrance point, is a low, grassy sandspit, 150 yards wide, rising gradually to the general level of the high land. The radio towers about 0.9 mile SW of Skiff Point are prominent from offshore.

(101) **Wing Point**, on the N side of the entrance to Eagle Harbor, is a narrow, bluff point 30 feet high, covered with trees to the edge. A flag pole is prominent on the point. A reef extends SSE for 0.5 mile from Wing Point and is generally marked by kelp. The S extremity of the reef is marked by a buoy. **Tyee Shoal**, 0.7 mile SSE of Wing Point, with a least depth of 14 feet, is marked by a light.

(102) Foul ground extends as much as 500 yards off the S point at the entrance; a light and buoy mark its outer limits.

(103) **Eagle Harbor** indents the E shore of Bainbridge Island opposite Elliott Bay. It is 2 miles long and affords excellent anchorage in 30 to 39 feet, muddy bottom. It narrows at the head to 300 yards.

(104) The entrance is deep, but caution is necessary in entering because the natural channel is only 200 yards wide between the reef S of Wing Point and the spit on the W side of the channel entrance. The channel is marked by lights and buoys. A wreck covered 18 feet is at 47°37'09"N., 122°31'11"W.

(105) **Winslow** is the largest town on Bainbridge Island. It is on the N shore of Eagle Harbor, and is a major ferry port on the cross-sound routes to and from downtown Seattle. About 0.2 mile W of the ferry slip is a large building and two piers which are used by the Washington State Ferry System for ferry mooring and maintenance. About 0.3 mile West of the ferry slip is a city park with a float that offers 48-hour free moorage. Immediately W of the float is a launching ramp.

(106) There are several marinas located on the shores of Eagle Harbor. Numerous small-craft are anchored in the upper half of Eagle Harbor.

(107) **Creosote**, a low flat extending 350 yards inland, then raising abruptly to over 200 feet, is on the S side of the entrance to Eagle Harbor. Two lights and a buoy mark shoals to the NW and E. **Eagledale**, is a small town with three marinas, on the S shore about 0.5 mile W of Creosote.

(108) **Blakely Rock**, the highest of four rocks, is prominent in approaching Blakely Harbor; it is 0.7 mile N of Restoration Point and at high water shows about 15 feet at its highest point. It is 300 yards long, with shoal water, well marked by kelp, extending over 250 yards N. A light is on the S side of the rock.

(109) **Blakely Harbor** is a small inlet on the E shore of Bainbridge Island near its S end. It is 1 mile long. Depths range from 145 feet at the entrance to 25 feet near the

head. The usual anchorage is near the entrance in 54 to 96 feet, sticky bottom, slightly favoring the S shore. There are many old pilings and dolphins in the shoal waters near the shores. There are no usable wharves in Blakely Harbor.

(110) **Restoration Point** is flat and about 10 feet high for 300 yards from the shore, then it rises abruptly to a wooded knoll about 100 feet high, on which a flagpole and a number of large buildings are prominent. **Decatur Reef**, partly bare, extends 300 yards E of Restoration Point. The outer end of the reef is marked by a lighted buoy.

Charts 18449, 18446, 18447, 18474

(111) **Shilshole Bay** is between Meadow Point and West Point. It is an open bight from which the Lake Washington Ship Canal is entered, and is the site of the largest marina in the Seattle area. Clay cliffs extend for about 0.5 mile S of the canal entrance. Golden Gardens Park, Seattle Department of Parks and Recreation is N of the marina and extends up to and includes Meadow Point.

(112) **Shilshole Bay Marina**, the small-craft basin just N of the canal entrance, is administered by the Port of Seattle. A 4,400-foot breakwater, marked at each end by a light, protects the basin on its W side. The basin has two entrances. In 2009, the controlling depths were 14 feet in the S entrances, and 15 feet in the N entrance.

(113) There are berths at the concrete floats for 1,400 craft to 250 feet long, including a guest pier and transient berths. The marina can provide electricity, gasoline, bio-diesel (#1 and #2), diesel fuel, water, ice, marine supplies, and a pump-out station at the 600-foot pier at the midpoint of the basin. Two 3-ton hoists are at the S end, and one 3-ton and one 4-ton hoists are at the N end of the basin. A 55-ton marine travel lift, for haul-out, is available at the boatyard at the S end of the basin. Dry storage is available for 82 boats on movable trailers at the N end of the marina. A boat launching ramp is located immediately N of the marina in Golden Gardens Park. The marina can be contacted on VHF-FM channel 17.

(114) **West Point**, at the N entrance to Elliott Bay, is a low, sandy point which rises abruptly to an elevation of over 300 feet 0.5 mile from its tip. The edge of the shoal extending WSW from the point is marked by a lighted buoy. **West Point Light** (47°39'43"N., 122°26'09"W.), 27 feet above the water, is shown from a 30-foot white octagonal tower attached to a building on the end of the point; a mariner radio activated sound signal is at the station, initiated by keying the microphone five times on VHF-FM channel 81A. Prominent in the area are the sump tanks of a sewage treatment plant about 0.1 mile E of the light, a VTS antenna tower between the plant and the light, and a large white dome about 1 mile ESE of the light.

(115) **Alki Point**, at the S entrance to Elliott Bay, is low with a small prominent wooded knoll about 80 feet high immediately back of it. E of the knoll, lowland extends for nearly 0.4 mile before rising to the high land extending S from Duwamish Head. **Alki Point Light** (47°34'35"N., 122°25'14"W.), 39 feet above the water, is shown from a 37-foot white octagonal tower attached to a building on the end of the point.

(116) **Elliott Bay** indents the E shore of Puget Sound just N of Duwamish Head. The entrance is between West Point on the N and Alki Point 5 miles S. The bay proper, lying E of a line between Magnolia Bluff and Duwamish Head, has a width of about 2 miles and extends SE for nearly the same distance. The bay is deep throughout most of its area.

(117) **Magnolia Bluff**, largely bare, light-colored, and rising in places to nearly 300 feet, extends along the N shore from West Point to Smith Cove. **Fourmile Rock** is 60 yards offshore, 1.7 miles SSE of West Point Light. A light is on the rock. A wreck, covered 56 feet, is about 0.5 mile W of Magnolia Bluff in about 47°38'25"N., 122°25'35"W.

(118) Elliott Bay Marina is located just W of Smith Cove (Pier 91) below Magnolia Bluff. A 2,700-foot breakwater, marked by private lights, protects the basin on its S side. The basin has entrances on the E and W ends and has a reported depth 23 feet in the approach with a depth of 10 feet alongside the berths. The marina can accommodate 1,200 vessels up to 200 feet long, including 20 transient berths; larger vessel moorage is at the E pier. Services available include: electricity, gasoline, diesel fuel, water, ice, pump-out facility, engine and electrical repair. A yacht chartering firm is on site. VHF-FM channel 78A is monitored and a heliport is located at the center of the breakwater. No commercial vessels, commercial work or major boat repairs are allowed.

(119) **Duwamish Head**, 1.8 miles NE of Alki Point and rising to over 260 feet from the point, bounds Elliott Bay to the S. The bluff is tree covered, but is interspersed with houses. The lights of the houses along the beach and on the bluff are conspicuous at night. A shoal, extending over 0.2 mile N of the point, is marked by **Duwamish Head Light** and a mariner radio activated sound signal, initiated by keying the microphone five times on VHF-FM channel 83A.

Chart 18450

(120) **Seattle**, the largest and most important city in the Northwest and one of the major ports of the Pacific Coast, extends as a densely populated greater metropolitan area from Everett, the city to its N, almost to Tacoma, the major city to the S, and E beyond the limits of Lake Washington and its shores. Seattle has many modern, fully equipped ocean terminals, excellent transportation facilities, several large shipyards, and numerous large marine supply houses.

Seattle, Washington
Image courtesy U.S. Army Corps of Engineers (2002)

(121) Much of Seattle's shipping is in the Pacific Rim trade, and the city is a major industrial center. Seattle handles most of the waterborne commerce to Alaska Ports, and is the terminus of several shipping lines operating to Alaska as well as other parts of the world. Almost 22 per cent of Seattle's commerce is in the foreign trade, with British Columbia, Japan, Asia, and Europe forming the cornerstone of the overseas commerce. Principal exports are grain and grain mill products, logs, petroleum products, food and vegetable products, lumber, waste and scrap, chemicals, cement, wood chips and fuel wood, fabricated metal products, and sulfur. The principal imports are logs, lumber, sand and gravel, iron and steel, petroleum products, newsprint, bananas, cement, canned fish and shellfish, limestone, machinery, pulp and paper, asphalt and tar, radio and TV products, and clay.

(122) The **Port of Seattle** includes an outer and inner harbor. The outer saltwater harbor includes Elliott Bay; East, West, and Duwamish Waterways; Shilshole Bay, and the portions of Puget Sound adjacent to Ballard on the N and West Seattle to the S of the entrance of Elliott Bay. Seattle's freshwater inner harbor consists of Lakes Union and Washington, which are connected with each other and with Puget Sound by the Lake Washington Ship Canal. Most of the waterfront facilities of the inner harbor are privately owned.

(123) Of the nearly 60 piers and terminals in the outer harbor, the Port of Seattle owns more than 25, operating three and leasing out the others. These properties include 10 general cargo handling facilities and 1 major container handling terminal. The port also has four fully developed marine terminals, and a fifth in the construction phase, on the Duwamish Waterway S of Harbor Island in the Lower Duwamish Development District, a project which provides lease-sites for terminal facilities and water-oriented industries. The Port of Seattle also operates Seattle-Tacoma International Airport, which is located about midway between Seattle and Tacoma.

(124) Although there are several deep-draft terminals on Elliott Bay, many of the piers and wharves are used by fisheries, ferry and tour boat operators and for entertainment facilities.

(125) **East Waterway** is separated from West Waterway by **Harbor Island**. Several important terminals are on the waterway. Most of the N side of Harbor Island is occupied by the piers and drydocks of a shipyard. A private light, shown from the NE corner of Terminal 18, marks the W side of the entrance to East Waterway.

(126) **Note:** Vessels are cautioned against anchoring in the vicinity of pipeline and cable areas shown on the charts.

(127) Most of the E side of **West Waterway** and the area W of the entrance are occupied by the facilities of two large shipyards. The SW side of the waterway is the site of the Port of Seattle's Terminal 5, which receives considerable deep-draft traffic. Several other wharves on

(128) **Duwamish Waterway, extending** S from West Waterway, is fronted by factories and industrial plants for more than 4 miles. A number of log rafts are often anchored along the waterway around Kellogg Island and S of the 1st Avenue South Bridge.

Prominent features

(129) In clear weather the skyline of Seattle itself is unmistakable. From N to S the conspicuous features are: the "Space Needle," a legacy from the 1962 World Fair; the red lighted "E" sign at pier 67; the Washington Building, of light sandstone, usually illuminated at night; the Columbia Center building, distinguishable from other skyscrapers by its greater height; the Seattle Tower; and the square-topped Seattle First National Bank building, distinguished from two other skyscrapers by its slightly taller height and black color.

Channels

(130) Depths of 34 feet or more are available to the Seattle waterfront in Elliott Bay. A **Federal project** provides for a depth of 34 feet in East and West Waterways. (See latest edition of charts for depths in East and West Waterways.) The project for Duwamish Waterway provides for a 30-foot channel from the S end of West Waterway to the 1st Avenue South Bridge, thence 20 feet for about 0.65 mile to 8th Avenue South, thence 15 feet to a point about 1.2 miles S of the 14th Avenue South Bridge, the end of the project. (See Notice to Mariners and latest editions of charts for controlling depths.)

Anchorages

(131) Four general anchorages are in Elliott Bay. (See **110.1 and 110.230**, chapter 2, for limits and regulations.)

Regulated Navigation Areas

(132) A **security zone** has been established at Pier 36 in Elliott Bay. (See **33 CFR 165.1 through 165.9, 165.30, 165.33, and 165.1334**, chapter 2, for limits and regulations.)

(133) Two regulated areas have been established in Elliott Bay: southeast of Duwamish Head and on the east side of West Waterway. (See **33 CFR 165.1 through 165.13 and 165.1336**, chapter 2, for limits and regulations.)

Bridges

(134) There are no bridges over the Seattle waterfront in Elliott Bay, and none over East and West Waterways. The 4.5-mile-long Duwamish Waterway is crossed at Mile 0.2 by the SW Spokane Street swing bridge, with a clearance of 44 feet (55 feet at center); thence a fixed bridge with a clearance of 140 feet just above the swing bridge; thence at Mile 0.3, the Burlington Northern Railroad bascule bridge with a clearance of 7 feet; thence at Mile 2.1, the 1st Avenue S dual bascule bridges with a clearance of 22 feet (32 feet at the central 100 feet); thence at Mile 3.3, the 16th Avenue S bascule bridge with a clearance of 21 feet (34 feet at center.) (See **117.1 through 117.59 and 117.1041**, chapter 2, for drawbridge regulations.) The power cables in the waterway have a least clearance of 90 feet (at Mile 3.5.)

Currents

(135) As a rule, the tidal **currents** in the harbor have little velocity. At times, however, with a falling tide an appreciable current will be found setting NW along the waterfront. (See Tidal Current Charts for Puget Sound, Northern Part.)

Weather, Seattle and vicinity

(136) Seattle is on a hilly stretch of land overlooking the salt-waters of Puget Sound to the W, and in an E direction, the waters of Lake Washington, an 18-mile-long (33 km) freshwater lake. The Lake Washington shoreline roughly parallels that of Puget Sound at distances varying from about 2.5 to 6 miles (5 to 11 km). Hills rise rather abruptly from both shorelines and reach elevations of more than 300 feet (92 m) in the central sections and more than 500 feet (153 m) in the extreme Northern and the Southwestern sections. The general N-S trend of the city is paralleled on the E by the Cascade Mountains, while to the W and NW, at somewhat greater distance, the Olympic Mountains rise abruptly. The main commercial section of the city is along the E shore of Elliott Bay, an indentation in the Puget Sound shoreline.

(137) The climate is mild and moderately moist due to the prevailing W air currents, which advance inland from the Pacific Ocean, and to the shielding effects of the Cascade Mountains, which serve to exclude and deflect the cold continental air toward the E. Although the city is 90 miles distant from the ocean at the nearest point, the marine air penetrates readily inland, an effect that is aided by the extensive water surface of Puget Sound. The prevailing W air currents cross vast reaches of ocean, acquiring much water vapor and a temperature near that of the sea. This effect is received from the general currents of the ocean rather than from the Japanese Current which curves far N into Alaskan waters. As a result of the rather steady influx of marine air, winters are comparatively warm and summers cool. Extremes of heat or cold are moderate and usually of short duration, and the daily range in temperature small.

(138) The warmest summer and the coldest winter days come with N to E winds which have traveled under land influences from British Columbia or eastern Washington. In the summer, the number of days having maximum temperatures of 90°F (32.2°C) or above averages less than three but these extreme temperatures have occurred in each month between May and September. Only once during the entire period of record has the

temperature reached 100°F (37.8°C, July 1994). The average annual temperature is 52°F (11.1°C) with an average maximum of 59°F (15°C) and an average minimum of 44°F (6.7°C). Nighttime temperatures during the warmest months usually reach comfortable levels, and very seldom remain about 65°F (18.3°C). During the winter, daily maximum temperatures fail to rise above the freezing point (0°C) on an average of only about two days per year, while the number of days having minimum temperatures of 32°F (0°C) or below averages only 15 per year. However, each month, October through May, has recorded sub-freezing temperatures and single-digit temperatures have been recorded in each month from November through February. An extreme low temperature of 0°F (-17.8°C) was recorded in January 1950. In general, temperatures may vary by several degrees at any one time throughout the city, depending on wind direction, distance from shoreline, and elevation.

(139) The normal precipitation of 38 inches (965 mm) is moderate compared with many points along the north Pacific Coast. Primarily this is due to the location of the city, which lies in the lee or dry side of the Olympic Mountains. The W or windward slopes of these mountains cause the moist marine winds to rise to cooler levels with heavy precipitation on the seaward slopes and diminished amounts E of the summits. A winter seasonal wet period along the Pacific Coast coincides with and is caused by the Aleutian Low. In summer this low pressure recedes N with higher pressures off the coast and results eventually in clear weather, rising temperatures, and decreased humidities. The area has, therefore, a pronounced but not sharply defined wet season extending usually from October through April, a period in which about 82 percent of the total precipitation occurs, and a dry season, May through September, with 18 percent. Excessive precipitation is rare and the 24-hour extreme precipitation event is only 3.41 inches (86.6 mm), but in the wet season the continuance of light or moderate amounts is rather persistent. The average winter snowfall totals about 12 inches (305 mm), and snow seldom remains on the ground for more than 1 or 2 days at a time. Maximum recorded snow depths have ranged from as little as a trace in several instances to over 21 inches (533 mm). The occurrence of light fog is most frequent during late fall and winter where, on average, 19 days report fog during the October through January period. Thunderstorms average about eight per year, lightning damage is very infrequent, and tornadoes have never been reported in the city.

(140) The National Weather Service maintains an office in Seattle. **Barometers** may be compared there or by telephone. (See Appendix A for address.)

(141) (See Appendix B for **Seattle climatological table.)**

Routes

(142) Vessels bound for the Strait of Georgia from Seattle can use the following routes: **via Rosario Strait**–an approximate midchannel course using the vessel traffic system outbound lane (see the beginning of chapter 12 for Traffic Separation Scheme information), through Puget Sound and Admiralty Inlet to the precautionary area N of Point Wilson, thence E of Partridge Bank, Smith Island, and Davidson Rock to the precautionary area at the S end of Rosario Strait, thence N passing E of Belle Rock, Lydia Shoal, and Peapod Rocks, thence leaving the vessel traffic system lanes at the precautionary area just N of Clark Island, and proceeding into the Strait of Georgia either N or S of Alden Bank; **via Haro Strait**–from Admiralty Inlet using the vessel traffic system outbound lane to the precautionary area N of Point Wilson, thence W of Partridge Bank leaving the vessel traffic system lanes at the precautionary area just SE of Hein Bank, thence through Haro Strait and Boundary Pass to the Strait of Georgia.

(143) These routes are available for vessels of any draft. A range should be steered where available to ensure making the courses good.

(144) Between Admiralty Inlet and the entrance to Rosario Strait, the current on the flood has a tendency to set a vessel E toward Whidbey Island; it also sets strongly through Deception Pass and up Rosario Strait. There is a strong W set in this area on the ebb tide. Through Rosario Strait the currents run with considerable velocity. Heavy tide rips and swirls are found off Black Rock, Obstruction Pass, Peapod Rocks, and Lawrence Point.

(145) In crossing from Admiralty Inlet to the entrance of Haro Strait, the tidal currents setting to and from Rosario Strait and San Juan Channel, with estimated velocities of 2 to 3 knots, should be kept in mind. From Henry Island to around Turn Point, heavy tide rips are found on the ebb. Particularly heavy and dangerous tide rips occur on the ebb between East Point and Patos Island and for 2 miles N in the Strait of Georgia. The flood from Rosario Strait, which is felt as soon as the passage between Orcas and Sucia Islands is open, is apt to set a vessel toward East Point. The ebb in this vicinity sets to the E even before the Strait of Georgia is well open.

Pilotage, Seattle

(146) Pilotage is compulsory for all vessels except those under enrollment or engaged exclusively in the coasting trade on the W coast of the continental United States (including Alaska) and/or British Columbia. Pilotage for Puget Sound is provided by the Puget Sound Pilots. (See Pilotage, Strait of Juan de Fuca and Puget Sound, indexed as such, chapter 12, for detail.)

Towage

(147) Tugs up to 5,000 hp are available in Seattle. Arrangements should be made in advance through ship's agent.

				Facilities in the Port of Seattle			
Name	Location	Berthing Space (feet)	Depths* (feet)	Deck Height (feet)	Mechanical Handling Facilities and Storage	Purpose	Owned/ Operated by:
Facilities on Elliott Bay							
Port of Seattle Terminal 91, Pier 91	47°37'35"N., 122°22'58"W.	2,495 (W side) 1,875 (E side) 357 (face)	16-30	18	• Open storage (45 acres) • Cold storage (4.5 million feet³)	Receipt of general cargo, automobiles, and seafood (Note 3)	Port of Seattle
Port of Seattle Terminal 91, Pier 90	47°37'35"N., 122°22'48"W.	1,875 (W side) 2,222 (E side) 295 (face)	22-30	18	• Covered storage (138,000 sq. feet) • Tank storage (198,000 barrels)	Receipt and shipment of fruit and petroleum products (Note 3)	Port of Seattle
Louis Dreyfus Corp. Terminal 86	47°37'24"N., 122°22'12"W.	1,400	70	20	• Grain elevator (4.2 million bushels) • Vessel loading spouts • Belt conveyors	Shipment of grain	Port of Seattle/ Louis Dreyfus Corp.
Total Terminals Terminal 46	47°35'48"N., 122°20'28"W.	1,874	39-43	18.5	• Open storage (70 acres) • Gantry cranes (40 tons)	Receipt and shipment of general cargo	Port of Seattle/ Total Terminals, Inc.
SSA Terminals Terminal 37	47°37'32"N., 122°20'33"W.	850	50	18.5 / 21	• Open storage (12 acres) • Lifts (15 tons)	Receipt and shipment of general cargo and steel products	Port of Seattle/ SSA Terminals, Inc.
Rainier Petroleum Corp. Equilon Enterprises	47°35'20"N., 122°21'12"W.	460 (W side) 460 (E side)	35-40	19	Tank storage (550,000 barrels)	Receipt and shipment of petroleum products	ExxonMobil Corp./ Rainier Petroleum and Equilon Enterprises, LLC
Facilities on East Waterway							
SSA Terminals Terminal 18 (Berths 1 to 5)	47°35'20"N., 122°21'12"W.	6,000	49	17	• Open storage (196 acres) • Tank storage (850,000 barrels) • Traveling cranes (50 tons)	Receipt and shipment of general cargo and Petroleum products	Port of Seattle/ SSA Terminals and Kinder Morgan Energy Partners
Trans Pacific Container Service Corp. Terminal 30	47°34'49"N., 122°20'35"W.	1,812	40–44	18.5	• Open storage (45 acres) • Container cranes (50 tons)	Receipt and shipment of general cargo	Port of Seattle/ Trans Pacific Container Service Corp.
SSA Terminals Terminal 25	47°34'32"N., 122°20'35"W.	1,580	42-44	18.5	• Open storage (37 acres) • Container cranes (40 tons)	Receipt and shipment of general cargo	Port of Seattle/ SSA Terminals
Facilities on West Waterway							
BP Oil Company Seattle Terminal (Pier 11)	47°34'57"N., 122°21'30"W.	460	32	20	Tank storage (617,800 barrels)	Receipt and shipment of petroleum products	BP Oil Company
American President Lines Terminal 5 Wharf	47°34'37"N., 122°21'41"W.	2,900	45-50 (Note 1)	19	• Open storage (130 acres) • Container cranes (50 ton)	Receipt and shipment of general cargo	Port of Seattle/ American President Lines
Pacific Terminals East and West Wharves	47°34'25"N., 122°21'35"W.	670	15	19	Covered storage	Receipt and occasional shipment of lumber; receipt of wood pulp and paper products (Note 2)	Puget Sound Freight Lines/Pacific Terminals, Ltd.
Facilities on Duwamish Waterway							
Ash Grove Cement Co. North Wharf	47°34'06"N., 122°20'44"W.	600	25	20	• Silo storage (54,500 tons) • Pneumatic pipelines	Occasional shipment of bulk cement	Ash Grove Cement Co.
Ash Grove Cement Co. South Wharf	47°34'03"N., 122°20'45"W.	360	25	20	• Open storage • Silo storage	Receipt of coal, gypsum, gravel, and limestone	Ash Grove Cement Co.
Birmingham Steel Corp. Terminal 105	47°33'54"N., 122°20'56"W.	660	40	17	Open storage (3.7 acres)	Receipt of scrap metal by barge	Port of Seattle/ Birmingham Steel Corp.
Lafarge Corporation Cement Wharf	47°33'19"N., 122°20'42"W.	645	32	25	Silo storage (68,250 tons)	Receipt and shipment of bulk cement	Lafarge Corp.
Lafarge Corporation Raw Materials Wharf	47°33'14"N., 122°20'35"W.	1,100	30	20	• Open storage (50,000 tons) • One traveling crane	Receipt of limestone, shale, coal, and slag	Lafarge Corp.
Glacier Northwest West Terminal Wharf	47°32'56"N., 122°20'25"W.	467	34	20	• Silo storage (50,000 tons) • Traveling cement unloader	Receipt of bulk cement	Glacier Northwest
Glacier Northwest Slip No. 2 Wharf	47°32'49"N., 122°20'16"W.	325	16–17	15	• Open storage (13,000 tons) • Belt conveyor system	Receipt of sand and gravel	Glacier Northwest
International Terminal Co. Terminal 115	47°32'54"N., 122°20'24"W.	925	30	20	• Open storage (6.4 acres) • One 50-ton gantry crane	Receipt and shipment of general cargo and forest products; receipt of steel products	Port of Seattle/ various operators

				Facilities in the Port of Seattle			
Name	Location	Berthing Space (feet)	Depths* (feet)	Deck Height (feet)	Mechanical Handling Facilities and Storage	Purpose	Owned/ Operated by:
Northland Services 8th Avenue Terminal Wharf	47°32'05"N., 122°19'16"W.	1,035	13–15	18	• Open storage (20 acres) • Cranes to 150 tons	Receipt and shipment of general cargo	Crowley Marine Services/ Northland Services Inc.

* The depths given above are reported. For information on the latest depths contact the port authorities or the private operators.

Note 1 – Mariners are advised to use caution when using this wharf as the South Berth shallows rapidly from the 250-foot mark to the end of the pier.
Note 2 – Two tugs are recommended when docking at East Wharf.
Note 3 – Safety and Security Zone, See **33 CFR §165.1324**, chapter 2, for limits and regulations.

Quarantine, customs, immigration, and agricultural quarantine

(148) (See chapter 3, Vessel Arrival Inspections, and Appendix A for addresses.)

(149) **Quarantine** is enforced in accordance with regulations of the U.S. Public Health Service. (See Public Health Service, chapter 1.) The quarantine anchorage is just N of Harbor Island.

(150) Seattle is a **customs port of entry**.

Coast Guard

(151) The Thirteenth Coast Guard District Office and Sector Puget Sound is located in the Federal Building in downtown Seattle. (See Appendix A for addresses.) The Coast Guard moors vessels at the Pier 36 Slip (47°35'24"N., 122°20'31"W.)

Harbor regulations

(152) Harbor regulations are enforced by the Harbor Patrol Unit of the Seattle Police Department. The unit has two patrol boats to aid in the enforcement of the city ordinance prohibiting unlawful destruction by excessive speeds, disorderly behavior, or unsafe seamanship. They maintain constant radio contact with each other and the police "land cruisers" on 24-hour patrol. The police patrol all waters of the harbor.

Wharves

(153) The Port of Seattle has numerous piers and wharves on both the outer harbor (Elliot Bay, East, West, and Duwamish Waterways) and the inner harbor (Lake Washington Ship Canal, Lake Union, and Lake Washington.) Of the facilities listed in the table, nearly half are owned by the Port of Seattle and leased to private operators, including eight large general cargo facilities, a grain elevator, and a large terminal for handling automobiles. Most of the facilities in the inner harbor are privately owned and handle barge traffic almost exclusively. Only the major deep-draft facilities are listed. For a complete description of the port facilities refer to Port Series No. 36, published and sold by the U.S. Army Corps of Engineers. (See Appendix A for address.) The alongside depths given in the table are reported. (For information on the latest depths contact the port authorities or the private operators.)

(154) All facilities described have direct highway connections and most have plant trackage with direct railroad connections. Water is available at most of the wharves, but electrical shore power connections are available at less than half of the wharves. General cargo at the port is usually handled by ships' tackle. Mechanical handling equipment, if available, is mentioned in the table. Shore-based hoisting equipment with capacities up to 200 tons and floating cranes with capacities to 400 tons are available to the public at Port of Seattle.

Supplies

(155) Marine supplies of all kinds are available in Seattle. Bunker fuel, diesel oil, and lubricants are available. Large vessels can be bunkered at Pier 91, Pier 15 (Rainer Petroleum Corp. and Equilon Enterprises) and at Pier 11 (BP Oil Co.). Bunkering may be done at other berths by tank barges. Water is available at most berths. N of Seattle, vessels may bunker at Point Wells or Edwards Point.

Repairs

(156) There are two large shipyards in the Seattle area, both on Harbor Island at the S end of Elliott Bay. The largest floating drydock, at a shipyard just E of the entrance to West Waterway, has a capacity of 40,000 tons, an overall length of 873 feet, a minimum clear inside width of 137 feet and a depth over the keel blocks of 30 feet. Gantry cranes to 150-ton capacity are available at the yard. Another shipyard, at the NW end of Harbor Island, has a drydock which is only slightly smaller. Smaller shipyards are on the Duwamish River and on Lake Union, in the inner harbor. There are larger drydocks at the Puget Sound Naval Shipyard in Bremerton, available for private use under certain conditions when not required by the Government.

Small-craft facilities

(157) In addition to the large Shilshole Bay Marina, mentioned earlier in this chapter, numerous small-craft facilities line the shores of Lake Union, Lake Washington, Lake Washington Ship Canal, Elliott Bay, and Duwamish Waterway. (See the small-craft facilities tabulation on charts 18445 and 18447 for services and supplies available.)

Lake Washington Ship Canal, Washington
Image courtesy U.S. Army Corps of Engineers

Ferries

(158) **Washington State Ferries** operates three ferry slips at the **Colman Ferry Terminal (Pier 52)** in about 47°36'09"N., 122°20'22"W. Ferries operate between Seattle/Winslow and Seattle/Bremerton 24 hours a day. For information on routes or schedules, see http://www.wsdot.wa.gov/ferries or call 206–464–6400.

Communications

(159) Ferry service for passengers and automobiles is available to many points on Puget Sound. Seattle is served by two important railroads, and by many steamship and towing companies. Many airlines have passenger and freight service to Seattle-Tacoma International Airport. Seattle is the major port for Alaska commerce, by both water and air carriers.

Chart 18447

(160) **Lake Washington Ship Canal** extends from Puget Sound through Shilshole Bay, Salmon Bay, Lake Union, Portage Bay, and Union Bay to deep water in Lake Washington. The canal is the only entrance from Puget Sound to Lake Union and Lake Washington and is highly trafficked by recreational boats, fishing vessels, and commercial vessels. **Federal project** depth through the canal is 30 feet, which is generally maintained. (See Notice to Mariners and latest editions of charts for controlling depths.) The entrance to Lake Washington Ship Canal is marked by a lighted range, lights, and buoys.

(161) A **speed limit** of 4 knots is enforced within the guide piers of the Hiram M. Chittenden Locks. A **speed limit** of 7 knots is enforced elsewhere in the Lake Washington Ship Canal, except in an area marked by four private buoys in the N part of Lake Union.

(162) The **Hiram M. Chittenden Locks**, a government owned and operated double lock, and a fixed dam are at the narrows of the entrance to Salmon Bay, 1.2 miles in from the sound. The large lock, a two-chamber structure, has a clear length of 760 feet, width of 80 feet, lift of 26 feet, and depth over the lower miter sill of 29 feet. The small lock has a clear length of 123 feet, width of 28 feet, lift of 26 feet, and depth over the lower sill of 16 feet. Passage time is less than 30 minutes for large vessels and 5 to 10 minutes for small vessels. The lock tenders monitor VHF-FM channel 13, and can be contacted at 206–783–7000 for additional information.

(163) A saltwater barrier extends across the E end of the E chamber of the large lock to reduce the intrusion of saltwater into Lake Washington and to conserve water. (See **207.750**, chapter 2, for navigation regulations for Lake Washington Ship Canal, the Hiram M. Chittenden Locks, and the saltwater barrier.)

Depths

(164) Depths above Hiram M. Chittenden Locks are referred to low water of the lakes which is 20 feet above the plane of mean lower low water of Puget Sound.

Heights

(165) Vertical clearances above Hiram M. Chittenden Locks are referred to the mean water level of the lakes, which is 21 feet above mean lower low water of Puget Sound.

(166) **Salmon Bay** extends for about 0.8 mile from the E end of the locks to the Ballard (15th Avenue) Bridge. There are numerous piers and floats with extensive small-craft facilities on the bay. Fishermen's Terminal, operated by the Port of Seattle, is immediately W of the Ballard Bridge. The terminal is the home port of a large commercial fishing fleet. Depths of 14 to 28 feet are alongside the piers. There are 700 berths for craft 27 to 176 feet long. Complete facilities for fishing boats are available at the 54-acre terminal, including electricity, gasoline, diesel fuel, water, net repair yards, and all types of marine supplies. Marine railways at the terminal can handle craft to 300 tons for complete repairs. A travel lift to 46 feet is also available at the terminal.

(167) From Salmon Bay the canal leads SE to **Lake Union**, which is about 1 mile long in a N-S direction and about 0.5 mile wide. Depths in the lake range generally from 37 to 41 feet. There is an 11-foot shoal about 200 yards offshore from the SW end of the lake; it is marked by a buoy. Four private buoys in the N part of Lake Union mark an unrestricted speed zone, which is used by boat builders around the lake as a testing area. The buoys are frequently repositioned; caution is advised when transiting the area. Seaplane takeoff and landings are frequent on the E and W sides of the lake. The lake is heavily utilized by recreational boaters, especially during the summer months.

(168) There are numerous marinas and repair facilities, and several commercial wharves from which various commodities are shipped by barge. A drydock company has several floating drydocks, the largest of which has a lifting capacity of 3,600 tons.

(169) **Portage Bay**, E of Lake Union has many slips and finger piers for small-craft; hull and engine repairs are available on the NE shore.

(170) **Montlake Cut (Portage Cut)** leads from Portage Bay past the conspicuous buildings and athletic stadium of **University of Washington**, on the N side, thence into **Union Bay**, and thence into Lake Washington.

(171) Lake Washington Ship Canal is crossed by five bascule bridges and two fixed bridges. Clearances of the drawspans are 14 to 43 feet. (See **117.1 through 117.59 and 117.1051**, chapter 2, for drawbridge regulations.) The bridgetenders of the drawbridges monitor VHF-FM channel 16 and 13, and works on channel 13. The call signs are as follows:

(172) Burlington Northern Railroad, KCE-201;
(173) Ballard (15th Avenue), KJA-445;
(174) Fremont Avenue, KJA-442;
(175) University, KJA-441;
(176) Montlake, KJA-438.

(177) The fixed bridges have a least clearance of 127 feet. Cables crossing the canal have a least clearance of 155 feet.

(178) **Lake Washington**, the large freshwater lake on Seattle's E side, provides deep and protected water over most of its length of nearly 16 miles. Significant bands of submerged aquatic vegetation exist around the periphery of the lake in the 10 to 20-foot depth range. These beds are particularly thick in the relatively flat, shoal areas at the N end of the lake and in the various coves and bays along the eastern shore. The shores of the lake are studded with private piers and landings, and there are marinas and small-craft repair places at many locations. Gasoline and diesel fuel are available at a yacht basin just S of Newport Shores on the E side of Lake Washington.

(179) There are few commercial installations. Except for a few oil wharves, commercial shipments are by barge. A large offshore wharf of a tar and creosote company is at **May Creek (Port Quendall)** on the E side of the lake opposite the S end of Mercer Island. A lumber mill and creosoting plant are here. A large log storage area is at May Creek.

(180) State Route 520 pontoon bridge crossing the lake between Seattle and Evergreen Point has a fixed span at the E and W ends. The clearances are 57 feet at the E end and 44 feet at the W end. The floating drawspans at the center of the bridge provide an opening 100 feet wide. (See **117.1 through 117.59 and 117.1049**, chapter 2, for drawbridge regulations.) The Interstate Route 90 pontoon bridges between Seattle and East Seattle, on the N end of **Mercer Island**, has fixed spans at the E and W ends with clearances of 29 feet. The fixed highway (Interstate Route 90) bridge on the E side of Mercer Island, from Barnabie Point to the mainland, has a clearance of 71 feet. The underwater remains of the E and W piers of a former fixed bridge are just SE of the Interstate Route 90 bridge. Mariners should use caution when outside the main navigation channel.

(181) A **091°55'-271°55' measured nautical mile** has been established along the pontoon bridge to Mercer Island. The targets are painted on both sides of the bridge so that the courses can be run either N or S of the bridge.

(182) Combined **measured half nautical mile, nautical mile**, and **2,000-meter measured courses** have been established along the pontoon bridge from Foster Island to Evergreen Point on a bearing of **102°30'-282°30'**. The half nautical mile and nautical mile courses are marked on the S side of the bridge by 18-inch circles resembling an engineers target; the half nautical mile markers have green and white quadrants, and the nautical mile markers have red and white quadrants. The 2,000-meter course is marked by 1- by 3-foot green

(183) markers with 3-inch white vertical stripes on both sides of the bridge.

(183) **Houghton**, at the NE side of the lake just S of Kirkland, is the site of a former shipyard. There are several marinas catering to yachtsmen.

(184) **Juanita Bay**, N of Kirkland, is a summer recreational area with several small piers.

(185) Offices and storage facilities of the National Oceanic and Atmospheric Administration are at **Sand Point** on the W shore of the lake just NE of Union Bay.

(186) **Kenmore**, at the N end of Lake Washington about 4.4 miles N of Sand Point, is the site of several marinas and a barge loading facility. A dredged channel, marked by lighted buoys, leads across the flats to a turning basin. In 2010, the controlling depth was 11 feet in the dredged channel. A submerged wreck covered 16 feet is near the approach to the dredged channel in about 47°44'51"N., 122°15'58"W.

(187) A seaplane base is at Kenmore.

(188) **Sammamish River**, about 0.1 mile S of Kenmore, is entered through a dredged channel that branches NE from the Kenmore channel. In 2001, the controlling depth was 2.8 feet in the N half with shoaling to bare in the S half. About 0.3 mile above the mouth of the river is a highway bridge with a 47-foot fixed span and a clearance of 12 feet.

Chart 18441

(189) **Possession Sound** joins Puget Sound at the S point of Whidbey Island and extends in a general N direction for 10 miles to its junction with Saratoga Passage and Port Susan. From the entrance it extends for 3.5 miles with an average width of 2 miles, and then expands into an irregular basin about 6 miles in diameter.

(190) The E part of this basin is filled with extensive flats, many of which uncover and rise abruptly from deep water. These flats are intersected by several shifting channels, forming the mouth of the Snohomish River. The waters of the sound are generally deep, and the only anchorage used by large vessels is off the town of Everett, close inshore, in 10 to 15 fathoms.

(191) **Meadowdale**, a residential area on Browns Bay, is on the E side of the sound about 4 miles S of Possession Point. There is a large dry storage boathouse here with a hoist that can handle craft to 24 feet. Several floats are available during the summer months; gasoline and covered storage for about 40 craft are also available. Reported depths of 5 feet can be carried to the hoist on the NW face of the wharf. Norma Beach, about 3 miles S of Possesion Point, is on the E side of the sound. A boathouse with a marine railway that can handle small craft to 20 feet; gasoline and dry storage are available.

Chart 18443

(192) **Elliot Point**, on the E side of Possession Sound 4 miles NE of Possession Point, is a low spit projecting some 200 yards from the high land. **Mukilteo Light** (47°56'55"N., 122°18'22"W.), 33 feet above the water, is shown from a 33-foot white octagonal tower on the point; a mariner radio activated sound signal is at the station, initiated by keying the microphone five times on VHF-FM channel 83A.

(193) **Mukilteo** is a town E of Elliot Point. An automobile ferry runs between Mukilteo and Clinton on Whidbey Island. A light about 300 yards NE of Mukilteo Light marks the approach to the ferry dock. A wharf for deep-draft vessels is 0.4 mile E of Mukilteo Light. A rail/barge transfer facility (Mount Baker Terminal) at 47°57'15"N., 122°17'19"W., is marked by two private lights.

(194) **Gedney Island**, 3.5 miles N of Elliot Point, is about 1.5 miles long in an SE direction, high, wooded, and prominent. From its SE point, a shoal extends SE, the 5-fathom curve being at a distance of 0.8 mile. Foul ground extends 0.2 mile from the S side of the E half of the island. A light is on the N side of the shoal area.

(195) A fish haven is about 0.5 mile S of Gedney Island in about 47°59'48"N., 122°18'30"W. A marina, protected by a breakwater, is on the NE side of the island. The breakwater is marked by private lights.

(196) **Clinton**, a village on **Randall Point**, is the Whidbey Island terminus of the ferry from Mukilteo. The town has several stores; a restaurant is near the ferry slip. Gasoline is available.

Chart 18444

(197) **Everett**, an important wood products shipping port, is on the E side of **Port Gardner**, 4 miles NE of Elliot Point. A tall pulpmill chimney and the Port of Everett's large alumina silo are prominent along the water.

Channels

(198) A dredged channel with two settling basins extends inside a training dike along the E side of **Jetty Island** and in the Snohomish River around the N half of the city to a lumbermill 6 miles above Port Gardner. The channel is marked by lights, buoys, and lighted and unlighted ranges. The second settling basin is subject to continual shoaling. (See Notice to Mariners and latest editions of charts for controlling depths.)

Anchorages

(199) The general anchorage area is W of the waterfront. (See **110.1 and 110.230**, chapter 2, for limits and regulations.) Vessels usually proceed to the wharves. A buoy marks a submerged obstruction near the center of the anchorage.

Pilotage, Everett

(200) Pilotage is compulsory for all vessels except those under enrollment or engaged exclusively in the coasting trade on the W coast of the continental United States (including Alaska) and/or British Columbia. Pilotage for Puget Sound is provided by the Puget Sound Pilots. (See Pilotage, Strait of Juan de Fuca and Puget Sound, indexed as such, chapter 12, for details.)

Towage

(201) Tugs up to 3,000 hp are available at Everett, and larger tugs may be obtained from Seattle. Arrangements should be made in advance through ships' agents.

Quarantine, customs, immigration, and agricultural quarantine

(202) (See chapter 3, Vessel Arrival Inspections, and Appendix A for addresses.)

(203) **Quarantine** is enforced in accordance with regulations of the U.S. Public Health Service. (See Public Health Service, chapter 1.)

(204) Everett is a **customs port of entry**.

Harbor regulations

(205) Harbor regulations are enforced by the manager of the Port of Everett, who serves as **harbormaster** and port warden.

(206) **Naval Station Everett** is on the W and N end of the harbor. A naval restricted area, marked by a floating barrier and private lights, surrounds the docking facilities. (See **334.1215**, chapter 2, for limits and regulations.)

Wharves

(207) The Port of Everett operates three deep-draft piers on Port Gardner and only the deep-draft facilities on those piers are described. For a complete description of the port facilities refer to Port Series No. 37, published and sold by the U.S. Army Corps of Engineers. (See Appendix A for address.) The alongside depths are reported. (For information on the latest depths, contact port authorities or the private operators.) All the facilities described have both direct highway and railroad connections. Water is available at most of the wharves and electrical shore power is available at all except Hewitt Wharf. General cargo at the port is usually handled by ships' tackle. Special handling equipment, if available, is mentioned in the description of the particular facility.

(208) **Port of Everett, South Terminal, Berth No. 1 and Dolphin Berth** (47°58'31"N., 122°13'38"W.): depth alongside, 38 feet; deck height, 20 feet; berthing space, 1,555 feet; 30 acres of paved open storage; receipt and shipment of conventional general cargo; shipment of logs; owned and operated by Port of Everett.

(209) **Port of Everett, Pacific Terminal Wharf** (47°58'47"N., 122°13'25"W.): depth alongside, 32 to 37 feet; deck height, 18 feet; berthing space, 600 feet; 8 acres of open storage; receipt and shipment of conventional and containerized general cargo in foreign and domestic trade; receipt and shipment of lumber and steel products; owned and operated by Port of Everett.

(210) **Port of Everett, Hewitt Avenue Terminal, Pier No. 1** (47°58'42"N., 122°13'22"W.): depth alongside, 38 feet (N side) and 42 feet (S side); deck height, 18 feet; berthing space, 140 feet (face), 600 feet (N side), 600 feet (S side); one 35-ton diesel crawler crane for handling containers; receipt and shipment of conventional and containerized general cargo; receipt and shipment of lumber and steel products; shipment of perishable food commodities; owned and operated by Port of Everett.

(211) **Port of Everett, Hewitt Wharf** (47°58'47"N., 122°13'12"W.): depth alongside, 20 feet; deck height, 18 feet; berthing space, 830 feet; one 36,000-square foot refrigerated building; shipment of perishable food commodities; owned and operated by Port of Everett.

(212) **Port of Everett, Hewitt Avenue Terminal, Pier No. 3** (47°58'53"N., 122°13'16"W.): depth alongside, 38 feet; deck height, 19 feet; berthing space, 120 feet (face), 800 feet (S side), 900 feet (N side); 15 acres of open storage, 55,000-ton covered storage dome, one mobile pneumatic unloader (rate of 600 tons per hour), 35-ton diesel crawler crane; receipt and shipment of conventional general cargo; shipment of lumber and logs; receipt of alumina; owned and operated by Port of Everett.

Supplies

(213) Water, provisions, and some marine supplies can be obtained. Gasoline and diesel fuel are available for small craft at Everett Yacht Harbor. Fuel oil for large vessels is available only by Seattle-based tank barges.

Repairs

(214) There are no facilities for repairs to deep-draft vessels in Everett; the nearest such facilities are in Seattle.

(215) The **Port of Everett Marina** is about a mile above the mouth of and on the E side of the Snohomish River Channel. The marina consists of two separate N and S basins and has berths for more than 2,200 small craft including about 45 transient berths. The reported depths in the entrance to the S basin are 10 with 13 feet alongside and 12 feet in the entrance and alongside the berths in the N basin. Services available include; electricity, gasoline, diesel fuel, water, ice, marine supplies, pump-out facility, launching ramps, full repairs (hull, engine, electrical) and a 75-ton marine lift. A harbormaster, whose office is on the S side of the harbor, assigns all berths.

Communications

(216) Everett is served by a railroad. The county airport, Paine Field, is 6 miles SSW of the city.

(217) **Snohomish River**, once heavily traveled by the light-draft river steamers and loggers, flows down through the dredged channel and settling basin near

the yacht harbor and empties into Port Gardner just W of East Waterway. Traffic on the river above the yacht harbor consists of log tows, tugs and barges, and pleasure boats. Several pulp, plywood, and lumber mills are along the river.

(218) The Snohomish River is crossed by a railroad swing bridge with a least clearance of 9 feet about 0.6 mile E of Preston Point. U.S. Highway 529 crosses the river just above the railroad bridge and has a lift bridge with a least clearance of 38 feet. Interstate 5 crosses the river about 1.6 miles above the U.S. Highway 529 bridge; this fixed bridge has a clearance of 66 feet. (See **117.1 through 117.59 and 117.1059**, chapter 2, for drawbridge regulations.) A marina is 0.5 mile upstream from the U.S. 529 highway bridge. There is dry storage for over 1,000 craft to 40 feet long; transient mooring floats are available for visiting craft. Gasoline, water, ice, limited marine supplies, and hull and engine repairs are available. A city park with a launching ramp is 1.2 miles upstream from the U.S. 529 highway bridge. The practical limit of navigation on the Snohomish River is 0.8 mile above the Interstate 5 highway bridge.

Chart 18443

(219) The flats N of Everett at the mouths of **Steamboat Slough** and **Ebey Slough** are used for log storage. Steamboat Slough is crossed by a fixed bridge with a clearance of 41 feet and by three swing bridges with a least clearance of 7 feet. Ebey Slough is crossed by two fixed bridges and two swing bridges. Clearances on the fixed bridges are 41 feet; clearances on the swing bridges are 5 feet. The bridgetender of the drawbridge at Marysville monitors VHF-FM channel 16 and works on channel 13; call sign KZ-2475. (See **117.1 through 117.59 and 117.1059**, chapter 2, for drawbridge regulations.) Overhead power cables with a least clearance of 53 feet cross Steamboat Slough. Navigation across the shallow flats should not be attempted without local knowledge. Local small craft navigate Ebey Slough to **Marysville**. A marina and boatyard are just E of the railroad bridge in the town. Marine supplies, winter boat storage, engine and hull repairs, a 4-ton hoist, and launching ramp are available. There is a public launching ramp just W of the Interstate 5 highway bridge at Marysville.

(220) **Sandy Point**, the S point at the entrance to Saratoga Passage, is a low spit rising abruptly to 100 feet, with bluffs on each side; it is marked by a light.

(221) **Camano Head**, 1.5 miles NNE of Sandy Point, is the SE point of Camano Island. A shoal, with a rock bare at low tide, extends nearly 0.2 mile SE from the point, and is marked by a light.

(222) **Tulalip Bay**, 4 miles NW of Everett, is a small cove on the mainland. On the N side are the village of **Tulalip** and the agency buildings of the Tulalip Indian Reservation. The bay is shoal, with rocks extending more than 300 yards S and W from the point on the N side of the entrance. A light marks the edge of the shoal water W of the point at the S side of the entrance. Several small wharves and landing floats, mostly dry at low water, are at Tulalip; however, it has no public facilities. There are log-booming grounds in the S part of the bay. Mission Beach, immediately S of the bay, has several private boathouses and float landings.

Chart 18441

(223) **Camano Island** extends between Port Susan and Saratoga Passage. It is irregular in shape and 14 miles in length; the S portion consists of a long, narrow tongue that terminates in Camano Head, 340 feet high. At its N end it is separated from the mainland by **Davis Slough**, and South Pass and West Pass of the Stillaguamish River, all dry at low water. On the shores of the island are several resorts and unincorporated residential tracts.

(224) **Port Susan**, on the E side of Camano Island, extends about 11 miles in a NW direction, terminating in flats which bare and extend over 3 miles wide at its head. There are several resort settlements. Deep water is throughout until nearing the head, where anchorage may be had off the extreme W edge of the flats in about 10 fathoms. Care should be used in approaching and anchoring, as the flats rise abruptly from deep water.

(225) **Stanwood** is in a dairying and farming district on the N side of the **Stillaguamish River** at the junction of **South Pass** and **West Pass**.

(226) **Saratoga Passage**, on the W side of Camano Island, extends some 18 miles in a NW direction from its entrance between Sandy Point and Camano Head. At its N end it connects with Penn Cove and Crescent Harbor, and leads E into Skagit Bay. Depths in the passage are from 100 fathoms at the entrance to 15 fathoms at the Crescent Harbor entrance. There are few outlying dangers, and a midchannel course is clear.

(227) There is considerable traffic in these waters, mostly pleasure and fishing craft, with occasional tugs bound to or from Deception Pass. This is a resort area; along the shores of the islands are several small marinas which provide gasoline, limited berths, launching ramps, and lodgings. Principal commercial products are lumber and fish.

(228) **Langley** is a small town on Whidbey Island about 1.2 miles W of Sandy Point. Tugs often anchor off the beach between Langley and Sandy Point. The South Whidbey Harbor at Langley is protected on the N and E sides by a timber breakwater marked by private lights. Transient berths, water, electricity, launching ramp, and pump-out facility are available. In 2010, 12 feet was reported alongside the berths. The harbormaster monitors VHF channels 16 and 66A; telephone: 360–221–1120. The stores of the town business district are nearby, supplies may be obtained.

(229) **East Point**, 6 miles NW of Sandy Point, is a low sandspit about 300 yards long. It is marked by a light.

(230)　**Elger Bay**, on the W shore of Camano Island across Saratoga Passage from East Point, is an open bight 1 mile wide. Tugs anchor here in W and NW winds.

(231)　**Holmes Harbor**, entered 8 miles NW of Sandy Point, indents Whidbey Island 5 miles in a S direction. Except for a sand and gravel wharf and a large private boathouse at the head of the harbor, only private pleasure piers are on the shores of Holmes Harbor. Depths range from 30 to 40 fathoms off the entrance to 17 fathoms near the head, where good anchorage, except from N weather, may be had in mud bottom. A **general anchorage** is in Holmes Harbor. (See **110.1 and 110.230**, chapter 2, for anchorage limits and regulations.) **Rocky Point**, at the E side of the entrance, is low but rises abruptly to 500 feet. **Baby Island** is a small islet 0.2 mile off the point. Shoals, marked by a buoy, extend NW from the island.

(232)　**Greenbank**, a small farming settlement, is on the W side of Holmes Harbor at the entrance. It has a store and service station. Anchorage against W weather is available off Greenbank in 12 to 18 fathoms, muddy bottom. **Freeland**, the business center for this area, is a small town at the head of Holmes Harbor.

(233)　**Camano**, a settlement on the E side of Saratoga Passage, is 3.5 miles NW of **Lowell Point**. A light is on **Onamac Point**, 0.8 mile N of Camano. A fish haven is NW of the point.

(234)　**Penn Cove** indents the W shore of the basin at the head of Saratoga Passage and extends W for about 3.5 miles. In most weather, the cove affords good protection in 5 to 15 fathoms, good holding ground.

(235)　Off **Snatelum Point**, the S point at the entrance to Penn Cove, is a narrow spit extending N 0.5 mile, with ½ fathom near its end. The spit is marked by a buoy.

(236)　**Blowers Bluff**, the N point at the entrance to Penn Cove, is bare, light-colored, high, and rounding. Rocks lie offshore 200 yards at places along the bluff. The shoal extending off the SW end of the bluff reaches almost one-third the distance across Penn Cove. Vessels should favor the S shore when passing this shoal.

(237)　**Coupeville**, the county seat of Island County, is on the S shore of Penn Cove, about 2 miles from the head. The town has stores and service stations. A wharf here extends to about 12 feet. Berthage is available at floats attached to the E side of the wharf. Gasoline, diesel fuel, and pump-out station are available at a fuel dock on the N side. A rock covered 15 feet is about 300 yards NE of the wharf. A launching ramp is about 0.3 mile E of the wharf.

Chart 18428

(238)　**Oak Harbor**, which indents the N shore of Saratoga Passage W of Crescent Harbor, is a semicircular cove about 1 mile in diameter with depths of 20 to 9 feet. **Maylor Point**, the E point of the entrance, is foul with several rocks, awash at low water, 0.5 mile SE from the point. The natural entrance channel is marked by lights, lighted, and unlighted buoys. The town of Oak Harbor is on the N shore of the harbor and has a seasonal dock with entrance channel marked by pilings. A marina operated by the town is on the E side. The marina is protected on the W side by a breakwater marked by lights. Services available at the marina include: electricity, gasoline, diesel fuel, water, ice, pump-out facility, surfaced launch ramp, and complete (hull, engine, electrical) repairs can be made. The marina also has a 30-ton marine lift and about 15 transient berths.

(239)　**Crescent Harbor**, immediately E of Oak Harbor, is a semicircular bight 2 miles in diameter, between **Forbes Point** and **Polnell Point**. Polnell Point is wooded and rather bold, and connected to the main island by low ground, giving the point the appearance of an island from a distance off. A shoal extends about 0.9 mile W of Polnell Point; another shoal extends about 0.2 mile S from this point. Shoals extend about 0.7 mile S and E from Forbes Point; the S shoal is marked by a lighted buoy. Foul ground surrounds these points, but otherwise the harbor is clear, affording anchorage in 10 to 11 fathoms, muddy bottom. The harbor is exposed to the S. The large pier of the U.S. Naval Air Station, Whidbey Island, extends from the W side of the harbor. Depths of 26 feet are alongside the outer two-thirds of the pier. This pier can be used only with permission. Services and/or provisions cannot be provided, and ships' own power must be relied upon. A 183-foot T-pier used for fueling Naval vessels is on the N side of the main pier near the shoreward end.

Charts 18421, 18441, 18400

(240)　The entrance to **Skagit Bay**, southern part, lies between Polnell Point and Rocky Point. The bay is about 12 miles long in a WNW direction. The greater portion of it is filled with flats, bare at low water, and intersected by numerous channels discharging the waters of Skagit River.

(241)　A natural channel varying in width from 0.2 to 0.6 mile and marked by lights and buoys follows the E shoreline of Whidbey Island to the N end of the bay. Shoal water extends off for some 100 to 300 yards from the E shore of the island. The N part of Skagit Bay is described in chapter 12.

(242)　The controlling elevation of the flats at the mouth of South Fork is about 2.5 feet above mean lower low water, and the controlling depth at low tide depends on the river stage, probably not exceeding 1 foot during periods of minimum flow. The diurnal range at the mouth of the river is 11.3 feet. The extreme range at this point is estimated to be 20 feet.

(243)　A fixed highway bridge with a clearance of 10 feet crosses the South Fork at **Conway**, 4.8 miles above the mouth.

(244)　**Utsalady**, a small village on the N shore of Camano Island about 1.2 miles E of Rocky Point, has a store.

Vessels may anchor just E of **Utsalady Point** in a small inlet between the shoal water of the flats and the shore in 3 to 6 fathoms, muddy bottom, with shelter from S winds. In the 1860's Utsalady became the first shipbuilding port in Puget Sound.

(245) **Strawberry Point**, about 2.5 miles N of Utsalady Point, is marked by a light. SW of the light, dredged canals give access to private moorings.

(246) The **South Fork** channel leading into Skagit River winds through the flats N of Camano Island. Because of shoaling, however, the channel has largely been abandoned by boat traffic to Mount Vernon except for local outboard boats; **North Fork** is used instead. In 1971, the mouth of the North Fork bared 2 feet at MLLW. There are several small-boat moorings along the banks of the river at **Mount Vernon**.

Charts 18440, 18477, 18476

(247) The entrance to **Hood Canal** is at the lower end of Admiralty Inlet, between Foulweather Bluff and Tala Point, about 10 miles S of Marrowstone Point. It extends in a general S direction for about 44 miles and then bends sharply NE for 11 miles, terminating in flats bare at low water. The head of Case Inlet, in the S part of Puget Sound, is less than 2 miles from the head of Hood Canal. The shores are high, bold, and wooded, and the water is deep, except at the heads of the bays and at the mouths of the streams. Many small craft ply these waters. There are mostly small float-landings and private docks in the canal.

(248) U.S. Highway 101 follows much of the W shore of Hood Canal, and connecting highways to Port Orchard follow the S shore of the S part of the canal around The Great Bend. There are road connections with Port Orchard and with the Puget Sound highway system from all the settlements on the E shore of the canal.

(249) Water traffic in general is confined to tugs with log rafts, naval vessels in the upper part, and many pleasure craft. Hood Canal is a vacation area. Numerous private houses and summer cottages with small piers, mooring buoys, and floats are on both sides of the canal. There are relatively few public floats or piers, and the only commercial activities are logging and some oystering.

Tides and currents.

(250) The **tidal currents** in Hood Canal at times attain velocities exceeding 1.5 knots. In some places in the canal the currents are too weak and variable to predict. At times there are heavy tide rips N of and around Foulweather Bluff, sufficiently heavy to be dangerous to small boats and to break up log rafts. This is most pronounced when the ebb current from the main body of Puget Sound meets that from Hood Canal off the point, and particularly so with the ebb against a strong N or NW wind. Off Point Hannon and Hazel Point, tide rips occur at times sufficiently strong to be troublesome to tugs with log tows. Current observations taken at a station in midchannel E of Hazel Point show that directions of both flood and ebb vary considerably at that location. At times SW winds from Hood Canal and N winds from Dabob Bay cause a chop dangerous for small boats. Under these conditions smoother water is found near either shore.

(251) The dangers are few and generally close inshore. A few low sandspits from 100 to 300 yards long are difficult to see at night, but most of them have been made into resorts and the buildings nearby show up well against the background of trees. Flats off the mouths of streams extend as much as 0.5 mile offshore and are extensive at the heads of some of the bays. A midchannel course is clear until reaching The Great Bend, where Hood Canal turns E. Here the N shore just E of Ayres Point should be favored to clear the flats extending from the E part of Annas Bay.

Chart 18477

(252) **Twin Spits** are two long, low, sand points, 0.5 mile and 1 mile S of Foulweather Bluff. When waiting for smooth weather to round Foulweather Bluff, tugs with log tows often anchor in 50 feet 1 mile SE of the S spit, in a bight known locally as **Races Cove**, with Colvos Rocks Light slightly clear of the end of the S point of Twin Spits.

(253) **Hood Head**, on the W side of Hood Canal about 3 miles S of the entrance, is almost an island, having only a narrow strip of low sand connecting it with the W shore. The head is 220 feet high, steep and wooded, and is a prominent feature in the entrance.

(254) A rocky ledge, marked by some kelp and covered 4 to 26 feet, extends more than 500 yards S of Hood Head; rocks covered 4 feet are near the S end of this ledge about 325 yards S of Hood Head. An aquaculture site, marked by lighted private buoys, is about 0.4 mile S of Hood Head.

(255) **Coon Bay**, 2.5 miles S of Foulweather Bluff, is a small, nearly landlocked harbor offering excellent protection to small craft during periods of rough weather. The privately dredged entrance channel is narrow and has a reported controlling depth of about 3 feet. There are several private piers inside the entrance, but no facilities are available.

(256) **Point Hannon** is at the E extension of Hood Head; it is marked by a light. A low sandy spit with shoal water extends about 200 yards E of the light.

Local magnetic disturbance

(257) Differences of more than 2° from normal variation have been observed in Hood Canal at Point Hannon.

(258) **Termination Point**, 1.6 miles E of the village of **Shine**, is 1.7 miles SW of Point Hannon. A lighted transformer substation is on Termination Point.

(259) **Hood Canal Bridge**, a pontoon highway bridge crossing the canal between Termination Point and Salsbury Point W of Port Gamble has two fixed openings; the clearance of the W opening is 35 feet, and that of the E opening is 50 feet (at all tide levels). In the 600-foot center opening there are pontoons which are retracted for larger vessels. The bridgetender monitors VHF-FM channel 16 and works on channel 13; call sign, WHD-721. (See **117.1 through 117.59 and 117.1045**, chapter 2, for drawbridge regulations.) Anchor cables, extending from the bridge pontoons to the canal bottom, extend nearly 500 yards both N and S of the bridge; anchoring should not be attempted in this area.

(260) **Sisters**, two rocks 200 yards apart, 0.5 mile S of Termination Point, are awash at about half tide. A light is on the S rock, 0.4 mile from the N entrance point to **Squamish Harbor**, an open bight just SW of Termination Point. Tugs frequently anchor near the head of the harbor in about 6 fathoms, muddy bottom.

(261) **Case Shoal**, partly bare at low water, is about 0.6 mile from and parallel with the W shore of Squamish Harbor. The shoal is marked at its N end by a daybeacon and on its SE side by a light. A clam tract, marked at the N and S ends by private buoys, is in the SW part of the harbor between Case Shoal and the W shore.

(262) **Port Gamble Bay** is a small bay on the E shore of Hood Canal 5 miles from the entrance. It is 2 miles long with a narrow entrance.

(263) A dredged entrance channel leads from deep water in Hood Canal into deep water in Port Gamble Bay. In 1986, the controlling depth was 23 feet. The channel is marked by a **001°-181°** unlighted range, lights, and lighted buoys.

(264) **Port Gamble**. the town on the W shore at the entrance, is owned by the lumber company which maintains all facilities including the local housing, church, and store. The mill has been in operation for more than a century. The white church steeple and flagpole in the town are prominent. A shoal covered 4 feet is about 500 yards NE from the N end of the lumbermill wharf. The lumbermill wharf has a 385-foot face with reported depths of 29 to 35 feet alongside, a 400-foot berth at the S end of the wharf with 36 feet reported alongside and a 170-foot berth at the NW end of the wharf with 24 to 29 feet reported alongside. All deck heights are 14½ feet. Strong currents on both flood and ebb tide are experienced through the entrance channel to Port Gamble Bay. Vessels should dock against the current. Local knowledge and careful, precise piloting are essential in docking at this wharf.

(265) Excellent anchorage may be had in the bay in 24 to 54 feet, muddy bottom.

(266) Vessels should hold a midchannel course on entering Port Gamble Bay until 200 yards or more past the S light, and then head for the wharf, keeping the long E face open to avoid shoal water on the W side of the channel.

Caution

(267) The entrance channel to Port Gamble Bay is quite constricted by shoals on both sides of the channel. The two lights on the E side of the channel are in shoal water and do not mark the edge of the channel.

(268) A bridge pontoon storage area is on the W side of Port Gamble Bay about 0.4 mile S of Port Gamble.

Charts 18458, 18476, 18477, 18441

(269) **Thorndyke Bay** is a small bight on the W side of Hood Canal about 4 miles S of Squamish Harbor. An **explosives anchorage** is S of the bay. (See **110.1 and 110.230**, chapter 2, for limits and regulations.)

(270) **Bangor Wharf** on the E side of the canal, 3.5 miles S of Thorndyke Bay, is the property of the Bangor U.S. Naval Submarine Base. A naval restricted area, marked by a floating barrier and private lights, surrounds the wharf and other naval docking facilities along the E side of Hood Canal. Keyport Naval Undersea Warfare Engineering Station, 0.9 mile SSW of Bangor Wharf, is also within the restricted area. (See **334.1220**, chapter 2, for limits and regulations.) Naval security zones are adjacent to the Naval Submarine Base. (See **165.1302 and 165.1311**, chapter 2, for limits and regulations.) A 500-foot radio tower, marked by red aircraft warning lights, is on Bangor Wharf and is prominent. A 459-foot red and white radio tower, marked by red aircraft warning lights, is on the wharf 0.3 mile NNE of Bangor Wharf; this tower is also prominent. It is reported that vessels southbound from Hood Canal Bridge can use the towers as a **200.6°** range. Strong currents are in the vicinity of the piers at Keyport Naval Undersea Warfare Engineering Station.

(271) A **naval operating area** is in the S part of Hood Canal. (See **334.1190**, chapter 2, for limits and regulations.) A **naval exercise area** extends N from the N boundary of the operating area to just off **South Point**, about 2.3 miles NE of Thorndyke Bay.

(272) **Bangor**, a small residential community about 2 miles S of Bangor Wharf, has no facilities.

(273) **Seabeck**, about 6 miles SW of Bangor, is a settlement and resort at the head of **Seabeck Bay**, a small cove on the E shore. A marina, protected by a breakwater awash at high water, is on the S side of the bay. Berths, gasoline, diesel fuel, water, ice, supplies, and a 1½-ton hoist are available. In 2005, the marina was reported to be closed. Shoal water extends 0.5 mile from the head of the bay. Good anchorage, well protected from SE to SW weather, is available in the bay in 35 to 50 feet. Shoal water extends more than 200 yards off **Misery Point**, at the W side of the entrance of the bay. A light is about

(274) 300 yards NE of Misery Point, and a fish haven is close NW of the light.

Oak Head, 2 miles NNE of Misery Point and marked by a light, is the S point of **Toandos Peninsula. Hazel Point**, 1.8 miles ENE of Oak Head, is the turning point where the canal bends sharply from S to SW.

(275) **Fisherman Harbor** is a cove on the S end of Toandos Peninsula, just E of Oak Head. It is very narrow, with a constricted entrance which is practically bare at low water. A sandspit extends partly across the entrance from the W shore.

(276) **Brinnon** is a village on the S side of Dosewallips River, 3.5 miles W of Oak Head, at the entrance of Dabob Bay. It has a general store and service station. Gasoline, water, and ice are available, but there is no landing pier. A log booming ground is close offshore at Brinnon.

(277) **Dabob Bay**, the largest inlet in the canal and separated from it by Toandos Peninsula, extends 9 miles in a N direction. The entrance is between **Tskutsko Point** and **Sylopash Point** just N of the mouth of Dosewallips River. A light is off Tskutsko Point. The W shore of Dabob Bay is particularly steep and bold, reaching an elevation of over 2,600 feet in less than 2 miles from the coast.

(278) A **naval operating area** is in the bay. Unlighted spherical yellow mooring buoys may be temporarily established within the bay. Navy–maintained warning lights are shown from **Whitney Point**, Pulali Point, and Sylopash Point on the W side of the bay, from **Zelatched Point** on the E side of the bay, and on the SE side of Bolton Peninsula on the N side of the bay. Flashing amber lights indicate that naval operations are in progress and all craft should keep well clear of vessels engaged in testing. Flashing red lights will be shown when naval operations close the area to navigation. Craft on the bay during these periods should stop their screws and secure their engines and depth sounders. Mariners are advised to pass no closer than 1 mile of naval vessels engaged in bottom operations unless directed otherwise by radiotelephone or other signal from the shore, picket boat, or surveillance aircraft. (See **334.1190**, chapter 2, for limits and regulations.)

(279) A **restricted area** is off Whitney Point. (See **334.1260**, chapter 2, for limits and regulations.)

(280) **Quilcene Bay** is a small inlet on the W side of Dabob Bay N of Whitney Point. A light marks the E side of the entrance to the bay. The N half of the bay is filled with flats which bare. This part of the bay has two log booms and log storage areas. An oyster farm is on the E side of the bay just inside the entrance. Floats with mooring buoys evenly spaced along the E edge mark the oyster farm. **Quilcene**, a small town on the W side and near the head of the bay, is about 0.5 mile inland. The town has hotels, restaurants, and stores.

(281) **Quilcene Boat Haven**, is on the W side of the bay about 1.4 miles S of the town. The entrance to the haven is protected by a stone breakwater; mooring floats for over 50 small craft and gasoline are available. The basin has a reported controlling depth of 10 feet. Two oyster farms are near the haven.

(282) **Pleasant Harbor** is a small cove on the W shore of Hood Canal about 3 miles W of Misery Point. It is about 300 yards wide, and has a narrow shallow entrance. Owing to the narrowness of the entrance, boats should keep in midchannel until clear of the 6-foot shoal. Two marinas in the harbor have berths for about 250 craft, and can provide electricity, gasoline, diesel fuel, water, ice, pump-out, and limited marine supplies. Anchorage in about 36 feet, mud bottom is available inside the harbor. A state park pier is in the harbor.

(283) **Triton Head**, on the W shore, is 8.2 miles SW of Oak Head. It is low, rocky, and timbered, with a reef that bares extending 200 yards N from the point. **Triton Cove** is a small cove formed by the head and the W shore, which affords anchorage for small craft against S winds. Oyster beds, marked by stakes and brush, are about 0.8 mile N from Triton Head on the flat which extends off the mouth of **Fulton Creek**. Two resorts just S of Triton Head have berths, gasoline, diesel fuel, water, ice, dry storage, and marine supplies. Hoists and railways to 10 tons are available, and outboard engine repairs can be made.

Charts 18448, 18476

(284) **Holly** (47°33.5'N., 122°58.6'W.), on the E shore of Hood Canal, is a settlement on the S side of a small bight about 10 miles SW of Oak Head. There are no facilities here. Shoal water extends about 300 yards N and E from the S shore of the bight. **Anderson Cove** is the shallow cove directly N of Holly.

(285) **Eldon** is a W shore settlement on the S bank of **Hamma Hamma River**, about 3 miles SW of Holly. The delta flats of the Hamma Hamma River extend nearly 0.5 mile from shore. Unmarked jetties extend from the river through the flats into Hood Canal and constitute a potential hazard to small craft.

(286) **Lilliwaup** is a village on the S shore of **Lilliwaup Bay**, a small shallow cove on the W shore of Hood Canal about 6 miles SW of Eldon.

(287) About 1 mile S, there is a resort at which berths, water, ice, and marine supplies are available. A 3-ton elevator at the resort can handle craft to 19 feet long for hull and engine repairs.

(288) **Dewatto** is a small settlement on the S side of **Dewatto Bay**, a small, shallow cove on the E shore opposite Lilliwaup.

(289) **Hoodsport**, the largest town on Hood Canal, is on the W shore 4 miles SW of Dewatto. It has a State fish hatchery and a public pier with floats.

(290) **Potlatch** is a small town on the W side of the canal about 2 miles S of Hoodsport and opposite **The Great Bend**, where Hood Canal turns NE. The large gray building of a hydroelectric powerplant, connected to a standpipe on the mountain above by three pipelines, is

very prominent on the W shore 0.5 mile S of the town. **Potlatch State Park**, just S of the powerplant, has a small-craft launching ramp, mooring buoys, and water.

(291) **Union** is a town with several stores on the S shore of The Great Bend. A marina here can handle craft to 30 feet for minor repairs; berths, electricity, gasoline, water, ice, and marine supplies are available. Depths alongside the floats are reported sufficient for small craft at all stages of the tide, however, the marina should be approached from the NE to avoid shoal water and snags. A large resort in the cove on the S shore 1.3 miles E of Union has a T-pier with a 600-foot face and reported depths of 15 feet alongside. Berths, electricity, and water are available at the resort. A large motel and restaurant are here.

(292) **Annas Bay**, immediately W of Union, is a broad, open bight; the E half is flat and bare at low water. This flat extends about 0.2 mile into the canal immediately W of Union and is formed by the **Skokomish River**, which empties at the head of the bay.

(293) **Tahuya**, a small town on the N shore of The Great Bend 1.8 miles NE of Union, has a resort with a pier and floats, about 0.75 mile W of the town; water and a launching ramp are available. Reported depths of 2½ feet are off the floats.

(294) Hood Canal terminates in **Lynch Cove**. Flats, mostly bare at low tide, extend for about 2.2 miles from the head of the cove.

Charts 18446, 18449

(295) **Port Orchard** is an extensive body of water, W of **Bainbridge Island**, 15 miles long. Its N end connects with Port Madison through Agate Passage. At its S end Port Orchard connects with Puget Sound through Rich Passage. The depths in the main body of Port Orchard range from 36 to 150 feet with few dangers and these, as a rule, are close inshore. The shores are moderately low and wooded. Villages and numerous cottages line the shores with many having private docks, moorings, and platforms.

Current

(296) Current observations taken in midchannel about 1 mile S of **Tolo** indicate that the tidal current in that locality is very weak.

Chart 18446

(297) **Agate Passage** is the N entrance to Port Orchard and connects it with Port Madison. The channel extends about 1 mile in a SW direction. The depth is about 20 feet. The passage is straight; the shores are wooded and fairly steep-to; the shoreline is mostly rocky and fringed with kelp to Point Bolin. The currents have velocities up to 6 knots; the flood sets SW and the ebb NE.

(298) The passage is partially obstructed by a shoal near the middle of the N end with depths of 9 to 10 feet, and there are other depths of 14 to 18 feet almost in midchannel.

(299) The N entrance is marked by a light on the W side of the channel opposite **Agate Point**; a lighted buoy marks the channel through the passage and a light marks a shoal NE of **Point Bolin**.

(300) A fixed highway bridge, 0.7 mile S of Agate Point, has a clearance of 75 feet for a midwidth of 300 feet. Overhead power cables cross the passage on both sides of the bridge; least clearance is 96 feet.

(301) **Liberty Bay** is a narrow inlet extending about 4 miles in a N direction from the NW part of Port Orchard. The SE half of the bay is narrow and tortuous. The shores are low and wooded; the shoreline is mostly sand and gravel. There are mud flats at the head of the bay and in the small bight on the S side of the bay. Mud is the predominating bottom characteristic. The current velocity is 0.8 knot N of Keyport, in the narrow entrance to the bay. Velocities exceeding 1 knot occur at times.

(302) **The Keyport Naval Undersea Warfare Center (NUWC)** is on the W side of the entrance to Liberty Bay. A seaplane float extends 100 feet NW from the end of the pier and mariners are requested not to exceed 3 knots when passing it. Several buildings are prominent at the station.

(303) A **torpedo test area** extends off the shore between Brownsville and Keyport NUWC. Flashing red lights on Navy range vessels between Keyport and Brownsville and atop a building at the seaward end of the southern building at Keyport NUWC indicate torpedo firings, or that noise measurement tests are in progress, or that conditions are generally hazardous to mariners. When lights are flashing, mariners should not enter the test area. Mariners near the area should stop engines, or other equipment generating underwater noise, such as depth sounders, because some torpedoes are guided by noise and may be attracted to the boat noises. (See **334.1230**, chapter 2, for limits and regulations of the restricted area.)

(304) **Keyport** is on the S side of the passage leading to Liberty Bay. A power cable with a clearance of 90 feet crosses the passage at Keyport. There are two piers with floats that can accommodate about 42 small craft. A store with gasoline pumps is about a half block from the Keyport launching ramp. A marine railway that can handle craft to 42 feet is available for repairs; a 7-ton hoist is also available. Engine and hull repairs and salvage and towing services are available at Keyport.

(305) **Poulsbo**. a fishing and pleasure resort on the E shore at the head of Liberty Bay, is the principal town of the area. The small-craft harbor at Poulsbo, protected on the S and W sides by an angled timbered breakwater, can accommodate about 400 fishing boats and pleasure craft. The breakwater is well marked by private lights. Piers and floats are in the harbor with reported depths of 7 feet alongside. Supplies and services available at

(306) the harbor are: electricity, gasoline, diesel fuel, water, a pump-out facility and electrical/engine repairs. A float with the edges painted yellow is on the NE side of the harbor and has been reserved as a seaplane dock. A yacht club and marina are about 0.4 and 0.6 mile SSE of the small-craft harbor, respectively. Supplies of all types may be obtained in town. A tall church steeple on the hill NE of the harbor is prominent.

(306) **Manzanita** is a settlement on the W side of Bainbridge Island in a small cove about 2 miles S from Agate Passage. **Manzanita Bay**, S of the town, affords an excellent anchorage for small craft in 27 feet, mud bottom. There are several private wharves, buoys and floats in the bay. Caution is urged to avoid rows of submerged piling on each side of the bay, about midway in from the entrance.

(307) **Battle Point**, a sandy spit on the E side of Port Orchard about 1.7 miles S of Point Bolin, marks the turn in the direction of the channel from SW to S. A light is off the end of the spit.

(308) **Brownsville**, on the W shore of Port Orchard, is on the N shore of **Burke Bay**, about 1.2 miles SW of Battle Point. Brownsville has a marina with 310 berths, 35 transient berths, and an additional 1,000 linear feet of guest moorage. The reported depth alongside is 8 feet with 20 feet in the approach. The marina can provide gasoline, diesel fuel, electricity, water, ice, marine supplies, and a pump-out facility. The **harbormaster's** office is on the second floor of the town store. All of Burke Bay bares, but it may be entered by small craft at about half tide.

Chart 18449

(309) **Illahee** is a small settlement on the W shore of Port Orchard about 3.0 miles S of Battle Point. The town has a wharf and stores. A fish haven, extending about 140 feet from the outer end of the wharf, provides marine habitat improvement for scuba diving and public fishing; mariners are advised to use caution. About 1 mile S of Illahee at **Illahee State Park** is a public pier with floats for small craft and a launching ramp. A rock awash was reported about 50 yards SE of the pier in about 47°35'59.8"N., 122°35'32.1"W.; caution is advised in the area.

(310) **Fletcher Bay** is a village on the E shore of Port Orchard about 1.2 miles S of Battle Point. Small boats can enter the bay at three-quarter tide and find anchorage in 12 feet, mud bottom; the swinging area is limited. The bar across the entrance bares at half tide.

(311) The E and principal approach to Port Orchard from Puget Sound is S of Bainbridge Island through Rich Passage, between Restoration Point and Blake Island. It is deep and almost free from dangers, except for **Bainbridge Reef**, covered 35 to 55 feet, and currents in the constricted W part of Rich Passage. Bainbridge Reef is marked at the SW end by a lighted buoy.

(312) **Orchard Point**, the S point at the entrance to Rich Passage, is marked by a mariner radio activated sound signal, initiated by keying the microphone five times on VHF-FM channel 81A. A **naval restricted area** is on the S side of the point, surrounding the pier projecting S from the shoreline. (See **§334.1244**, chapter 2, for limits and regulations.) A **general anchorage** is in the vicinity of the point. (See **110.1 and 110.230**, chapter 2, for limits and regulations.)

(313) **Rich Passage** is about 3 miles long, with a sharp bend near its W end, where it narrows to 0.2 mile. **Orchard Rocks**, some 400 yards in extent, are on the N side of the channel just inside the E entrance. A small area near the center of the reef, which uncovers, is marked by a daybeacon. The rocks are marked off their S end by a lighted buoy. The reef off **Point Glover** is marked by a light and a mariner radio activated sound signal, initiated by keying the microphone five times on VHF-FM channel 83A. **Waterman Point**, at the W entrance, is marked by a light and a mariner radio activated sound signal, initiated by keying the microphone five times on VHF-FM channel 81A. A light marks the S edge of the shoal extending from **Point White**, the N point at the W entrance. The town of **Waterman** has a pier and float in deep water about 1 mile SW of Waterman Point.

Currents

(314) Continuous observations in midchannel between Point Glover and Point White and at other points in the passage indicate that: Current velocities increase from E to W in Rich Passage reaching a maximum average velocity of 2.4 knots on the flood and 3.1 knots on the ebb at the W end off Point White. The strongest observed currents were 4 knots on the flood and 5 knots on the ebb. Ferry pilots on the regular daily run between Seattle and Bremerton advised that on rare occasions they have experienced ebb currents of "at least" 6 knots in the vicinity of Light 10.

(315) Near the time of slack, the average period when the velocity does not exceed 0.2 knot is about 20 minutes. For strong currents these periods will be decreased; for weak currents they will be increased.

(316) In the channel off Orchard Point, at the E end of Rich Passage, the velocity of the flood is 0.8 knot and on the ebb, 1.1 knots. Off Pleasant Beach the velocity of the flood is 1.3 knots and on the ebb, 2.8 knots.

(317) On the flood, the lines of stream flow are nearly uniform except off the bight just NW of Middle Point and in the large cove on the N shore opposite Point Glover. Eddies do form in those two places, but they do not extend outward to the usual vessel track. On the ebb, however, extensive eddies and countercurrents do occur, owing to the funnel-shaped configuration of the passage.

(318) Between Middle Point and Point Glover, an extensive eddy extends from shore almost to midchannel, and will frequently be encountered by vessels on the track between Orchard Rocks and Point Glover buoys.

(319) An eddy fills the cove on the N shore opposite Point Glover, but does not extend outward to the vessel track.

(320) An eddy occurs about 0.2 mile SSW of Point White and a little N of midchannel at the W entrance to the passage. A weak countercurrent occurs inshore along the SE side of Point White.

(321) These eddies and countercurrents on the ebb greatly diminish the effective width of the passage, and so increase the velocities in the channel.

(322) Mariners unfamiliar with the area should not attempt to navigate Port Orchard, and particularly Rich Passage, in thick weather because of the strong tidal currents. In clear weather, however, the navigation of these waters presents no unusual difficulty.

Caution

(323) **Rich Passage**, because of activities of the Puget Sound Naval Shipyard, has a large volume of traffic. Many ferries a day each way, tugs with hawser tows, and various types of naval craft, all contribute to create a considerable collision hazard in the passage, particularly at the sharp bend off Point Glover. Strong tidal conditions prevail in this vicinity, and deep-draft outbound vessels making the sharp turn may be unavoidably set well over toward the E shore, necessitating a two-blast, starboard-to-starboard meeting with inbound vessels. Vessels approaching Point Glover from either direction should sound one long blast when within 0.5 mile of the point as a warning to any vessel approaching from the opposite direction.

(324) **Fort Ward**, formerly a military post and now a State park on Bainbridge Island, is near the E entrance to Rich Passage, just inside Beans Point. There is a wharf here built out to 18 feet. A fish pen off the end of the wharf is marked by private lights. An aquaculture site, marked by private lights, is about 300 yards SSW of the wharf in about 47°34'30.5"N., 122°31'29.5"W. A rocky patch covered 11 feet, 150 yards S of the wharf, is dangerous to vessels approaching from southward. A radio tower just NE of Fort Ward and a large white house on **Beans Point** are prominent from the E end of Rich Passage.

Chart 18452

(325) **Sinclair Inlet**, site of the city of Bremerton and the Puget Sound Naval Shipyard, is entered from Rich Passage and Port Orchard on the E, and Port Washington Narrows on the N. The inlet is 3.5 miles long, extending in a WSW direction from **Point Herron**, which is at the junction of Port Washington Narrows and Port Orchard; the point is marked by a light. Several Navy-maintained unlighted mooring buoys, used at times by unlighted craft, are in Sinclair Inlet. Mariners are advised to exercise caution at night.

(326) **East Bremerton** is the community back of Point Herron, on the E side of the Port Washington Narrows entrance. The fixed highway bridge crossing the narrows here has a clearance of 82 feet.

(327) Sinclair Inlet is a **naval restricted area.** (See **334.1240,** chapter 2, for limits and regulations.)

(328) **Annapolis** is a village on the S shore of Sinclair Inlet directly S of Point Herron. A foot pier extends out to a float which is used by a passenger ferry between the village and Bremerton. E of the ferry pier is a public float and launching ramp. The float grounds at low water. The buildings of a veterans' home on the bluff above the town are prominent.

(329) A flat that bares extends about 0.2 mile from shore in the bight between Annapolis and Port Orchard.

(330) The town of **Port Orchard** is on the S shore about 0.5 mile W of Annapolis. It has a ferry pier, float landing, and a marina. Passenger ferry service is maintained with Bremerton every 15 minutes from 1600 to 2400 daily. A marina, protected on the W, N, and E sides by a floating breakwater, is just W of the ferry pier. The entrance is at the NW corner and is marked by private lights. There are covered and open berths for about 600 small craft. A yacht club has its moorings just inside the W breakwater. Transient berths for 50 small-craft are on the E side of the marina; larger transient craft can moor on the inside or outside of the N and E parts of the breakwater. Gasoline, diesel fuel, electricity, water, ice, pumpout facilities and full repairs are available at the marina. The stores of the town business district are nearby and all types of supplies may be obtained.

(331) A marina and boatyard are on the W side of town; water, ice, limited marine supplies, and diesel fuel are available. The yard has a marine railway that can handle craft up to 75 feet and a floating drydock with a 25-ton capacity. Hull and engine repairs can be done at the boatyard; a machine shop and carpentry shop are available. Port Orchard Yacht Club has its moorings W of the boatyard. A floating breakwater in ruins, a wreck, and other sunken debris are about 75 yards off the ends of the Yacht Club floats. Another marina and boatyard, just W of Port Orchard Yacht Club, can accommodate about 25 vessels. A mobile hoist with a 30-ton capacity can handle craft up to 55 feet.

(332) A marina and boatyard, about 1.5 miles W of Port Orchard, has berths for about 50 fishing boats and small craft. Electricity, gasoline, water, and limited marine supplies are available. The boatyard has three marine railways, the largest of which can handle craft to 30 tons for hull repairs.

(333) **Puget Sound Naval Shipyard** occupies most of the N shore of the inlet. The hammerhead crane near the offshore end of Pier 6 of the yard is one of the most conspicuous objects from any direction. The ends of Pier 4, Pier 5 and Pier 6 are equipped with radar reflectors. A floating security barrier, marked by lighted buoys, surrounds the waterfront of the naval shipyard.

(334) Navy Drydock No. 6 is one of the largest in the world. Its inside dimensions are 1,152 feet long, 165 feet wide at the entrance measured 6 feet over sill, and

53 feet over the sill at mean high water. This facility was built to accommodate the largest supercarrier. When not committed to Navy use, and under certain conditions, the drydock may be used by other ships that are too large for commercial docks.

(335) **Bremerton** adjoins the shipyard, and most of the city's business and affairs are keyed to the needs of the Navy establishment. The city limits include East Bremerton and Point Herron. Frequent ferry service connects with Seattle. Floats for small craft are adjacent to the N ferry slip. The floats are managed by the Port of Bremerton; water, electricity, and overnight moorage are available.

Chart 18449

(336) **Port Washington Narrows**, 3 miles long, joins Sinclair and Dyes Inlets. Tidal currents in the narrows attain velocities in excess of 4 knots at times. (See Tidal Current Tables and Tidal Current Charts for detailed information.)

(337) There are a number of petroleum distribution facilities with storage tanks and receiving wharves along the W shore of Port Washington Narrows between the S bridge over the narrows and Phinney Bay.

(338) Two fixed highway bridges and two power cables cross the narrows. In 2011, the Bremerton-East Bremerton Bridge, the S bridge, was under consturction and being replaced; consult Local Notice to Mariners for lastest conditions. A power cable with a clearance of 90 feet is about 0.3 mile N of the bridge, and a second power cable with a clearance of 80 feet is close E of the N highway bridge. The N bridge has a clearance of 80 feet.

(339) **Anderson Cove** is a small bight on the S shore about 1.5 miles above the East Bremerton Bridge. The cove is shoal; however, it has several private piers and a public launching ramp. A small-craft moorage is 250 yards E of Anderson Cove. Oil wharves are on both sides of the moorage.

(340) **Phinney Bay**, 0.8 mile long, makes into the W shore near the N end of the narrows. Bremerton Yacht Club has its moorage with floats on the W side of the bay. **Rocky Point** is on the W side of the N entrance of the narrows. There are tide rips off this point.

(341) **Dyes Inlet** extends about 3 miles NNW from the N end of the narrows to the village of **Silverdale** on the W side of the head of the inlet. The inlet is used by fishing boats and pleasure craft. There are several villages and many houses on its shores. A dock here has electricity, water, a pump-out station, and limited marine supplies available. The facility is managed by the Port of Silverdale at the Silverdale Waterfront Park. Some local fishing boats are hauled out by crane for repairs. The village of **Tracyton** is on the E shore just N of the narrows. The village has a public boat launching ramp.

(342) **Chico** is a small residential town on the SW side of Dyes Inlet, close W of Chico Bay; the log dump wharf here is in ruins.

(343) **Ostrich Bay** is an inlet in the SW part of Dyes Inlet. A covered rock is reported in Ostrich Bay 500 yards S of **Elwood Point** inside the breakwater extending S of the point.

(344) That part of the W shore of Ostrich Bay extending about 0.5 mile S from Elwood Point is an annex of the Puget Sound Naval Shipyard. The wharves and shops are no longer used and are in ruins.

(345) A depth of 6 feet can be carried from Ostrich Bay into **Oyster Bay** on midchannel courses. There is 4 feet or more in Oyster Bay.

Charts 18448, 18449, 18474

(346) **East Passage**, on the E side of Vashon and Maury Islands, extends from Alki Point SSE for 12.5 miles to Point Robinson, and thence SW for 6 miles to Browns Point. The waters throughout are deep and free from dangers, which in no case extend as much as 0.5 mile from shore.

(347) **Fauntleroy Cove**, 3.5 miles S of Alki Point, is the site of the landing for the automobile ferry plying from there to Vashon Heights and Point Southworth.

(348) **Blake Island**, about 1 mile long, 249 feet high, and covered with trees, is off the N entrance to Colvos Passage. Heavy tide rips, strongest with a flood current and strong S winds, are encountered at the N entrance to Colvos Passage S of Blake Island. Shallow, irregular bottom extends about 0.5 mile off the N shore of the island. A light is on the NE point of the island. Just S of the NE point of the island are the ruins of a wharf. A State marine park small-craft basin, protected by a breakwater, is at the NE end of the island. The entrance to the basin is marked by a private light and daybeacons; a pump-out station is available. Several public mooring buoys are along the W, N, and E sides of the island.

(349) **Yukon Harbor** is about 2 miles SW of Blake Island and can afford anchorage in 30 to 50 feet, sticky mud and pebble bottom. The harbor is protected from S winds and can be used for anchorage in a variety of conditions. Much of the head of the harbor is bare at low tides. Several settlements and resort villages are along the shores of Yukon Harbor; mostly fishermen and pleasure boaters use these waterfront facilities. **Manchester** has a short wharf with a float landing and a launching ramp. A large fuel pier, just S of Orchard Point, is part of the U.S. Navy's Manchester Fuel Depot. The pier is a major fueling station for U.S. Government deep-draft vessels. A **naval restricted area** surrounds the fuel pier (See §334.1244, chapter 2, for limits and regulations.) A **general anchorage** is between Blake Island and Manchester. (See 110.1 and 110.230, chapter 2, for limits and regulations.) **Harper**, a mile WNW of Point Southworth, is the site of a former ferry pier. A ferry now

operates from a pier on Point Southworth to Seattle, Fauntleroy and Vashon Island.

(350) **Vashon Island** is 11 miles long in a N direction. **Maury Island**, actually a peninsula of Vashon Island at its SE extremity, is connected to it by a highway on a narrow neck of land. Maury Island is about 5 miles long.

(351) On these islands the land is of moderate rolling elevation and in places rugged, and most of the country is heavily wooded. The islands have numerous orchards and houses. There is some farming, and cattle and poultry are raised. The transmitting towers of Seattle broadcasting stations are on the islands; two groups of towers are on Vashon Island and two on Maury Island. The shores on all sides have numerous settlements. The county wharves, formerly used to ship farm produce, are no longer kept in repair, and shipments are now by truck.

(352) **Point Vashon**, the NW tip of Vashon Island, is 305 feet high, steep, and wooded. Shoal water extends 0.2 mile N from the point and nearly as far along the N shore as **Dolphin Point**, 1 mile E. A light is 300 yards N of Point Vashon.

(353) **Vashon Heights Landing**, 0.5 mile ESE of Point Vashon, has a combination ferry slip and landing wharf built out to 14 feet. An automobile ferry runs to Point Southworth and Fauntleroy.

(354) The tall radio towers of station KOMO are on Point Beals. The town of **Vashon** is on high land 1.5 miles SW of Point Beals.

(355) A **159°58'-339°58' measured nautical mile** is E of Point Beals. The range markers are steel towers with round orange targets.

(356) **Three Tree Point**, about 7.8 miles S of Alki Point, is a sharp low spit, projecting 300 yards from the high land which in 1 mile rises to an elevation of 430 feet. On the low part of the point is a grassy knoll, 30 feet high, with several trees on it. A light and a mariner radio activated sound signal are on the point, initiated by keying the microphone five times on VHF-FM channel 83A.

(357) **Tramp Harbor**, formed by the easternmost part of Vashon Island and the N end of Maury Island, has shoal water extending about 0.2 mile out from shore along its entire length. It is bounded on the N by **Point Heyer**, a sandspit behind which the ground rises rapidly. A shoal extends 0.2 mile SE from the point. A radio tower on this point is about 450 feet high.

(358) **Portage** is a village extending over both sides of the low isthmus that connects Vashon and Maury Islands. Two radio towers about 526 feet high are 0.6 mile S of the isthmus, and three other radio towers are one mile SE of the isthmus.

(359) The city of **Des Moines**, on the E shore of East Passage, operates a small-craft marina about 3.7 miles SE of Three Tree Point. The marina, protected by a rock breakwater, offers shelter for over 700 craft including 50 transient berths. The entrance to the marina is from the W around the N end of the breakwater. Lights mark the N end and SW corner of the breakwater. Services available include electricity, gasoline, diesel fuel, water, ice, pump-out station, wet and dry storage, marine supplies, and a 25-ton marine lift; full repairs can be made.

(360) **Point Robinson**, the easternmost end of Maury Island and the major turning point in the passage, is a low spit projecting 140 yards from the wooded high land. **Robinson Point Light** (47°23'17"N., 122°22'28"W.), 40 feet above the water, is shown from a 40-foot white octagonal tower on the point; a mariner radio activated sound signal is at the station, initiated by keying the microphone five times on VHF-FM channel 81A.

(361) There are two barge-loading berths at the gravel pits about 1 mile SW of Point Robinson. Conveyors load the barges. The gravel pits are prominent from the S end of East Passage. These facilities are the only commercial wharves on Vashon and Maury Islands, except for oil receiving wharves.

(362) **Redondo**, on **Poverty Bay**, about 6.8 miles SSE of Three Tree Point, is a suburban village. **Dumas Bay**, 2 miles W of Redondo, has a small wharf which bares alongside at low water.

(363) **Quartermaster Harbor** extends 5 miles NNE between the S parts of Vashon and Maury Islands, opposite Commencement Bay. The entrance is between **Neill Point** to the W and **Piner Point** to the E. Its shores are low and wooded, with numerous clearings, and several landings and private piers.

(364) Quartermaster Harbor affords excellent anchorage about 2 miles inside the entrance in 5 to 10 fathoms, muddy bottom. The harbor provides easy access, however caution is advised to avoid charted obstructions and wrecks.

(365) A shoal just inside the entrance extends 300 yards from the E shore and is marked by a buoy. Several shoal areas with depths of 2 to 2¾ fathoms extend up to 400 yards off the W shore between Neill Point and Harbor Heights. Shoal areas with depths of 4¼ fathoms are near midchannel W of **Manzanita** and W of Dockton. In 2007, a wreck covered 8¾ fathoms was in this vicinity at 47°20'59"N., 122°29'01"W.

(366) Many settlements and summer resorts are along the shores of the harbor, but the landing wharves, for the most part, are in disrepair. There are several submerged hazards in the vicinity of the wharves.

(367) **Burton** is a town on **Burton Peninsula** which projects E from the W side about 3 miles from the entrance. The town has several stores and some marine supplies are available. There are numerous private mooring buoys in the harbor.

(368) An oil-receiving wharf and storage tanks are on the W side of the harbor about 0.7 mile N of Burton at the mouth of Judd Creek. The storage tanks are on the hill N of the harbor.

(369) The village of **Dockton** is in the bight on the E side about 2.5 miles from the entrance. A county park on the E side of the bight has a public dock with several piers and a boat ramp. There is a large mooring field off the village; numerous submerged obstructions, small

wrecks, and scattered debris litter the bottom in this area.

(370) In the upper part of the harbor, N of the Burton Peninsula, are several private wharves and floats.

(371) **Colvos Passage**, on the W side of Vashon Island, extends about 11 miles in a general S direction, with an average width of 1 mile. The passage is free of dangers. The N entrance is about 4.5 miles SW of Alki Point, and the S entrance is abreast Point Defiance. The passage is used principally by tugs hauling logs for sawmills and by medium-sized vessels departing Tacoma. A midchannel course can be followed with safety. The passage is marked by lights.

(372) The current in Colvos Passage sets N on the ebb and flood, and at times advantage is taken of this fact by vessels bound from Tacoma to Seattle. The current in the middle of Dalco Passage and along the SW shore of Commencement Bay sets W or NW almost continuously.

(373) **Point Southworth**, on the W side of the N entrance, is high and wooded. A ferry slip is 0.2 mile NW of the point. An automobile ferry runs to Fauntleroy and Vashon Heights.

(374) **Fragaria** and **Olalla**, on the W shore of Colvos Passage, are small residential communities. Only isolated pilings remain of their former wharves. A rock which bares at half tide is 400 yards N of the former wharf at Olalla. Olalla has a small-craft float landing and a general store. Gasoline, water, ice, and some marine supplies are available.

(375) **Cove** and **Lisabeula**, on the E shore, are summer resort areas. There are no facilities at either area. The wharf at Cove is in ruins. Several pilings, formerly used as moorings for log rafts, are adjacent to the wharf. Lisabeula consists of a single waterfront resort with no facilities for small craft.

(376) **Tahlequah** is a small residential community on the S shore of Vashon Island between Neill Point and Point Dalco. A ferry operates between Tahlequah and Tacoma.

(377) **Gig Harbor** is an inlet about 1 mile long on the W side of the S entrance to Colvos Passage abreast Point Defiance. A private light is on the S end of the sandspit, at the E side of the entrance, which makes out for 220 yards and constricts the entrance to less than 100 yards wide. A narrow 10-foot channel in the middle has currents of considerable velocity. Inside the entrance the basin has from 3 to 5 fathoms. An obstruction with a least depth of 8 feet was reported in the harbor in about 47°20'14"N., 122°35'06"W. The surrounding land, partially cleared of timber, slopes gently toward the shores and is thickly settled.

(378) The town of **Gig Harbor** extends along the W shore and the head of the harbor. It is the home port of many pleasure craft and fishing boats. The town has a boatyard with three marine railways and one crane. The larger of the three railways can handle craft to 150 tons for hull and engine repairs. There are many private piers and wharves, including one gasoline float. There are many marinas here. Berths, gasoline, diesel fuel, water, ice, launching ramps, and marine supplies are available in the harbor. Most of the pleasure craft moor at one of the marinas at the head of the harbor.

(379) On entering Gig Harbor, hold midway between the spit on the E side and the W shore until just inside the entrance. Then swing right toward the E shore until past the short spit extending from the W shore, and steer a course just S of midchannel into the harbor.

Chart 18453

(380) **Dash Point**, the E entrance of Commencement Bay, and the village of **Dash Point** are 1 mile NE of Browns Point. There is a restaurant at the foot of the long pier which extends out from the N side of the point to a depth of 20 feet.

(381) **Point Defiance**, the W entrance of Commencement Bay, terminates in a very prominent dirt bluff, 160 feet high. A light is just W of the point. The terminal for the Point Defiance/Tahlequah ferry is approximately 1.8 miles SSE of the Point. A small boat launch ramp is just S of the terminal adjacent to a small-craft boat basin formed by a manmade peninsula. **Point Defiance Park** is wooded along its northeastern shore for 3.8 miles from the end of the point.

(382) **Commencement Bay** entrance lies 18 miles S of Alki Point and 56 miles S of Point Wilson. The bay is about 2.5 miles in length, easy of access, and free of dangers. Log storage grounds are off the NE shore of the bay.

(383) **Tacoma**, the second city in size and importance on the sound, occupies the S and SW shores of Commencement Bay, and its residential area has grown N into Seattle's S suburbs, and to Steilacoom on the SW.

(384) The **Port of Tacoma** is a rapidly expanding major port, second only to Seattle in maritime importance on Puget Sound. Its exports include lumber and other wood products, grain, refined metals, machinery, general and containerized cargo; imports include alumina, and refined steel, automobiles, electronic equipment, rubber, and meat. Much of the Alaska trade originates here.

Prominent features

(385) On entering Commencement Bay, either from the N via East Passage or Colvos Passage or from the S via The Narrows and Dalco Passage, Dash Point, Browns Point, and Point Defiance are prominent. **Browns Point Light** (47°18'21"N., 122°26'39"W.), 38 feet above the water, is shown from a 35-foot white concrete house on Browns Point. Once inside the bay, numerous stacks, tanks, and towers are visible.

(386) A **132°05' - 312°05' measured nautical mile** is along the SW shore of the bay about midway between Ruston and Tacoma.

(387) A fishing reef is along the SW shore of the bay about midway between Ruston and Tacoma. In the same vicinity, a line of mooring buoys extends 0.7 mile along the SW shore of the bay.

(388) From the SE corner of Commencement Bay, the city waterfront extends NW to the SE corner of Point Defiance Park. Along here are numerous industrial plants with wharves to accommodate vessels drawing 30 feet or more.

(389) **Thea Foss Waterway** is the westernmost of the channels at the head of the bay; a light is on the E side of the entrance. In 2007, an 11-foot obstruction was midchannel (47°14'57"N., 122°25'58"W.). Two deep-draft wharves and many oil storage tanks are on the E side.

(390) There are two bridges over the waterway. The South 11th Street vertical lift bridge, 0.5 mile from the entrance to the waterway, has a clearance of 64 feet down and 139 feet up. A fixed highway bridge near the head of the waterway has a clearance of 28 feet (36 feet at the center).

(391) **Middle Waterway**, NE of Thea Foss Waterway, and **St. Paul Waterway**, NE of Middle Waterway, are not **Federal projects**. The inner parts of both waterways have shoaled and are not navigable; there is no deep-draft traffic. St. Paul Waterway is used for log storage by the large papermill which occupies the land on the NE side.

(392) **Puyallup Waterway**, NE of St. Paul Waterway, discharges the water of **Puyallup River.** The waterway has shoaled to such an extent that it cannot be used commercially. A lighted buoy marks a shoal area extending about 500 yards NW of the entrance. A fixed bridge, with a clearance of 29 feet, crosses the waterway about 0.7 mile above the mouth. An overhead cable, just SE of the bridge, has a clearance of 46 feet.

(393) **Sitcum Waterway**, NE of Puyallup Waterway, is maintained at more than the project depth of 40 feet. The Port of Tacoma's Pier 7 is on the E side. A private light is just off the NW end of Pier 7; it marks the NE side of the entrance to Sitcum Waterway.

(394) The next two channels to the NE of Sitcum Waterway, **Blair Waterway and Hylebos Waterway,** are maintained as **Federal projects**. A lighted buoy is off a shoal on the N side of the entrance and a private light is on the S side at the NW end of Pier 25; these aids mark the entrance to Hylebos Waterway. The entrance to Blair Waterway is marked by a private lighted buoy on the SW side. Project depths in Hylebos Waterway are 30 feet in the waterway and basins. The project depth in Blair Waterway is 51 feet in the waterway and basin. (See Notice to Mariners and latest editions of charts for controlling depths.)

(395) The 11th Street bascule bridge over Hylebos Waterway has a clearance of 21 feet. (See **117.1 through 117.59 and 117.1061**, chapter 2, for drawbridge regulations.) The bridgetender monitors VHF-FM channel 16 and works on channel 13. Call signs: KZN-574, Hylebos Bridge. A power cable at the bridge has a clearance of 173 feet.

(396) **Security zones** are in the Sitcum Waterway and Blair Waterway areas. (See **165.1 through 165.8, 165.30 and 165.1321**, chapter 2, for limits and regulations.) **Regulated navigation areas** are in the Thea Foss Waterway. (See **33 CFR 165.1 through 165.13 and 165.1329**, chapter 2, for limits and regulations.)

Anchorage

(397) A **general anchorage** is off the N shore of Commencement Bay. (See **110.1 and 110.230**, chapter 2, for limits and regulations.) The depths elsewhere in the bay, as a rule, are too great for convenient anchorage. In 2010, a wreck covered 54 feet (47°17'36"N., 122°26'06"W.) and a submerged obstruction (47°17'33"N., 122°26'00"W.) were reported near the NW corner of the anchorage area.

(398) City regulations permit anchorage in any part of the bay outside the harbor lines so as not to interfere with vessels arriving or departing from their docks.

Currents

(399) The tidal currents in the harbor have little velocity, except in Hylebos Waterway where the NOAA Ship McARTHUR reported estimated currents of up to 2 knots in 1994.

Pilotage, Tacoma

(400) Pilotage is compulsory for all vessels except those under enrollment or engaged exclusively in the coasting trade on the W coast of the continental United States (including Alaska) and/or British Columbia. Pilotage for Puget Sound is provided by the Puget Sound Pilots. (See Pilotage, Strait of Juan de Fuca and Puget Sound, indexed as such, chapter 12 for details.)

Towage

(401) Tugs up to 5,000 hp are available at Tacoma, and larger tugs may be obtained from Seattle. Arrangements should be made in advance through ships' agents.

Quarantine, customs, immigration, and agricultural quarantine

(402) (See chapter 3, Vessel Arrival Inspections, and Appendix A for addresses.)

(403) **Quarantine** is enforced in accordance with regulations of the U.S. Public Health Service. (See Public Health Service, chapter 1.)

(404) Tacoma is a **customs port of entry**.

Harbor regulation

(405) Harbor regulations are administered by the **harbormaster**, whose headquarters are at the fire station at 901 South Fawcett Street. The general offices of the Port of Tacoma are in the Tacoma Building at the corner of

Name	Location	Berthing Space (feet)	Depths* (feet)	Deck Height (feet)	Mechanical Handling Facilities and Storage	Purpose	Owned/ Operated by:
Facilities on Hylebos Waterway							
Trident Seafoods Corporation (Berths C and D)	47°16'58"N., 122°24'27"W.	1,258	18-25	18	• Open storage (4 acres) • Three gantry cranes	Receipt of frozen seafood	Port of Tacoma/ Trident Seafoods Corp.
Pioneer Americas (Docks 1 and 2)	47°16'49"N., 122°24'13"W.	940	25-28	19	• Tank storage (1.6 million gallons) • Open storage	• Receipt of bulk salt • Receipt and shipment of caustic soda	Pioneer Americas Inc.
City of Tacoma Coal Dock	47°16'36"N., 122°23'36"W.	250	30	-	Open storage (12,000 tons coal)	Receipt of coal by barge	City of Tacoma
Sound Refining	47°16'36"N., 122°23'10"W.	770	27	19	Tank storage (700,000 barrels)	Receipt and shipment of petroleum products	Sound Refining, Inc.
Atofina Chemicals	47°16'09"N., 122°22'28"W.	645	30	18	• Tank storage (5,360 tons) • Crane (½ ton)	Shipment of caustic soda and sodium chlorate	Atofina Chemicals, Inc.
Schnitzer Steel	47°16'05"N., 122°22'08"W.	850	32-35	18	• Open storage (26 acres) • Cranes to 250 tons	Receipt and shipment of scrap metal	Schnitzer Steel of Tacoma
Weyerhaeuser Company	47°15'48"N., 122°21'55"W.	1,100	34-37	19	Open storage (18 acres)	Receipt and shipment of logs	Weyerhaeuser Co.
Manke Lumber Company	47°15'52"N., 122°21'41"W.	320	30	18	• Open storage (10 million board feet) • Tank storage (21,360 tons)	• Receipt and shipment of lumber • Shipment of tallow	Manke Lumber Co. Inc./ Manke Lumber Co. Inc. and Pacific Northwest Terminals Inc.
Facilities on Blair Waterway							
Totem Ocean Trailer Express	47°16'28"N., 122°24'18"W.	790	40	11	Open storage (41 acres)	Receipt and shipment of general cargo	Port of Tacoma/ Totem Ocean Trailer Express
Tru-Grit	47°16'18"N., 122°24'02"W.	160	15-20	18	• Open storage (10,000 tons) • Belt conveyor	• Receipt of copper slag • Shipment of fabricated steel products	A.H. Powers Inc./ Jesse Engineering and Tru-Grit, Inc.
Graymont Western U.S.	47°16'11"N., 122°23'52"W.	335	32	20	• Open storage (15,000 tons) • Tank storage (1.3 million gallons) • Belt conveyor	• Receipt of limestone • Occasional shipment of calcium carbonate slurry	Graymont Western U.S., Inc.
Georgia-Pacific Gypsum Corperation	47°16'07"N., 122°23'45"W.	700	35	18	• Covered storage (32,000 tons) • Belt conveyor	Receipt of gypsum	Port of Tacoma/ Georgia-Pacific Gypsum Corp.
Weyerhaeuser Paper Company	47°15'43"N., 122°23'05"W.	800	40-51	20	• Open storage (185,000 tons) • Belt conveyors	Receipt and shipment of wood chips	Port of Tacoma/ Weyerhaeuser Paper Co.
Port of Tacoma (Berths A and B)	47°15'14"N., 122°22'42"W.	1,400	51	22	• Open storage (80 acres) • Covered storage (102,400 square feet)	• Receipt of automobiles • Receipt and shipment of lumber and general cargo	Port of Tacoma
Port of Tacoma Blair Waterway Terminal	47°15'35"N., 122°23'04"W.	1,200	51	22	Open storage (2 acres)	Shipment of logs	Port of Tacoma
Washington United Terminals	47°15'45"N., 122°23'23"W.	2,000	51	21.5	• Open storage (80 acres) • Four container cranes	Receipt and shipment of general cargo	Port of Tacoma/ Washington United Terminals
U.S. Oil & Refining Company (Docks 1 and 2)	47°16'04"N., 122°23'59"W.	1,095	40	18	Tank storage (2 million barrels)	Receipt and shipment of petroleum products	U.S. Oil & Refining Co.
Port of Tacoma (Terminal 4)	47°16'21"N., 122°24'21"W.	1,900	51	18	• Open storage (75 acres) • Six container cranes	Receipt and shipment of general cargo	Port of Tacoma/ Marine Terminals Corp.
Facilities on Sitcum Waterway							
Port of Tacoma (Terminal 7D)	47°16'16"N., 122°25'06"W.	900	51	18	• Open storage (33 acres) • Six container cranes	Receipt and shipment of general cargo	Port of Tacoma/ Husky Terminal & Stevedoring, Inc.
Port of Tacoma (Terminal 7C)	47°16'10"N., 122°24'58"W.	600	48	18	• Open storage (5 acres) • Covered storage (150,000 tons) • One 40-ton gantry crane	Receipt and shipment of miscellaneous bulk materials	Port of Tacoma/ Kaiser Aluminum & Chemical Corp.
Port of Tacoma (Terminals 7A and 7B)	47°16'04"N., 122°24'50"W.	1,200	48	18	• Open storage (6 acres) • Covered storage (180,000 square feet)	Receipt and shipment of containerized general cargo	Port of Tacoma

		Facilities in the Port of Tacoma					
Name	Location	Berthing Space (feet)	Depths* (feet)	Deck Height (feet)	Mechanical Handling Facilities and Storage	Purpose	Owned/ Operated by:
Maersk Pacific, APM Terminals	47°16'03"N., 122°24'58"W.	2,200	46	20	• Open storage (135 acres) • Five container cranes	Receipt and shipment of containerized general cargo	Port of Tacoma/ Maersk Pacific, Ltd.
Facilities on Thea Foss Waterway							
ST Services/Shore Terminals	47°15'38"N., 122°26'09"W.	600	26	20	Tank storage (500,000 barrels)	Receipt and shipment of petroleum products	ST Services/Shore Terminals, LLC
Tosco Corporation	47°15'30"N., 122°26'03"W.	660	24-30	20	Tank storage (280,000 barrels)	Receipt of petroleum products	Tosco Corp
Tacoma Export Marketing Corporation	47°15'59"N., 122°26'35"W.	910	65	19.5	• Silo storage (3 million bushels) • Belt conveyor	Shipment of grain	Port of Tacoma/ Tacoma Export Marketing Co.

* The depths given above are reported. For information on the latest depths contact the port authorities or the private operators.

11th and A Streets; the Port of Tacoma terminal offices are at Pier 2.

Speed

(406) A city ordinance prohibits speeds in excess of 5 knots on any of the waterways and within 200 yards of any shore or pier in the harbor.

Wharves

(407) The Port of Tacoma operates three marine terminals and owns ten which are privately operated. In addition to the port-owned facilities listed in the table, there are several private deep-draft piers and wharves. Only the major deep-draft facilities are listed. For a complete description of the port facilities refer to Port Series No. 35, published and sold by the U.S. Army Corps of Engineers. (See Appendix A for address.) The alongside depths given in the table are reported. (For information on the latest depths contact the Port of Tacoma general office or the individual operators.) All the facilities listed have direct highway connections, and most have plant trackage with railroad connections. Water and electrical shore power connections are available at about 80 percent of the wharves. General cargo is usually handled by ships' tackle. Mechanical handling equipment, if available, is mentioned in the table. The Port of Tacoma operates its own belt line railroad with switching connections to two major railroads and has a 200-ton mobile crane and a 300-ton floating crane.

Supplies

(408) Most marine supplies and services are available at Tacoma. Bunker fuel, diesel oil, and lubricants are available. Gasoline and diesel fuel are available at the oil docks on Thea Foss Waterway. Large vessels are bunkered at their berths by barge. Water is available at most of the berths.

Repairs

(409) There are no facilities for major repairs to large oceangoing vessels in Tacoma; the nearest such facilities are in Seattle, WA. The largest marine railway in Tacoma is at a repair yard on the NE side of the upper turning basin in Hylebos Waterway; the railway here is certified for 1,000 tons.

Small-craft facilities

(410) A public pier, owned by the city of Tacoma, is 0.6 mile SE of the S marker of the measured mile course on the SW side of Commencement Bay; small craft moor here temporarily. There are numerous other small-craft facilities on Hylebos, Blair, and Thea Foss Waterways, and on the NE and SW shores of Commencement Bay.

Communications

(411) Tacoma is served by two major railroads, Seattle-Tacoma Airport, and Tacoma Narrows Industrial Airport.

Chart 18448

(412) S of Point Defiance are numerous inlets, passages, and islands. At many of the towns the landing wharves have fallen into ruins, all transportation following the highways. These waters are navigated by log tows and by pleasure craft. Deep-draft vessels call at Olympia for lumber and other forest products. The depths are generally great, and the dangers are few. The shores are well wooded and moderately low. The beaches are sand and gravel, with boulders in places, and are often backed by steep, bare sand and gravel bluffs. Olympia and Shelton are the only cities, but there are many towns. Strangers bound through these waters at night are advised to take a pilot.

Currents

(413) In The Narrows current velocities exceed 5 knots at times. At the N end of The Narrows the current sets N most of the time on the E side of the passage and S

most of the time on the W side. (See Tidal Current Tables for daily current predictions for a midstream position near the N end of The Narrows and details of the current movement at other locations; these tables and the Tidal Current Charts, Puget Sound, Southern Part, should both be consulted for details of the complicated currents of this area.)

(414) From Point Defiance to near Days Island, the E shore of **The Narrows** consists of high, bold bluffs. A tunnel is 1.7 miles SE of Point Defiance; from it a railroad track follows the shoreline to Nisqually River.

(415) **Point Evans**, 2 miles S of Point Defiance on the W side of The Narrows, is marked by a light. Power cables with a clearance of 200 feet cross 200 yards S of the point. **Tacoma Narrows Bridge**, a dual-span highway suspension bridge, crosses The Narrows a mile S of Point Evans. The clearance is 160 feet at the piers and 180 feet at the center.

(416) **Days Island** is about 4.5 miles S of Point Defiance. The ferry slip and wharf here are in ruins. There are three marinas here, one on the E side of Days Island and two in the cove 150 yards E of the N end of the island. A total of about 200 berths are at the marinas; electricity, gasoline, diesel fuel, water, ice, dry storage for over 500 craft, and marine supplies are available. A 15-ton crane and hoists to 3 tons are available to handle craft for hull and engine repair. Obstructions covered 1 to 2¼ fathoms are 230 yards W of the former ferry slip.

(417) A small-boat channel, 1 foot deep, leads into **Days Island Lagoon**. The channel favors the Days Island side and under the bridge is 30 yards from the island shore. Local boats anchor in 3 feet in the lagoon. The floats of a private yacht club are on the S and W sides of the lagoon. Anchorage for small-craft may be had E of the N end of Days Island.

(418) Three miles S of Days Island, the shores consist of bare bluffs which are prominent from S.

(419) From here the route to Olympia continues SW and W through **Balch Passage**, Drayton Passage, and Dana Passage, thence S into Budd Inlet. This route is deep and generally free of dangers.

Caution
(420) The channel through Balch Passage is only about 100 yards wide between the 10-fathom curves, and the scale of the chart is small. Vessels should stay carefully in midchannel, traffic permitting.

(421) **Hale Passage**, between **Fox Island** and the mainland, enters on the W shore 5 miles S of Point Defiance. It is 4 miles to its junction with Carr Inlet. Near the W end the passage is crossed by a fixed highway bridge with a clearance of 31 feet. A shoal, marked on its NE side by a buoy, is 350 yards SE of the bridge and near the middle of the passage; the shoal is boulder-strewn and bares. The channel is on the NE side of the buoy. A good small-craft anchorage is on either side of Tanglewood Island. The current in Hale Passage attains a velocity in excess of 3 knots at times. The E (ebb) current is stronger than the W (flood) current. (See Tidal Current Tables for current predictions.)

(422) **Fox Island** is a village in the small cove near the NE end of Fox Island. It has a store and service station. **Tanglewood Island**, in the center of the cove, has a boys' camp, the buildings of which are prominent.

(423) **Wollochet Bay** is a small inlet about 2 miles long extending N from Hale Passage, about 1 mile inside the E entrance. The upper part is narrow and shoal. It affords an anchorage in midchannel about 0.3 mile inside the entrance in 11 to 12 fathoms, sticky bottom. There are many private piers and mooring buoys in the bay. A small-boat launching ramp is on the E side of the bay near the entrance.

(424) **Gibson Point**, the S tip of Fox Island and the N entrance point of Carr Inlet, is marked by a light. **Toliva Shoal**, nearly in midchannel 0.9 mile S of Gibson Point, consists of two rocks covered 3½ fathoms and is marked by a lighted bell buoy. An unmarked fish haven extends about 0.25 mile N from the shoal.

(425) **Carr Inlet** enters the W shore of the sound about 7½ miles SSW of Point Defiance. From the entrance, between Fox and McNeil Islands, it extends about 6 miles NW and then trends NNE for 8 miles terminating in flats at the head. Good anchorage is available in the upper reaches in 6 to 15 fathoms, soft bottom, and in several small coves on its S and E shores. From the entrance, a midchannel course is safe.

(426) A **naval restricted area** is in the S part of Carr Inlet. (See **334.1250**, chapter 2, for limits and regulations.)

(427) A **298°23'-118°23' measured nautical mile** has been established on the NE shore of McNeil Island. Range markers, consisting of white diamond daymarks with red vertical stripes, mark the ends of the measured course; the daymarks are reported to be partially obscured and not maintained.

(428) The Washington State penitentiary, on the SE side of **McNeil Island** about 0.8 mile SW of **Hyde Point**, is prominent from offshore. Vessel traffic is restricted within 100 yards of McNeil Island, which is prison property. The island is served by a ferry from Steilacoom which lands at the terminal on the S shore about a mile inside the E end of Balch Passage.

(429) **Wyckoff Shoal**, part of which bares, extends 0.8 mile NW from the NW part of McNeil Island. Lights on the W side of the shoal mark the E side of the channel leading into Pitt Passage.

(430) **Pitt Passage**, between Key Peninsula and McNeil Island, connects Drayton Passage and Carr Inlet. It is obstructed about midway of its length by **Pitt Island** and its surrounding rocks and shoals. Only the passage E of Pitt Island is used by small craft with local knowledge. In this passage the ebb (N current) is stronger than the flood and attains a velocity of 2.5 knots or more at times.

(431) **Lakebay**, at the head of **Mayo Cove** on the SW shore of Carr Inlet, is a village with a store and several small private piers. A marina here has a long pier and floats with berthage for about 35 craft; electricity, gasoline, water, and ice are available. About 7 feet can be carried to the marina pier, but the channel to the pier is difficult to navigate; strangers are advised to proceed cautiously and obtain local advice. On the E side of Mayo Cove, along **Penrose Point**, a State park has a small float with moorage for about 10 small craft. Water and a pump-out station are available at the State park.

(432) **Home**, a village on the W side of **Von Geldern Cove**, has a store and service station. A bridge crosses the cove at its head. A shoal extends from the N shore at the entrance to the cove.

(433) **Glencove** is a small settlement in Glen Cove on the W side of Carr Inlet, about 5 miles N of South Head. It is a summer recreational area with a private wharf and float. A small marina here has berths and gasoline.

(434) **Wauna** is a village at the head of Carr Inlet, where the spit enclosing **Burley Lagoon** joins the mainland. A county road extends along the spit and across the entrance to the lagoon over a fixed highway bridge to Rosedale and Gig Harbor. The bridge has a clearance of 12 feet (23 feet at center). A boat launching ramp is at Wauna just W of the bridge.

(435) **Rosedale** is a residential community on the cove on the E side of Carr Inlet and 180-foot-high **Raft Island**. There is an extensive shoal area around and between Raft Island and **Cutts Island**. Cutts Island is part of a state park. The shores of these islands are strewn with boulders. A fixed highway bridge and overhead cable extend from the S side of Raft Island to the mainland. The bridge clearance is 17 feet, and the cable, 48 feet.

(436) **Horsehead Bay**, about 1 mile long, is directly N of Green Point, at the W extremity of Hale Passage. This is a residential area with many private wharves.

(437) **Eagle Island**, small and wooded, is near the middle of Balch Passage, 0.2 mile from **Anderson Island**, and is marked on its N end by a light. Eagle Island is a State park.

(438) **Eagle Island Reef**, 300 yards W of Eagle Island, bares at low water at the S end and has a depth of 2 feet at the N end.

(439) **Drayton Passage**, between Key Peninsula and Anderson Island, is about 3 miles long in a N direction; at its N end, it connects with Pitt Passage and Balch Passage, and at its S end joins the W part of Nisqually Reach. With the exception of a spit extending 0.2 mile from the W shore, marked by a light, the waters are deep and free of dangers. A small-boat launching ramp is 0.25 mile N of the light. Estimated current velocities of 1 to 2 knots occur at the SW end of the passage.

(440) **Filucy Bay**, on the W shore opposite Balch Passage, is about 1.5 miles long and irregular in shape; it is 0.4 mile wide at the entrance. Good anchorage in 7 to 8 fathoms, muddy bottom, is available. There are numerous houses around the shores of this bay. **Longbranch**, a village in the small cove opposite the entrance, has a pier and floats for about 30 fishing and pleasure craft.

(441) **Steilacoom** is on the mainland about 9 miles SSW of Point Defiance. The town is of little commercial importance and has no waterfront facilities except for the ferry terminal which maintains service to Anderson, McNeil and Ketron Islands. Limited berthage for small craft, gasoline, water, ice, and a hoist are available at the terminal. Limited engine repairs can be made. Indifferent anchorage may be had along the waterfront close inshore, but it is not recommended as the holding ground is poor and the currents have considerable velocity. Off Steilacoom there are tide rips which, with a wind opposing the current, are dangerous to small boats.

(442) There are two large, conspicuous sand and gravel pits on the bluffs about 1.5 miles NNE of Steilacoom. A pier is at the N pit and is served by a conveyor belt used for the shipment of sand and gravel. The pier is 520 feet long, 20 to 30 feet reported alongside, and has a deck height of 14 feet. Another pier, just N of the mouth of Chambers Creek, has been abandoned and is in ruins.

(443) **Ketron Island**, 10 miles SSW of Point Defiance and privately owned and heavily wooded. A ferry from Steilacoom lands at the terminal on the NW shore three times a day. **Cormorant Passage**, 0.5 mile wide, separates the island from the mainland S. The passage is clear, but is little used.

(444) **Nisqually Reach** trends S and W around Anderson Island. The S shore is occupied for nearly 1 mile offshore by **Nisqually Flats**, the delta formed by the **Nisqually River**. The flats are very soft mud and bare at low water. A major portion is designated a National Wildlife Refuge, the boundaries are marked by signs. A section is also used for commercial aquaculture. A boat ramp at Nisqually Head is accessible only at high water. Two lights mark the steep N edge of the flats and are supplemented by a series of piles. A light marks the S tip of Anderson Island at Lyle Point. **Thompson Cove** on the W side of the point is a cable area and should not be used as an anchorage. An artificial reef is at the State park 2.7 miles W of Nisqually Head. The reef is marked by a private buoy.

(445) **Oro Bay**, in the SE part of Anderson Island, is an irregular bight between **Cole Point** and **Lyle Point**. Most of the bay is shallow; it affords an indifferent anchorage in about 10 fathoms, but is affected by the currents and affords little protection. A small shallow arm extends about 1 mile NW on the W side of the bay and is marked by private buoys. An anchorage for small craft is here.

(446) **Devils Head**, the S point of Key Peninsula, is 280 feet high and heavily wooded. A light is shown off the S tip of Devils Head.

(447) **Johnson Point**, 2 miles W of Devils Head, is 90 feet high. A light is on the sandspit at the end of the point.

(448) A marina is on the W shore of Nisqually Reach about 0.8 mile SSE of Johnson Point. The marina provides open and covered berths with 6 transient berths.

Services available include: electricity, gasoline, diesel fuel, water, ice, marine supplies, launching ramp, pump-out station, and a 3-ton marine lift.

Local magnetic disturbance

(449) Differences of as much as 3° from normal variation have been observed along Henderson Inlet.

(450) **Itsami Ledge**, covered 1 fathom, lies 1 mile WSW of Johnson Point. It is surrounded by kelp and marked by a light. This is a danger in entering Henderson Inlet or Dana Passage. A fish haven is close N of the light.

(451) **Henderson Inlet**, locally known as **South Bay**, immediately W of Johnson Point, extends about 4.5 miles in a S direction; the S part is an extensive flat. Good anchorage is inside the entrance in 5 to 6 fathoms, muddy bottom. A spit makes out about 0.2 mile N from the W point at the entrance; on the W shore, 0.8 mile S of the entrance point, is a long sandspit. Oyster beds abound in the S area of the bay.

(452) **Case Inlet**, a popular sport fishing and resort area, extends some 14 miles N from Johnson Point. The flats at its head are only 2 miles from the head of Hood Canal. Depths are irregular, from 10 to 30 fathoms, but there are no off-lying dangers.

(453) **Harstine Island** forms the W side of the S part of the inlet.

(454) A facility in Whiteman Cove, on the E side of the inlet about 3.7 miles N of Devils Head, has berthing, water, and a launching ramp.

(455) A marina in Jarrell Cove at the N end of the island has berths, electricity, gasoline, diesel fuel, water, ice, and some groceries. The pier here has 10 feet reported alongside. The 200-foot Jarrell Cove State Park pier is directly across the cove from the marina. A State park float, with a pump-out station, is farther up the cove.

(456) **Herron Island**, about 4 miles N of the entrance and 0.3 mile W of the E side, is a private island, with moorings for small craft. A ferry connects with the mainland at the village of **Herron**. The bar between the N end of Herron Island and the E shore has a least depth of about 13 feet, but with local knowledge a depth of 21 feet can be carried through by rounding the NE tip of Herron Island some 300 to 500 yards off.

(457) **McMicken Island**, 1.1 miles SW of Herron Island, is connected to Harstine Island by a sandpit which bares at low water. Anchorage with a rocky bottom and protection from S winds is on the NW side of the island.

(458) **Pickering Passage** indents the W shore of Case Inlet, about 2 miles N of Herron Island. The passage extends in a general S direction for 8 miles, connecting at its S end with Peale Passage and Totten Inlet. The shores are generally low and wooded, and the depths vary from 4½ to 15 fathoms. Except for the shoals extending E from the mouth of Hammersley Inlet, the passage is free of outlying dangers, and a midchannel course is safe. In Pickering Passage the flood current sets from Case Inlet toward Hammersley Inlet and the ebb in the opposite direction. The strongest currents are near the S end where velocities reach 2.5 knots at times. The settlements are served by highway. A fixed highway bridge with a clearance of 31 feet crosses the passage from Graham Point to Harstine Island, about 2.6 miles N of the entrance to Hammersley Inlet.

(459) **Stretch Island** is near the W shore of Case Inlet, just N of the entrance to Pickering Passage. There is no through channel W of this island. The N part of this island is partly cleared of trees and laid out in orchards; a winery and several grape juice factories, no longer operating, are here. There is a private landing wharf built out to 12 feet on the N end of the island. A fixed highway bridge with a clearance of 14 feet connects the mainland. **Grapeview** is a village opposite Stretch Island.

(460) **Reach Island**, 0.2 mile N of Stretch Island, has been subdivided for homesites and is known as **Treasure Island**. It is separated from the W shore by a shallow channel known locally as **Fair Harbor**. The channel is spanned by a fixed bridge with a clearance of 16 feet. There is a marina on the mainland 0.3 mile S of the bridge with about 70 berths, electricity, gasoline, water, ice, nautical supplies, hull and engine repair, and a launching ramp. Approaches to the marina are recommended from the S. The remainder of the channel has reported depths of 2 feet when favoring the W shore. Caution is advised when navigating more than 150 feet N of the marina.

(461) **Vaughn** is a village on the N shore of **Vaughn Bay**, which lies on the E side of Case Inlet about 4 miles from the head. There is a public launching ramp here. The combined civic center for all the small towns on the entire peninsula is at Vaughn. A channel 1½ feet deep leads to deeper water in the bay. Follow the N shore for 200 yards after entering in midchannel off the end of the spit; then cross the bay parallel with the spit at a distance of 200 yards, heading toward the S shore; then follow the S shore at a distance of 200 yards, steering toward the head of the bay. Around the shores are numerous houses and orchards, and a little-used log booming area.

(462) **Rocky Bay** is the shallow inlet N of Vaughn Bay. A channel 3 feet deep leads to the lagoon back of the sandspit near **Windy Bluff**. It is necessary to come around the small sand island N of the spit. Oysterbeds are in the E side of the bay N of the spit.

(463) **Allyn** is a village on the W side of Case Inlet near the head about 0.5 mile N of **Sherwood Creek**. A public pier and launching ramp are here. An oyster wharf is just N of Allyn.

(464) Good anchorage may be had anywhere N of Harstine Island, in 6 to 15 fathoms, muddy bottom.

(465) There are numerous farms and several small settlements whose chief industries are oyster culture, farming, and some logging. The flats near the head of the inlet are largely covered with oysterbeds.

(466) **Peale Passage**, about 4 miles long, extends NW between Harstine and Squaxin Islands, and connects with Pickering Passage. It has a controlling depth of about 10 feet. Strangers should not attempt it. The current at times attains a velocity of 2.0 knots in the narrow part of the passage, and sets N on the flood.

Chart 18456

(467) **Dana Passage**, between **Brisco Point**, the S point of Harstine Island, and the mainland, is about 2 miles long. It is the main route to Budd Inlet and Olympia, and also joins with three other bodies of water: Eld Inlet, Squaxin Passage, and Peale Passage. Squaxin Passage leads to Totten and Hammersley Inlets, and Peale Passage leads to Pickering Passage.

(468) With the exception of Itsami Ledge near its E end and a fish haven about 0.3 mile N of Itsami Ledge Light 7, Dana Passage is clear and a midchannel course may be safely followed. The currents in Dana Passage frequently attain velocities of 3 knots or more.

(469) **Boston Harbor**, a village in the cove of the same name just E of Dofflemyer Point, has a marina with berthage for about 100 craft, gasoline, diesel fuel, water, ice, limited supplies, and a launching ramp.

(470) **Budd Inlet**, 29 miles by water from Tacoma, is about 6 miles long, extending S from Dana Passage and terminating in flats that bare at the head of **East Bay** and **West Bay**. The entrance is between Cooper Point and **Dofflemyer Point**; the latter is marked by a light. The entrance to Budd Inlet is deep except for a 27-foot shoal in the middle of the entrance. The shores are comparatively low and wooded, and the depths shoal less abruptly on the E than on the W side of the inlet. East Bay and West Bay are obstructed by flats and shoals that bare for about 0.8 mile, through which channels have been dredged to the Olympia waterfront.

(471) **Olympia**, the capital of the State of Washington is at the head of East and West bays at the S end of Budd Inlet. Traffic in the port is composed primarily of container vessels, roll-on/roll-off, and break bulk.

Prominent features

(472) The capitol dome and the radio tower on the N end of the port fill area are prominent landmarks from outside the entrance channel.

Channels

(473) A **Federal project** provides for a 30-foot channel from deepwater in Budd Inlet to a 30-foot turning basin off the W side of the port terminal near the head of West Bay. The channel is marked by lighted and unlighted buoys, lights, and lighted ranges.

(474) A dredged channel with a project depth of 13 feet leads SE from the 30-foot outer channel to a mooring basin on the E side of the peninsula at the head of East Bay; the channel is marked by a lights. (See Notice to Mariners and latest editions of charts for controlling depths.)

Anchorage

(475) Good anchorage may be had anywhere inside the entrance in muddy bottom.

Dangers

(476) **Olympia Shoal**, which bares, is about 0.4 mile off the W shore, 3 miles inside the entrance. A light is on the E side of the shoal, and on its W side are lights marking the approach to the dredged channel. There are numerous shoals, piles, dolphins, and log booms on the E side of the harbor. A visible wreck, in about 47°05'14"N., 122°55'49"W., is near the approach to the dredged entrance channel to Olympia; the wreck is marked by an orange buoy.

Regulated navigation area

(477) A security zone has been established in the turning basin of West Bay. (See **33 CFR 165.1321**, chapter 2, for limits and regulations.)

Pilotage, Olympia

(478) Pilotage is compulsory for all vessels except those under enrollment or engaged exclusively in the coasting trade on the W coast of the continental United States (including Alaska) and/or British Columbia. Pilotage for Puget Sound is provided by the Puget Sound Pilots. (See Pilotage, Strait of Juan de Fuca and Puget Sound, indexed as such, chapter 12 for detail.)

Towage

(479) Tugs to 5,000 hp are available from Tacoma and Seattle. No large tugs are stationed in Olympia.

Quarantine, customs, immigration, and agricultural quarantine

(480) (See chapter 3, Vessel Arrival Inspections, and Appendix A for addresses.)

(481) **Quarantine** is enforced in accordance with regulations of the U.S. Public Health Service. (See Public Health Service, chapter 1.)

(482) Olympia is a **customs port of entry**.

(483) There are two hospitals in Olympia.

Wharves

(484) The port terminal, owned and operated by the Port of Olympia, is on the E side of the turning basin near the head of West Bay; it is the only deep-draft facility in Olympia Harbor. The terminal has a 1,750-foot face with a deck height of 20 feet and alongside depths of 35 to 40 feet; contact the Port of Olympia (360–528–8000) for the latest depths. The terminal is served by two container gantry cranes, container toplifts, a rail car switcher, and other cargo handling equipment. More than 59 acres of paved open storage is available.

Supplies

(485) Water, ice, groceries, and some marine supplies can be obtained. Diesel fuel, gasoline, and lubricants are available.

Repairs

(486) Only small craft can be repaired in Olympia. A large marina in the East Bay has a 77-ton lift that can handle craft up to 90 feet long. Machine shops are in the city. For repairs to larger vessels, the nearest facilities are in Seattle, WA.

Small-craft facilities

(487) There are many marinas at Olympia. Berths, electricity, gasoline, diesel fuel, water, ice, launching ramps, storage, and marine supplies are available. Hull and engine repairs can be made at a marina just S of the port wharf. A private yacht club has its moorings at the head of West Bay 0.3 mile S of the turning basin.

Communications

(488) Olympia is served by two major railroads. Olympia Airport is 4.5 miles S of the city.

Chart 18448

(489) **Eld Inlet**, locally known as **Mud Bay**, immediately W of Budd Inlet, is of little commercial importance. It affords good anchorage inside the entrance in 24 to 42 feet, soft bottom. A midchannel course is clear to the flats at its head. In entering, **Cooper Point**, the E point at the entrance, should be given a berth of not less than 0.2 mile. Some logging and oystering are done here.

(490) **Squaxin Passage** (see also chart 18457), S of **Squaxin Island** and **Hope Island**, is about 1 mile long and leads to Totten and Hammersley Inlets. A light on Hunter Point marks the SW entrance point of the passage. The N shore is foul; a shoal covered 19 feet is 150 yards off the W shore of Hope Island abreast Steamboat Island.

(491) The passage is narrow, and strangers should proceed with caution. The S shore should be favored, and, at the W end, the N point of Steamboat Island should be favored. The principal danger in the passage is a reef which bares at extreme low water, SE of Hope Island; a buoy is near its S end. This reef is easily avoided by keeping the N point of Steamboat Island well open of the S point of Hope Island. Tide rips are said to occur in Squaxin Passage. The usual velocity of the current is about 1.5 knots.

(492) The passage between Hope and Squaxin Islands has a least depth of 9 feet in the middle; greater depths can be carried in the passage with local knowledge.

(493) **Steamboat Island**, covered with private homes, is connected with **Carlyon Beach** on the mainland by a roadway on piling. The island, practically a part of the mainland, has abrupt shores and is heavily wooded. The NW end of the island terminates in a long sandspit marked on the end by a daybeacon. A private pier is on the NW side of the island, and a pier and large building of a private yacht club are on Carlyon Beach just E of the roadway on piling.

(494) **Totten Inlet** extends 9 miles SW from the W end of Squaxin Passage. A depth of 30 feet can be carried to a point off the entrance to Skookum Inlet. A 3½-fathom shoal is about in midchannel at the entrance, 620 yards SW of the S end of Steamboat Island. A spit extends W for about 100 yards from Steamboat Island. In entering, favor the W shore to avoid the spit and shoal. The inlet shoals gradually to near **Burns Point**, 100 feet high, on the S shore, where it bares at low tide.

(495) **Oyster Bay**, S of Burns Point, is an extensive mudflat; oysters are grown in this area, and there are log booms. S of the entrance to **Little Skookum Inlet**, along the shores of Totten Inlet, are rock or concrete walls enclosing the oysterbeds. The walls are a danger to navigation, and the oyster industry discourages boatmen from entering these waters. Oyster-processing wharves are on the N side of the inlet. Local knowledge is required to get to them. Good anchorage may be had anywhere inside the entrance of Little Skookum Inlet.

Chart 18457

(496) **Hammersley Inlet** indents the W shore of the sound about 1 mile N of the W end of Squaxin Passage. It is about 6 miles long, expanding at its head into **Oakland Bay**, which is 3.5 miles long in a NE direction. The inlet is obstructed by shoals, particularly at its mouth, where there is an extensive bar. The rocky shoals have been partly removed. The channel, marked by lights on **Libby Point** and **Church Point** has a controlling depth of about 8 feet to the town of Shelton on Oakland Bay. It is navigated only by small craft, and by tugs with log rafts and railroad car floats; local knowledge is required. Tidal current velocities may reach 5 knots at times in the constricted parts of the inlet. (See Tidal Current Tables for current predictions.) Vessels enter on the flood, usually after half tide, and leave on the ebb, usually before maximum strength. Hammersley Inlet is considered dangerous for strangers.

(497) Vessels with sharp rise of bilge should avoid the inlet as there is danger of capsizing in the strong current in case of grounding.

(498) **Arcadia** is a small settlement on the S point of the entrance of Hammersley Inlet. It has a public ramp for launching small pleasure craft.

(499) **Shelton**, at the head of the inlet, is a town of some commercial importance. Extensive logging, lumber, and lumber product manufacturing interests are centered here. The W end of **Oakland Bay** is used primarily as a storage area for logs trucked in from the Olympic Peninsula to be used by the mills at Shelton. Hammersly Inlet receives little commercial traffic. Shelton is on

a branch of the Burlington Northern Railroad; lumber is shipped largely by rail, however, some railroad car ferrying is done. Railway trestles used as log dumps extend E across the flats from the Shelton waterfront. The Port of Shelton marina, 0.3 mile from the head of the Shelton waterfront and on the N shore, has berths, electricity, gasoline, and water. A yacht club has its facilities at the marina. Some marine supplies are available in the town. There are no haulout or repair facilities at Shelton. Oysters are cultivated in the shoal portions of Oakland Bay.

| TIDAL INFORMATION ||||||
Chart	Station	LAT/LONG	Mean Higher High Water*	Mean High Water*	Mean Low Water*
18421	Patos Island Wharf, Haro Strait	48°47'N/122°58'W	8.6	7.9	2.6
18421	Bellingham, Bellingham Bay	48°45'N/122°30'W	8.5	7.8	2.4
18421	Blaine, Semiahmoo Bay, Strait of Georgia	49°00'N/122°46'W	9.5	8.7	2.7
18421	Roche Harbor, San Juan Island	48°37'N/123°09'W	7.6	7.0	2.5
18428	Crescent Harbor	48°17'N/122°37'W	11.4	10.6	2.8
18440	Ediz Hook, Port Angeles, Strait of Juan de Fuca	48°08'N/123°25'W	7.0	6.3	2.2
18444	Everett, Possession Sound	47°59'N/122°13'W	11.1	10.2	2.8
18446	Brownsville, Port Orchard, Puget Sound	47°39'N/122°37'W	11.8	10.9	2.9
18446	Poulsbo, Liberty Bay, Puget Sound	47°44'N/122°38'W	11.7	10.8	2.9
18446	Port Madison, Puget Sound	47°42'N/122°32'W	11.4	10.5	2.8
18446	Edmonds, Puget Sound	47°49'N/122°23'W	10.9	10.1	2.8
18448	Steilacoom, Cormorant Passage	47°10'N/122°36'W	13.5	12.6	3.0
18449	Port Blakely, Puget Sound	47°36'N/122°31'W	11.5	10.6	2.8
18450	Duwamish Waterway, Puget Sound	47°32'N/122°19'W	11.1	10.2	2.7
18450	Seattle, Puget Sound	47°36'N/122°20'W	11.4	10.5	2.8
18452	Bremerton, Sinclair Inlet, Port Orchard	47°34'N/122°37'W	11.7	10.9	2.9
18453	Tacoma, Commencement Bay, Sitcum Waterway	47°16'N/122°25'W	11.8	10.9	2.9
18456	Dofflemeyer Point, Boston Harbor (Budd Inlet)	47°09'N/122°54'W	14.4	13.4	3.1
18456	Olympia Budd Inlet, Puget Sound	47°07'N/122°54'W	14.6	13.6	3.1
18457	Shelton, Oakland Bay, Puget Sound	47°13'N/123°05'W	14.2	13.2	2.6
18457	Arcadia, Totten Inlet, Puget Sound	47°12'N/122°56'W	14.4	13.4	3.0
18458	Seabeck, Seabeck Bay, Hood Canal	47°39'N/122°50'W	11.5	10.6	3.0
18458	Bangor Wharf, Hood Canal	47°45'N/122°44'W	11.1	10.2	2.9
18458	Zelatched Point, Dabob Bay, Hood Canal	47°43'N/122°49'W	11.5	10.5	2.9
18464	Port Townsend (Point Hudson)	48°07'N/122°45'W	8.6	7.9	2.6
18464	Oak Bay, Admiralty Inlet	48°01'N/122°43'W	9.4	8.6	2.6
18471	Port Townsend, Admiralty Inlet	48°07'N/122°45'W	8.5	7.8	2.5
18474	Gig Harbor, Puget Sound	47°20'N/122°35'W	11.8	11.0	2.8
18476	Lofall, Hood Canal	47°49'N/122°39'W	10.7	9.8	2.9
18476	Union, Hood Canal	47°22'N/123°06'W	11.8	10.9	3.0
18477	Port Ludlow, Hood Canal	47°56'N/122°41'W	9.9	9.1	2.7
18477	Port Gamble, Hood Canal	47°52'N/122°35'W	10.3	9.4	2.7

* Heights in feet referred to datum of sounding MLLW.
Real-time water levels, tide predictions, and tidal current predictions are available at:
http://tidesandcurrents.noaa.gov
To determine mean tide range subtract Mean Low Water from Mean High Water.
Data as of October 2012

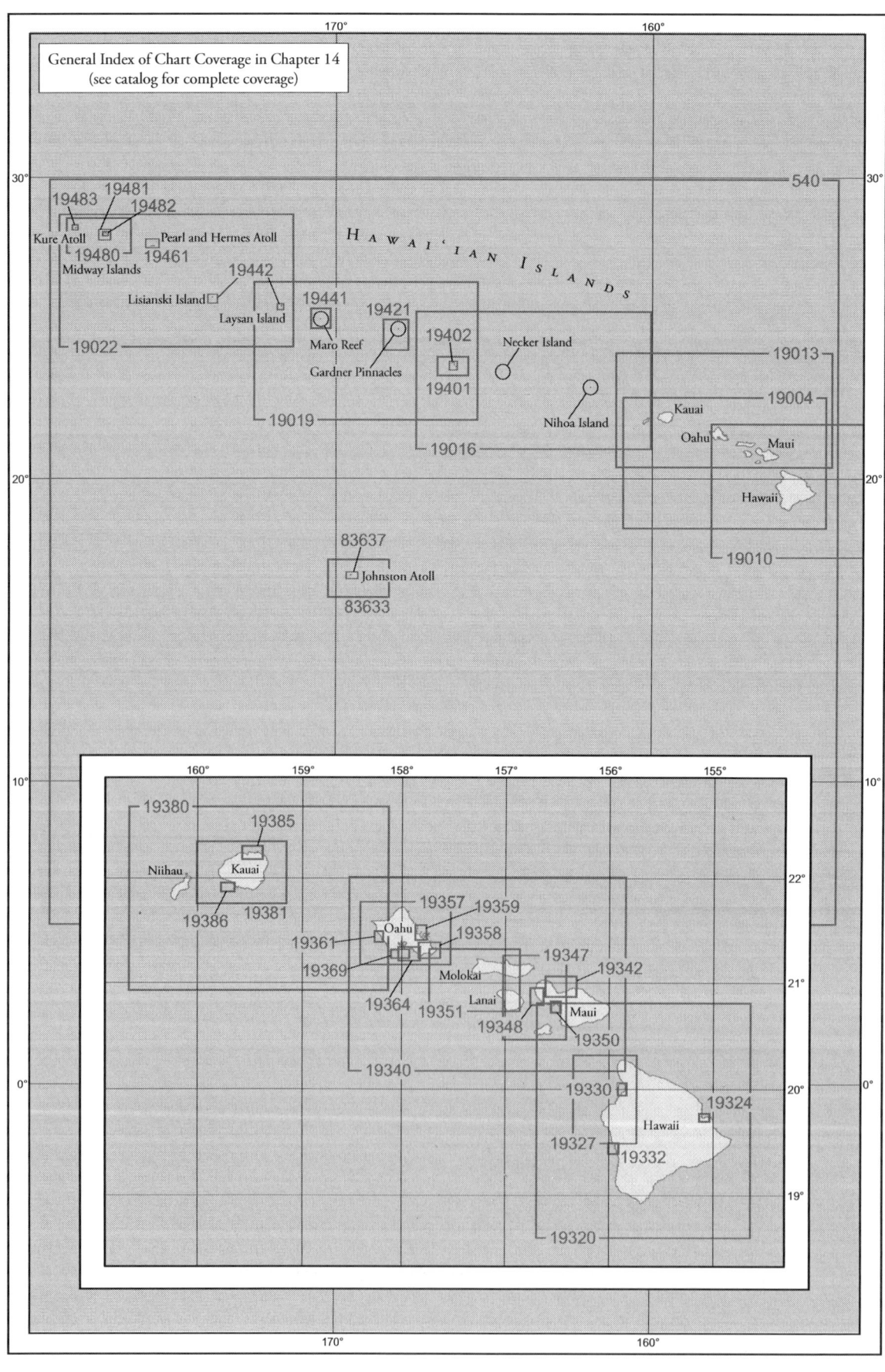

Hawaii

Chart 540

(1) **Hawaii**, a Polynesian kingdom until 1893 and then briefly a republic, requested and was granted annexation to the United States in 1898 and was given a territorial form of government in 1900. By Presidential proclamation of August 21, 1959, Hawaii officially became the 50th of the United States.

(2) The **Hawai'ian Islands**, an archipelago, consist of eight large islands, plus many islets, reefs, and shoals, strung out from SE to NW for 1,400 nautical miles in the north-central Pacific Ocean. The archipelago extends from 18°55'N. to 28°25'N., and from 154°49'W. to 178°20'W., straddling the Tropic of Cancer. All the islands of the archipelago, except 2-square-mile Midway, are part of the State of Hawaii.

(3) The capital and chief population center of the State is Honolulu on the island of O'ahu; the port is 2,091 nautical miles from San Francisco, 4,685 miles from the Panama Canal, and 2,477 miles from Anchorage, AK. Land area of the State totals 6,425 square statute miles, of which the "Big Island" of Hawaii alone accounts for nearly 63 percent. The other seven large islands are, in order of size, Maui, O'ahu, Kauai, Moloka'i, Lanai, Ni'ihau, and Kahoolawe.

(4) The major islands are mountainous and of volcanic origin; the Island of Hawaii has two volcanoes that are still active. Elevations range from sea level to nearly 14,000 feet, with many peaks in excess of 2,500 feet. Although coastal plains, valley floors, and certain plateaus are relatively flat, much of the surface is quite rugged, with high ranges and deep ravines or gorges.

(5) Nearly all of the island streams may be classified as mountain torrents, although some of them can be navigated for short distances by small boats. Most of the streams are on the N and E coasts, where rainfall generally is heaviest.

(6) The 20-fathom depth curve is seldom more than 1 mile from shore and usually is not far from the coral reefs that fringe much of the island coastline. The bottom generally pitches off rapidly to great depths from a narrow coastal shelf, and the few off-lying dangers usually are indicated by breakers or by a change in color of the water. Under normal conditions the color of the water changes from a deep blue in the open ocean to a blue-green between the 10- and 15-fathom curves; bottom features become visible at 6 to 7 fathoms.

(7) **Tourism** is Hawaii's bedrock industry accounting for the largest portion of the state's economy with over 6 million visitors arriving annually. All branches of the military maintain a large presence in the islands, specifically on Oahu, due to Hawaii's strategic location. Hawaii, once dominated by sugar and pineapple production, has seen those crops diminish, and now has committed itself to diversified agriculture such as seed corn, floriculture, unprocessed sugar, macadamia nuts, coffee and cattle. Science and technology, film and television production, sports, and ocean research and development round out the state's economy.

(8) **Fish Aggregating Devices** (FADs) along the coastal waters of the main Hawai'ian Islands make the area very popular with commercial and recreational fishermen. For reasons unknown, fish in the N and W Pacific Ocean frequently gather in schools under floating objects. FADs may be as sophisticated as floating devices, often buoys, with electronic equipment attached for tracking or as crude as floating logs or other objects. The FADs in Hawai'ian waters, established by the state, are yellow, 6 feet across at the base, and show a quick flashing yellow light atop a 5-foot steel pole. The buoys display 12-inch white letters. These buoys frequently break loose and/or become unlighted. Mariners are advised to use caution when in the vicinity of the FADs.

Polynesian-English Geographic Glossary (English meanings of Polynesian words used frequently in Hawaiian geographic names)	
Akau – north	**Kowa** – channel, strait, sound
Ana – cave	**Lae** – cape, point
Awa – bay, cove	**Lapa** – ridge
Hale – house	**Loko** – pond
Hana – bay	**Lua** – crater, pit
Heiau – place of worship, temple	**Mauna** – mountain, hill, peak
Hema – south	**Moana** – ocean
Hikina – east	**Moku** – islet, island, rock
Hono – bay, cove	**Pali** – cliff, peak, point
Kai – sea	**Pele** – volcano
Kapu – prohibited	**Pohaku** – rock
Komohana – west	**Puu** – hill(s), mountain, peak
Kona – leeward	**Wai** – water
Koolau – north	**Wailele** – waterfall

Emergency signal flag

(9) The State of Hawaii has adopted an emergency signal flag as one of the signals that may be used or displayed when a vessel is in need of assistance; the flag should be at least **2 feet square** and **international orange**

in color. This distress signal is authorized by the Hawaii Boating Law.

Harbors and ports

(10) Honolulu is by far the largest commercial deepwater facility in Hawaii. Other commercial deepwater harbors are Hilo and Kawaihae on Hawaii Island, Kahului on Maui, and Nawiliwili and Port Allen on Kauai. These ports service both overseas and interisland shipping.

(11) Hawaii has several commercial barge harbors engaged in interisland shipping. Some of the more important are at Kaumalaupau on Lanai, and Kaunakakai, Haleolono, and Kalaupapa on Moloka'i. These harbors service only light-draft vessels.

Marine radio communications

(12) Honolulu is the only port that maintains a commercial radio communication watch. Vessels desiring services at other Hawai'ian ports must make arrangements in advance.

COLREGS Demarcation Lines

(13) The lines established for the Hawai'ian Islands and United States Pacific Island Possessions are described in **80.1410 through 80.1495**, chapter 2.

Control over movement of vessels

(14) Regulations require advance notice of vessel's time of arrival to Captain of the Port. (See **160.1 through 160.201**, chapter 2, for regulations.)

(15) Submerged submarine operations are conducted at various times in this area; proceed with caution. (For information on submarine emergency identification signals, see chapter 1.)

Anchorages

(16) Anchorages are numerous except on the N and E sides of the islands where shelter from the trade winds is a major requirement. The anchorages on the S and W sides of the islands are unsafe during kona weather.

Regulated Navigation Area

(17) A security zone has been established for all waters within 1,000 yards of any U.S. Navy submarine that is operating in the Sector Honolulu Captain of the Port Zone and that is being escorted by the U.S. Coast Guard. (See **165.1 through 165.13 and 165.1412**, chapter 2, for limits and regulations.)

Tides

(18) The periodic tides around Hawaii average only 1 to 2 feet. The tides along the N coasts usually occur about 1 to 1½ hours earlier than the tides along the S coasts. (See Tide Tables for daily predictions of times and heights of high and low waters for Honolulu.)

(19) The effect of strong winds added to normal tidal action may cause water level to fall considerably below chart datum and/or rise considerably above mean higher high water. A heavy surf, particularly from N, gives the impression of higher tides on the exposed beaches; there is usually little actual increase under such conditions. On the S side of O'ahu, where the trades usually blow directly off the land, a shift to kona winds or to a calm has been observed to raise the tide level a few tenths of a foot.

Currents

(20) The variable oceanic currents in the vicinity of Hawaii are believed to depend mostly upon the velocity and direction of the wind, but there are many reports of strong NE currents setting against the prevailing trades. There is a prevailing W oceanic drift in the vicinity of the larger islands and as far W as Necker Island.

(21) The tidal currents are generally rather weak and are influenced by winds and oceanic movements. Such currents are mainly reversing in the channels between the larger islands, but they are rotary in more open waters, particularly around the W islets, and shift direction continuously in a clockwise movement.

Tsunami (seismic sea wave)

(22) The Hawai'ian Archipelago has been visited from time to time by tsunami, which causes enormous destruction. Loss of life and property can be lessened by intelligent response to warnings that such waves are imminent. (See chapter 1 for basic discussion.)

(23) The National Oceanic and Atmospheric Administration administers a tsunami warning system that alerts the Hawai'ian Islands, other Pacific islands, and most of the countries bordering the Pacific. The system has an operating center at the Pacific Tsunami Warning Center, Ewa Beach, O'ahu, and includes scattered seismograph stations for quick detection and location of submarine earthquakes, a network of wave-detecting and reporting stations throughout the Pacific, a high-priority communication setup, and an extensive international arrangement for broadcasting warnings of possible sea waves.

(24) Military authorities in Honolulu will issue warnings to all military bases that might be affected. Local base commanders will put into effect any precautions deemed necessary. Elsewhere warnings will be broadcast by civilian authorities. Disaster committees have been set up on all the major islands to alert the population and to assist in evacuation and rescue as needed. In Honolulu and Hilo, former air raid sirens now operated by the police department will be used. On O'ahu, Civil Air Patrol planes equipped with sirens will fly the shoreline and sound the alarm. This service will later be extended to the other islands. On all the major islands, police cars equipped with sirens will patrol the coastal areas. Local commercial broadcasting stations will interrupt all programs to give the latest information and instructions.

(25) All warnings will also be broadcast by the National Weather Service on NOAA Weather Radio. (See Appendix A for locations and frequencies of the stations.)

(26) Should a warning occur when a radio station is closed down, it will come on the air immediately and remain on until the all clear is sounded. When an alarm is given, all persons are warned to turn on their radios to a local broadcasting station for information and instructions. If they have no radio and cannot find access to one nearby, they should seek high ground. Telephones are apt to be flooded with calls and therefore cannot be relied on during a warning.

(27) When a warning is received, persons should vacate waterfront areas and seek high ground. The safest procedure for ships will depend upon the amount of time available, and this may not always be known. A ship well out at sea would ride such waves safely, and hence, if time is available to put to sea, that would be the safest action. During the 1946 wave, the master of a ship lying offshore near Hilo felt no unusual waves, though he could see great waves breaking on the shore. Crews of fishing boats in the Hawaiʻian area also reported no unusual conditions at that time. On the other hand, the crew of a ship in the harbor may have a difficult time averting serious damage.

(28) The destructive force is usually greater on the sides of the islands facing the oncoming waves, but this directional effect is frequently lacking and the waves may reach their greatest heights on the leeward sides of the islands. The waves may also attain great heights in funnel-shaped bays and at capes or other places where a submarine ridge projects seaward toward the oncoming wave. Unusual heights may be attained at any place where two waves traveling different paths arrive at the same time to reinforce each other. There is still much to be learned about these waves, and the best policy is to avoid them in any way possible.

Weather, Hawaii

(29) The climate of the Hawaiʻian Islands is unusually pleasant for a tropical area, the result principally of the marked marine influence and the persistent trade winds. Considering the latitude of the islands, there is relatively little uncomfortable heat. The discomfort that is occasionally experienced usually occurs when the trades are temporarily displaced by light variable or south winds, which are accompanied by comparatively higher humidities. The outstanding climatic features of the islands are the dominant trade-wind influences throughout all seasons, the remarkable variation in rainfall over adjacent areas, and the uniform temperature regime which varies slightly throughout the year.

(30) During the summer season the trades blow with a high degree of persistency. As a result, uncomfortable periods are usually delayed until fall, and thus follow by weeks or possibly as much as two months the period when the highest temperatures occur. Rains most frequently fall at night.

(31) Thunderstorms are infrequent and practically never severe. Hail seldom occurs. Occasionally local storms are accompanied by winds of sufficient force to do limited damage, but severe storms such as hurricanes or tornadoes are rare. So-called thick weather is almost unknown to the extent of seriously interfering with shipping, and is usually confined to mist and rain, rather than being in the form of fog. Interference to shipping or travel because of bad weather is almost unknown.

(32) The strongest influence in the pressure pattern underlying the general circulation of air over the Hawaiʻian Islands area is the persistent and semipermanent high-pressure cell known as the Pacific high. The clockwise circulation around this cell, coupled with a slight deflection of the surface winds away from the high pressure, result in the NE trades that are the dominant winds of the area.

(33) The trade-wind influence is dominant in all seasons throughout the greater part of all the islands. In some local areas, winds deviate from the general pattern because of topography. In coastal areas where mountains to the E project high above sea level, as they do in the kona districts of the Island of Hawaii, the trades are cut off, resulting in prevalent SW winds with land and sea breezes in evidence. Such effects may be rather general in some areas and extremely local in others.

(34) The Hawaiʻian Islands lie on the extremities of both the Western North Pacific typhoon area and the Eastern North Pacific hurricane area. Therefore, a tropical cyclone from either region is rare. **Typhoons** can form in any month, but they rarely cross 180°; when they do they are usually extratropical and well N of the islands. It is not impossible, but highly improbable, that a typhoon will move through the Hawaiʻian Islands.

(35) It is more probable that an Eastern North Pacific hurricane would hit the islands. These storms, prevalent from May through November, originate from the North American coast W between 10°N and 20°N. Most hurricanes either recurve or dissipate before reaching the Hawaiʻian Islands. August is the most favorable month for one of these storms to reach the area, although they have occurred from July through November. Since 1842 at least six storms have hit the Big Island. However, all six storms were in the dissipation stage and no major damage was reported.

(36) It is a different case however, for the western islands especially Kauai. Since 1842, Kauai has had a direct impact from a northeast Pacific hurricane at least four times. Perhaps the most noteworthy storms were Hurricane Dot on August 7, 1959. Dot was a minimal hurricane with only 75-knot winds. Hurricane Iniki, with maximum winds estimated at 125 knots and gusts estimated at 150 knots slammed into Kauai early on September 12, 1992. Damage was extensive throughout Kauai. Damage from the ocean was heaviest along the south shore of Kauai and affected shoreline hotels and condominiums. Wind damage was extremely heavy

throughout Kauai, as many houses or buildings were flattened or lost their roofs. Iniki left 14,350 damaged or destroyed homes on the island. Electric and telephone services were lost throughout the island and only 20% of the power had been restored four weeks after the event. Crop damage was extensive, especially to fruit trees and sugar cane. The monetary value of the damage caused by Iniki on Kauai was estimated at $1.8 billion. Six deaths were connected to the storm.

(37) The word "kona" is of Polynesian origin and means leeward. It refers to the S winds and accompanying weather on the normally leeward slopes of the principal Hawai'ian Islands which, because of the wind shift, have temporarily become the windward slopes.

(38) The konas, which occur most frequently during October through April, provide the major climatic variations of the Hawai'ian Islands. During these storms, heavy rainfall and cloudiness can be expected on the lee sides of coasts and slopes, which, under the usual wind pattern, receive less cloudiness and may have almost no rain. Near gales may occur, especially near points where the air tends to funnel into sharp mountain passes near the coasts. At such times leeward anchorages may become unsafe for smaller craft.

(39) The complicated rainfall pattern over the islands results chiefly from the effects of the rugged terrain on the persistent trade winds. Frequent and heavy showers fall almost daily on windward and upland areas, while rains of sufficient intensity and duration to cause more than temporary inconvenience are infrequent over the lower sections of leeward areas.

(40) In the districts where the trade winds are dominant, rains are decidedly heavier at night than during the day. This applies generally to the greater part of the islands. Daytime showers, usually light, often occur while the sun continues to shine.

(41) Considerably more rain falls from November through April over the islands as a whole than from May through October. It is not unusual for an entire summer month to go by without measurable rain falling at some points on the Maui isthmus; at times considerably longer dry periods may occur in that locality.

(42) Elevation is the major control factor in determining temperatures, although location, whether in a leeward or windward position, is also a noticeable factor. The highest temperatures reached during the day in leeward districts are usually higher than those attained in windward areas. The daily range is also greater over leeward districts where, because of less cloudiness, the maximum temperatures are higher and the minimum temperatures usually lower.

(43) August and September are the warmest months, and January and February are the coldest. At Honolulu there is an average monthly range between a low of 73.0°F (22.8°C) in January and February, and a high of 81.3°F (27.4°C) in August. The extreme range of temperature at Honolulu for the 46-year period of record is from a low of 52°F for January 1969, to a high of 95°F recorded in September 1994. This spread of only 43°F (24°C) between the extreme high and extreme low temperatures is small when compared with ranges at Pacific coast ports.

(44) All coastal areas are subject to the relatively high humidities associated with a marine climate. Humidities, however, vary considerably, with high percentages over and near the windward slopes to low percentages on the leeward sides of the higher elevations.

(45) At Honolulu the normally warm months of August and September are usually comfortable because of the persistency of the NE trades which bring moderate humidities. Unpleasant weather is more likely later during the autumn or early winter when the trades may diminish and give way to S winds. During these periods known locally as "kona weather" ("kona storms" when stormy), the humidity may become oppressively high.

Routes

(46) Between the islands, proceed on rhumb lines as direct as safe navigation permits.

Honolulu to Panama

(47) Rhumb lines through 21°14'N., 157°39'W., and 21°18'N., 157°00'W.; thence great circle to 8°40'N., 88°00'W., off shoals reported S of Guardian Bank; thence rhumb lines through 7°05'N., 81°45'W.

Honolulu to San Diego, Los Angeles, San Francisco, and Strait of Juan de Fuca

(48) (See routes in chapter 3.)

Honolulu to Anchorage

(49) Rhumb lines through 21°19'N., 157°36'W., and 59°00'N., 151°20'W.

Radar

(50) Most mariners rely on a combination of visual and radar piloting for interisland navigation. It is reported that landfall at a distance of 20 to 30 miles is not uncommon. The generally high, rugged coastline of the islands provide good and well-defined radar returns; some navigators have reported radar contact at 40 miles.

Pilotage, Hawaii, General

(51) Pilotage is compulsory for all foreign vessels and for U.S. vessels under register in the foreign trade; it is optional for U.S. vessels in the coastwise trade. Hawaii Pilots provide pilotage service to several ports in the islands, namely, Honolulu Harbor, Hilo Harbor, Kahului Harbor, Port Allen Harbor, Nawiliwili Harbor, and Kawaihae Harbor. Specific information is given in the description of the various ports.

Towage

(52) Tugs are available at the more important ports. (See description of port for further information.) Honolulu has some salvage equipment.

Quarantine, customs, immigration, and agricultural quarantine

(53) (See chapter 3, Vessel Arrival Inspections, and Appendix A for addresses.)

(54) **Quarantine** is enforced in accordance with regulations of the U.S. Public Health Service. (See Public Health Service, chapter 1.) There are good hospitals on Hawaii, Moloka'i, Maui, Lanai, O'ahu, and Kauai.

(55) Honolulu is a **customs port of entry**. (See Appendix A for lists of other ports of entry.)

Harbor regulations

(56) These are established by the Harbors Division, Hawaii Department of Transportation, which also assigns harbormasters to the deepwater ports and the commercial barge harbors.

Supplies

(57) Honolulu is the principal supply center for the State. Water is available at most of the wharves and piers at the deepwater ports. Gasoline, diesel fuel, ice and minor items of marine supplies are available at the smaller ports.

Repairs

(58) Honolulu has a floating drydock that can handle medium-size vessels. The other ports have only minor facilities for small vessels.

Communications

(59) Honolulu is a major port of call for transpacific passenger and cargo vessels; air service, passenger and freight, includes scheduled flights to the other islands, to the mainland, and to W and SW Pacific areas. The other deepwater ports have regular interisland barge service and are irregular ports of call for transpacific vessels; interisland passenger travel is almost entirely by air.

Standard Time

(60) The State of Hawaii uses Hawaii-Aleutian standard time, which is 10 hours slow of Greenwich mean time. Example: When it is 1200 at Greenwich, it is 0200 in Honolulu. Midway Islands use Samoa standard time, which is 11 hours slow of Greenwich mean time. Example: When it is 1200 at Greenwich, it is 0100 at Midway Islands.

Daylight saving time

(61) Daylight saving time is not observed in the State of Hawaii.

Chart 19320

(62) **Hawaii**, at the SE end of the archipelago, is the "Big Island"; its area of 4,021 square statute miles is twice that of all the other islands in Hawaii State combined. The island is roughly triangular in shape, 82 nautical miles N to S and 72 miles E to W.

(63) Hawaii is also the **Volcano Island**; it has five volcanoes, two of which–Mauna Loa and Kilauea–are still active. **Mauna Kea** and **Mauna Loa**, the two volcanoes that dominate the island, rise to heights of nearly 14,000 feet and are the highest in the State; from their summits, the land descends gradually with occasional cinder cones and lesser peaks dotting the slopes. Lava flows are numerous, and some reach the coast. **Kilauea**, 20 miles E of Mauna Loa and 9 miles from the SE coast, appears to be a crater in the side of its towering neighbor, but is really a separate peak with an elevation of more than 4,000 feet.

(64) **Hualalai**, a volcano dormant since 1801, rises to an elevation of 8,269 feet near the middle of the W coast. A peak of the **Kohala Mountains** rises to an elevation of 5,505 feet from the **Kohala Peninsula** at the NW end of the island.

(65) A highway encircles the island, and another leads from Hilo to Waimea by way of the pass between Mauna Kea and Mauna Loa.

Anchorages

(66) There is little shelter from the NE trades along the NE and SE sides of the island. Good anchorage is available along much of the W coast, but there are some areas so steep-to that anchorage is not practicable.

Currents

(67) The currents generally follow the NE trade wind, but occasionally set against it. One current follows the coast NW from Cape Kumukahi, the E extremity of Hawaii, and around Upolu Point, the N extremity. Another current follows the coast SW from Cape Kumukahi around Kalae, the S extremity, and thence N to Upolu Point; the latter flow is accompanied by an inshore counter current which sets SE from Hanamalo Point around Kalae and thence NE to Keauhou Point. An inshore current sets N from Hanamalo Point and sometimes attains considerable velocity. There are reports of strong NE currents off Makolea Point and strong N currents at Mahukona; another report states that currents offshore from Makolea Point set E toward the coast. Currents are weak at Kawaihae; SW currents with velocities of 0.5 knot have been observed in Honokaope and Kiholo Bays.

Weather, The Big Island

(68) The NE trade winds seem to divide at Cape Kumukahi, one part following the coast Northwestward and losing its force when it rounds Upolu Point, the other

part following the coast Southwestward and around Kalae. On the W coast of Hawaii, except at Mahukona, the sea breeze sets in about 0900 and continues until displaced by the land breeze that usually springs up after sundown. Vessels bound E to ports on the windward side of the island should pass Upolu Point close-to and avoid the heavier offshore winds.

(69) During the trades, the NE coast frequently is clouded over in early morning, but there is clear weather 1 or 2 miles (2 to 4 km) offshore; when the breeze picks up about 0900 the clouds are driven inland. Rainfall varies greatly with locality; the greatest amount is along the windward side, the kona highlands get a moderate amount, and a little reaches the Kau District and the W coast.

(70) The NE coast of Hawaii Island has a length of about 77 miles between Upolu Point, the N extremity, and Cape Kumukahi, the E extremity. This coast is mostly bold, and all dangers can be avoided by giving it a berth of 2 miles. Hilo Bay is the only sheltered harbor or anchorage.

Chart 19327

(71) The numerous bluffs in the vicinity of **Upolu Point** appear quite similar from seaward. Several structures are prominent on the point: two buildings on the S side of Upolu Point Airport, an aerobeacon atop a wooden tripod, and three blue silos with white tops S of the airport. A wind farm with several large wind turbines, adjacent to the silos and centered at 20°15'31"N., 155°51'16"W., is very prominet on Upolu Point. The country back of the point is cattle range; the camps and villages are generally situated high on the bluffs and among the occasional clumps of trees.

(72) **Kauhola Point Light** (20°14'47"N., 155°46'17"W.), 108 feet above the water, is shown from a 86-foot white cylindrical concrete tower on the low point 5 miles E of Upolu Point. A dangerous reef, usually marked by breakers, extends 0.3 mile from Kauhola Point; passing vessels should give the point a berth of 2 miles.

(73) Local vessels sometimes anchor in **Keawaeli Bay**, on the W side of Kauhola Point, in depths of about 4 fathoms with the light 0.3 mile distant on bearing 090°. Protection is afforded vessels forced to leave anchorage on the W coast during kona storms. **Halaula**, the principal village in the vicinity, is 1 mile inland from the light.

(74) **Akoakoa Point** is 2.8 miles SE of Kauhola Point. The country SE of Akoakoa Point rises gradually to the **Kohala Mountains**, which are heavily wooded to their summits.

Chart 19320

(75) The 10-mile stretch of coast between Akoakoa Point and Waipio Valley is backed by cliffs ranging up to 1,300 feet in height, and deep gorges that extend well inland. Waterfalls are numerous. The cliff faces have a general brownish appearance, but in some places they are covered with vegetation from top to bottom.

(76) **Honokane Iki Stream** empties into a narrow bay about 9.2 miles SE of Upolu Point. The bay affords fair protection and possible landing places for small boats. A rock awash, 0.5 mile offshore from the stream, is surrounded by depths of 12 to 14 fathoms. A rock, covered 2 fathoms, is about 0.75 mile E of the bay in about 20°12'01"N., 155°42'20"W.

(77) Three rocky islets, the largest 230 feet high, are about 300 yards offshore 0.8 mile SE of Honokane Iki Stream. Between Akoakoa Point and the islets, the bottom is fairly regular and slopes gradually to the 20-fathom depth curve, which is about 0.7 mile offshore.

(78) **Waimanu Valley**, 14.5 miles SE of Upolu Point, splits the highest cliffs in the vicinity and is the second largest ravine along this coast. Waimanu Bay may be used as an anchorage in favorable weather; there are depths of 7 fathoms 0.2 mile offshore from the ravine.

(79) **Waipio Valley**, the largest ravine along this coast, is 17.5 miles SE of Upolu Point. The valley is a remarkable cleft in the bluffs and is easily recognized. Taro is grown in the vicinity of **Waipio**, a small village near the mouth of the valley. In favorable weather, anchorage may be found in depths of 7 to 9 fathoms 0.3 mile off the valley or under the bluffs to the E.

(80) From Waipio Valley E the cliffs become lower, and at Kukuihaele the coast is a comparatively low bluff 30 to 300 feet high. The slopes between Waipio Valley and Hilo are covered in patches of feral sugarcane mixed with thick vegetation to an elevation of about 2,000 feet; continuing upward toward Mauna Kea, the slopes are wooded to about 2,600 feet and then present a barren appearance. Mauna Kea is frequently snowcapped during the winter.

Chart 19322

(81) **Kukuihaele Point Light** (20°07'41"N., 155°33'22"W.), 154 feet above the water, is shown from a 27-foot white concrete tower at **Kukuihaele**, 19 miles SE of Upolu Point.

(82) **Honokaa** is 24 miles SE of Upolu Point. A power plant (Hamakua Energy) with two storage tanks, two stacks, and a cooling tower is prominent just N of Honokaa in about 20°05'38"N., 155°28'13"W. A reef that usually breaks extends 170 yards N from the landing and is marked by several bare rocks. No shelter is available during normal weather, as the landing is open to the N and E.

Chart 19326

(83) **Paauhau**, 26 miles SE of Upolu Point, is marked by the masonry of the abandoned inclined railway that leads to the top of the bluff. The shore at the foot of the

bluff consists of rocks and ledges over which the sea breaks constantly. The small concrete landing at the foot of the masonry incline offers little protection from the NE trades.

Chart 19320

(84) **Paauilo** is 31 miles SE of Upolu Point and a mile inland.

(85) **Ookala**, about 36 miles SE of Upolu Point, is on the edge of a bluff on the S side of a deep gulch. A lighted microwave tower is prominent.

(86) **Kaawalii Gulch** is about 1.5 miles SE of Ookala. In this locality the country back of the coast changes slightly in appearance; hummocky fields are noticeable.

(87) **Laupāhoehoe Point,** 39 miles SE of Upolu Point, is low and flat and makes out about 0.3 mile from a deep gulch. **Laupāhoehoe Point Light** (19°59'37"N., 155°14'26"W.), 39 feet above the water, is shown from a pole with a black and white diamond-shaped daymark on the point. The outer end of the point is a mass of black lava rock which is broken into detached ledges that extend 250 yards seaward from the light. The seas usually break with considerable force over the ledges.

(88) **Laupāhoehoe** is at the inner end of the point. A boat ramp is in a 30-foot opening in the rock on the SE side of the point. A breakwater, marked by a light, offers some protection for small boats in the area.

(89) **Maulua Bay**, 1.7 miles SE of Papaaloa, is a 0.3-mile indentation in the coast at the mouth of a gulch which is spanned by a high bridge. In favorable weather, small boats can be beached on the shingle at the head of the bay. Only slight protection is afforded from the NE trades. **Ninole** is 1.5 miles SE of the bay.

(90) **Honohina**, 6.5 miles SE of Laupāhoehoe Point, is a settlement on the plain between two gulches. No stacks or prominent buildings are to be seen from seaward. The land has lost its hummocky appearance, and the cane-covered fields are more uniform, although still broken by gulches. Between Honohina and Hilo the bluffs gradually decrease in height and finally disappear.

(91) **Hakalau Bay**, 8.5 miles SE of Laupāhoehoe Point, lies at the mouth of **Hakalau Gulch**. Prominent from offshore are a high trestle spanning the gulch and several buildings on the highland just S of the gulch and quite close to the edge of the bluff. At night, a row of prominent lights extends from the highland down to the gulch.

(92) **Wailea** is a small settlement a mile S of Hakalau Bay and just N of **Kolekole Gulch.**

(93) **Honomu** is at the mouth of a gulch 10.5 miles SE of Laupāhoehoe Point.

(94) **Pepeekeo Point**, 52 miles SE of Upolu Point and 25 miles NW of Cape Kumukahi, is the most prominent point in the vicinity. **Pepeekeo Point Light** (19°50'50"N., 155°04'58"W.) 147 feet above the water, is shown from a 72-foot steel pole with a black and white diamond-shaped dayboard on the N side of the entrance to Hilo Bay. During the day, the light tower is obscured by trees. **Papaikou**, 4 miles S of Pepeekeo Point, is on the W side of Hilo Bay.

Chart 19324

(95) **Hilo Bay** has an entrance width of 8 miles between Pepeekeo Point on the N and Leleiwi Point on the SE; the head of the bay is 4 miles inland. **Hilo**, on the SW side of the bay, is second in importance of the commercial deepwater harbors in the State of Hawaii.

(96) The W shore of Hilo Bay is bluff, but the S and SE shores are low. The outer bay is exposed to the NE trades, but the inner harbor is protected by a breakwater on Blonde Reef. There is frequently a heavy swell which is deflected E by the W shore and causes considerable surge at the wharves behind the breakwater. The W end of the breakwater is marked by a light.

Prominent features

(97) **Paukaa Point Light** (19°45'44"N., 155°05'23"W.) 145 feet above the water, is shown from a white pyramidal concrete tower about 2 miles N of Hilo. A lighted red and white water tank is on the SE side of Kuhio Bay.

(98) The marine terminal is in **Kuhio Bay**, behind the inner end of the breakwater. S of the terminal is a large commercial airport; the aero light at the airport can be seen many miles at sea.

(99) A flashing amber warning light, privately maintained and shown 2 feet above the SW corner of the roof of the shed on Pier 2, is activated when there is a gas leak or the likelihood thereof. Anyone observing the light flashing should remain well clear and upwind, and sources of ignition should be secured.

COLREGS Demarcation Lines

(100) The lines established for Hilo Harbor are described in **80.1480**, chapter 2.

Channels

(101) From deep water on the N, the channel to the inner harbor leads between the breakwater and the W shore, then turns sharply E and follows the S edge of Blonde Reef to the wharves in Kuhio Bay. A **Federal project** provides for an entrance channel 35 feet deep and a harbor basin of same depth in Kuhio Bay. Channel and basin are maintained at or near the project depth. The entrance and channel to the basin are marked by a directional light on **Coconut Point**, lighted and unlighted buoys, and a **097.5°** lighted range leading into Kuhio Bay. The range may be obscured by vessels moored at Pier 1.

Anchorages

(102) Anchorages may be obtained anywhere under the lee of the breakwater where depths are suitable. Good anchorage is available W of Kaulainaiwi Island in depths

of 25 to 35 feet over good holding ground. Well protected small-craft anchorages with fair holding ground may be found in S of Kuhio Bay, and in **Radio Bay** E of Pier 1. The Hilo harbormaster usually assigns deep-draft anchorages.

(103) **Special anchorages** are on the S side of Hilo Bay and in the E part of Kuhio Bay at the S end of the breakwater. (See **110.1 and 110.128b**, chapter 2, for limits and regulations.)

Dangers

(104) **Blonde Reef** has depths of 4 to 25 feet and extends 1.5 miles in a NW direction from the SE side of Hilo Bay. In general, the shoaling is abrupt on all sides of the reef. A lighted buoy is off the outer end of the breakwater, which extends the length of the reef.

(105) Opposite Blonde Reef are two small islands on a reef that makes out 0.3 mile from the S shore; bare **Kaulainaiwi Island** is near the outer end of the reef and wooded **Coconut Island**, connected to the mainland by a footbridge, is close to shore. A lighted buoy marks the outer end of the reef.

(106) A large fleet of fishing boats operates in the outer part of Hilo Bay; the movements of these boats are uncertain, and approaching vessels should maintain a sharp lookout. The approach should be made from N, favoring the W shore and avoiding the NW part of Blonde Reef; vessels have gone aground on the N side of the breakwater.

Currents

(107) A NNW current of about 1 knot has been reported in the approach to the harbor. After heavy rains, currents from **Wailoa River** and **Wailuku River** set N in the inner harbor.

Weather, Hilo

(108) Hawaii lies well within the belt of NE trade winds generated by the semipermanent Pacific high-pressure cell to the N and E. The climate of the island is greatly influenced by terrain. Its outstanding features are the marked variations in rainfall with elevation and from place to place, the persistent NE trade winds in areas exposed to them, and the equable temperatures from day to day and season to season in localities near sea level.

(109) Over the island's windward slopes, rainfall occurs principally in the form of showers within the ascending moist trade winds. Mean annual rainfall increases from 100 inches or more (>2540 mm) along the coasts, to a maximum of over 300 inches (>7620 mm) at elevations of 2,000 to 3,000 feet (610 to 915 m), and then declines to about 15 inches (381 mm) at the summits of Mauna Kea and Mauna Loa. In general, leeward (south and west) areas are topographically sheltered from the trades, hence from trade-wind showers and are therefore drier; although sea breezes created by daytime heating of the land move onshore and upslope, causing afternoon and evening cloudiness and showers. Where mountain slopes are steeper, mean annual rainfall may range from 30 inches (762 mm) along the coast to 120 inches (3048 mm) at elevations of 2,500 to 3,000 feet (763 to 915 m). The driest locality on the island and in the State, with an average annual rainfall of less than 10 inches (254 mm), is the coastal strip just leeward of the south portion of the Kohala Mountains and of the saddle between the Kohalas and Mauna Kea.

(110) These marked contrasts in rainfall are reflected in soil and vegetation, with frequent abrupt transitions from lush tropical growth to near-desert conditions, such as occurs between Kilauea's wet windward slopes and the Kau Desert just to the S.

(111) Within the city of Hilo itself, average rainfall varies from about 130 inches (3302 mm) a year near the shore to as much as 200 inches (5080 mm) in mountain sections. The wettest part of the island, with a mean annual rainfall exceeding 300 inches (7620 mm), is about 6 miles (11 km) upslope from the city limits. Rain falls on about 280 days a year in the Hilo area. At the Hilo airport, the average precipitation is 130 inches (3302 mm) annually and has ranged from 211 inches (5360 mm) in 1990 to 68 inches (1727 mm) in 1983. The mean number of days with precipitation is 314. The wettest month is November with 15.35 inches (390 mm) and the driest month June, with a mean amount of 6.44 inches (164 mm). On 20 February 1979, 16.87 inches of rainfall fell at the Hilo airport; the wettest 24-hour period on record for the site. Snowfall has never been documented at Hilo.

(112) Hawaii's equable temperatures are associated with its mid-ocean location and the small seasonal variation in the amount of energy received from the sun. At Hilo, the range in average temperature from February, the coldest month, to August, the warmest, is only 4.9°F (2.7°C) and the average daily range, 14.4°F (8°C). The highest temperature of record at Hilo Airport is 94°F (34.4°C) recorded in May 1966; the lowest 53°F (11.7°C) recorded in February 1962. Greater variations occur in localities with less rain and cloud cover, but temperatures in the mid-nineties (33.9° to 36.1°C) and low fifties (10.6° to 11.1°) are uncommon anywhere on the island near sea level. Every month except April and July (more cloud cover) have seen extreme maximum temperatures of 90°F (32.2°C) or greater and each month from November through May has recorded extreme minimum temperatures below 60°F (15.6°C).

(113) The trade winds prevail throughout the year (although they may be absent for days or even weeks at a time) and profoundly influence the climate. However, the island's entire W coast is sheltered from the trades by high mountains, except that unusually strong trade winds may sweep through the relatively low (2,600-foot, (793 m)) saddle between the Kohala Mountains and Mauna Kea and reach the areas to the lee. But even places exposed to the trades may be affected by local mountain circulations. For example, the prevailing

Hilo Harbor, Hawaii
2004

wind at Hilo Airport is not the NE trade, but the SW wind that drifts downslope off Mauna Loa during the night and early morning hours.

(114) Except for heavy rain, really bad weather seldom occurs. Thunderstorms average only ten per year, most likely in March, and are rarely severe. During the winter, cold fronts or the cyclonic storms of subtropical origin (the so-called kona storms) may bring blizzards to the upper slopes of Mauna Loa and Mauna Kea, with snow extending at times to 9,000 feet (2745 m) or below and icing nearer the summit.

(115) Storms crossing the Pacific a thousand miles to the N, or kona storms closer by, may generate seas that cause heavy swell and surf along the N, E, and SW shores of the island.

(116) The National Weather Service office is at the Hilo Airport; **barometers** may be compared there or by telephone.

(117) (See Appendix B for **Hilo climatological table.**)

Pilotage, Hilo

(118) Pilotage is compulsory for all foreign vessels and for U.S. vessels under register in the foreign trade; it is optional for U.S. vessels in the coastwise trade with a Federal licensed pilot on board.

(119) Pilots are available through the Hawaii Pilots Association. Mariners are requested to give 24 hours advance notice of arrival, gross tonnage, length, and draft of vessel by telephone (808-537-4169) or by e-mail at dispatch@hawaiipilots.net. The 31-foot long pilot boat PAUKAA has a black hull with yellow superstructure and displays the words 'HAWAII PILOTS' in large white letters on the sides of the cabin. The pilot boat displays the International Code Flag 'H' by day and shows the standard pilot lights at night, white over red. The pilot boat monitors VHF-FM channels 12 and 16 and can be reached by "HILO PILOTS". Additionally, vessels are requested to rig a pilot ladder 1 meter above the water on the leeward side. The pilot boarding area is about 1 mile E of Paukaa Point Light.

Towage

(120) One diesel-powered tug up to 1,600 hp is based in Hilo. A second assist tug from another island may be arranged with advance notice. This may require a minimum of 12 to 24 hours transit time to get to the Port of Hilo from either Maui or Oʻahu.

Quarantine, customs, immigration, and agricultural quarantine

(121) (See chapter 3, Vessel Arrival Inspections, and Appendix A for addresses.)

(122) **Quarantine** is enforced in accordance with regulations of the U.S. Public Health Service. (See Public Health Service, chapter 1.)

(123) Hilo is a **customs port of entry**.

(124) A Coast Guard patrol boat moors in the basin E of Pier 1.

Harbor regulations

(125) **Harbor regulations** are established by the Harbors Division of the Hawaii Department of Transportation. There is a vessel draft restriction of 32½ feet in Hilo Harbor. The **harbormaster** enforces the regulations and assigns anchorages.

Wharves

(126) The State-owned and operated piers are on the E side of Kuhio Bay. General cargo is usually handled by ships' tackle; fork lift trucks, a 20-ton mobile hoist, and two electric traveling bulk sugar loading towers are available. Transit sheds with 103,000 square feet of covered space, and 7.5 acres of open storage space are also available. For a complete description of the port facilities refer to Port Series No. 50, published and sold by the U.S. Army Corps of Engineers. (See Appendix A for address.)

(127) **Pier 1:** 1,255 feet of berthing space, 34 feet reported alongside; deck height, 9 feet; receipt of dry bulk fertilizer, and lumber; shipment of bulk raw sugar and molasses; receipt and shipment of general and containerized cargo.

(128) **Pier 2:** 722 feet of berthing space, 35 feet reported alongside; deck height, 10 feet; receipt and shipment of general and containerized cargo by barge; receipt of bulk cement and lumber.

(129) **Pier 3:** 636 feet of berthing space, 35 feet reported alongside; deck height, 9½ feet; receipt of occasional cruise ships, petroleum products, liquefied petroleum gas, and lumber; shipment of molasses; and occasional receipt and shipment of general and containerized cargo by barge.

(130) Hilo Bay is subject to heavy surge, particularly between October and mid-April. Large vessels make fast to mooring buoys when coming alongside Pier 1; this is necessary to assist in leaving the pier and for breasting off when the surge is excessive. The use of wire mooring lines is not advised.

(131) Most of the small craft of the area berth at **Wailoa River Small Boat Harbor**, 0.1 miles S of Wailoa River mouth; lights mark the entrance to the river. In 2001, the reported depths were 9 feet in the river channel and 7 to 10 feet in the berthing area. The Wailoa River mouth is subject to extensive shoaling, especially during the winter months. In 2006, extensive flooding created further shoaling within the channel. Local boaters have reported depths of 2.5 feet within the channel. A precautionary sign with a flashing red light has been posted at the entrance to the harbor alerting mariners to the shoaling and advises them to use caution. Vessels drafting more than 4 feet should not attempt to enter the river. The fixed highway bridge at the entrance has a clearance of 12 feet.

Supplies

(132) Gasoline, diesel fuel, bunker C, and water are available at the State piers; all fuels must be trucked in. Ice and some marine supplies are available in Hilo.

Repairs

(133) Hilo has no facilities for drydocking or making repairs to deep-draft vessels, the nearest facilities are in Honolulu. A marine railway at Hilo has a capacity of 50 tons. Several machine, electrical, and welding shops off the waterfront are available for making above-waterline repairs to vessels at the port.

Communications

(134) Hilo has regular interisland barge service and is a port of call for trans-pacific vessels. Inter-island passenger travel is available by air and through two cruise ships that make weekly calls in Hilo. Telephone communication is available to the other islands and to the mainland.

Chart 19320

(135) **Leleiwi Point**, on the SE side of the entrance to Hilo Bay, is marked by a mass of bare, black lava rock about 20 feet high that extends 100 yards seaward from the tree line; the low point is difficult to identify at night.

(136) The 17-mile stretch of coast between Leleiwi Point and Cape Kumukahi is a series of low bluffs meeting the ocean with abrupt descents of 10 to 40 feet. The shoreline is a jumble of lava boulders. **Keaau**, 6 miles S of Leleiwi Point and 3 miles inland, is marked by two mill stacks and a water tank; the seaward stack is the most prominent. The Olaa plantations rise to an elevation of about 2,000 feet, above which the forest may be seen. An old lava flow reaches the sea 4 miles NW of Cape Kumukahi and is marked by two black hills, about 50 feet high, lying close together at its seaward end.

(137) **Cape Kumukahi Light** (19°30'59"N., 154°48'39"W.), 156 feet above the water, is shown from a 115-foot white pyramidal skeleton tower on the E extremity of Hawaii Island. The cape is a low mass of bare, black lava with a jagged top and is clearly defined from all sides; sharp pinnacles mark the end of the point. A chain of old craters, or cinder cones, extends 7 miles SW from the cape. The nearest cone (Kapoho crater), 1.4 miles from the cape, is 245 feet high and is heavily covered with vegetation.

(138) The SE coast of Hawaii Island is 63 miles long between Cape Kumukahi, the E extremity, and Kalae, the S extremity. This coast is mostly bold, but passing vessels are advised to keep at least 1 mile offshore. There are no all-weather harbors or anchorages.

(139) The country SW of Cape Kumukahi is heavily wooded, and there are numerous coconut groves along the beach. Characteristic of this coast are the lava flows, bare and rough in appearance, which extend from the

hills to the sea. The old craters SW from the cape join the ridge which forms the divide between the **Puna District** and **Kau District.**

(140)   **Pohoiki**, a small village 4 miles SW of Cape Kumukahi, has a boat launching ramp on the N shore of a small bight. The bight is protected by a breakwater marked by a light.

(141)   **Puu Honuaula**, 5 miles SW of Cape Kumukahi and 3 miles inland, is 844 feet high and quite prominent. The SE side is blown out, but the remaining slopes are covered with vegetation and the rim is fringed with trees.

(142)   **Opihikao**, a village 7 miles SW of Cape Kumukahi, is marked by a prominent grass-covered mound, 125 feet high, near its NE beach.

(143)   The shoreline between **Waipuku Point** and **Kupapau Point**, 11 to 17 miles SW of Cape Kumukahi, was reported in 2001 to be constantly changing and extending further seaward due to steady lava flows.

(144)   **Apua Point**, 27 miles SW of the cape, is low and bare; shallow water extends 300 yards or more offshore. **Keauhou Point**, 2 miles W of Apua Point, is another prominent feature.

(145)   From 3 miles SW of Kupapau Point to Keauhou Point, the coastal plain and the lower slopes of the mountains are devoid of vegetation; higher up the mountains are wooded. Beginning 2 miles W of Kupapau Point is a series of bluffs several hundred feet high and 1 to 3 miles back of the shore. The bluffs are marked by numerous lava flows. The crater of **Kilauea** cannot be seen from seaward, but its location, when active, is indicated in daytime by the smoke that it discharges and at night by the glare on the clouds.

(146)   At Keauhou Point the bluffs are yellow, steeper, and near the beach. The plain at the foot of the bluffs is low, and on a dark night the beach is hard to see. A small shallow bay just W of Keauhou Point is the only area between Pohoiki and Punaluu that offers small craft protection from the seas; it offers little protection from the winds. **Keauhou Landing** is along the shallow bay just W of Keauhou Point. When entering the bay, favor the W shore to avoid a reef, covered 2 feet, in the entrance. The reported depth in the entrance channel along the W shore is 6 feet. An anchorage, with a restricted swinging area and a reported depth of 9 feet, is inside the reef in the entrance. **Puu Kapukapu**, about 2 miles W of Keauhou Point, is a yellow bluff about 1,053 feet high at its NE end. This bluff is the most prominent landmark near the beach on this part of the coast.

(147)   About 1.5 miles W of Keauhou Point is **Keaoi Island**, which is low, close inshore, and separated from the mainland at its E extremity only by shoal water. Small boats find shelter behind this islet by entering from the W.

(148)   **Kau Desert**, the country S of Kilauea volcano, is devoid of vegetation. The **Great Crack**, on the W side of the 1823 lava flow from Mauna Loa, marks the W limits of the desert. The Great Crack, which is visible from seaward, passes along the E side of **Puu Ulaula**. The hill is 1.5 miles inland and 994 feet high. A sharply defined, low, black cone is about 5 miles inland and on the E side of the lava flow at an elevation of about 1,800 feet. A prominent fence, which extends from just E of Puu Ulaula to the shore 8 miles W of Puu Kapukapu, marks the W edge of Hawaii Volcanoes National Park.

(149)   The country between the Great Crack and Punaluu is covered with sugarcane to an elevation of about 2,000 feet; thence the slopes are wooded to within about 6,000 feet of the summit of Mauna Loa. Here and there, bare lava flows cut up the canefields. Cane in the Kau District extends as far W as Waiohinu.

Chart 19322

(150)   **Punaluu**, 17 miles NE from Kalae, is a small bight with a black sand beach at its head. It was a former shipping point for the town of **Pahala**, 3 miles inland, but the landing is no longer used and is in disrepair; a surfaced ramp is just N of the landing. Small boats find some protection in depths of 6 to 11 feet close to the E shore of the bight.

(151)   The SW part of the bight is foul. A rock, awash at half tide, is 260 yards SSE of the landing; another, with 8 feet of water over it, is 40 yards farther offshore in the same direction. The entrance is between these rocks and the shore to the N. A rock, with 3 feet of water over it, is 0.2 mile E of the entrance and 80 yards offshore. The NE trades tend to haul more offshore in the vicinity of Punaluu Harbor, but in rough weather breakers extend completely across the entrance and passage is impossible.

Chart 19320

(152)   The church and houses of **Hilea**, 1.7 miles W of Punaluu and 1.5 miles inland, can be seen from seaward. Back of the landing at Punaluu, and up to an elevation of about 3,500 feet, the slopes are broken; above this they appear regular and gradual to the summit of Mauna Loa. The upper slopes of Mauna Loa can only be seen from several miles offshore.

(153)   **Puu Enuhe**, 3 miles NW of Punaluu, is the seaward end of **Enuhe Ridge**. The butte is a conspicuous flat-topped cone with an elevation of 2,327 feet. **Kaiholena, Pakua,** and **Makanau** are promontories on **Kaiholena Ridge**, which extends 3 miles NW from the village of Hilea. **Ninole Gulch** lies between the two ridges, making the region extremely rugged, with the buttes standing out boldly. The buttes are prominent from either the SW or NE.

(154)   **Kaumaikeohu Peak**, about 5 miles N of Punaluu, is a prominent cone, 3,430 feet high, on the SE boundary of the Kau Forest Reserve.

(155)   Between Punaluu Harbor and Honuapo Bay, the shore is composed of masses of black lava rock which project out into deep water. About 1 and 3 miles SW of

Punaluu are two conspicuous lava flows which reach the shore. Some of the slopes back of Honuapo Bay are covered with cane.

Chart 19322

(156) **Honuapo Bay** is a slight coastal indentation 13 miles NE of Kalae. Most prominent from offshore is the 236-foot cliff 0.5 mile SW of the bay; the upper half of the cliff shows black against the light-brown background of the hills, and the lower half is a grass-covered slide. The Honuapo pier is in ruins. The bay offers good anchorage in about 20 fathoms for deep-draft vessels. The bay is exposed to the trades and offers little protection for small craft.

Chart 19320

(157) **Naalehu**, 11 miles NE of Kalae and 2 miles inland, is on the S side of the base of **Puu Hoomaha**, which is 2,109 feet high. The country between Naalehu and Kalae is a grassy plain on which cattle range.

(158) **Maniania Pali** begins at **Kimo Point**, 11 miles NE of Kalae, and ends at **Waikapuna Bay**, 9 miles from Kalae; the black coastal cliff is 100 to 200 feet high and has a band of yellow clay on top. From Waikapuna Bay to Kamilo Point, the coast is low and rocky.

(159) **Kamilo Point**, 6 miles NE of Kalae, is a low, dark, lava mass on which is a black lava monument with a square base. A reef over which the sea generally breaks extends about 0.3 mile from the point.

(160) **Kaalualu Bay**, 1 mile W of Kamilo Point, affords good shelter for small craft during NE trades, but is exposed during kona weather. Anchorage can be found in depths of about 10 fathoms 200 yards due W of the point on the E side of the entrance. The submerged coral reefs between the anchorage and the NE part of the bay should be avoided, especially during periods of heavy swells.

(161) Between Kaalualu Bay and Kalae, the grassy plain is occasionally broken by bare lava. About 2.5 miles SW of Kaalualu Bay, the low coastline is broken by a grayish cinder cone.

(162) **Kaulana Bay**, 0.9 mile NE of Kalae, is a small bay that offers excellent protection from the trades. It is best approached from SW to avoid the submerged rocks extending offshore from a lava flow spit that makes up the E shore of the bay. A boat ramp, used by local fishermen, is on the N shore of the bay.

(163) **Kalae** is the S extremity of Hawaii Island. **Ka Lae Light** (18°54'44"N., 155°40'55"W.), 60 feet above the water, is shown from a 28-foot white concrete post with a black and white diamond-shaped dayboard on the outer end of the cape. The SE side of the point is low; the bluff on the W side rises gently from the point to a height of 335 feet, 2 miles to the N. The bluff then leaves the shore and trends inland for several miles, increasing in height and forming the **Pali o Mamalu**, extends 0.6 mile S of the point; all vessels should keep 1 mile off to avoid possible dangers. The shore current setting NE against the trade wind frequently produces a rough sea on the E side of the cape. Offshore the current sets SW.

(164) From Kalae to Upolu Point, a distance of about 95 miles, the coast has a general N trend and is mostly bold. The largest reef extends about 0.6 mile from shore in Kawaihae Bay; few of the others off the numerous capes and points make out more than 0.3 mile. All dangers can be avoided by staying at least 1 mile offshore.

(165) **Honokohau Small-Boat Harbor** and **Kawaihae** are the only sheltered harbors along the W coast of Hawaii; all others are smooth during regular NE trades, but are exposed during kona weather. The trade winds draw around Kalae and hold N offshore for about 3 miles, generally causing a rough sea from Kalae to Kauna Point. At Kauna Point, the complexion of the sea changes abruptly, the sea being considerably smoother to the N.

(166) Storms from the SW to NW are most frequent in January and February. Some protection for small craft may be found in Keauhou, Honokohau, and Kawaihae Bays, but anchorage space is limited. Boats sometimes seek shelter along the SE side of the island during these storms.

(167) Gasoline and a limited supply of water are available at Keauhou, Kailua Kona, and Kawaihae along the W coast. Supplies are mostly obtained from the stores on the main highway inland from the coast.

(168) The section of the W coast between Kalae and Kawaihae Bay, 79 miles N, is known as the **Kona Coast**. The country along this coast is broken up by numerous lava flows, varying in length from a few hundred yards to 30 miles, that have broken out from Mauna Loa and Hualalai. Between these flows are areas that are heavily wooded and covered with vegetation above an elevation of 1,500 feet, and there are large areas planted in coffee. Many of the lava flows reach the coast and terminate in bluffs, some fairly high and others only a few feet above the water. Scattered trees and bushes can be seen between many of the flows.

(169) From Pali o Mamalu to Hanamalo Point, about 16 miles NW, are lowlands several miles wide, which rise gradually to the mountains. The country is extremely desolate, with its grayish-black slopes of bare lava. A particularly black flow lies at the base of the lighter colored cliffs of Pali o Mamalu.

(170) At an elevation of 2,000 feet the kona region is known for its cool and bracing climate and plentiful rain. Little variation in weather is experienced; there is generally a land and sea breeze, except during kona winds. This condition, however, does not apply between Kawaihae Bay and Upolu Point, since the region is affected by the winds which draw across the island.

(171) **Waiahukini**, a small fishing village at the base of **Pali o Kulani**, is marked by a patch of white sand. **Kāʻilikiʻi (Kailikii Shoal)** extends about 0.5 mile offshore to the W and N of the landing.

(172) **Puu Hou**, a black, well-defined cone 273 feet high, is close to the beach 1.6 miles NW of Waiahukini.

(173) **Pohue Bay**, 9 miles NW of Kalae, has a sand beach at its head where landings can be made.

(174) **Na Puu a Pele** are cones near the beach 12 miles NW of Kalae. The cones are prominent landmarks, and at the summit of the highest is a black stone cairn.

(175) **Kauna Point**, 13.5 miles NW of Kalae, is low, flat, and somewhat grassy, with a small hummock of graying lava 0.5 mile inland. The concrete base of a former light, nearly flush with the ground, is visible on the point. A 160-foot tower (19°03′01″N., 155°52′32″W.) is conspicuous just NNW of the point.

(176) **Kamoi Point**, 16.3 miles NW of Kalae, is a low jumble of lava rock. A small bight, S of the point, has a sand beach at its NE extremity where small boats can land. A small shack and a skeleton tower at the head of the bight are conspicuous from seaward.

(177) **Kanewaa Point** is 18.5 miles NW of Kalae.

(178) **Okoe** is at the head of **Okoe Bay**, a cove immediately S of Hanamalo Point. The cove indents the shore more than any other in the vicinity and has a little more sand on the beach. Anchorage can be found in depths of 7 to 15 fathoms. Larger vessels can anchor in 20 fathoms by entering the bay from due W and dropping anchor with Milolii Point Light bearing **022°**.

(179) **Hanamalo Point**, 21 miles NW of Kalae, is a low mass of lava with no prominent features. Unless close inshore, the point is difficult to distinguish from other points in the vicinity. S of Hanamalo Point, an inshore current sets S around Kalae and thence NE along the shore to the vicinity of Keauhou Point.

(180) **Milolii Point Light** (19°11′13″N., 155°54′29″W.), 44 feet above the water, is shown from a 20-foot white steel pole with a black and white diamond-shaped dayboard.

(181) **Milolii**, a village 2 miles N of Hanamalo Point, has a concrete boat landing with a depth of 7 feet alongside. A hoist on the landing has a maximum capacity of 2,000 pounds. The current off the landing has a prevailing N set which sometimes reaches a velocity of 2 knots. A dangerous reef extends about 400 yards offshore at the S end of the village.

(182) A large open-air shelter with a bright roof amongst several trees is visible from the NW, about 250 yards S of Milolii landing. Much of the area around the landing and shelter is covered with vegetation, however, farther outside this area the countryside is a barren mass of black lava. There is no protected anchorage off the landing. Storms occur most frequently in January and February.

(183) The lava flow of 1926 from the slopes of **Puu o Keokeo** entirely destroyed the village of **Hoopuloa**, 1 mile N of Milolii. The same flow nearly engulfed Milolii.

(184) **Papa Bay**, 3 miles N of Milolii, is a coastal indentation to the S of a prominent black lava flow of 1919. The ruins of an ancient Hawai'ian civilization are at the N end of the bay.

(185) Three lava flows of 1950 are prominent 4.3, 7.7, and 9.3 miles N of Milolii Point Light. These flows emanating from the SW rift zone of Mauna Loa extend into the sea, forming precipitous cliffs.

(186) **Auau Point**, 8.6 miles N of Hanamalo Point, is the crescent-shaped rim of an old crater that has had its seaward face blown out.

(187) **Lepeamoa Rock**, 11 miles N of Hanamalo Point, is close offshore from the island. The rock, 95 feet high, is the crescent-shaped rim of an old crater that has had its seaward face blown out. About 1.5 miles inland from the rock is the 1,766-foot peak of **Haleili**. Small villages of a few houses each are scattered along the coast, 1 or 2 miles apart, between Milolii and Lepeamoa Rock. The highway, which is 2 miles inland at Milolli, draws nearer the coast until at Lepeamoa Rock it is only 0.5 mile inland.

(188) **Kauhako Bay**, 34 miles NW of Kalae, is a small cove which has at its head a pali, or cliff, about 0.5 mile long and 120 feet high. **Hookena** is a small village at the foot of the N end of the pali. There is a heavy concentration of coconut and shade trees along with large amounts of vegetation around the village. Anchorage can be found in depths of 15 fathoms, sandy bottom, about 300 yards off Hookena. A landing near the N end of the sand beach is in ruins and unusable.

(189) The bluffs along the coast N of Hookena lose their height. The slope up to the interior is not so steep as to the S, and the country is covered with brush and coffee plantations.

(190) **Loa Point**, about 35.5 miles NW of Kalae, is flat and low, and green to within 40 yards of the water, then rocky.

(191) Between Loa Point and Hookena is the settlement of **Kealia**, which is at the N end of a long white sand and coral rubble beach. The villages along this section of the coast usually have a few houses on the beach, but most of the houses are on the highway 1 or 2 miles inland.

Chart 19332

(192) **Honaunau Bay**, 37 miles NW of Kalae, indents the coast about 500 yards and is about 500 yards in width. The bay lies between two flat lava points. **Puuhonua Point**, on the S, is lower and smaller and is marked by the 12-foot-high stone walls of the **City of Refuge** and by a grove of tall coconut trees. The City of Refuge is of historic interest and is now maintained as a National Historical Park of about 182 acres. In former times, criminals or refugees reaching the place were safe until such a time as the king of the land took action. Vessels anchor in depths of 4 to 8 fathoms 150 yards from the S shore. A surfaced ramp (19°25′24″N., 155°54′41″W.) is just N of the sand beach on the SE side of the bay. Small boats can easily land on the beach during normal weather.

(193) **Palemano Point**, on the S side of the entrance to Kealakekua Bay, is low and flat, with scattered coconut trees and temple ruins near its outer end. The buildings

of a resort camp on the point are prominent. A mass of bare rocks extends 125 yards off the N side of the point. About 0.4 mile N of the point, an old lava flow reaches the shore.

(194) **Kealakekua Bay**, 40 miles NW of Kalae, is marked on its N side by a light on Cook Point. The bay is about 2 miles wide between Palemano Point and Keawekaheka Point, and indents the coast about 1 mile. The shore is low, except on the NE side where a precipitous cliff between 400 and 600 feet high extends about 0.5 mile. A narrow reef fringes the shore between the S end of the cliff and Palemano Point. The bay is free of obstructions, affords good anchorage in all but strong SW winds, and is by far the best anchorage along this coast. In choosing an anchorage it is well to remember that in the daytime a sea breeze will prevail, shifting to a land breeze at night. The bottom is of coral and sand and is only fair holding ground.

(195) **Kaawaloa Cove** is the N part of Kealakekua Bay and lies between the high cliff and Cook Point. It was here that Captain James Cook was killed by the native Hawaiians in 1779. **Cook's Monument** is a concrete shaft, 25 feet high, near the shore of the inner side of Cook Point. A concrete landing, with a depth of about 6 feet alongside, affords a means for visitors to reach the monument. Kaawaloa Cove is within the boundary of Kealakekua Bay Marine Life Conservation District and State Park. State regulations forbid anchoring, except in an emergency, and overnight mooring at other than designated locations within the park boundaries. A copy of the regulations can be obtained from the Department of Land and Natural Resources.

(196) The village of **Napoopoo** consists of a few houses scattered among the coconut trees just S of the cliff. Water and provisions are scarce. The landing, which has a depth of about 4 feet alongside, is in the middle of the village. A church spire is fairly prominent from offshore.

(197) **Keawekaheka Point**, on the N side of the entrance to Kealakekua Bay, is a low, bare, lava point. An extensive lava flow reaches from the point to the high cliff at the head of the bay.

Chart 19327

(198) **Puu Ohau**, 1.5 miles N of Keawekaheka Point, is a green cone, 231 feet high, near the beach. The cone has a blowhole in the middle, and its seaward side is blown out, forming a red cliff.

(199) **Keikiwaha Point**, 2 miles N of Keawekaheka Point, is low, black, and jagged, with coconut trees on it. About 2 miles inland from the point, and on the highway, are a stack, a church, and the buildings of **Kainaliu**.

(200) From Napoopoo to Kailua Kona is the most thickly settled section of the coast; cultivated fields of coffee extend both ways from the highway that parallels the shore 1 to 2 miles inland.

(201) **Kaukalaelae Point**, 4.4 miles N of Keawekaheka Point, is low and flat. The white hotel on the point is one of the most prominent landmarks along this coast.

(202) **Keauhou Bay**, 45 miles NW of Kalae, indents the coast 0.3 mile and is 300 yards wide between entrance points. The bay is between two lava flows at the foot of a gentle slope and, though small, is one of the best protected along the Kona coast. **Keauhou Bay Entrance Directional Light** (19°33'44"N., 155°57'43"W.), 25 feet above the water, is shown from a post at the head of the bay. The **Keauhou** schoolhouse on the highway 1.5 miles inland is fairly prominent from offshore. The bottom is extremely irregular and has many coral heads with depths of 5 to 6 feet over them. A reef extends 100 yards off the N entrance point. By maintaining a lookout for coral heads, boats of 4-foot draft can enter the bay for anchorage. Breakers frequently extend across the mouth of the bay. Launching ramps are near the light at the head of the bay and on the SE side. A pier used mainly for embarking and disembarking passengers for excursion cruises is at the SE end of the bay, near the launching ramp. Fuel is available in limited quantities and is trucked in; there is no fuel dock. Several mooring buoys are in the bay.

(203) **Kahalu'u** is a small village about 1 mile N of Keauhou.

(204) **Hualalai**, in the central W part of the island, is a conical peak 8,269 feet high, covered with vegetation to its summit and prominent from any point of approach. Its W slopes terminate in a bare lava plain about 4 miles wide. The plain forms a low beach consisting of sand in some places and lava rocks in others.

Chart 19331

(205) **Kailua Bay**, 50 miles NW of Kalae, is a dent in the coast at the S end of the flat plain which extends N to Kawaihae Bay.

(206) **Kailua**, on the N side of the bay, formerly a barge terminal, is now used by cruise and charter boats. Large ships anchor offshore and ships' tenders are used for transportation to shore. **Kailua Light** (19°38'16"N., 156°00'03"W.), 32 feet above the water, is shown from a white pyramidal concrete tower on **Kukailimoku Point**, which is on the NW side of the bay entrance. Also prominent is the church spire E of Kailua pier and the radio tower NW of the pier.

(207) No breakwater protects this small exposed harbor. Access is good, and no channel is required to reach open water. The turning basin E of the pier is 12 to 20 feet deep and about 500 feet square. The approach to the pier is marked by a **023°** directional light. The W side of the pier has a surfaced boat-launching ramp. The E side of the pier has a pump-out station and a marine hoist with a maximum capacity of 2,000 pounds.

Chart 19327

(208) The coast between Kailua Bay and Kawaihae Bay is a black, jagged mass of lava. The numerous capes and indentations are caused by the lava flows over the level country. Between Keahole and Upolu Points, the trade winds draw over the mountains, at times causing a very strong offshore wind. Vessels anchoring in this vicinity should be prepared to use both anchors, as the prevailing N current prevents laying to the wind.

(209) **Kaiwi Point**, about 2 miles NW of Kailua, is low and black, with some small patches of white sand. Shoal water extends about 0.3 mile offshore on the S side of the point, but on the W side the 100-fathom curve is only 0.3 mile offshore.

(210) **Honokohau Small-Boat Harbor**, at the head of **Honokohau Bay**, about 1 mile N of Kaiwi Point, is entered through a marked dredged channel that leads to two basins in the harbor. In 2010, the controlling depths were 12.5 feet from the bay to the W basin, thence 13 feet in the W basin, except for lesser depths along the S side. In 2005-2010, the reported controlling depths were 7 feet in the channel along the N side of the harbor, with 6 feet in the E basin. Two boat ramps, a haul-out ramp, and moorings are available in the harbor. A wharfinger is available on weekdays from 0630 to 1730 and can assist in arranging delivery of petroleum products by tank truck. A fuel facility and oil disposal shed are available. The harbor office phone number is 808–329–4215.

(211) **Keahole Point**, 57 miles NW of Kalae, is the W extremity of Hawaii Island. **Keahole Point Light** (19°43'40"N., 156°03'40"W.), 43 feet above the water, is shown from a post with a black and white diamond-shaped dayboard. Kona International Airport, 1.2 miles ENE of the point, is prominent when transiting along the coast. An aerobeacon atop the 65-foot control tower is more prominent at night than Keahole Point Light. The point is low and well defined, and consists of black lava with some small vegetation. White patches of sand may be seen between the fingers of the lava. A N current sets past Keahole Point. Frequently there are small tide rips near the point, and 2 miles to the N the rips are violent when the NE trade winds are strong. A berth of 0.5 mile clears the point in deep water. Mariners should not anchor within 1 mile offshore or 500 yards N and 1000 yards S of Keahole Point because of submerged pipelines.

(212) **Puu Waawaa** (see chart 19320), 13 miles E of Keahole Point, is prominent and can often be seen when Hualalai is hidden by the clouds. The mountain, 3,971 feet high, is dome-shaped, with deep gorges on its side, and rises about 1,000 feet above the slope on which it stands.

(213) Between **Makolea Point** and **Kawili Point**, 3 and 4 miles N of Keahole Point, shoal water extends about 0.7 mile offshore. The sand and coral bottom is plainly visible. A current sets NE along this coast, and there are tide rips off Makolea Point. Offshore, beyond the 2,000-fathom curve, the current has been observed to set E toward the coast. When a heavy swell is running, breakers extend about 0.5 mile offshore. Strangers should give these points a berth of 1.5 miles. The village of **Mahaiula** is at the head of the unimportant bay between the two points. Between Keahole and Mano Points are several small bays that are rarely used.

(214) **Kuili**, 5 miles N of Keahole Point and 0.3 mile inland, is a brown crater 342 feet high. The hill marks the seaward end of a series of cones on the ridge extending from the NW slope of Hualalai. An extensive shoal extends about 0.5 mile offshore about 2 miles N of Kuili and between the villages of **Kukio** and **Kaupulehu**.

(215) **Mano Point**, 9 miles NE of Keahole Point, is a poorly defined, rounded, flat mass of lava.

(216) **Kiholo Bay**, 11 miles NE of Keahole Point, indents the coast 0.5 mile and is 1 mile wide. The head of the bay is foul, but local vessels have anchored close to the black lava shore on the S side. A SW current, with an average velocity of about 0.5 knot, has been observed in Kiholo Bay. The village of **Kiholo** consists of a few houses in a coconut grove at the head of the bay.

(217) **Puu Anahulu** (see chart 19320), 4 miles E of Kiholo, is a prominent yellowish cone, 1,523 feet high, with lava flows on three sides.

(218) **Kapalaoa** is a village on the S side of a small bight 3.5 miles NE of Kiholo. The bight is foul and can only be used by small boats with local knowledge.

Charts 19330, 19327

(219) **Puako Bay** is a small indentation in the coast 20 miles NE of Keahole Point. There is no protection for large vessels, and very little is available for small craft. The bay is open to W and NW winds and is foul with coral heads and reefs. The shores are mostly black, smooth lava extending into the water on a gentle slope, with many detached rocks of the same material. A small landing is at **Puako**, on the SE side of the bay, and many houses are along the S shore.

(220) Small boats can approach the landing on a course of 137° until within 250 yards of it, where the channel is marked by private buoys; a private light is on shore near the landing. A reef off **Waima Point**, 1 mile SW of Puako, is easily recognized from a safe distance offshore. Anchorage can be found about 0.8 mile NW of Puako in depths of 12 to 15 fathoms, sand and coral bottom.

(221) A large hotel and golf course can be seen at **Kaunaoa Beach**, 2.7 miles NE of Waima Point and a cluster of three tanks, about 0.5 mile inland from Puako Bay, are prominent.

(222) The coast, which has a NE trend to Puako, turns N for 3 miles, then gradually recurves to the NW, forming **Kawaihae Bay**. The black lava flows are no longer characteristic, and the back country, with its extensive slopes, is some of the best grazing land in the State.

Kawaihae Bay and Harbor, Hawaii
2004

(223) **Kawaihae**, 3.5 miles N of Puako, is a commercial deepwater harbor in the N part of Kawaihae Bay. The harbor is protected by stone revetment and fill on the S and by a breakwater on the W; the entrance is from NW.

Prominent features

(224) **Kawaihae Light** (20°02'29"N., 155°49'58"W.), 59 feet above the water, is shown from a 34-foot white pyramidal concrete tower on the NW side of Kawaihae. Deep and heavily wooded **Honokoa Gulch** is NW of the harbor, and **Puukohola Heiau** is a square of dark rocks on a 50-foot knoll SE of the breakwater. **Puu Kamalii**, 1 mile NE of Kawaihae, is 690 feet high and fairly conspicuous.

COLREGS Demarcation Lines

(225) The lines established for Kawaihae Harbor are described in **80.1470**, chapter 2.

Channels

(226) In 2003, the controlling depth was 38 feet in the entrance channel (except for shoaling to 26 feet in the left outside quarter in about 20°02'19"N., 155°49'57"W.), thence depths of 34 to 35 feet were available in the basin. A lighted **120°** entrance range and lighted and unlighted buoys mark the channel. The N end of the breakwater is marked by a light. A small-boat basin, just N of the main basin, had a controlling depth of 4 feet in 2003. The breakwater on the W side of the small-boat basin is marked by a light at the S end. A dock and surfaced ramp are in the basin.

Anchorages

(227) Good anchorage, except in kona weather, may be found in 4 to 8 fathoms between Honokoa Gulch and the outer end of the entrance channel.

Dangers

(228) Reefs that bare in places extend as much as 0.5 mile from the outer side of the breakwater and from the shore to the S.

Currents

(229) The strong N current felt off Keahole Point and Makolea Point passes offshore at Kawaihae, where there is practically no current.

Weather, Kawaihae and vicinity

(230) This subject has been discussed on previous pages, but vessels maneuvering in Kawaihae Harbor are again warned to be on the alert for sudden strong offshore gusts caused by the trade winds drawing over the mountains.

Pilotage, Kawaihae

(231) Pilotage is compulsory for all foreign vessels and for U.S. vessels under register in the foreign trade; it is optional for U.S. vessels in the coastwise trade with a Federal licensed pilot on board.

(232) The pilot boat, NININI, is yellow and 22 feet long with the word "PILOT" written in black letters on the hull. The boat displays the standard pilot lights at night and the International Code flag "H" by day. The pilot boarding station is 1 mile seaward of the NW end of the breakwater on the entrance channel rangeline. The pilots monitor and work VHF-FM channel 12. Mariners are requested to give at least 24 hours advance notice of arrival with gross tonnage, length, and draft of vessel; telephone (808–537–4169). Additionally, vessels are requested to rig the pilot ladder 2 feet above the water on the lee side and maintain a speed of not more than 5 knots.

Towage

(233) Tug service must be arranged for in advance; there are no tugs available in the harbor.

Quarantine, customs, immigration, and agricultural quarantine

(234) (See chapter 3, Vessel Arrival Inspections, and Appendix A for addresses.)

(235) **Quarantine** is enforced in accordance with regulations of the U.S. Public Health Service. (See Public Health Service, chapter 1.)

Harbor regulations

(236) These are established by the Harbors Division of the Hawaii Department of Transportation and are enforced by the **harbormaster**.

Wharves

(237) The State-owned waterfront facilities are on the NE side of the harbor basin. General cargo is usually handled by ships' tackle, and cargo to and from barges by forklift trucks. For a complete description of the port facilities refer to Port Series No. 50, published and sold by the U.S. Army Corps of Engineers. (See Appendix A for address.)

(238) **Kawaihae Pier 1**: Just inside harbor basin; 410-foot face, 20 to 24 feet reported alongside; deck height, 8 feet; 8,700 square feet covered storage; 20 refrigerated container positions; receipt and shipment of general and containerized cargo by barge; receipt of bulk cement and lumber; operated by State of Hawaii, Department of Transportation, Harbors Division; and others.

(239) **Kawaihae Pier 2**: 200 yards SE of barge wharf; 1,152-foot face with 38-foot ends; 35 feet reported alongside; deck height, 8 feet; 12,000 square feet covered storage; pipelines extending from wharf to 5 steel storage tanks in rear with 41,000 barrel capacity; receipt and shipment of general cargo and automobiles; shipment of aggregate; receipt of petroleum products; operated by State of Hawaii, Department of Transportation, Harbors Division; and others.

(240) A 100-foot-wide concrete ramp with mooring dolphins, used exclusively for handling military cargo to and from U.S. Government-owned landing craft, is at the SW end of the harbor.

Supplies

(241) Water and limited amounts of fuel oil and diesel oil are available.

Communications

(242) Kawaihae has interisland barge and air service and is a port of call for transpacific vessels.

Chart 19327

(243) Between Kawaihae and Mahukona, the country is uncultivated grazing land. Mountain slopes terminate in cliffs at the coast and are cut intermittently by ravines.

Chart 19329

(244) **Mahukona Harbor** is a small, open bight 10 miles NW of Kawaihae and 6 miles SW of Upolu Point. There are several abandoned warehouses and oil tanks around the harbor. The shore is rocky and the slopes back of the village are partially covered with algaroba trees.

(245) **Mahukona Light** (20°10'49"N., 155°54'05"W.), 64 feet above the water, is shown from a 22-foot white pyramidal concrete tower on Kaoma Point, S of the village.

Magnetic disturbance

(246) Differences of as much as 3° from normal variation have been observed in the vicinity of Kauili Point about 0.7 mile N of Mahukona.

(247) Anchorage may be selected 0.2 mile SW of Makaohule Point, in depths of 10 to 15 fathoms, sand and coral bottom. An anchorage with less wind can be found 0.3 mile NW of the point and about 400 yards off the beach.

(248) Reports indicate that the inshore current usually sets N with considerable velocity. However, during the period of current observations the average N drift was about 0.2 knot, both N and S velocities of nearly 1 knot were measured, and the tidal current averaged less than 0.2 knot at strength. During the observations, winds were light to moderate and variable in direction. Strong offshore winds, accompanied by violent gusts from varying directions, are frequently experienced during the normal NE trades. Because of these conditions, vessels should anchor with plenty of cable and have a second anchor ready to let go.

(249) A public landing is at the head of the bight which has a hoist that is poor condition. The private landing on the N side is in ruins. Both landings are for small boats only.

Chart 19327

(250)　The coast between Mahukona and Upolu Point is a series of low, black bluffs. Back of the bluffs, the country is marked by many cinder cones and rises gently to the Kohala Mountains. The cuts and fills of the railroad that formerly skirted the coast from Mahukona to Kohala may be seen when close inshore.

Chart 19320

(251)　**Alenuihaha Channel**, between the islands of Hawaii and Maui, is 26 miles wide in its narrowest part, between Upolu Point and Puhilele Point. The channel is free of obstructions and is deep close to the shores.

(252)　Strong trade winds usually prevail, causing the channel to be very rough and a current of 1 to 2 knots to set W. Passage is very difficult for smaller vessels, especially when going E. During the calms that frequently follow, there is at times an E set of about 1 knot, and during kona winds the E set may reach a velocity of 2 or 3 knots. The channel is roughest and the W current strongest when the wind is between NNE and ENE. During periods of strong NE trades, violent tide rips may be encountered 2 miles N of Keahole Point, probably caused by the meeting of the SW offshore current with the N inshore current. When bound from Upolu Point to Alalakeiki Channel, an onshore set is sometimes felt when reaching the lee of Maui.

Chart 19340

(253)　**Maui**, 26 miles NW of Hawaii, has an area of 728 square statute miles and is second in size of the eight large islands. The island is 42 miles long in a NW-SE direction and 23 miles in greatest width. A low, flat isthmus joins the two distinct mountain masses that make up the island. The crater of **Haleakala** (house of the sun), 10,025 feet high, is near the center of the E and larger part of the island. On the NW side of the crater the land slopes gently, while on the S and E sides, it is much steeper and in some places precipitous. **Koolau Gap** on the N side, and **Kaupo Gap** on the SE side, are two large openings in the side of the crater. **Puu Kukui**, 5,788 feet high, is near the center of the W and smaller part of the island, which is cut up by rugged peaks and deep valleys and gulches.

Anchorages

(254)　Anchorages are numerous on the SW side of Maui; the first requirement under ordinary conditions is shelter from the trade winds.

Currents

(255)　In the vicinity of Maui, currents are variable, depending to a great extent upon the velocity and direction of the wind. Usually there is a W flow in the offshore areas along the N and S coasts, which is part of the general W oceanic drift accompanying the prevailing NE trade winds. Much of the flow along the S coast appears to continue W past the S coast of Kahoolawe. Weak, variable currents are reported in Alalakeiki Channel, and there is a N flow in Auau Channel. Near the shores of the island the currents are complicated by tidal effects, wind, and counter currents.

Weather, Maui and vicinity

(256)　The trade winds divide at Kauiki Head, one part following the trend of the coast NW and the other part following the S coast. The winds following the NW coast divide again at the isthmus, one part drawing S and often reaching great force in the vicinity of Maalaea Bay, and the other part following the trend of the coast around the NW end of Maui and through Pailolo Channel, with the greater force on the Moloka'i side of the channel. That part of the trades following the trend of the S coast of Maui divides, with part continuing along the S shore of Kahoolawe and the other part drawing through Alalakeiki Channel, around the N end of Kahoolawe and W through Kealaikahiki Channel.

(257)　On the S coast of Maui, a sea breeze frequently sets in about 0900 and continues until after sundown, when the land breeze springs up. Light airs or calms are generally found in the vicinity of Molokini Islet and again along the W shore of Maui between Hekili and Kekaa Points. In the vicinity of Lahaina a light onshore breeze is generally felt, while farther out in Auau Channel the NE trades are noticed.

(258)　Rainfall is quite heavy on the windward side of the island and light on the lee side.

Quarantine, customs, immigration, and agricultural quarantine.

(259)　(See chapter 3, Vessel Arrival Inspections, and Appendix A for addresses.)

(260)　**Quarantine** is enforced in accordance with regulations of the U.S. Public Health Service. (See Public Health Service, chapter 1.)

Supplies

(261)　Marine supplies are available in limited quantities for small craft at Kahului, Wailuku, Lahaina, and Maalaea. Fuel and water are available at Kahului, Maalaea, and Lahaina.

Repairs

(262)　Some machine repairs can be made at Kahului. Minor repairs of small craft can be accomplished at Maalaea.

Communications

(263)　Maui has telephone communication with the other islands and with the mainland. Passenger and freight service travels over good to fair highways that extend to most parts of the island. Kahului is a port of call for interisland and transpacific shipping. The island has regularly scheduled air service.

(264) From Hana Bay to Cape Hanamanioa, the coast has a generally WSW trend. Between Hana Bay and Nuu Landing the coast consists of high, rough bluffs, broken up by numerous small capes and indentations. Vegetation may be seen as far as Kaupo Gap. The entire S face of Haleakala is steep and eroded, presenting a reddish-brown appearance, dotted here and there with green patches. The slopes become less steep as the shore is approached. From Nuu Landing to Cape Hanamanioa the coast is bare, with practically no sign of habitation. Dangers lie offshore in the vicinity of Alau Island, Ahole Rock, and between Pohakueaea Point and Cape Hanamanioa. Otherwise, the 10-fathom curve lies within 0.2 mile of the shore. Landings can be made during tradewind weather in the numerous coves along the coast between Muolea Point and Nuu Landing. There are no suitable anchorages between Nuu Landing and Cape Hanamanioa.

Chart 19341

(265) **Hana Bay** lies between Kauiki Head and Nanualele Point at the E end of Maui. The bay is about 0.4 mile in diameter and is open to the E. **Hana** is on the S side of the bay.

(266) **Kauiki Head**, on the S side of Hana Bay entrance, is a crater 390 feet high; the outer half of the crater has eroded, leaving the inner side exposed. Because it is joined to the rest of Maui by a comparatively low neck of land, Kauiki Head has the appearance from a distance of a separate island. **Kauiki Head Light** (20°45'26"N., 155°58'46"W.), 85 feet above the water, is shown from a 9-foot white pyramidal concrete tower on an islet close to the NE side of the crater.

(267) The shores of Hana Bay are rocky except for two short beaches, one at the S end of the bay and the other on the NW side. A shoal, usually marked by breakers, extends halfway across the bay from the middle of the N shore. A small 16-foot rocky spot is 350 yards N of the light. Numerous rocks, some bare at all tides, extend for 200 yards off **Nanualele Point**. The point is low, flat lava on the N side of Hana Bay. **Twin Rocks** are two bare rocks, with deep water close-to, about 300 yards NE of the light; the inner and larger rock is 15 feet high. About 200 yards S and 300 yards SE of outer Twin Rock are **Inner Pinnacle Rock**, about 3 feet high, and **Outer Pinnacle Rock**, about 5 feet high.

(268) The entrance channel to Hana Bay is between Twin Rocks and the 16-foot shoal and is unmarked. A local rule is to avoid entering the harbor when the seas are breaking at the entrance.

(269) The bay does not afford a desirable anchorage. Small vessels sometimes anchor in the SW portion of the bay, but swinging room is limited. Anchorages in the bay are exposed to NE winds and sea, and during strong SW blows vessels are apt to drag anchor. In the absence of local knowledge, anchorage should be attempted only by small craft.

Currents

(270) Just outside the bay a tidal current reaches its S strength when the tide at Honolulu is rising and its N strength when the Honolulu tide is falling. S and N velocities of about 1 knot and 1.5 knots, respectively, have been observed. Farther offshore, a strong N or NE current has been reported. Off Kauiki Head and Nanualele Point, rough seas occur when a NE wind blows against the NE current.

(271) No breakwater protects this small, exposed harbor. The turning basin is 20 to 30 feet deep and about 600 feet by 800 feet. The State-owned T-pier is in poor condition and has been condemned. A surfaced ramp for launching small boats is adjacent to the T-pier, however, its' orientation leaves it open to swells from the N which can make launching extremely difficult. Small boats can also be launched from the sand beach at the S end of the bay.

Chart 19340

(272) **Puu o Kahaula**, 545 feet high, is the highest of five hills 0.7 mile inland from Hana; the stone memorial cross atop the hill is sometimes lighted at night.

(273) **Alau Island**, 1.5 miles S of Kauiki Head and 0.4 mile offshore, is 100 yards in diameter and 150 feet high, is grass covered and has a few coconut palms. Between the island and Maui is an extensive reef. Tidal currents of 0.5 knot, setting N and S, have been observed near Alau Island. Off the island is a strong NE current, and there is an eddy between the island and Kauiki Head.

(274) Two rocks with about 9 feet of water over them are close together about 0.7 mile SE of Alau Island. Under favorable conditions, these rocks appear as small, yellowish-brown spots in the water. However, they are seldom seen and do not break in moderate seas. Vessels may avoid the rocks by giving Alau Island a berth of about 1.5 miles in passing.

(275) **Iwiopele**, about 1.5 miles S of Hana Bay, is a formation similar to Kauiki Head and resembles the latter in size and appearance.

(276) **Mokae Cove**, almost 1 mile S of Iwiopele, affords a landing for small boats in NE weather. S currents with velocities up to 0.5 knot have been observed 0.5 mile from the shore in this locality.

(277) From **Makaalae Point**, 3 miles S of Kauiki Head, the coastal trend is SW. There are several villages between Mokae Cove and Wailua Cove. A church spire is prominent on the bluff at **Puuiki**, 3.5 miles SW from Kauiki Head.

(278) **Wailua Cove** is at the mouth of a valley 5.5 miles SW from Kauiki Head. Inland from the cove and halfway up

(279) the mountain is a high waterfall that is usually conspicuous from offshore. A white cross, below the waterfall, is visible. Landings may be made during normal tradewind weather in almost any of the coves along the coast, although the swell enters all of them. **Muolea Point**, a mile E of Wailua Cove, is rounded and rocky.

(279) **Kipahulu**, 8 miles SW of Kauiki Head and 0.5 mile W of **Puhilele Point**, is a ranch settlement on the W side of deep **Kipahulu Valley**. **Ahole Rock**, about 0.3 mile off the shore below Kipahulu, is low and flat, and has a bare appearance; anchorage in the vicinity is not recommended.

(280) **Kaapahu Bay**, 1.5 miles W of Kipahulu, is a small coastal dent which sometimes can be used for small-boat anchorage in trade-wind weather; there are depths of 4 fathoms about 200 yards off the pebble beach.

(281) **Kaupo Landing**, 11 miles SW of Kauiki Head, is the best in the vicinity during trade-wind weather. Adjacent land is divided into small homesteads, and cattle raising is the principal occupation. Vessels anchor well off and E of the landing. Strong E winds make landings difficult.

(282) **Kailio Point**, 13 miles SW of Kauiki Head, is 73 feet high, narrow, and at the E end of **Mamalu Bay**. A prominent church is on the highway directly N of the point. Trade-wind anchorage may be found about 300 yards from the head of the bay in depths of 10 fathoms, sandy bottom.

(283) **Kaupo Gap** is the large opening, about 1.3 miles wide, in the SE side of Haleakala Crater. An immense old lava flow slopes gradually from the gap to the coast. The wide U-shaped gap at the top is a good landmark, day or night, for Kailio Point. The brush-covered lava flow is the dividing line between the forest and brush of the E part and the barren W part of the S coast. Waterfalls are numerous E of the gap.

(284) Low **Apole Point**, 15 miles SW of Kauiki Head, is composed of black, jagged rock. The point marks the seaward end of the Kaupo lava flow.

(285) **Nuu Landing** is a small bight on the W side of Apole Point. Small vessels can find anchorage in depths of about 8 fathoms.

(286) From Nuu Landing to **Pohakueaea Point**, 12 miles to the W, the coast is barren and deep water is close-to. All dangers are close to the bluffs. A few homesteads may be seen on the slopes that rise to the rim of Haleakala. The slopes are cut by gulches and are barren except for a scattering of trees about halfway up. At Pohakueaea Point, the 20-fathom curve begins to trend offshore.

(287) A pinnacle rock with depths of less than 12 feet over it is reported to exist within 0.5 mile of the shore somewhere between Pohakueaea Point and La Perouse Bay. The rock may be off Pohakueaea Point as an extension of the lava flow that forms the point. Vessels making the run along this coast in recent years have observed no indication of an offshore danger; however, they give Cape Kinau a berth of about 1 mile, as it is known that a steamer struck bottom in the vicinity of the cape, probably about 0.2 mile offshore.

(288) **Lualailua Hills**, 6 miles W of Nuu Landing and 2 miles inland, are a group of red mounds about 2,000 feet high.

(289) **Hokukano**, 1 mile SW of Lualailua Hills, is a conspicuous red cone with a lava flow reaching the sea in a high black mass.

(290) **Pimoe**, 2.4 miles W of Hokukano, is a red dome, irregular in shape, with its E side broken. The dome, 1,766 feet high, is the crater from which the large, fan-shaped lava flow in the vicinity of Pohakueaea Point had its origin.

Chart 19347

(291) **Cape Hanamanioa**, the SW extremity of Maui, is a black lava mass. **Hanamanioa Point Light** (20°35'00"N., 156°24'43"W.), 73 feet above the water, is shown from a 21-foot post with a black and white diamond-shaped dayboard on the cape. A current is reported to set constantly NW past the cape; however, a short series of observations a mile SE of the light indicates a tidal current with a velocity of 0.8 knot at strength.

(292) **La Perouse Bay**, between Cape Hanamanioa and Cape Kinau, is about 0.7 mile wide and indents the coast about 0.5 mile. On the NW side of the bay is **Puu o Kanaloa**, a low yellowish-brown cone at the water's edge, with its seaward side blown out. The crater is surrounded by a lava flow from **Kalua o Lapa**, a small, black cone about 1 mile N of the bay. A rock covered 10 feet is in the middle of the entrance to the bay. A rocky outcrop is on the NW side of the bay. Strangers are advised to exercise extreme caution in the bay.

(293) **Cape Kinau**, 1.5 miles NW of Cape Hanamanioa, is a broad, low, black, lava point and a **protected area** of a Natural Area Reserve. A rock with 4½ feet of water over it is 400 yards offshore near the N end of the cape.

(294) **Puu Olai**, about 2.5 miles N of Cape Kinau, is the most prominent landmark in this vicinity. The hill is brown in color, 367 feet high, and consists of three bare knolls, of which the southernmost is the highest.

(295) **Molokini**, 5.5 miles NW of Cape Hanamanioa, is a small crescent-shaped islet about 0.3 mile long and 156 feet high. The islet is the bare rim of a crater, the N part of which is submerged. **Molokini Island Light** (20°37'50"N., 156°29'51"W.), 186 feet above the water, is shown from a 30-foot pole with a red and white diamond-shaped dayboard. A reef extends 300 yards N from the NW end of the islet; there is deep water close to the S side. Vessels pass on either side of the islet. In 1984, unexploded ordnance was reported in the vicinity of the islet; caution is advised.

(296) **Makena Anchorage**, 1 mile N of Puu Olai, is exposed to kona weather, but affords good holding ground during the trades. Anchorage can be had in depths of 12 to 15 fathoms off **Nahuna Point**, with a fairly prominent church bearing 100°. A few houses may be seen among the trees on the rocky point at the N side of the bight,

and a prominent house is at the S end of the sand beach. The strong trade winds that are felt farther N in Maalaea Bay are not pronounced at Makena. Secondary roads lead along the coast and inland from the village. Anchorage can also be found in **Ahihi Bay**, just S of Puu Olai.

(297) The country back of Makena rises gently to the mountains. The lower slopes are covered with cactus, while the slopes higher up are wooded in places. From Makena to Kihei the coast has a general N trend and is heavily developed with beach homes and hotels. The country back of the coast is like that in the vicinity of Makena.

(298) **Keawakapu** is 8 miles N of Cape Hanamanioa. An apartment building on the small point at Keawakapu is the most prominent landmark along this coast. A fish haven, 200 yards by 1,150 yards, is 0.7 mile SW of Keawakapu.

Chart 19350

(299) **Maalaea Bay** is a large bight midway along the SW coast of Maui. The shores are low, mostly sandy, and fringed with algaroba trees. The isthmus behind the bay and the slopes on either side are cultivated in sugarcane. Several hotels and resort developments can be seen along the E side of the bay and three stacks are prominent in about 20°48'02"N., 156°29'37"W.

(300) Maalaea Bay is only a fair anchorage. Fresh winds sweep across the isthmus during the trades, and the bay is completely exposed to kona storms. The holding quality of the ground is poor. A N current has been reported in the bay. In the central and E portions the bottom is very irregular. A reef fringes the shore for a distance of 3.5 miles S of Kihei. Off Kalepolepo, where the reef is widest, a 14-foot spot is 0.5 mile offshore along the edge of the reef. Broken ground with a least depth of 3 fathoms lies about 0.7 mile WSW of the Kihei wharf. A shoal with a least depth of 7 fathoms is in the center of the bay; shoals with 3¾ and 4½ fathoms are NE of this shoal. Strangers should pass well offshore.

(301) **Kalepolepo**, is on the E side of Maalaea Bay, 11 miles N of Cape Hanamanioa. A large old fishpond extends 0.2 mile from shore. Local vessels anchor behind the reefs in depths of 3 to 4 feet.

(302) **Kihei** is on the E side of Maalaea Bay 12 miles N of Cape Hanamanioa. A settlement is scattered among the trees and along the beach in the vicinity of the remains of a wharf.

(303) **Kealia Pond**, just NW of Kihei, is separated from the bay by a narrow sand strip over which the shore highway passes.

(304) **Maalaea** is a village on the NW shore of Maalaea Bay. A few buildings can be seen among the algaroba trees. The boat harbor at the village is about 500 yards long E to W, about 200 yards across, and is protected by breakwaters. Depths in the harbor are about 7 feet in the W basin and about 10 feet in the NE basin, mud bottom. In 2009, a reported depth of 8 feet was available in the entrance channel. The entrance channel is marked by a **339°** lighted range and private buoys. Inside the harbor, a reef and shoal area extends into the center of the harbor. Care must be taken to avoid these areas when approaching the slips on the N side of the harbor. Gasoline, diesel fuel (by fuel truck) and a launching ramp are available; engine repairs can be made. The harbormaster can be contacted on VHF-FM channel 68 or by phone at 808–243–5818. The harbor office is at the head of the harbor. The harbor experiences considerable surge during all but calm weather.

Coast Guard Station

(305) Coast Guard Station Maui is just inside the breakwaters of Maalaea Village and can be contacted at 1-808–986–0023.

Chart 19347

(306) **McGregor Point Light** (20°46'39"N., 156°31'22"W.), 72 feet above the water, is shown from a 20-foot white tower on McGregor Point on the W side of Maalea Bay. The coast between McGregor Point and Olowalu is broken by low bluffs rising from the water's edge, behind which the country presents a barren appearance. The mountains have sharp jagged peaks and are cut by deep gorges.

(307) **Papawai Point**, 0.9 mile W of McGregor Point, is the southernmost point of W Maui. Deep water is close inshore at the point.

(308) **Olowalu** is on **Hekili Point**, 18 miles NW of Cape Hanamanioa. The deep gulch of **Olowalu Stream** appears as a gap in the mountains when abreast of the point and is an excellent night mark.

(309) **Launiupoko Point**, about 2 miles NW of Olowalu, is low and rounding. About 0.8 mile inland from the point is an 808-foot hill that has a mottled, grayish-brown appearance. Shoal water extends about 0.2 mile offshore from the point NW to Lahaina. The highway skirts the shore between these points, and automobile lights along the road are usually the only lights seen along the coast.

Chart 19348

(310) **Lahaina** is 23 miles NW of Cape Hanamanioa. Once the whaling capital of the mid-Pacific, Lahaina is now a colorful resort town and a favorite port of call of yachtsmen and boating enthusiasts. In the vicinity of Lahaina, canefields extend along the coast and for several miles inland on the ridges that lead to high, rugged mountains. A mill stack near the center of Lahaina is very prominent and a spire is visible on Puunoa Point. A reef, over which the sea generally breaks, extends about 350 yards offshore from Makila Point, 1 mile SE of Lahaina, to Puunoa Point, a mile NW of Lahaina. **Mala** is a small

(311) settlement on the N side of **Puunoa Point**. The concrete wharf at Mala is in poor condition and is no longer in use. A breakwater extends along the NE side of the Mala wharf. A launching ramp is between the inner end of the breakwater and a short groin that protects the ramp on its N side.

(311) **Lahaina Light** (20°52'20"N., 156°40'43"W.), 44 feet above the water, is shown from a 39-foot white pyramidal concrete tower at the inner end of the Lahaina small-boat wharf.

(312) S of Lahaina wharf is a boat basin, about 200 by 800 feet, protected by breakwaters. The approach to the basin is marked by a lighted buoy. The entrance channel is marked by lighted buoys and a **044.4°** lighted range. In 1979, the controlling depth was reported to be 8 feet in the channel. In 2009, reported depths in the basin were 6 to 8 feet. Vessels entering or leaving the boat basin should exercise caution as the combined effects of the swell and the 90° turn into the basin can set vessels onto the shoal opposite the basin entrance.

(313) Gasoline and diesel fuel are available at Lahaina, but must be obtained through the harbormaster (VHF-FM channel 68 or 808–662–4060). Some small-craft supplies may be obtained at Lahaina and a 1-ton hoist is available on the small-boat wharf.

(314) Good anchorage can be had off Lahaina. Calm water will generally be found even though strong trade winds are blowing elsewhere, however, the anchorage is exposed in kona weather. In approaching the anchorage, vessels should keep about one mile offshore until the light bears **056°**, then head in on this course and anchor in depths of 9 to 15 fathoms. Anchorage can be had anywhere in the bight N of Mala wharf, 0.6 mile offshore in depths of about 12 fathoms, sandy bottom. Offshore mooring buoys for up to 72 hours are available by permit only.

(315) Lahaina has become a destination for both foreign and domestic cruise ships. From fall to spring, passenger and crew counts in excess of 300 can be expected. Ships anchor out and ferry passengers into the harbor by small boat. When ships are present, a 300-yard security zone exists around the ship. For foreign vessels, a customs station is set up at the harbor. The Harbor Master acts as a VTS for the duration of the cruise ship port call. All traffic must check in and out of the harbor on VHF-FM channel 68.

Currents

(316) The current off Lahaina usually sets N and reaches a maximum velocity of 1 or 2 knots before low water. Before high water the current is normally quite weak and may set either N or S.

(317) It is reported that the current near the wharf at Mala sets S most of the time.

(318) The coast between Mala and Kekaa Point consists of a low, sandy beach with a fringe of coconut and algaroba trees, back of which the canefields extend inland for about 2 miles. Buildings can be seen along the coast among the trees.

(319) **Puu Laina**, 1.2 miles NE of Mala, is a prominent cone 650 feet high. The lower slopes of the hill are covered with cane.

(320) **Hanakaoo Point**, 2 miles N of Mala, is rounding and not conspicuous from offshore. The 10-fathom curve is about 500 yards off this point, and the bottom slopes gradually to the sandy beach. Several hotels line the shore N and S of the point.

Chart 19347

(321) **Kekaa Point** (20°55.8'N., 156°42.0'W.), 26 miles NW of Cape Hanamanioa, is the westernmost extremity of Maui and is known locally as Black Point. The point is a dark, rocky promontory, 85 feet high, which appears detached from a distance; there are no offshore dangers. A hotel is on the point.

(322) A northward current is reported off Kekaa Point. A tidal current of 0.5 knot, setting N and S, was observed 0.5 mile from the shore.

(323) From Kekaa Point to Lipoa Point, the coast consists of low bluffs and stretches of sand beach along which may be seen clumps of algaroba trees and several resort hotel complexes. The gently sloping country is cut by shallow gulches and is covered with cane and pineapple which extend well up the mountain slopes.

(324) **Napili Bay**, 4.5 miles N of Kekaa Point, is a small bight between two coral reefs. Anchorage can be found about 0.5 mile offshore in depths of 5 fathoms, but it is seldom used. N currents are reported off the bay. Small boats can land in Napili Bay during tradewind weather. Breakers extend 0.2 mile offshore for a distance of 1.5 miles S of the bay.

(325) **Hawea Point Light** (21°00'14"N., 156°39'59"W.), 75 feet above the water, is shown from a post with a diamond-shaped black and white dayboard 5 miles N of Kekaa Point.

(326) **Honolua Bay** is the open bight on the S side of **Lipoa Point**, which is 7 miles NE of Kekaa Point. Smaller vessels can find fair anchorage in the bay, and boats can land in the cove at the NE end.

(327) In the vicinity of Lipoa Point, the bluffs along the N shore of Maui become higher and more precipitous. Also, the bluffs are cut up by more bights and headlands. The country is more rolling and is cut by deeper gulches. The mountains are steeper and greener. Near their tops the mountains are wooded in places. Patches of black rocks, awash at high water, are found close inshore off several of the points in the vicinity. Vessels should give this coast a berth of at least 0.8 mile.

(328) **Kanounou Point**, about 2 miles ENE of Lipoa Point, has several bare, black rocks a short distance offshore.

(329) **Honokohau**, on the W side of Kanounou Point, consists of a few houses at the mouth of **Honokohau Stream**. There is little protection off the village.

(330) **Nakalele Point** is three miles ENE of Lipoa Point. Close off Nakalele Point are several bare, black rocks; blowholes can be seen along the SE face of the point. **Nakalele Point Light** (21°01'45"N., 156°35'26"W.), 142 feet above the water, is shown from a 21-foot pile with a black and white diamond-shaped dayboard.

Chart 19342

(331) **Kahakuloa Head**, 3 miles SE of Nakalele Point, is the seaward end of one of the numerous abrupt capes in this general vicinity. **Puʻu Koaʻe (Sugarloaf)**, a dark bare, conical mound 634 feet high, is on Kahakuloa Head; this feature is one of the most conspicuous landmarks on the island of Maui. E and close to Puʻu Koaʻe, on the same ridge, is a low and more rounded dome. **Kahakuloa** is a small village in **Kahakuloa Bay**, just W of Kahakuloa Head. A spire can be seen in the village. Kahakuloa is the last settlement on the paved road that skirts the W and N shores of Maui. Deep water is found close to the head, although there are numerous breakers and covered rocks just offshore. A rock, covered 4½ feet, in surrounding depths of 15 to 20 fathoms, is 0.4 mile off the head of the cove between Puʻu Koaʻe and Mokeehia Island.

(332) **Mokeehia Island**, 1.4 miles SE of Puʻu Koaʻe, is a large, bare rock 170 feet high, just off the outer end of **Hakuhee Point**. Caverns can be seen in the faces of the cliffs on both sides of the island.

(333) **Puu Olai**, 0.7 miles inland from Mokeehia Island, is 1,002 feet high.

(334) **Hulu Island**, 95 feet high and close to shore, is 2 miles S of Mokeehia Island. Several rocks are close S of the island.

(335) **Waihee Point** is 2.6 miles S of Mokeehia Island. SE of the point is extensive **Waihee Reef**, and back of the point is deep and precipitous **Waihee Valley**, which is quite prominent.

(336) **Iao Valley**, also deep and precipitous, is 6 miles S of Mokeehia Island; some of the finest scenery on Maui is found in this vicinity.

(337) **Wailuku** at the mouth of Iao Valley and 1.5 miles from the coast, is the seat of Maui County and is the largest town on the island. The town has a hospital, hotels, and numerous stores; a white multistory building in the center of the town is prominent. There is a direct highway to Kahului.

(338) **Kahului Harbor**, on the S side of **Kahului Bay** 6 miles SE of Mokeehia Island, is protected by breakwaters which extend outward from the W and E shores. On the SE side of the harbor is the commercial deepwater port of **Kahului**.

Prominent features

(339) **Pauwela Point Light** (20°56'44"N., 156°19'17"W.), 161 feet above the water, is shown from a 40-foot white post 9 miles ENE of Kahului Harbor and is the principal mark for the approach. Other marks are an aero light at the airport E of Kahului, the breakwater lights, the lighted entrance range, the powerplant stacks E of the piers, the radio tower 0.8 mile W of the rear range, and the Wailuku spire and stack 2 miles W of the harbor.

COLREGS Demarcation Lines

(340) The lines established for Kahului Harbor are described in **80.1460**, chapter 2.

Channels

(341) From deep water on the N, the channel leads between the breakwaters, then turns sharply SE to the Kahului piers. A **Federal project** provides for an entrance channel 35 feet deep and a harbor basin of the same depth. Channel and basin are maintained at or near project depth. Navigational aids include lighted and unlighted buoys, breakwater lights, and a **177°** lighted range. A channel, marked by private buoys and an unlighted range, leads to a launching ramp at the W end of the harbor.

Anchorages

(342) Swinging room inside the breakwaters is too restricted for large vessels, which may anchor E of the sea buoy, but caution is necessary to avoid dragging by the prevailing NE trades. Small craft have plenty of anchorage room in the unimproved areas behind the breakwaters.

Dangers

(343) **Waihee Reef**, NW of the breakwaters, and **Spartan Reef**, NE of the breakwaters, extend 0.7 mile and 1.2 miles offshore, respectively. Vessels approaching the harbor entrance range from either direction should avoid the reefs. The W part of the inner harbor is shallow. There is a buildup of silt and marine debris (old tires) that creates a shallow area in the SE corner of the commercial harbor in about 20°53'44"N., 156°27'56"W.

Currents

(344) Harbor currents are weak.

Weather

(345) The prevailing winds are the NE trades.

Pilotage, Kahului

(346) Pilotage is compulsory for all foreign vessels and for U.S. vessels under register in the foreign trade; it is optional for U.S. vessels in the coastwise trade with a Federal licensed pilot on board. Pilotage is available through the Hawaii Pilots Association. Mariners are requested to give 24 hours advance notice of arrival, gross tonnage, length, and draft of vessel by telephone (808–537–4169) or by e-mail at dispatch@hawaiipilots.net. The 31-foot long pilot boat PAUWELA has a black hull with yellow superstructure and displays the

Kahului Bay and Harbor, Maui
2004

word 'PILOT' in large white letters on the sides of the cabin. The pilot boat displays the International Code Flag 'H' by day and shows the standard pilot lights at night, white over red. The pilot boat monitors VHF-FM channels 12 and 16 and can be reached by "KAHULUI PILOTS". Additionally, vessels are requested to rig a pilot ladder 1 meter above the water on the leeward side. The pilot boarding area is about 1.5 miles N of Kahului Entrance Breakwater Light 3.

Towage

(347)   A 3,400 hp tug and a 4,400 hp assist tug are available at the port.

Quarantine, customs, immigration, and agricultural quarantine

(348)   (See chapter 3, Vessel Arrival Inspections, and Appendix A for addresses.)

(349)   **Quarantine** is enforced in accordance with regulations of the U.S. Public Health Service. (See Public Health Service, chapter 1.) There is a public hospital between Kahului and Wailuku.

(350)   Kahului is a **customs port of entry**.

Harbor regulations

(351)   These are established by the Harbor Division of the Hawaii Department of Transportation. The harbormaster enforces the regulations and assigns berths and anchorages. The harbormasters' office hours are from 0745-1630 and can be contacted at 808–873–3350; 808–357–0665 (after-hours) and (emergency only).

Wharves

(352)   The State-owned and operated piers are on the SE side of the harbor. General cargo is usually handled by ships' tackle, and cargo to and from barges by forklift trucks; crawler and truck cranes are available. Transit sheds with 78,000 square feet of covered storage space and 21 acres of open storage space are available at the piers. Truck lines serve the piers. For a complete description of the port facilities refer to Port Series No. 50, published and sold by the U.S. Army Corps of Engineers. (See Appendix A for address.)

(353)   **Pier 1:** 1,350 feet of berthing space along the SW side; 35 feet reported alongside; deck height, 9 feet; two traveling bulk sugar loading towers with conveyors and loading spouts, loading rate 800 tons per hour; receipt and shipment of general and containerized cargo; receipt of automobiles; receipt of petroleum products, coal, lumber, and steel products; shipment of raw sugar and molasses; boarding passengers.

(354)   **Pier 2:** 894 feet of berthing space along the NE side, 27 feet reported alongside; deck height, 9½ feet; 288 feet of berthing space along the outer end, 27 feet reported alongside; receipt and shipment of conventional and

containerized cargo and automobiles; receipt of lumber, bulk cement, and liquefield petroleum gases.

(355) **Pier 3:** extends NE from the foot of Pier 2; 500 feet of berthing space along NW side, 18 feet reported alongside; deck height, 9 feet; receipt and shipment of general and containerized cargo and automobiles; receipt of petroleum products, sand, lumber, and steel products; boarding passengers; mooring towboats.

(356) There is a surge at the piers during periods of heavy N swells; this occurs about 10 times a year. Departing vessels may have some difficulties in breasting off from Pier 1 during kona weather.

Supplies

(357) Gasoline, diesel fuel, and water are available at all piers; gasoline and diesel fuel are trucked in. Bunker C fuel can be obtained in limited quantities by truck. Ice and some marine supplies are available.

Repairs

(358) Kahului has no facilities for making repairs or drydocking deep-draft vessels. The nearest such facilities are in Honolulu. There are machine, electrical, and welding concerns off the waterfront for making above-the-waterline repairs to vessels.

Communications

(359) Kahului has regular interisland barge service and is a port of call for transpacific vessels, but interisland passenger travel is almost entirely by air. Telephone communication is available to the other islands and to the mainland.

(360) The coast is low between Kahului Harbor and Pauwela Point. The back country is planted in sugarcane.

(361) **Paia** is 6 miles E of Kahului Harbor and 1 mile inland. An opening in Spartan Reef off Paia is sometimes used by local craft seeking anchorage behind the reef.

(362) **Maliko Bay**, 8 miles ENE of Kahului Harbor, is a narrow opening with steep, rocky sides. The bay provides fair anchorage for small craft in depths of 1½ to 5¼ fathoms, rocky bottom, when the trade winds are blowing. Rocks and foul ground, which extend from the E side of the entrance to the bay to about halfway across, form a natural breakwater. Rocks on the W side of the entrance restrict the channel to a width of about 100 yards. A reef that bares is on the SW side of the bay about 0.1 mile inside the entrance. Small craft can be launched from a boat ramp at the head of the bay.

(363) **Pauwela Point**, 9 miles ENE of Kahului Harbor, is marked by a prominent light which has already been described. An E current is reported off the point.

Chart 19340

(364) Paralleling the NE coast of Maui is a State highway which is the main link between Kahului and Hana. From Pauwela E the road is a succession of sharp turns and steep grades as it winds from and toward the shore in crossing the numerous gulches. Sections of the highway can be seen from seaward, but it disappears as it follows the gulches inland.

(365) Between Pauwela and Nahiku, a distance of about 15 miles, the bluffs reach heights of 300 to 400 feet, then gradually lose elevation to the SE, and are low in the vicinity of Hana. The back country is generally green, and the higher slopes are heavily wooded. Because of the heavy rains, waterfalls are numerous in the many gulches that lead to the sea. Very little of this NE coast is planted in sugarcane. From Pauwela Point to Waipio Bay the land on the seaward side of the coastal highway is under pineapple cultivation, and there are many taro patches at Keanae and Nahiku. The slopes SE of Nahiku are grazing areas for cattle. There are many inshore rocks between Pauwela Point and Hana, but all such dangers can be avoided by keeping a mile offshore.

(366) **Uaoa Bay**, 3 miles E of Pauwela Point and just E of **Opana Point**, indents the coast about 0.4 mile. Fair anchorage during S winds can be had 0.3 mile offshore in depths of 12 to 16 fathoms, sandy bottom. A large detached rock off Opana Point marks the W side of the bay.

(367) **Pilale Bay**, 4 miles E of Pauwela Point, is a small opening at the mouth of a deep valley. Small boats can find fair anchorage during tradewind weather in depths of 4 to 7 fathoms a short distance off the beach.

(368) **Waipio Bay**, 6 miles E of Pauwela Point, lies between **Honokala Point** and **Huelo Point** and is open to the NE. **Huelo** is a small village along the highway 0.5 mile inland.

(369) **Hoalua Bay**, 7 miles SE of Pauwela Point is small and too exposed for anything but emergency anchorage. Under favorable conditions landings can be made at the head of the bay.

(370) **Oopuola Cove**, 8 miles SE of Pauwela Point, is narrow and steepsided. A reef lies just N of the point on the W side of the entrance. Beach landings can be made at times, and small boats can find anchorage in depths of 3 to 6 fathoms near the center of the cove. **Puu Kukai**, 574 feet high, is 0.5 miles W of the cove.

(371) **Keopuka Rock**, 141 feet high, is 9.5 miles SE of Pauwela Point and close to shore. The rock's double-humped top is distinctive from E or W, but from directly offshore it blends into the cliffs behind it.

(372) **Honomanu Bay**, 10 miles SE of Pauwela Point, is a good landing place and a fair small-boat anchorage during the trades, although the swell is felt in the bay. Anchorage can be found in depths of 2 to 3 fathoms about 200 yards from the black shingle beach at the head of the bay. The E side of the bay is shallow. **Puu o Kohola**, 844 feet high, is 0.5 mile W of the bay.

(373) **Nuaailua Bay**, close E of Honomanu Bay and on the W side of Keanae Point, is the only suitable anchorage for moderate-size vessels along this NE coast. The bay is somewhat exposed to the NE trades, but is partly protected by Keanae Point. A 250-foot vessel can anchor in

depths of 13 to 15 fathoms in the middle of the main bay; the bottom is quite even and has good holding qualities. Approach from seaward should be made on a due S course, keeping about 0.3 mile off the W shore and well clear of the 15-foot lone, black rock which is 0.3 mile off the E shore.

(374) **Keanae Point**, 11 miles SE of Pauwela Point, is a low, flat peninsula that juts out 0.3 mile from the bluff line. Landings should not be attempted on the point proper because of the covered rocks and ledges on all sides. A scattering of houses can be seen on the point.

(375) **Keanae Valley** is the largest and most prominent valley on this part of Maui. The valley leads inland 7 miles from the vicinity of Keanae Point to **Koolau Gap**, the large opening in the N rim of Haleakala Crater.

(376) **Pauwalu Point** is 1 mile SE of Keanae Point. **Mokumana Rock**, close off Pauwalu Point, is 77 feet high and flat-topped; the rock is particularly outstanding when approached from the E, but from some directions it appears to be a continuation of the point although there is a separation of some 50 yards.

(377) **Aluea Rock**, 2 miles SE of Keanae Point and about 0.2 mile offshore, is only a few feet high and has the appearance of a reef awash as the seas break over it continuously and covered rocks extend another 300 yards from shore. This area should be avoided by all boats.

(378) **Wailua** consists of a few houses along the shore of the small bight immediately SW of Aluea Rock. On the E side of the bight is a high wooded bluff, and the W side is low and grass-covered. The highway leading to Hana leaves the shore W of the bight and from seaward it may be seen high up on the ridges as it winds its way SE.

(379) **Nahiku**, 15 miles SE of Pauwela Point, is a small settlement on the E side of an open bight. Anchorage can be found in depths of 7 fathoms close to shore, but strangers should not attempt it because of the two covered rocks near shore. A SE current is reported off Nahiku, and the inshore current between Nahiku and Kauiki Head is said to be weak. **Kuhiwa Gulch** extends inland from the vicinity of Nahiku and is visible from seaward.

(380) **Opikoula Point** is a low, rocky bluff on the E side of the Nahiku anchorage. Similar bluffs extend 5 miles SE to Pukaulua Point, and there are no easily recognized landmarks. This reef-fringed stretch of coast is not recommended for small-boat landings.

(381) Low **Pukaulua Point** is 2.5 miles NNW of Hana Bay and Kauiki Head. **Hana Airport** is 0.5 mile NW of the point; the main runway is laid out in an E-W direction and is close to the bluffs.

Chart 19347

(382) **Alalakeiki Channel**, between Maui and Kahoolawe, is about 6 miles wide. The channel is clear of dangers, with the exception of Molokini, which is marked by a light.

(383) Observations show that the **current** usually flows NW with a maximum velocity of 0.7 knot on the W side of the channel near Kahoolawe Island, and SSE with a maximum velocity of 0.4 knot along the E side of the channel near Maui Island. Velocities up to 1 knot have been observed in the channel.

(384) The trade winds draw through the channel, hauling around the N end of Kahoolawe. The trades blow with much force at the E entrance to the channel, but in the vicinity of Molokini it is generally calm.

(385) **Auau Channel**, between Maui and Lanai, is about 8 miles wide. With the exception of a reef about 3 miles long, which extends not more than 0.5 mile offshore N of Kikoa Point, Lanai, the channel is free from obstructions. The aerolight at Moloka'i airport can be seen when passing through Auau Channel.

(386) Observations in Auau Channel show that the **current** seldom floods, but that the flow is mainly in the ebb direction; ebb is E with a velocity of 1.1 knots. Beginning with maximum ebb, the current decreases to a minimum ebb or slack and then increases to a maximum ebb without a significant flow in the flood direction. Maximum velocities of 2 knots have been observed. (For predictions see the Tidal Current Tables.) During trade winds it is often calm in the channel.

(387) **Pailolo Channel**, between Maui and Moloka'i, is about 7.5 miles wide. The channel is clear of obstructions with the exception of Mokuho'oniki and Kanaha Rock, near the E end of Moloka'i, and a reef about 0.8 mile wide which fringes the shore of Moloka'i.

(388) Observations show the **current** in the channel to set NE with a velocity of about 0.3 knot. The maximum velocity observed was 0.6 knot.

(389) In navigating this channel, the tanks on Moloka'i and Maui will prove useful landmarks; those on Moloka'i are on the SE shore, near Pukoo, and those on Maui are on its WNW side, near Kekaa Point.

(390) It is reported that the junction of Pailolo, Auau, and Kalohi Channels, locally known as **The Slot**, is subject to high winds and dangerous currents.

(391) **Kahoolawe**, 6 miles SW across Alalakeiki Channel from the SW extremity of Maui, has an area of 45 square statute miles and is the smallest of the eight major islands. Kahoolawe is about 10 miles long and 6 miles wide, and from a distance has an even, unbroken appearance. The high cliffs on the E and S sides are grayish-black; the soil of the mountain tops and the gentle slopes of the N and W sides are reddish. The island has scarcely any rainfall, and the huge clouds of red dust which trail to leeward during strong winds can be seen for many miles. **Puu Moaulaiki (Moaula)**, a brown dome 1,444 feet high near the E end of the island, is the most prominent landmark.

Warning

(392) Kahoolawe is under Naval jurisdiction. The island was previously used as a military target area for bombing and gunnery training. Large amounts of unexploded

(392) ordnance are present on the island and in its adjacent waters. Entry onto the island or in its adjacent waters is prohibited without the consent of Commander, Third Fleet, Pearl Harbor, HI 96860. Entry regulations are contained in **32 CFR 763.1 through 763.6** (not carried in this Coast Pilot). A **danger zone** extends 2 miles from all sides of the island. (See **334.1340**, chapter 2, for limits and regulations.)

(393) From **Lae o Kuikui (Cape Kuikui)**, the most N point of the island, to Kanapou Bay, the coast is rocky and the bluffs gradually increase to cliffs several hundred feet high at the bay.

(394) **Lae 'O Kaule (Ule Point)**, 2.8 miles SE of Lae o Kuikui, is on the N side of Kanapou Bay.

(395) **Kanapou Bay** 2 miles wide between Lae 'O Kaule and **Lae o Halona (Halona Point)**, offers protection in kona weather. Anchorage is available for small vessels in **Keoneuli (Beck Cove)** on the SW side of the bay. The bay should be entered on a SW course, heading for the middle of the cove, and anchorage should be made in depths of 15 to 20 fathoms off the mouth of the cove and midway between the sides. The bottom shoals rapidly from depths of 12 to 3 fathoms about 0.2 mile from the sandy beach at the head of the cove. W winds draw down the canyon at the head of the cove with considerable force.

(396) From **Lae o Kaka (Kaka Point)**, the SE point of Kahoolawe, to within 1 mile of Honokanaia on the SW side, the coast consists of sheer cliffs which reach a maximum height of 800 feet at Kamohio Bay. There are no offlying dangers except Puu Koae.

(397) **Kamohio Bay** and **Waikahalulu Bay**, 3 and 6 miles W of Lae o Kaka, respectively, each indent the coast about 0.7 mile. Neither bay can be recommended as an anchorage because of the deep water close to the shores. The bays are subject to strong gusts of wind that sweep down over the high cliffs when the trades are blowing. On the W side of Kamohio Bay is **Puu Koae**, a black mass of rocks 378 feet high and about 100 yards offshore.

(398) **Kahoolawe Southwest Point Light** (20°30'08"N., 156°39'59"W.), 120 feet above the water, is shown from a 20-foot white skeleton tower near the SW end of Kahoolawe.

(399) The prevailing current along the S coast of Kahoolawe is W.

(400) **Honokanaia** is 1 mile SE of **Lae 'O Kealaikahiki (Kealaikahiki Point)**, the westernmost point of the island. The cove is the best anchorage on the island except during W or S weather. Anchorage can be had in depths of 10 to 12 fathoms 0.5 mile off the sand beach. The prevailing current at the anchorage is NW. The best landing is on the sand beach close to the conspicuous black rock at the head of the cove. The shore is low and has alternate stretches of sand and rocks. A stream, which is usually dry, and a clump of algaroba trees may be seen. As many as five buildings may be seen on the shore above the beach.

(401) **Kuia Shoal**, with a least depth of 1 fathom, extends 0.7 mile W from Lae 'O Kealaikahiki. A shoal with a least depth of 3 fathoms is about 0.5 mile SW of Kuia Shoal. Vessels should give the point a berth of at least 1.5 miles. The country slopes up evenly from Lae 'O Kealaikahiki to the E.

(402) The NW coast is rocky and has a line of low bluffs from which the country slopes gently up to the reddish hills in the center of the island. There are scarcely any distinguishing marks and no off-lying dangers.

(403) **Kuheeia Bay (Kuheia Bay)**, 2 miles SW of Lae o Kuikui, is a very small bight where boats can land at times.

(404) **Kealaikahiki Channel**, between Kahoolawe and Lanai, is about 15 miles wide. The channel is free from obstructions. Currents in the channel are weak and variable and are influenced by the wind. A maximum velocity of 0.5 knot in a general NE direction was observed in 1962. Sailing craft should avoid this channel during trade winds, as long periods of calms sometimes occur S and W of Kahoolawe and Lanai.

Chart 19340

(405) **Lanai**, 8 miles W across Auau Channel from Maui and the same distance S across Kalohi Channel from Moloka'i, has an area of 141 square statute miles and ranks sixth in size of the eight major islands. Lanai is about 15 miles long in a NW direction and about 10 miles wide near its S end, gradually narrowing toward its NW end. The highest point on Lanai is **Lanaihale**, 3,370 feet high and 3.5 miles inland from the SE side of the island. The slopes on the E side of the mountain are steep and cut by gulches; those on the W side are more gradual, terminating in a rolling plain between the 1,000- and 2,000-foot levels. There is little rainfall and, in general, the island has a barren appearance. The local economy is driven mostly by tourism, although some livestock is raised. **Lanai City**, the only large community, is in the center of the island.

Chart 19347

(406) The coast is low, sandy, and brush-covered from **Kikoa Point**, the easternmost point of Lanai, to **Kamaiki Point**, 3.1 miles SSW. A coral reef and shoal water fringe the shore from 200 to 400 yards off the beach. Low bluffs appear to Kamaiki Point, gradually increasing in height until close to Manele Bay, where they reach a maximum of about 400 feet.

(407) **Manele Bay** is a small indentation in the S coast of Lanai, 3 miles SW of Kaimaiki Point; a lighted buoy is off the entrance, the ruins of a cattle loading ramp, resembling a fisherman's scaffolding, are on the SW point of the bay, and the wreckage of a barge is on the N shore.

(408) **Manele Small-Boat Harbor**, protected by a breakwater on the S side, is in the NW corner of the bay. A

light marks the end of the breakwater. A dredged channel, marked by private buoys, leads from Manele Bay N of the breakwater thence SW to a mooring basin. In 1997, the midchannel controlling depth was 7 feet in the dredged channel, with depths of 6 to 8 feet in the basin; general depths of 4 to 6 feet are available in the boat slips. When entering the harbor, local conditions dictate staying well to the right side of the entrance channel. The prevailing winds blow from the E and there are numerous coral heads near the left edge of the channel, just off the end of the breakwater. In 1981, a rock covered 3 feet and marked by a buoy, was reported about 30 yards NW of the breakwater light in about 20°44'34"N., 156°53'13"W. A fishing pier and launching ramp are at the head of the harbor.

(409) A low rock, over which the sea usually breaks, is 300 yards seaward from the entrance point on the E side of Manele Bay. Small local vessels have anchored in depths of 14 fathoms about 350 yards SW of the rock.

(410) **Puupehe Island (Puupehe Rock)**, locally known as Sweetheart Rock, is 0.5 mile SW of Manele Bay. The island is 110 feet high, brown on its steep sides, flat and grass-covered on its top. It is separated from the shore by a short, low sandspit. The island is the most prominent landmark along this section of the coast. Rocks, over which the sea usually breaks, extend 300 yards E and S from Puupehe. **Hulopoe Bay**, just W of the island has a sandy beach and a prominent large hotel complex at its head. Squalls are less pronounced in Hulopoe Bay than in Manele Bay.

(411) Hulopoe Bay is within the boundary of Manele-Hulopoe Marine Life Conservation District. State regulations forbid operating, mooring, or anchoring any power-driven vessel within Hulopoe Bay. A copy of the regulations can be obtained from the State of Hawaii, Department of Land and Natural Resources, P.O. Box 621, Honolulu, HI 96809.

(412) From Manele Bay to Palaoa Point, the coast consists of low bluffs, behind which the land rises in steep slopes to the tableland above. It is reported that the currents are weak along the S coast of Lanai. A high, detached, grass-covered rock is close to the shore 1.8 miles W of Puupehe. Many small rocks are close to the shore; one, awash at times, is 400 yards offshore and about 2 miles E of Palaoa Point.

(413) **Palaoa Point Light** (20°43'56"N., 156°57'53"W.), 91 feet above the water, is shown from a white skeleton tower on the E prong of a double point at the SW extremity of Lanai. A small bight, with a rocky shore on which small boats can usually land during trade-wind weather, is between the double points. A large rock, known locally as Shark Fin Rock, is about 0.3 mile NNW of the point in about 20°44'15"N., 156°58'08"W.

(414) Beyond Palaoa Point, the coast has a NNW trend. Between the point and Kaumalapau Harbor, the sheer coastal bluffs of **Kaholo Pali** are more than 1,000 feet high in some places. The bluffs are marked by two landslides; one about 1.5 miles N of Palaoa Point, consists of dark material and is very large and conspicuous; the other, about 1.8 miles N of the point, has a gravelly appearance and is covered with vegetation.

(415) **Puu Ulaula**, 1,271 feet high, is 2 miles N of Palaoa Point and a mile inland from Kaholo Pali. There is an air-navigation installation on the summit.

Chart 19351

(416) **Kaumalapau Harbor**, 3.5 miles N of Palaoa Point, is the best harbor on Lanai in all but W and kona weather. The harbor is a small bight at the mouth of the most prominent gulch in the vicinity. A shoal area, marked by unlighted buoys at the outer extremity, extends along the S and E sides of the harbor. Many local fishing craft moor to unlighted mooring buoys in the harbor.

(417) **Kaumalapau** is a commercial barge landing on the N side of the harbor.

(418) **Kaumalapau Light** (20°46'59"N., 156°59'30"W.), 68 feet above the water, is shown from a post with a black and white diamond-shaped dayboard on the S side of the harbor entrance. Oil tanks are prominent on the high ground back of the wharf. A private aerolight is about 2.3 miles E of the harbor.

(419) A 250-foot breakwater with a distinctive white appearance is on the N side of the entrance, is about 50 yards WSW of the outer end of the breakwater. There is no entrance channel but a 600-foot opening leads to a turning basin which is 30 to 50 feet deep and about 500 feet by 800 feet. The wharf provides cargo sheds and about 400 feet of berthing space. The facilities also include two 35-ton and one 30-ton cranes, bulk-handling and storage for petroleum products. A barge makes weekly (Wednesday) calls on the harbor, at which time the harbor becomes a security zone. If a fuel barge is present, there is no admittance.

(420) Gasoline, diesel fuel, and water can be obtained on the Kaumalapau wharf. Small craft up to 40 feet can be handled by a derrick to the deck of the wharf, and small machine repairs can be made at a nearby shop.

(421) Between Kaumalapau Harbor and Ka'ena Point, the coast is a series of bluffs, in some places precipitous and 300 to 400 feet high. The shore is rocky, with a few short stretches of sand. In general, the bottom is fairly steep-to, but small vessels can find anchorage with sufficient swinging room in some places. At times, when the trades are blowing, the wind sweeps down the gulches in heavy gusts which are felt for a mile or more offshore. There are no houses or trees of any size along this coast, which has a barren appearance.

(422) **Nanahoa (Five Needles)**, about 2.3 miles N of Kaumalapau Harbor and near the middle of the W side of the island, are a group of detached pinnacle rocks. The outermost rock is about 300 yards offshore and 32 feet high, and the inner pinnacle is 120 feet high. The rocks are of the same material as the higher cliffs of the shore and are therefore not easily recognized from

offshore. Good anchorage for small-craft can be had in the vicinity.

(423) **Keanapapa Point**, 7.5 miles NW of Kaumalapau Harbor, is the westernmost point of Lanai. The point is low and rocky and is marked by a small knoll 150 yards inland from the shore. A small detached rock, 8 feet high and 150 yards offshore, is 1.9 miles SE of Keanapapa Point. The cliffs, which are 200 feet high in the vicinity of this rock, gradually diminish in height until they are only 20 or 30 feet high 0.5 mile S of Keanapapa Point.

(424) **Ka'ena Point**, 1 mile N of Keanapapa Point, is low and rocky and is hard to distinguish from the other points in the vicinity. The low, rounding, unlighted, NW coast of Lanai is not easily seen at night, and vessels should give it a berth of at least 1 mile, although 0.5 mile will clear all dangers. There are many small, rocky points and short, sandy indentations in this vicinity, and boats can land in the lee of the points at times.

(425) About 1.5 miles ENE of Ka'ena Point is a 1-mile-long stretch of sand beach, with no fringing reef, that provides easy landing for small boats. E of this beach the coral reef fringes the N and E sides of Lanai to a width of as much as 0.3 mile. In general, the beach is backed by a low, narrow strip of land that rises gently to the tableland. Vegetation consists of cactus, low brush, and a few small trees.

Chart 19347

(426) **Pohakuloa Point**, marked by a light, 4 miles ENE of Ka'ena Point, is so low and rounding that it is difficult to recognize as the N extremity of Lanai. A 150-yard opening in the reef 0.4 mile E of the point affords small-boat access to the sand beach. Two wrecks on the reef that fringes the N coast are very prominent. One wreck is 0.7 mile W of Pohakuloa Point; the other wreck is 4.4 miles E of the point.

(427) **Maunalei Gulch**, 6 miles E of Pohakuloa Point, is forked and should not be confused with deep **Hauola Gulch**, 2 miles farther to the SE. A hard-surface highway leads from Lanai City to the mouth of Maunalei Gulch; a group of beach houses, probably **Kahokunui**, is 0.8 mile NW of the gulch.

(428) **Keomuku**, 10 miles SE of Pohakuloa Point, is an abandoned village in an extensive coconut grove. There is a shallow opening in the reef off the village, and boats of less than 4-foot draft find anchorage behind and S of the entrance.

(429) The NE coast of Lanai should be given a berth of at least 0.8 mile. Prevailing E winds tend to set vessels to the W. Current information for this coast is included in the discussion of Auau Channel.

(430) **Kalohi Channel**, 8 miles wide between Lanai and Moloka'i, is free of dangers except for the marginal reefs around the two islands.

Currents

(431) Observations made in Kalohi Channel show reversing currents with average maximum velocities of 0.5 knot. The flood sets NE, and the ebb sets SW. (See Tidal Current Tables for predictions.)

Chart 19340

(432) **Moloka'i**, 7.5 miles NW across Pailolo Channel from Maui and 8 miles N across Kalohi Channel from Lanai, has an area of 259 square statute miles and ranks fifth in size of the eight major islands. More or less rectangular in shape, Moloka'i is about 34 miles long in a W direction and about 7 miles wide. The E end is mountainous; its summit is **Kamakou**, 4,970 feet high. On the N side, the mountain slopes are very steep, in many places almost perpendicular, and numerous deep gorges with precipitous sides can be seen. On the S side, the slopes are gradual, cut by gorges, and terminate in a narrow strip of rolling land near the coast. On the W side, the land slopes gently and is cut by gulches; here and there the crater of an extinct volcano can be seen. About 10 miles from the W end of the island the plain is only a few hundred feet high and is marked here and there by prominent blowholes. The entire W end of the island is a bare table land cut by small gulches and rising gradually to **Mauna Loa**, 1,400 feet high. From seaward this part of the island presents a smooth and rolling appearance.

(433) The island's rural economy includes tourism, cattle ranching, irrigated fruit and vegetable farming, and coffee.

Anchorage

(434) Depths along the S and W coasts of Moloka'i are such that vessels may anchor at will, having due regard for the abrupt shoaling inside the 10-fathom curve. The bottom is mostly coral and sand. The E end of the island is exposed to the NE trades, and the N coast is exposed and offers very little protection. The only traffic along the N coast is the twice-yearly supply barge that calls on Kalaupapa, a community of Hansen's Disease patients. Kamalo Harbor and the boat lagoon in Puko'o Harbor are the only harbors on the S side of the island considered safe during kona storms. Local knowledge is advised when entering Puko'o Harbor.

Currents

(435) Current observations have been made at several places along the S shore of Moloka'i between Kamalo and Laau Point. They indicate, in general, an E flow along the shore in the vicinities of Kaunakakai and Kamalo and a W flow near Laau Point. Combined with these movements are tidal currents which usually reach an E maximum velocity about the time of low water at Honolulu and a W maximum about the time of high water. The W flow near Laau Point is reported to turn

sharply N at the point, and vessels should guard against a set toward the point. Currents are said to set W along the entire N coast of Moloka'i and NE along the E coast. (For further current information covering waters adjacent to Moloka'i, see the discussions of Pailolo, Kalohi, and Kaiwi Channels.)

Weather, Molokai

(436) The trade winds divide at Cape Halawa; one part follows the N shore and another part follows the S shore. Because of the topography of the island the trade wind is frequently a little S of E along the S coast of Moloka'i. The wind is usually light in the early morning, but blows with considerable strength in the middle of the day. During strong trades, dust clouds appear over the W end of the island. Very heavy rainfall is found on the NE side of the island; the S and W sides have very little rainfall.

Supplies

(437) Provisions and some marine supplies are available at Kaunakakai. Gasoline and diesel fuel can be delivered by truck to the Kaunakakai pier. There are no other sources of provisions on Moloka'i. The harbor agent may be contacted at 808–553–1742.

Communications

(438) The island has telephone communication with the other islands and with the mainland. Good roads extend from Kaunakakai, on the S coast, to Moloka'i Airport, in the W central part of the island, and to Kamalo and other small towns. Interisland air and barge service are available.

(439) From Cape Halawa, the E part of the island, to Kamalo, a distance of about 12 miles, the coast has a general SW trend; thence to Laau Point, a distance of about 25 miles, the trend is W. A reef about 1 mile wide fringes almost the entire coast, the widest part being in the bight about 13 miles E of Laau Point. During the day the limits of the reef can generally be determined by the breakers, but, at night, vessels are cautioned to give this coast a good berth.

Chart 19347

(440) **Cape Halawa**, the E point of Moloka'i, is a brown cliff about 300 feet high. Breakers extend about 300 yards off the point and a rock, which bares at times, is 250 yards offshore. During the heavy E sea, it is apt to be quite choppy off this point and vessels should give the cape a berth of about 1.5 miles.

(441) **Cape Halawa Light** (21°09'33"N., 156°42'45"W.), 321 feet above the water, is shown from a steel pole with a concrete base.

(442) **Koali'i**, 1 mile W of the cape, is a hill 794 feet high. In general, the coast between Cape Halawa and Kaunakakai Harbor is low, but rises, first gently, then rapidly, to high, rugged mountains that are cut by many gulches.

(443) **Mokuho'oniki**, a small, yellow, bare, rocky islet, 198 feet high and with almost perpendicular sides, is 0.9 mile offshore and 1.6 miles S of Cape Halawa. **Kanaha Rock**, 95 feet high, is about 50 yards SW of Mokuho'oniki. Midway between the rocks and Moloka'i are depths of about 15 fathoms. The two islets together are locally known as Turtle Rock.

(444) **Honouliwai**, 3.5 miles SW of Cape Halawa, is a small indentation in the coast and offers small boats a little protection from the trades. It should be entered only with local knowledge. About 0.3 mile NE of Honouliwai is **Honoulimaloo**, a small bight in the coast. The coral reef trends farther offshore from Honouliwai SW.

(445) **Waialua**, 4.6 miles SW of Cape Halawa, consists of a few houses at the mouth of a gulch.

(446) **Pauwalu Harbor**, 5 miles SW of Cape Halawa, is a double opening in the reef. The W opening is about 200 yards wide and is usually marked by breakers on either side. Within the entrance is a small pocket with depths of about 2 fathoms, where a few local vessels find some shelter. A house and tank near the beach are partly hidden by trees. The reef extends 0.6 mile offshore, and the 10-fathom curve is about 0.7 mile offshore.

(447) About a mile SW of Pauwalu Harbor is another opening in the reef near **Kainalu**.

Chart 19353

(448) **Pukoo Harbor**, 7.4 miles SW of Cape Halawa is a pocket in the reef some 800 yards long and 250 yards wide. The entrance is through a break in the reef from the SE. A privately dredged channel continues from the harbor to a three-fingered boat lagoon called **Pukoo Lagoon**. The entrance to the lagoon is a 60-yard opening through a rock seawall. A depth of 12 feet can be carried across the harbor entrance to the lagoon channel. The lagoon channel has a depth of 6 feet with a depth of 4 feet inside. The lagoon offers excellent protection to small craft in all weather. The outer harbor is smooth during the trades, although the wind sweeps across it with full force. The passage through the reef is marked on either side by breakers. During kona storms, breakers extend across the passage. Boats entering the harbor should start their approach midway between the breakers and steer for the opening in the seawall of the boat lagoon. Caution should be exercised as there are no navigation aids, and numerous coral heads and submerged rocks are on both sides of the channel; local knowledge is advised. The village of **Pukoo** consists of a few houses on the lowland near the beach in front of a steep-sided gorge that extends well back into the mountain. The reef at Pukoo extends 0.6 mile offshore.

Chart 19347

(449) There are many old fishponds in the vicinity of Pukoo and along the coast for 10 miles W. About 1 mile W of Pukoo is the village of **Kaluaʻaha.**

(450) **Kalaeloa Harbor**, 3.2 miles W of Pukoo Harbor, is the largest and best protected harbor along the coast, but its use is limited by the bar across the entrance, which is an unmarked opening in the reef.

Chart 19353

(451) **Kamalo Harbor**, 5 miles SW of Pukoo Harbor, is the E of two pockets opening S in the reef at the most S point on Molokaʻi. The harbor, excluding the entrance, is about 150 yards wide, and extends more than 0.5 mile into the reef. The entrance to the harbor is through a break in an outer reef. The outer reef has general depths of 1 to 6 feet and the entrance through the break has a least depth of 11 feet. A lighted buoy is off the entrance. The coral reef marking the limits of deep water within the harbor usually are easily seen by day. The village of **Kamalo** consists of a few houses at the mouth of a gulch back of the harbor. The ruins of an old wharf are at the head of the harbor and an A-frame house is visible from seaward.

(452) Kamalo Harbor offers good protection from W to N winds. The soft gray mud bottom has good holding quality. The harbor is used by small boats, but seldom by larger vessels. The swell is not felt within the harbor. Current observations a mile off Kamalo show velocities of about 1 knot. Water, fuel, and supplies are available in the village.

Chart 19351

(453) **Puu Papai**, 830 feet high, is 2 miles NW of Kamalo Harbor and 0.6 mile inland. Deep **Kamalo Gulch** is 1 mile E of the hill and 2.5 miles W of the hill is **Kawela Gulch**, which extends well inland from the small village of **Kawela.**

(454) From Kamalo Harbor the coast has a W trend and the reef extends as much as 1 mile from shore.

Chart 19353

(455) **Kaunakakai Harbor**, 9 miles W of Kamalo Harbor and 16 miles from the W extremity of Molokaʻi, is a commercial barge harbor in the reef off **Kaunakakai**. The harbor is about 600 feet wide by 1,500 feet long and is open to the S. The approach to the basin is marked by lighted and unlighted buoys and a **033.7°** lighted range.

(456) The State-owned wharf, lit by floodlights at night, provides a cargo shed and 500 feet of berthing space. A 700-yard-long mole extends NE from wharf to shore. The mole protects small craft from the trade winds. Barges can lie at the wharf except during the two or three severe kona storms of the winter season. Kamalo Harbor offers better protection for small craft during the konas. When barges are present, the wharf is a secure area and proper identification is required for access. Water is piped to the wharf; gasoline and diesel fuel can be delivered by tank truck. Some marine supplies may be obtained in Kaunakakai.

(457) A boat ramp and mooring area for small craft are just off the N end of the wharf. A channel, marked by private buoys, leads to a small-boat harbor off the SE side of the wharf. With local knowledge, 10 feet can be carried into the harbor. The SE side of the channel and E side of the harbor are extremely shoal; caution is advised. The harbor is protected on its E side by a detached breakwater. There are 29 slips that are reserved for regular occupancy; no visitor slips are available.

(458) The coastal reef extends more than a mile from shore on both sides of the Kaunakakai entrance. Vessels can anchor temporarily in depths of about 15 fathoms off the entrance, but there is little shelter from the NE trades or the konas.

(459) Current observations a mile off Kaunakakai indicate an E set most of the time. Maximum velocities observed were 1 knot E and 0.5 knot W. E and W maximums occur at about the times of low water and high water, respectively, at Honolulu.

Chart 19351

(460) For 3 miles W from Kaunakakai the lowlands extend much farther inland than along any other section of the coast. The reef extends more than a mile from shore and is mostly covered 1 to 3 feet, but has many coral heads that bare at low water. The country between Kaunakakai and Kolo is bare and rocky and is cut by numerous small gulches. The sandy beach is fringed with algaroba trees.

(461) The aerolight of Molokaʻi Airport and the aero obstruction lights on the surrounding hills are visible off the S shore of the island.

Chart 19353

(462) **Kolo Harbor**, about 10 miles W of Kaunakakai, is a large pocket in the reef with a narrow entrance from S. Two private white markers on shore about 300 yards W of Kolo wharf provide a **007°** range, which marks the channel through the reef. The channel and the harbor have depths of about 8 feet; the harbor is subject to shoaling. A moderately heavy swell causes heavy surf on the entrance bar, and the combination of surf and current often creates a hazardous condition. Kolo Harbor affords anchorage with limited swinging room, but the swell is felt even though its full force is broken by the outer reefs. The harbor is not recommended for strangers. The ruins of an old wharf are at the head of the harbor.

Chart 19351

(463) From Kolo Harbor W to Laau Point, the coast is low and has a narrow sand beach, broken here and there by short stretches of rocky shore. The coral reef gradually becomes narrower until it disappears at Laau Point.

(464) **Haleolono Point**, 13 miles W of Kaunakakai and 3.5 miles E of Laau Point, is a conspicuous brown bluff, 50 feet high, that extends 0.2 mile along the water's edge.

Chart 19353

(465) An abandoned barge harbor (**Lono Harbor**) is at Haleolono Point. The entrance is marked by a **345°** private unlighted range. Two breakwaters provide protection for the harbor. Local knowledge is advisable for entering.

Chart 19351

(466) **Waieli** is a prominent, bare hill, 625 feet high, 1 mile NE of Haleolono Point.

(467) **Laau Point**, the SW extremity of Moloka'i, is low and rocky; the 10-fathom curve is about 0.5 mile offshore. **Laau Point Light** (21°05'59"N., 157°18'18"W.), 151 feet above the water, is shown from an 18-foot pole with a black and white diamond-shaped dayboard on a bluff near the point. The prevailing current off Laau Point is N, and vessels are cautioned against a set onto the point.

(468) **Penguin Bank**, an extensive shelf, makes out from the W end of Moloka'i in a general WSW direction for a distance of 28 miles from Laau Point. The bank is fairly flat and consists of sand and coral at depths of 21 to 30 fathoms. Along the N, W, and S edges, the bank drops off very abruptly into depths of more than 100 fathoms.

(469) In the vicinity of Laau Point currents are strong and likely to be erratic. Usually flowing along the W part of the S coast of Moloka'i is a W current that turns sharply to the N as it rounds the point. A strong tide rip W and N of the point forms breakers when the wind is N. A NE set over Penguin Bank joins the N current along the W coast of Moloka'i. This current is not felt in the deep water W of Penguin Bank but is apparent at the edge of the bank when passing inside the 100-fathom curve. There is no apparent connection between this current and the tides, and the trade winds appear to have little effect upon it, although it appears to be stronger or weaker according to whether there is a barometric depression N or S of the islands.

(470) Between Laau Point and Ilio Point, a distance of about 8 miles, the W coast of Moloka'i is bare, low, and rolling, and cut up by a few small gulches. The beach is marked by low bluffs and short stretches of sand, back of which the land rises gently.

(471) **Ilio Point**, 8 miles from Laau Point, is the NW extremity of Moloka'i. Breakers have been observed about 0.3 mile off Ilio Point during heavy weather. A 293-foot hill is 0.8 mile inland. During the trades, small craft can find fair anchorage 1.5 miles S of the point.

(472) The N coast of Moloka'i is mostly bold, but deep-draft vessels should not stand close to the shore. This N coast has no harbor or anchorage that affords shelter in all winds. Kalaupapa is the only port of call for local vessels.

(473) **Mokio Point**, 3 miles E of Ilio Point, is a low, rocky bluff with a detached rock just offshore.

(474) Five miles E of Ilio Point is **Hauakea Pali**, a low cliff that extends inland at right angles to the beach. The seaward end resembles a large, white sandbank and is the most conspicuous landmark in the vicinity. The cliff is the W boundary of the low plain that extends across the island.

(475) E of Hauakea Pali the coastal bluffs gradually rise to precipitous cliffs which are 2,000 to 3,000 feet high in some places.

(476) **Kalaupapa Peninsula**, 16 miles E of Ilio Point, is a low point of land that juts out 2 miles from the face of a high cliff. **Moloka'i Light** (21°12'34"N., 156°58'11"W.), 213 feet above the water, is shown from a 138-foot white tower on the outer part of the peninsula. There is deep water close to the peninsula except for the marginal reef just N of Kalaupapa.

(477) **Kalaupapa** on the W side of Kalaupapa Peninsula is the commercial barge harbor for the community of Hansen's Disease patients which occupies the peninsula. Special permit is required to land unless on State business. This open harbor has a small breakwater on the N side. The State landing provides 56 feet of berthing space and has depths of 2 to 4 feet alongside. Access is good, and no channel is needed to reach open water. Anchorage can be found in depths of 12 fathoms, 0.2 mile off the landing. A steeple is prominent on the approach from the W.

Chart 19347

(478) The country between Kalaupapa Peninsula and Cape Halawa has a very irregular and jagged appearance and is more or less covered with vegetation. The coastal cliffs are broken by headlands, bights, and deep gulches. There are no landing places other than the few debris piles in front of the cliffs and the few level spots in the mouths of the gulches.

(479) **Kalawao**, on the SE side of Kalaupapa Peninsula is a part of the community of Hansen's Disease patients.

(480) **Mokapu Island**, 360 feet high, is 3 miles SE of Moloka'i Light and 0.7 mile offshore. The island is the outermost of two; **Okala Island**, 370 feet high, is close to shore.

(481) **Pahu Point**, 5 miles SE of Moloka'i Light, is a bold, pyramidal headland 1,022 feet high. The point is the seaward end of a sharp ridge that extends inland along

the W side of a deep gulch. **Mokolea Rock**, over which the sea always breaks, is 0.6 mile NE of the point.

(482) **Umilehi Point**, 1 mile E of Pahu Point, is particularly conspicuous and appears to be a small crater with the entire seaward side blown out. **Mokohola Island**, 20 feet high, is a dark rock 0.3 mile off Umilehi Point.

(483) The E half of Molokaʻi's N coast is noted for its rugged scenery and high waterfalls. **Papalaua Falls**, 10 miles E of Kalaupapa Peninsula and 5 miles W of Cape Halawa, start from an elevation of about 2,000 feet at the head of a deep gulch and have a 500-foot drop in one place.

(484) **Halawa Bay** is between **Lamaloa Head**, an 837-foot cliff, and Cape Halawa, the E extremity of Molokaʻi. The bay, which is about 1.5 miles wide between Lamaloa Head and Cape Halawa extends about 0.7 mile inland, affords no shelter from the trades, but indifferent anchorage can be found in depths of 5 fathoms about 0.3 mile from the head. The shores of the bay are mostly backed by high cliffs; there are two black rocks close to the S shore.

(485) **Halawa** consists of a few houses at the mouth of a deep gulch on the SW side of Halawa Bay. The gulch penetrates W, and a waterfall is visible 1 mile from the mouth. A triangular cliff, 300 feet high, is conspicuous about 0.5 mile E of Halawa.

Chart 19340

(486) **Kaiwi Channel**, between Molokaʻi and Oʻahu, is about 22 miles wide and is clear of obstructions. A general N drift is reported over Penguin Bank and in the vicinity of Laau Point; elsewhere in the channel the currents appear variable, depending mainly upon the direction and velocity of the wind. The trade winds that follow the N and S shores of Molokaʻi draw across Kaiwi Channel toward Makapuu Point.

Chart 19357

(487) **Oahu**, 22 miles WNW across Kaiwi Channel from Molokaʻi, has an area of 604 square statute miles and is third largest of the eight major islands. Oʻahu measures 39 nautical miles SE-NW between Makapuʻu and Kaʻena Points and 26 miles S-N between Kalaeloa and Kahuku Point. The island has two prominent mountain ranges, and its skyline is rough and jagged.

(488) **Koʻolau Range** parallels the NE coast for nearly its entire length. The part of the range between Makapuʻu Point and Kaneʻohe Bay has on its seaward side a sheer, rocky cliff, or pali, nearly 2,000 feet high in some places. NW of Kaneʻohe Bay, the cliffs give way to steep, rugged slopes. From offshore, the NW half of the range appears as a long ridge, sloping gradually downward, and ending in low bluffs near Kahuku Point. The crest of the ridge and about half the seaward slope are wooded; the lower part of the slope is grass-covered. The entire range has a very jagged appearance and is cut up on its inland side by deep gorges and valleys. The greatest elevation in Koʻolau Range is at **Puu Konahuanui**, 3,150 feet high and 5 miles back of Honolulu; the peak is on the E side of Nuuanu Valley and overlooks the famous **Nuʻuanu Pali** at the head of the valley. Two miles closer to Honolulu is **Tantalus**, a rounded peak, 2,013 feet high, with a heavily wooded summit. On the seaward side of Koʻolau Range the land is mostly low and rolling; it is cut by a few sharp hills, and is under cultivation.

(489) **Waianae Mountains** parallel the SW coast for nearly the entire distance between Kaʻena Point and Kalaeloa. Several spurs extending from the range toward the shore form short valleys. The range has numerous high peaks; **Kaala**, 4,046 feet high, is the highest.

(490) Between the two mountain ranges is an extensive plain which extends from Pearl Harbor on the S to Haleiwa on the N; the plain rises to an elevation of about 1,000 feet at Wahiawa. There are low, flat, coastal plains between Honolulu and Kalaeloa, in the vicinity of Waianae, Haleiwa, and Kahuku Point, and between Kaneʻohe Bay and Waimanalo.

(491) Prominent headlands on Oʻahu are Makapuʻu Head, Koko Head, Diamond Head, Kaʻena Point, Kahuku Point, Kualoa Point, and Mokapu Peninsula. The entire coast of the island is fringed with coral reefs 0.5 to 1 mile in width, except along parts of the W shore between Kalaeloa and Kaʻena Point. From Kaʻena Point to Kahuku Point, the reefs are not so continuous as along other parts of the island.

Harbors and ports

(492) The largest harbors on Oʻahu are Kaneʻohe Bay and Pearl Harbor; the latter is a prohibited area. Small-craft harbors include Maunalua Bay, Honolulu's Ala Wai Boat Harbor and Kewalo Basin, Waianae Harbor, and Haleiwa Small-Boat Harbor in Waialua Bay. The NE coast is exposed to the trade winds during most of the year, and the only small-craft shelter available is in Kaneʻohe Bay.

Currents

(493) The currents around Oʻahu depend largely upon the winds and are variable in velocity and direction. The general tendency is a W or N flow along the coast. Tidal currents and eddies are noticeable in some places.

Weather, Oʻahu

(494) Thanks largely to the marked marine influence and the persistent trade winds, the climate of Oʻahu is unusually pleasant for the tropics. Records at the International Airport at Honolulu, on the leeward side of the island, show a lowest temperature of 52°F (11.1°C) and a highest of 95°F (35°C). August is the warmest month with an average temperature of 81.3°F (27.4°C). January and February are the coolest with an average temperature of 73.0°F (22.8°C). Each month, May through November, has recorded maximum temperatures in excess of 90°F (32.2°C) while each month from November

through May has recorded minimum temperatures of 60°F (15.6°C) or lower. Throughout the year, the average daily range in temperature is about 14°F (8°C).

(495) In some parts of the Koʻolau Range the annual rainfall is as much as 300 inches (7620 mm). The driest region is the southwest where rainfall drops to below 20 inches (508 mm) a year. At the International Airport, the average annual precipitation is only about 22 inches (559 mm) ranging from about 3.5 inches (89 mm) in December to about one-third of an inch (9.7 mm) in June.

Supplies and repairs

(496) All kinds of supplies are available at Honolulu, and medium-size vessels can be handled for repairs.

Communications

(497) Oʻahu has a good network of hard-surfaced highways. Air and sea transportation is available from Honolulu to the other islands and to the mainland.

(498) Honolulu is the only port in the Hawaiʻian Islands that maintains a commercial radio communication watch.

Chart 19358

(499) **Makapuʻu Head**, the E extremity of Oʻahu, is a bold, barren, rocky headland 647 feet high. **Makapuu Point Light** (21°18'36"N., 157°38'59"W.), 420 feet above the water, is shown from a 49-foot white cylindrical concrete tower on the head.

(500) The seaward side of Makapuʻu Head is a dark cliff; the inland side slopes rapidly to the valley which separates it from the Koʻolau Range. The headland is the landfall for vessels inbound to Honolulu from the mainland.

(501) There is deep water close to the outer end of the headland, but shallower water is found along the N and E sides. Deep-draft vessels should give Makapuʻu Head a berth of about 1 mile and/or stay in depths greater than 20 fathoms.

(502) The **restricted area** of the Makai Undersea Test Range extends NW and NE from Makapuʻu Point. (See **334.1410**, chapter 2, for limits and regulations.)

(503) **Koko Crater**, 2.6 miles SW of Makapuʻu Head and 0.5 mile from the beach, is a sharp, brown cone 1,204 feet high. The coast between Makapuʻu Head and Koko Crater is low sand, rock, and shingle; from Koko Crater to Koko Head the coast is rocky, precipitous, and somewhat irregular.

(504) **Hanauma Bay**, 3.5 miles SW of Makapuʻu Head, is 0.3 mile wide and extends 0.5 mile inland. The waters off the entrance are very choppy during S and E winds. Across the head of the bay is a sand beach that is fringed by 150 yards of coral reefs. The bay is a nature preserve and is a popular snorkeling and scuba diving site. State regulations do not permit boats to enter the bay.

(505) **Koko Head**, 4 miles SW of Makapuʻu Head, is a bold promontory 640 feet high; the seaward side is precipitous, the top is flat, and it slopes off rapidly on the inland side. The headland is developed on its lower W slopes with residential homes, but its general appearance is mostly brown and barren. There is deep water close to Koko Head. Strong W currents have been reported offshore.

(506) **Maunalua Bay** is an open bight that extends W from Koko Head to Diamond Head; coral reefs fringe most of the shore. On the W side of Koko Head, a channel, marked by a light and private daybeacons, leads through the reef to a private marina in Kuapa Pond and to a public launching ramp behind the reef. The channel has a least depth of 5 feet, except at the entrance where it shoals to a depth of 3 feet on the E side near Daybeacon 2. Behind the Koko Head reefs is one of the few anchorages that offer small-craft shelter in all weather except kona storms. Although depths are 13 feet, only small craft familiar with the area should venture behind the reefs. Tidal currents in Maunalua Bay flood W and ebb E; slack waters occur at about the times of high and low waters at Honolulu.

Caution

(507) Vessels approaching Honolulu from the E at night should not mistake the lights between Koko Head and Diamond Head for the lights of Waikiki Beach. Commercial and residential development of the coast along Maunalua Bay has resulted in an increase of background lighting. Vessels have mistaken Makapuu Point Light for Diamond Head Light and run aground on the reef W of Koko Head.

(508) **Wailupe**, 2.7 miles W of Koko Head, is a residential area with a seawall and private piers. A channel, reported dredged to 12 feet, leads through the reefs to Wailupe. Several pipes mark the W side of the entrance channel.

(509) **Diamond Head**, 9 miles WSW of Makapuʻu Head, is an extinct volcano 761 feet high. The steep slopes and the top of the crater are bare and brown; the base is brush covered. **Diamond Head Light** (21°15'21"N., 157°48'34"W.), 147 feet above the water, is shown from a 64-foot white concrete tower near the beach. A lighted buoy is moored in 150 feet of water 0.6 mile off the light. Currents setting in various directions with velocities up to 1 knot were noted about 3 miles SW of Diamond Head.

Chart 19369

(510) The low coast between Diamond Head and Honolulu Harbor is thickly developed, and palm trees are numerous. Along this stretch is world-famous **Waikiki Beach** with its big hotels, surfboarding, outrigger canoe races, and sunbathers. The Waikiki Shore Water Restricted Zone is an area extending about 0.4 mile

offshore along Waikiki Beach. Boating is prohibited in this area, except by permit issued by the Harbors Division, Hawaii Department of Transportation.

Anchorage

(511) A **special anchorage** is in **Kapua Entrance**, about 0.9 mile S of Waikiki Beach. (See **110.1 and 110.128d(d)**, chapter 2, for limits and regulations.)

(512) **Ala Wai Boat Harbor** is 2.5 miles NW of Diamond Head Light. A dredged channel leads from Mamala Bay through the reefs to the basins inside the harbor. In 1967, the channel was dredged to 22 feet. Depths inside the harbor are 8 to 20 feet. The approach to the channel is marked by lighted buoys and the channel is marked by private buoys, daybeacons, and a **013°30'** lighted range. Mariners are advised to line up on the range before entering or exiting the harbor at night.

(513) During the trades, the winds within the harbor are distorted by the nearby tall buildings. Vessels maneuvering in the harbor under sail should beware of sudden changes in the direction and velocity of the wind. The harbor can be entered in all weather except during kona storms. During the summer months, very large swells can be found outside Ala Wai Harbor; mariners should navigate with the utmost caution during those times.

(514) The harbor is one of the most popular places for small-boat activity on O'ahu, and yacht clubs in the harbor are the host for the famed transpacific yacht race. The harbor attendant controls the berthing and mooring facilities.

(515) Marine supplies and complete repair facilities are availabe in the harbor including a sailmaker, radio repairs, and a marine railway that can handle craft up to 45 feet.

(516) **Kewalo Basin**, 3.5 miles NW of Diamond Head Light, is used exclusively by cruise boats, and charter and commercial fishing vessels. A dredged channel leads from Mamala Bay through the reefs to the basin. The channel has a controlling depth of 19 feet. Depths in the basin are from 18 to 22 feet for the most part with shallow depths of less than 4 feet along the edges of the entrance channel. The channel is marked by lighted buoys and a directional light.

(517) At times when stormy S or SW (kona) winds create high swells, the channel becomes extremely hazardous. There is usually a strong rip current crossing the channel at this time.

Charts 19367, 19369, 19362

(518) **Honolulu Harbor** is 5 miles NW of Diamond Head and midway along the S coast of O'ahu; the harbor is protected from all winds and is usually free of surge. **Honolulu** is the capital and the principal deepwater port of the State of Hawaii.

Prominent features

(519) **Honolulu Harbor Entrance Light** (21°17'45"N., 157°52'08"W.), 95 feet above the water, is shown from a white post on the SE point of the entrance channel. The flashing green light can be easily identified against the background of Honolulu lights.

(520) **Sand Island**, which borders the seaward side of Honolulu Harbor, is Government-owned and has been built up mostly from harbor dredging. The Coast Guard base is on the NE side of the island.

(521) **Aloha Tower**, a 193-foot cream-colored, square clock tower on Pier 10, is one of the most conspicuous objects in the harbor. The tall, square, twin white office buildings 300 yards E of Aloha Tower are prominent and provide an excellent reference to ships approaching the harbor by day. **Punchbowl Hill**, 500 feet high and flat topped, is 1 mile inland from Aloha Tower. The horizontal blue lights of the Ala Moana Tower restaurant (21°17.8'N., 157°50.7'W.), 1.5 miles E of Honolulu Harbor entrance, are easily distinguished at night and provide an excellent navigation aid.

Caution

(522) Vessels approaching the harbor from the W at night should not mistake the lights between Pearl Harbor and Honolulu for the lights of Honolulu, or the lighted buoys off Kalihi Channel for the lighted buoys off the main entrance. Vessels have mistaken these lights and gone aground off Keehi Lagoon. From the E the lights N of Diamond Head should not be confused with those of Honolulu, or the lighted aids of Kewalo Basin with those of Honolulu Harbor. Also from the E, vessels should not mistake the lights between Koko Head and Diamond Head for the lights of Waikiki Beach. Commercial and residential development of the coast along Maunalua Bay has resulted in an increase of background lighting. Vessels have mistaken Makapuu Point Light for Diamond Head Light and run aground on the reef W of Koko Head.

COLREGS Demarcation Lines

(523) The lines established for Mamala Bay are described in **80.1420**, chapter 2.

Channels

(524) A **Federal project** provides for a 45-foot Honolulu Entrance Channel from **Mamala Bay**, thence 40 feet in the main harbor basin. The project also provides for a 23-foot channel leading from seaward in Mamala Bay through Kalihi Channel on the W side of Sand Island to Kapalama Basin. The connecting channel between main harbor basin and Kapalama Basin has a 40-foot project depth with 40 feet in the Kapalama Basin. (See Notice to Mariners and the latest editions of charts for controlling depths.)

(525) **Honolulu Entrance Channel** is marked by lights, buoys, and a **027.9°** lighted range. The rear light and marker of the range is sometimes obscured when large

ships are moored at Berth 8. **Kalihi Channel** is marked by lights, buoys, and a **007°** lighted range.

(526) The John H. Slattery (Sand Island) highway bridge over the harbor end of Kalihi Channel has fixed spans with a clearance of 14 feet.

Anchorages

(527) General anchorages for commercial vessels are in Mamala Bay, W and SE of Kalihi Channel Entrance, sand and coral bottom. (See **110.1** and **110.235**, chapter 2, for limits and regulations.) Mariners are advised not to use this anchorage or to leave the anchorage during periods of large S swell or strong kona winds. Use of the anchorages is controlled by the Honolulu harbormaster; any vessel that wishes to use an assigned anchorage is required to obtain permission from the harbormaster's office. Vessels entering the anchorage area are required to seek traffic clearance from Aloha Tower traffic control on VHF-FM channel 12; call sign, WHX-528. Vessels are also required to advise Aloha Tower of their departure time from the anchorages. All vessels must monitor VHF-FM channels 16 and 12 while they are in the anchorages. Anchorage is not practical in the harbor basins because of the limited swinging room. Sewer outfall lines extend SW from a point on Sand Island; mariners are cautioned not to anchor within 600 yards of the sewer line.

Regulated navigation areas

(528) A **Security Zone** has been established in Honolulu Harbor and entrance channel. (See **33 CFR 165.1407**, chapter 2, for limits and regulations.)

Currents

(529) It is reported that a tidal current floods W and ebbs E along the coast between Makapu'u Point and Honolulu. In the vicinity of Honolulu, an E counterflow along the edge of the reef is reported to accompany the W flood. Strong W currents have been reported off Honolulu. Currents setting toward all four quadrants and having velocities up to 1 knot have been noted about 3 miles SW of Diamond Head.

Tsunami (seismic sea waves)

(530) The size of a predicted tsunami cannot be estimated in advance. Most of them felt in Honolulu Harbor have been relatively small; the largest of record was 10 feet high in 1960. However, it is prudent to anticipate that even greater ones may strike.

(531) Honolulu Harbor authorities require all ships to vacate the harbor prior to the estimated time of arrival of a sea wave if possible. If a long engine-warmup is necessary, it should be started at the first alert so the vessel may be ready to proceed in time.

(532) Telephone notification will be given by the Captain of the Port to vessel agents who must, in turn, notify their respective ships. Messengers will be used to the extent available to supplement the telephone warnings.

(533) When ready to depart, each ship should obtain clearance from the harbormaster. The Aloha Tower, traffic control, can be contacted on VHF-FM channel 12, call sign WHX-528. The traffic controller will assign each vessel a departure time in accordance with harbor regulations, depending on vessel size, type, location in the harbor, and vessel type priority. Once a vessel has checked in with Aloha Tower traffic control, they are required to monitor VHF-FM channel 12 at all times.

(534) The **harbormaster** will assign the departure time in accordance with assigned priorities and in consideration of the time each vessel becomes ready to move. The assigned priorities for vessels ready to depart are: Government vessels, passenger vessels, tankers, vessels with explosive cargo, and freighters.

(535) Vessels unable to move in time should take adequate precautions against damage during the tsunami due to the expected rise and fall of the water.

(536) (See discussions of tsunamis at beginning of this chapter and in chapter 1.)

Weather, Honolulu and vicinity

(537) The climate of Hawaii is unusually pleasant for the tropics. Its outstanding features are (1) the persistence of the trade winds, where not disrupted by high mountains; (2) the remarkable variability in rainfall over short distances; (3) the sunniness of the leeward lowlands, in contrast to the persistent cloudiness over nearby mountain crests; (4) the equable temperature from day to day and season to season; and (5) the infrequency of severe storms.

(538) The prevailing wind throughout the year is the NE trade wind, although its average frequency varies from more than 90 percent during the summer to only 50 percent in January.

(539) Annual rainfall in the Honolulu area averages less than 30 inches along the coast (22 inches at the airport, 24 inches in the downtown area (559 mm and 610 mm, respectively)), but increases inland at about 30 inches (762 mm) a mile. The mean annual number of days with precipitation totals 220. The wettest year on record, 1965, saw nearly 43 inches (1092 mm) while the driest year, 1983, saw only five inches (127 mm) of precipitation. In March 1958, over 15 inches (381 mm) of precipitation fell in one 24-hour period. Parts of the Ko'olau Range average 300 inches (7620 mm) or more a year. This heavy mountain rainfall sustains extensive irrigation of cane fields and the water supply for Honolulu. East (windward) of the Ko'olaus, coastal areas receive 30 to 50 inches (762 to 1270 mm) annually; cane and pineapple fields in central O'ahu get about 35 to 40 inches (889 to 1016 mm). O'ahu is driest along the coast west of the Waianaes where rainfall drops to about 20 inches (508 mm) a year. However, variations from month to month and year to year are considerable; more so during the cooler season, when occasional major storms provide much of the rain, than in the summer, when rain occurs primarily as showers

that form within the moist trade winds as they override the mountains. Thus, March rainfall at Honolulu Airport has ranged from more than 20 inches (508 mm) to as little as 0.001 of an inch (0.03 mm, in effect, a trace). In the mean, about a third of the airport's annual total occurs during its two wettest months, December and January. Trade-wind rainfall is more frequent at night. Daytime showers, usually light, often occur while the sun continues to shine, a phenomenon referred to locally as "liquid sunshine."

(540) Average water temperatures at Waikiki Beach vary from 75°F (23.9°C) in the morning to 77°F (25°C) in the afternoon during March, and from 77°F (25°C) in the morning to 82°F (27.8°C) in the afternoon during August.

(541) Because of the persistence and moderate humidity of the NE trade winds, even the warmest months are usually comfortable. But when the trades diminish or give way to S winds, a situation known locally as "kona weather" ("kona storms" when stormy), the humidity may become oppressively high.

(542) Weather severe enough to interfere with shipping or travel is uncommon. Intense rains of the October to April "winter" season sometimes causes serious, but local, flash flooding. Thunderstorms are infrequent and usually mild, as compared with those of the midwestern United States. Hail seldom occurs, and when it does it is small and rarely damaging to crops. At great intervals a small tornado or a waterspout moving onshore may do some slight damage. Four hurricanes have struck Hawaii since 1950, but several times that many, and a number of less intense tropical cyclones, most of them drifting W from their breeding grounds off the Mexican coast, have approached near enough for their outlying winds, clouds, and rain to affect the islands.

(543) The National Weather Service office is at the airport; **barometers** may be compared there or by telephone. (See Appendix A for address.)

(544) (See Appendix B for **Honolulu climatological table.)**

Pilotage, Honolulu

(545) Pilotage is compulsory for all foreign vessels and U.S. vessels under register in foreign trade; it is optional for U.S. vessels in coastwise trade with a Federal licensed pilot on board. Pilots are available through the Hawaii Pilots Association. Mariners are requested to give 24 hours advance notice of arrival, gross tonnage, length, and draft of vessel by telephone (808–537–4169) or by e-mail at dispatch@hawaiipilots.net. The 41-foot long pilot boat HONOLULU has a black hull with yellow superstructure and displays the words 'HAWAII PILOTS' in large white letters on the sides of the cabin. The pilot boat displays the International Code Flag 'H' by day and shows the standard pilot lights at night, white over red. The pilot boat monitors VHF-FM channels 12 and 16 and can be reached by "HONOLULU PILOTS" call sign, WXZ-456. Additionally, vessels are requested to rig a pilot ladder 1 meter above the water on the leeward side. The pilot boarding area is about 1 mile seaward of the sea buoy on the entrance channel range line. The pilot station is at pier 19 and monitors VHF-FM channels 12 and 16. When pilots are boarding incoming vessels from the pilot boat, the vessel should maintain a speed of about 5 knots. Foreign and U.S. vessels under registry in foreign trade, and U.S. vessels in coastwise trade without a licensed Federal pilot on board must acquire pilot service before entering the anchorages.

(546) In addition to the above, the State of Hawaii has established **special pilotage regulations** for all **tankers, tanker barges**, and **tankerlike vessels**. In general the regulations require these vessels to have on board a Honolulu Port Pilot when entering or departing Honolulu Harbor for any reason. Exempt from this requirement are tankerlike vessels and vessels towing tanker barges when under the control and direction of a person duly licensed as a pilot by the U. S. Coast Guard for the Port of Honolulu, and tankers when departing from anchorage. A copy of the rules and regulations affecting such vessels may be obtained from the Department of Transportation of the State of Hawaii, Harbors Division, Honolulu, or at the office of the harbormaster.

(547) All mariners are advised to monitor Honolulu harbor traffic movements on VHF-FM channel 12 at all times when approaching or transiting the waters of Mamala Bay.

Towage

(548) Tugs up to 4,000 hp, including several z-drive type tractor tugs, are available in Honolulu. Salvage equipment is also available.

Quarantine, customs, immigration, and agricultural quarantine

(549) (See chapter 3, Vessel Arrival Inspections, and Appendix A for addresses.)

(550) **Quarantine** is enforced in accordance with regulations of the U.S. Public Health Service. (See Public Health Service, chapter 1.)

(551) Honolulu is a **customs port of entry**.

Coast Guard

(552) **Honolulu Coast Guard Base** is on the NE side of Sand Island. The Fourteenth Coast Guard District Office and Sector Office Honolulu are located in Honolulu. (See Appendix A for address.)

Harbor regulations

(553) Harbor regulations are established by the Harbors Division, Hawaii Department of Transportation, and are enforced by the harbormaster. Prior to entry, all vessels must establish communications with Aloha Tower traffic control on VHF-FM channels 12 or 16; call sign, WHX-528. The phone number for Aloha Tower is 808–587–2076. **Traffic control** in Honolulu is controlled by amber lights on the tower at night. The lower light,

Facilities in the Port of Honolulu

Name	Location	Berthing Space (feet)	Depths* (feet)	Deck Height (feet)	Mechanical Handling Facilities and Storage	Purpose	Owned/ Operated by:
State of Hawaii Diamond Head Terminal (Piers 1 and 2)	21°18'00"N., 157°52'01"W.	2,967	34-39	7.25	• Open storage (29 acres) • Covered storage (318,610 square feet)	• Receipt and shipment of conventioanl and containerized general cargo • Receipt of automobiles, lumber and paper products	State of Hawaii
State of Hawaii (Piers 22 and 23)	21°18'40"N., 157°52'10"W.	800	30	6	Grain elevator with 20 silos (26,000 tons) served by underground conveyor	Receipt of grain	State of Hawaii/ Hawaiian Flour Mills
State of Hawaii (Piers 24 and 25)	21°18'38"N., 157°52'13"W.	935	23-30	6	Covered storage (70,000 square feet)	Receipt and shipment of conventioanl, containerized and roll-on/roll-off general cargo and automobiles	State of Hawaii/ Young Brothers, Ltd.
State of Hawaii (Pier 26)	21°18'37"N., 157°52'14"W.	695	22-29	6	Covered storage (35,000 square feet)	Receipt and shipment of conventioanl, containerized and roll-on/roll-off general cargo and automobiles	State of Hawaii/ Young Brothers, Ltd.
State of Hawaii (Pier 27)	21°18'35"N., 157°52'14"W.	885	29	7	Covered storage (64,450 square feet)	Receipt and shipment of conventioanl, containerized and roll-on/roll-off general cargo and automobiles	State of Hawaii/ Young Brothers, Ltd.
State of Hawaii (Piers 28 and 29)	21°18'35"N., 157°52'19"W.	1,290	28-30	7	Covered storage (102,175 square feet)	Receipt and shipment of conventioanl, containerized and roll-on/roll-off general cargo and automobiles	State of Hawaii/ Young Brothers, Ltd.
Chevron Products Co. Honolulu Pier 30	21°18'41"N., 157°52'26"W.	270	30	6-7	28 storage tanks with a total capacity of 370,000 barrels	Receipt and shipment of petroleum products	Chevron Products Co., Inc.
State of Hawaii (Piers 31A, 31, 32 and 33)	21°18'45"N., 157°52'35"W.	1,440	34	7	• Open storage (5 acres) • Covered storage (200,000 square feet) • Tank storage: (302,000 barrels) (600,000 gal. caustic soda	• Receipt and shipment of conventional genral cargo • Receipt of lumber, automobiles, caustic soda and miscellaneous bulk commodities	State of Hawaii
State of Hawaii (Pier 34)	21°18'53"N., 157°52'40"W.	550	34	7	Tank storage: (18,000 tons of cement) (508,000 barrels of petroleum)	• Receipt of petroleum products • Shipment of bulk cement	State of Hawaii/ Tosco Distribution Co.; Tesoro Petroleum Corp.; Hawaiian Cement Corp.
State of Hawaii (Pier 39)	21°19'03"N., 157°52'50"W.	2,238	24-33	8	• Open storage (9.5 acres) • Covered storage (90,000 square feet)	Receipt and shipment of conventional, containerized and roll-on/roll-off general cargo and automobiles	State of Hawaii/ Young Brothers, Ltd.
State of Hawaii (Pier 40)	21°19'02"N., 157°52'54"W.	2,010	25-33	8	• Open storage (13 acres) • Covered storage (46,800 square feet)	Receipt and shipment of conventional, containerized and roll-on/roll-off general cargo and automobiles	State of Hawaii/ Young Brothers, Ltd.
State of Hawaii (Pier 51A)	21°18'51"N., 157°53'07"W.	556	39	8	• Open storage (39.9 acres) • Tank storage (840,000 barrels) • Two 37½-ton container cranes	Receipt and shipment of containerized general cargo	State of Hawaii/ Sea Land Service, Inc.; Airport Group International, Inc.
State of Hawaii (Piers 51B and 51C)	21°18'50"N., 157°53'00"W.	1,000	39	8	• Covered storage (49,741 square feet) • Tank storage (72,000 gallons)	Receipt and shipment of containerized and roll-on/ roll-off general cargo, automobiles and molasses	State of Hawaii/ Matson Terminals, Inc.
State of Hawaii (Piers 52A, 52B and 53)	21°18'40"N., 157°52'37"W.	3,000	40	8.2	• Open storage (40.3 acres) • Tank storage (4 million gal.) • Seven container cranes to 45 tons	Receipt and shipment of containerized and roll-on/ roll-off general cargo, automobiles and molasses	State of Hawaii/ Matson Terminals, Inc.; Alexander & Baldwin, Inc.

* The depths given above are reported. For information on the latest depths contact the port authorities or the private operators.

showing fixed, is 143 feet above the water; the upper flashing light is 152 feet above the water. The lights are visible 5 miles from 320° to 062°; flashing light on, incoming traffic only; fixed light on, outgoing traffic only; both lights on or no lights showing, harbor closed to all traffic. To pass visual messages, contact Pearl Harbor Navy Signal Tower, call H-1.

(554) The **speed limit** in Honolulu Harbor is 5 knots for all vessels and tows and 10 knots for motorboats, and other small craft.

(555) A flashing amber warning light, privately maintained and shown about 22 feet above the water from a pole about 70 yards SSW of Pier 38, is activated when there is a gas leak or the likelihood thereof. Anyone observing the light flashing should remain well clear and upwind, and sources of ignition should be secured.

Wharves

(556) Honolulu has several piers and wharves around its harbor waterfront. Only the deep-draft facilities are listed in the facilities table. For a complete description of the port facilities refer to Port Series No. 50, published and sold by the U.S. Army Corps of Engineers. (See Appendix A for address.) The alongside depths for the facilities listed are reported; for information on the latest depths, contact the State of Hawaii, Department of Transportation, Harbors Division or the private operators. All facilities have direct highway connections. Water is available at the berths and most have electrical connections. General cargo at the port is usually handled by ship's tackle; special handling equipment, if available, is mentioned in the table under 'Mechanical Handling Facilities and Storage'. Several cranes to 200 tons can be rented and numerous warehouses/cold storage facilities adjacent to the waterfront are available.

Supplies

(557) Vessels are usually bunkered at berth by tank barges. Vessels usually receive bunker fuel at Piers 30 through 34. Other operators at the port provide bunker fuel solely to vessels using their particular facility.

Repairs

(558) Above and below the waterline repairs of any nature can be made at Honolulu. Two floating drydocks are available; the largest has a lifting capacity of 8,000 tons, 463-foot length over the keel blocks, 78-foot width between the wing walls (maximum width of 101 feet), and a 20-foot depth over the blocks. A large marine railway is available in the port with a lifting capacity of 400 tons, 222-foot length, 63-foot width, and 10-foot depth. In an emergency large commercial vessels have been handled at the Pearl Harbor Naval Shipyard.

Communications

(559) Honolulu is a major port of call for transpacific vessels, and there is commercial barge service to and from the other islands. Air service, passenger and freight, includes scheduled flights to the other islands, to the mainland, and to W and SW Pacific areas.

Chart 19369

(560) **Keehi Lagoon**, 6 miles NW of Diamond Head is triangular in shape and is fronted by coral reefs. The cuts through the lagoon are former seaplane landing areas. Kalihi Channel, previously mentioned, cuts through the SE part of the lagoon. A privately dredged channel branches NW from Kalihi Channel to a small-boat harbor and a barge harbor and turning basin on the E side of the landing areas. In 2009, the controlling depth was 18 feet in the channel to the turning basin; thence in 13 feet was in the basin. The barge channel is marked by a private **334°** lighted range.

Anchorage

(561) A **special anchorage** is in Keehi Lagoon on the W side of the barge channel. (See **110.1 and 110.128d(c)**, chapter 2, for limits and regulations.)

(562) Submerged pipelines, centered about 160 yards NE from the N corner of the special anchorage, extend from the SE to the NW side of Keehi Lagoon; mariners should avoid anchoring in the pipeline area.

Regulated navigation areas

(563) A **Security Zone** has been established in Kalihi Channel and Keehi Lagoon. (See **33 CFR 165.1407**, chapter 2, for limits and regulations.)

(564) **Honolulu International Airport**, on the N shore of Keehi Lagoon, is the largest commercial airport in the State. The control tower (21°19'14"N., 157°55'38"W.) is prominent from seaward.

Charts 19357, 19369, 19366

(565) A low, flat plain, 3 to 5 miles wide, borders the sandy shore between Keehi Lagoon and Kalaeloa. The area includes Pearl Harbor and several airfields. W of Pearl Harbor, most of the area is developed with residential communities.

(566) **Pearl Harbor**, 9.5 miles WNW of Diamond Head, is a **Defensive Sea Area** established by Executive Order No. 8143 of May 26, 1939. The order says in part:

(567) "The area of water in Pearl Harbor, Island of O'ahu, Territory of Hawaii, lying between extreme high-water mark and the sea, and in and about the entrance channel to said harbor, within an area bounded by the extreme high-water mark, a line bearing S from the SW corner of the Puuloa Naval Reservation, a line bearing S from Ahua Point, and a line bearing W from a point 3 miles due S from Ahua Point, has been established as a defensive sea area for purposes of national defense, and no persons (other than persons on public vessels of the United States) are permitted to enter this defensive sea area, and no vessels or other craft (other than public vessels of the United States) are permitted to navigate in this area, except by authority of the Secretary of the Navy."

(568) Permission to enter Pearl Harbor must be obtained in advance from Commander, Navy Region Hawaii 96860.

Pilotage, Pearl Harbor

(569) All vessels, except commissioned ships of the U.S. Navy and U.S. Coast Guard, are required to take a pilot when entering or departing Pearl Harbor. Pilots meet vessels at Approach Point PAPA HOTEL (21°16'06"N., 157°56'23"W.), about 2 miles SE of the entrance buoys.

All vessels destined for Pearl Harbor must pass through this point, which is not marked by any navigational aid.

(570) Pearl Harbor Control maintains a 24 hour guard on VHF-FM channel 69. It is requested that vessels guard VHF-FM channel 69, 1 hour before entrance, and continuously thereafter unless guard for this circuitry is arranged after arrival. The voice call of Pearl Harbor Port Control is "Pearl Harbor Control;" ships use own ship's name as voice call. Pearl Harbor Control also guards the Bridge-to-Bridge frequency VHF-FM channel 13.

(571) The fan-shaped harbor has an entrance width of 400 yards and a greatest inland extent of 5 miles. The entrance channel is marked by lights, a lighted range, lighted and unlighted buoys. The main basin is divided by two peninsulas and an island into four smaller basins known as **West Loch**, **Middle Loch**, **East Loch**, and **Southeast Loch**. Tidal currents are generally weak, but the ebb sometimes exceeds 0.5 knot. A dangerous W set may be experienced in the vicinity of the entrance to Pearl Harbor Channel.

Anchorages

(572) **Special anchorages** are on the E side of the Pearl Harbor Entrance Channel near Kumumau Point; on the W side of the channel in the lagoon S of Iroquois Point; and in Aiea Bay on the E side of East Loch. (See **110.1 and 110.128d (e) through (h)**, chapter 2, for limits and regulations.)

Chart 19362

(573) **Kalaeloa**, 17 miles W of Diamond Head, is the SW extremity of Oʻahu. The low land back of the rounding point extends 3 miles N to the foothills of the Waianae Mountains; the hill slopes are steep and partly brush covered but the bare soil that shows in places gives them a reddish appearance.

(574) **Barbers Point Light** (21°17'47"N., 158°06'22"W.), 85 feet above the water, is shown from a 75-foot white cylindrical concrete tower. A reef extends 0.6 mile off the light.

(575) In 1996, Captain of the Port Honolulu amended federal **pilotage waters** in the vicinity of the offshore pipeline terminal off Kalaeloa. The area was expanded to be identical to that designated in 1995 for vessels engaged in foreign commerce and is defined by the following points:

(576) 21°17'47"N., 158°06'23"W.; thence to
(577) 21°14'49"N., 158°06'23"W.; thence to
(578) 21°14'49"N., 158°03'10"W.; thence to
(579) 21°15'26"N., 158°00'57"W.; thence to
(580) 21°18'18"N., 158°01'49"W.; thence along the shoreline to the point of beginning.

(581) All foreign trade vessels, U.S. vessels under registry, and U.S. vessels engaged in coastwise trade operating within this area must be under the direction and control of a first class pilot.

(582) Two naval **danger zones** and a **restricted area** have been established between Kalaeloa and the entrance to Pearl Harbor. (See **334.1360, 334.1370, and 334.1400**, chapter 2, for limits and regulations.)

(583) Three offshore oil tanker mooring terminals and their submarine pipelines are located within a **restricted anchorage area** and **security zone** off Kalaeloa. (See 33 **CFR 110.236** and **165.1407**, chapter 2, for limits and regulations.) All vessels, except for vessels with official business at the tanker terminals, should stay well S of these areas in order to avoid the unlit mooring buoys located there.

Currents

(584) There is a general W current along the coast between Honolulu and Kalaeloa. Velocities up to 0.8 knot, setting W, have been measured off the point, and greater velocities have been reported.

Chart 19357

(585) The coast has a general NW trend between Kalaeloa and Kaena Point, a distance of about 20 miles, and consists of alternating ledges of rock and stretches of white sand. Spurs of the Waianae Mountains extend to most of the points. Between the spurs and ridges are heavily wooded valleys that contrast with the rocky and bare mountains. A highway follows the coast from just N of Kalaeloa to Kaena Point.

(586) Much of the shoreline is fringed with rocks and reefs, but they are mostly close to the shore. The 3-fathom curve is within 0.5 mile of the shore, and the 10-fathom curve is within 1 mile. Vessels can avoid all outlying dangers by giving the coast a berth of 1 to 1.5 miles. Other than Pokai Bay, there are no harbors or anchorages along the W coast that afford shelter in all winds.

(587) **Barbers Point Harbor** is about 2 miles NW of Kalaeloa. A dredged channel leads NE to a basin in the harbor. In June 2007, the controlling depth was 38 feet in the entrance channel to the basin, thence 36 to 38 feet in the basin. The channel is marked by lighted buoys, lights, and a **045°** lighted range. A **security zone** has been established in the harbor. (See **33 CFR 165.1407**, chapter 2, for limits and regulations.)

(588) The basin has a 1,600-foot dock with a 30-acre paved backup area and 120 acres for cargo handling and storage. A ship repair company has an 18,000-ton drydock capable of handling vessels over 600 feet long and 94 feet wide. Vessels entering the harbor during the winter months should be aware of large swells coming from the N.

Pilotage, Barbers Point Harbor

(589) A state licensed pilot is required to enter the harbor. Pilots are available through the Hawaii Pilots Association. Mariners are requested to give 24 hours advance

notice of arrival, gross tonnage, length and draft of vessel by telephone (809–537–4169) or by e-mail at dispatch@hawaiipilots.net. The 31-foot long pilot boat IWA has a black hull with yellow superstructure and displays the word 'PILOTS' in large white letters on the sides of the cabin. The pilot boat displays the International Code Flag 'H' by day and shows the standard pilot lights at night, white over red. The pilot boat monitors VHF-FM channels 12 and 16 and can be reached by "BARBERS POINT PILOTS". Additionally, vessels are requested to rig a pilot ladder 1 meter above the water on the leeward side.

(590) A marina harbor entrance, marked by lights, is in the NW portion of the basin. Gasoline, diesel fuel, 267 slips, electricity, water, pump-out, marine supplies, and a public boat ramp are available at the marina. In 2003, the harbormaster reported that the marina could accommodate vessels up to 150 feet in length with a draft of 13 feet.

(591) A flashing amber warning light, privately maintained and shown from a pole about 22 feet high on the S side of the harbor, is activated when there is a gas leak or the likelihood thereof. Anyone observing the light flashing should remain well clear and upwind, and sources of ignition should be secured.

(592) Barbers Point Harbor is a **customs port of entry**.

(593) **Kahe Point**, 3.5 miles N of Kalaeloa, is the seaward end of a mountain spur. A large power plant is prominent on the point. The largest stack is 485 feet high with a strobe light on top. Two short boulder groins extending from the shore protect the intake of the plant's cooling system. The outfall is about 250 yards offshore with 9 feet of water over it.

(594) **Nanakuli**, 5.5 miles N of Kalaeloa, is a homestead area near the shore.

(595) **Puu o Hulu**, about 7 miles NW of Kalaeloa, is a narrow rocky, barren ridge, 1.5 miles long. A large water tank is on the saddle of the S slope. The ridge is on **Maili Point**, the S of the two important projecting points of this coast, and is the most conspicuous landmark in this vicinity. The W end of the ridge is close to the shore and has an elevation of 856 feet; it is precipitous on its seaward side.

Chart 19361

(596) **Lualuaei Homestead** tracts are N and NE of Puu o Hulu. Two 1,500-foot radio towers are prominent in the valley. **Puu Mailiilii**, about 2 miles N of Puu o Hulu, is a narrow, rocky ridge, 723 feet high, near the shore and approximately at right angles with it.

(597) Low **Kaneilio Point**, 10 miles NW of Kalaeloa, projects 0.2 mile from the general coastline. A fish haven consisting of old auto bodies is 1 mile S of the point. Between Puu o Hulu and Kaneilio Point the light-colored buildings of a limekiln 0.3 mile inland show up against a dark background. In 1999, suspected live ordnance was reported about 2 miles SW of Kaneilio Point inside the following coordinates: 21°26'23"N., 158°12'11"W.; 21°26'23"N., 158°12'38"W.; 21°25'26"N., 158°12'38"W.; 21°25'26"N., 158°12'11"W.

(598) **Pokai Bay**, on the NW side of Kaneilio Point, is the seaward approach to **Waianae**. Shallow water extends 0.3 mile from the inner shore of the bay. The breakwater extending N from Kaneilio Point and the opposing boulder groin from the inner shore form a State water recreation area. Piles are about midway between the breakwater and the shore. The area E of the piles is for swimming, and the area between the piles and the breakwater is for outrigger canoes. No person shall operate, anchor or moor any other vessel in the area between the piles and the breakwater except in adverse weather conditions when emergency anchoring is permitted.

(599) **Waianae Boat Harbor**, 0.5 mile NW of Kaneilio Point, is owned and operated by the State of Hawaii. The harbor is used primarily by fishing boats. The harbor is entered from the SE between two breakwaters. The harbor is protected on the W side by a 1,690-foot-long L-shaped breakwater, marked on its seaward end by a light, and on the NE side at the entrance by a 220-foot-long stub breakwater. A **003°-183°** lighted range marks the entrance approach. In 2006, the controlling depths were 8 feet in the entrance channel to a turning basin, thence 12 feet was available in the basin (except for lesser depths to 10 feet in the NE corner), thence 11 feet in the main access channel along the L-shaped breakwater. Berthage, water, and two double launching ramps are available at the harbor. Waianae harbormaster has scheduled daytime hours (0745 to 1630) Tuesdays through Saturdays; phone numbers are: 808–697–7095 (business) and 808–851–1839 or 808–696–9921 (emergency or after hours); 808–594–0849 (fax).

Local magnetic disturbance

(600) Differences of 2° or more from normal variation may be expected in Pokai Bay.

(601) A deep valley extends about 4 miles inland between Puu o Hulu and Lahilahi Point and is the largest valley on this side of the Waianae Range. The broken ridge which makes down to Puu Paheehee divides the valley. **Puu Paheehee**, 652 feet high, is about 1 mile inland from Waianae.

(602) **Lahilahi Point**, 1.7 miles NW of Kaneilio Point, is a detached, steep ridge of dark rock, 234 feet high. This narrow, conspicuous point, projecting seaward about 0.2 mile, has the appearance of an islet from a distance and is known to local fishermen as **Black Rock**. An apartment building on the beach 250 yards N of the point and a hotel about 1.2 miles NNE of the point are good landmarks.

(603) **Kepuhi Point**, 13 miles NW of Kalaeloa, is a few hundred yards from the seaward end of a bold, rocky, mountain spur.

Chart 19357

(604) The coastal bight between Kepuhi Point and Ka'ena Point, 7 miles to the NW, is backed mostly by ridges of the Waianae Mountains. Midway along the bight is a sand beach in front of a small valley; small boats can make beach landings when the sea is smooth and can anchor in depths of 4 to 6 fathoms about 0.2 mile offshore.

(605) **Ka'ena Point**, the NW extremity of O'ahu, is low and rocky and is only a few hundred yards from the foot of Kuaokala Ridge. **Kaena Point Light** (21°34'20"N., 158°15'50"W.), 931 feet above the water, is shown on top of a 25-foot building on Kuaokala Ridge. Another light is 0.9 mile W of Kaena Point Light on the lower W end of the Point. Off the end of the point are several low, jagged rocks, over which the sea washes, and breakers extend about 0.4 mile from shore. The 10-fathom curve is 0.8 mile W of the point.

(606) The **danger zone** of a firing area covers a wide sector N of Ka'ena Point. (See **334.1350**, chapter 2, for limits and regulations.)

Currents

(607) A continuous NW current and moderate tide rips are reported off Ka'ena Point. Observations over a 24-hour period at a location 0.8 mile S of Kaena Point Light show a NW current averaging 0.8 knot; the greatest velocity measured was 1 knot.

(608) The N coast of O'ahu trends E for 9 miles from Ka'ena Point to Waialua, thence NE for another 11 miles to Kahuku Point; rock ledges alternate with stretches of white sand beach. The broad valley back of Waialua spreads to the coastal plain, which narrows as it approaches Ka'ena and Kahuku Points; most of the valley is cultivated in sugarcane. From Ka'ena Point to Waialua the mountains have a rugged appearance; from Waialua to Kahuku Point the hills resemble a continuous plateau. A hard-surface highway parallels the coast.

(609) Most of the N coast is fringed with reefs as much as 0.5 mile in width, but all dangers can be avoided by staying at least 1 mile from shore. Haleiwa Small-Boat Harbor is the only harbor along the N coast.

(610) **Kuaokala Ridge**, back of Ka'ena Point, is high, and its seaward end breaks off rather abruptly. White domes and telemetry antennas are conspicuous along the ridge. The scattered beach houses between Ka'ena Point and Waialua are backed by cultivated fields that extend to the mountains.

(611) **Kaiaka Bay** is a small coastal dent 9 miles E of Ka'ena Point; **Kiikii Stream** and **Paukauila Stream** empty into the head of the bay. Prominent from offshore is the mill stack in **Waialua**, 0.5 mile back of the beach.

A depth of 3 feet can be carried halfway into the bay by passing between the **Kaiaka Point** reefs, on the NE side, and the reef in midentrance.

(612) **Waialua Bay**, 1 mile NE of Kaiaka Bay, is a small dent at the bend in the middle of the N coast. The bay shores are low, black rock, with sand patches in the bights and fringed by large algaroba trees. The low land back of the beach slopes gently to a tableland with mountain ranges on either side. **Haleiwa** is at the head of Waialua Bay.

(613) **Haleiwa Small-Boat Harbor**, at the head of Waialua Bay is protected by a breakwater on the W and a mole; both are marked by lights on the outer ends. The entrance channel is marked by lighted and unlighted buoys, lights, and by a **129°** lighted range. In 1999, the midchannel controlling depth in the entrance channel was 9 feet. Depths are reported to be 11 feet in the outer harbor and 4 feet near the S part of the harbor. The harbor has 64 slips and 24 moorings available for vessels up to 50 feet, boat ramps, and water at most of the slips. The harbor can be entered in all but the most violent storms, at which time good anchorage can be found about 1 mile offshore in 20 to 30 fathoms. Night entry is not recommended without local knowledge. The harbor office can be reached at 808–637–8246.

(614) **Anahulu River** empties into the SW corner of Waialua Bay. River navigation is restricted by the fixed bridge over the mouth; the clearance is 8 feet for a channel width of 14 feet.

(615) The narrow coastal plain between Waialua and Kahuku Point is backed by a vegetation-covered tableland with steep seaward slopes that are cut by deep gorges.

(616) **Waimea Bay**, 5 miles NE of Waialua, is a small coastal dent at the mouth of the **Waimea River** gorge. The highway bridge over the river can be seen from seaward. A yellow-brown tower and scattered buildings are visible on the N side of the bay.

(617) **Wananapaoa Islet**, the outer of two ragged masses of black rock off the S point of Waimea Bay, has deep water close to its seaward sides. The submerged rocks near the point on the NE side of the bay are usually marked by breakers.

(618) Waimea Bay affords little shelter, and beach landings can be made only in very smooth weather. There is a wide beach at the head of the bay, but both sides of the entrance are fringed with rocky ledges. Indifferent anchorage is available in depths of 9 or 10 fathoms, sand bottom, 0.3 mile W of the river mouth.

(619) **Waialee** is 4 miles NE of Waimea Bay. A group of large conspicuous buildings is at the foot of a bluff a few hundred yards inland. Also prominent are two large dish antennas atop a ridge about 1.3 miles SW of Waialee and a windmill with a strobe light about 2.0 miles ESE. Low **Kuilima Point**, 5.4 miles NE of Waimea Bay, has a resort hotel complex on the point.

(620) **Kahuku Point**, the N extremity of O'ahu, is low and sandy; the dunes are partly overgrown with vegetation, and there are few scattered trees. The coast rounds

gradually at Kahuku Point, and there are several small black rocks close to shore. The land rises gently from the low bluffs near the point to the mountains of Koʻolau Range. The 10-fathom curve draws in to within 0.4 mile of the point. The breakers afford sufficient daytime warning of coastal dangers, but the low, unmarked point is difficult to locate at night. Currents off Kahuku Point set W or NW, but are sometimes negligible; tide rips have been reported 1 mile E of the point.

(621) The coast between Kahuku Point and Makapuʻu Point, 30 miles to the SE, is known as **Windward Oʻahu** and is more productive than other parts of the island because of its greater rainfall. Paralleling this coast is the Koʻolau Range from which several spurs reach shore between Laie Bay and Kaneʻohe Bay. The shore is low and sandy with patches of black rock outcrop, particularly at the headlands and most of the points. Between the shore and Koʻolau Range is a narrow strip of cultivated land; this coastal area widens between Kaneʻohe Bay and Waimanalo and is one of the principal agricultural areas of Oʻahu. There are good highways along the entire coast.

(622) Nearly all of this NE coast is fringed by coral reefs with little or no water over them at low tide, and the area is exposed throughout most of the year to the sea and swell built up by the NE trades. The numerous small openings in the reefs can be navigated by local craft; wider openings lead to Kahana, Kaneʻohe, Kailua, and Waimanalo Bays. The 10-fathom curve is no farther than 1.6 miles from shore except in Kaneʻohe Bay.

(623) **Kahuku**, 3 miles SE of Kahuku Point, is marked by a mill stack which is a half mile from the beach.

(624) Low **Makahoa Point** projects 0.2 mile from the general coast 3.5 miles SE of Kahuku Point. **Kihewamoku**, an islet 24 feet high, is 0.5 mile off Makahoa Point; 0.2 mile N of the islet is a rock that covers 4 feet and sometimes breaks.

(625) Wooded **Kalanai Point**, 4 miles SE of Kahuku Point is on the N side of Laie Bay. **Mokuauia**, an island 0.2 mile long and 23 feet high, is 0.2 mile off the point; between the island and the point are depths of only 1 or 2 feet. A rock 0.2 mile seaward of the island is covered 10 feet.

(626) **Pulemoku**, a rock 30 feet high, is 0.4 mile SE of Mokuauia. A 2-foot-high rock is close to the S side of Pulemoku.

(627) **Laie Bay** has outer depths of 3 to 7 fathoms, and a narrow reef opening affords access to shelter and landing for local small craft. **Laie**, at the head of the bay, has a Mormon Temple, a large, flat-roofed building that is visible from seaward.

(628) **Laniloa** a narrow peninsula with white sandy beaches on either side and covered with homes is on the S side of Laie Bay. Off the outer end of Laniloa are two small rocky islets; **Kukuihoolua**, 30 feet high and **Mokualai**, 33 feet high.

(629) **Kaipapau Hill**, about 700 feet high, is 2 miles S of Laniloa and 0.5 mile inland; the hill has a pyramidal, grass-covered top.

(630) **Hauula** is a beach settlement 2.5 miles S of Laniloa. **Punaluu** 4 miles S of Laniloa, is a beach settlement with a prominent apartment building near the beach.

(631) **Kahana Bay**, 11 miles SE of Kahuku Point, has an entrance width of 1 mile between **Makalii Point** on the N and **Mahie Point** on the SE; inland extent is 0.6 mile. Local small craft make the narrow passage through the reef and find limited shelter behind it. A breakwater protects a launching ramp on the W side of the bay. The breakers on both sides of the bay are the only guides for entering.

Chart 19359

(632) **Kualoa Point**, 15 miles SE of Kahuku Point, is on the NW side of the entrance to Kaneʻohe Bay. **Mokoliʻi Island**, 206 feet high, is a conspicuous conical islet 0.3 mile seaward of Kualoa Point.

(633) **Kaneʻohe Bay** has an entrance width of 4.6 miles between Kualoa Point on the NW and Mokapu Peninsula on the SE; greatest inland extent is 3 miles. The bay has low sand and coral beaches along which are many of the old diked fishponds, some which are still in use. Islands, coral reefs, and sand shoals are numerous throughout the bay. Mokoliʻi Island, **Kapapa Island**, about 2.8 miles SE of Kualoa Point and in the center of Kaneʻohe Bay, and **Kekepa Island**, mushroom-shaped and 4.4 miles SE of Kualoa Point, are easy to identify from seaward. These islands make for poor landfall. **Moku o Loe Island (Coconut Island)**, in the SW part of the bay, is the largest of the islands with reports of significant uncharted coral shoaling on all sides; the majority being found S of the island.

(634) The University of Hawaii operates a launch that ferries university personnel to and from the Hawaii Institute of Marine Biology on the island of Moku o Loe. The launch runs from the island to a nearby pier on the SW side of Kaneʻohe Bay.

(635) **Kaneʻohe Bay** is a **Naval Defensive Sea Area**. established by Executive Order No. 8681 of February 14, 1941. The order says in part:

(636) "The territorial waters within Kaneʻohe Bay between extreme high-water mark and the sea and in and about the entrance channel within a line extending 3 miles NE from Kaʻoʻio Point, a line extending 4 miles NE from Kapaho Point, and a line joining the seaward extremities of the two above-described bearing lines, are hereby established and reserved as a naval defensive sea area for purposes of national defense, such area to be known as Kaneʻohe Bay Naval Defensive Sea Area; and the airspace over the said territorial waters is hereby set apart and reserved as a naval airspace reservation for purposes of national defense, such reservation to be known as Kaneʻohe Bay Naval Airspace Reservation."

(637) "At no time shall any person, other than persons on public vessels of the United States, enter Kaneʻohe Bay Naval Defensive Sea Area, nor shall any vessel or other

craft, other than public vessels of the United States, be navigated into said area unless authorized by the Secretary of the Navy."

(638) "At no time shall any aircraft, other than public aircraft of the United States, be navigated into Kaneʻohe Bay Naval Airspace Reservation, unless authorized by the Secretary of the Navy."

(639) **Note:** Naval control over entry into Kaneʻohe Bay Naval Defensive Sea Area has been suspended, except for a 500-yard **prohibited area** around the perimeter of Mokapu Peninsula where only authorized vessels may enter. Naval control may, however, be reinstated without notice at any time.

(640) **Kaneohe Marine Corps Air Station** is on Mokapu Peninsula. Mariners are advised that field operations are conducted throughout the year and divers, rafts and aircraft may be operating in the bay. Additionally, Military Amphibious/Search and Rescue operations may be underway at any time, day or night, in the vicinity of 21°26'06"N., 157°46'11"W. and 21°26'45"N., 157°46'55"W. Surface support craft will be marked with appropriate day and night time markings/signals and can be reached via MARBAND 82A for any reason. Request that vessels using sonar contact Water Front Operations via MARBAND 82A or 808–257–2941 to avoid injury to divers that may be in the area. Caution should be exercised when operating near the air station runway.

COLREGS Demarcation Lines

(641) The lines established for Kaneʻohe Bay are described in **80.1430**, chapter 2.

(642) Two channels lead through the reefs to the SE end of the bay. The deeper approach from the N end of the bay is through a dredged channel entered about 2 miles E of Kualoa Point. The channel is marked by lights, buoys, daybeacons, and a **227°** and a **349°30'** lighted range with the front range tower common to both. Sampan Channel (Kaneohe Passage) to the SE, is entered about 0.8 mile NW of the N extremity of Mokapu Peninsula. This channel intersects the deeper channel about 0.9 mile W of Mokapu Peninsula and is marked by a **217°15'** lighted range, daybeacons, and lighted and unlighted buoys.

(643) **Crashboat Channel**, about 0.4 mile W of Mokapu Peninsula, has been dredged by the Navy for search and rescue vessels. This channel is within the prohibited area and should not be used by pleasure craft as it may hamper aid to a needy vessel or downed pilot. The Navy monitors VHF-FM channels 16 and 82A at its search and rescue facility on the SW side of Mokapu Peninsula; telephone number (808–257–2941).

Anchorages

(644) **Special anchorages** are in the SE and W parts of Kaneʻohe Bay. (See **110.1 and 110.128d (a) and (b)**, chapter 2, for limits and regulations.) Anchoring in Kaneʻohe Bay outside of these areas is limited to 72 hours. To obtain authorization for longer durations, contact the Harbor Master at 808–233–3603.

Dangers

(645) Mariners are advised to exercise caution as the channels and other dredged areas in the bay have not been dragged or swept. Numerous coral heads are along the sides of the channels, especially in the vicinity of Moku o Loe Island. Many of these are marked by privately maintained pipes extending 3 to 5 feet above the water.

(646) The bay is by far the best locality for the operation of small craft on Oʻahu. Many permits are being obtained by property owners to dredge small-boat basins and channels through the reefs. Numerous docks, including the Kaneohe Yacht Club, are in the bay. In addition, many uncharted private floats and buoys, used to mark race courses, moorings, and fish and lobster pots are throughout the bay.

(647) **A 015°–195° measured course**, 3,038 feet long, is SE of Moku o Loe Island in Kaneʻohe Bay. The range markers are 30-by 40-inch white daymarks with orange borders set on coral reefs about 0.4 mile off the SE shore of the bay.

(648) **Kaneʻohe** near the SE end of the bay is the principal community in the area. Radio towers are prominent at **Heʻeia**, a mile NW of Kaneʻohe.

(649) **Heʻeia Kea Small-Boat Harbor**, just N of Kealohi Point about 0.9 mile N of Heʻeia, is open to the public. In 1999, the controlling depth in the harbor was 6½ feet. The fuel pier has a reported depth of 10 feet alongside. Gasoline, diesel fuel, berths, water, ice, and launching ramps are available. Anchorage in the harbor is by permit only. The Harbor Master can be contacted at 808–233–3603.

Chart 19357

(650) **Mokapu Peninsula**, 20 miles SE of Kahuku Point, has a greatest elevation of 683 feet. **Pyramid Rock**, on the NW point of the peninsula, is black and has a sharp summit. **Pyramid Rock Light** (21°27'44"N., 157°45'49"W.), 101 feet above the water, is shown from a white square concrete house with black diagonal stripes. **Puu Hawaiiloa** is a 337–foot hill near the center of the peninsula. A red and white skeleton tower and a nearby aerobeacon atop the hill are the most prominent navigation aids on the peninsula.

Danger zone

(651) A weapons training range **danger zone**, marked by lighted and unlighted buoys, extends NNE from Mokapu Point. (See **334.1380**, chapter 2, for limits and regulations.)

(652) **Ulupau Crater**, part of an old crater rim, is a rocky headland at the NE end of Mokapu Peninsula. **Mokumanu Islands**, two islets with vertical sides 202 feet and 132

feet high, are 0.7 mile N of the headland. The passage between the islets and the peninsula has midchannel depths of 3½ to 8½ fathoms, but is not recommended for strangers. An E current is reported in the vicinity of Mokumanu Islands.

(653) The beach between Mokapu Peninsula and Makapu'u Point, 10 miles to the SE, is mostly low and sandy, with black rocks showing in some places. Between the beach and the cliffs of the Ko'olau Range is a narrow strip of land developed with residential communities. The cliffs are characteristic of Ko'olau Range from behind Kane'ohe Bay to rugged Makapu'u Head.

(654) **Mokolea Rock**, is about 1 mile off the SE side of Mokapu Peninsula; the black rock is 20 feet high, has a submerged edge that extends 0.15 mile W, and has depths of 6 to 8 fathoms around it.

(655) **Kailua Bay**, S of Mokapu Peninsula, is an open bight which affords no shelter from the trades. The N part of the bay is free of the usual fringing reefs, and there is a sand beach at the head of the bay.

(656) **Alala Point**, on the S side of Kailua Bay, is a low bluff with a 25-foot white stone monument that resembles a lighthouse. A public launching ramp is on the W side of the point.

(657) **Popoia Island** is a small, flat, low-lying island 0.2 mile N of Alala Point.

(658) **Mokulua Islands**, 0.7 mile from shore and midway between Mokapu Peninsula and Makapu'u Head, are steep, rocky, grass covered, and locally known as **Twin Peaks**. Elevations are 206 feet for the N islet and 182 feet for the S islet. On the shore side of the islets is an extensive reef; between the reef and the shore is a small-boat passage that leads to private landings.

Chart 19358

(659) **Wailea Point**, 5 miles NW of Makapu'u Head, is the NW point of Waimanalo Bay. An inactive airfield occupies a large area S of the point.

(660) **Waimanalo Bay**, between Wailea Point and Makapu'u Head, affords all-weather shelter for small craft behind the barrier reefs that parallel much of the bay's shore. A 2-mile stretch off midbay has no fringing coral reef; in its S part, the reef gets closer to shore and disappears near Makapu'u Head. Depths of 10 feet can be carried into the bay except during strong trades when the entrance is closed by breakers. **Waimanalo** is on the coastal highway that skirts the head of the bay.

(661) **Manana Island**, 361 feet high, is 1 mile NNW of Makapuu Point Light. The island is part of an old crater and has a lighter shade of rock than any other in the vicinity. The sides are bluff except on the W where there is a short sloping point. The water is deep on the seaward side of Manana Island, and there are depths of 4 fathoms between the island and the mainland; the 4-fathom passage is not recommended for strangers.

(662) **Kaohikaipu Island**, 80 feet high, is a flat, black mass of rock midway between Manana Island and Makapu'u Head. A double rock, 10 feet high, is 200 yards NE of Kaohikaipu, and a small black rock, barely above water, is about the same distance SW of the island. There are depths of 5 fathoms between Manana and Kaohikaipu Islands, but passage is not recommended for strangers because reefs make off from both islands. Depths are 4 to 6 fathoms in the bight between Kaohikaipu Island and Makapu'u Head; passage is not recommended.

(663) About 1.2 miles NW of Makapu'u Point is a privately operated ocean research facility. An L-shaped pier, protected by a breakwater, extends 700 feet into the bay. In 2000, the basin and channel leading to the facility had a reported depth of 12 feet. The channel and basin are privately marked by daybeacons. A **restricted area** of the Makai Undersea Test Range extends about 2.5 miles offshore. (See **334.1410**, chapter 2, for limits and regulations.)

Chart 19380

(664) **Kauai Channel**, NW of O'ahu, is wide, deep, and clear. During the trades the current usually sets W across the channel and divides at Kauai, part following the N side of the island and the other part following the S side. Strong S or SW winds cause the current to set in the opposite direction to that produced by the trades.

Chart 19381

(665) **Kauai**, 63 miles NW across Kauai Channel from O'ahu, has an area of 555 square statute miles and is fourth largest of the eight major islands. Kauai measures 29 nautical miles E-W by 23 miles N-S and slopes from centrally located **Kawaikini**, a 5,170-foot peak. **Lihue**, the seat of Kauai County, is 2 miles inland from the east-coast port of Nawiliwili.

(666) The mountains on the W and N sides of Kauai descend in steep, jagged ridges; the gentle slopes on the E and S sides are cut by numerous gulches. The peaks are nearly always cloud covered, making them difficult to see from any great distance. Dome-shaped **Haupu**, 2,290 feet high, is prominent in the SE part of the island. The entire NW coast is backed by high bluffs; the rest of the coast is mostly low and rocky with some scattered sand beaches. A low coastal plain extends W from the town of Waimea. The few outlying dangers can be avoided by giving the coast a berth of 2 miles.

Harbors and ports

(667) Nawiliwili, on the E coast, and Port Allen, on the S coast, are the only commercial harbors on Kauai and are the only places that afford shelter in almost all weather.

(668) Small craft planning to visit Kauai should carry two good holding anchors, because mooring space is scarce and there are few well-protected anchorages. Advance

Nawiliwili Bay and Harbor, Kauai
2004

arrangements with the Kauai District Manager, Harbors Division of the Hawaii Department of Transportation, are advised.

Currents

(669) The oceanic currents in the vicinity of Kauai generally follow the winds. The available local information relative to currents is given in the discussions of the various localities.

Weather, Kauai

(670) The trade winds divide on the E side of Kauai, one part follows the N coast and one part the S coast, and unite again some distance W of the island. On the W side, between Mana Point and Makaha Point, calm or light variable airs prevail. A moderate SW wind is sometimes felt at Waimea Bay, while a strong E wind is blowing about 2 miles (4 km) offshore. Along the N and S shores the early morning trade wind is usually light until about 0900 and again decreases in strength about 1600. Occasionally kona winds, starting in the SE, displace the normal trades; this condition occurs more often during the winter.

(671) The E and N, or windward, sides of the island are noted for their heavy rainfall, which reaches a maximum yearly average of more than 400 inches (10160 mm) on 5,080-foot-high (1550 m) **Waialeale**. The lower slopes have much less rain, and along the S side the fall seldom exceeds 20 inches. The winter, from December to March, produces the strongest winds, which sometimes reach gale force and are accompanied by more rain than is usual at other times of the year. Precipitation averages over 42 inches (1067 mm) at the Lihue airport and has ranged from 74.4 inches (1890 mm) in 1982 to 16.4 inches (417 mm) the very next year. Precipitation falls, on average, 275 days each year. December is the wettest month and June, the driest.

(672) The National Weather Service office located at the Lihue Airport has an average annual temperature of 75.6°F (24.2°C). The average maximum is 81.1°F (27.3°C) while the average minimum is 69.7°F (20.9°C). Annual extremes are 90°F (32.2°C) recorded in August 1981, September 1993 and 1995, and October 1957, and 50°F (10°C) recorded in January 1969. August is the warmest month with an average temperature of 79.3°F (26.3°C) while January and February each have an average temperature of 71.6°F (22°C).

(673) (See Appendix B for **Lihue climatological table**.)

Supplies and repairs

(674) Food supplies are obtainable at the various towns on the island, particularly at Lihue, the county seat. Marine supplies are limited to small-craft requirements and occasionally must be ordered from Honolulu. Fuel and water are available at Nawiliwili and Port Allen; limited bunker C oil is available at Port Allen. The island

has no repair facilities for medium or large vessels, but minor repairs can be made at Nawiliwili and Port Allen.

Communications

(675) Port Allen and Nawiliwili are ports for a few interisland barges and transpacific vessels. Interisland passenger traffic is by air. Telephone communication is available to the other islands and to the mainland. A good highway skirts the island except on the NW side.

Chart 19383

(676) **Nawiliwili Bay**, on the SE side of Kauai, has an entrance width of 0.8 mile between Carter and Ninini Points and an inland extent of about 1 mile. **Nawiliwili**, on the N side of the bay, is one of the two commercial deepwater ports on Kauai and is protected by a breakwater, marked at the end by a light, extending NE from Carter Point, and by a jetty in the inner harbor. SE winds produce some surge, but the harbor is otherwise secure.

Prominent features

(677) The shore consists of rocky bluffs, except at the mouth of Huleia Stream and in the vicinity of Nawiliwili. The jagged, mountainous coast extending SW from the bay is in marked contrast with the lowlands of Huleia Stream, on the SW side of the bay, and affords a means of fixing the entrance from well offshore. A water tank on the wharf and a large white bulk sugar warehouse on the hill overlooking the wharf are conspicuous.

(678) A flashing amber warning light, privately maintained and shown about 4 feet above the roof on the SW corner of the shed (largest shed on the N piers) on Pier 2, is activated when there is a gas leak or the likelihood thereof. Anyone observing the light flashing should remain well clear and upwind, and sources of ignition should be secured.

(679) **Ninini Point**, on the N side of the entrance, is low, flat, and rocky, and is backed by land planted in cane. A rocky ledge with a depth of 12 feet at the outer end extends about 100 yards S of the point. **Nawiliwili Harbor Light** (21°57'18"N., 159°20'09"W.), 110 feet above the water, is shown from a 73-foot buff-colored cylindrical concrete tower on the point. The loom of the light is frequently seen by vessels 40 miles away. **Lihue Airport** is along the coast, north of the light.

(680) **Kukii Point**, 0.7 mile W of Ninini Point and the N entrance point of the inner harbor, is a high bluff with a low, rocky shelf at the base. There is a light on the point.

(681) **Carter Point**, on the S side of the entrance to Nawiliwili Bay, is rocky and rises rapidly to **Kalanipuu**; the hill is marked by an aviation obstruction light 799 feet high. The mountain spur that extends inland rises to Haupu, the most prominent feature of SE Kauai.

(682) **Kawai Point**, 0.5 mile S of Carter Point, is a bold rocky headland, 525 feet high, very irregular and jagged in appearance.

COLREGS Demarcation Lines

(683) The lines established for Nawiliwili Harbor are described in **80.1450**, chapter 2.

Channels

(684) A **Federal project** provides for an entrance channel which leads between the outer end of the breakwater and Kukii Point, thence turns SW before entering the harbor basin. The Federal project depths are 40 feet in the entrance channel and 35 feet in the harbor basin. The entrance channel is marked by lights, buoys, and a lighted range.

Anchorage

(685) Anchorage in the vicinity of Nawiliwili Bay, outside the breakwater, is not recommended. Commercial vessels are not allowed to anchor within the harbor basin, except by permission from the harbormaster. Swinging room is limited. An anchorage area for small boats is within the mouth of **Huleia Stream**, adjacent to the small boat harbor basin.

(686) A **special anchorage** is N of the Nawiliwili Small-Boat Harbor. (See **110.1 and 110.128c**, chapter 2, for limits and regulations.)

Caution

(687) Generally, the current offshore of Ninini Point is from north to south. However, deep-draft vessels have reported a northerly set as they get closer to the point, while on the range line. The transit of the entrance into Nawiliwili Harbor is difficult for large vessels in all but calm weather. The turn around the outer breakwater, then immediately turning in the opposite direction around the inner jetty, is made difficult by the combined effects of the winds and seas. Vessels must contend with large quartering swells and brisk tradewinds on the stern, while approaching the outer breakwater. While turning around the inner jetty into the main basin, the fresh tradewinds generally are on the beam. Local pilots require an assist tug to escort all medium to large size vessels inbound and outbound from Nawiliwili. Vessels berthing at pier 3 are advised to consider laying out an anchor to assist in undocking during moderate to heavy tradewinds weather conditions.

Pilotage, Nawiliwili

(688) Pilotage is compulsory for all foreign vessels and for U.S. vessels under register in the foreign trade; it is optional for coastwise vessels who have on board a pilot licensed by the Federal government.

(689) Pilots are available through the Hawaii Pilots Association. Mariners are requested to give 24 hours advance notice of arrival, gross tonnage, length, and draft

of vessel by telephone (808–537–4169) or by e-mail at dispatch@hawaiipilots.net. The 31-foot long pilot boat NININI has a black hull with yellow superstructure and displays the word 'PILOTS' in large white letters on the sides of the cabin. The pilot boat displays the International Code Flag 'H' by day and shows the standard pilot lights at night, white over red. The pilot boat monitors VHF-FM channels 12 and 16 and can be reached by "NAWILIWILI PILOTS". Additionally, vessels are requested to rig a pilot ladder 1 meter above the water on the leeward side. The pilot boarding area is about 1 mile ESE of Nawiliwili Harbor Light. The boarding area is generally very rough, open sea conditions. Vessel masters are advised that boarding a pilot in these conditions may take some time. They should not allow their vessel to stand in towards shore W of Ninini Point until a local pilot is on the bridge.

Towage

(690)   Two tugs are available for hire based in Nawiliwili Harbor. Local pilots advise which combination of tugs is necessary for safe transit of ships.

Quarantine, customs, immigration, and agricultural quarantine

(691)   (See chapter 3, Vessel Arrival Inspections, and Appendix A for addresses.)

(692)   **Quarantine** is enforced in accordance with regulations of the U.S. Public Health Service. (See Public Health Service, chapter 1.) A private hospital is at Lihue.

(693)   Nawiliwili is a **customs port of entry.**

Harbor regulations

(694)   Harbor regulations are established by the Harbors Division of the Hawaii Department of Transportation and enforced by the harbormaster.

(695)   The harbor has a **security zone** when the fuel barge is in port, generally each Friday to Saturday. (See **165.1 through 165.40**, chapter 2, for regulations.)

(696)   The **speed limit** in the harbor is 5 m.p.h.

Wharves

(697)   The **State of Hawaii, Nawiliwili Piers 1 and 2** (21°57'15"N., 159°21'18"W.): 1,285 feet of berthing space with a depth of 35 feet alongside and deck height of 8.8 feet; receipt and shipment of conventional and containerized general cargo; receipt of petroleum products, cement, and bulk fertilizer; shipment of bulk raw sugar and molasses; owned and operated by the State of Hawaii.

(698)   The **State of Hawaii, Nawiliwili Pier 3** (21°57'07"N., 159°21'31"W.): 627 feet of berthing space with a depth of 35 feet alongside and a deck height of 8 feet; receipt and shipment of conventional and containerized general cargo and automobiles; receipt of liquefied petroleum gas, lumber, and dry bulk fertilizer; owned and operated by the State of Hawaii.

Supplies

(699)   Gasoline, kerosene, fuel oil, and diesel fuel are available by tank truck, and water is piped to the pier. Some provisions and supplies are available at Lihue. Marine supplies are limited to items for small craft.

Repairs

(700)   There are no facilities available at Nawiliwili for making major repairs or for drydocking large, deep-draft vessels. Several machine, electrical, and welding concerns off the waterfront in Nawiliwili and in Honolulu are available for making above-waterline repairs to vessels berthed at the port.

(701)   **Nawiliwili Small-Boat Harbor** is on the SW side of Nawiliwili Harbor. Two jetties protect the harbor and are marked by lights on the outer ends at the entrance. Private lights mark the channel inside the harbor. The harbor has three piers, 85 berths, a launching ramp on the N side of the harbor, and a pump-out station. In 1999-2003, the controlling depths were 9 feet for a mid-width of 30 yards; thence in 2003, 12 feet in the basin (except for lesser depths along the S edge), thence 7 feet in the channel along the S side of the harbor.

Chart 19381

(702)   **Kawelikoa Point**, 4 miles SW of Nawiliwili Bay, is a dark, rocky headland 691 feet high. The point is at the seaward end of a ridge which extends N to a 2,297-foot-high peak of Haupu.

(703)   From about 1.5 miles SW of Kawelikoa Point to Hanapepe Bay, the coast is a series of low bluffs and beaches; the back country is mostly under cultivation, and the cane fields extend well up the slopes in some places.

(704)   **Makawehi Bluff**, 3.5 miles SW of Kawelikoa Point, stands on the E side of **Shipwreck Beach**. The beach extends for 0.25 mile and fronts a conspicuous hotel with distinctive green roofs.

(705)   **Makahuena Point**, 7 miles SW of Nawiliwili Bay, is the S extremity of Kauai. The low, flat point has a rocky shore with bluffs 20 to 50 feet in height. The land near the point is sandy and rolling, and there are short stretches of sand beach both NE and W of the point. A hotel is prominent on the W side of the point. **Makahuena Point Light** (21°52'08"N., 159°26'39"W.), 80 feet above the water, is shown from a 17-foot pole with a black and white diamond-shaped daymark on the point. The bottom slopes gradually to a depth of 7 fathoms about 0.5 mile off the point. Several reefs extend about 300 yards offshore between the point and Koloa Landing.

(706)   There is a conspicuous mill stack at **Koloa**, 2 miles inland from Makahuena Point. The stack is visible all along this coast except for the short distance where it is hidden by **Paa Cones**, which are on a long, low ridge that extends inland from the point.

(707) **Koloa Landing**, 1.5 miles W of Makahuena Point, has a landing slip for small, flat-bottom boats and outrigger canoes. The landing slip is treacherous, and only persons familiar with the landing should attempt to land a small boat. Anchorage is available in depths of 12 fathoms, rocky bottom, about 400 yards S of the landing. A road leads inland to Koloa.

(708) **Kuhio Park** is 0.5 mile W of Koloa Landing and on the shore road. There are several beach houses between the landing and the park.

(709) **Kukuiula Bay**, 3 miles W of Makahuena Point, has an entrance width of 150 yards and an inland extent of 300 yards. There is a small boat harbor with ramp and moorings; considerable protection is afforded except in S winds. A wreck (21°52'54"N., 159°29'36"W.), covered 25 feet, is about 0.3 mile S of the breakwater. **Kukuiula** is a settlement at the head of the bay. About 500 yards W of Kukuiula is the **Spouting Horn**, a seawater spout which is active even in smooth weather.

(710) **Lawai Bay**, 3.5 miles W of Makahuena Point, has an entrance width of 300 yards and an inland extent of 0.2 mile; fair protection is afforded small craft except in S winds. The side shores of the bay are low and rocky, but there is a wide sand beach at the head. A grass-topped rock, 70 feet high, stands at the upper edge of the sand on the W side of the bay.

(711) **Makaokahai Point**, 4.6 miles W of Makahuena Point, is easily recognized because of the several hills extending N from it. One particularly prominent hill, 0.5 mile inland, is 436 feet high and well rounded, has canefields on the lower slopes, and is evenly capped with trees. The first low hills on the point are the walls of a water-filled crater.

(712) **Ioleau**, 1.1 miles N of Makaokahai Point, is a flat-topped 625-foot hill. A Vortac station on the hill is a good landmark.

(713) **Kalanipuao Rock**, with 2 feet of water over it, is about 0.3 mile SE of Makaokahai Point and is marked by a buoy. Vessels should not attempt to pass N of the buoy.

(714) **Koheo Point**, 1.4 miles W of Makaokahai Point, is level and covered with vegetation. A radio tower is on the W side of the point. A radar tower (21°53'38"N., 159°33'09"W.), on the grounds of the Kauai Coffee plantation, is the most conspicuous landmark on the south shore and is visible from Makahuena Point.

Chart 19382

(715) **Wahiawa Bay**, 2.8 miles W of Makaokahai Point and 1 mile E of Port Allen, is 170 yards wide at the entrance and indents the coast about 0.2 mile. Excellent protection is afforded small craft in all but S winds. Boats anchor in depths of 5 to 10 feet, sandy bottom. The sides of the bay are rocky. The seas usually break over the shoal 100 yards off **Weli Point** on the SE side of the bay.

(716) **Hanapepe Bay**, midway along the S coast of Kauai, is the approach to **Port Allen**. The bay is about 0.6 mile wide and about 0.4 mile long, and is protected from the SE by a breakwater marked near the end by a light. The shores are low, rocky bluffs except at the head of the bay, where there is a sandy beach.

Local magnetic disturbance

(717) Differences of as much as 2¼° from normal variation have been observed at Hanapepe Bay.

Prominent features

(718) The E side of the bay has several oil tanks and warehouses. A light is on low, flat, and rocky **Puolo Point** on the W side of the bay. A landing strip, used by tour helicopters and occasionally small planes, is back of the point.

COLREGS Demarcation Lines

(719) The lines established for Port Allen Harbor are described in **80.1440**, chapter 2.

Channels

(720) A **Federal project** provides for an entrance channel which leads N past the outer end of the breakwater to a harbor basin in Hanapepe Bay with a project depth of 35 feet in the entrance channel and basin. The harbor basin is marked by lighted and unlighted buoys on the N and W sides.

Dangers

(721) A reef extends about 200 yards from the shore E of the inner end of the breakwater. In heavy weather breakers extend 350 yards offshore on the NW side of the bay and 50 to 150 yards off the SE side of Puolo Point.

Anchorage

(722) There is little shelter for vessels intending to anchor off Port Allen. In order for a vessel to get in the lee of the bluffs, located on the E shore, the vessel would be positioned dangerously close to shallow water near the breakwater. Fresh tradewinds generally make this area a poor anchorage. The harbor is congested with small commercial charter boats. There is little swinging room within the basin. Port Allen is known for surge conditions. At times, the surge is severe enough to discourage commercial vessels from mooring at the S face of the main pier.

Currents

(723) The prevailing current off Puolo Point is W.

Pilotage, Port Allen

(724) Pilotage is compulsory for all foreign vessels and U.S. vessels under register in the foreign trade; it is optional for coastwise vessels who have on board a pilot licensed by the Federal government. The pilot boat, IWA,

Hanapepe Bay and Port Allen, Kauai
2004

is a yellow 35-foot catamaran with the word PILOT in black letters on the side of the cabin. The boat displays the International Code flag "H" by day and the white and red signal lights at night. The pilot boarding ground is 0.75 mile S of the outer end of the breakwater. The pilots monitor and use VHF-FM channel 12. Mariners are advised to give at least 24 hours advance notice of arrival with overall length, gross tonnage, and draft of vessel; telephone 808–537–4169. Vessels are requested to rig a ladder no more than one meter on the lee side and to maintain a "dead slow ahead" speed, between 5 and 10 knots.

Towage

(725) Two tugs from Nawiliwili Harbor are available to service vessels entering and exiting Port Allen.

Quarantine, customs, immigration, and agricultural quarantine

(726) (See chapter 3, Vessel Arrival Inspections, and Appendix A for addresses.)

(727) **Quarantine** is enforced in accordance with regulations of the U.S. Public Health Service. (See Public Health Service, chapter 1.) A private hospital is at Waimea.

(728) Port Allen is a **customs port of entry**.

Harbor regulations

(729) Harbor regulations are established by the Hawaii Department of Transportation, Harbors Division and enforced by the **harbormaster**.

(730) The harbor has a **security zone** when the fuel barge is in port, regularly scheduled for every Monday. (See **165.1 through 165.40**, chapter 2, for regulations.)

(731) The **speed limit** in the harbor is 5 m.p.h.

Wharves

(732) The State pier in the E part of the harbor provides 600 feet of berthing space along both the N and S sides, and 124 feet along the W face. In 1999, depths to 25 feet were available along the N side, 33 feet on the S side and 28 feet on the W face; deck height, 11 feet. A transit shed with 24,000 square feet of covered storage space, and open storage are available. Pipelines are on the wharf, and bulk handling and storage facilities for molasses, liquid fertilizer, and petroleum products are in the port. General cargo, and barge and tanker traffic are handled at the pier.

(733) Vessels are advised to drop an anchor when approaching the pier. This assists in maneuvering to a berth as well as getting away in an emergency. During and after strong winds some surge is experienced at the pier. This condition may require small and medium craft to cast off and sometimes interferes with the cargo handling of large vessels.

Supplies

(734) Gasoline, fuel oil, and diesel fuel are available by tank truck, and water is piped to the wharf. Provisions are available in the principal towns on the island. Marine supplies are limited to small-craft items.

Repairs

(735) Facilities for minor repairs to vessels are available.

(736) **Port Allen Small Boat Harbor** is N of the State pier on the E side of the bay. The harbor has 3 launching ramps, 38 berths, 6 mooring buoys, and a small pier.

Communications

(737) Port Allen has highway and telephone communication with other parts of the island and radiotelephone and air communication with the other islands of the group. The town is a port of call for interisland barge and transpacific vessels.

Chart 19386

(738) **Kaumakani** is 2 miles NW of Puolo Point and a half mile inland. A mill stack is prominent.

(739) **Robinson Landing**, 1 mile NW of Kaumakani, is a small-boat harbor with a dredged entrance that accommodates drafts of 2 to 4 feet. A stone wall has been built around the harbor edges, and a marine railway is available for handling small craft. This is a private landing and cannot be used without the owner's permission.

(740) **Hoanuanu Bay**, 2 miles NW of Kaumakani, has depths of 2 to 3 fathoms and affords good protection from trade winds for small craft. The E side of the bay is rocky; the NW side is a sand beach.

(741) A breaking area extends 0.5 mile off **Poo Point**, which is on the NW side of Hoanuanu Bay.

(742) **Waimea Bay**, an open bight 3 miles NW of Kaumakani, is the approach to **Waimea**, which is the place where Captain James Cook, R.N., made his first (January 1778) landing in the islands.

Anchorages

(743) A **naval anchorage** is off Waimea Bay. (See **110.1 and 110.237**, chapter 2, for limits and regulations.) Good anchorage, for other vessels, can be found in and off Waimea Bay during ordinary weather in depths of 3 to 20 fathoms, sand bottom. Small boats usually shift anchorage to Hoanuanu Bay for better protection when the trades are strong. Depths of 5 to 18 feet extend 0.3 mile from the shore of Waimea Bay. The Waimea pier, 0.3 mile NW of the Waimea River, is a former inter-island steamer landing that is used as a state recreational pier, primarily for fishing. The town has a hospital.

(744) **Waimea River**, which empties into Waimea Bay along the E side of Waimea, is navigable only for pulling boats because of the bar across the mouth; the river descends from the mountains through the deepest gorge on this part of Kauai. The ruins of a Russian fort are on the E side of the river's mouth; the fort was built in 1815 and abandoned in 1817.

(745) Between Waimea River and **Oomano Point**, 2.3 miles to the W, a reef extends 0.4 mile from shore and breaks in heavy weather. **Kikiaola Boat Harbor**, 1.6 miles W of the river, is entered over the reef and is protected by breakwaters. The end of the west breakwater is marked by a privately maintained light. The harbor has a launching ramp and loading piers; the entrance is marked by a privately maintained lighted range. In 2010, the controlling depth over the bar was 1¼ fathoms, with shoaling to ¾ fathom in the basin. Caution should be exercised when entering or leaving the harbor due to the combined effects of the breakers and the 90° turn in the basin.

Chart 19381

(746) A low plain, about 2 miles wide, extends W from Waimea River around Kokole Point and N to Barking Sands beyond Nohili Point. The shore side of the plain has a growth of algaroba trees, behind which are occasional sand dunes.

(747) **Kekaha** is a plantation settlement on the NW side of Oomano Point and 2.5 miles from Waimea River. A mill stack is prominent.

(748) **Kokole Point**, 5 miles WNW of Waimea River, is low, rounding, and wooded. **Kokole Light** (21°58'44"N., 159°45'22"W.), 58 feet above the water, is shown from a three-legged tower with a black and white diamond-shaped daymark on the point. The transmitting antenna of Radio Station **WWVH** (National Bureau of Standards) is about 0.7 mile NW of Kokole Light.

(749) **Mana Point**, about 3.5 miles N of Kokole Point, is the W extremity of the island. Along the water's edge is a strip of sand that extends 2 miles on either side of the point, but the sea breaks on a lava ledge at the edge of the sand, making the beaching of boats dangerous except when the sea is smooth. The aviation control tower at Barking Sands Pacific Missile Range Facility Airport is prominent.

(750) Current observations taken during a 24-hour period 0.5 mile off Mana Point show a tidal current of 0.8 knot velocity at strength setting S and N along the coast. The S maximum occurs about 3 hours after low water at Honolulu, and the N maximum 3 hours after high water. Similar observations taken near the coast about 3.8 miles NNE of Nohili Point show a tidal current with velocities generally less than 0.5 knot. Discolored water, caused by the drainage canals and the undertow from the beach, is often noted as far as 2 miles off Mana and Kokole Points.

Safety zone

(751) A safety zone extends northward from Mana Point to Polihale. (See **165.1406**, chapter 2, for limits and regulations.)safety zone

Danger zone

(752) A danger zone is between Mana Point and Nohili Point. (See **334.1390**, chapter 2, for limits and regulations.)

(753) **Nohili Point**, about 6 miles N of Kokole Point, is marked by **Nohili Dune**, 100 feet high, and the highest and southernmost of a chain of sand dunes extending along the coast for 2.5 miles to the NE. The dunes are known as **Barking Sands**. A road continues to Polihale. A light is on the point.

(754) A narrow sand shoal, with depths of 7 to 10 fathoms, extends from Nohili Point to **Alapii Point**, 7.5 miles to the NE. The shoal, which appears to be a succession of E-W sand ridges, is 1 to 2 miles from shore. A depth of 3 fathoms is 0.5 mile W of Alapii Point; from there to Kailiu Point, 7 miles farther to the NE, the 15-fathom curve is at an average distance of 1 mile from shore. A navy aerolight and radar dome antenna are about 2.5 miles SW of Alapii Point, and a conspicuous radar dome antenna is on top of a high ridge about 3 miles ESE of Alapii Point.

(755) From Barking Sands NE to Kailiu Point, the coast is rocky and precipitous. The section between Alapii and Kailiu Points consists of a series of cliffs known as **Na Pali (Napali)**. These cliffs are 2,000 feet high in some places, and are cut up by numerous streams which form small waterfalls. The S part of this section is practically bare, but the N part is wooded.

(756) **Kalalau Valley**, 2.5 miles NE of Alapii Point, is the broadest and deepest valley along the NW coast and is easily distinguished from seaward.

(757) **Kailiu Point**, on the N coast of Kauai, is the seaward end of a jagged ridge that ends abruptly in a sharp peak 1,200 feet high. There is a narrow strip of lowland at the point.

Chart 19385

(758) **Haena Point**, 1.2 miles E of Kailiu Point, is low and rounding. A reef, which bares at low water, extends 0.3 mile NW from the point. The **Haena Caves**, which cannot be seen from seaward, are 0.2 mile inland under the bold face of the mountains; the caves are near the W end of the highway that skirts the N shore of Kauai.

(759) **Wainiha Bay**, 1.3 miles E of Haena Point, has an entrance width of 0.5 miles between the extensive **Kepuhi Point** reef on the W and **Kolokolo Point** on the E; inland extent is 0.4 mile. The bay is an open bight that affords little protection except in kona weather. **Wainiha River** empties into the head of the bay from the most W of the deep valleys along the N coast of Kauai.

(760) **Lumahai River**, which is unnavigable, empties into the sea on the E side of Kolokolo Point; E of the river mouth is a sandy beach with a few rocky patches.

(761) **Makahoa Point**, 2 miles ESE of Haena Point, is black and rocky. A half mile inland is Puu Ka Manu, a 714-foot hill.

(762) **Hanalei Bay** has an entrance width of a mile between Makahoa Point on the W and the extensive Puu Poa Point reef on the NE; inland extent is nearly a mile. Breaking coral reefs fringe the shores on both sides of the entrance. Seas break across the entire entrance during N or NW gales. During the winter and spring, the entire bay is subject to high surf, but when the sea is calm good protection is afforded from the trades. Midbay anchorage is in depths of 6 fathoms, sandy bottom.

(763) Along the sandy beach at the head of Hanalei Bay are clumps of ironwood and coconut trees and the houses of **Hanalei**. The highway is close to the shore. Three miles inland the mountains attain heights of more than 4,000 feet.

(764) **Hanalei River**, which empties into the E side of the bay, is navigable for shallow-draft boats for a distance of 2 or 3 miles. A privately dredged channel passes close to the reef on the NE side of the bay and leads to the river mouth. At high water, a depth of 4½ feet can be carried over the bar at the mouth and about 4 feet to the bridge 1.8 miles above the mouth. A launching ramp is on the S side of the river, 0.1 mile above the mouth. A clump of ironwood trees is prominent on the N side of the river's mouth.

(765) Overhead power and telephone cables with a clearance of 27 feet cross Hanalei River at its mouth.

(766) A 300-foot long concrete pier, used as a shore recreation site for swimming and fishing, is on the E side of the bay and 200 yards S of the Hanalei River. A prominent large resort complex is on the bluff on the N side of the river near the entrance.

(767) **Waioli Stream** and **Waipa Stream** which empty into the head of Hanalei Bay, are not navigable.

(768) **Puu Poa Point**, on the E side of Hanalei Bay, is a bluff about 50 feet high, back of which a green ridge extends inland.

(769) From offshore the N side of Kauai presents a very irregular and jagged skyline, with ridges extending in all directions. In the NW part of the island these ridges often end abruptly at the sea. The mountains are heavily wooded. The coast between Hanalei and Kalihiwai Bays is a series of more or less wooded bluffs cut up by gulches back of which a rolling plain extends to the mountains. Between the shore and the highway, 1 mile inland, is a resort community with homes, condominiums, and golf courses.

(770) **Anini Beach**, to the west of Kalihiwai Bay, is a long stretch of sandy beach with a boat ramp.

(771) **Kalihiwai Bay**, 4.5 miles E of Hanalei Bay, is about 0.5 mile wide and is a popular surfing site. **Kapukaamoi Point**, a red precipitous bluff about 150 feet high, is on the E side of the entrance. Several houses are scattered along the sand beach at the head of the bay, which is backed by a wooded gulch. Indifferent anchorage, with poor holding ground, can be found in depths of 5 fathoms in the center of the bay, but a heavy swell sets in during N winds. A rock awash is 150 yards N of Kapukaamoi Point. A reef, 0.2 mile wide and bare at low water,

fringes the shore for 2.5 miles W from Kalihiwai Bay, and vessels should stay at least 0.8 mile offshore. A shore road, with beach houses along it, extends W from the bay for 1.5 miles.

(772) **Kilauea Point**, the N extremity of Kauai Island, is a grass-covered bluff about 165 feet high. **Kilauea Point Light** (22°13'53"N., 159°24'07"W.), 174 feet above the water, is shown from a white concrete pole. **Mokuaeae Island**, 200 yards off Kilauea Point, is a black, flat, grass-topped rock about 200 yards in diameter and 92 feet high. The island is the most prominent feature in the vicinity to coasting vessels.

(773) **Kilauea**, 1.3 miles inland from Kilauea Point, is the site of a sugarmill, but is not easily seen when close to the shore. The sugar of the district is trucked to Nawiliwili for shipment.

(774) Between Kilauea Point and Mokolea Point the coast is bluff, rising gradually from each point to an elevation of about 570 feet midway between them.

(775) **Makapili Rock**, 0.8 mile SE of Kilauea Point, is 156 feet high, black, and prominent. The rock is on the outer end of a narrow neck of land that juts out 200 yards from the general coastline.

(776) **Mokolea Point**, 1.2 miles SE of Kilauea Point, is narrow and 140 feet high, and projects out 0.3 mile from the general coastline. The point is on the NW side of Kilauea Bay and has two old buildings near its outer end. An abandoned rock quarry is on the E side of the point.

(777) **Kilauea Bay** has an entrance width of 0.5 mile and an inland extent of 0.5 mile. The bay is subject to high surf, especially in the winter and spring. The bay is open to the trades, but offers some protection in W weather. A narrow coral reef fringes the shore, and **Kilauea Stream** empties into the head of the bay. Anchorage can be found in depths of 6 fathoms, rocky bottom, near the center of the bay.

(778) Low **Kepuhi Point** is 2 miles E of Mokolea Point. The low coast between the two points is fringed with a narrow coral reef.

Chart 19381

(779) **Moloaa Bay** (22°12'N., 159°20'W.), 4.5 miles SE of Kilauea Point, has an entrance width of 0.3 mile and extends the same distance inland to the mouth of a gulch. Little protection is afforded from the heavy swell that sets into the bay during the trades, but anchorage is possible during S winds in depths of 3 to 6 fathoms in midbay. There are a few houses along the sand beach at the head of the bay, and rice is grown in the gulch. The interior between Moloaa and Anahola Bays is used for pineapple cultivation and for grazing.

(780) **Papaa Bay**, 6 miles SE of Kilauea Point, is a small bight that is wide open to the trades. The central part of the bay is foul, and there is a rock awash 300 yards from shore. A coral reef fringes the S shore.

(781) **Anahola Bay**, 7.5 miles SE of Kilauea Point, is a small bight exposed to the trades. **Kahala Point**, a low bluff with a grove of ironwood trees near the outer end is on the SE side of the bay. **Kahala Point Light** (22°08'48"N., 159°17'43"W.), 40 feet above the water, is shown from an 21-foot steel pole with a black and white diamond-shaped daymark on the point. A water tank 1 mile W of the light is prominent. Discolored water frequently extends for a considerable distance off **Kuaehu Point** on the NW side of the bay. A reef extends about 0.3 mile from Kuaehu Point. Because of the numerous reefs, strangers should not attempt to enter the bay. In moderately smooth weather small vessels can find anchorage well inside the bay in depths of 4 to 6 fathoms, mud bottom.

(782) **Puu Konanae**, 1.3 miles inland from Anahola Bay, is a tall, dark spire, with green slopes, that stands out more prominently than any other land feature on this part of the island.

(783) Between Kahala Point and Kealia are low coastal bluffs and a rocky shore with some patches of sand.

(784) **Kealia**, 3 miles S of Kahala Point, is a plantation village. A short breakwater, extending SE from the shore, affords some protection from N weather for shallow-draft boats. The breakwater is not kept in repair, and portions have been carried away by the sea. Vessels should not approach the village without local knowledge. About 0.8 mile S of Kealia, and 0.3 mile inshore, the stack of the Samuel Mahelona Memorial Hospital is prominent.

(785) **Kapaa**, 4.5 miles S of Kahala Point, is scattered along the beach. A reef, which is 0.3 mile wide in some places, extends alongshore from N of Kapaa to Hanamaulu Bay. An opening in the reef at Kapaa is usually marked by breakers on either side. Small craft find anchorage in depths of about 2 fathoms behind the reef and about 150 yards off the N side of the village. At **Waipouli Beach Park** an opening in the reef with a marked channel, and spanned by a foot bridge, leads to a sheltered boat ramp. The village of **Waipouli** is just S of Kapaa along the highway.

(786) **Wailua** is a settlement at the mouth of **Wailua River** which empties into small **Lehuawehe Bay** 6.5 miles S of Kahala Point. The river, which is spanned by a bridge at its mouth, is navigable for small boats for several miles, once a shifting bar at the mouth is passed. Only very shallow draft vessels can cross the bar even at high tide, and only during calm weather. A public marina is 0.3 mile above the mouth. Vessels may find unprotected anchorage off Wailua in depths of 10 to 15 fathoms, rocky bottom, but like the whole NE coast of the island, anchorage is not safe when the trade winds are blowing.

(787) **Nounou**, 1.3 miles NW of Wailua and 1,241 feet high, is the northernmost and highest of the low mountains near the coast.

(788) **Kalepa Ridge** is 1 mile inland and parallels the coast from Wailua to Hanamaulu Bay. The S end of the ridge, which is about 700 feet high, is marked by

several buildings high on the seaward face of the bluff. The buildings can be seen for many miles offshore and are a good leading mark for Hanamaulu Bay.

Chart 19384

(789) **Hanamaulu Bay**, 10 miles S of Kahala Point and 2.6 miles N of Nawiliwili, is about 0.3 mile wide and indents the coast about 0.5 mile. **Ahukini Landing** is on the point on the S side of the entrance. Only the outer third of the bay has deep water; the sand and coral bottom slopes gradually from the 18-foot curve to the beach at the head of the bay. The shores of the bay are low, rocky bluffs, about 40 feet high, except for the white sand beach at the head. A fringe of trees on the bluffs forms a windbreak for the extensive cane fields on either side of the bay. **Hanamaulu Stream**, which empties into the head of the bay, is not navigable.

(790) The 20-foot concrete tower of an abandoned lighthouse is on the outer end of the 300-foot stone breakwater that projects from the S point of Hanamaulu Bay entrance; the pilings and ruins of a small wooden pier are at the inner end of the breakwater. The bay is no longer used by large vessels. Only the concrete piling remains of the former wharf at Ahukini Landing, and most of the port installations are in ruins. A heavy outside swell causes a heavy surge in the harbor.

Chart 19381

(791) From Hanamaulu Bay to Nawiliwili the coast is a series of low bluffs with occasional stretches of sand beach; there are no off-lying dangers. Sugarcane is grown extensively on the land back of the beach. An aerolight at Lihue Airport is 0.7 mile S of Hanamaulu Bay.

Chart 19380

(792) **Kaulakahi Channel**, between Kauai and Niʻihau, is about 15 miles wide and clear of obstructions. Off Mana Point the trade wind following the S coast of Kauai meets the air current that has followed around the N side. The trades blow directly across the lowlands of Niʻihau, but part is deflected S and around the SE point of the island.

Currents

(793) Little is known of the current in Kaulakahi Channel, but presumably it is variable depending mainly upon the velocity and direction of the wind. There appears to be a general NW flow along the SW coast of Kauai. It is reported that a current sometimes sets S along the E coast of Niʻihau at the same time that the current is setting NW along the Kauai coast. There are noticeable tidal currents near the W extremity of Kauai.

(794) **Niʻihau**, 15 miles W across Kaulakahi Channel from Kauai, is seventh in size and westernmost of the eight major islands. Niʻihau has an area of 72 square statute miles, a NE-SW length of 16 nautical miles, and an average width of 3.5 miles. Near the middle of the island is a high tableland with occasional rises or cones, the highest of which is 1,281-foot **Pānīʻau**. The N and E ends of the tableland are precipitous and vary in height from 600 to 1,000 feet; the S and W slopes are gradual. An unpaved road follows the W coast of Niʻihau for most of its length. The island lies in the rain shadow of Kauai and is a semi-arid island with no streams.

(795) The population of Niʻihau was 230 in 1990. One family owns the entire island and operates it as a cattle ranch. There are no scheduled communications with the island.

(796) **Lehua**, about 0.6 mile off the N end of Niʻihau, is a small rocky, crescent-shaped island, with the crescent open to the N. The E and W points are low, rising gradually to an elevation of about 700 feet near the center of the island. On the W point is a natural arch. **Lehua Rock Light** (22°01'12"N., 160°05'51"W.), 704 feet above the water, is shown from a 10-foot post on the summit of Lehua.

(797) **Lehua Channel**, between Niʻihau and Lehua, is restricted on its S side by rocks that show above water and extend about halfway across it. A depth of 9 fathoms can be carried through the channel by staying within about 350 yards of the Lehua shore. In heavy NW weather the swell almost breaks in the passage, and, as little is to be gained by using the channel, vessels should pass N of Lehua Island. The current through the channel varies with the tide and sets in both directions with a velocity of about 1.5 knots.

(798) To the E of Lehua Channel vessels should give the N coast of Niʻihau a berth of 0.5 mile; to the W the clearance should be about 1 mile.

(799) **Puu Kole (Puukole Point)**, on the N end of Niʻihau, is low, as is **Kikepa Point**, 1 mile to the E. Between the points and the high bluff on the N side of the tableland, the land is low and grass covered, with a few low hills. From a distance this lowland is not visible and Lehua appears to be about 3.5 miles from Niʻihau.

(800) **Kaunuopou**, 1.8 miles SE of Kikepa Point, is the easternmost point of Niʻihau. **Kaunuopou Rocks**, over which the sea breaks, are 300 yards off the point. Another rock, about 0.4 mile off the S side of the point, usually breaks and should be given a good berth by vessels approaching Kiʻi.

(801) **Kiʻi (Kiʻi Landing)**, a small bight about 0.7 mile W of Kaunuopou, is only slightly protected from the trade winds. The landing is usable in ordinary weather, but not in S weather. The landing is built on beach boulders and has depths of only 2 or 3 feet alongside. Anchorage can be had in depths of about 8 fathoms, coral bottom, about 0.6 mile off the landing.

(802) About 1.3 miles S of Kiʻi, a reef with about 1 fathom of water over it and usually breaking, extends 0.5 mile

(803) offshore. The 10-fathom curve is about 1 mile offshore. From the vicinity of the reef to Pueo Point the coastline consists of cliffs reaching a height of 1,000 feet.

(803) **Pueo Point**, 5 miles S of Kaunuopou, is a prominent brown, precipitous bluff about 800 feet high. SW from the point for a distance of about 4.5 miles the coastline consists of bluffs that gradually diminish in height toward the lowlands of the S half of the island. The bluffs are broken by small bights, most of which have short sand or pebble beaches where boats could land during smooth weather. Beyond the bluffs to Kawaihoa, a distance of about 6 miles, the coast consists of a series of low bluffs about 15 feet high, with stretches of sand beach, a few sand dunes, and scattered trees. Between Pueo Point and Kawaihoa are no known outlying dangers; the few isolated rocks are very close to the shore.

(804) The lowland of the S part of the island is broken by two hills, one on Kawaihoa and the other, **Kawaewae**, a gently rounded hill 315 feet high, which is 4 miles N of the cape and 1.3 miles inland from the W coast.

(805) **Kawaihoa (Kawaihoa Point)**, the southernmost point of Niʻihau, is formed by a hill 548 feet high, the seaward face of which is steep. From a distance the hill has the appearance of an island and can easily be mistaken for Kaʻula. Deep water is close to the point. About 2 miles S of the point there is a prevailing W current which reaches a velocity of about 1.5 knots.

(806) Beyond Kawaihoa the coast gradually curves NW and N and is low and rocky with occasional short sand beaches. At **Leʻahi (Leʻahi Point)**, 1.7 miles W of Kawaihoa, the 10-fathom curve is 0.6 mile offshore. A road skirts the W shore.

(807) The coast between **Kamalino**, a former village 4 miles NW of Kawaihoa and Puu Kole, is practically one low, continuous beach, with an occasional group of rocks. Near the beach are numerous sand dunes covered with sparse vegetation. In the vicinity of Kamalino, weak currents have been reported setting N and S along the coast.

(808) **Nonopapa Landing**, 5.5 miles NW of Kawaihoa, is the principal landing on the island. Local vessels call occasionally for the island's cattle. The landing is used only from May to September, as there is often a heavy N swell during the winter. The landing is marked by a shed and derrick on a short concrete retaining wall at the N end of a long sand beach. **Kaeo**, a cone 1,018 feet high and near the center of the tableland, shows on the skyline from the anchorage.

(809) Anchorage is available in depths of 8 fathoms, coral and sand bottom, about 660 yards off the derrick, with the landing shed and Kaeo in range and bearing 070°. Kawaewae is 1.5 miles 135° from the anchorage. The landing is somewhat protected by a small reef extending about 75 yards SW from the end of the retaining wall. Small boats approaching the landing head S of it until the reef is rounded. **Puʻuwai**, the principal village of the island, is about 2.5 miles NE of the landing.

(810) **Kuakamoku Rock**, 1.6 miles N of Nonopapa Landing, is a large, single rock about 4 feet above water and near the center of a reef some 200 yards in diameter and 500 yards offshore. The reef should be given a berth of 0.5 mile, and only small craft should attempt the passage between the reef and the shore. Other reefs extend about 0.5 mile offshore 0.5 mile S, and 3 miles NE of Kuakamoku Rock.

(811) **Kaununui (Kaununui Point)**, 4.5 miles NE of Kuakamoku Rock, is marked by a group of rocks a few feet high and close to the shore. A coral reef with depths of 6¼ fathoms over it is 1.5 miles off the point. It is reported that the reef breaks in heavy weather. The passage inside the reef is not recommended except for small boats.

(812) **Keawanui Bay**, is no more than a slight curve in the shoreline that extends NE from Kaununui for 3 miles. The bay has a sand and coral bottom and a sandy shore. A rock with 2 feet of water over it is in the S part of the bay, 0.8 mile N of Kaununui and 0.5 mile offshore.

(813) From the N side of the bay to Puu Kole the coast is foul for a distance of about a mile offshore. Vessels should give this section of the coast a berth of at least 1 mile. About 2 miles W of Puu Kole and 0.9 mile offshore is a reef with reported depths of 12 feet over it. A mile S of this reef and 0.8 mile offshore is a rock with 5 feet of water over it.

(814) **Kaʻula**, 19 miles SW of Niʻihau, is a small, bare, rocky islet, 550 feet high. Vessels have anchored close to both the S and E sides of Kaʻula in depths of about 20 fathoms, but as the islet is only 0.7 mile long, little protection is afforded. A rock with a least depth of 5 fathoms is 3.8 miles 300° from the highest point on Kaʻula. A bank with depths of 30 to 40 fathoms extends 5 miles NW from the islet.

Danger zone

(815) The **danger zone** of an aerial bombing and strafing target is centered on Kaʻula. (See **334.1340**, chapter 2, for limits and regulations.)

Chart 540

(816) **Outer Islands**. The small rocky islands, reefs, and atolls WNW from Niʻihau form a well-defined chain in the Hawaiʻian Archipelago. Between Niʻihau and Gardner Pinnacles, 480 miles distant, are several widely separated high barren rocks; continuing W are the coral reefs and atolls.

(817) The Hawaiʻian Archipelago from longitude 161°W. to 176°W. is part of the **Hawaiʻian Islands National Wildlife Refuge**, and under the jurisdiction of the U.S. Fish and Wildlife Service, Department of Interior. The islands and atolls in the refuge include Nihoa, Necker Island, French Frigate Shoals, Gardner Pinnacles, Maro Reef, Laysan Island, Lisianski Island, Pearl and Hermes

Reef, and all intervening reefs and shoals, which are also part of the so-called Leeward Islands.

(818) The refuge was established in 1909 in order to preserve wildlife including very rare forms, found in the area. All fish and wildlife are protected. Federal laws governing wildlife and national wildlife refuges are in force. Sharks are abundant throughout the refuge. Entry to the refuge is **prohibited** except by permit issued by the Refuge Manager, Hawai'ian/Pacific Islands National Wildlife Refuge Complex, U.S. Fish and Wildlife Service, 300 Ala Moana Boulevard, P.O. Box 50167, Honolulu, HI 96850. Entry upon Tern Island of French Frigate Shoals and Green Island, Kure Atoll, must be also by approval Commander, 14th U.S. Coast Guard District, Honolulu. The restrictions apply to all civilian and military agencies, as well as individuals. Because of the extreme fragilities of the refuge islands ecosystems general public use is not permitted. Entry to the entire refuge is restricted to scientists on previously U.S. Fish and Wildlife approved research projects.

(819) The Hawai'ian Archipelago and surrounding waters between Nihoa Island and Kure Atoll have been designated as the **Northwestern Hawai'ian Islands (Papahanaumokuakea) Marine National Monument** by Presidential Proclamation 8031 of June 15, 2006. Within this Monument are three areas to be noted: a Particularly Sensitive Sea Area (PSSA), Areas to be Avoided, and a Ship Reporting Area. These areas are described in detail below.

(820) The Northwestern Hawai'ian Islands (Papahanaumokuakea) Marine National Monument encompasses an area of the marine waters and submerged lands of the Northwestern Hawai'ian Islands. The seaward boundary of the reserve is 50 miles from the approximate geographical center of Nihoa Island, Necker Island, French Frigate Shoals, Gardner Pinnacles, Maro Reef, Laysan Island, Lisianski Island, Pearl and Hermes Reef, Midway Atoll, and Kure Atoll and includes all areas of the Hawai'ian Islands National Wildlife Refuge and Midway Atoll National Wildlife Refuge. (See **50 CFR 404.1 through 404.12**, chapter 2, for limits and regulations.)

(821) The **Particularly Sensitive Sea Area (PSSA)** is an IMO-designated zone sharing the same boundary as the Monument. The area encompasses a 1,200-mile stretch of coral islands, seamounts, banks, and shoals. It is home to more than 7,000 marine species and contains 4,500 square miles of coral reefs. Ship traffic has been identified as one of the primary anthropogenic threats to the vulnerable and valuable natural and cultural resources of the area. PSSA designation augments domestic protective measures by alerting mariners to exercise extreme caution when navigating through the area.

(822) The International Maritime Organization (IMO) has adopted certain **Areas to be Avoided** in the region of the Northwestern Hawai'ian Islands (Papahanaumokuakea) Marine National Monument. Given the magnitude of obstacles that make navigation in these areas hazardous and in order to increase: maritime safety, protection of the environment, preservation of cultural resources and areas of cultural importance significant to Native Hawai'ians, and facilitate the ability to respond to developing maritime emergencies in the Monument, all ships solely in transit should avoid the following areas contained within a circle having a radius of 50 nautical miles centered upon the following geographical positions:

(823) (1) 28°25.18'N., 178°19.75'W. (Kure Atoll)
(824) (2) 28°14.20'N., 177°22.10'W. (Midway Atoll)
(825) (3) 27°50.62'N., 175°50.53'W. (Pearl and Hermes Atoll)
(826) (4) 26°03.82'N., 173°58.00'W. (Lisianski Island)
(827) (5) 25°46.18'N., 171°43.95'W. (Laysan Island)
(828) (6) 25°25.45'N., 170°35.32'W. (Maro Reef)
(829) (7) 25°19.50'N., 170°00.88'W. (Between Maro Reef and Raita Bank)
(830) (8) 25°00.00'N., 167°59.92'W. (Gardner Pinnacles)
(831) (9) 23°45.52'N., 166°14.62'W. (French Frigate Shoals)
(832) (10) 23°34.60'N., 164°42.02'W. (Necker Island)
(833) (11) 23°03.38'N., 161°55.32'W. (Nihoa Island)
(834) and the areas encompassed by the following geographical positions:
(835) Area 1
(836) (1) 26°53.22'N., 173°49.64'W.
(837) (2) 26°35.58'N., 171°35.60'W.
(838) (3) 24°57.63'N., 171°57.07'W.
(839) (4) 25°14.42'N., 174°06.36'W.
(840) Area 2
(841) (1) 25°38.90'N., 167°25.31'W.
(842) (2) 24°24.80'N., 165°40.89'W.
(843) (3) 23°05.84'N., 166°47.81'W.
(844) (4) 24°14.27'N., 168°22.13'W.

(845) A mandatory **Ship Reporting System (CORAL SHIPREP)** has been established in the Northwestern Hawai'ian Islands (Papahanaumokuakea) Marine National Monument Particularly Sensitive Sea Area for the following vessels entering or departing any U.S. port or place and in transit through the reporting area:

(846) (1) All vessels 300 gross tons or greater
(847) (2) All vessels experiencing an emergency in the Reporting Area
(848) Vessels other than those described above, including sovereign immune vessels, are encouraged to participate. The current notification requirements described in **50 CFR 404.4** for U.S. flagged vessels passing through the Monument remain in effect.

(849) The reporting area boundary adopted by the IMO generally extends 10 miles out and entirely around the Monument boundary and includes three transit corridors through the Monument PSSA. Vessels using these corridors are asked to report only twice, once when entering the reporting area and once when leaving. These transit corridors are between the designated Areas to be Avoided around:

(850) (1) Pearl & Hermes Atoll and Lisianski Island
(851) (2) Maro Reef and Gardner Pinnacles
(852) (3) Necker Island and Nihoa Island
(853) The reporting area does not include the Areas to be Avoided within the Monument. A vessel that passes through an Area to be Avoided shall notify the shore-based authority when:
(854) (1) entering the reporting area
(855) (2) leaving the reporting area to enter an Area to be Avoided
(856) (3) exiting the Area to be Avoided to enter the reporting area on the other side of the Area
(857) (4) leaving the reporting area.
(858) The potential burden of reporting four times is justified by the navigation hazards that exist within the Areas to be Avoided. (See **50 CFR 404-Appendix E**, chapter 2, for reporting requirements.)

Atolls

(859) An atoll may comprise one or more low coral islands situated on a strip or ring of coral surrounding a central lagoon. Many of these atolls have openings in the coral ring that permit passage of small boats, and sometimes large vessels, to anchorage in the enclosed lagoon.

Reefs

(860) Successful navigation through or among coral reefs often depends on the eye. They are always more plainly seen from the masthead than from the deck or bridge. The best observing conditions are with the sun high and behind the observer, and with the sea slightly ruffled; reefs are extremely difficult to distinguish if the sea is glassy calm.

(861) Reefs with about 3 feet of water over them appear light brownish in color; those with a fathom or more appear light green, deepening to dark green and finally deep blue. Under favorable circumstances, a reef with depths of 3 or 4 fathoms over it can be seen from aloft for a considerable distance; in greater depths, the reef can only be seen when nearly over it. Polarized glasses have been found of great help in navigating among reefs.

Vigias

(862) A vigia is an indication on a chart that a dangerous rock or shoal is thought to be near the spot indicated. Doubtful navigation and strong currents account for a large proportion of the vigias that encumber or have encumbered the charts of the Pacific Ocean. Phosphorescence, seaweed scum, and shoals of fish often resemble reefs and breakers so closely as to deceive the most experienced. Many vigias have been disproved by extensive investigation, but many others are still on the charts and remain a source of annoyance to the navigator.

Chart 19016

(863) **Nihoa** (23°03'N., 161°55'W.), a barren, rocky, and uninhabited island, is about 120 miles NW of Ni'ihau. The island was discovered by Captain Douglas of the British vessel IPHIGENIA on April 13, 1790. The low, stone walls of ancient Polynesian ceremonial sites still remain on the island. The island is inhabited by a number of species of sea birds and two extremely rare land birds.

(864) Nihoa is about 0.8 mile long and 0.2 mile wide. The E, N, and W sides are high and precipitous; the S side is much lower and its slopes are more gradual. **Millers Peak**, 910 feet high and the highest point on the island, is near the NW end. **Tanager Peak**, 874 feet high, is near the NE end. The SE and SW sides of the island terminate at points on either side of **Adams Bay**. In the bay are three small bights; the westernmost has a sand beach, and the shores of the other two are rocky ledges. There is deep water, close to all sides of the island.

(865) The safest anchorages are between the 15-and 20-fathom curves W and SW of the island, but the holding ground is poor. The middle cove of Adams Bay probably affords the best landing, but the surge is considerable and great care must be taken in landing anywhere on the island. During heavy NW weather landing is very dangerous. A steep trail leads from the middle cove to the top of the bluff. At the foot of the bluff is a seepage of water that is not suitable for drinking purposes except in emergencies.

Currents

(866) The prevailing current sets W in the vicinity of Nihoa. Current observations taken about 0.2 mile W of the island show a nontidal flow of about 0.2 knot setting WSW combined with a tidal current of nearly 0.5 knot at strength setting N and S. The N strength of the tidal current occurs about 6 hours after the local transit of the moon and the S strength at about the time of local transit. The velocity measured was nearly 2 knots and set S.

Local magnetic disturbance

(867) Differences from normal variation of as much as 33° have been observed on Nihoa.

(868) Nihoa is near the SW end of a bank which is about 18 miles long in a NE-SW direction 10 miles wide and has depths of 14 to 36 fathoms, except for a reported depth of 6½ fathoms at the westernmost extremity. Another bank, the center of which is about 18 miles WSW from Nihoa, is about 14 miles long in an E-W direction, 9 miles wide, and has depths of 15 to 25 fathoms, except for an 11-fathom depth about 2 miles SE of its center, and a 14-fathom depth about 6 miles SSE of its center, reported in 1968. A bank about 54 miles SE of Nihoa has a least depth of 32 fathoms except for a reported depth of 19 fathoms at its S end; the positions of the reported

depths are approximate and caution is advised. The two banks 57 and 70 miles W of Nihoa have least depths of 29 and 33 fathoms, respectively. The edges of the bank slope steeply to much greater depths. A 9-fathom shoal is about 5 miles NW of the E bank.

(869) **Necker Island** (23°34'N., 164°42'W.) is 158 miles W from Nihoa. It was discovered by La Perouse on November 1, 1786, and was annexed to Hawaii in 1895. The island, which might well be called a rock, is uninhabited, but, like Nihoa, shows unmistakable evidence of ancient habitation. It is the home of countless sea birds.

(870) About 0.7 mile long and less than 0.2 mile wide, Necker Island is made up entirely of lava. There are four peaks or hills, one near each end and two between. The highest, **Summit Hill**, 277 feet high, is near the middle of the island. **Annexation Hill**, 249 feet high, at the W end of the island, is separated from the other hills by a low saddle and, when seen from a distance appears detached. There is a sparse growth of low brush on the upper slopes of the hills.

(871) **Northwest Cape**, a rocky spur extending N from the W end of the island, is joined to the rest of the island by a low isthmus over which the seas break in rough weather. On the W side of the cape is **West Cove**, and on the E side is **Shark Bay**. Off the E end of the island are several low, detached rocks. A depth of 5 fathoms has been reported 0.5 mile S of Necker Island where general depths are 10 to 12 fathoms.

(872) Vessels can anchor in depths of about 12 fathoms 0.5 mile S of the SW point of the island, but the island is so small that it affords little protection. West Cove and Shark Bay are the landing places, and are usually very hazardous and there are times when it is impossible to land anywhere on the island. During heavy NW weather landing at West Cove is very dangerous. Shark Bay, open to the NE trades, is usually filled with breakers. Small seepages of unpalatable water have been found on the island.

Currents

(873) The prevailing current sets W, but countercurrents may be expected close to the island. Four days of current observations taken 0.2 mile WNW of the W end of Necker Island show a W nontidal flow of about 0.5 knot, combined with a tidal current of about 0.8 knot at strength. E trade winds prevailed during the observations.

Weather, Necker Island

(874) September is reported to be the calmest month of the year; strong N and NE winds prevail during the other months.

Local magnetic disturbance

(875) Differences from the normal variation of as much as 22° have been observed on Necker Island.

(876) Necker Island is near the N end of a bank about 40 miles long in a NW-SE direction. The bank is about 15 miles wide and has depths of 8 to 23 fathoms except for a reported 5-fathom depth 0.5 mile S of Necker Island and a 5-fathom depth reported in 1968 about 5 miles N of Necker Island. The sand and coral bottom is plainly visible. A 10-fathom shoal has been reported about 19 miles NE of Necker Island.

Charts 19401, 19402

(877) **French Frigate Shoals**, about 85 miles W from Necker Island, is a crescent-shaped atoll about 17 miles long in a NNW direction. It was discovered by La Perouse on November 6, 1786, the day after leaving Necker Island, and like that island, was annexed to Hawaii in 1895. The atoll consists of a coral reef with a number of small, bare, sand islets on it, and is flanked by a volcanic rock and numerous coral heads and reefs. It is home to many sea birds, seals, turtles and other fish and wildlife all protected by Federal Law.

(878) La Perouse Pinnacle and Tern Island are the best landmarks. The other islands are of little assistance in navigation due to their constantly changing size and shape and low elevations. Shark Island has been observed to be particularly unreliable in this regard.

(879) The crescent reef is double, and the outer and inner arcs bound a lagoon that is 1 to 6 miles wide. At its midpoint the windward reef lies about 8 miles from a line joining the tips of the crescent; the leeward reef is about 5 miles from this line. The windward reef is nearly continuous and can be plainly seen in the daytime for a considerable distance by vessels approaching from the N, E or SE. The sea practically always breaks over the reef, and during the few times it is not breaking, the green shoal water inside the reef is seen in ample time to avoid danger. The bottom slopes uniformly from the reef to the 100-fathom curve 1 to 2 miles off, and there are no known dangers from N through E to S of the windward reef.

(880) The leeward or inner reef, however, is broken in many places and in normal weather is seldom marked by breakers. The lagoon between the reefs is very foul with numerous coral heads, some just under the surface of the water.

(881) **La Perouse Pinnacle** (23°46'08"N., 166°15'39"W.), a volcanic rock about 60 yards long, 20 yards wide, and 122 feet high, lies about midway between the tips of the crescent and W of the leeward arc of the reef. The rock is so steep and rugged that is almost inaccessible. From a distance its guano-coated outline resembles a brig under sail. A small detached lava rock about 9 feet high lies off the W side of the pinnacle. The points of the crescent reef, as indicated by the ends of the line of breakers, bear about 170° and 310° from La Perouse Pinnacle. La Perouse Pinnacle is reported to be the first object sighted, generally, when approaching the atoll, and that it is usually picked up on radar at 12 to 15 miles.

(882) **Shark Island**, the northwesternmost of the sand islets, lies 6 miles NW of La Perouse Pinnacle. A coral reef fringes the island. **Tern Island**, about 2 miles ENE of Shark Island, is marked by two 40-foot towers, low concrete buildings, a wooden telegraph pole, and four large trees. The island and buildings are visible at 8 and 5 miles, respectively. There are no facilities on the island.

(883) **East Island**, 3 miles ENE of La Perouse Pinnacle, is a low sand bar 600 yards long in a NW direction and about 100 yards across. Reefs that are awash most of the time extend a mile W and 0.2 mile S from the island; the S reef seldom breaks. A coral head that sometimes breaks is 0.6 mile S of East Island. NE and E of the island are numerous coral heads and reefs.

(884) Extreme caution must be exercised when navigating in the vicinity of these islets because of the numerous coral heads.

Channels

(885) The principal approach to Tern Island is through a natural channel that leads to a lagoon and anchorage SE of the island. Entry into the lagoon is through an opening in the reef indicated by the 3¼-fathom sounding in 23°51'09"N., 166°16'27"W., on chart 19402. Mariners are advised that attempting entry into the lagoon requires extensive local knowledge, good sea and weather conditions, and the sound judgment to recognize when conditions allow committing the vessel to a course through the reef opening.

Anchorages

(886) The best holding ground SW of French Frigate Shoals is in depths of 13 to 15 fathoms, sand bottom; in lesser depths the bottom is mostly coral. There are no all-weather anchorages for large vessels, but the conformation of the reef is such that some protection can be found from choppy seas and ground swell. Small vessels can find good protection from most weather behind the shoals and coral heads.

Routes

(887) Vessels approaching French Frigate Shoals from the N, E, or SE in the daytime should have no difficulty in picking out the outer reef from a considerable distance off. La Perouse Pinnacle, plainly visible from outside the reefs in clear weather, is reported to make a good radar target at 19 miles. From the S, the reef is not so easily seen. The sea may not break over the shoals, and although the bottom is plainly visible close in, the shoals might not be detected from a short distance. The 100-fathom curve is only about 0.5 mile from the shoals.

Currents

(888) A prevailing current sets W in the vicinity of French Frigate Shoals, but variable currents have been noted. A SW current of 2 knots has been measured. A 1-day series of half-hourly current observations taken 0.7 mile W of the S end of the shoal during a period of small wind velocity shows practically no current.

Weather, French Frigate Shoals and vicinity

(889) The NE trades prevail throughout the year, but W blows can be expected during the winter. The average wind velocity is 12 knots, with monthly averages of about 16 knots in December to 9.5 knots in August. Gales have been experienced in July and September. Occasional heavy showers of short duration cut visibility to about 2 miles (4 km).

Chart 19019

(890) **Brooks Banks** and **St. Rogatien Bank** are a group of five coral banks between French Frigate Shoals and Gardner Pinnacles. The banks extend 50 miles in a NW direction, have depths of 11 to 59 fathoms, and are separated by channels several miles wide and more than 100 fathoms deep. The largest of these banks lies 60 miles 305° from La Perouse Pinnacle, is about 12 miles in diameter, and has depths of 12 to 56 fathoms. The southeasternmost bank, the smallest in the group, is 27 miles 297° from La Perouse Pinnacle, is about 2 miles in diameter, and has depths of 28 fathoms. The northwesternmost bank is 75 miles 311° from La Perouse Pinnacle, is about 6 miles long and 4 miles wide, and has depths of 30 to 43 fathoms.

(891) Unprotected anchorage can be had on the shoaler areas, but the holding ground is only fair. The sand and coral bottom is plainly visible. There are no known dangers.

Currents

(892) The oceanic flow is variable, but usually sets W. Sixty half-hourly current observations indicate a NW nontidal current of about 0.5 knot, combined with a tidal current of 0.8 knot at strength. The tidal current is somewhat rotary, turning clockwise. The largest velocity observed was nearly 1.5 knots setting W.

Chart 19421

(893) **Gardner Pinnacles** (25°00'N., 168°00'W.) are 120 miles NW of La Perouse Pinnacle. They were discovered by Captain Allen of the whaler MARO in June 1820. The pinnacles are solid, volcanic, rocky islets; the larger pinnacle is 190 feet high and about 200 yards in diameter, and the smaller about 100 yards from the NW side of the larger. The rocks are barren of vegetation and are covered with guano, giving them a snow-capped appearance. The only off-lying dangers are a small rock just off the NW side of the larger pinnacle and two 20-foot patches, one of which is about 100 yards S of the larger pinnacle and the other just N of the smaller pinnacle.

From an E approach, the pinnacles are reported visible at a distance of 20 miles.

(894) Anchorage can be had anywhere on the bank which surrounds the pinnacles, but there is no protection; in general, the holding ground is poor. In comparatively smooth weather, landings can be made just N of the bight on the W side of the larger pinnacle. Because of its exposed position, most times the surf breaks high up its sides and landings are extremely hazardous and generally impossible. Some sea birds nest on its higher elevations.

Currents

(895) Current observations taken at a number of locations in the vicinity of Gardner Pinnacles show a WNW oceanic drift of about 0.2 knot combined with a rotary tidal current, turning clockwise, of 0.2 knot at strength. Velocities of about 2 knots setting WSW were measured during E winds.

(896) Gardner Pinnacles lie near the NE side of a bank about 50 miles long, in a N-S direction, and about 20 miles wide near the N end. The bank has depths of 10 to 25 fathoms, and the sand and coral bottom is plainly visible.

Chart 19019

(897) **Raita Bank** (25°32'N., 169°28'W.), is about 85 miles 291° from Gardner Pinnacles. It was discovered in 1921 by the French schooner RAITA. The bank is about 20 miles long in a NNE direction and has a maximum width of about 10 miles. Depths range from 9 to 20 fathoms, and the sand and coral bottom is plainly visible under ordinary weather conditions. At the 20-fathom curve, the bottom drops off rapidly to great depths. In heavy weather, the swells seem to lump up slightly over the shoaler areas, but there are no known dangers. Large schools of ulua fish and sharks have been observed on the bank. Anchorage can be had on the bank in the open sea with fair holding ground.

Currents

(898) Variable currents are reported in the vicinity of Raita Bank. Observations in the vicinity indicate a rotary tidal current turning clockwise.

Chart 19441

(899) **Maro Reef** (25°25'N., 170°35'W.), is about 60 miles W of Raita Bank. It was discovered by Captain Allen of the whaler MARO in June 1820. The large, oval-shaped, coral bank is about 31 miles long in a NW direction and about 18 miles wide. The center of the bank is a large area of reefs awash. This broken area, about 12 miles long in a NW direction and 5 miles wide, is extremely foul, with many coral heads awash and channels of deep water between. Only one very small rock, about 2 feet high and on the N side of the reef, shows above high water. The broken part of the reef is practically always marked by breakers. The wide shelf of the bank is outside the broken part of the reef.

(900) Breakers, or the light blue-green color of the area within the broken portions of the reef, give the first warning of the proximity of danger. All maneuvering in the vicinity of the broken area must be done with extreme caution and with the sea and light such that shoal spots can be seen and avoided. Ordinarily, spots with less than 6 fathoms of water are plainly visible.

(901) There are no known dangers more than 3.3 miles from the general outline of broken portions of Maro Reef, thus leaving a navigable shelf with depths of 12 to 20 fathoms on all sides but the NE where depths of 7 to 10 fathoms are found.

Currents

(902) In the vicinity of Maro Reef the prevailing current sets W, but variable currents have been noted. Over the bank a rotary tidal current, turning clockwise, has been reported.

Charts 19442, 19019

(903) **Laysan Island** (25°46'N., 171°44'W.) is a low sand island about 65 miles WNW of Maro Reef. The island is 1.6 miles long in a N-S direction, about 1 mile wide, and 35 feet in elevation at its highest point near the N end. In the center of the island is an extremely hypersaline, foul-smelling lake about 0.9 mile long. The island, mostly soft white sand, is partly covered with low vines and grass, and walking over it is tiring because of innumerable sea-bird nesting holes. The island is marked by an ironwood tree behind a wooden refuge warning sign on the W side of the island, and by a grove of coconut palms on the N edge of the lake. The rock which bares about 3 feet, located on the reef NW of the island presents a good radar target in mild weather. The wreck of a steel fishing boat is on the S shore of the island in 25°45.4'N., 171°44.4'W., but does not present a good radar target. Water can be obtained by digging shallow wells. The island is uninhabited and is seldom visited. As with other islands in the Leeward Islands, an entry permit is required. It is home to countless sea birds. Millions of flies make a visit there unpleasant most of the year.

(904) A coral reef, a few hundred yards wide, fringes the island. About 0.3 mile off the NW shore is a small, sharp rock, about 3 feet high. Coral heads, covered with 4 to 7 fathoms of water, are numerous in the area within 1 mile of the island. The sand and coral bottom can usually be seen in depths less than 10 fathoms, and often in greater depths. When approaching closer than 1 mile, a sharp lookout must be maintained to detect the coral heads.

(905) Vessels can anchor in depths of 8 to 15 fathoms 1 to 1.5 miles off the island on all sides, depending upon which side affords the best protection. During the trades, anchorage can be had 0.5 to 1 mile off the W side in depths of 8 to 15 fathoms, fair holding ground. In 1976, the Coast Guard Cutter MALLOW found good anchorage in 45 feet of water, sand and coral bottom, in 25°46'22"N., 171°45'15"W., with the ironwood tree bearing 084°, 1,390 yards. However, the anchor chain is subject to fouling on the coral heads because of the rotary currents. The coral heads are large and present a problem to vessels as they can foul ground tackle. It may be advisable to remain underway while attempting to land a small boat. Small craft drawing not over 12 feet can lie at anchor inside the reef and off the ironwood tree on the W side of the island, but this anchorage affords no protection from W winds. In 1978, the NOAA Ship TOWNSEND CROMWELL found anchorage with good holding ground, sand and coral bottom, and fair protection from strong W and NW winds accompanied by heavy seas and swell in 25°46.3'N., 171°43.0'W. and 25°45.8'N., 171°43.5'W. Surf of 10 to 15 feet was observed breaking on the W side of the island, and a 3- to 5-foot surf was observed on the reefs on the E and NE side.

(906) During NE and SE weather, the best landing can be made off the ironwood tree on the W side of the island on a sloping sandy beach. An alternate landing site on the W side of the island is about 0.5 mile S of the primary landing site, where the reef narrows close to shore. A poor landing can be made near the NE end of the island during light W winds. Caution is advised when attempting a landing on this side of the island. Clear sand beaches are almost nonexistent, and approaches to the beach must be made between breakers on the outer reef and the shore. Summer is the best for landing, as the NE trades prevail during this period.

Currents

(907) A current velocity of about 1 knot and a rotary tidal current, turning clockwise, have been reported. The current is believed to depend to a great extent upon the wind. In 1976, the Coast Guard Cutter MALLOW observed the current to round the S side of the island in a clockwise direction on the flood; and to round the N tip of the island in a counterclockwise direction on the ebb.

(908) Laysan Island is just SE of the center of a circular bank 14 miles in diameter, with depths of 9 to 23 fathoms, beyond which the water deepens rapidly.

(909) **Northampton Seamounts**, unsurveyed seamounts with a least known depth of 15 fathoms, are about 35 miles SW of Laysan Island.

Charts 19442, 19022

(910) **Lisianski Island** (26°04'N., 173°58'W.) is a small, low, sandy island, about 120 miles W of Laysan Island. Captain Lisianski, of the Russian ship NEVA, discovered the island on October 15, 1805, when his ship grounded on the reef and was nearly wrecked. The island is about 1.2 miles long in a NNW direction, 0.5 mile wide, and 20 feet in elevation at its highest point on the NE side. The shores are white sand except for two stretches of rock ledge at the waterline on the E side of the island. Behind the sand beach, the island is overgrown with vines and bushes. One coconut palm tree in the NE part of the island is prominent from N. In 1976, a small boat was reported wrecked on the NE end of the island and two groves of palm trees were observed near the middle of the island. Brackish water may be obtained by digging shallow wells. Large numbers of sea birds nest on the island, and, as at Laysan, large numbers of flies make a stay there unpleasant. Although the island is uninhabited and seldom visited, a permit is required for landing as the Hawaiian Monk seal is protected here. Visits should be made during the summer, when the NE trades prevail, but small-boat landings have been made on the E side of the island at other times, although this is very risky.

(911) A reef circles around to the SW from off the N side of the island. It is marked near its offshore end by a coral ledge that bares at times and over which the seas break. The S end of this ledge is 1.7 miles 260° from the N end of the island. About 0.5 mile SW of this point is another ledge which is marked by a breaker in most weather. Midway between these ledges or breakers is a passage leading to the lagoon between the island and the reef. The passage has an uneven bottom with depths of 11 to 22 feet. About 350 yards SW of the N ledge is a small shoal with a depth of 3 feet over it. These shoal spots are easily seen and avoided by small boats making the passage into the lagoon, but vessels should not enter without local knowledge. Once inside, anchorage can be had in depths of 3 to 6 fathoms, taking care to avoid the scattered coral heads with only a few feet of water over them. The coral heads are large and vessels anchoring here are cautioned because of the danger of fouling the ground tackle. Landing can be made on the W side and S end of the island in all but SW and W weather.

(912) **Neva Shoal**, with innumerable coral ledges, extends about 8 miles SE from Lisianski Island. This reef, which is about 4 miles wide, has its W extremity about 4 miles SSW of the island. The S end of the reef is usually marked by breakers, and many of the ledges break in almost all weather. The shoal has areas of deeper water between the ledges, and small boats can maneuver but with difficulty over many parts of the reef. It must be avoided entirely by larger vessels.

(913) In addition to Neva Shoal, there are many coral heads with depths of 3 to 6 fathoms over them within 3

miles of all sides of the island. A small coral ledge, with an islet on it and nearly always marked by breakers, is 2.7 miles 254° from the S end of the island. Between this ledge and the island are depths as great as 8 fathoms and a scattering of coral heads, some of which are nearly awash. The lagoon could be entered between this ledge and the ledge marking the S side of the previously described opening 1 mile N. A rock covered 14 feet, about 1.5 miles NNE of the island, is marked by breakers only during heavy weather. Under favorable conditions dangerous coral heads can be seen for several hundred yards.

Anchorage

(914) Anchorage can be had in trade-wind weather about 3 miles W of the island in depths of 11 to 15 fathoms, sand and coral bottom, with the N end of the island bearing 080°. During SW weather, vessels can find anchorage 3 to 4 miles E of the N end of the island in depths of 8 to 15 fathoms. Small boats can anchor in the lagoon, as described previously.

(915) Vessels may approach to within 3 miles of Lisianski Island from the N on courses between 270° and 090°. The island and Neva Shoal should be given a wide berth when passing S of them, as the island is seldom seen from the S limits of the shoal. Vessels approaching from the SW should keep about 5 miles W of the meridian of the island until the island bears 090°, and then approach the anchorage.

Currents

(916) One-half day of current observations taken 3 miles W of Lisianski Island indicate a rotary tidal current, turning clockwise, of 0.8 knot velocity at strength. A prevailing NW current is reported in the vicinity of the island.

(917) Lisianski Island and Neva Shoal lie just SE of the center of a bank about 25 miles long in a NW direction and about 15 miles wide. Outside the reefs, general depths on the bank are 9 to 47 fathoms.

(918) **Pioneer Bank** (26°02'N., 173°26'W.) is about 30 miles E of Lisianski Island. The bank is about 8 miles in diameter, and soundings of 18 fathoms have been obtained near its center. No breakers or dangers were observed during a preliminary survey, but, as the least depth may not have been obtained, vessels should avoid the area.

(919) An unsurveyed bank with least known depths of 30 fathoms is reported to be about 36 miles NW of Lisianski Island.

Chart 19461

(920) **Pearl and Hermes Atoll**, about 145 miles NW of Lisianski Island, is an extensive oval-shaped atoll about 40 miles in circumference, 17 miles long in a NE direction, and 9 miles wide. The reef was discovered on April 26, 1822, by the British whalers PEARL and HERMES, which were wrecked on the same night within 10 miles of each other. Within the outer reef is a lagoon in which are numerous coral reefs with deep water between. The remains of a wreck stranded on the E side of the reef are still visible, but over the years most have been beaten down by breakers. There are no known dangers outside the heavy breakers on the outer reef.

(921) Within the outer fringing reef are several small islets, most of which are on the S side; the exception is **North Island**. There are also several sandbanks that are awash at high water. **Southeast Island** (27°47'N., 175°49'W.) is the largest of the group; five other named islands are scattered along a 7-mile stretch to W. Though uninhabited and vegetated by low plants and shrubs, a permit is required for landing as the Hawaiian Monk seal is protected here. Large numbers of sea birds nest on the island.

(922) The 6-mile opening on the NW side of the outer reef has depths of 1 to 6 feet between the numerous coral heads, and is hazardous to negotiate with a small boat. The small-boat channel between Southeast Island and **Bird Island**, next islet to the W, has a least depth of 4 feet; the channel between Bird Island and **Sand Island** has 19 feet. The eastern portion of the lagoon is maze-like and could be dangerous to the navigator without local knowledge. Caution is advised when making entry.

Anchorage

(923) Anchorage can be had off the W entrance to the lagoon in depths of 8 to 12 fathoms, or on the E side of the reef. Vessels have anchored midway between the S entrances and about 0.6 mile off Bird Island in depths of 25 fathoms.

Currents

(924) The current appears to set N between Lisianski Island and Pearl and Hermes Atoll.

Chart 19022

(925) **Salmon Bank** is about 60 miles SW from Southeast Island on Pearl and Hermes Atoll. The least known depth on the bank is 30 fathoms.

(926) **Gambia Shoal**, position doubtful, is about 50 miles WNW of Southeast Island on Pearl and Hermes Atoll. The shoal has a depth of 14 fathoms, and the bottom can be plainly seen. About 25 miles N of the charted position of Gambia Shoal is **Ladd Seamount**, a bank with a least known depth of 35 fathoms.

Charts 19480, 19481, 19482

(927) **Midway Islands**, 1,150 miles WNW of Honolulu, were discovered in 1859 by Captain N. C. Brooks, an American shipmaster on the Hawai'ian vessel GAMBIA; possession was taken on behalf of the United States on

September 30, 1867, by Captain William Reynolds of the U.S.S. LACKAWANNA. The circular atoll is 6 miles in diameter and encloses two islands. The coral reef does not completely enclose the lagoon; there is a natural opening on the W side, and another opening has been dredged on the S side. The reef rises abruptly from deep water and there are no off-lying rocks or shoals; breakers mark all seaward sides of the reef. The enclosed islands average 12 feet high with a maximum height of 45 feet. Numerous birds, especially albatross, nest on the islands and are sometimes a hazard to landing or departing airplanes.

(928) The Midway Islands, not part of the State of Hawaii, are under the administration of the Department of the Interior **Midway Atoll National Wildlife Refuge** established by Executive Order No. 13022 of October 31, 1996. Copies of the Executive Order directing the **Management** and **General Public Use** of the National Wildlife Refuge System can be obtained from Refuge Manager, Hawai'ian/Pacific Islands National Wildlife Refuge Complex, U.S. Fish and Wildlife Service, 300 Ala Moana Boulevard, P.O. Box 50167, Honolulu, HI 96850.

(929) Requests for emergency entry of vessels in distress should be made by any means possible to the Joint Rescue Coordination Center (JRCC), Honolulu, Hawaii (808–535–3333). JRCC will then obtain entry approval or denial from the USFWS Refuge Manager and provide a response to the requester.

(930) Non-emergency entry requests must be approved in advance by contacting the USFWS Refuge Manager. Additionally, the Midway harbormaster can be reached by VHF-FM radio channel 16.

(931) **Eastern Island**, at the SE end of the atoll, is triangular in shape, about 1.2 miles long, and 6 to 12 feet high.

(932) **Sand Island**, on the S side of the atoll, is about 2 miles long in a SW direction and is composed of white coral sand. Prominent from offshore are the towers, tanks, and radio masts of the naval installations and a group of trees on the N side of the island. An aerolight is on top of the tallest tank in the N central part of the island.

(933) **Welles Harbor** is the area inside the gap in the barrier reef on the W side of the atoll. The harbor was formerly used to a considerable extent as an anchorage by ships calling at Midway, but since the dredging of the ship channel and harbor between Sand and Eastern Islands, Welles Harbor is little used. Navigation in this area should not be attempted.

Channels

(934) Marked dredged channels through the S reef lead to deepwater basins on the E and NE sides of Sand Island, and to a small-craft basin on the W side of Eastern Island. The entrance channel is marked by a lighted buoy, unlighted buoys, and a **359.5°** lighted range. (Consult the United States Fish and Wildlife Service, Notice to Mariners, and latest editions of charts for controlling depths.)

Anchorages

(935) The established anchorage area is NE of Sand Island. Outside anchorage is available in depths of 15 to 25 fathoms E of the main channel sea buoy; this anchorage is fair during NE winds, but should not be attempted during winds from other quadrants. Anchorage S of Sand Island is prohibited to avoid possible fouling of the San Francisco-Honolulu-Midway-Guam-Manila cable.

Routes

(936) Vessels approaching Midway Islands are reminded that entry into the Midway Atoll National Wildlife Refuge is prohibited without prior approval. In approaching from any direction, vessels will remain 3 miles off until S of the entrance. Then vessels should steer a course to pass through a position (28°09'25"N., 177°21'15"W.) about 2 miles S of Midway Channel Entrance Lighted Buoy 1, then steer a N course heading directly between Sand and Eastern Islands until the channel is made out, then steer on the range. Due to the prevailing E winds and W set of current, caution must be exercised in entering. Drift and leeway should be anticipated, and sufficient speed should be maintained at all times to control the vessel. (See discussion of currents in the channel.)

Radar Navigation

(937) Radar and visual contact have been frequently made with the radio towers on Sand Island at distances in excess of 20 miles.

(938) The best radar returns are the SE edge of Sand Island, the stranded wreck on E edge of the entrance channel, the radio towers on Sand Island, an unlighted platform on the N side of the atoll, and the W tip of Eastern Island.

Currents

(939) The current off the main entrance channel usually sets W with a velocity of about 2 knots. Within the channels, the current changes direction with velocities of 2 to 8 knots, depending on the weather; extreme caution is necessary to avoid being carried outside the channel limits. It is reported that during heavy gales Welles Harbor is full of strong currents caused by the sea forced over the reefs.

Weather, Midway Islands and vicinity

(940) During the summer the winds are generally variable and light, either from NE, SE, or SW until about the middle of July, when fresh to strong NE trades set in, continuing through July and August. SW winds are always accompanied with a low barometer, rain, and squalls. Rain also comes occasionally with NE and SE winds and a high barometer. NW winds following SW storms generally indicate clearing weather.

(941) During the winter from October to April, gales frequently occur, working around from SE through SW to NW. Occasionally a few days of fine weather will prevail, but a rough W sea is always present.

(942) The average temperature at Midway is 73°F (22.8°C). The average maximum is 76°F (24.4°C) while the average minimum is 68°F (20°C). The record high is 92°F (33.3°C) recorded in September 1979, July and August 1984, and August 1987. The record low is 49°F (9.4°C) recorded in January 1980. On average, only one day each year is 90°F (32.2°C) or warmer and 137 days each year are 80°F (26.7°C) or warmer.

(943) Precipitation is moderate at Midway and averages 41.3 inches (1050 mm) each year. June is the driest month and January the wettest. On average, six thunderstorms each year affect Midway.

Pilotage, Midway Islands

(944) Vessels required by law to have a licensed master should consult the Captain of the Port, Honolulu (808–842–2640) to determine specific pilotage requirements. Pilots are not required for public vessels of the United States.

Harbor facilities

(945) Two deepwater piers are on the NE side, and one smaller pier is in the inner harbor on the E side of Sand Island; a small-craft pier is on the W side of Eastern Island.

(946) Provisions, jet fuel (JP–5), and water are not available for commercial use, except in case of emergency. Limited emergency repairs can be made to vessels, but there are no drydocking facilities. Tugs are available; there is a 20-ton mobile crane for use in emergencies.

Chart 19480

(947) **Nero Seamount** is about 30 miles WSW from Midway Islands. Nero Seamount, formerly Pogy Bank, extends about 8.5 miles in an E-W direction, about 7 miles in a N-S direction, and has a least depth of 37 fathoms.

Chart 19483

(948) **Kure Atoll** (28°25'N., 178°20'W.) is 50 miles WNW of Midway Islands, which it closely resembles both in formation and appearance. Kure Atoll is 4.5 miles in diameter, and a nearly continuous coral reef encloses a lagoon in which reefs and coral heads alternate with deep water. A mile-wide break in the SW side of the barrier reef provides an entrance of sorts to the lagoon.

Anchorage

(949) Good anchorage in 15 fathoms may be found on the NW side of the atoll.

(950) Entry upon Kure Atoll must be approved by the State of Hawaii, Department of Land and Natural Resources and Commander, 14th Coast Guard District, Honolulu, HI. These restrictions apply to all civilian and military agencies as well as individuals.

(951) **Green Island**, on the SE side of the atoll, has a highest elevation of 20 feet and is covered with scaevola brush.

(952) The island is a wildlife refuge and entry upon the island must be by approval of the State of Hawaii Department of Land and Natural Resources. This restriction applies to civilian and military agencies as well as individuals. The Coast Guard has reported that Green Island presents a good radar target at 22 miles and the reef line presents a good target at 7.5 miles. Another good radar target, reported by NOAA Ship TOWNSEND CROMWELL, is a large wreck in about 28°27.0'N., 178°18.9'W., on the NE side of the atoll. W of Green Island are small sand islets, the largest of which is 8- to 10-foot-high **Sand Island**. These islands continually shift and change with weather and sea action.

(953) The best anchorage is on the W side, at the SW corner of the atoll with depth of 8 to 15 fathoms, rocky bottom. Boats may then be taken to a concrete pier with 3 to 5 feet alongside, located at about the midpoint of the lagoon side of Green Island. Vessels also anchor about 0.3 to 0.5 mile SSW of the S tip of Green Island in depths up to 15 fathoms. Landings can be made in good weather through a break in the reef to a sand beach at the SW tip of Green Island; depths to the landing are 5 to 6 feet between small coral heads and ledges.

(954) A bank with depths of 20 to 30 fathoms surrounds Kure Atoll. No dangers have been observed outside the reef; however, the reef is inadequately surveyed. From the appearance of the islands, it may be assumed that they are sometimes visited by severe storms, the sand being thrown into numerous cones and pyramids.

Currents

(955) A set to the S has been observed between Kure Atoll and Midway Islands. In the vicinity of Kure Atoll a continuous E current of about 2 knots during W weather has been reported.

Weather

(956) Weather for Kure Atoll is similar to that for the Midway Islands.

Chart 19022

(957) In 1923, breakers were reported observed about 180 miles S of Kure Atoll in about 25°23'N., 178°04'W., by the American vessel ETHAN ALLEN. The master reported that the swell appeared to mount up and occasionally break as though over a shoal extending for about 2 or 3 miles in an E-W direction.

Charts 83633, 83637

(958) **Johnston Atoll** (16°45'N., 169°31'W.) is about 780 miles WSW of the island of Hawaii. Johnston Atoll consists of four islets that lie on a reef about 9 miles long in a NE-SW direction. Johnston Island, the largest island, lies about 2 miles inside the SW end of the reef. **Sand Island** and **Hikina Island** lie about 1 and 2 miles NE of Johnston Island, respectively; **Akau Island** is about 1.5 miles N of Sand Island.

(959) Johnston Atoll is a possession of the United States and has been designated a National Wildlife Refuge. The administration of the atoll is split between the U.S. Air Force and the U.S. Fish and Wildlife Service (USFWS). Entry onto the atoll is prohibited unless authorized by a USFWS permit.

Prominent features

(960) The large multi-story Joint Operations Building stands on the NE end of Johnston Island and is very prominent. The outline of the island does not show until within 10 miles of the island.

Channels

(961) The main entrance channel is entered S of Johnston Island and leads to the harbor. The harbor consists of a turning basin within the lagoon about midway between Johnston and Sand Islands. In 1964, the entrance channel was dredged to a depth of 35 feet. The turning basin and harbor area have a depth of 35 feet. The berthing area alongside the main pier has a depth of 29.8 feet. Maximum draft for vessels entering the harbor under normal conditions is 28 feet. The largest vessel to enter was 656 feet long. Vessels should not enter at night or when cross channel winds exceed 25 knots.

Anchorage

(962) Vessels drawing more than 28 feet should anchor in the channel approach area S of the channel entrance. Anchorage is prohibited within the area of an arc extending 1.5 miles S and SE from 16°42'44"N., 169°31'01"W, and in an area situated near the center of the turning basin.

Dangers

(963) A barrier reef surrounds Johnston Island, and extends in an arc from about 2 miles W to about 7 miles NE of the island. Depths outside the reef drop off to 100 fathoms about 0.4 mile off. With heavy breakers on the reef, a 2 to 3-foot surge exists inside the lagoon. From the NE, via S to SW is a foul area with a very irregular bottom. The 100-fathom curve lies 4 miles S of the center of Johnston Island; however, there are 5-fathom shoals lying as close as 0.3 mile inside the curve and depths shallower than 10 fathoms can be found as far as 10 miles E and 6 miles SE of the Johnston Island.

Weather

(964) Winds average 10 to 15 knots in summer and 15 to 25 knots in winter. They are from the E to NE about 90 percent of the time. The occasional Hawai'ian Island storms are characterized by stormy S or SW winds and heavy rains. Brief showers occur frequently, but protracted bad weather is rare. Visibility is good, usually over 12 miles.

TIDAL INFORMATION					
Chart	Station	LAT/LONG	Mean Higher High Water*	Mean High Water*	Mean Low Water*
19322	Honuapo, Hawaii Island	19°05'N/155°33'W	2.5	2.0	0.3
19324	Hilo, Kuhio Bay	19°43'N/155°03'W	2.4	2.0	0.3
19329	Mahukona, Hawaii Island	20°11'N/155°54'W	2.1	1.6	0.2
19330	Kawaihae, Hawaii Island	20°02'N/155°50'W	2.1	1.6	0.2
19331	Kailua Kona, Hawaii Island	19°39'N/156°00'W	2.1	1.6	0.2
19332	Napoopoo, Kealakekua Bay, Hawaii Island	19°28'N/155°55'W	2.1	1.6	0.2
19341	Hana, Maui Island	20°46'N/155°59'W	2.5	2.0	0.2
19342	Kahului, Kahului Harbor, Maui Island	20°54'N/156°28'W	2.2	1.9	0.3
19347	Kaumalapau, Lanai Island	20°47'N/157°00'W	2.2	1.7	0.2
19348	Lahaina, Maui Island	20°53'N/156°41'W	2.2	1.7	0.3
19350	Kihei, Maalaea Bay	20°47'N/156°28'W	2.3	1.8	0.2
19353	Kolo, Molokai Isalnd	21°06'N/157°12'W	2.0	1.5	0.2
19353	Kaunakakai Harbor, Molokai Isalnd	21°05'N/157°02'W	2.1	1.6	0.2
19353	Kamalo Harbor, Molokai Island	21°03'N/156°53'W	2.1	1.6	0.2
19353	Pukoo Harbor, Molokai Island	21°04'N/156°48'W	2.1	1.6	0.2
19357	Haleiwa, Waialua Bay, Oahu Island	21°36'N/158°07'W	1.6	--.--	--.--
19357	Laie Bay, Oahu Isalnd	21°39'N/157°56'W	2.2	1.6	0.3
19358	Hanauma Bay, Oahu Island	21°17'N/157°42'W	1.9	1.5	0.2
19358	Waimanalo, Oahu Island	21°20'N/157°42'W	1.8	1.4	0.3
19359	Waikane, Kaneohe Bay, Oahu Island	21°30'N/157°51'W	2.2	1.8	0.4
19359	Moku O Loe, Oahu Island	21°26'N/157°48'W	2.1	1.8	0.3
19361	Waianae, Oahu Island	21°27'N/158°12'W	1.8	1.4	0.2
19366	Pearl Harbor, Oahu Island	21°22'N/157°57'W	2.0	1.5	0.2
19367	Honolulu, Oahu Island	21°19'N/157°52'W	1.9	1.4	0.2
19382	Port Allen, Hanapepe Bay, Kauai Island	21°54'N/159°36'W	1.8	1.4	0.2
19383	Nawiliwili, Nawiliwili Bay, Kauai Island	21°57'N/159°21'W	1.8	1.4	0.2
19384	Hanamaulu Bay, Kauai Island	22°00'N/159°20'W	1.8	1.4	0.2
19385	Hanalei Bay, Kauai Island	22°13'N/159°30'W	1.8	1.5	0.2
19386	Waimea Bay, Kauai Island	21°57'N/159°40'W	1.6	1.2	0.2
19402	East Island Frigate Shoals	23°47'N/166°13'W	1.4	1.1	0.2
19442	Lisianski Island	26°04'N/173°58'W	0.8	0.6	0.1
19442	Laysan Island	25°46'N/171°45'W	1.0	0.8	0.1
19482	Sand Island, Midway Islands	28°13'N/177°21'W	1.2	1.1	0.2
19483	Midway Islands	28°13'N/177°22'W	1.2	1.0	0.2
83637	Johnston Atoll	16°44'N/169°32'W	2.2	2.0	0.1

* Heights in feet referred to datum of sounding MLLW.
Real-time water levels, tide predictions, and tidal current predictions are available at: http://tidesandcurrents.noaa.gov
To determine mean tide range subtract Mean Low Water from Mean High Water.
Data as of October 2012

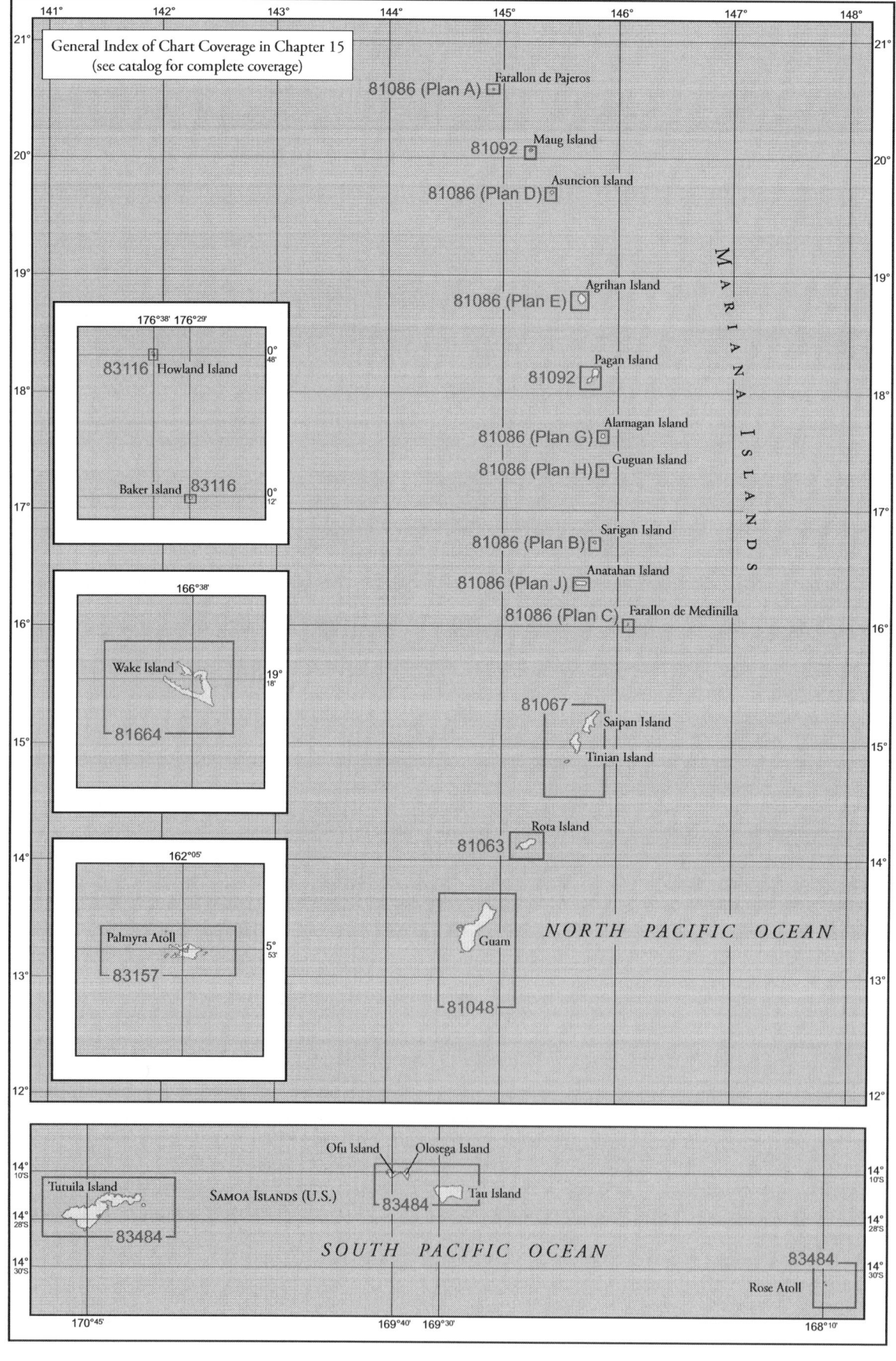

Pacific Islands

(1) Islands and Pacific waters discussed in this chapter are other than those of the Hawai'ian Archipelago. See chapter 14, Hawaii, for the latter.

National Wildlife Refuges

(2) The National Wildlife Refuges of Rose Atoll (American Samoa), Howland Island, Baker Island, Jarvis Island, Kingman Reef, and Palmyra Atoll are administered by the U.S. Fish and Wildlife Service, Department of the Interior. The refuge boundaries extend outward 12 nautical miles. Entry into the refuge without a permit is prohibited, except in an emergency. An entry permit is obtained from Refuge Manager, Hawai'ian/Pacific Islands National Wildlife Refuge Complex (see Appendix A, Department of Interior, for address).

Pacific Marine National Monuments

(3) The **Pacific Marine National Monuments**, Marianas Trench, Pacific Remote Islands and Rose Atoll were established by Presidential Proclamation in January 2009.

(4) The **Marianas Trench Marine National Monument** includes the waters and submerged lands of the three northernmost Mariana Islands (the Islands Unit), and only the submerged lands of designated volcanic sites (the Volcanic Units) and the Mariana Trench (the Trench Unit). The seaward boundary of the Islands Unit extends from the mean low water line of the islands of Farallon de Pajaros, Maug and Asuncion, out to approximately 50 nautical miles.

(5) The **Pacific Remote Islands National Monument** includes the waters and submerged lands out to approximately 50 nautical miles from the mean low water line around the islands of Wake, Baker, Howland, and Jarvis Islands, Johnston and Palmyra Atolls, and Kingman Reef.

(6) The **Rose Atoll Marine National Monument** consists of Rose Atoll and lands and interests in lands that lie 50 nautical miles from the mean low water line of the atoll.

(7) For more information visit the NOAA Fisheries Marine National Monument Program website http://www.fpir.noaa.gov/MNM/mnm_index.html

Chart 83484

(8) The **Samoa Islands** (Navigator Islands) (13°25'S. to 14°30'S.; 168°00'W. to 173°00'W.) consists of two groups of islands, which are commonly referred to as **American Samoa** and **Western Samoa**. The islands comprising American Samoa are **Tutuila Island, Aunuu Island, Ofu Island, Olosega Island, Ta'u Island**, and **Rose Atoll**. Western Samoa comprises the islands of **Upolu Island** and **Savai'i Island**.

(9) The Samoa Islands have been populated for 3,000 years, but known to the western world for little more than two centuries. American Samoa, the only U.S. territory S of the equator, consists of five rugged, highly eroded volcanic islands, and two coral atolls. The land area of the territory is 76 square miles. The islands have a population of approximately 65,000, with most people living on the main island of Tutuila. Tuna fishing and canning are the major industries.

(10) The **National Marine Sanctuary of American Samoa**, established in 1986 and expanded in 2012, consists of six distinct units. These units include Larsen Bay (Fagalua/Fogama'a), Fagatele Bay and the waters surrounding Swains Island, Rose Atoll (Muliava), Annu'u Island (partial) and Ta'u Island (partial). The precise boundaries are defined by regulation. The Sanctuary contains a unique and vast array of tropical marine organisms, including corals and a diverse tropical reef ecosystem with endangered and threatened species. The Sanctuary also contains areas such as near-shore, mid-shore, deep reef, seamount, open pelagic waters and other habitats and areas of historical and cultural significance. (See **15 CFR 922.1** through **922.50** and **Subpart J**, chapter 2, for limits and regulations.)

COLREGS Demarcation Lines

(11) The lines established for U.S. Pacific Island Possessions are described in **80.1495**, chapter 2.

Weather, Samoa Islands

(12) The prevailing winds, or so called trade winds, come from a direction more nearly E, blowing between ESE and NNE. They are fairly constant through the dry season, but during the wet season they are fitful, and are frequently broken by periods of calm. The islands lie within the typhoon area of the W Pacific. Typhoons occur from January to March, and occasionally up to the middle of April. The year divides itself distinctly, but not sharply into a dry season (May to November) and a wet season (November to April.) The wettest month, January, has a range of 5 to 65 inches of precipitation. The annual rainfall has also varied this much. The climate varies little from year to year, because of the great area of water surrounding the group. December is the hottest

month, with an average excess of only about 2° over the mean temperature for July, the coldest month.

Caution

(13) Caution should be exercised in the vicinity of American Samoa, as several Fish Aggregating Devices have been moored at off-lying, deep-water locations around Tutuila, and other positions around the group. The devices may drift off position, and/or concentrations of fishing vessels may be found in their vicinity. The devices are comprised of aluminum catamaran floats painted orange and white. Each device carries a white daymark, fitted with the letter designation of the device, and a flashing white light. The devices offer good radar returns.

(14) **Rose Atoll** (14°33'S., 168°09'W.), the farthest E of the Samoa Islands, is nearly square in shape; its sides are about 1.5 miles in length. Sand Island, inside the reef on the N extremity, is merely a sand spot. A large clump of trees, 65 feet high, stands on Rose Island. There is a boat channel into the lagoon, close W of the N extremity of the reef. Rose Atoll is a U.S. National Wildlife Refuge, Marine National Monument and National Marine Sanctuary. (See National Wildlife Refuges, Pacific Marine National Monuments and National Marine Sanctuary of American Samoa, this chapter.)

Tides and currents

(15) Tidal currents off Rose Atoll are reported to set NE and SW, with the SW or ebb current being the stronger.

(16) The **Manua Islands** (14°13'S., 169°33'W.) consists of three islands, Ofu, Olosega, and Ta'u, which extend over an area of about 17 miles in an ESE-WNW direction. The islands are about 60 miles E of Tutuila. Ofu and Olosega are joined by a bridge. These islands are sparsely populated. The villages on the islands have only a few hundred people. There is a national park on Ofu and Ta'u.

(17) **Ta'u Island** (14°15'S., 169°28'W.) is the farthest of the three islands which comprise the Manua Islands. The island is about 5.8 miles long E-W, is dome-shaped, and rises to a height of 3,170 feet. It is covered with vegetation. **Maafee Islet** is located close offshore, about 0.3 mile S of the W extremity of the island.

(18) **Ta'u Harbor** (14°14.5'S., 169°30.6'W.), on the W shore, should only be entered by flat bottom boats; caution is advised. An entrance channel, marked by a **045°** unlighted range, leads NE to a turning basin in the harbor. In 2005, the controlling depth was 9 feet in the entrance channel, thence depths of 9 to 13 feet were available in the basin (except for lesser depths to 6 feet in the N corner.) The dock is poorly maintained and should be avoided. Permission to enter the harbor along with directions must be obtained from the harbormaster in Pago Pago Harbor.

(19) **Faleasao Harbor** (14°13.02'S., 169°30.10'W.) is located at the NW point of Ta'u Island. Severe storms have damaged the jetty and mariners are advised to avoid the jetty while transiting the channel. Numerous coral heads and a shallow bottom present a danger to navigation. In 2005, the controlling depth was 10 feet in the entrance channel (except for lesser depths to 7 feet along the edges), thence the harbor basin had depths of 9 to 10 feet with lesser depths in the NW corner. The entrance is marked by a **200.5°** unlighted range. Permission to enter the harbor along with directions must be obtained from the harbormater in Pago Pago Harbor.

Anchorage

(20) **Faleasau (Faleasao)**, on the NW side of the island, affords sheltered anchorage, in 14.5 fathoms, during the trade winds, but a vessel should be prepared to weigh anchor with any change. Anchorage may be obtained, in 13 fathoms, coral, 0.4 mile W of **Fitiuta Point**, the NE extremity of the island.

Caution

(21) An area with a least depth of 24 fathoms, is about 1.3 miles W from the NW extremity of Ta'u Island. This area has experienced submarine volcanic activity.

Currents

(22) The tidal currents at the Faleasau anchorage flow SW on the ebb at 1 to 2 knots, and the flood flows NW at 1 to 2 knots.

(23) **Olosega Island** (14°11'S., 169°37'W.), 6 miles NW of Ta'u Island, rises nearly perpendicular on its W side to a height of 2,095 feet. The coral reef surrounding the island consists of two regular shelves, one beyond the other. There is fair anchorage, except during the trade winds, in 18 fathoms, coral, S of the W extremity of Olosega Island, and in 14.5 fathoms, sand, NE of the W extremity of the island.

(24) **Ofu Island** (14°11'S., 169°39'W.) is separated from Olosega Island by Asaga Strait, which is about 0.2 mile wide. Ofu Island is nearly 3 miles long in an E-W direction, and about 1.5 miles at its widest point. The island rises to 1,621 feet on its SE part. Two islets lie off the W side of the island. The coastal reef extends about 0.2 mile from Ofu Island to these islets. Lights are on the NW end of the island. There is good anchorage, except during strong trade winds, in 17 fathoms, sand, NW of **Sunuitao Peak**, at the E end of the island.

(25) **Ofu Harbor** (14°09.8'S., 169°40.9'W.) is on the NW point of Ofu Island. A dredged entrance channel leads E to a turning basin inside the harbor. In 2005, the controlling depth was 11 feet in the entrance channel to the basin, thence depths of 11 to 16 feet were available in the basin with lesser depths in the NW and SE corners. Storms have damaged the seawalls and mariners are advised to stay clear. Offloading and loading of cargo is

not advised during high tide. Permission to enter the harbor along with directions must be obtained from the harbormaster in Pago Pago Harbor.

(26) **Tutuila Island** (14°19'S., 170°42'W.) is about 17 miles long in an ENE-WSW direction, 5 miles wide, and rises to a height of 2,142 feet. A wooded mountain ridge extends nearly the entire length of the island and is extremely rugged, especially in the E. The N coast is bold and precipitous. The 100-fathom curve lies from 0.1 to 2.3 miles off the S coast, about 4.3 miles off the W extremity, and from 1.3 to 2.5 miles off the N coast. There are several shoal areas, especially off the S coast, which are best seen on the chart. The S coast of the island extends from **Cape Matatula**, the E extremity of the island, in a WSW direction about 14 miles to **Steps Point**, the S extremity, and then about 5.8 miles NW to **Cape Taputapu**, the W extremity. From **Cape Matatula** to **Matuli Point**, 1.5 miles S, the coast is fronted by a reef which extends about 0.1 mile offshore.

(27) **Auasi Harbor**, about 0.5 mile WSW of Matuli Point, is protected by a jetty on the SW side and a breakwater to the NE. An entrance channel leads NW, between the jetty and breakwater, into the harbor to a turning basin. In 2005, the controlling depths were 9 feet in the left half and 3 feet in the right half of the entrance channel, thence depths of 5 to 8 feet were available in the basin.

Currents

(28) Currents near the coast set SSW, particularly with NE winds; velocities of 4 knots have been observed. Between Tutuila Island and Upolo Island (Western Samoa), a NW current with a velocity of less than 0.5 knot has been found to exist. A current setting SW from Cape Taputapu is said to produce overfalls.

(29) **Aunuu Island** (14°17'S., 170°33'W.) is 0.7 mile SSE of Matuli Point. The island has two peaks, and there is a village at its W end. Lights are on the NE side and off the NW corner.

(30) **Aunuu Harbor** is located on the west side of Aunuu Island. Aunuu Harbor is a feeder port for the island. Small boats from **Auasi Harbor** on Tutuila Island frequently transit between the islands. Mariners should be aware that the light off the NW corner of the island, near the harbor, marks the entrance and is on the S jetty, not the N jetty. Permission to enter the harbor along with directions must be obtained from the harbormaster in Pago Pago Harbor.

(31) A dredged entrance channel leads E between a revetted mole on the N and a breakwater on the S to a mooring basin. In 2005, the controlling depth was 9 feet in the entrance channel (except for lesser depths to 4 feet in the NE corner), thence depths of 7 to 8 feet were in the basin.

Caution

(32) A cable area extends across the channel between Aunuu and Tutuila Islands and is best seen on the chart; vessels should avoid anchoring in the vicinity. **Nafanua Bank**, with a least charted depth of 3½ fathoms, extends 1.5 miles in a SW direction from Aunuu Island. A rock, covered 1¾ fathom, is about 0.4 mile SSE of **Cape Fogausa**. A rock, covered 3 fathoms, is about 1.2 miles SW of Cape Fogausa between **Fagaitua Bay** and **Narragansett Passage**. The chart should be consulted for other depths.

(33) **Breakers Point** (14°17.4'S., 170°39.8'W.), 3.5 miles WSW of Cape Fogausa, is the E entrance point to Pago Pago Harbor and is marked by a light. In 1989, discolored water was reported in the S approach to the harbor in about 14°22.2'S., 170°40.7'W. **Taema Bank**, with a least depth of 4 fathoms, lies about 1.6 miles SSE of the entrance to Pago Pago Harbor. The bank is about 2.3 miles long in an ENE-WSW direction and is marked on the W end by a lighted buoy. Narragansett Passage is between Taema Bank and Nafanua Bank to the E. There are several banks in the vicinity of the passage whose positions may best be seen on the chart. The passage is not recommended due to the age of survey.

(34) **Pago Pago Harbor** (14°17'S., 170°40'W.), a natural harbor located on the S shore of Tutuila Island, is entered between Breakers Point and **Niuloa Point**. **Pago Pago**, on the NW side of the harbor is the largest village on the island and is the capital of American Samoa; it is the only port of entry for American Samoa. The village of **Utulei** is close SE of the government administration buildings, and the village of **Fagatogo** is close W of the same buildings.

Prominent Features

(35) Easily identified landmarks include Aunuu Island; Steps Point, the S extremity of the island marked by a light; the sharp peak of **Matafao**, 2,142 feet high, 1.3 miles S of Pago Pago; the flat, dome shape of **North Pioa Mountain**, 1,718 feet high, on the E side of the harbor; and **Fatu Rock**, 102 feet high, 0.2 mile S of Niuloa Point. **Tauga Rock**, about 1 mile E of Breakers Point, is 89 feet high and prominent.

Routes

(36) Vessels approaching from the E should pass about 2 miles E and 1.5 miles SE of Aunuu Island, thence a course of **256°** should be steered until **Breakers Point Light** (14°17'23"S., 170°39'49"W.) bears about **025°**, thence alter course to the N to pass W of Taema Bank. When clear of the bank, steer a NE course to intersect the entrance range, thence steer **342°** and enter the harbor the range. This range line passes E of **Whale Rock** and W of **Toasa Rock**. Vessels and deep-draft vessels approaching from the W or S should keep outside the 100-fathom line until reaching 14°21.0'S., 170°41.5'W.,

thence steer **025°** to clear the W end of Taema Bank, then proceed as directed above. Mariners should stay well clear of Taema Bank. Locals have noted breakers over Taema Bank during rough weather.

Anchorage

(37) There is good anchorage in the inner harbor, in 6 to 25 fathoms, mud and sand. The best anchorage for large vessels is at midchannel off the Main Dock. Vessels of 1,000 gross tons or more should not anchor in less than 15¾ fathoms, as the harbor becomes narrow and there is no room to swing.

Dangers

(38) The shores of the harbor are fringed by reefs, which on the W and E sides of the entrance extend up to 0.3 mile offshore. In most parts the reefs are steep-to and their edges are marked by surf. The depths in the harbor are from 17 to 37 fathoms. A dangerous submerged wreck is about 0.1 mile S of Breakers Point. **Whale Rock**, covered 2 fathoms and marked by a lighted buoy on the E side and Toasa Rock covered 2 feet and marked by a buoy on the SW side, are the two principal dangers in the harbor.

Pilotage

(39) Pilotage is not compulsory, but is advisable; a pilot is available day or night. Pilotage fees are charged whether or not a pilot is used. It is recommended that large vessels request a pilot if docking in inclement weather. A radio request for a pilot should be made 24 hours prior to the ETA. The pilot prefers to embark close to the dock, but in good weather will embark off Fatu Rock. Entrance at night is not encouraged; however, if previous arrangements are made and weather permits, a pilot will embark during hours of darkness. Port officials board incoming ships alongside the dock.

Harbormaster

(40) Pago Pago Control and the harbormaster may be contacted on VHF-FM channel 16. Pago Pago Harbor Control also monitors 2182 kHz. Required notifications to the Officer in Charge, Marine Inspection and/or the Captain of the Port, Honolulu, may be made in American Samoa to:

(41) U.S. Coast Guard Liaison Office, American Samoa
(42) P.O. Box 249
(43) Pago Pago, AS 96799

Wharves

(44) Station Wharf (Main Wharf), on the S side of the inner harbor, has depths of 5¼ to 6 fathoms alongside, however, in 1987, a vessel reported a least depth of 5 fathoms alongside. A deep draft container wharf, 787 feet long, is situated between Station Wharf and the oil dock. The oil dock has depths of 5¼ fathoms alongside. In 1992, Station Wharf and the oil dock were reported to be in poor condition. The customs pier has a depth of 1½ fathoms at the SW end and 3¾ fathoms at the NE end. The facilities on the N shore of the inner harbor are reserved for the fishing fleet serving the canneries.

(45) From Pago Pago Harbor, the shore trends SW 6.8 miles to **Steps Point** (14°22.4'S., 170°45.6'W.) Midway along this stretch of shore, near the airport, a reef extends about 0.3 mile offshore; the sea breaks continuously on this reef.

(46) The shore from Steps Point to **Papualoa Point**, about 2 miles NW, is formed partly by perpendicular rocks and partly by blocks of lava, which extend some distance seaward and upon which the sea breaks. **Leone Bay** is entered between Papualoa Point and **Fagaone Point**, and is open to the SSW. There is anchorage W of the village of **Leone**, in 15 to 20 fathoms, but it is dangerous when winds are from the S or SSW.

(47) **Cape Taputapu** (14°19'S., 170°51'W.), the W extremity of Tutuila, lies 1.5 miles WNW of Fagaone Point. It is a mass of high, steep rocks, fronted by some rocky islets. Taputapu Island lies on the reef close SW of Cape Taputapu. The following banks, with the indicated least depths, lie in the approach to Cape Taputapu:

(48) a. 14 fathoms – 3.3 miles SE.
(49) b. 11 fathoms – 2.3 miles SSE.
(50) c. 15 fathoms – 3.8 miles SW.
(51) d. 18 fathoms – 3.5 miles W.

(52) The N coast of Tutuila is described from E to W. From Cape Matatula to **Pola Island**, 6.5 miles W, the coast is indented by numerous bays. The coast then trends WSW 11 miles to Cape Taputapu. This coast is also indented with bays. **Aoa Bay** (14°15.0'S., 170°35.4'W.), affords anchorage, in 16 fathoms, midway between the entrance points. **Masefau Bay**, entered W of **Tiapea Point**, 1.5 miles W of Aoa Bay, affords anchorage, in 17 fathoms. The surrounding reefs and **Nuusetoga Island**, off the W entrance point, narrow the anchorage. **Afono Bay**, 1.5 miles W of Nuusetoga Island, is reported to provide good anchorage, in 14 fathoms, coral, except in N winds.

(53) **Pola Island** (14°14.0'S., 170°40.2'W.), 1.5 miles NW of Afona Bay, is located off the N extremity of Tutuila Island. **Cockscomb Point**, the N extremity of Pola Island is formed by a ridge of rocks, which are high, indented, and steep. An area with a least depth of 13 fathoms is just over 1 mile ENE of Cockscomb Point and an area with a least depth of 15 fathoms is about 1.5 miles W of the point. **Fagasa Bay** is about 4 miles SW of Cockscomb Point. Anchorage, protected from the trades, can be had in 13 fathoms between the E and W points of the bay. Between Fagasa Bay and **Aoloau Bay**, 3 miles WSW, there are two small bays backed by mountains. Aoloau Bay affords good anchorage, in 14 fathoms in mid-bay, but vessels should be prepared to leave on short notice when the winds shift to the N. Aoloau Bay is small and surrounded by high mountains. A 12-fathom area is 1.5 miles NNE of Aoloau Bay. Similar depths are charted to

a distance of 4.8 miles W of the 12-fathom depth. **Poloa Bay** (14°19.0'S., 170°50.6'W.), 4 miles SW of Aoloau Bay, affords good anchorage during E winds, in 16 fathoms, midway between the entrance points. Vessels should be prepared to leave on short notice when the wind shifts to the W. In this bay there is a 1 to 4 knot current that runs in a SW direction. Cape Taputapu is located close SW of Poloa Bay.

(54) **Swains Island** (11°03'S., 171°04'W.), about 195 miles NNW of Tutuila Island (American Samoa), is a circular-shaped island, with a diameter of about 1.5 miles. A steep reef surrounds the island and uncovers at low water. The island is covered with heavy vegetation including palm trees reaching 100 feet at the NW corner and 70 to 80 feet on the E side.

(55) Swains Island provides no sheltered anchorage; deep-draft vessels are advised to remain at least 0.4 mile offshore as depths shoal rapidly. The fringing coral reef surrounding the island may make landing difficult. There are two charted landings, one on the W side and one on the SE side of the island. The landing on the W side is marked by a flagpole.

Chart 83157

(56) **Palmyra Atoll** (5°53'N., 162°05'W.), about 870 miles SSW of the island of Hawaii, is an atoll which consists of many small islets lying on a barrier reef enclosing three distinct lagoons. The reef surrounding the atoll is 5 miles long, E to W, and 2 miles at its widest part. Shoal water extends 1.8 miles E from the SE end of the reef and the same distance from the NW and SW ends. The islets are low, about 6 feet high, and covered with coconut and other trees reaching heights of 98 feet and visible 12 to 15 miles.

Prominent features

(57) Two radio towers stand as a good landmark on Paradise Island at the SW part of the atoll.

Channels

(58) A dredged entrance channel leads through the SW side of the atoll to West Lagoon; it is the only entrance to the atoll. In 2006, a depth of 18 feet was reported in the channel. Depths in the lagoon vary from 10 to 174 feet. Reefs and shoals within the lagoon are shown on the chart. A pier along the NE edge of West Lagoon is in poor condition with depths of 19 to 23 feet alongside. A current is reported to set W in the entrance channel. It is not advisable to enter the channel between sunset and sunrise.

Anchorage

(59) The atoll should be approached from the W. Anchorage may be had on the bank between 2 and 2.5 miles from the NW end of the atoll in about 5°53'00"N., 162°08'55"W., sand and coral. It is not advisable to anchor between sunset and sunrise. In 1988, a 2-knot current setting S was observed during a NW fresh at the anchorage.

Caution

(60) An explosive dumping area is situated with its center about 15 miles WSW of Palmyra Atoll.

Currents

(61) Strong and variable currents can be expected in the vicinity of the atoll. Caution is advised if approaching the atoll from the SW as dangerous tide rips have been reported 5 miles SW of the atoll.

Weather

(62) Palmyra Atoll has unfavorable weather and is the only island/atoll in its latitude where fresh W winds occur. A tropical front, a result of the Northeast and Southeast Trades converging, hovers in the vicinity of the atoll. Northeast Trades prevail, with an average velocity of 10 to 12 knots. There are frequent squalls of short duration and occasional winds up to 22 knots; typhoons are infrequent. Rainfall is heavy and humidity high, ranging from 100 to 180 inches annually. Rain occurs almost daily and heavy squalls come up suddenly from the SW, but there are no severe storms.

(63) Palmyra Atoll is a U.S. possession and National Wildlife Refuge. It is under the jurisdiction of the U.S. Fish and Wildlife Service (see National Refuges, this chapter.) Cooper Island is owned and administered by the Nature Conservancy. Nature Conservancy personnel on the island monitor VHF-FM channel 16.

Chart 83153

(64) **Kingman Reef** (6°25'N., 162°26'W.) is located about 33 miles NNW of Palmyra Atoll. It is triangular in shape with its apex to the N and is about 9 miles Long E-W and 5 miles N-S. The reef dries on its NE, E, and SE edges with small islets, reported to not be permanent, forming on these sides. The remainder of the atoll is contained within the ridge with depths of 10 to 20 fathoms. Breaks in the reef are on the N and S sides. Outside the ridge the bottom slopes steeply to over 100 fathoms.

(65) The reef has been reported to be difficult to identify, both visually and by radar. It has also been reported to be visible at 7 miles with optimal conditions; in weather it is very difficult to see. In 2007, with 8 to 10-foot seas, an island was sighted at about 3 miles out.

(66) Kingman Reef is within the belt traversed by the equatorial countercurrent which sets E at a rate of 1.3 to 1.8 knots in this area.

(67) Kingman Reef is a U.S. possession and a National Wildlife Refuge. It is under the jurisdiction of the U.S. Fish and Wildlife Service (see National Wildlife Refuges, this chapter.) The reef is also a Defensive Sea Area and

Airspace Reservation and is closed to the public. The airspace entry control has been suspended but is subject to immediate reinstatement without notice.

Chart 83116

(68) **Jarvis Island** (0°22'S., 160°00'W.), an island of sand and coral formation, is located about 460 miles SSE of Palmyra Atoll. The island is 1.8 miles long E-W and about 1 mile wide; it rises to a height of 20 feet. A narrow fringing reef, which dries in places and has breakers along the S shore, encircles the island. There are two breaks in the reef on the W side. A daybeacon is near the middle of the W shore.

(69) A shoal with a least depth of 2½ fathoms extends about 0.6 mile from the E side of the island. The depths drop rapidly outside the shoal area. The highest ground lies on the W end of the island. Low shrubs cover most of the island, however, it has been observed without much vegetation.

(70) Jarvis Island has been reported to lie 1 mile NE (1991), 1.6 miles E (1992), and 1.3 miles ENE (1996) of its charted position.

(71) Jarvis Island is a U.S. possession and a National Wildlife Refuge. It is under the jurisdiction of the U.S. Fish and Wildlife Service (see National Wildlife Refuges, this chapter.)

(72) **Baker Island** (0°12'N., 176°29'W.) is nearly flat but rises to an elevation of 20 feet at its SW end. At this point there is a steep, sandy beach which extends some distance N; elsewhere, the island is fringed by a coral reef. An extensive shoal with depths of 3 to 7 fathoms extends about 0.8 mile from the island on the N and E sides. The surf breaks heavily on the E side and the SW extremity of the island.

(73) Baker Island is a National Wildlife Refuge and under the jurisdiction of the U.S. Fish and Wildlife Service (see National Wildlife Refuges, this chapter.)

Anchorage

(74) There is no sheltered anchorage. Vessels lie off the island and discharge to landing craft. The fringing coral reef surrounding Baker Island makes landing difficult. The S point of the island can be used for landing when winds are from the NE. A daybeacon is near the middle of the W shore. Tangent bearings of the island are unreliable.

Weather

(75) The W side of the island is leeward of prevailing wind conditions. Winds from the E predominate throughout the year. From December to May, the prevailing winds are sometimes interrupted by W winds and bad weather.

(76) **Howland Island** (0°48'N., 176°37'W.), about 38 miles NNW of Baker Island, is a low, flat island devoid of vegetation other than a few stunted trees. It is ringed by a relatively flat coral reef almost completely exposed at low water extending out to about 0.1 mile, except on the W side where the reef averages about 80 yards in width. Outside this reef is a coral shelf extending about 0.3 to 0.5 mile on the N, E, and S sides, and about 0.1 mile on the W side. The depths on this shelf vary between 2 and 15 fathoms.

(77) A broad, sandy, and in some places, gravelly beach slopes upward at a slight angle on the W side of the island. On the windward or E side, there is practically no beach and the island rises abruptly from the reef to an average height of 12 feet, with the highest point about 18 feet in the N part. Amelia Earhart Daybeacon is situated near the center of the W side of the island.

(78) Howland Island is a National Wildlife Refuge and under the jurisdiction of the U.S. Fish and Wildlife Service (see National Wildlife Refuges, this chapter.)

Anchorage

(79) In 1966, a vessel anchored 0.4 mile from the N end of the island in 30 fathoms, with the E tangent of the island bearing **144°**, the W tangent bearing **185°**, and the daybeacon bearing **167.5°**. In 1967, a vessel anchored about 0.3 mile NNE of the N end of the island in 13 fathoms, with the E tangent of the island bearing **153°**, the W tangent bearing **213°**, and the daybeacon bearing **176°**, distance 1 mile. If an easterly swell is present, anchorage is not advisable at the N end of the island.

Weather

(80) Winds from the E predominate throughout the year. From December to May, the prevailing winds are sometimes interrupted by W winds and bad weather.

Chart 81664

(81) **Wake Island** (19°17'N., 166° 37'E.) lies in the Pacific Ocean on the direct route from Hawaii to Hong Kong. It is a U.S. possession with an area of only 3 square miles, consisting of three islands about 21 feet high. The islands form all but the NW side of an atoll enclosing a shallow lagoon. The higher parts of the islands are covered with fairly heavy growth of scrub brush. The entire island group is surrounded by a shallow reef interspersed with coral pinnacles. There is no natural freshwater.

(82) Wake Island is administered by the Department of the Interior and activities on the island are managed by the US Army under a US Air Force permit. The restrictions imposed upon the entry into the Wake Island Naval Defensive Sea Area have been suspended, except for the entry of foreign flag vessels and foreign nationals. The restrictions may be re-established without notice at any time.

Prominent Features

(83) A conspicuous concrete structure with storage tanks in the background is situated near the W end of Wake Island. A prominent tower stands on Peale Island. An aero light is shown from an abandoned control tower situated 0.6 mile NW of Peacock Point, the SE extremity of Wake Island. It was reported that a ship obtained radar contact with Wake Island from a distance of 35 miles. The complete outline of the island was observed from a distance of 25 miles.

Channels

(84) On the seaward side, between Wake Island and Wilkes Island, there is a channel leading to a boat basin at the W extremity of Wake Island. In 1970, the channel and boat basin had controlling depths of 12 feet.

(85) The boat basin can accommodate three small-craft, which may serve as tugs or cargo lighters. Ships should radio their ETA 48 hours in advance. An unloading wharf is situated on the SW side of the basin and a boat landing is at the head of the basin. Two mooring buoys are just outside the boat basin entrance channel. Cargo is discharged at the moorings. Sea conditions often permit a vessel to lie offshore and discharge dry cargo; this reported to be the safest and best method for large vessels. Oil is discharged through a floating hose which is floated out on barrels and connected to a fuel jetty at the E entrance point of the boat channel.

Anchorage

(86) The depths drop off sharply outside the atoll reef making it unsuitable for anchorage. The lagoon itself is inaccessible. The mooring facility outside the boat basin is available to all vessels having permission to call at Wake Island, but is considered hazardous. The use of an anchor is not recommended when using the mooring buoys. Vessels should not attempt to secure at the mooring buoys in an onshore or S wind. If secured to one buoy when the wind shifts to blow onshore, slip the mooring and leave the area. Any vessels moored to only one buoy must have engines on standby. Vessels should be secured to the mooring buoys with the bow headed ESE. Small-craft usually assist in mooring operations with the best times being at either high water or low water slack.

Currents

(87) A SSW current of 0.5 to 1 knot has been observed in the vicinity of Wake Island. There have been occasions when the currents are erratic and onshore sets have been observed. Vessels should carefully note the set and the drift of the tidal currents before attempting to moor. The tidal currents in the vicinity of the mooring buoys have been observed to set parallel to the shore at a rate of about 0.8 knot.

Weather

(88) Winds from the E and NE prevail throughout the year, with average velocities of 10 to 13 knots. Gales occur on an average of 10 days a year. By reason of its position, the atoll is subject to typhoons and tropical storms; thunderstorms seldom occur.

(89) At Wake Island, the influence of the higher latitude is noticeable and the means vary between a low of 77°F in January and February and a high of 82°F in September. In August the mean maximum reaches 88°F. Extremes above 95°F are rare.

(90) The annual average rainfall is only 37 inches, showing a great decrease in precipitation from that occurring in the lower latitudes. The monthly totals range from a January average of 1 inch in the dry season to 7 inches in August.

Chart 81004

Mariana Islands

(91) Mariana Islands are comprised of the **Northern Marianas** and **Guam**. The Northern Marianas, a self-governing U. S. commonwealth consists of a chain of 16 volcanic islands, which extend in a N and S direction for a distance of about 450 miles. The islands in the group from N to S are Farallon de Pajaros, Maug, Asuncion, Agrihan, Pagan, Alamagan, Guguan, Sarigan, Anatahan, Farallon de Medinilla, Saipan, Tinian, Aguijan, and Rota. Except for Maug, which is a cluster of three tiny islands, all are single islands which rise precipitously as mountain peaks of rocky, volcanic material and are conspicuous from the offing. They are a good radar target from a distance of 14 miles, but are reported to give a poor return from a distance of 28 miles. Their total area is approximately 184 square miles. The three principal islands, Saipan (47 square miles), Tinian (39 square miles) and Rota (32 square miles) form two-thirds of the land area of the group.

Weather, Pacific Islands

(92) The islands of the Marianas Archipelago have similar weather conditions. Under ordinary circumstances, the wind and seas in the vicinity of Guam are easterly due to the Northeast Trades. Westerly winds are at times experienced during the summer months as Guam is barely within the limits of the Southwest Monsoon. These winds are light as a rule. In the vicinity of Guam, northeasterly and east-northeasterly winds prevail for 6 months of the year. These winds blow from the northeast to east 65% of the time between December and May, and are strongest during these months. Between June and November, the surface winds are quite variable; calms are rare. In the southerly islands, the winds show a slight southerly trend as early as May.

(93) In the vicinity of the islands of Saipan and Tinian, the steadiest winds occur when the winter monsoon and

the NE Trades reinforce each other. Between November and April, NE and easterly winds prevail 70% of the time at rates of 10 to 12 knots. During the summer monsoon (May to October) easterly winds predominate, but southerly to westerly winds also occur. Wind velocities are about 10 to 11 knots from May to July, and 8 knots from August to October. Land mass effect modifies the maritime diurnal variations so that the surface winds are strongest at 0300 and weakest at 1400.

(94) In the vicinity of Pagan Island, the winds are steadiest during the Northeast Monsoon (November through March). They blow mostly from the NE at an average rate of 15 knots. From April through June, the monsoon weakens and the prevailing winds become more easterly. During the wet season (June through November), easterly winds continue to predominate, but with considerable percentages from southerly to westerly directions. The winds are mostly light; the only strong winds occurring with typhoons.

(95) Precipitation increases decidedly during the summer months, especially in the southern islands. The wet season (July through October) has a mean monthly average of 10 inches (254 mm) or more. The major rainfall consists of heavy showers. As a rule, the rainfall diminishes as the latitude increases.

(96) The rainy season at Guam is from the first of July until the early part of November, with a monthly average of 11 to 15 inches (279 to 381 mm). January through June is the driest period, with an average monthly fall of 3.9 to 6.5 inches (99 to 165 mm). March is the driest month with an average precipitation amount of 3.9 inches (99 mm). The mean average rainfall is about 101 inches annually (2565 mm) but has ranged from 165 inches (4191 mm) in 1976 to 67 inches (1702 mm) in 1973. An average of 30 thunderstorms each year effect the island of Guam. The most active month is August.

(97) The rainy season at the islands of Saipan and Tinian is from July to November; the dry season lasts from December through June. During the rainy season, with the doldrums belt lying almost directly over these islands, there are increased showers and numerous thunderstorms and squalls. The dry season is characterized by fair weather, interrupted by fronts associated with northerly low pressure centers and some showers. Saipan Island has an average rainfall of 86 inches (2184 mm) per year with a monthly average of 13 inches (330 mm). During the rainy season (July through October) it averages 13 inches (330 mm) per month. Throughout the rest of the year, the average is about 4 inches (102 mm) per month. April is the driest month with an average of about 2¾ inches (70 mm).

(98) Typhoons frequently form south and east of the Mariana Archipelago and routinely pass in the vicinity of these islands. They are apt to occur more often during the summer months and are accompanied by high winds and torrential rains. They seldom occur during the winter months.

(99) Tropical disturbances often occur in the vicinity of Guam. Since 1842, at least 51 tropical cyclones have come within 25 miles (46 km) of Guam and another 49 have come within 50 miles (93 km) of the island. Since 1980, nine tropical cyclones have come within 25 miles (46 km) of the island and another 11 within 50 miles (93 km) of the island. As recently as August 1992, before attaining super typhoon status, Typhoon Omar raked the island with winds of 105 knots and gusts in excess of 140 knots. Omar was the most damaging typhoon to strike Guam since Typhoon Pamela in 1976. Omar caused an estimated $457 million of damage and destroyed or severely damaged over 2,158 homes.

(100) Tropical disturbances occur between August and January in the vicinity of the islands of Saipan and Tinian. Since 1842, at least 51 tropical cyclones have come within 25 miles (46 km) of Saipan and another 53 have come within 50 miles (93 km) of the island. Since 1980, 15 tropical cyclones have come within 25 miles (46 km) of the island while an additional 15 have come within 50 miles (93 km) of the island. As recently as December 3, 1986, Super Typhoon Kim passed only 18 miles (33 km) north of Saipan and raked the island with 135 knot winds and record rainfall.

(101) Tropical disturbances usually pass well to the south of Pagan Island, but several have been experienced. August, September and October are the most likely months. January through April is the only period believed to be entirely free of such storms. Probably not more than one a year pass close enough to affect Pagan Island.

(102) Gales, other than those of tropical origination, seldom occur in the vicinity of the islands of Tinian and Saipan. Winds reach gale force in the vicinity of Pagan Island from 2 to 4% of the time.

(103) Thunderstorms occur frequently from July to the early part of November. December through May are the months that are relatively free from thunderstorms.

(104) In Guam, the mean temperature is 79°F (26.1°C), the mean maximum is 86°F (30°C), and the mean minimum is 72°F (22.2°C). The temperatures for the rest of the Mariana Islands are quite uniform throughout the year. January and February are the coolest months. The nights are cooler in the northern islands. Temperatures above 85°F (29.4°C) normally occur from 25 to 28 days a month between April and August. The daily minimums seldom fall below 74°F (23.3°C) during the summer months. The yearly RANGE of temperatures is 3°F (2°C) in the south and 7°F (4°C) in the north. The daily RAnge is about 10°F (6°C). The extreme maximum temperature on Guam is 95°F (35°C) recorded in September 1957 and the extreme minimum is 54°F (12.8°C) recorded in March 1965.

(105) In Saipan, the mean temperature is 82°F (27.8°C), the mean maximum is 86° (30°C), and the mean minimum is 77°F (25°C). Extremes include a maximum of 104°F (40°C) recorded in May 1977 and September 1987

and an extreme minimum of 60°F (15.6°C) recorded in March 1975.

(106)   Humidity is high throughout the year, but there is somewhat less humidity from December through May. The yearly average is about 76%. The January average is 68% and the June average is 84%.

(107)   Fog and mist are rarely reported in the Guam, Saipan-Tinian areas. Visibility of less than ¼ miles (2 km) can be expected on less than one day per month. The occurrence of fog averages only one to two days each year.

(108)   The yearly average cloud cover is about 7/10 (70%). The maximum coverage of 8/10 to 9/10 occurs during the summer months (July to October). Cloudiness is higher over the islands than over the adjacent seas. Clouds are more frequent during the daytime.

Tides and currents

(109)   See Sailing Directions (Planning Guide) for the South Pacific Ocean (Pub. 122), for general information on tides, currents, and tidal currents in the region.

(110)   Currents in the vicinity of the Mariana Islands are for the most part westerly. They are strongest near to and south of Saipan Island, and gradually become weaker north of that island. In June, the Equatorial Drift Current was reported to be strongest during that season in the parallel of 13° N. and to run to the northwest at a maximum rate of 1 knot. In October, a westerly current of 1 knot to 1½ knots was reported to have been experienced up to 20 miles east of Guguan Island, but little or no current was experienced north of that island.

(111)   Variable currents are sometimes encountered near the islands. These are caused by the physical makeup of the island and by the additional force of the tidal currents.

(112)   An almost constant southwesterly set has been reported along the northwest coast of Guam during the Northeast Trades. This current has been felt up to 10 miles offshore.

(113)   In the vicinity of the Mariana Islands, the flood current usually sets westerly and ebb easterly; the tidal currents turn at the approximate times of high and low water. These currents are usually weak, except in narrow passages, and their directions and rates are sometimes variable. The tidal currents are usually confused and irregular off the east sides of these islands, due to the configuration of the land.

Charts 81048, 81054

(114)   **Guam** (13°25'N., 144°44'E.), a U.S. territory since 1898, is not included in the Commonwealth of the Northern Marianas. The largest and southernmost island of the Marianas Archipelago, Guam is about 30 miles long and varies from 4 to 8 miles in width. The N end of the island is a plateau of rolling hills set on vertical cliffs rising to about 490 feet above sea level. The S end of the island consists of high volcanic hills. The plateau is covered with a thick growth of jungle; the volcanic hills support mainly sword grass. The highest hills are found in the central and S parts of the island.

(115)   **Apra Harbor**, situated midway along the W coast of Guam, is the main berthing facility on the island, consisting of a commercial harbor, a naval complex, and a repair facility. The harbor is comprised of two main areas; **Apra Inner Harbor** and Apra Outer Harbor. **Apra Outer Harbor** is the principal commercial port for the island. Apra Inner Harbor houses the U.S. Naval facility and a commercial ship repair facility. **Glass Breakwater** forms the N and NW sides of Apra Outer Harbor and acts as a barrier against most ocean swells from the N and W. The seaward end of the breakwater is marked by a light. The harbor is extensive and safe, except during typhoon season. During this time, vessels should be prepared to get underway at short notice.

Prominent features

(116)   **Orote Point**, the W end of **Orote Peninsula**, is a sharp bluff about 210 feet high. **Orote Island** lies close off the N side of the point. **Orote Point Light** (13°26'47"N., 144°37'11"E.), 226 feet above the water is shown from a concrete tower with a black and white diamond-shaped dayboard on Orote Point. The light may be obscured by land features on a southern approach. A 200-foot radio tower is SW of Orote Point Light in about 13°26'45"N., 144°37'10"E.

COLREGS Demarcation Lines

(117)   The lines established for Apra Harbor are described in **80.1490**, chapter 2.

Anchorages

(118)   There are **naval, explosive, and general anchorages** that have been designated within Apra Outer Harbor. (See **33 CFR 110.1 and 110.238**, chapter 2, for limits and regulations.)

(119)   There are also **special anchorage areas** in Apra Outer Harbor. (See **33 CFR 110.1** and **110.129a**, chapter 2, for limits and regulations.)

Channels

(120)   The approaches to the harbor are free and deep, as is the channel between the breakwaters. The entrance to Apra Outer Harbor is marked by lights, lighted buoys, and a **083.6°** lighted range. The entrance to Apra Inner Harbor is marked by lighted buoys and a **141°** lighted range and a **176°** lighted range.

Regulated navigation areas

(121)   **Regulated navigation areas** have been established in the approach to and in Apra Outer Harbor. (See **33 CFR 165.1402** and **165.1405**, chapter 2, for limits and regulations.)

(122) **Safety zones** and **security zones** have been established in Apra Outer Harbor. (See **33 CFR 165.1401** and **165.1404**, chapter 2, for limits and regulations.)

(123) Apra Inner Harbor and an area just W of the entrance to the Inner Harbor are included in a **restricted area**. (See **33 CFR 334.1 through 334.6 and 334.1430**, chapter 2, for limits and regulations.) A **harbor security barrier gate**, marked by two uncharted buoys, has been installed across the entrance to Apra Inner Harbor between the outermost ends of Wharves L and B.

Caution

(124) The restricted area of a **Firing Danger Zone** extends offshore about 1 mile S of Orote Point and off the SW coast of the island. (See **33 CFR 334.1420**, chapter 2, for limits and regulations.) An acoustic range facility is S of the restricted area and a submarine operating area surrounds most of the island. Submerged submarine operations are conducted at various times in these waters; proceed with caution. (For information on submarine emergency identification signals, see chapter 1.)

Currents

(125) On the approach to Orote Point, the SW current associated with the Northeast Trades tends to curve to the S and SE. The rate of the current is greatly affected by the force of the wind. During the typhoon season, the outgoing current from the harbor augments the SW current and reduces any NE current that may occur. Strong rips may be observed under these conditions. The prevalent set of the current at the harbor entrance is usually S or SW regardless of the tidal currents, but a set to the N or NE may be experienced, especially during the summer months. The flood current in the harbor entrance sets N to NNE at a maximum rate of 1.5 knots. The ebb current sometimes attains a maximum rate of 3 knots. Slack water occurs 30 minutes before low water and 45 minutes before high water. Heavy W swells sometimes make the entrance of Apra Outer Harbor dangerous. This condition occurs when a typhoon builds up in the area, progresses to the NW, and then curves NE. Beacons and buoys are sometimes destroyed or carried away at such times. The currents and tidal currents within the harbor are weak and variable.

Pilotage

(126) Pilotage is compulsory for vessels over 500 gross tons and all vessels entering the port for the first time and after daylight hours. Pilot services are available on a 24-hour basis for Apra Harbor. Pilots are required to board inbound vessels and leave outbound vessels at Alpha Hotel Pilot Station (13°26'52"N., 144°35'16"E.), about 2 miles W of Orote Point, to insure that the vessel is properly aligned on the entrance range; the station is unmarked.

Towage

(127) Tugs to 3,200 hp are available in Apra Harbor.

Quarantine, customs, immigration, and agricultural quarantine

(128) Apra Harbor is a customs and U.S. immigration port of entry. U.S. immigration regulations apply and are enforced by U.S. Customs and Border Protection; telephone 671–472–7138, fax 671–472–7139. U.S. Customs regulations are enforced by:

(129) Department of Customs, Government of Guam
(130) Customs and Quarantine Agency
(131) PO Box 21828
(132) GMF, Barrigada, GU 96921
(133) telephone 671–475–6202

Coast Guard

(134) The Coast Guard Communications Center is a full-service communications station. The center is monitored 24 hours and can be contacted on VHF-FM channel 16 or 9, call sign **NRV**. A Sector Office and Station are located on the U.S. Naval base and can also be contacted on VHF-FM channel 16 or 9 (24 hours); telephone 671–355–4821.

Harbor Regulations

(135) All operations in Apra Outer Harbor are under the jurisdiction of The Port Authority of Guam and The United States Coast Guard. Prior to entry all vessels must establish communications with Guam Port Control Harbormaster's office on VHF-FM channels 12, 13 or 16; call sign WRV-574. The phone number for Guam Port Control Harbormaster's Office is 671–477–8697.

(136) All operations in Apra Inner Harbor are under the jurisdiction of the U.S. Navy Port Control Harbormaster's Office with communication on VHF-FM channels 14 and 16. The phone number is 671–339–6141.

(137) Vessels entering, leaving or shifting berth are required to give a minimum of 24 hours notice to **The Port Authority of Guam Harbor Master and US Coast Guard Captain of the Port**. Failure to give such notice is a basis for denying entry. No vessel shall enter or leave the harbor without radio clearance from the Harbormaster. Vessels must be ISPS/MTSA compliant.

(138) A tug boat (or tugs) shall be used by all commercial vessels, exceeding 250 feet in overall length entering, leaving, or operating within the harbor, except research vessels and vessels up to 300 feet in overall length equipped with an operational bow thruster. A fishing vessel's use of a skiff boat in lieu of a tug boat is permitted provided there is constant communication between the skiff operator and the vessel Master.

(139) Speed is limited to no more than 12 knots in Outer Harbor and no more than 5 knots in Inner Harbor, except in emergency situations.

Wharves

(140) The commercial port, situated on **Cabras Island**, handles general cargo, passengers, and inter-island transshipments. Three 30 to 40-ton gantry cranes, three hoists, and one 150-ton crane are available at the port. The Inner Harbor is under the jurisdiction of the Navy, but certain berths are available through the Port Authority upon special request.

Supplies

(141) Apra Harbor is the principal supply center for the region. Water is available at most wharves. Bunker fuel is available at Golf Pier, Berths F-1 and F-3 and by tanker truck.

Repairs

(142) Apra Harbor has a floating dry dock that can handle a maximum LOA of 700 feet. Guam Shipyard, PO Box 13010, Bldg. 20 Comnavmar, Santa Rita, GU 96915-3010; telephone 671–339–1101 or 671–339–5258.

Chart 81063

(143) **Rota Island** (14°10'N., 145°12'E.), of volcanic formation, is about 32 miles northeast of Guam. The northeast part consists of a plateau 522 feet high; southwesterly part is a low sandy isthmus. The shore of Rota is generally steep and rocky except at the southwest tip; a narrow coral reef nearly fringes the entire island. Rota rises to 1,611 feet in its west-central part.

Caution

(144) A naval operating area is off the northeast shore of Rota.

Tidal currents

(145) The diurnal inequality is considerable. The flood attains a rate of ½ knot. The flood sets southerly, the ebb northerly; turning at about the time of high and low water.

(146) **Harnom Point (Puntan Taipingot)** (14°07'N., 145°07'E.) is the south end of **Taipingot**, a prominent headland with a distinct 'wedding cake' shape, which forms the southwesterly end of Rota Island.

(147) **Sasanlagu**, situated on the NW side of the Taipingot Peninsula, affords some shelter during southeasterly winds. **Rota West Harbor**, on the SE side of Sasanlagu and 0.5 mile SW of the village of Rota (Song Song), is the only commercial port serving the Commonwealth of the Northern Mariana Islands. An entrance channel, marked by a **118°** lighted range, leads SE to a turning basin inside the harbor. In 2007, the entrance channel had a controlling depth of 18 feet and the turning basin had depths of 11 to 14 feet except for shoaling to 6 feet in the E corner of the basin.) A strong current runs along the coast in a SW direction. It is funneled between Mafuiion Rock and the fringing reef causing extreme difficulties in bringing vessels into the port. Entering the port except at slack tide is not recommended without local knowledge.

(148) Pilotage is compulsory for vessels greater than 300 gross tonnage. There are no pilots in Rota but pilotage can be arranged by contacting Saipan Marine Corporation at 670–322–7345/46/51. Arrival at night is not permitted. There is no anchorage inside Rota West Harbor, however, anchorage can be permitted outside the harbor by contacting Rota Port Control on VHF-FM channels 13 or 16. Tugs and barges are not available in Rota. Pilots require a vessel with twin screws or a single screw with strong bowthruster to enter the harbor. Vessels over 236 feet do not have swinging room inside the basin.

(149) Rota West Harbor has two berthing facilities: Berth 1 is 150 feet in length, 16 feet alongside and Berth 2 is 100 feet in length, 11 feet alongside. Forklifts to 3 tons and an 80-ton crane are available at the harbor. Stevedoring services are available by Rota Terminal & Transfer (RT&T), Monday-Saturday, and can be contacted at 670–532–3117 or 670–532–5270. The harbor is owned and operated by the Commonwealth Ports Authority (CPA). Hours of operation are Monday-Saturday 0730 to 1630. Other times may be arranged by contacting the CPA (670–532–9497/89) and other agencies needed to provide port services. Advance notice of at least 24 hours is required to provide adequate services. A boat ramp and several small boat slips are available in the harbor.

Quarantine, customs, immigration, and agricultural quarantine

(150) Customs, quarantine, and immigration offices are in Rota West Harbor. Hours of operation are Monday-Saturday 0730 to 1630 for customs and quarantine, Monday-Friday 0730 to 1630 for immigration. Other times may be arranged by calling: customs office 670–532–9484/88, quarantine office 670–532–3415/9494, immigration office 670–532–9436.

(151) **Sasanhaya** is a bay on the east side of Taipingot and south of the village of Rota. Anchorage can be had in Sasanhaya, however, a swell sets in with winds from any direction except NE. When northeasterly winds are strong, they often blow down from the steep slopes at the inner part of the bay. Anchorage may be found in depths of 16 fathoms, about 0.4 mile south of the village of Rota (Song Song). During northeasterly winds, good anchorage may be found on the east side of the bay.

Off-lying Danger

(152) A bank with a depth of 22 fathoms is about 120 miles, 273° from Harnom Point (Puntan Taipingot).

Tinian Harbor, Northern Mariana Islands
2004

Charts 81004, 81067

(153) **Aguijan Island** (14°51'N., 145°33'E.) is about 022°, 42 miles from Rota Island, and it has steep, cliffy and inaccessible shores. Naftan Rock is about ½ mile southwest of the island's southwest end.

Off-lying banks and dangers

(154) **Esmeralda Bank**, about 17 miles northwest of Aguijan Island, has a least depth of about 33 fathoms, and can be recognized by the discoloration of the water, which has the appearance of sulphur being emitted. A 30 fathom bank, marked by boiling sulphur, is about 20 miles northwest of Aguijan Island. Other banks with greater depths are charted in this vicinity.

(155) A bank, with a depth of 19 fathoms over it, is about 5 miles southwest of Aguijan Island.

(156) **Tatsumi Reef**, centered about 2 miles southeast of the southern end of Tinian Island, is on the northeast side of Tinian Channel. A patch with a depth of 13 fathoms over it is 14 miles west of the north end of Tinian Island.

Charts 81067, 81071

(157) **Tinian Island** (15°00'N., 145°38'E.) is northeast of Aguijan Island and it is separated from it by Tinian Channel. The north end of the island is low and flat.

(158) Tinian Island is an experimental cattle raising center. The island is extensively cultivated; vegetables and produce are shipped to Guam. Tinian is a transfer point for tuna purse seiners. An inter-island tug and barge reportedly visits the island several times a week. The population was 3,540 (2000).

Prominent features

(159) **Lasso Hill**, 564 feet high, is the summit of the island and lies about 3¾ miles south of the north end of Tinian Island. **Maga Hill**, a mile northwest of Lasso Hill, is joined to the latter by a ridge. The land south of this ridge is sloping and for the most part cultivated. Several radio towers are prominent on the slope W of Maga Hill.

(160) An extensive ridge is located along the east side of the south part of the island, between **Puntan Carolinas** and **Puntan Masalok**. The coast between these points is faced by a sheer cliff. The broad and cultivated land in the central part of the island gives way to narrow and successively lower terraces near the coast. These levels are separated by steep slopes or cliffs. Sandy beaches are found near the town of Tinian and in the bay between Puntan Masalok and Puntan Asiga.

Saipan Harbor, Northern Mariana Islands
2004

(161) Many charted landmarks were either nonexistent or were overgrown with foliage (1963).

(162) **Tinian Harbor** is the name given to the area lying off the southwestern shore of Tinian Island, fronting the town, and including the swept area best shown on the chart.

(163) The inner harbor area off Tinian is protected from the sea by a breakwater constructed on the reef that fronts the town. The north end of the breakwater was in ruins (2005). An entrance channel, marked by lighted and unlighted buoys, is entered about ½ mile S of the head of the breakwater and leads NE and NW to a basin off the town of Tinian. In 2007, the controlling depths were 28 feet in the entrance channel with lesser depths to 26 feet along the edges of the channel, thence 24 feet in the basin. A smokestack is about 0.6 mile NNW of the inner harbor in about 14°58'25"N., 145°36'55"E.

Routes

(164) A course of **035°** leads through the first leg of the channel to a position southeast of the outer end of the breakwater, then a course of **336°** leads to the main quay.

Anchorages

(165) Anchorage may be found, in depths of 10 to 20 fathoms, sand and coral, good holding ground, off Tinian; however, it is unsafe during the Southwest Monsoon. During westerly winds anchorage may be found in a bay on the northeast side of Tinian Island between Puntan Masalok and Puntan Asiga, in depths of 15 to 25 fathoms; however, this anchorage is reported untenable during strong easterly and northeasterly winds.

(166) **Explosive anchorages** are off the west shore of Tinian Island, off **Puntan Diapblo** (see **110.239**, chapter 2, for limits and regulations.)

(167) A **security zone** is off the west shore of Tinian Island, between Puntan Diapblo and the village of Tinian (see **165.1403**, chapter 2, for limits and regulations).

Tides and Currents

(168) At times the tides will become diurnal around the time of the moon's maximum declination. The currents set northwest on the flood and southeast on the ebb; attaining rates of about a knot and turning at about the times of high and low water.

Pilotage

(169) Vessels must obtain permission and acquire a pilot from the authorities at Saipan before entering the harbor. Entering and exiting port is permitted only during daylight hours and "Tinian Port Control" monitors VHF-FM channel 16.

Wharves

(170) The Main Quay has a length 2,000 feet with depths of 17 to 20 feet alongside. Pier 1 and Pier 2, off the NW side of Main Quay, were reported in ruins and unserviceable in 2005.

Charts 81067, 81071, 81076

(171) **Saipan Island** (15°10'N., 145°45'E.), the second largest of the Mariana Islands, is northeast of Tinian Island and is separated from it by **Saipan Channel**. Saipan Channel is deep and clear of known dangers.

Prominent features

(172) A chain of mountains, the summit of which is **Ogsoʻ Takpochao**, 1,555 feet high, a conspicuous, conical, extinct volcano, lines the center of the island in a north-south direction. The east peninsula and the south part of the island are low flat plateaus. Some relatively level areas are found on the north end and northwest and west sides of the island, between the coast and the lower slopes of the ridge. These areas are, for the most part, cultivated. The land on the west and northwest sides slopes down to the beaches. The northeast and southeast shores of the island are formed by rugged, rocky cliffs.

(173) The west and northwest shores are fronted by barrier reefs, within which are shallow lagoons. Detached dangers and foul ground containing many coral heads, with depths of 3 fathoms or less, extend about a mile southwest from the southwest extremity of the barrier reef that fronts the northwesterly end of the island. A number of detached dangers lie south of this foul ground, along the edges of the swept anchorages areas.

(174) Vessels approaching the island will first sight Ogsoʻ Takpochao. Vessels passing S of the island will next sight **Finaʻ Sisu**, the 295-foot summit, located 2¾ miles south-southwest of the above peak. This summit, when first seen, appears as a detached island. **Isleta Managaha (Maniagassa Island)**, located off the northwest coast, appears as a destroyer when viewed from the west.

(175) An abandoned lighthouse, 43 feet high, white circular concrete structure, stands at an elevation of 375 feet, about a mile northeastward of the pier at Garapan. Two radio masts, marked by obstruction lights, are close to the abandoned lighthouse. Five radio towers are on **Puntan Agingan** and are reported to serve as one of the most visible landmarks on Saipan.

(176) Saipan Harbor is reported to be radar conspicuous at a distance of about 20 miles.

(177) **Saipan Harbor** (15°12'N., 145°41'E.), lying on the west side of Saipan Island, includes the outer anchorage, **Garapan Anchorage** and the inner harbor, **Puetton Tanapag**.

Routes

(178) Vessels entering Puetton Tanapag should make the approach with the light on Managaha ahead bearing **044°**, passing on either side of the fairway buoy. When approaching Lighted Buoy No. 3, course should be altered to **088°** with the harbor entrance lighted range lined up. This course leads into and through the harbor.

Channels

(179) The northern part of Saipan Harbor, **Puetton Tanapag**, is entered through a dredged channel that leads NE then turns E to a turning basin. In 2009-2010, the controlling depth was 36 feet in the channel to the basin, thence depths of 32 of 40 feet were available in the basin.

Anchorages

(180) The outer anchorage affords shelter during prevailing easterly winds, but none during infrequent westerly storms. This anchorage, which lies from 3 to 5 miles offshore, is suitable only as a temporary anchorage for large vessels. The inner anchorage, which includes Garapan Anchorage, contains numerous berths with depths ranging from 25 to 100 feet, holding ground fair to good, with coarse coral sand. This anchorage lies from 1 to 2 miles offshore. Vessels can anchor in 10 fathoms, sand bottom, about 0.8 mile offshore, abreast **Finaʻ Sisu**, off the village of **Chalan Kanoa**. Vessels can anchor in 12 to 14 fathoms, coral bottom, in a position about 1.5 miles off **Garapan**. The anchorage area in Puetton Tanapag has depths ranging from 12 to 30 feet. A seaplane landing area is northward of the anchorage area.

Regulated navigation area

(181) A security zone has been established in Saipan Harbor. (See **33 CFR 165.1405**, chapter 2, for limits and regulations.)

Caution

(182) A sewer outfall extends from a position about 200 yards southwest of the southwest corner of Pier C to a position about 600 yards north-northwest of the northwest corner of the same pier.

(183) Unexploded ordnance has been reported to lie within Anchorage Berth L8.

(184) **Okino Reef** (15°12'41"N., 145°41'48"E.), an isolated shallow area in Garapan Anchorage, has a least depth of 6 feet and is marked by a buoy on the W side.

(185) Some mooring buoys and many wrecks are in the harbor.

(186) Two mooring buoys are just outside the reef off **Puntan Susupi**.

Tidal Currents

(187) Tidal currents in Saipan Channel set northwesterly at a rate of 2½ knots on the flood and southeasterly at

1¼ knots on the ebb; turning at about the times of high and low water. In the outer anchorage of Saipan Harbor, the tidal currents are irregular, with a maximum west-northwest set of about 2 knots during the flood. In Garapan Anchorage, the tidal currents set northerly at rates of ½ to 1 knot during the flood and southwesterly at rates of ½ to ¾ knot during the ebb. In Puetton Tanapag the tidal currents set north on the flood and south on the ebb, neither exceeding a rate of ¾ knot. They appear to turn at times of high and low water.

Pilotage

(188) Pilotage is compulsory; pilots board vessels in the vicinity of Tanapag Harbor Approach Lighted Buoy T.

Wharves

(189) The port provides 2,600 linear feet of berthing space, and a 22-acre container yard. Water, fuel, electricity, and sewage pump-out are available. A marina is about 0.5 mile SW of the port facilities.

(190) **Bahia Laolao** (Bahia Laulau) is on the southeast side of Saipan Island affording the only shelter with the wind between west and north, but due to excessive depths it can not be recommended. Vessels may obtain anchorage in a depth of about 30 fathoms, about 600 yards offshore, south of the village of Laulau.

Off-lying banks and dangers

(191) A bank, with a depth of 26 fathoms is about 9½ miles north-northeast of **Puntan Sabaneta** (15°17'N., 145°49'E.).

Charts 81004, 81086, 81092

(192) **Arakane Reef** (15°38'N., 145°45'E.),. about 175 miles west of Saipan Island, is a coral reef with a least depth of 30 feet over it. In 1945, a heavy swell was observed over Arakane Reef; discoloration was very noticeable. In 1969, mooring buoys were reported to be upon this reef.

(193) **Farallon de Medinilla** (16°01'N., 146°05'E.) 265 feet high, and guano-covered, has steep coasts forming precipes. Deep caves are found on the south and west shores. A chasm, located in the southern part of the island, separates that part from the north. Farallon de Medinilla was reported to be radar conspicuous from a distance of 23 miles.

(194) A rocky bank, with a least depth of 8.7 fathoms, is about 0.3 mile northeast of the north end of the island. Another bank with least depth of 3.9 fathoms is about 1.3 miles north of the island; the bank is marked by breakers in heavy weather. In 1964, a depth of 10 fathoms was reported about 9 miles west-northwest of the north end of Farallon de Medinilla.

Caution

(195) Farallon de Medinilla is used as a bombing and strafing target complex by the U.S. Navy. Mariners are advised to avoid the area by as wide a margin as is practicable.

(196) **Anatahan Island** (16°22'N., 145°40'E), 2,585 feet high, is about 20 miles northwest of Farallon de Medinilla, and is of volcanic formation. The crater of a dormant volcano, which contains a wide grass-covered field, forms the summit of the island. The crater wall has a peak on its east and west sides; the west one being quite sharp.

(197) Small vessels can anchor off the northern part of the west coast of Anatahan Island, about 600 yards offshore. A bank, with a depth of 37 fathoms over it, is about 18 miles east of Anatahan Island. In 1974, another bank with a depth of 35 fathom was reported to lie about 10 miles farther north-northeast of the island.

(198) In 1967, a depth of 12 fathoms was reported in 17°08'N., 143°15'E. An 8 fathom patch has been reported to be in 16°31'N., 143°08'E.

(199) **Sarigan Island** (16°43'N., 145°47'E.), lying about 20 miles northeast of Anatahan Island, is cone-shaped, wooded, and of volcanic origin; rising to a height of 1,801 feet in its southern part.

(200) A bank, with a depth of 12 fathoms is 5 miles north of Sarigan Island.

(201) **Zealandia Bank**, about 11 miles north-northeast of Sarigan Island, is comprised of two rocks that dry, lying ½ mile apart. The sea breaks on these rocks at all times and the breakers can be seen from a distance. It was reported that there was a depth of 11 fathoms around both rocks, and that there are no other dangers. A bank, with a depth of 51 fathoms over it, is 9 miles northwest of Zealandia Bank.

(202) **Guguan Island** (17°19'N., 145°51'E.), lying about 35 miles north of Sarigan Island, has two summits; the southern is 988 feet, the north is 814 feet high, and is an active volcano. Guguan Island is reported to be a good radar target from a distance of 27 miles. A large quantity of sulphur covers the ground around the crater. When seen from east or west, the northern summit appears to be covered with snow. The coasts are steep, and there is vegetation and breadfruit trees.

(203) **Alamagan Island** (17°36'N., 145°50'E.), lying 15 miles north of Guguan Island, is an inactive volcano with two peaks; the higher being 2,441 feet. The island is reported to be radar conspicuous at a distance of 31 miles. The shores are lined with rocks and the southeast side is a steep slope of bare lava. There is a hot spring at the north end of the west coast.

(204) Shoals with depths 35 and 26 fathoms were reported (1946 and 1970, respectively) to lie about 165 miles west of Alamagan Island. A bank, with a least depth of 4 fathoms over it, is in about 18°05'58"N., 143°07'36"E.

Anchorage

(205) Anchorage may be found, during northeasterly winds, off the southwest side of Alamagan Island, about 600 yards offshore, in 12 fathoms, sand bottom.

(206) **Pagan Island** (18°07'N., 145°47'E.) lying about 30 miles north of Alamagan Island, has two active volcanoes. **Mount Pagan**, 1,870 feet high, rises in the northern and larger segment of the island. Several volcanic cones, some of which give off steam, are located in the southern part of the island. A hot spring lies on the eastern side of the southern part of the island. The two parts of the island are connected by a narrow, but high, isthmus. The island is rugged, except for a low level marshland lying south of Mount Pagan. Two lakes are located between the mountain and the northwest coast. The western lake, which is separated from the sea by a sand bar, 50 yards wide, is salty. The shores of the island are steep and rocky, except for some sandy beaches along Apaan Bay. Casuarina and coconut trees grow along most of the coastline and lower slopes, but the upper and steeper slopes of the volcanoes appear almost barren. **Apaan Bay** is an open bight off the middle of the west side of Pagan Island. The beach is for the most part steep, exposed to surf, and has a thick growth of shrubs. **Shomushon**, a settlement which contains most of the population of the island, is located at the head of a small inlet that indents the northern end of the bay.

Anchorage

(207) Anchorage may be found in Apaan Bay in a depth of about 60 feet, southwest of **Bandeera Rock**. Bandeera is a prominent rock, 161 feet high, lying 600 yards northwest of Shomushon. This anchorage is sheltered from winds between northeasterly and easterly, but during westerly winds heavy seas set in, making the anchorage dangerous.

(208) A 24-foot shoal is about 800 yards south-southwest of Bandeera Rock. A shoal, with depths less than 36 feet over it, projects 400 yards south-southwest from the 24-foot shoal.

(209) **Agrihan Island** (18°46'N., 145°40'E.), lying about 33 miles north of Pagan Island, has two peaks. The highest peak rises to 3,166 feet. The island is of volcanic origin and has a large crater. The southwest side forms a gentle slope with a shore of black sand. **Agrihan**, a small settlement, is located near the southwest end of the island. A prominent church is about a mile northwest of the southern extremity of Agrihan Island. It was reported that the island was visible from a distance of 26 miles. Agrihan Island serves as a good radar target from a distance of 31 miles. A westerly current with a rate of 1¼ knots was observed in August, in a position about 6 miles northwesterly of Agrihan Island.

Anchorage

(210) Anchorage may be taken in 14 fathoms, sand and gravel bottom, about 650 yards off the beach fronting the settlement of Agrihan; however, it is unsafe during strong southerly or westerly winds, when there is a heavy swell.

(211) **Asuncion Island** (19°40'N., 145°24'E.), lying about 55 miles north of Agrihan Island, is a volcanic cone rising steeply to a height of 2,923 feet. White smoke occasionally emits from this cone. On the northeast and east sides there are some prominent crevices and broken cliffs, from the cracks in which smoke emits. The slope is gentle at the southwestern foot of the mountain, and coconut palms grow sparsely amongst dense stunted trees. The south coast is fronted by a pebble beach; the remaining coasts are precipitous.

(212) In 1955, breakers and discolored water were reported to extend about ½ mile offshore from the northeast end of the island.

(213) Asuncion Island is reported to be radar conspicuous from a distance of up to 48 miles.

(214) In 1969, it was reported that Asuncion Island lay 2 miles north of its charted position.

(215) In 1953, a bank, with a depth of 27 fathoms over it was reported to lie about 5½ miles southeast, and another, with a depth of 58 fathoms over it lies 16 miles south, of Asuncion Island.

(216) In 1945, depths of 52 and 60 fathoms were reported to lie about 85 miles west-southwest of Asuncion Island.

(217) **Maug Islands** (20°01'N., 145°14'E.), lying about 24 miles north-northwest of Asuncion Island, are comprised of three rocky, uninhabited islands; named North, East and West. This group has the appearance of a conical volcanic peak that has partially collapsed. **North Island**, 748 feet high, is the highest but smallest. This island, together with **East Island**, and **West Island**, form a circle that encloses a lagoon. The steep sides of East Island are covered with grass and low bushes, and the higher slopes are covered with trees and coconut palms. A tower is on the summit of East Island. In 1958, the ruins of what appeared to be a fishing station were reported on the north end of the same island. In 1977, Maug Island was reported to be a fair radar target from distances up to 38 miles.

Local magnetic anomaly

(218) A local magnetic anomaly amounting to 3°W has been observed near East Island, and up to 7° near West Island.

(219) Tidal currents set easterly across the south entrance of the lagoon at a rate of ¾ knot during the flood. They set north through the entrance at a rate of ¼ knot during the ebb.

Depths-Limitations

(220) South Passage, about 600 yards wide and swept to depths of 59 feet and 48 feet, is the best passage leading into the lagoon. The northeast passage, which has been swept to 15 feet over a width of 150 yards, is not recommended, as it is fully exposed to the prevailing winds. The northwest passage is foul.

Anchorages

(221) In 1941, it was reported that safe anchorage could be found, in depths of 20 to 40 fathoms, about halfway between the west end of North Island and the southwest end of East Island; rock bottom.

(222) Vessels can anchor off the northern part of the west side of East Island.

(223) A vessel reported anchoring in 16 fathoms, black sand bottom, with the northern point of East Island bearing 056°. However, this anchorage was reported unsafe due to swells rolling in through the northeast passage.

(224) **Supply Reef**, with a depth of 27 feet over it, lies about 10 miles northwest of North Island. Supply Reef is reported to be a circular reef of about 300-yard diameter, marked by discolored water and by breaking seas.

Chart 81086

(225) **Farallon de Pajaros** (20°32'N., 144°54'E.), lying about 36 miles north-northwest of Maug Islands, is the most northern of the Mariana Islands and it is an active volcano; its summit forming a regular cone of ashes 1,047 feet high.

(226) In 1974, a shoal, with a depth of 10 feet over it, was reported to lie 115 miles northwest of Farallon de Pajaros. Submarine volcanic activity has been reported in this vicinity.

(227) Farallon de Pajaros is reported to be visible from a distance of 40 miles; at night the crater glow can be seen for 15 miles. In 1967, it was reported that the volcano appeared as a well defined shadow at night from a distance of 27 miles. Farallon de Pajaros is radar conspicuous from a distance of 29 miles. The northern, southern, and eastern coast are precipitous. All coasts are rocky and steep-to. There is no anchorage. The island is barren, except near the high rock on the southeast side, where there is some coarse grass.

(228) A high rock is connected to the southeast side of the island. Several smaller rocks, one of which is prominent, are located about 150 yards southeast of the high rock. A rock lies about 300 yards offshore of a position located about 600 yards southeast of the southwestern end of the island. There is a depth of less than 6 feet over this rock.

(229) **Stingray Shoal**, having a depth of 8 fathoms, is located in approximate position 20°30'N., 142°26'E. The shoal has not been examined, and should be given a wide berth.

| TIDAL INFORMATION ||||||
Chart	Station	LAT/LONG	Mean Higher High Water*	Mean High Water*	Mean Low Water*
81054	Apra Harbor, Guam	13°27'N/144°40'E	2.4	2.2	0.6
81063	Rota Island, Marianas	14°08'N/145°08'E	2.3	2.1	0.9
81071	Tinian Island, Marianas	14°58'N/145°37'E	1.8	1.7	0.2
81076	Saipan Harbor, Saipan Island, Marianas	15°12'N/145°43'E	1.9	1.8	0.5
83484	Tau Island, Manua Islands, Samoa Islands	14°13'S/169°32'W	--.--	3.7	--.--

* Heights in feet referred to datum of sounding MLLW.
Real-time water levels, tide predictions, and tidal current predictions are available at:
http://tidesandcurrents.noaa.gov
To determine mean tide range subtract Mean Low Water from Mean High Water.
Data as of October 2012

Appendix A

Sales Information

(1) NOAA publications, nautical charts and unclassified National Geospatial-Intelligence Agency (NGA) nautical charts are sold by authorized sales agents in many U.S. ports and in some foreign ports. Information on obtaining charting products and a listing of authorized agents can be found at http://nauticalcharts.noaa.gov.

Charts, Publications, and Services–NOAA

Reporting corrections to Nautical Charts and Coast Pilots

(2) Users are requested to report all significant discrepancies or additions to NOAA charts and Coast Pilots, including depth information in privately maintained channels and basins; obstructions, wrecks, and other dangers; new, relocated, or demolished landmarks; uncharted fixed private aids to navigation; deletions or additions of small-craft facilities and any other information pertinent to safe navigation. This information may be submitted using the NOAA Office of Coast Survey website: http://nauticalcharts.noaa.gov/discrepancy. All correspondence should be addressed to:

(3) Department of Commerce, NOAA
(4) Nautical Data Branch
(5) N/CS261, Station 7331
(6) 1315 East-West Highway
(7) Silver Spring, MD 20910

Nautical Charts

(8) United States Coastal and Intracoastal waters, and possessions.
(9) Great Lakes, Lake Champlain, New York State Canals, and the St. Lawrence River-St. Regis to Cornwall, Canada
(10) Catalogs of Charts and Publications:
(11) Catalog 1–Atlantic Coast
(12) Catalog 2–Pacific Coast
(13) Catalog 3–Alaska
(14) Catalog 4–Great Lakes
(15) Catalog 5–Gulf Coast

Dates of Latest Editions

(16) Information concerning the dates of latest editions for the full suite of NOAA's nautical charts and U.S. Coast Pilot volumes can be found at: http://www.nauticalcharts.noaa.gov/mcd/dole.htm

Chart validity

(17) **CAUTION: A NOAA nautical chart is not a valid document until its publication is announced in the NGA Weekly Notice to Mariners. This also applies to NOAA nautical publications such as Coast Pilot. The date of a chart** is also of vital importance to the navigator. When charted information becomes obsolete, further use of the chart for navigation may be dangerous.

Coast Pilots

(18) U.S. Coast Pilot 1, Atlantic Coast, Eastport to Cape Cod.
(19) U.S. Coast Pilot 2, Atlantic Coast, Cape Cod to Sandy Hook.
(20) U.S. Coast Pilot 3, Atlantic Coast, Sandy Hook to Cape Henry.
(21) U.S. Coast Pilot 4, Atlantic Coast, Cape Henry to Key West.
(22) U.S. Coast Pilot 5, Atlantic Coast–Gulf of Mexico, Puerto Rico, and Virgin Islands.
(23) U.S. Coast Pilot 6, Great Lakes, Lakes Ontario, Erie, Huron, Michigan and Superior, and St. Lawrence River.
(24) U.S. Coast Pilot 7, Pacific Coast, California, Oregon, Washington, and Hawaii.
(25) U.S. Coast Pilot 8, Pacific Coast Alaska, Dixon Entrance to Cape Spencer.
(26) U.S. Coast Pilot 9, Pacific and Arctic Coasts, Alaska–Cape Spencer to Beaufort Sea.

Distance Tables

(27) Distances Between United States Ports (available at: http://nauticalcharts.noaa.gov/nsd/distances-ports).

Tide Tables

(28) East Coast of North and South America, including Greenland.
(29) West Coast of North and South America, including Hawaii.
(30) Central and Western Pacific and Indian Oceans.
(31) Europe and West Coast of Africa, including the Mediterranean Sea.

Tidal Current Tables

(32) Atlantic Coast, North America.
(33) Pacific Coast, North America and Asia.

National Ocean Service Center for Operational Oceanographic Products and Services

For Tide and Tidal Current Observations and Predictions, PORTS® data, Tidal Datums, Levels and Bench Mark Sheets:

(34) Oceanographic Division (N/OPS3)
(35) 1305 East-West Highway, 7th floor
(36) Silver Spring, MD 20912-3281
(37) Tel: 301–713–2815 Ext. 0
(38) Fax: 301–713–4500 (24 hours)
(39) Email: tide.predictions@noaa.gov
(40) Web: http://www.tidesandcurrents.noaa.gov

National Weather Service Offices

(41) The following offices provide marine weather forecasts and warnings by telephone: refer to the local telephone directions for numbers.
(42) Eureka, CA: 300 Startare Drive, Eureka, CA 95501 Tel: 707–443–6484
(43) Los Angeles, CA: 520 North Elevar Street, Oxnard, CA 93030 Tel: 805–988–6610
(44) San Diego, CA: 11440 W. Bernardo Court, Suite 230, San Diego, CA 92127 Tel: 858–675–8700
(45) San Francisco, CA: 21 Grace Hopper Avenue, Stop 5, Monterey, CA 93943-5505 Tel: 831–656–1725
(46) San Joaquin Valley, CA: 900 Foggy Bottom Road, Hanford, CA 93230-5236 Tel: 559–584–3752
(47) Honolulu, HI: 2525 Correa Road, Ste 250, Honolulu, HI 96822 Tel: 808–973–5286
(48) Medford, OR: 4003 Cirrus Drive, Medford, OR 97504-4198 Tel: 541–773–1067
(49) Pendleton, OR: 2001 NW 56th Drive, Pendleton, OR 97801 Tel: 541–276–7832
(50) Portland, OR: 5241 NE 122nd Avenue, Portland, OR 97230-1089 Tel: 503–261–9246
(51) Seattle, WA: 7600 Sandpoint Way NE, Seattle, WA 98115-6349 Tel: 206–526–6976
(52) Spokane, WA: 2601 N. Rambo Road, Spokane, WA 99224 Tel: 509–244–0110

Marine Weather Services Charts

(53) Published by the National Weather Service (available at http://www.weather.gov/om/marine/pub-htm).

NOAA Weather Radio

(54) National Weather Service VHF-FM radio stations provide mariners with continuous FM broadcasts of weather warnings, forecasts, radar reports, and surface weather observations. Reception range is up to 40 miles from the antenna site, depending on the terrain, type of receiver, and antenna used. The VHF-FM radio stations with location of antenna in or near the area covered by this Coast Pilot are listed in the table.

(55) The National Weather Service provides **Radio facsimile Weather Information** for Hawaiian waters through Coast Guard Communications Station Pt. Reyes (NMC) and DOD Communication Station Honolulu (KVM70). Broadcasts are made on the following frequencies:

(56) Pt. Reyes (NMC)-4346 (except 19z, 23z), 8682, 12590.5, 17151.2, 22527 (19z, 23z) kHz.
(57) Honolulu-9982.5 (11z), 11090 (except 23z), 16135 (except 11z), 23331.5 (23z) KHz.
(58) For carrier frequency, subtract 1.9 kHz. Fax schedules are transmitted at 1104 and 2324 GMT (Pt. Reyes), 1045 and 2018 GMT (Honolulu), providing area coverage and descriptions of services. For further information, go to: http://www.nws.noaa.gov/om/marine/radiofax.htm.

Marine Weather Forecasts

(59) Scheduled coastal marine forecasts are issued four times daily by National Weather Service Offices. For further information on coastal marine forecasts as well as additional types of forecasts, go to: http://www.nws.noaa.gov/om/marine/forecast.htm.

Call Sign	Station	Location	Frequency (MHz)
KEC-62	San Diego, CA	33°01'N., 116°57'W.	162.40
WWG-21	Santa Ana, CA	33°50'N., 117°36'W.	162.45
KWO-37	Los Angeles, CA	34°13'N., 118°03'W.	162.55
KIH-34	Santa Barbara, CA	34°26'N., 119°46'W.	162.40
WWF-62	Santa Barbara, CA	34°31'N., 119°58'W.	162.475
KIH-31	San Luis Obispo, CA	35°21'N., 120°39'W.	162.55
KEC-49	Monterey, CA,	37°11'N., 121°54'W.	162.55
KHB-49	San Francisco, CA	37°27'N., 122°30'W.	162.40
KIH-30	Point Arena, CA	39°01'N., 123°31'W.	162.40
KEC-82	Eureka, CA	40°25'N., 124°07'W.	162.40
KIH-37	Brookings, OR	42°07'N., 124°12'W.	162.55
WNG-596	Port Orford, OR	42°42'N., 124°27'W.	162.425
KIH-32	Coos Bay, OR	43°23'N., 124°07'W.	162.40
WNG-674	Florence, OR	44°03'N., 124°02'W.	162.50
KIH-33	Newport, OR	44°45'N., 124°02'W.	162.55
WWF-95	Tillamook, OR	45°28'N., 123°56'W.	162.475
KIG-98	Portland, OR	45°34'N., 122°47'W.	162.55
KEC-91	Astoria, OR	46°22'N., 123°48'W.	162.40
KXI-27	Forks, WA	47°50'N., 124°23'W.	162.425
KIH-36	Neah Bay, WA	48°22'N., 124°40'W.	162.55
WWG-24	Puget Sound, WA	48°02'N., 122°58'W.	162.425
KHB-60	Seattle, WA	47°32'N., 121°55'W.	162.55
WXM-62	Olympia, WA	46°33'N., 122°55'W.	162.475
CFA-240	Mt Tuam, BC*	48°43'N., 123°29'W.	162.4
KBA-99	Hilo, HI	19°44'N., 155°05'W.	162.55
KBA-99	Maui, HI	20°43'N., 156°16'W.	162.40
KBA-99	Honolulu, HI	21°31'N., 158°09'W.	162.55
KBA-99	Kauai, HI	22°07'N., 159°40'W.	162.40

* Canadian Government weather radio station

Space Environment Center (SEC)

(60) The Space Environment Center disseminates space weather alerts and forecasts (information concerning solar activity, radio propagation, etc.).
(61) For general information write or call;
(62) NOAA, National Weather Service
(63) National Center for Environmental Prediction

(64) Space Environment Center, W/NP9
(65) 325 Broadway
(66) Boulder, CO 80305
(67) Telephone 303–497–3171
(68) Website: http://www.sec.noaa.gov/.

Charts and Publications–Other U.S. Government Agencies

(69) A partial list of publications and charts considered of navigational value is included for the ready reference of the mariner. In addition to the agents located in the principal seaports handling publication sales, certain libraries have been designated by the Congress of the United States to receive the publications as issued for public review.

Government Printing Office

(70) Publications of the U.S. Government Printing Office may be ordered at http://bookstore.gpo.gov. Orders may also be placed by phone (866–512–1800; 202–512–1800 in the DC area), FAX (202–512–2104), or mail (U.S. Government Printing Office, P.O. Box 979050, St. Louis, MO 63197-9000).

National Geospatial-Intelligence Agency Procurement Information

(71) Unclassified publications produced by the National Geospatial-Intelligence Agency (NGA) are available from the U.S. Government Printing Office, Superintendent of Documents, P.O. Box 371954, Pittsburgh, PA 15250-1954. Orders can be placed on the U.S. Government Online Bookstore (http://bookstore.gpo. gov), by phone (202–512–1800) or by FAX (202–512–2250). Classified NGA publications and charts are available to authorized users from the Defense Supply Center Richmond (attn: JNAA), 8000 Jefferson Davis Highway, Richmond, VA 23297-5336. Defense Supply Center Richmond, Customer Assistance office may be contacted at 800–826–0342.

Nautical Charts

(72) **U.S. Waters:**

(73) **Apalachicola, Chattahoochee and Flint Rivers Navigation Charts, Alabama River Charts, and Black Warrior-Tombigbee Rivers River Charts:** Published and for sale by U.S. Army Engineer District Mobile, P.O. Box 2288, AL 36602, Attn: Map Sales, LM-SR; telephone, 251–441–5631.

(74) **Flood Control and Navigation Maps of the Mississippi River, Cairo, IL to the Gulf of Mexico:** Published by Mississippi River Commission and for sale by U.S. Army Engineer District Vicksburg, 4155 Clay Street, Vicksburg, MS 39183-3435, Attn: Map Sales; telephone: 601–631–5042.

(75) **Upper Mississippi River Navigation Charts (Mississippi River, Cairo, IL to Minneapolis, MN):** Published and for sale by U.S. Army Engineer District Rock Island, Clock Tower Bldg., P.O. Box 2004, Rock Island, IL 61204-2004; telephone, 309–794–5338.

(76) **Charts of the Illinois Waterway, from Mississippi River at Grafton, IL to Lake Michigan at Chicago and Calumet Harbors:** Published and for sale by U.S. Army Engineer District Rock Island, Clock Tower Bldg., P.O. Box 2004, Rock Island, IL 61204-2004; telephone, 309–794–5338.

(77) **Foreign Waters:** Published by National Geospatial-Intelligence Agency (see National Geospatial-Intelligence Agency Procurement Information above).

Publications

(78) **Notices to Mariners:**

(79) Local Notices to Mariners are posted weekly by the U.S. Coast Guard Navigation Center at http://www.navcen. uscg.gov/. The National Geospatial-Intelligence Agency, U.S. Notice to Mariners are available at: http://msi.nga.mil/ NGAPortal/MSI.portal.

(80) **Special Notice to Mariners** are published annually in National Geospatial-Intelligence Agency Notice to Mariners 1. These notices contain important information of considerable interest to all mariners. Interested parties are advised to read these notices.

(81) **Light Lists (United States and Possessions):** Published by U.S. Coast Guard; for sale by the Government Printing Office. (See Government Printing Office, early this Appendix A.)

(82) **List of Lights (Foreign Countries):** Published by National Geospatial-Intelligence Agency (see National Geospatial-Intelligence Agency Procurement Information above).

(83) **Sailing Directions (Foreign Countries):** Published by the National Geospatial-Intelligence Agency (see National Geospatial-Intelligence Agency Procurement Information above).

(84) **Radio Navigational Aids,** Pub. 117: Published by the National Geospatial-Intelligence Agency (see National Geospatial-Intelligence Agency Procurement Information above).

(85) The **Nautical Almanac,** the **Air Almanac,** and **Astronomical Almanac:** Published by U.S. Naval Observatory; for sale by Government Printing Office. (see Government Printing Office, early this Appendix A.)

(86) **American Practical Navigator Bowditch** Pub. 9: Published by the National Geospatial-Intelligence Agency (see National Geospatial-Intelligence Agency Procurement Information above).

(87) **International Code of Signals,** Pub. 102: Published by National Geospatial-Intelligence Agency (see National Geospatial-Intelligence Agency Procurement Information above).

(88) **Marine Product Dissemination Information:** maintained by the National Weather Service; http://www.nws. noaa.gov/om/marine/home htm.

(89) **Navigation Rules:** Navigation Rules, International-alInland (COMDTINST M16672.2 series): Published by

the U.S. Coast Guard; for sale by Government Printing Office. (see Government Printing Office, early this Appendix A.)

(90) **Federal Requirements for Recreational Boats:** Published by U.S. Coast Guard; http://www.uscgboating.org.

(91) **Port Series of the United States:** Published and sold by U.S. Army Corps of Engineers, Institute for Water Resources, Navigation Data Center, (CEIWR-NDC-N), 7701 Telegraph Road, Casey Building, Alexandria, VA 22315-3868; telephone 703–428–8059

Offices and Services-Other U.S. Government Agencies

U.S. Army Corps of Engineers (USACE) Offices

(92) **Pacific Ocean Division Office:** Bldg. 230, Fort Shafter, HI 96858-5440.

(93) The Pacific Ocean Division includes the State of Hawaii. The division also performs protection and preservation works at the islands of Guam and American Samoa.

(94) **Los Angeles District Office:** 300 North Los Angeles Street, Los Angeles, CA 90012.

(95) The Los Angeles District includes the coastal waters and tributaries of California from the Mexican boundary to Cape San Martin (35°54'N., 121°27'W.).

(96) **Portland District Office:** Duncan Plaza, 333 S.W. First Avenue, P.O. Box 2946, Portland, OR 97208.

(97) The Portland District includes the coastal waters and tributaries of Oregon, and the waters and tributaries of the Columbia River as far as the bridge at Umatilla, OR, just below McNary Dam.

(98) **Sacramento District Office:** 650 Capitol Mall, Federal and Court Bldg., Sacramento, CA 95814-4794.

(99) The Sacramento District includes Suisun Bay, and the Sacramento and San Joaquin Rivers and their tributaries.

(100) **San Francisco District Office:** 211 Main Street, San Francisco, CA 94105-1905.

(101) The San Francisco District includes the coastal waters and tributaries from Cape San Martin to the Oregon boundary, including San Francisco Bay but not Suisun Bay and the Sacramento and San Joaquin Rivers and their tributaries.

(102) **Seattle District Office:** 4735 East Marginal Way South, Seattle, WA 98134.

(103) The Seattle District includes the coastal waters and tributaries of Washington except the Columbia River.

(104) **Walla Walla District Office:** Bldg. 602, City-County Airport, Walla Walla, WA 99362-9265.

(105) The Walla Walla District includes the Columbia River and tributaries above the bridge at Umatilla, OR, just below McNary Dam.

Environmental Protection Agency (EPA) Offices

(106) Regional offices and States in the EPA coastal regions:

(107) **Region I** (New Hampshire, Vermont, Maine, Massachusetts, Connecticut, Rhode Island): J. F. Kennedy Federal Bldg., Boston, MA 02203.

(108) **Region II** (New Jersey, New York, Puerto Rico, Virgin Islands): 26 Federal Plaza, New York, NY 10278.

(109) **Region III** (Delaware, Maryland, Virginia, District of Columbia, Pennsylvania): 841 Chestnut Street, Philadelphia, PA 19107.

(110) **Region IV** (Alabama, Florida, Georgia, Mississippi, South Carolina, North Carolina): 345 Courtland Street, NE., Atlanta, GA 30365.

(111) **Region V** (Illinois, Indiana, Michigan, Minnesota, Ohio, Wisconsin): 230 South Dearborn Street, Chicago, IL 60604.

(112) **Region VI** (Louisiana, Texas): 1445 Ross Avenue, Dallas, TX 75270.

(113) **Region IX** (California, Hawaii, Guam): 215 Fremont Street, San Francisco, CA 94105.

(114) **Region X** (Alaska, Oregon, Washington): 1200 Sixth Avenue, Seattle, WA, 98101.

U.S. Coast Guard Navigation Center (NAVCEN)

(115) The Coast Guard Navigation Center provides cutting edge services for safe, secure, and efficient maritime transportation. The center operates the Navigation Information Service (NIS), the Maritime Differential GPS (DGPS) and the developing Nationwide Differential Global Positioning System (NDGPS). In addition, NAVCEN serves as the civilian interface for the Global Positioning System and manages other navigation-related projects.

(116) For further information and/or operational questions regarding GPS and DGPS, visit:

(117) http://www.navcen.uscg.gov/, or contact:
(118) Commanding Officer
(119) U.S. Coast Guard Navigation Center
(120) 7323 Telegraph Road
(121) Alexandria, VA 22315
(122) TEL: 703-313-5900; FAX: 703-313-5920
(123) Email: NISWS@navcen.uscg.mil

Coast Guard District Offices

(124) Commander, Eleventh Coast Guard District, Coast Guard Island, Building 50-6, Alameda, CA 94501-5100. Arizona; Utah; Nevada; California; and the ocean area bounded by a line from the California-Oregon state line westerly to 40°N., 150°W., thence southeasterly to 5°S., 100°W., thence northeasterly to the border between Guatemala and Mexico on the Pacific Coast (14°38'N., 92°19'W.).

(125) Commander, Thirteenth Coast Guard District, 915 Second Avenue, Jackson Federal Building, Seattle, WA 98174-1067. The coastal waters and tributaries in Oregon, Washington, Idaho, and Montana.

(126) Commander, Fourteenth Coast Guard District, Prince Kalanianaole Federal Building, 300 Ala Moana Boulevard, Honolulu, HI 96850-4982. The State of Hawaii and the Pacific Islands belonging to the United States west of 150°W., and south of 40°N.

Coast Guard Sector/Sector Field Offices

(127) Note: A Sector Office combines the functions of the Captain of the Port and Marine Inspection Office.

(128) Sector Columbia River - 2185 SE Airport Road, Warrenton, OR 97146-9693

(129) Sector Guam - Victor Pier, CO US Naval Forces, Santa Rita, GU 96915

(130) Sector Honolulu - 400 Sand Island Parkway Honolulu, HI 96819-4398

(131) Sector/Air Station Humboldt Bay, 1001 Lycoming Way, McKinleyville, CA 95519-9309

(132) Sector Los Angeles-Long Beach - 1001 S. Seaside Avenue, Bldg. 20, San Pedro, CA 90731-0208

(133) Sector/Air Station North Bend - 2000 Connecticut Avenue, North Bend, OR 97459-2399

(134) Air Station/Sector Field Office Port Angeles, 1 Ediz Hook Road, Port Angeles, WA 98362-0159

(135) Sector Puget Sound - 1519 Alaskan Way South, Seattle, WA 98134-1192

(136) Sector San Diego - 2710 Harbor Drive, North San Diego, CA 92101-1028

(137) Sector San Francisco - 1 Yerba Buena Island San Francisco, CA 94130-9309

Coast Guard Marine Safety Unit

(138) Portland, 6767 North Basin Avenue, Portland, OR 97217-3992

Coast Guard Marine Safety Detachments

(139) American Samoa, Pago Plaza Suite 215, Pago Pago, AS, 96799

(140) Saipan, 1 Kopa Di Oru Dr. Horiguchi Bldg 5th Floor, Saipan, MP 96950

(141) Santa Barbara, 111 Harbor Way, Santa Barbara, CA 93109-2397

Coast Guard Stations

(142) The stations listed are in the area covered by this Coast Pilot. They have search and rescue capabilities and may provide lookout, communication, and/or patrol functions to assist vessels in distress. The National VHF-FM Distress System provides continuous coastal radio coverage outwards to 20 miles on channel 16. After contact on channel 16, communications with the Coast Guard should be on channel 22. If channel 22 is not available to the mariner, communications may be made on channel 12. Selected stations guard the International Radiotelephone Distress, Safety and Calling Frequencies.

(143) **California:**

(144) Humboldt Bay Air Station (40°59'N., 124°06'W.). At McKinleyville.

(145) Bodega Bay (38°18.7'N., 123°03.0'W.). On E side of channel 0.8 mile inside Bodega Harbor.

(146) Channel Islands Harbor (34°09.7'N., 119°13.3'W.). On the E side of the harbor about 0.4 mile above the entrance.

(147) Golden Gate (37°49'54"N., 122°28'30"W.). At entrance to Horseshoe Bay, about 0.4 mile NNE of Golden Gate Bridge.

(148) Humboldt Bay (40°45'59"N., 124°13'02"W.). E side of North Spit at the entrance to Humboldt Bay.

(149) Lake Tahoe (39°10.8'N., 120°07.1'W.). On W shore of the lake, about 1.3 miles W of Dollar Point.

(150) Los Angeles/Long Beach (33°43'26"N., 118°16'06"W.). On the W side of Reservation Point.

(151) Los Angeles Air Station (33°57'N., 118°24'W.). At Los Angeles International Airport.

(152) Vallejo (38°06'38"N., 122°16'12"W.) 2.5 miles above the entrance to Mare Island Strait just below the Vallejo-Mare Island causeway lift bridge.

(153) Rio Vista (38°08.8'N., 121°41.5'W.). On the W side of the Sacramento River, 0.9 mile below bridge.

(154) Sacramento Air Station (38°40'N., 121°24'W.). NE of the city at McClellan Air Force Base.

(155) San Diego (32°43.6'N., 117°10.9'W.). In North San Diego Bay, 700 yards NE of E end of Harbor Island.

(156) San Diego Air Station (32°43.6'N., 117°10.9'W.). In North San Diego Bay.

(157) San Francisco Base and Station (37°48.7'N., 122°21.6'W.). On the E side of Yerba Buena Island.

(158) San Francisco Air Station (37°38'N., 122°23'W.). At San Francisco International Airport.

(159) **Hawaii:**

(160) Barbers Point Air Station (21°18.8'N., 128°04.4'W.). At Barbers Point Naval Air Station.

(161) Honolulu Base (21°18.6'N., 157°52.6'W.). On Sand Island, 0.8 mile from harbor entrance.

(162) Maui (20°47.5'N., 156°30.6'W.). At Maalaea Village in Maalaea Bay.

(163) **Oregon:**

(164) Astoria Air Station (46°10'N., 123°53'W.). At Clatsop County Airport.

(165) Chetco River (42°02.8'N., 124°16.0'W.). On E side of river, about 450 yards above the entrance.

(166) Coos Bay (43°20.7'N., 124°19.3'W.). S side of Charleston Boat Basin.

(167) Depoe Bay (44°48.6'N., 124°03.5'W.). On E side of bay.

(168) North Bend Air Station (43°25'N., 124°15'W.). At North Bend Municipal Airport.

(169) Portland (45°34.2'N., 122°43.3'W.). On N side near entrance of Swan Island Basin.

(170) Siuslaw River (44°00.1'N., 124°07.2'W.). On E side of river, about 1.3 mile above the entrance.

(171) Tillamook Bay (45°33.5'N., 123°55.2'W.). On N shore at Garibaldi.

(172) Umpqua River (43°40.9'N., 124°10.9'W.). In Winchester Bay, 2 miles above the mouth.

(173) Yaquina Bay (44°37.6'N., 124°03.3'W.). Newport waterfront, N side of bay near bridge.
(174) **Washington:**
(175) Bellingham (48°45.4'N., 122°30.4'W.). In Squalicum small-boat harbor.
(176) Cape Disappointment (46°16.8'N., 124°02.7'W.). At Fort Canby on SW side of Baker Bay.
(177) Grays Harbor (46°54.3'N., 124°06.1'W.). On the S side of Westhaven Cove.
(178) Neah Bay (48°22.3'N., 124°35.8'W.). About 0.5 mile S of Waadah Island.
(179) Port Angeles Air Station (48°08.4'N., 123°24.5'W.). On Ediz Hook about 0.3 mile W of the E extremity of the hook.
(180) Quillayute River (47°54.5'N., 124°38.2'W.). At La Push.
(181) Seattle (47°39.8'N., 122°23.5'W.). On S side Lake Washington Ship Canal, 0.8 mile from W entrance.

Coast Guard Radio Broadcasts

(182) Urgent, safety, and scheduled marine information broadcasts are made by Coast Guard radio stations. In general, these broadcasts provide information vital to vessels operating in the approaches and coastal waters of the United States including Puerto Rico and U.S. Virgin Islands. Transmissions are as follows:
(183) **By radiotelephone:** (a) upon receipt; (b) repeated 15 minutes later, (for urgent messages only); (c) text only on the first scheduled broadcast unless canceled; (d) additional broadcasts at the discretion of the originator.
(184) **Urgent broadcasts** are preceded by the urgent signal PAN-PAN. Both the urgent signal and message are transmitted on 2182 kHz, and VHF-FM channel 16.
(185) **Safety broadcasts** are preceded by the safety signal SECURITY. After the preliminary safety signal is broadcast on 2182 kHz and VHF-FM channel 16, broadcast stations will shift to 2670 kHz and VHF-FM channel 22A, respectively.
(186) Up-to-date U.S. Coast Guard radio broadcast schedules may be found at http: www.nws.noaa.gov/om/marine/home.htm.

Radio Weather Broadcasts

(187) Taped or direct broadcasts of marine weather forecasts and storm warnings are made by commercial and Coast Guard radio stations in the area covered by this Coast Pilot. These broadcasts usually are made several times a day; the transmission schedules are shown on the **Marine Weather Services Chart** for the following areas:
(188) Mexican Border to Point Conception, CA.
(189) Point Conception, CA to Point St. George, CA.
(190) Point St. George, CA to Canadian Border.
(191) Hawai'ian Waters.
(192) The weather broadcasts schedules of Coast Guard radio stations are also listed in the descriptions of Coast Guard marine services found elsewhere in this appendix.

U.S. NAVTEX Transmitting Stations

(193) NAVTEX coverage is reasonably continuous to 200 NM off the U.S. East, Gulf and West Coasts; Puerto Rico; Southwest Alaska; Hawaii; and 100 NM off Guam. U.S. Coast Guard NAVTEX broadcast stations and message content for the West Coast are as follows:

Station	ID	Broadcast Schedule (UTC)
Kodiak	J	0130, 0530, 0930*, 1330, 1730, 2130*
Kodiak	X	0350, 0750, 1150*, 1550, 1950, 2350*
Astoria	W	0340*, 0740, 1140, 1540*, 1940, 2340
San Francisco	C	0020, 0420*, 0820, 1220, 1620*, 2020
Cambria	Q	0240*, 0640, 1040, 1440*, 1840, 2240
Guam	V	0330, 0730, 1130, 1530, 1930, 2330
Honolulu	O	0220, 0620, 1020*, 1420, 1820, 2220*

*Routine weather forecasts are broadcast four times per day with these being the normal times when repeats of Notices to Mariners are broadcast in lieu of weather. Weather warnings may be broadcast at any time.

(194) **Cambria (NMC) (Station Q)**
(195) Eleventh Coast Guard District Broadcast Notices to Mariners.
(196) Distress, Urgent, and Safety messages.
(197) Gale, storm, and Hurricane warnings.
(198) Coastal weather forecasts for Point St George to Guadalupe Island and 60 NM offshore.
(199) **San Francisco (NMC) (Station C)**
(200) Eleventh Coast Guard District Broadcast Notices to Mariners.
(201) Distress, Urgent, and Safety messages.
(202) Gale, storm, and hurricane warnings.
(203) Offshore marine weather forecasts for:
(204) North of 30 N., East of 160 E.;
(205) South of 30 N., East of 140 W.
(206) **Astoria (NMW) (Station W)**
(207) Thirteenth Coast Guard District Broadcast Notice to Mariners.
(208) Distress, Urgent, and Safety messages.
(209) Gale, storm, and hurricane warnings.
(210) Offshore marine weather forecasts for the Canadian border to Point St. George and 250 NM offshore.
(211) **Kodiak (NOJ) (Station J)**
(212) Seventeenth Coast Guard District Broadcast Notice to Mariners.
(213) Distress, Urgent, and Safety messages.
(214) Gale, storm, and hurricane warnings.
(215) Offshore marine weather forecasts for the Canadian border to 85 N including the Aleutian Chain.
(216) **Kodiak (NOJ) (Station X)**
(217) Seventeenth Coast Guard District Broadcast Notice to Mariners.
(218) Distress, Urgent, and Safety messages.
(219) Gale, storm, and hurricane warnings.
(220) Coastal weather forecasts for the Andreanof Island vicinity.
(221) **Honolulu (NMO) (Station O)**
(222) Fourteenth Coast Guard District Broadcast Notice to Mariners.

(223) Distress, Urgent, and Safety messages.
(224) Gale, storm, tropical storm, and typhoon warnings.
(225) Offshore marine weather forecasts for:
(226) North Pacific to 50 N. and 160 E. to 140 W.;
(227) South Pacific to 25 S. and 160 E. to 110 W.
(228) **Marianas (NRV) (Station V)**
(229) Sector Guam Broadcast Notice to Mariners.
(230) Distress, Urgent, and Safety messages.
(231) Gale, storm, tropical storm, and typhoon warnings.
(232) Offshore marine weather forecasts.

Customs Ports of Entry and Stations

(233) Vessels may be entered and cleared at any port of entry or customs station, but at the latter only with advance authorization from the Customs Service district director.
(234) **Pacific Region**
(235) **San Diego District:**
(236) Port of Entry: San Diego.
(237) Los Angeles District:
(238) Ports of Entry: Los Angeles-Long Beach, Port San Luis.
(239) Customs Station: Port Hueneme.
(240) **San Francisco District:**
(241) Ports of Entry: San Francisco-Oakland, Eureka.
(242) Customs Station: Monterey.
(243) Columbia-Snake (at Portland) District:
(244) Ports of Entry: Astoria, Coos Bay, Longview, Newport.
(245) **Seattle District:**
(246) Ports of Entry: Aberdeen, Blaine, Point Roberts, Puget Sound (includes Anacortes, Bellingham, Everett, Friday Harbor, Neah Bay, Olympia, Port Angeles, Port Townsend, and Tacoma).
(247) **Honolulu District:**
(248) Ports of Entry: Barbers Point, Hilo, Honolulu, Kahului, Nawiliwili-Port Allen.

Public Health Service Quarantine Stations

(249) Stations where quarantine examinations are performed:
(250) Honolulu: U.S. Quarantine Station, Honolulu International Airport, Terminal Box #67, Honolulu, HI 96819-1832.
(251) Los Angeles: U.S. Quarantine Station, P.O. Box 90834, Los Angeles, CA 90009-0834.
(252) San Francisco: U.S. Quarantine Station, P.O. Box 8548 SFIA, San Francisco, CA 94128-0548.
(253) Seattle: U.S. Quarantine Station, Room S-212, Seattle-Tacoma International Airport, Seattle, WA 98158-1720.
(254) At other ports, quarantine and/or medical examinations are usually performed by Public Health Service contract personnel or by quarantine inspectors from the nearest quarantine station. Inquiries concerning quarantine matters should be directed to the nearest quarantine station.

Food and Drug Administration (FDA) Regional Offices

(255) **Northeast Region** (New York, Maine, Connecticut, New Hampshire, Vermont, Rhode Island): 830 Third Avenue, Brooklyn, NY 11232.
(256) **Mid-Atlantic Region** (Delaware, Pennsylvania, Virginia, Maryland, Ohio, New Jersey): U.S. Customhouse, 2nd and Chestnut Streets, Philadelphia, PA 19106.
(257) **Southeast Region** (South Carolina, North Carolina, Georgia, Alabama, Louisiana, Mississippi, Florida, Puerto Rico): 60 Eighth Street, N.E., Atlanta, GA 30309. Midwest Region (Illinois, Indiana, Michigan, Wisconsin): 20 N. Michigan Avenue, Chicago, IL 60602.
(258) **Southwest Region (Texas)**: 3032 Bryan Street, Dallas, TX 75204.
(259) **Pacific Region** (California, Hawaii, Alaska, Washington, Oregon): 50 U.N. Plaza, San Francisco, CA 94102.

Department of Agriculture, Animal and Plant Health Inspection Service (APHIS) Offices

(260) Listed below are ports covered by this volume where APHIS inspectors are available to inspect plants, and plant and animal products, and locations of Animal Import Centers where livestock and birds are inspected.
(261) Information on importation of plants, animals, and plant and animal products is available from APHIS, Department of Agriculture, 4700 River Road, Riverdale, MD 20737.
(262) Telephone: 301–374–0841 (plant related); 301–734–7833 (animal related).
(263) Visit http://www.aphis.usda.gov for more information.
(264) **California:**
(265) Los Angeles: Bldg. D North, 9650 La Cienega Boulevard, Inglewood 90301.
(266) Los Angeles: International Arrivals Area, Satellite 2, World Way Center Post Office, Los Angeles International Airport, 90009.
(267) San Diego: U.S. Border Station, San Ysidro 92073.
(268) San Francisco: Agriculture Bldg., Embarcadero and Mission Streets 94120.
(269) San Francisco: Airport Station, San Francisco International Airport 94128.
(270) **Hawaii:**
(271) Hilo: General Lyman Field 96720.
(272) Honolulu: International Arrivals Bldg., Honolulu International Airport 96820.
(273) Wailuku: Federal Post Office Bldg., 96793.
(274) **Oregon:**
(275) Astoria: Port Docks 97103.
(276) Coos Bay: U.S. Postal Service Bldg., 235 West Anderson Street 97420.
(277) Portland: Federal Bldg., 511 Northwest Broadway 97209.
(278) **Washington:**
(279) Blaine: U.S. Customs House, 98230.

(280) Seattle: Federal Office Bldg., 909 First Avenue 98174.
(281) Seattle: Seattle-Tacoma International Airport 98158.
(282) **Animal Import Centers:**
(283) Honolulu, HI: 300 Ala Moana Boulevard, 96850.
(284) Miami, FL: 8120 N.W. 53rd Street, 33166.
(285) Rock Tavern, NY, New York Animal Import Center, Stewart Airport, Rural Route 1, Box 74, 12575.

Immigration and Naturalization Service Offices
(286) **California:**
(287) Los Angeles: 300 North Los Angeles Street 90012.
(288) Sacramento: Federal and U.S. Courthouse Bldg., 650 Capitol Mall 95814.
(289) San Diego: 880 Front Street 92188.
(290) San Francisco: Appraisers Bldg., 630 Sansome Street 94111.
(291) San Luis Obispo: Frontage Road South Highway 101, 93406.
(292) San Pedro: Terminal Island 90731.
(293) Stockton: U.S. Post Office Bldg., 401 North San Joaquin Street 95202.
(294) **Hawaii:**
(295) Honolulu: 595 Ala Moana Boulevard 96809.
(296) **Oregon:**
(297) Portland: Federal Office Bldg., 511 Northwest Broadway 97209.
(298) **Washington:**
(299) Bellingham: Federal Bldg., Magnolia and Cornwall Streets 98227.
(300) Blaine: Peace Arch Inspection Station 98230.
(301) Longview: U.S. Postal Service Bldg., 1603 Larch Street 98632.
(302) Port Angeles: U.S. Post Office Bldg., First and Oak Streets 98362.
(303) Seattle: 815 Airport Way South 98134.
(304) Tacoma: U.S. Post Office Bldg., 11th and A Streets 98401.

Department of Interior, U.S. Fish and Wildlife Service
(305) Interior, Department of Refuge Manager, Hawai'ian/Pacific Islands National Wildlife Complex, U.S. Fish and Wildlife Service, 300 Ala Moana Boulevard, P.O. Box 50167, Honolulu, HI 96850. See National Wildlife Refuges (indexed as such), chapter 15.

Federal Communications Commission Offices
(306) **District field offices:**
(307) San Diego, CA: Interstate Office Park, 4542 Ruffner St., Room 370 San Diego, CA 92111-2216.
(308) Los Angeles, CA: Cerritos Corporate Tower, 18000 Studebaker Rd., Room 660, Cerritos, CA 90701-3684.
(309) San Francisco, CA: 5653 Stoneridge Drive, Suite 105, Pleasanton, CA 94588-8543.
(310) Seattle WA: 11410 NE 122nd Way, Room 312, Kirkland, WA 98034-6927.
(311) Telephone toll-free: 888–225–5322: (888–CALLFCC) to report radio communications interference issues.

Radio shore stations providing medical advice
(312) Messages to shore stations may be transmitted in code groups or plain language; messages should be signed by the master and be prefixed: "RADIOMEDICAL". The following stations will provide radio services for medical advice. (See Medical advice, chapter 1.)
(313) **NMC**, San Francisco, CA, U.S. Coast Guard, and
(314) **NMO**, Honolulu, HI, U.S. Coast Guard on HF single-sideband radiotelephone channels 424(4134 kHz), 601(6200 kHz), 816(8340 kHz), or 1205(12242 kHz).
(315) **NOJ**, Kodiak, AK, U.S. Coast Guard, and
(316) **KLB**, Seattle, WA, Mobile Marine Radio, Inc.

Measured Courses
(317) The positions of measured courses are shown on the chart and their description is included in the Coast Pilots when information is reported to the National Ocean Service. Courses are located in the following places covered by this Coast Pilot.
(318) Carr Inlet, on the NE shore of McNeil Island; 18448.
(319) Channel Islands Harbor, on the breakwater N of the entrance; 18725.
(320) Commencement Bay, on the SW shore between Ruston and Tacoma; 18474.
(321) Dungeness Bay, on the strait side of Dungeness Spit; 18465.
(322) Edmonds, N of Edwards Point on the E shore of Puget Sound; 18473.
(323) Kaneohe Bay, SE of Moku o Loe Island in S part of bay; 19359.
(324) Lake Washington, on pontoon bridge from Foster Island to Evergreen Point; 18447.
(325) Lake Washington, on pontoon bridge to Mercer Island; 18447.
(326) Long Beach Harbor, on Long Beach Breakwater; 18751.
(327) Marina del Rey, just N of entrance; 18744.
(328) Newport Harbor, W side of harbor entrance; 18754.
(329) Pacific Beach, just N of Scripps Institution of Oceanography; 18765.
(330) Parry Bay, on the NW shore of the bay; 18465.
(331) Port Angeles, in SW part of the harbor; 18468.
(332) Sacramento River, on NE side of river N of Walnut Grove; 18662.
(333) San Clemente Island, S of West Cove; 18763.
(334) San Diego Bay, on W side of North Island; 18773.
(335) San Diego Bay, on S side of Harbor Island; 18773 (not charted).
(336) Sinclair Inlet, S of Bremerton naval shipyard; 18452.
(337) Vashon Island, E of Point Beals; 18448.
(338) The pages in the text describing the courses can be obtained by referring to the index for the geographic places; the chart number follows the names.

Appendix B

- Climatological Data
- Meteorological Data
- Atmospheric Pressure Conversion
- Mean Surface Water Temperatures and Densities
- Table for Estimating Time of Transit
- Determination of Wind Speed by Sea Condition
- Distances Between Ports
- Distances of Visibility for Objects Having Various Elevations
- Conversion of Degrees to Points
- Standard Abbreviations Used in Broadcasts
- Conversion Factors
- Measurements and Equivalencies
- Tips for Boating Clean and Green

CLIMATOLOGICAL DATA – SAN DIEGO, CA (32°44'N, 117°10'W) 13 feet (4 m)

WEATHER ELEMENTS	JAN	FEB	MAR	APR	MAY	JUN	JUL	AUG	SEP	OCT	NOV	DEC	YEAR	YEARS OF RECORD
SEA LEVEL PRESSURE*														
Mean (millibars)	1018.5	1017.9	1016.6	1015.5	1014.5	1013.0	1013.3	1013.1	1012.2	1014.3	1016.8	1018.2	1015.3	48
TEMPERATURE (°F)														
Mean	57.1	58.4	59.5	62.1	64.1	66.8	70.7	72.2	71.2	67.4	62.1	57.7	64.1	48
Mean daily maximum	65.4	66.2	66.3	68.4	69.2	71.8	75.9	77.5	77.1	74.2	70.5	66.3	70.8	48
Mean daily minimum	48.3	50.0	52.2	55.3	58.4	61.4	65.1	66.5	64.8	60.2	53.2	48.5	57.0	48
Extreme (highest)	88	90	93	98	96	101	95	98	111	107	97	88	111	48
Extreme (lowest)	29	36	39	44	48	51	55	58	51	43	38	34	29	48
RELATIVE HUMIDITY														
Average percentage	60.5	54.0	41.0	29.7	19.7	5.3	7.7	6.3	-3.2	18.2	43.4	56.6	28.1	48
CLOUD COVER														
Percent of time clear	36.4	33.7	28.2	26.9	22.6	23.6	29.3	30.8	37.2	33.4	42.8	39.1	32.0	48
Percent of time scattered	18.3	17.6	19.5	19.2	17.5	16.7	20.1	20.9	18.8	18.6	18.5	19.8	18.8	48
Percent of time broken	17.7	19.1	21.0	19.8	16.3	12.4	13.6	13.9	12.5	15.3	16.4	17.0	16.2	48
Percent of time overcast	27.6	29.5	31.4	34.1	43.7	47.3	36.9	34.4	31.5	32.8	22.3	24.0	32.9	48
PRECIPITATION (inches)														
Mean amount	2.1	1.6	1.9	0.7	0.1	0.0	0.0	0.0	0.1	0.3	1.1	1.4	9.9	48
Greatest amount	9.0	5.4	6.9	3.7	1.7	0.8	0.2	2.1	1.9	1.7	5.8	6.6	19.4	48
Least amount	T	0.0	T	0.0	0.0	0.0	0.0	0.0	0.0	0.0	0.0	0.0	3.4	48
Maximum amount (24 hours)	2.5	1.7	2.1	1.4	1.4	0.4	0.2	1.4	0.9	1.0	2.0	2.1	2.5	48
Mean number of days	9	8	10	7	7	5	3	2	3	4	6	7	71	48
SNOW														
Mean amount	T	0.0	0.0	0.0	0.0	0.0	0.0	0.0	0.0	0.0	0.0	T	T	48
Greatest amount	T	0.0	0.0	0.0	0.0	0.0	0.0	0.0	0.0	0.0	0.0	T	T	48
Least amount	0.0	0.0	0.0	0.0	0.0	0.0	0.0	0.0	0.0	0.0	0.0	0.0	0.0	48
Maximum amount (24 hours)	T	0.0	0.0	0.0	0.0	0.0	0.0	0.0	0.0	0.0	0.0	T	T	48
Mean number of days	Miss	0.0	0.0	0.0	0.0	0.0	0.0	0.0	0.0	0.0	0.0	Miss	Miss	48
WIND														
Percentage with gales	0.00	0.00	0.00	0.00	0.00	0.00	0.00	0.00	0.00	0.00	0.00	0.00	0.00	48
Mean wind speed (knots)	5.3	5.7	6.6	6.9	7.0	6.8	6.6	6.5	6.3	5.7	5.2	4.9	6.1	48
Direction (percentage of observations)														
North	6.7	6.4	5.5	4.9	3.9	4.5	5.8	6.5	7.0	7.8	7.1	7.4	6.1	48
North Northeast	4.6	4.5	3.8	3.6	3.2	3.2	3.8	4.5	5.5	5.4	5.2	4.9	4.4	48
Northeast	5.5	5.2	4.3	3.4	2.3	2.1	2.1	2.9	3.3	4.8	5.2	5.3	3.9	48
East Northeast	4.9	4.5	3.8	2.7	1.8	1.0	0.7	1.2	1.8	3.5	4.7	4.6	2.9	48
East	4.2	3.9	3.6	2.5	1.3	0.8	0.4	0.7	1.5	2.4	4.4	4.2	2.5	48
East Southeast	4.0	3.8	3.6	2.5	1.5	0.8	0.4	0.5	0.9	1.9	3.7	3.8	2.3	48
Southeast	3.5	3.1	2.6	1.9	1.0	0.7	0.4	0.5	0.8	1.7	2.4	3.3	1.8	48
South Southeast	4.6	3.7	3.3	2.9	2.5	2.2	1.6	1.5	2.2	2.4	3.6	3.5	2.8	48
South	6.0	5.9	6.2	6.6	8.2	8.5	7.2	6.1	5.7	5.1	5.0	5.1	6.3	48
South Southwest	4.6	5.2	6.0	7.4	10.2	10.9	10.3	8.1	6.4	5.4	4.1	4.2	6.9	48
Southwest	4.0	4.3	5.8	7.4	10.0	10.3	9.2	7.5	5.9	5.2	4.1	3.8	6.5	48
West Southwest	3.6	4.5	6.5	7.1	10.5	9.2	7.2	6.9	5.1	4.7	3.8	3.4	6.1	48
West	4.8	5.4	7.4	8.6	9.5	8.2	8.1	7.3	4.5	5.9	4.5	4.3	6.8	48
West Northwest	10.1	11.8	14.7	17.3	16.9	18.1	20.4	21.3	18.3	14.7	11.9	9.6	15.5	48
Northwest	10.4	11.4	10.9	11.6	10.9	12.6	14.5	15.3	17.0	14.0	11.5	10.8	12.6	48
North Northwest	6.6	6.8	5.6	5.5	4.5	5.7	7.0	7.1	8.9	7.8	7.2	7.4	6.7	48
Calm	12.0	10.0	6.7	4.5	2.3	1.8	1.4	1.6	3.5	7.3	11.6	14.6	6.4	48
Direction (mean speed, knots)														
North	4.2	4.3	4.5	4.5	4.5	4.9	4.7	4.6	4.5	4.3	4.1	4.2	4.4	48
North Northeast	4.5	4.6	4.6	4.5	4.6	4.5	4.7	4.5	4.5	4.4	4.2	4.5	4.5	48
Northeast	4.6	4.2	4.3	4.3	4.3	4.1	4.2	4.1	4.3	4.2	4.3	4.7	4.3	48
East Northeast	4.4	4.5	4.4	4.1	4.3	4.1	3.9	3.7	4.0	4.2	4.3	4.6	4.3	48
East	4.1	4.1	4.0	4.1	3.7	3.4	3.1	3.7	3.8	3.8	3.9	4.3	4.0	48
East Southeast	5.2	5.3	5.3	5.4	5.1	4.5	4.1	4.5	4.8	5.4	5.1	5.0	5.1	48
Southeast	6.1	6.4	6.5	6.3	5.9	5.4	4.8	5.6	5.2	5.4	5.7	5.8	6.0	48
South Southeast	7.9	8.3	8.7	7.9	6.9	7.1	6.6	6.7	7.1	6.4	6.9	7.0	7.4	48
South	7.1	8.0	8.0	7.4	7.0	6.9	6.3	6.5	6.6	6.1	6.5	6.2	6.9	48
South Southwest	6.6	6.8	7.7	7.7	7.3	7.4	6.7	6.6	6.4	6.6	6.5	6.1	6.9	48
Southwest	6.2	7.1	7.6	7.6	7.6	7.4	6.9	7.0	6.8	7.0	6.4	5.9	7.1	48
West Southwest	6.5	6.9	7.9	7.9	7.7	7.1	6.6	6.7	6.8	7.0	6.4	5.8	7.1	48
West	6.3	6.9	8.1	7.9	7.6	6.9	6.8	6.7	6.7	7.0	6.2	6.3	7.1	48
West Northwest	7.6	7.9	8.8	8.7	8.1	8.0	7.8	8.0	8.0	7.9	7.7	7.5	8.0	48
Northwest	7.0	7.6	8.0	8.2	8.0	7.5	7.3	7.2	7.3	7.4	7.3	7.0	7.5	48
North Northwest	5.3	5.7	5.8	6.1	6.0	5.8	5.6	5.4	5.7	5.5	5.3	5.4	5.6	48
VISIBILITY														
Mean number of days with fog	11	9	8	6	6	7	6	7	9	11	11	11	102	48

* Sea level pressure is station pressure reduced to sea level
T = trace (not measurable) amount of precipitation
Miss or blank is a missing value
These tables were prepared by the National Climatic Data Center (NCDC), National Environmental Satellite, Data & Information Service (NESDIS), NOAA

CLIMATOLOGICAL DATA – LOS ANGELES, CA (33°56'N, 118°23'W) 100 feet (30.5 m)													
WEATHER ELEMENTS	JAN	FEB	MAR	APR	MAY	JUN	JUL	AUG	SEP	OCT	NOV	DEC	YEAR	YEARS OF RECORD
SEA LEVEL PRESSURE*														
Mean (millibars)	1018.5	1017.8	1016.4	1015.5	1014.3	1013.1	1013.3	1013.1	1012.4	1014.5	1017.0	1018.2	1015.3	44
TEMPERATURE (°F)														
Mean	56.2	57.5	58.1	60.6	62.8	66.0	69.3	70.4	69.7	66.6	61.7	57.3	63.0	49
Mean daily maximum	64.8	65.6	65.4	67.6	69.1	72.0	75.3	76.5	76.3	74.1	70.6	66.2	70.3	49
Mean daily minimum	47.1	48.9	50.3	53.0	56.1	59.5	62.7	63.8	62.6	58.7	52.4	47.9	55.3	49
Extreme (highest)	88	92	95	102	97	104	97	98	110	106	101	94	110	49
Extreme (lowest)	27	34	37	43	45	48	52	51	47	43	38	32	27	49
RELATIVE HUMIDITY														
Average percentage	59.8	52.6	39.1	29.9	17.8	5.6	8.3	6.2	-1.1	20.5	45.3	57.2	28.3	44
CLOUD COVER														
Percent of time clear	33.9	33.2	31.5	34.4	31.3	34.2	36.9	38.4	38.3	35.5	39.1	37.6	35.4	44
Percent of time scattered	19.3	18.5	21.0	20.0	17.8	16.4	20.9	21.1	19.2	20.5	20.7	20.0	19.6	44
Percent of time broken	16.1	16.2	16.6	15.7	13.9	11.9	14.2	13.8	13.0	14.5	15.7	15.4	14.7	44
Percent of time overcast	30.7	32.1	30.9	29.9	36.9	37.5	28.0	26.8	29.5	29.5	24.6	27.0	30.3	44
PRECIPITATION (inches)														
Mean amount	2.8	2.4	1.9	0.7	0.1	0.0	0.0	0.1	0.2	0.2	1.3	1.6	11.8	49
Greatest amount	12.7	11.0	6.3	4.5	2.5	0.7	0.3	2.4	1.9	1.7	7.4	5.7	29.4	49
Least amount	0.0	0.0	0.0	0.0	0.0	0.0	0.0	0.0	0.0	0.0	0.0	0.0	3.1	49
Maximum amount (24 hours)	4.5	3.9	3.1	1.2	1.6	0.7	0.2	2.1	1.6	1.7	5.6	2.8	5.6	49
Mean number of days	8	7	8	6	5	4	2	2	3	4	5	6	60	49
SNOW														
Mean amount	T	0.0	0.0	0.0	0.0	0.0	0.0	0.0	0.0	0.0	0.0	0.0	T	49
Greatest amount	T	0.0	0.0	0.0	0.0	0.0	0.0	0.0	0.0	0.0	0.0	0.0	T	49
Least amount	0.0	0.0	0.0	0.0	0.0	0.0	0.0	0.0	0.0	0.0	0.0	0.0	0.0	49
Maximum amount (24 hours)	T	0.0	0.0	0.0	0.0	0.0	0.0	0.0	0.0	0.0	0.0	0.0	T	49
Mean number of days	Miss	0.0	0.0	0.0	0.0	0.0	0.0	0.0	0.0	0.0	0.0	0.0	Miss	49
WIND														
Percentage with gales	0.00	0.00	0.01	0.00	0.00	0.00	0.00	0.00	0.00	0.00	0.01	0.00	0.00	44
Mean wind speed (knots)	5.8	6.5	7.0	7.4	7.2	6.9	6.7	6.6	6.3	6.0	5.8	5.7	6.5	44
Direction (percentage of observations)														
North	4.7	4.0	3.0	2.1	1.3	0.7	1.1	1.3	1.3	2.5	4.5	5.0	2.6	44
North Northeast	5.5	3.6	2.5	1.3	0.8	0.6	0.6	0.7	1.2	2.0	4.4	5.7	2.4	44
Northeast	7.9	5.6	4.0	2.3	1.4	1.1	0.7	1.0	1.7	3.2	6.3	8.3	3.6	44
East Northeast	9.6	7.3	6.2	4.8	3.2	2.0	1.5	1.6	2.6	5.2	8.4	9.3	5.1	44
East	11.5	10.5	8.8	7.5	5.8	4.2	3.3	3.7	5.3	8.0	10.5	11.1	7.5	44
East Southeast	8.0	7.8	6.2	5.9	4.3	4.0	3.2	3.1	4.5	6.2	7.6	8.2	5.7	44
Southeast	4.1	4.8	4.3	4.0	3.7	4.1	3.3	3.3	3.9	4.1	3.8	3.8	3.9	44
South Southeast	2.2	2.4	2.4	2.3	2.3	2.5	2.2	2.0	2.5	2.2	2.2	2.0	2.3	44
South	2.0	2.5	2.2	2.7	2.4	2.7	2.9	2.5	3.2	2.3	2.0	1.6	2.4	44
South Southwest	1.8	2.0	2.2	2.0	2.2	2.2	2.0	2.3	2.3	1.8	1.6	1.5	2.0	44
Southwest	3.9	5.2	6.3	7.4	9.2	9.8	8.3	8.5	7.4	6.5	4.3	3.3	6.7	44
West Southwest	12.2	15.7	21.6	26.6	31.7	33.9	34.8	33.7	29.4	23.4	14.9	11.3	24.1	44
West	11.0	13.4	16.7	19.3	21.3	20.9	23.3	22.7	20.5	17.5	13.4	10.9	17.6	44
West Northwest	3.1	3.1	3.7	3.6	3.5	3.6	3.8	3.7	3.2	3.7	3.0	3.0	3.4	44
Northwest	2.3	2.0	1.7	1.7	1.2	1.3	2.0	1.9	1.7	1.6	2.0	2.7	1.8	44
North Northwest	3.0	3.0	2.4	2.0	0.9	0.9	1.2	1.4	1.3	1.8	3.0	4.0	2.1	44
Calm	7.4	7.1	6.0	4.7	5.0	5.7	5.9	6.7	8.0	8.3	8.1	8.4	6.8	44
Direction (mean speed, knots)														
North	6.3	6.9	6.3	5.9	4.2	3.1	3.3	3.6	3.5	4.8	5.8	6.5	5.7	44
North Northeast	5.5	6.1	5.1	4.7	4.7	3.9	3.6	4.2	4.3	5.0	5.3	5.8	5.3	44
Northeast	5.4	5.5	5.2	5.2	4.5	4.3	3.9	3.7	4.3	4.9	5.2	5.4	5.2	44
East Northeast	5.4	5.2	5.0	5.1	4.7	4.4	4.3	4.5	4.4	4.7	5.0	5.2	5.0	44
East	5.4	5.4	5.3	5.0	4.8	4.6	4.5	4.4	4.6	4.5	5.0	5.1	5.0	44
East Southeast	5.3	5.7	5.4	5.2	5.1	5.0	4.7	4.9	4.9	4.5	5.1	5.1	5.1	44
Southeast	5.8	5.9	6.0	5.5	5.4	5.2	5.1	4.9	4.9	4.8	5.2	5.3	5.4	44
South Southeast	5.3	5.8	5.7	5.6	5.0	4.9	4.8	4.6	4.5	4.3	5.0	5.2	5.1	44
South	5.4	5.9	5.1	5.1	4.5	4.4	4.3	4.2	4.3	4.2	4.6	5.0	4.7	44
South Southwest	7.1	8.4	7.0	6.6	5.9	5.3	4.8	5.0	5.2	5.2	6.4	6.1	6.0	44
Southwest	6.9	7.4	7.9	7.6	7.6	7.2	6.9	6.6	6.8	6.6	6.7	6.4	7.1	44
West Southwest	7.6	8.3	9.2	9.2	8.9	8.6	8.4	8.4	8.4	8.1	7.7	7.4	8.5	44
West	8.1	8.9	9.8	9.9	9.1	8.6	8.3	8.4	8.3	8.4	8.2	7.8	8.7	44
West Northwest	7.1	7.5	8.3	8.3	7.4	6.6	5.9	6.0	6.3	6.5	7.4	6.9	7.0	44
Northwest	7.1	7.8	6.9	6.6	5.4	4.7	4.5	4.4	4.8	5.1	7.0	7.3	6.1	44
North Northwest	7.3	10.0	8.7	9.5	5.9	4.4	4.1	4.0	4.3	6.3	7.9	8.5	7.5	44
VISIBILITY														
Mean number of days with fog	11	10	8	7	6	6	7	8	9	11	11	11	105	49

* Sea level pressure is station pressure reduced to sea level
T = trace (not measurable) amount of precipitation
Miss or blank is a missing value
These tables were prepared by the National Climatic Data Center (NCDC), National Environmental Satellite, Data & Information Service (NESDIS), NOAA

CLIMATOLOGICAL DATA – SAN FRANCISCO, CA (37°37'N, 122°23'W) 8 feet (2.4 m)

WEATHER ELEMENTS	JAN	FEB	MAR	APR	MAY	JUN	JUL	AUG	SEP	OCT	NOV	DEC	YEAR	YEARS OF RECORD
SEA LEVEL PRESSURE*														
Mean (millibars)	1020.1	1019.3	1018.0	1017.5	1016.1	1014.5	1014.7	1014.7	1014.1	1016.6	1019.0	1020.3	1017.1	43
TEMPERATURE (°F)														
Mean	48.9	51.9	53.5	55.7	58.3	61.4	62.7	63.4	64.1	61.1	55.0	49.7	57.2	50
Mean daily maximum	55.6	59.1	60.8	63.7	66.4	69.9	71.3	71.9	73.3	70.2	62.9	56.2	65.2	50
Mean daily minimum	41.6	44.3	45.7	47.2	49.7	52.4	53.7	54.5	54.3	51.5	46.7	42.6	48.7	50
Extreme (highest)	72	77	85	92	97	106	105	100	103	99	85	75	106	50
Extreme (lowest)	26	30	31	36	39	43	44	45	41	37	31	24	24	50
RELATIVE HUMIDITY														
Average percentage	75.6	67.7	55.4	49.8	36.0	20.2	21.7	22.3	15.5	40.8	64.8	77.8	45.6	43
CLOUD COVER														
Percent of time clear	25.7	28.8	26.6	31.5	36.8	43.1	49.8	44.8	50.3	43.8	32.6	27.6	36.8	43
Percent of time scattered	16.3	16.2	19.0	20.4	20.6	20.1	19.6	20.6	17.7	18.4	18.0	16.6	18.6	43
Percent of time broken	17.1	18.2	21.0	20.2	18.1	14.3	13.7	15.1	14.1	16.1	18.8	17.0	17.0	43
Percent of time overcast	40.8	36.8	33.3	27.9	24.6	22.5	16.9	19.5	17.9	21.7	30.5	38.8	27.6	43
PRECIPITATION (inches)														
Mean amount	4.2	3.1	3.0	1.2	0.3	0.1	0.0	0.0	0.2	1.0	2.3	3.4	19.2	50
Greatest amount	11.2	9.5	9.0	6.3	3.8	0.8	0.3	0.6	2.3	7.3	7.9	12.3	38.3	50
Least amount	0.2	T	0.0	T	T	T	0.0	T	T	T	T	0.0	8.6	50
Maximum amount (24 hours)	5.5	2.2	1.9	2.3	1.5	0.8	0.3	0.3	2.2	2.6	2.3	3.1	5.5	50
Mean number of days	14	12	15	11	9	7	6	8	6	8	11	13	120	50
SNOW														
Mean amount	0.0	T	T	0.0	0.0	0.0	0.0	0.0	0.0	0.0	0.0	T	0.0	50
Greatest amount	1.5	T	T	0.0	0.0	0.0	0.0	0.0	0.0	0.0	0.0	T	1.5	50
Least amount	0.0	0.0	0.0	0.0	0.0	0.0	0.0	0.0	0.0	0.0	0.0	0.0	0.0	50
Maximum amount (24 hours)	1.5	T	T	0.0	0.0	0.0	0.0	0.0	0.0	0.0	0.0	T	1.5	50
Mean number of days	Miss	Miss	Miss	0	0	0	0	0	0	0	0	Miss	Miss	50
WIND														
Percentage with gales	0.08	0.06	0.04	0.04	0.08	0.04	0.03	0.00	0.00	0.02	0.04	0.12	0.09	43
Mean wind speed (knots)	6.7	7.7	9.4	10.8	11.8	12.0	11.7	11.0	9.8	8.3	6.9	6.8	9.4	43
Direction (percentage of observations)														
North	4.3	3.3	2.5	1.5	0.8	1.0	1.0	0.9	1.3	2.2	3.5	4.7	2.2	43
North Northeast	5.6	3.8	2.3	1.3	1.0	1.2	1.2	1.1	1.9	2.7	3.2	5.0	2.5	43
Northeast	6.0	4.2	2.7	1.8	1.6	1.7	1.8	1.7	2.6	3.7	4.7	5.7	3.2	43
East Northeast	5.8	4.1	2.4	1.8	1.5	1.1	1.1	1.3	1.9	2.7	4.1	6.4	2.8	43
East	5.4	4.1	2.4	1.1	0.7	0.5	0.3	0.4	1.0	1.9	3.6	5.8	2.3	43
East Southeast	6.5	4.5	2.2	0.9	0.5	0.3	0.2	0.2	0.4	1.5	4.4	6.4	2.3	43
Southeast	9.4	6.6	4.2	2.0	0.7	0.5	0.2	0.3	0.7	2.2	6.6	8.9	3.5	43
South Southeast	6.8	5.2	3.9	2.2	1.1	0.5	0.2	0.5	1.0	2.6	5.4	6.9	3.0	43
South	7.2	6.2	5.5	3.7	2.4	1.4	0.8	1.2	2.3	4.2	6.5	7.4	4.1	43
South Southwest	5.1	5.4	4.7	3.8	2.9	2.4	1.0	1.5	2.3	3.6	5.0	4.5	3.5	43
Southwest	4.1	4.6	5.4	4.7	4.3	2.8	2.2	2.2	3.6	3.9	4.5	3.9	3.8	43
West Southwest	3.8	5.1	6.2	7.3	8.9	8.8	6.3	6.5	6.4	5.1	4.1	3.4	6.0	43
West	5.5	8.8	14.5	20.0	24.7	26.5	18.3	19.2	16.2	12.8	7.1	4.9	14.9	43
West Northwest	8.9	17.3	26.4	33.5	33.6	33.3	33.5	32.1	32.5	28.6	17.6	9.5	25.6	43
Northwest	3.7	6.5	7.9	9.9	12.0	15.0	26.7	25.3	20.2	13.3	7.5	4.4	12.7	43
North Northwest	1.5	2.0	1.8	1.2	1.0	1.5	3.1	3.1	2.5	1.8	1.7	1.7	1.9	43
Calm	10.9	8.2	5.0	3.5	2.8	2.1	2.7	3.0	3.8	7.5	10.6	10.6	5.9	43
Direction (mean speed, knots)														
North	7.6	8.1	8.3	8.2	6.2	5.5	6.4	6.5	6.7	8.9	7.3	8.5	7.8	43
North Northeast	6.4	6.7	7.8	7.1	6.8	7.0	6.7	6.8	6.3	6.6	6.5	7.0	6.8	43
Northeast	6.2	6.0	6.1	5.9	6.3	6.8	7.1	6.8	6.1	5.7	6.0	6.4	6.2	43
East Northeast	6.1	6.0	5.6	5.7	5.9	5.8	6.0	5.9	5.6	5.3	6.0	6.6	6.0	43
East	6.0	5.5	5.9	5.5	5.1	4.9	5.2	5.3	5.4	5.4	5.6	5.8	5.7	43
East Southeast	6.3	6.4	7.4	7.6	5.3	4.5	4.1	6.0	5.9	6.1	6.4	6.2	6.4	43
Southeast	7.6	8.0	8.9	9.1	6.5	5.7	5.8	5.8	5.9	7.1	7.2	7.5	7.6	43
South Southeast	7.1	7.1	7.8	8.3	7.1	7.4	5.8	5.7	5.6	6.8	6.7	6.8	7.1	43
South	8.0	8.4	8.7	8.6	7.0	6.2	5.9	5.3	5.6	6.9	6.7	7.4	7.5	43
South Southwest	8.8	9.8	9.0	9.1	10.0	8.9	8.3	7.6	7.4	6.7	7.0	8.2	8.5	43
Southwest	8.4	8.3	8.1	9.1	10.1	10.1	9.3	8.3	7.9	6.8	7.3	8.2	8.4	43
West Southwest	8.0	7.8	8.5	9.2	10.2	10.6	10.3	9.7	8.4	7.3	7.1	8.2	9.1	43
West	8.3	9.9	11.2	12.7	13.9	13.8	13.0	12.3	11.3	10.0	8.5	8.3	12.0	43
West Northwest	9.3	10.7	12.4	13.1	13.8	13.5	12.7	12.0	11.4	10.8	9.9	9.4	12.0	43
Northwest	8.2	9.4	10.5	11.4	11.9	12.3	12.8	12.4	11.5	10.3	8.9	9.0	11.4	43
North Northwest	7.1	7.7	8.1	8.0	8.0	8.7	10.0	9.9	9.2	8.3	7.0	8.5	8.6	43
VISIBILITY														
Mean number of days with fog	17	12	7	4	4	3	4	4	6	9	12	17	99	50

* Sea level pressure is station pressure reduced to sea level
T = trace (not measurable) amount of precipitation
Miss or blank is a missing value
These tables were prepared by the National Climatic Data Center (NCDC), National Environmental Satellite, Data & Information Service (NESDIS), NOAA

CLIMATOLOGICAL DATA – SACRAMENTO, CA (38°31'N, 121°30'W) 18 feet (5.5 m)														
WEATHER ELEMENTS	JAN	FEB	MAR	APR	MAY	JUN	JUL	AUG	SEP	OCT	NOV	DEC	YEAR	YEARS OF RECORD
SEA LEVEL PRESSURE*														
Mean (millibars)	1020.7	1019.1	1017.2	1015.9	1014.0	1012.0	1011.8	1012.2	1012.2	1015.3	1019.0	1020.7	1015.8	47
TEMPERATURE (°F)														
Mean	45.7	50.7	53.8	58.8	65.2	71.5	75.6	74.8	71.8	64.4	53.4	45.8	61.0	48
Mean daily maximum	53.0	59.8	64.1	71.4	79.8	87.3	92.9	91.5	87.5	77.9	63.6	53.2	73.6	48
Mean daily minimum	37.8	41.0	43.0	45.8	50.2	55.1	57.9	57.6	55.7	50.3	42.7	37.9	48.0	48
Extreme (highest)	70	76	88	93	105	115	114	109	108	101	87	72	115	48
Extreme (lowest)	20	23	26	32	34	41	48	48	43	35	26	18	18	48
RELATIVE HUMIDITY														
Average percentage	82.2	66.1	47.0	34.1	14.6	-5.4	-6.7	-2.5	-3.4	28.3	65.2	82.5	33.3	48
CLOUD COVER														
Percent of time clear	22.8	31.4	34.1	39.2	46.9	63.3	78.5	76.3	71.1	55.2	38	22.3	48.5	47
Percent of time scattered	12.9	16.4	18.6	19.8	21.5	19.0	13.1	13.7	15.2	18.5	17.6	14.1	16.7	47
Percent of time broken	12.4	16.3	17.4	18.7	17.5	11.4	6.3	7.4	8.7	12.3	14.4	12.4	12.8	47
Percent of time overcast	51.9	35.9	29.9	22.3	14.1	6.3	2.1	2.5	5.0	13.9	29.9	51.2	22.0	47
PRECIPITATION (inches)														
Mean amount	3.7	2.8	2.5	1.2	0.4	0.1	0.0	0.0	0.3	0.9	2.2	2.8	17.3	48
Greatest amount	9.6	8.7	8.1	4.2	3.1	1.2	0.7	0.6	2.7	7.5	7.4	12.6	33.4	48
Least amount	0.1	0.1	0.0	0.0	0.0	0.0	0.0	0.0	0.0	0.0	T	0.0	5.5	48
Maximum amount (24 hours)	3.0	2.6	1.8	2.1	1.5	1.1	0.7	0.6	1.7	3.7	2.4	2.8	3.7	48
Mean number of days	13	11	11	7	4	2	1	1	2	5	9	12	78	49
SNOW														
Mean amount	T	0.0	T	T	0.0	0.0	0.0	0.0	0.0	0.0	0.0	T	0.0	48
Greatest amount	T	2.0	T	T	0.0	0.0	0.0	0.0	0.0	0.0	0.0	T	2.0	48
Least amount	0.0	0.0	0.0	0.0	0.0	0.0	0.0	0.0	0.0	0.0	0.0	0.0	0.0	48
Maximum amount (24 hours)	T	2.0	T	T	0.0	0.0	0.0	0.0	0.0	0.0	0.0	T	2.0	48
Mean number of days	Miss	Miss	0	0	0	0	0	0	0	0	0	Miss	Miss	49
WIND														
Percentage with gales	0.15	0.05	0.05	0.01	0.01	0.00	0.00	0.01	0.02	0.02	0.03	0.09	0.04	48
Mean wind speed (knots)	6.2	6.5	7.4	7.5	7.9	8.4	7.8	7.4	6.4	5.6	5.3	5.8	6.8	48
Direction (percentage of observations)														
North	5.9	5.1	3.7	3.0	2.8	2.0	0.9	1.2	3.2	5.3	5.8	5.8	3.7	48
North Northeast	1.8	1.6	1.3	0.7	0.6	0.4	0.4	0.3	0.8	1.4	1.6	2.1	1.1	48
Northeast	1.8	1.7	1.1	0.8	0.6	0.4	0.2	0.2	0.6	1.3	1.7	1.7	1.0	48
East Northeast	1.4	1.4	0.8	0.7	0.4	0.3	0.1	0.1	0.6	0.8	1.2	1.6	0.8	48
East	3.5	3.2	2.3	1.8	1.0	0.6	0.4	0.4	1.0	2.0	2.9	3.5	1.9	48
East Southeast	5.7	5.2	4.6	3.5	2.1	1.7	1.5	1.7	2.3	3.8	4.6	5.3	3.5	48
Southeast	13.5	11.1	10.0	7.9	6.1	5.0	5.7	6.5	7.1	7.2	9.4	11.5	8.4	48
South Southeast	11.6	10.2	9.2	7.1	6.4	7.8	10.0	9.9	8.0	6.3	8.0	10.9	8.8	48
South	7.0	8.3	9.6	10.2	12.3	14.6	18.3	17.5	12.1	8.3	6.1	6.3	10.9	48
South Southwest	3.4	5.3	9.5	12.6	17.7	21.2	25.0	23.2	15.7	8.4	4.0	2.9	12.5	48
Southwest	2.8	4.8	10.8	16.1	20.5	21.9	21.3	19.7	15.6	9.2	3.8	2.7	12.5	48
West Southwest	1.6	2.2	3.8	4.9	4.8	4.2	4.5	5.0	4.0	3.5	2.1	1.4	3.5	48
West	2.0	2.9	2.9	3.0	2.8	2.5	2.3	2.7	2.8	2.5	2.0	2.1	2.5	48
West Northwest	3.0	3.6	3.8	3.6	3.2	2.8	2.2	2.2	3.1	3.0	3.3	2.8	3.0	48
Northwest	7.4	8.4	8.2	7.9	6.7	5.4	2.5	2.6	5.0	7.7	9.0	8.2	6.6	48
North Northwest	10.1	9.9	9.0	8.8	6.6	5.4	1.7	1.9	6.6	10.2	11.6	11.0	7.7	48
Calm	17.9	15.3	10.0	8.0	6.0	4.5	3.7	5.4	11.3	19.3	23.1	20.3	12.1	48
Direction (mean speed, knots)														
North	6.9	7.1	8.2	7.8	8.0	7.3	5.6	5.4	6.7	6.8	6.8	6.6	7.0	48
North Northeast	5.4	5.5	6.1	6.6	6.0	6.9	4.5	5.2	5.1	5.6	5.5	5.6	5.6	48
Northeast	4.6	4.5	4.4	4.9	5.0	5.4	4.2	4.2	4.4	4.5	4.3	4.3	4.5	48
East Northeast	4.3	4.7	5.2	4.9	4.8	4.9	5.3	4.3	4.4	4.4	4.3	4.5	4.6	48
East	4.4	4.4	4.7	4.7	4.0	4.6	3.8	3.8	4.4	4.2	4.4	4.4	4.4	48
East Southeast	5.7	5.7	5.7	5.4	5.1	5.2	4.6	4.9	4.8	4.7	5.0	5.6	5.3	48
Southeast	8.4	8.1	7.8	6.6	5.9	5.8	5.8	5.7	5.7	5.8	7.2	7.9	7.0	48
South Southeast	10.1	9.6	8.8	7.5	6.5	6.4	6.3	6.5	6.1	6.7	8.3	9.9	7.9	48
South	7.4	7.2	7.4	7.1	7.4	8.0	7.5	7.4	6.6	6.2	6.4	6.8	7.2	48
South Southwest	7.8	8.2	8.6	9.1	9.6	10.1	9.4	9.1	8.5	7.9	7.7	7.2	9.0	48
Southwest	7.4	8.5	9.3	9.3	10.0	10.5	9.8	9.4	9.0	8.4	7.4	7.0	9.4	48
West Southwest	6.0	6.4	7.2	7.6	7.9	8.0	7.3	6.9	6.5	6.4	5.3	5.7	7.0	48
West	5.0	4.5	5.8	5.8	5.7	5.9	5.6	5.6	5.1	4.6	4.4	4.4	5.2	48
West Northwest	5.6	6.1	7.0	7.5	7.0	7.0	6.2	6.1	5.5	5.6	5.6	5.5	6.3	48
Northwest	7.3	8.3	9.6	9.6	9.0	8.8	6.8	6.7	7.2	7.3	7.3	7.3	8.1	48
North Northwest	8.7	9.8	10.5	10.6	9.8	9.6	7.0	6.8	8.4	9.1	8.3	8.7	9.2	48
VISIBILITY														
Mean number of days with fog	22	14	8	3	1	Miss	Miss	1	2	7	16	22	96	49

* Sea level pressure is station pressure reduced to sea level
T = trace (not measurable) amount of precipitation
Miss or blank is a missing value
These tables were prepared by the National Climatic Data Center (NCDC), National Environmental Satellite, Data & Information Service (NESDIS), NOAA

CLIMATOLOGICAL DATA – EUREKA, CA (40°48'N, 124°07'W) 59 feet (18 m)

WEATHER ELEMENTS	JAN	FEB	MAR	APR	MAY	JUN	JUL	AUG	SEP	OCT	NOV	DEC	YEAR	YEARS OF RECORD
TEMPERATURE (°F)														
Mean	48.0	49.3	49.4	50.6	53.2	55.7	57.0	58.0	57.4	55.0	51.8	48.7	52.9	47
Mean daily maximum	54.1	55.3	55.2	56.0	58.1	60.2	61.4	62.4	62.8	60.9	58	54.9	58.3	47
Mean daily minimum	41.4	42.8	43.2	44.7	47.8	50.6	52.2	53.1	51.6	48.6	45.1	42.1	46.9	47
Extreme (highest)	78	80	76	80	82	81	76	82	86	87	78	77	87	47
Extreme (lowest)	26	27	30	34	36	41	46	47	42	32	29	21	21	47
PRECIPITATION (inches)														
Mean amount	6.6	5.0	5.3	2.8	1.6	0.6	0.1	0.3	0.7	2.7	5.6	6.4	38.1	47
Greatest amount	13.9	10.8	11.1	10.6	6.0	2.5	1.1	3.4	3.3	13.0	16.5	14.1	67.2	47
Least amount	0.6	0.1	1.1	0.3	0.0	T	0.0	T	T	0.0	0.2	0.5	21.0	47
Maximum amount (24 hours)	3.7	4.8	2.9	2.3	1.4	1.1	0.8	1.5	1.4	5.0	2.7	3.3	5.0	47
Mean number of days	17	16	19	14	12	9	7	7	8	12	15	16	152	32
SNOW														
Mean amount	0.1	0.1	0.0	T	0.0	0.0	0.0	0.0	0.0	0.0	0.0	0.1	0.4	47
Greatest amount	2.8	3.5	1.0	T	0.0	0.0	0.0	0.0	0.0	0.0	0.1	1.9	3.5	47
Least amount	0.0	0.0	0.0	0.0	0.0	0.0	0.0	0.0	0.0	0.0	0.0	0.0	0.0	47
Maximum amount (24 hours)	1.5	2.0	0.9	T	0.0	0.0	0.0	0.0	0.0	0.0	0.1	1.9	2.0	47
Mean number of days	1	1	Miss	Miss	0	0	0	0	0	0	0	Miss	2	32
VISIBILITY														
Mean number of days with fog	13	11	10	12	13	16	22	23	21	21	15	15	192	32

* Sea level pressure is station pressure reduced to sea level
T = trace (not measurable) amount of precipitation
Miss or blank is a missing value
These tables were prepared by the National Climatic Data Center (NCDC), National Environmental Satellite, Data & Information Service (NESDIS), NOAA

CLIMATOLOGICAL DATA – SEATTLE (PORTAGE BAY), WA (47°39'N, 122°18'W) 20 feet (6.1 m)

WEATHER ELEMENTS	JAN	FEB	MAR	APR	MAY	JUN	JUL	AUG	SEP	OCT	NOV	DEC	YEAR	YEARS OF RECORD
TEMPERATURE (°F)														
Mean	41.1	43.7	46.5	51.0	56.5	61.1	65.2	65.0	60.7	53.8	46.8	42.7	52.9	92
Mean daily maximum	45.3	48.9	52.7	58.3	64.3	69.0	74.1	73.5	68.1	59.6	51.4	46.7	59.4	92
Mean daily minimum	36.4	38.0	39.8	43.2	48.3	52.7	55.8	56.1	52.8	47.5	41.7	38.2	45.9	92
Extreme (highest)	67	70	76	87	92	100	100	97	92	82	73	65	100	92
Extreme (lowest)	0	1	22	30	35	40	44	46	36	19	0	9	0	92
PRECIPITATION (inches)														
Mean amount	5.0	3.7	3.2	2.1	1.6	1.4	0.6	0.8	1.6	2.9	5.1	5.3	33.9	92
Greatest amount	10.9	8.1	7.2	5.2	4.6	3.7	2.1	5.4	5.6	8.0	11.2	15.3	48.1	92
Least amount	0.6	0.3	0.4	0.1	0.3	0.0	0.0	T	0.0	0.1	0.5	1.0	19.5	92
Maximum amount (24 hours)	4.2	2.2	2.5	2.0	1.1	1.4	0.9	1.5	1.7	2.5	2.6	3.4	4.2	92
Mean number of days	28	25	27	24	23	23	17	19	20	25	26	28	285	25
SNOW														
Mean amount	4.0	1.9	0.6	0.1	0.0	0.0	0.0	0.0	0.0	T	0.6	1.4	8.5	92
Greatest amount	31.0	35.4	8.6	2.4	0.0	0.0	0.0	0.0	0.0	T	9.6	13.5	63.6	92
Least amount	0.0	0.0	0.0	0.0	0.0	0.0	0.0	0.0	0.0	0.0	0.0	0.0	0.0	92
Maximum amount (24 hours)	11.5	21.5	5.5	1.5	0.0	0.0	0.0	0.0	0.0	T	6.0	10.0	21.5	92
Mean number of days	7	4	3	1	0	0	0	0	0	Miss	1	3	19	25
VISIBILITY														
Mean number of days with fog	3	2	1	1	1	1	1	3	4	3	3	3	26	25

* Sea level pressure is station pressure reduced to sea level
T = trace (not measurable) amount of precipitation
Miss or blank is a missing value
These tables were prepared by the National Climatic Data Center (NCDC), National Environmental Satellite, Data & Information Service (NESDIS), NOAA

CLIMATOLOGICAL DATA – PORTLAND, OR (45°36'N, 122°36'W) 21 feet (6.4 m)														
WEATHER ELEMENTS	JAN	FEB	MAR	APR	MAY	JUN	JUL	AUG	SEP	OCT	NOV	DEC	YEAR	YEARS OF RECORD
SEA LEVEL PRESSURE*														
Mean (millibars)	1019.4	1018.2	1016.9	1018.0	1017.5	1017.3	1017.5	1016.7	1016.6	1018.1	1018.8	1019.4	1017.9	47
TEMPERATURE (°F)														
Mean	39.5	43.3	47.5	52.0	57.9	63.4	68.3	68.4	63.6	55.1	46.2	41.4	53.9	62
Mean daily maximum	44.7	50.0	55.6	61.2	67.7	73.2	79.5	79.5	74.5	64.0	52.4	46.3	62.5	62
Mean daily minimum	33.8	36.1	38.9	42.3	47.6	53.0	56.6	56.7	52.3	45.7	39.5	36.0	44.9	62
Extreme (highest)	65	71	83	90	100	102	107	107	105	92	73	65	107	62
Extreme (lowest)	-2	-3	19	29	29	39	43	44	34	26	13	6	-3	62
RELATIVE HUMIDITY														
Average percentage	69.2	56.9	43.5	55.1	50.5	48.1	49.5	42.3	40.6	55.7	62.8	68.6	53.7	47
CLOUD COVER														
Percent of time clear	11.6	11.3	10.2	12.1	14.0	19.0	37.8	33.4	33.9	18.9	10.4	7.9	18.4	47
Percent of time scattered	8.6	10.5	12.2	13.8	15.9	17.1	17.2	19.1	17.6	15.4	10.4	9.1	13.9	47
Percent of time broken	12.9	15.8	19.2	21.0	22.9	21.5	16.3	16.5	16.8	18.1	15.9	14.4	17.6	47
Percent of time overcast	66.8	62.4	58.4	53.2	47.2	42.3	28.8	31.0	31.7	47.5	63.3	68.5	50.2	47
PRECIPITATION (inches)														
Mean amount	5.3	4.0	3.7	2.4	2.0	1.5	0.5	0.8	1.6	3.0	5.3	6.5	37.3	62
Greatest amount	12.8	11.4	8.1	6.2	4.3	4.0	2.6	4.5	4.3	8.4	14.4	17.4	55.4	62
Least amount	0.0	0.6	1.1	0.5	0.1	0.0	0.0	T	T	0.1	0.3	1.3	22.4	62
Maximum amount (24 hours)	2.4	1.8	2.0	1.8	1.4	1.9	1.0	1.4	2.2	2.4	2.4	3.9	2.4	62
Mean number of days	22	19	21	19	16	13	7	8	11	16	21	23	196	48
SNOW														
Mean amount	3.3	1.3	0.5	T	T	0.0	0.0	0.0	0.0	0.0	0.5	1.5	7.0	48
Greatest amount	41.4	13.2	12.9	T	T	0.0	0.0	0.0	0.0	0.0	8.2	15.7	44.3	48
Least amount	0.0	0.0	0.0	0.0	0.0	0.0	0.0	0.0	0.0	0.0	0.0	0.0	T	48
Maximum amount (24 hours)	9.3	6.1	7.6	T	T	0.0	0.0	0.0	0.0	0.0	7.0	8.0	9.3	48
Mean number of days	6	3	2	1	Miss	0	0	0	0	0	1	4	17	48
WIND														
Percentage with gales	0.04	0.04	0.02	0.01	0.00	0.00	0.00	0.00	0.00	0.00	0.02	0.03	0.09	47
Mean wind speed (knots)	8.6	8.0	7.2	6.4	6.2	6.2	6.6	6.1	5.7	5.7	7.5	8.4	6.9	47
Direction (percentage of observations)														
North	1.3	1.6	2.6	3.8	5.7	8.2	9.6	8.2	5.3	2.9	1.5	1.5	4.4	47
North Northeast	0.8	0.8	1.1	1.2	2.0	2.2	2.7	2.4	2.1	1.3	0.8	0.9	1.5	47
Northeast	1.0	1.0	1.1	2.0	1.8	1.8	1.7	1.8	1.5	1.3	1.0	0.9	1.4	47
East Northeast	2.1	2.1	2.4	2.3	2.2	1.8	1.6	1.5	2.0	1.5	1.3	1.5	1.8	47
East	8.3	7.5	6.1	4.8	3.7	2.4	1.7	1.8	3.8	4.2	5.1	6.8	4.7	47
East Southeast	25.4	22.7	15.0	8.5	4.8	3.4	1.8	2.5	6.2	12.5	20.6	24.8	12.3	47
Southeast	13.7	12.0	7.6	4.4	3.0	1.8	1.1	2.3	4.4	8.6	12.8	14.3	7.1	47
South Southeast	3.8	3.5	3.6	3.1	2.3	1.9	1.4	1.8	2.9	4.1	4.8	3.9	3.1	47
South	8.1	7.6	8.5	7.9	5.8	5.1	2.7	3.8	5.0	7.1	9.0	7.8	6.5	47
South Southwest	8.6	9.3	9.6	7.9	5.6	4.9	2.1	2.8	4.6	6.2	8.8	9.0	6.6	47
Southwest	1.2	4.4	5.1	5.2	4.2	3.0	1.6	2.1	3.4	3.9	4.5	4.5	3.8	47
West Southwest	2.6	2.5	4.0	4.6	3.9	2.9	2.3	2.1	3.7	3.6	3.1	2.7	3.2	47
West	2.8	3.5	4.8	5.7	5.7	5.2	4.5	4.8	6.4	5.8	4.1	3.0	4.7	47
West Northwest	3.7	4.8	7.2	9.6	12.0	11.6	12.3	12.4	11.8	8.2	5.0	3.5	8.5	47
Northwest	2.9	3.8	6.0	10.6	16.0	19.2	25.2	23.7	15.1	8.4	4.3	3.1	11.6	47
North Northwest	1.5	2.0	3.6	6.9	12.1	16.1	22.1	18.6	10.2	5.0	2.1	1.9	8.6	47
Calm	9.5	11.2	11.7	11.6	9.4	8.7	6	7.7	11.8	15.6	11.6	10.1	10.4	47
Direction (mean speed, knots)														
North	3.8	3.9	4.8	5.1	5.6	6.2	6.0	5.7	5.3	4.8	4.5	4.2	5.5	47
North Northeast	4.4	4.4	4.7	4.7	4.8	5.0	4.9	4.8	5.0	4.8	4.6	4.8	4.8	47
Northeast	4.7	4.7	4.9	4.6	4.8	4.7	4.8	4.7	5.6	4.6	4.5	5.0	4.8	47
East Northeast	9.3	6.9	6.2	5.8	5.6	5.3	5.6	5.8	8.1	6.5	6.7	7.3	6.6	47
East	11.6	9.9	8.2	7.0	5.6	4.9	5.3	5.1	8.6	8.0	10.4	11.1	8.9	47
East Southeast	10.6	9.9	8.6	7.3	6.4	5.7	5.8	5.9	6.7	8.0	10	10.8	9.3	47
Southeast	9.1	9.2	8.1	6.5	6.0	5.8	5.9	5.4	5.6	6.8	8.3	9.0	8.0	47
South Southeast	7.6	8.0	7.6	6.8	6.8	6.1	6.3	5.8	5.6	6.3	7.0	7.1	6.9	47
South	10.5	9.9	9.6	8.7	7.6	6.8	6.6	6.4	6.6	7.9	9.4	9.9	8.7	47
South Southwest	12.4	12.4	11.4	10.1	8.6	8.5	8.5	7.6	8.4	9.5	11.1	12.3	10.7	47
Southwest	10.2	10.6	10.0	9.0	8.2	7.9	7.3	7.2	6.8	7.3	9.0	9.9	8.9	47
West Southwest	7.4	7.6	7.8	7.4	7.1	7.1	6.3	5.9	5.6	5.2	6.4	6.8	6.7	47
West	4.9	5.7	6.2	6.3	6.1	6.0	5.6	5.5	5.0	4.7	5.1	5.3	5.5	47
West Northwest	5.5	6.0	6.6	6.8	6.8	7.0	7.1	6.7	6.3	5.6	5.8	5.6	6.5	47
Northwest	5.7	6.2	6.8	7.0	7.2	7.3	7.6	7.2	6.7	6.0	5.8	6.0	7.0	47
North Northwest	5.6	5.3	6.2	6.9	7.2	7.5	7.8	7.4	6.9	6.2	5.5	5.7	7.2	47
VISIBILITY														
Mean number of days with fog	15	12	9	7	5	4	3	5	12	18	17	16	123	48

* Sea level pressure is station pressure reduced to sea level
T = trace (not measurable) amount of precipitation
Miss or blank is a missing value
These tables were prepared by the National Climatic Data Center (NCDC), National Environmental Satellite, Data & Information Service (NESDIS), NOAA

CLIMATOLOGICAL DATA – ASTORIA, OR (46°09'N, 123°53'W) 8 feet (2.4 m)

WEATHER ELEMENTS	JAN	FEB	MAR	APR	MAY	JUN	JUL	AUG	SEP	OCT	NOV	DEC	YEAR	YEARS OF RECORD
SEA LEVEL PRESSURE*														
Mean (millibars)	1017.6	1017.5	1015.9	1018.0	1018.0	1018.1	1018.9	1018.0	1017.3	1017.7	1017.2	1018.1	1017.7	43
TEMPERATURE (°F)														
Mean	42.3	44.4	45.7	48.3	52.8	57.1	60.3	60.9	58.7	52.9	46.9	43.0	51.2	43
Mean daily maximum	47.9	51.0	53.0	55.8	60.4	64.1	67.6	68.7	67.7	61.2	53.4	48.6	58.3	43
Mean daily minimum	36.2	37.3	37.8	40.3	44.7	49.5	52.5	52.6	49.2	44.2	39.9	36.9	43.5	43
Extreme (highest)	67	72	73	83	87	93	100	96	95	85	71	64	100	43
Extreme (lowest)	11	9	22	29	30	37	39	39	33	26	15	6	6	43
RELATIVE HUMIDITY														
Average percentage	51.4	49.8	34.1	54.5	54.8	55.9	63.7	54.8	47.6	52.0	46.7	56.5	51.9	47
CLOUD COVER														
Percent of time clear	11.5	11.7	9.3	10.1	10.1	9.8	18.3	16.9	23.5	16.5	10.8	10.0	13.3	40
Percent of time scattered	10.2	11.0	12.9	14.1	15.8	15.9	16.3	18.2	18.9	17.0	12.6	12.6	14.6	40
Percent of time broken	13.1	14.6	17.5	19.0	20.9	18.2	15.5	15.8	16.1	15.6	16.1	15.2	16.4	40
Percent of time overcast	65.2	62.7	60.4	56.9	53.2	56.2	49.9	49.1	41.6	50.9	60.5	62.2	55.6	40
PRECIPITATION (inches)														
Mean amount	9.9	7.5	7.0	4.9	2.9	2.5	1.1	1.3	2.7	5.9	10.3	10.5	67.0	43
Greatest amount	18.9	21.8	13.4	9.4	6.6	5.4	4.3	5.2	6.9	12.5	17.4	16.5	87.3	43
Least amount	0.6	1.3	0.9	1.3	0.3	0.5	0.0	0.0	0.0	0.5	1.4	2.6	41.5	43
Maximum amount (24 hours)	4.5	2.8	2.5	2.7	1.7	2.0	1.7	1.6	2.4	3.5	3.6	3.5	4.5	43
Mean number of days	23	21	23	22	20	19	16	15	15	19	23	24	240	43
SNOW														
Mean amount	2.1	0.4	0.5	0.0	T	0.0	0.0	0.0	0.0	T	0.2	1.1	4.3	42
Greatest amount	26.3	4.0	6.7	1.1	T	0.0	0.0	0.0	0.0	T	4.6	19.0	27.3	42
Least amount	0.0	0.0	0.0	0.0	0.0	0.0	0.0	0.0	0.0	0.0	0.0	0.0	0.0	42
Maximum amount (24 hours)	10.8	4.0	4.5	1.0	T	0.0	0.0	0.0	0.0	T	4.3	5.7	10.8	42
Mean number of days	4	2	2	1	Miss	0	0	0	0	Miss	1	3	13	43
WIND														
Percentage with gales	0.12	0.05	0.03	0.01	0.00	0.00	0.00	0.00	0.00	0.03	0.08	0.09	0.13	45
Mean wind speed (knots)	8.0	7.7	7.7	7.5	7.4	7.4	7.5	7.0	6.5	6.4	7.5	7.8	7.4	45
Direction (percentage of observations)														
North	1.3	1.9	2.2	2.1	2.4	2.2	2.3	2.3	2.5	2.1	1.2	1.0	1.9	45
North Northeast	1.6	1.5	1.7	1.3	1.0	0.8	0.4	0.8	2.0	1.8	1.4	1.1	1.3	45
Northeast	4.9	4.4	3.3	1.8	1.3	0.9	0.6	0.7	2.8	3.9	4.1	4.5	2.7	45
East Northeast	11.4	10.1	4.9	2.7	1.5	1.0	0.7	0.7	3.2	6.0	9.2	11.5	5.2	45
East	16.5	12.5	7.6	5.2	2.8	2.1	1.2	1.9	4.4	8.2	13.7	16.2	7.7	45
East Southeast	11.5	10.4	9.1	7.4	5.5	4.1	3.4	4.8	7.7	11.1	13.0	13.9	8.5	45
Southeast	7.1	7.3	9.6	8.4	6.6	5.7	4.7	6.5	9.3	11.1	9.6	8.5	7.9	45
South Southeast	4.0	4.7	5.5	5.0	3.9	3.8	3.0	3.7	5.2	5.7	5.8	4.5	4.5	45
South	7.8	8.6	8.6	6.6	5.5	5.1	4.3	5.4	6.4	7.7	8.4	7.5	6.8	45
South Southwest	7.7	8.0	8.0	7.4	6.3	6.6	5.4	6.7	7.6	7.8	7.4	6.5	7.1	45
Southwest	5.8	6.3	7.8	9.5	10.2	11.3	10.4	11.3	9.4	6.9	5.2	4.9	8.3	45
West Southwest	4.1	4.3	5.6	8.6	9.6	9.6	9.2	9.6	6.7	4.3	3.8	4.0	6.6	45
West	3.9	4.4	6.2	8.3	10.4	10.3	10.3	8.6	5.2	3.4	3.2	3.7	6.5	45
West Northwest	2.3	3.0	5.6	8.4	11.1	12.2	14.2	10.9	6.4	3.4	2.7	2.8	7.0	45
Northwest	1.4	2.6	5.1	8.0	12.0	13.9	18.3	14.5	8.8	4.5	1.8	1.2	7.7	45
North Northwest	0.9	1.5	2.5	3.3	4.2	5.9	7.4	5.5	4.1	2.4	0.8	0.7	3.3	45
Calm	7.7	8.6	6.9	6.3	6.3	5.5	5.4	6.8	8.8	10.2	8.3	7.8	7.4	45
Direction (mean speed, knots)														
North	4.5	4.9	5.5	6.1	6.1	6.7	6.7	6.1	5.7	5.5	5.0	5.2	5.8	45
North Northeast	6.1	6.1	6.9	6.9	6.7	6.0	7.6	6.2	7.4	7.0	6.5	6.2	6.7	45
Northeast	7.1	7.5	7.9	7.9	7.0	6.9	7.4	7.1	8.6	8.2	7.5	7.9	7.7	45
East Northeast	7.6	7.6	7.5	7.1	6.3	5.6	5.8	6.3	7.5	7.1	7.2	7.5	7.3	45
East	7.1	6.7	5.9	5.3	4.2	4.0	4.1	4.0	5.3	5.7	6.4	6.8	6.2	45
East Southeast	6.6	6.1	5.5	5.1	4.4	4.3	4.3	4.2	4.6	5.0	5.8	6.3	5.5	45
Southeast	5.8	5.9	5.5	5.0	4.7	4.4	4.3	4.4	4.5	4.8	5.6	6.1	5.1	45
South Southeast	8.4	8.2	7.5	6.5	5.7	5.4	5.2	5.1	5.5	6.9	8.2	8.4	6.9	45
South	13.1	12.4	10.9	9.3	7.2	6.7	6.3	6.4	7.5	9.4	12.1	12.9	10.0	45
South Southwest	14.0	12.9	11.7	10.2	8.8	8.0	7.4	7.6	8.7	10.2	13.2	13.7	10.7	45
Southwest	11.9	10.8	10.2	9.4	8.6	8.0	7.0	7.2	7.7	8.7	11.2	11.8	8.9	45
West Southwest	10.5	9.5	8.9	8.5	7.8	7.4	6.8	6.7	6.8	7.5	9.1	10.1	7.9	45
West	9.3	8.5	8.7	8.1	7.8	7.5	7.3	6.8	6.6	6.6	8.8	9.6	7.8	45
West Northwest	10.1	9.7	10.2	9.5	9.4	9.2	9.5	9.5	9.0	8.2	10.6	10.7	9.5	45
Northwest	8.6	8.7	9.9	10.7	10.6	10.5	10.5	10.3	9.8	8.7	9.9	10.3	10.2	45
North Northwest	6.1	7.0	7.9	8.6	9.0	9.6	9.3	9.1	8.5	7.5	7.9	7.5	8.7	45
VISIBILITY														
Mean number of days with fog	18	16	15	14	12	13	13	17	18	20	17	18	191	43

* Sea level pressure is station pressure reduced to sea level
T = trace (not measurable) amount of precipitation
Miss or blank is a missing value
These tables were prepared by the National Climatic Data Center (NCDC), National Environmental Satellite, Data & Information Service (NESDIS), NOAA

CLIMATOLOGICAL DATA – SEATTLE-TACOMA, WA (47°27'N, 122°18'W) 450 feet (137 m)															
WEATHER ELEMENTS	JAN	FEB	MAR	APR	MAY	JUN	JUL	AUG	SEP	OCT	NOV	DEC	YEAR	YEARS OF RECORD
SEA LEVEL PRESSURE*														
Mean (millibars)	1017.5	1016.9	1016	1017.3	1017.3	1017.2	1017.9	1017	1017	1017.8	1017.3	1017.5	1017.2	48
TEMPERATURE (°F)														
Mean	39.7	42.9	45.3	49.4	55.6	60.7	65.0	64.9	60.5	52.6	45.2	40.9	51.9	48
Mean daily maximum	44.5	48.8	52.2	57.3	64.3	69.6	75.1	74.6	69.4	59.5	50.4	45.4	59.3	48
Mean daily minimum	34.5	36.6	37.9	41.0	46.3	51.3	54.4	54.7	51.2	45.3	39.5	35.8	44.1	48
Extreme (highest)	64	70	75	85	93	96	100	99	98	89	74	64	100	48
Extreme (lowest)	0	1	11	29	28	38	43	44	35	28	6	6	0	48
RELATIVE HUMIDITY														
Average percentage	49.7	44.5	35.3	47.7	48.3	46.8	53.6	45.2	44.6	53.2	48	49.6	47.2	48
CLOUD COVER														
Percent of time clear	9.5	10.6	11.2	11.1	12.9	15.5	31.5	28.4	27.7	15.0	8.9	7.9	15.9	48
Percent of time scattered	9.3	11.2	14.1	15.2	18.7	18.5	18.5	19.0	17.7	15.4	11.1	9.7	14.9	48
Percent of time broken	13.6	15.7	19.2	21.7	23.5	23	17.9	18.1	17.9	19.1	16.1	15.3	18.4	48
Percent of time overcast	67.6	62.4	55.5	52.0	44.9	43.0	32.1	34.6	36.7	50.4	63.9	67.1	50.8	48
PRECIPITATION (inches)														
Mean amount	5.6	4.1	3.7	2.5	1.6	1.4	0.7	1.1	1.8	3.4	5.9	5.8	38.0	48
Greatest amount	12.9	9.1	8.4	6.5	4.7	3.8	2.3	4.5	5.9	7.7	10.7	11.8	55.1	48
Least amount	0.5	0.3	0.5	0.3	0.1	0.1	T	0.0	T	0.3	0.7	1.3	23.7	48
Maximum amount (24 hours)	2.9	2.9	2.7	2.6	1.8	1.7	0.8	1.6	1.6	2.7	3.4	2.1	3.4	48
Mean number of days	23	19	21	19	16	14	10	11	12	17	22	23	207	48
SNOW														
Mean amount	4.9	1.7	1.3	0.1	T	0.0	0.0	0.0	0.0	0.0	0.9	2.6	11.6	48
Greatest amount	57.2	13.1	18.2	2.3	T	0.0	0.0	0.0	0.0	2.0	17.5	22.1	60.6	48
Least amount	0.0	0.0	0.0	0.0	0.0	0.0	0.0	0.0	0.0	0.0	0.0	0.0	T	48
Maximum amount (24 hours)	20.0	7.0	6.0	1.2	T	0.0	0.0	0.0	0.0	2.0	7.8	9.3	20.0	48
Mean number of days	7	4	3	1	Miss	0	0	0	0	Miss	2	5	22	48
WIND														
Percentage with gales	0.03	0.01	0.01	0.01	0.00	0.00	0.00	0.00	0.00	0.00	0.03	0.03	0.13	48
Mean wind speed (knots)	8.4	8.3	8.4	8.2	7.7	7.6	7.2	6.9	7.1	7.4	8.2	8.4	7.8	48
Direction (percentage of observations)														
North	6.4	7.2	7.5	6.7	8.3	9.2	9.9	10.2	12.8	9.8	6.7	6.0	8.4	48
North Northeast	7.6	7.8	7.2	6.6	7.9	8.3	10.3	9.0	10.9	9.1	6.9	7.4	8.3	48
Northeast	4.8	4.2	4.1	4.2	4.6	4.3	5.0	5.1	5.4	4.2	3.8	4.0	4.5	48
East Northeast	2.8	2.9	2.1	1.5	1.2	1.0	1.3	1.2	1.8	1.6	2.3	2.6	1.8	48
East	6.5	5.3	4.0	2.6	1.5	1.0	0.8	1.1	2.2	3.0	4.6	6.0	3.2	48
East Southeast	9.5	7.8	6.2	3.6	2.3	1.4	0.8	1.5	3.0	6.2	8.3	9.7	5.0	48
Southeast	9.3	7.9	6.9	5.8	3.6	2.7	1.9	2.9	5.4	8.6	11.0	10.8	6.4	48
South Southeast	7.2	7.5	6.7	5.7	4.6	3.5	2.8	3.7	4.7	7.1	8.6	8.5	5.9	48
South	14.1	13.7	12.7	12.4	10.6	10.1	8.1	9.7	10.4	13.3	16.1	15.5	12.2	48
South Southwest	13.7	13.7	15.1	15.9	14.9	15.2	13.1	12.5	11.0	11.5	12.4	13.1	13.5	48
Southwest	0.9	8.1	10.7	13.3	13.4	15.2	13.2	11.3	7.7	7.0	6.3	6.5	10.0	48
West Southwest	1.9	2.5	4.0	5.6	6.4	6.9	7.0	6.6	3.8	2.7	2.0	1.9	4.3	48
West	1.0	1.5	1.9	3.2	4.2	4.9	5.8	5.5	3.2	2.1	1.3	1.0	3.0	48
West Northwest	0.6	1.1	1.7	2.5	3.8	4.0	4.6	4.7	3.1	2.3	0.8	0.7	2.5	48
Northwest	0.8	1.2	2.0	2.5	3.4	3.4	4.1	3.8	2.6	2.1	1.0	0.6	2.3	48
North Northwest	1.7	2.7	3.7	3.9	5.6	5.2	7.2	6.2	6.1	3.8	2.2	1.5	4.1	48
Calm	5.5	5.5	4.3	4.4	4.2	3.9	4.3	5.0	6.2	6.1	5.9	5.0	5.0	48
Direction (mean speed, knots)														
North	8.3	8.3	8.4	8.6	8.5	8.3	8.2	7.8	8.3	7.8	8.2	7.8	8.2	48
North Northeast	7.9	7.9	8.0	8.2	8.2	8.1	8.0	7.7	8.0	8.3	7.8	7.8	8.0	48
Northeast	7.1	7.4	7.2	7.9	8.1	8.0	7.9	7.5	7.5	7.2	7.3	7.0	7.5	48
East Northeast	7.1	6.8	7.0	6.8	6.5	5.9	6.5	6.0	5.5	5.7	6.4	6.6	6.5	48
East	7.3	7.2	6.5	6.4	5.3	5.2	4.0	4.4	5.3	6.0	6.6	7.0	6.5	48
East Southeast	7.7	7.4	7.0	6.4	5.8	5.5	5.4	5.2	5.7	6.5	7.7	7.6	7.0	48
Southeast	7.0	6.9	6.9	6.8	6.7	6.3	6.2	6.2	6.2	6.6	7.2	7.1	6.8	48
South Southeast	7.5	7.4	7.3	7.1	6.6	6.4	6.6	6.2	6.4	6.8	7.5	7.6	7.1	48
South	9.8	9.4	9.0	8.5	7.4	7.2	6.7	6.7	7.3	8.5	9.9	9.8	8.6	48
South Southwest	12.1	11.8	11.1	10.1	9.0	8.5	7.8	7.9	8.8	10.1	11.5	12.0	10.1	48
Southwest	12.8	12.4	12.0	11.1	9.8	9.3	8.3	8.2	9.2	10.4	11.7	13.0	10.4	48
West Southwest	8.9	8.7	9.6	8.7	8.1	7.8	7.1	7.1	7.0	7.4	8.9	8.9	8.0	48
West	4.3	5.5	6.3	6.6	6.3	6.3	6.3	6.1	5.9	4.8	5.2	4.5	6.0	48
West Northwest	5.4	5.5	6.1	6.3	6.3	6.5	6.8	6.5	5.9	5.6	4.8	5.1	6.2	48
Northwest	6.1	6.5	7.0	7.4	7.2	7.1	7.1	6.9	6.3	6.3	6.8	6.3	6.9	48
North Northwest	8.2	8.1	8.0	8.7	8.6	8.1	0.4	8.3	8.0	7.2	7.3	7.3	8.1	48
VISIBILITY														
Mean number of days with fog	18	15	13	10	8	8	8	11	16	19	19	19	164	48

* Sea level pressure is station pressure reduced to sea level
T = trace (not measurable) amount of precipitation
Miss or blank is a missing value
These tables were prepared by the National Climatic Data Center (NCDC), National Environmental Satellite, Data & Information Service (NESDIS), NOAA

CLIMATOLOGICAL DATA – QUILLAYUTE, WA (47°57'N, 124°33'W) 179 feet (54.6 m)

WEATHER ELEMENTS	JAN	FEB	MAR	APR	MAY	JUN	JUL	AUG	SEP	OCT	NOV	DEC	YEAR	YEARS OF RECORD
SEA LEVEL PRESSURE*														
Mean (millibars)	1016.6	1016.3	1014.8	1017.0	1017.5	1017.8	1018.9	1017.8	1017.8	1017.8	1015.4	1016.9	1017.1	29
TEMPERATURE (°F)														
Mean	40.4	42.4	44.0	46.7	51.7	55.9	59.3	59.7	57.1	50.4	44.3	40.7	49.4	29
Mean daily maximum	46.3	49.3	51.9	55.1	60.5	64.2	68.2	69.0	67.1	59.1	50.8	46.2	57.4	29
Mean daily minimum	34.1	34.9	35.7	37.8	42.4	46.9	49.8	49.9	46.6	41.2	37.4	34.6	41.0	29
Extreme (highest)	65	73	72	83	92	96	97	99	97	83	69	64	99	29
Extreme (lowest)	7	11	19	24	29	33	38	36	28	24	5	7	5	29
RELATIVE HUMIDITY														
Average percentage	41.3	37.8	22.8	45.4	50.1	53.0	64.3	53.4	52.5	52.9	29.2	44.4	45.7	29
CLOUD COVER														
Percent of time clear	12.0	13.2	11.9	9.8	10.4	10.9	16.3	20.0	25.0	16.8	8.8	12.5	14.0	29
Percent of time scattered	9.2	11.3	13.7	12.6	14.9	14.4	16.3	16.3	18.0	16.4	12.6	11.8	14.0	29
Percent of time broken	11.8	14.1	16.2	18.5	19.5	17.6	14.8	16.9	15.1	15.7	16.3	14.8	15.9	29
Percent of time overcast	67.1	61.3	58.1	59.1	55.2	57.1	52.7	46.8	41.8	51.1	62.3	60.8	56.0	29
PRECIPITATION (inches)														
Mean amount	13.7	12.0	10.9	7.7	5.2	3.1	2.3	2.8	4.6	10.0	14.2	14.8	101.7	29
Greatest amount	23.9	20.6	21.8	13.9	12.4	8.5	11.0	15.0	10.9	27.1	29.1	27.8	131.6	29
Least amount	1.2	0.8	1.8	2.9	1.0	0.4	0.3	0.3	0.1	1.3	4.4	3.6	60.2	29
Maximum amount (24 hours)	7.1	5.0	4.0	2.6	3.5	1.5	5.3	4.2	3.2	4.8	5.2	6.7	7.1	29
Mean number of days	23	20	22	22	20	19	16	15	15	20	23	24	239	29
SNOW														
Mean amount	4.6	2.9	1.6	0.3	T	0.0	0.0	0.0	T	T	1.0	2.7	13.1	29
Greatest amount	40.1	16.1	10.2	2.8	T	0.0	0.0	0.0	T	T	15.6	11.6	58.3	29
Least amount	0.0	0.0	0.0	0.0	0.0	0.0	0.0	0.0	0.0	0.0	0.0	0.0	0.5	29
Maximum amount (24 hours)	8.0	7.1	7.5	2.1	T	0.0	0.0	0.0	T	T	7.7	7.3	8.0	29
Mean number of days	5	4	4	3	Miss	0	0	0	Miss	Miss	2	5	23	29
WIND														
Percentage with gales	0.00	0.00	0.00	0.00	0.00	0.00	0.00	0.00	0.00	0.00	0.00	0.00	1.47	29
Mean wind speed (knots)	5.8	5.9	5.8	5.5	5.2	5.1	4.8	4.5	4.3	4.7	5.6	5.8	5.2	29
Direction (percentage of observations)														
North	2.2	2.4	2.9	2.3	3.2	2.9	3.3	4.2	4.2	3.2	2.4	2.3	3.0	29
North Northeast	3.9	4.0	4.0	2.6	2.4	1.9	2.4	2.3	4.1	4.4	3.5	3.7	3.3	29
Northeast	11.5	10.6	6.7	4.7	3.5	2.4	2.2	2.7	6.0	6.7	9.3	10.0	6.3	29
East Northeast	11.3	11.0	8.2	6.8	4.8	2.9	2.7	2.9	5.8	8.0	11.5	11.3	7.3	29
East	7.2	7.8	6.3	5.5	3.8	2.3	2.1	2.6	3.8	5.9	8.2	8.2	5.3	29
East Southeast	4.8	5.0	5.0	4.4	3.1	2.3	1.6	1.9	2.6	4.7	5.4	5.2	3.8	29
Southeast	6.6	7.1	6.8	5.1	3.4	2.7	2.1	2.0	3.0	5.9	7.7	7.8	5.0	29
South Southeast	10.0	10.0	9.0	7.0	5.5	5.3	3.6	4.8	6.2	9.1	10.5	11.1	7.7	29
South	8.1	9.6	9.3	9.1	8.3	9.0	7.4	8.8	8.7	9.5	8.6	7.6	8.7	29
South Southwest	4.5	4.5	5.5	6.1	6.5	6.8	6.3	6.6	5.7	4.2	4.2	3.9	5.4	29
Southwest	3.3	3.9	4.3	5.2	6.5	7.1	6.7	6.9	4.7	3.5	2.9	2.6	4.8	29
West Southwest	2.7	2.9	3.9	6.3	7.6	7.5	8.2	7.2	5.2	3.6	2.2	2.3	5.0	29
West	3.3	2.8	3.9	6.7	7.0	7.3	7.4	5.5	3.9	3.2	2.8	2.9	4.7	29
West Northwest	2.5	2.2	4.3	7.0	8.0	9.3	8.8	7.0	4.4	3.0	3.1	2.7	5.2	29
Northwest	1.3	1.4	2.9	3.9	6.3	8.3	9.7	7.2	3.8	2.0	1.6	1.5	4.2	29
North Northwest	1.1	1.5	1.9	2.6	4.2	5.0	6.0	5.2	3.9	2.1	1.2	1.2	3.0	29
Calm	15.8	13.7	14.8	14.8	16.4	17.6	19.5	22.4	24	20.9	14.8	15.9	17.6	29
Direction (mean speed, knots)														
North	3.9	4.2	4.4	4.4	4.3	4.5	4.7	4.3	4.4	4.0	4.1	4.1	4.3	29
North Northeast	5.8	5.8	5.7	5.2	5.0	5.0	4.4	4.6	5.2	5.2	5.4	5.6	5.3	29
Northeast	7.0	7.2	6.5	5.7	5.1	5.1	4.5	4.4	5.6	5.5	6.3	6.9	6.2	29
East Northeast	5.1	5.3	5.0	4.5	4.2	4.1	4.0	4.1	4.4	4.5	4.9	5.2	4.8	29
East	4.5	4.5	4.4	4.2	3.9	3.6	3.7	3.5	3.8	4.1	4.4	4.5	4.2	29
East Southeast	5.0	5.0	5.2	4.8	4.4	4.2	4.0	4.0	4.2	4.5	4.9	5.2	4.8	29
Southeast	7.3	7.4	7.4	6.9	5.9	5.5	5.5	5.4	5.8	6.9	7.5	7.7	7.0	29
South Southeast	8.5	8.5	8.3	7.3	6.8	6.1	5.8	6.2	6.4	7.7	8.4	8.6	7.7	29
South	8.3	8.1	8.1	7.4	6.7	6.0	5.8	5.8	6.2	7.2	8.3	8.5	7.2	29
South Southwest	8.9	8.3	8.1	7.5	7.1	6.7	6.4	6.0	6.1	7.0	8.7	9.0	7.3	29
Southwest	9.4	9.0	8.7	8.1	7.1	7.2	6.7	6.4	6.5	7.2	8.8	9.6	7.6	29
West Southwest	9.0	7.7	7.9	7.3	7.2	6.8	6.6	6.6	6.3	6.5	8.0	8.6	7.1	29
West	7.6	6.5	7.2	7.3	6.9	6.4	6.3	6.3	5.8	5.8	6.4	7.1	6.6	29
West Northwest	8.5	7.8	7.5	7.1	7.1	6.7	6.4	6.2	6.4	6.6	7.4	8.5	7.0	29
Northwest	7.0	7.5	7.5	7.3	7.0	6.8	6.5	6.5	6.4	6.5	6.8	7.9	6.8	29
North Northwest	5.7	5.1	6.5	6.3	6.4	6.0	6.3	6.1	5.5	5.1	6.0	5.4	6.0	29
VISIBILITY														
Mean number of days with fog	21	19	20	17	17	18	19	20	20	22	21	22	236	29

* Sea level pressure is station pressure reduced to sea level
T = trace (not measurable) amount of precipitation
Miss or blank is a missing value
These tables were prepared by the National Climatic Data Center (NCDC), National Environmental Satellite, Data & Information Service (NESDIS), NOAA

CLIMATOLOGICAL DATA – TATOOSH ISLAND, WA (48°23'N, 124°44'W) 115 feet (35.1 m)														
WEATHER ELEMENTS	JAN	FEB	MAR	APR	MAY	JUN	JUL	AUG	SEP	OCT	NOV	DEC	YEAR	YEARS OF RECORD
SEA LEVEL PRESSURE*														
Mean (millibars)	1015.6	1015.7	1014.8	1016.9	1017.6	1017.7	1018.5	1017.7	1016.5	1016.2	1015.8	1015.0	1016.5	19
TEMPERATURE (°F)														
Mean	41.4	43.3	43.5	46.9	50.6	53.4	55.4	56.2	55.1	52.0	47.3	44.1	49.1	18
Mean daily maximum	44.7	46.9	47.4	51.0	54.6	57.2	59.2	60.1	59.5	55.9	50.8	47.4	52.9	18
Mean daily minimum	37.6	39.2	39.1	42.4	46.1	49.2	51.1	51.8	50.2	47.7	43.3	40.3	44.8	18
Extreme (highest)	57	63	66	69	74	82	80	76	80	70	64	61	82	18
Extreme (lowest)	14	20	25	33	37	43	46	45	43	36	19	14	14	18
RELATIVE HUMIDITY														
Average percentage	30.9	31.9	23.2	44.4	51.4	52.0	60.5	52.1	40.1	36.7	32.5	24.9	40.1	19
CLOUD COVER														
Percent of time clear	11.0	11.3	9.2	10.1	10.3	9.6	15.9	13.5	20.1	13.8	10.5	7.4	11.9	19
Percent of time scattered	11.6	11.3	14.0	14.4	16.4	12.8	12.4	12.3	15.9	16.5	13.9	11.6	13.6	19
Percent of time broken	13.0	13.9	17.7	16.3	18.4	15.8	13.6	13.9	13.5	15.7	14.7	14.0	15.1	19
Percent of time overcast	64.4	63.6	59.1	59.2	55.0	61.7	58.1	60.3	50.5	54.0	60.9	67.1	59.5	19
PRECIPITATION (inches)														
Mean amount	10.9	9.5	7.9	5.4	2.6	2.5	2.0	2.3	3.3	8.6	11.5	12.5	79.6	18
Greatest amount	20.0	21.1	14.8	10.2	6.1	6.3	6.0	4.7	7.0	13.6	22.1	16.8	101.6	18
Least amount	1.8	4.2	2.9	0.6	0.8	0.4	0.0	0.1	1.1	2.5	4.4	7.2	68.7	18
Maximum amount (24 hours)	2.9	2.7	2.6	3.0	1.6	2.1	1.5	2.1	1.9	3.8	3.7	3.2	3.8	18
Mean number of days	25	22	24	20	19	19	18	19	16	20	23	26	251	18
SNOW														
Mean amount	4.4	2.1	3.4	0.0	0.0	0.0	0.0	0.0	0.0	0.0	0.6	3.0	13.5	17
Greatest amount	32.3	10.4	24.7	0.4	0.0	0.0	0.0	0.0	0.0	0.0	7.5	20.2	34.5	17
Least amount	0.0	0.0	T	0.0	0.0	0.0	0.0	0.0	0.0	0.0	0.0	0.0	T	17
Maximum amount (24 hours)	8.5	5.2	10.3	0.4	0.0	0.0	0.0	0.0	0.0	0.0	4.7	7.0	10.3	17
Mean number of days	6	4	4	Miss	0	0	0	0	0	0	1	4	19	18
WIND														
Percentage with gales	6.09	3.59	1.21	1.01	0.19	0.07	0.02	0.02	0.28	2.06	3.87	5.49	2.32	19
Mean wind speed (knots)	17.4	15.9	14.1	12.2	10.3	9.1	8.9	8.9	10.4	14.1	16.6	17.4	12.9	19
Direction (percentage of observations)														
North	0.8	1.5	1.9	2.1	1.7	1.5	1.2	1.7	2.9	1.4	0.8	1.0	1.5	19
North Northeast	0.4	0.3	0.4	0.4	0.6	0.7	0.7	0.7	1.1	0.5	0.7	0.4	0.6	19
Northeast	3.9	4.9	5.6	5.4	4.9	3.6	3.4	4.2	10.6	8.4	4.1	2.5	5.1	19
East Northeast	10.0	9.1	8.4	6.8	3.8	3.6	3.4	4.0	11.5	12.5	10.6	9.9	7.8	19
East	31.5	24.2	22.1	13.7	8.6	5.8	4.0	6.3	12.9	23.8	30.4	27.2	17.5	19
East Southeast	4.0	3.2	2.3	1.5	0.7	0.6	0.3	0.4	1.0	1.7	3.3	3.3	1.8	19
Southeast	6.5	5.7	5.3	4.3	2.4	1.4	1.4	1.8	2.2	4.8	6.9	6.3	4.1	19
South Southeast	5.6	6.1	5.7	3.5	3.0	3.5	2.7	3.5	4.3	6.1	5.6	6.3	4.6	19
South	13.0	13.8	12.6	14.2	15.5	19.5	24.1	30.6	20.9	15.2	12.9	14.5	17.2	19
South Southwest	3.1	2.5	3.6	5.4	5.9	9.1	12.6	11.8	6.1	4.1	2.7	2.9	5.8	19
Southwest	0.4	7.0	8.8	11.8	14.7	17.6	21.8	17.5	10.0	6.7	6.5	7.2	11.5	19
West Southwest	2.9	2.9	4.2	5.5	7.3	8.0	6.5	4.7	3.2	2.7	2.8	2.6	4.5	19
West	6.7	10.5	11.1	14.6	21.1	17.6	12.2	7.5	7.5	6.5	6.9	8.7	11.0	19
West Northwest	1.7	2.7	2.9	4.1	4.4	3.0	1.6	0.9	1.3	2.2	2.0	2.8	2.5	19
Northwest	1.5	3.1	3.1	4.0	2.7	1.6	1.2	1.4	1.5	1.4	2.2	2.5	2.2	19
North Northwest	0.4	0.4	0.4	0.5	0.4	0.4	0.3	0.2	0.3	0.2	0.4	0.3	0.3	19
Calm	1.3	1.3	1.8	2.4	2.4	2.7	2.8	2.8	2.7	1.9	1.1	1.6	2.1	19
Direction (mean speed, knots)														
North	8.1	6.6	6.7	5.8	5.3	5.2	5.8	4.7	5.3	5.2	8.1	7.2	5.9	19
North Northeast	11.0	7.5	10.0	7.9	8.4	6.6	6.7	6.4	7.7	6.6	11.1	10.1	8.2	19
Northeast	18.1	13.8	12.2	11.8	11.4	9.7	8.2	9.5	10.8	12.7	14.6	12.4	12.0	19
East Northeast	18.4	16.9	15.5	13.7	13.2	10.5	10.9	10.3	13.8	17.6	17.4	19.0	15.8	19
East	18.5	16.6	15.8	13.2	11.9	10.3	9.3	8.2	11.8	15.2	17.4	19.2	15.8	19
East Southeast	14.7	14.7	13.9	11.6	11.5	8.0	6.7	7.6	11.3	14.3	15.7	14.3	13.8	19
Southeast	12.9	13.4	11.8	11.5	8.4	8.2	8.3	8.9	9.5	12.0	13.3	13.9	12.0	19
South Southeast	15.8	16.4	15.2	14.5	12.9	11.3	11.2	11.3	12.9	16.3	16.1	17.9	14.9	19
South	19.1	17.9	14.8	14.3	11.8	10.9	10.6	10.8	11.6	15.0	19.0	20.1	13.9	19
South Southwest	22.9	18.9	15.5	14.4	11.9	10.3	11.1	9.5	10.5	14.4	22.2	21.7	13.1	19
Southwest	20.1	17.7	14.2	12.3	9.9	9.0	8.7	8.1	8.3	13.5	19.0	18.1	11.7	19
West Southwest	16.1	15.6	13.6	11.8	9.4	8.1	7.7	7.3	8.6	10.9	15.3	15.5	10.7	19
West	16.6	15.0	14.0	11.5	9.7	7.9	6.7	6.5	7.7	11.3	14.6	15.8	11.0	19
West Northwest	16.4	16.2	17.1	12.2	10.3	9.4	7.4	6.6	10.6	15.3	16.8	16.6	13.2	19
Northwest	13.8	13.4	10.1	10.3	8.0	7.7	6.3	5.5	6.5	11.6	14.4	13.1	10.4	19
North Northwest	10.8	10.5	7.1	6.0	6.3	7.3	6.6	5.2	5.2	5.5	11.1	8.8	7.8	19
VISIBILITY														
Mean number of days with fog	11	11	9	9	10	14	18	21	17	13	10	12	155	18

* Sea level pressure is station pressure reduced to sea level
T = trace (not measurable) amount of precipitation
Miss or blank is a missing value
These tables were prepared by the National Climatic Data Center (NCDC), National Environmental Satellite, Data & Information Service (NESDIS), NOAA

CLIMATOLOGICAL DATA – HILO, HI (19°43'N, 155°04'W) 36 feet (10.9 m)

WEATHER ELEMENTS	JAN	FEB	MAR	APR	MAY	JUN	JUL	AUG	SEP	OCT	NOV	DEC	YEAR	YEARS OF RECORD
SEA LEVEL PRESSURE*														
Mean (millibars)	1016.0	1016.0	1017.6	1017.8	1017.7	1017.5	1016.8	1016.3	1015.3	1015.6	1016.1	1016.2	1016.6	46
TEMPERATURE (°F)														
Mean	71.7	71.5	71.9	72.7	73.8	75.2	75.9	76.4	76.3	75.7	74.1	72.3	74.0	46
Mean daily maximum	79.5	79.3	79.2	79.5	80.9	82.4	82.8	83.4	83.7	83.0	81.0	79.6	81.2	46
Mean daily minimum	63.4	63.3	64.2	65.3	66.3	67.5	68.6	69.0	68.5	67.9	66.7	64.6	66.3	46
Extreme (highest)	91	92	93	89	94	90	89	93	92	91	90	93	94	46
Extreme (lowest)	54	53	54	59	59	61	62	63	61	62	58	55	53	46
RELATIVE HUMIDITY														
Average percentage	34.6	35.1	50.6	52.7	52.2	50.4	43.0	37.6	28.4	31.1	36.5	37.4	40.7	46
CLOUD COVER														
Percent of time clear	11.1	11.1	4.7	1.3	1.6	1.8	1.6	2.0	3.2	3.8	4.5	8.6	4.6	46
Percent of time scattered	27.1	25.4	22.2	17.1	17.5	22.8	21.1	22.1	25.8	24.3	21.3	24.6	22.6	46
Percent of time broken	26.1	25.8	28.5	30.5	30.6	34.0	33.8	33.7	32.4	31.8	29.1	28.5	30.4	46
Percent of time overcast	35.6	37.7	44.5	51.0	50.2	41.4	43.4	42.1	38.5	40.1	45.2	38.3	42.3	46
PRECIPITATION (inches)														
Mean amount	9.2	11.5	13.5	13.5	9.4	6.4	10.1	10.7	8.2	9.7	15.3	12.6	130.6	46
Greatest amount	32.2	45.5	49.9	43.2	25.0	13.2	28.5	26.9	21.8	26.1	45.7	50.8	211.2	46
Least amount	0.3	0.5	0.8	2.9	2.7	1.8	3.8	2.6	1.5	2.4	1.0	0.2	68.0	46
Maximum amount (24 hours)	9.5	16.8	15.6	9.6	7.8	2.8	5.9	9.6	8.6	8.6	15.4	9.3	16.8	46
Mean number of days	21	20	26	28	29	28	30	29	26	27	26	24	314	46
SNOW														
Mean amount	0	0	0	0	0	0	0	0	0	0	0	0	0	46
Greatest amount	0	0	0	0	0	0	0	0	0	0	0	0	0	46
Least amount	0	0	0	0	0	0	0	0	0	0	0	0	0	46
Maximum amount (24 hours)	0	0	0	0	0	0	0	0	0	0	0	0	0	46
Mean number of days	0	0	0	0	0	0	0	0	0	0	0	0	0	46
WIND														
Percentage with gales	0.00	0.00	0.00	0.00	0.00	0.00	0.00	0.00	0.00	0.00	0.00	0.00	0.93	46
Mean wind speed (knots)	6.5	6.7	6.7	6.5	6.4	6.1	6.0	5.9	5.9	5.8	5.9	6.3	6.2	46
Direction (percentage of observations)														
North	6.5	7.1	6.5	5.9	5.3	4.5	5.7	5.4	5.5	5.0	5.1	5.7	5.7	46
North Northeast	4.6	5.2	5.6	5.7	5.4	5.7	6.7	6.6	6.1	4.7	3.7	4.4	5.4	46
Northeast	3.5	4.7	5.8	7.1	6.8	8.1	8.5	8.2	6.5	5.8	4.8	3.7	6.1	46
East Northeast	3.4	3.9	6.1	7.4	7.0	8.6	8.0	7.9	6.1	5.6	4.9	4.0	6.1	46
East	4.1	4.4	6.0	6.1	6.9	7.2	5.9	5.8	5.1	5.0	4.8	3.9	5.4	46
East Southeast	5.5	5.6	5.9	5.2	5.9	4.6	3.6	3.5	4.1	4.8	5.4	5.5	5.0	46
Southeast	4.8	4.5	3.9	3.2	2.7	2.5	2.0	2.0	2.4	3.0	3.8	4.5	3.3	46
South Southeast	4.3	3.2	2.3	2.0	1.9	1.6	1.4	1.5	1.8	2.4	3.0	3.5	2.4	46
South	5.9	5.8	4.6	4.4	4.2	3.2	3.0	3.1	3.4	3.9	4.9	5.7	4.3	46
South Southwest	12.1	10.7	9.0	8.1	7.6	7.3	5.7	6.6	8.5	9.5	9.5	11.1	8.8	46
Southwest	18.3	17.0	15.0	14.1	14.3	15.2	13.8	14.8	18.4	18.9	19.0	18.6	16.4	46
West Southwest	9.9	9.3	10.7	11.8	11.8	13.2	13.6	13.1	13.7	13.8	12.4	11.4	12.1	46
West	4.3	5.0	5.4	6.4	6.8	6.8	7.6	7.5	6.7	5.7	5.8	4.7	6.1	46
West Northwest	1.9	2.4	2.6	2.9	3.2	2.8	3.3	3.7	2.5	2.6	2.8	2.5	2.8	46
Northwest	2.3	2.8	2.4	2.7	2.8	2.0	2.7	2.5	2.2	2.3	2.2	2.7	2.5	46
North Northwest	4.2	4.1	3.6	3.1	3.0	2.2	3.3	2.8	2.6	2.5	3.1	4.1	3.2	46
Calm	4.9	4.5	4.8	4.5	5.0	5.2	5.6	5.4	5.0	5.0	5.5	4.5	5.0	46
Direction (mean speed, knots)														
North	8.6	9.1	8.8	7.9	7.7	6.5	6.5	6.8	6.8	6.7	7.6	8.3	7.7	46
North Northeast	8.0	8.7	8.1	8.1	8.1	7.5	7.4	7.3	7.2	7.3	7.3	7.6	7.7	46
Northeast	7.5	8.3	8.2	7.9	7.8	7.9	7.7	7.4	7.3	7.1	7.0	7.7	7.7	46
East Northeast	7.5	8.2	8.1	8.3	8.3	8.2	8.1	8.1	7.7	7.3	7.5	7.7	8.0	46
East	7.9	8.3	8.7	8.6	8.7	8.4	8.1	8.0	8.0	7.8	7.5	7.4	8.2	46
East Southeast	9.4	9.7	9.7	9.7	9.1	9.1	8.5	8.5	8.4	8.6	8.0	8.6	9.0	46
Southeast	9.3	9.3	9.6	9.7	8.3	7.5	7.3	7.6	8.0	8.3	8.4	8.8	8.7	46
South Southeast	8.3	7.7	7.2	7.2	6.3	5.8	5.3	5.9	6.1	6.7	6.9	7.8	7.1	46
South	6.0	5.3	5.2	5.1	5.0	4.2	4.3	4.4	4.6	4.6	5.1	5.4	5.0	46
South Southwest	5.2	5.1	5.1	5.0	5.0	4.8	4.7	4.7	4.8	4.8	4.9	5.0	4.9	46
Southwest	5.4	5.5	5.4	5.2	5.3	5.2	5.2	5.1	5.3	5.3	5.3	5.4	5.3	46
West Southwest	5.8	5.7	5.7	5.6	5.7	5.6	5.5	5.5	5.7	5.5	5.5	5.7	5.6	46
West	5.4	5.5	5.4	5.4	5.5	5.4	5.4	5.5	5.5	5.3	5.4	5.4	5.4	46
West Northwest	5.8	5.8	5.5	5.6	5.5	5.3	5.3	5.3	5.3	5.4	5.6	5.5	5.5	46
Northwest	7.0	7.0	6.9	6.3	6.5	5.5	5.5	5.7	5.6	5.8	6.2	6.9	6.3	46
North Northwest	8.5	8.9	8.4	7.3	7.5	6.1	6.0	6.6	6.3	6.6	7.6	8.4	7.5	46
VISIBILITY														
Mean number of days with fog	Miss	Miss	Miss	Miss	0	Miss	Miss	Miss	Miss	Miss	Miss	Miss	1	46

* Sea level pressure is station pressure reduced to sea level
T = trace (not measurable) amount of precipitation
Miss or blank is a missing value
These tables were prepared by the National Climatic Data Center (NCDC), National Environmental Satellite, Data & Information Service (NESDIS), NOAA

CLIMATOLOGICAL DATA – HONOLULU, HI (21°20'N, 157°55'W) 7 feet (2.1 m)														
WEATHER ELEMENTS	JAN	FEB	MAR	APR	MAY	JUN	JUL	AUG	SEP	OCT	NOV	DEC	YEAR	YEARS OF RECORD
SEA LEVEL PRESSURE*														
Mean (millibars)	1015.6	1015.8	1017.3	1017.5	1017.4	1017.2	1016.5	1015.9	1015.0	1015.2	1015.7	1015.8	1016.2	46
TEMPERATURE (°F)														
Mean	73.0	73.0	74.2	75.7	77.4	79.4	80.4	81.3	81.0	79.6	77.3	74.5	77.2	46
Mean daily maximum	79.9	80.0	81.0	82.3	84.1	86.0	86.9	87.9	87.9	86.4	83.7	81.0	83.9	46
Mean daily minimum	65.5	65.5	67.0	68.6	70.2	72.2	73.4	74.2	73.5	72.3	70.4	67.5	70.0	46
Extreme (highest)	87	88	89	89	93	92	94	93	95	94	93	89	95	46
Extreme (lowest)	52	53	55	56	60	65	66	67	66	61	57	54	52	46
RELATIVE HUMIDITY														
Average percentage	31.3	32.9	48.3	49.6	48.8	46.6	39.9	33.8	25.4	27.5	32.1	33.4	37.5	46
CLOUD COVER														
Percent of time clear	12.4	10.7	7.4	4.4	3.6	3.2	2.9	3.3	5.9	5.9	6.5	9.9	6.3	46
Percent of time scattered	44.3	44.7	46.5	44.4	48.0	52.6	56.3	56.0	55.7	49.6	46.7	42.7	49.0	46
Percent of time broken	26.3	27.9	28.7	34.5	34.4	35.1	34.5	32.7	30.8	31.8	31.8	30.1	31.6	46
Percent of time overcast	17.0	16.7	17.4	16.7	14.0	9.0	6.3	7.9	7.5	12.8	15.0	17.3	13.1	46
PRECIPITATION (inches)														
Mean amount	3.3	2.6	2.8	1.3	0.9	0.3	0.5	0.5	0.7	2.0	2.5	3.5	21.5	46
Greatest amount	13.3	13.6	20.7	8.9	7.2	2.4	2.3	3.0	2.0	11.1	14.7	17.2	42.7	46
Least amount	0.1	0.0	0.0	0.0	0.0	T	0.0	T	0.0	0.1	0.0	0.0	5.0	46
Maximum amount (24 hours)	6.4	5.5	15.3	3.9	3.4	2.0	2.1	2.1	1.3	7.4	5.3	7.8	15.3	46
Mean number of days	17	16	19	20	19	19	20	18	17	18	19	18	220	46
SNOW														
Mean amount	0	0	0	0	0	0	0	0	0	0	0	0	0	46
Greatest amount	0	0	0	0	0	0	0	0	0	0	0	0	0	46
Least amount	0	0	0	0	0	0	0	0	0	0	0	0	0	46
Maximum amount (24 hours)	0	0	0	0	0	0	0	0	0	0	0	0	0	46
Mean number of days	0	0	0	0	0	0	0	0	0	0	0	0	0	46
WIND														
Percentage with gales	0.02	0.00	0.01	0.01	0.00	0.00	0.00	0.01	0.00	0.00	0.01	0.01	0.95	46
Mean wind speed (knots)	8.3	8.8	9.9	10.2	10.3	11.0	11.4	11.2	9.8	9.1	9.3	9.1	9.9	46
Direction (percentage of observations)														
North	5.8	5.4	5.1	4.4	3.0	1.4	0.9	1.3	2.5	3.8	4.6	5.0	3.6	46
North Northeast	5.1	4.7	4.9	4.6	4.1	2.7	2.4	2.5	3.7	4.3	4.5	4.7	4.0	46
Northeast	13.6	17.1	20.5	26.7	28.2	31.0	30.8	30.6	25.9	23.3	20.7	18.5	23.9	46
East Northeast	18.9	22.7	31.8	37.4	40.4	47.4	52.1	49.8	43.1	35.6	35.1	27.9	36.9	46
East	5.1	5.6	7.7	6.7	7.8	8.8	9.0	8.9	7.7	8.1	8.3	6.5	7.5	46
East Southeast	1.8	1.6	1.2	1.0	1.2	1.0	0.9	0.9	1.3	1.4	1.7	1.7	1.3	46
Southeast	3.0	2.8	2.3	1.8	1.6	0.8	0.7	1.1	1.7	2.5	2.2	2.8	1.9	46
South Southeast	4.2	3.0	2.7	2.1	1.7	1.1	0.5	0.7	1.9	2.3	2.6	3.3	2.2	46
South	5.5	4.1	3.1	2.1	1.9	0.9	0.4	0.6	1.8	2.4	2.5	3.5	2.4	46
South Southwest	4.2	3.1	2.2	1.3	1.0	0.6	0.1	0.2	0.8	1.5	1.5	2.3	1.6	46
Southwest	1.6	3.9	2.0	1.1	0.8	0.4	0.1	0.2	0.7	1.2	1.3	2.6	1.6	46
West Southwest	3.3	2.8	1.5	0.6	0.5	0.2	0.1	0.2	0.4	0.6	0.6	1.4	1.0	46
West	2.8	2.7	1.5	0.6	0.6	0.2	0.1	0.2	0.5	0.9	0.8	1.8	1.0	46
West Northwest	3.8	3.7	2.1	1.1	1.2	0.6	0.3	0.5	1.2	1.8	2.0	3.0	1.8	46
Northwest	7.8	7.4	5.1	3.5	2.6	1.1	0.8	1.1	2.6	4.0	5.0	6.6	4.0	46
North Northwest	6.0	6.0	4.3	3.3	2.2	1.0	0.6	0.8	2.2	3.4	4.0	5.3	3.3	46
Calm	5.1	3.9	2.5	2.2	1.8	1.2	0.7	1.0	2.4	3.2	2.9	3.4	2.5	46
Direction (mean speed, knots)														
North	5.8	6.1	6.4	5.9	5.7	4.7	5.0	4.9	4.9	5.0	5.6	6.0	5.7	46
North Northeast	7.4	7.8	8.4	8.3	8.8	8.1	8.9	8.2	7.4	7.4	7.7	7.7	8.0	46
Northeast	9.6	10.9	11.5	11.8	11.5	11.8	11.9	11.7	10.9	10.6	10.6	10.9	11.3	46
East Northeast	10.7	11.3	12.0	11.9	11.5	11.7	11.9	11.9	11.0	10.7	11.3	11.4	11.5	46
East	9.7	9.6	10.4	10.2	9.8	10.5	10.7	10.4	9.5	9.6	10.2	9.9	10.1	46
East Southeast	9.2	8.6	9.5	8.5	8.4	8.4	9.4	10.0	8.3	8.8	9.4	9.1	9.0	46
Southeast	9.9	10.3	11.1	9.4	10.3	10.1	10.7	11.6	11.1	10.6	10.5	10.3	10.4	46
South Southeast	9.9	9.6	9.8	10.1	9.3	10.5	9.8	9.9	9.0	9.5	10.1	9.7	9.7	46
South	8.8	7.9	7.9	7.7	7.2	7.6	7.1	8.2	7.6	7.6	7.6	8.3	8.0	46
South Southwest	9.3	8.2	8.4	8.2	7.8	7.8	6.2	9.0	8.2	7.9	7.5	8.8	8.4	46
Southwest	9.7	9.0	9.4	8.7	8.6	8.0	8.9	9.2	8.6	8.0	8.1	8.8	9.0	46
West Southwest	10.1	9.5	9.5	7.4	7.8	7.5	6.4	10.1	7.5	8.0	7.6	8.7	9.1	46
West	7.5	7.6	6.6	4.9	4.2	4.9	3.1	5.0	4.1	4.4	4.6	6.5	6.3	46
West Northwest	5.4	5.4	5.4	5.0	4.5	4.5	4.5	4.4	4.4	4.6	4.7	5.1	5.0	46
Northwest	5.6	5.8	5.8	5.5	5.3	5.2	5.2	5.1	4.9	5.0	5.5	5.5	5.5	46
North Northwest	6.0	6.2	5.7	5.8	5.5	4.8	4.9	4.9	4.8	5.0	5.5	5.9	5.7	46
VISIBILITY														
Mean number of days with fog	0	0	Miss	Miss	Miss	Miss	0	0	0	Miss	Miss	Miss	Miss	46

* Sea level pressure is station pressure reduced to sea level
T = trace (not measurable) amount of precipitation
Miss or blank is a missing value
These tables were prepared by the National Climatic Data Center (NCDC), National Environmental Satellite, Data & Information Service (NESDIS), NOAA

CLIMATOLOGICAL DATA – LIHUE, HI (21°59'N, 159°21'W) 103 feet (31.4 m)														
WEATHER ELEMENTS	JAN	FEB	MAR	APR	MAY	JUN	JUL	AUG	SEP	OCT	NOV	DEC	YEAR	YEARS OF RECORD
SEA LEVEL PRESSURE*														
Mean (millibars)	1015.9	1016.2	1017.8	1018.2	1018.2	1017.9	1017.4	1016.7	1015.7	1015.8	1016.2	1016.2	1016.8	45
TEMPERATURE (°F)														
Mean	71.6	71.6	72.5	73.9	75.7	77.8	78.9	79.6	79.3	77.8	75.7	73.1	75.6	46
Mean daily maximum	77.9	77.9	78.2	79.2	81.0	83.0	83.9	84.7	84.8	83.3	80.8	78.6	81.1	46
Mean daily minimum	64.8	64.8	66.3	68.0	69.9	72.1	73.3	74.0	73.3	71.8	70.0	67.1	69.7	46
Extreme (highest)	85	86	88	88	88	89	89	90	90	90	89	86	90	46
Extreme (lowest)	50	52	51	56	59	61	62	66	65	61	57	52	50	46
RELATIVE HUMIDITY														
Average percentage	34.1	36.7	53.1	56.5	56.6	54.2	48.8	42.5	31.9	33.4	37.0	37.0	43.4	45
CLOUD COVER														
Percent of time clear	16.1	15.9	9.2	4.1	3.1	3.2	1.8	2.5	4.9	6.4	7.1	11.8	7.1	45
Percent of time scattered	31.4	31.7	30.6	28.7	33.0	38.7	37.9	38.0	44.9	37.8	32.8	31.0	34.8	45
Percent of time broken	29.2	29.0	32.2	36.0	37.3	37.8	40.5	38.7	35.4	34.4	33.7	31.9	34.7	45
Percent of time overcast	23.4	23.4	28.0	31.2	26.6	20.4	19.8	20.8	14.8	21.3	26.4	25.4	23.4	45
PRECIPITATION (inches)														
Mean amount	5.4	3.6	4.2	3.0	2.6	1.5	2.1	1.9	2.2	4.4	5.4	5.5	42.3	46
Greatest amount	17.5	11.3	14.5	10.6	12.5	4.8	8.8	8.1	10.8	18.0	18.4	22.9	74.4	46
Least amount	0.3	T	0.3	0.3	0.4	0.4	0.7	0.7	0.4	1.0	0.5	0.5	16.4	46
Maximum amount (24 hours)	10.7	5.4	5.1	5.3	4.9	2.0	4.9	5.3	7.1	7.8	9.7	11.2	10.7	46
Mean number of days	20	19	23	24	23	23	26	25	22	24	24	22	275	46
SNOW														
Mean amount	0	0	0	0	0	0	0	0	0	0	0	0	0	46
Greatest amount	0	0	0	0	0	0	0	0	0	0	0	0	0	46
Least amount	0	0	0	0	0	0	0	0	0	0	0	0	0	46
Maximum amount (24 hours)	0	0	0	0	0	0	0	0	0	0	0	0	0	46
Mean number of days	0	0	0	0	0	0	0	0	0	0	0	0	0	46
WIND														
Percentage with gales	0.03	0.01	0.00	0.00	0.00	0.00	0.00	0.00	0.02	0.00	0.02	0.00	0.97	45
Mean wind speed (knots)	9.6	9.9	10.9	11.5	11	11.3	11.9	11.4	10.1	10.0	10.5	10.2	10.7	45
Direction (percentage of observations)														
North	4.9	5.5	4.5	4.3	2.9	1.1	1.0	1.3	2.1	3.6	4.9	5.2	3.4	45
North Northeast	6.5	6.6	7.2	7.7	7.0	4.5	5.7	5.4	5.5	7.0	7.2	7.0	6.4	45
Northeast	13.6	18.3	23.8	31.3	34.7	36.5	41.2	39.7	31.3	26.2	22.6	19.9	28.3	45
East Northeast	14.8	17.4	25.8	30.2	31.9	42.8	42.2	40.9	35.7	29.4	26.6	19.7	29.9	45
East	7.1	7.7	9.4	8.9	8.8	7.0	6.1	7.1	8.5	8.7	8.8	8.0	8.0	45
East Southeast	2.2	2.6	2.3	1.3	1.6	0.8	0.5	0.6	1.4	1.8	2.1	2.4	1.6	45
Southeast	1.3	1.4	0.8	0.7	0.7	0.4	0.2	0.3	0.5	1.1	1.1	1.6	0.8	45
South Southeast	2.2	1.6	1.1	0.9	0.6	0.3	0.1	0.3	0.4	1.0	1.3	1.7	1.0	45
South	4.5	2.9	2.0	1.7	0.8	0.6	0.2	0.4	0.7	1.6	2.6	3.3	1.8	45
South Southwest	4.4	3.0	1.5	0.6	0.4	0.1	0.0	0.1	0.4	0.8	1.2	2.6	1.2	45
Southwest	7.1	5.4	2.2	0.7	0.6	0.2	0.0	0.2	0.7	1.1	2.0	3.9	2.0	45
West Southwest	7.6	6.1	3.5	1.3	1.2	0.6	0.2	0.3	1.4	2.4	2.8	4.7	2.7	45
West	12.6	10.9	7.8	4.3	4.0	2.6	1.0	1.6	5.2	7.1	7.7	9.7	6.2	45
West Northwest	6.1	5.6	4.3	3.2	2.9	1.6	0.9	1.3	3.7	4.8	5.1	5.6	3.7	45
Northwest	1.9	1.9	1.5	1.0	1.0	0.6	0.5	0.4	1.1	1.3	1.4	1.6	1.2	45
North Northwest	3.1	3.0	2.6	1.7	1.2	0.7	0.6	0.6	1.2	1.9	2.5	2.8	1.8	45
Calm	0.4	0.6	0.4	0.4	0.4	0.2	0.1	0.1	0.4	0.6	0.3	0.4	0.4	45
Direction (mean speed, knots)														
North	9.0	8.7	8.8	8.1	7.7	5.8	6.6	5.9	6.2	7.2	8.9	8.4	8.1	45
North Northeast	12.1	12.0	11.9	11.6	11.0	9.7	10.4	10.3	9.8	10.7	11.6	11.7	11.1	45
Northeast	12.3	12.5	12.9	12.9	12.2	11.8	11.9	11.5	11.1	11.3	12.3	12.7	12.0	45
East Northeast	11.8	12.2	13.2	13.1	12.1	12.2	12.6	12.1	11.2	11.6	12.5	12.7	12.2	45
East	10.4	10.6	11.7	12.1	10.7	10.9	11.9	11.3	10.2	10.8	11.4	11.2	11.1	45
East Southeast	8.1	8.5	9.5	9.7	9.5	10.3	12.2	10.8	8.9	8.9	10.5	9.3	9.4	45
Southeast	8.5	8.4	8.3	8.5	7.9	8.6	10.2	9.9	8.9	8.8	8.7	8.6	8.6	45
South Southeast	9.4	9.7	9.5	10.1	8.5	10.6	9.1	10.4	8.6	9.7	9.9	10.7	9.8	45
South	9.8	9.1	9.1	9.5	8.1	8.0	8.0	9.6	7.5	8.4	9.6	9.9	9.3	45
South Southwest	10.7	10.1	10.1	9.1	8.6	9.4	8.0	12.5	8.7	9.5	9.4	10.5	10.1	45
Southwest	10.5	10.5	10.2	8.0	7.8	7.4	7.5	9.3	7.9	7.9	8.3	10.0	9.8	45
West Southwest	7.8	8.3	7.0	5.9	6.7	5.7	6.5	5.7	6.2	5.9	6.4	6.8	7.1	45
West	6.1	5.9	5.6	5.4	5.2	5.1	5.0	5.1	5.5	5.5	5.4	5.9	5.7	45
West Northwest	5.9	5.8	5.5	5.6	5.5	5.2	5.3	5.4	5.6	5.7	5.5	5.6	5.6	45
Northwest	5.9	6.4	5.8	6.2	5.7	5.0	5.1	5.4	5.5	5.7	6.0	6.3	5.9	45
North Northwest	7.1	7.8	7.7	7.1	6.4	5.8	6.0	6.3	5.9	6.2	7.2	7.4	7.0	45
VISIBILITY														
Mean number of days with fog	Miss	Miss	Miss	Miss	Miss	Miss	0	0	Miss	Miss	Miss	1	46	

* Sea level pressure is station pressure reduced to sea level
T = trace (not measurable) amount of precipitation
Miss or blank is a missing value
These tables were prepared by the National Climatic Data Center (NCDC), National Environmental Satellite, Data & Information Service (NESDIS), NOAA

METEOROLOGICAL TABLE – COASTAL AREA OFF SAN DIEGO, CA
Between 31°N to 34°N and 116°W to 120°W

WEATHER ELEMENTS	JAN	FEB	MAR	APR	MAY	JUN	JUL	AUG	SEP	OCT	NOV	DEC	YEARS OF RECORD
Wind > 33 knots [1]	0.4	0.5	0.4	0.4	0.3	0.1	0.0	0.0	0.1	0.1	0.2	0.5	48
Wave Height > 9 feet [1]	0.8	1.3	1.7	1.8	1.2	0.8	0.5	0.3	0.4	0.6	0.9	1.2	48
Visibility < 2 nautical miles [1]	4.4	4.5	2.8	2.4	1.5	3.2	2.9	2.2	3.0	4.7	3.3	4.0	48
Precipitation [1]	3.6	3.6	2.4	1.7	1.2	1.4	0.8	0.5	0.9	0.9	2.1	3.1	1.8
Temperature > 69° F	1.2	0.8	1.2	1.4	1.9	3.0	9.2	14.7	14.8	9.0	4.4	1.7	5.4
Mean Temperature (°F)	58.3	58.4	58.5	59.3	60.4	62.1	64.7	66.4	66.5	65.2	62.7	59.9	61.9
Temperature < 33° F [1]	0.0	0.0	0.0	0.0	0.0	0.0	0.0	0.0	0.0	0.0	0.0	0.0	0.0
Mean RH (%)	77	79	78	79	81	83	84	84	83	81	77	76	80
Overcast or Obscured [1]	19.4	21.4	22.2	25.7	37.9	48.1	45.7	38.8	31.4	26.3	15.4	16.7	29.3
Mean Cloud Cover (8ths)	3.8	3.9	4.1	4.2	5.0	5.5	5.6	5.3	4.6	4.2	3.4	3.5	4.4
Mean SLP (mbs)	1018	1018	1017	1015	1015	1013	1013	1013	1012	1014	1017	1018	1015
Ext. Max. SLP (mbs)	1040	1040	1037	1034	1030	1029	1027	1027	1028	1031	1035	1040	1040
Ext. Min. SLP (mbs)	996	996	995	998	999	998	999	998	997	997	999	995	995
Prevailing Wind Direction	NW	NW	NW	NW	NW	NW	NW	NW	NW	NW	NW	NW	NW
Thunder and Lightning [1]	0.1	0.1	0.2	0.1	0.0	0.1	0.2	0.1	0.3	0.2	0.1	0.1	0.1

METEOROLOGICAL TABLE – COASTAL AREA OFF POINT MUGU, CA
Between 34°N to 36°N and 119°W to 125°W

WEATHER ELEMENTS	JAN	FEB	MAR	APR	MAY	JUN	JUL	AUG	SEP	OCT	NOV	DEC	YEARS OF RECORD
Wind > 33 knots [1]	1.0	1.5	2.0	2.2	1.8	1.5	0.7	0.4	0.5	0.9	1.1	1.4	1.3
Wave Height > 9 feet [1]	4.4	6.0	8.1	10.4	10.6	8.1	5.3	4.4	3.9	3.8	4.6	6.4	6.4
Visibility < 2 nautical miles [1]	4.5	6.3	4.6	4.9	5.7	5.8	8.5	8.0	7.7	8.7	5.5	5.6	6.3
Precipitation [1]	5.5	5.8	5.0	3.2	1.6	1.7	1.5	1.6	1.4	1.4	3.4	4.8	3.0
Temperature > 69° F	0.6	0.5	0.5	0.5	0.7	1.4	3.4	3.6	4.2	2.6	1.5	0.8	1.7
Mean Temperature (°F)	55.5	55.8	55.9	56.7	57.6	59.4	61.1	62.1	62.8	61.7	59.5	57.4	58.8
Temperature < 33° F [1]	0.1	0.0	0.0	0.0	0.0	0.0	0.0	0.0	0.0	0.0	0.0	0.0	0.0
Mean RH (%)	79	79	80	80	82	84	86	86	85	84	81	79	82
Overcast or Obscured [1]	21.2	25.7	24.4	24.5	32.1	40.0	50.6	48.2	36.6	29.4	18.9	20.4	31.4
Mean Cloud Cover (8ths)	4.1	4.3	4.3	4.2	4.5	4.7	5.4	5.4	4.6	4.3	3.7	3.9	4.5
Mean SLP (mbs)	1019	1019	1018	1017	1016	1015	1015	1015	1014	1016	1018	1019	1017
Ext. Max. SLP (mbs)	1036	1036	1045	1043	1035	1031	1033	1030	1032	1034	1040	1039	1045
Ext. Min. SLP (mbs)	987	992	990	996	997	995	998	998	996	998	996	991	987
Prevailing Wind Direction	NW	NW	NW	NW	NW	NW	NW	NW	NW	NW	NW	NW	NW
Thunder and Lightning [1]	0.1	0.1	0.2	0.1	0.1	0.1	0.1	0.1	0.2	0.1	0.1	0.2	0.1

METEOROLOGICAL TABLE – COASTAL AREA OFF SAN FRANCISCO, CA
Between 36°N to 38°N and 121°W to 126°W

WEATHER ELEMENTS	JAN	FEB	MAR	APR	MAY	JUN	JUL	AUG	SEP	OCT	NOV	DEC	YEARS OF RECORD
Wind > 33 knots [1]	2.2	2.2	2.9	2.9	2.9	2.4	1.1	0.8	1.0	1.5	1.9	2.9	2.1
Wave Height > 9 feet [1]	6.2	5.9	7.8	9.1	9.8	7.4	5.8	4.8	4.2	3.8	5.3	7.1	6.5
Visibility < 2 nautical miles [1]	7.8	7.3	4.6	3.4	4.7	6.2	7.9	7.6	8.2	8.9	8.8	8.1	6.9
Precipitation [1]	9.4	7.4	6.9	3.8	2.7	2.6	2.0	2.0	2.0	2.6	5.2	7.7	4.4
Temperature > 69° F	0.2	0.1	0.2	0.2	0.4	0.7	1.1	2.0	2.4	1.3	0.5	0.3	0.8
Mean Temperature (°F)	53.7	53.9	54.1	54.2	55.6	57.6	59.2	60.5	61	59.7	57.4	55.2	56.9
Temperature < 33° F [1]	0.3	0.0	0.0	0.1	0.0	0.0	0.0	0.0	0.0	0.0	0.0	0.0	0.0
Mean RH (%)	82	83	81	81	83	85	86	87	85	85	83	81	84
Overcast or Obscured [1]	30.2	30.6	28.9	25.7	31.8	38.4	49.8	46.9	35.9	30.3	25.3	27.4	33.7
Mean Cloud Cover (8ths)	4.8	4.8	4.8	4.4	4.7	4.7	5.3	5.1	4.5	4.3	4.3	4.5	4.7
Mean SLP (mbs)	1019	1019	1018	1018	1017	1016	1016	1016	1015	1017	1019	1019	1017
Ext. Max. SLP (mbs)	1050	1051	1049	1041	1040	1042	1032	1031	1039	1033	1044	1042	1051
Ext. Min. SLP (mbs)	984	985	983	989	994	995	999	998	1000	997	996	989	983
Prevailing Wind Direction	NW	NW	NW	NW	NW	NW	NW	NW	NW	NW	NW	N	NW
Thunder and Lightning [1]	0.2	0.2	0.2	0.1	0.1	0.1	0.1	0.1	0.1	0.1	0.2	0.1	0.1

[1] Percentage Frequency
These data are based upon observations made by ships in transit. These ships tend to avoid bad weather when possible thus biasing the data toward good weather samples.

METEOROLOGICAL TABLE – COASTAL AREA OFF POINT ARENA, CA
Between 38°N to 40°N and 122°W to 127°W

WEATHER ELEMENTS	JAN	FEB	MAR	APR	MAY	JUN	JUL	AUG	SEP	OCT	NOV	DEC	YEARS OF RECORD
Wind > 33 knots [1]	3.6	3.1	3.3	4.1	6.1	4.8	4.0	2.4	2.6	2.8	2.6	3.4	3.6
Wave Height > 9 feet [1]	9.8	9.8	10.3	12.6	15.3	11.1	11.2	8.1	7.6	60	7.4	9.1	10.1
Visibility < 2 nautical miles [1]	8.0	8.6	5.7	4.1	5.2	7.0	9.4	10.0	11.8	9.7	9.4	10.4	8.2
Precipitation [1]	11.1	10.5	9.4	5.6	3.2	2.3	1.8	1.6	2.0	4.4	9.0	12.0	5.6
Temperature > 69° F	0.2	0.1	1.0	0.3	1.2	2.4	2.3	3.8	3.1	1.6	0.7	0.1	1.5
Mean Temperature (°F)	52.3	52.9	53.6	53.6	55.3	57.4	59.1	60.4	60.5	58.9	56.2	53.5	56.4
Temperature < 33° F [1]	0.1	0.0	0.0	0.0	0.0	0.0	0.0	0.0	0.0	0.0	0.0	0.0	0.0
Mean RH (%)	82	81	80	80	82	84	85	85	85	85	82	82	83
Overcast or Obscured [1]	33.6	34.2	29.5	25.1	26.3	31.2	39.2	38.6	34.2	29.0	31.4	34.9	32.3
Mean Cloud Cover (8ths)	5.0	5.0	4.7	4.4	4.2	4.3	4.7	4.6	4.3	4.2	4.6	5.0	4.6
Mean SLP (mbs)	1019	1019	1018	1018	1017	1016	1016	1015	1015	1017	1019	1019	1017
Ext. Max. SLP (mbs)	1047	1036	1041	1043	1043	1042	1035	1030	1030	1033	1041	1051	1051
Ext. Min. SLP (mbs)	985	984	982	994	993	996	998	997	1000	995	985	991	982
Prevailing Wind Direction	N	NW	NW	NW	NW	NW	NW	NW	NW	NW	N	N	NW
Thunder and Lightning [1]	0.2	0.2	0.2	0.1	0.1	0.1	0.1	0.0	0.2	0.2	0.1	0.3	0.2

METEOROLOGICAL TABLE – COASTAL AREA OFF EUREKA, CA
Between 40°N to 42°N and 124°W to 127°W

WEATHER ELEMENTS	JAN	FEB	MAR	APR	MAY	JUN	JUL	AUG	SEP	OCT	NOV	DEC	YEARS OF RECORD
Wind > 33 knots [1]	6.5	5.1	4.4	3.2	4.6	3.4	3.7	2.4	3.2	2.9	4.2	6.0	4.1
Wave Height > 9 feet [1]	10.8	8.8	10.7	5.5	9.9	7.4	8.8	5.9	6.9	5.0	7.7	11.3	8.2
Visibility < 2 nautical miles [1]	6.9	7.2	5.3	3.2	4.6	6.6	11.0	11.0	11.1	9.8	8.9	7.4	7.7
Precipitation [1]	15.1	12.9	12.2	8.2	4.3	3.2	2.1	3.2	3.3	6.1	12.3	15.0	7.6
Temperature > 69° F	0.0	0.0	0.0	0.1	0.2	0.8	0.9	2.2	1.7	0.8	0.2	0.0	0.6
Mean Temperature (°F)	51.7	51.8	52.1	52.6	54.2	56.7	58.2	59.5	59.5	57.6	55.0	52.5	55.3
Temperature < 33° F [1]	0.1	0.0	0.0	0.0	0.0	0.0	0.0	0.0	0.0	0.0	0.0	0.1	0.0
Mean RH (%)	84	83	82	81	83	84	86	87	86	85	83	83	84
Overcast or Obscured [1]	38.8	39.8	35.8	31.6	31.4	32.4	40.4	40.5	35.5	33.2	36.5	37.5	36.1
Mean Cloud Cover (8ths)	5.4	5.5	5.3	4.9	4.8	4.6	4.8	4.8	4.3	4.5	5.2	5.4	4.9
Mean SLP (mbs)	1018	1018	1018	1019	1019	1018	1017	1017	1015	1017	1018	1018	1018
Ext. Max. SLP (mbs)	1042	1060	1047	1036	1050	1045	1043	1042	1044	1043	1037	1038	1060
Ext. Min. SLP (mbs)	960	982	984	985	992	992	998	993	990	987	978	984	960
Prevailing Wind Direction	S	S	N	N	N	N	N	N	N	N	N	S	N
Thunder and Lightning [1]	0.3	0.8	0.2	0.3	0.1	0.2	0.1	0.0	0.2	0.4	0.5	0.4	0.3

METEOROLOGICAL TABLE – COASTAL AREA OFF NORTH BEND, OR
Between 42°N to 44°N and 124°W to 127°W

WEATHER ELEMENTS	JAN	FEB	MAR	APR	MAY	JUN	JUL	AUG	SEP	OCT	NOV	DEC	YEARS OF RECORD
Wind > 33 knots [1]	6.5	5.8	4.0	2.4	1.6	2.3	2.1	1.3	1.4	1.8	4.5	5.6	2.9
Wave Height > 9 feet [1]	11.9	11.4	9.8	5.5	5.4	4.7	5.2	3.2	3.3	4.9	11.3	12	6.5
Visibility < 2 nautical miles [1]	6.3	6.9	4.5	5.0	4.5	4.9	7.7	14.8	8.7	9.8	5.9	7.1	7.4
Precipitation [1]	18.7	17.7	15.9	10.1	7.6	5.7	3.6	4.0	4.6	6.8	15.2	18.2	9.3
Temperature > 69° F	0.0	0.0	0.0	0.1	0.3	0.7	1.3	1.5	1.2	0.4	0.1	0.1	0.6
Mean Temperature (°F)	49.7	50.0	50.3	51.5	53.6	56.5	58.9	59.3	59.8	57.0	54.0	51.1	55.0
Temperature < 33° F [1]	0.1	0.2	0.0	0.0	0.0	0.0	0.0	0.0	0.0	0.0	0.0	0.2	0.0
Mean RH (%)	83	82	82	81	82	84	86	87	86	85	83	83	84
Overcast or Obscured [1]	42.9	43.2	39.4	34.0	33.6	37.0	37.6	43.6	32.9	34.4	41.4	40.4	38.0
Mean Cloud Cover (8ths)	5.7	5.7	5.6	5.2	5.1	5.3	4.8	5.2	4.4	4.7	5.5	5.6	5.2
Mean SLP (mbs)	1018	1017	1017	1019	1019	1019	1019	1017	1016	1018	1018	1018	1018
Ext. Max. SLP (mbs)	1037	1051	1039	1043	1042	1046	1040	1037	1038	1050	1050	1045	1051
Ext. Min. SLP (mbs)	969	973	984	980	988	995	997	992	985	982	976	961	961
Prevailing Wind Direction	S	S	S	N	N	N	N	N	N	N	S	S	N
Thunder and Lightning [1]	0.4	0.7	0.1	0.2	0.2	0.1	0.1	0.1	0.3	0.3	0.6	0.5	0.3

[1] Percentage Frequency
These data are based upon observations made by ships in transit. These ships tend to avoid bad weather when possible thus biasing the data toward good weather samples.

METEOROLOGICAL TABLE – COASTAL AREA OFF NEWPORT, OR
Between 44°N to 46°N and 123°W to 127°W

WEATHER ELEMENTS	JAN	FEB	MAR	APR	MAY	JUN	JUL	AUG	SEP	OCT	NOV	DEC	YEARS OF RECORD
Wind > 33 knots [1]	6.0	3.8	3.2	1.2	0.6	0.5	0.4	0.3	0.4	2.0	4.6	7.9	2.0
Wave Height > 9 feet [1]	12.4	7.7	8.9	3.5	2.8	2.2	1.8	1.7	2.2	4.4	9.9	13.9	4.6
Visibility < 2 nautical miles [1]	6.1	8.0	4.5	3.4	4.2	4.0	4.4	7.5	6.5	7.1	6.5	7.3	5.7
Precipitation [1]	20.7	18.1	16.3	12.7	8.8	7.9	4.7	5.9	6.7	11.4	16.9	19.5	10.8
Temperature > 69° F	0.0	0.0	0.0	0.0	0.2	0.6	1.5	1.7	1.5	0.4	0.1	0.0	0.6
Mean Temperature (°F)	48.2	48.6	48.9	50.4	53.6	57.0	59.9	60.4	60.7	57.4	53	49.7	55.1
Temperature < 33° F [1]	0.5	0.3	0.1	0.1	0.0	0.0	0.0	0.0	0.0	0.0	0.1	0.5	0.1
Mean RH (%)	82	82	81	81	81	82	84	85	84	83	82	84	83
Overcast or Obscured [1]	44.8	42.6	39.4	34.6	35.5	40.6	40.0	40.1	34.0	33.6	40.4	44.1	38.8
Mean Cloud Cover (8ths)	6.0	5.8	5.7	5.5	5.5	5.8	5.5	5.5	4.8	5.0	5.7	5.9	5.5
Mean SLP (mbs)	1017	1017	1016	1019	1019	1019	1019	1018	1017	1018	1017	1017	1018
Ext. Max. SLP (mbs)	1040	1055	1042	1052	1049	1044	1042	1041	1055	1040	1043	1044	1055
Ext. Min. SLP (mbs)	970	960	972	986	993	990	996	992	985	966	981	964	960
Prevailing Wind Direction	S	S	S	N	N	N	N	N	N	N	S	S	N
Thunder and Lightning [1]	0.2	0.4	0.2	0.2	0.2	0.2	0.2	0.2	0.4	0.2	0.6	0.3	0.3

METEOROLOGICAL TABLE – COASTAL AREA OFF ASTORIA, OR
Between 46°N to 48°N and 122°W to 127°W

WEATHER ELEMENTS	JAN	FEB	MAR	APR	MAY	JUN	JUL	AUG	SEP	OCT	NOV	DEC	YEARS OF RECORD
Wind > 33 knots [1]	5.1	4.9	3.9	1.4	0.7	0.3	0.1	0.3	0.5	2.4	5.1	6.6	2.3
Wave Height > 9 feet [1]	8.0	6.9	5.9	3.4	1.9	1.7	1.3	0.9	1.3	4.0	8.7	9.3	4.0
Visibility < 2 nautical miles [1]	8.0	7.0	5.8	3.6	4.5	4.7	5.7	8.7	6.7	7.5	5.7	7.8	6.3
Precipitation [1]	21.1	19.7	17.6	13.1	10.9	8.6	5.1	6.5	7.8	12.5	20.0	22.0	13.0
Temperature > 69° F	0.0	0.0	0.0	0.0	0.2	0.6	2.1	2.0	1.2	0.2	0.0	0.0	0.6
Mean Temperature (°F)	45.6	47.0	47.7	49.6	52.9	56.4	59.5	60.3	59.8	56.1	50.9	47.6	53.4
Temperature < 33° F [1]	2.3	0.6	0.1	0.0	0.1	0.0	0.0	0.0	0.0	0.0	0.1	1.4	0.4
Mean RH (%)	84	84	82	82	84	84	85	87	85	84	83	84	84
Overcast or Obscured [1]	46.4	43.7	38.4	35.0	36.3	41.5	42.1	41.9	32.3	35.4	41.7	45.6	39.9
Mean Cloud Cover (8ths)	6.0	5.9	5.6	5.6	5.7	6.0	5.6	5.5	4.8	5.2	5.8	6.0	5.6
Mean SLP (mbs)	1017	1016	1016	1018	1018	1018	1019	1018	1017	1017	1016	1017	1017
Ext. Max. SLP (mbs)	1045	1041	1058	1040	1050	1043	1038	1037	1049	1040	1042	1050	1058
Ext. Min. SLP (mbs)	970	975	974	978	985	988	991	991	978	980	964	963	963
Prevailing Wind Direction	S	S	S	NW	NW	NW	NW	NW	N	S	S	S	NW
Thunder and Lightning [1]	0.2	0.3	0.3	0.1	0.2	0.1	0.1	0.2	0.3	0.3	0.5	0.3	0.2

METEOROLOGICAL TABLE – COASTAL AREA OFF SEATTLE, WA
Between 48°N to 50°N and 122°W to 129°W

WEATHER ELEMENTS	JAN	FEB	MAR	APR	MAY	JUN	JUL	AUG	SEP	OCT	NOV	DEC	YEARS OF RECORD
Wind > 33 knots [1]	3.6	2.8	2.3	1.2	0.8	0.6	0.3	0.3	0.5	1.7	3.1	3.4	1.6
Wave Height > 9 feet [1]	17.4	18.0	16.8	15.0	6.7	6.1	1.9	2.1	4.7	16.0	24.0	30.5	12.3
Visibility < 2 nautical miles [1]	11.4	10.4	8.1	7.1	6.6	6.7	9.2	14.0	12.0	13.2	11.7	12.1	10.3
Precipitation [1]	24.4	24.4	19.6	16.7	13.5	10.8	7.5	5.8	9.2	16.6	24.0	24.9	15.6
Temperature > 69° F	0.0	0.0	0.0	0.1	0.5	1.6	3.0	2.8	1.2	0.3	0.0	0.0	0.9
Mean Temperature (°F)	44.0	45.3	46.1	48.7	52.8	56.3	58.8	59.3	58.2	53.7	48.3	45.5	52.1
Temperature < 33° F [1]	3.3	0.8	0.2	0.0	0.0	0.0	0.0	0.0	0.0	0.0	0.6	0.9	0.4
Mean RH (%)	84	84	82	82	82	82	84	85	84	84	83	84	83
Overcast or Obscured [1]	46.3	43.3	34.5	32.8	32.7	33.1	32.6	32.9	30.6	36.5	38.4	41.3	35.8
Mean Cloud Cover (8ths)	6.2	6.0	5.5	5.5	5.4	5.5	5.1	5.0	4.7	5.4	5.9	6.0	5.5
Mean SLP (mbs)	1014	1015	1014	1016	1017	1017	1018	1017	1017	1016	1014	1014	1016
Ext. Max. SLP (mbs)	1041	1057	1041	1060	1044	1042	1048	1040	1050	1041	1043	1048	1060
Ext. Min. SLP (mbs)	951	974	967	977	987	988	993	990	973	967	966	964	951
Prevailing Wind Direction	SE	SE	SE	NW	NW	NW	NW	NW	NW	SE	SE	SE	NW
Thunder and Lightning [1]	0.3	0.2	0.2	0.1	0.1	0.1	0.1	0.2	0.3	0.3	0.3	0.2	0.2

[1] Percentage Frequency
These data are based upon observations made by ships in transit. These ships tend to avoid bad weather when possible thus biasing the data toward good weather samples.

METEOROLOGICAL TABLE – COASTAL AREA OFF HAWAI'IAN (WINDWARD) ISLANDS
Between 18°N to 22°N and 154°W to Island

WEATHER ELEMENTS	JAN	FEB	MAR	APR	MAY	JUN	JUL	AUG	SEP	OCT	NOV	DEC	YEARS OF RECORD
Wind > 33 knots [1]	1.4	0.8	1.3	0.4	0.0	0.1	0.2	0.2	0.1	0.2	1.1	1.9	0.6
Wave Height > 9 feet [1]	4.0	4.0	5.6	3.9	2.5	1.3	1.9	1.8	0.5	1.8	4.7	6.3	3.2
Visibility < 2 nautical miles [1]	1.2	0.6	0.3	0.5	0.2	0.3	0.2	1.0	0.6	0.4	0.6	0.3	0.5
Precipitation [1]	5.7	5.5	5.6	5.8	3.1	6.4	4.0	5.4	3.1	2.7	5.7	4.0	4.8
Temperature > 69° F	89.9	84.7	87.5	85.8	93.2	94.2	99.7	99.9	99.8	99.6	99.1	95.5	93.8
Mean Temperature (°F)	74.1	73.5	73.5	74.1	75.6	76.7	77.7	78.5	78.7	78.3	76.8	75.0	76.0
Temperature < 33° F [1]	0.0	0.0	0.0	0.0	0.0	0.0	0.0	0.0	0.0	0.0	0.0	0.0	0.0
Mean RH (%)	79	79	78	78	77	77	78	79	77	77	78	78	78
Overcast or Obscured [1]	12.5	13.0	14.7	13.2	7.6	7.1	6.9	7.0	5.7	8.4	11.9	11.0	9.9
Mean Cloud Cover (8^{ths})	4.1	4.2	4.5	4.5	4.1	4.3	4.2	4.1	3.9	4.0	4.4	4.1	4.2
Mean SLP (mbs)	1015	1016	1017	1017	1017	1017	1017	1016	1015	1015	1016	1016	1016
Ext. Max. SLP (mbs)	1030	1033	1038	1030	1028	1030	1030	1030	1031	1030	1033	1028	1038
Ext. Min. SLP (mbs)	998	996	997	1001	1002	1002	1002	1002	1001	999	1000	1001	996
Prevailing Wind Direction	E	E	E	E	E	E	E	E	E	E	E	E	E
Thunder and Lightning [1]	0.7	0.4	0.4	0.3	0.1	0.1	0.1	0.3	0.2	0.3	0.4	0.4	0.3

METEOROLOGICAL TABLE – COASTAL AREA OFF HAWAI'IAN (LEEWARD) ISLANDS
Between 18°N to 22°N and from Island to 160°W

WEATHER ELEMENTS	JAN	FEB	MAR	APR	MAY	JUN	JUL	AUG	SEP	OCT	NOV	DEC	YEARS OF RECORD
Wind > 33 knots [1]	0.5	0.4	0.8	0.4	0.1	0.1	0.1	0.2	0.1	0.2	0.4	0.9	0.3
Wave Height > 9 feet [1]	2.3	2.5	2.9	2.0	0.9	0.7	1.2	0.9	0.9	1.5	2.2	4.5	1.8
Visibility < 2 nautical miles [1]	0.7	0.7	0.3	0.5	0.3	0.3	0.2	0.2	0.2	0.3	0.5	0.4	0.4
Precipitation [1]	4.0	4.6	4.0	3.7	3.2	2.2	2.1	2.2	2.1	2.8	3.9	4.5	3.2
Temperature > 69° F	94.7	93.6	93.1	97.0	99.1	99.8	99.8	99.9	99.9	99.8	99.7	97.6	97.8
Mean Temperature (°F)	75.1	74.7	74.7	75.7	77.1	78.5	79.2	79.7	80	79.3	77.9	76.2	77.4
Temperature < 33° F [1]	0.0	0.0	0.0	0.0	0.0	0.0	0.0	0.0	0.0	0.0	0.0	0.0	0.0
Mean RH (%)	77	77	77	78	77	77	77	77	77	77	78	78	77
Overcast or Obscured [1]	9.0	10.4	11.9	11.6	7.0	5.4	4.1	4.2	4.8	7.4	9.6	10.4	8.0
Mean Cloud Cover (8^{ths})	3.7	3.8	4.1	4.2	4.0	4.0	3.8	3.6	3.6	3.9	4.0	4.0	3.9
Mean SLP (mbs)	1015	1015	1016	1017	1017	1016	1016	1016	1015	1015	1015	1015	1016
Ext. Max. SLP (mbs)	1032	1030	1037	1031	1031	1031	1031	1032	1031	1032	1032	1033	1037
Ext. Min. SLP (mbs)	993	998	1000	1000	1001	1002	1003	1001	1000	999	998	998	993
Prevailing Wind Direction	E	E	E	E	E	E	E	E	E	E	E	E	E
Thunder and Lightning [1]	0.4	0.5	0.5	0.3	0.2	0.1	0.2	0.1	0.2	0.4	0.7	0.5	0.3

METEOROLOGICAL TABLE – COASTAL AREA OFF BARKING SANDS, HI
Between 36°N to 38°N and 72°W to 76°W

WEATHER ELEMENTS	JAN	FEB	MAR	APR	MAY	JUN	JUL	AUG	SEP	OCT	NOV	DEC	YEARS OF RECORD
Wind > 33 knots [1]	0.6	0.4	0.6	0.2	0.1	0.3	0.2	0.1	0.0	0.2	0.8	0.7	0.3
Wave Height > 9 feet [1]	3.0	6.2	5.0	5.3	1.8	1.5	2.9	1.4	0.9	1.7	4.5	7.7	3.4
Visibility < 2 nautical miles [1]	0.7	0.4	0.3	0.3	0.2	0.1	0.1	0.2	0.5	0.4	0.4	0.6	0.3
Precipitation [1]	3.8	3.5	4.3	3.9	2.4	1.8	2.1	3.0	2.0	3.1	4.6	5.3	3.3
Temperature > 69° F	84.1	77.0	80.4	88.0	96.1	98.5	99.8	99.9	99.5	99.0	98.3	93.3	93.0
Mean Temperature (°F)	73.4	72.7	73.0	73.7	75.2	76.9	77.9	78.8	79.1	78.0	76.6	74.5	75.9
Temperature < 33° F [1]	0.0	0.0	0.0	0.0	0.0	0.0	0.0	0.0	0.0	0.0	0.0	0.0	0.0
Mean RH (%)	78	78	78	78	79	80	79	79	78	77	78	78	78
Overcast or Obscured [1]	11.3	13.9	13.5	12.4	8.7	5.1	4.6	4.7	3.6	8.7	11.9	14.7	9.3
Mean Cloud Cover (8^{ths})	3.9	4.2	4.3	4.4	4.2	3.9	4.0	4.0	3.7	3.9	4.1	4.3	4.1
Mean SLP (mbs)	1015	1016	1018	1018	1018	1018	1017	1017	1016	1016	1016	1016	1017
Ext. Max. SLP (mbs)	1028	1031	1031	1032	1030	1030	1027	1026	1030	1026	1032	1029	1032
Ext. Min. SLP (mbs)	997	999	998	1000	1007	1002	1004	1002	1002	1001	1002	995	995
Prevailing Wind Direction	E	E	E	E	E	E	E	E	E	E	E	E	E
Thunder and Lightning [1]	0.6	0.3	0.3	0.5	0.3	0.1	0.3	0.5	0.3	0.5	0.7	0.7	0.4

[1] Percentage Frequency
These data are based upon observations made by ships in transit. These ships tend to avoid bad weather when possible thus biasing the data toward good weather samples.

METEOROLOGICAL TABLE – COASTAL AREA OFF FRENCH FRIGATE SHOALS
Between 23°N to 25°N and 165°W to 168°W

WEATHER ELEMENTS	JAN	FEB	MAR	APR	MAY	JUN	JUL	AUG	SEP	OCT	NOV	DEC	YEARS OF RECORD
Wind > 33 knots [1]	1.7	1.3	0.4	0.9	0.2	0.0	0.3	0.0	0.1	0.3	1.6	1.4	0.7
Wave Height > 9 feet [1]	6.7	5.4	3.5	5.2	1.5	0.5	1.5	0.3	0.4	3.0	3.1	7.5	3.1
Visibility < 2 nautical miles [1]	1.1	0.9	0.8	0.3	0.3	0.2	0.4	0.4	0.0	0.3	0.6	0.6	0.5
Precipitation [1]	5.4	4.8	6.1	4.8	4.2	1.8	2.8	4.2	2.9	4.0	6.7	4.5	4.4
Temperature > 69° F	68.7	66.4	68.5	80.7	94.1	99.6	99.9	99.9	100	99.8	97.9	87.1	88.9
Mean Temperature (°F)	72.0	71.7	71.9	73.1	75.0	77.9	78.7	79.4	79.4	78.5	76.4	73.8	75.7
Temperature < 33° F [1]	0.0	0.0	0.0	0.0	0.0	0.0	0.0	0.0	0.0	0.0	0.0	0.0	0.0
Mean RH (%)	77	78	79	78	79	79	79	79	78	77	78	76	78
Overcast or Obscured [1]	16.8	14.1	16.1	16.1	10.8	3.9	4.4	7.0	5.0	9.5	14.9	13.6	11
Mean Cloud Cover (8ths)	4.6	4.2	4.6	4.8	4.3	3.9	4.2	4.2	3.9	4.3	4.5	4.4	4.3
Mean SLP (mbs)	1015	1016	1018	1019	1018	1018	1018	1017	1016	1016	1016	1016	1017
Ext. Max. SLP (mbs)	1029	1027	1030	1031	1026	1027	1029	1026	1022	1026	1029	1034	1034
Ext. Min. SLP (mbs)	991	1000	1001	998	1002	1004	1009	1007	1002	1004	1003	991	991
Prevailing Wind Direction	E	E	E	E	E	E	E	E	E	E	E	E	E
Thunder and Lightning [1]	0.1	0.3	0.4	0.4	0.1	0.2	0.2	0.4	0.2	0.6	0.7	0.5	0.4

METEOROLOGICAL TABLE – COASTAL AREA OFF MIDWAY ISLAND
Between 27°N to 28°N and 176°W to 179°W

WEATHER ELEMENTS	JAN	FEB	MAR	APR	MAY	JUN	JUL	AUG	SEP	OCT	NOV	DEC	YEARS OF RECORD
Wind > 33 knots [1]	4.1	3.0	2.2	0.8	0.1	0.0	0.2	0.0	0.1	0.3	1.3	3.4	1.4
Wave Height > 9 feet [1]	11.0	12.2	4.7	2.8	1.6	0.2	1.0	0.9	1.4	2.0	7.3	11.2	5.3
Visibility < 2 nautical miles [1]	0.9	0.4	0.6	0.8	0.7	1.1	0.1	0.0	0.1	0.2	1.1	0.8	0.6
Precipitation [1]	7.6	6.2	5.3	6.6	4.0	4.5	5.9	5.3	5.9	4.7	6.5	6.0	5.7
Temperature > 69° F	23.9	17.0	27.2	38.6	65.6	96.4	99.7	99.8	99.8	97.0	81.6	49.5	64.5
Mean Temperature (°F)	67.7	66.8	68.1	69.4	72.5	76.9	79.3	80.2	79.7	76.7	73.8	70.4	73.2
Temperature < 33° F [1]	0.0	0.0	0.0	0.0	0.0	0.0	0.0	0.0	0.0	0.0	0.0	0.0	0.0
Mean RH (%)	77	77	79	79	80	80	80	80	78	78	78	78	79
Overcast or Obscured [1]	24.3	21.9	22.6	22.0	16.6	13.3	7.4	9.4	13.2	12.8	17.3	21.2	17.1
Mean Cloud Cover (8ths)	5.3	5.0	5.0	5.1	4.9	4.5	4.3	4.5	4.5	4.6	4.8	5.0	4.8
Mean SLP (mbs)	1015	1016	1019	1021	1019	1019	1020	1019	1017	1018	1017	1017	1018
Ext. Max. SLP (mbs)	1030	1033	1032	1044	1030	1029	1032	1033	1035	1029	1030	1035	1044
Ext. Min. SLP (mbs)	987	998	993	1001	998	1002	1008	1002	1002	1002	1001	983	983
Prevailing Wind Direction	W	W	E	E	E	E	E	E	E	E	E	SW	E
Thunder and Lightning [1]	0.9	0.2	0.4	0.3	0.0	0.0	1.3	0.4	0.7	0.3	0.5	0.1	0.4

[1] Percentage Frequency
These data are based upon observations made by ships in transit. These ships tend to avoid bad weather when possible thus biasing the data toward good weather samples.

Atmospheric Pressure Conversion Table

Inches	Millibars	Inches	Millibars	Inches	Millibars
28.44	963	29.32	993	30.21	1023
28.53	966	29.41	996	30.30	1026
28.62	969	29.50	999	30.39	1029
28.70	972	29.59	1002	30.48	1032
28.79	975	29.68	1005	30.56	1035
28.88	978	29.77	1008	30.65	1038
28.97	981	29.86	1011	30.74	1041
29.06	984	29.94	1014	30.83	1044
29.15	987	30.03	1017	30.92	1047
29.24	990	30.12	1020	31.01	1050

Mean Surface Water Temperatures and Densities

		La Jolla, CA	Newport Bay, CA	Los Angeles (Outer Harbor), CA	Santa Monica, CA	Avila Beach, CA	Pacific Grove, CA	San Francisco (Fort Point), CA	Alameda, CA	Crescent City, CA	Astoria (Tongue Point), OR	Neah Bay, WA	Seattle (Elliot Bay), WA	Hilo, HI	Honolulu, HI	Kaneohe Bay, HI	Midway Island
Years of Record		56	17	49	27	27	51	51	33	37	48	37	50	26	28	16	28
Jan	Temp (°C)	13.9	14.0	13.9	13.5	12.4	11.8	10.4	10.3	9.6	4.7	7.3	8.6	22.3	24.4	22.7	19.7
	Density	24.9	24.4	24.7	24.9	24.5	24.7	21.1	17.3	20.8	0.1	22.4	20.4	19.6	25.4	25.3	26.4
Feb	Temp (°C)	13.9	14.5	14.2	13.7	12.5	12.0	10.9	11.9	9.9	5.4	7.4	8.2	22.2	24.3	22.7	19.5
	Density	24.8	24.4	24.6	24.9	24.4	24.6	20.0	15.6	20.7	-0.2	22.2	20.0	19.2	25.6	25.4	26.4
Mar	Temp (°C)	14.4	15.4	14.7	13.9	12.3	12.2	11.6	13.9	10.2	7.4	7.9	8.2	22.1	24.3	23.3	20.1
	Density	24.8	24.5	24.8	25.0	24.7	24.6	19.9	15.7	21.1	-0.5	22.5	19.9	19.0	25.6	25.1	26.5
Apr	Temp (°C)	15.4	16.6	15.4	14.7	12.5	12.4	12.4	16.1	10.7	10.5	9.1	8.9	22.2	24.7	23.8	21.0
	Density	24.9	24.5	24.9	25.0	24.9	24.7	20.0	16.5	21.8	-0.7	22.7	19.5	17.6	25.8	25.3	26.5
May	Temp (°C)	16.9	17.7	16.2	15.7	13.1	12.8	13.1	17.8	11.5	13.4	10.6	10.3	22.7	25.4	25.1	22.7
	Density	25.0	24.9	25.1	25.2	25.2	24.9	20.7	17.6	22.6	-0.7	23.2	19.5	18.2	25.8	25.4	26.6
Jun	Temp (°C)	18.4	19.0	17.7	17.5	14.1	13.4	13.9	19.4	12.5	15.8	11.6	11.9	23.3	26.0	26.2	25.1
	Density	25.0	25.0	25.1	25.2	25.4	25.0	21.5	18.7	23.3	-0.6	23.2	19.9	18.9	25.8	25.9	26.7
Jul	Temp (°C)	19.9	20.3	18.9	19.2	15.4	13.8	14.7	20.5	13.6	18.6	11.8	13.1	23.7	26.4	26.3	26.4
	Density	25.0	25.0	25.1	25.2	25.4	25.0	22.9	20.5	24.0	-0.5	23.7	20.7	18.5	25.9	25.9	26.7
Aug	Temp (°C)	20.8	21.2	19.7	19.9	15.9	13.9	15.2	20.5	14.3	19.3	11.6	13.4	23.9	26.8	26.6	26.9
	Density	25.0	25.0	25.1	25.2	25.3	25.0	23.7	21.8	24.1	-0.2	23.9	21.4	18.6	25.9	26.0	26.6
Sep	Temp (°C)	19.3	19.9	19.0	19.0	15.7	14.2	15.5	20.2	13.5	17.5	11.3	13.0	24.2	26.9	26.7	26.9
	Density	24.9	25.0	25.1	25.1	25.2	25.0	23.8	22.4	24.2	0.4	23.8	21.8	19.2	25.9	26.0	26.6
Oct	Temp (°C)	18.0	18.7	18.1	17.6	15.0	13.7	14.8	17.7	12.1	14.0	10.6	12.2	24.1	26.9	26.2	25.1
	Density	24.9	24.9	25.0	25.0	25.1	24.9	23.8	21.9	24.0	1.0	23.4	21.8	19.5	25.9	25.9	26.5
Nov	Temp (°C)	16.3	16.4	16.5	15.7	13.9	12.9	13.0	14.4	11.2	9.4	9.4	10.8	23.5	26.1	24.7	23.2
	Density	24.9	24.6	24.9	25.0	24.9	24.8	23.2	21.1	22.8	0.9	22.9	21.5	19.3	25.8	25.6	26.5
Dec	Temp (°C)	14.9	14.7	14.8	14.3	12.8	12.4	11.2	11.4	10.2	6.2	8.2	9.6	22.7	25.0	23.1	21.3
	Density	24.9	24.5	24.8	24.9	24.8	24.8	22.4	19.5	21.8	0.5	22.5	20.9	18.9	25.7	25.4	26.4
Mean	Temp (°C)	16.8	17.4	16.6	16.2	13.8	13.0	13.1	16.2	11.7	11.8	9.7	10.7	23.1	25.6	24.8	23.2
	Density	24.9	24.7	24.9	25.0	25.0	24.8	21.9	19.0	22.6	0.0	23.0	20.6	18.9	25.8	25.6	26.5

F (Fahrenheit) = 1.8C (Celsius) + 32

Density as used in this table is the specific gravity of the sea water or the ratio between the weight of a sea-water sample and the weight of an equal volume of distilled water at 15°C (59°F).

Table for Estimating Time of Transit

Distance (nautical miles)	Speed (knots)																		
	8	9	10	11	12	13	14	15	16	17	18	19	20	21	22	23	24	25	30
	days/hours	days/hours	days/hours	days/hours	days/hours	days/hours	days/hours	days/hours	days/hours	days/hours	days/hours	days/hours	days/hours	days/hours	days/hours	days/hours	days/hours	days/hours	days/hours
10	0/1	0/1	0/1	0/1	0/1	0/1	0/1	0/1	0/1	0/1	0/1	0/1	0/1	-	-	-	-	-	-
20	0/3	0/2	0/2	0/2	0/2	0/2	0/1	0/1	0/1	0/1	0/1	0/1	0/1	0/1	0/1	0/1	0/1	0/1	0/1
30	0/4	0/3	0/3	0/3	0/2	0/2	0/2	0/2	0/2	0/2	0/2	0/2	0/2	0/1	0/1	0/1	0/1	0/1	0/1
40	0/5	0/4	0/4	0/4	0/3	0/3	0/3	0/3	0/3	0/2	0/2	0/2	0/2	0/2	0/2	0/2	0/2	0/2	0/1
50	0/6	0/6	0/5	0/5	0/4	0/4	0/4	0/3	0/3	0/3	0/3	0/3	0/3	0/2	0/2	0/2	0/2	0/2	0/2
60	0/8	0/7	0/6	0/5	0/5	0/5	0/4	0/4	0/4	0/4	0/3	0/3	0/3	0/3	0/3	0/3	0/3	0/2	0/2
70	0/9	0/8	0/7	0/6	0/6	0/5	0/5	0/5	0/4	0/4	0/4	0/4	0/4	0/3	0/3	0/3	0/3	0/3	0/2
80	0/10	0/9	0/8	0/7	0/7	0/6	0/6	0/5	0/5	0/5	0/4	0/4	0/4	0/4	0/4	0/3	0/3	0/3	0/3
90	0/11	0/10	0/9	0/8	0/8	0/7	0/6	0/6	0/6	0/5	0/5	0/5	0/5	0/4	0/4	0/4	0/4	0/4	0/3
100	0/13	0/11	0/10	0/9	0/8	0/8	0/7	0/7	0/6	0/6	0/6	0/5	0/5	0/5	0/5	0/4	0/4	0/4	0/3
200	1/1	0/22	0/20	0/18	0/17	0/15	0/14	0/13	0/13	0/12	0/11	0/11	0/10	0/10	0/9	0/9	0/8	0/8	0/7
300	1/14	1/9	1/6	1/3	1/1	0/23	0/21	0/20	0/19	0/18	0/17	0/16	0/15	0/14	0/14	0/13	0/13	0/12	0/10
400	2/2	1/20	1/16	1/12	1/9	1/7	1/5	1/3	1/1	1/0	0/22	0/21	0/20	0/19	0/18	0/17	0/17	0/16	0/13
500	2/15	2/8	2/2	1/21	1/18	1/14	1/12	1/9	1/7	1/5	1/4	1/2	1/1	1/0	0/23	0/22	0/21	0/20	0/17
600	3/3	2/19	2/12	2/7	2/2	1/22	1/19	1/16	1/14	1/11	1/9	1/8	1/6	1/5	1/3	1/2	1/1	1/0	0/20
700	3/16	3/6	2/22	2/16	2/10	2/6	2/2	1/23	1/20	1/17	1/15	1/13	1/11	1/9	1/8	1/6	1/5	1/4	0/23
800	4/4	3/17	3/8	3/1	2/19	2/14	2/9	2/5	2/2	1/23	1/20	1/18	1/16	1/14	1/12	1/11	1/9	1/8	1/3
900	4/17	4/4	3/18	3/10	3/3	2/21	2/16	2/12	2/8	2/5	2/2	1/23	1/21	1/19	1/17	1/15	1/14	1/12	1/6
1000	5/5	4/15	4/4	3/19	3/11	3/5	2/23	2/19	2/15	2/11	2/8	2/5	2/2	2/0	1/21	1/19	1/18	1/16	1/9
2000	10/10	9/6	8/8	7/14	6/23	6/10	5/23	5/13	5/5	4/22	4/15	4/9	4/4	3/23	3/19	3/15	3/11	3/8	2/19
3000	15/15	13/21	12/12	11/9	10/10	9/15	8/22	8/8	7/20	7/8	6/23	6/14	6/6	5/23	5/16	5/10	5/5	5/0	4/4
4000	20/20	18/21	16/16	15/4	13/21	12/20	11/22	11/3	10/10	9/19	9/6	8/19	8/8	7/22	7/14	7/6	6/23	6/16	5/13
5000	26/1	23/4	20/20	18/23	17/9	16/1	14/21	13/21	13/1	12/6	11/14	10/23	10/10	9/22	9/11	9/1	8/16	8/8	6/23
6000	31/6	27/19	25/0	22/17	20/20	19/5	17/21	16/16	15/15	14/17	13/21	13/4	12/12	11/22	11/9	10/21	10/10	10/0	8/8

Determination of Wind Speed by Sea Condition

Miles per hour	Knots	Descriptive	Sea Conditions	Wind Force (Beaufort)	Probable Wave Height (feet)
0-1	0-1	Calm	Sea smooth and mirror like	0	-
1-3	1-3	Light Air	Scale-like ripples without foam crests	1	¼
4-7	4-6	Light Breeze	Small, short wavelets; crests have a glassy appearance and do not break.	2	½
8-12	7-10	Gentle Breeze	Large wavelets; some crests begin to break; foam has glassy appearance. Occasional white foam crests.	3	2
13-18	11-16	Moderate Breeze	Small waves, become longer; fairly frequent white foam crests.	4	4
19-24	17-21	Fresh Breeze	Moderate waves, taking a more pronounced long form; many white foam crests; there may be some spray.	5	6
25-31	22-27	Strong Breeze	Large waves begin to form; white foam crests are more extensive everywhere; there may be some spray.	6	10
32-38	28-33	Near Gale	Sea heaps up and white foam from breaking waves begin to be blown in streaks along the direction of the wind; spindrift begins.	7	14
39-46	34-40	Gale	Moderately high waves of greater length; edges of crests break into spindrift; foam is blown in well-marked streaks along the direction of the wind.	8	18
47-54	41-47	Strong Gale	High waves; dense streaks of foam along the direction of the wind; crests of waves begin to topple, tumble and roll over; spray may reduce visibility.	9	23
55-63	48-55	Storm	Very high waves with long overhanging crests. The resulting foam in great patches is blown in dense white streaks along the direction of the wind. On the whole, the surface of the sea is white in appearance. The tumbling of the sea becomes heavy and shock-like. Visibility is reduced.	10	29
64-72	56-63	Violent Storm	Exceptionally high waves that may obscure small and medium-sized ships. The sea is completely covered with long white patches of foam lying along the direction of the wind. Everywhere the edges of the wave crests are blown into froth. Visibility is reduced.	11	37
73+	64+	Hurricane	The air is filled with foam and spray. Sea completely white with driving spray; visibility is very much reduced.	12	45

Pacific Coast Distances
(nautical miles)

	Midway Island	Port Allen, HI	Nawiliwili, HI	Pearl Harbor, HI	Honolulu, HI	Kahalui, HI	Kawaihae, HI	Hilo, HI	Kuluk Bay, AK	Unimak Pass, AK	Kodiak, AK	Anchorage, AK	Seward, AK	Port Valdez, AK	Cape Spencer, AK	Sitka, AK	Ketchikan, AK	Seattle, WA	Swiftsure Bank, WA	Cape Flattery, WA	Portland, OR	Astoria, OR	San Francisco, CA	Los Angeles, CA	Long Beach, CA	San Diego, CA
Panama Canal 8°53.0'N., 79°31.0'W.	5707	4777	4767	4690	4685	4609	4594	4527	5604	5228	4924	5117	4940	4984	4603	4538	4387	4044	-	3920	3888	3803	3270	2939	2939	2867
San Diego, CA 32°43.0'N., 117°10.5'W.	3097	2347	2330	2283	2278	2212	2219	2175	2806	2412	2115	2303	2124	2174	1787	1723	1575	1228	-	1104	1074	989	455	95	94	-
Long Beach, CA 33°46.2'N., 118°13.3'W.	3034	2302	2284	2241	2236	2173	2183	2143	2725	2331	2034	2223	2043	2092	1707	1643	1497	1148	-	1024	992	908	374	3	-	
Los Angeles, CA 33°45.0'N., 118°16.2'W.	3031	2299	2281	2238	2233	2170	2180	2140	2722	2328	2031	2220	2040	2089	1703	1639	1493	1144	-	1020	989	904	371	-		
San Francisco, CA 37°48.5'N., 122°24.0'W.	2792	2146	2128	2096	2091	2036	2051	2019	2403	1990	1693	1882	1702	1745	1366	1302	1156	807	-	683	652	567	-			
Astoria, OR 46°11.7'N., 123°50.0'W.	2724	2281	2262	2251	2246	2207	2235	2214	2071	1626	1261	1435	1242	1239	883	815	660	278	-	153	85	-				
Portland, OR 45°33.0'N., 122°41.7'W.	2809	2366	2347	2336	2331	2292	2320	2299	2156	1711	1346	1520	1327	1324	968	900	745	362	-	238	-					
Cape Flattery, WA 48°26.0'N., 124°47.0'W.	2694	2308	2289	2290	2285	2245	2276	2260	-	-	-	-	-	-	-	-	-	124	10	-						
Swiftsure Bank, WA 48°31.0'N., 125°00.0'W.	-	-	-	-	-	-	-	1973	1510	1124	1294	1100	1100	739	681	518	134	-								
Seattle, WA 47°36.2'N., 122°20.3'W.	2818	2432	2413	2414	2409	2369	2400	2384	2107	1644	1258	1428	1234	1234	976*	815	659*	-								
Ketchikan, AK 55°20.5'N., 131°38.7'W.	2570	2387	2368	2388	2383	2361	2405	2398	1656	1193	742	892	682	713	307	224	-									
Sitka, AK 57°03.1'N., 135°20.5'W.	2481	2380	2361	2390	2385	2365	2412	2410	1490	1027	564	708	464	479	85	-										
Cape Spencer, AK 58°10.0'N., 136°38.3'W.	2472	2407	2388	2416	2411	2398	2445	2447	1450	987	505	641	422	400	-											
Port Valdez 61°06.0'N., 146°24.0'W.	2386	2445	2429	2473	2468	2463	2513	2524	1224	761	280	385	144	-												
Seward, AK 60°06.0'N., 149°26.0'W.	2250	2351	2332	2378	2373	2377	2432	2439	1115	652	175	274	-													
Anchorage, AK 61°14.2'N., 149°53.3'W.	2305	2459	2440	2482	2477	2479	2535	2542	1151	688	242	-														
Kodiak, AK 57°47.1'N., 152°25.1'W.	2088	2203	2184	2235	2230	2233	2289	2296	968	505	-															
Unimak Pass, AK 54°20.0'N., 164°45.0'W.	1680	1972	1963	2024	2028	2044	2110	2126	463	-																
Kuluk Bay, AK 51°51.6'N., 176°37.6'W.	1460	1990	1989	2057	2061	2099	2164	2198	-																	
Hilo, HI 19°44.1'N., 155°03.5'W.	1338	297	287	201	196	121	83	-																		
Kawaihae, HI 20°02.3'N., 155°49.9'W.	1278	240	230	145	140	85	-																			
Kahalui, HI 20°54.0'N., 156°28.2'W.	1232	193	181	94	89	-																				
Honolulu, HI 21°18.5'N., 157°52.3'W.	1150	106	96	9	-																					
Pearl Harbor, HI 21°20.0'N., 157°58.3'W.	1146	102	92	-																						
Nawiliwili, HI 21°57.4'N., 159°21.5'W.	1069	21	-																							
Port Allen, HI 24°51.1'N., 159°35.6'W.	1042	-																								
Midway Island 28°13.0'N., 177°22.0'W.	-																									

* via inside passage

Pacific Coast Distances – San Diego, California to Cape Flattery, Washington
(nautical miles)

	Cape Flattery, WA	Aberdeen, WA	South Bend, WA	Portland, OR	Vancouver, WA	Longview, WA	Astoria, OR	Garibaldi, OR	Depoe Bay, OR	Newport, OR	Florence, OR	Gardiner, OR	Coos Bay, OR	Crescent City, CA	Eureka, CA	Sacramento, CA	Stockton, CA	Oakland, CA	San Francisco, CA	Monterey, CA	Port San Luis, CA	Santa Barbara, CA	Port Hueneme, CA	Los Angeles, CA	Long Beach, CA	Newport Beach, CA
San Diego, CA 32°43.0'N., 117°10.5'W	1104	1031	1019	1074	1070	1034	989	937	891	881	848	832	817	704	653	530	526	458	455	370	259	174	147	95	94	78
Newport Beach, CA 33°37.1'N., 117°55.5'W.	1038	965	953	1007	1003	967	922	871	825	815	782	766	751	638	587	464	460	392	389	304	193	108	81	27	25	-
Long Beach, CA 33°46.2'N., 118°13.3'W.	1024	951	939	992	988	953	908	857	810	800	768	751	736	624	572	449	445	377	374	290	179	94	66	3	-	
Los Angeles, CA 33°45.0'N., 118°16.2'W.	1020	947	935	989	985	949	904	853	807	797	764	748	733	620	569	446	442	374	371	286	175	90	62	-		
Port Hueneme, CA 34°09.0'N., 119°12.4'W.	961	888	876	930	925	890	845	794	748	737	706	689	674	561	510	387	383	315	312	228	116	29	-			
Santa Barbara, CA 34°24.5'N., 119°41.1'W.	937	864	852	905	901	866	821	770	723	713	681	664	649	537	485	362	358	290	287	203	91	-				
Port San Luis, CA 35°10.4'N., 120°44.8'W.	854	781	769	823	819	783	739	687	641	631	599	582	567	455	403	280	276	208	205	121	-					
Monterey, CA 36°36.5'N., 121°53.0'W.	746	673	661	714	710	675	630	579	532	522	490	474	459	346	294	171	167	100	96	-						
San Francisco, CA 37°48.5'N., 122°24.0'W.	683	610	598	652	647	612	567	516	469	459	427	411	396	283	232	79	75	3	-							
Oakland, CA 37°48.2'N., 122°19.5'W.	686	613	601	655	651	615	570	520	473	463	430	414	399	287	235	82	78	-								
Stockton, CA 37°57.2'N., 121°18.8'W.	755	682	670	723	719	684	639	588	541	531	498	482	467	354	303	75	-									
Sacramento, CA 38°33.8'N., 121°33.0'W.	758	685	673	727	722	687	642	591	544	534	502	486	471	358	307	-										
Eureka, CA 40°47.8'N., 124°11.2'W.	468	395	383	436	432	397	352	301	254	244	212	195	180	64	-											
Crescent City, CA 41°44.5'N., 124°11.4'W.	411	339	327	381	377	341	296	245	199	188	156	140	125	-												
Coos Bay, OR 43°22.4'N., 124°12.5'W.	321	244	232	285	281	246	201	150	101	92	59	42	-													
Gardiner, OR 43°43.9'N., 124°06.8'W.	298	221	209	262	258	223	178	127	78	69	36	-														
Florence, OR 43°58.0'N., 124°08.3'W.	270	196	184	238	234	198	153	102	54	43	-															
Newport, OR 44°37.8'N., 124°03.1'W.	235	158	146	200	196	160	115	63	16	-																
Depoe Bay, OR 44°48.6'N., 124°03.6'W.	222	144	133	186	182	146	101	50	-																	
Garibaldi, OR 45°33.3'N., 123°55.1'W.	179	102	90	142	138	103	58	-																		
Astoria, OR 46°11.7'N., 123°50.0'W.	153	75	63	85	80	45	-																			
Longview, WA 46°06.3'N., 122°57.7'W.	198	119	108	39	34	-																				
Vancouver, WA 45°37.6'N., 122°41.3'W.	234	155	143	13	-																					
Portland, OR 45°33.0'N., 122°41.7'W.	238	159	147	-																						
South Bend, WA 46°40.1'N., 123°47.5'W.	131	53	-																							
Aberdeen, WA 46°58.4'N., 123°48.5'W.	117	-																								
Cape Flattery, WA 48°26.0'N., 124°47.0'W.	-																									

San Francisco Bay Area Distances
(nautical miles)

	San Francisco	Hunters Point	Redwood City	Oakland	Richmond	Sausalito	San Rafael	Petaluma	Vallejo	Napa	Benicia	Pittsburg	Antioch	Stockton	Hills Ferry	Rio Vista	Sacramento	Knights Landing	Colusa	Chico Landing
Chico Landing 39°42.6'N., 121°56.6'W.	197	203	219	200	194	196	192	204	178	193	171	159	163	174	246	146	119	89	42	-
Colusa 39°13.0'N., 122°00.0'W.	155	161	177	158	152	154	150	162	136	151	129	117	121	132	204	104	77	47	-	
Knights Landing 38°48.1'N., 121°43.1'W.	107	113	129	110	104	106	102	114	88	103	81	69	73	84	156	56	29	-		
Sacramento 38°33.8'N., 121°33.0'W.	78	84	100	81	75	77	73	85	59	74	52	40	44	75	127	27	-			
Rio Vista 38°09.3'N., 121°41.3'W.	52	58	73	55	49	51	47	58	33	48	26	14	17	48	100	-				
Hills Ferry 37°20.4'N., 120°58.5'W.	147	153	168	149	143	145	141	153	127	142	120	107	103	74	-					
Stockton 37°57.2'N., 121°18.8'W.	75	81	96	78	71	73	69	81	55	70	48	35	31	-						
Antioch 38°01.1'N., 121°48.7'W.	44	50	65	47	40	42	38	50	24	39	17	3	-							
Pittsburg 38°02.1'N., 121°52.6'W.	40	46	62	43	37	39	35	46	21	36	14	-								
Benicia 38°02.4'N., 122°08.2'W.	27	33	49	30	24	25	21	33	8	22	-									
Napa 38°17.7'N., 122°16.9'W.	37	43	58	40	34	36	32	43	15	-										
Vallejo 38°05.3'N., 122°15.3'W.	23	29	44	26	19	21	17	28	-											
Petaluma 38°14.1'N., 122°38.2'W.	33	39	54	36	29	31	27	-												
San Rafael 37°58.1'N., 122°30.7'W.	13	19	35	16	9	11	-													
Sausalito 37°51.6'N., 122°28.6'W.	5	11	27	8	7	-														
Richmond 37°54.6'N., 122°21.7'W.	11	17	32	14	-															
Oakland 37°54.6'N., 122°21.7'W.	3	7	22	-																
Redwood City 37°30.8'N., 122°12.5'W.	22	16	-																	
Hunters Point 37°43.5'N., 122°21.5'W.	6	-																		
San Francisco 37°48.5'N., 122°24.0'W.	-																			

Distances on Columbia River System
(nautical and statute miles)

	Johnson Bar Landing, ID	Lewiston, ID	Central Ferry, WA	Ice Harbor Dam, WA	Harrisburg, OR	Corvalis, OR	Albany, OR	Salem, OR	Oregon City, OR	Portland, OR	Richland, WA	Pasco, WA	Port of Walla Walla, WA	McNary Lock & Dam	Umatilla, OR	Arlington, OR	John Day Lock & Dam	The Dalles Lock & Dam	Hood River (town), OR	Bonneville Lock & Dam	Vancouver, WA	St. Helens, OR	Longview, WA	Astoria, OR	Warrenton, OR	Ilwaco, WA	Columbia River (mouth)
Columbia River (mouth)	483	404	354	291	230	203	192	162	110	97	293	285	276	254	251	210	188	166	148	126	92	75	58	12	11	6	•
Ilwaco, WA	484	404	355	292	230	203	193	163	111	98	294	286	276	254	252	211	189	167	149	127	93	76	59	13	12	•	7
Warrenton, OR	475	396	346	283	222	195	184	154	103	89	285	277	268	246	244	202	180	159	140	118	84	67	50	4	•	14	13
Astoria, OR	470	391	342	278	217	190	180	149	98	85	281	273	263	241	239	198	175	154	136	114	80	62	45	•	5	15	14
Longview, WA	425	345	296	233	171	144	134	104	52	39	235	227	217	195	193	152	130	108	90	68	34	17	•	52	58	68	67
St. Helens, OR	411	332	282	219	158	131	121	90	39	25	222	214	204	182	180	138	117	95	76	55	20	•	20	71	77	87	86
Vancouver, WA	391	312	262	199	145	118	108	77	26	13	202	193	184	162	160	118	96	75	56	35	•	23	39	92	97	107	106
Bonneville Lock & Dam	356	277	228	164	180	153	142	112	61	47	167	159	149	127	125	84	62	40	22	•	40	63	78	131	136	146	145
Hood River (town), OR	335	256	206	143	201	174	164	134	82	69	145	137	128	106	103	62	40	18	•	5	64	87	104	157	161	171	170
The Dalles Lock & Dam	316	237	188	124	220	193	183	152	101	87	127	119	109	87	85	44	22	•	21	46	86	109	124	177	183	192	191
John Day Lock & Dam	294	215	166	102	242	215	204	174	123	109	105	97	87	65	63	22	•	25	46	71	110	135	150	203	207	217	216
Arlington, OR	273	194	144	81	263	236	226	195	144	130	83	75	66	44	42	•	25	51	71	97	136	159	175	228	232	243	242
Umatilla, OR	231	152	103	39	305	278	268	237	186	172	42	34	24	2	•	48	72	98	119	144	184	207	222	275	281	290	289
McNary Lock & Dam	229	150	101	37	307	280	270	239	188	174	40	32	22	•	2	51	75	100	122	146	186	209	224	277	283	292	292
Port of Walla Walla, WA	207	128	79	15	329	302	292	261	210	196	18	10	•	25	28	76	100	125	147	171	212	235	250	303	308	318	318
Pasco, WA	204	125	75	12	339	312	301	271	220	206	8	•	12	37	39	86	112	137	158	183	222	246	261	314	319	329	328
Richland, WA	212	133	83	20	347	320	309	279	228	214	•	9	21	46	48	96	121	146	167	192	232	255	270	323	328	338	337
Portland, OR	403	324	275	211	133	106	96	65	14	•	246	237	226	200	198	150	125	100	79	54	15	29	45	98	102	113	112
Oregon City, OR	417	338	288	225	119	92	82	51	•	16	262	253	242	216	214	166	142	116	94	70	30	45	60	113	119	128	127
Salem, OR	468	389	340	276	68	41	31	•	59	75	321	312	300	275	273	224	200	175	154	129	89	104	120	171	177	188	186
Albany, OR	499	420	370	307	37	10	•	36	94	110	356	346	336	311	308	260	235	211	189	163	124	139	154	207	212	222	221
Corvalis, OR	509	430	380	317	27	•	12	47	106	122	368	359	348	322	320	272	247	222	200	176	136	151	166	219	224	234	234
Harrisburg, OR	536	457	407	344	•	31	43	78	137	153	399	390	379	353	351	303	278	253	231	207	167	182	197	250	255	265	265
Ice Harbor Dam, WA	192	113	63	•	396	365	353	318	259	243	23	14	17	43	45	93	117	143	165	189	229	252	268	320	326	336	335
Central Ferry, WA	129	50	•	72	468	437	426	391	331	316	96	86	91	116	119	166	191	216	237	262	302	325	341	394	398	409	407
Lewiston, ID	79	•	58	130	526	495	483	448	389	373	153	144	147	173	175	223	247	273	295	319	359	382	397	450	456	465	465
Johnson Bar Landing, ID	•	91	148	221	617	586	574	539	480	464	244	235	238	264	266	314	338	364	386	410	450	473	489	541	547	557	556

Distances in Strait of Juan de Fuca and Strait of Georgia
(nautical miles)

Location	Vancouver, BC, Canada	New Westminster, BC, Canada	Nanaimo, BC, Canada	Blaine, WA	Bellingham, WA	Anacortes, WA	Friday Harbor, WA	Roche Harbor, WA	Olympia, WA	Tacoma, WA	Bremerton, WA	Eagle Harbor, WA	Seattle, WA	Point Wells, WA	Everett, WA	Port Gamble, WA	Port Ludlow, WA	Port Townsend, WA	Victoria, BC, Canada	Port Angeles, WA	Neah Bay, WA	Swiftsure Bank, WA	Cape Flattery, WA
Cape Flattery, WA 48°26.0'N., 124°47.0'W.	141	139	145	112	108	93	87	83	168	143	131	123	124	111	117	104	100	86	62	61	10	10	-
Swiftsure Bank, WA 48°31.0'N., 125°00.0'W.	150	148	154	121	117	102	96	92	178	153	141	133	134	121	127	114	110	96	71	71	20	-	
Neah Bay, WA 48°22.4'N., 124°36.5'W.	133	132	138	105	101	86	80	76	160	136	124	115	116	103	110	97	93	79	55	54	-		
Port Angeles, WA 48°07.5'N., 123°26.4'W.	95	93	99	65	54	42	37	36	113	89	77	68	69	56	63	50	46	32	19	-			
Victoria, BC, Canada 48°25.0'N., 123°23.5'W.	83	82	89	55	50	36	30	25	115	91	80	71	72	59	66	53	48	34	-				
Port Townsend, WA 48°06.8'N., 122°45.2'W.	92	91	97	59	43	30	30	41	84	59	48	40	40	27	34	21	16	-					
Port Ludlow, WA 47°55.3'N., 122°41.0'W.	106	105	111	72	57	43	44	54	75	52	40	32	32	19	26	10	-						
Port Gamble, WA 47°51.3'N., 122°34.7'W.	110	109	115	76	61	47	48	58	78	53	42	34	34	21	28	-							
Everett, WA 47°59.3'N., 122°13.2'W.	115	114	118	80	63	49	62	71	73	49	38	29	30	16	-								
Point Wells, WA 47°47.1'N., 122°23.7'W.	117	116	121	83	68	54	54	64	59	34	23	14	14	-									
Seattle, WA 47°36.2'N., 122°20.3'W.	129	128	134	95	80	66	67	77	50	25	14	8	-										
Eagle Harbor, WA 47°34.2'N., 122°30.7'W.	129	128	134	95	80	66	67	76	50	25	13	-											
Bremerton, WA 47°33.5'N., 122°38.0'W.	138	137	142	104	88	74	76	85	50	29	-												
Tacoma, WA 47°16.0'N., 122°26.0'W.	149	148	154	115	100	86	86	96	34	-													
Olympia, WA 47°03.1'N., 122°54.3'W.	173	171	177	139	124	110	112	121	-														
Roche Harbor, WA 48°36.6'N., 123°09.1'W.	62	60	66	35	37	27	12	-															
Friday Harbor, WA 48°32.2'N., 123°00.9'W.	62	60	69	37	28	18	-																
Anacortes, WA 48°31.4'N., 122°36.7'W.	71	70	76	36	17	-																	
Bellingham, WA 48°45.1'N., 122°29.0'W.	72	71	75	38	-																		
Blaine, WA 48°59.5'N., 122°45.9'W.	48	48	55	-																			
Nanaimo, BC, Canada 49°10.1'N., 123°56.0'W.	36	48	-																				
New Westminster, BC, Canada 49°12.0'N., 122°54.5'W.	41	-																					
Vancouver, BC, Canada 49°17.4'N., 123°06.6'W.	-																						

Hawaii Distances
(nautical miles)

	Palmyra Island	Johnston Island	Midway Island	Nonopapa, Nihau	Hanalei, Kauai	Waimea, Kauai	Port Allen, Kauai	Nawiliwili, Kauai	Ahukini, Kauai	Pearl Harbor, Oahu	Honolulu, Oahu	Kalaupapa, Molokai	Haleolono, Molokai	Kaunakakai, Molokai	Kamalo, Molokai	Kaumalapau, Lanai	Kahalui, Maui	Lahaina (Mala), Maui	Hana, Maui	Mahukona, Hawai'i	Kawaihae, Hawai'i	Kailua, Hawai'i	Napoopoo, Hawai'i	Hilo, Hawai'i
Hilo, Hawai'i 19°44.1'N., 155°03.5'W.	959	905	1338	332	308	303	297	287	287	201	196	154	155	145	137	136	121	125	85	72	83	109	120	-
Napoopoo, Hawai'i 19°28.6'N., 155°55.3'W.	-	-	-	287	266	260	254	244	245	162	157	138	124	120	112	101	120	99	84	50	45	11	-	
Kailua, Hawai'i 19°38.6'N., 156°00.0'W.	-	-	-	278	257	251	245	235	236	152	147	127	114	109	102	91	110	88	73	39	34	-		
Kawaihae, Hawai'i 20°02.3'N., 155°49.9'W.	928	811	1278	277	251	246	240	230	230	145	140	110	103	93	86	82	85	72	48	12	-			
Mahukona, Hawai'i 20°11.2'N., 155°54.2'W.	-	-	-	272	244	239	233	223	223	138	133	102	95	85	77	76	74	63	36	-				
Hana, Maui 20°45.6'N., 155°59.1'W.	-	-	-	262	224	226	220	210	210	124	119	70	80	69	59	72	37	57	-					
Lahaina (Mala), Maui 20°53.5'N., 156°41.5'W.	-	-	-	214	186	182	177	165	165	78	73	39	34	23	15	25	27	-						
Kahalui, Maui 20°54.0'N., 156°28.2'W.	1010	798	1232	232	194	199	193	181	181	94	89	41	50	39	30	50	-							
Kaumalapau, Lanai 20°47.4'N., 156°59.7'W.	-	-	-	199	172	167	161	151	151	65	60	54	24	21	25	-								
Kamalo, Molokai 21°02.9'N., 156°52.7'W.	-	-	-	203	173	169	163	153	153	66	61	37	22	12	-									
Kaunakakai, Molokai 21°05.1'N., 157°02.0'W.	-	-	-	193	164	160	154	144	144	57	52	45	13	-										
Haleolono, Molokai 21°05.2'N., 157°15.2'W.	-	-	-	181	152	148	142	132	132	45	40	33	-											
Kalaupapa, Molokai 21°11.7'N., 156°59.3'W.	-	-	-	194	159	162	156	144	143	58	53	-												
Honolulu, Oahu 21°18.5'N., 157°52.3'W.	959	725	1150	147	116	112	106	96	96	9	-													
Pearl Harbor, Oahu 21°20.0'N., 157°58.3'W.	960	722	1146	143	112	108	102	92	92	-														
Ahukini, Kauai 21°59.7'N., 159°20.1'W.	-	-	-	65	29	29	23	5	-															
Nawiliwili, Kauai 21°57.4'N., 159°21.5'W.	986	668	1069	63	32	27	21	-																
Port Allen, Kauai 21°54.1'N., 159°35.6'W.	979	656	1042	45	42	8	-																	
Waimea, Kauai 21°57.4'N., 159°40.4'W.	-	-	-	40	35	-																		
Hanalei, Kauai 22°12.9'N., 159°30.1'W.	-	-	-	52	-																			
Nonopapa, Nihau 21°52.0'N., 160°14.1'W.	-	-	-	-																				
Midway Island 28°13.0'N., 177°22.0'W.	1606	825	-																					
Johnston Island 16°44.6'N., 169°31.2'W.	785	-																						
Palmyra Island 5°52.5'N., 162°08.0'W.	-																							

Distance of Visibility for Objects Having Various Elevations

Height (feet)	Distance (nautical miles)	Distance (statute miles)	Height (meters)	Height (feet)	Distance (nautical miles)	Distance (statute miles)	Height (meters)
1	1.2	1.3	0.3	120	12.8	14.7	36.6
2	1.7	1.9	0.6	125	13.1	15.1	38.1
3	2.0	2.3	0.9	130	13.3	15.4	39.6
4	2.3	2.7	1.2	135	13.6	15.6	41.2
5	2.6	3.0	1.5	140	13.8	15.9	42.7
6	2.9	3.3	1.8	145	14.1	16.2	44.2
7	3.1	3.6	2.1	150	14.3	16.5	45.7
8	3.3	3.8	2.4	160	14.8	17.0	48.8
9	3.5	4.0	2.7	170	15.3	17.6	51.8
10	3.7	4.3	3.1	180	15.7	18.1	54.9
11	3.9	4.5	3.4	190	16.1	18.6	57.9
12	4.1	4.7	3.7	200	16.5	19.0	61.0
13	4.2	4.9	4.0	210	17.0	19.5	64.0
14	4.4	5.0	4.3	220	17.4	20.0	67.1
15	4.5	5.2	4.6	230	17.7	20.4	70.1
16	4.7	5.4	4.9	240	18.1	20.9	73.2
17	4.8	5.6	5.2	250	18.5	21.3	76.2
18	5.0	5.7	5.5	260	18.9	21.7	79.3
19	5.1	5.9	5.8	270	19.2	22.1	82.3
20	5.2	6.0	6.1	280	19.6	22.5	85.3
21	5.4	6.2	6.4	290	19.9	22.9	88.4
22	5.5	6.3	6.7	300	20.3	23.3	91.4
23	5.6	6.5	7.0	310	20.6	23.7	94.5
24	5.7	6.6	7.3	320	20.9	24.1	97.5
25	5.9	6.7	7.6	330	21.3	24.5	100.6
26	6.0	6.9	7.9	340	21.6	24.8	103.6
27	6.1	7.0	8.2	350	21.9	25.2	106.7
28	6.2	7.1	8.5	360	22.2	25.5	109.7
29	6.3	7.3	8.8	370	22.5	25.9	112.8
30	6.4	7.4	9.1	380	22.8	26.2	115.8
31	6.5	7.5	9.5	390	23.1	26.6	118.9
32	6.6	7.6	9.8	400	23.4	26.9	121.9
33	6.7	7.7	10.1	410	23.7	27.3	125.0
34	6.8	7.9	10.4	420	24.0	27.6	128.0
35	6.9	8.0	10.7	430	24.3	27.9	131.1
36	7.0	8.1	11.0	440	24.5	28.2	134.1
37	7.1	8.2	11.3	450	24.8	28.6	137.2
38	7.2	8.3	11.6	460	25.1	28.9	140.2
39	7.3	8.4	11.9	470	25.4	29.2	143.3
40	7.4	8.5	12.2	480	25.6	29.5	146.3
41	7.5	8.6	12.5	490	25.9	29.8	149.4
42	7.6	8.7	12.8	500	26.2	30.1	152.4
43	7.7	8.8	13.1	510	26.4	30.4	155.5
44	7.8	8.9	13.4	520	26.7	30.7	158.5
45	7.8	9.0	13.7	530	26.9	31.0	161.5
46	7.9	9.1	14.0	540	27.2	31.3	164.6
47	8.0	9.2	14.3	550	27.4	31.6	167.6
48	8.1	9.3	14.6	560	27.7	31.9	170.7
49	8.2	9.4	14.9	570	27.9	32.1	173.7
50	8.3	9.5	15.2	580	28.2	32.4	176.8
55	8.7	10.0	16.8	590	28.4	32.7	179.8
60	9.1	10.4	18.3	600	28.7	33.0	182.9
65	9.4	10.9	19.8	620	29.1	33.5	189.0
70	9.8	11.3	21.3	640	29.5	34.1	195.1
75	10.1	11.7	22.9	660	30.1	34.6	201.2
80	10.5	12.0	24.4	680	30.5	35.1	207.3
85	10.8	12.4	25.9	700	31.0	35.6	213.4
90	11.1	12.8	27.4	720	31.4	36.1	219.5
95	11.4	13.1	29.0	740	31.8	36.6	225.6
100	11.7	13.5	30.5	760	32.3	37.1	231.7
105	12.0	13.8	32.0	780	32.7	37.6	237.7
110	12.3	14.1	33.5	800	33.1	38.1	243.8
115	12.5	14.4	33.1	820	33.5	38.6	249.9

This table gives the approximate geographic range of visibility for an object which may be seen by an observer. It is necessary to add to the distance for the height of any object the distance corresponding to the height of the observer's eye above sea level.

Conversion of Degrees to Points and Points to Degrees

Deg °	Min '	Points	Deg °	Min '	Points
000	00	N	180	00	S
002	49		182	49	
005	38	N ½ E	185	38	S ½ W
008	26		188	26	
011	15	N x E	191	15	S x W
014	04		194	04	
016	53	N x E ½ E	196	53	S x W ½ W
019	41		199	41	
022	30	NNE	202	30	SSW
025	19		205	19	
028	08	NNE ½ E	208	08	SSW ½ W
030	56		210	56	
033	45	NE x N	213	45	SW x W
036	34		216	34	
039	23	NE ½ N	219	23	SW ½ S
042	11		222	11	
045	00	NE	225	00	SW
047	49		227	49	
050	38	NE ½ E	230	38	SW ½ W
053	26		233	26	
056	15	NE x E	236	15	SW x W
059	04		239	04	
061	53	NE x E ½ E	241	53	SW x W ½ W
064	41		244	41	
067	30	ENE	247	30	WSW
070	19		250	19	
073	08	ENE ½ E	253	08	WSW ½ W
075	56		255	56	
078	45	E x N	258	45	W x S
081	34		261	34	
084	23	E ½ N	264	23	W ½ S
087	11		267	11	
090	00	E	270	00	W
092	49		272	49	
095	38	E ½ S	275	38	W ½ N
098	26		278	26	
101	15	E x S	281	15	W x N
104	04		284	04	
106	53	ESE ½ E	286	53	WNW ½ W
109	41		289	41	
112	30	ESE	292	30	WNW
115	19		295	19	
118	08	SE x E ½ E	298	08	NW x W ½ W
120	56		300	56	
123	45	SE x E	303	45	NW x W
126	34		306	34	
129	23	SE ½ E	309	23	NW ½ W
132	11		312	11	
135	00	SE	315	00	NW
137	49		317	49	
140	38	SE ½ S	320	38	NW ½ N
143	26		323	26	
146	15	SE x S	326	15	NW x N
149	04		329	04	
151	53	SSE ½ E	331	53	NNW ½ W
154	41		334	41	
157	30	SSE	337	30	NNW
160	19		340	19	
163	08	S x E ½ E	343	08	N x W ½ W
165	56		345	56	
168	45	S x E	348	45	N x W
171	34		351	34	
174	23	S ½ E	354	23	N ½ W
177	11		357	11	

Standard Abbreviations Used In Broadcasts

Aids to Navigation

Aeronautical Radiobeacon	AERO RBN
Articulated Daybeacon	ART DBN
Articulated Light	ART LT
Destroyed	DESTR
Discontinued	DISCONTD
Established	ESTAB
Exposed Location Buoy	ELB
Fog Signal Station	FOG SIG
Large Navigation Buoy	LNB
Light	LT
Light List Number	LLNR
Lighted Bell Buoy	LBB
Lighted Buoy	LB
Lighted Gong Buoy	LGB
Lighted Horn Buoy	LHB
Lighted Whistle Buoy	LWB
Ocean Data Acquisition System	ODAS
Privately Maintained	PRIV MAINTD
Radar Beacon	RACON
Radar Reflector	RA REF
Temporarily Replaced by Unlighted Buoy	TRUB
Temporarily Replaced by Lighted Buoy	TRLB
Whistle	WHIS

Light Characteristics

Alternating	AL
Characteristic	CHAR
Composite Group-Flashing	FL(2+1)
Composite Group-Occulting	OC(2+1)
Continuous Quick-Flashing	Q
Fixed and Flashing	FFL
Fixed	F
Group-Flashing	FL(3)
Group-Occulting	OC(2)
Interrupted Quick-Flashing	IQ
Isophase	ISO
Morse Code	MO(A)
Occulting	OC
Single-Flashing	FL

Colors[1]

Black	B
Blue	BU
Green	G
Orange	OR
Red	R
White	W
Yellow	Y

Organizations

Commander, Coast Guard District (#)	CCGD(#)
Coast Guard	CG
Corps of Engineers	COE
National Geospatial-Intelligence Agency	NGA
National Ocean Service	NOS
National Weather Service	NWS

Vessels

Aircraft	A/C
Fishing Vessel	F/V
Liquefied Natural Gas Carrier	LNG
Motor Vessel[2]	M/V
Pleasure Craft	P/C
Research Vessel	R/V
Sailing Vessel	S/V

Compass Directions

North	N
South	S
East	E
West	W
Northeast	NE
Northwest	NW
Southeast	SE
Southwest	SW

Months

January	JAN
February	FEB
March	MAR
April	APR
May	MAY
June	JUN
July	JUL
August	AUG
September	SEP
October	OCT
November	NOV
December	DEC

Days of the Week

Monday	MON
Tuesday	TUE
Wednesday	WED
Thursday	THU
Friday	FRI
Saturday	SAT
Sunday	SUN

[1] Color refers to light characteristics of Aids to Navigation only
[2] M/V includes: Steam Ship, Container Vessel, Cargo Vessel, etc.

Standard Abbreviations Used In Broadcasts (continued)

Countries and States	
Alabama	AL
Alaska	AK
American Samoa	AS
Arizona	AZ
Arkansas	AR
California	CA
Canada	CN
Colorado	CO
Connecticut	CT
Delaware	DE
District of Columbia	DC
Florida	FL
Georgia	GA
Guam	GU
Hawaii	HI
Idaho	ID
Illinois	IL
Indiana	IN
Iowa	IA
Kansas	KS
Kentucky	KY
Louisiana	LA
Maine	ME
Maryland	MD
Marshall Islands	MH
Massachusetts	MA
Mexico	MX
Michigan	MI
Minnesota	MN
Mississippi	MS
Missouri	MO
Montana	MT
Nebraska	NE
Nevada	NV
New Hampshire	NH
New Jersey	NJ
New Mexico	NM
New York	NY
North Carolina	NC
North Dakota	ND
Northern Mariana Islands	MP
Ohio	OH
Oklahoma	OK
Oregon	OR
Pennsylvania	PA
Puerto Rico	PR
Rhode Island	RI
South Carolina	SC
South Dakota	SD
Tennessee	TN
Texas	TX
United States	US
Utah	UT
Vermont	VT
Virgin Islands	VI
Virginia	VA
Washington	WA
West Virginia	WV
Wisconsin	WI
Wyoming	WY

Various	
Anchorage	ANCH
Anchorage Prohibited	ANCH PROHIB
Approximate	APPROX
Atlantic	ATLC
Authorized	AUTH
Average	AVG
Bearing	BRG
Breakwater	BKW
Broadcast Notice to Mariners	BNM
Channel	CHAN
Code of Federal Regulations	CFR
Continue	CONT
Degrees (temp; geo pos)	DEG
Diameter	DIA
Edition	ED
Effect/Effective	EFF
Entrance	ENTR
Explosive Anchorage	EXPLOS ANCH
Fathom(s)	FM(S)
Foot/Feet	FT
Harbor	HBR
Height	HT
Hertz	HZ
Horizontal Clearance	HOR CL
Hour	HR
International Regulations for Preventing Collisions at Sea	COLREGS
Kilohertz	KHZ
Kilometer	KM
Knot(s)	KT(S)
Latitude	LAT
Local Notice to Mariners	LNM
Longitude	LONG
Maintained	MAINTD
Maximum	MAX
Megahertz	MHZ
Millibar	MB

Standard Abbreviations Used In Broadcasts (continued)

Various (continued)	
Millimeter	MM
Minute (time; geographic position)	MIN
Moderate	MOD
Mountain, Mount	MT
Nautical Mile(s)	NM
Notice to Mariners	NTM
Obstruction	OBSTR
Occasion/Occasionally	OCCASION
Operating Area	OPAREA
Pacific	PAC
Point(s)	PT(S)
Position	POS
Position Approximate	PA
Pressure	PRES
Private/Privately	PRIV
Prohibited	PROHIB
Publication	PUB
Range	RGE
Reported	REP
Restricted	RESTR

Rock	RK
Saint	ST
Second (time; geographic position)	SEC
Signal Station	SIG STA
Station	STA
Statute Mile(s)	SM
Storm Signal Station	S SIG STA
Temporary	TEMP
Thunderstorm	TSTORM
Through	THRU
True	T
Uncovers; Dries	UNCOV
Universal Coordinate Time	UTC
Urgent Marine Information Broadcast	UMIB
Velocity	VEL
Vertical Clearance	VERT CL
Visibility	VIS
Yard(s)	YD
Warning	WARN
Weather	WX
Wreck	WK

www.TheBoatBookShop.com

Conversion Factors

	Known Value	Multiply By	Unknown Value
Linear	inches	25.40	millimeters
		2.540	centimeters
	centimeters	0.032808	feet
	feet	30.48	centimeters
		0.3048	meters
		0.00016458	nautical miles
	yard	0.9144	meters
	meters	3.2808	feet
		1.094	yards
		0.0005399	nautical miles
	statute miles	0.86897	nautical miles
		1.6093	kilometers
		1,609.3	meters
	nautical miles	1.151	statute miles
Area	square feet	0.0929	square meters
		0.00002296	acres
	square meters	10.764	square feet
		0.0002471	acres
	acres	4,046.9	square meters
		43,560	square feet
		0.404685	hectare
	hectare	2.471054	acres
		10,000	square meters
		1.07639×10^5	square feet
Depths	fathoms	1.8288	meters
	meters	0.54681	fathoms
		3.2808	feet
	feet	0.3048	meters
Rate	feet per second	0.5925	knots
		0.6818	miles per hour
		30.48	centimeters per second
	statute miles per hour	0.8689	knots
		1.467	feet per second
		0.447	meters per second
	knots	1.151	miles per hour
		0.5144	meters per second
		1.6878	feet per second
	centimeters per second	0.01944	knots
		0.02237	miles per hour
		0.032808	feet per second
Mass	grams	0.035275	ounces
		0.002205	pounds
	ounces	28.349	grams
	pounds	0.45359	kilograms
	short tons	2,000	pounds
		0.89286	long tons
		0.9072	metric tons
	long tons	2,240	pounds
		1.12	short tons
		1.016	metric tons
	metric tons	1,000	kilograms
		0.9842	long tons
		1.1023	short tons
		2,204.6	pounds
Volume	barrels (petroleum)	42	gallons (US)
		158.99	liters
	barrels (liquid, US)	31.5	gallons (US)
		26.229	gallons (British)
		119.24	liters
	gallons (US)	0.02381	barrels (petroleum)
		3.7854	liters
	liters	0.26417	gallons (US)

Measurements and Equivalencies

Unit	Equivalency
nautical mile	1,852 meters 6,076.12 feet
statute mile	5,280 feet 1,609.3 meters 1.6093 kilometers
cable	0.1 nautical mile (CN) 720 feet (US)
fathom	6 feet 1.8288 meters
foot	0.3048 meter
inch	2.54 centimeters
meter	39.37 inches 3.281 feet 1.0936 yards
kilometer	1,000 meters
knot	1.6877 feet per second 0.5144 meters per second
miles per hour (statute)	1.466 feet per second 0.44704 meters per second
acre	43,560 square feet 4,046.82 square meters
pound (avoirdupois)	453.59 gram
gram	0.0022046 pound (avoirdupois) 0.035274 ounce
short ton	2,000 pounds
long ton	2,240 pounds
metric ton	2,204.6 pounds
kilogram	2.2 pounds
liter	1.0567 quarts
barrel (petroleum)	42 gallons (US)

Tips for Boating Clean & Green

• Practice Preventive Engine Maintenance. Keep your engine well tuned and practice preventative engine maintenance by regularly checking hoses and lines for chaffing or deterioration.

• Use Oil Absorbents. Place and secure an oil absorbent under the engine and in the bilge. Avoid using bilge cleaners as they may get discharged overboard. It is illegal to use soap to disperse fuel and oil spills. Report oil and chemical spills by calling both the National Response Center (800) 424–8802 and 1–800–OILS–911

• Spill-Proof Your Fueling Practices. Use a spill proof system like a portable oil change pump to change your oil. Use oil absorbents when fueling and changing the oil. Do not top-off your fuel tank; leave it 10 percent empty to allow fuel to expand as it warms.

• Reduce Greywater Discharges. Use shore-side facilities for laundry, showers and dish washing whenever possible. Use only phosphate-free and biodegradable soaps. The legality of discharging greywater into a marina or within three miles off the coast varies from place to place. In some areas, there are local ordinances and codes that allow harbor patrol to issue citations for any discharge that is not "clean and clear". To avoid any potential fines and to protect the aquatic environment, do not discharge greywater overboard.

• Dispose of Hazardous Waste Properly: Recycle and properly dispose of absorbents, used oil, oil filters, paint, and batteries at your local household hazardous waste collection site.

• Minimize boat cleaning and maintenance conducted on the water. Use more elbow grease. Use products that are water-based, biodegradable, phosphate-free, and labeled as less toxic. Check out less toxic cleaning alternatives for all types of uses by visiting: http://www.coastal.ca.gov/ccbn/lesstoxic.html. Buy only the amount that you need and use products for spot cleaning only. Properly handle and store materials. Dispose of hazardous waste legally and safely.

• Reduce Discharges from Bottom Paints. Consider alternative, non-biocide hull coatings. Clean the bottom with a soft, non-abrasive sponge. Use hull cleaning companies who use green management practices such as monitoring their divers and using non-abrasive scrubbing agents that do not release paint into the water. For more information visit: http://www.ucanr.org/sites/coast.

• Stow it, Don't Throw it. Keep your trash on-board. Recycle plastic, glass, metal, and paper. Avoid excess packaging.

• Dump at the Pump! It is illegal to discharge untreated sewage anywhere within the three-mile territorial limit including lakes, rivers, reservoirs or coastal waters. Never discharge treated sewage into "restricted waters" such as a marina, swimming/wading areas, a sanctuary, poorly flushed areas, lakes, reservoirs, or freshwater impoundments and federal No Discharge Zones. Use sewage pumpouts, dump stations, or mobile-pumpout services.
For locations visit:
  CA – http://www.dbw.ca.gov
  WA – http://www.parks.wa.gov/boating/pumpout
  OR – http://www.boatoregon.com/OSMB/Clean/CVA.shtml

• Prevent the Spread of Aquatic Invasive Species. Before leaving any body of water, examine your boat and equipment and remove any visible mud, plants, or animals before transporting equipment. Never release plants or animals into a body of water or storm drains unless they came out of that body of water. Clean and dry anything that came in contact with the water. For cleaning procedures visit: http://www.protectyourwaters.net/

For hazardous waste recycling or collection centers call 1-800-CLEAN-UP or visit http://www.earth911.org

Made in the USA
Lexington, KY
12 August 2013